PAGE 48

ON THE ROAD

YOUR COMPLETE DESTINATION GUIDE
In-depth reviews, detailed listings and insider tips

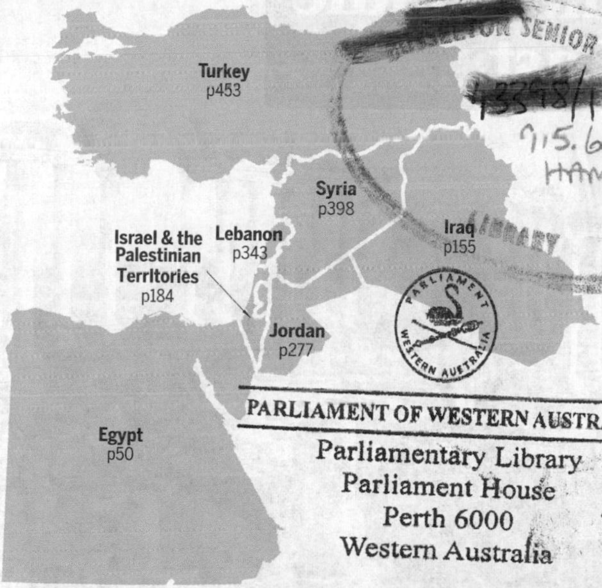

PAGE 613

SURVIVAL GUIDE

VITAL PRACTICAL INFORMATION TO HELP YOU HAVE A SMOOTH TRIP

THIS EDITION WRITTEN AND RESEARCHED BY
Anthony Ham
Stuart Butler, Zora O'Neill, Olivia Pozzan, Daniel Robinson,
Anthony Sattin, Paul Smith, Jenny Walker

welcome to the Middle East

History Writ Large

In the Middle East, history is not something you read about in books. Here, it's a story written on the stones that litter the region, from the flagstones of old Roman roads to the building blocks of Ancient Egypt and the delicately carved tombs and temples from Petra to Baalbek. This is where humankind first built cities and learned to write, and it was from here that Judaism, Christianity and Islam all arose. From wonderfully preserved ruined cities to modern settlements whose origins date back to the dawn of time, from the aspirational architecture of the great faiths to conversations that touch on the astonishing complexity of a region where the past is always present, history is the heart and soul of the Middle East.

Home of Hospitality

At some point on your visit to the Middle East, something will happen to challenge every stereotype you've ever heard about the region's people. You'll be sitting in a coffeehouse or looking lost in a labyrinth of narrow lanes when someone strikes up a conversation and, within minutes, invites you home to meet the family and share a meal. Or someone will simply approach and say with unmistakable warmth, 'Welcome'. These spontaneous, disarming and utterly genuine words of welcome can occur anywhere. And when they do, they

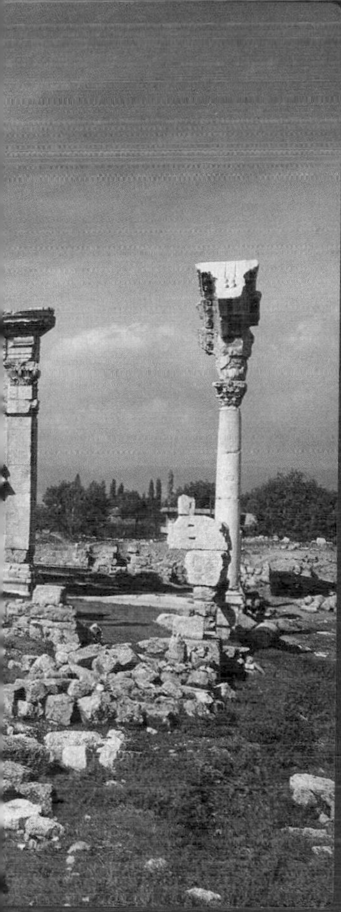

The Middle East is one of history's grand epics – a cradle of civilisations and a beautiful, complicated land that's home to some of the most hospitable people on the planet.

(left) Ruins of Baalbek (p377), Lebanon
(below) Muslim Quarter (p192), Jerusalem, Israel & the Palestinian Territories

can suddenly (and forever) change the way you see the Middle East. Put simply, in this land of historical, architectural and all manner of other treasures, it may just be the people who'll live longest in your memory.

Cities & Wilderness

The Middle East's cities read like a roll-call of historical heavyweights: Jerusalem, Damascus, Beirut, Cairo, İstanbul, Erbil. Aside from ranking among the oldest continuously inhabited cities on earth, these ancient-modern metropolises are places to take the pulse of a region, from the latest instalments in the gripping drama of the Arab Spring to Iraqi Kurdistan's headlong rush into the future. Beyond city limits, the Middle East is a land of mighty rivers (the Nile, Euphrates), even mightier deserts (the Sahara and peerless Wadi Rum) and green landscapes of exceptional beauty. Exploring these wilderness areas – from snow-capped summits in Turkey and Lebanon to the kaleidoscopic waters of the Red Sea – only adds to the appeal of the region. The message is simple. Forget the clichés that masquerade as Middle Eastern truth – a visit here is one of the most varied and soulful travel experiences on earth.

› Middle East

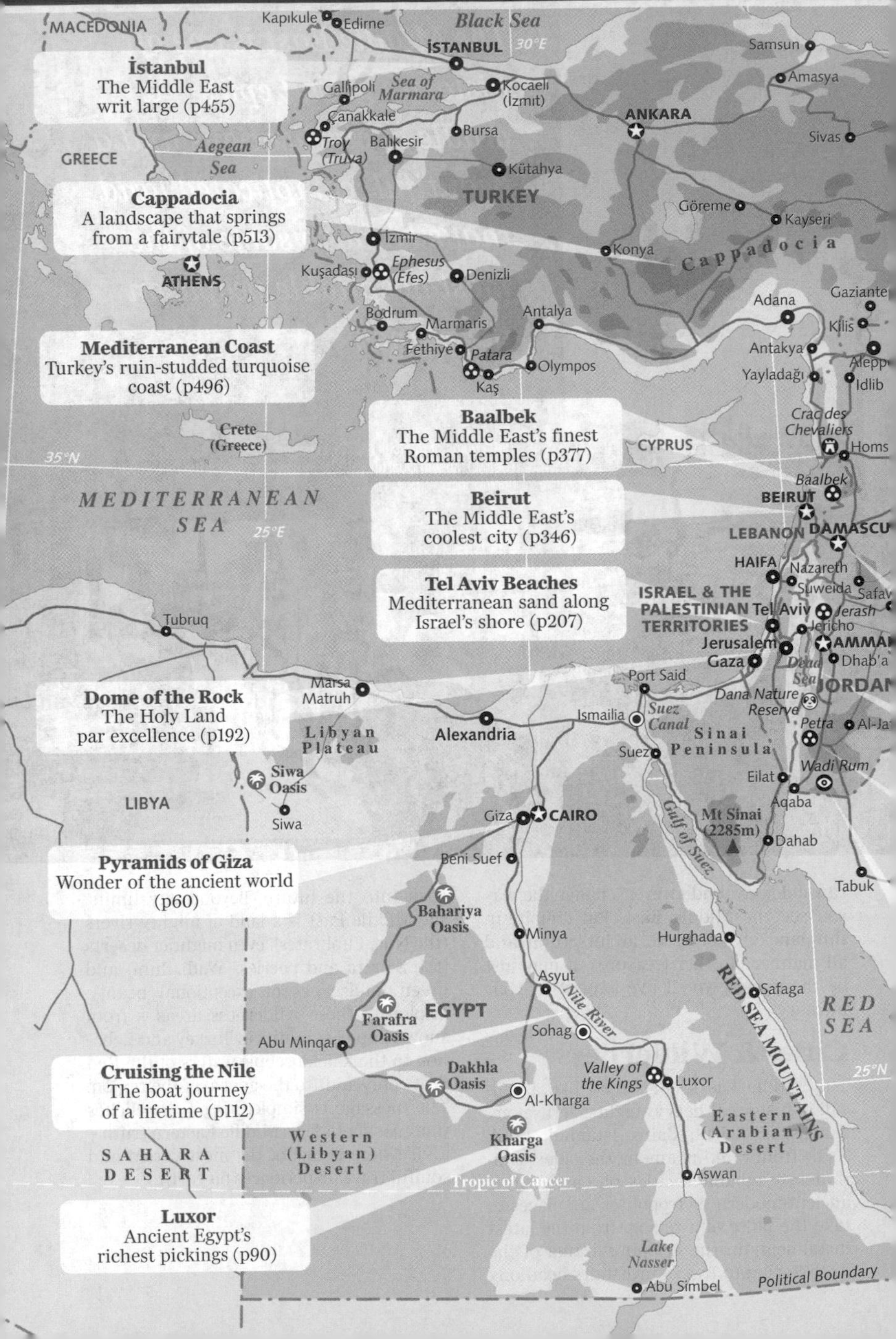

İstanbul
The Middle East writ large (p455)
Cappadocia
A landscape that springs from a fairytale (p513)
Mediterranean Coast
Turkey's ruin-studded turquoise coast (p496)
Baalbek
The Middle East's finest Roman temples (p377)
Beirut
The Middle East's coolest city (p346)
Tel Aviv Beaches
Mediterranean sand along Israel's shore (p207)
Dome of the Rock
The Holy Land par excellence (p192)
Pyramids of Giza
Wonder of the ancient world (p60)
Cruising the Nile
The boat journey of a lifetime (p112)
Luxor
Ancient Egypt's richest pickings (p90)
MACEDONIA
Kapıkule
Edirne
Black Sea
İSTANBUL
30°E
Samsun
Amasya
Gallipoli
Sea of Marmara
Kocaeli (İzmit)
Çanakkale
ANKARA
Troy (Truva)
Balıkesir
Bursa
Sivas
GREECE
Aegean Sea
Kütahya
TURKEY
Göreme
Kayseri
İzmir
Konya
Cappadocia
Kuşadası
Ephesus (Efes)
Denizli
ATHENS
Bodrum
Marmaris
Antalya
Adana
Gaziantep
Kilis
Fethiye
Patara
Olympos
Kaş
Antakya
Aleppo
Yayladağı
Idlib
Crac des Chevaliers
Homs
Crete (Greece)
CYPRUS
35°N
Baalbek
BEIRUT
MEDITERRANEAN SEA
25°E
LEBANON
DAMASCUS
HAIFA
Nazareth
Suweida
Safawi
ISRAEL & THE PALESTINIAN TERRITORIES
Tel Aviv
Jerash
Jericho
Jerusalem
AMMAN
Gaza
Dead Sea
Dhab'a
Tubruq
Port Said
JORDAN
Dana Nature Reserve
Marsa Matruh
Ismailia
Suez Canal
Petra
Al-Jafr
Libyan Plateau
Alexandria
Sinai Peninsula
Suez
Wadi Rum
Siwa Oasis
Eilat
LIBYA
Aqaba
Siwa
Giza
CAIRO
Mt Sinai (2285m)
Dahab
Gulf of Suez
Beni Suef
Tabuk
Bahariya Oasis
Minya
Hurghada
Asyut
Nile River
Safaga
RED SEA
Farafra Oasis
EGYPT
Sohag
RED SEA MOUNTAINS
Abu Minqar
Valley of the Kings
Luxor
25°N
Dakhla Oasis
Al-Kharga
Eastern (Arabian) Desert
Kharga Oasis
SAHARA DESERT
Western (Libyan) Desert
Tropic of Cancer
Aswan
Lake Nasser
Abu Simbel
Political Boundary

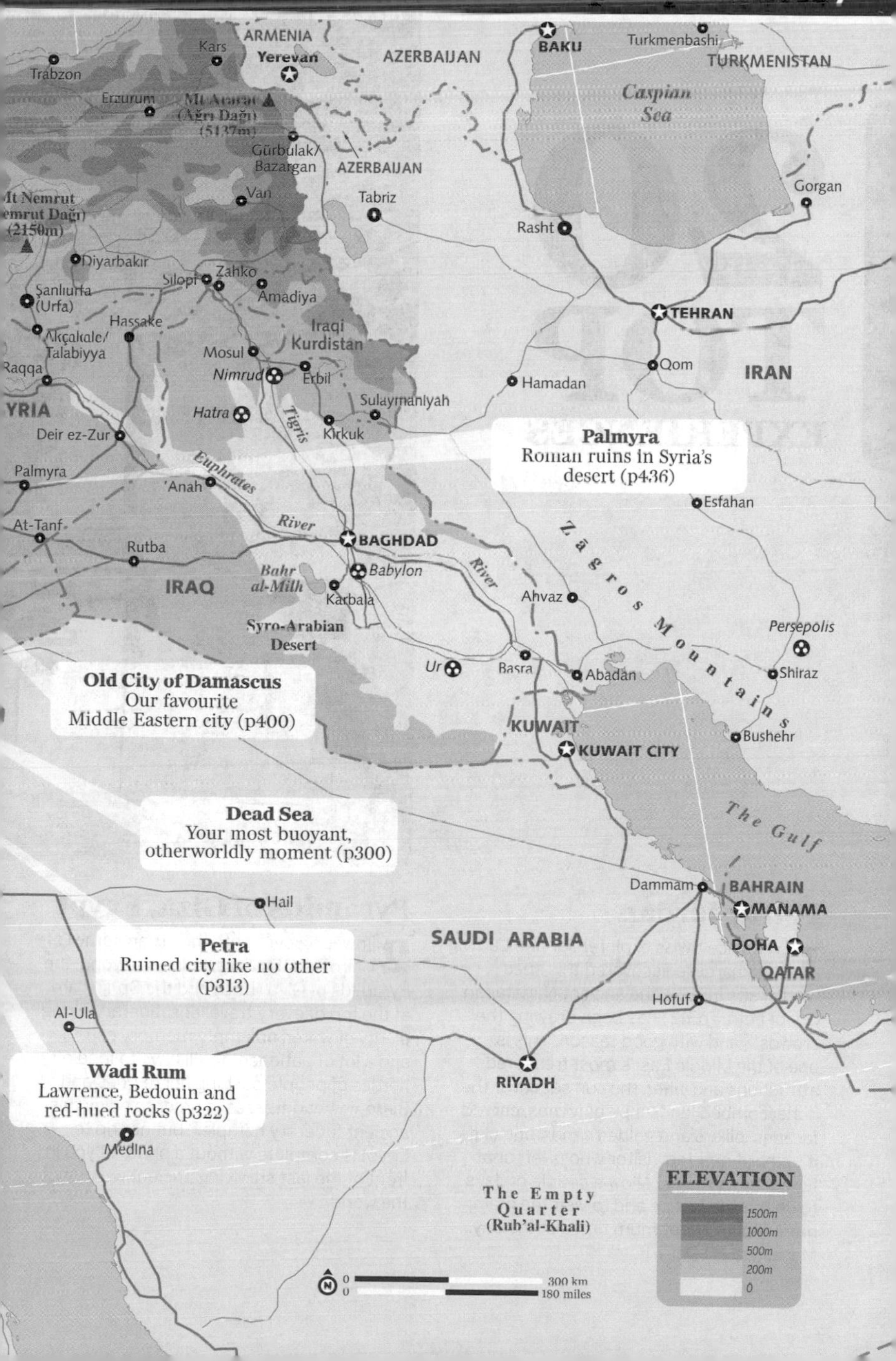

Palmyra
Roman ruins in Syria's desert (p436)
Old City of Damascus
Our favourite Middle Eastern city (p400)
Dead Sea
Your most buoyant, otherworldly moment (p300)
Petra
Ruined city like no other (p313)
Wadi Rum
Lawrence, Bedouin and red-hued rocks (p322)
ARMENIA
Yerevan
AZERBAIJAN
BAKU
Turkmenbashi
TURKMENISTAN
Caspian Sea
Kars
Trabzon
Erzurum
Mt Ararat (Ağrı Dağı) (5137m)
Gürbulak/Bazargan
AZERBAIJAN
Tabriz
Gorgan
Rasht
Van
Diyarbakır
Silopi
Zahko
Amadiya
Şanlıurfa (Urfa)
Hassake
Akçakale/Talabiyya
Raqqa
Iraqi Kurdistan
Mosul
Nimrud
Erbil
Hatra
Sulaymaniyah
Kirkuk
Tigris
TEHRAN
Qom
Hamadan
IRAN
Deir ez-Zur
Euphrates River
Palmyra
'Anah
At-Tanf
Rutba
BAGHDAD
Babylon
Bahr al-Milh
Karbala
IRAQ
Syro-Arabian Desert
Esfahan
Zāgros Mountains
Ahvaz
Persepolis
Shiraz
Ur
Basra
Abadan
KUWAIT
KUWAIT CITY
Bushehr
The Gulf
Dammam
BAHRAIN
MANAMA
DOHA
QATAR
Hail
SAUDI ARABIA
Hofuf
Al-Ula
RIYADH
Medina
The Empty Quarter (Rub'al-Khali)
ELEVATION
1500m
1000m
500m
200m
0
0
300 km
0
180 miles

20 TOP EXPERIENCES

Petra, Jordan

1 Ever since Swiss explorer Johann Ludwig Burckhardt rediscovered this spectacular site in 1812, the ancient Nabataean city of Petra (p313) has been drawing the crowds – and with good reason. This is one of the Middle East's most treasured attractions and when the sun sets over the honeycombed landscape of tombs, carved facades, pillars and golden sandstone cliffs, it's a hard-hearted visitor who is left unaffected by its magic. Allow a couple of days to do the site justice and to visit the main monuments at optimum times of the day.

Monastery (Al-Deir), Petra

Pyramids of Giza, Egypt

2 Towering over both the urban sprawl of Cairo and the desert plains beyond, the Pyramids of Giza (p60) and the Sphinx are at the top of every traveller's itinerary. Bring plenty of water, an empty memory card and a lot of patience! You'll have to fend off hordes of people pushing horse rides and Bedouin headdresses in order to enjoy this ancient funerary complex, but no trip to Egypt is complete without a photo of you in front of the last surviving ancient wonder of the world.

8

9

Palmyra, Syria

10 Every ancient city in the Middle East has its own calling card, and Palmyra's (p436) is an evocative desert location that harks back to its days as an oasis town along the great trade routes of antiquity. Palm trees and golden sands blend perfectly at sunrise and sunset with the sandstone used to build the hallmark monuments of urban Roman life. Throw in legends of a powerful desert queen and a hilltop castle with perfect views, and Palmyra is an unforgettable place. Palmyra ruins

İstanbul, Turkey

11 In İstanbul (p455), you can board a commuter ferry to flit between continents and be rewarded at sunset with the city's most magical sight, when the tapering minarets of the Old City are thrown into relief against a dusky pink sky. Elsewhere, history resonates with profound force amid the Ottoman and Byzantine glories of the Blue Mosque, Aya Sofya and Topkapı Palace. Such is İstanbul, a collision of continents and a glorious accumulation of civilisations. Little wonder, then, that locals call their city the greatest in the world. Blue Mosque (p458), İstanbul

BETHUNE CARMICHAEL/LONELY PLANET IMAGES©

JOHN ELK III/LONELY PLANET IMAGES©

HUW JONES/LONELY PLANET IMAGES©

Beirut, Lebanon

12 Few cities have the cachet of Beirut (p346) and few have earned it quite so tough. Battle-scarred yet perpetually brimming with optimism, this is a city at once Mediterranean and Middle Eastern. Beirut is both the sophisticated and hedonistic place that once partied under the sobriquet of the 'Paris of the Middle East', and a demographically diverse city that's rife with contradictions. Never is this more true than at sunset along the waterfront Corniche, where mini-skirted rollerbladers dodge veiled Shiite families intent on escaping the heat. Street cafe, Beirut

Luxor, Egypt

13 With the greatest concentration of ancient Egyptian monuments anywhere in Egypt, Luxor (p90) repays time. You can spend days or weeks around this town, walking through the columned halls of the great temples on the east bank of the Nile, such as the Ramesseum, or climbing down into the tombs of pharaohs in the Valley of the Kings on the west bank. Just watching the sun rise over the Nile or set behind the Theban hills count as two of Egypt's most unforgettable moments. Avenue of Sphinxes, Luxor Temple (p91), Luxor

Floating in the Dead Sea, Jordan

14 Floating in the Dead Sea (p300) is one of the world's great natural experiences. Floating is the right word for it: thanks to an eye-stingingly high salt content it is virtually impossible to swim in the viscous waters of a sea that is 1000ft lower than sea level. The experience is usually accompanied by a mud bath, a bake in the sun and a health-giving spa treatment at one of the modern pleasure palaces lined up along the Dead Sea's shores.

Aleppo Old City, Syria

15 The old city of Aleppo (p422) is the Middle East you always dreamed existed. Beneath the vaulted ceilings of its labyrinthine souq, the path lit by shafts of light filtering through the skylights, this is the Middle East of *The Thousand and One Nights*, a collision of cultures and a continual assault on the senses. Crowning the city and bathed in the clear light of northern Syria, the citadel provides the quintessential Middle Eastern vantage point, while the city's restaurants are some of the region's best. Souq, Aleppo

Golan Heights, Israel & the Palestinian Territories

16 From towering Nimrod Fortress, the 'Galilee Panhandle' spreads out before you like a topographical map, though when you turn around the looming flanks of Mt Hermon, snowcapped well into spring, dwarf even this Crusader-era stronghold. Hikers can take on the alpine peaks of Mt Hermon, or follow the wadis of the Banias and Yehudiya nature reserves on their way to the Jordan River and the Sea of Galilee. The Golan Height's (p238) basalt soils are ideal for growing grapes, so the local boutique wines are some of Israel's finest. Israel–Syria border from the Golan Heights

15

TIM BARKER/LONELY PLANET IMAGES©

16

17

KARSTEN BIDSTRUP/LONELY PLANET IMAGES©

18

ALI ABBAS/EPA/CORBIS©

Tel Aviv Beaches, Israel & the Palestinian Territories

17 Just over 100 years ago, Tel Aviv (p206) was little more than sand dunes. Nowadays it's a sprawling cosmopolitan city bursting with bars, bistros and boutiques, though the beach is still the epicentre of life. Here, sunbathers bronze their bodies, while the more athletic swim, surf and play intense games of *matkot* (beach raquetball). Each beach along the coast of Tel Aviv has its own personality – sporty, party, alternative, gay or religious – all set against the deep blue backdrop of the Mediterranean.

Park Life, Iraq

18 Nobody loves a picnic like an Iraqi Kurd and come summer weekends it can seem as if the entire population has descended on the nearest park. Some of these parks have to be seen to be believed: boating lakes and dancing fountains, enormous children's playgrounds, horse riding and amusement parks, plastic caves, glow-in-the-dark trees and even the odd cable car all feature. Throw in masses of picnicking locals, dozens of noisy wedding parties and coyly courting couples and you get the most fun in Iraq. Picnic lunch in a Baghdad park

Mediterranean Coast, Turkey

19 Welcome to one of the most beautiful coastlines on earth. Between the craggy mountains and the astonishing turquoise hue of the Mediterranean's waters, there are more than enough reasons to visit. The villages and ancient ruins that inhabit this space between mountain and sea add depth and personality to a coast as beloved by beachgoers looking for somewhere quiet to lay their towel as by travellers aboard traditional yachts, as well as those in search of more energetic aquatic pursuits. Coastline near Kalkan (p501)

Mt Sinai, Egypt

20 It may not be the highest of Sinai's craggy peaks, but Mt Sinai is the peninsula's most sacred. A place of pilgrimage for Jews, Christians and Muslims alike, the summit affords the magnificent spectacle of light washing over the sea of surrounding mountain tops. Down below, tucked into the mountain's base, is St Katherine's Monastery. Its sturdy Byzantine fortifications are built over the spot where Moses is believed to have witnessed the burning bush. St Katherine's Monastery (p137)

19

20

C-RIS MELLOR/LONELY PLANET IMAGES©

need to know

Currency

» Egyptian pound, Iraqi dinar, new Israeli shekel, Jordanian dinar, Lebanese lira, Syrian pound, Turkish lira

Language

» Arabic, Hebrew and Turkish; English widely spoken

When to Go

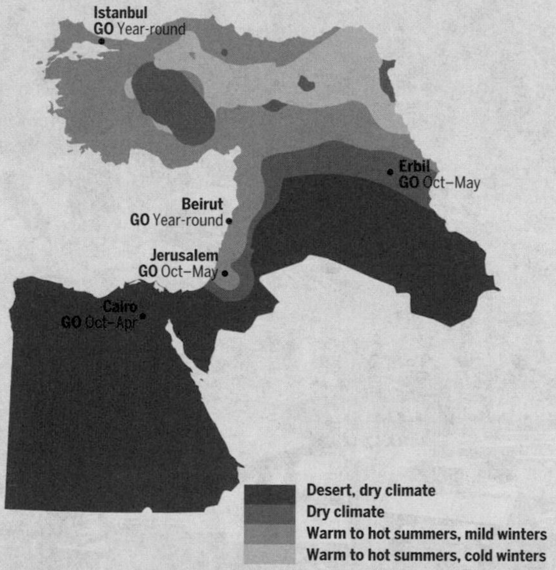

High Season (Jun–Aug)

» Mediterranean beaches and Turkish sites are extremely crowded in summer.

» Religious holidays represent mini high seasons.

» Prices are sky high; book accommodation well in advance.

Shoulder Season (May–Mar & Sep–Nov)

» Religious festivals aside, spring and autumn represent shoulder seasons in most countries.

» Weather is often agreeable and crowds are generally smaller at main sites.

Low Season (Jun–Aug & Dec–Feb)

» Egypt's Nile Valley and desert regions can be unbearably hot in summer.

» Turkey's Mediterranean and Aegean beaches are almost deserted in winter.

What to Take

» This book – what else could you possibly need?

» The latest travel advisory warnings – stay informed

» Travel insurance – accidents do happen

» Warm clothes for winter – the Middle East can be cold, desert nights can be freezing

» A universal bathplug: you'll thank us when you emerge from the desert

» Ear plugs – wake-up calls from nearby mosques can be *very* early

» A phrasebook – a '*salaam 'alaykum*' (peace be upon you) works wonders in turning suspicion into a smile

» Hiking boots – if you intend to get off the beaten track

» Patience – most things do run on time, but the timetable may be elusive to the uninitiated

Money

» ATMs and credit-card use widespread, except in Syria and Iraq; travellers cheques near useless; US dollars universally accepted, followed by euros and British pounds.

Visas

» Most visas available on arrival; an Israeli stamp will mean no entry to Iraq, Lebanon or Syria.

Mobile Phones

» Local SIM cards are widely available and can be used in most international mobile phones. Mobile coverage is widespread, but patchy in some areas.

Driving

» Driving is on the right (and steering wheel on the left) in all countries.

Websites

» **Lonely Planet** (www.lonelyplanet.com/middle-east) Destination information, hotel bookings, traveller forums and more.

» **Al-Ahram Weekly** (weekly.ahram.org.eg) Egypt's English-language newspaper.

» **Al-Bab** (www.al-bab.com) Portal covering the entire Arab world.

» **Al-Jazeera** (www.aljazeera.com/news/middleeast) CNN of the Arab world.

» **Bible Places** (www.bibleplaces.com) Biblical sites.

» **Jerusalem Post** (www.jpost.com) News from an Israeli perspective.

Exchange Rates

	Egypt	Turkey	Israel & the Palestinian Territories
Australia (A$1)	E£6.24	TL1.81	3.9NIS
Canada (C$1)	E£6.13	TL1.78	3.83NIS
Europe (€1)	E£8	TL2.32	5NIS
UK (UK£1)	E£9.8	TL2.84	6.13NIS
USA (USA$1)	E£6.04	TL1.75	3.78NIS

For current exchange rates see www.xe.com. Other currencies are covered in the individual country chapters.

Important Numbers

Country codes:

Egypt	☎20
Iraq	☎964
Israel & the Palestinian Territories	☎972
Jordan	☎962
Lebanon	☎961
Syria	☎963
Turkey	☎90

Arriving in the Middle East

» Cairo International Airport, Egypt (p151)

» Erbil International Airport, Iraq (p171)

» Ben-Gurion International Airport, Tel Aviv, Israel (p273)

» Queen Alia International Airport, Amman, Jordan (p339)

» Beirut Rafic Hariri International Airport, Lebanon (p394)

» Damascus International Airport, Syria (p450)

» İstanbul Atatürk International Airport, Turkey (p542)

Safe to Travel?

The simple answer to this fundamental question for travellers to the Middle East is a resounding yes, in most places most of the time. It's relatively easy to avoid known trouble spots – at the time of writing these included Arab Iraq, Syria and the Gaza Strip. This is also an area where things can change quickly: who would have thought a few years ago that Syria would be off-limits while Iraqi Kurdistan and Lebanon are relative beacons of peace and stability. The Arab Spring – that seismic eruption of people's power that overthrew the old order in Egypt – does make for some uncertainty; always keep your ear to the ground. But some things don't change – Jordan, Turkey and much of Israel continue to be safe, probably more so than many Western countries. For more detailed information, see p616.

if you like...

Ancient Cities

The cradle of civilisation, the crossroads of ancient empires...whatever true cliché you want to use to describe the region, the Middle East has ruins in abundance.

Petra Extraordinary tombs hewn from the rock by the Nabataeans (p313)

Luxor Ancient Egypt in all its glory, from the Temple of Karnak to the west bank temples (p90)

Ephesus An astonishing theatre and some wonderfully preserved temples (see the boxed text, p488)

Baalbek Perhaps the region's richest concentration of Roman temples (p377)

Palmyra Fabulous ruins in the Syrian desert (p436)

Caesarea An aqueduct, an amphitheatre and other Roman ruins spread out along the Mediterranean Coast (p218)

Jerash Temples, arches, a distinctive oval plaza and an outstanding colonnaded way in Jordan's north (p293)

Temple of Echmoun Unusually intact outpost of Phoenician culture in southern Lebanon (p372)

Pyramids of Giza Not exactly a city but worthy of one (p60)

Deserts & Oases

Deserts have always played a pivotal role in Middle Eastern life – it was from the desert that the great monotheistic faiths emerged – and the Middle East is still home to some of the most beautiful and soulful desert landscapes on earth.

Wadi Rum Exceptional rock formations, extraordinary colours, Bedouin companions and echoes of TE Lawrence (p322)

Western oases Egypt's remote oasis towns and gateways to the Sahara's White and Black Deserts (p114)

Ein Gedi Two spring-fed canyon oases are home to a profusion of plant and animal life (p240)

Eastern Desert Jordan's eastern wastes are home to a surprising collection of castles and wildlife sanctuaries (p302)

Palmyra An expansive oasis and ruined city that once drew ancient trade caravans (p436)

Sinai Peninsula Set out on camel with the Bedouin in the land of Moses (p141)

Mosques

Mosques stand at the very heart of Middle Eastern life and just about every Arab village, town and city has one as its architectural centrepiece. In many cases, the architecture speaks to the aesthetic aspirations of a people, with symmetrical forms and exquisite decorative features.

Dome of the Rock, Jerusalem One of Islam's holiest sites, with a graceful octagonal plan, gorgeous mosaic tiles and a gleaming gold dome (p192)

Blue Mosque, İstanbul The personification of Islamic architectural grace and perfect proportions (p458)

Süleymaniye Camii, İstanbul The highpoint of 16th-century Ottoman mosque design and İstanbul's grandest (p459)

Umayyad Mosque, Damascus Sublime mosaics, sacred shrines and a place to take the pulse of Damascus (p401)

Taynal Mosque, Tripoli Lebanon's most beautiful mosque in the country's Mamluk architectural heartland (p365)

Al-Azhar Mosque, Cairo One of the oldest mosques in Egypt and the world's oldest surviving university (p57)

» Yeni Cami (New Mosque; p459), İstanbul, Turkey

Souqs & Bazaars

The souqs and bazaars that snake through so many Middle Eastern towns provide many visitors with their most memorable experiences of the region. Indeed, some might even describe their sights, smells and sounds as the essence of the Middle East.

Khan al-Khalili, Cairo Cairo's Byzantine-era bazaar is a tourist cliché, but with very good reason (p57)

Qaysari Bazaar, Erbil One of the oldest souqs in the world (p169)

Jerusalem All the world's a bazaar in the Old City (p187)

Bethlehem Busy and colourful souq in the town of Jesus's birth (p252)

Tripoli, Lebanon Lebanon's finest bazaar with medieval Mamluk architecture (p364)

Aleppo, Syria Arguably the Middle East's most atmospheric souq with ancient vaulted ceilings and labyrinthine turns (p422)

Grand Bazaar, İstanbul The quintessential Turkish marketplace with carpets and controlled chaos (p459)

Castles & Fortresses

That the Middle East has been fought over for centuries is an understatement, and during the Crusades in particular, seemingly every conceivable hilltop was colonised by a defensive fortress. Many remain, in some cases beautifully preserved.

Crac des Chevaliers TE Lawrence called it 'the finest castle in the world' (p419)

Karak The most intact of Jordan's Crusader castles (p309)

Shobak Less well-preserved than Karak, but its equal in drama and beauty (p312)

Salahaddin's Fortress Turrets, stone walls and echoes of Saladin (Salah ad-Din) in Iraqi Kurdistan (p172)

İshak Paşa Palace Like the evocation of an Arabian fairy tale in Doğubayazıt in eastern Turkey (p524)

Nimrod Fortress Israel's best-preserved Crusader-era bastion (p239)

Fortress of Shali Melting mud-brick fortress rising from the Siwa Saharan oasis (p119)

Jordan's Desert Castles Seventh and 8th-century desert retreats in evocative desert location (p302)

Biblical Landmarks

The Bible – and before it the Torah, and after it the Quran – live and breathe in the cities and soil of the Middle East, particularly the Levantine arc. What follows is merely a starting point.

Jerusalem From Al-Haram ash-Sharif/Temple Mount to the Church of the Holy Sepulchre, Jerusalem is the Bible writ large (p187)

Bethlehem The Church of the Nativity stands on the site where Jesus is believed to have been born (p252)

Mt Sinai, Egypt Said to be where Moses received the Ten Commandments from God atop the summit (p140)

Bethany-Beyond-the-Jordan Jordanian site where Jesus was baptised (and the Pope agrees) (p299)

Machaerus, Jordan Herod the Great's castle where John the Baptist was martyred (p309)

Mt Nebo, Jordan Where Moses looked out over the Promised Land, now within sight of Jerusalem (p308)

Antakya, Turkey Saints Peter and Paul both preached here and there's a church to prove it (p509)

» Goods on display at Luxor Souq, Luxor (p90), Egypt

Hammams

One of the great sensual indulgences of the region, the hammam (hamam in Turkey) is an iconic Middle Eastern experience. You'll never forget the combination of robust massage on tiled slabs, sweltering steam-room sessions and hot tea.

Çemberlitaş Hamamı Sixteenth-century Ottoman hamam with an atmosphere to match in İstanbul (p463)

Cağaloğlu Hamamı Easily the Turkish capital's most beautiful hamam, albeit with a slightly touristy ambience; you can even have a sleep afterwards (p463)

Hammam Yalbougha an-Nasry Fifteenth-century but recently overhauled hammam showpiece in Aleppo (p426)

Hammam Nureddin Men-only hammam tucked away in the Damascus souq; it's the city's oldest (p405)

Al-Pasha Hammam A rare outpost of tradition in the modern Jordanian capital, Amman, with the full treatment (see the boxed text, p283)

Hammam Al-Hana This tourist-friendly place in Nablus offers a bath, steam room and massage (p255)

Hiking

The Middle East is – perhaps surprisingly for some – a top hiking destination, with Jordan and Israel in particular offering rewarding trails from short day-hikes to longer, multiday expeditions.

Dana Biosphere Reserve, Jordan Trek through one of the Middle East's most intact (and most beautiful) ecosystems (p311)

Makhtesh Ramon Hike through this vast desert crater, famous for its multicoloured sandstone (p244)

Ein Avdat National Park, Israel Trek through canyons and pools in the wonderful Negev Desert (p244)

Timna Park, Israel Stunning desert landscapes, enlivened with multicoloured rock formations (p249)

Petra, Jordan Hike through the main site, with intriguing trails leading further to little-known tombs (p313)

Qadisha Valley, Lebanon The starting point of hikes along the spine of Lebanon (see the boxed text, p368)

Mt Ararat, Turkey Climb to the summit of Turkey's highest peak in search of Noah's Ark – if you can cut through the red tape… (see the boxed text, p525)

Diving & Snorkelling

The Red Sea could just be the finest place to dive and snorkel on earth, its varied underwater topography wedded to one of the richest and most varied marine ecosystems on earth. The Turkish Mediterranean is possible, but not a patch on its southern rival.

Sharm el-Sheikh, Egypt Base for the *Thistlegorm*, a sunken WWII cargo ship that's the world's best wreck dive (p128)

Dahab, Egypt A place of Middle Eastern snorkelling legend and home to the famous Blue Hole (p132)

Ras Mohammed National Park, Egypt A national marine park teeming with more fish life than you can poke a regulator at (p128)

Aqaba, Jordan Jordan's wedge of the Red Sea has hundreds of coral species and around 1000 fish species (p324)

Marsa Alam, Egypt A remote and virgin reef offshore and the perfect place for shark spotting (p127)

Eilat, Israel Israel's best snorkelling, plus a chance to commune with fish without getting wet… (p245)

If you like... remote monasteries
Rabban Hormizd Monastery (p164) and Mar Mattai (p165) in Iraqi Kurdistan are ideal

If you like... hot-air ballooning over spectacular landscapes
Head for Cappadocia (p515) or Luxor (p95)

Urban Vibes

The Middle East is not just about religion, old stones and history lessons at every turn. The region's cities can be vibrant, exciting places where the young and young-at-heart race headlong towards the future.

Beirut One of the most resilient cities on earth, Beirut is also sassy, sophisticated and a daily contradiction between past and future (p346)

Tel Aviv Jerusalem's alter ego is dynamic, secular, international and more than a little hedonist (p206)

Erbil Few places capture the hope and excitement of the new Iraq quite like this irresistible Kurdish city (p167)

Amman Jordan's capital has some of the most enduring oases of urban cool in the region (p279)

Alexandria A culturally rich city as much Mediterranean as Egyptian (p83)

İstanbul One of the greatest cities on earth, at once ancient and very modern, European, Middle Eastern and Turkish all at once (p455)

Beaches

The Middle East is not most people's first thought when it comes to beach holidays, but there are some superb places to lay out your towel. You're most likely to feel comfortable doing so in Turkey and Israel. Parts of Egypt have also seen it all before.

ÖlüDeniz, Turkey Yes, it was long-ago discovered, but this lagoon beach is just gorgeous (p500)

Nuweiba, Egypt One of the quieter Egyptian Red Sea shores with plenty to do or lovely beaches on which to do nothing (p141)

Dahab, Egypt Yes, it's a scene, but the location is dramatic and you haven't lazed on a Middle Eastern beach unless you've done so at Dahab (p132)

Tel Aviv, Israel Long stretches of soft sand, with all the amenities of Israel's liveliest city right nearby (p207)

Coral Beach Nature Reserve, Israel Eilat's best beach is ideal for snorkellers (p247)

Dead Sea, Jordan Float to your heart's content in the Middle East's most buoyant experience (p300)

Wildlife

Much of the region's wildlife has been pushed to the brink of extinction, but vestiges of the wild somehow survive. Ecotourism projects and wildlife reserves now protect some of the Middle East's most charismatic fauna.

Yotvata Hai-Bar Nature Reserve, Israel Observe African asses, addax, ostriches and oryx in the wild (p249)

Ras Mohammed National Park, Egypt One of the Red Sea's few protected areas, it teems with marine life (p128)

Shaumari Wildlife Reserve, Jordan Arabian oryx, ostrich, gazelle and Persian onager bred for reintroduction to the wild in large enclosures (p304)

Mujib Biosphere Reserve, Jordan An enclosure for the Nubian ibex and the chance to see caracal (p301)

Chouf Cedar Reserve, Lebanon If you're (extremely) lucky, you might see wolves, wild cats, ibex and gazelle (p376)

Agamon HaHula, Israel Restored wetlands that let you see migrating cranes up close (p237)

month by month

Top Events

1 **Jerash Festival**, July

2 **Dahab Festival**, April

3 **Baalbek Festival**, July

4 **Akbank Jazz Festival**, October

5 **Arab Music Festival**, November

January

Much of the region, including desert regions at night, can be bitterly cold and there can be snow on the high peaks. Egypt and the Red Sea have relatively balmy temperatures.

Red Sea Snorkelling & Diving

Anywhere along the Red Sea coast is the place to be with warm winter sunshine. With clear blue skies and crystal clear waters, the winter months from December to March are the perfect time for an underwater adventure.

Christmas (Orthodox)

Orthodox Christians commemorate the birth of Jesus in Bethlehem (it's celebrated by Eastern Orthodox churches on 6 and 7 January and by Armenians in the Holy Land on 18 and 19 January). The date is also important among Christian communities in Lebanon, Egypt and Syria.

Prophet's Birthday

Moulid al-Nabi is a region-wide celebration with sweets and new clothes for kids and general merriment in all Muslim areas. In Cairo, the week before is an intense Sufi scene at Midan al-Hussein. For dates, see p624.

Luxor Marathon

Held in Luxor in Egypt's Nile Valley, this unusual marathon (www.egyptianmarathon.com) attracts competitors from around the world, drawn by the chance to get all hot and sweaty around the main antiquities sites on the West Bank of the Nile.

February

The winter chill continues throughout much of the region, though it's the perfect time of year in the south. Egypt's beaches and Nile Valley are packed, while Turkish mountain passes may be impassable.

Ascension of Ramses II

22 February is one of two dates each year (the other is 22 October) when the sun penetrates the inner sanctuary of the temple at Abu Simbel in southern Egypt, illuminating the statues of the gods within. The event draws a big crowd of theorists of all kinds.

Arab Music Festival

Early in the month, 10 days of classical, traditional and orchestral Arabic music are held at the Cairo Opera House and other venues. See www.cairoopera.org for the schedule.

March

In Egypt periodic, intense sandstorms can darken the horizon, but the hillsides and valleys of the Levant, Turkey and northern Iraq are green – it's a great time for hiking. Low-season room prices in most areas.

Purim

Purim celebrates the foiling of a plot to wipe out the Jews of ancient Persia. Children and adults put on costumes for an evening of revelry (23 and 24 February 2013, 15 and 16 March 2014, 4 and 5 March 2015; celebrated one day later in walled cities, including Jerusalem).

Nevruz

Kurds and Alevis celebrate the ancient Middle Eastern spring festival on 21 March with much jumping over bonfires and general jollity. Banned until a few years ago in Turkey, Nevruz is now an official holiday with huge parties, particularly in Diyarbakır.

April

A shoulder season for much of the Middle East, April is a wonderful time to visit with wild flowers in the Levant, tourist numbers at Egyptian archaeological sites drop off and good beach weather in southwest Turkey.

Passover

Known as Pesach, this week-long festival celebrates the liberation of the Israelites from slavery in Egypt with ritual family dinners and Shabbat-like closures on the first and seventh days. Lots of Israelis go on holiday so accommodation is scarce and room prices skyrocket.

Easter

During Holy Week, Catholic pilgrims throng Jerusalem's Via Dolorosa and the Church of the Holy Sepulchre, and many Protestants gather at the Garden Tomb. Dates for Orthodox celebrations differ slightly.

Dahab Festival

A mash-up of windsurfing contest, divers' meet, DJ party and Bedouin culture show, this week-long get-together is as groovy as its host town of Dahab. Oh, and camel races too! Details at www.dahabfestival.info.

Anzac Day

The WWI battles for the Dardanelles are commemorated on Gallipoli Peninsula on 25 April with an emphasis on the Allied soldiers. Antipodean pilgrims sleep at Anzac Cove before the dawn services; another busy time on the peninsula.

Palmyra Festival

Once peace returns to Syria, this fine folk festival is worth crossing the Middle East for. There's horse and camel racing, and live performances in the ancient theatre. It used to run most at the end of April or early May.

May

Still peak tourist season in the Levant with warm weather on the way. High season prices in coastal areas are yet to kick in, but it's good beach weather from the Red Sea to the Mediterranean.

Hiking & Camel-Trekking

It may be hotting up in Petra and Wadi Rum but May is the perfect time to experience the desert. With hot days and warm nights, you'll quickly slip into the rhythm of Bedouin life, rising early and napping after lunch.

June

You'll encounter long days and sunny, warm weather all across the region. The tourist high season draws large crowds and higher room prices in many areas, but it's unbearably hot in Egypt by the end of the month.

Israel Festival

Four weeks of music, theatre and dance performances, some of them free, in and around Jerusalem add a real spring to the step of the city in early summer. Check out the website (www.israel-festival.org.il) for dates and programs.

Dance with the Sufis

In Luxor in the third week of the Islamic month of Sha'aban, the Sufi festival of Moulid of Abu al-Haggag in Luxor offers a taste of rural religious tradition. Several smaller villages have *moulids* around the same time.

Oil Wrestling

In one of the Middle East's more unusual events, oil-coated men wrestle for the edification of huge crowds in a field near Edirne in Turkey's far northwest as part of the Kırkpınar Oil Wrestling Championship in late June or early July.

July

A great time for festivals, but the weather can be unpleasantly hot in most areas. It is, however, high season along Turkey's Aegean and Mediterranean coasts, while holidaying Europeans can push prices up anywhere.

Byblos Arts Festival

Lebanon kicks off the Levantine summer with pop, classic, opera and world music performances, many of which are staged among the ruins of Byblos' ancient harbour. This dynamic event can start in late June and continue on into August – check the website (www.byblosfestival.org) for details.

Jerash Festival

Hosted within world-class ruins, Jordan's best-loved cultural event brings ancient Jerash to life with plays, poetry recitals, opera and concerts. Held annually since 1981, the festival (www.jerashfestival.jo) is held over 17 days from mid-July to mid-August.

Ramadan

The holy month of dawn-to-dusk fasting by Muslims is offset by celebratory break-fast meals after sunset. Offices may have shorter hours, and restaurants may close during daylight. Foodies will love this time; ambitious sightseers may be frustrated. For forthcoming dates, see p624.

Eid al-Fitr

The Festival of Fast-Breaking that marks the end of Ramadan is celebrated with entirely understandable gusto throughout Muslim areas. It's generally a family-centric festival, but travellers will find themselves caught up in it all. For dates see p624.

Music Festivals

A string of summer music jamborees in Turkey; including İstanbul, İzmir and Bursa's highbrow international festivals, Aspendos Opera and Ballet Festival, plus multiple pop, rock, jazz and dance-music events.

Baalbek Festival

Lebanon hosts one of the region's most famous arts festivals (www.baalbeck.org.lb), evocatively staged in the Roman ruins deep in the Bekaa Valley. The full program includes opera, jazz, poetry and pop, and theatre productions.

Beiteddine Festival

Lebanon's full program of summer events continues with this terrific arts festival (www.beiteddine.org) with music, dance and theatre held in the beautiful courtyard of the Beiteddine Palace. It usually spills over into August.

August

The heat takes its toll everywhere; unless you've a particular festival in mind or you're by the beach in Turkey, it's a month to avoid. High-season rates (and overbooking) apply in many coastal areas.

Dance in the Desert

August is hot, so if you can't beat the heat, you may as well join it by building up a sweat at Jordan's annual Distant Heat festival (www.distantheat.com). This all-nighter takes place in Wadi Rum and features top international electronic-dance-music artists.

Red Sea Jazz

Eilat in August gives you the chance to combine long days by the water with some terrific jazz (www.redseajazzeilat.com). It draws international acts, takes place in the last week of August and it's probably the best jazz festival in the region.

Cappadocian Festivals

Two festivals take place in the land of fairy chimneys. A summer series of chamber music concerts is held in the valleys and, between the 16th and 18th, sleepy Hacıbektaş comes alive with the annual pilgrimage of Bektaşı dervishes (www.klasikkeyifler.org).

Bodrum International Ballet Festival

The 15th-century Castle of St Peter, as well as housing the Museum of Underwater Archaeology, is an atmospheric location for this two-week festival (www.bodrumballetfestival.gov.tr), which features Turkish and international ballet and opera performances.

September

Two of the most important Jewish holidays make for mini high seasons. Elsewhere, temperatures are starting to fall (only slightly in Egypt) and high-season crowds and prices start to ebb in Turkey.

Rosh Hashanah

The Jewish New Year causes Shabbat-like closures that last for two days. Some Israelis go on holiday so accommodation is scarce and room prices rise. Unless you're here for the ambience or for religious reasons, avoid this one.

Yom Kippur

The Jewish Day of Atonement is a solemn day

(Above) Diving off the Red Sea coast near Hurghada (p123), Egypt
(Below) Skiing at Uludağ National Park (p476), Turkey

of reflection and fasting – and cycling on the empty roads. In Jewish areas, all businesses shut and transportat (including by private car) completely ceases; Israel's airports and land borders close. Eerie.

International İstanbul Biennial

The city's major visual-arts shindig, considered to be one of the world's most prestigious biennials, takes place from mid-September to mid-November in odd-numbered years, with art ists and performers from around the world.

Silk Road Festival

Syria's late-September festival has Damascus, Aleppo and Palmyra as its focal points for celebrations of Syria's long cultural history. There are concerts and other live performances, assuming, of course, that the festival survives Syria's conflict.

October

As the summer heat finally breaks, Egypt comes back into play and the crowds have tapered off in Turkey. Elsewhere, it's a pleasant month with mild temperatures, although rain is possible. A great month for festivals.

Akbank Jazz Festival

From late September to mid-October, İstanbul celebrates its love of jazz with this eclectic line-up of local and international performers. Marking its 20th anniversary in 2010, the festival (www.akbanksanat.

com) is gaining in prestige every year.

Antalya Golden Orange Film Festival

Held in early October, Turkey's foremost film event (www.altinportakal.org.tr) features screenings, a parade of stars in cars and the obligatory controversy. At the award ceremony in Aspendos, the Golden Orange, nicknamed the Turkish Oscar, is awarded to film-makers.

Beirut International Film Festival

Beirut's contribution to the cinematic calendar is an increasingly high-profile film festival (www.beirutfilmfoundation.org) with a growing reputation as one of the best in the Middle East.

Desert Cheer

An oasis-wide celebration of the date harvest, the annual Siyaha get-together in the Egyptian oasis town of Siwa takes place around the full moon. Much like a *moulid*, though not as raucous, there's Sufi chanting and plenty of food.

Sukkot

The weeklong Feast of the Tabernacles holiday recollects the Israelites' 40 years of wandering in the desert. Families build *sukkot* (foliage-roofed booths) in which they dine and sometimes sleep. The first and seventh day are Shabbat-like public holidays.

Eid al-Adha

For the Feast of the Sacrifice, a four-day Muslim holiday, families slaughter sheep and goats at home, even in large cities. There's literally blood in the streets, and the air smells of roasting meat. In short, not for vegetarians. For forthcoming dates, see p624.

Egyptian Pilgrims

During the last week of October, almost a million pilgrims throng Tanta in the Nile Delta, where a 13th-century mystic founded an important Sufi order. Part family funfair, part intense ritual, Moulid of Al-Sayyed Badawi is worth a trip if you don't mind crowds.

Oktoberfest

Pints, Palestinians and lederhosen make for a fine if unlikely combination at this beer festival (www.taybehbeer.com) in the pretty Palestinian village of Taybeh, which just happens to be home to the Middle East's only microbrewery.

November

Good for sightseeing with surprisingly chilly weather and smallish crowds even at the more popular sights. Rain possibilities may deter hikers, but Saharan expeditions in Egypt again possible after the summer break.

Cairo International Film Festival

From the last weekend in November into December, this 10-day event (www.cairofilmfest.org) shows recent films from all over the world – all without censorship. Anything that sounds like it might contain scenes of exposed flesh sells out immediately.

December

The Middle East's winter begins in earnest, and low-season prices apply in most areas, except Christian areas at Christmas, ski resorts and in Egypt where Europeans flood in search of winter sun.

Hanukkah

The Jewish Festival of Lights celebrates the rededication of the Temple after the Maccabean revolt. Families light candles over eight nights using a nine-branched candelabra and waistlines bulge due to jelly doughnuts.

Christmas

Midnight Catholic Mass is celebrated in the Church of the Nativity in Bethlehem. Christmas is a public holiday in the West Bank but not in many other areas. Orthodox Christians must wait until early January for their Christmas.

Holiday of the Holy Days

Haifa's Wadi Nisnas neighbourhood celebrates Hanukkah, Christmas and Ramadan with art and music (HaChag shel HaChagim) on December weekends. It's one of the Middle East's more enlightened festivals, if only for its symbolism of shared celebration.

Ski Season

Hit the slopes at the beginning of the ski season at half a dozen resorts across Turkey, including Cappadocia's Erciyes Dağı (Mt Erciyes) and Uludağ, near Bursa. The season that starts in December will run, in most normal years, until April.

itineraries

Whether you've got six days or 60, these itineraries provide a starting point for the trip of a lifetime. Want more inspiration? Head online to lonelyplanet.com/thorntree to chat with other travellers.

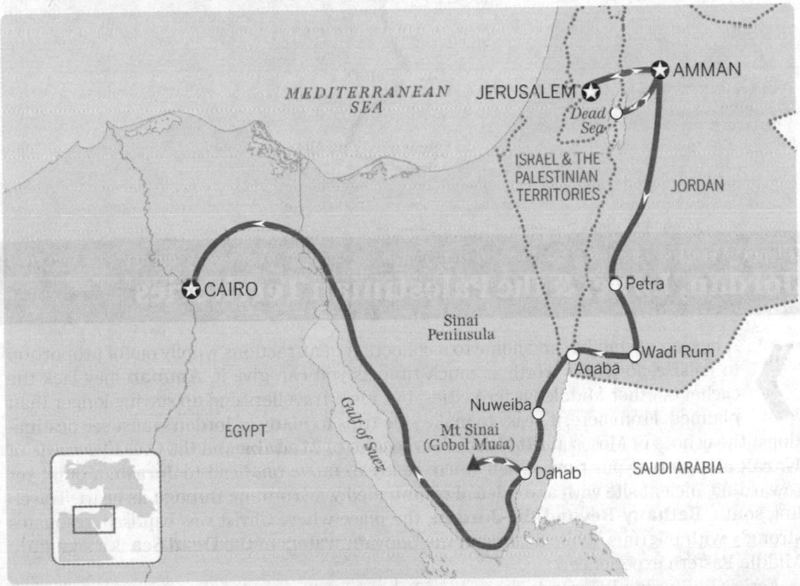

Two Weeks

Amman to Cairo

Your journey starts in **Amman**, an agreeably cosmopolitan city with a handful of Roman ruins offset by brilliant restaurants. Jordan may be small, but there's a lot to pack in, including a visit to the **Dead Sea** – it's an easy day trip from the capital. A detour to **Jerusalem** takes you to the Middle East's spiritual heart. Returning to Jordan, spend some time exploring fabulous **Petra**, arguably the Middle East's most beguiling ancient city. Futher south, Petra's rival to the title of Jordan's most spectacular site is **Wadi Rum**, a soulful red-hued desert landscape that rewards those who spend a couple of days exploring, either by camel or 4WD. From here, leave Jordan behind and cross the Red Sea at **Aqaba** to **Nueweiba** in Egypt, then continue on to **Dahab**, where just about every traveller pauses for at least a couple of days, including time for snorkelling in the Red Sea and sunrise at **Mt Sinai**. That should just leave enough time to make for **Cairo**, home to the Pyramids of Giza and the extraordinary Egyptian Museum, and the gateway to Egypt's many charms.

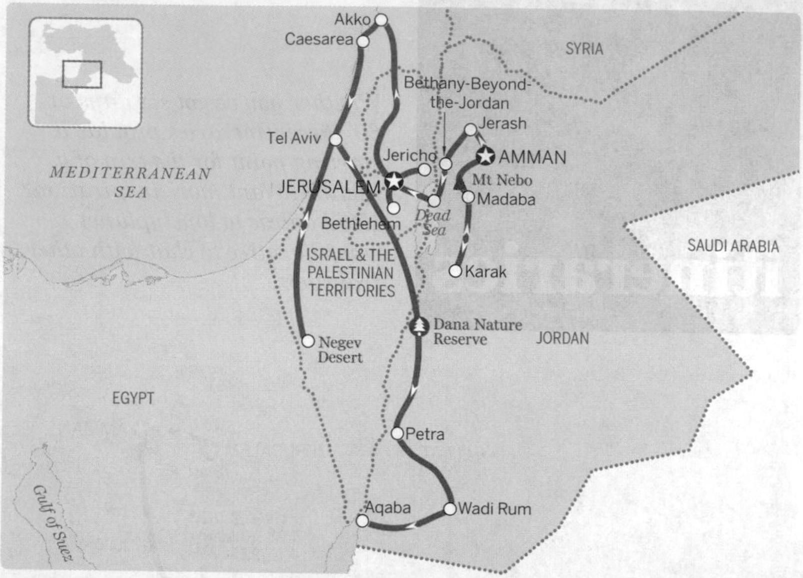

Three Weeks

Jordan, Israel & the Palestinian Territories

A beacon of stability and home to a collection of attractions wholly out of proportion to its size, Jordan is worth as much time as you can give it. **Amman** may lack the cachet of other Middle Eastern cities, but most travellers end up staying longer than planned. From here, it's easy to make side trips to many of Jordan's must-see destinations; the echoes of Moses at **Mt Nebo**, the mosaics of **Madaba** and the Crusader castle of **Karak** all deserve your time. When you're ready to move on, head to **Jerash**, a quiet yet rewarding ancient site with a wonderful colonnaded way running through its heart. Travelling south, **Bethany-Beyond-the-Jordan**, the place where Christ was baptised, resonates strongly with pilgrims, while floating in the buoyant waters of the **Dead Sea** is a signature Middle Eastern experience.

Across the Jordan River in Israel and the Palestinian Territories, beguiling **Jerusalem** is the site of so much Middle Eastern history that it can be difficult to believe you're actually there. From Jerusalem, your ability to visit the biblical towns of **Bethlehem** and **Jericho** will depend entirely on the prevailing security situation. In the north of the country, timeless **Akko** and the world-class ruins of **Caesarea** are worth as much time as you can give them. On your way back, don't miss **Tel Aviv**, a lively place to let your hair down and a chance to discover the other side of Israeli life that you rarely hear anything about. Its antithesis, the **Negev Desert**, is a wilderness area that you simply don't expect to find in this ever-crowded corner of the earth.

Crossing back into Jordan, the spectacular scenery of **Dana Nature Reserve** shouldn't be missed, while **Petra** is an astonishing place, one of those rare destinations where the reality outstrips even the most lofty of expectations. If time allows, plan to spend at least a couple of days here, so you can savour the main tombs as well as visit the more outlying areas of the site. The same applies to **Wadi Rum** – you could get a taste of this soulful place in a day, but you'll gain a deeper understanding of its gravitas if you sleep out under the stars for at least one night. The laid-back Red Sea port of **Aqaba**, with world-class diving and snorkelling, provides the perfect place to rest at journey's end.

» (above) Fishing port at Byblos (Jbail; p361), Lebanon
» (left) Wadi Rum (322), Jordan

MICHAEL BENANAV/LONELY PLANET IMAGES©

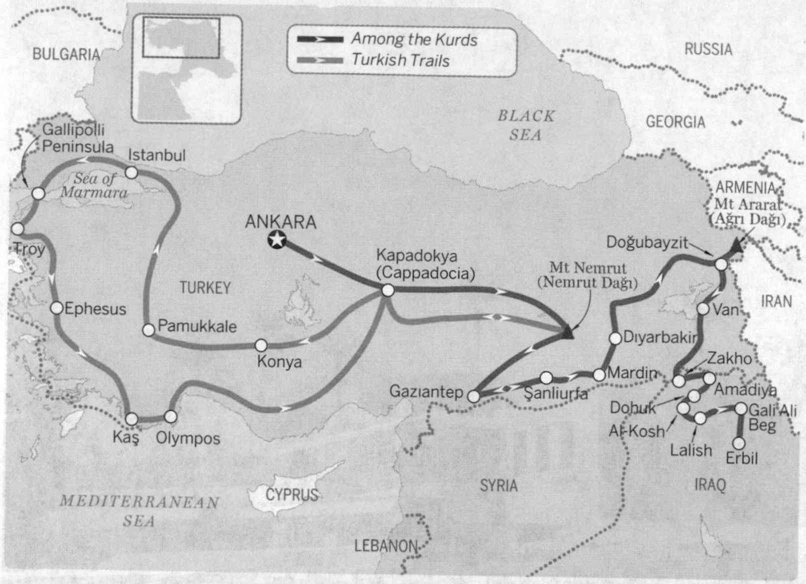

Three Weeks
Turkish Trails

İstanbul is at once a destination in its own right and the starting point of so many Turkish journeys. You could spend a week here, but three days should give you a taste before you move on to visit the **Gallipoli Peninsula**, with its poignant echoes of WWI, and **Troy**, where altogether more ancient battles took place. Work your way around the coast, pausing at the mighty ruins of **Ephesus**, which rank among the Middle East's most imposing, and lingering in the delightful Mediterranean villages of **Kaş** or **Olympos** where you'll wonder why life can't always be like this. On your way east, cut inland for long enough to marvel at the otherworldly landscapes of **Kapadokya (Cappadocia)** that seem to have sprung from a wonderfully childlike imagination. A detour to the east takes you to the brooding statues of **Mt Nemrut**, surely one of Turkey's most thought-provoking sights. On your way back to İstanbul, break up the journey in **Konya**, the spiritual home of the Sufis, and beautiful **Pamukkale**.

One Month
Among the Kurds

Begin in **Ankara**, the heart of Turkey's secularist Atatürk cult of personality, where you'll find a splendid museum and a fine citadel. On your way southeast into the Kurdish heartland, make the obligatory stop in **Cappadocia** and **Mt Nemrut** before exploring the rarely visited but always fascinating cities of **Gazıantep** and **Şanliurfa**. Nearby **Mardın** combines a beautiful setting with equally beautiful architecture and a fascinating cultural mix. By the time you reach **Dıyarbakir**, with its intriguing architecture, you're deep in Kurdish territory. Head for **Doğubayzit**, one of eastern Turkey's most extraordinary sights, with a legendary castle and stunning views of **Mt Ararat**; the mountain can be climbed, although most travellers content themselves with not-so-distant views from the town. Further south, **Van** is home to the lovely Armenian church on Akdamar Island. If you've come this far, it's likely you're en route to Iraq. If it's safe, cross into **Zakho** with its iconic bridge, then spend as long as they'll let you getting to know **Amadiya**, **Dohuk**, **Al-Kosh**, **Lalish** and **Gali Ali Beg**, before finishing up in **Erbil**, one of the oldest cities on earth, but one rushing headlong towards the future.

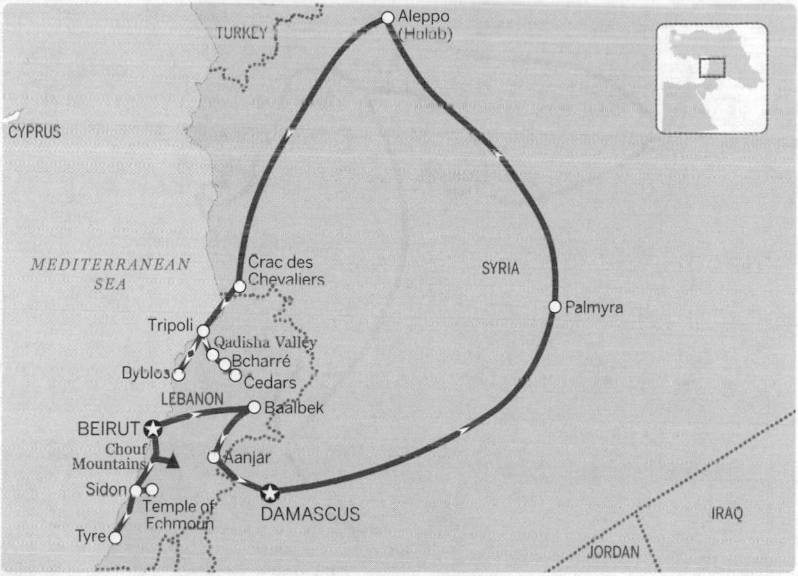

Two to Three Weeks

Lebanon & Syria

How much of this itinerary you're able to complete will depend entirely on whether Syria has returned to peace. If it remains unsafe, the Lebanon part of this itinerary could be completed in around 10 days, or a more leisurely two weeks. Either way, begin in that great survivor among Middle Eastern cities, **Beirut**, a glamorous metropolis that somehow manages to encapsulate the Middle East in complicated microcosm while also clinging to its Mediterranean joie de vivre – a stroll along the waterfront Corniche at sunset will show you what we mean. Check the security situation before setting out, and if it's OK, spend some time sweeping through the Phoenician heartland of the south – **Sidon**, the **Temple of Echmoun** and **Tyre** – where you'll see ruins that rank among the oldest traces of civilisation found in the Middle East. Save a couple of days for the wild landscapes, palaces and time-worn villages of the pretty **Chouf Mountains**. Returning north to the Bekaa Valley, **Baalbek** is one of the Middle East's premier Roman sites, an extraordinarily well-preserved proliferation of temples set against the distant backdrop of snow-capped mountains. Nearby **Aanjar** is a lesser-known Islamic archaeological jewel, with a walled Umayyad city that dates back 1300 years and bears traces of Roman town planning in its layout. If Syria is safe, cross to peerless **Damascus**, one of the oldest and most hospitable cities on earth. Spend a week or more taking in the desert ruins of **Palmyra**, the evocative souqs of **Aleppo** and the Crusader castle of **Crac des Chevaliers**. Back in Lebanon, **Tripoli** has some fabulous Mamluk architecture, not to mention a reputation for irresistible sweets. The pretty fishing port of **Byblos** contrasts nicely with the mountain drama around **Bcharré**. To really appreciate the landscape, go hiking through the **Qadisha Valley**, and then put on your skis at the **Cedars**.

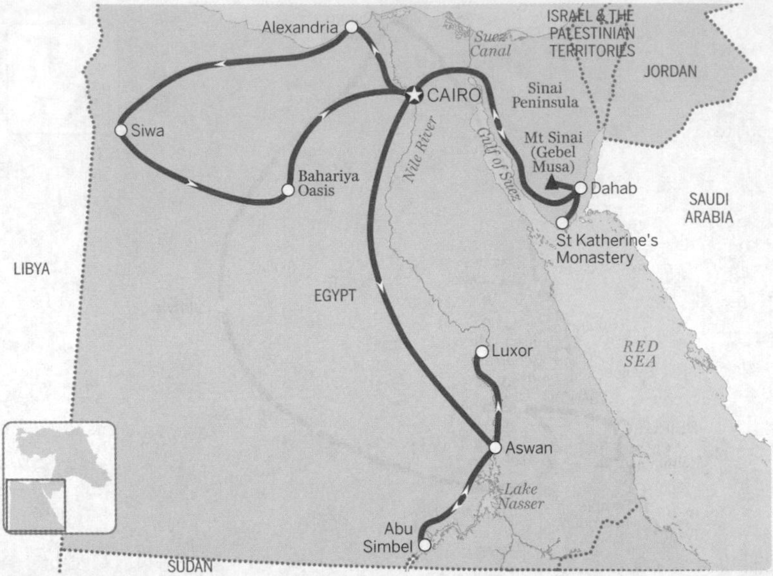

One Month
Land of the Pharaohs

All Egyptian journeys revolve around **Cairo**, and you'll return here again and again. Apart from being the Middle East's largest and most clamorous metropolis, Cairo is also home to the iconic Pyramids of Giza, the Egyptian Museum and a wonderful coffeehouse culture. If you can tear yourself away, begin by heading east to the Sinai Peninsula. Using utterly chilled **Dahab** as your base, climb **Mt Sinai**, visit **St Katherine's Monastery** and possibly take an excursion out into the desert with the Bedouin. Spend the remaining days, as many as you can spare, lounging in seaside restaurants and stirring only long enough to go for a long and lazy snorkel. But be warned – just about everyone who comes to Dahab ends up staying longer than they planned. Return to Cairo, then head north to **Alexandria**, Egypt's sophisticated and quintessentially Mediterranean city. It feels like nowhere else in the country, and a combination of terrific museums and great food gives you futher reason to visit. A *really* long journey west is worth it for your first sight of **Siwa**, one of the Sahara's great oasis outposts and home to an ancient temple in the sands. Dusty desert trails lead to the **Bahariya Oasis**, the starting point for expeditions into the White and Black Deserts. It's back to Cairo to enjoy the pleasures of civilisation for a day or two, then jump on a train south to **Aswan**, one of Africa's loveliest riverside spots. There's a monastery and museum to anchor your explorations of the city, but its real charm is its proximity to the Nile. Take the detour south into Nubia to **Abu Simbel**, one of Egypt's most extraordinary temples, then from Aswan sail slowly up the Nile aboard a felucca all the way to **Luxor**, home to the richest collection of Pharaonic sites in the country. Here you'll find so much of what drew you to Egypt in the first place, including the Temples of Karnak, the Valley of the Kings and the Valley of the Queens.

Visas & Border Crossings

Visas in Advance

Egypt – if entering overland from Israel
Jordan – if you need a multiple-entry visa
Syria – if there's a Syrian embassy in your country of residence/nationality
Arab Iraq – tourist visas not possible

Visas Available on Arrival

Egypt – except if crossing from Israel
Iraqi Kurdistan
Israel and the Palestinian Territories
Jordan – single-entry visas except if first entry on King Hussein/Allenby Bridge
Lebanon
Syria – if no Syrian representation in your home country
Turkey

Israeli Visa Stamp Allowed

Egypt
Jordan
Turkey

Israeli Visa Stamp Not Allowed

Iraq
Lebanon
Syria

Visas

If you do one piece of research before setting out on your trip, it should be to familiarise yourself with the requirements for obtaining visas for the countries that you intend to visit. For the unwary, it can be a minefield. For the well informed, it shouldn't pose too many difficulties.

The major issue arises if you plan to visit Israel and the Palestinian Territories. If you do, then you may need to think carefully about the order in which you visit the countries of the Middle East, or prepare for a little sleight of hand to ensure that an Israeli stamp in your passport doesn't limit the other countries that you're able visit.

Egypt

Most Egyptian tourist visas can be obtained on arrival. It couldn't be easier if you're arriving by air, while those travelling from Jordan can obtain a visa at the port in Aqaba before boarding the ferry. Visa fees vary by nationality and can usually be paid for in Egyptian pounds, US dollars or euros. Visas granted on arrival allow you to stay in Egypt for one month.

The only exception to these general rules is if you plan to enter Egypt from Israel via the Taba border crossing. In this case, we recommend that you apply for your Egyptian visa in advance in Tel Aviv or Eilat. If you just turn up at this border crossing

BANNED: ISRAELI PASSPORT STAMPS

Arab countries have widely varying policies on admitting travellers whose passports show evidence of a visit to Israel. Jordan and Egypt, with which Israel has peace treaties, have no problem at all, and the same goes for Tunisia, Morocco and many of the Gulf emirates (but not Saudi Arabia).

If there's any chance you'll be heading to Arab or Muslim countries during the life of your passport, your best bet is to make sure that it shows no indication that you've been to Israel. Fortunately, Israeli passport inspectors are usually amenable to issuing your entry stamp on a separate piece of paper. When you hand over your passport, just say 'no stamp, please' (make sure they've heard you!) and keep the insert until you depart.

Unfortunately, Egyptian and Jordanian officials are not so obliging about their own stamps, even though having a chop from one of those countries' land crossings to Israel or the West Bank may be no less 'incriminating' than having an Israeli one. This is especially true of Syria, Lebanon and Iran, which have been known to put travellers on the next plane out if they find even the slightest evidence of travel to Israel.

Some countries, including the United States, allow their citizens to carry more than one passport, but it can still be difficult to make this work without leaving unexplained gaps in the entry/exit paper trail.

without a visa in your passport, your visa must be guaranteed by an Egyptian travel agency – more trouble than it's worth.

For more information on Egyptian visas, see p150.

Iraq

Most nationalities can obtain a free, 10-day visa for Iraqi Kurdistan at the point of entry. This visa, which is not valid for the rest of the country, can be extended for a further 30 days in Erbil.

For everywhere outside of Iraqi Kurdistan, Iraqi embassies in your home country will only issue visas for those with official business in the country. Tourists need not apply.

For more information on Iraqi visas, see p181.

Israel & the Palestinian Territories

Tourist visas are issued to nationals of most Western countries at airports and land border crossings. Although most visas are for three-month periods, travellers arriving overland from Egypt or Jordan are sometimes given two-week or one-month visas. Some visas may also come with restrictions relating to travel inside the Palestinian Territories.

For more information on visas for Israel & the Palestinian Territories, see p272.

Jordan

Visitors to Jordan can obtain a one-month tourist visa at airports and *most* land borders. Such visas are single entry and cost JD20.

There are two exceptions. First, the only border crossing where visas are not available on arrival is the King Hussein/Allenby Bridge, which connects Jordan with Israel and the Palestinian Territories. This applies if you are entering Jordan for the first time. If, however, you are *returning* to Jordan after visiting Israel and the Palestinian Territories and you do so within the one-month validity of your original Jordanian visa, you may re-enter Jordan at this crossing without the need for a second visa.

The second exception applies if you are arriving in Aqaba. Because the city is located within a free-trade zone, arrivals are issued with a free, 15-day visa. If you wish to stay longer than this, you must register with the local authorities.

For more information on Jordanian visas, see p337.

Lebanon

One-month Lebanese tourist visas are available for most nationalities on arrival at airports and land borders. They're usually issued free of charge, although charges of LL50,000 are sometimes levied by immigration officials at land borders.

For more information on Lebanese visas, see p393.

Syria

Like most things in Syria, visa rules and requirements were in a state of flux at the time of writing. If the Assad regime survives the unrest, the following rules will *probably* apply. Either way, check with your nearest Syrian embassy.

Prior to the conflict in Syria, tourist visas were available at Syrian airports and land borders to travellers with no Syrian embassy or consulate in their country of nationality or residence. For everyone else, one-month tourist visas were available from Syrian embassies or consulates, and usually required a letter of recommendation from your own embassy if you applied outside your country of nationality/residence. Visas were rarely available in Amman, but were usually possible in Beirut and İstanbul. The cost of visas varied depending on your nationality.

For more information on Syrian visas, see p449.

Turkey

Three-month, multiple-entry tourist visas can be obtained on arrival at airports or land border crossings. The fee for this visa is US$20 (€15), except for Canadians who, for reasons unknown, pay US$60 (€45). Payment should be made in hard currency and no change is given. If you wish to stay for longer than three months, simply leave the country and return to obtain a new visa.

For more information on Turkish visas, see p541.

Border Crossings

Border crossings in the Middle East can be slow and it can take hours to pass through immigration and customs formalities, especially if you bring your own car. Showing patience, politeness and good humour *may* speed up the process.

If travelling overland to or from the Middle East, you can approach the region from Africa, the Caucasus, Iran or Europe.

For cross-border transport options for these entry points, please see p628.

Egypt

Sudan

The only border crossing between Egypt and Sudan is the ferry crossing between Aswan and Wadi Halfa. Before setting out, check the security situation in Sudan; many East African overlanders fly from Egypt to Addis Ababa in Ethiopia.

Libya

Egypt's only border crossing with Libya is at Amsaad, on the Mediterranean coast 12km west of Sallum. With the situation in Libya still in a state of flux at the time of writing, you should check the visa situation with the Libyan embassy in Cairo before setting out.

Iraq

Iran

Of the five major crossing points between Iraq and Iran, the only one that *may* be open to tourists is at the busy Iraqi border town of Haji Omaran, 180km northeast of Erbil. To cross here, you will need a prearranged Iranian visa. Check with the local authorities before travelling.

Turkey

Armenia

Turkey's border with Armenia has been closed for many years.

Bulgaria

There are three border crossings between Bulgaria and Turkey. The main border crossing is the busy Kapitan-Andreevo/Kapıkule, 18km west of Edirne on the E5. The closest town on the Bulgarian side is Svilengrad, some 10km from the border. This crossing is open 24 hours daily.

There's a second crossing at Lesovo-Hamzabeyli, some 25km north of Edirne; it's a quieter option during the busy summer months than Kapitan-Andreevo/Kapıkule, but takes a little longer to get to and there's no public transport.

The third crossing is at Malko Tărnovo-Kırıkkale, some 70km northeast of Edirne and 92km south of Burgas.

Georgia

The main border crossing is at Sarp on the Black Sea coast, between Hopa (Turkey) and Batum (Georgia). You can also cross inland at the Türkgözü border crossing near Posof, north of Kars (Turkey) and southwest of Akhaltsikhe (Georgia). The Sarp border crossing is open 24 hours a day; Türkgözü is open from 8am to 8pm, although in winter you might want to double check that it's open at all.

MIDDLE EAST BORDER CROSSINGS AT A GLANCE

TO/FROM	FROM/TO	BORDER CROSSINGS	FURTHER INFORMATION
Egypt	Israel & the Palestinian Territories	Taba	p152 and p274
Egypt	Jordan	Connected by ferry. Entry points at Nuweiba and Aqaba.	p152 and p340
Jordan	Israel & the Palestinian Territories	Crossings at: King Hussein Bridge/ Allenby Bridge (close to Jerusalem) Jordan River Bridge/Sheikh Hussein Bridge (close to Beit She'an/Irbid) Wadi Arabia/Yitzhak Rabin (close to Eilat/Aqaba).	p335 and p274
Jordan	Iraq	Karama/Tarbil crossing, 330km east of Amman. Not recommended.	p339
Jordan	Syria	Fastest of two crossings is at Ramtha/Deraa.	p335 and p450
Syria	Lebanon	Of four main crossings, the two main ones are the Beirut-Damascus Highway and the Tripoli-Tartus coastal road.	p450 and p395
Syria	Iraq	Only open crossing is south of Al-Bukamal in eastern Syria. Not recommended.	p450
Syria	Turkey	Most popular crossing is Bab al-Hawa between Antakya and Aleppo.	p451 and p543
Turkey	Iraq	Zakho	p543 and p182

Greece

The most popular ways of getting to Turkey from Europe are to make your way to Alexandroupolis in Greece and cross at Kipi–İpsala, 43km northeast of Alexandroupolis, or Kastanies–Pazarkule, 139km northeast, near the Turkish city of Edirne. Both borders are open 24 hours.

Iran

There are two border crossings between Iran and Turkey: the busier Gürbulak–Bazargan, near Doğubayazıt (Turkey) and Şahabat (Iran); and the Esendere–Sero border crossing, southeast of Van (Turkey). Gürbulak–Bazargan is open 24 hours and the crossing might take up to an hour. Esendere–Sero is open from 8am until midnight, but might be closed in winter. This second crossing has the added bonus of taking you through the breathtaking scenery of far southeastern Anatolia.

Activities

Best Desert Safaris
Location Wadi Rum
Country Jordan
Season October–May

Best Diving & Snorkelling
Location Red Sea
Country Egypt and Jordan
Season Year-round

Best Hiking
Location Dana Biosphere Reserve
Country Jordan
Season March–May and September–November

Best Sailing
Location Felucca ride, Aswan to Luxor
Country Egypt
Season Year-round

Best Snow Skiing
Location The Cedars
Country Lebanon
Season December–April

Best Sea Kayaking
Location Kaş
Country Turkey
Season May–September

Planning Your Trip

When to Go?

The Middle East is an excellent year-round activities destination, although some activities will require planning to make sure you're here at the right time. From June to September, and especially in July and August, desert expeditions in the Sahara and Wadi Rum may be too hot for comfort (and may even be impossible), while snow skiing also won't be possible; December to March is the best period for skiing. On the other hand, summer is the ideal time to enjoy diving, snorkelling and other water sports. Most non-snow-related activities are best enjoyed from September to November and March to May.

What to Take?

There are few requirements for most activities and those operators who organise activities (such as diving and snorkelling) will provide the necessary equipment. Bicycles and mountain bikes can be rented in the Middle East, but serious cyclists and bikers may want to bring their own bicycles. Most hikers head out onto the trail under their own steam, but even those who plan on joining an organised hike in the region with a guide will usually need to bring their own equipment.

PERSONAL EQUIPMENT CHECKLIST

- ☐ Sturdy hiking boots
- ☐ A high-quality sleeping bag – any time from October through to March can see overnight temperatures plummet in desert areas
- ☐ Warm clothing, including a jacket, jumper (sweater) or anorak (windbreaker) that can be added or removed
- ☐ A sturdy but lightweight tent
- ☐ Mosquito repellent
- ☐ A lightweight stove
- ☐ Trousers for walking, preferably made from breathable waterproof (and windproof) material such as Gore-Tex
- ☐ An air-filled sleeping pad
- ☐ Swiss Army knife
- ☐ Torch (flashlight) or headlamp, with extra batteries

Getting Active

From deep-desert safaris in the Sahara to snow-skiing in Lebanon, from hiking the high valleys of central Jordan to diving and snorkelling beneath the surface of the Red Sea, there aren't too many activities that you *can't* do in the Middle East.

For more details, see the Activities sections in each country's Directory.

Cycling & Mountain Biking

The Middle East offers some fantastic, if largely undeveloped, opportunities for cyclists. Unlike in Europe, you're likely to have many of the trails to yourself. However, the heat can be a killer (avoid June to September) and you'll need to be pretty self-sufficient, as spare parts can be extremely scarce. One of the highlights of travelling in this way is that locals in more out-of-the-way places will wonder what on earth you're doing – an ideal way to break the ice and meet new friends.

For information about cycling and mountain biking in **Lebanon**, turn to p392, while for general advice on cycling around the Middle East, see p630.

Desert Safaris

An expedition into the deserts of the Middle East will rank among your most memorable experiences of the region – the solitude, the gravitas of an empty landscape, the interplay of light and shadow on the sands. Various kinds of desert expeditions are possible, although they represent very different experiences. Camel trekking is environmentally friendly and slows you down to the pace of the deserts' traditional Bedouin inhabitants, but you'll be restricted to a fairly small corner of the desert. Travelling by 4WD allows you to cover greater distances but is usually more expensive.

Wadi Rum (p322) in Jordan has many calling cards: the orange sand, the improbable rocky mountains, the soulful Bedouin inhabitants who are the ideal companions around a desert campfire, and the haunting echoes of TE Lawrence. When you add to this the ease of getting here and exploring – it's accessible from major travel routes and is compact enough to visit within short time frames – and the professional operators that run expeditions here, it's hardly surprising that Wadi Rum is the desert experience that travellers to the Middle East love most. Everything is possible here, from afternoon camel treks to 4WD safaris and hikes lasting several days.

Other deserts where expeditions are possible include the **Sinai Peninsula**, Egypt (p141), for overnight, two- or three-day camel treks; the **Western Oases**, Egypt, for 4WD safaris into the Sahara from **Bahariya Oasis** (p118) and **Siwa Oasis** (p119); and the **Dead Sea**, Israel (p242), to explore the wild wadis and untamed mountains around the southern end of the Dead Sea.

Diving & Snorkelling

The **Red Sea** is one of the world's premier diving sites. Snorkellers heading out for the first time will be blown away by this dazzling underwater world of colourful coral and fish life, extensive reef systems and the occasional shipwreck. For experienced divers, there are plenty of sites to escape the wide-eyed newbies and see underwater landscapes that are both challenging and exceptionally beautiful.

Most dive centres offer every possible kind of dive course. The average open-water certification course for beginners, either with CMAS, PADI or NAUI, takes about five days and usually includes several dives. The total cost starts from around US$300; prices depend on the operator and location. A day's diving (two dives), including equipment and air fills, costs US$70 to US$125. An introductory dive is around US$75. Full equipment can be hired for about US$25 per day. Essential reading for anyone planning on taking a course is the boxed text on p136.

For our pick of the best dive sites in the Red Sea, see the boxed text, p130. Snorkelling and scuba diving is also possible at many points along Turkey's Mediterranean coast, although what's on offer doesn't come close to the Red Sea.

The following are the best bases for diving and snorkelling: **Sharm el-Sheikh** (p130), **Dahab** (p132), **Nuweiba** (p141) or **Marsa Alam** in Egypt (p127); **Aqaba** in Jordan (p324); or **Eilat** in Israel (p245).

Hiking

Israel & the Palestinian Territories

Israel in particular has some fabulous trekking possibilities, many of them in the **Upper Galilee** and **Golan** regions. For more information, see p267. In the Negev Desert, two spots stand out: the **Makhtesh Ramon** (p244), which is the Middle East's largest crater, and **Ein Avdat National Park** (p243), where you can trek through canyons and pools.

Jordan

Jordan is perhaps the Middle East's premier trekking destination, most notably in the spectacular landscapes of **Wadi Rum** (p322), **Dana Biosphere Reserve** (p311), **Wadi Mujib** (p301) and **Petra** (p313).

Lebanon & Turkey

In Lebanon, the **Qadisha Valley** offers the pick of the hiking possibilities (see the boxed text, p368).

In Turkey, some fine trails pass through the **Kaçkar Mountains**, the **Taurus Mountains** (near Niğde), the mountains of **Lycia** and **Cappadocia**, and **Mt Ararat** (5137m) near Doğubayazıt.

Horse Riding

The rocky trails of the Middle East lend themselves to exploration by horseback. There aren't many operators out here, least of all ones whom we recommend, but it is possible to visit some of the region's iconic attractions in this way, including the **West Bank tombs**, Luxor, Egypt (p98); the **Pyramids of Giza**, Cairo, Egypt (p66); and **Cappadocia**, Turkey (p514).

Sailing & Boat Trips

From the Nile to the Mediterranean, cruising the waters is a wonderfully laid-back way to travel.

Egypt

Drifting down the **Nile** aboard a felucca (traditional sailing boat) is one of the quintessential Middle Eastern experiences. Although trips are possible elsewhere, most take place between Aswan and Luxor and possibilities range from day trips to five-day expeditions with stops at some lesser-visited

OTHER ACTIVITIES

- **Archaeological digs: Israel** For details on archaeological digs that welcome paying volunteers, try the Biblical Archaeology Society (http://digs.bib-arch.org/digs), the Hebrew University of Jerusalem (http://archaeology.huji.ac.il/news/excavations.asp) and the Israeli Foreign Ministry (www.mfa.gov.il, search for 'Archaeological Excavations').
- **Caving: Lebanon** (p392)
- **Hot-air ballooning: Cappadocia, Turkey** (see the boxed text, p515) and **Luxor, Egypt** (p95)
- **Tandem paragliding or parasailing: Turkey** (p500)

riverside temples en route. For more information, see the boxed text on p112. Cairo is also possible for sunset trips (p61).

Turkey

With its whitewashed villages, idyllic ports and mountainous backdrop, Turkey's Mediterranean and Aegean coasts are ideal for yacht cruising, especially given its proximity to the Greek islands.

The most romantic option is to sail along the coast in a gület (traditional wooden yacht). The most popular excursion is a four-day, three-night trip from **Fethiye to Kale** (see the boxed text, p499). Other possibilities include everything from day trips to two-week luxury charters and you can hire crewless bareboats or flotilla boats, or take a cabin on a boat hired by an agency. Ask anywhere near the docks for details; the following towns have the largest number of options: **Kuşadası** (p489), **Bodrum** (p493), **Fethiye** (p498) and **Marmaris** (p496).

Skiing

'Snow sports in the Middle East' probably sounds like it belongs in the tall-tales-told-to-gullible-travellers category, but not if you're Lebanese. In the 1970s, Beirut was famous for the fact that you could swim in the Mediterranean waters of the Lebanese capital in the morning, then ski on the slopes of Jebel Makmel, northeast of Beirut, in the afternoon. No sooner had the guns of civil war fallen silent than the Lebanese once again reclaimed the slopes from the militias, and their infectious optimism has seen the ski resorts going from strength to strength.

For information on skiing in **Lebanon**, turn to p369.

Water Sports

Any Red Sea resort worth its salt – from the expensive package tour resorts of Sharm el-Sheikh (Egypt) to the chilled, backpacker-friendly Dahab (Egypt) – will let you indulge your passion for water sports from windsurfing to waterskiing.

In addition to the following, many of Turkey's Mediterranean beach resorts offer ample opportunities for waterskiing and windsurfing. **Eilat** (p249), in Israel, is arguably the Middle East's water-sports capital with waterskiing, parasailing and a host of other water-borne thrills on offer. Moon Beach is the region's best windsurfing spot at **Sharm el-Sheikh** (p128) in Egypt. **Hurghada** (p123) in Egypt is good for kitesurfing. **Aqaba** (p324) in Jordan offers a good range of sports, and **Beirut** and **Jounieh** (p392) in Lebanon have plenty of possibilities. For sea kayaking try **Kaş** (p502) in Turkey.

Travel with Children

Best Regions for Kids

Turkey

For the most part, travelling in Turkey is no different than anywhere else in Europe. The beach resorts of the Aegean and Mediterranean probably hold the greatest appeal, but don't forget the fairy-chimney landscape of Cappadocia. Public transport and road infrastructure is generally excellent, although distances between destinations can be long.

Jordan & Israel

Israel has terrific beaches, while Jordan boasts fabulous castles, camel trekking and the chance to float in the Dead Sea. An additional plus to travelling in these two compact countries is the short distances to get anywhere, while standards of food hygiene are relatively high.

Egypt

Despite large distances, train rides and sailing boats down the Nile go some way towards compensating. Throw in beaches, Red Sea snorkelling and *Tintin & the Pharaohs* come to life, and kids could easily fall in love with the country. For making even Cairo bearable with kids, see the boxed text, p61.

We have a simple message for those of you considering travelling with your children to the Middle East: go for it. If you don't believe us, look around – you won't see many families of travellers, but the ones you do see will probably be having a pretty good time.

The advantages of travelling with your kids are many. Not least among these, most people you'll meet in the region come from large extended families, love kids and will make sure that your children are made to feel welcome.

Middle East for Kids

Health & Safety

All travellers with children should know how to treat minor ailments and when to seek medical treatment. Make sure the children are up to date with routine vaccinations, and discuss possible travel vaccines well before departure as some vaccines are not suitable for children aged under one year.

On the all-important question of security, there are plenty of places in the Middle East that are extremely safe and any place that's safe for you to visit will generally be safe for your children.

Public transport is rarely easy with children: car sickness is a problem, they'll usually end up on your lap, functional seat belts are rare, even in taxis, and accidents are common.

For information on travelling safely in the region, see p616, while for general health advice see p638.

Eating Out

With the possible exception of Turkey, it's common for locals to eat out as a family. As a result, waiters are welcoming, or at least accepting of children. Best of all, the region's cuisine is generally child-friendly, being simple and varied, although you should always make sure the meat is well cooked. On the downside, Middle Eastern ice creams may be too much of a risk for tender young stomachs and, although some places have high chairs, they're in the minority. Kids' menus are rare except in Western-style hotel restaurants.

Beach Holidays

The beaches of the Middle East are ideal for families and factoring in some beach time to go with the region's more adult attractions can be an extremely wise move. The safest and most easily accessible place to begin is Turkey's Mediterranean coast, while Egypt, Jordan and Israel all have excellent beaches, many of which have a range of activities on offer, from boat rides to diving and snorkelling.

Cultures

Unlike any vaguely news-savvy adult, most children have yet to have their perceptions of the Middle East distorted by stereotypes. Discovering for themselves just how friendly the people of the Middle East can be is a lesson that will last a lifetime. More than that, your own chances of meeting locals (especially local families) is greatly enhanced if you're travelling as a family.

Children's Highlights

Temples & Castles

» Temple of Karnak – sound-and-light show that's a great alternative to history books.

» Petra – If they've seen *Indiana Jones,* watch them go wide-eyed with recognition.

» Crac des Chevaliers and Karak – castles filled with legends of knights and damsels in distress.

» Cappadocia – A fairy-tale landscape made for a child's fertile imagination.

Cities

» Jerusalem – child-friendly activities; brings Sunday school lessons to life.

» Aleppo – labyrinthine souqs evoking Ali Baba and Aladdin.

» İstanbul – make geography interesting by visiting two continents in one day.

Beaches & Activities

» Snorkelling the Red Sea – a whole new world to make *Nemo* look tame.

» Spending time on Turkey's beaches – gentle waters and family-friendly facilities.

» Sailing a felucca up the Nile from Aswan to Luxor – an unforgettable journey.

» Floating in the Dead Sea – yes, even Dad floats!

» Riding a camel through Wadi Rum – be Lawrence of Arabia for a day.

» Horse riding at the Pyramids – an original way to experience an iconic site.

Planning

What to Bring

Disposable nappies, powdered milk, formula and bottled water are widely available throughout the region in most large supermarkets; stock up in larger towns as some items won't be available elsewhere.

If you'll be travelling by taxi or minibus, you may consider bringing a child's seat-belt adjuster and/or a car seat; very few vehicles have the latter.

Other useful items to bring include child-friendly insect repellent and a blanket to spread out to use as a makeshift nappy-changing area.

When to Go

The best times to visit the Middle East are in autumn (September to November) or spring (March to May). Travel is certainly possible at other times, but winter (December to February) can be bitterly cold in the evenings and rain can be frequent. And unless you'll be spending all of your time in the water, avoid travel in the summer (especially in July and August) as the extreme heat can be quite uncomfortable and energy sapping.

Accommodation

Your chances of finding what you need (such as cots) increase the more you're willing to pay. And you'll almost certainly want something with a private bathroom and hot water, thereby precluding most budget accommodation. Hygiene standards at many budget establishments can also be poor.

Children under two usually stay for free in most hotels. There's usually a supplementary charge for squeezing in extra beds. Large family rooms or adjoining rooms with connecting doors are occasionally available.

regions at a glance

Every country in the region promises stirring historical landmarks – Egypt's date back to the Pharaohs, in Iraq it's Assyrians and Babylonians, Jordan boasts Nabataean Petra, while elsewhere it's mostly Greeks, Romans and Phoenicians. A choice of spectacular landscapes could similarly determine your route through the region, with Turkey, Iraq, Jordan and Egypt the highlights. If Red Sea diving and snorkelling appeal, it has to be Egypt (and, to a lesser extent, Jordan and Israel), while camel trekking is possible in both Jordan and Egypt. Turkey has the most beautiful beaches, while travellers for whom food is the main event will want to spend most of their time in Turkey, Syria – when tensions ease – and Lebanon.

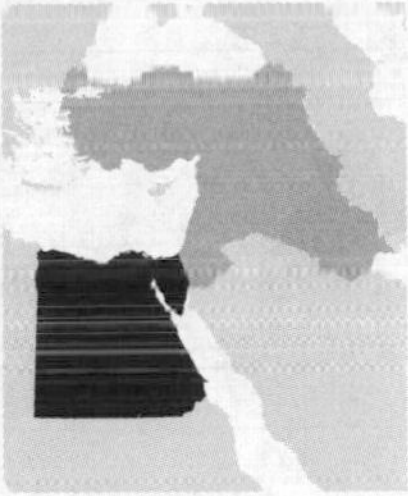

Egypt

Ruins ✓✓✓
Diving ✓✓✓
Landscapes ✓✓✓

Pharaohs
Few civilisations left an enduringly rich legacy quite like ancient Egypt. From the Pyramids of Giza in the north to Abu Simbel in the far south, the country's Nile Valley is an open-air museum to Egypt's glorious past.

Under the Red Sea
The waters off Egypt's Red Sea coast rank among the premier diving and snorkelling destinations on earth. Colourful corals and extraordinarily diverse marine life, accessible from delightfully laid-back resorts, will have you staying far longer than planned.

River, Desert & Mountain
With the longest river on earth (the Nile), the largest desert (the Sahara) and the mountain where the Ten Commandments were first proclaimed (Mt Sinai), Egypt's landscapes have the quality of an epic.

p50

Iraq

Landscapes ✓✓✓
Novelty ✓✓✓
Urban Life ✓✓✓

Northern Mountains

The safest corner of Iraq to visit is also its most beautiful. The far northeast of Iraqi Kurdistan is a mountainous realm of singular beauty, with villages perched atop precipices and Gali Ali Beg, the 'Grand Canyon of the Middle East'.

Traveller Cachet

Tell your friends back home that you visited Iraq without a bodyguard and your reputation for bravery is assured. They don't need to know that Iraqi Kurdistan is so safe nowadays as to be almost mainstream Middle Eastern travel.

A Region Reborn

The cities of Iraqi Kurdistan have a joie de vivre that can only come after emerging from long, dark decades of war and dictatorship. Erbil and Sulaymaniyah in particular, with their lively public parks, are prime examples of 'The Other Iraq'.

p155

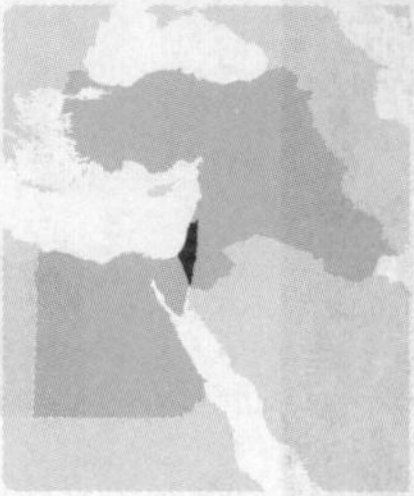

Israel & the Palestinian Territories

History ✓✓✓
Cities ✓✓✓
Activities ✓✓✓

Stones of Faith

The Bible, Torah and Quran come vividly to life here. Sacred ground to all three of the great monotheistic faiths, Israel and the Palestinian Territories are modern countries grafted onto a deeply spiritual land.

Old & New

Stunning Jerusalem is one of the holiest cities on earth, where seemingly every stone is at once contested and witness to ancient and modern history. Surprisingly close by, Tel Aviv is modern Israel writ large, the brash counterpoint to so much spirituality.

Diving & Hiking

Eilat is Israel's Red Sea foothold, with fabulous water sports to complement diving and snorkelling. On dry land, hiking is possible from the Golan Heights in the north to the Negev Desert in the south.

p184

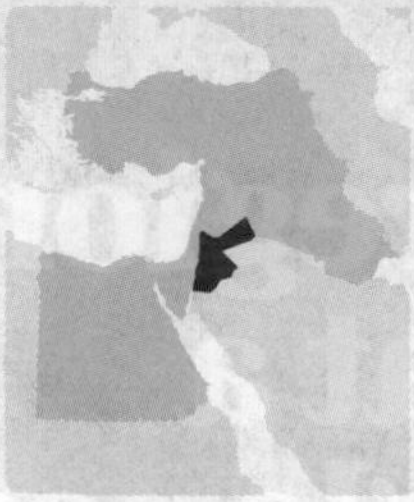

Jordan

Ruins ✓✓✓
Landscapes ✓✓✓
Activities ✓✓✓

Peerless Petra

Perhaps the Middle East's most extraordinary ancient city, Petra is unlike anywhere else on earth, a hidden world of rose-red tombs carved from the rock with astonishing delicacy. In the country's north, Jerash is an underrated Roman jewel, with abundant sites elsewhere.

Wadi Rum & Beyond

TE Lawrence, the Bedouin, red-walled canyons and the otherworldly rock formations of Wadi Rum add up to one of the Middle East's premier attractions. The Dead Sea and Dana Nature Reserve add depth and variety, if any were needed.

Diving & Desert Expeditions

Jordan's Red Sea coastline may be short, but it's an excellent gateway to the underwater landscapes for which the Red Sea is famed. Not far inland, camels and 4WDs take you out into the desert.

p277

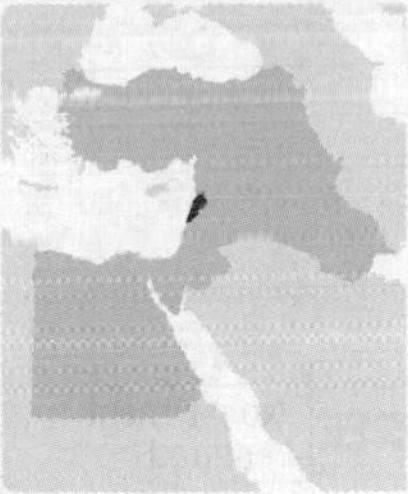

Lebanon

Ruins ✓✓✓
Landscapes ✓✓✓
Food ✓✓✓

Phoenicians & Romans

Tyre and Sidon in southern Lebanon gave birth to the seafaring Phoenicians, the first of the great Mediterranean civilisations, while Baalbek in Lebanon's Bekaa Valley has the Middle East's richest concentration of Roman temples.

Coast & Cedars

Lebanon may be tiny but its concentration of signature landscapes is without rival. Here, the rugged Mediterranean coast climbs steeply to snow-capped mountains strewn with ancient cedars.

Culinary Heaven

Think of all that's good about Middle Eastern cooking and you're probably thinking about Lebanon. Few countries can rival the sophistication of Lebanese cuisine, and Beirut's restaurants in particular offer the variety for which the region is rightly famed.

p343

Syria

Cities ✓✓✓
Ruins ✓✓✓
Food ✓✓✓

Damascus & Aleppo

Among the oldest continuously inhabited cities on earth, these two cities are soulful places. Damascus is a crossroad of cultures, home to storytellers, souqs and sublime mosques, while Aleppo's serpentine souq is the evocation of an Arabian fairy tale.

History's Canvas

Palmyra is one of the Middle East's most spectacular ancient cities, while Bosra and Apamea round out a splendid Roman heritage. And then there's the Crusader Crac des Chevaliers, intriguing Dead Cities and a village where the language of Jesus is still spoken.

The Middle East's Table

The Levantine obsession with food finds enticing expression throughout the country, but particularly in Damascus and Aleppo where the stars of the region's cuisine are celebrated daily.

p398

Turkey

Cities ✓✓✓
Beaches ✓✓✓
Ruins ✓✓✓

İstanbul

One of the most beautiful cities on earth, İstanbul spans two continents and many centuries, at once a modern touchstone of Turkish life and a gilded repository of historically significant palaces and mosques.

Natural Drama

Cappadocia is one of a kind, a breathtaking fusion of the human and natural worlds. Elsewhere, Turkey's coastline is one of the Mediterranean's prettiest, with quiet coves, beach resorts and numerous options for exploring the famously turquoise waters.

A Historical Journey

Roman Ephesus belongs to the elite of ancient Middle Eastern cities. Turkey also overflows with biblical signposts, while the solemn sculptures of Mt Nemrut live long in the memory of all who visit.

p453

❯ **Every listing is recommended by our authors, and their favourite places are listed first.**

❯ **Look out for these icons:**

TOP CHOICE Our author's top recommendation | A green or sustainable option | FREE No payment required

See the Index for a full list of destinations covered in this book.

On the Road

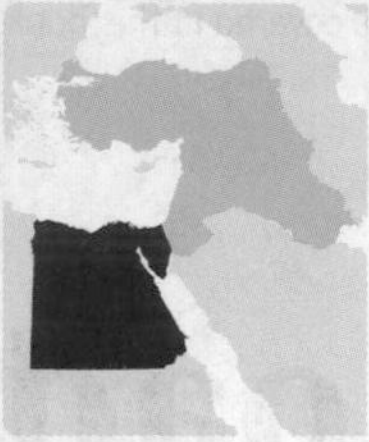

Egypt

Includes »

Best for Nature

» White Desert (p117)
» Ras Mohammed National Park (p128)
» Wadi Lahami Village (p128)
» Wilderness Ventures Egypt (p140)

Best for Culture

» Egyptian Museum (p55)
» Makan (p75)
» Bibliotheca Alexandrina (p83)
» Eskaleh (p114)

Why Go?

As Herodotus wrote in the 5th century BC, Egypt 'has more wonders in it than any other country in the world'. But the Pharaonic temples and pyramids that awed the Greek historian are just the beginning.

Egypt ruled the Islamic empire from Cairo, the City Victorious, where the medieval core is still a mesmerising warren. In desert monasteries, Egypt's native Christians, the Copts, preserve two-millennia-old rituals.

Out west, sand stretches to the Sahara, dotted with green oases and ghostly rock formations. To the east, the crystal waters of the Red Sea support a vivid frenzy of underwater life. On the Sinai peninsula, visitors can climb the mountain where God had words with Moses, and spend their remaining days at a beach camp Shangri-Las.

With cheap transport, beds and even cold beers, plus a borderline-overwhelming brand of hospitality, Egypt is the Middle East's most traveller-friendly country.

When to Go

Cairo

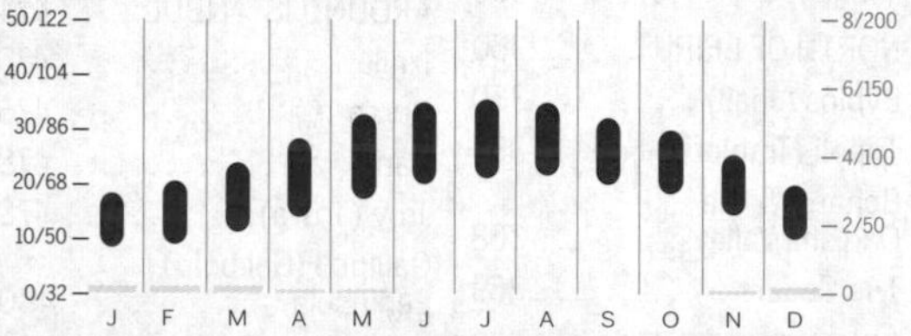

Dec–Feb Egypt's 'winter' high season is sunny and warm, with chilly nights.

Mar–May Spring brings occasional dust storms that can disrupt flight schedules.

Jun–Aug Scorching heat everywhere but the Mediterranean coast, which is balmy.

Connections

Egypt's borders are open to neighbouring countries: by bus to **Libya** and river ferry to **Sudan**, and, far more common, by bus to **Israel** (from Taba) and by ferry to Aqaba in **Jordan**. Both of these latter options are inexpensive and frequent. The border with **Gaza**, at Rafah, is technically open, but travellers can't carry on into Israel and must return to Egypt by the same border; delays and closures are common. By air, both Cairo and Alexandria receive numerous flights from neighbouring countries, with Alexandria often having cheaper fares.

ITINERARIES

One Week

If you only have a week, focus on **Cairo**'s attractions, such as the **Egyptian Museum** and the **Coptic Museum**, plus great coffeehouses, funky bars and live-music venues. Midweek, fly or take the train to **Luxor**, to admire the ancient ruins of Thebes. From there, you can hop a bus to Hurghada for the ferry to **Sharm el-Sheikh** in the Sinai – there are great snorkelling and diving options on either side of the Red Sea.

Two Weeks

In two weeks, you can cover Egypt's main sights. Head out from Cairo on the sleeper train to **Aswan**, where you can soak up Nubian culture. Sail back down the Nile to **Luxor** on a felucca. Train (or fly) back to Cairo, where you can spend two days seeing the **Pyramids of Giza**, the Egyptian Museum and the medieval souq of **Khan al-Khalili**. If you're continuing west towards Libya, stop in **Siwa Oasis** en route. If you're heading east, take a bus to the Sinai and hike up **Mt Sinai**, then spend a few days in **Dahab** to recharge. From here, it's easy to cross into Jordan and Israel.

Essential Food & Drink

» **Molokhiyya** A slippery, garlicky leafy green soup, served with rabbit.

» **Hamam mahshi** Roast pigeon stuffed with *fireek* (green wheat) and rice.

» **Kushari** A vegetarian's best friend: noodles, rice, black lentils, chickpeas and fried onions, with a tangy tomato sauce.

» **Fiteer** The Egyptian pizza, with a flaky pastry base and either sweet or savoury toppings.

» **Fuul** Slow-cooked fava beans, mashed more than in neighbouring countries.

» **Ta'amiya** What Cairenes call felafel, packed with herbs and shaped into flat patties.

AT A GLANCE

» **Currency** Egyptian pound (E£)

» **Mobile Phones** GSM phone network widespread

» **Money** ATMs are common

» **Visas** Available on arrival for many nationalities

Fast Facts

» **Capital** Cairo

» **Country code** ☎20

» **Language** Arabic

» **Official name** Arab Republic of Egypt

» **Population** 82 million

Exchange Rates

Australia	A$1	E£5.96
Euro Zone	€1	E£7.67
Israel	1NIS	E£1.58
Jordan	JD1	E£8.54
UK	£1	E£9.54
USA	US$1	E£6.05

For current exchange rates see www.xe.com.

Resources

» **Lonely Planet** (www.lonelyplanet.com/egypt) Destination info, hotel booking and forum

» **Egypt Tourism** (www.egypt.travel) Official tourism ministry site

» **Daily News Egypt** (www.thedailynewsegypt.com) Best English newspaper

» **Egypt Independent** (www.almasryalyoum.com/en) Respected online news

» **Theban Mapping Project** (www.thebanmappingproject.com) Archaeological database and news

Egypt Highlights

❶ Tip your head back and gape at the **Pyramids of Giza** (p60)

❷ Give your regards to Tutankhamun in the mazelike **Egyptian Museum** (p55)

❸ Explore ancient tombs and temples in the open-air museum that is **Luxor** (p90)

❹ Enjoy the ultimate 'away from it all' in western oases like **Siwa** (p119)

❺ Revel in the underwater wonderland that flourishes in **Ras Mohammed National Park** (p128)

❻ Thou shalt see the sun rise from **Mt Sinai** (p140)

❼ Marvel at Ramses II's colossal temple at far-flung **Abu Simbel** (p114)

❽ Watch the sun set over tranquil **Aswan**, the heart of Nubia (p107)

❾ Go Mediterranean in **Alexandria**, Egypt's cultural port city (p83)

❿ Kick back for a day or a month in **Dahab**, the ultimate beach hang-out (p132)

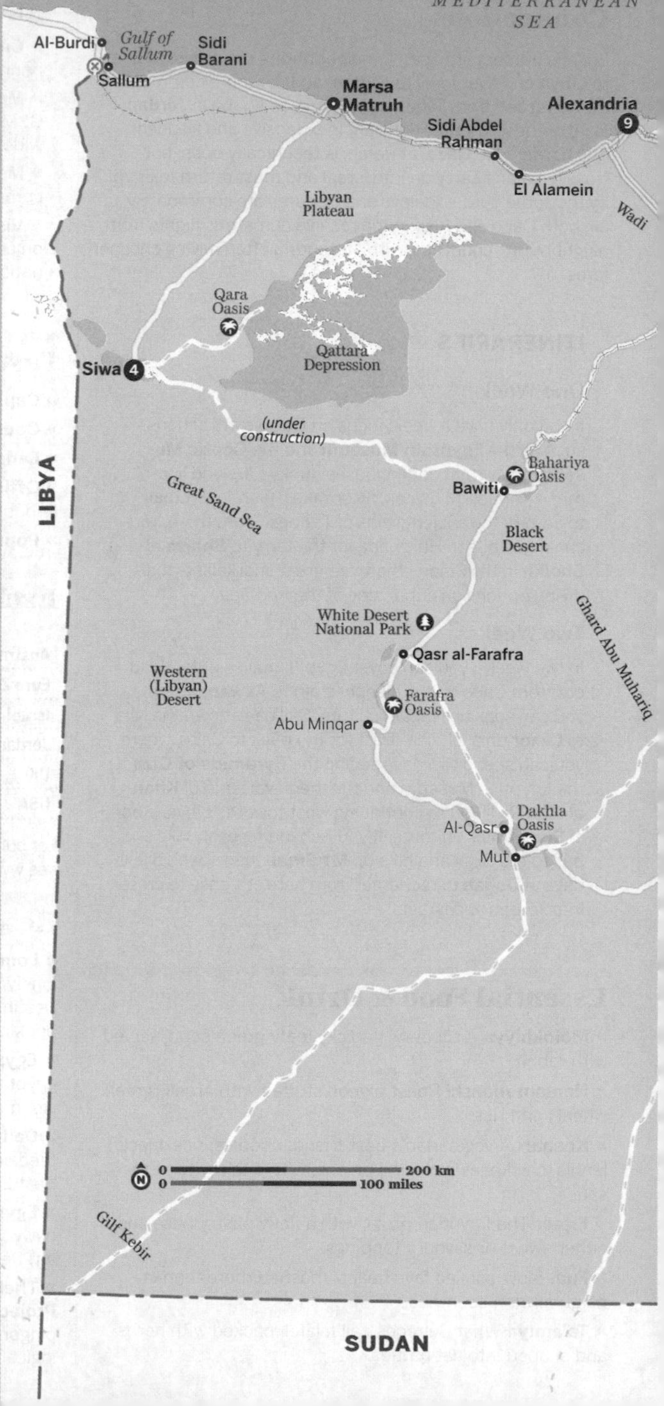

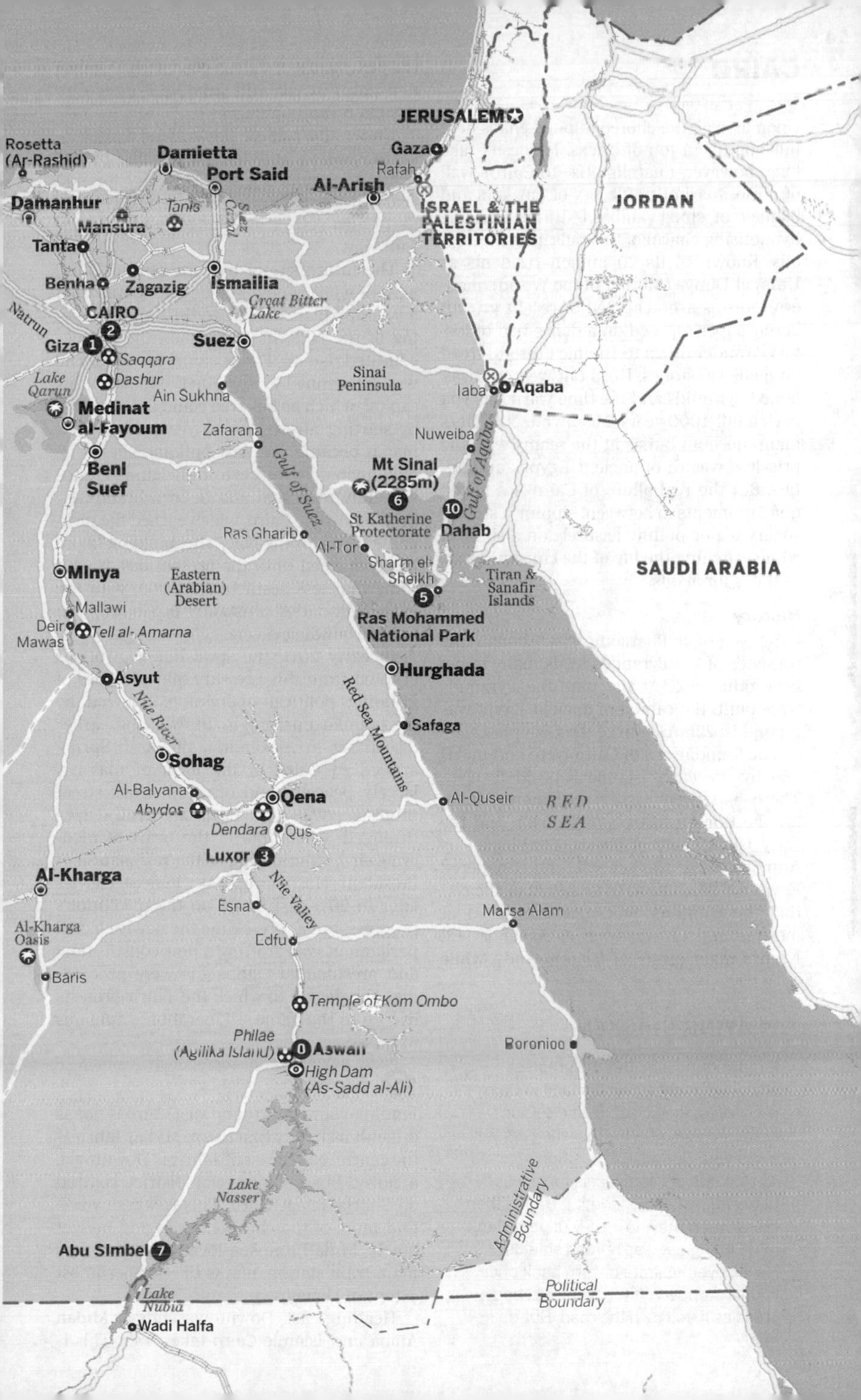
JERUSALEM
Gaza
Rafah
Al-Arish
ISRAEL & THE PALESTINIAN TERRITORIES
JORDAN
Rosetta (Ar-Rashid)
Damietta
Port Said
Damanhur
Tanis
Suez Canal
Mansura
Tanta
Zagazig
Ismailia
Benha
Great Bitter Lake
Natrun
CAIRO
2
Giza
1
Suez
Saqqara
Dashur
Lake Qarun
Ain Sukhna
Sinai Peninsula
Iaba
Aqaba
Medinat al-Fayoum
Zafarana
Nuweiba
Beni Suef
Gulf of Suez
Gulf of Aqaba
Mt Sinai (2285m)
6
10
St Katherine Protectorate
Dahab
Ras Gharib
Al-Tor
Sharm el-Sheikh
Minya
Eastern (Arabian) Desert
Tiran & Sanafir Islands
SAUDI ARABIA
5
Mallawi
Deir Mawas
Tell al-Amarna
Ras Mohammed National Park
Hurghada
Asyut
Nile River
Red Sea Mountains
Safaga
Sohag
Al-Balyana
Qena
Al-Quseir
RED SEA
Abydos
Dendara
Qus
Luxor
3
Al-Kharga
Nile Valley
Esna
Marsa Alam
Al-Kharga Oasis
Edfu
Baris
Temple of Kom Ombo
Philae (Agilika Island)
Aswan
High Dam (As-Sadd al-Ali)
Lake Nasser
Administrative Boundary
Abu Simbel
7
Political Boundary
Lake Nubia
Wadi Halfa

CAIRO القاهرة

☎02 / POP 20 MILLION

Upon arrival, the choreographed chaos here hits you like a ton of bricks. It doesn't take long, however, to acclimatise to Cairo's wall of noise, snarl of traffic, cry of hawkers and blanket of smog, and get drawn into the hypnotising charm of this pulsating metropolis. Known to its 20 million residents as Umm al-Dunya (Mother of the World), modern Cairo is a hotchpotch of recent growth barely superimposed on a dense bed of history. Wander down to Islamic Cairo to tread on medieval stones. Head out west to Giza's famed pyramids and the time warp sets you back a full 4000 years. Meanwhile, the city's main museum bursts at the seams with the priceless wealth of ancient Egypt's antiquities. But the real allure of Cairo lies in the quiet moments in between: sipping a strong, sugary tea or puffing leisurely on a sheesha while watching the life of the city whirl past as it has for aeons.

History

Cairo is not a Pharaonic city, though the presence of the Pyramids leads many to believe otherwise. At the time the Pyramids were built, the capital of ancient Egypt was Memphis, 22km south of the Giza plateau.

The foundations of Cairo were laid in AD 969 by the early Islamic Fatimid dynasty. There had been earlier settlements, notably the Roman fortress of Babylon and the early Islamic city of Fustat, established by Amr ibn al-As, the general who conquered Egypt for Islam in AD 642. Much of the city that the Fatimids built survives: the great mosque and university of Al-Azhar is still Egypt's main centre of Islamic study, while the great gates of Bab an-Nasr, Bab al-Futuh and Bab Zuweila still straddle Islamic Cairo's main thoroughfares.

Under the rule of subsequent dynasties, Cairo swelled and burst its walls, but at heart it remained a medieval city for 900 years. It wasn't until the mid-19th century that Cairo started to change in any significant way.

The future site of modern central Cairo, west of what is now Midan Opera, was then a swampy plain subject to the annual flooding of the Nile. In 1863, when the French-educated Ismail Pasha came to power, he was determined to upgrade the image of his capital, which he believed could only be done by starting afresh. For 10 years the former marsh became one vast building site as Ismail invited architects from Belgium, France and Italy to design and build a brand-new European-style Cairo, which earned the nickname 'Paris on the Nile'. This building boom has continued until the present day, if with somewhat less aesthetic cohesion, with the city's boundaries constantly expanding into the surrounding desert.

In early 2011, the sprawling metropolis erupted from this pressure, plus decades of grinding political oppression. Spurred by the popular uprising in Tunisia, and earlier discontent in Alexandria, the Arab Spring arrived in Cairo in the form of massive, largely peaceful and often hilarious street protests. For 18 days, Egyptians of all stripes thronged Midan Tahrir, the heart of modern Cairo, culminating in the resignation of President Hosni Mubarak. Violent clashes later in 2011 cast doubt on the revolution's progress, but at press time the newly elected parliament was drafting a new constitution, and presidential campaigns were proceeding. The degree to which the Tahrir protests live up to the name – 'Liberation' – remains to be seen.

PLAYING CHICKEN

It may sound silly, but the greatest challenge most travellers face in Cairo is crossing the street. Traffic seldom stops, so you have to trust the cars will avoid you. Our advice: position yourself so that one or more locals form a buffer between you and oncoming traffic, then cross when they do – they usually don't mind being used as human shields. Never, ever hesitate or turn back once you've stepped off the sidewalk, and cross as if you own the road. But do it fast!

Sights

Finding your way around vast Cairo is not as difficult as it may first seem. Midan Tahrir is the centre. Northeast of Tahrir is Downtown, a noisy, busy commercial district centred on Sharia Talaat Harb. This is where you'll find most of the cheap eateries and budget hotels. Midan Ramses, location of the city's main train station, marks the northernmost extent of Downtown.

Heading east, Downtown ends at Midan Ataba and Islamic Cairo takes over. This is

VISITING ISLAMIC CAIRO

» Dress modestly, with legs and shoulders covered. Wear sturdy shoes that are easily slipped off for entering mosques.

» Caretakers are usually around from 9am until early evening. Mosques are often closed to visitors during prayer times.

» Bring small change to tip caretakers at mosques for pointing out details or climbing a minaret. (See p148, for typical amounts.)

» With the exception of Sultan Hassan and Ar-Rifai, all mosques are free to enter, but some caretakers will try to sell you a ticket.

» Some caretakers have even claimed guidebooks aren't permitted in mosques, to prevent you from reading these very warnings.

» Closest metro stops are Ataba, about 1km away, and Bab al-Shaaria, 300m west of Bab al-Futuh. By taxi, ask for 'Al-Hussein', the name of the main square and mosque next to Khan al-Khalili.

the medieval heart of the city, and is still very much alive today. At its centre is the great bazaar of Khan al-Khalili.

Sitting in the middle of the Nile is the island neighbourhood of Zamalek, historically favoured by ruling elites and still a relatively upmarket enclave with many foreign residents, a few midrange hotels and plenty of restaurants and bars.

The west bank of the Nile is newer and more residential. The primary districts, north to south, are Mohandiseen, Agouza, Doqqi and Giza, all heavy on concrete and light on charm. The city stretches some 20km west either side of one long, straight road (Pyramids Rd, also known as Sharia al-Haram) that ends at the foot of the Pyramids.

DOWNTOWN

Midan Tahrir SQUARE

(Map p68) The world learned the name Midan Tahrir (Liberation Sq) in early 2011, when millions of Egyptians converged here in a peaceful revolution to oust then-president Hosni Mubarak. Visitors will likely make a beeline to this historic spot – on a regular day it's just your average giant traffic circle (albeit one where half-a-dozen major arteries converge), but it nonetheless resonates as the heart of the city.

Egyptian Museum MUSEUM

(Map p56; ☎2579 6948; www.egyptianmuseumcairo.org; Midan Tahrir, Downtown; adult/student E£60/30, royal mummy rooms adult/student E£100/50; ⏰9am-6pm Sat-Thu, 9am-4pm Fri) With one of the most significant collections of antiquities in the world crammed into one cavernous old building, the Egyptian Museum is not to be missed. With over 100,000 relics from almost every period of ancient Egyptian history, you'll need to pace yourself. A new Grand Museum of Egypt is allegedly under construction near the Giza Pyramids, though it is unlikely to be finished anytime soon. Until then, parts of this great but overflowing collection will have to be explored in their current location, poorly signed and stuffy as it is.

Last tickets are sold one hour before closing. Ideally visit around lunchtime to enjoy a break in the crowds. Guides cost E£60 per hour or so and congregate in the garden. You must check your cameras into the baggage room before entering the museum.

The museum occupies two storeys, with each room assigned a number, the same upstairs and down. The ground floor is arranged roughly chronologically, starting with the Old Kingdom in the centre atrium and progressing clockwise. Upstairs are special collections by theme – including jewellery, mummies and finds from particular tombs.

For highlights of the museum, see p57.

Townhouse Gallery GALLERY

(Map p68; ☎2576 8086; www.thetownhousegallery.com; 10 Sharia Nabrawy; ⏰10am-2pm & 6-9pm Sat-Wed, 6-9pm Fri) Set amid car-repair shops, Townhouse has launched many international Egyptian artists. Its workshop space, Rawabet, across the street, hosts performances.

COPTIC CAIRO

Once known as Babylon, this part of Cairo predates the coming of Islam and remains the seat of the Coptic Christian community. You can visit the **Coptic Museum** (Map p58; ☎2363 9742; Sharia Mar Girgis; adult/student E£50/25, audio guide E£10; ⏲9am-4pm), with its gorgeous mosaics, manuscripts, tapestries and Christian artwork, and the 9th-century **Hanging Church** (Al-Kineesa al-Mu'allaqa; Map p58; Sharia Mar Girgis; ⏲Coptic Mass 8-11am Wed & Fri, 9-11am Sun), suspended over Roman gates. Among the other churches and monasteries here, the **Church of St Sergius and Bacchus** (Abu Serga; Map p58; ⏲8am-4pm) is supposed to mark one of the resting places of the Holy Family on its flight from King

Egyptian Museum

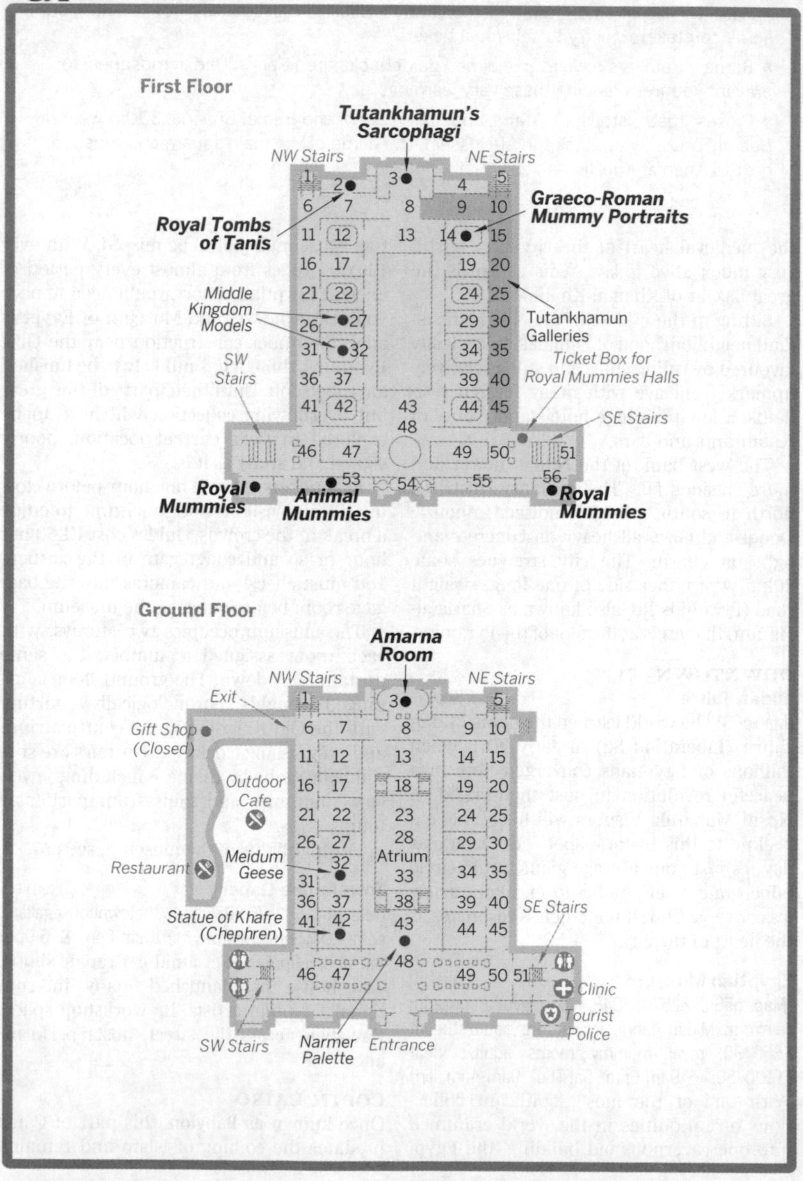

HIGHLIGHTS OF THE EGYPTIAN MUSEUM

The following are our favourite, must-see exhibits, for which you need at least half a day but preferably a little more.

Tutankhamun Galleries (1st fl, east side) Top on everyone's list, King Tut's treasures occupy a large chunk of the museum's upper floor. Go first to room 3 to see his sarcophagi while the crowds are light.

Old Kingdom Rooms (Ground fl, rooms 42, 37 & 32) After peeking at Tutankhamun, return to the ground floor for a chronological tour. Look out for the statue of well-muscled Khafre – you may also recognise him from the Sphinx.

Amarna Room (Ground fl, room 3) Stepping into this room feels like visiting another museum entirely – the artwork commissioned by Akhenaten for his new capital at Tell al-Amarna is dramatically different in style from his predecessors. Say hi to his wife, Nefertiti, while you're here.

Royal Tombs of Tanis (1st fl, room 2) While everyone else is gawking at Tutankhamun's treasure down the hall, this room of gem-encrusted gold jewellery, found at the largest ruined city in the Nile Delta, is often empty.

Graeco-Roman Mummy Portraits (1st fl, room 14) An odd interlude in mummy traditions, from very late in the ancient Egypt game, these wood-panel portraits were placed over the faces of embalmed dead, staring up in vividly realistic style.

Animal Mummies (1st fl, rooms 53 & 54) Tucked in an odd corner of the museum, this long, dim room contains the bundled remains of the ancients' beloved pets, honoured gods and even their last meals.

Middle Kingdom Models (1st fl, rooms 32 & 27) When you've had your fill of gold and other royal trappings, stop in these rooms to get a picture of common life in ancient Egypt, depicted in miniature dioramas made to accompany the pharaoh to the other world.

Royal Mummy Rooms (1st fl, rooms 56 & 46) Visit these around lunch or near closing time to avoid the crowds – they don't require more than half an hour, but they do put a human face on all the stunning objects you've seen. The ticket booth is on the east side of the museum, near room 56.

Herod. The **Ben Ezra Synagogue** (Map p58; admission free, donations welcome) also dates from the 9th century.

The easiest way to get here from Midan Tahrir is by metro (E£1) – get out at the Mar Girgis station.

ISLAMIC CAIRO

Despite the number of minarets on the skyline in this part of the city, 'Islamic' Cairo is not significantly more religious than other districts. But for many centuries, it was one of the power centres of the Islamic empire, and its monuments are some of the most resplendent architecture inspired by Islam.

Khan al-Khalili MARKET

(Map p72) The best place to start exploring is in the medieval cacophony of the great bazaar. Here, a maze of alleys meander their way past archaic gates, packed with shopkeepers selling everything from antiques and gaudy trinkets to pungent spices and everyday household wares. Bargaining is expected.

The bazaar is easy to find if you're walking from central Cairo: from Midan Ataba walk straight along Sharia al-Azhar under the elevated motorway, or along the parallel Sharia al-Muski, a lively market street.

Al-Azhar Mosque MOSQUE

(Gami' al-Azhar; Map p72; Sharia al-Azhar; ⌚24hr) One of Cairo's most historic institutions, founded in AD 970, and one of the world's oldest surviving universities. A lovely place to relax, along with Islamic students from all over the globe.

Mausoleum of Al-Ghouri MOSQUE, TOMB

(Map p72; Sharia al-Muizz li-Din Allah; adult/student E£25/15; ⌚9am-5pm) On the south side of Sharia al-Azhar, opposite the khan, two buildings loom over Sharia al-Mu'izz, both built by Qansuh al-Ghouri – the penultimate Mamluk sultan, who ruled for 16 years before being

Cairo

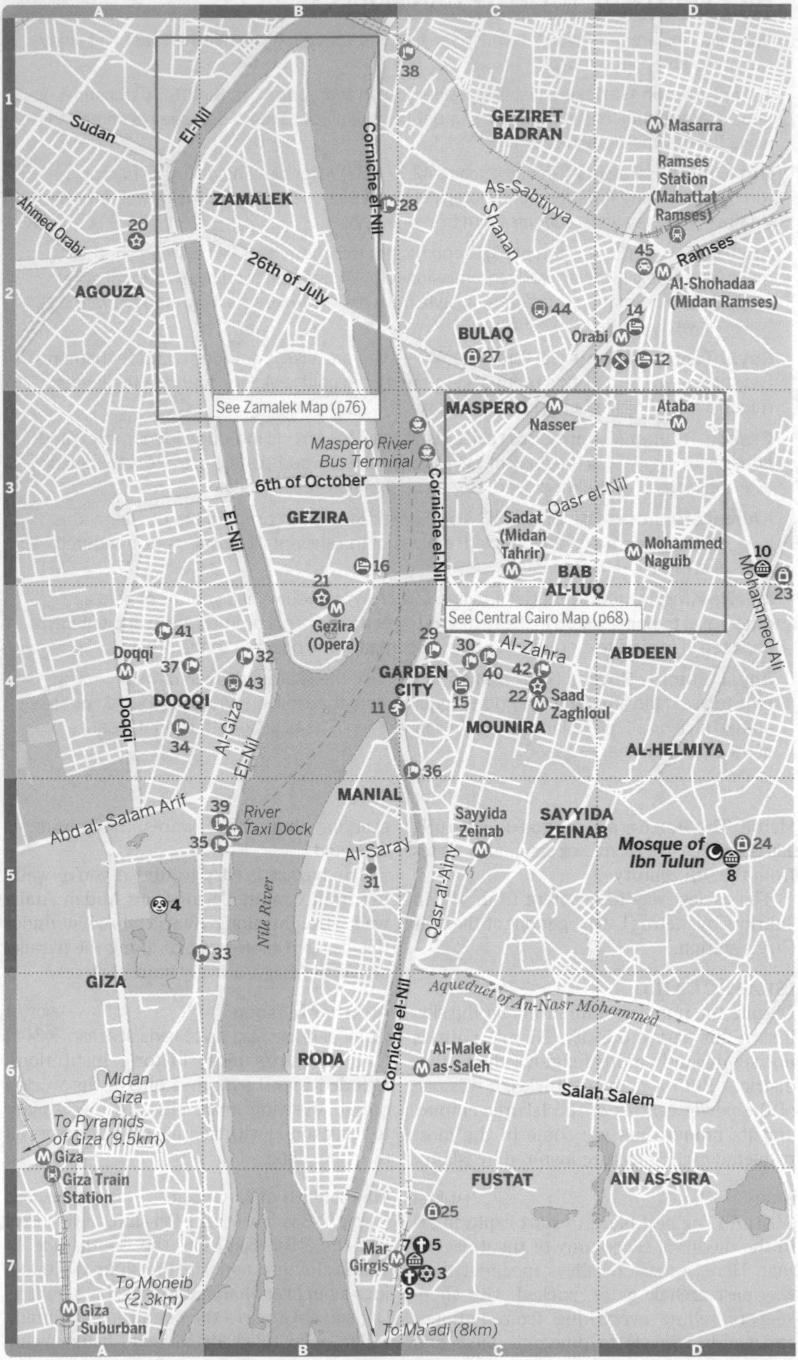
Sudan
El-Nil
Corniche el-Nil
GEZIRET BADRAN
Masarra
Ramses Station (Mahattat Ramses)
As-Sabtiyya
Shanan
Ahmed Orabi
ZAMALEK
26th of July
AGOUZA
Ramses
Al-Shohadaa (Midan Ramses)
BULAQ
Orabi
See Zamalek Map (p76)
MASPERO
Nasser
Ataba
Maspero River Bus Terminal
6th of October
GEZIRA
Qasr el-Nil
Sadat (Midan Tahrir)
Mohammed Naguib
BAB AL-LUQ
See Central Cairo Map (p68)
Mohammed Ali
Gezira (Opera)
Doqqi
DOQQI
GARDEN CITY
Al-Zahra
ABDEEN
Saad Zaghloul
MOUNIRA
Al-Giza
AL-HELMIYA
MANIAL
Abd al-Salam Arif
River Taxi Dock
Sayyida Zeinab
SAYYIDA ZEINAB
Mosque of Ibn Tulun
Al-Saray
Qasr al-Ainy
Nile River
GIZA
Aqueduct of An-Nasr Mohammed
RODA
Al-Malek as-Saleh
Midan Giza
Salah Salem
To Pyramids of Giza (9.5km)
Giza
Giza Train Station
FUSTAT
AIN AS-SIRA
Mar Girgis
To Moneib (2.3km)
Giza Suburban
To Ma'adi (8km)

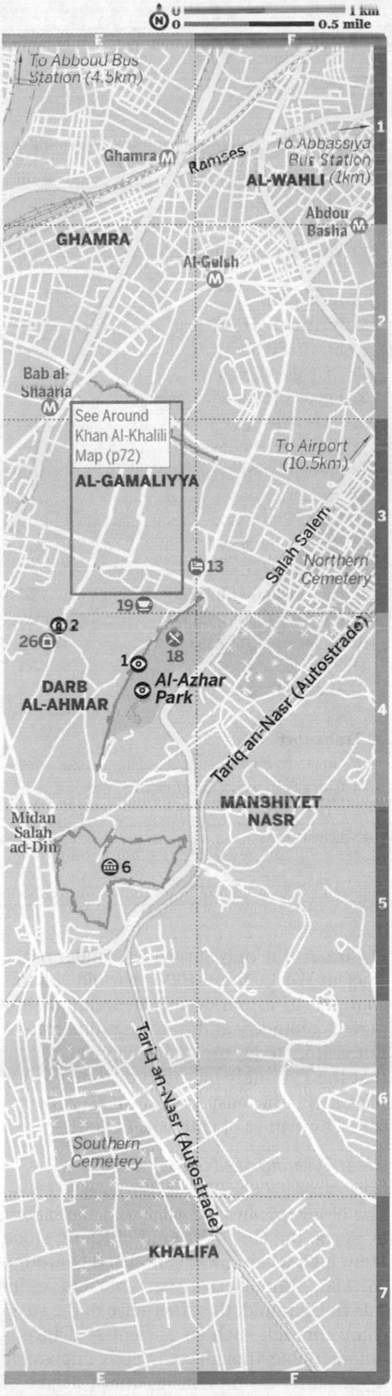

betrayed and beheaded. His mausoleum, on the east side of the street, holds his successor. To the west is his **mosque** (Map p72) with a red-chequered minaret.

The mausoleum hosts live music on Sundays at 9pm. This is not to be confused with the Sufi dance show (see p75) about 100m east along the street at the **Wikala of Al-Ghouri** (Map p72; adult/student E£20/10; ⌚9am-8pm Sat-Thu), another of the doomed sultan's legacies and more interesting to see at night for free.

Bab Zuweila GATE

(Map p58; adult/student E£15/8; ⌚8.30am-5pm) The only remaining southern gate of medieval Al-Qahira, Bab Zuweila offers a great view from its ramparts and attached minarets. There's also a nice small exhibit about the gate's history.

Museum of Islamic Art MUSEUM

(Map p58; ☎2390 1520; Sharia Bur Said; admission E£50; ⌚9am-5pm Sat-Thu, 9am-noon & 2-5pm Fri) Recently renovated, this museum on the edge of the medieval city holds one of the world's finest collections of Islamic applied art. English signage is somewhat limited, but the selected frescos, tiles, carpets and more speak for themselves. The museum is 500m due west from Bab Zuweila.

Al-Azhar Park PARK

(Map p58; ☎2510 7338; www.alazharpark.com; Sharia Salah Salem, admission Mon-Wed/Thu-Sun E£5/7; ⌚10am-10pm) Converted from a mountain of garbage, this green space is now the only park in Cairo of any size. It's most fun on weekends, when families make a day out with picnics. There's an entrance on the downhill side at **Bab al-Mahruq** (Map p58; ⌚10am-6pm), in the Darb al-Ahmar district. Otherwise, you'll need to take a microbus from Midan Opera, or a taxi.

Mosque of Ibn Tulun MOSQUE

(Map p58; Sharia al-Saliba; ⌚8am-4pm) One of Cairo's oldest mosques, and one of its largest, this 9th-century construction is quite unlike any other in the city, mainly because the inspiration is almost entirely Iraqi. The closest things to it are the ancient mosques of Samarra. While you're here, pop in to the **Gayer-Anderson Museum** (Beit al-Kritliyya; Map p58; Sharia ibn Tulun; adult/student E£35/20, video E£20; ⌚9am-4pm), two 16th-century houses restored and furnished by a British major between 1935 and 1942.

Cairo

Top Sights

	Al-Azhar Park	E4
	Mosque of Ibn Tulun	D5

Sights

1	Bab al-Mahruq	E4
2	Bab Zuweila	E4
3	Ben Ezra Synagogue	C7
4	Cairo Zoo	A5
5	Church of St Sergius & Bacchus	C7
6	Citadel	E5
7	Coptic Museum	C7
8	Gayer-Anderson Museum	D5
9	Hanging Church	C7
10	Museum of Islamic Art	D3

Activities, Courses & Tours

11	Dok Dok Landing Stage	B4

Sleeping

12	African House Hostel	D2
13	Arabian Nights	F3
14	Capsis Palace	D2
15	Hotel Juliana	C4
16	Novotel Cairo El Borg	B3

Eating

17	At-Tabei ad-Dumyati	D2
18	Citadel View	E4

Drinking

19	Coffeeshop Al-Khatoun	E3

Entertainment

20	Cairo Jazz Club	A2
21	Cairo Opera House	B4
22	Makan	C4

Shopping

23	Abd ar-Rahman Harraz	D3
24	Khan Misr Touloun	D5
25	Souq al-Fustat	C7
26	Tentmakers Bazaar	E4
27	Wikalat al-Balah	C2

Information

28	Australian Embassy	B2
29	British Embassy	C4
30	Canadian Embassy	C4
31	Egyptian Student Travel Services	B5
32	Ethiopian Embassy	B4
33	French Embassy	A5
34	Iranian Embassy	A4
35	Israeli Embassy	B5
36	Italian Embassy	C4
37	Jordanian Embassy	A4
38	New Zealand Embassy	C1
39	Saudi Arabian Embassy	B5
40	Sudanese Embassy	C4
41	Syrian Embassy	A4
42	Turkish Embassy	C4

Transport

43	Buses to Israel	B4
44	Cairo Gateway (Turgoman Garage)	C2
45	Ulali buses	D2

Citadel FORTRESS

(Al-Qala'a; Map p58; ☎2512 1735; Sharia Salah Salem; adult/student E£50/25; ⊙8am-4pm, mosques closed during Fri prayers) Commenced by Saladin (Salah ad-Din al-Ayyoub) back in the 12th century, the Citadel is one of the city's busiest tourist attractions – but we're not quite sure why. Its walls encircle an assortment of three very different and not terribly impressive mosques, and several palaces housing some fairly indifferent museums. The best part of any visit is marvelling at the view from the two terraces; on a clear day you can see all the way to the Pyramids of Giza.

GIZA

Pyramids of Giza ARCHAEOLOGICAL SITE

(Map p64; adult/student E£60/30; ⊙8am-4pm) Few superlatives do justice to the Pyramids of Giza. As the only surviving Wonder of the Ancient World, these 4000-year-old goliaths continue to astound with their impossibly perfect geometry and towering dimensions. But visitors today are often surprised to find that the Pyramids mushroom from a sandy plateau in the busy suburb of Giza, garrisoned by armies of enthusiastic touts.

Great Pyramid of Khufu (Cheops)

(adult/student E£100/50; ⊙8am-noon & 1-6pm) The oldest pyramid at Giza and the largest in Egypt, the Great Pyramid of Khufu stood 146m high when it was completed in around 2570 BC. Although there isn't much to see inside the pyramid, the experience of the steep climb through such an ancient structure is unforgettable, though completely impossible if you suffer from even the tiniest degree of claustrophobia. Cameras are not allowed into the pyramid; guards at the entrance will keep them for E£2 or so baksheesh.

Cheops Boat Museum
(adult/student E£50/25; 9am-4pm Oct-May, 9am-5pm Jun-Sep) Along the eastern and southern sides of the Great Pyramid are five long pits that once contained the pharaoh's funerary barques. One of these ancient wooden vessels, possibly the oldest boat in existence, was unearthed in 1954. It was restored and housed in a glass museum – well worth a look.

Pyramid of Khafre (Chephren)
(adult/student E£30/15; 8am-4pm, when open to visitors) Southwest of the Great Pyramid, and with almost the same dimensions, is the Pyramid of Khafre. At first it seems larger than that of Khufu, his father, because it stands on higher ground and its peak still has part of the original limestone casing that once covered the entire structure. This pyramid features the substantial remains of **Khafre's funerary temple**, located outside to the east.

Pyramid of Menkaure (Mycerinus)
(adult/student E£30/15; 8am-4pm, when open to visitors) At a height of 62m (originally 66.5m), this is the smallest of the three Pyramids. The gash in the exterior was made by a 12th-century caliph who wanted to demolish all the Pyramids, though he gave up after eight months, still far from his goal.

Sphinx
Known in Arabic as Abu al-Hol (Father of Terror), the Sphinx is carved almost entirely from one huge piece of limestone. The Sphinx was likely carved during the reign of Khafre to portray that pharaoh's features, framed by the *nemes* (royal headdress of Egypt). To get up close, you must pass through **Khafre's valley temple**, notable for its jigsaw-puzzle-like stonework – check the corners.

Sound & Light Show
(3386 3469; www.soundandlight.com.eg; admission E£75, plus E£10 for translation headset; 7pm & 8pm) Legions of tour groups converge on an area below the Sphinx for the nightly spectacular. It's rather low-tech, but fine if you're in the area. The first show is typically in English; the second varies.

Activities

Boat Trips

Cruising along the Nile on a traditional sail boat is lovely at dusk. You can hire **feluccas** for between E£50 and E£70 per hour (plus baksheesh for your captain) from the **Dok Dok landing stage** (Map p58), across from the Four Seasons. Once night falls, light-festooned **party boats** crowd the docks near the Maspero river bus terminal, on the east bank of the Nile north of 6th of October Bridge. A 45-minute or hour-long ride usually costs E£6 or so per person, and boats go whenever they're full.

Horse Riding

A desert horse ride at sunset, with the Pyramids as a background, is unforgettable. Stables are strung along the road south of the coach park by the Sphinx gate. Some of the best are **NB** (3382 0435), owned by Naser Breesh, who's praised for his healthy steeds and good guides; his place is just behind the Sphinx Club, further south than the others. **FB** (0106 507 0288) is also recommended. Expect to pay around E£100 per person per hour at a good place; a reputable operation won't ask for money till the end of the ride. Tip your guide an additional E£5 or E£10.

CAIRO FOR CHILDREN

The city can be exhausting, but there is plenty to keep children entertained. If the **Pyramids** and the **Egyptian Museum** aren't enough, they can play pirate on a **felucca ride**, frolic in the playground at **Al-Azhar Park**, or feed the camels at the dilapidated but popular **Cairo Zoo** (Guineenet al-Haywanat; Map p58; 3570 8895; Midan al-Gamaa, Giza; admission E£20; 9am-4pm), reachable by river bus.

For a special outing, the grand **Cairo Puppet Theatre** (Masrah al-Ara'is; Map p68; 2591 0954; Ezbekiyya; admission E£15; 6pm Thu-Sun) does shows in Arabic – colourful and animated enough to entertain all ages. The **National Circus** (Map p76; 3347 0612; Balloon Theatre, Sharia el-Nil, Agouza; admission E£30-50; box office 11am-10pm, performances 10pm-midnight) is a traditional one-ring show with clowns, acrobats, lions and lots of glitter, usually running during the cooler months. Go early for a good seat.

The Pyramids of Giza

Constructed more than 4000 years ago, the Pyramids are the last remaining wonder of the ancient world. The giant structures – the **Great Pyramid of Khufu** **1**, the smaller **Pyramid of Khafre** **2** and the **Pyramid of Menkaure** **3** – deservedly sit at the top of many travellers' to-do lists. But the site is challenging to explore, with everything, including the smaller **Queens' Pyramids** **4** and assorted tombs such as the **Tomb of Senegemib-Inti** **5**, spread out in the desert under the hot sun. And it all looks, at first glance, a bit smaller than you might have thought.

It helps to imagine them as they were: originally, the Pyramids gleamed in the sun, covered in a smooth white limestone casing. These enormous mausoleums, each devoted to a single pharaoh, were part of larger complexes. At the east base of each was a 'funerary temple', where the pharaoh was worshipped after his demise, with daily rounds of offerings to sustain his soul. In the ground around the pyramids, wooden boats – so-called solar barques – were buried with more supplies to transport the pharaoh's soul to the afterlife (one of these has been reconstructed and sits in the **Cheops Boat Museum** **6**). From each funerary temple, a long stone-paved causeway extended down the hill.

At the base of the plateau, a lake covered the land where the village of Nazlet as-Samaan is now – this was fed by a canal and enlarged with flood waters each year. At the end of each causeway, a 'valley temple' stood at the water's edge to greet visitors. Next to Khafre's valley temple, the lion-bodied **Sphinx** **7** stands guard.

So much about the Pyramids remains mysterious – including the whereabouts of the bodies of the pharaohs themselves. But there's still plenty for visitors to see. Here we show you both the big picture and the little details to look out for, starting with the **ticket booth and entrance** **8**.

Pyramid of Khafre
Khufu's son built this pyramid, which has some surviving limestone casing at the top. Scattered around the base are enormous granite stones that once added a snappy black stripe to the lowest level of the structure.

The Sphinx
This human-headed beast, thought to be a portrait of Khafre, guards the base of the plateau. The entrance is only through Khafre's valley temple. Come early or late in the day to avoid the long queue.

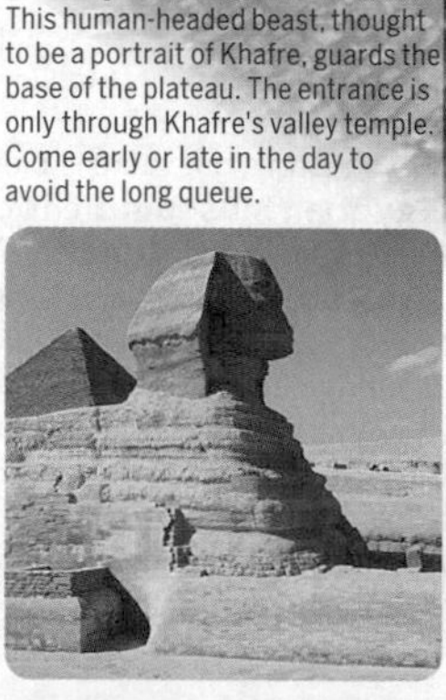

Cheops Boat Museum
Preserved in its own modern tomb, this 4500-year-old cedar barge was dug up from in front of the Great Pyramid and reassembled by expert craftsmen like a 1224-piece jigsaw puzzle.

ZORA O'NEILL

ZORA O'NEILL

3 Pyramid of Menkaure (Mycerinus)

This pyramid opens alternately with the Pyramid of Khafre. The gash in the exterior is the folly of Sultan al-Aziz Uthman, who tried to dismantle the pyramid in 1196.

Tomb of Senegemib-Inti

The Giza Plateau is dotted with small tombs like this one. Opening schedules vary each year. Duck inside to look for delicate wall carvings and enjoy a bit of shade.

Ticket Booth & Entrance

Buy tickets, marked with a hologram sticker, here and only here. All other options are counterfeit. Clean bathrooms, the only good facilities, are in a building just to the east.

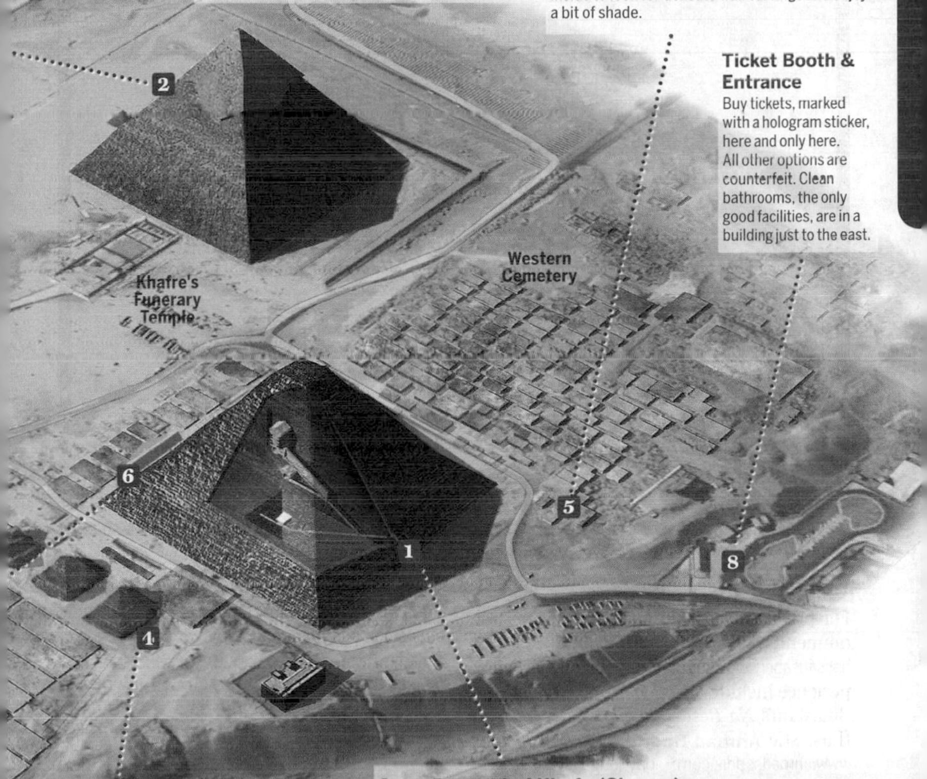

Great Pyramid of Khufu (Cheops)

Clamber inside the corridors to marvel at the precision engineering of the seamless stone blocks, each weighing 2.5 tonnes. Pause to consider the full weight of 2.3 million of them.

Queens' Pyramids

These smaller piles were built as the tombs of Khufu's sister, mother and wife. They're in bad shape, but some show the original limestone casing at the base – feel how smoothly the stones are fitted.

ZORA O'NEILL

ZORA O'NEILL

Giza Plateau

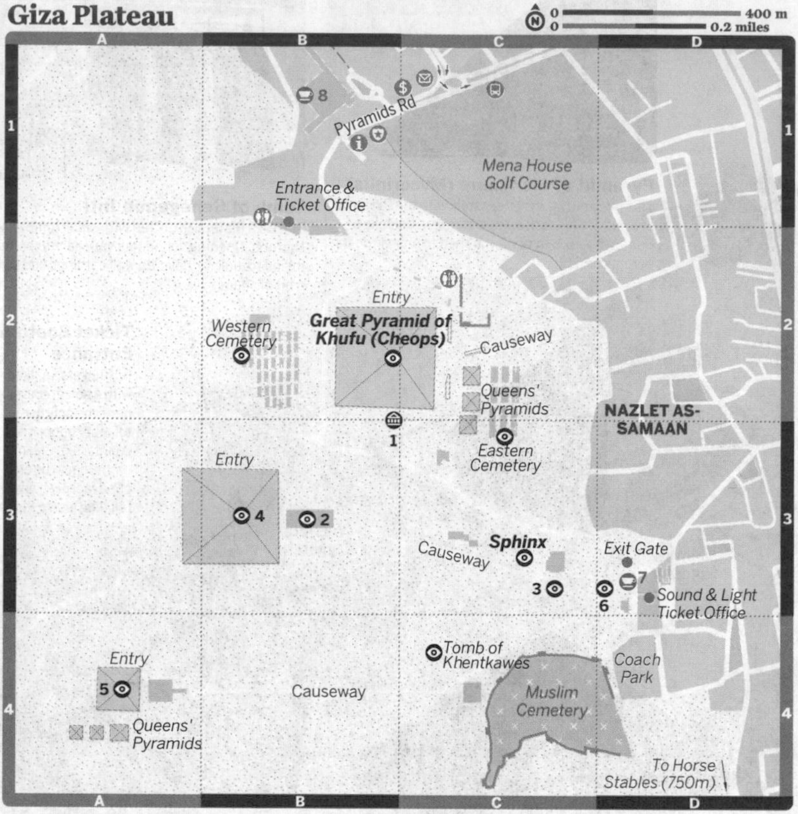

Tours

For private outings to ancient sites, we recommend **Hassan Saber** (☎0100 515 9857; hassansaber@hotmail.com), whose years of experience include an appearance on Anthony Bourdain's *No Reservations*. Witty and enthusiastic **Ahmed Seddik** (☎0100 676 8269; www.ahmedseddik.com; day-long tour E£200) runs a busy itinerary of group tours; his best are to the Egyptian Museum and Saqqara. **Samo Tours** (☎2299 1155; www.samoegypttours.com) is also reliable, with excellent English-speaking guides, Egyptologists and drivers.

To hire a taxi for the day and dispense with a guide, try **Aton Amon** (☎0100 621 7674; aton_manos@yahoo.com; full day E£300), who speaks English and French; he also does airport pickups. Friendly **Fathy el-Menesy** (☎2486 4251; full day E£300) owns a well-maintained Peugeot and speaks English.

Many taxi drivers factor commissions at dodgy papyrus and perfume shops into their earnings, so they really lay on the pressure. Be firm, and if you're truly desperate, offer to pay the difference yourself. It may be the only way to convey the message that tourists are often happier without shopping detours.

Sleeping

Cairo is chock-a-block with budget crash pads, including a few exceptionally good ones, but midrange gems are rarer. It pays to make reservations in advance – Cairo is no place to haul your luggage around while comparing room rates.

DOWNTOWN

Inexpensive hostels, hotels and pensions are concentrated in Downtown, mainly on the upper floors of buildings on and around Sharia Talaat Harb. Don't be alarmed by grimy stairs and shaky elevators – they

Giza Plateau

Top Sights

Great Pyramid of Khufu (Cheops) ... B2
Sphinx ... C3

Sights

1 Cheops Boat Museum ... B3
2 Khafre's Funerary Temple ... B3
3 Khafre's Valley Temple ... C3
4 Pyramid of Khafre (Chephren) ... B3
5 Pyramid of Menkaure (Mycerinus) ... A4
6 Sound & Light Show ... D3

Drinking

7 Cafe ... D3
8 Mena House Oberoi ... B1

aren't necessarily a reflection of the hotels above. All have at least a few rooms facing the busy street – request a rear room if you're a light sleeper.

TOP CHOICE **Pension Roma** HOTEL **$$**
(Map p68; ☎2391 1088; www.pensionroma.com.eg; 4th fl, 169 Sharia Mohammed Farid; s/d with fan E£80/127, with air-con E£165/253; ❄📶) Run by a French-Egyptian woman with impeccable standards, the Roma brings dignity, even elegance, to the budget-travel scene. You'll never be pressured to buy a tour here (they're not even an option), and the towering ceilings, antique furniture and filmy white curtains create a feeling of timeless calm. Most rooms have shared bathroom, though a few newer rooms have private facilities. Book ahead.

Berlin Hotel HOTEL **$$**
(Map p68; ☎2395 7502; berlinhotelcairo@hotmail.com; 4th fl, 2 Sharia Shawarby; s/d with fan E£100/130, s/d with air-con E£147/177; ❄📶) Like Pension Roma, Berlin is pleasantly old-fashioned and very low-pressure. Here, though, the knowledgeable owner can arrange airport pickup, reasonably priced tours and classes. Most of the 11 colour-saturated rooms (green! pink!) have air-con and private showers (but shared toilets); three rooms have fan only. There's a shared kitchen too. Booking ahead is wise, as the Berlin sees many repeat guests.

TOP CHOICE **Dina's** HOSTEL **$**
(Map p68; ☎2396 3902; www.dinashostel.com; 5th fl, 42 Sharia Abdel Khalek Sarwat; dm E£45, s/d with shared bathroom E£110/140, s/d with air-con E£140/200; ❄📶) Woman-owned and low-pressure, Dina's is tranquil and tidy, with warm colours, Egyptian appliqué pillows and soaring ceilings. The place has more private rooms than dorm beds, but it stays true to hostel roots with a gleaming shared kitchen. The building entrance is down a passage just east of Stephenson's pharmacy.

Hotel Royal BOUTIQUE HOTEL **$$**
(Map p68; ☎2391 7203; www.cairohotelroyal.com; 1st fl, 10 Sharia Elwy; s/d US$30/40; ❄📶) The only hotel in Cairo with a minimalist Scandinavian sensibility – brightened with just a touch of Egyptian glitzy gold trim. All rooms have niceties like mini-fridges, comfy office-style desk chairs and bunches of flowers on bedside tables. It's smack in the middle of a lively late-night cafe scene, but away from main-street traffic noise.

Hotel Luna HOTEL **$$**
(Map p68; ☎2396 1020; www.hotellunacairo.com; 5th fl, 27 Sharia Talaat Harb; s/d with shared bathroom E£100/140; with private bathroom from E£150/200; ❄📶) Modern, backpacker-friendly Luna offers three options: simple, slightly aged rooms with shared bathroom; basic private-bath rooms; and quieter 'Bella Luna' rooms with thicker mattresses and soothing pastel colour combos. Small comforts include bedside lamps and bath mats. Resident tour organiser Sam gets high marks from readers, and there's an excellent shared kitchen.

Hotel Osiris HOTEL **$$**
(Map p68; ☎2794 5728; http://hotelosiris.over-blog.com; 12th fl, 49 Sharia Nubar; s/d from €25/40; ❄📶) On the top floor of a commercial building, the Osiris' rooms enjoy views across the city. The French-Egyptian couple who run the place keep the tile floors and white walls spotless, and the pretty hand-sewn appliqué bedspreads tidily arranged on the plush mattresses. Breakfast involves fresh juice, crêpes and omelettes. Its location in Bab al-Luq is quiet at night.

Cairo City Center HOTEL **$$**
(Map p68; ☎0127 777 6383; www.cairocitycenterhotel.com; 14 Sharia Champollion; s/d US$30/40; ❄📶) Don't judge it by the dingy, claustrophobic lobby – rooms here are fine, with high ceilings, shiny tile floors, new bathrooms and good-quality mattresses. The sitting area has a beautiful terrace looking straight down Sharia Mahmoud Bassiouni.

PYRAMIDS PRACTICALITIES

Entrance & Tickets

The main **entrance** is at the end of Pyramids Rd (Sharia al-Haram). **Additional tickets** are required for the Cheops Boat Museum and the pyramid interiors. The Great Pyramid is always open, along with one of the other two. Tickets to the Great Pyramid (300 in summer, 500 in winter) are sold at the main ticket booth in two lots, starting at 8am and 1pm. In winter, you may need to queue. **Cameras** are not allowed inside pyramids and tombs.

Facilities & Food

Toilets are at the main entrance, in the Cheops Boat Museum and in a trailer near the Great Pyramid. For food, there's an expensive **cafe** (Map p64; drinks E£20, sandwiches E£25-55) by the Sphinx, but for the same amount, you can refresh at the nearby Pizza Hut or at the cafe at the opulent **Mena House Oberoi** (Map p64). For cheap eats, walk northeast on the main road through Nazlet as-Samaan. A short taxi ride away (around E£12), about 2km north on the Maryutia Canal, is the extremely popular **Andrea's** (☎3383 1133; 59 Tir'at al-Maryutia; entrées E£7-20, mains E£30-35; ⏲10am-midnight), famed for its succulent spit-roast chicken in a garden setting.

Horses & Camels

Prepare yourself for intense hustle – nearly everyone you meet, starting back at the Giza metro station, wants to sell you a horse or camel ride. Bargaining is required: at least E£50 for any distance and E£20 minimum for a short trot and photo op. For longer rides, it's better to hire a horse from one of the village stables. See p61.

Getting There & Away

Take the metro to Giza then go by taxi (about E£15), microbus (E£3) or bus (E£1 or E£2). Microbuses cluster outside the metro (drivers are yelling 'Haram'); get off where the van turns off Pyramids Rd and walk 1km straight to the entrance. Buses stop on the north side of Pyramids Rd; 355 and 357 (white with blue-and-red stripes) terminate in front of Mena House Oberoi, about 250m from the site entrance.

Sara Inn Hostel HOSTEL **$**
(Map p68; ☎2392 2940; www.sarainnhostel.com; 21 Sharia Youssef al-Guindi; dm E£50, s/d with shared bathroom E£80/115, with private bathroom from E£125/175; ❄📶) This is another decent option offering both dorms and private rooms for shoestring travellers. The Sara Inn is a small but personable place where you can easily get to know the staff. Plenty of well-strewn rugs and tapestries give a relaxed and cosy feel.

African House Hostel HOSTEL **$**
(Map p58; ☎2591 1744; www.africanhousehostel.com; 3rd fl, 15 Sharia Emad ad-Din; s/d/tr with shared bathroom US$17/19/25, s US$22; 📶) The African House offers an affordable way to stay in one of the city's most gorgeous mid-19th-century buildings. Rooms on the 4th floor have dimmer halls, but big balconies. The shared kitchen is a bit grotty, and the toilets occasionally run, but the staff are very nice.

Windsor Hotel HOTEL **$$**
(Map p68; ☎2591 5277; www.windsorcairo.com; 19 Sharia Alfy; s/d with shower & hand basin US$37/48, s/d full bathroom from US$46/59; ❄📶) Rooms at the Windsor are dim, many with low ceilings and noisy air-conditioners, and management is prone to adding surprise extra charges. But with the beautifully maintained elevator, worn stone stairs and a hotel restaurant, where the dinner bell chimes every evening at 7.30pm, the place is hard for nostalgia buffs to resist. The entrance is around the back, in the narrow street just south of Sharia Alfy.

Capsis Palace BUSINESS HOTEL **$$**
(Map p58; ☎2575 4029; 117 Sharia Ramses; s/d US$28/41; ❄📶) The Capsis is a thoroughly modern place with smallish but nicely kept rooms. By far the best option close to the train station. No wi-fi in rooms, though, and it costs to use it in the lobby.

GARDEN CITY

Just south of Midan Tahrir, this area is a lot quieter and has a lot of luxury palaces facing the Nile. There are a few more reasonable options.

Hotel Juliana HOTEL $$
(Map p58; ☎0122 424 9896; www.juliana-hotel.com; 3rd fl, 8 Sharia Ibrahim Naguib; s/d E£170/250; ❄📶) Not quite as sleek as its website suggests, but still showing a bit of style, with a red-and-gold colour scheme and balconies off every room. Perks include fridges and a small but functional shared kitchen. With only 18 rooms, it fills up fast – book ahead. Finding it in Garden City's web is a bit tricky – turn off Sharia Qasr el-Aini at the Co-op petrol station, and make the first left, and the next soft left after that. The hotel is in the same building as the Arab-African Bank.

Garden City House PENSION $$
(Map p68; ☎2794 8400; 23 Sharia Kamal ad-Din Salah; s/d with shared bathroom from E£97/143, s/d E£151/206; ❄) This pension is untouched by time – not great in some ways (rooms could use a fresh coat of paint), but a boon in others, such as the gentlemanly staff. The cheapest, fan-only rooms are small and stifling; those with en-suite bathroom are more spacious. Dinner is an option.

ISLAMIC CAIRO

The negatives: no immediate metro access, touts like locusts, nowhere to get a beer and more than the usual number of mosques with loudspeakers. But this is the place to plunge in at Cairo's deep end.

Arabian Nights HOTEL $$
(Map p58; ☎2589 4230; www.arabiannights.hostel.com; 10 Sharia al-Addad; s/d E£140/160; ❄📶) On a quiet street east of Midan al-Hussein, this midrange hotel is distinctly out of the tourist fray. Some rooms are quite dark and you need to check that the air-con works, but standards are generally good. The challenge is finding it: turn north on Sharia al-Mansouria (east along Sharia al-Azhar from Midan Hussein); 300m on, turn left at the ruined shell of a cinema (the Kawakeb cited as a landmark on the hotel's map).

ZAMALEK & GEZIRA

Relatively quiet Zamalek offers the best night's sleep in the city, if not the cheapest. Good restaurants, shops, bars and coffee shops are nearby, but most sights are a taxi ride away over traffic-jammed bridges.

Cairo Marriott LUXURY HOTEL $$$
(Map p76; ☎2728 3000; www.marriott.com/caieg, 16 Sharia Saray al-Gezira; r from US$219; ❄📶🏊) Historic atmosphere is thick in the lobby and other public areas, which all occupy a 19th-century palace. The rooms are all in two modern towers, and many have tiny bathrooms, but touches like plasma-screen TVs and extra-plush beds make up for it. It also has a popular garden cafe and a great pool.

Hotel Longchamps HOTEL $$
(Map p76; ☎2735 2311; www.hotellongchamps.com; 5th fl, 21 Sharia Ismail Mohammed; s/d from US$66/84; ❄📶) The old-European-style Longchamps has a residential feel. Rooms are spacious and well maintained, and guests gather to chat on the greenery-covered, peaceful rear balcony around sunset, or lounge in the restaurant. If you want your own balcony and a small bathtub, pay extra for an 'executive' room. Book well ahead.

Novotel Cairo El Borg BUSINESS HOTEL $$$
(Map p58; ☎2735 6725; www.novotel.com; 3 Sharia Saray al-Gezira; r from US$138; ❄📶🏊) Convenient location, sparkling new facilities and a pool are the selling points here, and more than make up for the somewhat generic chain feel. Midan Tahrir is just over the bridge; a metro stop is around the corner; and some of Gezira's prettiest gardens are just across the road.

Eating

DOWNTOWN

The best area for budget eats. If you're looking to self-cater, hit **Souq at-Tawfiqiyya** (Map p68), a blocks-long fruit-and-veg market that's open late, or **Souq Bab al-Luq** (Map p68), a covered market east of Midan Tahrir.

TOP CHOICE **At-Tabei ad-Dumyati** EGYPTIAN FAST FOOD $
Orabi (Map p54; 31 Sharia Orabi; dishes E£3-14; ⏰7am-1am); Talaat Harb (Map p68; Talaat Harb Complex, Sharia Talaat Harb; dishes E£3-10; ⏰9am-midnight) About 200m north of Midan Orabi, this place offers some of the cheapest meals in Cairo – and also some of the freshest and most delicious. Start by picking four salads from a large array, then order shwarma or ta'amiyya, along with some lentil soup or fuul. The entrance to the sit-down Orabi restaurant is set back from the street and signed only in Arabic; immediately north is the constantly thronged takeout window, where just

Central Cairo

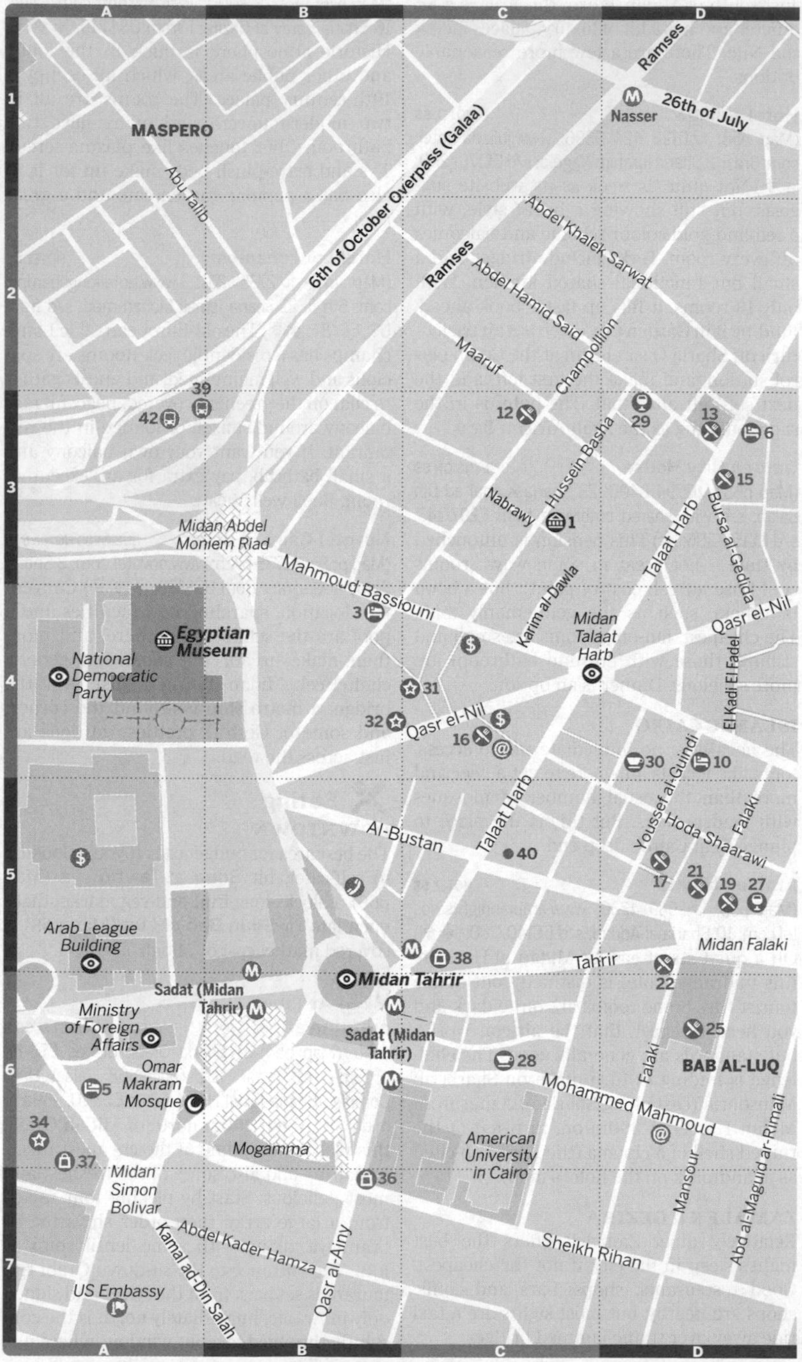
A
B
C
D
1
2
3
4
5
6
7
MASPERO
Abu Talib
6th of October Overpass (Galaa)
Ramses
26th of July
Nasser
Abdel Khalek Sarwat
Abdel Hamid Said
Champollion
Maaruf
12
29
13
6
15
Hussein Basha
Nabrawy
1
Talaat Harb
Bursa al-Gedida
39
42
Midan Abdel Moniem Riad
Mahmoud Bassiouni
3
Karim al-Dawla
Midan Talaat Harb
Qasr el-Nil
El Kadi El Fadel
Egyptian Museum
National Democratic Party
31
32
Qasr el-Nil
16
30
10
Youssef al-Guindi
Hoda Shaarawi
Falaki
Al-Bustan
Talaat Harb
40
17
21
19
27
Arab League Building
38
Midan Falaki
Tahrir
22
Sadat (Midan Tahrir)
Midan Tahrir
Ministry of Foreign Affairs
Sadat (Midan Tahrir)
25
Omar Makram Mosque
5
28
BAB AL-LUQ
Mohammed Mahmoud
Falaki
34
Mogamma
American University in Cairo
37
Midan Simon Bolivar
36
Mansour
Abd al-Maguid ar-Rimali
Abdel Kader Hamza
Kamal ad-Din Salah
Qasr al-Ainy
Sheikh Rihan
US Embassy

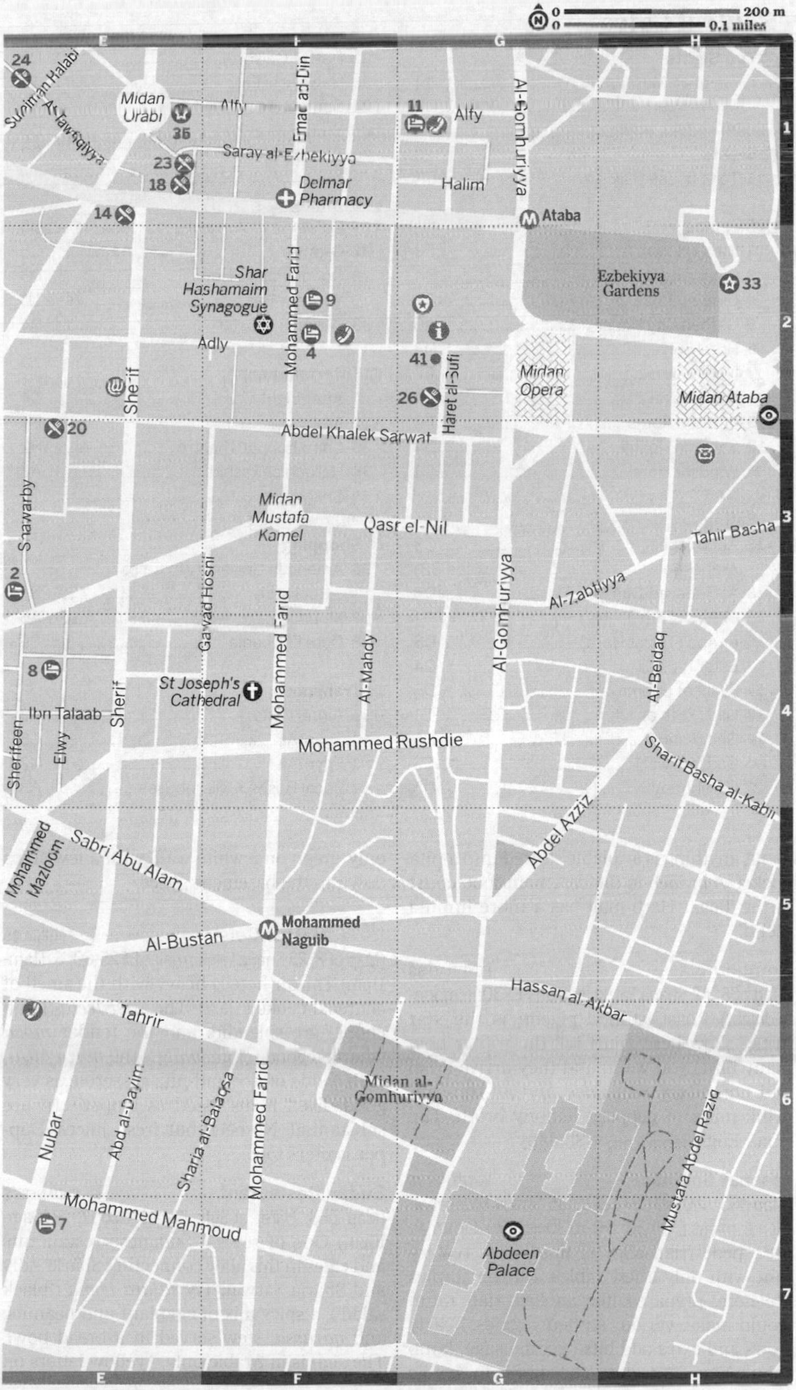
0
200 m
0
0.1 miles
E
F
G
H
1
2
3
4
5
6
7
24
Suleiman Halabi
Midan Urabi
35
Al-Tawfiqiyya
Alfy
Emad ad-Din
11
Alfy
Al-Gomhuriyya
Saray al-Ezbekiyya
23
18
Delmar Pharmacy
Halim
14
Ataba
Shar Hashamaim Synagogue
Mohammed Farid
9
Ezbekiyya Gardens
33
Adly
4
41
Haret al-Sufi
Midan Opera
26
Midan Ataba
Sherif
20
Abdel Khalek Sarwat
Shawarby
Midan Mustafa Kamel
Qasr el-Nil
Tahir Basha
2
Gawad Hosni
Al-Zabtiyya
Al-Mahdy
Al-Beidaq
8
St Joseph's Cathedral
Ibn Talaab
Sherifeen
Elwy
Mohammed Rushdie
Sharif Basha al-Kabir
Abdel Azziz
Mohammed Mazloom
Sabri Abu Alam
Mohammed Naguib
Al-Bustan
Hassan al-Akbar
Tahrir
Midan al-Gomhuriyya
Abd al-Dayim
Sharia al-Balaqsa
Nubar
Mustafa Abdel Raziq
Mohammed Mahmoud
7
Abdeen Palace

Central Cairo

Top Sights
- Egyptian Museum ... A4
- Midan Tahrir ... B6

Sights
- 1 Townhouse Gallery ... C3

Sleeping
- 2 Berlin Hotel ... E3
- 3 Cairo City Center ... B4
- 4 Dina's ... F2
- 5 Garden City House ... A6
- 6 Hotel Luna ... D3
- 7 Hotel Osiris ... E7
- 8 Hotel Royal ... E4
- 9 Pension Roma ... F2
- 10 Sara Inn Hostel ... D4
- 11 Windsor Hotel ... G1

Eating
- 12 Abou Tarek ... C3
- Arabesque ... (see 32)
- 13 At-Tabei ad-Dumyati ... D3
- 14 El-Abd (26th of July) ... E1
- 15 El-Abd (Talaat Harb) ... D3
- 16 Estoril ... C4
- 17 Fasahat Soumaya ... D5
- 18 Gad (26th of July) ... E1
- 19 Gad (Falaki) ... D5
- 20 Gad (Sarwat) ... E3
- 21 Gomhouriya ... D5
- 22 Hati al-Geish ... D5
- 23 Hawawshi Eid ... E1
- 24 Souq at-Tawfiqiyya ... E1
- 25 Souq Bab al-Luq ... D6
- 26 Sudan Restaurant ... G2

Drinking
- 27 Cafeteria El Horreya ... D5
- 28 Cilantro ... C6
- 29 Odeon Palace Hotel ... D3
- Windsor Bar ... (see 11)
- 30 Zahret al-Bustan ... D4

Entertainment
- 31 After Eight ... C4
- 32 Arabesque ... B4
- 33 Cairo Puppet Theatre ... H2
- 34 Haroun al-Rashid ... A6
- 35 Shahrazad ... E1

Shopping
- 36 American University in Cairo Bookstore ... B7
- 37 Mobaco ... A6
- 38 Oum El Dounia ... C5

Transport
- 39 Airport Bus ... A3
- 40 EgyptAir ... C5
- 41 EgyptAir ... G2
- 42 Local Buses & Microbuses ... A3

about anything is available stuffed into a pita pocket. A branch in the basement food court of the Talaat Harb mall has a more limited menu.

Gomhouriya EGYPTIAN **$$**
(Map p68; 42 Sharia Falaki; pigeons E£30; noon-midnight) Roast, stuffed pigeon is the star of the show here – just tell the waiter how many birds you want, and they arrive crisp and hot, along with salad and all-you-can-drink mugs of peppery, lemony broth. The small English sign says 'Shalapy'.

Fasahat Soumaya EGYPTIAN **$$**
(Map p68; 0100 9873 8637; 15 Sharia Youssef al-Guindi; mains E£15-30; 1-10.30pm;) Down a little pedestrian alley is this sweet restaurant with only a few tables. All the staples are here, prepared like an Egyptian mum would make: various stuffed veggies, hearty stews and extra odd bits (rice sausage, lamb shanks) on Thursdays. The sign is in Arabic only, green on a white wall, with a few steps down to the basement space.

TOP CHOICE **Hati al-Geish** GRILL **$$**
(Map p68; 23 Sharia Falaki; mains E£25-60; 11am-11pm) The air here is heavy with the smell of charcoal-cooked meat. The *kastileeta* (lamb chops) are splendid, and the tender *moza* (shanks) good for gnawing – the *moza fatta,* with a side of rice-and-pita casserole, is very good. Even items listed as 'Appetisers' are substantial. No beer, but fresh juices. Dapper waiters too.

Sudan Restaurant SUDANESE **$**
(Map p68; Haret al-Sufi; dishes E£6-17; 10am-10pm) One of several Sudanese restaurants and cafes in this alley connecting Sharia Adly and Sharia Sarwat. Try *salata iswid* ('black salad'), a spicy mix of eggplant and peanuts, and *qarassa,* stew served in a bread bowl. The sign is in Arabic only – yellow letters on

a red background; look for it in a courtyard off the southern end of the alley.

Gad EGYPTIAN FAST FOOD $
(Map p68; sandwiches E£2-15, mains E£20-50; 9am-2am) 26th of July (13 Sharia 26th of July); Sarwat (Sharia Abdel Khalek Sarwat at Shawarby); Falaki (North side Midan Falaki) Gad's lighthouse logo is fitting: it's a beacon in the night for hungry Cairenes. The ground floor is for takeaway, and arranged by type of food: *fiteer* (flaky pizza), shwarma, salads and more. Order and pay at the till first, then take the receipts to the relevant counters. You can also sit upstairs and order off the menu.

Abou Tarek EGYPTIAN FAST FOOD $
(Map p68; 40 Sharia Champollion; dishes E£3-10; 8am-midnight;) This temple of *kushari*, in the car-repair district, rises several storeys. It's worth eating in to check out the elaborate decor upstairs. You must pay in advance, either at the till downstairs (for takeaway) or with your waiter.

Hawawshi Eid EGYPTIAN FAST FOOD $
(Map p68; Sharia Saray al-Ezbekiyya; hawawshi E£6-8.50; 10am-4am) Just a few pounds gets you a huge round of bread filled with meat (spicy if you like) and baked in a paper wrapper until molten and delicious, plus pickles galore. There's no English sign – look for the oven out front, to the right of the counter.

Estoril EGYPTIAN $$
(Map p68; 2574 3102; off Sharia Talaat Harb; mezze E£10-35, mains E£35-65; noon-midnight) Very clubby, with clouds of cigarette smoke and tables crammed with Cairo's arts-and-letters set. Great for simple mezze and beer after beer. It's not uncommon to see women alone here. Look for it in the alley next to the Amex office.

El-Abd Bakery BAKERY $
(Map p68; pastries E£1-6; 8am-midnight) Talaat Harb (35 Sharia Talaat Harb); 26th of July (cnr Sharia 26th of July & Sharia Sherif) Cairo's most famous bakery, easily identified by the crowds outside tearing into croissants, sweets and savoury pies. It's a great place to augment your ho-hum hotel breakfast.

ISLAMIC CAIRO

There are plenty of fast-food joints around Midan al-Hussein but the restaurants in this part of town are limited – you really have to like grilled meat, and not be too squeamish about hygiene.

Farahat EGYPTIAN $$
(Map p72; 126A Sharia al-Azhar; pigeon E£30; noon-midnight) In an alley off Sharia Al-Azhar, this place is legendary for its pigeon, available stuffed or grilled. It doesn't look like much – just plastic chairs outside – but don't be fooled.

Citadel View MIDDLE EASTERN $$
(Map p58; 2510 9151; Sharia Salah Salem; entrées E£18-26, mains E£45-90; noon-midnight) Eating at this gorgeous restaurant in Al-Azhar Park, with the whole city sprawled below, is a treat, and less expensive than the surroundings suggest. Dishes include spicy sausage with pomegranate syrup and grilled fish with tahini. Skip it Friday, when there's only an expensive buffet (E£150). No alcohol.

Gad EGYPTIAN FAST FOOD $
(Map p72; Sharia al-Azhar; sandwiches E£2-15, mains E£20-50; 9am-2am) A branch of the Downtown snack experts.

Khan al-Khalili Restaurant & Mahfouz Coffee Shop EGYPTIAN $$
(Map p72; 2590 3788; 5 Sikket al-Badistan; snacks E£12-40, mains E£30-60; 10am-2am) Fairly sterile and touristy, but the food is decent, the air-con is strong and the toilets are clean. Look for the metal detector in the lane, immediately west of the medieval gate.

ZAMALEK

Cheap dining is not one of the island's fortes but hip hang-outs are.

Didos Al Dente ITALIAN $$
(Map p76; 26 Sharia Bahgat Ali; pasta E£32-47; 11am-2am) This cute eatery gets packed with students from the nearby AUC dorm, all clambering for a taste of the best pasta in town. It's tiny, so be prepared to wait on the street for a table.

La Taverna CAFE $$
(Map p76; 140 Sharia 26th of July; mains E£12-38; 8am-midnight) Thanks to its proximity to El Sawy cultural centre, there's usually an interesting crowd of Egyptians at this casual restaurant. The food itself (club sandwiches, pastas) isn't astounding, but it's reasonably priced for Zamalek, and there's outside seating or cool air-con indoors.

Abou El Sid EGYPTIAN $$
(Map p76; 2735 9640; 157 Sharia 26th of July; mezze E£12-25, mains E£25-70; noon-2am) Cairo's first hipster Egyptian restaurant (and now a national franchise), Abou El Sid is

Around Khan al-Khalili

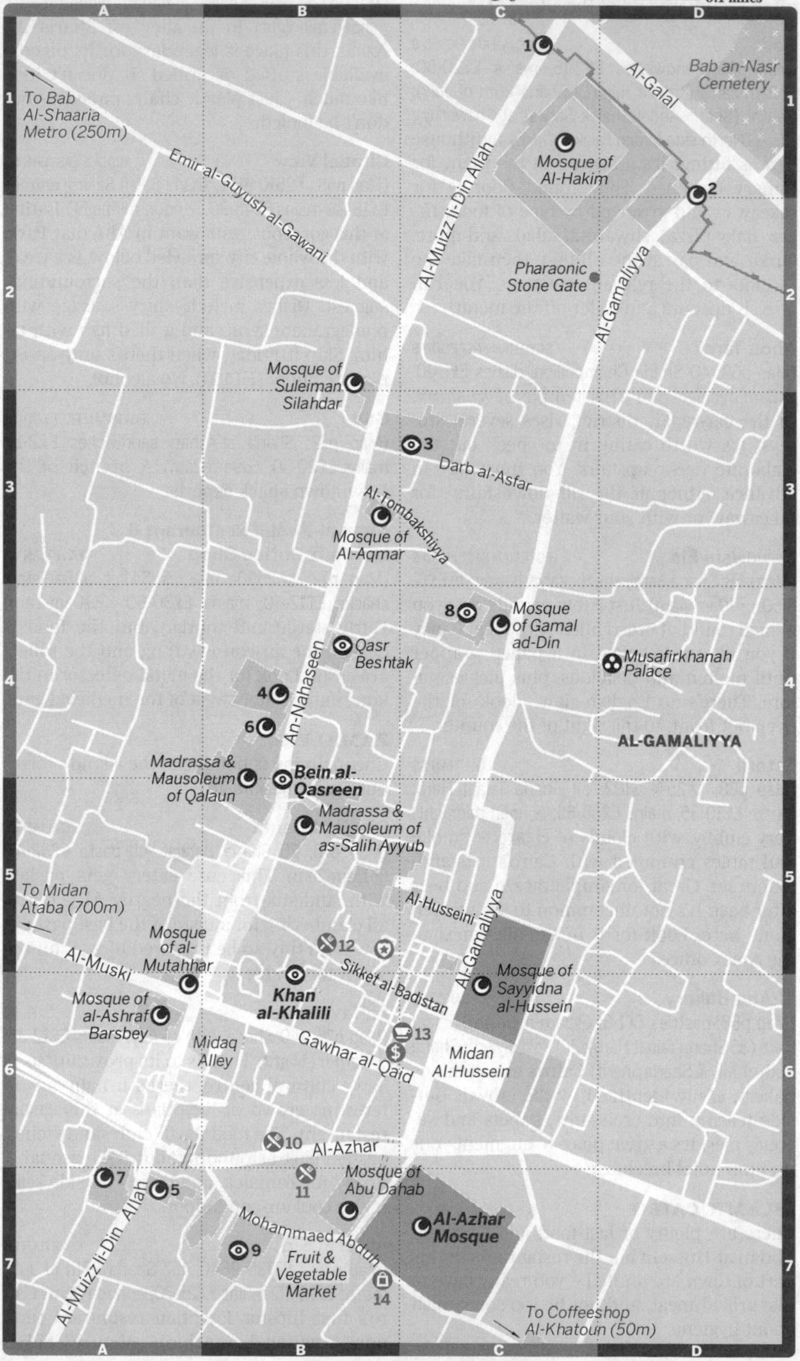

0 200 m
0 0.1 miles
To Bab Al-Shaaria Metro (250m)
Emir al-Guyush al-Gawani
Al-Muizz li-Din Allah
Al-Galal
Bab an-Nasr Cemetery
Mosque of Al-Hakim
Pharaonic Stone Gate
Al-Gamaliyya
Mosque of Suleiman Silahdar
Darb al-Asfar
Al-Tombakshiyya
Mosque of Al-Aqmar
Mosque of Gamal ad-Din
Qasr Beshtak
Musafirkhanah Palace
An-Nahaseen
AL-GAMALIYYA
Madrassa & Mausoleum of Qalaun
Bein al-Qasreen
Madrassa & Mausoleum of as-Salih Ayyub
To Midan Ataba (700m)
Al-Husseini
Mosque of al-Mutahhar
Al-Muski
Sikket al-Badistan
Mosque of Sayyidna al-Hussein
Mosque of al-Ashraf Barsbey
Khan al-Khalili
Midaq Alley
Gawhar al-Qaid
Midan Al-Hussein
Al-Azhar
Mosque of Abu Dahab
Al-Azhar Mosque
Mohammaed Abduh
Fruit & Vegetable Market
To Coffeeshop Al-Khatoun (50m)

Around Khan al-Khalili

Top Sights
- Al-Azhar Mosque C7
- Bein al-Qasreen B5
- Khan al-Khalili B6

Sights
1. Bab al-Futuh C1
2. Bab an-Nasr D1
3. Beit el-Suhaymi C3
4. Madrassa & Mausoleum of Barquq B4
5. Mausoleum of Al-Ghouri A7
6. Mausoleum of An-Nasir Mohammed B4
7. Mosque-Madrassa of Al-Ghouri A7
8. Wikala al-Bazara C4
9. Wikala of Al-Ghouri B7

Eating
10. Farahat B6
11. Gad B7
12. Khan al-Khalili Restaurant & Mahfouz Coffee Shop B5

Drinking
13. Fishawi's C6

Entertainment
- Al-Tannoura Egyptian Heritage Dance Troupe .... (see 9)

Shopping
14. Abd El Zaher B7

as popular with tourists as it is with upper class natives. You can get better *molokhiyya* (garlicky leaf soup) elsewhere, but here you wash it down with a cocktail and lounge on kitschy gilt 'Louis Farouk' furniture. The entrance is down a street off 26th of July; look for the tall wooden doors.

L'Aubergine BISTRO $$
(Map p76; ☎2738 0080; 5 Sharia Sayyed al-Bakry; entrées E£16-30, mains E£32-72; ⊙noon-2am; Ⓥ) This snug, white-walled, candlelit restaurant devotes half its menu to global vegetarian dishes, such as Turkish stewed aubergine and gnocchi with blue cheese.

Maison Thomas EUROPEAN $$
(Map p76; 157 Sharia 26th of July; sandwiches E£33-58, pizzas E£40-65; ⊙24hr) A little slice of the Continent, with waiters in long white aprons serving baguette sandwiches and pizza with generous toppings (including pork!).

Drinking

Cairo isn't a 'dry' city, but locals tend to run on caffeine by day, available at both traditional ahwas (cofeehouses) and European-style cafes. Drinking beer or spirits typically doesn't start till the evening, and then it's limited to Western-style bars, and some more locals-only dives. For the former, Zamalek is the best place to go boozing; the latter are all Downtown.

DOWNTOWN

Zahret al-Bustan COFFEEHOUSE
(Map p68; Sharia Talaat Harb; tea & sheesha E£9; ⊙8am-2am) This traditional ahwa is a bit of an intellectuals' and artists' haunt, though also firmly on many backpackers' lists, so be alert to scam artists. It's in the lane just behind Café Riche.

TOP CHOICE **Cafeteria El Horreya** BAR
(Map p68; Midan Falaki; ⊙8am-2am) A Cairo institution, and quite wholesome as *baladi* (local) bars go, as it's big, brightly lit and welcoming to women. No beer is served on the side with the chessboards.

Odeon Palace Hotel BAR
(Map p68; 6 Sharia Abdel Hamid Said; beer E£12; ⊙24hr) Its fake turf singed from sheesha coals, this slightly dilapidated rooftop bar is favoured by Cairo's heavy-drinking theatre and cinema clique, and is a great place to watch the sun go down (or come up).

Windsor Bar BAR
(Map p68; 19 Sharia Alfy; ⊙6pm-1am) Alas, most of the Windsor's regular clientele has passed on, leaving a few hotel guests, a cordial, polyglot bartender and a faint soundtrack of swing jazz and Umm Kolthum. Colonial history has settled in an almost palpable film on the taxidermist's antelope heads. Solo women will feel comfortable here.

Cilantro CAFE
(Map p68; 31 Sharia Mohammed Mahmoud; coffees & teas E£8-35, sandwiches E£12-45; ⊙9am-2am; 📶) Egypt's answer to Starbucks and Costa, this popular chain does all the usual coffee drinks, teas and juices, plus packaged sandwiches and cakes. If it weren't

A STROLL THROUGH HISTORY

One of the best walks in Islamic Cairo is a loop through the district north of Khan al-Khalili, which is undergoing massive restoration. From Midan Hussein, walk north up Sharia al-Gamaliyya, a major medieval thoroughfare for traders. After about 300m, on your left you will see the **Wikala al-Bazara** (Map p72; Sharia al-Tombakshiyya; adult/student E£20/10; ⏲8am-5pm), a beautifully restored caravanserai. Continue heading north until you hit the T-intersection of Sharia Al-Galal, marking the old **northern wall**. Pass through the square-towered **Bab an-Nasr** (Gate of Victory; Map p72) and walk left to the rounded **Bab al-Futuh** (Gate of Conquests; Map p72). Both were built in 1087 as the two northern entrances to the new walled Fatimid city of Al-Qahira.

From there, it's a straight walk back south via Sharia al-Muizz li-Din Allah. Don't miss the spectacular **Beit el-Suhaymi** (Map p72; Darb al-Asfar; adult/student E£30/15; ⏲9am-4.30pm), a complex of three houses. You'll find it tucked down a small alley on your left.

Just before you reach Khan al-Khalili again, you pass through the stretch known as **Bein al-Qasreen** (Map p72), or Palace Walk, the main drag of Fatimid Egypt. The buildings here have all been restored and are free to enter (tip the caretakers). The **Madrassa and Mausoleum of Barquq** (Map p72), with its black-and-white marble portal, is lavish inside, and the **Madrassa and Mausoleum of An-Nasir Mohammed** (Map p72) sports a plundered Gothic doorway from a church in Acre.

for the gaggles of headscarf-wearing teenage girls who crowd the banquettes after school, it would be easy to forget you're in Egypt. There are other branches just about everywhere you turn, including Zamalek (Map p76). All offer free wi-fi, strong air-con and usually clean restrooms.

ISLAMIC CAIRO

Fishawi's COFFEEHOUSE

(Map p72; off Midan al-Hussein; tea & sheesha around E£10; ⏲24hr, during Ramadan 5pm-3am) In action since 1773, this *shai*-sipping, sheesha-smoking institution is not to be missed. Filled with tourists and local shopkeepers in equal measure, this is a time capsule of the Cairo of bygone days. It's a few steps off Midan Hussein.

Coffeeshop Al-Khatoun COFFEEHOUSE

(off Map p72; Midan Al-Khatoun; tea & sheesha E£15; ⏲3pm-1am) Tucked away in a quiet square behind Al-Azhar, this outdoor modern ahwa is a great place to rest up after a walk, with tea and snacks and comfortable pillow-strewn benches. In the evenings, it attracts an arty crowd.

ZAMALEK

Arabica CAFE

(Map p76; 20 Sharia al-Marashly; cappuccino E£8, breakfast E£10-15, fiteer E£15-30; ⏲10am-midnight) This super-funky upstairs cafe is all 'Starbucks goes art house', with painting-draped walls and a dedicated following of hip young things doodling on the paper-topped tables. International tunes waft in the air, and you can munch on *fiteer,* soups, salads or wraps.

Simonds CAFE

(Map p76; 112 Sharia 26th of July; coffees & pastries from E£7; ⏲7am-10pm) A Zamalek institution, the barista here has been preparing cappuccino for over half a century – and judging by his grumpiness he hasn't taken a break in all that time. Pay at the till first.

Wel3a COFFEEHOUSE

(Map p76; 177 Sharia 26th of July; sheesha E£18-25, pot of tea E£22; ⏲24hr) A very upmarket ahwa specialising in the finest sheesha tobacco, imported from Jordan, the Gulf and beyond. Nice selection of sandwiches and snacks too.

La Bodega BAR

(Map p76; ☎2735 0543; 1st fl, Baehler's Mansions, 157 Sharia 26th of July; beer E£20, cocktails E£40; ⏲noon-2am) This vast, amber-lit lounge doubles as a restaurant, but it's the long brass-top bar and original cocktails that garner most of the attention. The place draws Cairo celebs, who look gorgeous against the belle-époque backdrop. Reservations recommended.

Sequoia LOUNGE

(Map p76; ☎2735 0014; www.sequoiaonline.net; 53 Sharia Abu al-Feda, beer E£28, cocktails E£50-60, mezze E£20-40, minimum Sun-Wed E£125, Thu-Sat E£150; ⏲11am-1am) At the very northern tip of Zamalek, this sprawling Nileside lounge is a swank scene, with low cushions for nursing a sheesha and sipping a cocktail. We don't recommend it for food. Bring an extra layer – evenings right on the water can be cool.

✪ Entertainment

For free fun after dark, street life can be entertainment enough. Stroll the pedestrian area around Midan Orabi, and also check out the Nile corniche downtown and Qasr el-Nil bridge.

Clubs & Live Music

Many venues are eclectic, changing musical styles and scenes every night. Many also start as restaurants and shift into club mode after midnight, at which point the door policy gets stricter. Big packs of men (and sometimes even single men) are always a no-no – go in a mixed group if you can, and ideally make reservations.

Cairo Jazz Club JAZZ, DJ
(Map p76; ☎3345 9939; www.cairojazzclub.com; 197 Sharia 26th of July, Agouza; ⏲5pm-3am) The city's liveliest stage, with modern Egyptian folk, electronica, fusion and more seven nights a week, from around 10pm. Book a table ahead (online is easiest); no one under 25 is admitted.

After Eight JAZZ, DJ
(Map p68; ☎2574 0855, 0100 339 8000; www.after8cairo.com; 6 Sharia Qasr el-Nil, Downtown; minimum Sun-Wed E£60, Thu-Sat E£100; ⏲8pm-4am) Everything from Nubian jazz to the wildly popular DJ Dina, who mixes James Brown, '70s Egyptian pop and the latest cab-driver favourites on Tuesdays. Reserve online (the website's style in no way reflects the club's).

Cairo Opera House CLASSICAL MUSIC, JAZZ
(Map p58; ☎2739 0144; www.cairoopera.org; Gezira Exhibition Grounds) Performances by the Cairo Opera and the Cairo Symphony Orchestra are held in the 1200-seat Main Hall, where jacket and tie are required for men (travellers have been known to borrow them from staff). The Small Hall is casual. Check the website for the schedule.

El Sawy Culture Wheel JAZZ, PERFORMING ARTS
(El Sakia; Map p76; ☎2736 8881; www.culturewheel.com; Sharia 26th of July, Zamalek; ⏲9am-9pm) The most popular young Egyptian rock and jazz bands play at this complex of a dozen performance spaces and galleries tucked under a bridge overpass. There's a nice Nileside cafe too.

TOP CHOICE **Makan** TRADITIONAL MUSIC
(off Map p68; ☎2792 0878; www.egyptmusic.org; 1 Sharia Saad Zaghloul, Mounira) An intimate space dedicated to folk music. Don't miss the traditional women's *zar*, a sort of musical trance and healing ritual (Wednesday, 9pm; E£20); Tuesday is usually Nass Makan, an Egyptian-Sudanese jam session. To find the space, walk south on Sharia Mansour.

FREE **Al-Tannoura Egyptian Heritage Dance Troupe** TRADITIONAL MUSIC
(Map p72; ☎2512 1735; ⏲8pm Mon, Wed & Sat) Egypt's premier Sufi dance troupe – more raucous and colourful than white-clad Turkish dervishes – puts on a mesmerising performance at the Wikala of Al-Ghouri near Al-Azhar. Arrive about an hour ahead to secure a seat.

Belly Dancing

If you see only one belly dancer in your life, it had better be in Cairo, the art form's true home. Many of them are Russian rather than Egyptian these days, but it doesn't mean they can't shake it. The best perform at Cairo's five-star hotels; at the other end are the dive halls where it's more about the seedy scene than dancing prowess.

Haroun al-Rashid CABARET
(Map p68; ☎2795 7171; Semiramis InterContinental, Corniche el-Nil, Garden City; ⏲11pm-4am Tue-Thu & Sun) This old-fashioned-looking five-star club – all red curtains and white marquee lights – is where the famous Dina has been known to undulate. Performances don't usually start till 1am.

TOP CHOICE **Shahrazad** CABARET
(Map p68; 1 Sharia Alfy, Downtown; admission E£5) Worth visiting for the gorgeous interior alone, this old-school hall got a makeover in recent years, and its Orientalist fantasia, complete with red velvet drapes, feels less sketchy than other downtown dives. Come armed with E£5 notes for tipping; expect to pay E£15 to E£20 for a beer. Occasionally the venue hosts a DJ night for an artier crowd.

Arabesque CLUB, LOUNGE
(Map p68; ☎2574 8677; www.arabesque-eg.com; 6 Qasr el-Nil, Downtown; ⏲7pm-2am) Book in advance for a table late on Thursday or Friday,

Zamalek

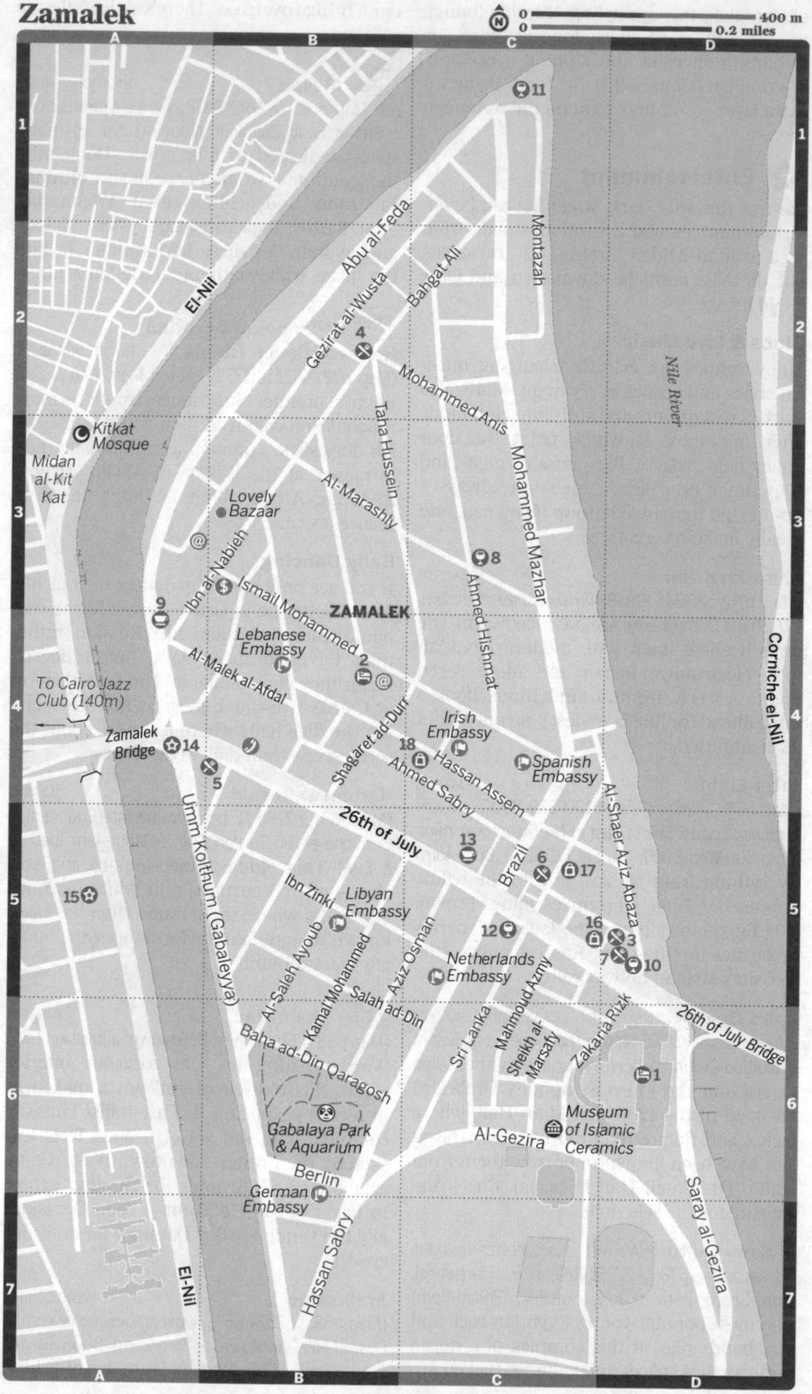
0 400 m
0 0.2 miles
A
B
C
D
1
2
3
4
5
6
7
El-Nil
Kitkat Mosque
Midan al-Kit Kat
Abu al-Feda
Gezirat al-Wusta
Bahgat Ali
Montazah
Nile River
Mohammed Anis
Taha Hussein
Al-Marashly
Mohammed Mazhar
Lovely Bazaar
Ibn al-Nabieh
Ismail Mohammed
ZAMALEK
Ahmed Hishmat
Lebanese Embassy
Al-Malek al-Afdal
To Cairo Jazz Club (140m)
Zamalek Bridge
Shagaret ad-Durr
Irish Embassy
Hassan Assem
Ahmed Sabry
Spanish Embassy
Corniche el-Nil
Al-Shaer Aziz Abaza
26th of July
Umm Kolthum (Gabaleyya)
Brazil
Ibn Zinki
Libyan Embassy
Al-Saleh Ayoub
Kamal Mohammed
Aziz Osman
Salah ad-Din
Netherlands Embassy
Mahmoud Azmy
Sri Lanka
Sheikh al-Marsafy
Zakaria Rizk
26th of July Bridge
Baha ad-Din Qaragosh
Gabalaya Park & Aquarium
Museum of Islamic Ceramics
Al-Gezira
Berlin
German Embassy
Hassan Sabry
Saray al-Gezira
1
2
3
4
5
6
7
8
9
10
11
12
13
14
15
16
17
18

Zamalek

Sleeping

1	Cairo Marriott	D6
2	Hotel Longchamps	B4

Eating

3	Abou El Sid	D5
4	Didos Al Dente	B2
5	La Taverna	B4
6	L'Aubergine	C5
7	Maison Thomas	D5

Drinking

8	Arabica	C3
	Cilantro	(see 7)
9	Cilantro	A4
10	La Bodega	D5
11	Sequoia	C1
12	Simonds	C5
13	Wel3a	C5

Entertainment

14	El Sawy Culture Wheel	A4
15	National Circus	A5

Shopping

16	Diwan	C5
17	Fair Trade Egypt	C5
18	Mobaco	C4

when a belly dancer performs. Other nights, this upper-crust place segues from tasty restaurant to chilled-out club with a house-music soundtrack.

Shopping

Egypt's best shopping is in Cairo, though you wouldn't know it on a first stroll through Khan al-Khalili, stocked with made-in-China tat – the trick is knowing where to look. For general gear, Downtown along Sharia Qasr el-Nil has cheap, mass-market fashion. Sharia al-Marashly and Sharia Mansour Mohammed in Zamalek have some gem boutiques, and not all of them are as expensive as you'd expect. For everything else, head to Citystars, Cairo's best mall, out east near the suburb of Heliopolis.

DOWNTOWN & GARDEN CITY

Oum El Dounia HANDICRAFTS
(Map p68; 1st fl, 3 Sharia Talaat Harb, Downtown; 10am-9pm) At a great central location, Oum El Dounia sells an exceptionally tasteful selection of locally made glassware, Bedouin jewellery, cotton clothes and other interesting trinkets. Illustrated postcards by cartoonist Golo make a nice change. Not especially cheap, but very good work, and open every day of the year.

American University in Cairo Bookstore BOOKS
(Map p68; 2797 5370; Sharia Sheikh Rihan, Downtown; 10am-6pm Sat-Thu) The best English-language bookshop in Egypt, with two floors of material on the politics, sociology and history of Cairo, Egypt and the Middle East. Plenty of guidebooks and maps, and some fiction.

Wikalat al-Balah CLOTHING, MARKET
(Souq Dulaq, Dulaq Market, Map p58, north of Sharia 26th of July, Bulaq) This street market specialises in secondhand clothing, mostly well organised, clean and with marked prices (especially on Sharia al-Wabur al-Fransawi). It starts a few blocks west of the 6th of October overpass.

COPTIC CAIRO

Souq al-Fustat HANDICRAFTS, MARKET
(Map p58; Sharia Mar Girgis, Old Cairo; 8am-4pm) A new market built for tourists, this is nonetheless a nice collection of shops, with respectable vendors of antique carpets, modern ceramics, spices, richly embroidered *galabiyyas* and wooden toys along with a branch of Abd El Zaher. Prices are marked (though occasionally negotiable), and sales pressure is pleasantly low.

ISLAMIC CAIRO

TOP CHOICE **Abd El Zaher** GIFTS
(Map p72; 31 Sharia Mohammed Abduh; 9am-11pm) Cairo's last working bookbinder also makes beautiful leather- and oil-paper-bound blank books, photo albums and diaries. Gold monogramming is included in the exceedingly reasonable prices.

Abd al-Rahman Harraz FOOD
(off Map p58; 1 Midan Bab al-Khalq; 10am-10pm) Since 1885, this has been one of the most esteemed spice traders in Cairo, with a brisk business in medicinal herbs as well. There's no English sign: look for dioramas of Egyptian village life in the corner shop windows. It's about 450m west of Bab Zuweila, and a couple of blocks east of the Museum of Islamic Art.

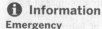

CAIRO CRAFTS: WHAT AND WHERE

In addition to shops, these are the best districts for certain goods.

Gold and silver The gold district is at the west end of Khan al-Khalili.

Backgammon and sheesha pipes Shops that stock ahwas line Sharia al-Muizz around Bein al-Qasreen.

Appliqué Best buys are at the **Tentmakers Bazaar** (Sharia al-Khayamiyya; Map p58).

Carpets The carpet bazaar south of the Mosque of al-Ghouri has imports; flat-weave Bedouin rugs are the only local style.

Spices Most dealers in the Khan are more trouble than they're worth. Try Harraz or shops around Midan Falaki.

Perfume In addition to the southwest corner of Khan al-Khalili, try shops around Midan Falaki.

Inlay Artisans in the Darb al-Ahmar neighbourhood at the bottom of Al-Azhar Park sell out of their workshops.

Khan Misr Touloun HANDICRAFTS
(Map p58; Midan ibn Tulun; ⏲10am-5pm Mon-Sat) This reasonably priced shop opposite the Mosque of Ibn Tulun is stacked with a desirable jumble of reasonably priced wooden chests, jewellery, pottery, puppets and scarves. Closes for vacation in August.

ZAMALEK

TOP CHOICE **Fair Trade Egypt** HANDICRAFTS
(Map p76; 1st fl, 27 Sharia Yehia Ibrahim; ⏲9am-8pm Sat-Thu, 10am-6pm Fri) Crafts sold here – Bedouin rugs, pottery, beaded jewellery – are produced in income-generating projects throughout the country. Very reasonable prices.

Diwan BOOKS, MUSIC
(Map p76; ☎2736 2578; 159 Sharia 26th of July; ⏲9am-11.30pm) Fabulous: English, French and German titles, from novels to travel guides to coffee-table books. It also has a kids' section, a large music wing and a small cafe.

Mobaco CLOTHING
(Map p76; 8 Sharia Ahmed Sabry) Sporty designs, inexpensive and with a great range of colours. There's always a flattering long skirt available, and men can choose from a rainbow of polo shirts sporting a camel logo. There are stores throughout the city, including at the Semiramis (Map p68).

Information

Emergency

Ambulance (☎123)

Fire service (☎180)

Police (☎122)

Tourist police (☎126) The **main tourist police office** (Map p68; ☎2390 6028; Sharia Alfy) is on the 1st floor of a building in the alley just left of the main tourist office in Downtown. There are other offices by the Pyramids (Map p64) and in Khan al-Khalili (Map p72).

Internet Access

The most conveniently located, all about E£5 per hour:

Concord (Map p68; 28 Sharia Mohammed Mahmoud, Downtown; ⏲10am-2am) Handy for southern Downtown.

InterClub (Map p68; 12 Sharia Talaat Harb, Downtown; ⏲8am-2am) In the alley next to Estoril restaurant.

Intr@net (Map p68; 1st fl, 36 Sharia Sherif, Downtown; ⏲24hr) Walk back into the shopping arcade and upstairs.

Sigma Net (Map p76; Sharia Gezirat al-Wusta, Zamalek; ⏲24hr) Opposite Golden Tulip Flamenco Hotel. Good air-con.

Zamalek Center (Map p76; 25 Sharia Ismail Mohammed, Zamalek; ⏲24hr)

Medical Services

Many of Cairo's hospitals suffer from antiquated equipment and a cavalier attitude to hygiene, but there are exceptions, including the Ma'adi branch of **As-Salam International Hospital** (☎2524 0250, emergency 19885; www.assih.com; Corniche el-Nil, Ma'adi).

Pharmacies abound in Cairo and almost anything can be obtained without a prescription. Pharmacies that operate 24 hours and deliver include **Delmar** (Map p68; ☎2575 1052; cnr Sharia 26th of July & Sharia Mohammed Farid, Downtown) and **Al-Ezaby** (☎19600), with numerous branches.

Money

Banks and forex bureaus are all over town, especially on Sharia Adly downtown and Sharia 26th of July in Zamalek – forex offices give slightly better rates on cash and are typically open till 8pm. There are oodles of ATMs throughout the city.

American Express (Amex; www.americanexpress.com.eg; ⊙9am-3pm Sat-Thu) Downtown (Map p68; ☎2574 7991; 15 Sharia Qasr el-Nil); Heliopolis (☎2480 1530; Citystars Centre)

Thomas Cook (☎emergency 0100 140 1367; www.thomascookegypt.com; ⊙8am-4.30pm Sat-Thu) Airport (☎2265 4447); Downtown (Map p68; ☎2574 3776; 17 Sharia Mahmoud Bassiouni); Heliopolis (☎2416 4000; 7 Sharia Baghdad, Korba); Heliopolis (☎0122 773 4609; Sheraton Heliopolis, 1229 Sharia al-Sheikh Ali Gad al-Haqq); Zamalek (Map p76; ☎2696 2101; 3A Sharia Ismail Mohammed)

Post

Main post office (Map p68; Midan Ataba; ⊙9am-6pm Sat-Thu) Stamps and letters at front entrance; parcels at the back (south) entrance. For parcels, leave your package unsealed for inspection; the staff will tape it up. Boxes are for sale; rates for slowest service are E£150 for the first kilo, E£40 for each thereafter.

Telephone

If you have your own mobile phone with you, you can purchase cheap, local pay-as-you-go SIM cards from dedicated Mobinil, Etisalat or Vodafone shops, or from many kiosks.

Telephone centrales Downtown (Map p68; fax 2578 0979; 13 Midan Tahrir; ⊙24hr); Downtown (Map p68; fax 2393 3909; 8 Sharia Adly; ⊙24hr); Downtown (Map p68; fax 2589 7635; Sharia Alfy; ⊙24hr); Downtown (Map p68; Sharia Tahrir; ⊙24hr); Zamalek (Map p76; Sharia 26th of July)

Tourist Information

Ministry of Tourism Downtown (Map p68; ☎2391 3454; 5 Sharia Adly; ⊙9am-6pm); Pyramids (Map p64; ☎3383 8823; Pyramids Rd, opposite Mena House Oberoi; ⊙8.30am-5pm); Ramses Station (Map p58; ☎2492 5985; ⊙9am-7pm) Not always equipped to answer questions, but can usually forward you to someone who can.

Travel Agencies

The streets around Midan Tahrir teem with travel agencies, but watch out for dodgy operators. Along with Amex and Thomas Cook, these are reliable:

Backpacker Concierge (☎0106 350 7118; www.backpackerconcierge.com) Culturally and environmentally responsible desert trips and Nile cruises, plus more focused custom trips such as food tours. No walk-in office, but can communicate via phone, email, Facebook and Twitter.

Egypt Panorama Tours (☎2359 0200; www.eptours.com; 4 Rd 79, Ma'adi; ⊙9am-5pm) Opposite Ma'adi metro station, this is one of the best-established agencies in town. It books tickets, tours and hotel rooms, and is good for four- and five-star hotel deals and tours within Egypt and around the Mediterranean. Note that separate departments handle flights and excursions.

FAVOURITE CAIRO SCAMS

Scams in Cairo are roughly divided into three types: overcharging on tours elsewhere in Egypt, hotel scams and shopping scams.

For tours, you are almost always better off booking in the place you'll be taking them. Stick with reputable agencies. Even your hotel is not a good place to book anything but typical day trips from Cairo. Never book with a random office downtown (many are fronts) or with the help of someone you meet on the street.

Favourite hotel scams involve diverting you from your lodging of choice. At the airport, a person with a badge saying 'Ministry of Tourism' may offer to confirm your hotel booking. They'll then tell you it's booked out, and offer one of their 'recommended' hotels (where they will earn a commission that is added to your bill). Another hustle involves a stranger chatting you up and asking where you'll be staying; when you arrive at your hotel, another person greets you outside and tells you your room is flooded/booked/closed by police, and reroutes you. Taxi drivers may claim your hotel is closed, or they have no idea where it is.

Finally, beware of chatty men around the Egyptian Museum, on Talaat Harb and in Khan al-Khalili. They'll often approach offering help or advice, but their end goal is to divert you (by telling you the museum is closed, there's a demonstration ahead, etc) and get you into a papyrus/perfume/souvenir shop where they'll earn commission.

Despite all of this, outside of tourist areas, Egyptians offering help typically have no ulterior motive.

Lovely Bazaar (Map p76; ☎2737 0223, 0111 861 2219; www.egyptbargaintours.com; Sharia Gezirat al-Wusta, Zamalek) Ibrahim's bargain tours in Cairo and beyond come recommended by travellers.

Getting There & Away

Air

Cairo is the hub for all flights within Egypt. For information on the airport see p153. For flight information call ☎0900 77777 from a landline in Egypt or ☎27777 from a mobile phone.

EgyptAir Airport Terminal 3 (☎2696 6798); Downtown (Map p68; ☎2393 0381; cnr Sharia Talaat Harb & Sharia al-Bustan); Downtown (Map p68; ☎2392 7680; 6 Sharia Adly)

Bus

The main bus station for all destinations in the Suez Canal area, Sinai, the deserts, Alexandria and Upper Egypt, is **Cairo Gateway** (Map p58; Mina al-Qahira, Turgoman Garage; Sharia al-Gisr, Bulaq; Ⓜ Orabi), 400m west of the Orabi metro stop.Tickets are sold at different windows according to company and destination.

Companies operating here are **East Delta Travel Co** (☎3262 3128) for Suez and the Sinai; **West & Mid Delta Bus Co** (☎2432 0049) for Alexandria, Marsa Matruh and Siwa; **Super Jet** (☎2290 9017) for some Sinai resort towns; and **Upper Egypt Travel Co** (☎2576 0261) to Western Desert oases and Luxor (though for the latter, the train is better). For information about buses to Libya, Israel and Jordan see p151.

A few smaller bus stations run more frequent services. Head here if the Cairo Gateway departure times aren't ideal.

Abbassiyya (Sinai Station; off Map p58; Sharia Ramses, Abbassiyya; Ⓜ Abbassiya) A few buses from Sinai still terminate here, 4km northeast of Ramses; take the nearby metro to the centre.

Abboud (off Map p58; Khazindar; Sharia al-Tir'a al-Boulaqia, Shubra; Ⓜ Mezallat) Services to the Delta and Wadi al-Natrun, 5km north of Ramses. Walk about 800m east from metro.

Al-Mazah (Sharia Abou Bakr al-Siddiq, Heli-

BUSES FROM CAIRO GATEWAY

DESTINATION	COMPANY	PRICE (E£)	DURATION (HR)	TIMES
Alexandria	West & Mid Delta	30	3	Hourly 4.45am–1.15am
Al-Kharga	Upper Egypt Travel Co	65	8-10	9.30pm, 10.30pm
Al-Quseir	Upper Egypt Travel Co	60-80	10	6.30am, 11pm, 1.30am
Bahariya (Bawiti)	Upper Egypt Travel Co	30	4-5	7am, 8am
Dahab	East Delta	90	9	8am, 1.30pm, 7.30pm, 11.45pm
Dakhla	Upper Egypt Travel Co	75	8-10	7.30pm, 8.30pm
Farafra	Upper Egypt Travel Co	45	8-10	7am, 8am
Hurghada	Super Jet	65	6	7.30am, 2.30pm, 11.10pm
Luxor	Upper Egypt Travel Co	100	11	9pm
Marsa Matruh	West & Mid Delta	60-70	5	6.45am, 8.45am, 11am, 4.30pm, 7.45pm, 10pm, 11.30pm
Port Said	East Delta	20-25	4	Hourly 6.30am–9.30pm
Sharm el-Sheikh	East Delta	60-80	7	6.30am, 10.30am, 4.30pm, 11pm, 1am
Sharm el-Sheikh	Super Jet	85	7	7.30am, 1.15pm, 10.45pm
Siwa	West Delta	70	11	7.45pm, 11.30pm
St Katherine's	East Delta	50	7	11am
Suez	East Delta	15-20	2	Every 30min 6am–7pm
Taba & Nuweiba	East Delta	60-100	8	6am, 9.30am, 11.30pm

opolis) Some international services, 3.5km northwest from the Korba area of Heliopolis; take a taxi.

Ulali (p58; Sharia Shurta al-Ezbekiyya, Ramses; Ⓜ Al-Shohadaa) No bus-station structure, just a ticket window for East Delta services to Tanta, Zagazig and canal-zone cities, and summer departures for Sinai, plus plenty of microbuses.

Servees & Microbus

You can get a seat in a microbus or taxi to most destinations from the blocks between Ramses Station and Midan Ulali, just to the southwest. For the Western Oases, head to Moneib, on Sharia el-Nil in Giza, under the ring road overpass (take a taxi or walk 800m east from the Sakkiat Mekki metro stop).

Train

Ramses Station (Mahattat Ramses; Map p58; ☎2575 3555; Midan Ramses) is Cairo's main train station. It was under renovation at the time of research, but should have a **left luggage office** (per piece per day E£2.50; ⏲24hr), a **post office** (⏲8am-8pm), ATMs and a **tourist information office** (⏲9am-7pm). Confirm times and train numbers first at the information desk, then head to the appropriate windows: Alexandra tickets are in the main building, while Upper Egypt tickets are across the tracks to the north.

Secondary stations include **Giza** (Map p58), for the sleeper to Upper Egypt, and Ain Shams, in the northeast part of the city, for Suez.

ALEXANDRIA Special and Spanish trains make fewer stops than the French ones. First class *(ula)* gets you a roomier, assigned seat and usually a much cleaner bathroom.

LUXOR & ASWAN Tourists can now take any train to Upper Egypt. If you do encounter a desk clerk who won't sell you a ticket, you can purchase one on board for a small additional fee, or in advance online.

The overnight wagon-lits service to Luxor and Aswan is operated by a private company, **Watania Sleeping Trains** (☎3748 9488; www.wataniasleepingtrains.com). You can purchase tickets at the point of departure, Giza Station or at Ramses. In high season (October to April), book several days in advance.

MARSA MATRUH Watania runs a train to the Mediterranean coast three times a week during the summer season.

SUEZ CANAL Delays on this route are common; going by bus is more efficient. If you're determined to travel by train, the best option is to Ismailia.

ℹ Getting Around

To/From the Airport

Cairo International Airport (www.cairo-airport.com) is 20km northeast of Cairo. **Terminal 1** (☎2265 5000) is three buildings, all within view of each other, though only arrival halls 1 and 3 receive commercial flights. Opened in 2009, **Terminal 3** (al-Matar al-Gideed; ☎2266 0508) is 2km south and handles all of EgyptAir's flights and other Star Alliance planes. A blue-and-white shuttle bus connects Terminals 1 and 3, though a shuttle train (called the APM) was scheduled to go into service soon after this book went to print. All buildings have ATMs after customs. There is no left-luggage service. For transport to the city, you have a few options.

BUS Air-con bus 27 or 356 (E£2, plus E£1 per large luggage item, one hour) runs every 20 minutes, 7am to midnight, to Midan Abdel Moniem Riad (behind the Egyptian Museum). After hours, the only option is bus 400 (50pt). You must take a blue-and-white shuttle bus from the terminals to the bus station; if the shuttle is headed for Terminal 3 (ie, has left Terminal 1), it will stop across the street from the bus station, not in it.

TAXI The going rate to central Cairo is between E£75 and E£100; you'll need to negotiate. (To the airport from the centre, you can easily get a meter taxi; you'll also pay the E£5 to enter the airport grounds.) Limousines (from car desks in the terminals) cost about E£110, and **Cairo Airport Shuttle Bus** (☎0128 911 1777; www.cairoshuttlebus.com; E£100 to Downtown) runs small vans and has a desk at Terminal 1, arrivals 1 (though it can pick you up anywhere).

Bus & Minibus

Cairo's main local bus and minibus stations are at Midan Abdel Moniem Riad and Midan Ataba (both Map p68). Fares range from 50pt to E£2. There is no known system map; buses are labelled in Arabic numerals only.

Metro

The metro system, now comprising three lines and expanding, is efficient, inexpensive (E£1 for any distance) and, outside rush hours, not too crowded. Given Cairo's traffic jams, if you can make even a portion of your journey on the metro, you'll save time. The two centre cars are typically reserved for women. Keep your ticket handy to feed into the machine on the way out.

Microbus

Private microbuses are hard to use unless you're familiar with their routes; you can flag them down anywhere by yelling out your destination. The most useful route for visitors is the one from the Giza metro stop to near the Pyramids. Fares range between 50pt to E£2 depending on distance, paid after you take your seat.

River Bus

Of limited utility, but scenic, the river bus runs from the **Maspero river bus terminal** (Map p58),

MAJOR TRAINS FROM CAIRO

Prices are for first-class service, all with air-con, unless otherwise noted.

DESTINATION	STATION	PRICE (E£)	DURATION (HR)	TIMES
Alexandria (direct)	Ramses	50	2½	8am, 9am, 11am, noon, 2pm, 6pm, 7pm, 9pm, 10.30pm
Alexandria (stopping)	Ramses	35	3-3½	8 daily, 6am–8.15pm
Aswan	Ramses	109	14	8am, noon, 7pm, 8pm, 1am
Ismailia	Ramses	15	3	6.15am, 1pm, 1.45pm, 2.45pm, 5.45pm, 7.50pm, 10pm
Luxor & Aswan (sleeper)	Giza	360	9½ (Luxor), 13 (Aswan)	8pm, 8.40pm
Luxor	Ramses	90	10½	8am, noon, 7pm, 8pm, 1am
Marsa Matruh (sleeper)	Giza	252	7	11pm Sat, Mon, Wed, mid-Jun–mid-Sep
Port Said	Ramses	21	4	6.15am, 1.45pm, 7.50pm
Suez (2nd class, fan only)	Ain Shams	15-18	2¼	6.15am, 9.20am, 1.10pm, 4.15pm, 6.45pm, 9.45pm
Tanta	Ramses	35-50	1-1½	6am, 8.15am, 10am, 11am, noon, 2.10pm, 3.10pm, 4pm, 5.15pm
Zagazig	Ramses	15	1½	5.15am, 6.15am, 1pm, 1.45pm, 3.40pm, 7.50pm, 10pm

north of the Ramses Hilton, to Giza by the zoo and Cairo University. Boats depart every 15 minutes; the trip takes 30 minutes and the fare is E£1.

Taxi

By far the easiest way of getting anywhere is by white taxi. They're easily flagged down at any time, and they use meters, starting at E£2.50, plus E£1.25 per kilometre and E£0.25 waiting. A tip of 10% or so is much appreciated. A few unmetered black-and-white taxis still ply the streets, but they're gradually aging out of the system.

Hiring a taxi for a longer period runs from E£25 to E£35 per hour, depending on your bargaining skills; E£300 for a full day is typical. One excellent service is **Blue Cab** (☎3760-9716, 0100 442 2008), which can be booked ahead.

AROUND CAIRO

Memphis, Saqqara & Dahshur ممفس سقارة & دهشور

There's little left of the former Pharaonic capital of **Memphis**, 24km south of Cairo. It's worth visiting, however, for the open-air **Mit Rahina Museum** (adult/student E£35/20; 8am-4pm, to 3pm during Ramadan), centred on a gigantic fallen statue of Ramses II, which gives a rare opportunity to inspect carving up close.

A few kilometres away is **Saqqara** (adult/student E£60/30; 8am-4pm, to 3pm during Ramadan), a massive necropolis covering 7 sq km of desert and strewn with pyramids, temples and tombs. Deceased pharaohs and their families, administrators, generals and sacred animals were interred here. The star attraction is the **Step Pyramid of Zoser**, the world's oldest stone monument and the first decent attempt at a pyramid. The excellent small **Imhotep Museum** showcases the best finds from the site.

Ten kilometres south of Saqqara is **Dahshur** (adult/student E£50/25; 8am-4pm, to 3pm during Ramadan), an impressive field of 4th- and 12th-dynasty pyramids, including the **Bent Pyramid** (unfortunately off limits to visitors) and the wonderful **Red Pyramid**, the oldest true pyramid in Egypt. It's arguably a better experience to clamber down into this than the Great Pyramid at Giza, because you'll almost certainly be alone here. And the ticket is far more reasonably priced.

It's possible to visit the three sites in five hours, but you will need your own transport to get here, travel around the sites (parking at each site costs E£2) and bring you back to Cairo. A taxi will cost around E£250 to E£300, or join a day tour (p64). In winter, visit Dahshur first, as it's furthest away; in warmer weather, start with Saqqara to avoid the worst heat.

MEDITERRANEAN COAST

Alexandria الإسكندرية

03 / POP 4.1 MILLION

Although Alexandria today has barely an ancient stone to show for its glorious past, it is in its cosmopolitan allure and Mediterranean pace of life that the magic lies. Sprawling necklace-like along a curving bay, this city offers a splendid cluster of restaurants, some moody, antediluvian cafes and a vibrant youth scene.

History

Established in 331 BC by Alexander the Great, the city became a major trade centre and focal point of learning for the entire Mediterranean world. Its ancient library held 500,000 volumes and the Pharos lighthouse was one of the Seven Wonders of the World. Alexandria continued as the capital of Egypt under the Roman Empire and its eastern offshoot, the Byzantine Empire. From the 4th century AD onwards, the city declined into insignificance. In 1798, Napoleon's arrival and Alexandria's subsequent redevelopment as a major port attracted people from all over the world, but Nasser's 1952 revolution put an end to much of the city's pluralistic charm. Most recently, Alexandria was where the 2011 revolution was sparked, after 28-year-old Khaled Said's beating death by the police sparked a protest movement on Facebook, then in the streets.

Sights

Alexandria is a true waterfront city, nearly 20km long from east to west and only about 3km wide. Its focal points are Midan Ramla (where the train terminates) and adjacent Midan Saad Zaghloul, around which are the main tourist office, restaurants, cafes and most of the cheaper hotels. To the west are the older quarters, such as Anfushi. To the east are newer, swisher suburbs stretching 15km along the coastline to easternmost Montazah.

Bibliotheca Alexandrina MUSEUM, LIBRARY
(Map p84; www.bibalex.org; Corniche al-Bahr, Shatby; adult/student E£10/5, for all museums E£45; 8am-4pm Sat-Thu) This boldly modern library and cultural centre seems a fitting 21st-century replacement for the near-mythical library of ancient times. The original was founded in the late 3rd century BC and was the pre-eminent centre of classical learning. The modern counterpart resembles a gigantic angled discus, with the ancient wealth lyrically evoked on the curved exterior by giant letters, hieroglyphs and symbols from every known alphabet. Inside is room for eight million books, as well as a **Manuscript Museum** (adult/student E£20/10), the excellent exhibition **Impressions of Alexandria** and a **Planetarium** (admission E£25; shows hourly from 11am-2pm, closed Tue & Fri).

Graeco-Roman Museum MUSEUM
(Map p84; 5 Al-Mathaf ar-Romani) A wonderful collection, but closed for renovation for an unspecified period. Worth checking with the tourist office.

Alexandria National Museum MUSEUM
(Map p84; www.alexmuseum.org.eg; 110 Tariq al-Horreyya; adult/student E£35/20; 9am-4.30pm) The excellent Alexandria National Museum sets new benchmarks for summing up Alexandria's impressive past. Its small, thoughtfully selected and well-labelled collection does a sterling job of relating the city's history, from antiquity to the modern period. Look for it in a beautifully restored Italianate villa.

Catacombs of Kom ash-Shuqqafa ARCHAEOLOGICAL SITE
(Carmous; adult/student E£35/20; 9am-5pm) Dating back to the 2nd century AD, these eerily fascinating tombs would have held about 300 corpses. The centrepiece of the catacombs, the **principal tomb**, is the prototype for a horror-film set, with a miniature funerary temple decorated with a weird synthesis of ancient Egyptian, Greek and Roman death iconography. No cameras are allowed. You'll find the catacombs about 2km southwest of the train station, and a short walk from the famed but misnamed

Central Alexandria

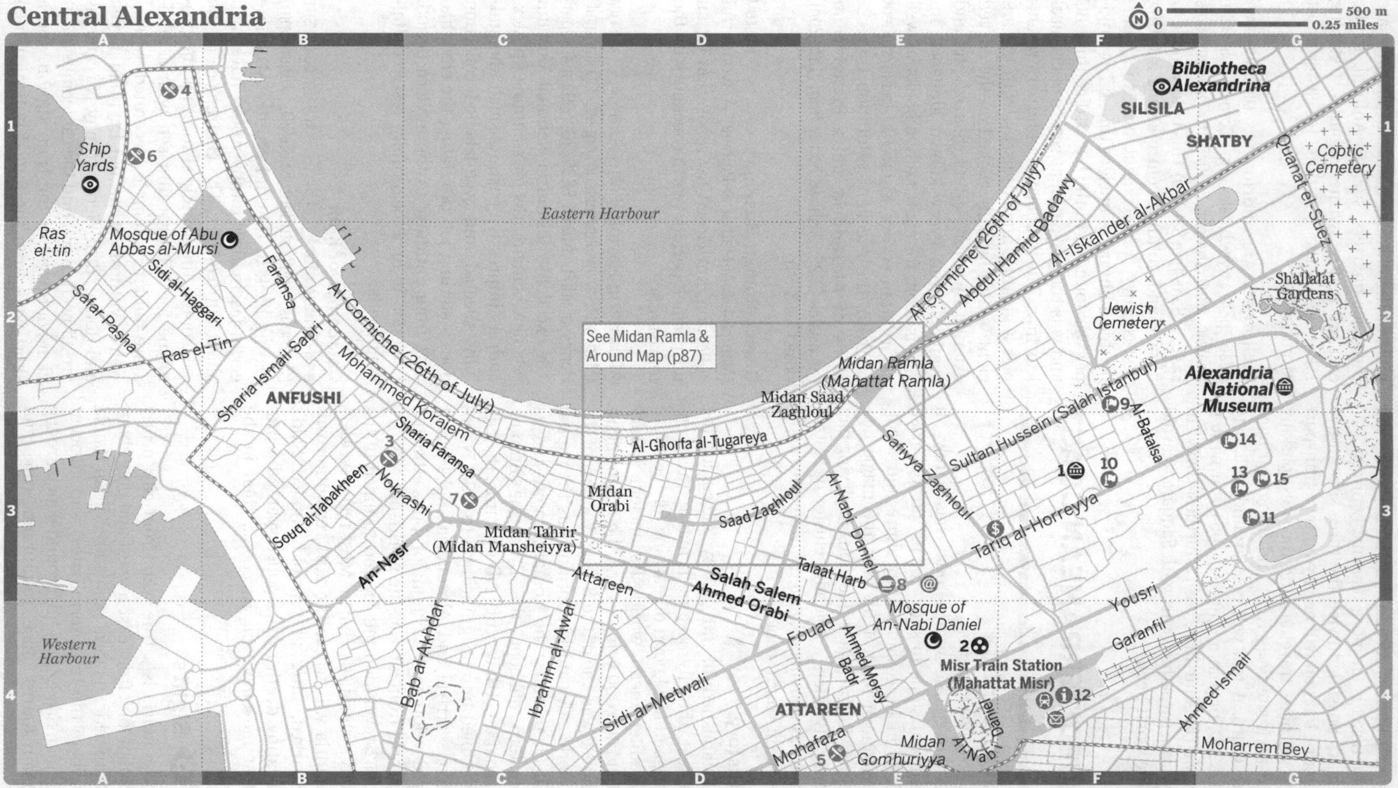
0 500 m
0 0.25 miles
Bibliotheca Alexandrina
SILSILA
SHATBY
Coptic Cemetery
Quanat el-Suez
Shallalat Gardens
Jewish Cemetery
Alexandria National Museum
Eastern Harbour
Ship Yards
Ras el-tin
Mosque of Abu Abbas al-Mursi
Sidi al-Haggari
Safar Pasha
Ras el-Tin
Faransa
Al-Corniche (26th of July)
Abdul Hamid Badawy
Al-Iskander al-Akbar
Sharia Ismail Sabri
ANFUSHI
Mohammed Koraiem
Sharia Faransa
Souq al-Tabakheen
Nokrashi
See Midan Ramla & Around Map (p87)
Midan Ramla (Mahattat Ramla)
Midan Saad Zaghloul
Al-Ghorfa al-Tugareya
Midan Orabi
Midan Tahrir (Midan Mansheiyya)
An-Nasr
Saad Zaghloul
Al-Nabi Daniel
Safiyya Zaghloul
Sultan Hussein (Salah Istanbul)
Al-Batalsa
Tariq al-Horreyya
Talaat Harb
Attareen
Salah Salem
Ahmed Orabi
Mosque of An-Nabi Daniel
Yousri
Garanfil
Fouad
Ahmed Morsy Badr
Misr Train Station (Mahattat Misr)
Western Harbour
Bab al-Akhdar
Ibrahim al-Awal
Sidi al-Metwali
ATTAREEN
Mohafaza
Midan Gomhuriyya
Al-Nabi Daniel
Ahmed Ismail
Moharrem Bey

Central Alexandria

Top Sights

Alexandria National Museum G2
Bibliotheca Alexandrina F1

Sights

1 Graeco-Roman Museum F3
2 Roman Amphitheatre (Kom al-Dikka) E4

Eating

3 Farag B3
4 Kadoura A1
5 Malek es Semon E4
6 Samakmak A1
7 Souq District C3

Drinking

8 Vinous E3

Information

9 German Consulate F2
10 Lebanese Consulate F3
11 Libyan Consulate G3
12 Mahaltat Misr Tourist Office F4
13 Saudi Arabian Consulate G3
14 Spanish Consulate G3
15 Turkish Consulate G3

Pompey's Pillar (Carmous; adult/student E£20/15; ◷9am-4.30pm), surrounded by a disappointing temple to Scrapis.

Roman Amphitheatre (Kom al-Dikka) ARCHAEOLOGICAL SITE
(Map p84; Sharia Yousef, off Midan Gomhuriyya; adult/student E£20/15; ◷9am-4.30pm) The 13 white marble terraces of the only Roman amphitheatre in Egypt were discovered in 1964. Worth visiting for the floor mosaics at the Villa of the Birds (adult/student E£15/8) in the complex.

Sleeping

June to September is Alexandria's high season, when you'll need to book in advance.

TOP CHOICE Windsor Palace Hotel HISTORIC HOTEL $$$
(Map p87; ☎480 8123; www.paradiseinnegypt.com; 17 Sharia ash-Shohada; r with sea view US$150; ❄@📶) This 1907 Edwardian gem is an institution unto itself, with wonderful old elevators and a grand lobby. The rooms sport an old-world, green-and-gold pizzazz; pricier ones have splendid sea views.

Metropole Hotel HISTORIC HOTEL $$$
(Map p87; ☎486 1467; www.paradiseinnegypt.com; 52 Sharia Saad Zaghloul; s/d US$100/$150; ❄@📶) The Metropole sits right in the thick of things, overlooking Midan Saad Zaghloul. Don't be put off by the magnificently tacky lobby with its fake Parthenon-style friezes – rooms are tastefully decorated with gigantic gilded doors and walls panelled like a St Petersburg palace.

Egypt Hotel HOTEL $$
(Map p87; ☎481 4483; 1 Sharia Degla; s US$50-60, d US$60-70; ❄📶) Filling a desperate need for decent midrange digs, the Egypt is a big step up from budget choices, in a renovated 100-year old Italian building. The lobby is floor-to-ceiling cream and brown tile, but the rooms have plush beds, wood floors, clean bathrooms, powerful air-con and small balconies with sea or street views. Wi-fi is in the lobby only.

Hotel Union HOTEL $$
(Map p87; ☎480 7312; 5th fl, Al-Cornich; s E£80-140, d E£120-160; ❄📶) One of the best budget choices in the centre, this busy place caters to foreigners and Egyptians. Simple rooms, in a bewildering range of bathroom/view/air-con options, are almost charming and relatively well maintained. Our rates quoted include a Byzantine mix of taxes, but no breakfast.

Hotel Crillon HOTEL $$
(Map p87; ☎480 0330; 3rd fl, 5 Sharia Adib Ishaq; s E£110-120, d E£150-180) Oodles of character, with high ceilings, but a little rough around the edges. Shared bathrooms could be cleaner, and there's no fan or air-con. Front-facing rooms are worth the extra, to enjoy traditional Egyptian breakfasts on your balcony overlooking the harbour.

Swiss Canal Hotel HOTEL $
(Map p87; ☎480 8373; 14 Sharia al-Bursa al-Qadima, s with/without air-con E£100/80, d with/without air-con E£120/100; ❄) The walls here are an iridescent shade of pink that really has to be seen to be believed, but the rooms are generally clean, with towering ceilings, mammoth wooden doors, spongy, soft beds, en-suite bathrooms, and windows overlooking a reasonably quiet souq area.

Triomphe Hotel HOTEL $$
(Map p87; ☎480 7585; 3rd fl, Sharia Gamal ad-Din Yassin; s/d E£90/140, without bathroom E£70/120) Quiet and good value old-timer with a tiled, leafy lobby. The rooms cling to shreds of

former elegance, with high ceilings, timber floors and handy washbasins, though some are aging more gracefully than others. Doubles have balconies with side sea view; singles have no view.

Sofitel Cecil Alexandria HISTORIC HOTEL $$$
(Cecil Hotel; Map p87; ☎487 7173; www.sofitel.com; 16 Midan Saad Zaghloul; s with/without sea view US$145/130, d with/without sea view US$185/165; ❄@📶) The Alexandria legend retains only a fraction of the lustre it had when Durrell and Churchill came to visit. The big consolation is the sweeping view over Eastern Harbour, plus fully equipped (if somewhat sombre) rooms.

Eating

The main place for cheap eats – fuul, ta'amiyya, sandwiches – is around where Sharia Safiyya Zaghloul meets Midan Ramla. Anfushi has some of Alexandria's best and freshest seafood.

TOP CHOICE **Mohammed Ahmed** FELAFEL $
(Map p87; 17 Sharia Shakor Pasha; mains E£2-5; ⏲24hr; 📝) Do not miss the undisputed king of fuul and felafel, filled day and night with locals downing small plates of spectacularly good and cheap Egyptian standards. Also try accompanying salads, such as tahini, *banga* (beetroot) or pickles. Note that the street sign on the corner of Saad Zaghloul calls this Abdel Fattah El Hadary St.

TOP CHOICE **Farag** SEAFOOD $$
(Map p84; 7 Souq al-Tabakheen, Manshey; mains E£35-75; ⏲lunch & dinner) Deep in the heart of the Anfushi souk, dine on perfectly cooked and seasoned seafood. This spot is very local and a bit hard to find – the sign is high above street level. Or just ask around; everyone knows it.

Malek es-Seman GRILL $$
(Map p84; 48 Midan el-Soriyin Masguid el-Attarine; two birds E£25; ⏲8pm-3am) Off Sharia Attareen, just south of the junction with Sharia Yousef, this open-air restaurant does one thing very, very well: quail. Birds are served grilled or stuffed; we especially like the slightly charred and crispy flavour of the grilled. Orders come with bread and six different salads. It's a bit hard to find, but look for a painted sign with a small bird. Serves beer.

Samakmak SEAFOOD $$
(Map p84; 42 Qasr Ras at-Tin; mains E£50-120; ⏲lunch & dinner) Samakmak is definitely one step up from the other fish eateries in the neighbourhood. Customers flock to this place for its specials, including crayfish, marvellous crab *tagen* (clay-pot stew) and a great spaghetti with clams.

Kadoura SEAFOOD $$
(Map p84; 33 Sharia Bairam at-Tonsi; mains E£35-80; ⏲lunch & dinner) This is one of Alexandria's most authentic fish restaurants. Pick your

CAFE CULTURE

In case you hadn't noticed, Alexandria is a cafe town – and we're not talking Starbucks double-decaf soy-vanilla grande lattes here. Ever since the first half of the 20th century, the city's diverse population has congregated to live out life's dramas over pastries and a cup of tea or coffee. Many of these old haunts are definitely worth a visit for historical associations and grand decor, but not always for the food.

As good a place to start as any is **Athineos** (Map p87; 21 Midan Saad Zaghloul), an establishment that lives and breathes nostalgia. The cafe part on the Midan Ramla side still has its original '40s fittings, period character, and quite possibly some of its original customers. Also facing Midan Ramla is **Trianon** (Map p87; 56 Midan Saad Zaghloul; ⏲from 7am; ❄), a favourite haunt of the Greek poet Cavafy, who worked in offices above. Stroll around the corner to check out **Délices** (Map p87; 46 Sharia Saad Zaghloul; ⏲from 7am; ❄). This enormous old tearoom drips with atmosphere and can actually whip up a decent breakfast.

Vinous (Map p84; cnr Sharia al-Nabi Daniel & Sharia Tariq al-Horreyya; ⏲7am-1am) is an old-school patisserie with more grand deco styling than you can poke a puff pastry at. From here you can make a historical detour to the now-closed **Pastroudis** (Tariq al-Horeyya), a meeting point for characters in Lawrence Durrell's *Alexandria Quartet*.

For one last pick-me-up coffee, head over to Sharia Saad Zaghloul and **Sofianopoulos Coffee Store** (Map p87; 21 Sharia Saad Zaghloul), a gorgeous coffee retailer that would be in a museum anywhere else in the world.

Midan Ramla & Around

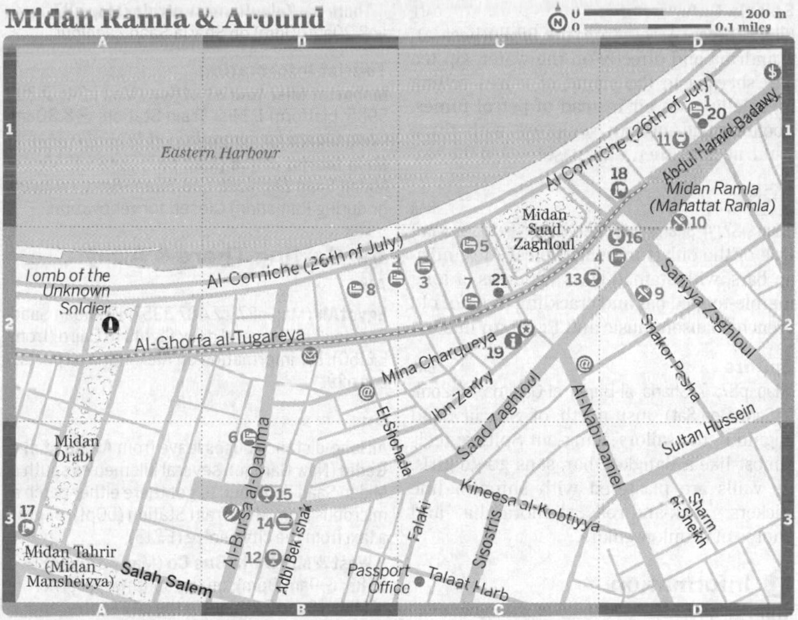

Midan Ramla & Around

Sleeping
- 1 Egypt Hotel D1
- 2 Hotel Crillon B2
- 3 Hotel Union C2
- 4 Metropole Hotel D2
- 5 Sofitel Cecil Alexandria C2
- 6 Swiss Canal Hotel B3
- 7 Triomphe Hotel C2
- 8 Windsor Palace Hotel B2

Eating
- 9 Mohammed Ahmed D2
- 10 Taverna D1

Drinking
- 11 Athineos D1
- 12 Cap d'Or B3
- 13 Délices C2
- 14 Sofianopoulos Coffee Store B3
- 15 Spitfire B3
- 16 Trianon D2

Information
- 17 French Consulate A3
- 18 Italian Consulate D1
- 19 Main Tourist Office C2

Transport
- 20 EgyptAir D1
- 21 West & Mid Delta Bus Co C2

fish from a huge ice-packed selection, which usually includes sea bass, red and grey mullet, bluefish, sole, squid, crab and shrimp, and often a lot more. A selection of mezze is served with all orders. Most fish average E£40 to E£80 per kilo; prawns E£180 per kilo.

Taverna EGYPTIAN FAST FOOD **$$**
(Map p87; Mahattat Ramla; mains E£9-30; ⏲breakfast, lunch & dinner) This deservedly popular establishment serves excellent hand-thrown sweet or savoury *fiteer*, pizza, and some of the best shwarma in town. Eat in or takeaway.

Drinking

Alexandria's corniche becomes one long ahwa in summertime, though many places tend to overcharge summer tourists. The city isn't much of a boozing town, with a few old exceptions.

Selsela Cafe CAFE
(Shatby Beach) Across from the Bibliotheca Alexandrina and directly on the water, sip tea and sheesha to the sound of waves rolling in, smelling sea air instead of petrol fumes. Look for the modern sculpture with three white needles, then walk past toward the sea.

TOP CHOICE **Cap d'Or** BAR
(Map p87; 4 Sharia Adbi Bek Ishak; ⏲10am-3am) One of the only surviving typical Alexandrian bars, with stained-glass windows, a long marble-topped bar and crackling tapes of old French chanson music and Egyptian hits.

Spitfire BAR
(Map p87; 7 Sharia al-Bursa al-Qadima; ⏲2pm-1.30am Mon-Sat) Just north of Sharia Saad Zaghloul, the sailors' hang-out Spitfire feels almost like a Bangkok bar, sans go-go girls. Its walls are plastered with shipping-line stickers, rock-and-roll memorabilia and photos of drunk regulars.

Information

Emergency

Tourist police (Map p87; ☎485 0507) Upstairs from the main tourist office.

Internet Access

Internet cafes open and close in the blink of an eye in Alexandria. A few of the more reliable:

Farous Net Cafe (Map p84; Tariq al- Horreyya; per hr E£3; ⏲10am-midnight)

Hightop Internet Cafe (Map p87; 71 Sharia al-Nabi Daniel; per hr E£3; ⏲10am-midnight)

MG@Net (Map p87; 10 Sharia el-Shohada; per hr E£3; ⏲7am-2am)

Medical Services

Al-Madina at-Tibiya (Alexandria Medical City Hospital; ☎543 2150/7402; Sharia Ahmed Shawky, Rushdy; ⏲24hr)

Money

For changing cash, the simplest option is to use one of the many exchange bureaus on the side streets between Midan Ramla and the Corniche. Otherwise:

American Express (Amex; ☎420 2288; www.americanexpress.com.eg; Elsaladya Bldg, Sharia 14th Mai, Smouha; ⏲9am-4pm Sun-Thu) Also a travel agency.

Thomas Cook (Map p87; www.thomascookegypt.com; 15 Midan Saad Zaghloul; ⏲8am-5pm)

Post & Telephone

The **main post office** (Map p87; Sharia al-Bursa al Qadima; ⏲8.30am-3pm Sat-Thu) is two blocks east of Midan Orabi.

There is a **Telephone centrale** (Map p87; ⏲8.30am-10pm) on Sharia Saad Zaghloul.

Tourist Information

Mahattat Misr tourist office (Map p84; ☎392 5985; platform 1, Misr Train Station; ⏲8.30am-6pm) Closed for renovation at time of research.

Main tourist office (Map p87; ☎485 1556; Midan Saad Zaghloul; ⏲8.30am-6pm, reduced hr during Ramadan) Closed for renovation.

Getting There & Away

Air

EgyptAir (Map p87; ☎487 3357; 19 Midan Saad Zaghloul) has several daily flights to Cairo (from E£150). For information on Alexandria airports, see p89.

Bus

All long-distance buses leave from **Al-Mo'af al-Gedid** (New Garage), several kilometres south of Midan Saad Zaghloul; to get there either catch a microbus from Misr Train Station (50pt), or grab a taxi from the city centre (E£15).

West & Mid Delta Bus Co (Map p87; ☎480 9685; ⏲9am-9pm), on the southwest corner of Midan Saad Zaghloul in the city centre, and considerably nicer **Super Jet** (☎543 5222; ⏲8am-10pm), opposite Sidi Gaber Train Station, next to the fountain, operate from here.

CAIRO Super Jet and West & Mid Delta both have hourly buses to Cairo (E£30, 2½ hours), also stopping at Cairo airport (E£35), from early morning.

NORTH COAST & SIWA West & Mid Delta has hourly departures to Marsa Matruh (E£25 to E£35, four hours); a few continue on to Sallum (nine hours) on the border with Libya. For Siwa (E£38, nine hours), buses go at 8.30am, 11am and 10pm; or just take any Marsa Matruh bus and change to a microbus there.

Super Jet runs five buses to Marsa Matruh (E£35) daily during summer (June to September), the last leaving in the late afternoon. Most Marsa Matruh buses stop in El Alamein (one hour), and will stop at Sidi Abdel Rahman on request, though you will have to pay the full Marsa Matruh fare.

SINAI West & Mid Delta has one daily service to Sharm el-Sheikh (E£110, eight to 10 hours) at 9pm.

SUEZ CANAL & RED SEA COAST Super Jet has a daily evening service to Hurghada (E£100, nine hours). West & Mid Delta has several services a day to Port Said (E£30, four to five hours) and four to Suez (E£35, five hours). It also has two buses to Hurghada and Port Safaga (E£90). The Upper Egypt Bus Co has three daily Hurghada buses (E£90) that continue to Port Safaga.

WORTH A TRIP

EL ALAMEIN

In June 1942 the Afrika Korps, headed by German Field Marshal Erwin Rommel, the celebrated 'Desert Fox', launched an all-out offensive from Tobruk, Libya, determined to take the strategically important Suez Canal. The Axis powers and their 500 tanks came within nearly 100km of their goal before the Allies, under the command of General Bernard Montgomery, stopped their advance at El Alamein. In October 1942 Montgomery's 8th Army swooped down from Alexandria with 1000 tanks, and within two weeks routed the Axis forces. More than 80,000 soldiers were killed or wounded at El Alamein and in subsequent battles for North Africa.

Today, El Alamein is noted more for its fine beaches, and it makes a good day trip from Alexandria. A **war museum** (adult/student E£20/10; ⏲9am-4pm) and the Commonwealth, German and Italian **war cemeteries** (admission free; ⏲7am-2.30pm, key available outside of these hr) mark the scene of one of the biggest tank battles in history.

The easiest way to visit is to organise a car and English speaking driver from **Mena Tours** (☎480 9676; menatoursalx@yahoo.com; ⏲9am-5pm Sat-Thu) for approximately E£500. Otherwise, a private taxi will charge between E£300 and E£400 to take you to the museum and cemeteries and bring you back to Alexandria.

Alternatively, you can catch any of the Marsa Matruh buses from Al-Mo'af Al-Gedid station in Alexandria. You'll be dropped on the main road about 200m down the hill from the museum.

Servees & Microbus

Service taxis and microbuses for Cairo (E£25) depart from outside Misr Train Station. All others go from Al-Mo'af al-Gedid (New Garage) bus station at Moharrem Bey.

Train

The main terminal is **Mahattat Misr** (Misr Train Station; Map p84; ☎426 3207), about 1km south of Midan Ramla in the city centre. **Mahattat Sidi Gaber** (Sidi Gaber Train Station; ☎426 3953) serves the eastern suburbs. Trains from Cairo stop at Sidi Gaber first, and most locals get off here.

There are more than 15 trains daily between Cairo and Alexandria, from 6am to 10pm. There are two train types: Spanish *(esbani)* and French *(faransawi)*. Spanish trains (1st/2nd class E£50/35, 2½ hours) are better and make fewer stops. The French train (1st/2nd class E£35/19, 3½ to four hours) makes multiple stops. There are two daily trains to Luxor at 5pm and 10pm (1st/2nd class E£129/69), with the 5pm train continuing to Aswan (1st/2nd class E£148/77).

At Mahattat Misr, 1st- and 2nd-class tickets to Cairo are sold at the ticket office along platform 1; 3rd- and 2nd-class ordinary tickets are in the front hall.

Getting Around

To/From the Airport

All flights to Alexandria arrive at **Burg al-Arab** (HBE) airport, about 45km southwest of the city. Smaller **Nouzha** (ALY) airport, 7km southeast, was being renovated at the time of research, to reopen at the end of 2012; domestic flights may be routed here.

For Burg al-Arab, an air-conditioned bus (one way E£6 plus E£1 per bag, one hour) leaves from the Sofitel Cecil hotel, three hours before all departures; confirm the exact time at the Cecil. A taxi to/from the airport should cost between E£100 and E£150. You can also catch bus 475 (one hour) from Misr Train Station.

If you do need to get to/from Nouzha, a taxi should cost no more than E£20.

Microbus

The most useful are the ones zooming along the Corniche. There are no set departure points or stops, so when one passes, wave and shout your destination; if it's heading that way it will stop. It's anywhere from 50pt for a short trip to E£1.50 to Montazah.

Red Bus

An air-conditioned red double-decker bus (E£3) plies the Corniche every 15 to 30 minutes between Ras el-Tin and the Sheraton in Montazah. It's worth riding the length of the Corniche on the upper deck, just for the views.

Taxi

There are no working taxi meters in Alexandria, though the possibility was being discussed at the time of research. Some sample fares: Midan Ramla to Misr Train Station E£5; Midan Saad Zaghloul to Fort Qaitbey (west edge of the harbour) or the Bibliotheca Alexandrina (east end) E£5; Cecil Hotel to Montazah (eastern suburbs) E£25.

Tram

Alexandria's old trams are fun to ride, but very slow. Midan Ramla is the main station. Lime-yellow-coloured trams go west and blue-coloured ones travel east. The fare is 25pt.

Tram 14 goes to Misr Train Station; tram 15 goes through Anfushi; trams 1 and 25 go to Sidi Gaber.

Rosetta (Ar-Rashid) الرشيد

☎045 / POP 69,000

It is hard to believe that this dusty town on the western branch of the Nile was Egypt's most significant port in the 18th century. Today, it's a contrast with modern Alex: the streets are packed with donkey carts, basket-weavers and blacksmiths. Rosetta is also famous as the discovery place of the stone stele that provided the key to deciphering hieroglyphics (see below).

The other major draws here are the beautifully crafted Ottoman-era **merchants' houses**, built in the traditional Delta style with flat bricks painted red and black. Many of these three-storey structures are adorned with ornate carved-wood *mashrabiyya* screens over the windows. Among the 22 impressive buildings hiding along Rosetta's streets, several have been restored and are open to the public. These include the **House of Amasyali**, the **House of Abu Shaheen** (adult/student E£15/10), and the wonderful **Hammam Azouz**, a 19th-century bath-house. Buildings are open from 9am to 4pm, and tickets purchased at the House of Abu Shaheen are good for all of the open monuments in the town centre.

The skinny 11-storey **Rasheed International Hotel** (☎045 293 4399; www.rosettahotel.jeeran.com; Museum Garden Sq; s/d/tr E£100/130/160; ❄) has plainly decorated but spotless rooms, all with satellite TV, minibar and balconies with top views – on a clear day you can see the Mediterranean from the higher floors. Its **restaurant** serves some of the better food in town.

The easiest way to make the 65km trip from Alexandria is by **microbus** (E£4, one hour) from Al-Mo'af Al-Gedid, the long-distance bus station. Coming back it's easy to get a microbus from Rosetta's main roundabout, at the southwest entrance to town. A **private taxi** from Alexandria to Rosetta costs about E£150, including waiting time.

NILE VALLEY وادي النيل

In this part of the country, the life-giving Nile snakes its way through Egypt's desolate belly. An abundance of ancient riches lines its green shores.

Luxor الأقصر

☎095 / POP 484,132

Built on the once-brilliant 4000-year-old city of ancient Thebes, modern-day Luxor inherited the relics of one of history's most prosperous and powerful empires. Many of these relics seem to mushroom directly from the sprawl of this bustling modern Egyptian town. For most visitors, the opulent cache of tombs and funerary temples scattered across the west bank make this Egypt's must-see destination.

History

Following the collapse of centralised control at the end of the Old Kingdom, the small village of Thebes emerged as the main power in Upper Egypt under the 11th- and 12th-dynasty pharaohs. Rising against the northern capital of Heracleopolis, Thebes reunited the country under its political, religious and

ROSETTA STONE

The Rosetta Stone is the most significant find in the history of Egyptology. Unearthed in 1799 by a French soldier near Rosetta, this dark granitic stele records a decree issued by the priests of Memphis in 196 BC, on the anniversary of the coronation of Ptolemy V (205–180 BC). In order to be understood by Egyptians, Greeks and others living in Egypt, it was written in the three scripts current at the time: hieroglyphic, demotic (a cursive form of hieroglyphs) and Greek. At the time of its discovery scholars had still not managed to decipher hieroglyphs, and it was quickly realised that these three scripts would help crack the hieroglyph code and recover the lost world of the ancient Egyptians.

When the British defeated Napoleon's army in 1801, the original Rosetta Stone was taken as a spoil of war and shipped to London, where it can still be seen at the British Museum.

administrative control and ushered in the Middle Kingdom. The strength of Thebes' government also enabled it to re-establish control after a second period of decline, liberate the country from foreign rule and bring in the New Kingdom dynasties.

At the height of their glory and opulence, from 1550 to 1069 BC, all the New Kingdom pharaohs (with the exception of Akhenaten, who moved to Tell al-Amarna) made Thebes their permanent residence. The city had a population of nearly a million, and the architectural activity was astounding.

Sights

Luxor consists of three separate areas: the town of Luxor itself on the east bank of the Nile; the village of Karnak, 2km to the northeast; and the towns of Gurna, New Gurna and Al-Gezira near the monuments and necropolis of ancient Thebes, all on the west bank of the Nile.

EAST BANK

Temples of Karnak TEMPLES
(off Map p92; Sharia Maabad al-Karnak; adult/student E£65/40; ⏲6am-6pm) Simply referred to as Karnak, the vast complex of extraordinary temples, pylons, obelisks and sanctuaries is quite possibly the most incredible sight in all of Egypt. A stunning representation of the power and prestige of the pharaohs and their Theban gods, one can only feel Lilliputian when confronted with this sprawling 2-sq-km site. Built, modified, enlarged and restored over a period of 1500 years, this was the most important place of worship in Egypt during the New Kingdom, and the main structure, the **Temple of Amun**, is considered to be the largest religious building ever built.

A **sphinx-lined path** that once went to the Nile takes you to the massive **1st Pylon**, from where you end up in the **Great Court**. To the left is the **Temple of Seti II**, dedicated to the triad of Theban gods – Amun, Mut and Khons. In the centre of the court is the one remaining column of the **Kiosk of Taharqa**, a 25th-dynasty Ethiopian pharaoh.

Beyond the **2nd Pylon** is the unforgettable 6000-sq-metre **Great Hypostyle Hall**. Built by Amenhotep III, Seti I and Ramses II, this hall is a pylon garden of 134 gargantuan, papyrus-shaped stone pillars that can only be described as humbling.

Off to the left of the first court, an **open-air museum** (adult/student E£25/15) displays a collection of statuary found in the complex, as well as three well-preserved chapels.

> **KARNAK PRACTICALITIES**
>
> » Buy tickets to the museum at the main entrance.
>
> » Tour groups descend on the site daily, usually around 10am. Come in the early morning, the late afternoon or around lunchtime.
>
> » Microbuses make the short run to the temples from Luxor's centre for 50pt. A *calèche* (horse-drawn carriage) costs E£10 from Luxor Temple; a taxi costs E£10 to E£15.
>
> » The requisite **sound-and-light show** (☎238 6000, 238 2777; www.soundandlight.com.eg; adult/student E£100/60, video camera E£35) runs two or three times each evening.

Luxor Temple TEMPLE
(Map p92; Corniche an-Nil; adult/student E£50/30; ⏲6am-9pm Oct-Apr, to 10pm May-Sep) Built on the site of an older sanctuary dedicated to the gods Amun, Mut and Khons, this is a striking piece of Nileside architecture. Largely built by the New Kingdom pharaohs Amenhotep III and Ramses II, it was expanded and altered over the centuries by Nectanebo, Alexander the Great and various Romans. Not to be outdone, the Arabs also built a mosque in an interior court in the 13th century. Be sure to return at night when the temple is lit up.

Luxor Museum MUSEUM
(Map p92; Corniche an-Nil; adult/student E£80/40; ⏲8.30am-2pm) Definitely worth a peek for its selective and excellently displayed collection, dating from the Old Kingdom to the Mamluk period. In the main downstairs hall, don't miss the finely crafted and well-preserved **relief of Tuthmosis III**, **statue of Thuthmosis III**, alabaster **figure of Amenhotep III**, and rare **Theban relief** dating from the Old Kingdom of Unas-ankh. The newest wing of the museum showcases the splendour of Thebes during the New Kingdom, with the highlight being two royal mummies of **Amhose I** and possibly **Ramses I**, eerily presented unwrapped in darkened rooms.

Mummification Museum MUSEUM
(Map p92; ☎238 1501; Corniche an-Nil; adult/student E£50/25; ⏲9am-2pm) For mummy buffs (and who isn't one?), visit this small

Luxor – East Bank

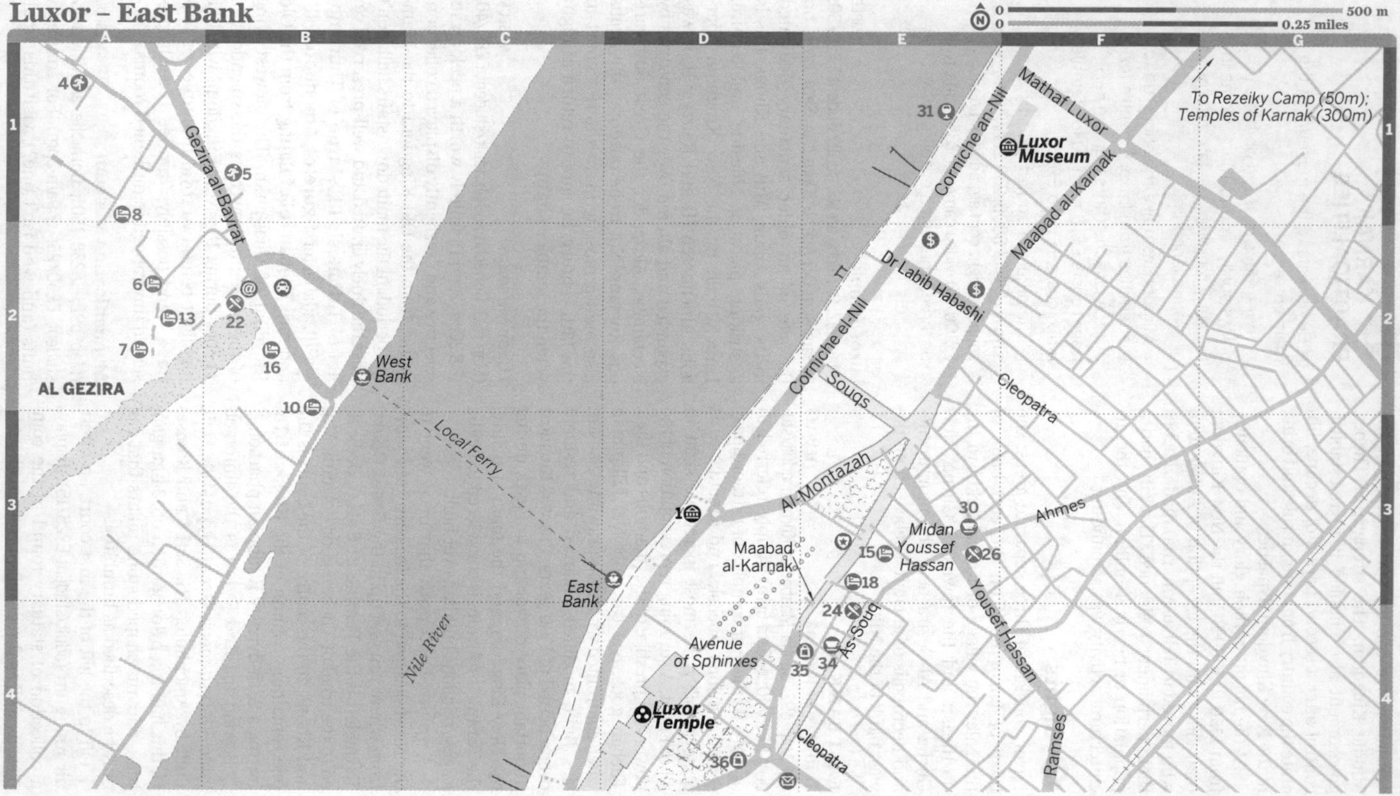

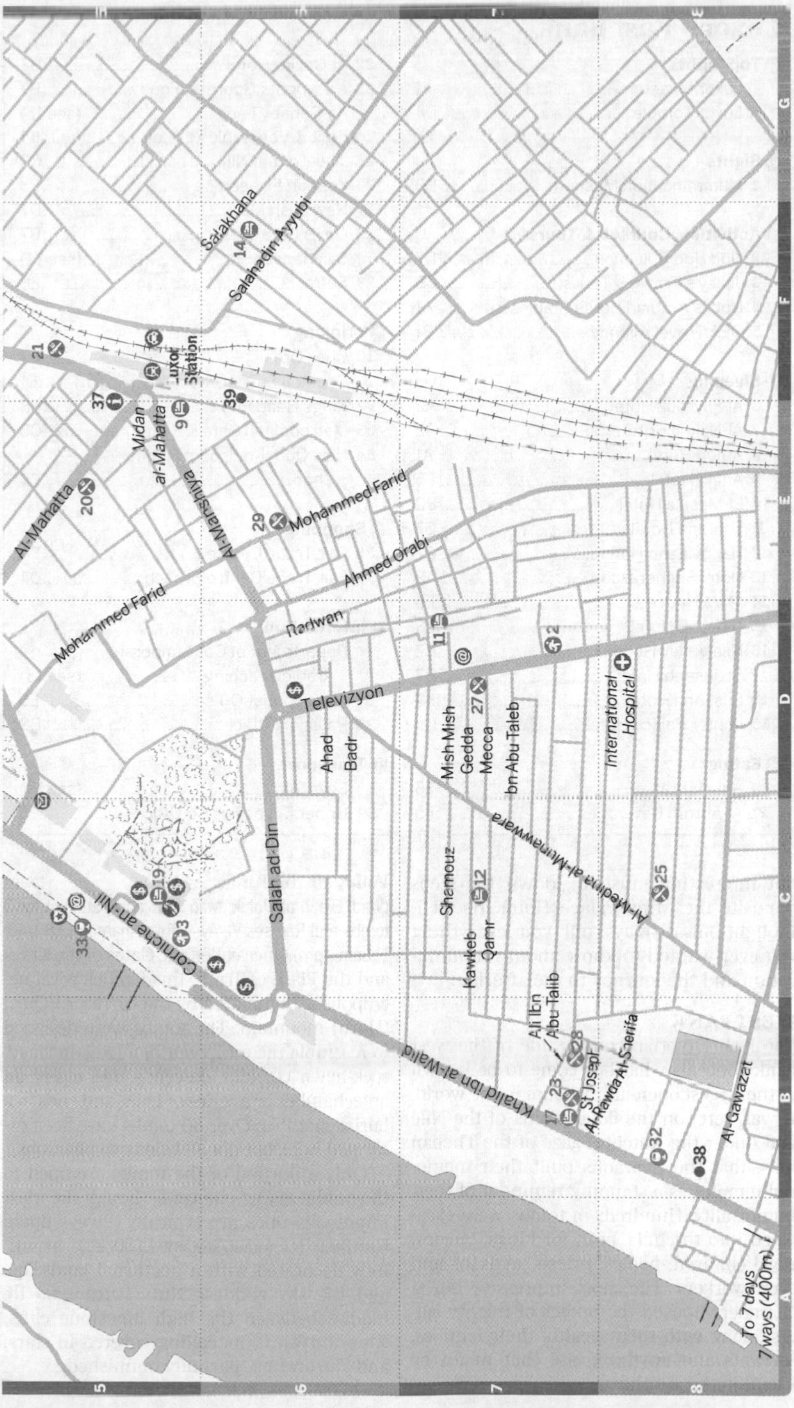
Salakhana
Salahadin Ayyubi
Luxor Station
Midan al-Mahatta
Al-Mahatta
Al-Manshiya
Mohammed Farid
Ahmed Orabi
Radwan
Televizyon
Salah ad-Din
Ahad
Badr
Mish Mish
Gedda
Mecca
Ibn Abu Taleb
International Hospital
Al-Medina al-Munawwara
Shemouz
Kawkeb
Qamr
Ali Ibn Abu Talib
St Joseph
Al-Rawda Al-Sherifa
Al-Gawazat
Corniche an-Nil
Khalid ibn al-Walid
To 7 days 7 ways (400m)
2
3
9
11
12
14
17
19
20
21
23
25
27
28
29
32
33
37
38
39
E
F
G
A
B
C
D
5
6
7
8

Luxor – East Bank

but interesting museum, down the steps opposite the Mina Palace Hotel. Its well-thought-out displays tell you everything you ever wanted to know about mummification and the journey to the afterlife.

WEST BANK

The lush Egyptian countryside of the west bank conceals what has come to be known as the largest open-air museum in the world. It was here, on the flood plains of the Nile and under the watchful gaze of the Theban hills, that the pharaohs built their memorial temples as a standing reminder of their immortality. Hundreds of tombs were excavated into the hills, built for kings, queens, royal children, nobles, priests, artisans and even workers. The most impressive burial chambers housed the bodies of mighty rulers, along with their wealth, their families, servants and anything else that might be useful in the afterlife.

Valley of the Kings TOMBS

(Wadi Biban al-Muluk; Map p98; adult/student for 3 tombs excl Ramses VI, Ay & Tutankhamun E£80/40; 6am-4pm) Once called the Gates of the Kings and the Place of Truth, this famous royal necropolis is dominated by the barren **Al-Qurn** (Horn) mountain. The tombs were designed to resemble the underworld; a long, inclined, rock-hewn corridor descends into either an antechamber or a series of halls, and ends in a burial chamber. Over 60 tombs have been excavated here, but not all belong to pharaohs.

Only a portion of the tombs are open to the public at any one time, though the most impressive ones are typically always open: **Ramses VI** (adult/student E£50/25), beautifully decorated with a nocturnal landscape and the sky goddess Nut; **Tuthmosis III**, hidden between the high limestone cliffs; **Amenhotep II**, its ceiling covered in stars; and **Horemheb**, partially unfinished.

Other tombs open to visitors at the time of research include **Ramses VII**, **Ramses IV**, **Ramses IX**, **Ramses II**, **Merenptah**, **Ramses III**, and more than five others past the tomb of Tuthmosis III.

The **Tomb of Tutankhamun** (adult/student E£100/60) is the supposed main attraction, and conveniently reached by miniature train (E£10). Howard Carter's 1922 discovery is actually one of the least interesting tombs. Only Tutankhamun's mummy in its gilded wood coffin is in situ, and everything else is in Cairo's Egyptian Museum or the Luxor Museum.

Deir al-Bahri TEMPLE

(Funerary Temple of Hatshepsut; Map p98; adult/student E£30/15; ⌚6am-5pm) Rising out of the desert plain in a series of terraces, Hatshepsut's funerary temple merges with the sheer limestone cliffs of the eastern face of the Theban mountain. It was desecrated and vandalised by her bitter successor, Tuthmosis III, but retains much of its original magnificence, including some fascinating reliefs.

Tombs of the Nobles TOMBS

(Map p98; per group of tombs adult E£15-30, student E£10-15; ⌚6am-5pm) For intriguing artwork, these are some of the best tombs on the west bank, but also the least visited. The most colourful of the 400 or so are those of **Ramose**, which shows two different styles from the periods of Amenhotep III and Akhenaten; **Sennofer**, who oversaw the Garden of Amun and whose tomb is fittingly adorned with paintings of grapes and vines; and **Nakht**, where there's a small museum and some of the best-known tomb paintings. Tombs are clustered together in twos or threes, with a ticket for each group – each of these three is in a separate cluster, so you'll have to buy three tickets to see them all.

Valley of the Queens TOMBS

(Biban al Harim; Map p98; adult/student E£35/20; ⌚6am-5pm) The 75-odd tombs in this valley belong to queens and other royal family members from the 19th and 20th dynasties. Only three – the tombs of **Amunherkhepshef** (the finest), **Khaemwaset**, and **Titi** – are currently open to the public. The crowning glory of the site, the **Tomb of Nefertari**, is still closed to the public until further notice.

Medinat Habu TEMPLE

(Map p98; adult/student E£30/15; ⌚6am-5pm) One of the more underrated sites on the west bank, the temple complex of Medinat Habu is dominated by the enormous **Funerary Temple of Ramses III**. The largest temple after Karnak, it has an enthralling mountain backdrop and some fascinating reliefs. The best time to visit is in the late afternoon, when the setting sun interacts amazingly with the golden stone.

Temple of Seti I TEMPLE

(Map p98; adult/student E£30/15; ⌚6am-5pm) This pharaoh expanded the Egyptian empire to include Cyprus and parts of Mesopotamia. The temple is seldom visited, but it's in a picturesque location and was very nicely restored in the 1990s.

Ramesseum TEMPLE

(Tomb of Ozymandias; Map p98; adult/student E£35/20; ⌚6am-5pm) Ramses II's funerary temple now lies mostly in ruins, but its scattered remains inspired the English poet Shelley's work 'Ozymandias', mocking the pharaoh's aspirations to immortality.

FREE **Colossi of Memnon** ARCHAEOLOGICAL SITE

(Map p98) These 18m-high statues are all that remain of a temple built by Amenhotep III, once the largest in Egypt. The Greeks believed that they were statues of Memnon, who was slain by Achilles in the Trojan War.

Deir al-Medina ARCHAEOLOGICAL SITE

(Map p98; adult/student E£30/15; ⌚6am-5pm) This small Ptolemaic temple, dedicated to the goddesses Hathor and Maat, was later occupied by Christian monks. The **Tomb of Sennedjem** is especially fine, befitting his status as an artist under Seti I and Ramses II.

Activities

Felucca Rides

Feluccas cruise the Nile throughout the day, and cost between E£30 and E£50 per hour per boat, depending on your bargaining skills. The most popular trip is to Banana Island, a tiny, palm-dotted isle about 5km upriver. The trip takes between two and three hours, ideally timed to watch the sunset from the boat.

Hot-Air Ballooning

Sunrise balloon rides are offered by several companies, including **Horus** (☎228 2670, 0111 015 12 41; www.horusballoon.com) and **Hod Hod Suleiman** (Map p92; ☎227 1116/0122 115 8593; Sharia Omar Ali, off Sharia Televizyon). Expect to pay from €80 to €150 per person.

Luxor

There's usually no way around the crowds of visitors and hawkers in the Valley of the Kings, but try to go early, before it gets hot. Stop off at the **Colossi of Memnon** **1** as you pass them, taking a look at the ongoing excavation of the ruins of the Temple of Amenhotep III, whose entrance they once flanked. From the royal tombs, drive around the hillside to visit the massive terraced **Temple of Hatshepsut** **2**, almost entirely reconstructed but still good to see as it is the best surviving example of classical-style Egyptian architecture in Luxor.

The Theban hillside further to the south is pitted with thousands of tomb openings. The Tombs of the Nobles in what was **Gurna Village** **3** and the nearby **Workers' Tombs** **4** at Deir al-Medina are very different in style and construction from the royal burials. In some ways, their views of everyday life are more impressive than the more orthodox scenes on the walls of the royal tombs.

In the afternoon, drop down towards the line between desert and agriculture to see two royal temples. The Ramesseum is dedicated to the memory of Ramses II and contains the upper half of a massive statue of the pharaoh. In midafternoon, when the light starts to soften, head over to **Medinat Habu** **5**, the temple of Ramses III. The last of the great imperial temples built during the New Kingdom, the temple has retained much of its grandeur, as well as extensive (and often exaggerated) records of the king's reign.

TOP TIPS

- **Allow** at least one day.
- **Tickets** for everything except the Valley of the Kings must be bought at the ticket office.
- **Bring** a hat, sunscreen and plenty of water.
- **Photography** is not allowed inside the tombs, but there is plenty to see – and photograph – outside.

Medinat Habu
Original paintwork, applied more than 3000 years ago, can still be seen on lintels and inner columns. Some of this was preserved by the mudbrick houses and chapels of early Christians (since destroyed).

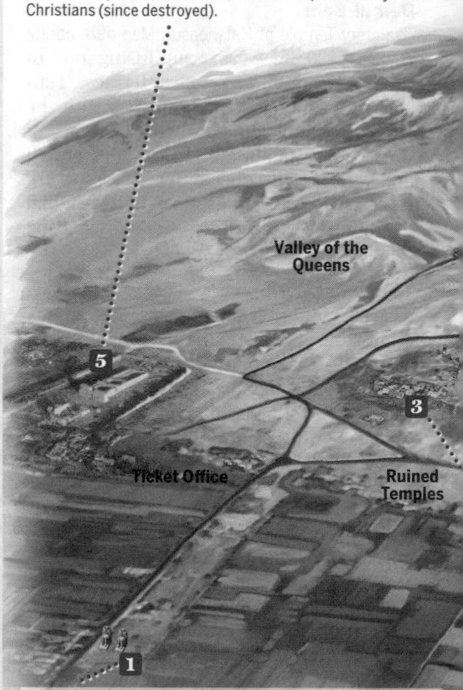

Colossi of Memnon
Although the Greeks called him Memnon, the colossi were built for Pharaoh Amenhotep III, who built the largest of all funerary temples here on the west bank (its ruins are only now being excavated).

Workers' Tombs (Deir al-Medina)

What to do with your spare time if you were an ancient Egyptian tomb worker? Cut a tomb and decorate it with things you didn't have in this life, including ceilings decorated with rug patterns.

Temple of Hatshepsut

Hatshepsut's funerary temple is unlike any other in Luxor. Built on three terraces with its back to the hill that contains the Valley of the Kings, it was once as grand as the pharaoh-queen.

Gurna Village

Rumours of treasure beneath houses in Gurna led the government to move the villagers and demolish their houses in the early 2000s. Some Gurna houses dated back to at least the beginning of the 19th century.

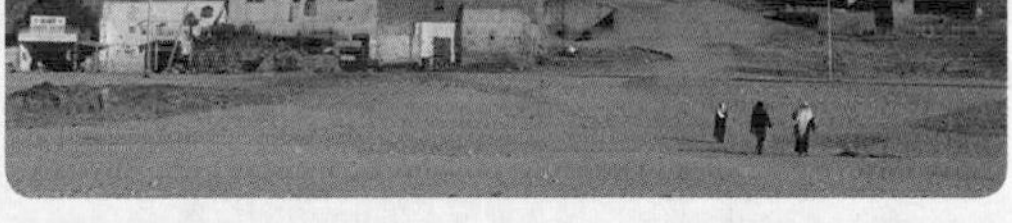

Luxor – West Bank

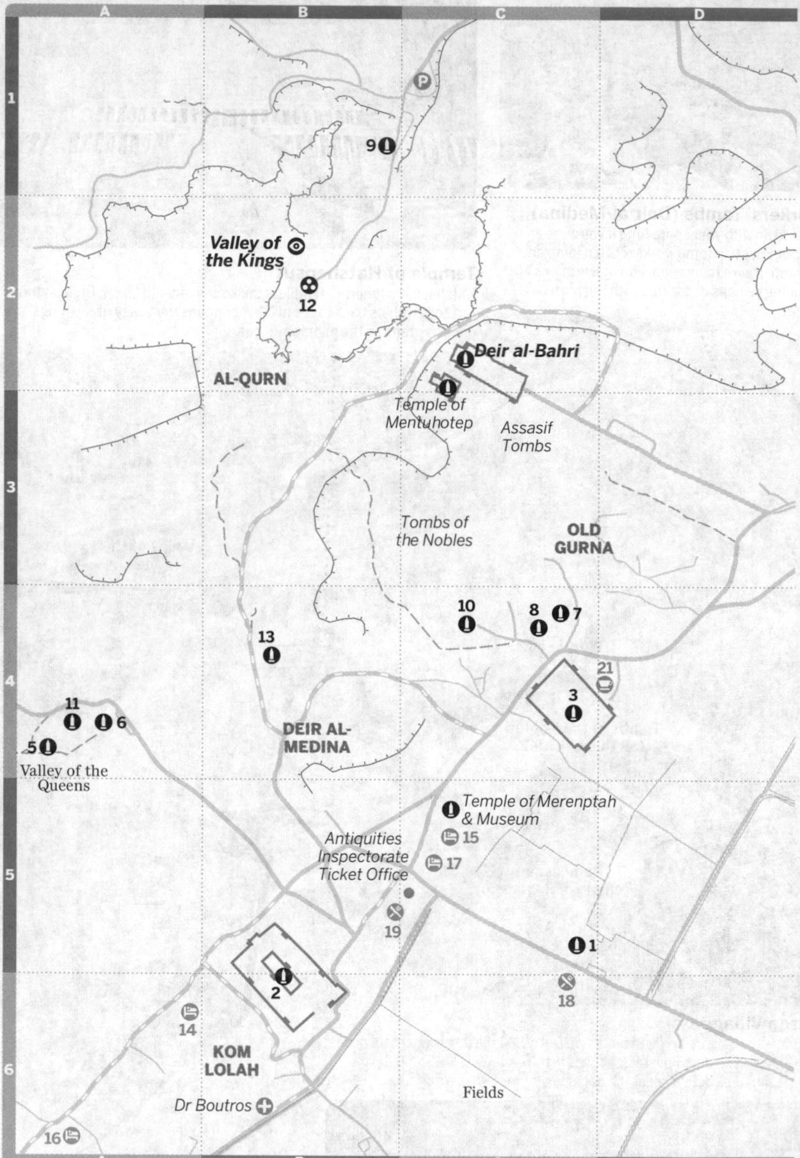

Horse Riding

A sunset ride around the west-bank temples is an unforgettable experience. Two stables offer guided horse rides, the better being **Nobi's Arabian Horse Stables** (Map p92; ☎231 0024, 0100 504 8558; www.luxorstables.com; approx per hr E£30; ⏲7am-sunset), which is known for its well-kept horses and tackle. If you phone ahead to book, staff will collect you from the east bank in a launch. Rides usually take three hours. It also offers camel and donkey rides.

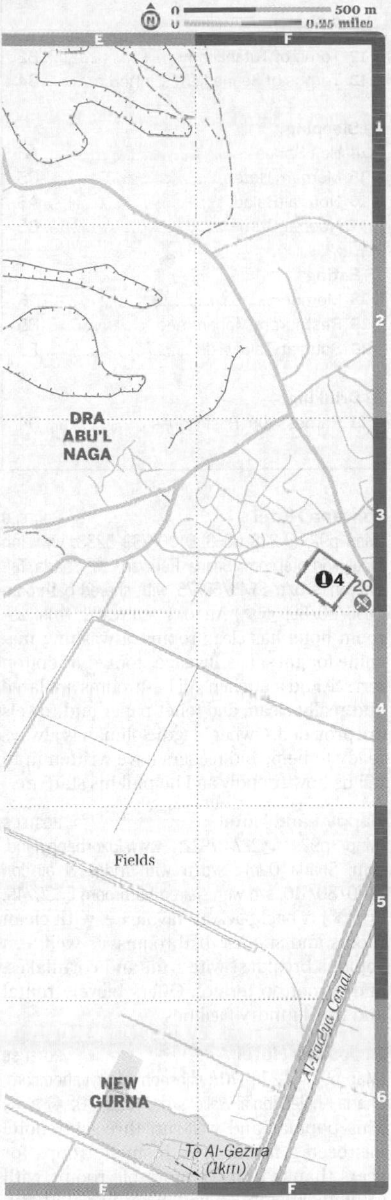

Tours

Most small budget hotels aggressively promote their own tours (E£75 to E£100 is the going rate), but often they lead only to papyrus shops and alabaster factories. On the upper end, American Express and Thomas Cook (see p105) arrange tours for around E£250 to E£400 per half-day.

Jolley's Travel & Tours CULTURAL
(Map p92; ☎237 2262; www.jolleys.com; ⊙9am-10pm) This reputable company, next to the Winter Palace Hotel, runs day trips to the main sites, including boats to Dendara.

QEA Travel Agency CULTURAL
(Map p92; ☎0100 2943169; http://questforegyptianadventure.com; Gezira al-Bayrat) This British-run agency does tailor-made tours in and around Luxor, as well as further afield. A percentage of its profits go to charitable projects in Egypt.

Sleeping

The cost of Luxor accommodation is a rollercoaster driven by demand. May to September is the low season, when hotels drop their charges by nearly 50%, but the second half of January is a premium as Egyptians travel over the school holidays – book ahead.

It's best to decide whether to stay on the east or the west bank before you arrive, as getting between the two is not easy. The west bank is quieter, has fewer touts and is closer to Luxor's main tombs and temples. There is a great selection of midrange accommodation but eating options are limited. The east bank is where most of the shopping and entertainment action is, as well as most of Luxor's budget hotels and cheap eateries. It's home to the Karnak and Luxor temples, Luxor Museum and a battery of touts who seem to revel in hassling tourists. (The hotel hustlers specialise in telling fibs about hotels that refuse to pay them commission – ignore them.)

EAST BANK

Nefertiti Hotel GUESTHOUSE $$
(Map p92; ☎237 2386; www.nefertitihotel.com; Sharia as-Sahabi, btwn Sharia Maabad al-Karnak & Sharia as-Souq; s/d/tr E£120/160/200, f E£220; ❄📶) Right in the thick of the market action, this splendid budget option has unfussy but faultlessly maintained rooms, with small private bathrooms and air-con. Larger new rooms on the top floors are decorated in local style. The roof terrace has views over to the west bank.

TOP CHOICE **La Maison de Pythagore** GUESTHOUSE $$
(☎0100 535 0532; www.lamaisondepythagore.com, in French; Al-Awamiya; s/d/tr €35/50/60;

Luxor – West Bank

Top Sights

Sights

Sleeping

Eating

Drinking

❄@) This seven-room Belgian-run guesthouse is tucked away in a tiny village behind the Sheraton Hotel, about 1km south of the centre. The soft traditional architecture encloses simple but cosy rooms in earthy colours mixed with turquoise and blue. Some rooms have air-con, others fans. The garden is a small oasis with date palms, flowers and fruit trees. Lunch (E£40) and dinner (E£55) are made with local seasonal produce. Look for it along the outside of the Sheraton's back wall – head toward the palm trees.

Winter Palace Hotel HISTORIC HOTEL **$$$**
(Map p92; ☎237 1197; www.sofitel.com; Corniche an-Nil; old wing r €180-320, ste €450-900; ❄≋) One of Egypt's most famous historic hotels, this Victorian pile has high ceilings, lots of gorgeous textiles, fabulous views over the Nile, an enormous garden with exotic trees and a huge swimming pool. The hotel is undergoing a major renovation, but remains open, so it may be a bit noisier than usual.

Mara House GUESTHOUSE **$$**
(Map p92; ☎236 5081, 0100 757 1855; www.egyptwithmara.com; Sharia Salahadin Ayyubi, off Sharia Salakhana; per person US$50; ❄📶) Irish Mara wanted to open a home for travellers and seems to have succeeded with spacious rooms, each decorated in local style with a sitting area and clean bathroom. Some of the accommodation is small flats, particularly good for families. This is a very popular option so book well ahead in the winter season.

Fontana Hotel HOSTEL **$**
(Map p92; ☎228 0663, 0100 733 3238; www.fontanaluxorhotel.com; Sharia Radwan, off Sharia Televizyon; s/d/tr E£45/60/75, with shared bathroom E£35/50/65; ❄📶) An old stalwart, this 25-room hotel has clean rooms, a washing machine for guest use, luggage storage, a rooftop terrace and a kitchen. All bathrooms are large and really clean, and toilet paper and towels are provided. Owner Magdi Soliman is always ready to help, and readers have written in to tell us how friendly and helpful his staff are.

Happy Land Hotel HOSTEL **$**
(Map p92; ☎227 7922; www.luxorhappyland.com; Sharia Qamr; s/d/tr with fridge & air-con E£70/80/110, s/d with shared bathroom E£30/45; ❄@📶) A backpackers' favourite, with clean rooms and spotless bathrooms, as well as a copious breakfast with fruit and cornflakes, and a rooftop terrace. Offers bicycle rental and free laundry facilities.

St Joseph Hotel HOTEL **$$**
(Map p92; ☎238 1707; stjosephhotel@yahoo.com; Sharia Khaled ibn al-Walid; s/d US$25/30; ❄📶≋) This popular and well-run three-star hotel has been a favourite with small groups for years thanks to its comfortable rooms with satellite TV, air-con and clean private bathrooms. All rooms have some Nile views, although the front rooms are quite noisy, and the breakfast buffet is quite basic.

Susanna Hotel HOTEL **$$**
(Map p92; ☎236 9915; www.susannahotelluxor.com; 52 Sharia Maabad al-Karnak; s/d/tr city view

US$30/35/50, Nile view US$40/45/60; ❄︎≋) Set between the Luxor Temple and the souq, this modern hotel has 45 spacious rooms with comfortable beds and great views. There is a good rooftop terrace where alcohol is available.

Anglo Hotel HOTEL $

(Map p92; ☎238 1679; Midan al-Mahatta; s/d/tr E£70/100/120; ❄︎) Next to the train station, so a bit noisy at times, but right in the centre of town. The spacious old-style rooms are excellent value, clean and well maintained, with satellite TV and private bathroom. The bar in the basement is popular with locals.

Rezeiky Camp CAMPGROUND $

(off Map p92; ☎238 1334; www.rezeikycamp.com.eg; Sharia Maabad al-Karnak; campsite per person E£25, vehicle E£20, s/d with fan E£55/110, with air-con E£65/120; ❄︎@≋) The only place to pitch a tent in town, and pleasant enough, though the motel-style rooms are not nice enough to make up for the inconvenient location north of town. There is a large garden with a restaurant and bar, and internet access. The place is popular with overland groups, so call ahead.

WEST BANK

Marsam Hotel GUESTHOUSE $$

(Map p98; ☎237 2403, 231 1603; www.luxor-westbank.com/marsam_e_az.htm; Gurna; s/d E£75/150, with shared bathroom E£50/100) Built for American archaeologists in the 1920s, the Marsam is charming, with 30 simple rooms set around a lovely courtyard, ceiling fans and traditional palm-reed beds. A delicious breakfast with home-baked bread is served in the garden. Book ahead during the winter dig season.

TOP CHOICE **Beit Sabée** GUESTHOUSE $$

(Map p98; ☎0100 632 4926, 0100 570 5341; www.beitsabee.com; Kom Lolah; d €40-70, with air-con €50-80; ❄︎) With eight rooms in a traditional-style two-storey mud-brick house, Beit Sabée has appeared in design magazines for its cool use of Nubian colours and local furnishings with a twist. Near the farms around Medinat Habu, it offers quiet accommodation and a closer contact to rural Egypt.

El-Mesala Hotel GUESTHOUSE $$

(Map p92; ☎231 4004, 0100 441 6741; www.hotelelmesala.com; Al-Gezira; s/d/tr/flat €18/28/35/45; ❄︎) Very welcome newcomer on the scene of small family-oriented hotels, with just 12 rooms with comfortable beds. Near the ferry landing, it's perfectly located for visits on both banks, as well as for magnificent views of the Nile and Luxor Temple. The staff and the manager, Mr Ahmed, are all extremely welcoming, and there's a great rooftop terrace for sunbathing.

Nile Valley Hotel HOTEL $$

(Map p92; ☎231 1477, 0122 796 4473; www.nilevalley.nl; Al-Gezira; s/d E£178/238, 2-room flat E£510; ❄︎) Pleasant Dutch-Egyptian-run hotel in a modern block right near the ferry landing. Some rooms have Nile views but those overlooking the rear garden are quieter and slightly bigger. This hotel is particularly family-friendly, with a separate children's pool in the garden, in addition to the regular one (E£50 for non-residents).

Amon Hotel GUESTHOUSE $$

(Map p92; ☎231 0912, 0100 639 4585; www.amonhotel.com; Al Gezira; s/d/tr E£200/250/300; ❄︎) Charming family-run hotel in a modern building with spotless rooms, a lush exotic garden, extremely helpful staff and delicious home-cooked meals. In the new wing the rooms are large with private bathrooms, ceiling fans, air-con and balconies overlooking the courtyard. In the old wing, some of the small rooms have private bathrooms. This hotel is popular with archaeologists in winter, so book ahead.

Al-Fayrouz Hotel HOTEL $$

(Map p92; ☎231 2709, 0122 277 0565; www.elfayrouz.com; Al-Gezira; s/d/tr/q E£95/150/190/240; ❄︎) Overlooking green fields, this tranquil hotel has 17 brightly painted rooms, which are simple, nicely decorated and spotless. The more expensive rooms have a sitting area and a bit more atmosphere. Meals can be had on the comfortable roof terrace or in the popular garden restaurant.

Hotel Sheherazade HOTEL $$

(Map p92; ☎231 1228, 0122 212 3719; www.hotelsheherazade.com; Al-Gezira; s/d/tr E£180/250/330, flat E£450, 3-course meals per person E£45; ❄︎) Mohammed Sanusy takes great pride in his Moorish-style hotel. Its 28 spacious rooms are decorated with local colour and furnishings and surrounded by a garden. A pool is planned.

Al-Nakhil Hotel HOTEL $$

(Map p92; ☎231 3922, 0122 382 1007; www.el-nakhil.com; Al-Gezira; s/d/tr €25/35/40; ❄︎) Nestled in a palm grove, this resort-style hotel has 17 spotless, well-finished domed rooms.

WEST BANK PRACTICALITIES

» Pace yourself – it's impossible to see everything (and it would cost nearly E£500 besides).

» All sites are open 6am to 5pm daily.

» Tickets for Deir al-Bahri (Temple of Hatshepsut), the Assassif Tombs, the Valley of the Kings and the Valley of the Queens are sold at the sites.

» All other tickets are sold at the **Antiquities Inspectorate Ticket Office** (Map p98; ⌚6am-5pm) on Main Rd, 3km inland from the ferry landing.

» Tickets are valid only for the day of purchase and no refunds are given.

» Photography is strictly forbidden in tombs, and guards will confiscate film or memory cards.

» Distances are large: 3km to the antiquities office, and another 1km to the Valley of the Queens, and 5km to the Valley of the Kings.

» From the west bank ferry landing, a taxi around the sites should cost E£150 to E£250, or hire a bicycle for the day for E£20. Otherwise, pickup trucks (50pt) provide some local transport, but you'll still have to walk quite a bit to each site.

» Tour groups visit Deir al-Bahri and the Valley of the Kings in the morning. Hit exceptionally hot Deir al-Bahri as early as possible, to beat the heat and crowds, but you can leave the tombs till the afternoon.

» Carry plenty of water, a hat, small change and a torch.

» A picnic lunch is a good idea, though you can get a good snack at the Ramesseum Rest House (Map p98), opposite the Ramesseum, and a cafe in front of Medinat Habu.

Cots are available for children, and three rooms cater for disabled guests. There's a large restaurant on the roof terrace with great views over the Nile.

Nour al-Gurna GUESTHOUSE **$$**
(Map p98; ☎231 1430, 0100 129 5812; Old Gurna; s E£150, d E£200-250, ste E£300) This mud-brick, thatch-roofed little hotel is opposite the Antiquities Inspectorate office. Rooms are stylishly decorated (some even have air-con) and there's a great shaded and cushioned indoor-outdoor restaurant serving food made from home-grown ingredients. Its sister hotel, **Nour al-Balad** (Map p98; ☎242 6111; Ezbet Bisily; s/d/ste E£200/250/300; ❄), is quieter but further from the sights.

Eating

EAST BANK

Sharia al-Mahatta has a number of fine sandwich stands, juice stands and other cheap-eat possibilities.

TOP CHOICE **Sofra** EGYPTIAN **$$**
(Map p92; ☎235 9752; www.sofra.com.eg; Sharia al-Mahdy, 90 Sharia Mohammed Farid; mains E£20-60; ⌚11am-midnight) For pasha-style dining that won't cost an arm and a leg, do not miss this treat of a place, set in a 1930s house and adorned with wrought-iron lamps, handcarved wooden furniture and enormous painted trays for tables. The menu comprises traditional Egyptian dishes such as excellent duck, and a large selection of mezze. No alcohol, but you can relax over tea and sheesha after.

Oasis Café MEDITERRANEAN **$$**
(Map p92; ☎0111 140 0557; Sharia Dr Labib Habashi; mains E£15-60; ⌚10am-10pm; ❄) Very Western, but in a nice way: art on the brightly coloured walls, soft jazz wafting through the air, smoking and nonsmoking rooms and copies of *New Yorker* magazine. Come for the enticing pastas, succulent grilled meats or hearty sandwiches, then linger a while over the selection of pastries and excellent coffee.

As-Sahaby Lane EGYPTIAN **$$**
(Map p92; ☎236 5509; www.nefertitihotel.com/sahabi.htm; Sharia as-Sahaby, off Sharia as-Souq; mains E£35-60; ⌚9am-11.30pm) Great easy-going alfresco restaurant in the lane running between the souq and the street to Karnak Temple. Fresh and well-prepared Egyptian dishes like *tagen* (stew cooked in earthenware pots) are served as well as good pizzas and salads. The same food is served on the hotel's rooftop terrace, with great views.

Salahadeen EGYPTIAN $$
(Map p92; ☎0100 757 1855; www.salahadeen.com; Mara House, Sharia Salahadin Ayyubi, off Sharia Salakhana; dishes E£18-60; ⏰6pm-midnight; ❄✍) Food here is served as in an Egyptian home: knives and forks are offered but guests are encouraged to eat by dipping bread in the various dishes. Dinner starts promptly at 7pm, but the bar opens for pre-dinner drinks at 6pm. Best deal and experience: the set menu (E£100) includes three courses with 15 dishes to share. The vegetarian options are not cooked in a meat broth, as in so many other places.

Jewel of the Nile EGYPTIAN, BRITISH $$
(Map p92; ☎0106 252 2394; Sharia al-Rawda al-Sherifa; mains E£30-45, set menu E£60-70; ⏰10am-midnight winter, 1pm-midnight summer; ❄📶✍) Laura and Mahmud offer traditional Egyptian food using organic vegetables from their own farm, as well as well-prepared British food like steaks, cottage pie, apple crumble and an all-day English breakfast (E£25). The menu features a good selection of vegetarian dishes. Alcohol available. Turn inland one block south of the St Joseph hotel and cross Sharia al-Medina al-Munawwara.

Gerda's Garden EGYPTIAN, EUROPEAN $$
(☎235 8688, 0122 5348 326; opposite Hilton Luxor, New Karnak; www.luxor-german-restaurant.com; dishes E£15-45; ⏰6.30pm-11pm; ❄) This German-Egyptian operation, out east on the road to the airport, is more provincial European bistro than Egyptian, but the menu features both Egyptian specials like kebab and delicious grilled pigeon, and very European comfort food such as goulash and potato salad.

Abu Ashraf EGYPTIAN FAST FOOD $$
(Map p92; ☎237 5936; Sharia al-Mahatta; dishes E£4-20; ⏰8am-11pm) This large, popular restaurant and takeaway is just down from the train station. It serves roast chicken, pizzas, good *kushari* and kebabs.

Koshari Elzaeem EGYPTIAN FAST FOOD $
(Map p92; Midan Hussain; dishes E£5-20; ⏰24hr) Popular *kushari* restaurant that also serves an Egyptian version of spaghetti. There are a few tables but they fill up fast.

New Mish Mish EGYPTIAN FAST FOOD $$
(Map p92; ☎228 1756, 0100 810 5862; Sharia Televizyon; mains E£20-30; ⏰8am-midnight; ❄) This long-standing budget-traveller haunt has a swish contemporary and air-conditioned fast-food-style interior, serving good sandwiches, salads and grilled meats and fish. There's no alcohol, but there is a selection of fresh fruit juices.

WEST BANK

Restaurant Mohammed EGYPTIAN $$
(Map p98; ☎0120 385 0227; Kom Lolah; set menu E£25-60) This laid-back family restaurant is set in and around the peaceful courtyard of Mohammed Abdel Lahi's mud-brick house, fronted by a 600-year-old tree. Mohammed's mum cooks up a yummy *kofta tagen* (meatball stew), served with home-grown salad leaves; it goes down a treat with a cold Stella (E£12).

TOP CHOICE **Al-Moudira** MEDITERRANEAN $$$
(☎0120 325 1307; Daba'iyya; mains E£75-110; ⏰8am-midnight) In keeping with its flamboyant decor, the glamorous hotel Al-Moudira has the most sophisticated food on the west bank, with great salads and grills and other Mediterranean-Lebanese cuisine. This is a great place for a romantic dinner in the courtyard, or by the fire in winter. Call ahead for reservations and directions; it's about 6km southwest of Medinat Habu, on the edge of the desert.

Al-Gezira Hotel EGYPTIAN $
(Map p92; ☎231 0034; Al-Gezira) This comfortable rooftop restaurant serves a set menu with Egyptian specialities, such as *molokhiyya* (garlicky green soup) and *mahshi kurumb* (stuffed cabbage leaves) that must be ordered in advance. There are great views over the Nile. Cool beers are on offer (E£12) as well as Egyptian wine (E£85).

Memnon EGYPTIAN $$
(Map p98; ☎012 327 8747; opposite Colossi of Memnon; dishes E£25-500; ⏰8am-11pm, later in summer) Excellent, laid-back restaurant with simple but very well prepared Egyptian fare, and if you want a change from that, there are some equally good Indian and Chinese dishes on the menu.

Self-Catering

On the east bank, the **fruit-and-veg market** (Map p92) on Sharia as-Souq is best in the early morning.

Arkwrights Gourmet Food SUPERMARKET $
(Map p92; ☎228 2335, 0100 334 5312; Sharia St Joseph, off Sharia Khaled ibn al-Walid, near St Joseph Hotel; ⏰6am-midnight) This is the place to stock up for a more sophisticated picnic;

LIFE AFTER DEATH

Ancient Egyptians developed an intricate belief system around death and the afterlife. Life in the beyond was believed to be a vast improvement on life on earth, and you literally could take everything with you. Burial chambers were packed with life's necessities: household goods, riches and even family members and slaves – anything that might come in handy for a long and comfy life ever after. Corpses were ritually cleaned, hollowed out and mummified to create a body that would be useful for an eternity on the other side.

Belief had it that after death the deceased would travel along a treacherous river to the Hall of Final Judgement, where one's life would be reviewed by Anubis, god of mummification. A scale was used to measure the weight of one's heart against the 'feather of truth'. The heart was thought to hold a record of all the deeds of one's life, and if a heart was lighter than the feather (and thus chaste), eternal life with the gods was granted. If the heart was heavy with guilt and outweighed the feather, the deceased was consumed by Ammit, a hybrid crocodile, lion and hippopotamus creature, to disappear forever.

freshly made sandwiches and salads are an option.

Al-Ahram Beverages LIQUOR STORE **$**
(Map p92; ☎237 2445; Sharia Ramses) Beer and wine.

Souq at-Talaat MARKET
(Map p98; ⏲Tue mornings) Wonderful weekly market in Taref, on the west bank, opposite the Temple of Seti I.

Drinking

Metropolitan Café & Restaurant BAR
(Map p92; lower level, Corniche an-Nil) A pleasant, popular outdoor cafe, right on the Nile, the Metropolitan sits in front of the Winter Palace. A wide selection of cocktails are available, served on a terrace with rattan furniture and mist machines. The perfect place to enjoy a sundowner.

New Oum Koulsoum Coffee Shop COFFEEHOUSE
(Map p92; Sharia as-Souq; ⏲24hr) A people-watching haven, this is deservedly the most popular ahwa in town. It's next to the Nefertiti Hotel.

Chez Omar COFFEEHOUSE
(Map p92; Midan Youssef Hassan) A relaxed cafe terrace in a small garden off the main souq, as good for a snack as it is for a sheesha. Inside is Chez Omar II, a cool laid-back eatery with Egyptian dishes like kebab and pigeon stew (E£30).

Kings Head Pub PUB
(Map p92; ☎228 0489; Sharia Khaled ibn al-Walid; ❄) A relaxed and perennially popular place to have a drink and shoot pool, the Kings Head has a laid-back atmosphere that's welcoming to solo women.

Cocktail Sunset COCKTAIL BAR
(Map p92; ☎238 0524; ❄) Look for this funky pontoon boat – it was closed at the time of writing, but rumoured to be reopening, hopefully with its congenial, retro atmosphere intact.

Shopping

All the usual souvenirs can be had in Luxor, but alabaster is ubiquitous – it's mined about 80km northwest. Head for the west bank, where factories near the Ramesseum and Deir al-Bahri sell a range of products. Also seek out **Fair Trade Centre** (Map p92; Sharia Maabad al-Karnak; ⏲9am-10.30pm); there's a branch (Map p92; Sharia Maabad Luxor, next to Mc Donalds; ⏲9am-10.30pm) behind Luxor Temple.

Beware of a common scam in which horse-cart drivers offer to take you to a less-touristy souq than the one behind Luxor Temple, then drive around in circles and drop you off at the same (and, in truth, *only*) souq.

Information

Dangers & Annoyances

Luxor is perhaps the hassle capital of Egypt – if you can make it here, you can make it anywhere. Breathe deep and smile. Unless you're a woman, in which case be reserved. Due to a minor trend of female sex tourism in Luxor, women are often seen as possible customers of another sort.

Internet Access

Gamil Centre (Map p92; lower level, Corniche an-Nil; ⏲24hr) In front of the Winter Palace Hotel.

Heroes Internet (Map p92; Sharia Televizyon; ⏲24hr)

Pono Internet (Map p92; main street, Al-Gezira; ⌚8am-2am) On the west bank; very fast.

Medical Services

Dr Boutros (Map p98; ☎231 0851; Kom Lolah) Excellent English- and French-speaking doctor, who works on the west bank.

International Hospital (Map p92; ☎228 0192; Sharia Televizyon) The best place in town.

Money

Most banks have branches in Luxor offering ATMs and foreign exchange services. Money can be changed at a slew of forex offices around town.

American Express (Map p92; ☎237 8333; Corniche an-Nil; ⌚9am-4.30pm) Beside the Winter Palace Hotel.

Thomas Cook (Map p92; ☎237 2190; Corniche an-Nil; ⌚8am-8pm) Below the Winter Palace Hotel.

Post

Main post office (Map p92; Sharia al-Mahatta; ⌚8.30am-2.30pm Sat-Thu)

Telephone

Cardphones are scattered around town, and mobile phone shops are concentrated along Sharias al-Mahatta and Televizyon.

Telephone centrale (Map p92; Corniche an-Nil; ⌚8am-8pm) Below the Winter Palace.

Tourist Information

Main tourist office (Map p92; Midan al-Mahatta; ⌚8am-8pm) Very helpful and well-informed tourist information, particularly Mourad Gamil (moro_2004@yahoo.com), opposite the train station.

Getting There & Away

Air

EgyptAir (Map p92; ☎238 0580; Corniche el-Nil; ⌚8am-8pm) Flies to Cairo several times daily. At the time of writing, services to Abu Simbel (via Aswan) and Sharm el-Sheikh were suspended due to low demand. Even if the Abu Simbel service is restored, there is a long wait in Aswan.

Bus

Super Jet (☎236 7732) Goes only from Luxor bus station at 8pm to Cairo (E£130, eight to nine hours) via Hurghada (E£45, four hours).

Upper Egypt Bus Co ticket office (Map p92; ☎237 2118; Midan al-Mahatta) Just south of the train station; a few buses leave from here.

Zanakta bus station (☎232 3218; Sharia al-Karnak) Way out of town, close to the airport. A taxi from the town costs around E£25 to E£35.

Cruises

The best times of the year for cruising are October/November and April/May. During the high season (November to March), an armada of cruise boats travels the Nile between Aswan and Esna (for Luxor), stopping at Edfu and Kom Ombo en route. You can often make deals directly with the boat captains in Esna, rather than through a travel agency. Feluccas can also be organised from Esna, but most travellers prefer to go the other way (Aswan to Luxor), as this is how the current runs. See p112 for more information.

Servees & Microbus

The **servees and microbus station** (Map p92) is behind the train station. Big Peugeots and mini-vans run from Luxor to Aswan (E£18 to E£20) via Esna (E£5), Edfu (E£9) and Kom Ombo (E£15), as well as to Hurghada (E£20) via Qena (E£4). There is no service to Asyut.

The drivers are always ready to privatise the car to make special trips up the Nile to Aswan, stopping at the sights on the way; expect to pay about E£450 to E£500. To Asyut or to Hurghada, the going rate is about E£450. It is possible to take a private *servees* to Al-Kharga via the direct road, avoiding Asyut, at E£700 for the car (maximum seven people).

Train

Luxor Station (Map p92; ☎237 2018; Midan al-Mahatta) has left-luggage facilities and a post office.

The **Watania Sleeping Trains** (☎237 2015, in Cairo 02-3748 9488; www.wataniasleepingtrains.com) go daily to Cairo at 7.15pm and 10.30pm (single/double including dinner and breakfast US$80/120, child four to nine years US$45, nine hours).

For day trains headed north to Cairo (1st/2nd class E£90/46), the best are 981, at 8.25am, stopping at Qena (for Dendara; 1st/2nd class E£28/19) and Asyut (for the Western Desert; E£53/30).The slower 983 leaves at 10.30am, and the 935 at noon.

There are several trains to Aswan (adult 1st/2nd class E£41/25, three hours): the 996 at 7.30am, the 1902 at 9.30am and the 980 at 6pm. All train tickets are better bought in advance, but if you buy your ticket on the train there is a charge of E£6.

Getting Around

To/From the Airport

Luxor International Airport (☎237 4655) is 7km east of town. A taxi will cost between E£70 to E£100 to east bank destinations. There is no bus.

Bicycle

Easily the most pleasant way to get around, bicycles can be rented on the west bank and from most hotels for around E£12 to E£15 per day. One good place to rent is from restaurant **7 days 7 ways** (off Map p92; ☎012 020 1876;

BUSES FROM LUXOR

For Al-Quseir and Marsa Alam, change at Safaga. For Qena, it's cheaper to take a *servees*. At the time of writing, there were no buses between Luxor and Aswan. For the Western Desert, take a train to Asyut, then one of several daily buses to Al-Kharga (E£18) and Dakhla (E£30).

DESTINATION	PRICE (E£)	DURATION (HR)	TIMES
Cairo	100	10-11	7pm
Cairo (Super Jet)	130	9	8pm
Dahab	140	16-17	4.30pm
Hurghada	35-40	5	5 daily, 8.30am-8pm
Hurghada (Super Jet)	45	4	8pm
Luxor	130	18	4pm
Nuweiba	15	1	10.30am
Port Said	80	12	7.30pm
Qena	8	1-2	Frequently, 6.30am-8pm
Safaga	30-35	4½	5 daily, 8.30am-8pm
Sharm el-Sheikh	130	12	4.30pm

www.rentabikeluxor.com; Sharia Sheraton; ⏲8am-11pm), which also organises cycling tours around Luxor. You can take a bicycle on the ferry connecting the east and west banks.

Ferry & Boat

The *baladi* (municipal) ferry (E£1) runs to the west bank from the dock in front of Luxor Temple. Private launches charge E£10 to E£20 per boat each way for the same trip.

Hantour

The most interesting way to get around town is by horse and carriage, also called a *calèche*. Rates range from E£20 to E£50 per hour depending on your haggling skills. Expect to pay about E£20 to Karnak.

Pick-Up Taxis

Kabout (pick-up trucks) and microbuses can be the quickest and easiest way to get about in Luxor. They ply fixed routes and will stop whenever flagged down. To get to the Temples of Karnak, take a microbus from Luxor station or from behind Luxor Temple for 50pt. Other routes run inside the town. On the west bank, trucks wait in the lot by the ferry landing, with drivers shouting out the villages they're headed for; the Gurna route passes the antiquities ticket office.

North of Luxor

DENDARA دندرة

☎096

The wonderfully preserved **Temple of Hathor** (adult/student E£35/20; ⏲8am-5pm) at Dendara is one of the most impressive temples in Egypt. Built at the very end of the Pharaonic period, its main building is still virtually intact, with a great stone roof and columns, dark chambers, underground crypts and twisting stairways, all carved with hieroglyphs. The head of Hathor, the goddess of pleasure and love, is carved on six of the 24 columns of the outer hypostyle hall, and on the walls are scenes of Roman emperors as pharaohs.

Dendara is 4km southwest of Qena on the west side of the Nile and an easy day trip from Luxor. A return taxi will cost about E£200. There are also day boat trips to Dendara and nearby Abydos, best arranged through a tour agency in Luxor. If you arrive in Qena by train, you will need to take a taxi to the temple (E£25 to E£35 to the temple and back with some waiting time).

South of Luxor

ESNA إسنا

The hypostyle hall, with its 24 columns still supporting a roof, is all that remains of the **Temple of Khnum** (adult/student E£20/15; ⏲6am-5pm), constructed by Egypt's Ptolemaic rulers. Dedicated to the ram-headed creator god who fashioned humankind on his potter's wheel using Nile clay, its pillars are decorated with hieroglyphic accounts of temple ceremonies.

Trains between Luxor and Aswan stop here, but the station is on the opposite side of the Nile; so is the drop-off point if you arrive in a *servees*. Hop a *kabout* from by the canal. It's much easier to take a day tour or travel in a private taxi (E£150 return or E£450 to Aswan with stops en route).

EDFU إدفو

The **Temple of Horus** (adult/student E£50/25; 7am-7pm) is the star attraction here, 53km south of Esna, as the most completely preserved Ptolemaic temple in Egypt. It was one of the last great Egyptian attempts at monument building on a grand scale (it took about 200 years to complete) and was dedicated to the falcon-headed son of Osiris. Walking through this awesome temple's halls, many filled with detailed inscriptions of temple rituals and priesthood rites, is both mesmerising and eerie.

Trains running between Luxor and Aswan stop here, but the station is approximately 4km from the temple. Pickups travel between the station and town for E£8 (for the whole truck). Again, it's easier to take a day tour or travel in a private taxi from Luxor (E£200 return or E£450 to Aswan with stops en route).

KOM OMBO كوم أمبو

The **Temple of Kom Ombo** (adult/student E£30/20; 7am-7pm), spectacularly crowning an outcrop at a bend in the Nile, is unique for its dual dedication to the crocodile and falcon gods Sobek and Haroeris. The symmetrical main temple dates from the Ptolemaic times, and among the halls and shrines inside you can view the remains of mummified crocodiles, which were once plentiful here as they basked on the Nile's shores.

The easiest way to visit Kom Ombo is to take a day tour or travel by private taxi, from about E£450 round-trip from Luxor, with a stop at Edfu, or onward to Aswan. By train (50pt), you'll need to take a *kabout* to the boat landing on the Nile, about 800m north of the temple, then walk the rest of the way.

Aswan أسوان

097 / POP 265,004

With a pace of life as slow as the meandering Nile in this part of Egypt, picturesque Aswan will have you reaching for your point-and-shoot every few minutes. Just north of the first cataract and the southernmost boundary of ancient Egypt's empire, contemporary Aswan is a sleepy Nileside town fringed by palms and sandy expanses and the river is dotted with flocks of graceful feluccas. Outside the summer months, when daily temperatures soar to 50°C, Aswan is an ideal place to sail the Nile the ancient way or to base yourself as you explore the fantastic ruins of nearby Abu Simbel.

Sights

Aswan's sights are spread out, mostly to the south and west of the town. The souq cuts right through the centre of town, parallel to the Nile. The Nubia Museum is within walking distance, just, but all other sights require transport. The sites on the islands and on the west bank involve a short boat trip.

Nubia Museum MUSEUM

(Map p108; Sharia Abtal at-Tahrir; adult/student E£50/25; 9am-5pm) This little-visited but fascinating museum showcases the history, art and culture of Nubia, and the collection ranges from prehistoric times to the present day. The extensive and clearly labelled collection includes highlights such as horse armour from the 7th century BC. Make sure you have a good look at the 'Nubia Submerged' exhibition, which includes photographs of Philae, Abu Simbel and Kalabsha before they were resited. The museum is a 15-minute walk from the town centre.

Fatimid Cemetery CEMETERY

(Map p108) Behind the Nubia Museum, this vast cemetery has tombs dating back to the 9th century, many built with distinctive mud-brick domes, and burial spots for local saints, decorated with flags.

DON'T MISS

ANIMALIA

Mohamed Sobhi, a passionate and knowledgeable Nubian guide, and his family maintain a sort of unofficial Nubian Museum called **Animalia** (Map p108; 231 4152, 0100 545 6420; main st, Siou; admission E£5, incl guided tour E£10; 8am-7pm). They have dedicated part of their large house to the traditions, flora and fauna and the history of Nubia. Sobhi also has a small shop selling crafts at fixed prices and a lovely roof terrace for drinks and lunch.

Aswan

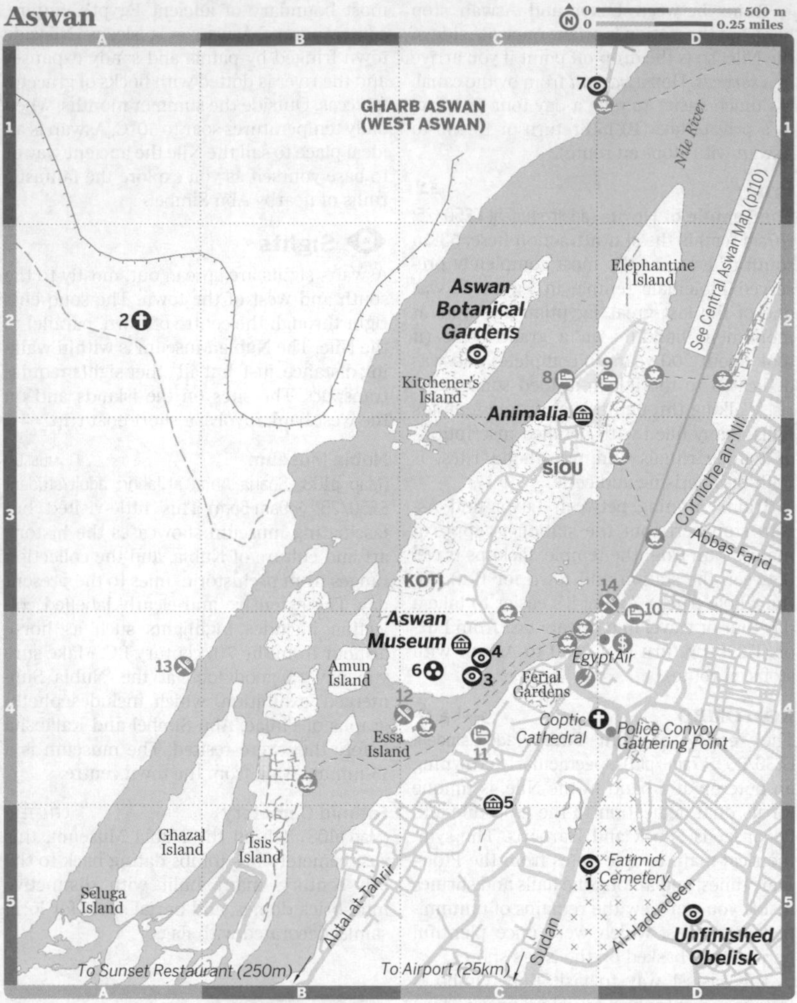

Unfinished Obelisk ARCHAEOLOGICAL SITE

(Map p108; adult/student E£30/20; ⏲8am-5pm) This huge discarded obelisk lies on the edge of the northern granite quarries that supplied the ancient Egyptians with most of the hard stone used in pyramids and temples. Three sides of the 42m-long, 1168-tonne shaft were completed before a flaw was revealed in the rock. If it had been completed, it would have been the largest single piece of stone ever handled. Private taxis charge around E£15 to bring you here from the centre of town.

Elephantine Island ISLAND

(Map p108) Aswan's earliest settlement, over 5000 years ago, was on this Nile island, which still holds two **Nubian villages** with shady alleys and gardens. The traces of Elephantine's ancient community, the **ruins of Abu** (adult/student E£30/15; ⏲8am-5pm) occupy the southern part of the island. You can see two impressive **Nilometers**, and your ticket also gives entrance to the fascinating **Aswan Museum**. Ferries (E£1) run regularly to the island; see p113.

Aswan

Top Sights

	Animalia	C2
	Aswan Botanical Gardens	C2
	Aswan Museum	C4
	Unfinished Obelisk	D5

Sights

1	Fatimid Cemetery Entrance	C5
2	Monastery of St Simeon	A2
3	Nilometer & Temple of Khnum	C4
4	Nilometer of Satet	C4
5	Nubia Museum	C4
6	Ruins of Abu	C4
7	Tombs of the Nobles	D1

Sleeping

8	Baaba Dool	C2
9	Mövenpick Resort Aswan	D2
10	Nile Hotel	D4
11	Sofitel Old Cataract Hotel & Spa	C4

Eating

12	Al-Dakka	C4
13	Nubian Beach	A4
14	Panorama	D3

Aswan Botanical Gardens GARDENS

(Map p108; admission E£20; 8am-6pm) West of Elephantine Island, this spot was where Lord Kitchener built a lush palm garden while he was commander of the Egyptian army in the 1890s. The island is most easily seen as part of a felucca tour, but you can also walk across Elephantine Island and take a short felucca from there (E£20 to E£25 for a round trip).

Monastery of St Simeon MONASTERY

(Map p108; Deir Amba Samaan; adult/student E£25/15; 8am-4pm) This 7th-century mud-brick Coptic monastery looks like a fortress, with 10m-high walls surrounding a stone-and-mud-brick structure. It no longer functions, however – it was destroyed by Saladin (Salah ad-Din) in 1173. The basilica shows traces of frescos, and one monk's cell shows graffiti from Muslim pilgrims en route to Mecca.

Take a private boat to the monastery, then scramble up the desert track on foot (about 25 minutes) or hire a camel to take you up (about E£30). Alternatively, you can take the ferry to the Tombs of the Nobles and ride a camel or donkey from there – remember to bring water.

Tombs of the Nobles TOMBS

(Map p108; adult/student E£25/15; 8am-4pm) A few of the Old and Middle Kingdom tombs of local dignitaries are worth exploring for their wall paintings and biographical hieroglyphics.

Activities

Top of the priority list for most visitors is a quick sluice between Aswan's many islands on a felucca. The afternoon is the ideal time to do this, as the fiery sun plonks itself down over Aswan's dunes. The trustworthy **Gelal** (0122 415 4902), who hangs out near Panorama Restaurant and the ferry landing, offers hassle-free tours on his family's feluccas at a fixed price (E£30 to E£40 per boat for an hour, E£35 to E£45 for a motor boat). According to the tourist office, a three- or four-hour tour costs at least E£100 to E£150. A two- to three-hour trip down to Seheyl Island costs about E£120.

Sleeping

Aswan's accommodation scene isn't nearly as good value as Luxor's. Be warned that hotels in the centre of town, particularly those on the Corniche, can be noisy at night.

TOP CHOICE **Philae Hotel** HOTEL $$

(Map p110; 231 2090; philaehotel@gmail.com; 79 Corniche an-Nil; s/d/tr/family apt US$60/70/90/250;) After a serious revamp, this is now by far the best midrange hotel in town. The tasteful and cosy rooms are decorated with calligraphy-adorned fabrics and elegant local furnishings. The hotel **restaurant** (mains E£20-40) serves mainly vegetarian organic food from its own gardens at reasonable prices. Book ahead.

Nile Hotel HOTEL $$

(Map p108; 231 4222; www.nilehotel-aswan.com; Corniche an-Nil; s/d/tr US$40/55/73;) Spotless private bathrooms, satellite TV and minibar, all with a window or balcony overlooking the Nile. The staff speak English and are very friendly and helpful. There is a restaurant, a small library with foreign novels and books about Egypt, and a business centre.

Baaba Dool B&B $

(Map p108; 0100 497 2608; Siou, Elephantine Island; r without bathroom per person €10) A great place to unwind for a few days. A few rooms in this beautiful mud-brick house are painted in Nubian style, and have superb Nile views. Rooms are very basic but clean

Central Aswan

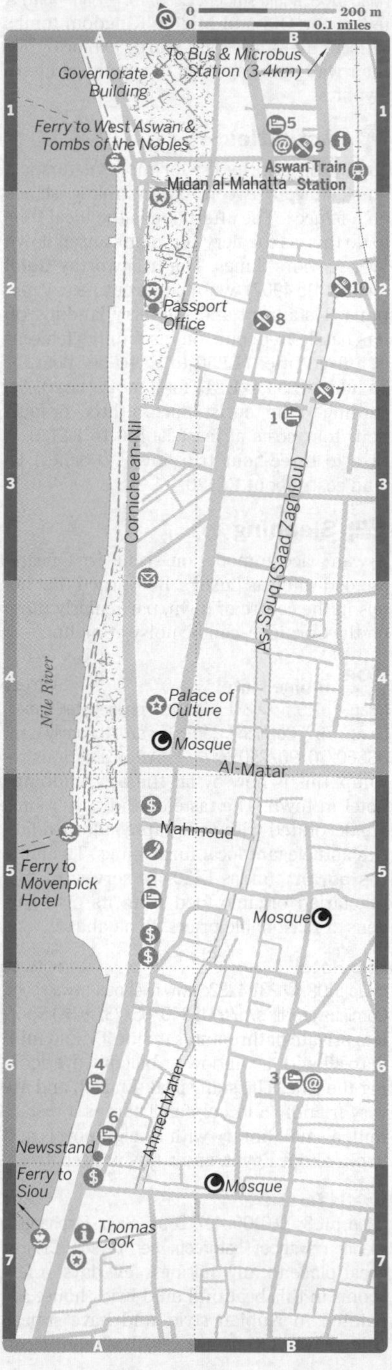

Central Aswan

Sleeping

1 Cleopatra Hotel........B3
2 Hathor Hotel........A5
3 Keylany Hotel........B6
4 Memnon Hotel........A6
5 Nuba Nile Hotel........B1
6 Philae Hotel........A6

Eating

7 Al-Madina........B3
8 Al-Makka........B2
9 Biti Pizza........B1
10 Chef Khalil........B2

(bring a sleeping bag) and there are shared hot showers. Mustapha can arrange meals. Book ahead.

Keylany Hotel HOTEL $$
(Map p110; ☎231 7332; www.keylanyhotel.com; 25 Sharia Keylany; s/d/tr US$24/34/45;) This great little hotel has simple pine furniture and spotless bathrooms with proper showers and hot water. The management and staff are friendly and endlessly helpful. The roof terrace has no Nile view, but with ample shade, it's a great place to hang out.

Nuba Nile Hotel HOTEL $
(Map p110; ☎231 3267; www.nubanile.com; Sharia Abtal at-Tahrir; s/d E£60/75;) A solid budget option, with clean, comfortable rooms, conveniently located just north of the square in front of the train station. Check the room before you agree, as they vary considerably: some are tiny and others have no windows or hot water.

Hathor Hotel HOTEL $
(Map p110; ☎231 4580; www.hathorhotel.com; Corniche an-Nil; s/d/tr E£85/110/140;) What this hotel lacks in charisma it makes up for in cleanliness. The sometimes gloomy rooms are covered in bleach-cleaned tiles and proffer boxy bathrooms and air-con. A big bonus here is the small pool on the rooftop with breathtaking Nile vistas.

Memnon Hotel HOTEL $
(Map p110; ☎230 0483, 0100 193 5639; www.memnonhotel-aswan.com; Corniche an-Nil; s/d E£70/100;) The Memnon has been around for a few years and it shows, but the clean, good-sized rooms have great Nile views. The rooftop has a small, not-very-attractive pool and no shade. The shabby

hotel entrance is easily missed, on a dusty street off the Corniche, south of the Aswan Moon Restaurant.

Cleopatra Hotel HOTEL **$$**
(Map p110; ☎231 400; Sharia as-Souq; s/d US$50/70; ❄@☒) Very central and well kept, the Cleopatra has 109 spacious, clean, albeit rather dark, rooms, in need of some updating. It is popular with groups on cut-price package tours, because of its convenient location and the reasonably sized (but overlooked) rooftop pool.

Mövenpick Resort Aswan RESORT **$$$**
(Map p108; ☎230 3455; www.moevenpick-aswan.com; Elephantine Island; s/d from US$170/230; ❄@☒) Hidden in a large garden on the northern end of Elephantine Island, the Mövenpick has simple but very comfortable rooms, decorated in Nubian style and colours. It has a great swimming pool. Guests are transported to and from the town centre by a free ferry.

TOP CHOICE **Sofitel Old Cataract Hotel & Spa** HISTORIC HOTEL **$$$**
(Map p108; ☎231 6000; www.sofitel-legend.com; Sharia Abtal at-Tahrir; r/ste from US$368/568; ❄☒) Likely out of the budget for many long-haul travellers, the Old Cataract nonetheless deserves mention as it's the grande dame of hotels on the Nile and a destination in itself. Agatha Christie is said to have written part of *Death on the Nile* here, and it was featured in the movie. The splendid building is surrounded by exotic gardens with fantastic views of the river. The hotel was completely rehabbed in 2011 and is the pinnacle of luxury.

Eating

Along Sharia as-Souq and Sharia Abtal at-Tahrir there are plenty of small restaurants and cafes, good for taking in the lively souq atmosphere.

Sunset PIZZERIA **$$**
(off Map p108; ☎233 0601, 012 166 1480; Sharia Abtal at-Tahrir, Nasr City; set menus E£45-60; ⏲9am-3am) This great cafe terrace and restaurant is the place to be at sunset, with spectacular views over the First Cataract. Sit on the huge shady terrace for a mint tea, or enjoy the small selection of excellent grills or pizzas (E£40 to E£50). Very popular with locals at night.

Nubian Beach EGYPTIAN **$$**
(Map p108; west bank, past the Aga Khan Mausoleum; set menus per person E£55) Wonderful Nubian cafe-restaurant set in a quiet garden on the west bank of the Nile, against the backdrop of a towering sand dune. During the heat of the day or on cold winter nights, there is a beautifully painted room indoors. The food is simple but good, and alcohol is served – sometimes with live Nubian music.

Ad-Dukka EGYPTIAN **$$**
(Map p108; Essa Island; mains E£35-50; ⏲6.30-10pm) This restaurant set on an island just beyond Elephantine serves excellent Nubian food, in large portions. It comes recommended by our readers. To get here, there's a free ferry from the dock opposite the Egypt Air office.

Panorama EGYPTIAN **$**
(Map p108; Corniche an-Nil; dishes E£8-20) With its pleasant Nileside terrace, this is a great place to chill and sip a herbal tea or fresh juice. It also serves simple Egyptian stews cooked in clay pots, with salad, mezze and rice or chips, or an all-day breakfast.

Al-Makka GRILL **$$**
(Map p110; ☎230 3232; Sharia Abtal at-Tahrir, opposite Ramses Hotel; mains E£35-50; ⏲noon-2am) Popular with meat-eating local families, this place is famous for its excellent fresh kebabs and *kofta* (mincemeat and spices grilled on a skewer), as well as pigeon and chicken, all served with bread, salad and tahini. There is a sister store, **Al-Madina** (Map p110), with a similar menu, on Sharia as-Souq.

Biti Pizza PIZZERIA **$$**
(Map p110; Midan al-Mahatta; dishes E£23-38; ⏲10am-midnight; ❄) Biti is a popular air-conditioned restaurant that serves good Western-style pizzas, but more recommended are the delicious *fiteer* (flaky Egyptian pizza), including the excellent tuna option, and a fruit-and-nut dessert version. Watch out for the more expensive English-language tourist menu with the offer of any topping for E£38. The main menu is cheaper.

Chef Khalil EGYPTIAN **$**
(Map p110; ☎231 0142; Sharia as-Souq; meals E£25-60) This tiny but busy seafood eatery grills delicious fresh fish from Lake Nasser and the Red Sea over coals and serves it up with salads, and rice or French fries.

Information

Internet Access

Internet prices range from E£10 to E£15 per hour.

Aswanet Internet Café (Map p110; ☎231 7332; 25 Sharia Keylany; ⏲9am-11pm) Next to Keylany Hotel.

Nuba Nile Internet (Map p110; Sharia Abtal at-Tahrir; ⏲24hr) Next to Nuba Nile Hotel.

Money

The main banks all have branches (with ATMs) on the Corniche.

American Express (Map p108; ☎230 6983; Corniche an-Nil; ⏲9am-5pm Sun-Thu, to 2pm Fri & Sat)

Banque Misr (Map p110; ⏲8am-3pm & 5-8pm) Has a foreign-exchange booth in its main building.

Thomas Cook (Map p110; ☎230 4011; www.thomascook.com.eg; Corniche an-Nil; ⏲8am-2pm & 5-9pm)

Post

Main post office (Map p110; Corniche an-Nil; ⏲8am-8pm Sat-Thu, 1-5pm Fri)

Telephone

There are cardphones along the Corniche and at the train station.

Telephone centrale (Map p108; Corniche an-Nil; ⏲24hr)

Tourist Information

Tourist office (Map p110; ☎231 2811, 0100 576 7594; Midan al-Mahatta; ⏲8am-3pm & 7-9pm Sat-Thu, 9am-3pm & 6-8pm Fri) Very little printed material, but can advise on timetables and prices for taxis and feluccas.

Getting There & Away

Air

EgyptAir (Map p108; ☎231 5000; Corniche el-Nil; ⏲8am-8pm) offers several daily flights between Aswan and Cairo (E£320 to E£896, 1¼ hours). If tourist demand increases, the 30-minute flight to Luxor may be reinstated. Flights to Abu Simbel were also on hold at the time of writing.

Bus

The **bus station** (off Map p110) is 3.5km north of the train station. As of late 2011, there were no buses to Luxor and travel to Abu Simbel was restricted to four foreigners per bus. **Upper Egypt Bus Co** has two buses to Abu Simbel (E£35, four hours), departing 8am and 5pm. A direct bus to Cairo (E£150, 14 hours) leaves at 6am and 3pm daily.

Felucca

Aswan is the best place to arrange overnight felucca trips (see also boxed text below). The most popular trips are to Kom Ombo (one night, two days) or Edfu (two to three nights, three to four days), but some people go on to Esna (four

CRUISING THE NILE FELUCCA STYLE

It wasn't so long ago that the Nile was swarming with the white-tipped sails of feluccas, the traditional wooden boats that have been cruising this river for eons. Motorised barges and colossal cruise boats may have taken some of the wind out of the felucca's sails, but this time-tested craft remains an idyllic way to travel.

Around Aswan, a flock of some 3400 swan-like vessels ply the river's gently sluicing waters. Trust us when we say the best way to experience this river is from the bow of a felucca as it lazily meanders its way from bank to bank. One Egyptian proverb advises, 'The one who voyages the Nile must have sails made of patience'. But that's exactly the appeal. At the leisurely pace of the wind, you pass within arm's reach of river-bank villages, fishermen plying their trade and palms swaying leisurely as the desert sunset burns bright. On an overnight trip, you'll be rewarded with the blinding vista of the stars.

With so many boats and boat captains around, it's not hard to find an eager skipper willing to organise a multiday trip towards Luxor (currents will propel you if the wind fails). Feluccas are decked out in comfy cushions and usually hold six to eight passengers, making for a far more intimate experience than large cruise boats. Trips can be arranged from Aswan to the temples at Kom Ombo, Edfu or Esna and last between two and five days. Each evening, feluccas moor and set up camp either on the shore or on the boat. Food is prepared on the boat, and often captains and crew burst into song and dance at the slightest provocation. Best of all, the fast-flowing bits of water south of Luxor are less likely to contain the nasty bug bilharzia (see p637), making a post-temple dip in the cool Nile a joy. For prices and practicalities, see the next page.

nights, five days). Boats don't go beyond to Luxor due to locks at Esna.

Expect to pay at least E£100 per person to Kom Ombo, E£130 to Edfu and E£160 to Esna, including food. On top of this, add E£5 to E£10 per person for the captain to arrange the police registration. You can get boats for less, but take care; if it's much cheaper you'll either have a resentful captain and crew, or you'll be eating little more than bread and beans. Do not hand out the whole amount until you get to your destination because there have been several reports of trips being stopped prematurely due to 'breakdowns'.

Many of the better felucca captains can be found in Nileside restaurants such as the Aswan Moon or Emy, or on Elephantine Island. Meet a few – and inspect boats – before choosing.

Servees & Microbus

Servees cars and microbuses leave from the bus station, 3.5km north of the train station. A taxi there will cost E£15, or 50pt in a communal taxi. To Luxor costs E£18, to Kom Ombo E£7 and to Edfu E£15.

Train

From **Aswan Train Station** (Map p110; ☎231 4754) a number of daily trains run north to Cairo from 5am to 9.10pm (E£175, 14 hours). Tickets should be bought in advance, but can be bought on the train for an additional E£6. Student discounts are available. All trains stop at Kom Ombo (E£24/17, one hour), Edfu (E£28/19, two hours), Esna (E£38/23, 2½ hours) and Luxor (E£45/29, three hours).

Watania Sleeping Trains (☎230 2124; www.wataniasleepingtrains.com) has two daily services to Cairo at 5pm and 7pm (single/double cabin per person including dinner and breakfast US$60/120, children aged four to nine years US$45, 14 hours).

Getting Around

To/From the Airport

Aswan International Airport (☎248 0333) lies about 25km southwest of town; a taxi into town costs about E£50 to E£80.

Ferry

Two public ferries (E£1) run to Elephantine Island; the one across from EgyptAir goes to the Aswan Museum, while the one across from Thomas Cook goes to Siou. A third ferry (E£1) goes from the landing across from the train station to West Aswan and the Tombs of the Nobles.

Taxi

A taxi tour that includes Philae, the High Dam and the Unfinished Obelisk costs around E£150 to E£200. Taxis can also take you on day trips to Kom Ombo for about E£250. A taxi anywhere in town costs E£5 to E£10.

Around Aswan

PHILAE (AGILIKA ISLAND) فيلة معبد

The dreamy **Temple of Isis** (Temple of Philae; adult/child E£50/25; ⏰7am-4pm Oct-May, to 5pm Jun-Sep), just south of Aswan, was dedicated to Isis, who found the heart of her slain brother, Osiris, on Philae Island. Before Philae was submerged under the High Dam floods in the 1970s, the temple was relocated stone by stone to nearby Agilika Island, and the area landscaped to resemble its old home. Most of the temple was built by the Ptolemaic dynasty and the Romans. Early Christians later turned the hypostyle hall into a chapel, defacing some of the reliefs – this, in turn, was vandalised by early Muslims.

You must purchase tickets before you get on the boat to the island. The office is just before the boat landing at Shellal, south of the old Aswan Dam. You'll pay around E£60 for a taxi to bring you here, wait for an hour or so and then bring you back to town. You'll need to negotiate a price for a boat; theoretically, it's not more than E£10 per person return, but you'll have to haggle. Regardless, tip your boatman a couple of pounds.

A nightly **sound-and-light show** (www.soundandlight.com.eg; adult/child E£70/50; ⏰6.30pm, 7.45pm & 9.00pm Oct-May, 7pm, 8.15pm & 9.30pm May-Sep), lasting 1½ hours, is held at the temple. Check the website or the tourist office (p112) in Aswan for performance times and languages.

HIGH DAM السد العالي

Egypt's modern example of construction on a monumental scale, the controversial **Aswan High Dam** (As-Sadd al-Ali; adult/child E£20/10; ⏰8am-5pm) contains 18 times the amount of material used in the Great Pyramid of Khufu and created Lake Nasser, the world's largest artificial lake.

Most people visit the High Dam, 13km south of Aswan, as part of an organised trip to sights south of Aswan. There is a small pavilion with displays detailing the dimensions and the construction of the dam, and on the western side is a monument honouring Soviet-Egyptian friendship and cooperation. Video cameras and zoom lenses cannot be used, although nobody seems to police this. A taxi from Aswan is about E£25.

ABU SIMBEL أبو سمبل

☎097

Laid-back and quiet, the town of Abu Simbel lies 280km south of Aswan and only 40km north of the Sudanese border. Few tourists linger more than the few hours needed to visit the temples, but anyone interested in peace and tranquility, and Nubian culture, might choose to hang around for a few days. There are banks in town, but no ATMs.

Abu Simbel's temples alone are certainly worth the trip. They are remarkable not only in and of themselves, but also for their recent history. Between 1964 and 1968, both temples (consisting of more than 2000 blocks, each weighing 10 to 40 tonnes) were relocated to escape the High Dam flood. The temples were carefully oriented to face their original direction, though the original alignment – in which the rising sun flooded the sanctuary on Ramses' birth and coronation days – is now slightly off. Since the temples were moved, this phenomenon happens one day later, on February 22 and October 22.

Sights & Activities

The two temples of Abu Simbel are reached by road or, if you are on a cruise boat, from one of the jetties leading directly into the fenced temple compound.

Great Temple of Ramses II TEMPLE

(adult/student E£90/48.50 incl guide fee; 6am-5pm Oct-Apr, to 6pm May-Sep) Ramses II managed to surpass even himself when he had this magnificent temple carved out of a mountainside. The temple was dedicated to the gods Ra-Horakhty, Amun and Ptah as much as to the deified pharaoh himself. Four colossal statues of Ramses II – three intact, one half-collapsed – sit majestically, more than 20m tall, watching over the sands to the south, like a warning to would-be invaders.

Temple of Hathor TEMPLE

The other temple at the Abu Simbel complex (same ticket) is the rock-cut Temple of Hathor, fronted by six 10m-high standing statues. Four represent Ramses; the other two are Nefertari. Unusually, she is portrayed as the same height as her husband (instead of only up to his knees, like most consorts).

Sound-and-Light Shows SHOW

(www.soundandlight.com.eg; adult/child E£80/45; shows 7pm, 8pm & 9pm Oct-Apr, 8pm, 9pm & 10pm May-Sep) Performed in front each night. The text is flowery, but the laser show projected onto the temples is stunning.

> **POLICE CONVOYS**
>
> Driving north to Luxor from Aswan no longer needs to be done in a convoy, but the trip to Abu Simbel (at least three hours) does. Departures are twice daily, at 4.30am and 11am. Armed convoys congregate at the beginning of Sharia Sadat, near the Coptic Cathedral. Be there at least 15 minutes in advance.

Sleeping & Eating

Abu Simbel Village HOTEL $

(☎340 0092; s/d E£90/120; ❄) Abu Simbel's cheapest option, the faded Abu Simbel Village has basic vaulted rooms centred on a concrete courtyard.

TOP CHOICE **Eskaleh** HOTEL $$

(Beit an-Nubi; ☎0122 368 0521; www.eskaleh.net; d €60-70; ❄@) A self-styled Nubian cultural centre, this sensational little hotel is housed in traditionally constructed mud-brick buildings and filled with local furniture and crafts. Rooms are simple, but the modern tiled bathrooms are a welcome addition. There's a lovely **restaurant-lounge** (organic meals E£70-75) and a roof terrace with views over the lake. The friendly owner, Fikry el-Kashef, is a musician and occasionally hosts performances.

Toya CAFE $

(☎012 357 7539; Tariq al-Mabad; breakfasts E£8, mains E£15) New place in town serving breakfast for early arrivals, or simple local cuisine in either a lovely garden or madly painted rooms inside. A good place to stop for a drink or to smoke a sheesha.

Getting There & Away

AIR EgyptAir flies to Abu Simbel from Cairo; if tourist demand increases, flights from Aswan may be restored.

BUS From Abu Simbel to Aswan (four hours), buses leave at 8am, 9.30am, 1pm and 4pm from the Wadi el-Nil Restaurant on the main road. There is no advance booking, and tickets (E£25) are purchased on board. **Microbuses** make the same journey in three hours (E£30).

WESTERN OASES

الواحات الغربية

The vast sandy expanses west of the Nile, all the way to the Great Sand Sea, make up the Western Desert, a natural wonder as unfathomable as it is inhospitable. Five major oases lie in this formidable khaki ocean. In these islands of fresh water and greenery, you can explore crumbling Roman forts, flourishing palm plantations and medieval fortified towns. It's also here that you'll find the eerie rock formations of the White and Black Deserts, a dreamscape of pinnacles eroded into surreal shapes, as well as the exceptionally tranquil oasis of Siwa.

Travel in this region takes time, but the Western Desert vaunts some of the most jaw-dropping scenery in all of Egypt.

Al-Kharga Oasis الواحات الخارجة

☎092 / POP 100,000

The largest of the oases and the closest to the Nile Valley, Al-Kharga hides its attractions under a veneer of provincial busy-ness. A trade-route waypoint since ancient times, it has enough gently crumbling sights to merit a stopover. Police escorts have been notoriously heavy-handed, though at the time of writing they were no longer common; if they start up again, you should be able to shake them by signing a waiver at the tourist office.

The main town of Al-Kharga is fairly spread out, with the bus station in the south-central part of town, the minibus stand in the southeast near the souq, and most hotels a fair hike away from both.

Sights

If you really dig archaeology, contact guide **Sameh Abdel Rihem** (☎0100 296 2192), an expert on Kharga's antiquities.

Necropolis of Al-Bagawat ARCHAEOLOGICAL SITE
(adult/student E£30/15; ⏰8am-5pm Oct-Apr, to 6pm May-Sep) One of the earliest surviving and best-preserved Christian cemeteries in the world, 3km north of town. Most of the 263 mud-brick tombs date from the 4th to the 6th centuries AD. Tip the guardian E£5.

Al-Kharga Museum of Antiquities MUSEUM
(Sharia Gamal Abdel Nasser; adult/student E£30/15; ⏰8am-5pm) A small but interesting selection of archaeological finds from around the oases: tools, jewellery, textiles and other objects that sketch out the cultural history of the region.

Qasr al-Ghueita FORTRESS
(adult/student E£25/15; ⏰8am-5pm Oct-Apr) A Roman mud-brick fortress dominating the road to Baris, 18km south of Al-Kharga. The walls enclose a 25th-dynasty sandstone temple, dedicated to the Theban triad Amun, Mut and Khons. To get here, take a bus for Baris or pickup toward Bulaq, then walk 2km up a paved road.

Sleeping & Eating

Choose dirty budget digs or full luxury – there's nothing in between. Mohsen at the tourist office says **Kharga Oasis Hotel** (Midan Nasser) should be reopening soon under government management with rooms from about E£120 per night; call him for details.

There's a smattering of basic eateries around Midan Sho'ala, Sharia al-Adel and near Midan Basateen.

Pioneers Hotel HOTEL $$
(☎792 0751; www.solymar.com; Sharia Gamal Abdel Nasser; s/d half board from €66/84; ❄@≋) While the salmon-pink, low-rise construction is reminiscent of a hollowed-out sponge cake, the hotel does offer surprising comforts: a swimming pool, fitness area, Bedouin cafe, ATM, billiards and a children's playground all connected by lush grass. It is the only place in Al-Kharga with alcohol.

Hamadalla Hotel HOTEL $
(☎0122 831 3776; off Sharia Abdel Moniem Riad; s/d E£80/100, without air-con E£50/70; ❄) With torn carpeting, cracked plaster, occasionally clean rooms and an obvious rodent issue, Hamadalla is one of the better budget choices in Al-Kharga. It's only a minute's walk from some good felafel and streetside cafes (around the midan by the main post office).

Dar al-Bida Hotel HOTEL $
(☎792 9393; Midan Sho'ala; s/d/tr E£65/85/125, without air-con E£50/60/80; ❄) Dar al-Bida is convenient if you're arriving late or leaving early by minibus. Rooms are cramped but vie for cleanest budget digs in town – which isn't saying much. Those with private and shared bathrooms are the same price. The family that runs this place is quite sweet.

Information

National Bank of Egypt (Sharia Gamal Abdel Nasser) Has an ATM.

New Valley Tourist Office (☎792 1206; Midan Nasser; ⏰9am-2pm Sat-Thu) Find Mohsen Abd Al Moneam, a motherlode of knowledge, here or on his mobile (☎0100 180 6127).

Getting There & Away

AIR The airport is 5km north of town. The Petroleum Service Company (usually) has Sunday flights on a 15-seat plane, leaving Cairo at 8am and returning from Al-Kharga at 3pm (E£600 one way, 1½ hours). Contact the tourist office for schedules and bookings.

BUS Upper Egypt Bus Co (Sharia Mohammed Farid) operates buses to Cairo (E£65, eight to 10 hours) at 9pm and 10pm. There's one departure each to Asyut (E£15, three to four hours, 7pm), Baris (E£7, one hour, 6pm) and Dakhla Oasis (E£15, three hours, 2pm). For Luxor, either change in Asyut or hire a private taxi.

MICROBUS The most convenient way to get to Dakhla (E£15, three hours) or Asyut (E£15, three to four hours), minivans leave from the microbus station at Midan Sho'ala.

TAXI Taxis can get you to Luxor (via Jaja) in three hours, but will set you back about E£400. Cairo (seven hours) costs E£1000 for the whole car (maximum seven people).

Dakhla Oasis الواحات الداخلة

☎092 / POP 75,000

Shaded by swaying palms and studded with traditional villages and ancient mud-brick forts, Dakhla exemplifies oasis life. The main town is modern Mut, with most of the hotels and other services, but medieval Al-Qasr is more enchanting.

Sights & Activities

The biggest highlight is the thoughtfully restored Ottoman-era buildings of **Al-Qasr**, a village inside a mud-brick fortress. Antiquities police will show you through the narrow covered lanes and into half-hidden buildings ('donate' E£10). It hosts a small **Ethnographic Museum** (Sharia as-Salam; admission E£5; ⏲by request).

Eager explorers will find over 600 **hot springs** in the oases – be sure to investigate.

Sleeping

El-Forsan Hotel HOTEL $

(☎782 1343; Sharia al-Wadi, Mut; s/d E£90/110, without air-con E£70/90; ❄@📶) The main building is a typical concrete confabulation; the domed mud-brick bungalows out back are a more stylish, if worn, option. There's a garden cafe, manager Zaqaria has a wry sense of humour and breakfast is huge.

El Badawiya BOUTIQUE HOTEL $$

(☎772 7451; www.badawiya.com; near Al-Qasr; s/d €50/64; ❄@🏊) Perched above the fork in the road to Bir al-Gebel, this luxurious hotel features comfortable domed rooms of stone, mud and tile, most with awesome balconies with mesmerizing views of the oasis and desert. The sweet spot is the swimming pool. This is a great choice for families.

El-Negoom Hotel HOTEL $

(☎782 0014; north of Sharia as-Sawra al-Khadra, Mut; s/d E£80/100, without air-con E£60/70; ❄@📶) On a quiet street behind the tourist office and near a selection of restaurants, this friendly hotel has a span of trim little abodes. One of the most dependable options in town.

Al-Qasr Hotel HOTEL $

(☎787 6013; Al-Qasr; r E£30) This old backpacker favourite sits above a cafe/restaurant near the old town. The simple rooms with shared bathroom are fine for the price, or for E£5 you can sleep on a mattress on the roof. There's a breezy upstairs communal sitting area. Owner Mohamed has a long history of fine hospitality.

Desert Lodge BOUTIQUE HOTEL $$$

(☎772 7061; www.desertlodge.net; s/d/tr half board €75/120/175; ❄@🏊) This thoughtfully designed, ecofriendly mud-brick lodge crowns a hilltop overlooking the old town of Al-Qasr. The restaurant is adequate, and there is also a bar, a private hot spring, a painting studio on the desert's edge, and many of the services you'd expect for the price.

Eating

Said Shihad GRILL $$

(Sharia as-Sawra al-Khadra, Mut; meals E£20-35; ⏲dinner) Owner Said is onto a great thing here: grilling up a meat-centric dinner nightly to a dedicated following of hungry locals. The lamb shish kebab is the thing to go for – yum!

Ahmed Hamdy's Restaurant EGYPTIAN $$

(Sharia as-Sawra al-Khadra; meals E£20-30; ⏲lunch & dinner) On the main road west of Mut, this popular restaurant serves delicious chicken, kebabs, vegetables and a few other small dishes. The freshly squeezed lime juice is excellent and you can request beer (E£12) and sheesha.

Information

Banque Misr (Sharia al-Wadi, Mut; ⏲8.30am-2pm Sun-Thu) Has an ATM and will change cash and give advances on Visa and MasterCard.

Internet Cafe (Sharia Basateen, Mut; per hr E£2; ⌚11am-midnight) Gets you online at carrier-pigeon speeds.

Tourist office (☎782 1685; Sharia as-Sawra al-Khadra, Mut; ⌚8am-3pm & some evenings) Run by Omar Ahmad, a mine of knowledge; he can be contacted anytime on his mobile (☎0122 179 6467).

Getting There & Around

BUS **Upper Egypt Bus Co** (☎782 4366; Sharia al-Wadi, Mut) runs buses at 7pm and 8pm to Cairo (E£75, eight to 10 hours) via Al-Kharga Oasis (E£20, one to two hours) and Asyut (E£40, four to five hours). Additional buses head to Al-Kharga at 6am and 10pm. You can also go to Cairo via Farafra Oasis (E£25, four hours) and Bahariya Oasis (E£50, seven hours) at 6am and 5pm. There's a **ticket office** at Midan al-Tahrir, and buses stop to pick up passengers across the circle from the kiosk.

SERVEES & MICROBUS Microbuses leave when full from the old part of Mut, near the mosque, and cost E£14 to Al-Kharga, E£20 to Farafra and E£80 to Cairo (nights only). Pickups, Peugeots and microbuses run from Mut to Al-Qasr (E£1.50) from Sharia as-Sawra al-Khadra.

Farafra Oasis واحة الفرافرة

☎092 / POP 17,000

Blink and you'll miss the smallest, and probably dustiest, of the oases. Farafra can be an alternative setting-off point for trips into the spectacular White Desert (see below), but otherwise, **Badr's Museum** (donation E£10; ⌚8.30am-sunset) is the only attraction in town. We salute the effort put into this place by self-taught local artist Badr Abdel Moghny.

Desert tours are arranged through the few hotels.

Sleeping & Eating

Dining choices are limited to hotels (Al-Badawiya is solid) and a trio of grill joints in the centre of town. Alcohol isn't available.

Al-Badawiya Safari & Hotel BOUTIQUE HOTEL **$$**
(☎751 0060; www.badawiya.com; s/d €20/25, ste with air-con €35/50; @✻) Al-Badawiya dominates Farafra tourism with its hotel and thoroughly professional safari outfit. Immaculate, comfortable rooms have a Bedouin theme, there's a refreshing pool, and plenty of arches and domes. Reservations are recommended in winter.

Al-Waha Hotel HOTEL **$**
(☎0122 720 0387; wahafarafra@yahoo.com; d with shared bathroom E£60, r E£75) A small, spartan hotel opposite Badr's Museum, Al-Waha is the only real budget choice in town. The rooms, with faux-oriental rugs, are well-worn but acceptably clean. In summer, the cement walls throb with heat.

Getting There & Away

BUS **Upper Egypt Bus Co** goes from Farafra to Cairo (E£45, eight to 10 hours) via Bahariya (E£25, three hours) at 10am and 10pm. Buses from Farafra to Dakhla (E£25, four hours) originate in Cairo and leave around 2pm to 3pm and around 2am. Tickets are bought from the

WHITE & BLACK DESERTS

Upon first glimpse of the **White Desert** (Sahra al-Beida), you'll feel like Alice fallen through the desert looking glass. Beginning 20km northeast of Farafra, the yellow desert sands are pierced by chalky rock formations, sprouting almost supernaturally from the ground. Blindingly white spires reach for the sky, like frost-coloured lollipop licked into shapes – some surreal, some familiar as chickens or camels – by the dry desert winds. They are best viewed at sunrise or sunset, when the sun turns them pink and orange, or under a full moon, which gives the landscape a ghostly arctic appearance. A few kilometres north, the desert is littered with quartz crystals, best viewed at the famous Crystal Mountain.

Further north, closer to Bawiti, the change in the desert floor from beige to black signals the beginning of the **Black Desert** (Sahara Suda). Here, layers of black powder and rubble, eroded from former mountains, lie strewn all over the sandy earth.

Only 4WD vehicles can enter deep into the deserts, so you'll need to arrange a tour to get the most out of your visit. Bahariya Oasis is the more popular starting point for tours, though they can be less expensive from Farafra. For an overnight camping trip, expect to pay between E£400 and E£800 per vehicle, plus US$5 national park fee per person.

conductor. Buses stop across from Al-Abeyt restaurant and at the petrol station.

MICROBUS To Dakhla (E£20, three to four hours) and Bahariya (E£20, three hours); microbuses leave from the town's main intersection when full (not often).

Bahariya Oasis الواحات البحرية

☎02 / POP 35,000

Just 365km from Cairo, Bahariya is the Western Desert's most bustling and visited oasis. Set among hills and thick with date palms and springs, Bahariya is also the most convenient jumping-off point for the White and Black Deserts (see boxed text, p117). Buses drop you at Bawiti, the dusty main village.

Sights & Activities

Attractions in and around Bawiti include the **Temple of Alexander**, the 26th-dynasty tombs at **Qarat Qasr Salim** and the 10 famous Graeco-Roman **Golden Mummies** on show near the **Antiquities Inspectorate Ticket Office** (admission to 5 sites adult/student E£45/25; ⏲8am-4pm), just south of the main road in Bawiti.

There is ferocious competition among tour guides offering trips into the deserts. Visit the helpful tourist office if you feel overwhelmed. Well-established local safari outfits include **Eden Garden Tours** (☎0100 071 0707; www.edengardentours.com); **Helal Travel** (☎0122 423 6580; www.helaltravel.com); and **White Desert Tours** (☎0122 321 2179, www.whitedeserttours.com). Many freelance guides are also good, and slightly less expensive.

Sleeping & Eating

Sort out accommodation in Bawiti before you arrive, especially in high season, to avoid dealing with the frenzy of touts that swarm each arriving bus.

Food options are limited to the hotels, roast chicken in the market area and the aptly named **Popular Restaurant** (meals E£25; ⏲5.30am-10pm), which serves set meals and cold beer.

BAWITI

Old Oasis Hotel HOTEL $$

(☎3847 3028; www.oldoasissafari.com; by El-Beshmo spring; s/d/tr E£120/180/220, without air-con E£90/120/180; ❄@📶🏊) One of the most charming places to stay in Bawiti, with a garden and 13 simple but impeccable fan rooms, plus a few fancier stone-wall air-con rooms. A large pool receives steaming hot water from the nearby spring; the run-off waters the garden, where there's a shady restaurant/cafe.

New Oasis Hotel HOTEL $

(☎0122 847 4171; max _rfs@hotmail.com; by El-Beshmo spring; s/d E£70/120, without air-con E£50/100; ❄) This small homey hotel has several teardrop-shaped rooms, some with balconies overlooking the expansive palm groves nearby. Inside, the rooms are in good shape, though heavy on powder-blue paint.

Alpenblick Hotel HOTEL $$

(☎3847 2184; www.alpenblick-hotel-oasis.com; near Telephone centrale; s/d E£70/140, without air-con E£60/120; ❄) This granddaddy of the Bahariya hotel scene keeps getting dragged out of retirement by its consecutive owners; the current ones give a warm welcome. The rooms are characterless but clean.

AROUND BAWITI

Nature Camp BUNGALOW $$

(☎0122 337 5097; nature camps@hotmail.com; Bir al-Ghaba; r half board per person E£150) At the foot of Gebel Dist, Nature Camp sets new standards for environmentally focused budget accommodation with a peaceful cluster of candlelit and intricately designed thatch huts. The food is very good (meals E£25) and the owner, Ashraf Lotfe, is a skilled desert hand. Staff will drive you the 17km to and from Bawiti if you arrive without transport.

Eden Garden Camp HUT $

(☎0100 071 0707; www.edengardentours.com; huts with fan per person E£55, full board E£105) Located 7km east of Bawiti, in the small, serene oasis of El Jaffara, Eden Garden features simple huts, shaded lounge areas, fresh food and hot and cold springs just outside its gates. Its desert safaris have a good reputation, and pickups from Bawiti are free.

Badr's Sahara Camp HUT $

(☎0122 792 2728; www.badrysaharacamp.com; huts per person E£50) A couple of kilometres from town, Badr's Sahara Camp has a handful of bucolic, African-influenced huts, each with two beds and small patios. Hot water and electricity can't always be counted on, but cool desert breezes and knockout views of the oasis valley can. Free pickups available.

Information

National Bank for Development (⊙9am-2pm Sun-Thu) In the first street on the right after the tourist office; has an ATM and changes cash.

Sebt Internet (off Sharia Misr; per hr E£5; ⊙8am-3am)

Tourist office (☎3847 3035/9; ⊙8am-2pm Sat-Thu, plus 7-9pm Sat-Thu Nov-Apr) On the town's main roundabout; helpful manager Mohamed Abd el-Kader can also be contacted on his mobile (☎0122 373 6567).

Getting There & Away

Bus

Upper Egypt Bus Co (☎3847 3610; Sharia Misr; ⊙roughly 9am-1pm & 7-11pm) runs to Cairo (E£30, four to five hours) at 6.30am, 10am and 3pm from the kiosk near the post office. Buy tickets the day before travelling. Two more Cairo-bound buses originate in Dakhla and pass through Bawiti around noon and midnight, stopping at the Hilal Coffeehouse at the western end of town.

For Farafra (E£20, two hours) and Dakhla (E£40, four to five hours), hop on one of the buses that leave Bahariya around noon and 11.30pm from the Upper Egypt Bus Co kiosk and Hilal Coffeehouse.

Microbus

Minibuses run from Bawiti to Cairo (E£25), near the Moneib metro station in Giza. Minibuses to Farafra (E£20) and Dakhla (E£45) are rare, best caught an hour or so before the night bus departs. All leave from Hilal Coffeehouse.

4WD

There is no public transport to Siwa, so you will have to hire a private 4WD for the journey (see p120). If there's a 4WD from Siwa that's returning empty, you might be able to ride with it for half the usual E£1500. Permits (US$5 per person) are required and easy to get from the bank.

Siwa Oasis واحة سيوة

☎046 / POP 23,000

Easily the prettiest, and most remote, of Egypt's oases, sleepy Siwa is the perfect antidote to the commotion of bustling Egyptian cities. Isolated for centuries from the rest of the country, Siwa today hasn't strayed from its traditional roots – donkeys work alongside combustion engines and Siwi, the local Berber language, dominates. A long detour from the Nile Valley, Siwa rewards those who trek out here with gorgeous freshwater springs, a dash of ancient history, and generous helpings of tranquillity among palm-shaded streets.

Sights & Activities

The town centre is marked by the jagged remnants of the medieval mud-brick **Fortress of Shali**, and the only proper attraction is the **House of Siwa Museum** (adult/student E£10/5; ⊙9am-2.30pm Sun-Thu), worth a peek for the embroidered wedding dresses. Beyond this are acres of date-palm groves and a profusion of dazzling, freshwater **springs**. The remains of the **Temple of the Oracle** (adult/student E£25/15; ⊙9am-5pm), which once housed the famed oracle of Amun, and some Graeco-Roman **tombs** can easily be visited on a day trip. At the edge of town are the towering dunes of the **Great Sand Sea**.

The innumerable safari companies in Siwa charge around E£30 for a tour of town and environs and E£50 for a half-day trip to various springs. For an overnight desert trip, it's E£400 or so per vehicle, plus permits (US$5 per day plus E£11 service charge, arranged by your guide). We highly recommend **Ghazal Safari** (☎0100 277 1234); driver/guide Abd El-Rahman Azmy has a kick-ass vehicle and a love for Siwa that's contagious.

Sleeping

Make sure your hotel room has screened windows; the mosquitoes in Siwa are particularly insatiable.

Shali Lodge BOUTIQUE HOTEL **$$**
(☎460 1299; www.siwa.com/accommodations.html; Sharia Subukha; s/d/tr E£285/365/450) This tiny, beautiful mud-brick hotel, owned by environmentalist Mounir Neamatallah,

RESPECTING LOCAL CUSTOMS

Siwa may seem more laid-back than other parts of Egypt, but modesty is perhaps even more serious business here. When western women (or men, for that matter) wear shorts and tank tops, it's about the same as walking naked around a stranger's home. Keep your skin covered – as with anywhere in the country, showing respect earns respect.

nestles in a lush palm grove about 100m from the main square. The large, extremely comfortable rooms have exposed palm beams, rock-walled bathrooms and cushioned sitting nooks.

Al-Babinshal BOUTIQUE HOTEL $$
(☎460 1499; www.siwa.com/accommodations.html; s/d/tr E£275/375/450) Literally attached to the fortress of Shali, Al-Babinshal is a maze of tunnels and stairways connecting spacious and cool, cavelike rooms. Entirely made from the same materials as the original fort, each intimate abode has wood floors, traditional shuttered windows and exposed palm-log supports.

Kelany Hotel HOTEL $
(☎460 1052, 0122 403 9218; zaitsafari@yahoo.com; Azmi Kiliani; s/d E£120/150, without air-con E£70/100; ❄) Kelany has decent rooms that are beginning to show their age. If you're looking for air-con, this is your best budget bet. The rooftop restaurant features views of Shali Fortress, Gebel Dakrur and everything in between.

Desert Rose HOTEL $$
(☎0122 440 8164; ali_siwa@hotmail.com; s/d/tr E£120/200/280, without bathroom E£80/150/180; ≋) Overlooking the magnificent dunes southeast of Siwa, this friendly, cosy hotel has creatively decorated, spotless rooms in a funky octagonal building. Its pool is natural spring water. There are no electric lights, but there is a small generator to charge camera and phone batteries.

Palm Trees Hotel HOTEL $
(☎460 1703, 0122 104 6652; m_s_siwa@yahoo.com; Sharia Torrar; s/d E£35/50, without bathroom E£25/35, bungalows s/d E£50/70, r with air-con E£75; ❄) This deservedly popular budget hotel has sufficiently tidy rooms, all with screened windows, fans and balconies. The shady, tranquil garden with date-palm furniture is delightful (but mosquito-intensive), and the few ground-level bungalows have porches.

Yousef Hotel HOTEL $
(☎460 0678; central market sq; s/d E£30/40, without bathroom E£20/30) With the cheapest beds in town, Yousef is perennially full with backpacking budgeters. The rooms are a bit tattered and hot in summer, but the four-storey rooftop has great views of the oasis. Noise can be an issue.

Eating & Drinking

No alcohol is served in Siwa restaurants.

Abdu's Restaurant INTERNATIONAL $
(central market sq; mains E£5-30; ⏲8.30am-midnight) Before internet and mobile phones, there were places like Abdu's – a village hub where people gathered nightly to catch up and swap stories. This is the longest-running restaurant in town and remains the best, with a huge menu that includes traditional dishes, vegetable stews and fantastic pizza.

Kenooz Siwa EGYPTIAN $$
(Shali Lodge, Sharia Subukha; mains E£15-25) On the roof terrace of Shali Lodge, this is a great place to hang out while enjoying a mint tea or a cold drink. Mains include some unique Siwan specialties, like baked lentils and eggplant with pomegranate sauce.

Abo Ayman Restaurant GRILL $$
(meals E£13-23) Roasted on a hand-turned spit over coals in an old oil drum, the chickens at Abo Ayman are the juiciest in Siwa. They're served with salad, tahini and bread.

Nour al-Waha INTERNATIONAL $
(☎460 0293; Sharia Subukha; mains E£5-20) A popular hang-out in a palm grove opposite Shali Lodge, Nour al-Waha has shady tables and plenty of games on hand for those who just want to while away the day in the shade. The food is generally fresh and good.

Information

Al-Waha Internet (per day E£10-15) Wi-fi connection works all around the centre of town.

Banque due Caire (⏲8.30am-2pm, plus 5-8pm Oct-Apr) Branch with ATM, to the north of the main square.

Desert Net Cafe (per hr E£3; ⏲11am-3pm & 7pm-3am) Has the cheapest internet access.

Post office (⏲8am-2pm Sat-Thu) Behind Arous al-Waha Hotel.

Tourist office (☎460 1338; mahdi _hweiti@yahoo.com; ⏲9am-2pm Sat-Thu, plus 5-8pm Oct-Apr) Siwa's tourist officer, Mahdi Hweiti, is very knowledgeable and can help arrange trips to surrounding villages or the desert. His mobile number is ☎0100 546 1992.

Getting There & Away

Bus

West & Mid Delta Bus Co operates and sells tickets from the bus stop opposite the tourist police station, although when you arrive you'll be let off near the central market square. Buy your ticket ahead, as buses are often full.

There are three daily buses to Alexandria (E£37, eight hours), stopping at Marsa Matruh (E£17, four hours); these leave at 7am, 10am and 10pm. There's one daily departure to Cairo (E£70) at 8pm, except when there's not.

Microbus

Microbuses going to Marsa Matruh leave from the main square near the King Fuad Mosque. They are more frequent and much more comfortable than the West & Mid Delta bus; tickets cost the same.

4WD

A new road linking Siwa and Bahariya is about half-finished, and the whole distance (about 400km) can be crossed in five hours. A 4WD is necessary (there is no bus or *servees*), and drivers and the required permits are easy to arrange on either end. You'll pay about E£1500 per car.

Getting Around

BICYCLE One of the best ways to get around and can be rented from several sources; bicycle repair shops are best. The going rate is E£15 to E£20 per day.

DONKEY CARTS Otherwise known as *caretas*, donkey carts are a much used mode of transport for Siwans and can be a more amusing, if slower, way to get around. After haggling, expect to pay about E£30 for two to three hours or E£10 for a short trip.

SERVEES Pickup trucks (50pt to E£1) link Siwa town with the surrounding villages. For private hire, a reliable, English-speaking driver is **Anwar Mohammed** (☎0122 687 3261).

SUEZ CANAL السويس قناة

An engineering marvel by any measure, the 1869-built canal that severs Africa from Asia is darned impressive. Though the region is hardly geared for tourists, intrepid travellers are rewarded not only with a couple of picturesque colonial-built cities, but also the unforgettable sight of behemoth supertankers virtually gliding through the deserts that make up the Isthmus of Suez.

Port Said بورسعيد

☎066 / POP 570,600

At the mouth of the Suez Canal's Mediterranean entrance, wealthy Port Said tips its hat to a prosperous past. Abuzz with the energy of a lively port city, its muddle of grand but faded wooden buildings still manages to cling to some colonial charm. Visit for the yesteryear allure and the modern canal. A boardwalk provides up-close views, and a free ferry that crosses the canal gives casual visitors a chance to ride the waters of this manmade marvel. In the two days before the spring holiday of Sham el-Nessim, the city hosts the bizarre effigy-burning festival called El-Limbo.

The town is effectively built as an island, connected to the mainland by a bridge to the south and a causeway to the west. Most services are on Sharia al-Gomhuriyya, two blocks inland from the canal.

SUEZ CANAL: FAST FACTS

- **Construction** Begun 1859, completed 1869
- **Length** 190km
- **Surface width** 280–345m
- **Depth** 22.5m
- **Speed limit** 11–14kph
- **World trade passing through canal** 14%
- **Vessels passing annually** Over 20,000

Sights & Activities

The easiest way to explore the canal is to take the **free public ferry** from near the tourist office across to Port Fuad and back. Keep an eye out for the striking green domes of **Suez Canal House**, built for the channel's inauguration in 1869. It's currently fenced off, so the only way to peek at it is from the water. Back on land, stroll the boardwalk on Sharia Palestine and then amble down Sharia Memphis, with its old **Woolworth's**, Sharia al-Gomhuriyya, and around the streets just north of the Commercial Basin for some wonderfully odd colonial remnants.

You could also peek into the **Military Museum** (☎322 4657; Sharia 23rd of July; admission E£5; ⏱10am-3pm Sat-Thu), for its information on the canal and also some rather curious exhibits (complete with toy soldiers) documenting the 1956 Suez Crisis and the 1967 and 1973 wars with Israel.

Sleeping

TOP CHOICE **Hotel de la Poste** HISTORIC HOTEL $
(☎322 4048; 42 Sharia al-Gomhuriyya; s/d E£75/95; ❄) Port Said's best budget option,

this faded classic still manages to maintain a hint of its original charm. Clean and comfortable rooms and a decent on-site restaurant are good perks, in addition to the faint whiff of colonial history.

New Continental HOTEL $$
(☎322 5024; 30 Sharia al-Gomhuriyya; s/d E£110/183; ❄) Efficient, friendly management makes this typical Egyptian midrange hotel stand out from the crowd. Light-filled rooms, over-cluttered with furniture, come in a range of sizes, so ask to see a few.

Mereland Hotel HOTEL $
(☎322 7020; Sharia Digla; s/d E£67/79, without bathroom E£30/42) This shabby place has seen better days but the fan-only rooms have clean linen and friendly manager Ahmed tries hard to help. Shell out for en-suite facilities, as the shared ones leave a lot to be desired.

Eating

Self-caterers will find all the groceries they need at **Metro Supermarket** on Sharia al-Geish. For fruit and vegetables, try the lively **market** on Sharia Souq, three blocks north of Sharia al-Gomhuriyya.

Abou Essam SEAFOOD $$
(☎323 2776; Sharia Atef as-Sadat; mains E£30-60) This flashy glass-fronted place does a great selection of fish, pasta and grilled meat and has a popular serve-yourself salad bar.

Pizza Pino ITALIAN $$
(☎323 9949; Sharia al-Gomhuriyya; mains E£20-50) Moodily lit and decked out in comfy seats, it's no wonder people linger here well after dinner is over. Friendly service, good Italian-influenced food and fresh juice draws crowds.

Information

The main **banks** all have branches with ATMs in town, mostly along Sharia al-Gomhuriyya.

Mody Net (☎324 4202; Sharia Salah Salem; per hr E£3; ⏲9am-midnight) Internet access.

Tourist office (☎323 5289; 8 Sharia Palestine; ⏲10am-7pm Sat-Thu) Enthusiastic staff and good maps of town, near the ferry to Port Fuad.

Getting There & Away

BOAT For details of boats from Port Said to Cyprus and Syria, see p628.

BUS The bus station is about 3km from the town centre at the beginning of the road to Cairo (about E£5 in a taxi). **Super Jet** (☎372 1779) and **East Delta Travel Co** (☎372 9883) run from here. Bookings are advisable.

SERVEES The *servees* station is next door to the train station. Sample fares: Cairo (E£20), Ismailia (E£10), Suez (E£12).

TRAIN To Cairo (1st-/2nd-class E£21/11, five hours), via Ismailia (E£11/4) services run at 5.30am, 1pm and 5.30pm. There's also a 2nd-class-only service at 7.30pm. Delays are common and buses are, in general, quicker and more comfortable.

Suez السويس

☎062 / POP 500,000

Poor Suez. Thanks to a heavy thumping delivered during the 1967 and 1973 wars, it has none of the nostalgic appeal of Port Said or Ismailia, and overzealous security measures have made canal-viewing here a no-go, with plenty of barbed wire and bored guards to stop you from snapping photos. We mention the place only because it's a transit hub.

The town is in two parts: Suez proper, the chaotic main settlement, and Port Tawfiq, a catatonic suburb at the mouth of the canal.

There are ATMs at **Banque Misr** and **Union National Bank**, on Sharia al-Geish. For

BUSES FROM PORT SAID

DESTINATION	PRICE (E£)	DURATION (HR)	TIMES
Alexandria (Super Jet)	30	4	4.30pm
Alexandria (East Delta)	25	4-5	7am, 11am, 2pm, 4pm, 6pm, 8pm
Cairo (Super Jet)	25	4	Every 30min
Cairo (East Delta)	23	4	Hourly 5am-9pm
Ismailia	6	1½	Hourly 6am-6pm
Suez	11	2½-3	6am, 10am, 2pm, 4pm

BUSES FROM SUEZ

All services are on East Delta.

DESTINATION	PRICE (E£)	DURATION (HR)	TIMES
Al-Tor	25-30	4½	8.30am, 11am, 1.30pm, 3pm, 4.30pm, 5.15pm, 6pm
Cairo	15-20	2	Every 30min
Dahab	40	7	11am
Hurghada	35-40	4	Hourly 5am-11pm
Ismailia	6	1½	Every 30min 6am-4pm
Luxor	60-70	9-10	8am, 2pm, 8pm
Nuweiba	45-50	8	3pm, 5pm
Port Said	14	2½	7am, 9am, 11am, 12.15pm, 3.30pm
Sharm el-Sheikh	35-40	6	8.30am, 11am, 1.30pm, 3pm, 4.30pm, 5.15pm, 6pm
St Katherine	25	4	2pm
Taba	45-50	9	3pm, 5pm

internet, try **CACE** (Sharia al-Geish; per hr E£4; ⏰9am-8pm).

If you do get stuck here, **Medina Hotel** (☎322 4056; Sharia Talaat Harb; s/d E£75/125; ❄) is your best bet, just off the main drag and perfectly clean, though short on windows. For inexpensive food, wander around the Sharia Talaat Harb area.

Getting There & Away

BUS The bus station is 5km out of town along the road to Cairo. **East Delta Travel Co** (☎356 4853) services the Sinai, and **Upper Egypt Bus Co** (☎356 4258) handles the Red Sea coast and the Nile Valley.

SERVEES The *servees* station is beside the bus station and prices are similar to the buses. The only place in the Sinai they serve is Al-Tor (E£15).

TRAIN Six uncomfortable 2nd-class Cairo-bound trains depart Suez daily (E£15 to E£18, three hours) going only as far as Ain Shams, 10km northeast of central Cairo; the first Cairo-bound train leaves at 5.30am. There are also eight slow trains to Ismailia.

RED SEA COAST

ساحل البحر الاحمر

The long stretch of Egyptian coastline that meets the Red Sea, extending from Suez to Sudan, is fringed by world-class coral reefs and clear aqua waters. It is here that Moses parted the waters and early Christians established the first monasteries. These days, however, the legions of holidaymakers that descend en masse are keener on sunbathing than biblical history.

In Hurghada, heart of the European package tourist scene, ravenous development has steamrolled its way through, while the political unrest in Egypt has stalled further plans, leaving the concrete husks of unfinished future resorts. Further south, Marsa Alam, so close to the Red Sea's most beautiful reefs, has received a bit of the 'developer's touch', but the time-warp town of Al-Quseir remains a picturesque, if not very lively, waypoint.

Hurghada

الغردقة

☎065 / POP 160,900

Hailed by Egyptian tourist authorities as a success story, Hurghada is a poster child for everything that can go wrong with mass tourism. Uninhibited growth over the years has disfigured this part of the Red Sea coast with its relentless concrete spread, destroying much of the fringing reef ecosystems along the way. Nevertheless, there are a few low-key resorts that manage to retain shreds of calm, and for many touring the Nile Valley it remains the most accessible part of the Red Sea. At press time, boats were set to begin running between Hurghada and Sharm el-Sheikh in the Sinai, a convenient shortcut. For details of the somewhat belated efforts to rescue the region's green credentials, see p608.

A main road connects Ad-Dahar, the main town area, with Sigala, where the port is. South of Sigala, a road winds 15km down along the coast through the 'resort strip', the town's upmarket tourism enclave.

⊙ Sights & Activities

There's little to do in Hurghada itself other than sit on a beach and dream of more secluded places. The **public beach** (admission E£2; ⊙8am-sunset) in Sigala is less than appealing, though many resorts offer preferable sun-and-sand options (nonguest access charges range from E£25 to E£75).

If you go diving or snorkelling, arrange with a specific operator, rather than through your hotel, as those trips often go to the closest, over-dived reefs. **Jasmin Diving Centre** (☑346 0334; www.jasmin-diving.com; Grand Seas Resort Hostmark, resort strip, Hurghada) has an excellent reputation.

🛏 Sleeping

Most budget hotels are in Ad-Dahar, at the northern end of a long stretch of resorts. Don't immediately rule out higher-end resorts – fantastic deals can be had in low seasons, so long as you book ahead online.

AD-DAHAR

TOP CHOICE 4 Seasons Hotel HOSTEL $
(☑0122 704 3917; fourseasonshurghada@hotmail.com; off Sharia Sayyed al-Qorayem; s/d E£60/80; ✳) A real old-school hostel with bags of character. Manager Mohammad is always on hand to dish out advice and help. The rooms, though nothing special, are clean and great value. For E£20 guests get beach access at the nearby Sandbeach Hotel.

Luxor Hotel HOTEL $$
(☑354 2877; www.luxorhotel-eg.com; off Sharia Sayyed al-Qorayem; s/d €20/30; ✳🛜) Some of the rooms may be on the small side and the furnishings are a bit bland, but still a solid midrange choice. Management are eager to help, there's a pleasant terrace and it's surprisingly quiet.

El-Arosa Hotel HOTEL $$
(☑354 8434; elarosahotel@yahoo.com; off Corniche; s/d E£125/180; ✳✳) El-Arosa overlooks the sea in the distance from the inland side of the Corniche. Cosy rooms have decent amenities and there's even a pool (albeit located in the dining room).

Geisum Village RESORT $$
(☑354 6692; Corniche; s/d E£180/300; ✳@✳) The gloomy corridors don't inspire confidence but the rooms are surprisingly tidy and bright. The centre of the action is the large swimming pool surrounded by a lawn, and you can always take a dip in the ocean or lie on the beach (er, spot of sand).

Happy Land HOTEL $
(☑354 7373; Sharia Sheikh Sebak; s/d from E£45/75) Better named 'Grumpy Land' as management seem to have misplaced their Prozac, but the dingy, noisy rooms will suffice if 4 Seasons is full.

SIGALA

Bella Vista Resort RESORT $$
(☑344 6012; www.bellavista-hurghada.com; Sharia Sheraton; s/d €55/70; ✳@✳) This large midrange option may be a little dated but pleasant management, well-cared-for grounds and a wee patch of private beach make up for it. The rooms here are airy and decorated in soothing neutrals.

White Albatross HOTEL $$
(☑344 2519; walbatros53@hotmail.com; Sharia Sheraton; s/d/tr US$25/30/35; ✳) Well-run, with spic-and-span rooms, the White Albatross is slap in the centre of the Sigala action. Top-floor doubles give some respite from street noise. There's no beach but you can drop into any of the nearby resorts for a small fee.

RESORT STRIP

TOP CHOICE Oberoi Sahl Hasheesh RESORT $$$
(☑344 0777; www.oberoihotels.com; Sahl Hasheesh; ste from €200; ✳@✳) Justifiably advertised as the most luxurious destination on the Red Sea, the Oberoi features palatial suites decorated in minimalist Moorish style.

Hurghada Marriott Beach Resort RESORT $$
(☑344 6950; www.marriott.com; resort strip; s/d US$95/105; ✳@✳) Within walking distance of the resort strip's nightlife and restaurants, the well-kept rooms here exude a modern, beachy feel. The beach is small, but if you want the freedom to choose where to eat it's a good choice.

✕ Eating

Ad-Dahar and Sigala have dozens of inexpensive local-style restaurants.

AD-DAHAR

Red Sea I SEAFOOD $$

(☎354 9630; off Sharia an-Nasr; mains E£30-70; ❄) Slap in the souq, Red Sea I has a wide selection of seafood, plus Egyptian and international dishes, all at decent prices. Choose from fairy-light-strewn rooftop seating or pavement dining.

El Taybeen GRILL $$

(Sharia Soliman Mazhar; meals E£30-50; ❄) All the usual kebab favourites are dished up at this no-nonsense restaurant. Service can be a bit slow but meals are tasty and filling.

SIGALA

Kastan SEAFOOD $$

(Arena Mall, Sharia Sheraton; meals E£40-100) Affordable, fresh seafood with an Egyptian twist. We love the hearty and filling seafood soup and cheap shrimp curry. Never mind the mall location – the quality and service here make it stick out from the crowd.

Al-Araby EGYPTIAN $$

(Sharia Sheraton; mains E£25-50) This popular place, with street-side seating in the heart of downtown, serves up a satisfying menu of Egyptian classics. If you're hankering for *shish tawooq* (grilled chicken) or a snack of *baba ganoog* (eggplant dip) Al-Araby is a decent bet.

Abu Khadigah EGYPTIAN $

(Sharia Sheraton; meals E£10-20) This no-frills place is known for its *kofta* (mincemeat and spices grilled on a skewer), stuffed cabbage leaves and other Egyptian staples.

Shade Bar and Grill INTERNATIONAL $$$

(Marina Rd; mains E£50-95) If you're pining for a steak look no further. Sprawl out on the terrace beanbags and order your red-meat fix. For those too lazy to bar-hop, Shade conveniently turns into a popular bar late at night.

Gad EGYPTIAN FAST FOOD $$

(Sharia Sheraton; dishes E£15-45) With a menu that covers all bases you simply can't go wrong at Egypt's favourite fast-food restaurant. Come here for Egyptian comfort-food like *fiteer* (Egyptian-style pizza) and baked macaroni.

Drinking & Entertainment

In addition to the more casual places below, the major clubs are franchises of internationally renowned **Ministry of Sound** (www.ministryofsoundegypt.com) and **HedKandi** (www.hedkandibeachbar.com), with admission prices up to E£100.

Retro LIVE MUSIC

(Sharia Sheraton, Sigala) This relaxed pub dishes up live rock, blues and soul every Sunday and Wednesday. An easy-going vibe, decent bar menu and pool table make it an all-round winner.

Papas Bar CLUB

(www.papasbar.com; New Marina Rd, Sigala) Probably the most popular hang-out in Hurghada, this Dutch-run bar has loads of atmosphere and is packed nightly with diving instructors and other foreign residents. There's a Papas II located in Ad-Dahar.

BUSES FROM HURGHADA

DESTINATION	PRICE (E£)	DURATION (HR)	TIMES
Al-Quseir (Upper Egypt Bus)	20	1½	5.30am, 4pm, 8pm, 1.30am
Alexandria (Super Jet)	95	9	2.30pm
Aswan (Upper Egypt Bus)	45-50	7	10.30pm, 12.30am
Cairo (Super Jet)	65	6	9.30am, noon, 2.30pm, 5pm, 12.30am, 2.30am
Cairo (Upper Egypt Bus)	65	6	10.30am, 3pm, 5.30pm, 1am
Luxor (Super Jet)	45	4	8.30am
Luxor (Upper Egypt Bus)	30	5	8pm, 10.30pm, 12.30am, 1.30am, 2am, 3am, 3.30am
Marsa Alam (Upper Egypt Bus)	35	4	4pm, 8pm, 1.30am
Suez (Upper Egypt Bus)	50	4-5	7am, 11am, 12.30pm, 3pm, 4pm, 5.30pm, 11.30pm

Memories BAR
(Corniche, Ad-Dahar) Good for early evening drinks on the outside terrace, this casual, friendly place has a dark wood interior, blissfully cold beer and regular live music.

Information

There are internet cafes all over the city and in many hotels, most charging between E£5 and E£10 per hour. Banks are scattered all over Hurghada: most have ATMs. Many upmarket hotels also have ATMs in their lobbies.

Estenv Internet (Sharia Sheikh Sabak, Ad-Dahar; 24hr)

02 Internet (Sharia Sheraton, Sigala; 10.15am-11.15pm)

Post office (Sharia al-Mustashfa, Ad-Dahar) Toward the southern end of Ad-Dahar.

Telephone centrale (Sharia an-Nasr; 24hr) Northwest of the post office.

Thomas Cook Ad-Dahar (354 1870/1; Sharia an-Nasr; 9am-2pm & 6-10pm); Sigala (344 3338; Sharia Sheraton; 9am-3pm & 4-10pm); Resort Strip (344 6830; 9am-5pm)

Getting There & Away

AIR EgyptAir (344 3592/3; www.egyptair.com; resort strip) has daily flights to Cairo.

BOAT During research for this book a new ferry between Hurghada and Sharm el-Sheikh was announced but had yet to begin operation. The proposed schedule has departures for Sharm el-Sheikh at 9am every Tuesday, Thursday and Saturday (child/adult E£150/250, two hours). Enquire at any of the hotels for up-to-date information; if you're staying in Ad-Dahar, 4 Seasons Hotel is a good contact point.

BUS Upper Egypt Bus Co (354 7582; off Sharia an-Nasr, Ad-Dahar) has a station at the southern end of Ad-Dahar. **Super Jet** (354 4722; Sharia an-Nasr, Ad-Dahar) is 500m south of the Upper Egypt station. Ideally, book ahead for long-distance such as to Luxor and Cairo.

SERVEES The *servees* station, off Sharia an-Nasr in Ad-Dahar, has cars to Cairo (E£55 to E£60, six hours), Safaga (E£10, one hour) and Al-Quseir (E£10, 1½ hours). It is also possible to take one to Luxor (E£25, five hours).

Getting Around

TO/FROM THE AIRPORT Hurghada International Airport (344 2592) is located 6km southwest of town. A taxi to downtown Ad-Dahar costs between E£25 and E£30.

MICROBUS Microbuses run from central Ad-Dahar south along the resort strip (50pt to E£1), and along Sharia an-Nasr and other major routes. **El-Gouna Transport** operates a more comfortable route (E£5 to E£10) from El-Gouna (to the north) to Ad-Dahar and the end of Sharia Sheraton in Sigala about every half-hour. You can flag the bus down at any point along the way and pay on board.

TAXI Taxis from Ad-Dahar to the start of the resort strip (around the Marriott hotel) charge about E£15. Travelling from the bus station to the centre of Ad-Dahar, expect to pay between E£5 and E£10.

Al-Quseir القصير

065 / POP 35,045

It's hard not to fall in love with this sleepy Red Sea port, passed by most tourists. Beautiful Ottoman-era coral-block buildings line the waterfront and a maze of dusty laneways snake inland. It's worth a stopover to soak up some ocean-side serenity and get a glimpse of the region before tourism took over.

In Pharaonic times, the port was the departure point for boats heading south to the fabled East African kingdom of Punt, and until the 10th century, Al-Quseir was one of the most important exit points for pilgrims travelling to Mecca. Later, it became an important import channel for Indian spices destined for Europe.

The town has a 24-hour **telephone centrale**, a **National Bank of Egypt** branch with an ATM, and a **post office**.

Sights

The only formal sight in town is the 16th-century **Ottoman Fortress** (admission E£15; 9am-5pm), still largely intact, though later modified (with cannonballs) by French and British colonials. Just across from the fortress is the 19th-century **shrine** of a Yemeni sheikh, Abdel Ghaffaar al-Yemeni, marked by an old gravestone in a niche in the wall.

Sleeping & Eating

Dining options are limited. There are the usual ta'amiyya and fish stands around the seafront and the bus station.

TOP CHOICE **Al-Quseir Hotel** HISTORIC HOTEL $$
(333 2301; www.alquseirhotel.com; Sharia Port Said; s/d without bathroom E£150/180) If you're looking for atmosphere rather than amenities this renovated 1920s merchant's house on the seafront is a delightful place to stay. Six simple but spacious rooms shine with high wooden ceilings and latticework on the windows. If you order ahead they can provide meals.

Rocky Valley Beach Camp BEACH CAMP $$
(☎333 5247; www.rockyvalleydiverscamp.com; 4/8-day all-inclusive diving package €200/350) About 10km north of town, this camp is a veritable paradise for shoestringing scuba aficionados, with Bedouin-style tents, beach-side barbecues, late-night parties and some incredible reefs right off shore.

Mövenpick Sirena Beach RESORT $$$
(☎333 2100; www.moevenpick-quseir.com; s/d US$125/175; ❄@≋) This low-set, domed ensemble, 7km north of town, is top of the line in Al-Quseir, and one of the most laid-back resorts along the coast. There are restaurants, a Subex diving centre and a refreshing absence of glitz.

Restaurant Marianne EGYPTIAN $$
(☎333 4386; Sharia Port Said; mains E£20-40) The most popular place in town, serving yummy grilled fish on beachside tables.

Getting There & Around

The bus and *servees* stations are next to each other about 3km northwest of the Safaga road. A taxi from the bus station to the waterfront costs E£5.

BUS Buses run to Cairo (E£60 to E£80, 10 hours) via Hurghada (E£20 to E£25, 1½ to two hours), departing at 8.30am, 1pm, 3.30pm and 10pm. Buses to Marsa Alam (E£15, two hours) are at 4am, 6pm and 10pm but the schedule changes frequently so check beforehand.

MICROBUS Microbuses go along Sharia al-Gomhuriyya, with some also going to the bus and *servees* stations. Fares are between 50pt and E£1.

SERVEES Sample fares: Hurghada (E£10, 1½ hours) and Marsa Alam (E£10, two hours).

Marsa Alam مرسى علم

☎065

The Red Sea off the coast of Marsa Alam shelters some of the most impressive diving in the world. While just a decade ago these sites were accessible only by boat from Hurghada and Sharm el-Sheikh, new development has made this area an easier jumping-off point. Despite a construction drive of slick resorts north and south of town, the area is still a diving aficionado's dream, and some long-standing beach camps here cater to those who want to spend most of their time underwater.

The town of Marsa Alam itself is rather nondescript. Just south of the main junction is a modest collection of shops, a **pharmacy**, a **telephone centrale** and a bustling **market**.

Sights & Activities

Dive camps have their own operators, but you could also organise a trip through **Red Sea Diving Safari** (☎02-337 1833/9942; www.redsea-divingsafari.com; Marsa Shagra), run by environmentalist Hossam Hassan, who pioneered diving in the Red Sea's deep south.

Back on land, **Red Sea Desert Adventures** (☎0122 399 3860; www.redseadesertadventures.com; Marsa Shagra) is highly recommended for tailored walking, camel and jeep safaris through the fascinating Eastern Desert, studded with Roman traces. Prices start at approximately €60 per person per day; they vary considerably depending on mode of transport, length of trip and number of people travelling. For multiday safaris, try to book at least one month in advance so the necessary permits can be arranged.

Sleeping & Eating

There are few places to stay in Marsa Alam village itself, but north and south along the coast there's an ever-growing number of all-inclusive resorts, plus a handful of simpler, diver-oriented camps, many of which focus on sustainable tourism practises.

Most visitors to Marsa Alam eat at their resorts. In town, there's a small **supermarket** with the basics, and a couple of cafes at the junction where you can find ta'amiyya and similar fare. The only restaurant worth seeking out is **Dolce & Salato** (68 St, Marsa Alam; mains E£18-35), a little gem in the centre of town that dishes up surprisingly authentic pizza and pasta. It's one block down from the mosque.

Marsa Shagra Village BEACH CAMP $$
(☎023-337 1833; www.redsea-divingsafari.com; tent/royal tent/chalet full board per person €40/45/55) One of the first eco-minded dive places to open up on the Red Sea and, despite the development that has gone on nearby, it has stayed true to its sustainable tourism credentials. Marsa Shagra has rigorous environmental standards and offers excellent snorkelling just offshore. Lodging is in two-bed tents with shared bath or stone chalets with private facilities. It's 24km north of Marsa Alam along the main road.

TOP CHOICE **Wadi Lahami Village** BEACH CAMP $$
(☎023-337 1833; www.redsea-divingsafari.com; Wadi Lahami; tent/royal tent/chalet full board per person €40/45/55) With a similar set-up and environmental standards to Marsa Shagra, this is a more remote alternative, set on a bird-filled mangrove bay near Fury Shoals reefs, 120km south along the main road from Marsa Alam. Worth the extra distance if you have the time.

Oasis Resort RESORT $$$
(☎0100 505 2855; www.oasis-marsaalam.de; s/d half board €68/112) Smaller than many of the mega-resorts along this stretch of sand, Oasis is unique for utilising local materials and traditional architecture rather than the usual concrete. Rooms here are spacious, airy and comfortable with great sea views. It's 24km north of Marsa Alam along the main road.

Um Tondoba BEACH CAMP $$
(☎0100 191 1414; www.ecolodge-redsea.com; hut/chalet full board per person €25/35) Stripping it right back to the basics of sun, sea and sand, Um Tondoba offers palm-thatch beach huts (across the road from the beach rather than on the shore), good diving packages and an exceptionally mellow atmosphere. Find it 14km south of Marsa Alam along the main road.

Getting There & Away

AIR EgyptAir flies from Cairo to **Marsa Alam International Airport** (☎370 0005), 67km north of Marsa Alam along the Al-Quseir road. There is no public transport, so you'll need to arrange a transfer in advance with your hotel.

BUS Marsa Alam bus station is just past the T-junction along the Edfu road. Buses to Cairo (E£85 to E£90, 10 to 11 hours) via Al-Quseir (E£10 to E£15, two hours) and Hurghada (E£25 to E£35, 3½ to four hours) depart at 1.30pm and 8.30pm, but check beforehand as timetables change frequently. There are also a couple of services per day to Shalatein (E£20 to E£25, four hours).

SINAI سيناء

The breathtaking region of Sinai is famed as the place where Moses received the Ten Commandments from the big man in the sky. It's also here that ancient and modern armies fought and Bedouin tribes established their homes. This striking desertscape rolls straight into the turquoise waters of the Red Sea, offering countless opportunities for exploration of both the mountainous desert and pristine underwater ecosystems. Visitors can take their pick of places to stay while exploring the peninsula: the glitzy resorts of Sharm el-Sheikh, the chilled-out vibes of Dahab or the remote and low-key Nuweiba and St Katherine Protectorate.

In part due to their popularity with Israeli tourists, Sinai resorts have been the targets of terrorist bombs, though not since 2006. Since then, millions of holidaymakers (though significantly fewer Israelis) have enjoyed their stay here without incident – but it is worth checking current warnings.

Ras Mohammed National Park محمية رأس محمد

Declared a **national marine park** (admission per person €5, plus per vehicle €5; ⏰8am-5pm) in 1988, the headland of Ras Mohammed lies about 20km west of Sharm el-Sheikh. The waters surrounding the peninsula are considered the jewel in the crown of the Red Sea, and the park is inundated with more than 50,000 visitors annually, enticed by the prospect of marvelling at some of the world's most spectacular coral-reef ecosystems.

Camping (€5 per person) is allowed in designated areas. Take all supplies and your passport with you; it is not possible to enter the park if you have only a Sinai permit and not a full visa.

Many people visit the reefs to **dive** on day-boats or live-aboards, but walk-in **snorkelling** is excellent too (bring your own gear). You can hire a taxi from Sharm el-Sheikh for around E£150 for the day or join one of the many day tours by 4WD or bus from Sharm el-Sheikh. They will drop you at the best beaches and snorkelling sites. Expect to pay from E£150.

To move around the park you'll need a vehicle. Access is restricted to certain parts of the park and, for conservation reasons, it's forbidden to leave the official tracks.

Sharm el-Sheikh شرم الشيخ

☎069 / POP 38,478

Sharm is the main jumping-off point for spectacular, world-class diving. Alas, in recent years a development frenzy has turned this once-sleepy fishing village into a major package-tour destination. With most traces of Egypt sanitised for Western

Sinai

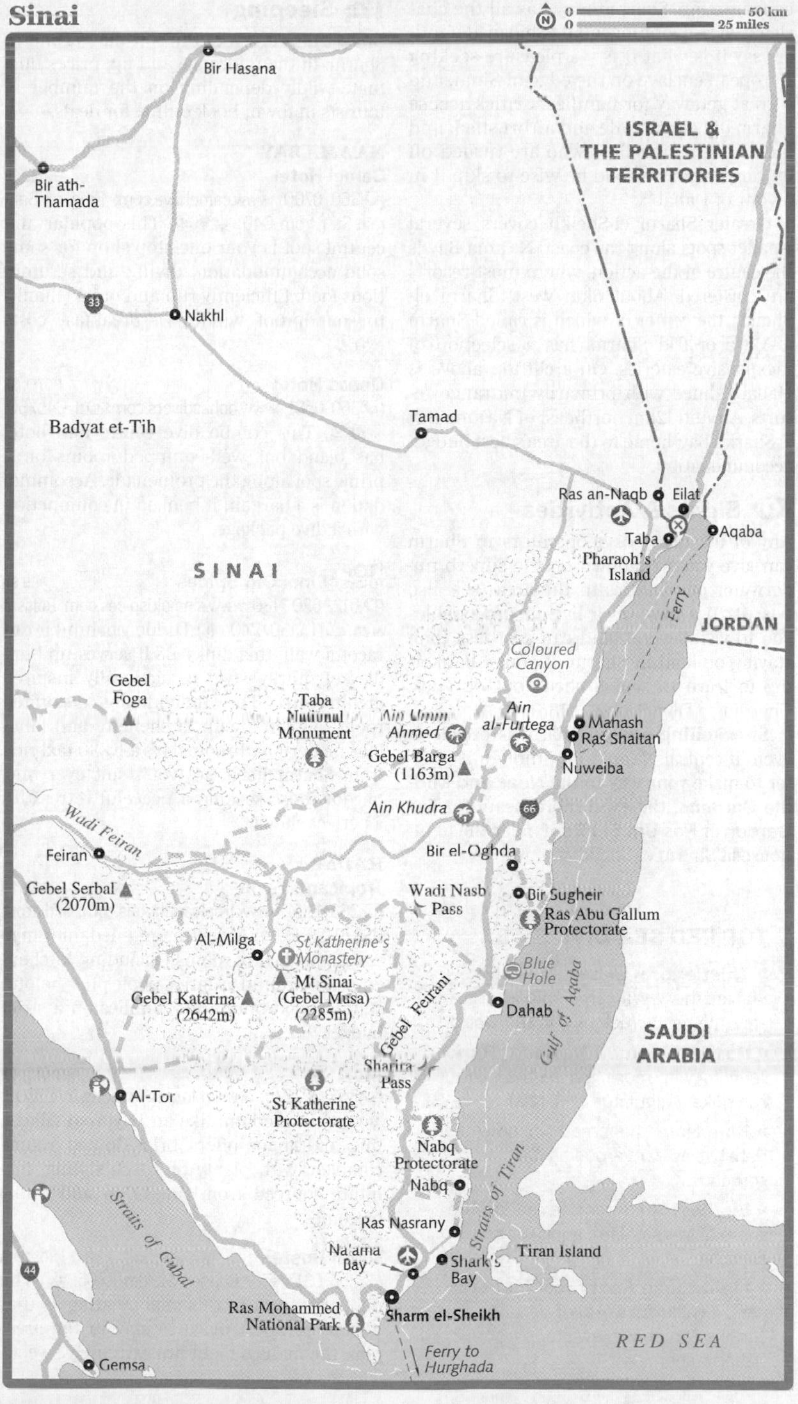
N
0 50 km
0 25 miles
Bir Hasana
Bir ath-Thamada
33
Nakhl
ISRAEL & THE PALESTINIAN TERRITORIES
Tamad
Badyat et-Tih
Ras an-Naqb
Eilat
Taba
Aqaba
Pharaoh's Island
SINAI
Ferry
JORDAN
Coloured Canyon
Gebel Foga
Taba National Monument
Ain Umm Ahmed
Ain al-Furtega
Mahash
Ras Shaitan
Gebel Barga (1163m)
Nuweiba
Ain Khudra
66
Wadi Feiran
Feiran
Bir el-Oghda
Gebel Serbal (2070m)
Wadi Nasb Pass
Bir Sugheir
Ras Abu Gallum Protectorate
Al-Milga
St Katherine's Monastery
Mt Sinai (Gebel Musa) (2285m)
Gebel Katarina (2642m)
Blue Hole
Gebel Feirani
Dahab
Gulf of Aqaba
SAUDI ARABIA
Sharira Pass
Al-Tor
St Katherine Protectorate
Nabq Protectorate
Nabq
Straits of Gubal
Straits of Tiran
Ras Nasrany
Tiran Island
Na'ama Bay
Shark's Bay
44
Ras Mohammed National Park
Sharm el-Sheikh
RED SEA
Gemsa
Ferry to Hurghada

consumption, Sharm today has all the charisma of a shopping mall. Sharm defenders say it is what it is – a pleasure-seeking European enclave on the edge of Sinai, and a great getaway for families. Critics accuse Sharm of being sterile and airbrushed, and independent travellers who are turned off by gated resorts would be wise to skip it in favour of Dahab.

Greater Sharm el-Sheikh covers several smaller spots along the coast. Na'ama Bay is the centre of the action, where most resorts are clustered. About 6km west, Sharm el-Sheikh, the center of which is called Sharm al-Maya or Old Sharm, has a selection of inexpensive eateries. On a clifftop above is Hadaba, lined with primarily midrange resorts. Around 12km northeast of Na'ama Bay is Shark's Bay, home to the area's best budget accommodation.

Sights & Activities

Any of the many **dive** operators in Sharm can give you a rundown on the superb underwater possibilities in the area (see also box p130). Going on a live-aboard enables you to visit several, and can cost less than staying on land in Sharm. If you're hankering to learn to scuba, check out our box, Choosing a Dive School (p136).

Snorkelling around Sharm is excellent, even in central Na'ama Bay, though it's better to make your way to the **Near and Middle Gardens**, the even more beautiful **Far Garden** or **Ras Um Sid Reef**, near the lighthouse at Sharm el-Sheikh.

TOP RED SEA DIVE SITES

» **Thistlegorm** Closest to Sharm el-Sheikh, this WWII cargo ship is, arguably, the best wreck dive in the world.

» **Ras Mohammed National Park** Teeming with more fish life than you can poke a regulator at (p128).

» **Blue Hole** The famed sinkhole near Dahab is as dangerous as it is gorgeous.

» **Elphinstone** A remote reef off the shore of Marsa Alam, good for shark spotting.

» **Lighthouse Reef** Great for beginners, a colourful world of darting, curious fish only a few steps from Dahab's shore.

Sleeping

Budget digs are very thin on the ground in Sharm. In the midrange and up, prices fluctuate wildly depending on the number of tourists in town; book online for deals.

NA'AMA BAY

Camel Hotel HOTEL $$
(☎360 0700; www.cameldive.com; King of Bahrain St; r from €40; ❄📶🏊) This popular and central spot is your one-stop shop for some solid accommodation, diving and scrumptious food. Efficiently run and quiet (thanks to soundproof windows). Breakfast costs extra.

Oonas Hotel HOTEL $$
(☎360 0581; www.oonasdivers.com; s/d €45/60; ❄@🏊) This combo dive centre and hotel has bland but well-equipped rooms on a prime spot along the promenade. Accommodation is a bargain if booked in conjunction with a dive package.

TOP CHOICE **Sinai Old Spices** B&B $$
(☎0122 680 3130; www.sinaioldspices.com; Roissat area; s/d E£150/240; ❄) Hidden behind a terracotta wall, this dinky B&B serves up bundles of quirky style using locally inspired architecture. The individually decorated rooms all come with kitchenette and fabulous modern bathrooms. It's a E£30 taxi ride from Sharm itself, so won't suit everyone, but for those seeking a peaceful retreat it's a perfect choice.

HADABA

Tropicana Tivoli HOTEL $$
(☎366 1384; www.tropicanahotels.com; s/d from US$70/80; ❄🏊) A well-maintained midrange winner with tidy rooms (including kitchenette) set around a large pool, plus helpful staff. A good option for families on a strict budget.

Amar Sina HOTEL $$
(☎366 2222/9; www.minasegypt.com; r E£300; ❄@🏊) Decked out like an Egyptian village, this midranger offers brick-domed rooms complete with plenty of kitsch styling, furniture sourced from the 1970s and dinky balconies.

Youth Hostel HOSTEL $
(☎366 0317; City Council St; dm E£65; ❄) The only attraction of this shabby affair is that it's the cheapest place to stay in the area; plus, the management are extremely sweet.

SHARK'S BAY

Shark's Bay Umbi Diving Village BEACH CAMP $$
(☎360 0942; www.sharksbay.com; s/d huts without bathroom €17/20, s/d beach cabins €24/35, s/d room €35/45; ❄📶) This long-standing Bedouin owned place is a clutch of cute chalets and pine beach cabins, all spic-and-span if a bit of a squeeze. Larger rooms are built into the cliff above. On the clifftop, spartan huts have just mattress and mosquito net. Taxi is about E£25 from Na'ama Bay and E£35 to E£45 from the bus station.

Eating

Cheap eats are clustered around Sharm Old Market, while Na'ama Bay is graced with higher-end places. Approach the promenade here with caution – not all the food is as good as the view.

SHARM EL-SHEIKH

El-Masrien EGYPTIAN $$
(dishes E£25-40) El-Masrien's continued success is due to the fact it delivers succulent kebabs and *kofta* that perfectly hit the spot, without hiking its prices to try and compete with fancier Sharm restaurants. It's an old-fashioned neighbourhood place with tables pouring out onto the pavement, perfect for people-watching.

Safsafa Restaurant SEAFOOD $$
(mains E£20-50; ❄) This tiny, cheerful restaurant manages to serve up fresh seafood platters, *tagens* (clay-pot stews), and pasta at budget-friendly prices.

Koshary el-Sheikh EGYPTIAN FAST FOOD $
(meals E£5-10) Egypt's favourite carbohydrate-fuelled feast, *kushari* (a blend of pasta, rice, lentils and fried onion smothered in a tomato sauce) is dished up here.

NA'AMA BAY

TOP CHOICE Fairuz LEBANESE $$$
(King of Bahrain St, mezze dishes E£18, mains E£80-100; ❄) A mouth-watering journey through the subtle flavours of the Middle East, with dishes such as *batingan bi laban* (aubergine in garlicky yoghurt), *makinek* (spicy sausages) and *loubieh* (a green bean stew). The mezze set menu (E£105 per person, minimum two people) is great value.

Pomodoro ITALIAN $$
(King of Bahrain St; dishes E£40-80; ⏲from 6.30pm) Hearty portions of Italian classics keep this place full of customers most evenings. Risottos, pasta and a fair whack of seafood are all featured on the menu as well as favourites like pepper steak.

Tam Tam EGYPTIAN $$
(Na'ama Bay promenade; dishes E£20-60) Great for those who want to sample a range of Egyptian fare. This laid-back waterfront restaurant is the place to while away a few hours while relaxing on cushions overlooking the beach and puffing on a sheesha.

Abou El Sid EGYPTIAN $$$
(Sultan Qabos St; dishes E£30-100; ❄) This branch of the famous Cairo restaurant is one of the few places in Sharm where you can experience the full gamut of Egypt's national dishes: stuffed pigeon and *kirsha* (spicy lentil stew) are menu highlights, as are the mezze.

Little Buddha ASIAN $$$
(Sultan Qabos St, mains E£45-115; ❄) One of the most popular Asian restaurants in Sharm, Little Buddha serves excellent Asian fusion cuisine alongside a fresh and varied sushi bar. Later in the night it turns into a loungey bar.

Self-Catering

Panorama Market SUPERMARKET $
(cnr Sultan Qabos & King of Bahrain Sts, Na'ama Bay; ⏲9am-2am) Very well-stocked grocery store.

Sharm Express SUPERMARKET $
(Sharm el-Sheikh; ⏲8am-2am) This reasonably priced supermarket, in front of the Old Market, sells a decent range of toiletries, drinks and food.

Al-Ahram Beverages LIQUOR STORE $
(Sharm el-Sheikh; ☎366 3133) For all your beer and wine needs.

Drinking & Entertainment

Compared with the rest of relatively conservative Egypt, Sharm el-Sheikh nightlife can either be a shock to the senses or a welcome relief. All the action is in Na'ama Bay.

Camel Roof Bar BAR
(Camel Hotel, King of Bahrain St; ⏲3pm-2.30am) A favourite among dive instructors for its relaxed, casual vibe – a good place to swap stories from down under.

Pacha CLUB
(☎360 0197; www.pachasharm.com; King of Bahrain St; admission Fri-Wed E£85, Thu E£155; ⏲10pm-4am) If you're up for some serious clubbing, this is the most popular option. It absolutely

heaves on Thursday nights. International DJs demand a heftier entrance fee. Pacha's mellower cousin, the Bus Stop Lounge, is open next door from 4pm, with a pool table and happy hour from 8pm to 9pm.

Pirates' Bar BAR
(Hilton Fayrouz Resort) A cosy pub where divers congregate for an early evening drink or bar meal. Happy hour is 5.30pm to 7.30pm.

Little Buddha LOUNGE
(Sultan Qabos St) DJs spin those proprietary Buddha Bar sounds well into the night.

Information

Many restaurants offer wi-fi, and internet cafes dotted around town charge between E£5 and E£10 per hour. There are ATMs every few metres in Na'ama Bay.

Naama Internet (Na'ama Centre, Na'ama Bay; ⌚noon-3am)

Post office (Bank St, Hadaba; ⌚8am-3pm Sat-Thu) On the hill.

Telephone centrale (Bank St, Hadaba; ⌚24hr) Near the post office.

Thomas Cook (☎360 1808/9; Gafy Mall, Sharm–Na'ama Bay Rd, Na'ama Bay; ⌚9am-2pm & 6-10pm) Bank, just west of Sinai Star hotel.

Tiba Net (Sharm Old Market; ⌚24hr)

Getting There & Away

AIR Egypt Air (☎366 1056; www.egyptair.com; Sharm al-Maya; ⌚9am-9pm) has several flights per day to Cairo and five per week direct to Luxor. For international flights, see p151.

BOAT During the course of research for this book a new ferry between Sharm el-Sheikh and Hurghada was announced but had yet to begin operation. The proposed schedule has departures for Hurghada at 5pm every Tuesday, Thursday and Saturday (adult/child E£250/150, two hours). Enquire at any of the hotels and travel agencies in Sharm el-Sheikh for up-to-date information or contact the **Sharm el-Sheikh Port Office** (☎366 0217; Sharm el-Sheikh Port). If you do arrive by ferry, don't be pressured into a taxi close to the ferry building's exit. If you walk up the hill to the gates, you'll be able to pick up a taxi for half the price (E£20 to the bus station, E£35 to Na'ama Bay).

BUS The bus station is along the Sharm–Na'ama Bay road, behind the Mobil petrol station. **Super Jet** (☎366 1622, in Cairo 02-2290 9017) and **East Delta Travel Co** (☎366 0660) are the two operators. Seats on Cairo buses should be reserved in advance.

Getting Around

TO/FROM THE AIRPORT Sharm el-Sheikh Airport (☎360 1140; www.sharm-el-sheikh.airport-authority.com) is about 10km north of Na'ama Bay at Ras Nasrany; taxis generally charge from E£20 to E£25 to Sharm or Na'ama Bay. Prepare to bargain hard.

MICROBUS & TAXI Blue-and-white microbuses (E£2) connect Na'ama Bay and Sharm el-Sheikh. Taxis charge a minimum of E£10 between the two centres, and between Hadaba and Na'ama Bay, and from E£5 within Na'ama Bay.

Dahab دهب

☎069

Little Dahab has come a long way from its origins as a stop on the overland hippie trail. Even though prices have crept up,

BUSES FROM SHARM EL-SHEIKH

All services are on East Delta unless marked otherwise.

DESTINATION	PRICE (E£)	DURATION (HR)	TIMES
Al-Tor	11	1-2	7.30am, 9.30am, 12.30pm, 3.30pm, 8pm, 9.30pm, 1am
Alexandria (Super Jet)	110	8-9	3pm
Cairo (Super Jet)	85	6-7	11am, 1pm, 3pm, 11.30pm
Cairo	60-80	6-7	7.30am, 9.30am, 11am, 12.30pm, 2.30pm, 3.30pm, 8pm, 9.30pm, 11pm, midnight, 1am
Dahab	15-20	1-2	6am, 7am, 9am, 3pm, 5pm, 9pm
Nuweiba	25-30	2-3	9am, 5pm
Suez	80	6-7	7am, 10am
Taba	30-35	3-4	9am

the promenade has been paved and there's even a Hilton, Dahab manages to cling to its 'chill or be chilled' roots. Backed by dramatic desert cliffs and fronted by unforgettable dive sites, Dahab's laid-back appeal has been known to suck in travellers for weeks or months at a time. You have been warned.

There are two parts to Dahab: the small and newer area of Dahab City to the south, with a smattering of resort hotels, the bus station and other services; and beachfront Assalah, originally a Bedouin village and now the major tourist stretch to the north. Assalah is further divided into three areas. The northernmost point, where most locals live, is still known as Assalah. Starting at the lighthouse, the Masbat area is a stretch of 'camps', hotels and laid-back restaurants. Further south, starting roughly at the ruins (no entry), is the slightly more staid Mashraba. In the centre of Masbat is a small pedestrian bridge, which makes a convenient landmark and is a good place to find taxis.

Sights & Activities

The most popular activity in Dahab is loafing. Those who manage to drag themselves away from the beachside couches, however, will also find some of the best and most accessible dive sites in the Red Sea, including the (in)famous **Blue Hole**, a 130m-deep sinkhole that has claimed a few lives. Despite its intimidating reputation, the top of the reef here is good for snorkelling when the sea is calm. Nearly 100 dive shops in Dahab offer all manner of diving possibilities.

For above-the-water adventures, there are loads of options for camel and jeep safaris, including day trips to the heavily touristed **Coloured Canyon** (Map p129; quieter alternatives are preferable) or the fascinating **Ras Abu Gallum Protectorate** (Map p129). Any hotel can help arrange trips, though prices vary considerably. Have your bargaining hat on; expect to pay between E£300 and E£400 per day, all-inclusive.

Sleeping

Lower-end hotel rates in Dahab typically do not include breakfast.

TOP CHOICE Alaska Camp & Hotel HOSTEL $
(☎364 1004; www.dahabescape.com; Masbat; r with/without air-con E£200/100; ❄📶) Easy on the wallet without sacrificing the small comforts, Alaska has spacious, bright and sparkling-clean rooms with comfortable beds. The courtyard garden is a welcoming shady spot to relax and the central location puts you just steps from the promenade bustle.

TOP CHOICE Sunrise Lodge GUESTHOUSE $
(☎0109 057 4242; www.sunrisedahab.com; Masbat; r E£120; ❄📶) Down a sandy alley just off the beachfront, this welcoming home-from-home has just five large, spotless rooms (one fan-only room is a cheaper E£80) around a sandy, palm-shaded courtyard. There's free tea and coffee, hammocks and a cushion area to lounge in, plus a small play area for children.

Dahab Paradise RESORT $$
(☎0100 700 4133; www.dahabparadise.com; s/d US$58/68; ❄📶🏊) This low-key resort on a secluded sweep of bay on the main road to the Blue Hole is the perfect get-away-from-it-all. Decorated in warm earthy tones, the charming rooms have an understated beach-chic elegance. The bright lights of Masbat are a 10-minute taxi ride away.

Red Sea Relax HOTEL $$
(☎364 1309; www.red-sea-relax.com; Masbat; dm/s/d €8/37/46; ❄@🏊) With rooms wrapped around a glistening pool, Red Sea Relax dishes up resort-like facilities for bargain prices. Large rooms have tea-making facilities and TV. It's a well-organised set-up with free water fill-ups, a beckoning rooftop bar and an excellent dive centre.

Seven Heaven HOSTEL $
(☎364 0080; www.7heavenhotel.com; Masbat; dm E£20, r with/without air-con E£80/60, without bathroom E£30; ❄📶) This bustling long-time favourite is popular for its range of budget digs, from rustic, but, clean thatch huts to more robust and good-value concrete air-con rooms. The six-bed air-con dorms are a bargain. Amenities include a busy dive shop and tour booking centre.

Alf Leila B&B $$
(☎364 0595; www.alfleila.com; cnr Peace Rd & Sharia al-Fanar, Masbat; s/d €30/36; ❄📶) Seven rooms are a daydream of gorgeous tile-work and traditional textiles in earthy colours, stone and wood. The location (on the main road) isn't the best, but if you don't mind a walk to the beach and a bit of traffic noise, for its sheer style this place is still worth it.

Dahab Coach House GUESTHOUSE $$
(☎364 1027; www.dahabcoachhouse.dk; Masbat; s/d €38/40; ❄📶) What this place lacks in

Dahab

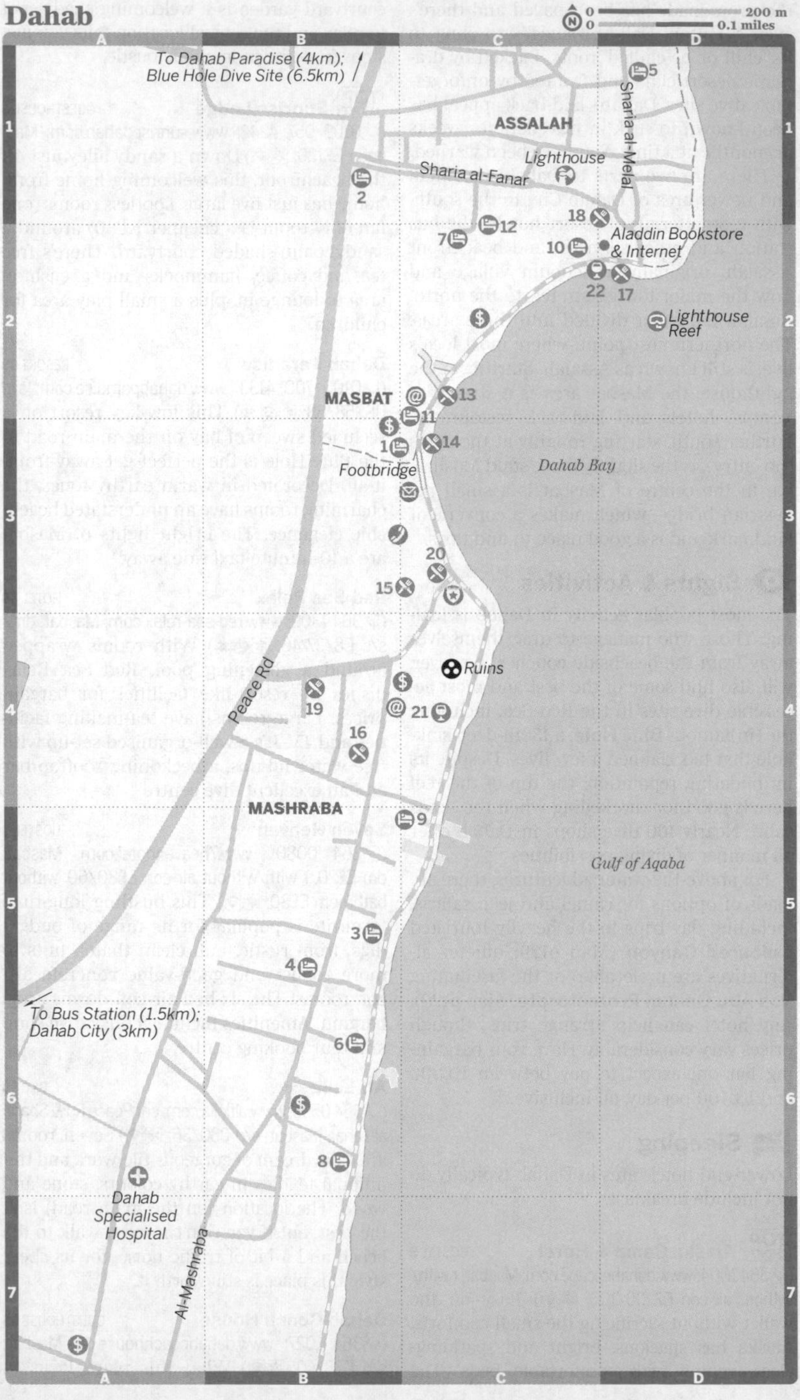
0 200 m
0 0.1 miles
A
B
C
D
1
2
3
4
5
6
7
To Dahab Paradise (4km);
Blue Hole Dive Site (6.5km)
5
Sharia al-Melal
ASSALAH
Lighthouse
Sharia al-Fanar
2
18
12
7
10
Aladdin Bookstore
& Internet
22
17
Lighthouse
Reef
MASBAT
13
11
1
14
Footbridge
Dahab Bay
20
15
Ruins
Peace Rd
19
21
16
MASHRABA
9
Gulf of Aqaba
3
4
To Bus Station (1.5km);
Dahab City (3km)
6
8
Dahab
Specialised
Hospital
Al-Mashraba

Dahab

Sleeping

1	Alaska Camp & Hotel	B3
2	Alf Leila	B1
3	Bedouin Lodge	B5
4	Bishbishi Garden Village	B5
5	Blue Beach Club	D1
6	Christina Beach Palace & Christina Pool	B6
7	Dahab Coach House	C2
8	Ghazala Hotel	B6
9	Nesima Resort	C5
10	Red Sea Relax	C2
11	Seven Heaven	C2
12	Sunrise Lodge	C2

Eating

13	Ali Baba	C2
	Blue House	(see 11)
14	Fighting Kangaroo	C3
15	Ghazala Supermarket	C3
16	King Chicken	B4
17	Nirvana	D2
	Ralph's German Bakery	(see 15)
18	Ralph's German Bakery	D1
19	Seabride	B4
20	The Kitchen	C3

Drinking

21	Tree Bar	C4
22	Yalla Bar	C2

resort facilities, it more than makes up for with hugely helpful management and a genuine welcoming feel. The rooms are simple but comfortable and the courtyard is the perfect place to chill out after a long day's diving.

Nesima Resort RESORT $$
(☎364 0320; www.nesima-resort.com; Mashraba; s/d/ste €47/61/84;) A lovely compromise if you want resort living without being isolated from town. Set amid a mature garden of blooming bougainvillea, Nesima's cosy cottages have pleasing stone and wood overtones, domed ceilings and dinky terraces.

Ghazala Hotel HOTEL $$
(☎364 2414; www.ghazaladahab.com; Mashraba; s/d E£100/140;) Ghazala's cute white-domed rooms surround a narrow courtyard set with colourful mosaic tiles. Some are larger than others so ask to see a few before you decide. There are a couple of cheaper fan-only rooms as well.

Christina Beach Palace & Christina Pool HOTEL $$
(☎364 0390; www.christinahotels.com; Mashraba; s/d with air-con US$62/83, without air-con US$55/76;) This small Swiss-run hotel offers a degree of efficiency unmatched in town. Depending on your preference, Beach Palace rooms have lovely sea views, while the recently renovated Pool-side ones are more luxurious.

Bishbishi Garden Village HOSTEL $
(☎364 0727; www.bishbishi.com; Sharia al-Mashraba; s/d without bathroom €5/8;) Classic of the Dahab camp scene, Bishbishi continues to offer a winning mix of easy-on-the-wallet rooms and lots of shaded communal areas for socialising.

Blue Beach Club RESORT $$
(☎364 0411; www.bluebeachclub.com; Assalah; s/d/ste €28/36/44;) Blue Beach's recently renovated annex rooms (across the road from the main resort) are bright, comfortably outfitted and boast the snazziest modern bathrooms in Dahab.

Bedouin Lodge GUESTHOUSE $
(☎364 1125; www.bedouin-lodge-dahab.com; Mashraba; s/d with air-con €17/25, without air-con €14/20) A local Bedouin family runs this simple but highly friendly hotel.

Eating

The long curve of Dahab Bay is a string of waterside restaurants with groovy cushioned seats, mood lighting and funky tunes. It's hard to recommend one over the other: they typically have the same slightly pricey menu of passable food. The restaurants mentioned below stand out from the crowd.

If you're after a cheap, filling lunch look out for **Ali's Kushari Cart**, which makes the rounds up and down the beachfront roughly between noon and 1pm.

TOP CHOICE **Seabride** SEAFOOD $$
(Mashraba; meals E£40-60) Locals' favourite for seafood, serving up startling good value. All meals come loaded with fish soup, rice, salad, *baba ghanoog,* a delectably tangy tahini and bread. Order the spicy Bedouin calamari to sample seafood Dahab-style.

CHOOSING A DIVE SCHOOL

Here's some advice for when considering donning flippers for the first time.

» Do your homework. You're about to spend a chunk of money and put your life in a stranger's hands, so it pays to visit several outfits.

» Check to see how well the equipment is treated and stored. Stay away from shops with BCDs and regulators left out in the sun or strewn about their equipment room.

» Big schools have lots of instructors and shiny equipment, but they can feel like impersonal diving factories. Some smaller outfits can offer a more personal touch.

» Try to find an instructor who speaks your native language. Ask other travellers for recommendations, talk to several instructors and go with the one you feel most comfortable with.

» Check whether your travel insurance covers diving accidents. If not, see what sort of insurance the school provides. Find the location of the nearest hyperbaric chamber, just in case.

The Kitchen INTERNATIONAL **$$$**
(Masbat; mains E£60-95) With a menu offering a choice of Indian, Chinese, Thai and Japanese and superb service this is as close as Dahab gets to fine dining. The Indian is the real standout. If you've got a sweet tooth you won't be able to resist the fried pineapple and ice cream dessert.

Blue House THAI **$$**
(Masbat; mains E£35-60) An inspiring selection of authentic Thai cuisine keeps this breezy upstairs terrace packed with diners. Tuck into the flavour-filled curries or the zingy papaya salad and you'll understand why this place has so many fans.

Ali Baba INTERNATIONAL **$$**
(Masbat; mains E£30-80) One of the most popular restaurants along the waterfront for good reason, this place adds flair to its seafood. Great service and twinkly fairy lights add to the relaxed ambience.

Fighting Kangaroo EGYPTIAN **$**
(Masbat; meals E£15-20) Despite the unfortunate name this narrow waterfront restaurant should be commended for serving Egyptian-style feasts at bargain-basement prices. Simple and hearty meals (pick from fish, *kofte,* chicken or vegetarian) all come with soup, salad and tahini.

Ralph's German Bakery BAKERY **$**
(Ghazala Supermarket courtyard, Masbat; sandwiches E£18-25, pastries E£4-15; ⌚7am-6pm) Caffeine heaven, plus particularly tempting calorific pastries and excellent sandwiches. A second outlet on Sharia Sharia al-Fanar also does some original breakfast dishes.

King Chicken EGYPTIAN **$**
(Sharia al-Mashraba; dishes E£15-25) Always crowded with locals, this cheap and cheerful little place hits the spot for a budget chicken dinner.

Nirvana INDIAN **$$**
(Masbat; dishes E£45-75) A slice of the subcontinent complete with direct beach access and sun-loungers. Although not particularly authentic, the meals are tasty and the ice cream, with homemade waffle cone, is perfect for a promenade stroll after dinner.

Ghazala Supermarket SUPERMARKET
(Masbat; ⌚8am-2am) A good option for self-caterers, near the main junction at the southern end of Masbat.

Drinking

Dahab is fairly quiet at night, but there is a good selection of lively bars, some of which turn into discos if the atmosphere is right.

Tree Bar BAR
(Mashraba; ⌚10pm-late) Two-for-one cocktail deals and a thumping soundtrack of house and R&B make this open-air beachfront bar Dahab's top late-night party venue.

Yalla Bar BAR
(Masbat; beer E£10-12) This popular waterfront bar-restaurant has a winning formula of friendly staff and excellent happy-hour beer prices from 5pm to 9pm.

Information

Free wi-fi is widely available at most hotels and many of the restaurants. There are plenty of ATMs scattered along the waterfront throughout

Mashat, and a handy post office/bookshop on the waterfront in Masbat, next to Bamboo House Hotel, where you can also place calls.

Aladdin Bookstore & Internet (Masbat; per hr E£5)

Banque du Caire (Sharia al-Mashraba & Masbat) Near the bridge, has an ATM.

Dr Haikal (☎010 143 3325; lagoon, Dahab City) Local doctor whose surgery also has a hyperbaric chamber.

National Bank of Egypt (Sharia al-Mashraba & Masbat)

Net Internet Cafe (Sharia al-Mashraba; per hr E£5; ⊙24hr)

Getting There & Around

BUS From the bus station in Dahab City, **East Delta Travel Co** (☎364 1808) runs to other Sinai beach towns and elsewhere in Egypt. In addition, **Bedouin Bus** (☎0101 668 4274; www.bedouinbus.com) connects Dahab to St Katherine on Tuesday and Friday (E£50, two hours); confirm the schedule on the website.

TAXI Taxi drivers at the bus station (and around town) charge E£100 to Sharm el-Sheikh and E£250 to St Katherine. A taxi (usually a pickup truck) between Assalah and Dahab City costs E£5.

St Katherine Protectorate

محمية كاترينا القديسة

☎069

The 4350-sq-km national park protects a unique high-desert ecosystem, as well as St Katherine's Monastery and the adjacent Mt Sinai, both sacred to the world's three main monotheistic religions. Although it can be difficult to pry yourself away from Sinai's beaches, a visit to the St Katherine Protectorate is not to be missed.

Sights

St Katherine's Monastery is tucked at the foot of Mt Sinai (locally called Gebel Musa). Approximately 3.5km west from here is the small town of Al-Milga, also called Katreen, where most tourist services are available.

FREE **St Katherine's Monastery** MONASTERY (⊙9am-noon Mon-Thu & Sat, except religious holidays) This monastery, home to some 20 Greek Orthodox monks, traces its roots back to AD 330, when Byzantine empress Helena built a small chapel and refuge here – on the supposed site of the biblical burning bush where God first had words with Moses. The grounds, which have been declared a Unesco World Heritage Site, hold some beautiful and rare Byzantine icons, hidden here during the 8th-century iconoclasm.

In the 6th century, Emperor Justinian had a fortress built around the original chapel, also throwing in a monastery, dedicated to St Katherine, who was martyred in Alexandria on a spiked wheel. Look in the apse of the Justinian-built **Church of the Transfiguration** for a 6th-century mosaic, and enter the monastery's museum, the **Sacred Sacristy** (Monastery Museum; adult/student E£25/10), to see the best painted icons.

BUSES FROM DAHAB

Be sure to check departure times with hotel staff, as they're subject to change, especially in the low season.

DESTINATION	PRICE (E£)	DURATION (HR)	TIMES
Al-Tor	25-30	4	8am, 10am, 8.30pm, 9.30pm, 10.30pm
Cairo	90	9	9am, 12.30pm, 3pm, 10pm
Hurghada	105	10	4pm
Ismailia	60	7	10am, 8.30pm, 9.30pm, 10.30pm
Luxor	130	18	4pm
Nuweiba	15	1	10.30am
Sharm el-Sheikh	15-20	2	9am, 12.30pm, 3pm, 5.30pm, 10pm
Suez	45	7	8am
Taba	35	2	10.30am

St Katherine's Monastery

A HISTORY OF THE MONASTERY

4th Century With hermetic communities congregating in the area, a chapel is established around the site of Moses' miraculous **Burning Bush** 1.

6th Century In a show of might, Emperor Justinian adds the monastery **fortifications** 2 and orders the building of the basilica, which is graced by Byzantine art, including the **Mosaic of the Transfiguration** 3.

7th Century The prophet Mohammed signs the **Ahtiname** 4, a declaration of his protection of the monastery. When the Arab armies conquer Egypt in AD 641, the monastery is left untouched. Despite the era's tumultuous times, monastery abbot St John Klimakos writes his famed **Ladder of Divine Ascent** 5 treatise, depicted in the Sacred Sacristy.

9th Century Extraordinary happenings surround the monastery when, according to tradition, a monk discovers the body of St Katherine on a mountain summit.

11th Century To escape the wrath of Fatimid caliph Al-Hakim, wily monks build a mosque within the monastery grounds.

15th Century Frequent raids and attacks on the monastery lead the monks to build the **Ancient Gate** 6 to prevent the ransacking of church treasures and to keep the monastic community safe.

19th Century In 1859 biblical scholar Constantin von Tischendorf borrows 347 pages of the **Codex Sinaiticus** 7 from the monastery, but fails to get his library books back on time. Greek artisans travel from the island of Tinos in 1871 to help construct the **bell tower** 8.

20th Century Renovations inside the monastery reveal 18 more missing parchment leaves from the Codex Sinaiticus, proving that all the secrets hidden within these ancient walls may not yet be revealed.

SIMON BALSON/ALAMY ©

Fortifications

The formidable walls are 2m thick and 11m high. Justinian sent a Balkan garrison to watch over the newly fortified monastery, and today's local Jabaleyya tribe are said to be their descendents.

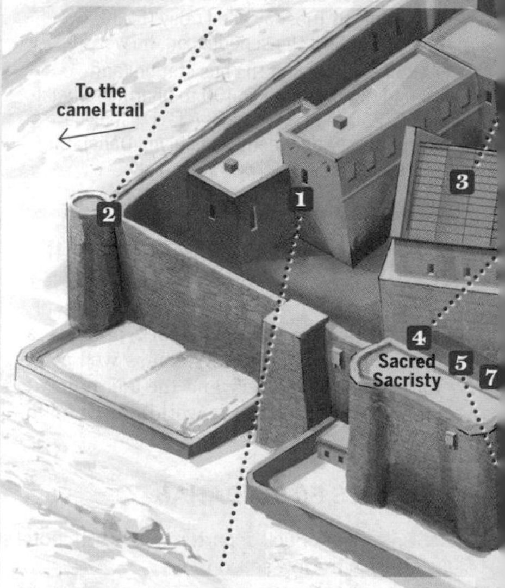

The Burning Bush

This flourishing bramble (the endemic Sinai shrub *Rubus Sanctus*) was transplanted in the 10th century to its present location. Tradition states that cuttings of the plant refuse to grow outside the monastery walls.

JESSICA LESS

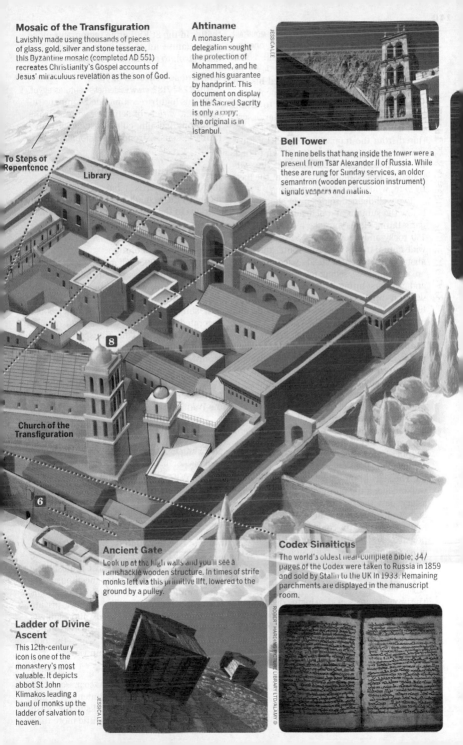

Mosaic of the Transfiguration

Lavishly made using thousands of pieces of glass, gold, silver and stone tesserae, this Byzantine mosaic (completed AD 551) recreates Christianity's Gospel accounts of Jesus' miraculous revelation as the son of God.

Ahtiname

A monastery delegation sought the protection of Mohammed, and he signed his guarantee by handprint. This document on display in the Sacred Sacrity is only a copy; the original is in Istanbul.

JESSICA LEE

Bell Tower

The nine bells that hang inside the tower were a present from Tsar Alexander II of Russia. While these are rung for Sunday services, an older semantron (wooden percussion instrument) signals vespers and matins.

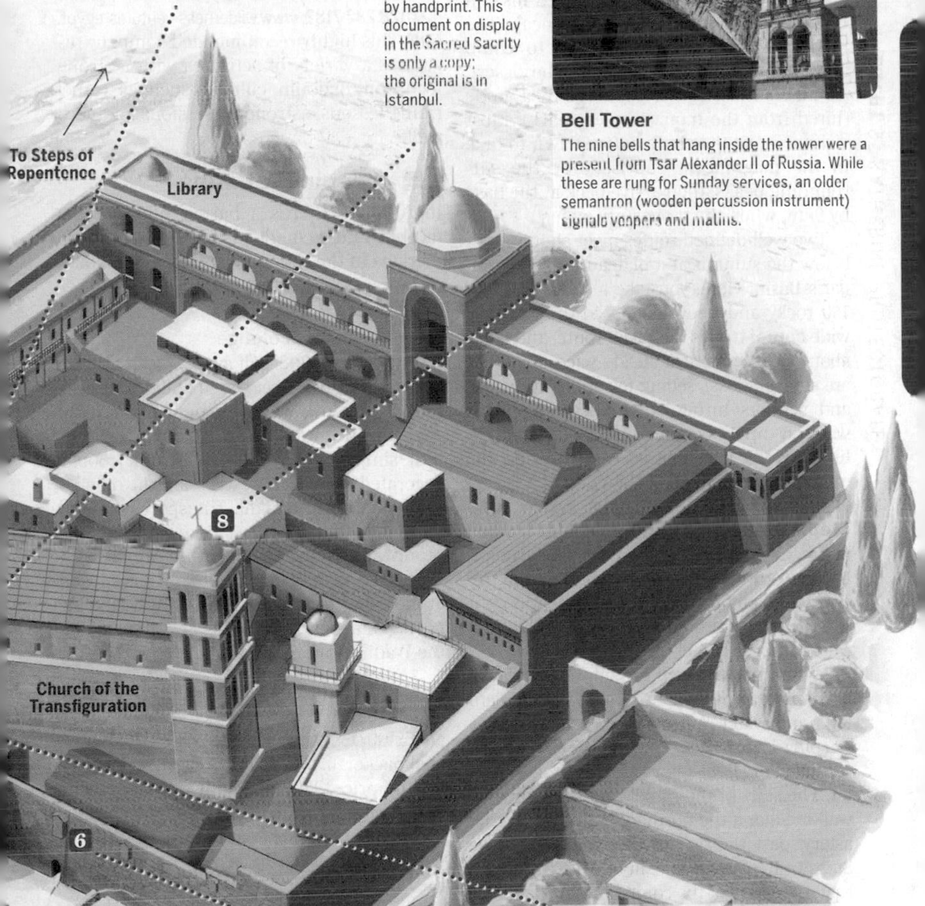

Ancient Gate

Look up at the high walls and you'll see a ramshackle wooden structure. In times of strife monks left via this primitive lift, lowered to the ground by a pulley.

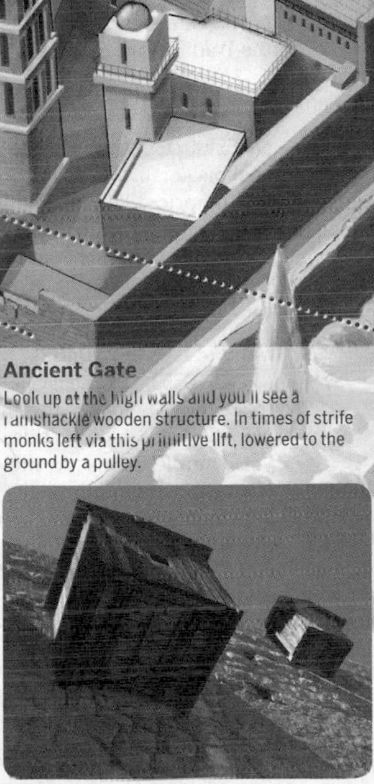

JESSICA LEE

Codex Sinaiticus

The world's oldest near-complete bible; 347 pages of the Codex were taken to Russia in 1859 and sold by Stalin to the UK in 1933. Remaining parchments are displayed in the manuscript room.

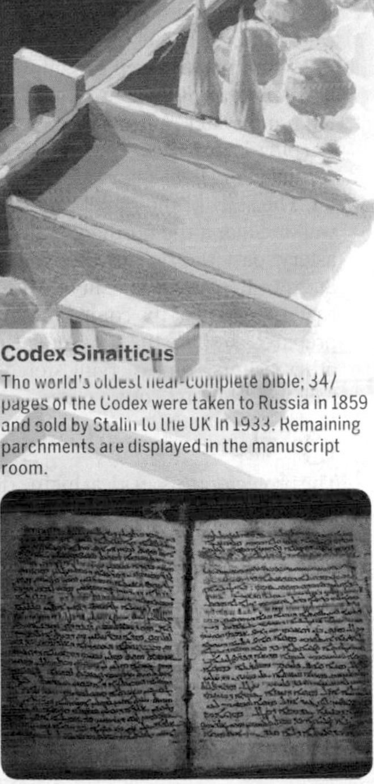

ROBERT HARDING PICTURE LIBRARY LTD/ALAMY ©

Ladder of Divine Ascent

This 12th-century icon is one of the monastery's most valuable. It depicts abbot St John Klimakos leading a band of monks up the ladder of salvation to heaven.

Mt Sinai MOUNTAIN
(Gebel Musa; guide E£125, camel ride one-way E£125) Jutting up 2285m, Mt Sinai is revered by Christians, Muslims and Jews, all of whom believe that God delivered his Ten Commandments to Moses at the peak. The mountain is beautiful and easy to climb and offers striking views across the desert. All hikers must be accompanied by a guide (hired from the monastery car park). Most visitors make the climb before dawn to take in the magnificent sunrise over the surrounding peaks, then arrive back at the base by 9am, when the monastery opens.

Two well-defined routes meet about 300m below the summit at a plateau known as Elijah's Basin. Here, you take a steep series of 750 rocky and uneven steps to the top. The wide **camel trail** is the easier route, and takes about two hours at a steady pace. En route are several kiosks selling tea and soft drinks, and vendors hiring out blankets (E£5) to ward off the chill at the top. If you do want to hire a camel, note that it's easier to ride one up the mountain, rather than down.

The alternative path, the harsh 3750 **Steps of Repentance**, was laid by one monk as a form of penance. The rough-hewn stone steps are steep and uneven, requiring strong knees and concentration – it can't feasibly be done in the dark. The typical strategy is camel trail up, steps down.

In summer, to reach the summit by dawn, be on the trail by 3am. Bring a torch, sufficient food and water, warm clothes and, ideally, a sleeping bag. It gets cold and windy, even in summer, and light snows are common in winter. The start of the camel trail is reached by walking along the northern wall of the monastery, past the end of the compound. The Steps of Repentance begin outside the south-eastern corner of the compound. At dawn, be prepared to share the summit with up to 500 other visitors, some carrying stereos, Bibles or well-worn hymn books.

Tours

The protectorate is an ideal hiking destination, and activities are easy to organise independently. Guided hikes typically start at around €50 per day, including food and equipment. Whoever you go with, be sure to register with the police prior to leaving, and make sure you bring water-purification tablets.

Mountain Tours Office HIKING
(☎347 0457; www.sheikmousa.com; El-Malga Bedouin Camp) The main hub for trekking activities in the St Katherine region, this office can organise anything from a short afternoon stroll to a multiday itinerary.

Wilderness Ventures Egypt HIKING
(☎0128 282 7182; www.wilderness-ventures-egypt.com) This highly recommended company organises a variety of activities with a strong focus on Bedouin culture, such as camel riding lessons, astronomy sessions and herb walks.

Sleeping & Eating

In Al-Milga there's a bakery opposite the mosque and a couple of well-stocked supermarkets in the shopping arcade. A few small restaurants are just behind the bakery.

TOP CHOICE **Al-Karm Ecolodge** LODGE $
(☎0100 132 4693; Sheikh Awaad; r without bathroom, half/full board per person E£100/120) Surrounded by lush walled gardens in a remote wadi, this Bedouin-owned ecolodge has beautiful simple stone and palm-trunk rooms, decorated with local textiles and lit only by candlelight in the night. Transport here and lodge booking is easiest done through the **Mountain Tours Office** at Al-Milga in St Katherine as only minimal English is spoken at the lodge itself. The lodge is only accessible by 4WD, about 20km from St Katherine on the Wadi Feiran road.

El-Malga Bedouin Camp HOSTEL $
(☎0100 641 3575; www.sheikmousa.com; dm E£25, s/d E£100/150, without bathroom E£55/85; wifi) A backpacker favourite with excellent quality for the price. The new-built en-suite rooms are large and comfortable while the cheaper rooms all share excellent bathroom facilities with hot water. It's an easy 500m walk from the bus stand.

Monastery Guesthouse GUESTHOUSE $$
(☎347 0353; St Katherine's Monastery; s/d US$35/60) Definitely the most atmospheric place to bed down, this guesthouse lets you sample monastic life. Spartan rooms (request a mountain view) all have private bathrooms, comfortable beds and blankets for cold mountain nights. The reasonable restaurant serves beer and wine; the outdoor cafe has primo mountain views.

Desert Fox Camp HOSTEL $
(☎347 0344; www.desertfoxcamp.com; s/d without bathroom E£30/60) This rudimentary camp can't be missed at night thanks to the brash neon sign. Rooms here offer little more than

a bed, some heavy blankets and four walls, and the communal toilets are a bit whiffy. Still, there are campfires at night and they cook up breakfast (E£10) and other meals (E£20 to E£30) on request.

Shopping

Fansina HANDICRAFTS
(347 0155; Al-Milga; 10am-3pm Sat-Thu) This Bedouin women's cooperative works with over 300 local women and displays a huge range of their textiles and local handicrafts. It's signposted on the first left-hand turn coming into town from Desert Fox Camp.

Information

The **St Katherine Protectorate Office** (347 0032), near the entrance to Al-Milga, sometimes has informative guide booklets. In the village of Al-Milga, there's a **post office, telephone centrale,** and an **internet cafe**. The **Banque Misr** here will change cash and give Visa and MasterCard advances. The only **ATM** is near the entrance to the monastery.

Getting There & Away

BUS East Delta Travel Co (347 0250) has its station and ticket office just off the main road in Al-Milga, behind the mosque. There is a daily bus to Cairo (E£50, seven hours) at 6am, via Wadi Feiran and Suez (E£40, five hours). Local transport initiative **Bedouin Bus** (0101 668 4274; www.bedouinbus.com) runs between Al-Milga and Dahab and Nuweiba. To Dahab the bus departs every Tuesday and Friday at 11am, and to Nuweiba at 8am every Wednesday and Sunday. Both cost E£50 and take two hours. The bus leaves from next to the bakery (opposite the mosque).

SERVEES Taxis and pickups wait at the monastery car park for people coming down from Mt Sinai in the morning, and then again around noon when visiting hours end. A lift to the village costs E£10 to E£15. The rate per car to Dahab or Sharm el-Sheikh is E£250.

Nuweiba نويبع

069

Like Dahab, the beaches here are golden, the water crystal clear, the desert mountains shimmering pink. And yet Nuweiba has the catatonic feel of a post-apocalyptic beach resort – perhaps because it's stretched randomly over about 15km, without a clear centre. If you want to avoid the scenes at Sharm and Dahab and just relax solo on a tranquil beach, it could well be the place for you. Also check out some of the beach camps north of Nuweiba, remote getaways where the hippy vibe soldiers on.

The bus station and port area is on the south edge. About 8km north is Nuweiba City, a small but spread-out settlement with a few accommodation options, a small bazaar and several cheap places to eat. About a 10-minute walk further north along the beach is Tarabin, a rustic backpacker site that would be like Dahab of yesteryear, if it were maintained properly.

Sights & Activities

Apart from lazing on the beach and soaking in the plentiful peace, underwater delights are the feature attraction, with scuba diving and snorkelling keeping many visitors busy. **Sinai Dolphin Divers** (350 0879; www.sinaidolphindivers.com; Nakhil Inn, Tarabin) and **Emperor Divers** (352 0321; www.emperordivers.com; Nuweiba Hilton) have solid reputations.

Nuweiba is the place to organise 4WDs or camel treks to sights such as **Coloured Canyon**, **Ain Khudra**, **Ain Umm Ahmed** (the largest oasis in eastern Sinai) and **Ain al-Furtega** (another palm-filled oasis). Most hotels and beach camps along the coast will be able to organise a trip for you, with all-inclusive camel treks costing around E£300 to E£400 per day.

Sleeping

NUWEIBA CITY & TARABIN

TOP CHOICE **Nakhil Inn** INN $$
(350 0879; www.nakhil-inn.com; Tarabin; s/d US$46/56;) A cosy compromise of hotel comforts without the crowds. Communal areas are all local textiles and dark wood, while the studio-style wooden cabins exude simple beach-chic. Guests can snorkel the reef just a few metres from the shore.

Petra Camp BEACH CAMP $
(350 0855; www.petra-camp.com; Tarabin; s/d hut E£40/80) One of the nicest camps in Tarabin, with a good open-air restaurant constructed from recycled wood salvaged from a defunct Cairo theatre. Huts are simple but well cared for and most have air-con. The communal bathrooms are clean.

Big Dune BEACH CAMP $
(0100 610 8731; Nuweiba City; hut E£25) Chilled out to the max and reminiscent of the hippy beach camps of old, this is one of the few Nuweiba camps that still uses traditional

JUST ACROSS THE BORDER: WADI RUM & PETRA, JORDAN

If you're in the Sinai region of Egypt, it would be criminal not to hop across the border to Jordan and check out the beautiful desert valley of Wadi Rum or the breathtaking spectacle that is the lost city of Petra. Both can be visited easily over a few days from Sinai.

To get to Jordan, catch an early bus to connect with the 3.30pm ferry (p152) from Nuweiba to Aqaba, Jordan. Free Jordanian visas are organised on the boat for most nationalities.

From the ferry terminal, grab a taxi into Aqaba, where you'll have to stay the night if you want to make the trip by public transport to either Wadi Rum or Wadi Mousa (for Petra). Or, if funds allow, you can charter a taxi and head there directly – it's one hour to Wadi Rum and a little less than two to Wadi Mousa, where you'll want to get a good night's rest before visiting Petra early the next morning.

hoosha (palm-thatch) huts. Bare-bones basic, but a great beach setting.

Habiba Village INN $$
(☎0122 217 6624; habiba@sinai4you.com; Nuweiba City; s/d US$20/30; ❄) The rooms are a little rough around the edges but set around a quiet courtyard a hop, skip and jump from a nice beach with a good snorkelling reef. Management are engaged in a local permaculture project and have set up an organic farm where interested long-stayers can volunteer.

Saraya Beach BEACH CAMP $
(☎0109 198 7803; Tarabin; hut/r E£30/80) This well-looked-after Tarabin camp has a wide variety of accommodation ranging from rustic wooden huts with fan through to more expensive air-con rooms (E£100).

NORTH OF NUWEIBA

TOP CHOICE **Sawa Camp** BEACH CAMP $
(☎0111 322 7554; www.sawacamp.com; Mahash area; s/d hut E£50/60) A strip of perfect white beach, hammocks on your hut porch to swing in, solar-powered showers and a restaurant dishing up delicious meals: Sawa is our idea of heaven. Bedouin owner Salama has got all the little touches right. Huts have electricity at night, the communal bathrooms win our award for most spotless toilets in Egypt and the welcome makes you instantly feel at home.

Basata BEACH CAMP $$
(☎350 0480; www.basata.com; Ras Burgaa area; camping per person €14, s/d hut €23/42, 3-person chalets €80) This German-run, commune-esque ecolodge offers very basic huts as well as curvy walled chalets. The owners sell organic produce and guests can use the well-stocked kitchen. Basata ('simplicity' in Arabic) recycles waste, does beach clean-ups, desalinates its own water and actively supports the local community.

Eating

Eating options in Nuweiba are limited. Fuul and ta'amiyya places cluster at the port. There's a supermarket in Nuweiba City, and a sprinkling of open-air eateries among the camps on Tarabin's promenade.

Cleopatra Restaurant SEAFOOD $$
(Nuweiba City; dishes E£20-50) One of the more popular tourist restaurants in Nuweiba City, Cleopatra offers up the bounty of the sea along with a few Western fast-food favourites.

Dr Shishkebab GRILL $$
(Bazaar, Nuweiba City; dishes E£10-30) The place to head to for filling and tasty kebab meals.

Information

The **post** and **telephone** offices are next to the tiny bus station in the Nuweiba Port area. Near the port and bus station, the Banque Misr, Banque du Caire and National Bank of Egypt branches have ATMs but will not change Jordanian dinars. In Nuweiba City, the **National Bank of Egypt** (Helnan Nuweiba) has an ATM. The **Almostakbal Internet Café** (per hr E£4; ⏲9am-3am) is behind Dr Shishkebab in Nuweiba City.

Getting There & Away

BOAT For information on ferries to Aqaba in Jordan, see p152.

BUS Buses going to or from Taba stop at both the port and its nearby bus station. You can also request that they stop outside the hospital in Nuweiba City, but this is on the whim of the driver. Buses don't stop at Tarabin. A seat in a *servees* from the bus station to Tarabin costs

E£5; the whole taxi will cost E£15. The drivers will always try to charge more, so be ready to haggle. **East Delta Travel Co** (☎352 0371) has buses at 9am and 3pm to Cairo (E£60 to E£100, eight hours) via Taba (E£15, one hour); there is also a noon service to Taba only. Buses to Sharm el-Sheikh (E£25, three to four hours) via Dahab (E£15, one hour) leave at 6.30am and 4pm. For St Katherine, **Bedouin Bus** (☎0101 668 4274; www.bedouinbus.com) runs every Wednesday and Sunday (E£50).

SERVEES Taxis and a couple of *servees* cars hang out by the port. Unless you get there when the ferry has arrived from Aqaba, you'll have to wait a long time for a *servees* to fill up. A taxi to Dahab costs about E£150 and roughly E£100 to the beach camps on the Nuweiba–Taba road.

Taba طابا

☎069

This busy border crossing between Egypt and Israel is open 24 hours. Just inside the border are an ATM and several foreign-exchange booths. Cash and travellers cheques can also be exchanged at the Taba Hilton. The town has a couple of banks, a small hospital and various shops.

Taxis and minibuses wait just past the border on the Egypt side. Per-person fares are about E£15 to Nuweiba, E£30 to Dahab, E£45 to Sharm el-Sheikh and E£55 to Cairo. But if business is slack, you may have a long wait for the vehicle to fill up. You could pay for the remaining seats, or head for the bus station, about 800m straight ahead. **East Delta Travel Co** (☎353 0250) has buses to Nuweiba (E£11, one hour) at 3pm and 4pm; the 3pm bus carries on to Dahab (E£25, 2½ hours) and Sharm el-Sheikh (E£30, four hours). To Cairo (E£60 to E£80, six to seven hours) there are two buses daily at 10.30am and 4.30pm.

UNDERSTAND EGYPT

Egypt Today

The January 2011 revolution, the 18-day popular uprising that ousted President Hosni Mubarak, seemed to create a blank slate for contemporary Egypt. But the initial euphoria of the Arab Spring has dissipated in the face of reality. The supposedly temporary ruling Supreme Council of Armed Forces (SCAF) has resorted to violence to quell dissent, and Islamist parties won a significant share of seats in parliamentary elections, causing worries about sectarian strife. Meanwhile, the economy, so dependent on tourism, has been on shakier ground than ever, and the majority of Egyptians still live in a grinding poverty. The threat of a hard-line Islamist regime seems remote, but uncertainty and deep dissatisfaction continue.

On the bright side, Egyptians have revelled in their hard-earned freedom for more than a year, and there is at least consensus that they will not let the country slip into oppressive rule again. Just what form the new government will take is yet to be seen, but the country is engaged and invigorated as never before.

History

Ancient Egypt

For centuries before 3000 BC, the fertility and regularity of the annual Nile floods supported communities along the Nile valley. These small kingdoms eventually coalesced into two important states, one covering the valley, the other consisting of the Delta itself.

The pharaoh Menes' (Narmer's) unification of these two states in about 3100 BC set the scene for the greatest civilisation of ancient times.

Little is known of the immediate successors of Menes except that, attributed with divine ancestry, they promoted the development of a highly stratified society, patronised the arts and built numerous temples and public works. In the 27th century BC, Egypt's pyramids began to materialise. Ruling from nearby Memphis, the Pharaoh Zoser and his chief architect, Imhotep, built what may have been the first – the Step Pyramid at Saqqara.

For the next three dynasties and 500 years (a period called the Old Kingdom), the power

ESSENTIAL EGYPTIAN VOCAB

Mafeesh Mushkila No problem, dude!

Malish Whatever, don't worry about it.

Khalas It's over, finished, okay, understand?

Mumkin Possibly or please or maybe.

of Egypt's pharaohs, and the size and scale of their pyramids and temples increased dramatically. The immense dimensions of these buildings served as a reminder of the pharaoh's importance and power over his people. The last three pharaohs of the 4th dynasty, Khufu (Cheops), Khafre (Chephren) and Menkaure (Mycerinus), left their legendary mark by commissioning the three Great Pyramids of Giza.

By the beginning of the 5th dynasty (about 2494–2345 BC), the pharaohs had ceded some of their power to a rising class of nobles. In the following centuries Egypt broke down into several squabbling principalities. The rise of Thebes (Luxor) saw an end to the turmoil, and Egypt was reunited under Montuhotep II, marking the beginning of the Middle Kingdom. For 250 years all was well, but more internal fighting and 100 years of occupation by the Hyksos, invaders from the northeast, cast a shadow over the country.

The New Kingdom, its capital at Thebes and later Memphis, represented a renaissance of art and empire in Pharaonic Egypt. For almost 400 years, from the 18th to the 20th dynasties (1550–1069 BC), Egypt was a formidable power in northeast Africa and the eastern Mediterranean. But by the time Ramses III came to power (1184 BC) as the second pharaoh of the 20th dynasty, disunity had again become the norm. Taking advantage of this, the army of Alexander the Great took control of Egypt in the 4th century BC.

Alexander founded a new capital, Alexandria, on the Mediterranean coast, and for the next 300 years the land of the Nile was ruled by a dynasty established by one of the Macedonian's generals, Ptolemy. Romans followed the Ptolemaic dynasty, during which time Christianity took hold. Then came Islam and the Arabs, conquering Egypt in AD 640. In due course, rule by the Ottoman Turks and the Europeans followed (the French under Napoleon, then the British) – shifts of power common to much of the Middle East.

SILENT COMMUNICATION

» As elsewhere in the Middle East, 'no' is often communicated with a quick upward nod or a brusque *tsk*. Use it casually with touts and they're more likely to leave you alone.

» A loud hiss doesn't necessarily mean a guy is commenting on your hot bod – it's also used by anyone moving a load to say 'Heads up – comin' through'.

» To request your bill at a restaurant, hold out your hand palm up, then make a quick chopping motion across it with the side of your other hand, as if to say 'Cut me off'.

Modern Egypt

Egyptian self-rule was restored through the Revolution of 1952, led by the Free Officers. Colonel Gamal Abdel Nasser, the coalition's leader, was confirmed as president in elections in 1956 and successfully faced down Britain, France and Israel to reclaim the Suez Canal. Nasser was unsuccessful, however, in the 1967 war with Israel, and died shortly after of heart failure. Anwar Sadat, his successor, also fought Israel, in 1973. The eventual outcome of the so-called October War was the 1979 Camp David Agreement, which established peace with Israel. In certain quarters, Camp David was viewed as treacherous abandonment of Nasser's pan-Arab principles; it ultimately cost Sadat his life at the hands of an assassin in 1981.

Sadat's murderer was a member of the terrorist organisation Islamic Jihad. Mass round-ups of Islamists were immediately carried out on the orders of Sadat's successor, Hosni Mubarak. He also reinstated emergency law (instituted during the 1967 war, and lifted only in 1980). It continues to this day, despite the 2011 revolution.

For almost a decade, Mubarak and his National Democratic Party (NDP) managed to keep the domestic political situation calm – with the constant presence of the armed forces always in the background. But discontent brewed among the poorer sections of society as the country's economic situation worsened. Frequent attempts were made on the life of the president and his ministers, and the government responded by arresting thousands and continuing to outlaw the most popular Islamist opposition group, the Muslim Brotherhood. In 1997, members of the Gama'a al-Islamiyya carried out a bloody massacre of 58 holidaymakers at the Funerary Temple of Hatshepsut in Luxor. The massacre crippled the economy and destroyed grassroots support for militant groups. The Muslim Brotherhood declared a ceasefire the following year.

Uprising

Things were relatively quiet until October 2004, when a bomb at Taba, on the border with Israel, killed 34. In early 2005, President Mubarak bowed to pressure and introduced competitive presidential elections, but voter intimidation and boycotts by opposition parties rendered Mubarak's victory meaningless to most Egyptians. Opposition leaders were jailed on questionable charges, while bombings in Sharm el-Sheikh and Dahab took a total of 122 lives, many of them Egyptian.

For 2008 council elections, a further 800 members of the Muslim Brotherhood were jailed, and few voters even bothered to turn up. Food prices spiralled, Mubarak intimated he was grooming his son Gamal to replace him and anyone even remotely suspected of opposition activity suffered torture at the hands of the police. It all came together to inspire an uprising on 25 January 2011.

People

With 82 million people, Egypt has the third-largest population in Africa (after Nigeria and Ethiopia) and is also the most populous country in the Arab world.

The blood of the pharaohs flows in the veins of many Egyptians today, but centuries of invading Libyans, Persians, Greeks, Romans, Arabs and Turks have added to the mix. Some independent indigenous groups persist: the nomadic Bedouin tribes, now for the most part settled in Sinai and Egypt's deserts; the Berbers of Siwa Oasis; and dark-skinned Nubians from the regions south of Aswan that were swallowed up by the High Dam.

About 90% of Egypt's population is Muslim; much of the remainder is Coptic Christian. Most of the time, the two communities peacefully coexist, although sectarian concerns come to the fore periodically. Islam permeates most aspects of Egypt's culture, from laws and mores to social norms, but more fundamentalist varieties are still a minority.

Arts

Literature

Egypt's literary pride is Naguib Mahfouz (1911–2006), awarded the Nobel Prize for literature in 1988; his Cairo Trilogy was some of the first work to sympathetically portray working-class Egyptians. Other notable Egyptian writers include feminist Nawal al-Saadawi, an outspoken critic on behalf of women; her nonfiction book *The Hidden Face of Eve* is still banned in Egypt. As interested with workaday Egyptians as Mahfouz and as outspoken as al-Saadawi, Alaa al-Aswany is best known for his soap-operatic but enthralling novel *The Yacoubian Building*, the world's best-selling novel in Arabic.

Cinema

Egypt's golden years were the 1940s and 1950s, when Cairo studios turned out more than 100 movies a year, filling cinemas throughout the Arab world with charming musicals that are still classics of regional cinema. Egypt's best-known director is Youssef Chahine (1926–2008), honoured at Cannes in 1997 with a lifetime achievement award.

Music

Alongside cinema, classical Arabic music peaked in the 1950s, the prime years of iconic diva Umm Kolthum. The country came to a standstill during her weekly live radio broadcast of lovelorn songs, some upwards of an hour long. Contemporary music is more lightweight, in the form of pop stars like Amr Diab, known across the Arab world for catchy choruses and loads of synthesisers. During the 2011 revolution, protest songs filled the air, and hip hop has inspired many working-class performers.

Food & Drink

Egyptian food is an earthy variant of Middle Eastern cuisine – a mix of dishes from Turkish, Levantine, Greek and ancient Egyptian traditions. Compared with its neighbours, Egyptian cuisine might seem to lack refinement and diversity, but the food here is good, honest peasant fare that packs an occasional sensational punch. High points include seafood on the Mediterranean coast, pickled vegetables with loads of garlic, succulent mangos in summer and fresh dates in autumn. Wash it down with ubiquitous tea or an ice-cold beer.

SURVIVAL GUIDE

Directory A–Z

Accommodation

Good hostels in Egypt are rare, but there are loads of excellent budget hotels. Decent midrange hotels are harder to find. At the top end, the major international chains are represented in the larger cities.

Winter (December to February) is high season, with higher hotel rates; June to August is the low season, except on the coasts, and to a lesser degree in Cairo.

Prices in this book are for rooms in the winter high season, and include breakfast unless otherwise indicated. For budget and most midrange hotels, taxes are included. For high-end hotels, tax is typically separate.

$ less than E£125 (US$25)

$$ E£125 to E£600 (US$25 to US$120)

$$$ more than E£600 (US$120)

Rates at budget and midrange places can be negotiable in off-peak seasons and during the middle of the week.

Many hotels will take US dollars or euros in payment, and some higher-end places even request it, though officially this is illegal. Lower-end hotels are usually cash only, though it's not a given that all upmarket hotels accept credit cards.

Activities

See destinations for specific options. For extended wilderness trips, you may need military permits. They are required for the Eastern Desert south of Shams Allam (50km south of Marsa Allam), around Lake Nasser, between Bahariyya and Siwa and off-road in the Western Desert. Safari companies can usually obtain them with two weeks' notice.

Business Hours

The weekend is Friday and Saturday; some businesses close Sunday. During Ramadan, offices, museums and tourist sites keep shorter hours.

Banks 8.30am-2.30pm Sun-Thu

Bars and clubs Early evening until 3am, often later (particularly in Cairo)

Cafes 7am-1am

Government offices 8am-2pm Sun-Thu. Tourist offices are generally open longer.

Post offices 8.30am-2pm Sat-Thu

Private offices 10am-2pm and 4-9pm Sat-Thu

Restaurants Noon-midnight

Shops 9am-1pm and 5-10pm Jun-Sep, 10am-6pm Oct-May

Children

» Egyptians are extraordinarily welcoming to children, but Egypt's budget and midrange hotels rarely have child-friendly facilities. Cots, babysitting services and other amenities are usually available only in top-end hotels.

» Restaurants everywhere are very welcoming to families, and high chairs are sometimes available.

PRACTICALITIES

» Tap water in Egypt is not considered safe to drink, with the exception of Cairo, where it's drinkable but not palatable.

» Egypt uses the metric system for weights and measures.

» Security checkpoints are common on highways outside Cairo. Carry your passport with you.

» Smoking is common in Egypt, including in restaurants and bars. Sheesha (hookah or water pipe) is a common social pastime. It delivers substantially more nicotine than a cigarette.

» Alcohol is available, typically only at higher-end restaurants. Drinking on the street is taboo, as is public drunkenness.

» International English-language TV news such as CNN and BBC World can be accessed in hotel rooms throughout the country.

» BBC World Service (www.bbc.co.uk/worldservice) is on the Middle East short-wave schedule, broadcasting from Cyprus. In Cairo, European-program 95.4 FM/557AM runs news in English at 7.30am, 2.30pm and 8pm. The English newspaper is the *Daily News Egypt*, an insert in the *International Herald-Tribune* (E£14).

» Monthly *Egypt Today* (E£15; also online at www.egypttoday.com) covers social and economic issues.

» Towns and cities have few parks with playground equipment. Fortunately, there are other things kids find cool: felucca and camel rides, exploring the interiors of pyramids and snorkelling on Sinai reefs are only a few.

» Formula is readily available in pharmacies, and supermarkets stock disposable nappies.

Discount Cards

The International Student Identity Card (ISIC) gives deep discounts on museum and site entries. Some travellers have also been able to get the discount with HI cards and Eurail cards.

To get an ISIC in Cairo, visit **Egyptian Student Travel Services** (off Map p58; www.estsegypt.com; 23 Sharia al-Manial). You'll need a university ID card, a photocopy of your passport and one photo; the cost is E£90. Beware counterfeit operations in Downtown Cairo.

Embassies & Consulates

Australia (Map p58; ☎02-2575 0444; www.egypt.embassy.gov.au; 11th fl, World Trade Centre, 1191 Corniche el-Nil, Cairo)

Canada (Map p58; ☎02-2791 8700; www.egypt.gc.ca; Sharia Ahmed Raghab, Garden City, Cairo)

Ethiopia (Map p58; ☎02-3335 3696; 21 Sharia Mohammed al-Ghazali, off Sharia al-Musaddeq, Doqqi, Cairo)

France Cairo (Map p58; ☎02-3567 3200; www.ambafrance-eg.org; 29 Sharia Charles de Gaulle, Giza); Alexandria (Map p87; ☎03-484 7950; 2 Midan Orabi)

Germany Cairo (Map p76; ☎02-2728 2000; www.kairo.diplo.de; 2 Sharia Berlin, Zamalek); Alexandria (Map p84; ☎03-486 7503; 9 Sharia el-Fawatem, Bab Sharqi); Hurghada (☎065-344 3605; 365 Sharia al-Gabal al-Shamali)

Iran (Map p58; ☎02-3348 6492; 12 Sharia Refa'a, off Midan al-Misaha, Doqqi, Cairo)

Ireland (Map p76, ☎02-2735 8264; www.embassyofireland.org.eg; 22 Hassan Assem, Zamalek, Cairo)

Israel Cairo (Map p58; ☎02-3332 1500; 6 Sharia Ibn Malek, Giza); Alexandria (☎03-544 9501; 15 Sharia Mena, Rushdy)

Italy Cairo (Map p58; ☎02-2794 3194; www.ambilcairo.esteri.it; 15 Sharia Abd al-Rahman Fahmy, Garden City); Alexandria (Map p87; ☎03-487 9470; 25 Midan Saad Zaghloul)

Jordan (Map p58; ☎02-3749 9912; 6 Sharia Gohainy, Cairo)

Lebanon Cairo (Map p76; ☎02-2738 2823; 22 Sharia Mansour Mohammed, Zamalek); Alexandria (Map p84; ☎03-484 6589; 64 Sharia Tariq al-Horreyya)

Libya Cairo (Map p76; ☎02-2735 1269; 7 Sharia al-Saleh Ayoub, Zamalek); Alexandria (Map p84; ☎03-494 0877; 4 Sharia Batris Lumomba, Bab Sharqi)

Netherlands (Map p76; ☎02-2739 5500; http://egypt.nlembassy.org; 18 Sharia Hassan Sabry, Zamalek, Cairo)

New Zealand (Map p58; ☎02-2461 6000; www.nzembassy.com; lvl 8, North Tower, Nile City Towers, 2005 Corniche el-Nil, Cairo)

Saudi Arabia Cairo (Map p58; ☎02-3761 4308; 2 Sharia Ahmed Nessim, Giza); Alexandria (Map p84; ☎03-497 7951; 12 Sharia Jabarti); Suez (☎062-333 4016; 10 Sharia Abbas al-Akkad, Port Tawfiq)

Spain Cairo (Map p76; ☎02-2735 6462; embespeg@mail.mae.es; 41 Sharia Ismail Mohammed, Zamalek); Alexandria (Map p84; ☎0100 340 7177, 101 Sharia Tariq al-Horreyya)

Sudan Cairo (Map p58; ☎02-2794 9661; 3 Sharia al-Ibrahimi, Garden City); Aswan (☎097-230 7231; bldg 20, Atlas, north of the train station about 1km, then west; ⏲9am-3pm)

Syria (Map p58; ☎02-3335 8805; 18 Abdel Rahim Sabry, Doqqi, Cairo)

Turkey Cairo (Map p58; ☎02-2797 8400; 25 Sharia Falaki, Mounira); Alexandria (Map p84; ☎03-399 0700; 11 Sharia Kamel el-Kilany)

UK Cairo (Map p58; ☎02-2791 6000; www.ukinegypt.fco.gov.uk; 7 Sharia Ahmed Ragheb, Garden City); Alexandria (☎03-546 7001; Sharia Mena, Rushdy)

USA (Map p68; ☎02-2797 3300; www.egypt.usembassy.gov; 5 Sharia Tawfiq Diab, Garden City, Cairo)

Food

Prices in this book represent the cost of a standard main-course dish.

$ less than E£15 (US$2.50)

$$ E£15 to E£75 (US$2.50 to US$12.50)

$$$ more than E£75 (US$12.50)

Many restaurants do not quote taxes (10%) in the menu prices, and will also add 12% for 'service', but this is typically used to cover wait-staff salaries and is not strictly a bonus. So an additional cash tip, paid directly to your server, is nice.

For more information about eating out in Egypt, see p145.

Gay & Lesbian Travellers

Homosexuality is not strictly criminalised, but statutes against obscenity and public indecency have been used to prosecute gay men. Despite a few visibly gay protesters during the 2011 revolution, the situation remains tense. The main gay and lesbian Egypt site is www.gayegypt.com, though its guide info is not kept up to date.

Language Courses

Egyptian Arabic dialect is understood throughout the Arab world, and classes are plentiful and inexpensive.

Department of Contemporary Arabic Teaching (DEAC; Map p92; ☎0100 639 3466; www.cfcc-eg.com; Gezira al-Bayrat; 2-week course E£2300) A range of Arabic courses at the Hotel Sheherazade in Luxor.

International Language Institute (ILI; ☎02-3346 3087; www.arabicegypt.com; 4 Sharia Mahmoud Azmi, Mohandiseen; 4-week courses from €245) The largest school in Cairo, so able to offer the widest range of levels. Two-week and four-week sessions.

Kalimat (☎02-3761 8136; www.kalimategypt.com; 22 Sharia Mohammed Mahmoud Shaaban, Mohandiseen; 4-week courses from E£1440) Smaller than ILI, but more convenient Cairo location.

Magana Camp (www.almagana.de) This beach camp between Taba and Nuweiba in Sinai runs summer and winter programs. See the Magana Camp group on Facebook.

Money

Change There is a severe shortage of small change, which is invaluable for tips, taxi fares and more. Withdraw odd amounts from ATMs to avoid a stack of unwieldy E£200 notes, hoard small bills and always try to break big bills at fancier establishments.

Currency Egyptian pound (E£), *guinay* in Arabic, divided into 100 piastres (pt).

Exchange rate The government sets the exchange rate, and it is fairly stable, changing incrementally only every few years. Rates are given at the beginning of this chapter.

Notes and coins 5pt, 10pt and 25pt are basically extinct; 50pt notes and coins are on their way. E£1 coins are the most commonly used small change, while E£5, E£10, E£20, E£50, E£100 and E£200 notes are commonly used.

Prices Produce markets and some other venues sometimes write prices in piastres: E£3.50 as 350pt, for example.

ATMS

Cash machines are common, except in Middle Egypt and the oases, where you may find only one. Then you'd be stuck if there's a technical problem, so load up before going somewhere remote. Banque Misr, CIB, Egyptian American Bank and HSBC are the most reliable.

CREDIT CARDS

All major cards are accepted in midrange-and-up establishments. In remote areas they remain useless. You may be charged a percentage of the sale (anywhere between 3% and 10%).

MONEYCHANGERS

Money can be changed at Amex and Thomas Cook offices, as well as commercial banks, foreign exchange (forex) bureaus and some hotels. Rates don't vary much, but forex bureaus usually don't charge commission. Don't accept bills that are badly defaced, shabby or torn because you'll have difficulty offloading them later.

TIPPING & BARGAINING

Bargaining is a part of everyday life in Egypt and people haggle for everything from hotel rooms to clothes. (The exceptions are places like supermarkets, and among friends.) Tipping, called baksheesh, is another fact of life. Salaries are extremely low and are supplemented by tips. In hotels and restaurants the 12% service charge goes into the till; an additional tip of between 10% and 15% is expected for the waiter. When in doubt, tip.

SERVICE	TIP
Ahwa or cafe	E£1 or E£2
Hotel staff (collective)	E£5-10 per guest per day
Informal mosque or monument guide	E£5-10 (more if you climb a minaret)
Meter taxi	10%
Restaurant	10%
Shoe attendant in mosque	E£1
Toilet attendant	E£1 or E£2

TRAVELLERS CHEQUES

The only reliable place to cash travellers cheques in Egypt is at the issuing office – Amex or Thomas Cook – in Cairo, Alexandria, Luxor, Aswan, Hurghada and Sharm el-Sheikh. Forex bureaus don't handle them, and even major banks are unreliable.

Post

Parcels Surface mail to the USA, Australia or Europe costs E£150 for the first kilo, E£40 for each thereafter. Usually only the main post office in a city will handle parcels; bring them unsealed so the contents can be inspected for customs. Clerks usually have cartons and tape on hand.

Poste restante The service functions well and is free.

Service Egypt Post (☎0800 800 2800; www.egyptpost.org) is reasonably reliable. The express service (EMS) is downright speedy.

Stamps Available at yellow-and-green-signed post offices and some shops and hotels.

Public Holidays

In addition to the main Islamic holidays (p624), Egypt celebrates the following public holidays:

New Year's Day 1 January – Official holiday but many businesses stay open.

Coptic Christmas 7 January – Most government offices and all Coptic businesses close.

National Police Day 25 January – Now overshadowed by the 2011 uprising, which began on this day.

Sham an-Nessim March/April – First Monday after Coptic Easter, this tradition with Pharaonic roots is celebrated by all Egyptians, with family picnics. Few businesses close.

Sinai Liberation Day 25 April

May Day 1 May – Labour Day

Revolution Day 23 July – Date of the 1952 coup

Armed Forces Day 6 October

Safe Travel

You're generally safe walking around Egypt day or night. Since 2011, bag and wallet snatchings have been reported, usually as drive-bys on mopeds. Carry your bag across your body, and keep it looped around a chair leg in restaurants. Don't walk on empty streets past 1am or 2am.

More common theft, such as items stolen from locked hotel rooms and even from safes, is a possibility, so secure your belongings in a locked suitcase.

Generally, unwary visitors are parted from their money through scams; see p79 for more.

Telephone

Area codes Listed at the start of each city or town section. Leave off the initial zero when calling from outside Egypt.

SHOPPING

So great is the quantity of junk souvenirs in Egypt that it can easily hide the good stuff – but if you persist, you'll find some treasures. Look out for modern housewares using traditional techniques, and Siwan, Bedouin and Nubian handicrafts.

The most popular items, available in every tourist destination in the country:

Perfume Essential oils are often diluted with vegetable oil. Watch when your bottles are packed up – make sure they're filled from the stock you sampled.

Papyrus True papyrus is heavy and difficult to tear, and veins should be visible in the light. A small painting on faux papyrus (made from banana leaves) can goes for just E£10; a good-quality piece can easily be 10 times as much.

Spices Buy whole spices, never ground, for freshness, and skip the 'saffron' – it's really safflower and tastes of little more than dust.

Gold and silver Gold and silver are sold by weight. Check the international market price before you buy, then add in a bit extra for work.

Appliqué and fabric On geometric and figurative tablecloths, pillowcases and more, stitches should be barely visible. Printed fabric used for tents is inexpensive when sold by the metre (about E£10).

Country code ☎20

Directory assistance ☎140 or ☎141

International access code from Egypt ☎00

MOBILE PHONES

Egypt's GSM network (on the 900MHz/1800MHz band) has thorough coverage, at least in urban areas. SIM cards from any of the three carriers (Vodafone, the largest; Mobinil; Etisalat) cost E£15. You can buy them and top-up cards from most kiosks, and you may be asked to show a passport. For pay-as-you-go data service (about E£5 per day or E£50 per month), register at a company phone shop.

PUBLIC PHONES

Pay phones (from yellow-and-green Menatel and red-and-blue Nile Tel) are card-operated. Cards are sold at shops and kiosks. After you insert the card into the telephone, press the flag in the top left corner to get instructions in English.

Alternatively, telephone centrales are offices where you book a call at the desk, pay in advance for three minutes, then take your call in a booth. Centrales also offer fax services.

Time

Egypt is two hours ahead of GMT/UTC.

In 2011, Egypt did not observe daylight saving time in order to cut the day short for Ramadan observers. This is expected to continue at least through 2014 as Ramadan continues to fall in the summer months.

Tourist Information

The **Egyptian Tourist Authority** (www.egypt.travel) has offices throughout the country. Individual staff members may be helpful, but often they're doling out rather dated maps and brochures. Smaller towns and oases tend to have better offices than big cities. In short, don't rely on these offices, but don't rule them out either.

Travellers with Disabilities

Egypt for All (www.egyptforall.com; 334 Sharia Sudan, Mohandiseen, Cairo) specialises in organising travel arrangements for travellers who are mobility impaired.

Visas

Visas are required for most foreigners, although travel in Sinai between Sharm el-Sheikh and Taba (including St Katherine's Monastery but not Ras Mohammed National Park) requires no visa, only a free entry stamp, good for a 15-day stay.

PLACES OF ISSUE

Visas are available for most nationalities at the airport on arrival (though check before departure), and are typically valid for 30 days. If you want more time, apply in advance or get an extension once in Egypt. Payment is accepted in US$, UK£ and €.

If travelling overland from Jordan, visas are available at the port in Aqaba.

If travelling overland from Israel, visas at available at the border only if guaranteed by an Egyptian travel agency; otherwise, apply in advance in Tel Aviv or at the consulate in Eilat (65NIS for US or German citizens; 100NIS for others).

COST

Australia	A$35
Canada	C$25
Euro Zone	€25
Israel	65NIS
Japan	¥5,500
New Zealand	NZ$45
UK	UK£15
USA	US$15

EXTENSIONS

Visa extensions used to be routine, but are now subject to scrutiny, especially after repeat extensions. The fee is E£11 to E£15, depending where you apply. There's a 14-day grace period for extension application, with E£100 late fee. If you leave during this time, you must pay a E£135 fine at the airport. Most large cities have passport offices for extensions.

Al-Tor Mogamma (main road, town centre) The only place in Sinai to get an extension; 90km from Sharm el-Sheikh.

Alexandria Passport office (Map p87; ☎482 7873; 28 Sharia Talaat Harb; ⏲8am-1.30pm Sat-Thu) Off Sharia Salah Salem.

Aswan Passport office (off Map p110; ☎231 2238; Corniche an-Nil; ⏲8.30am-1pm Sat-Thu) On the 1st floor of the police building on the Corniche.

Cairo Mogamma (Map p68; Midan Tahrir, Downtown; ⏲8am-1.30pm Sat-Wed) Get form from window 12, 1st floor, then stamps from window 43 and file all back at window 12; next-day pickup is at window 38.

Hurghada Passport Office (☎446 727; Sharia an-Nasr, Ad-Dahar; ⏰8am-2pm Sat-Thu)

Luxor Passport office (off Map p92; ☎238 0885; Sharia Khalid Ibn al-Walid; ⏰8am-2pm Sat-Thu) Almost opposite the Isis Pyramisa Hotel, south of the centre. There's a branch in the west bank, near the Antiquities Inspectorate Ticket Office.

Women Travellers

In public at least, Egypt is a man's world, and solo women will certainly receive comments in the street – some polite, others less so – and possible groping. As small consolation, street harassment is a major problem for Egyptian women as well. With basic smarts, the constant male attention can be at least relegated to background irritation.

» Wear a sturdy bra, long sleeves and pants or skirts. Sunglasses also deflect attention.

» Carry a scarf to cover your head inside mosques.

» Outside of Red Sea resorts, swim in shorts and a T-shirt at least.

» A wedding ring sometimes helps, but it's more effective if your 'husband' (any male travel companion) is present. Most effective: travel with a child.

» Keep your distance. Even innocent, friendly talk can be misconstrued as flirtation, as can any physical contact.

» Ignore obnoxious comments – if you respond to every one, you'll wear yourself out, and public shaming seldom gets satisfying results.

» Avoid city buses at peak times; the crowds make them prime groping zones.

» Bring tampons and contraceptives with you; outside of Cairo, they can be expensive.

Getting There & Away

Entering Egypt

At Cairo International Airport or Burg al-Arab Airport (Alexandria), the main formality is getting a visa, if you haven't arranged one in advance. Visas are sold at a row of bank booths in every arrivals terminal. Pay cash, then present the sticker with your arrival form and passport at the immigration desks. By land or sea, the process is similar. Your passport must be valid for at least six months from your date of entry.

Israeli stamps in your passport (and Israeli passports, for that matter) are not a problem.

Air

Aswan, Hurghada and Marsa Alam handle international charter flights.

Alexandria Has become a viable alternate airport, especially for low-cost carriers **Air Arabia** (www.airarabia.com) and **flydubai** (www.flydubai.com).

Cairo Served by all the major international carriers, including good-value **EgyptAir** (www.egyptair.com). **Air Sinai** (really just EgyptAir in disguise) flies from Tel Aviv; buy tickets at the unmarked office at Ben Yehuda and Allenby.

Luxor Receives one commercial international flight, by **EasyJet** (www.easyjet.com) from London Gatwick.

Sharm el-Sheikh Served by a number of European and Middle Eastern budget airlines. Arrive here only if you'll be spending time in the Sinai and Jordan; otherwise, it's an eight-hour bus ride to Cairo.

Land

BORDER CROSSINGS

The only land border shared by the rest of the Middle East is with Israel and the Palestinian Territories.

Rafah

The border crossing to the Gaza Strip is officially open Saturday to Thursday, but can be closed for days at a time for security reasons. As Gaza's border with Israel is closed, you likely won't be entering from Gaza, nor can you exit this way and carry on to Israel.

If you do want to visit Gaza, you must also return to Egypt, and you must have special permission from the Palestinian Affairs division of the **Ministry of Foreign Affairs** (☎02-2574 9682; ⏰noon-3pm) in Cairo. Be prepared to wait for approval (perhaps for weeks) to re-enter Egypt.

DEPARTURE TAX

Airline tickets include Egypt's exit tax in the price. If you're leaving by ferry to Jordan, expect to pay E£50/US$10 port tax. Crossing overland to Libya, there was no exit tax at the time of research.

Taba

The border at Taba is open 24 hours.

Entering Egypt Advance visa required, unless you're only visiting eastern Sinai. Israeli exit tax is 101NIS, and Egyptian entry tax is E£46, paid at a booth 1km south of the border on the main road. Entry to eastern Sinai only, with a travel permit, is free.

Exiting Egypt Israeli visa not required for most nationalities. Taxis or city bus number 15 (7.5NIS) run 4km to Eilat, for buses onward to Jerusalem or Tel Aviv. Note that no buses operate in Israel and the Palestinian Territories from Friday evening to Saturday sundown. Only Israeli-registered cars can cross here.

Bus service **Mazada Tours** (www.mazada.co.il) operates a bus between Cairo and Jerusalem (US$145, 24 hours) via Tel Aviv, though service can be cancelled if there are not enough passengers. In Cairo, bookings are handled by Misr Travel in the Pyramisa Hotel in Doqqi; the office will likely relocate to the Cairo Sheraton when renovation is complete in late 2012.

Sea

For information on ferries between Egypt and Cyprus, Saudi Arabia or Sudan, see p628.

ISRAEL & THE PALESTINIAN TERRITORIES

There's been talk about resuming the boat service from Port Said to Haifa. At the time of writing, this service was still non-existent. Contact **Varianos Travel** (www.varianostravel.com) in Cyprus.

JORDAN

Public Ferries

AB Maritime (☎069-352 0365; www.abmaritime.com.jo; one-way economy/1st class US$75/95) runs a fast ferry between Nuweiba in Egypt and Aqaba in Jordan. It leaves Nuweiba at 3.30pm daily (except Saturday) and takes two hours. Delays are common, but you nonetheless must be at the ferry terminal building at least two hours before departure to go through shambolic formalities.

Tickets can be purchased in US dollars or Egyptian pounds. Except for during the hajj, when you must book weeks in advance through a travel agent, tickets can purchased only on the day of departure at the **ferry ticket office** (☎352 0427; ⏲9am-3pm). To find the office, turn right when you exit the bus station, walking towards the water, and turn right again after the National Bank of Egypt. Continue one long block, and you'll see the ticket-office building ahead to your left.

There's also a slow ferry (US$65 to US$75, five hours) leaving at 2pm daily, though the more comfortable fast ferry is worth every cent.

Tourist Ferry

Meenagate Marine (☎03 2013100; www.meenagate.com; one-way/return US$85/125) in Aqaba runs a new tourist-only ferry. It leaves Nuweiba Port at 6.30am and has a sailing time of 1½ hours. You must be at the port one hour earlier. Heading back to Nuweiba, the ferry leaves from Aqaba's Royal Yacht Club (rather than the public port) at 7pm. Meenagate intends to open a ticket office in Nuweiba; until then, tickets are best booked by emailing the company directly, 48 hours prior to sailing.

Visas

Most nationalities are entitled to receive a free Jordanian visa upon arrival in Aqaba. You hand in your passport to the immigration officials onboard the ferry and collect it in the immigration building in Aqaba.

Bus Connections

From Cairo, a **Super Jet** (☎02-2266 2252; superjet.eg@hotmail.com) service to Amman (US$65/E£220, 15 hours) uses the public ferry, but the boat ticket must be purchased separately. The bus runs Tuesday and Saturday at 10pm from Al-Mazah; tickets can be purchased at Cairo Gateway.

SAUDI ARABIA

Ferries run from Hurghada to Duba, though they are not recommended due to erratic schedules, which fluctuate according to work and hajj seasons. Note that tourist visas are not available for Saudi Arabia, though there is an elusive tourist transit visa, which you must apply for well in advance.

> **PORT TAX**
>
> All Egyptian international ferries charge US$10/E£50 port tax per person on top of the ticket price.

SYRIA

Passenger service between Alexandria and Tartous was cancelled in 2011 due to the political situation. It may be restored. Check with **Visemar Line** (www.visemarline.com).

Getting Around

Air

EgyptAir (www.egyptair.com) is the only domestic carrier, and fares can be surprisingly cheap, though they vary considerably depending on season. Domestic one-way fares can be less than US$100.

Bicycle

Cairo-based club **Cycle Egypt** (www.cycle-egypt.com), and its very active Facebook group, is a good starting point for making local contacts and getting advice on shops and gear. Also check the Thorn Tree travel forum on www.lonelyplanet.com, where there's a dedicated section for cyclists.

Boat

No trip to Egypt is complete without a trip down the Nile. You can take the trip on a felucca (a traditional sailboat) or opt for a modern steamer or cruise ship. For information on Nile cruises and felucca trips, see p112.

At the time of research, a new boat service from Hurghada to Sharm el-Sheikh was in the works. For more information on the ferry, see p126.

Bus

You can get to just about every city, town and village in Egypt on a bus, at a very reasonable price. Buses aren't necessarily fast, though, and if you're going to or from Cairo, you'll lose at least an hour just in city traffic. For trips under two or three hours, a microbus or *servees* is preferable.

Air-con 'deluxe' buses connect the biggest destinations; tickets cost a bit more than those for standard buses (which may also make more stops along the way) but they're still cheap.

Buy tickets at bus stations or on the bus. Hang on to your ticket until you get off as inspectors almost always board to check fares. You should also always carry your passport as buses are often stopped at military checkpoints for random identity checks.

It is advisable to book in advance, especially Cairo-to-Sinai service and to the Western Desert, where buses run infrequently. An International Student Identity Card (ISIC) gives discounts on some bus routes.

Some companies:

Bedouin Bus (☎0101 668 4274; www.bedouinbus.com) Private start-up within the Sinai; runs services between Dahab, Nuweiba and St Katherine's.

East Delta Travel Co (☎02-3262 3128; www.eastdeltatravel.com) For the Sinai, East Delta is comparable to Super Jet.

Super Jet (☎02-2266 2252; superjet.eg@hotmail.com) Tends to be most reliable.

Upper Egypt Bus Co (☎02-2576 0261; www.uppereg.com) Serves most of the oases and the Nile Valley, though for the latter destinations, the train is preferable.

West & Mid Delta Bus Co (☎03-427 0916; www.westmidbus-eg.com) To Alexandria and to Marsa Matruh and beyond; showing substantially worse service.

Car & Motorcycle

Proceed with caution. Driving in Cairo is a crazy affair, and only slightly less nerve-racking in other parts of the country (night driving should be completely avoided). But some intrepid readers have reported that driving is a wonderful way to leave the tour buses in the dust.

A motorcycle would be a good way to travel around Egypt, but you must bring your own, and the red tape is extensive. Ask your country's automobile association and Egyptian embassy about regulations.

An International Driving Permit is required to drive in Egypt, and you risk a heavy fine if you're caught without one. Likewise, ensure that you always have all car registration papers with you while driving.

RENTING

Finding a cheap deal with local agencies is virtually impossible – it's advisable to make arrangements with an international agency online before you arrive. Read insurance terms carefully to see whether lower-quality roads are ruled out.

Local Transport

BUS

Several of the biggest Egyptian cities have bus systems. Practically speaking, you might use them only in Cairo and Alexandria. They're often overcrowded and rarely roll to a complete stop. Buy your ticket from the conductor.

MICROBUS

These 14-seat minivans run informally alongside city bus systems, or sometimes in lieu of them. For the average traveller they can be difficult to use, as they are unmarked. Typically you pay the driver as you're getting out.

PICKUP

Toyota and Chevrolet pickup trucks cover some routes between smaller towns and villages off the main roads, especially where passengers might have cargo. Trucks are also sometimes used within towns. To indicate that you want to get out, pound on the floor with your foot; pay your fare to the driver when you get out.

TAXI

Even the smallest cities in Cairo have taxis. They're inexpensive and efficient, even if the cars themselves have seen better days.

Fares In Cairo metered taxis are taking over, but everywhere else, locals know the accepted price and pay it without (much) negotiation. This book gives guidelines on taxi rates, but check with locals, as fares change as petrol prices rise.

Negotiating For short fares, setting a price beforehand reveals you don't know the system. But for long distances – from the airport to the city centre, for instance – you should agree on a price before getting in.

Paying In unmetered taxis, get out first, then hand money through the window. If a driver suspects you don't know the correct fare, you'll get an aghast 'How could you possibly pay me so little?' look, if not a full-on argument. Don't be drawn in if you're sure of your position, but remember E£5 makes a far greater difference to your driver than it does to you.

TUK-TUK

These clever scooters-with-seats, ubiquitous in Thailand and India, have arrived in Egypt. They're typically the same price or cheaper than taxis (E£10, say, for a 15-minute ride). Negotiate a price before getting in.

Microbus & Servees

The microbus (pronounced 'meekrobas'), often also called a micro or a minibus, is a Toyota van with seats for 14 passengers. (In some areas, the *servees*, a big Peugeot 504 station wagon with seats for seven, is more common.) They run most of the same routes that buses do, for a bit cheaper. They also stop anywhere on request, and will pick up riders along the way if there's a free seat. You can usually find one headed where you want to go, no matter the time of day.

Microbuses run on no schedule – they just wait until they're full, then take off. If you're in a hurry or just want more room, you can buy an extra seat. They usually congregate outside bus and train stations, or at major highway intersections on the edges of cities. Drivers shout their destinations; just shout yours back, and eventually you'll wind up in the right zone.

Pay the driver once you're underway. This involves passing your money up hand-to-hand through the rows; your change will be returned the same way.

Train

Egypt's British-built rail system comprises more than 5000km of track to almost every major city and town, but not to the Sinai. The system is antiquated, and cars are often grubby and battered. Aside from two main routes (Cairo–Alexandria, Cairo–Aswan), you have to be fond of trains to prefer them to a deluxe bus, though 1st class is usually fine and still inexpensive. For destinations near Cairo, however, trains win because they don't get stuck in traffic.

To check schedules of 1st-class trains and buy tickets for trips along the main Alexandria–Aswan line, visit **Egyptian Railways** (www.enr.gov.eg) online.

CAIRO–ALEXANDRIA

The best trains on the Cairo–Alexandria route are speedy 'Spanish' (*esbani*) trains. Almost all go direct, or with just one stop, in 2½ hours. 'French' (*faransawi*) trains are less comfortable and make more stops. Ordinary trains on this route are basic and slow.

CAIRO–ASWAN

The private company **Watania Sleeping Trains** (www.wataniasleepingtrains.com) runs daily services from Cairo to Luxor and Aswan. Tickets include two meals; reservations should be made a few days in advance.

Tourists can now ride regular day trains south of Cairo. The best is number 980, the express departing Cairo at 8am, with an enjoyable 10 hours to Luxor and 13 to Aswan, and views of lush plantations and villages along the way.

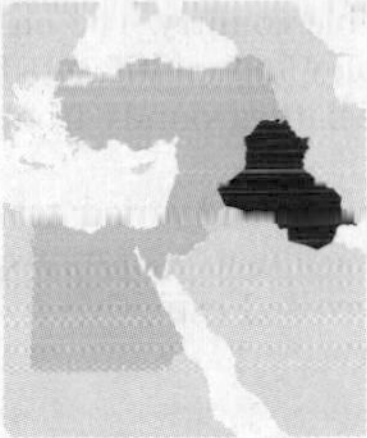

Iraq

Includes »

Best for Nature

- The Hamilton Road (p166)
- Amadiya (p164)
- Ahmadawa (p175)

Best for Culture

- Martyr Sami Abdul-Rahman Park (p169)
- Family Mall (p171)
- Al-Kosh (p164)
- Grand Bazaar (p173)
- Amna Suraka (p172)
- Lalish (p163)

Why Go?

Torn between its glorious past and the turmoil of its recent bloody history, Iraq is a country of contradictions. It is the birthplace of writing and the legendary home of the Garden of Eden, Hanging Gardens of Babylon and the Epic of Gilgamesh. But it is also a place of unimaginable horrors.

Since the 2003 US-led invasion, Iraq has been caught in a cycle of violence. Although there is finally some light at the end of the long, black tunnel, with the exception of Iraqi Kurdistan much of Iraq remains too dangerous for independent travellers. The future is far from certain, but with its rich history and warm hospitality, Iraq could soon become one of the great travel destinations of the Middle East, *insha' Allah*.

Due to the unstable security situation, we were unable to independently travel outside of Iraqi Kurdistan to update this chapter. Arab Iraq is currently off limits to independent travellers, so research for this part of the country was done using local contacts, the internet and other sources.

When to Go

Baghdad

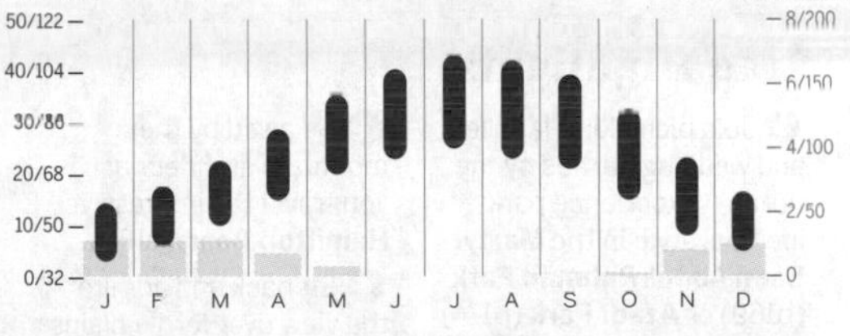

Mar Join the locals in welcoming in the Kurdish New Year with bonfires, picnics and dancing.

Apr Mountains dusted in snow, valleys carpeted in wild flowers. Iraqi Kurdistan looks good right now!

Oct Goodbye summer heat, hello autumnal colours and the first snowfall in the mountains.

Warning

Iraq is a war zone. The majority of the country has been in a state of war since the US-led invasion of Iraq in 2003. Although the security situation across much of the country has improved considerably in the last couple of years, Iraq remains a dangerous, volatile and unpredictable country. The ongoing conflict is a complex and multifaceted war with no discernible battlegrounds, front lines or combatants.

The risks are omnipresent and varied: terrorist attacks, military combat operations, suicide bombings, improvised explosive de-

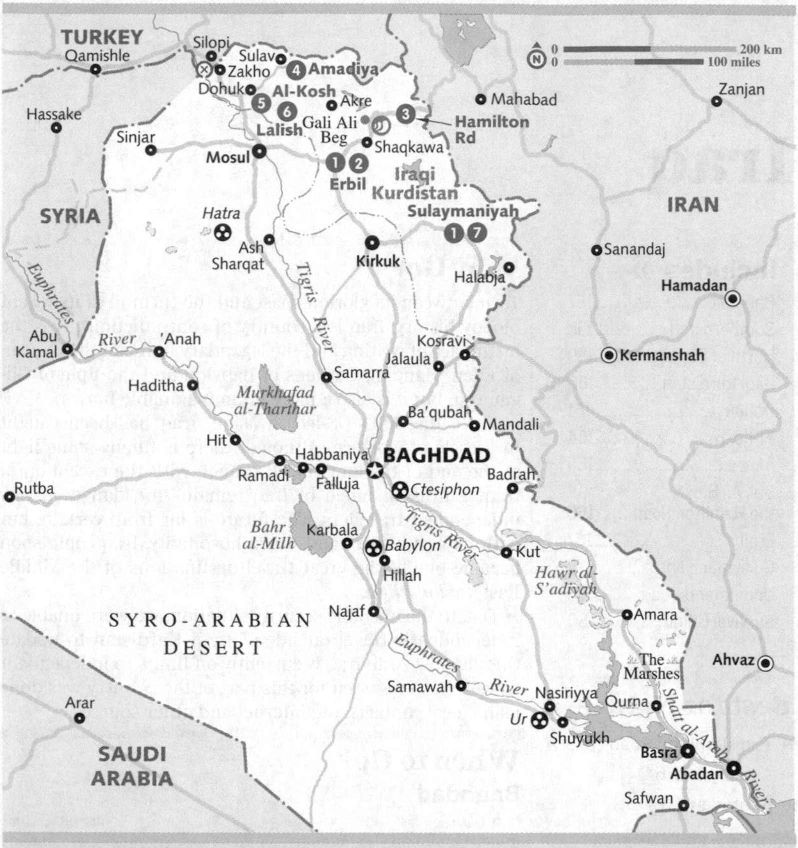

Iraq Highlights

1 Join picnicking families and wedding parties by the dozen – experience park life Iraqi style in the **Martyr Sami Abdul-Rahman Park** (p169) or **Azadi Park** (p174)

2 Visit one of the glossy **shopping malls** (p171) and understand why Erbil is being touted as the 'new' Dubai

3 Be awed by the mountain grandeur as you travel the impressive **Hamilton Road** (p166)

4 Sit back and admire the view over fertile plains and snowy mountains from the lofty village of **Amadiya** (p164)

5 Scramble up the steps to the **Rabban Hormizd Monastery** (p164), set like an eagle's nest high in a cliff face

6 Tie knots and pray for a better future for Iraq in the Yazidi holy site of **Lalish** (p163)

7 Reflect on the horrors of the recent past in Sulaymaniyah's **Amna Suraka** (p172), a former Saddam-era prison turned war-crimes museum

vices (IEDs), land mines, sectarian violence, kidnappings, highway robberies and petty crime. Foreigners are the primary targets of militant groups such as Al-Qaeda in Iraq. Attacks can occur anywhere, at any time.

The majority of violence in Iraq is concentrated in the southern two-thirds of the country, which has a predominantly Arab population; particularly in the so-called 'Sunni Triangle'. Consequently, Arab Iraq should be considered completely off limits to independent travellers. Especially dangerous areas include Mosul, Kirkuk and Baghdad. Nationwide, the security situation may have improved dramatically since a US troop surge in mid-2007 but it still has a long way to go before the bulk of the country is open for business. As if to emphasis this point, at the time of writing, levels of violence had increased again after the last US troops left in late 2011.

Iraqi Kurdistan – 'The Other Iraq' – is the only area of the country currently safe for travel. The pro-Western, Kurdish Regional Government–controlled provinces of Dohuk, Erbil and Sulaymaniyah are stable and peaceful with a growing tourism industry. Violence is rare, but not unheard of. Suicide bombers struck government offices in Erbil in 2004 and 2007, killing at least 54 people. In March 2008 a small bomb exploded outside Sulaymaniyah's Palace Hotel, killing one. Turkish and Iranian forces occasionally bomb the remote and mountainous border areas of northern Iraq in their fight against Kurdistan Workers' Party (PKK) militant separatists (there had been a spate of Turkish air bombings in late 2011/early 2012; though these were well away from tourist areas).

No matter how safe Iraqi Kurdistan appears to be you should always remember that you are still in Iraq and the situation could change for the worse very fast. You should also check that your travel insurance covers you for Iraqi Kurdistan before venturing there.

FAST FACTS

- **Area** 437,072 sq km
- **Capital** Baghdad
- **Country code** ☎964
- **Languages** Arabic, Kurdish (Kurmanji and Sorani)
- **Money** Iraqi dinar (ID); US$1 = ID1165; €1 = ID1549 (unofficial street rates are slightly higher)
- **Official name** Republic of Iraq
- **Population** 32 million

BAGHDAD بغداد

☎01 / POP 7 MILLION

All roads lead to Baghdad, the capital of Iraq and once the centre of the Islamic world. Baghdad's very name once invoked images of golden domes, towering minarets, sunlight filtering through exotic bazaars and tales of Ali Baba, Sinbad and *The 1001 Nights*. Today, the harsh reality is that Baghdad is now a city in ashes, ravaged by nearly three decades of war and neglect.

As the seat of Iraq's new government and former headquarters of the US military, Baghdad has been the focal point of the 2003 war. Suicide bombings, mortar attacks, kidnappings, murder and crime continue to be a daily fact of life. Despite a slowly improving security situation (not withstanding the spike in attacks as this book was being researched) Baghdad remains unsafe for independent travellers.

Sights

National Museum of Iraq MUSEUM

Founded in 1923, this museum once housed a world-class collection dating from the dawn of man. In the chaotic days after Baghdad fell to US forces, looters robbed the museum of 15,000 priceless artefacts; most were recovered or returned, but about 5000 items remain missing.

Green Zone NEIGHBOURHOOD

Officially, it's called the International Zone, a 12-sq-km, heavily fortified compound that houses Iraqi government offices, military bases and the largest US embassy in the world. Attractions within its walls include **Zawra Park**, **Baghdad Zoo**, Saddam Hussein's gaudy **Republican Palace**, **Martyr's Monument**, **Monument to the Unknown Soldier** and the **Swords of Qadisiyah** – also known as the Hands of Victory – commemorating Saddam's 'victory' over Iran.

Abbasid Palace PALACE

Perched imposingly on the banks of the Tigris River, in the Old City (Sheikh Omar), the 13th-century palace is one of Baghdad's architectural wonders, with detailed brickwork and arches.

Baghdad

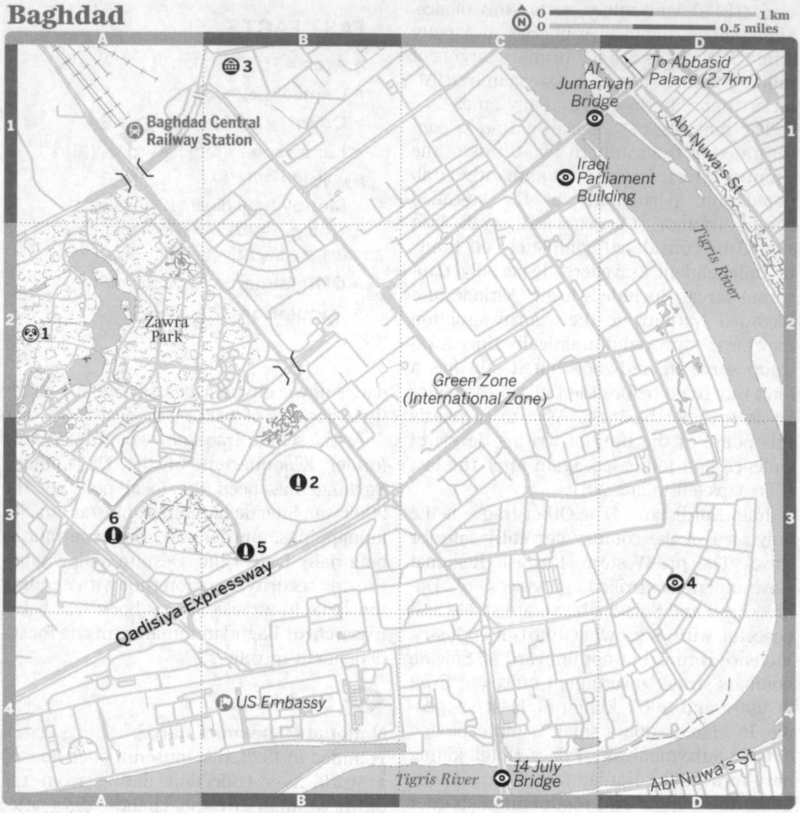

Baghdad

Sights

1 Baghdad Zoo....A2
2 Monument to the Unknown Soldier....B3
3 National Museum of Iraq....B1
4 Republican Palace....D3
5 Swords of Qadisiyah (Hands of Victory Statue)....B3
6 Swords of Qadisiyah (Hands of Victory Statue)....A3

SOUTHERN IRAQ

Southern Iraq is the spiritual homeland of the Shiites. The sacred cities of Najaf and Karbala attract pilgrims from around the world. The region is also awash with legends of the past, from the port city of Basra – where Sinbad the Sailor set out on his epic journeys – to the ancient sites of Babylon, Ur and the Garden of Eden. The Marsh Arabs, whose culture has changed little in millennia, make their homes among the reeds of the marshlands.

Babylon بابل

Babylon is Iraq's most famous archaeological site, and one of the most important in the world. Babylon dates back to at least 2300 BC. It was the capital city of two of the most famous kings of antiquity: Hammurabi (1792–1750 BC), who introduced the world's first law code, and Nebuchadnezzar (604–562 BC), who built the Hanging Gardens of Babylon, one of the Seven Wonders of the Ancient World.

Today, little remains of ancient Babylon except for several mounds and the famous Lion of Babylon, a basalt statue carved more than 2500 years ago. In the 1980s, Saddam Hussein rebuilt the Ishtar Gate and several palaces, stamping his name into every brick.

TOURISM IN ARAB IRAQ

We don't yet recommend it and almost every Western government advices against it, but should you really feel the need to visit 'Arab Iraq' then a couple of pioneering tour operators are running scheduled tours.

» **Hinterland Travel** (www.hinterlandtravel.com) UK-based tour company with years of experience in Iraq. Current tours feature Baghdad, Tikrit, Samarra and Babylon among others as well as Iraqi Kurdistan.

» **Terre Entiére** (www.terreentiere.com) Well-respected French-based tour company offering tours of many of the main historical sites across Iraq.

» **Babel Tours** (www.babel-tours.com) This Iraqi-based tour company is one of the pioneers of travel to southern Iraq.

Independent travel to Arab Iraq is currently neither possible (tourist visas are not issued to independent travellers) nor advisable. However, visa issues aside, if the security situation continues to improve it isn't totally beyond the realms of possibility that some parts of 'Arab Iraq' may become possible to visit again during the lifetime of this book.

Karbala كربلاء

☎032 / POP 572,300

Karbala is one of Shiite Islam's holiest sites and of great significance to all Muslims. It's best known for the Battle of Karbala in AD 680, whereafter Islam would forever be divided between Sunni and Shiite sects. The city attracts millions of pilgrims every year, particularly on the Day of Ashura.

Najaf النجف

☎033 / POP 506,000

The holy Shiite city of Najaf was once a major centre of learning with many madrassas (religious schools) and libraries. In the middle of the city stands the **Shrine of Ali ibn Abi Talib** (AD 600–61), who was the cousin and son-in-law of the Prophet Mohammed. The other major attraction is the **Wadi al-Salam Cemetery**, the largest cemetery in the world. Both attract millions of pilgrims every year.

Ur أور

The ancient Sumerian city of Ur, 15km south of Nasiriyya, is one of the most impressive archaeological sites in Iraq. Some believe it is the Ur of the Chaldees mentioned in the Bible as the birthplace of Abraham.

Ur dates back to at least 4000 BC but reached its heyday during the third and last Sumerian dynasty (2112–2004 BC). The dynasty's founder, Ur Namma, built the **Great Ziggurat of Ur** to honour the Sumerian moon god Nanna.

Basra البصرة

POP 1.76 MILLION

Iraq's third-largest city was once known as the 'Venice of the Middle East' for its canal waterways and location on the Shatt al-Arab River. The fictional voyages of Sinbad the Sailor began here, but modern reality is less inspiring.

In the 2003 invasion, the British occupied Basra, where they repeatedly clashed with Shiite militias and insurgents. In December 2007, the British relinquished the city to Iraqi officials. Chaos followed as Islamic fundamentalists battled each other for control of the city. Basra's security has improved, but it remains a dangerous city.

NORTH OF BAGHDAD

Northern Iraq is caught between a rock and a hard place. To its south lies the volatile Sunni Triangle; to the north and east lies the Kurdish Regional Government (KRG), which is slowly annexing Arab lands into its territory. It is home to a complicated ethnic mix of Arabs, Christians, Kurds and smaller minorities who have lived together peacefully for centuries – until now. The two major cities, Mosul and Kirkuk, might sit close to safe and stable Iraqi Kurdistan, but they are both extremely dangerous no-go areas.

Kirkuk كركوك

☎050 / POP 755,700

The oil-rich city of Kirkuk is a kaleidoscope of ethnic groups, and a tinderbox waiting to explode. Kurds, Arabs and Turkmen all lay claim to Kirkuk. Kurds consider it part of their historical homeland and are seeking to make it the capital of the Kurdish Regional Government. Arabs and most Turkomans want the city and its oil wealth to remain under central government control.

Mosul الموصل

POP 3 MILLION

Mosul is Iraq's second-largest city, and its most ethnically diverse. It has the country's largest number of Christians and significant numbers of Kurds, Assyrians, Turkomans and Yazidis.

Since the 2003 war, Mosul has been a hotbed of insurgency activity in northern Iraq. Thousands of minorities have fled the predominantly Arab city to escape violence and ethnic strife. As of early 2012 Mosul remains one of the most dangerous cities on earth.

IRAQI KURDISTAN

Leave your misconceptions behind and discover the newest travel destination in the Middle East – Iraqi Kurdistan. The region's slogan, 'The Other Iraq', could not be more fitting. This is the Iraq you don't see in the news. It's a safe and tranquil oasis with happening cities, soaring mountains and warm, welcoming people.

Iraqi Kurdistan is technically part of Iraq, but it might as well be a separate country. It has its own prime minister and parliament, its own passport stamps, its own languages and culture and its own army – the Peshmerga. The red, white and green Kurdish flag, with its blazing yellow sun in the centre, seems to flutter from every building, car and hilltop.

The semi-autonomous Kurdish Regional Government administers the Iraqi provinces of Dohuk, Erbil, Sulaymaniyah and a few northern bits of Ninawa and Tamim. The region has enjoyed de facto autonomy since 1991, when the US military established a no-flight zone to protect the long-oppressed Kurds from Saddam Hussein's brutal regime. The status was formalised in 2005 when the new Iraqi Constitution recognised Iraqi Kurdish sovereignty.

For early visitors to Iraqi Kurdistan, it's a chance to witness nation building first-hand. In the cosmopolitan cities of Erbil and Sulaymaniyah, cranes outnumber minarets as

THE BIG DIG

'I think it's true to say that Iraq, more than anywhere else, is the cradle of civilisation and the country is one vast archaeological site,' says Dr John Curtis, keeper of the British Museum's Middle East department. Just how many sites there are is impossible to quantify, he says. 'With the exception of the desert, anywhere you dig in Iraq you will find an archaeological site. That reflects the fact that there have been continuous civilisations and settlements here for 8000 years and it was very prosperous in antiquity,' says Dr Curtis.

The most important archaeological sites in Iraq are Ashur, Babylon, Hatra, Khorsabad, Nimrud, Nineveh, Samarra and Ur. The three that follow are in and around Mosul.

Nineveh

The ancient ruins of Nineveh are on the outskirts of modern-day Mosul. Some historians now believe the fabled Hanging Gardens of Babylon may have been confused with gardens that actually did exist in Nineveh.

Nimrud

Nimrud, the second capital of Assyria, is 37km southeast of Mosul and contains several buildings, the most impressive being King Ashurnasirpal II's palace and the Temple of Nabu, the God of Writing.

Hatra

Hatra, 110km southwest of Mosul, is one of the best preserved and youngest of Iraq's archaeological sites, dating to the 1st century AD. A Unesco World Heritage Site, it's covered by dozens of temples, tombs and columns.

Iraqi Kurdistan

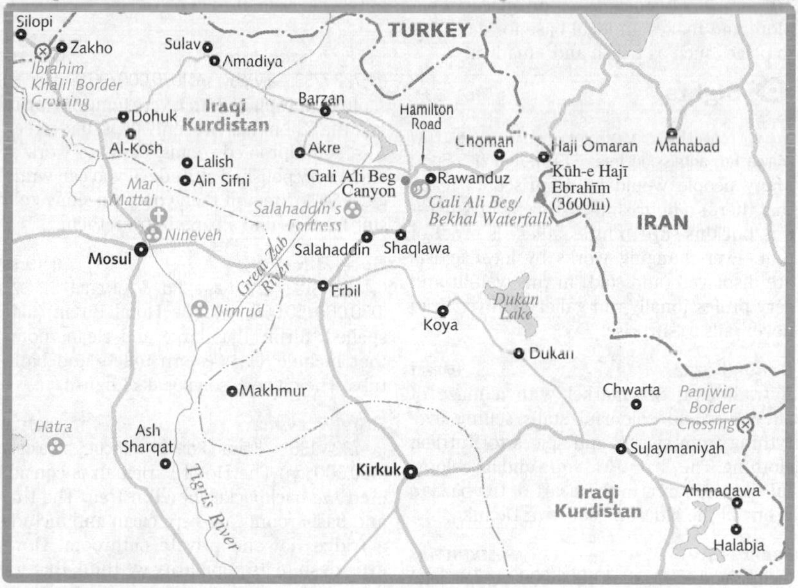

a construction boom gives rise to new luxury hotels, museums, shiny malls and tourist resorts. Iraqi Kurdistan's real attractions though are its stunning natural beauty – snow-capped mountains, deep canyons, gorgeous waterfalls and raging rivers – and its people, whose generosity and warmth never fail to capture the hearts of all visitors.

Zakho زاخو

☎062 / POP 90,000

Sooner or later, everyone ends up in Zakho. This hustling, bustling border town is just a hop from the **Ibrahim Khalil Border**, the main crossing point between Turkey and Iraq. Like many border towns around the world, trade is the lifeblood of the local economy, but while Zakho is pleasant enough there is little of interest for tourists.

Sights

Delal Bridge BRIDGE

Zakho's most famous attraction is this ancient bridge, a beautiful stone arch over the Khabur River. Unfortunately, the history of the old bridge has been forgotten over time. Near the bridge, you'll find a small **amusement park** and pleasant cafes overlooking the river.

Sleeping & Eating

There are dozens of hotel and restaurant options along Bederkhan St. Hotel prices are often quoted in US dollars, but you can pay in dinar.

Bazaz Hotel HOTEL $$

(☎770 2685; Bederkhan St; s/d ID30,500/61,000; ❄) Not the friendliest place, and the lobby stinks of cigarette smoke, but otherwise this place has very good value rooms with huge beds, Western toilets and a decent but pricey restaurant.

Information

If heading to Turkey change remaining Iraqi dinar here as the rates on the Turkish side are appalling.

Getting There & Away

Share taxis travel between Zakho and Dohuk and cost ID7000 per person. A private taxi to the Iraq-Turkey border costs ID5000. For more info on crossing this border see p182.

Dohuk دهوك

☎062 / POP 130,000

Cradled by two mountain ranges about 40km southeast of Zakho, Dohuk is a busy, energetic and curiously appealing place. This university town is a fun place to explore and makes an ideal base for day trips to places such as Lalish and Amadiya.

Sights

TOP CHOICE Dohuk Art Gallery GALLERY
(Kawa Rd; admission free; 9am-1pm & 3-6pm) Many people would be surprised to learn that there's a flourishing art scene in Kurdistan, but this superb little gallery is proof of that. Ever-changing works by local artists are displayed (and sold) in this well-lit and very professionally run gallery. Oh yes, Iraq never fails to surprise!

Dohuk Bazaar MARKET
A traditional old market with a maze of alleyways and colourful stalls selling everything from sweets and spices to Kurdish clothing. The **Grand Mosque** and its colourful tiled minaret, in the heart of the bazaar, is one of the oldest mosques in Dohuk.

Dream City AMUSEMENT PARK
(admission ID1500, rides ID1000-2000; 7pm-late) Dohuk's most popular attraction with Iraqis, this is a large amusement park/resort with a towering Ferris wheel and other thrill rides, plus a video arcade, bowling, swimming, restaurants, hotels and holiday homes. The place really gets cranking on Thursday and Friday nights, when local women turn out in their dazzling colourful traditional dresses.

Corniche Promenade PARK
This is a popular walking path and people-watching spot, especially in the late afternoon and early evening and weekends. The Corniche Promenade has inviting benches, water fountains, sculptures, cafes and an outdoor amphitheatre.

Church of St Ith Llaha CHURCH
This domed church is on a hill in west Dohuk and dates back to the 6th century AD. The current building is clearly newer and includes a cute little blue-and-beige outdoor chapel dedicated to the Virgin Mary.

Dohuk Dam VIEWPOINT
Just north of downtown, the dam and its man-made lake and waterfall is a popular family picnic spot and offers lovely views.

Sleeping & Eating

You'll find dozens of budget and midrange restaurants and hotels along Kawa Rd. Modern and pricier hotels and restaurants are on Zakho Way near Dream City. Most budget hotels have squat toilets.

TOP CHOICE Khani Hotel HOTEL $$$
(722 7733; Galy Way; s/d ID70,000/90,000;) A plush new place with a very tempting price tag, the Khani has heavenly beds, flat-screen TVs, soundproofed rooms, desks to work at and a very polished attitude. If you can wrangle a 30% discount then you get a shiny gold star from us and a bargain from them.

Hotel Bircin HOTEL $$
(722 8182; cnr Kawa Rd & Cinema St; s/d ID30,000/50,000;) The Hotel Bircin (also spelled 'Birjin') has large and clean rooms that include TV, Western toilets and bathtubs. The owner's son speaks English.

Hotel Parleman HOTEL $
(722 1361; Kawa Rd; r without breakfast ID20,000;) The Hotel Parleman is considered *the* backpacker hotel in Iraq. The tiny and basic rooms are kept clean and include a fridge, TV and private bathroom. However, despite its popularity we think that for just a little more money you can get a whole lot more elsewhere in town. Note that some people are charged by the room, others by the person.

Dolphin Hotel HOTEL $$
(0750 855 2841; Kawa Rd; per person ID40,000;) A large, new hotel that's much cheaper than its flash, mirrored-glass exterior leads you to expect. The massive rooms are filled with conservative dark-wood furnishings and all up it's something of a bargain.

Al-Sadeer Palace Rest IRAQI $$
(Galy Way; mains ID7000-10,000; 10am-midnight) Ask a local where to eat in Dohuk and there's a pretty good chance they'll send you here. In truth the food is fairly similar to many other places (kebab anyone?), but the views from the 1st-floor dining room and the marginally more extensive menu certainly give it an edge over the competition.

Mankal Restaurant IRAQI $$
(cnr Zakho Way & Kawa Rd; mains ID5000-10,000; 10am-midnight) Come here hungry, because the portions are absolutely huge. The lamb *quzi* is the house speciality, and big enough to feed an army.

Getting There & Away

Share taxis travel between Dohuk and Zakho and cost ID7000 per person. Going the opposite way

Dohuk

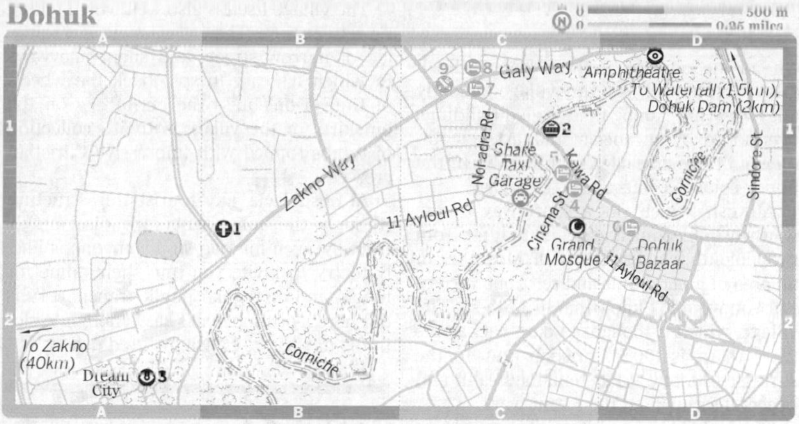

to Erbil costs ID15,000. Note that many (but not all) share taxis travel to Erbil via the outskirts of the city of Mosul. This takes you into something of a 'grey' area where security is shared between the Kurds and the Iraqi army and whether you are still completely in Kurdish-controlled Iraq is somewhat open to debate (the area is outside the autonomous region as recognised in 2005 by the government in Baghdad and venturing here may make your travel insurance invalid). Despite Mosul being one of the most dangerous cities on earth, the route is generally considered safe, but you'd only need to venture a very short way off this road to potentially find yourself in very big trouble. For this reason we'd recommend that you request the driver to travel the alternative route via Bardarash, which some drivers take anyway.

The share-taxi garage is in the dry river bed (wadi) just below Kawa Rd.

Dohuk

Sights

1 Church of St Ith Llaha B2
2 Dohuk Art Gallery C1
3 Dream City A2

Sleeping

4 Dolphin Hotel C1
5 Hotel Bircin C1
6 Hotel Parleman D2
7 Khani Hotel C1

Eating

8 Al-Sadeer Palace Rest C1
9 Mankal Restaurant C1

Lalish لاليش

Hidden in a deep, green valley, Lalish is the most sacred place on earth for practitioners of the Yazidi faith. At least once in their lifetime, each Yazidi must make a pilgrimage to Lalish, where their chief deity Malak Taus – the peacock angel – first landed. Some also believe Noah's Ark came to rest here. Visitors must walk barefoot through the complex.

The focal point of Lalish is the **Sanctuary**, a temple topped by two large pyramids. The entrance is guarded by a stone relief of a black snake slithering into a hole in the wall, which some believe symbolises a snake that used his body to plug a leak in Noah's Ark. The interior of the temple contains several tombs; the most important is the **tomb of Sheikh Adi ibn Mustafa**, a Yazidi reformer. The tombs and walls are wrapped in colourful silks; visitors tie and untie knots to make a wish. Other sights at Lalish include the **White Spring**, a crystal-clear baptismal pool fed by waters from the underground spring.

Lalish is about 30km southeast of Dohuk and 10km north of Ain Sifni, in the Kurdish Peshmerga-controlled territory of Ninawa Province. The best days to visit are on the Yazidi holy day of Wednesday and on Saturday, the day of rest, when hundreds of traditionally dressed Yazidi families come to pray and picnic on the hillsides.

There's no public transport to Lalish so you'll need to hire a taxi. A day trip from Dohuk, including a visit to A-Kosh, should cost around US$100.

Al-Kosh الكوش

One of the gems of northern Iraq, Al-Kosh (also spelt alqosh) is a tiny village of shady alleyways and flaking mud-walled buildings overlooked by an ancient monastery complex built like an eagle's nest high up in the honey-coloured cliffs above the village.

Al-Kosh, which sits a short way to the southeast of Dohuk and not all that far from the violently contested city of Mosul, is in an area of great ethnic and religious variety. But you wouldn't know that in Al-Kosh. The village, which is thought to date back some 2500 years, is 100% Christian and, to the surprise of many, it has remained calm and peaceful throughout the recent wars.

The highlight of a visit is without a doubt the 7th-century **Rabban Hormizd Monastery** (Sant Hormizd Monastery). To get there head north 1km or so out of the village and there it is in front of you. See it? No? OK, we'll give you a clue. Look up and scour the cliff face and there it is melting like a chameleon into the rocks. A new sealed road runs right up to the monastery entrance but it's much more authentic to struggle up the steps to it. The large complex is still occupied by a handful of Chaldean Monks and as such a large chunk of it is out of bounds, but you can visit the chapel (which was being renovated at the time of research), pay your respects at the tomb of Abba Gabriel Darnbo, who did much to revitalise the monastery after it was largely abandoned in the 19th century, and explore the web of tunnels, caves and shrines that lead off from the back of the chapel. The surrounding cliffs are also full of little caves, some of which were once used to house shrines.

Down at ground level is the monastery of **Notre Dame des Semences**, a large complex built in 1859.

The village itself is also well worth taking time to explore. The **old quarter** is a squiggle of narrow streets and silent alleyways in which it's easy to spin back the wheels of time. Don't miss the **cemetery** on the outskirts of the village with it's collection of tombs topped with impressive Christian crosses.

Al-Kosh lacks any tourist infrastructure (though the inhabitants are disarmingly friendly, even for Iraq, and someone is likely to try to invite you into their home for lunch) and no regular public transport runs out here. Fortunately it's easy enough to slot into a day trip to Lalish by hired taxi.

Amadiya العمادية

Like a village in the clouds, amazing Amadiya – or Amedi – is built on a high plateau 1200m above sea level. The village setting is fabulously picturesque, surrounded by magnificent mountains and endless green valleys. The city is a mix of Muslims and Christians, and there are several fine churches in town.

The most visible landmark is the 30m-high **minaret** of **Amadiya Mosque**, near the centre of town and built by Sultan Hussein Wali. It's about 400 years old and pockmarked with bullet holes from the Kurdish Civil War. It's possible to climb the spiral staircase to the top of the minaret, if you can find the imam who holds the key. The city was once a high-walled citadel, but all that remains is the huge, marble **Eastern Gate**. The gate is 4m wide and carved with intricate bas-reliefs. There's a small **cemetery** just to the left of the main entrance into town, containing the remains of several Amadiya royal-family members.

There are no hotels and few services here, but you'll find everything you need in near-

WHO ARE THE YAZIDIS?

The Yazidis is a misunderstood, long-persecuted Kurdish sect that practises Yazidism, a religion that is an amalgam of Islam, Christianity, Judaism and Zoroastrian. There are about 500,000 Yazidis in the world, most in Iraqi Kurdistan. Most speak Kurdish Kurmanji. The Yazidis believe a supreme god created the universe with seven angels, the chief among them Malak Taus, the peacock angel. He fell from grace but was later pardoned, leading many people to unfairly label Yazidis as 'devil worshippers'. Yazidis regard themselves as descendents of Adam, not Eve. Like Muslims, Yazidis pray five times a day.

Yazidis believe they will be reincarnated until they reach soul purity to enter heaven. They have two holy books, the Mishefa Res (black book) and the Kitab al-Jilwa (Book of Revelation).

WORTH A TRIP

MAR MATTAI

Long ago the plains of Nineveh were filled with Assyrian Christian monasteries and churches, but the tide of time hasn't been kind to them and over the past millennium most have been destroyed and faded away to dust. But some have survived and Mar Mattai (St Matthew's Monastery), which is spirited away halfway up the face of Jebel Maqlub (Mt Maqlub), is not just the most important Assyrian monastery in Iraq, but also the oldest and one of its largest and certainly most spectacular.

A monastery in some form or another has existed at this remote site since the 4th century when Saint Mattai, fleeing persecution, settled on the slopes of Jebel Maqlub and set about curing the inhabitants of the nearby villages of their ailments. Much of the vast 50-room structure that stands today is considerably newer, dating back to just 1845, but parts of the walls are thought to date back to the 12th century and some claim that the inner part of the church stretches right back to the days of Saint Mattai himself.

Today this breathtaking complex is home to just six monks, a bishop and a number of trainee monks. This might not sound like many but the situation is a lot better than it was in 2003 when just two monks lived here. At its peak in the 9th century the monastery was home to around 7000 monks.

Getting to Mar Mattai isn't all that easy. No public transport runs here so you'll need to hire a car from Dohuk (or Erbil) for around US$100 to US$150. A visit can be combined with one to Al-Kosh and Lalish but that makes for a very long day trip (set off at the crack of dawn). It's worth noting that though Mar Mattai is still within the safe Kurdish controlled areas it is situated very close to Mosul (you can look down at Mosul's radio masts and factory chimneys from the monastery) and security around the monastery is tight. Getting here from Erbil presents no major security issues, but coming from Dohuk you have a choice of two roads. The older, better-known road, passes right through the suburbs of Mosul and though police and army at the numerous checkpoints will assure you that it's safe there is a very distinct change in atmosphere and you suddenly start to feel mighty close to the war in Iraq. Fortunately, a new road running just to the north of the monastery now provides a quicker, prettier and much less tense approach to Mar Mattai.

by Sulav. To get here taxis (ID25,000 one way) can be hired in Dohuk.

Sulav سولاف

Tiny Sulav is a mountain resort town overlooking Amadiya, a hop and a skip to the northwest. The crisp, cool climate attracts tourists from hotter parts of the country. A 1km-long, cobblestone **hiking trail** leads to a small **waterfall** and a **stone arch bridge**. The path begins near the Sulav Hotel, behind the cheesy man-made waterfall.

Sleeping & Eating

There are several hotels, restaurants, cafes and shops along the one and only road through Sulav.

Sulav Hotel & Restaurant HOTEL **$$**
(r per person US$40; closed Nov-Feb) A small, family-run hotel with rooms that have balconies and shared bathrooms. One room has a small, babbling brook running through it. The terraced restaurant offers magnificent views of Amadiya and the valley below.

Baper Restaurant IRAQI **$**
(mains ID7000-9000) It's at times like this, sitting in the sun, enjoying a long, lazy lunch of traditional Kurdish dishes served up with a breathtaking view over Amadiya and the mountain hulks beyond, that you have to pinch yourself and say 'Yes, I am in Iraq'.

Akre عقره

The ancient city of Akre (also spelled Aqrah) is built into a steep hillside above a thriving old market. Located about 23km south of Barzan along a scenic mountain road, Akre once had a substantial Jewish population. The mountain overlooking Akre has a flat plateau called **Zarvia Dji**, meaning Land of the Jews, and was once used for Jewish celebrations. Today it is the site of the region's largest **Nowruz festival**, celebrating the Kurdish New Year on 21 March, when huge bonfires and fireworks light up the night skies around Akre.

The best way to explore the town is on foot. Narrow alleyways and hidden staircases climb past clusters of colourful houses. The opposite hill contains an old **cemetery** with great views of old Akre.

The valley floor at the base of the old city houses the town's two focal points, the **bazaar** and the white-and-green-trimmed **Akre mosque**. The crumbling **town hall** in the city centre has seen better days, but it's a fine example of British colonial architecture. Just north of the city centre, a hiking path leads to **Sipa Waterfall**.

As there is no real tourism industry here, sleeping and eating options are limited. **Jar Jra Motel** (☎0750 464 2320; New Akre; r ID84,000; ❄) is on the noisy main drag and has large apartments which can sleep four, but the staff don't appear to own a brush and mop so it's all quite shabby. There are a couple of other options in town but all are equally unappealing.

Gali Ali Beg & the Hamilton Road

قلي علي بيك

Prepare yourself for one of the most amazing sights in the Middle East. The northeast corner of Iraqi Kurdistan is an unheralded area of beauty marked by cascading waterfalls, soaring snow-capped mountains, deep gorges cut by raging rivers, rolling green hills and lush valleys. It is, without a doubt, the most beautiful and awe-inspiring place in Iraq.

In 1928 New Zealand engineer Sir Archibald Milne Hamilton was commissioned to build a road from the Kurdish capital of Erbil to Haji Omaran on the Iranian border. This 'short cut' allowed the creation of a strategic and direct overland route from the Mediterranean cities of Beirut and Alexandretta (now Iskenderun) to the Caspian Sea, Tehran and on to India. Hamilton completed his road in 1932 and detailed its construction in his travelogue, *Road Through Kurdistan*.

Named for its builder, the **Hamilton Road** remains a remarkable feat of engineering through some of the world's most impassable and inhospitable terrain. Kurds also call it the Haji Omaran road, and it crosses at least five mountain ranges and rises from 409m in Erbil to about 1850m on the Iranian border. The most scenic portion of the drive is the 55km stretch from Gali Ali Beg to Haji Omaran.

Sights

In *Road Through Kurdistan,* Hamilton called **Gali Ali Beg Canyon** 'one of the grandest formations of nature to be found in the world'. This Grand Canyon of the Middle East extends 12km between the Korak and Bradost mountains and is cut by two rivers that form to create the **Great Zab River**. The Hamilton Road traverses the canyon from west to east. At the western entrance to the canyon the road splits into upper and lower halves.

The **Lower Hamilton Road** runs parallel to the river past high, red limestone walls that rise almost vertically from the canyon floor. Halfway along the canyon is **Gali Ali Beg Waterfall**. The waterfall is Iraq's most famous, appearing on the back of the ID5000 note, and the falls tumble 80m into a frigid tidal pool that offers wading possibilities.

Upper Hamilton Road hugs the rim of the canyon along a series of hairpin turns. The road eventually arrives at **Bekhal Waterfall** – white-water falls that appear to pour straight out of the side of a mountain and down several steps.

The roads meet again in the dusty town of **Rawanduz**, a former British colonial outpost with few facilities. From here, Hamilton Road begins its most dramatic climb, running parallel to the Choman River. The regional market town of **Choman** is a city of about 10,000 people surrounded by unparalleled beauty and snow-capped mountains, but once again there are no tourist facilities.

The Hamilton Road ends at the border town of **Haji Omaran**, the last city before the Iranian frontier (for details on this border crossing see p182). It's a major point of legal and not-so-legal trade. Iranian and Kurdish men in traditional clothing haggle over goods on the roadside. At 1828m above sea level, the air here is cold and crisp and surrounded by mountains that are covered in snow even in the summer. Some reach peaks of 3600m. In another time and place, this could be a ski resort or busy hiking region. But for now, there is little of consequence in Haji Omaran apart from its natural beauty. Here, one can truly appreciate the Kurdish proverb, 'No friends but the mountains'.

Sleeping & Eating

There are cafes at the Bekhal falls – so many that they've virtually swallowed up the waterfalls themselves! And, just a little further up the road from the falls, a cable car was under construction at the time of research.

Pank Resort RESORT $$$
(☎066-353 0105, 0750 412 8910; www.rawandoz.com; admission ID3000, cottage from US$125; ⊙8am-midnight) Siting atop a plateau above the village of Rawanduz, Pank features a roller coaster, Ferris wheel, minigolf, restaurants and three helicopter landing pads.

Lawin Restaurant KURDISH $$
(Rawanduz; meals ID9000) Don't miss lunch at the Lawin which has fan-fracking-tastic lamb *quzi* and even better mountain vistas.

Getting Around

Getting around the Hamilton Road without your own transport is problematic. Share taxis are very few and far between, so some people end up hitching; as in other parts of the world, hitching is never entirely safe, and we don't recommend it. Those travellers who decide to hitch should understand that they are taking a potentially serious risk. The other option is to hire a taxi for the day from Erbil – this will cost you. Plan on somewhere between US$150 and US$200. An excellent, English-speaking Erbil-based driver is **Haval Quaraman Rwandzy** (☎0750 4858 186; haval_aaaa42@yahoo.com).

Shaqlawa شقلاوة

About 50km northeast of Erbil at the base of Safeen Mountain is the resort town of Shaqlawa. At 966m above sea level, the cool temperatures and lush, green environment have long attracted wealthy Iraqi tourists from the hotter Arab regions of the country. Shaqlawa is a predominantly Assyrian Christian town with several new churches.

A strenuous one hour hike leads up into a canyon on the side of Safeen Mountain. Hidden in a rock crevice near the top of the mountain are the ruins of the **Rabban Beya Monastery**. Dating to the 4th century AD, the ruins consist of a stone arch and three crumbling, small rooms. The real reward here is the stunning view of the Beya Valley and Shaqlawa below.

Shaqlawa has several hotels, restaurants, falafel shops and supermarkets.

The **Stars Hotel and Swedish Village** (☎0750 746 6283; www.starshotelshaqlawa.com; r/cottage with breakfast US$120/180; @☎❄) is great value if there are two or three of you. The business-class rooms are pretty plush and there are fully equipped cottages with small kitchens. The receptionist speaks superb English.

A place in a share taxi to Erbil is ID5000.

Erbil أربيل

☎066 / POP 1 MILLION

Erbil (Irbil; Kurdish: Hawler) is the capital of the Kurdish Regional Government and the largest city in Iraqi Kurdistan. It is one of the oldest continuously inhabited cities in the world. Today, Erbil is where it's all happening. It's the fastest-growing city in Iraq, with dozens of glossy shopping malls, amusement parks, five-star hotels, glass office blocks and a flash new airport.

Billboards advertise luxury Western-style homes in posh subdivisions with names such as 'Dream City' or 'English Village'. Erbil's master plan even calls for championship golf courses, a wildlife safari park and a Grand Prix racetrack. Clearly Erbil thinks itself the new Dubai and with the energy on the streets and the money to back it all up, who's to say it's not. This tolerant, diverse city full of big dreams and optimism should serve as a model for all of Iraq.

History

There is archaeological evidence that Neolithic peoples roamed the area 10,000 years ago. The first written record of Erbil dates back to 2000 BC when it was called Arbilum. The city was consecutively invaded by Akkadians, Sumerians, Assyrians, Persians and Greeks. Around 100 AD, Erbil became a centre of Christianity until Muslims conquered it in 642 AD. Over the next several hundred years, Erbil passed through many powerful hands, including the Abbasids, Moguls, Turkomans, Persians, Ottomans and British.

During the mid-1990s, Erbil was caught in the middle of the Iraqi Kurdish Civil War between the armies of the two major political parties, the Kurdish Democratic Party (KDP) and the Patriotic Union of Kurdistan (PUK). Erbil was PUK territory until it was captured by the KDP in 1996. Thousands were killed during the fighting until the parties signed a peace treaty in 1998.

Since the 2003 US-led invasion, Erbil has enjoyed relative peace and stability, but there has been a handful of attacks.

Erbil

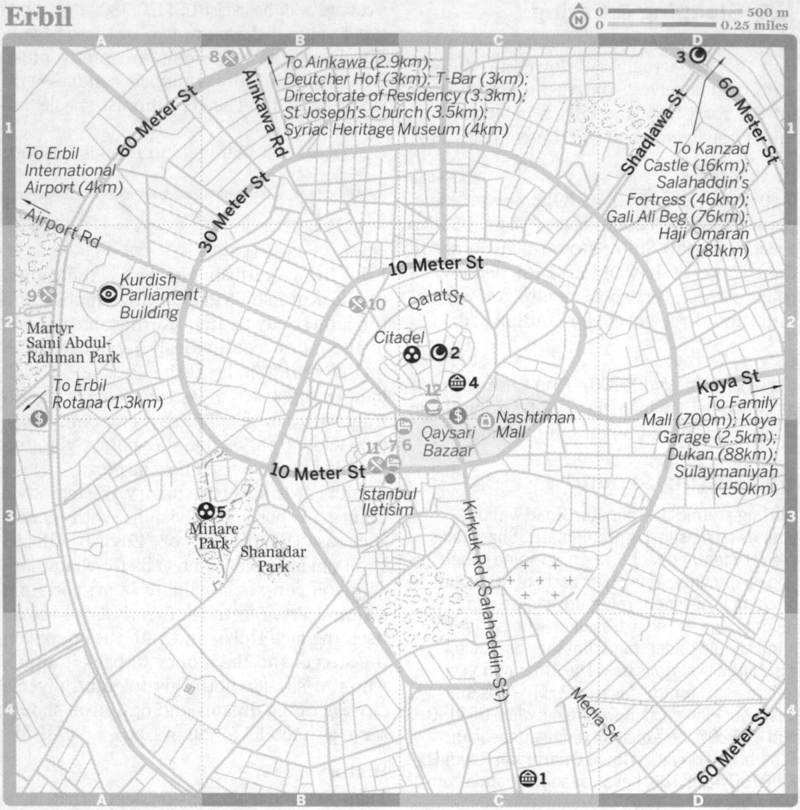

Erbil

Sights

Antikqala .... (see 4)
1 Erbil Civilization Museum C4
2 Grand Mosque & Citadel Bath C2
3 Jalil Khayat Mosque D1
4 Kurdish Textile Museum C2
5 Sheik Chooli Minaret B3

Sleeping

6 Bekhal Hotel C3
7 Peace Pigeon Hotel B3
Saira Miss Hotel .... (see 6)

Eating

8 Abu Shahab Restaurant B1
9 Dowa 2 Restaurant A2
10 Pushi B2
11 Tajryan Restaurant B3

Drinking

12 Machko Chai Khana C2

Sights

Erbil has more mosques than any city in Iraqi Kurdistan. The Christian neighbourhood of Ainkawa has several churches. The largest is **St Joseph's Church**, a Chaldean Christian church built in 1978.

Citadel

OLD TOWN

The heart of Erbil is the citadel (Qalat Hawler in Kurdish), claimed (along with a number of other Middle Eastern cities) to be the longest continuously inhabited urban area on earth. This imposing tell, or mound, covers an area of 102,000 sq metres and rises 32m above street level, built on layers of successive settlements.

A ring of fortified honey-yellow walls tops the citadel. Inside this city within a city are hundreds of little stone and mud-brick homes, many built directly into the walls. In the centre of town is the **Grand Mosque** and **Citadel Bath**, built in 1775 on top of an older structure and featuring a colourfully tiled minaret.

The citadel has been continuously inhabited for at least 8000 years – sort of. Until recently, it was home to more than 3000 of Erbil's poorest people, many of them refugees who had fled war-torn regions of Iraq. Human action was wreaking havoc on the citadel. So in a controversial November 2006 move, the KRG paid off and resettled residents to make way for redevelopment. Most of the citadel is now an eerie, crumbling ghost town, but one family remains in order to not break the continuous habitation streak. Unesco and the KRG are currently undertaking extensive renovation works which have left much of the citadel closed to the public, but it was still possible to walk up and down the 'main' street.

The main entrance into the citadel is the **South Gate**, guarded by a **colossal statue** of 12th-century historian Mubarek Ahmed Sharafaddin.

FREE Kurdish Textile Museum MUSEUM
(www.kurdishtextilemuseum.com; ⌚9am-7pm Sat-Thu) This museum contains a colourful collection of Kurdish carpets, clothing and other goods. Next door, **Antikqala** is an eclectic and pricey antiques shop.

TOP CHOICE Martyr Sami Abdul-Rahman Park PARK
(60 Meter St; admission free; ⌚8am-midnight) Also known as Erbil Park, Martyr Sami Abdul-Rahman Park, across from the Kurdish Parliament Building, is one of the most beautiful urban spaces in Iraq. This oasis of fountains, lakes and gardens was built over what was previously a military base for Saddam Hussein's feared 5th Corps Army. On Fridays, the park is packed with young couples, families enjoying picnics and lots and lots of boisterous wedding parties. The large lake in the centre of the park rents swan-shaped paddleboats and speedboat rides and nearby is a huge children's playground. Off to one side are football pitches and a skateboard/BMX park.

Qaysari Bazaar BAZAAR
(⌚8am-late Sat-Thu) Erbil's huge bazaar is one of the oldest in the world. It wraps around the entire southern half of the citadel, where you can literally find anything. It's a maze of narrow alleys and streets, much of it covered by a corrugated metal roof to protect shoppers from the blazing Iraqi sun. The bazaar is divided into various sections. The western side has many book stalls. The south side is filled with clothing stores and shops selling fresh yogurt and honey and cheese. The east side contains hardware, electronics and bootleg DVDs and video games.

Minare Park & Shanadar Park PARK
Standing at the heart of the Minare Park is the 36m-tall **Sheik Chooli Minaret**, all that remains of a grand mosque. The broken, leaning minaret was built between 1190 and 1232 during the reign of Sultan Mudhafaraddin Kokburi.

The minaret stands on a 14.5m octagonal base and is made of baked bricks and gypsum with highly detailed tiled ornamentation.

On the opposite side of the road from the Minare Park is the Shanadar Park, which contains a lake with dancing fountains and a fake cave which is home to an art gallery. Crossing over the top of the park, but starting in the Minare Park, is the huge **Erbil Teleferique** (cable car; ID5000). Both parks are packed on Fridays.

FREE Syriac Heritage Museum MUSEUM
(Ainkawa Museum; Ainkawa; ⌚9am-8pm Sun-Fri) In the almost entirely Christian suburb of Ainkawa, this worthwhile little museum showcases the culture and history of the Syriac Christian peoples of Kurdistan. The collection consists of displays of traditional dress, household utensils and farming implements.

FREE Erbil Civilization Museum MUSEUM
(Ministry of Antiques, Salahaddin St; ⌚9am-1.30pm Sat-Thu) This small museum inside the Ministry of Antiques houses a collection of Iraqi archaeological finds, some dating back to 6000 BC.

Jalil Khayat Mosque MOSQUE
Driving into the city from Shaqlawa, you can't miss Erbil's largest and grandest mosque, the Jalil Khayat Mosque. Opened in 2007, it's inspired by İstanbul's famed Blue Mosque. The main dome is 45m high, flanked by two 65m-tall minarets. Non-Muslim visitors are normally welcome to look around outside prayer time.

Sleeping

There are many budget hotels in and around the bazaar and it's really just a case of checking out a few until you find something that suits. Most have squat toilets unless otherwise noted.

Peace Pigeon Hotel HOTEL $$$
(Kotri Salam Hotel; ☎0750 7754 949, 0662 221 776; 10 Metre St; s/d/tr US$60/75/100; ❄📶) The smartest option in the bazaar district, this modern hotel overlooking a statue of a white (ish!) dove has large, tiled and comfortable rooms, some insulation from road noise, hot water spurting out of the taps and an eager-to-please owner.

Saira Miss Hotel HOTEL $
(☎0770 4686 337; Bazaar; per person without breakfast ID20,000; ❄) Located in the bazaar about a block southwest of the Citadel, this basic hotel has small but well-maintained rooms with hot-water bathrooms. The cheerful receptionist speaks some English. Like most cheap Iraqi hotels this one has several beds per room and pricing is by the bed rather than by the room.

Erbil Rotana HOTEL $$$
(☎210 5555; www.rotana.com; Gulin St; r from US$270; ❄@📶🏊) The business person's choice; the Rotana is currently the most sophisticated hotel in Erbil, though with the speed at which new five-star hotels are cropping up you can be certain it'll have some competition soon! Amenities include swimming pools and several bars and restaurants (including excellent Italian and Lebanese ones). It's just beyond the western edge of the Martyr Sami Abdul-Rahman Park.

Bekhal Hotel HOTEL $
(☎0750 4467 515, 0662 510 538; Bazaar; per person without breakfast ID15,000; ❄) Spacious but otherwise fairly gloomy rooms which feel kind of neglected. However, it's about as cheap as you'll find in Erbil. The owner speaks basic English. It's a door or so up from the Saira Miss Hotel.

Eating

Many budget kebab shops and food vendors can be found in the bazaar and in fact Erbil considers itself the kebab capital of Iraq!

Abu Shahab Restaurant IRAQI $$
(60 Metre St; mains ID8000-10,000) If you want to sample high-class Kurdish food the Abu Shahab is generally considered the place to go by both locals and expats. It's a large and fairly formal place but still manages to have something of a shopping-mall look to it. The special is *quzi-sham,* a biryani-like dish covered in fried pastry. Don't get it confused with the fast-food joint with the same name that sits opposite.

Tajryan Restaurant IRAQI $
(10 Meter St; mains ID4000-5000) The best-loved restaurant in the bazaar area; come at Friday lunchtime and you might have to queue for a table. It serves all the Kurdish Iraqi basics of kebabs in myriad (though normally identically tasting) forms, spit-roasted chickens and aubergine in a tomato sauce. Finish your meal with a sweet tea from the stall outside. There are several similar places nearby.

Pushi KURDISH $$
(Ainkawa Rd; mains ID8000-12,000; ⏲noon-midnight) Pushi Restaurant is an Erbil institution, and due to serving up Turkish and Kurdish specialties such as *İskender kebaps* and fish dishes, it's a perfect place to sample some high-class local fare in a relaxed atmosphere.

Dowa 2 Restaurant TURKISH $$$
(☎0750 4452 303; Martyr Sami Abdul-Rahman Park; set menu ID25,000; ⏲11am-midnight) For excellent Turkish food this large restaurant, popular with the movers and shakers of Erbil society, is a good choice. Its multi-course set menu is comprised of classic Turkish dishes expertly produced. It's on the edge of the Martyr Sami Abdul-Rahman Park and is very popular on Fridays for a posh lunch followed by a stroll in the park.

Drinking

Machko Chai Khana CAFE
(Citadel) This legendry teashop, which is virtually built into the walls of the Citadel, has been a haunt of writers, intellectuals and arty types for decades. It's also the backgammon, card-playing and tea-sipping hang-out of choice for dozens of old men.

Entertainment

Deutscher Hof BAR
(Ainkawa; mains ID10,000-20,000; ⏲noon-midnight) The Christian suburb of Ainkawa is home to a bunch of bars, including this one. It's always full of expats and serves typical German dishes such as bratwurst, schnitzel and steak.

T-Bar BAR
(Ainkawa; ⊙noon-midnight) Cheaper beer is available at the T-Bar, which is an equally popular expat hang-out with a quiz night on Mondays.

TOP CHOICE **Family Mall** ICE SKATING
(100 Metre St; ⊙9am-11pm) 'So, what did you do in Iraq?'. 'I went ice-skating!' Yes, not the sort of thing that instantly springs to mind when you think of Iraq but the hyper-glossy, hyper-huge Family Mall contains an **ice-skating rink** (admission ID6000). When you've twirled yourself dizzy (or broken an arm trying) you can shoot things on the **arcade games**, visit a **5D cinema** (that's 3D with added movement and rain showers) or even a **9D cinema** (that's, well, we've no idea really) or head outside to the roller coasters and big wheels. Failing all that you can fill your shopping bags at **Mango** or any other of the numerous brand-name shops, or fill your tummy in one of the Western-style (and priced) coffee shops. Put simply, this is the face of modern Iraqi Kurdistan and therefore shouldn't be missed.

Information

The **Central Bank of Kurdistan** (cnr 60 Meter & Qamishly Sts) and **Rasheed Bank** (Qalat St) can wire money anywhere in the world. Rasheed Bank offers MoneyGram services. Moneychangers can be found opposite the Peace Pigeon Hotel.

Getting There & Away

International flights arrive at **Erbil International Airport** (www.erbilairport.net), 6km northwest of the city centre.

Share taxis to Dohuk cost ID15,000 per person. See the Dohuk section for important safety information on this route. North to Shaqlawa costs ID5000.

Direct share taxis to Sulaymaniyah (ID15,000) travel via the outskirts of the dangerous city of Kirkuk. As with the Erbil–Dohuk route you are in something of a grey area here with security shared between the Kurds and the Iraqi army. Some travellers do take this route and although 99% of the time you'll encounter no problems, things only have to go wrong once for you to find yourself in a very serious situation. For the sake of saving half-an-hour and ID2000 we'd highly recommend that you avoid the Kirkuk route and take the safer northern road via Koya (which is also much more scenic!). Start by taking a share taxi to Koya (ID7000), where you can catch another to Sulaymaniyah (ID10,000).

Getting Around

Taxis within Erbil are cheap and plentiful. A short ride in town should cost between ID3000 to ID5000 and a bit more to the suburbs of Ainkawa.

Taxis from the airport charge US$15 to the city centre. Taxis aren't generally allowed to drive right up to the airport so when you come out of the arrivals hall hop on the free shuttle bus to the check point 1km or so away where you'll find dozens of waiting taxis.

Around Erbil

Sights

Khanzad Castle CASTLE
Located 15km north of Erbil on the road to Shaqlawa, Khanzad Castle dates back to the Soran Period. The stone castle features a squat turret on each of its four corners. Sawtoothed battlements top the turret and main building of the castle. The castle was recently renovated and now looks a little too new.

WORTH A TRIP

KOYA

For most people the small market town of Koya, on the edge of the mountains roughly halfway between Erbil and Sulaymaniyah, is little more than a transit point on the back road between those two cities, but it well rewards a couple of hours further investigation.

On the hill at the top of town are the remains of an Ottoman era **fort**. The high defensive walls are in excellent condition. There's a small **museum** inside, although we can't tell you much about it because when we were here last nobody was able to get the door key to turn in the lock!

Down in the town the traditional covered **souq** (⊙closed Fri & lunchtime) is arguably one of the most interesting in Iraqi Kurdistan. Don't miss the tumbledown **caravanserai** (you'll need some one to point out the entrance to you).

The town has a couple of scrappy places to eat and a cheap hotel.

Salahaddin's Fortress CASTLE
Salahaddin's Fortress (Kurdish: Qalat Salahaddin) is a spectacular ruin perched on a high ridge overlooking two valleys. A small path leads up to several stone walls and five turrets that survive intact. The history of this fortress, also called Deween Castle, is open to debate. According to the KRG Tourism Ministry, it was established by princes of the Zarzariya Tribe, who were associates of Shadi bin Marwan, the grandfather of 12th-century Kurdish conqueror Saladin (Salah ad-Din).

Getting here is the hard part; there are no signs and even locals have never heard of the fortress. It's about 15km north of the city of Salahaddin, itself about 30km northeast of Erbil. From Salahaddin, a scenic drive traverses through a goat-herding region of tiny villages with mud-brick homes.

Warning: the last 5km to the fortress is a gravel road lined by minefields, identified by piles of rocks painted red. Never venture off hard surfaces.

Dukan دوكان

Dukan, 65km northwest of Sulaymaniyah, is a resort town on the banks of the Dukan Lake, the largest man-made lake in Iraq. The lake is a popular place for swimming and boating. Several hotels and holiday cabins have been built around the southern shores of the lake. On Fridays, the banks of the river below are swarming with families enjoying the Kurdish national pastime of picnicking.

Sulaymaniyah السليمانية

053 / POP 700,000

Cosmopolitan Sulaymaniyah (Kurdish: Slemani) is Iraqi Kurdistan's second-largest city, and the most liberal and Westernised city in Iraq. Born in 1784, Sulaymaniyah is a young city by Mesopotamian standards, and that youthful vibrancy shows – by Iraqi standards this city is trendy, fashion forward, chic, sophisticated and free spirited. It has a strong arts and cultural scene with great museums and several universities.

Spread-out Sulaymaniyah feels much bigger than compact Erbil, and aside from the central core you'll probably want to take a taxi everywhere.

History

If Iraq is the cradle of civilisation, Sulaymaniyah is a newborn baby. It was founded in 1784 by Kurdish prince Ibrahim Pasha Babanm. During WWI, the city was the centre of Kurdish nationalism.

The PUK, one of two major political parties in Iraqi Kurdistan, was founded in Sulaymaniyah in 1975. During and after the Iran-Iraq war, Saddam Hussein brutalised Sulaymaniyah's residents until the Kurdish uprising of 1991.

In 1994 civil war broke out between forces of the PUK and the KDP. The fighting between the two went nowhere until 1996, when the KDP made a deal with the devil: with the help of Saddam's Iraqi forces, the KDP captured the PUK-held cities of Erbil and Sulaymaniyah, driving the PUK into Iran. Much of Sulaymaniyah was destroyed in the fighting. Peace finally prevailed in 1998 when Washington mediated a power-sharing deal between KDP leader Massoud Barzani and PUK leader Jalal Talabani.

Today, 'Sulay' as it's called by locals, has been rebuilt into a model city. It is the provincial capital of Sulaymaniyah (the capital and province go by the same name), the cultural centre of the Sorani-speaking Kurds, and an important economic centre of Iraqi Kurdistan.

Sights

TOP CHOICE **Amna Suraka (Red Security)** MUSEUM
(21st St; admission free; 9am-noon & 2-4pm Sat-Thu) The Amna Suraka, Kurdish for Red Security, was once a house of unspeakable horrors. Under Saddam Hussein's regime, this imposing red building served as the northern headquarters of the notorious Iraqi Intelligence Service, or the Mukhabarat. Thousands of people, mainly Kurds, were imprisoned and tortured here. Many more simply vanished. In 1991 the Kurdish Peshmerga attacked and liberated the prison. In 2003 Hero Ibrahim Ahmed, wife of Iraqi President Jalal Talabani, spearheaded a plan to turn the building into the country's first war-crimes museum. The Amna Suraka now stands out as the most impressive museum in Iraq.

Upon entering the complex gates, the first thing you notice is the **Amna Suraka** building itself. Its red facade has been kept exactly as it appeared after the 1991 uprising, pockmarked from bullet holes, shattered windows and blackened from fires. The courtyard contains a **weapons display** of Iraqi tanks, artillery, mortars and other instruments of death. The first stop indoors is the **Hall of Mirrors**, a 50m-long narrow hallway lined by 182,000 shards of mirrored glass, one for every victim of Saddam's Anfal campaign. The ceiling twinkles with around 4500 lights, one for every Kurdish village destroyed under Saddam. The next room features a replica of a traditional **Kurdish village home**.

Passing through exterior corridors covered by barbed wire, you enter the main building that contains several **prison cells** and **torture chambers**. Many rooms contain gruesome life-like sculptures of Kurdish prisoners, created by local artist Kamaran Omer. In one, a Kurdish man is hanging by his wrists from a metal hook, and in another a man is having the soles of his feet beaten. In one of the prison cells is a sculpture of two frightened children. Saddam's henchmen tortured children in order to extract information on their parents. The basement of the museum is a graphic **photo gallery** showing the aftermath of Saddam's chemical attack on Halabja.

Museum guides (one or two speak English) conduct free tours of the complex.

FREE **Slemani Museum** MUSEUM
(Sulaymaniyah Museum; Salim St; ⌚9am-2pm Sat-Thu) This superb museum is a timeline of Mesopotamian history dating back to the Palaeolithic Age from 15,000 BC. The museum is divided into several galleries featuring an array of archaeological artefacts. Some of the more interesting finds include a ceramic coffin containing the skeleton of a 6000-year-old woman found near Dohuk, and a Greek statue of Hercules dating to 334 BC. There is also a fine display of Islamic ceramic arts from the Islamic Golden Age. Most of the exhibits have Kurdish and English signs. At the time of research some renovation work was underway which promised to make the museum even more visitor friendly.

Grand Bazaar MARKET
(along Malawi St; ⌚8am-6pm) Sulaymaniyah's bazaar may be the largest traditional market

Sulaymaniyah

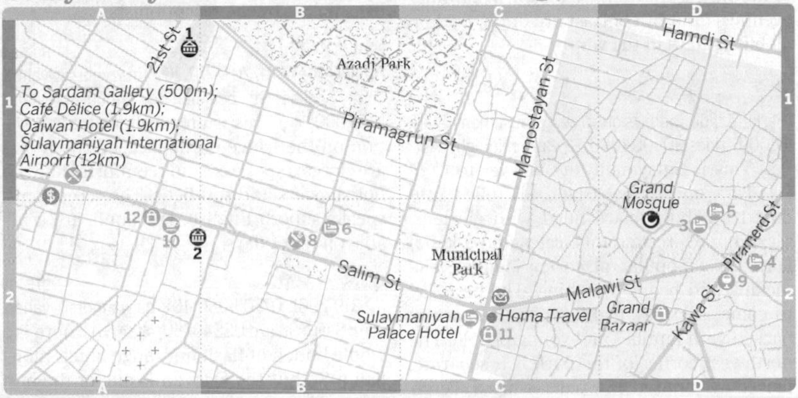

Sulaymaniyah

Sights
1 Amna Suraka A1
2 Slemani Museum A2

Sleeping
3 Hotel Mazy Plaza D2
4 Molawy Hotel D2
5 Pesha Hotel D2
6 Shwan Hotel B2

Eating
7 Pizza & Kebab Shops A1
8 Zalu B2

Drinking
9 Sha'ab Chai Khana D2
10 Zewe Cafeteria A2

Shopping
11 Carpet Jehan Show C2
12 World of Heritages A2

in Iraqi Kurdistan. You can find anything here including and up to the proverbial kitchen sink. This place is huge, stretching nearly 1.5km along Malawi and Goran Sts from the Sulaymaniyah Palace Hotel to Ibrahim Pasha St. The bazaar is an intermingled mix of tiny shops, traditional market stalls and street vendors.

The real heart of the market is the **covered bazaar** between Malawi and Kawa Sts – a chaotic and colourful treat for all five senses. The smells of spices and kebabs waft through the dark narrow alleys, beckoning shoppers into the depths of the bazaar.

FREE **Sardam Gallery** GALLERY
(Salim St; 9am-6pm Sun-Thu) This art gallery, inside the Sardam Publishing House, features rotating exhibits by local Kurdish artists. Most of the work is modern abstract. It's a great place to bump into local, often English-speaking, artists.

PARKS OF SULAYMANIYAH

Sulaymaniyah is a green city blessed with many beautiful public parks, which come to life with a festive buzz on warm summer evenings (and by contrast are quite dead on all but Fridays in the winter).

TOP CHOICE **Azadi Park** PARK
(Parki Azadi; admission free, amusement park ID1000, rides ID500-1000; 8am-midnight Apr-Oct) This is Sulaymaniyah's answer to Central Park and Coney Island all rolled into one. It's a huge place filled with gardens, playgrounds, restaurants, cafes and a small lake. It's a popular place for jogging, picnicking and people-watching. The best day to come is Friday night, when the park is packed with families and young people. The northwest corner of the park is a separate, fenced-in amusement park with a Ferris wheel, kiddie rides and plenty of junk-food vendors.

Municipal Park PARK
(Salim St at Sulaymaniyah Circle) This is a small park popular with the lunchtime crowd from nearby Sulaymaniyah University.

Sarchnar Park PARK
(admission ID1000; 8am-midnight) Northwest of the city, just outside the ring road, this is a large family park with outdoor garden restaurants, a small amusement park with the obligatory Ferris wheel, and a sad little zoo containing such 'exotic' caged animals as dogs, pigeons, squirrels and goats. Most of the amusement park attractions are open only in summer.

Azmar Mountain MOUNTAIN
Further afield, about 6km northeast and above the city, is a stunning picnic spot with million-dinar views.

Sleeping

Sulaymaniyah has an impressive array of places to stay and more are springing up all the time. In general you get more for your money here than in Erbil. There are quite a few budget choices in the bazaar, particularly near the roundabout that intersects Kawa, Malawi, Goran and Piramerd Sts. Plusher midrange hotels are along Salim St.

Pesha Hotel HOTEL $$
(0750 1195 722; off Beekas St; per person ID25,000;) With wardrobes in the rooms and pictures on the wall, this is a step up from the standard cheap Iraqi hotel. Throw in free internet and a very garish reception area and you get an all-round great deal. The only drawback is the lack of English spoken by the receptionists.

Hotel Mazy Plaza HOTEL $
(320 4292, 0770 7772 165; mazyplaza@yahoo.com; Beekas St; per person without breakfast ID20,000;) This is an excellent budget option on the fringe of the bazaar. The rooms are large, spotless and comfortable with hot showers and soft beds. The receptionist speaks superb English. Discounts are available on quiet days.

Qaiwan Hotel HOTEL $$
(319 2961, 0770 5060 401; qaiwanhotel@yahoo.com; Salim St; s/d US$40/50;) There is a whole bunch of flash midrange hotels along Salim St, but the Qaiwan is one of the best value. The rooms are huge and clean with sofas, armchairs and hot water splashing out of the showers. The staff are friendly and all the food in the restaurant (except breakfast) appears to come from local takeaways! It's a five-minute taxi ride from the bazaar.

Molawy Hotel HOTEL $
(312 0147, 0770 8698 373; cnr Malawi & Kawa Sts; per person without breakfast ID15,000;) This ageing but passably clean hotel is in the heart of the bazaar. The surprisingly quiet rooms won't make you scream with joy, but they won't make you recoil in horror either.

Shwan Hotel HOTEL $$
(☎312 2877, 0770 8172 233; hotel.shwan@yahoo.com; off Salim St; d & tw ID50,000; ❄📶) The rooms here are small, but the welcome is big and hearty. Everything is kept spick and span and it's on a quiet side street.

Eating

Many fast-food restaurants serving doughy pizzas and greasy burgers are on Salim St. The **bazaar** is the place to go for cheap grub and there are so many near-identical possibilities selling kebabs and spit-roasted chicken that it would be unfair for us to recommend one over another. There's also a small strip mall of **pizza and kebab shops** near the corner of Salim and 21st Sts that is popular in the evenings.

Café Délice INTERNATIONAL $$
(Salim St; mains ID7000; ⏲9am-9pm) Head down the stairs to this chilled-out cafe-restaurant with its big, soft sofa chairs. It's run by a Kurdish woman who lived in Belgium, and European influences show in the range of pastas, salads and curries that fill the menu (although it's best not to expect them to taste as they do back home). There are also fresh juices, sheesha pipes and fruit teas. It's opposite the Sulaimani Mall Palace.

Zatu IRAQI $
(cnr Salim & 15th Sts; mains ID3000-5000; ⏲noon-midnight) This place, which is directly under the Chrakan Hotel, is famous for its tasty kebabs. Other menu options include shwarmas, grilled chicken and pizza.

Drinking

TOP CHOICE **Sha'ab Chai Khana** CAFE
(Kawa St; ⏲6am-7pm) Follow the stream of local men through the unmarked door of the most famous teahouse in town. It's a traditional smoky establishment where old guys slap dominos loudly on the table and young blokes watch football on the telly. Peruse through the many old books and photos of Sulaymaniyah while drinking tiny, tulip-shaped cups of sweet tea. A local lady wouldn't dream of entering this strictly male-only domain but Western women are generally made very welcome.

Zewe Cafeteria CAFE
(Salim St; ⏲9am-10pm) Relax with a sheesha pipe and some sweet, black tea at this modern 1st-floor teashop. It's next to the Slemani Museum.

Entertainment

Bowling Centre BOWLING
(Malik Mahmoud St; bowling ID5000; ⏲noon-midnight) This mammoth 10-pin bowling alley has 16 lanes, a bar, snack shop and outdoor cafe. The huge upstairs hall contains a video arcade, pool tables, foosball (table football), air hockey and bumper cars.

Shopping

You can find almost anything under the sun at the Grand Bazaar.

World of Heritages ARTS & CRAFTS
(Salim St; ⏲9am-noon & 3-7pm, closed Fri) For something different, this is an eccentric shop selling unique antiques, souvenirs and trinkets.

Carpet Jehan Show ARTS & CRAFTS
(Mamostayan St; ⏲8am-8pm) Has a nice selection of handmade carpets at reasonable prices. It's across from the Sulaymaniyah Palace Hotel.

Information

Money

Most banks can wire money internationally. **Warka Bank** (Salim St; ⏲9am-4pm, closed Fri) offers Western Union services.

Travel Agencies

Homa Travel (☎0770 1534 861; Mamostayan St; ⏲10am-6pm, closed Fri) Agent for Best Van bus tickets to Turkey.

Getting There & Away

International flights arrive at **Sulaymaniyah International Airport** (www.sulairport.net), about 15km west of the city.

Long-distance shared taxis and buses arrive and depart from **Sulaymaniyah Garage**, in the southwest corner of the city just outside the ring road. Drivers will be standing outside their vehicles, yelling the name of their destinations. For important information on the route to Erbil see p171.

Getting Around

Taxis around town are cheap and plentiful and should cost between ID2000 and ID5000 depending on time and destination.

Ahmadawa احمداواه

The resort village of Ahmadawa, 62km southeast of Sulaymaniyah near the Iranian border, is a wonderful place of natural beauty with plenty of opportunities for hiking, swimming and picnicking. Hidden in a deep and narrow green gorge, the resort is surrounded by walnut, pomegranate and fig trees, attracting visitors to their cool shade. A small cascading river runs along the base of the canyon. From the entrance of the gorge, hike up the 3km very rough dirt road to reach a spectacular 30m-high **waterfall**.

On Fridays in spring, summer and autumn, busloads of Kurds in colourful traditional dress descend on Ahmadawa to enjoy weekend picnics, filling the canyon with Kurdish music and the smells of barbecues. There are several kebab restaurants at the entrance to the gorge.

Be very cautious of doing any more ambitious walks around here; the three American hikers infamously arrested and jailed by Iranian authorities in 2009 after walking illegally into Iranian territory and accused of being spies set off from here.

Halabja حلبجة

Mention the name 'Halabja' to Iraqi Kurds and you'll be met with looks of sadness and sorrow. What happened in Halabja on 16 March 1988 was one of the darkest days in Kurdish history.

Halabja was once a bustling city. In the final days of the Iran–Iraq war, it found itself on the front line, occupied by Iranian troops and Kurdish Peshmerga forces allied with Iran. On the morning of 16 March 1988, Saddam Hussein's Ba'athist forces launched a counter strike, bombarding the city with conventional air strikes and artillery. At about 3pm, Iraqi jets flying low overhead began dropping an unusual kind of bomb that left a smell of sweet apples – chemical weapons. In less than 30 minutes, 5000 men, women and children were dead and 7000 injured. Human Rights Watch has declared the massacre an act of genocide.

Nearly 25 years on, Halabja has never fully recovered. It's a poor, run-down village with high rates of poverty and unemployment. As you enter the town, the first thing you'll notice is a small roadside **statue** modelled on the most famous photograph of the massacre, depicting a lifeless elderly man on the ground shielding his dead grandson. The road behind the statue leads to the controversial **Monument of Halabja Martyrs**, a 30m-tall cenotaph and museum. In 2006 villagers stormed the monument and set it on fire, angry that the government was spending money on the dead instead of helping the living. The monument has since been rebuilt.

In **Halabja Cemetery**, thousands of victims of the chemical attack are buried in **mass graves** under giant, black-and-white marble blocks. Nearby, a grassy field contains hundreds of neatly arranged white **headstones** bearing the names of the dead. A sign at the entrance of the cemetery is unforgiving: 'It is not allowed for Ba'athists to enter'.

A new **museum**, which portrays the horror of that day and commemorates those who died, has recently opened. It is not made for pleasant viewing.

UNDERSTAND IRAQ

Iraq Today

Despite uncertainty about its future, Iraq is sowing some seeds of optimism. In 2005 Iraqis elected a transitional government and ratified a new constitution. In 2006 the country held elections to form Iraq's first permanent democratic government, led by Prime Minister Nouri al-Maliki. He has led the country ever since.

In 2007 the tide began to turn against the insurgency. The US deployed 20,000 more troops to quell the violence. Iraqis began to reject the insurgency and by the time the last US servicemen and women left Iraq at the end of 2011 violence had fallen dramatically.

Despite the reduction in violence, Iraq continues to face many obstacles. The fragile coalition government came close to collapse in early 2012; the semi-autonomous Kurdish-controlled area in the north is increasingly going its own sweet way, the status of Kirkuk (which the Kurds want as their capital) remains unsolved and the infrastructure of all but Iraqi Kurdistan remains dilapidated. But despite all these things the very fact that Iraq seems to be putting the years of violence and bloodshed behind it means that Iraqis are now finally starting to look to the future with more confidence than they have had in decades.

History

Ancient Mesopotamia

Iraq's story begins with the Sumerians who flourished in the rich agricultural lands surrounding the Tigris and Euphrates Rivers from around 4000 BC. In 1750 BC, Hammurabi seized power and went on to dominate the annals of the Babylonian empire. He developed the Code of Hammurabi, the first written codes of law in recorded history. Despite constant attacks from the Hittites and other neighbouring powers, Babylon would dominate the region until the 12th century BC, after which it went into a slow decline.

By the 7th century BC, the rival Assyrian civilisation had reached its high point under Ashurbanipal, whose capital at Nineveh was one of the great cities of the world with cuneiform libraries, luxurious royal courts and magnificent bas reliefs that survive to this day. But his expensive military campaigns against Babylonia and other neighbours drained the kingdom of its wealth and manpower. In 612 BC, Nineveh and the Assyrian Empire fell to Babylonian King Nabopolassar.

The Neo-Babylonian Empire returned Babylon to its former glory. Nabopolassar's son, Nebuchadnezzar II, built the famous Hanging Gardens of Babylon and conquered Jerusalem. In 539 BC, Babylon finally fell to the Persian Empire of Cyrus the Great. The Persians were in turn defeated by Alexander the Great, who died in Babylon in 323 BC. For the next 1000 years, Mesopotamia was ruled by a string of empires, among them the Seleucid, Parthian and Sassanid.

Islamic Iraq

In AD 637 the Arab armies of Islam swept north from the Arabian Peninsula and occupied Iraq. Their most important centres became Al-Kufa, Baghdad and Mosul.

In 749 the first Abbasid caliph was proclaimed at Al-Kufa and the Abbasids would go on to make Iraq their own. The founding of Baghdad by Al-Mansur saw the city become, by some accounts, the greatest city in the world (see p554). In 1258 Hulagu – grandson of the feared Mongol ruler Chingiz (Genghis) Khan – laid waste to Baghdad and killed the last Abbasid caliph. Political power in the Muslim world shifted elsewhere.

By 1638, Iraq had come under Ottoman rule. After a period of relative autonomy, the Ottomans centralised their rule in the 19th century, where after Iraqi resentment against foreign occupation crystallised even as the Ottomans undertook a massive program of modernisation. The Ottomans held on until 1920, when the arrival of the British saw Iraq submit to yet another occupying force, which was first welcomed then resented by the Iraqis.

Independent Iraq

Iraq gained its independence from the British in 1932. The period that followed was distinguished by a succession of coups, counter-coups and by the discovery of massive reserves of oil. During WWII, the British again occupied Iraq over fears that the pro-German government would cut oil supplies to Allied forces. On 14 July 1958, the pro-British monarchy was overthrown in a military coup and Iraq became a republic. In 1968 a bloodless coup brought the Ba'ath Party to power.

The 1970s marked a glory decade for Iraq. The oil boom of the 1970s brought wealth and prosperity. Oil profits were heavily invested in education, health care and infrastructure.

Iraq's heyday ended on 16 July 1979, when an ambitious Ba'ath official named Saddam Hussein Abd al-Majid al-Tikriti worked his way into power. Saddam's first action as president was to secure his power by executing political and religious opponents.

Iran–Iraq War

Meanwhile, next door, the Islamic Revolution was busy toppling Iran's pro-Western government. Saddam – a secular Sunni Muslim – became increasingly concerned about the threat of a Shiite revolution in his own country. After several months of sabre rattling, Iraq invaded Iran on 22 September 1980 with the full support of the USA, the Soviet Union and several Arab and European states.

At first, Iraq had the upper hand but soon found itself at an impasse. The eight years of war were characterised by Iranian human-wave infantry attacks and Iraq's use of chemical weapons against Iranian troops and civilians. The Iran–Iraq war ended as a stalemate on 20 August 1988. Each side suffered at least 200,000 deaths and US$100 billion in war debts.

In the closing months of the war, Saddam launched *al-Anfal,* a genocidal campaign against the ethnic Kurds of northern Iraq who had long opposed his regime. The exact number of dead has never been fully ascertained but Iraqi prosecutors put the figure at 182,000 (other sources give a significantly higher figure). In addition around 4500 Kurdish villages were destroyed.

Gulf War & Sanctions

The wounds of the Iran-Iraq war had barely healed when Saddam turned his attention to Kuwait. In July 1990 Saddam accused the Kuwaitis (with some justification) of waging 'economic warfare' against Iraq by attempting to artificially hold down the price of oil and of stealing oil by slant-drilling into the Iraq side of the border. On 2 August 1990, Iraq invaded Kuwait, whose small armed forces were quickly overrun. Six days later, Iraq annexed Kuwait as its 19th province. It was a costly miscalculation.

Led by the US President George W Bush Snr, an international coalition of nearly one million troops from 34 countries amassed on Iraq's borders. On 17 January 1991, Operation Desert Storm began with a massive five-week bombing campaign, followed by a ground offensive that drove Iraqi forces from Kuwait. Widely varied figures estimate that between 20,000 and 100,000 Iraqis were killed. As part of the ceasefire agreement, the UN ordered Iraq to destroy all chemical, nuclear and biological weapons and long-range missile programs.

Shortly before the war ended, Iraqi Shiites and Kurds took up arms against Saddam, encouraged by the impending victory and promises of coalition support. But help never arrived. Saddam's forces quickly crushed the rebellion, leaving thousands more dead. Other Saddam opponents were imprisoned, tortured or simply vanished. Coalition forces later established no-fly zones in southern and northern Iraq to protect the Shiites and Kurds.

In the meantime the UN had imposed a stringent sanctions regime on Iraq. First enforced in August 1990, their original stated purpose was to compel Iraq to withdraw from Kuwait, pay reparations and disclose any weapons of mass destruction. The removal of Saddam, although never officially a goal, was believed by many to be a non-express aim of the sanctions. Whether this is true or not, the sanctions did little to undermine Saddam's regime; they did bring untold misery to the people of Iraq in the form of malnutrition, poverty, inadequate medical care and lack of clean water. The most hard hit group was children. Estimates of the number of children who died due to the effects of the sanctions and collateral effects of war vary hugely, but Unicef estimated the figure to be around 500,000. When Madeleine Albright (at the time US ambassador to the UN) was questioned in 1996 about whether the death of so many children was a price worth paying for the removal of Saddam Hussein she replied, 'I think this is a very hard choice but the price, we think the price is worth it'.

2003 Iraq War

In a 12 September 2002 speech to the UN General Assembly, US President George W Bush Jnr set the stage for war by declaring that Iraq was manufacturing weapons of mass destruction (WMDs) and harbouring Al-Qaeda terrorists, among other claims. Saddam disputed the claims but reluctantly agreed to allow weapons inspectors back into the country. UN inspectors concluded that Iraq had failed to account for all its weapons, but insisted there was no evidence WMDs had existed. Meanwhile, a 'coalition of the willing' led by American and British troops was massing in Kuwait. On 20 March 2003 – without UN authority – the coalition launched its second war on Iraq. Allied forces easily overran Iraqi forces, with relatively few casualties. Baghdad fell on 9 April 2003, but Saddam escaped. On 1 May 2003, Bush declared victory under a banner that read 'Mission Accomplished'. But the war was just beginning.

Allied forces were at first welcomed by Iraqis as liberators. But initial optimism quickly vanished, and it soon became clear that planning for postwar Iraq had been woefully inadequate. Iraq descended into chaos and anarchy. The Iraqi army was disbanded and former Ba'ath party members were excluded from the new Iraqi government, suddenly leaving millions of unemployed men on the streets. The country was spiralling into a guerrilla war with a growing insurgency.

In December 2003, a dishevelled and bearded Saddam was found cowering in a spider hole near his hometown of Tikrit. Saddam was executed in December 2006 for crimes against humanity.

In 2004 things went from bad to worse. The insurgency exploded, led by such groups as Al-Qaeda in Iraq. That same year, photos emerged of American soldiers abusing Iraqi prisoners at Abu Ghraib prison, creating an international backlash against the occupation. Two major battles in the Sunni city of Fallujah did little to stem the bloodshed. On 22 February 2006, the holy Shiite shrine in Samarra was bombed, kicking off a wave of sectarian violence that pitched Iraqi Sunnis and Shiites against one and other and left thousands dead.

The tide finally started to turn in 2007 when the US launched a troop surge that saw an extra 20,000 troops being sent to Iraq. Since then the levels of violence have fallen hugely and foreign troops began to leave. Britain ended its combat operations in 2009 and the US in 2010 with the last US troops leaving at the end of 2011.

By the time of the final US withdrawal, the death toll from the war and subsequent insurgency in Iraq had reached an estimated 105,000 to 115,000 Iraqi civilians (based on figures provided by Iraq Body Count – other sources give a different figure), 10,125 Iraqi soldiers and police, 4800 coalition soldiers (mostly from the US) and 150 journalists. Tens of thousands more have been injured or maimed. The UN High Commissioner on Refugees estimates at least 3.4 million Iraqis have either fled the country or are internally displaced.

LONELY PLANET & THE IRAQ WAR

In a 2007 BBC documentary, former US ambassador Barbara Bodine said that an outdated copy of Lonely Planet's *Middle East* guide was used during the planning stages of the Iraq invasion and postwar reconstruction. 'It's a great guidebook, but it shouldn't be the basis of an occupation', she told the BBC.

People & Society

National Psyche

Iraq is one of the most multicultural and socially diverse countries in the Middle East. About 75% to 80% of the population is Arab, 15% to 20% Kurdish and the rest is made up of Turkomans, Assyrians, Persians, Chaldeans, Palestinians, Yazidis and nomadic Bedouins. Islam is the official religion of Iraq. Muslims make up 97% of the population – about 60% to 65% Shiite and 35% to 40% Sunni. There are also small but historically significant communities of Christians who belong to various sects including Chaldeans, Assyrians, Syrian and Roman Catholics. Other religious minorities are the Yazidis, Sabeans, the Mandeans (followers of John the Baptist) and a handful of Jews.

No matter what the ethnic and religious background, you would think that decades of war would have left all Iraqis demoralised and bitter. On the contrary, Iraqis are resilient, warm and welcoming people. Nowhere is this truer than in Iraqi Kurdistan, where the Kurds are renowned for their hospitality.

Iraqis are well known for their sense of humour, even in the face of suffering and misery and they have an acute sense of pride and honour. It is a country where formality and politeness are all important.

Arabic and Kurdish are the official languages of Iraq. Arabic is spoken by 80% of the population. The Kurds speak a language that is widely known as Kurdish, but in reality Kurds speak one of two Indo-European languages: Kurmanji and Sorani. In Iraqi Kurdistan, English education is now compulsory, so many young people understand at least a bit of English.

Democracy has brought capitalism – and materialism – to the country. Iraqis have embraced Western pop culture and there's nothing many of them like better than an evening out in a flash shopping mall full of Western designer goods (or a pretty good imitation of them anyway!). With the grip of violence now loosening and the economy improving, Iraqis are looking to the future with a guarded sense of optimism.

Daily Life

Iraqi life revolves around the family and extended family, a bond that took on added significance during years of war, sanctions and international isolation. Family dominates all aspects of Iraqi life, with great importance on honour and reputation. It's a paternalistic, patriarchal and conservative society, especially in rural areas. Iraq is primarily a tribal society. Allegiance to one's ethnic group often takes precedent over any party, provincial or national loyalties, and ethnic interests play an important role in the shaping of government and public policy.

The role of women is complex. Legally, men and women have the same rights. Women are commonplace in government, politics, media, private business and universities. Nevertheless, women are still expected to take on the traditional role as wife and mother. Arranged marriages are the norm, usually between first cousins. So-called honour killings are not uncommon. The sectarian violence that has swept through 'Arab Iraq' has forced many women back into the home and to adopt a more conservative style of dress. In the cities of Iraqi Kurdistan things are more relaxed and women play a bigger part in daily street life. Wherever they are in Iraq, men and women who are not related socialise separately.

Many an Iraqi's favourite pastime is picnicking. The Kurds in particular have turned the humble picnic into an art form and every Friday throughout the warmer months of the year Kurds descend en masse to the nearest park or beauty spot for a family picnic.

SURVIVAL GUIDE

Directory A–Z

Accommodation

For a developing country emerging from decades of war, Iraq is a surprisingly expensive place. Hotel rooms that went for US$5 before the war are now going for US$50. It all comes down to supply and demand.

For the purpose of this guide, we are assuming that readers are only travelling to Iraqi Kurdistan.

The Kurdish Regional Government is focusing all its energies on building four- and five-star luxury hotels. Thankfully, family-run budget hotels are quite common. Older hotels usually have squat toilets, but Western toilets are increasingly common, especially in newer midrange and top-end establishments.

Prices in this book are for double rooms in high season and include bathrooms, breakfast and taxes unless otherwise indicated.

$ less than ID40,000 (US$35)

$$ ID40,000 to ID80,000 (US$35 to US$70)

$$$ more than ID80,000 (US$70)

PRACTICALITIES

» Iraq uses the metric system for weights and measures.

» The electrical current is 230V AC, 50Hz. Wall sockets are generally the round, two-pin European type, but expect to encounter some three-prong, British-type plugs in southern Iraq.

» For the news in English, check out the independent *Aswat al-Iraq* (www.aswataliraq.info).

» Of the international news broadcasters *Al-Jazeera* (www.aljazeera.com) is the best for Iraqi-based news and features in English.

Business Hours

Officially, government offices, banks and private businesses are usually open 8am to 6pm Sunday to Wednesday and until 1.30pm on Thursday. Unofficially, business hours in Iraq are whenever the employees feel like showing up to work.

Embassies & Consulates

Most countries strongly advise their citizens not to travel to anywhere in Iraq except Iraqi Kurdistan (though some also advise against this and if your country is one of these your travel insurance will be invalid – take a special Iraq policy). Foreign embassies in Iraq can only provide limited consular services, if any.

Australia (☎01 538 2104; www.iraq.embassy.gov.au; Baghdad International Zone)

France (☎071 819 96; www.ambafrance-iq.org; Baghdad)

Germany (☎01-543 1470; www.bagdad.diplo.de; al-Mansour district, Baghdad)

Netherlands (☎01-778 2571; iraq.nlembassy.org; Baghdad International Zone)

UK (☎0790 191 1684; http://ukiniraq.fco.gov.uk/en; Baghdad International Zone)

USA (Map p158; ☎0760 030 3000; iraq.usembassy.gov; Baghdad International Zone)

Food

Prices in this book represent the cost of a standard main-course dish.

$ less than ID5000 (US$4)

$$ ID5000 to ID10,000 (US$4 to US$8)

$$$ more than ID10,000 (US$8)

Internet Access

Most big-city internet cafes, which typically keep very long hours, are filled with cigarette smoke and charge about ID1500 to ID2000 per hour. In Iraqi Kurdistan an increasing number of midrange and top-end hotels provide wireless internet access.

Money

With a few rare exceptions, Iraq is a cash country. You should plan to bring enough cash – preferably US dollars – to last your entire trip.

The official unit of currency is the Iraqi dinar (ID). Current banknotes include 50, 250, 500, 1000, 5000, 10,000 and 25,000 dinars. Coins are no longer used. US dollars are also widely accepted. Businesses often list prices in both dinars and dollars. US notes should be undamaged and printed after 2003.

In Iraqi Kurdistan, as in the rest of Iraq, dollars are king, but euros, British pounds and Turkish lira can usually be changed in larger centres. Money can be changed in banks, but for the best exchange rate, hit one of the street-corner exchange stands and look for the guys holding giant wads of cash.

ATMs are starting to pop up, but at the time of writing, most only work for accounts held in Iraq or, more likely, they just don't work at all. Credit cards and travellers cheques are even more useless. Many banks now offer international transfers. MoneyGram and Western Union money wire services can be found in Baghdad, Erbil and Sulaymaniyah.

BUDGET

Prices in Iraqi Kurdistan are reasonable. A basic room with attached bathroom can always be found for ID20,000 or even less and a cheap meal consisting of various salads, kebabs, bread and tea can be had for ID7000 to ID9000. The one thing that isn't that cheap is transport, but as distances in Iraqi Kurdistan are short even this isn't going to break the bank. A seat in a share taxi between Erbil to Sulayamaniya is ID15,000.

Public Holidays

In addition to the main Islamic holidays (p624), Shiite Muslims also observe a number of other religious holidays. Iraq also observes the following:

Nowruz (21 March) Kurdish New Year, Iraqi Kurdistan only.

Baghdad Liberation Day (9 April) Anniversary of the fall of Saddam Hussein's regime in 2003.

Ceasefire Day (8 August) End of Iran-Iraq war.

Safe Travel

We've said it once (p156) and we'll say it again: Iraq is a war zone. In Iraqi Kurdistan, violence and crime are rare, but not unheard of. Take the same precautions you'd take anywhere. Open hostility towards Western visitors – including Americans – is rare in Iraqi Kurdistan. Check points are common, so you should carry your passport with you at all times.

Telephone

The country code for Iraq is ☎964, followed by the local area code (minus the zero), then the subscriber number. Due to the poor state of Iraq's landline telephones, most residents and businesses rely on mobile phones. Considering the mobile phone has only been around since 2003, Iraq has a surprisingly reliable and widespread network. The main service providers are Iraqna, AsiaCell and Korek. SIM cards and pay-as-you-go phones are widely available.

Visas

Visas are required for everyone entering Iraq.

The Republic of Iraq issues visas for Arab regions of the country such as Baghdad and Basra, and they are only available to people with official business in the country such as journalists, diplomats, contractors and aid workers. Visas must be obtained prior to departing your home country.

The Kurdish Regional Government issues its own tourist visa, good for travelling within Iraqi Kurdistan only. Citizens of most countries, including Australia, the EU, New Zealand and USA, are automatically issued free, 10-day tourist visas at the point of entry. Thirty-day visa extensions can be obtained in Erbil at the **Directorate of Residency** (Shlama Rd, Ainkawa; ⏰8am-3pm, closed Fri). in the Ministry of Interior satellite building.

Women Travellers

Iraqi Kurdistan is safe for female travellers, and women are generally treated with courtesy and respect. Still, we recommend that it is best to always travel in pairs or groups. As in most parts of the Middle East, it's im portant to dress conservatively – no bare shoulders or legs, cleavage or other excessive skin should be on display. Iraqi Kurdistan is a secular society, so there is no need to cover your hair. Western clothing is common throughout Iraq.

Getting There & Away

Air

Iraqi Kurdistan has two international airports: Erbil and Sulaymaniyah. Only those

USEFUL WEBSITES

The **Thorn Tree** (www.lonelyplanet.com) travel forum on Lonely Planet's website is easily the best place to go (even if we do say so!) for bang-up-to-date information on Iraqi travel.

Joe's Trippin': Iraq (http://joestrippin.blogspot.com/search/label/iraq) Blog of a ridiculously well-travelled Canadian living in Iraqi Kurdistan. Full of great ideas of things to see and do.

British Museum Iraq Project (www.britishmuseum.org/iraq) The British Museum's project to protect and preserve Iraq's cultural heritage.

Iraq Updates (http://iraqupdates.com) Excellent pay-for website with the latest news and incident reports.

Iraqi Kurdistan Tourism Ministry (http://tourismkurdistan.com)

Iraqi Ministry of Foreign Affairs (http://mofa.gov.iq) Includes news and listings of Iraqi embassies abroad.

Kurdish Regional Government (http://krg.org)

The Other Iraq (http://theotheriraq.com) Focusing on all things Kurdish.

UNAMI (www.uniraq.org) UN Assistance Mission for Iraq.

who absolutely *must* fly into Baghdad should do so. Flying anywhere into Iraq except Iraqi Kurdistan is very expensive due to high insurance costs and limited competition.

Austrian Airlines (www.aua.com) Flies from Vienna to Erbil and Baghdad.

Emirates (www.emirates.com) Flies from Amman and Dubai to Baghdad, Erbil, Sulaymaniyah and Basra.

Iraqi Airways (www.iraqiairways.co.uk) Connects Baghdad to a number of Middle Eastern cities as well as London – reliability is not its forte.

Lufthansa (www.lufthansa.com) Flies from Frankfurt to Erbil.

Pegasus (www.flypgs.com) One of the cheapest ways of getting to Iraqi Kurdistan by air is by flying first to İstanbul (Turkey) and then on to Erbil with this Turkish budget airline.

Royal Jordanian (www.rj.com) Flies from Amman and Dubai to Baghdad, Erbil, Sulaymaniyah and Basra.

Turkish Airlines (www.thy.com) Flies between İstanbul and Baghdad, Erbil and Sulaymaniyah.

Land

BORDER CROSSINGS

Iraq is bordered by six countries. At the time of writing, the only safe overland crossings are the Ibrahim Khalil border crossing between Silopi, Turkey and Zakho, Iraq and the Iran-Iraq border crossings at Haji Omaran and Panjwin (note that you can only enter Iran with a pre-arranged visa). Of the Iranian border crossings, (which are much less used by foreign tourists), the Haji Omaran crossing is by far the easiest of the two in regards to transport connections, but whichever you use it's likely to involve some hitching (note that hitching is never completely safe in any country and we do not recommend it). All other borders are dangerous no-go zones.

Note that you cannot cross from Iraqi Kurdistan into the rest of Iraq without a valid Iraqi visa, which independent travellers are highly unlikely to get and even if you did, the overland crossing would be very dangerous.

Ibrahim Khalil

This very busy border crossing can be quite slow to get across (allow an hour for crossing into Iraq and up to three hours crossing into Turkey), but it's otherwise a breeze. Taxis in Silopi will take you to the Iraqi side of the border and handle all formalities for you. The price is set at US$50 per taxi. From the Iraqi side of the border taxis are available into Zakho.

A note of caution. When crossing from Iraq into Turkey taxi drivers will do their utmost to get you to smuggle boxes of cigarettes over the border for them. It goes without saying that agreeing to do this isn't a very clever idea. You should never for an instant leave your bags unattended or the driver is likely to stuff ciggies into your baggage. They will also hide packets of cigarettes all over the car which the Turkish customs officials, who know perfectly well what is going on, will largely pretend not to notice.

It's also possible to travel direct from Erbil to Diyarbakir in southeast Turkey in one clean sweep by bus. **Best Van** (US$30) buses leave Erbil daily at 4pm. Tickets can be bought from a number of agents around Erbil, including from **İstanbul Iletisim** (10 Metre St) opposite the Peace Pigeon Hotel.

Getting Around

Air

Iraqi Airways flies several domestic routes, but it is so unreliable it's not worth it.

Bus

Iraq's bus transport network is very poor. The few routes that exist are crowded and unsafe.

Local Transport

Taxis are the main mode of public transport in Iraq. In cities, they are cheap and plentiful, usually costing no more than ID5000. For intercity travel within Iraqi Kurdistan, you have two choices: private taxi or cheaper, shared taxis. Shared taxis depart and arrive from a city 'garage', or large parking lot; drivers will be standing outside their vehicle, yelling the name of their destination. Shared taxis leave when they are full. Expect to pay between ID5000 to ID20,000. When travelling between major cities in Iraqi Kurdistan, ensure you stay within Kurdish Peshmerga-controlled territory. Agree on price and route before getting in.

Israel & the Palestinian Territories

Includes »

Best for Nature

- » Ein Gedi (p240)
- » Makhtesh Ramon (p244)
- » Hula Valley (p237)
- » Red Sea Snorkelling (p247)

Best for Culture

- » Israel Museum (p198)
- » Tel Aviv's theatres (p213)
- » Tsfat's art galleries (p235)
- » Ramallah (p250)

Why Go?

At the intersection of Asia, Europe and Africa – geographically, culturally and even botanically – Israel and the Palestinian Territories have been a meeting place of cultures, empires and religions since the dawn of history. Cradle of Judaism and Christianity, and sacred to Muslims and Baha'is, the Holy Land offers visitors the opportunity to immerse themselves in the richness and variety of their own religious traditions, as well as to discover the beliefs, rituals and architecture of other faiths. Distances are short, so you can relax on a Mediterranean beach one day, spend the next floating in the mineral-rich waters of the Dead Sea or rafting down the Jordan River, and the day after that scuba diving in the Red Sea. Hikers can follow spring-fed streams as they tumble towards the Jordan, discover verdant oases tucked away in the arid bluffs above the Dead Sea, and explore the multicoloured sandstone formations of Makhtesh Ramon.

When to Go

Jerusalem

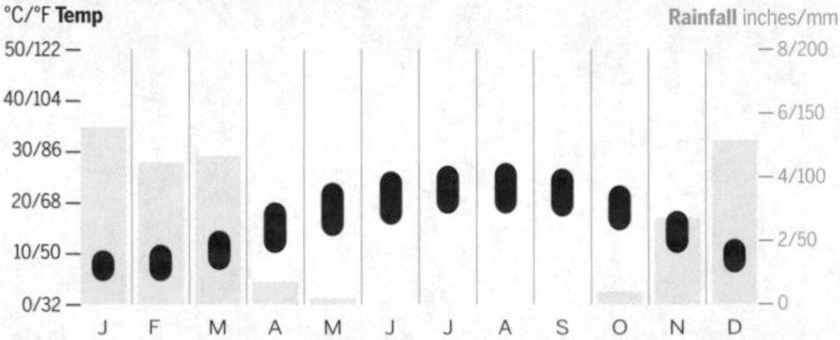

Feb–Apr Hillsides and valleys are carpeted with wildflowers; the ideal season for hiking.

Jul–Aug Warm and dry in Jerusalem, humid in Tel Aviv, infernal at the Dead Sea and Eilat.

Sep–Oct Jewish holidays generate a spike in domestic tourism – and room prices.

Connections

For onward travel to Egypt, the only crossing currently open to travellers is at Taba, on the Red Sea 7km south of Eilat. If you're heading to Jordan, you have three options: Allenby/King Hussein Bridge, just east of Jericho; the Jordan River/Sheikh Hussein crossing, 30km south of the Sea of Galilee; or the Yitzhak Rabin/Wadi Araba crossing, 4km northeast of Eilat/Aqaba. Travel to the Gaza Strip may be possible from Egypt.

ITINERARIES

Ten Days

Spend three days exploring the wonders of **Jerusalem**, then take the slow train to **Tel Aviv** and spend a couple of days in cafes, at museums, cycling, and on the beach. Rent a car, if you can, and head north, spending two days at the **Sea of Galilee** and hiking at **Yehudiya** or **Banias**. Finally, drive west to **Haifa** to visit the gorgeous **Baha'i Gardens**, then down the coast to the ancient ruins of **Caesarea**. From Tel Aviv, fly home or head by bus to **Eilat** and, via the Taba border crossing, to **Sinai**, Egypt.

Two Weeks

From **Jerusalem** take a day trip below sea level to **Qumran**, where the Essenes hid the Dead Sea Scrolls, and to **Masada**, where Jewish Zealots defied the Roman legions. Then head south to friendly, engaging **Bethlehem** and the troubled city of **Hebron**. To the northeast there's **Mt Tabor**, with its inspirational views, and **Nazareth**, Jesus' boyhood stomping ground. Continue northeast to the **Sea of Galilee** and to spiritual **Tsfat** (Safed), centre of Kabbalah (Jewish mysticism).

Essential Food & Drink

» **Amba** Iraqi-style mango chutney

» **Bourekas** Flaky Balkan pastries filled with Bulgarian cheese, spinach or mushrooms

» **Challah** Braided bread traditionally eaten by Jews on the Sabbath

» **Cholent** A heavy meat and potato stew simmered overnight and served for Sabbath lunch

» **Labneh** Thick, creamy yoghurt cheese, often smothered in olive oil and sprinkled with zaatar

» **Sabich** A pita pocket filled with fried eggplant, boiled potato, hard-boiled egg, tahina, amba and freshly chopped vegies

» **Schug** Yemenite hot chili paste

» **Zaatar** A spice blend that includes hyssop, sumac and sesame seeds

AT A GLANCE

» **Currency** Israeli new shekel (NIS or ILS)

» **Mobile Phones** Generally excellent 900/1800 MHz cell-phone coverage

» **Money** ATMs widely available in Israel, less so in the Palestinian Territories

» **Visas** On-arrival visas available to most nationalities

Fast Facts

» **Capitals** Jerusalem (I), Ramallah (PT)

» **Country Codes** ☎972 (I), ☎972 or ☎970 (PT)

» **Languages** Hebrew and Arabic (I), Arabic (PT)

» **Official Names** State of Israel, Palestinian National Authority

» **Populations** Israel 7.8 million, West Bank 2.7 million, Gaza 1.7 million

Exchange Rates

Australia	A$1	3.90NIS
Euro Zone	€1	5.0NIS
Jordan	JD1	5.33NIS
UK	UK£1	6.12NIS
USA	US$1	3.78NIS

For current exchange rates see www.xe.com.

Resources

» **Israel Nature & Parks Authority** (www.parks.org.il)

» **This Week in Palestine** (www.thisweekinpalestine.com)

» **Israel Ministry of Tourism** (www.goisrael.com)

Israel & the Palestinian Territories Highlights

1. Gaze at the architectural magnificence of the **Dome of the Rock** (p192), Jerusalem's most recognisable symbol
2. Visit the **Church of the Holy Sepulchre** (p191), Christendom's holiest site and a unique piece of architecture built over a period of centuries
3. Ascend the Snake Path before dawn and watch the sun rise from atop **Masada** (p241)
4. Swim in the warm Mediterranean and watch the bods at Tel Aviv's **beaches** (p207)
5. Explore the nooks and crannies of the **Church of the Nativity** (p253) in Bethlehem
6. Float in the briny, soothing waters of the **Dead Sea** (p240)
7. Wander the underground passages of **Akko**, an extraordinary walled city-on-the-sea (p223)
8. Take a refreshing dip in the spring-water pools of **Ein Gedi** oasis (p240)
9. Stop to smell the roses in Haifa's spectacular **Baha'i Gardens** (p219)
10. Hike amid the sheer cliffs and coloured sands of **Makhtesh Ramon** (p244)

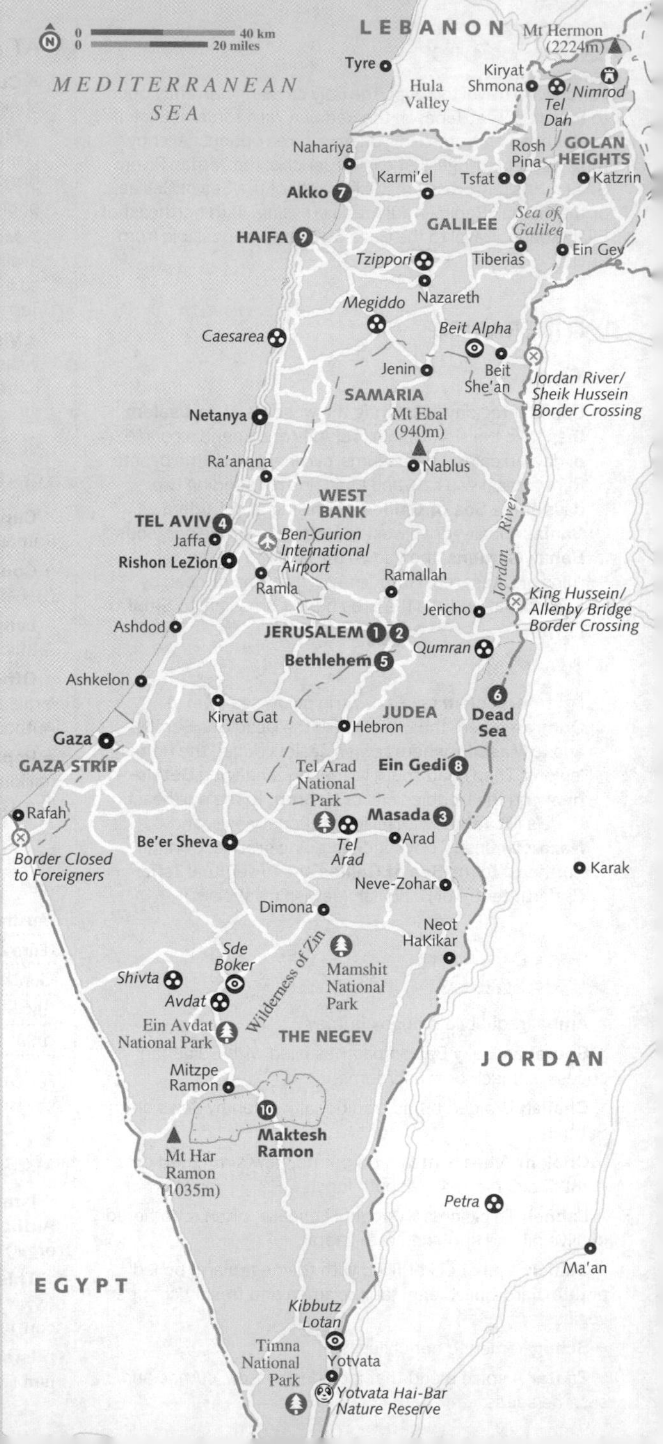

JERUSALEM

القدس ירושלים

02 / POP 729,100

Jerusalem has been seducing travellers, pilgrims and curiosity seekers since time immemorial. Holy to Jews, Christians and Muslims, the city is overflowing with sites of intense religious importance, not the least of which are the Dome of the Rock, the Western Wall and the Church of the Holy Sepulchre. Even for the nonreligious, it's hard not to be moved by the emotions and history that come alive in the narrow alleyways of the Old City.

History

According to the American historian Eric H Cline (in his 2004 book *Jerusalem Besieged*), Jerusalem has been destroyed at least twice, placed under siege 23 times, attacked another 52 times and captured and recaptured 44 times.

The first settlement on the site of Jerusalem was a small Jebusite village situated south of Mt Moriah (today Al-Haram ash-Sharif/Temple Mount), where the Bible says Abraham almost sacrificed his son Isaac. In 997 BC King David captured the city and made it his capital. His son, King Solomon, built the First Temple. This was destroyed in 586 BC by the Babylonian king Nebuchadnezzar, who exiled the Jews to Babylonia. In 538 BC they were allowed to return by Cyrus the Great, and almost immediately began construction of the Second Temple, which was consecrated in 516 BC.

Power in Jerusalem shifted between Jewish rulers, such as the Maccabees, and various regional empires, until the Romans took control in 63 BC, installing Herod the Great as king of Judea. He launched a massive building campaign, significantly expanding the Second Temple. The city was then ruled by a series of procurators; it was the fifth of these, Pontius Pilate, who ordered the crucifixion of Jesus.

Growing Jewish discontent with Roman rule exploded in AD 66 with the Great Jewish Revolt (the First Jewish–Roman War), which ended with the sacking of Jerusalem and the destruction of the Second Temple in AD 70. After the Bar Kochba Rebellion (AD 132–35), the Jews were banished from Jerusalem. Emperor Hadrian razed the city and rebuilt it as Aelia Capitolina – the street grid forms the basis of today's Old City.

During the Byzantine era (4th to early 7th century AD), Christianity became the official state religion, forcing the conversion of many local Jews and Samaritans. Many Christian shrines were built; work on the Church of the Holy Sepulchre, for instance, commenced in AD 326.

In AD 638 Byzantine Jerusalem fell to a new power, Islam, and came under the sway of Arab civilisation. The Dome of the Rock, instantly recognisable thanks to its gleaming gold dome, was completed in AD 691. But despite its significance to Islam, Jerusalem's political and economic fortunes fell into decline, the result of the city's distance from the imperial capitals of Damascus and Cairo.

In the 11th century, Palestine fell to the Seljuk Turks, who stopped Christian pilgrims from visiting Jerusalem. The response of Western European Christians was a series of Crusades – and Crusader kingdoms – that lasted from 1095 to 1270. The Crusaders took Jerusalem in 1099, but lost it in 1187 to Saladin (Salah ad-Din), Kurdish founder of the Muslim Ayyubid dynasty.

In 1250 the city came under the influence of the Mamluks, successors to the Ayyubids, who ruled from Egypt and turned the city into a centre of Islamic learning. In 1517 the Ottoman Turks absorbed Jerusalem into their expanding empire, where it would remain, something of a backwater, for the next 400 years. Sultan Süleyman the Magnificent (r 1520–66) built the walls that still surround the Old City.

In the 19th century the first road linking Jerusalem with Jaffa was built, greatly increasing the number of Jewish and Christian pilgrims. By about 1850, Jews constituted the majority of the city's 25,000 residents. The first neighbourhood built outside the walls of the Old City was Yemin Moshe, established in 1860. Access to the city became quick and easy with the completion of the Jaffa–Jerusalem rail line in 1892.

The British captured Jerusalem from the Ottomans in December 1917 and later made it the capital of the British Mandate of Palestine. Tensions between Jews and Arabs flared in the 1920s and 1930s. After the British left Palestine in 1948, fighting between the new State of Israel and Jordan's Arab Legion resulted in the city partition. West Jerusalem became the capital of Israel; East Jerusalem, including the entire Old City, was annexed by Jordan.

Jerusalem was reunified after Israel captured the eastern part of the city during the 1967 Six Day War. Shortly after the war, Israel annexed East Jerusalem, declaring the entire city to be its 'eternal capital'. The Palestinians claim East Jerusalem as the capital of a future independent state of Palestine. Israel's Separation Fence – in many places around Jerusalem an 8m-high cement wall – cuts East Jerusalem off from the West Bank.

Sights

Jerusalem is divided into three distinct parts: the walled Old City, with its four quarters; the predominantly Arab neighbourhoods of East Jerusalem; and the Israeli New City, also known as West Jerusalem.

Jerusalem

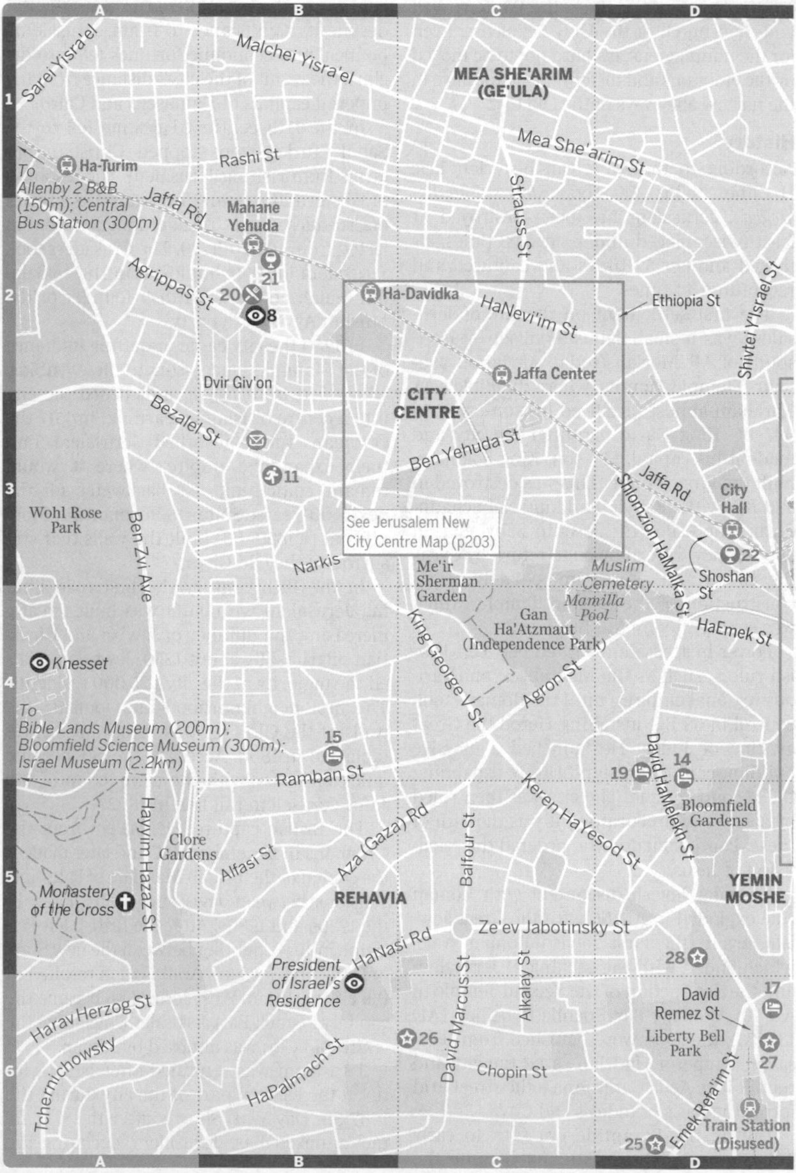

OLD CITY

Protected by 16th-century stone ramparts, the magical, mysterious Old City is divided into Jewish, Muslim, Christian and Armenian quarters, each with a distinct and intoxicating atmosphere. The sturdy Old City walls are the legacy of Süleyman the Magnificent, who built them between 1537 and 1542.

Above all, the Old City is a holy place – the Western Wall, the Dome of the Rock and the Church of the Holy Sepulchre are hardly more than a stone's throw from each other.

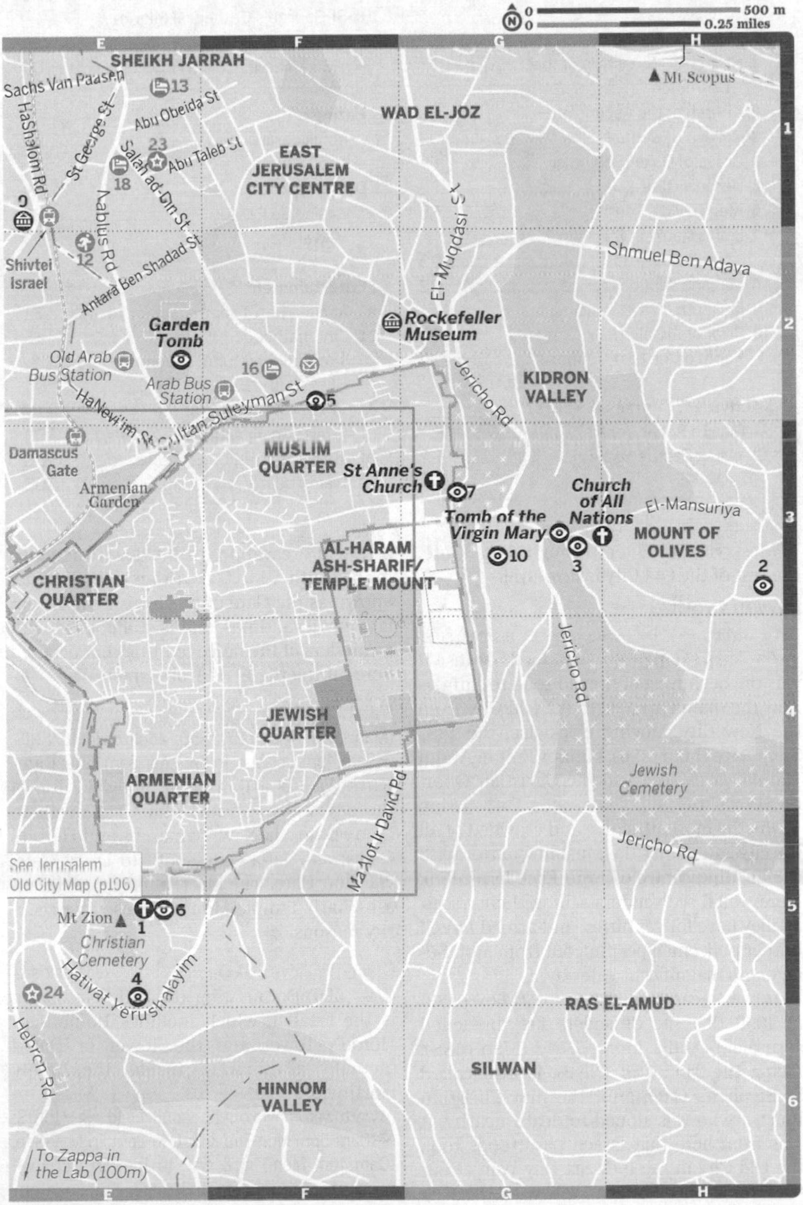

Jerusalem

Top Sights

Church of All Nations	H3
Garden Tomb	E2
Rockefeller Museum	F2
St Anne's Church	G3
Tomb of the Virgin Mary	G3

Sights

1	Church & Monastery of the Dormition	E5
2	Church of the Ascension	H3
3	Garden of Gethsemane	G3
4	Grave of Oskar Schindler	E5
5	Herod's Gate	F2
6	King David's Tomb	E5
7	Lion's Gate (St Stephen's Gate)	G3
8	Mahane Yehuda Market	B2
9	Museum on the Seam	E1
10	Pillar of Absalom	G3
	Room of the Last Supper	(see 6)

Activities, Courses & Tours

11	Gerard Behar Centre	B3
12	YMCA East Jerusalem	E2

Sleeping

13	American Colony Hotel	E1
14	King David Hotel	D4
15	Little House in Rehavia	B4
16	Rivoli Hotel	F2
17	St Andrew's Guesthouse	D6
18	St George's Cathedral Pilgrim Guesthouse	E1
19	YMCA Three Arches Hotel	D4

Eating

20	Itchikidana	B2

Drinking

21	Casino de Paris	B2
22	Mikveh	D3

Entertainment

23	Al-Hakawati Theatre	E1
24	Cinematheque	E5
25	International Cultural Centre for Youth	D6
26	Jerusalem Centre for the Performing Arts	C6
27	Khan Theatre	D6
28	Train Theatre	D5

Most visitors enter through Jaffa Gate; the rest of the Old City is downhill.

CITY WALLS & GATES

City Gates HISTORIC SITES

Jaffa Gate (Map p196), so named because it was the beginning of the old road to Jaffa, is now the main entrance to the Old City from the New City. Moving clockwise, the 1887 **New Gate** (Map p196), built by Sultan Abdul Hamid, gives access to the Christian Quarter. Down the hill, **Damascus Gate** (Map p196), the most attractive and crowded of all the city gates, links the Muslim Quarter with the bustling centre of Arab East Jerusalem. Here, you'll see vendors selling their wares, as they have for centuries, and armed Israeli border policemen peeping out from atop Süleyman's magnificent gateway.

It was near **Herod's Gate** (Map p188) in 1099 that the Crusaders first breached Jerusalem's walls. **Lion's Gate** (Map p188), facing the Mount of Olives, is also called St Stephen's Gate, after the first Christian martyr, who was stoned to death nearby. It was from here that Israeli paratroops took the Old City in the 1967 Six Day War. **Dung Gate** links the Western Wall with the City of David excavations, a bit down the slope to the south. **Zion Gate** (Map p196) became known as the Gate of the Jewish Quarter in late medieval times, and is still pocked with reminders of the fierce fighting that occured here during the 1948 Arab–Israeli War.

Ramparts Walk WALK

(Map p196; 02-627 7550; adult/child 16/8NIS; 9am-4pm Oct-Mar, to 5pm Apr-Sep) The Ramparts Walk is a 1km jaunt along the top of the city walls – from Jaffa Gate north to Lion's Gate, via New, Damascus and Herod's Gates; and Jaffa Gate south to Dung Gate, via Zion Gate. The stretch along Al-Haram ash-Sharif/Temple Mount is closed for security reasons.

Citadel (Tower of David) HISTORIC SITE

(Map p196) Dominating the Jaffa Gate area is the Citadel, which includes Roman-era Herod's Tower and the Tower of David (actually a minaret). Inside, the highly worthwhile **Tower of David Museum** (www.towerofdavid.org.il; adult/child 30/15NIS; 10am-5pm Mon-Thu & Sat, to 2pm Fri May-Sep, 10am-4pm Mon-Thu & Sat, to 1pm Fri Oct-Apr), presents the entire history of Jerusalem in a concise and easily digestible format. Among the highlights: a scale model of Jerusalem, made in the late 19th century and discovered almost 100 years later, forgotten in a Geneva warehouse.

CHRISTIAN QUARTER

Jerusalem's Christian Quarter, to the left as you enter Jaffa Gate, is an attractive blend of clean streets, souvenir stalls, hospices and religious institutions belonging to 20 different Christian denominations.

Church of the Holy Sepulchre CHURCH
(Map p196; ⌚4.30am-8pm) The centrepiece of the Christian Quarter is this sombre, exuberantly decorated church, at the site also known as Calvary or Golgotha – this is where the Catholic, Greek Orthodox, Ethiopian and Coptic churches believe Jesus was crucified, buried and resurrected. The Via Dolorosa (see p193) ends here. The original Byzantine church was destroyed by the mad Caliph Hakim in 1009, extensively rebuilt by the Crusaders, and tweaked by numerous others over the years. To keep the peace between the church's notoriously fractious Christian denominations, a Muslim family keeps the keys, unlocking the doors each morning and securing them again at night. Open daily to anyone who's modestly dressed.

Ethiopian Monastery CHURCH
(Map p196; ⌚daylight hr) Located in the northwest corner of the Holy Sepulchre complex, where a few Ethiopian monks reside in a highly atmospheric medieval cloister.

Lutheran Church of the Redeemer CHURCH
(Map p196; ⌚9am-1pm & 1.30-5pm Mon-Sat) Built in 1898, this church is famed for its excellent views over the Old City (from the tower).

ARMENIAN QUARTER & MT ZION

Armenia was the first nation to officially embrace Christianity when their king converted in AD 303. When the Armenians' kingdom disappeared at the end of the 4th century, they adopted Jerusalem as their spiritual capital and have had an uninterrupted presence here ever since. The city's Armenian population, now numbered at about 1500, grew significantly in the early 1900s, when immigrants arrived – both to work on re-tiling the Dome of the Rock and to escape Ottoman Turkish persecution.

St James' (Jacques') Cathedral CHURCH
(Map p196; Armenian Orthodox Patriarchate Rd; ⌚6-7.30am & 3-3.30pm Mon-Fri, 2.30-3pm Sat & Sun) The glowing lamps that hang from the ceiling and the richly patterned carpets strewn across the floors give St James' Cathedral a palpable aura of mystery. The cathedral is only open for services; the most impressive are held on Sunday when nine hooded priests take part.

FREE Room of the Last Supper RELIGIOUS SITE
(Map p188; ⌚8.30am-5.30pm) From the Armenian Quarter, Zion Gate leads out to Mt Zion, where you'll find a room believed to be where Jesus' last supper took place.

FREE King David's Tomb RELIGIOUS SITE
(Map p196; ⌚8am-6pm Sun-Thu, to 2pm Fri) At the back of the same building as the Room of the Last Supper.

Church & Monastery of the Dormition CHURCH
(Map p196; ⌚8am-noon & 2-6pm) Where Jesus' mother Mary fell into 'eternal sleep'. Around the corner from the Room of the Last Supper.

Grave of Oskar Schindler CEMETERY
(Map p196; ⌚8am-5pm Mon-Thu, to 1pm Fri) The Austrian industrialist who saved more than 1200 Jews from the gas chambers (and whose story was captured by filmmaker Steven Spielberg in the Oscar-winning film *Schindler's List*) is buried on Mt Zion, downhill and bearing left at the fork as you exit Zion Gate.

JEWISH QUARTER

Largely residential, the wheelchair-friendly Jewish Quarter was almost entirely flattened during and after the 1948 fighting, and was reconstructed following its capture by Israel in 1967. Consequently, there are few historic monuments above ground level, but excavations have unearthed a number of archaeological sites.

Western Wall RELIGIOUS SITE
(HaKotel; Map p196) Judaism's holiest site was built about 2000 years ago as a simple retaining wall for the Temple Mount, upon which stood the Second Temple. It became a place of pilgrimage during the Ottoman period – Jews would come to mourn the destruction of the temple, which is why the site came to be known as the Wailing Wall (a name that Jews themselves tend to avoid). The area immediately in front of the wall now serves as an open-air synagogue;

the right side is for women (who must dress modestly, covering their arms and legs), and the larger left side for men (who must wear a kippa; paper ones are provided). It's accessible 24 hours a day; up-to-the-minute live pictures can be viewed online at www.aish.com/wallcam. Look out for the prayers on slips of paper stuffed into cracks in the wall, which are thought to have a better chance than others of being answered.

Western Wall Tunnels HISTORIC SITE
(Map p196; ☎02-627 1333; www.thekotel.org; adult/child 30/15IS; ⏰7am-6pm Sun-Thu, to 12.30pm Fri) This fascinating 488m passage, excavated by archaeologists, follows the northern continuation of the Western Wall. The foundation stones here are enormous – one is a 570-ton monster the size of a small bus. Visitable only on a 75-minute guided tour that must be booked in advance, a week ahead if possible.

Jerusalem Archaeological Park & Davidson Centre HISTORIC SITE
(Map p196; www.archpark.org.il; adult/concession 30/16NIS; ⏰8am-5pm Sun-Thu, to 2pm Fri) A bit south of the Western Wall, this area's streets, columns, walls and plazas offer a peek into the history of the Temple Mount.

Cardo Maximus STREET
(Map p196) Cutting a broad north–south swath, the Cardo Maximus is the reconstructed main street of Roman and Byzantine Jerusalem. At one time it would have run the whole breadth of the city, up to what's now Damascus Gate. Part of the street has been restored to approximate its original appearance, while another section has been turned into a shopping arcade with thoroughly modern gift and souvenir shops. Close to the large menorah (seven-branched candelabra) near the southern end of the Cardo, the **Alone on the Walls Museum** (Map p196; adult/senior/student 12/6/10NIS; ⏰9am-5pm Sun-Thu, to 1pm Fri) documents the Jews' unsuccessful 1948 campaign for control of the city.

Wohl Archaeological Museum (Herodian Quarter) ARCHAEOLOGICAL SITE
(Map p196; 1 HaKara'im St; adult/senior/student 18/9/13NIS; ⏰9am-5pm Sun-Thu, to 1pm Fri) Features a 1st-century home and several Herodian archaeological sites, plus interpretive displays detailing the lavish lifestyle enjoyed in the Jewish neighbourhood of Herod's city.

Hurva Synagogue SYNAGOGUE
(Map p196; ☎02-626 5900; adult/student 25/15NIS; ⏰8am-6pm Sun-Thu, 9am-1pm Fri) Built in the early 1700s, rebuilt in 1864 and destroyed by the Jordanians after a pitched battle in 1948, this synagogue underwent a lengthy post-1967 reconstruction and re opened in 2009.

MUSLIM QUARTER

Running from Damascus Gate south and southeast towards the Temple Mount, this is the most visually stimulating area of the Old City; it's also the most claustrophobic, confusing and crowded. You'll inevitably get lost in the tangle of trade and teeming humanity and be enchanted by the tempting aromas emanating from spice merchants, coffee shops, bakeries and tiny restaurants. Wander its Mamluk and medieval alleyways and you'll be transported back to a different century.

FREE **Al-Haram ash-Sharif/ Temple Mount** ANCIENT SITE
(Map p196; www.noblesanctuary.com, www.templemount.org; ⏰7.30-11am & 1.30-2.30pm Sat-Thu Apr-Sep, 7.30-10am & 12.30-1.30pm Sat-Thu Oct-Mar) There are few patches of ground as holy, or as disputed, as this one.

The huge, open stone plaza, dotted with cypress trees, was built over the biblical Mt Moriah, the location, according to Jewish tradition, of the foundation stone of the world itself. It was here, says the Talmud, that Adam, Cain, Abel and Noah performed ritual sacrifices, and where Abraham offered his son Isaac to God in a supreme test of faith. It was also the site of Solomon's First Temple, where the Ark of the Covenant was housed, and the Second Temple, destroyed by the Romans in AD 70. The Romans subsequently erected a temple to Zeus on the site, which later served as a Christian church.

There are nine gates to the enclosure, but though you can leave the compound by most of them, non-Muslims are allowed to enter only at the Bab al-Maghariba/Sha'ar HaMugrabim (Gate of the Moors), reached from the Western Wall plaza. Line up early for security checks and bear in mind that the Mount closes on Muslim holidays. Modest dress is required. Non-Muslims can walk around the Temple Mount, but are barred from entering the Dome of the Rock.

The centrepiece of the Temple Mount today is the gilded, mosaic-adorned **Dome of the Rock**, completed in AD 691, which covers the slab of stone on which, according to the Quran, Abraham prepared to sacrifice his son Ishmael, and from which Mohammed ascended to heaven.

Al-Aqsa Mosque is a functioning house of worship believed to be a partial conversion of a 6th-century Byzantine church, with columns donated – oddly enough – by Benito Mussolini. For Muslims, Al-Haram ash-Sharif is Islam's third-holiest site, after Mecca and Medina.

Via Dolorosa RELIGIOUS SITE

(Map p196) The road leading from Lion's Gate into the heart of the Old City is known as Via Dolorosa (Way of Sorrows) or the Stations of the Cross. It's the route that many Christians believe was taken by the condemned Jesus as he carried his heavy cross to Calvary. At 3pm on Fridays, the Franciscan Fathers lead a solemn procession here; you're also likely to encounter groups of Italian or Spanish pilgrims lugging their own huge (rented) crosses up the hill. Explanations on plaques at each of the nine 'stations' along the way illuminate the New Testament story (the final five stations are in the Church of the Holy Sepulchre, p191).

St Anne's Church CHURCH

(Map p188; admission 7NIS; ⌚8am-noon & 2-5pm Mon-Sat Apr-Sep, 8am-noon & 2-5pm Mon-Sat Oct-Mar) Near Lion's Gate, this church – famed for its superb acoustics – is perhaps the finest example of Crusader architecture in Jerusalem. It is traditionally thought to have been the home of Joachim and Anne, parents of the Virgin Mary.

CITY OF DAVID & KIDRON VALLEY

To the east of the Old City, outside Lion's Gate, the land drops away into the Kidron Valley, then rises again up the slopes of the Mount of Olives.

The Kidron Valley has over four millennia of archaeological remains. Because of the steep terrain, it's more isolated than other areas of Jerusalem, making it all the more worth exploring.

City of David ARCHAEOLOGICAL SITE

(Map p196; www.cityofdavid.org.il; adult/student 27/14NIS, guided tour 60NIS, movie 13NIS; ⌚8am-5pm Sun-Thu, to 2am Fri) The oldest part of Jerusalem, the City of David was the Canaanite settlement captured by King David some 3000 years ago. The excavations are the result of work, still ongoing, started in 1850.

From Dung Gate, head east (downhill) and take the road to the right. At the visitors centre you can watch a 3D movie about the city. The site is spread out and contains numerous paths, so signing up for the guided tour (10am or 2pm, Friday 10am only) is recommended.

If you intend to walk through the extraordinary 500m-long, water-filled **Hezekiah's Tunnel** you can change into swimming trunks in the bathrooms and leave your gear in a locker (10NIS).

From the bottom of the hill you can walk back up or take the shuttle bus (5NIS) to the top.

Pillar of Absalom TOMB

(Map p188) At the top of the Kidron Valley sits the legendary tomb of David's son (II Samuel 18:17).

MOUNT OF OLIVES

For Christians, this hillside holds special significance as the site where it is believed Jesus took on the sins of the world, was arrested and later ascended to heaven. According to the Book of Zechariah, this is where God will redeem the dead on the Day of Judgement (that's why much of the Mt of Olives is covered with a Jewish cemetery). Keep yourself busy exploring the half-dozen churches, most commemorating events in Jesus' life. The panorama of the Old City from the summit is spectacular – visit early in the morning for the best light.

Church of the Ascension CHURCH

(Map p196; admission 5NIS; ⌚8am-1pm Mon-Sat) This church has stunning views from its 45m-high tower.

Church of All Nations CHURCH

(Map p196; ⌚8.30-11.30am & 2.30-4pm) Situated amid the Gardens of Gethsemane, this church has glistening golden mosaics on its facade.

Garden of Gethsemane GARDENS

(Map p188; ⌚8am-noon & 2-6pm) This is the garden where Jesus is believed to have been arrested (Mark 14:32-50). It contains several ancient olive trees that were probably already standing during Jesus' lifetime.

Tomb of the Virgin Mary RELIGIOUS SITE

(Map p188; ⌚6am-noon & 2.30-5pm) One of the holiest sites in Christianity, the Tomb of the Virgin Mary is a dim and somewhat forlorn place, owned by the Greek Orthodox Church.

Al-Haram ash-Sharif/ Temple Mount

A TOUR OF THE TEMPLE MOUNT

The Temple Mount encompasses multiple sites that span an area the size of one or two city blocks. A visit requires a little planning and may need to be accomplished over a couple of days.

Ascend the rickety wooden ramp at the Western Wall plaza to reach the Temple Mount at the Bab al-Maghariba (Gate of the Moors). Passing through the gate, continue ahead to view the understated facade of the **Al-Aqsa Mosque** **1** and the sumptuous detail of the **Dome of the Rock** **2**. Take a slow turn around the Dome to admire its surrounding structures, including the curious **Dome of the Chain** **3** and the elegant **Sabil of Qaitbay** **4**. Don't miss the stunning view of the Mount of Olives seen through the stone arches known as the **Scales of Souls** **5**.

Exit the Temple Mount at the **Bab al-Qattanin (Gate of Cotton Merchants)** **6**; and return to the Western Wall plaza where you can spend some time at the **Western Wall** **7** and visit the **Jerusalem Archaeological Park & Davidson Centre** **8**.

TOP TIPS

» **Get in Early** Opening hours for the Temple Mount are limited and lines can be long during the busy summer season, so queue early (gates open at 7.30am).

» **Go Underground** An interesting way to reach the Jerusalem Archaeological Park is to take the underground tunnel that starts 600m away in the City of David (tickets for the park are sold at the City of David).

MICHAEL KOHN

Scales of Souls

Muslims believe that scales will be hung from the column-supported arches to weigh the souls of the dead.

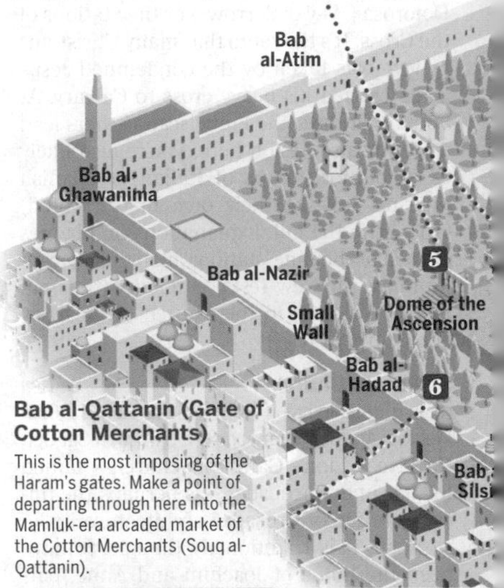

Bab al-Qattanin (Gate of Cotton Merchants)

This is the most imposing of the Haram's gates. Make a point of departing through here into the Mamluk-era arcaded market of the Cotton Merchants (Souq al-Qattanin).

MICHAEL KOHN

Sabil of Qaitbay

This three-tiered, 13m-high structure is one of the finest pieces of architecture on the Temple Mount. It was built by Egyptians in 1482 as a charitable act to please Allah and features the only carved-stone dome outside Cairo.

MICHAEL KOHN

MICHAEL KOHN

Dome of the Chain

Some believe this structure was built as a model for the Dome of the Rock. Legend has it that Solomon hung a chain from the dome and those who swore falsely while holding it were struck by lightning.

MICHAEL KOHN

Dome of the Rock

The crown jewel of Israel's architectural heritage, the Dome famously contains the enormous foundation stone that Jews believe is the centre of the earth and Muslims say is the spot where Mohammed made his ascent.

Al-Aqsa Mosque

One of the world's oldest mosques, Al-Aqsa (the Furthest Mosque) is 75m long and has a capacity for more than 5000 worshippers. The Crusaders called it Solomon's Temple and used it as a royal palace and stable for their horses.

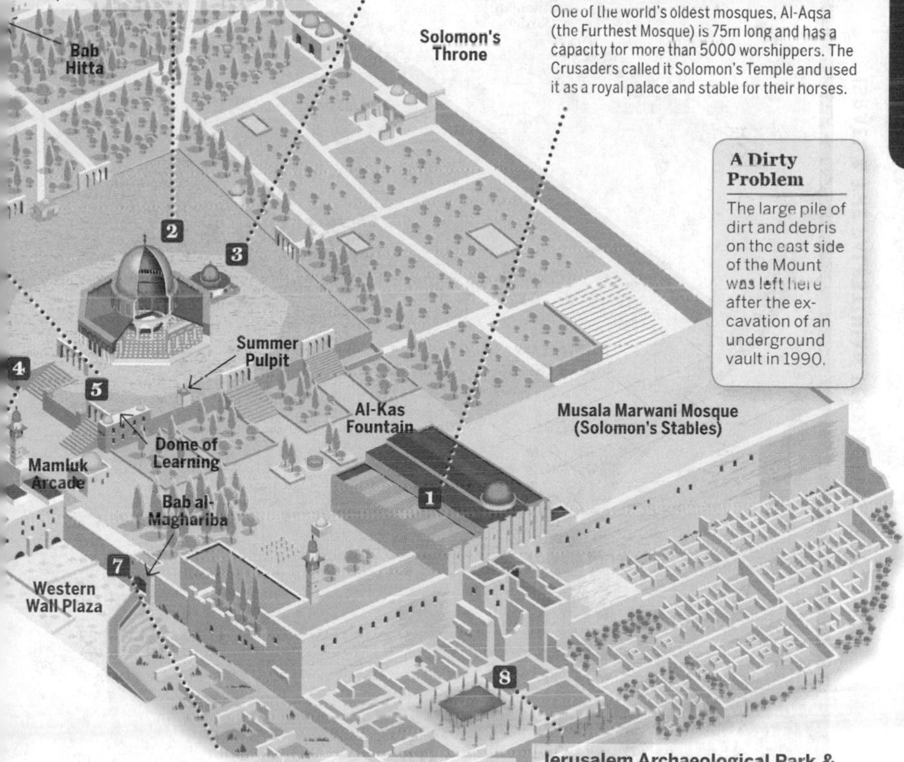

A Dirty Problem

The large pile of dirt and debris on the east side of the Mount was left here after the excavation of an underground vault in 1990.

Western Wall

Today it's the holiest place on earth for Jews and an important cultural nexus on Shabbat, when Jews from around the city come to sing, dance and pray by the Wall.

Jerusalem Archaeological Park & Davidson Centre

This is the place to see Robinson's Arch, the steps that led up to the Temple Mount and ancient *mikveh* (Jewish ritual bath) where pilgrims washed prior to entering the holy temple.

Coming Clean

Al-Kas Fountain, located between Al-Aqsa Mosque and the Dome of the Rock, is used for ritual washing before prayers.

MICHAEL KOHN

MICHAEL KOHN

Jerusalem Old City

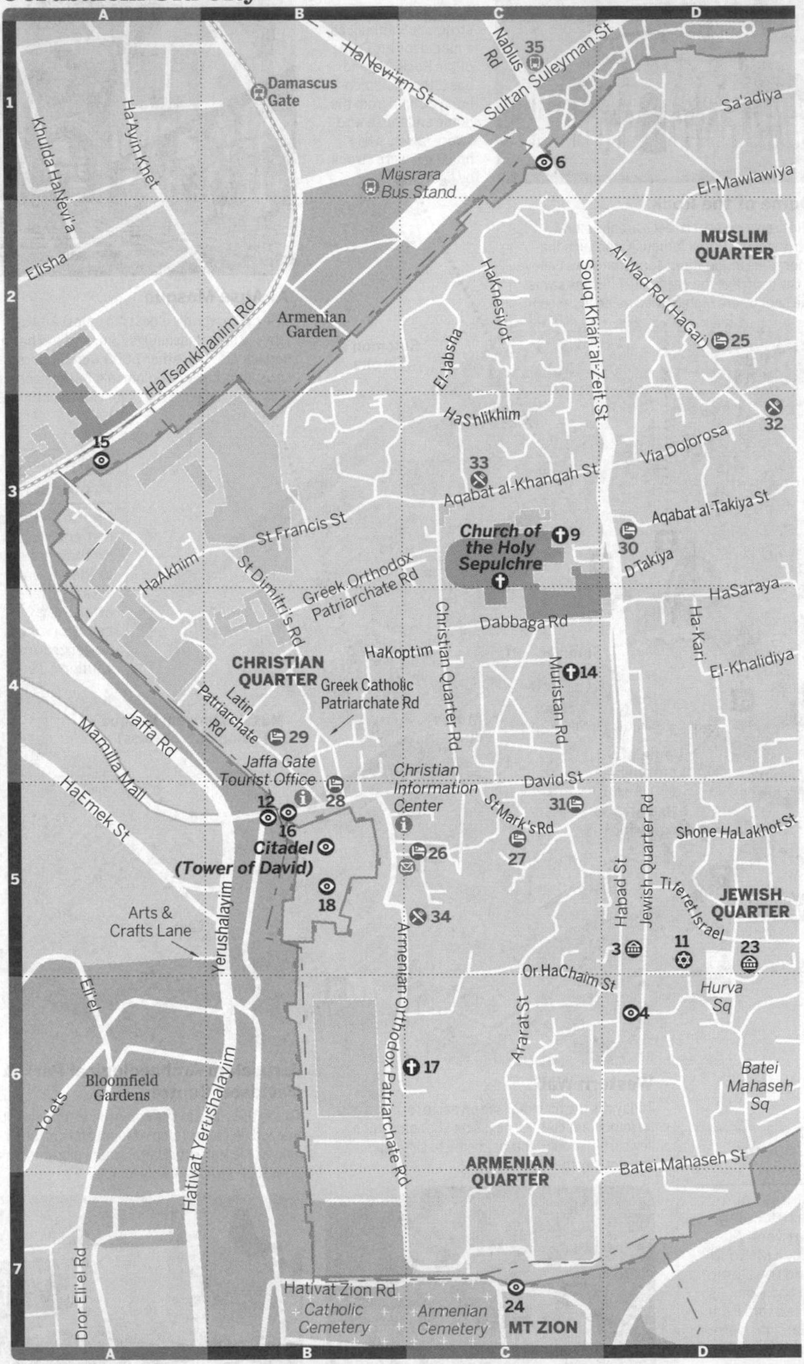
A
B
C
D
1
2
3
4
5
6
7
HaNevi'im St
Nablus Rd
35
Sultan Suleyman St
Damascus Gate
Sa'adiya
Khulda HaNevi'a
Ha'Ayin Khet
Musrara Bus Stand
6
El-Mawlawiya
MUSLIM QUARTER
Elisha
HaKnesiyot
Souq Khan al-Zeit St
Al-Wad Rd (HaGai)
Armenian Garden
HaTsankhanim Rd
25
El-Jabsha
HaShlikhim
32
15
33
Via Dolorosa
Aqabat al-Khanqah St
Aqabat al-Takiya St
St Francis St
Church of the Holy Sepulchre
9
30
D Takiya
HaAkhim
St Dimitris Rd
Greek Orthodox Patriarchate Rd
Christian Quarter Rd
HaSaraya
Ha-Kari
Dabbaga Rd
HaKoptim
CHRISTIAN QUARTER
Greek Catholic Patriarchate Rd
Muristan Rd
14
El-Khalidiya
Latin Patriarchate Rd
Jaffa Rd
Mamilla Mall
29
Jaffa Gate Tourist Office
28
Christian Information Center
David St
HaEmek St
12
16
31
St Mark's Rd
Habad St
Jewish Quarter Rd
Shone HaLakhot St
Citadel (Tower of David)
26
27
18
Tiferet Israel
JEWISH QUARTER
Arts & Crafts Lane
Yerushalayim
34
Armenian Orthodox Patriarchate Rd
3
11
23
Or HaChaim St
Hurva Sq
Eli'el
Ararat St
4
17
Bloomfield Gardens
Yo'ets
Hativat Yerushalayim
Batei Mahaseh Sq
ARMENIAN QUARTER
Batei Mahaseh St
Dror Eli'el Rd
Hativat Zion Rd
Catholic Cemetery
Armenian Cemetery
24
MT ZION

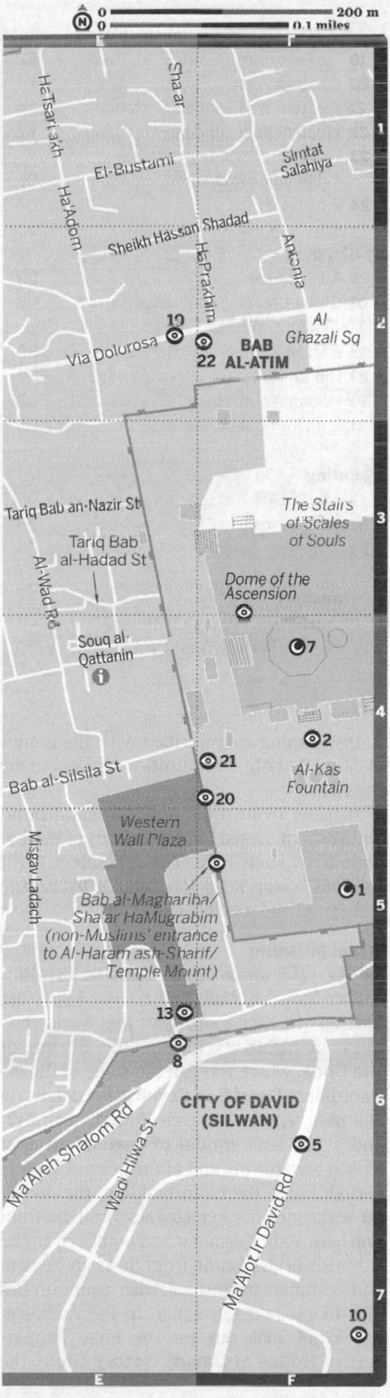

EAST JERUSALEM

Modern, workaday, predominantly Arab East Jerusalem is filled with plenty of hustle and bustle, some lovely (if crumbling) architecture, and a number of worthwhile sights.

FREE Rockefeller Museum MUSEUM

(Map p188; Sultan Suleyman St; ⌚10am-3pm Sun, Mon, Wed & Thu, to 2pm Fri) Archaeology buffs who do not get their fill at the Israel Museum should drop by this octagonal building, established thanks to a US$2 million donation from the Rockefeller family in 1927.

FREE Garden Tomb GARDENS

(Map p188; ☎02-627 2745; www.gardentomb.org; ⌚9am-noon & 2-5.30pm Mon-Sat) Behind a heavy stone wall on Nablus Rd, this garden and ancient stone tomb may have once been the property of Joseph of Arimathaea. It's believed by some to be the site of Jesus' crucifixion and resurrection, an alternative location to the Church of the Holy Sepulchre.

Museum on the Seam MUSEUM

(Map p188; www.mots.org.il; 4 Hel Handasa Rd; adult/concession 25/20NIS; ⌚10am-5pm Sun-Thu, to 2pm Fri; 🚋Shivtei Israel) Conflict, prejudice and racism (and occasional coexistence) are on display at the Museum on the Seam, a sociopolitical/contemporary-art museum that speaks to issues both global and local. It's located on the Green Line, which divided East and West Jerusalem from 1948 to 1967.

NEW CITY

The New City is centred on the triangle formed by Jaffa Rd, King George V St and the pedestrianised Ben Yehuda St. The latter two are good bets for shopping, as is nearby Yoel Solomon St.

Mahane Yehuda Market MARKET

(Map p188; ⌚8am-sunset Sun-Thu, 9am-2pm Fri; 🚋Mahane Yehuda) Jerusalem's bustling main market is crammed with fresh, delicious edibles. Creative types and gourmets have discovered the area in recent years, opening up trendy restaurants, bars and art galleries.

Mea She'arim NEIGHBOURHOOD

(Map p188) One of the world's most reluctant tourist attractions, the ultra-Orthodox Jewish neighbourhood of Mea She'arim is reminiscent of a *shtetl* (ghetto) in pre-Holocaust Eastern Europe, with the customs and dress-code to go with it. Dress conservatively (crucial if you're female – women should wear long skirts and long-sleeve shirts), don't

Jerusalem Old City

take photos without permission and avoid the area during Shabbat – though Thursday night and Friday daytime before Shabbat are particularly lively times to visit.

In 2011 extremist groups tried to segregate some of Mea She'arim's sidewalks – men on one side, women on the other. The campaign, opposed by many mainstream ultra-Orthodox Jews, was declared unconstitutional by Israel's Supreme Court.

HAR HAZIKARON & MUSEUM ROW

FREE Yad Vashem MEMORIAL

(www.yadvashem.org; 9am-5pm Sun-Thu, to 2pm Fri; Mount Herzl) This moving museum is Israel's official memorial to the six million victims of the Holocaust. The centrepiece is a prism-like **history museum** illustrating not only how Jews died during WWII but also how they lived before the Nazis' onslaught. In the underground **Children's Memorial**, a solitary flame commemorates the 1.5 million Jewish children who perished in the Holocaust. The **Avenue of the Righteous** is lined with trees dedicated to the Gentiles who risked their own lives to save Jews. Down the hill, in the **Valley of the Communities**, columns of stone are inscribed with the names of 5000 Jewish communities wiped out by the Nazis.

It takes about three hours to get around Yad Vashem. Egged bus 99 (as part of its city-wide tour) stops here. The Jerusalem Light Rail has a stop near Mt Herzl, a 10-minute walk from Yad Vashem.

Israel Museum MUSEUM

(off Map p188; www.imj.org.il; adult/child 48/24NIS; 10am-5pm Sun, Mon, Wed & Thu, 4-9pm Tue, 10am-2pm Fri, 10am-5pm Sat) At this world-class museum highlights include the **Shrine of the Book**, where you can see some of the extraordinary **Dead Sea Scrolls** (for details on Qumran, where they were found, see p242) and a 1:50 scale **model of Jerusalem** as it looked towards the end of the Second Temple period. Inside the main building, the **Judaica wing** includes synagogues brought from northern Italy, Germany and southern India; a Jewish bride's outfit from San'a in Yemen; and costumes from the Jewish communities of Ethiopia and Kurdistan. In the Archaeology Wing, look out for the First Temple-period **'House of David' Victory Stele**, the only contemporary, extra-biblical reference to the Davidic dynasty; a superb bronze bust of Hadrian from the 2nd century AD, found at Beit She'an; and a replica of a nail pierced through a human anklebone, dated to the first century BC: a victim of Roman crucifixion. The **Israeli Art** pavilion has striking paintings and sculptures. Don't forget to pick up a complimentary audio guide from the visitors centre. The Israel Museum, situated about 2.5km west of the Old City (on foot, take Agron, Ramban and Rupin Sts), is adjacent to the Hebrew University's Givat Ram campus and is served by buses 9, 14, 17 and 99.

Bible Lands Museum MUSEUM

(off Map p188; www.blmj.org; 25 Granot St, Givat Ram; adult/student/senior 40/20/30NIS; ⏲9.30am-5.30pm Sun-Tue & Thu, 9.30am-2pm Fri & Sat, 9.30am-9.30pm Wed) This museum presents the material culture and history of both the Holy Land and neighbouring civilisations, with a wealth of well-displayed artefacts and background information. Situated across the parking lot from the Israel Museum.

Courses

Gerard Behar Centre HEBREW LANGUAGE

(Map p188; ☎02-624 0034; 11 Bezalel St) Morning and evening Hebrew-language classes with ongoing enrolment. Five days a week costs 920NIS per month, three days a week 613NIS.

YMCA East Jerusalem ARABIC LANGUAGE

(Map p188; ☎02-628 5210, 054 920 3932; 29 Nablus Rd) Offers three-month Arabic-language courses for 1200NIS. Classes meet twice weekly in the evenings. Contact Malda.

Tours

Egged 99 Circular Line BUS TOUR

(☎02-530 4704; www.egged.co.il/eng; non-stop tour adult/child 60/48NIS, hop-on hop off tour 80/68NIS) A good introduction to the city, this open-air coach service cruises past 35 of Jerusalem's major sites, providing commentary in eight languages along the way. The first bus leaves the central bus station at 9am; stops include Jaffa Gate, the King David Hotel, Yad Vashem and the Israel Museum. The Egged website (click the Tourism link) lists the stops and times.

Abraham Hostel WALKING TOUR

(☎02-650 2200; www.abraham-hostel-jerusalem.com; 67 HaNevi'im St; day tour 120NIS) Jerusalem's most popular hostel offers highly recommended tours of Jerusalem as well as places further afield

Sleeping

Most budget accommodation is located in the Old City or in the city centre along Jaffa Rd. There are some great midrange options, including atmospheric Christian hospices in the Old City and boutique hotels in the city centre. High-end category picks are found in Mamilla and East Jerusalem.

While the Old City hotels offer much in the way of rustic atmosphere and access to Jerusalem's historic places of interest, the area is crowded and filled with steps and narrow streets, inconvenient if you have a car or lots of luggage.

For a list of B&Bs, check out www.bnb.co.il.

OLD CITY

TOP CHOICE **Austrian Hospice** GUESTHOUSE $$

(Map p196; ☎02-626 5800; www.austrianhospice.com; 37 Via Dolorosa; dm/s/d/tr €22/62/104/135; @📶) This castle-like guesthouse, opened in 1863, has a leafy garden and rooms that are simply furnished but comfortable. Non-guests can enjoy the wonderful cafe (open 10am to 10pm), which serves Austrian cakes, soups, pastries and sausages.

Lutheran Guest House GUESTHOUSE $$

(Map p196; ☎02-626 6888; www.luth-guesthouse-jerusalem.com; St Mark's Rd; s/d/tr €53/82/105; ❄) Downstairs is a bright, welcoming lobby; upstairs is a gorgeous reading room where you can pull a book off the shelf and enjoy views of the Church of the Holy Sepulchre. The modern double rooms are simply furnished but comfortable. To get here from Jaffa Gate walk down David St, then take the first right up a narrow staircase; the guesthouse is about 100m down on the left.

Christ Church Guesthouse GUESTHOUSE $$

(Map p196; ☎02-627 7727; www.cmj-israel.org; Omar Ibn al-Khattab Sq, Jaffa Gate; s/d/ste 295/465/525NIS; 📶) This wonderfully maintained hospice gets high marks for its period atmosphere, prime location and welcoming staff. Simply furnished rooms have stone floors and domed ceilings. The staff comprises Christians, Jews and Muslims, all hired as a way to promote intercultural understanding.

Gloria HOTEL $$

(Map p196; ☎02-628 2431; www.gloria-hotel.com; 33 Latin Patriarchate Rd; s/d/tr US$120/150/180;

JERUSALEM FOR CHILDREN

Biblical Zoo (www.jerusalemzoo.org.il; Zoo Rd; admission adult/child 47/37NIS; ⌚9am-6pm Sun-Thu, to 4.30pm Fri, 10am-6pm Sat) An excellent, innovative animal park in the southwest of the city, contains animals mentioned in the Bible, a petting zoo, a great playground and plenty of space for a picnic. To get there, take the light rail to Mt Herzl, where you can pick up bus 33 to the zoo.

Bloomfield Science Museum (off Map p188; www.mada.org.il; Hebrew University, Ruppin Blvd; admission 34NIS, under 5yr free; ⌚9am-6pm Sun-Thu, to 4.30pm Fri, 10am-6pm Sat) Kids will love this museum, which has loads of hands-on activities and introductory science exhibits. Situated 10 minutes on foot northwest of the Israel Museum (take Rupin Ave), or a 10-minute walk southeast from the Kiryat Moshe light rail stop.

Train Theater (Map p188; ☎02-561 8514; www.traintheater.co.il; Liberty Bell Park; admission 15-60NIS) Puts on occasional puppet performances.

City of David (p193) Good for older kids as they can make like Indiana Jones and wade through a spooky, water-filled tunnel.

❄📶) A hidden gem of a hotel, the 100-room Gloria offers clean and well-maintained single, double and triple rooms. About 100m uphill from Jaffa Gate.

Hebron Youth Hostel GUESTHOUSE $
(Map p188; ☎02-628 1101; ashraftabasco@hotmail.com; 8 Aqabat al-Takiya St; dm 60-70NIS, d 250NIS, without bathroom 200NIS; @📶) One of the longest-running hostels in the Old City, Hebron is a character-filled place with stone walls, arches and Arab decor. The rooftop additions are not as nice, but do offer a little more sunlight. On the downside, the share dorm bathroom gets busy in the mornings.

Citadel Youth Hostel HOSTEL $
(Map p196; ☎02-628 5253, 054 580 5085; citadelhostel@mail.com; 20 St Mark's Rd; dm 65NIS, d 180-210NIS, without bathroom 140-180NIS; @📶) This quirky hostel has ancient walls of stone, a twisting staircase and great views from the roof. Upper level rooms are poorly insulated. The owner is friendly, but the kitchen facilities and showers are a tad basic.

East New Imperial Hotel HISTORIC HOTEL $
(Map p196; ☎02-628 2261; www.newimperial.com; Jaffa Gate; s/d/tr US$70/100/120; @📶) Recent improvements have given the rooms here a clean, fresh look, but without ruining the historic atmosphere. On the downside, the plumbing is a bit erratic. Located just inside Jaffa Gate, and thus accessible by taxi.

EAST JERUSALEM

American Colony Hotel HISTORIC HOTEL $$$
(Map p188; ☎02-627 9777; www.amcol.co.il; 23 Nablus Rd, Sheikh Jarah; s/d/ste from US$235/315/900; ❄@📶🏊) Luxurious but unpretentious, the renowned American Colony has long been a favourite with journalists, scholars and celebrities. Former guests include Winston Churchill, Mikhail Gorbachev, Jimmy Carter, Bob Dylan, Ingrid Bergman and John Steinbeck. If the sky-high room rates are too much, head here for a courtyard lunch or afternoon tea – or to prop up the Cellar Bar.

St George's Cathedral Pilgrim Guesthouse GUESTHOUSE $$
(Map p188; ☎02-628 3302; stgeorges.gh@j-diocese.org; 20 Nablus Rd; s/d/tr US$110/150/190; ❄@📶) Located on the property of a 110-year-old Anglican church, this tranquil guesthouse has simply furnished guest quarters and a lovely garden. The distinguished reading room is a nice place to relax with a thick novel.

Rivoli Hotel HOTEL $
(Map p188; ☎02-628 4871; 3 Salah ad-Din St; s/d US$70/85; 📶; 🚊Damascus Gate) A no-frills place just a few steps away from Herod's Gate. Rooms are simple, if a little bland, but there is a small lounge.

NEW CITY

King David Hotel HOTEL $$$
(Map p188; ☎02-620 8888; www.danhotels.com; 23 King David St; r US$470-600, ste $960; ❄@📶🏊) Built in the 1930s in the presumed style of King David's palace, this landmark hotel – a favourite of presidents and prime ministers – is both grandiose and charming. The extraordinary lobby is furnished with velvet couches, gold drapery and marble-top tables. Meals are taken in a grand ballroom

down the hall, or out on the back patio, which overlooks a lawn and pool.

TOP CHOICE Abraham Hostel HOSTEL $
(Map p203; ☎02-650 2200; www.abraham-hostel-jerusalem.com; 67 Hanevi'im St; dm 70-100NIS, s 240NIS, d 270-360NIS, tr 400NIS; ❄@🛜; 🚊Ha-Davidka) Hugely (and justifiably) popular with budget travellers, this super-central place has 77 clean, functional rooms, all with private bathroom and shower. The ever-busy lounge/bar has an attached kitchen for communal cooking. A great place to meet other travellers.

YMCA Three Arches Hotel HOTEL $$$
(Map p188; ☎02-569 2692; www.ymca3arch.co.il; 26 King David St; s/d/tr US$150/164/242; @🛜🏊) A hard-to-miss local landmark (thanks to the tower) and a great place to spend a few nights. The hotel's 56 rooms are simply furnished; you're paying more for the atmosphere and the location than the quality of rooms. Guests can use the gym and pool.

Jerusalem Hostel & Guest House HOSTEL $
(Map p203; ☎02-623 6102; www.jerusalem-hostel.com; 44 Jaffa Rd, Zion Sq; dm 80NIS, s 200-260NIS, d 250-280NIS, tr 360NIS; ❄@🛜; 🚊Jaffa Center) With a prime location overlooking Zion Sq, this is a fine option for budget travellers looking for a place in the city centre. Rooms are clean and there is a good traveller vibe. In summer it offers basic accommodation on the roof for 80NIS.

TOP CHOICE St Andrew's Guesthouse GUESTHOUSE $$
(Map p188; ☎02-673 1711; www.scotsguesthouse.com; 1 David Remez St; s/d/tr US$120/160/180; @🛜) St Andrew's feels like a bit of Scotland transported to the Middle East, with colonial charm aplenty. Rooms are plainly furnished with desk, phone, heater and fan. Some rooms include balconies; those that don't still have access to a large sun deck.

Allenby 2 B&B B&B $$
(off Map p188; ☎052 257 8493, 534 4113; www.bnb.co.il/allenby; Allenby Sq 2, Romema; s US$25-55, d US$35-70; ❄@🛜; 🚊Central Station) A nine-room B&B that combines a warm atmosphere with excellent service. Enthusiastic owner Danny Flax is a mine of information and a keen cyclist who can offer great advice on offbeat trips. There is no reception, so advanced bookings are essential. Situated half a block northeast of (ie behind) the Central Bus Station.

Little House in Rehavia HOTEL $$
(Map p188; ☎02-563 3344; www.jerusalem-hotel.co.il; 20 Ibn Ezra St, Rehavia; s/tw/q US$119/149/229; @🛜) Quaint set-up in Rehavia with a relaxing garden in the back. It's located in one of Jerusalem's prettiest neighbourhoods, a 1.5km walk to the Old City.

Little House in the Colony HOTEL $$
(☎02-566 2424; www.jerusalem-hotel.co.il; 4a Lloyd George St, German Colony; s/tw/q US$119/149/229; @🛜) A renovated Templar building located on a quiet lane in the German Colony. Rooms are charmingly antiquated but comfortable. Situated about 1.5km southwest of the Old City's Jaffa Gate, just off Emeq Refa'im St.

Hotel Palatin HOTEL $$
(Map p203; ☎02-623 1141; www.palatinhotel.com; 4 Agrippas St; s 350-450NIS, d 380-480NIS; 🛜; 🚊Jaffa Center) Superbly central, with 29 smallish but comfortable rooms. The newly renovated rooms (100NIS extra) have a fresh, boutique-hotel feel.

Hotel Kaplan HOTEL $
(Map p203; ☎02-625 4591; natrade@netvision.net.il; 1 HaHavatzelet St; s/d/tr US$45/65/75; ❄@; 🚊Jaffa Center) Rooms here are basic and the furniture is a little ragged, but you do get a private bathroom and views of Jaffa Rd. No breakfast, but guests can cook in the small kitchen.

Eating

Jerusalem is home to an array of restaurants in all categories – from your basic hole-in-the-wall shwarma joints all the way up to sushi bars and haute cuisine taken in the leafy gardens of a historic home. Befitting Jerusalem's religious nature, a significant percentage of restaurants are kosher; when almost everything in Jerusalem's Jewish neighbourhoods shuts down for Shabbat, head to East Jerusalem. For a self-catering extravaganza, visit the Mahane Yehuda Market.

OLD CITY

For quick eats in the Old City, head to the Muslim Quarter, where there are hole-in-the-wall stores aplenty vending felafel, freshly ground coffee, shwarma, cookies and pastries, while stalls and stands sell mountains of fresh fruit and vegetables, olives and pickles.

TOP CHOICE Amigo Emil MIDDLE EASTERN $$
(Map p196; Aqabat al-Khanqah St; dishes from 40NIS; ⏲10.30am-9.30pm Mon-Sat) In a 400-year-old stone building, this place has some nice appetisers, including mezze. The house speciality is *musakhan,* a dish of spiced chicken and onions stuffed into Bedouin bread (40NIS).

Armenian Tavern ARMENIAN $$
(Map p196; 79 Armenian Orthodox Patriarchate Rd; meat dishes 55-70NIS; ⏲11am-10.30pm Tue-Sun) Walk down a flight of stairs near Jaffa Gate to find a beautiful stone-and-tile interior complete with a gently splashing fountain. Try the *khaghoghi derev,* a spiced minced-meat mixture bundled in vine leaves, or the excellent Armenian pizza.

Abu Shukri HUMMUS $
(Map p196; 63 Al-Wad Rd; hummus platters 20NIS; ⏲8am-4pm; 🅥) Our search to find the best hummus in Jerusalem landed us at this place, as recommended by many a local. Add 10NIS for a cup of freshly squeezed OJ. It's located near the Fifth Station of the Cross.

NEW CITY

The New City offers diners a world of choice. To find your own dining gems, go wandering: Jaffa Rd has a number of trendy, loungey places; Yoel Solomon St has a string of simple, tourist-orientated choices; the upscale, heavily English-speaking German Colony has lots of informal cafes; and Aza Rd hosts some funky places popular with students.

Barud MIDDLE EAST $$$
(Map p203; 31 Jaffa Rd, Feingold Courtyard; dishes 65-85NIS; ⏲12.30pm-1am Mon-Sat; 🚊Jaffa Center) Come to Barud for the cosy atmosphere and dazzling Sephardic cooking. Meatballs with eggplant is a speciality, as well as *pastalikos* (a pastry with pine nuts, minced meat and onion; 59NIS). Live jazz is played once or twice a week. Not kosher.

T'mol Shilshom CAFE $$
(Map p203; 5 Yoel Solomon St; salads 45-56NIS, mains 56-83NIS; ⏲8.30am-midnight Sun-Thu; 📶; 🚊Jaffa Center) This legendary boho-style place is more cafe than restaurant, but serves great, light, kosher meals – and strong coffee – to a distinctly literary set. Gay- and lesbian-friendly.

Pinati HUMMUS $
(Map p203; 13 King George V St; hummus 17NIS; ⏲9am-7pm Sun-Thu, to 4pm Fri; 🅥; 🚊Jaffa Center) The old photos of loyal customers that cover the walls are a testament to the longevity of this popular hummus joint.

Itchikidana INDIAN $
(Map p188; Rehov HaEshkol 4; 🅥) This colourful Indian vegetarian cafe near Mahane Yehuda specialises in thali (set meal with dhal, rice and vegetables; 39NIS to 64NIS) and masala dosa (22NIS). It opens at 9am for chai (tea), but food is not served till noon.

TOP CHOICE Focaccio Bar MEDITERRANEAN $
(Map p203; 4 Rabbi Akiva St; dishes 30-50NIS; ⏲10am-1am; 🅥; 🚊Jaffa Center) One of the most popular restaurants in town. The speciality of course is focaccia, baked fresh in the *taboun* (clay oven).

Drinking

Jerusalem's city centre is well set up for pub crawling, with a number of bars clustered in close proximity, especially on Rivlin and Yoel Solomon Sts. They tend to be crowded with American teenagers on study breaks, but there are a few local places among them. East Jerusalem bars tend to be inside hotels, while the Old City is almost as dry as the Negev.

Uganda BAR
(Map p203; 4 Aristobulos St; ⏲noon-3am; 🚊Jaffa Center) An alternative bar named after the alternative territory offered by the British to Herzl. West Bank–brewed Taybeh beer is available, as is East Jerusalem hummus. Comfy chairs, a relaxed vibe and good music go down well with locals and visitors alike.

Casino de Paris BAR
(Map p188; Georgian Market ; ⏲noon-3am; 🚊Mahane Yehuda) During the British Mandate this building used to be an Officer's Club for British soldiers. Known as the Casino de Paris, it housed a bar downstairs and a brothel on the 2nd floor. It reopened in 2011 as a tapas bar, serving up tasty Spanish snacks and 25 types of Israeli boutique beers such as Negev, Shapira and Malka. Come around midnight and see the place in full swing.

Mikveh GAY & LESBIAN BAR
(Map p188; 4 Shoshan St; ⏲9pm-late Mon-Sat; 🚊City Hall) Attracts peoples of various religions and ethnicities. Drag shows on Mondays from 11pm, parties on Thursday and Friday. Situated on a quiet alley south of Safra Sq.

Jerusalem New City Centre

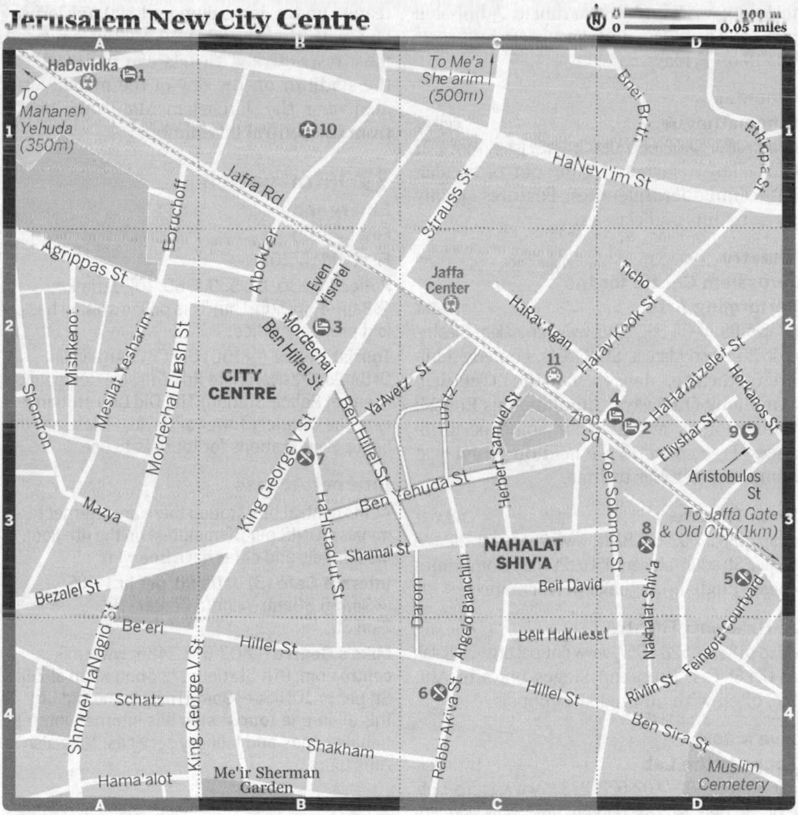

Jerusalem New City Centre

Sleeping

1 Abraham Hostel A1
2 Hotel Kaplan D3
3 Hotel Palatin B2
4 Jerusalem Hostel & Guest House D2

Eating

5 Barud D3
6 Focaccio Bar C4
7 Pinati B3
8 T'mol Shilshom D3

Drinking

9 Uganda D3

Entertainment

10 Wallenberg B1

Transport

11 Service Taxis for Tel Aviv C2

☆ Entertainment

Nightclubs

Yellow Submarine CLUB

(☎02-570 4646; www.yellowsubmarine.org.il; 13 HaRechavim St, Talpiot; ⊙11pm-late Thu & Fri) Usually a venue for live music, the Yellow Submarine also hosts DJs and dance parties. It's best to call first to see what's on, as you may need to order tickets in advance. Situated 3.5km southwest of Jaffa Gate; from the southern end of Emeq Refa'im St, head south on Pierre Koenig St for about 700m.

Wallenberg CLUB

(Map p188; 6 Raul Wallenberg St; ⊙9pm-late Thu-Sat; ⓜHa-Davidka) This centrally located nightclub, popular with the 30s crowd, plays techno, Israeli and house music. Admission is free Thursday and Saturday but costs 20NIS on Fridays.

Cinemas

Cinematheque CINEMA
(Map p188; ☎02-606 0800; www.jer-cin.org.il; 11 Hebron Rd) A favoured hang-out of secular, left-leaning Jerusalemites. Features quality foreign films and classics.

Theatre

Jerusalem Centre for the Performing Arts THEATRE
(Map p188; ☎02-560 5755; www.jerusalem-theatre.co.il; 20 David Marcus St) Hosts comedy, children's theatre, dance, and the Jerusalem Symphony Orchestra. Simultaneous English translation is available for some performances. Free concerts are held on Monday at 5pm from October to June.

Khan Theatre THEATRE
(Map p188; ☎02-671 8281; www.khan.co.il; 2 David Remez St; adult/student 150/120NIS) Sometimes stages English-language performances.

Al-Hakawati Theatre THEATRE
(Map p188; ☎628 0957; www.pnt-pal.org; Off Salah ad-Din St, East Jerusalem) Stages plays in Arabic, often with an English synopsis.

Live Music

Zappa in the Lab LIVE MUSIC
(off Map p188; ☎02-622 2333; www.zappa-club.co.il, in Hebrew; 28 Hebron Rd; admission 80-160NIS) Crafted out of a disused railway warehouse, this innovative live-music venue stages local talent for a sophisticated crowd. Doors open at 8.30pm and shows start at 10pm. Open most days of the week – check the website or call for upcoming events.

Dancing

International Cultural Centre for Youth CULTURAL CENTRE
(ICCY; Map p188; ☎02-566 4144; 12 Emek Refa'im St) Hosts folk dancing on Tuesdays (25NIS) from 10.30am to 12.30pm. It's not a performance – it's locals coming to dance, and you can join in (an instructor is available at the beginning of the session). Thursday night is an all-ages dance party. There are dances most nights – call ahead to find out what's on.

Sport

Teddy Kollek Stadium FOOTBALL
(Malha) Seating a respectable 20,000, this stadium is home to the two Jerusalem football teams, Beitar Jerusalem and HaPo'el Jerusalem, with their rowdy and relatively relaxed fans, respectively. Tickets can be bought at the stadium on the day of the match. Situated near the Jerusalem Mall; take bus 6 from the central bus station.

Information

Emergency

Fire (☎102)

First aid (☎101)

Police (☎100, 02-539 1360; 107 Jaffa Rd; 8am-4pm Sun-Thu) This police station has a lost property office.

Tourist police (☎100) Old City (Armenian Orthodox Patriarchate Rd); Russian Compound (Central Police Station) The Old City station is near the Citadel (Tower of David). These are the best police stations for tourists to use.

Internet Access

At the central bus station there are internet terminals (10NIS per 30 minutes) on the 4th floor. Most hotels and cafes have free wi-fi.

Internet Café (31 Jaffa Rd; per hr 14NIS; 9am-5.30am; Jaffa Center) Near Zion Sq.

Mike's Centre (☎02-628 2486; www.mikes-centre.com; 9th Station, 172 Souq Khan al-Zeit St; per hr 10NIS; 9am-11pm) In the Old City, this all-in-one tourist stop has internet, international phones and laundry services. Mike also runs tours.

Medical Services

Hadassah Medical Centre (☎02-677 7111; www.hadassah.org.il) Above Ein Kerem.

Terem (☎1 599 520 520; www.terem.com; 80 Yirmiyahu St, Romema; 24hr; Central Station) Efficient walk-in medical clinic that handles everything from minor ailments to emergencies. A consultation with a doctor costs 400NIS. It's a five-minute walk from Central Bus Station.

Money

The best deals for changing money are at the private, commission-free change offices in the New City (around Zion Sq), East Jerusalem (Salah ad-Din St) and in the Old City (Jaffa Gate). Some moneychangers, especially around Ben Yehuda St, will also change travellers cheques. Note that they close early on Friday and remain closed all day Saturday.

Banks with ATMs, such as Mizrahi and Leumi, are found on every block in the city centre.

American Express (☎02-623 8000; 18 Shlomzion HaMalka St; City Hall) Cashes travellers cheques (3% commission) but cannot replace lost cheques.

Post

Main post office (Map p188; ☎02-624 4745; main section, 23 Jaffa Rd; ⏰7am-7pm Sun-Thu, to noon Fri)

Tourist Information

Christian Information Centre (Map p196; ☎02-627 2692; www.cicts.org; Omar ibn al-Khattab Sq; ⏰8.30am-5.30pm Mon-Fri, to 12.30pm Sat) Opposite the entrance to the Citadel; provides information on the city's Christian sites. Also gives out handy maps that detail walking tours around the Old City.

Jaffa Gate Tourist Office (Map p196; ☎02 627 1422; www.tourism.gov.il; Jaffa Gate; ⏰8.30am-5pm Sat-Thu, to 1.30pm Fri) Has free maps and reams of literature on sites around town. Don't confuse it with the 'Jerusalem Tourist Information Center', a private tourist company next door.

Travel Agencies

ISSTA HaNevi'im St (☎02-621 3600; 31 HaNevi'im St); Herbert Samuel St (☎02-621 1188; 4 Herbert Samuel St; 🚊Jaffa Center) Israel's student travel agency. Organises inexpensive flight tickets.

Websites

Go Jerusalem (www.gojerusalem.com) Useful website with everything from car rental and bus schedules to hotel reviews and festival dates.

Jerusalem.com (www.jerusalem.com) Excellent overview of the city, its attractions and events. Virtual tours of important sites and even an application that allows you to leave prayers at holy places!

Jerusalem Municipality (www.jerusalem.muni.il) Has thorough and up-to-date pages on events and festivals. It also has a list of art exhibits and cultural institutes.

Getting There & Away

Bus

For details on making a day trip to the Dead Sea, see p240.

Central bus station (off Map p188; www.bus.co.il; Jaffa Rd; 🚊Central Station) From here you can get to all major cities and towns in Israel. Buses travel to Tel Aviv (bus 405, 20NIS, one hour, every 15 minutes), Haifa (bus 940 or 960, 40NIS, two hours, every 15 minutes), Tiberias (bus 962, 40NIS, 2½ hours, hourly), Be'er Sheva (bus 446 or 470, 32.50NIS, 90 minutes, twice hourly) and Eilat (bus 444, 75NIS, 4½ hours, four daily).

Damascus Gate bus station (Map p196) For Bethlehem, take bus 21 (7NIS). For Hebron, change in Bethlehem. For Nablus, change in Ramallah.

Arab bus station (Map p188; Sultan Suleyman St) Come here to get to parts of East Jerusalem such as Abu Dis (7NIS) and Mount of Olives (5NIS). For Jericho, take a bus to Abu Dis and change for a sherut (shared taxi) to Jericho. Alternatively, take a bus to Ramallah and change there.

Old Arab bus station (Map p188; Nablus Rd) For northern areas of the West Bank such as Ramallah (7NIS). Opposite the Garden Tomb.

Car

Most Jerusalem-based rental-car agencies forbid you to take their cars into the Palestinian Territories (Rte 1 to the Dead Sea is generally not a problem). An exception is **Green Peace** (☎02-585 9756; www.greenpeace.co.il; Shu'fat, East Jerusalem).

Sherut (Shared Taxi)

Sheruts (shared taxis, *servees* in Arabic) are much faster than buses, depart more frequently and cost only a few shekels more; on Shabbat they're the only public transport to destinations in Israel. Service taxis for Tel Aviv (23NIS per person on weekdays, 33NIS on Friday and Saturday) depart from the corner of HaRav Kook St and Jaffa Rd, near Zion Sq (Map p203). Service taxis for all destinations in the West Bank depart from the ranks opposite Damascus Gate, in East Jerusalem (Map p196).

Train

Jerusalem's **railway station** (Jerusalem Malcha; ☎02-577 4000; www.rail.co.il) is located in the southwest of the city, near the Jerusalem Mall; to get there, take bus 6 from the central bus station. Trains to Tel Aviv (adult/child 22/17.50NIS, 1¾ hours) depart every hour or two between 5.43am and 9.43pm Sunday to Thursday.

Getting Around

To/From the Airport

Ben-Gurion airport is 51km west of Jerusalem, just off Rte 1 to Tel Aviv. Bus 947 links the central bus station with the Airport City Commercial Complex (23NIS, 40 minutes, twice hourly), from where you have to switch to bus 5 (6.40NIS) to reach Terminal 3. Alternatively, **Nesher service taxis** (☎02-625 7227, 1 599 500 205) pick up booked passengers from their accommodation 24 hours a day (60NIS).

Bicycle

The hills of Jerusalem make biking tough going, but if you want a bike try **Nitzan Bike Shop** (☎02-623 5976; 137 Jaffa Rd; 🚊Mahane Yehuda), which rents out bikes for a pricey 100NIS per day.

If you are serious about cycling and want a good quality, well-maintained bike, contact **EcoBike** (☎077-450 1650; www.ecobike.co.il), which rents out top-of-the-line hybrids for $25 a day or $125 per week (available to pick up at the Abraham Hostel, p201).

Bus

Jerusalem is laced with a good network of city bus routes (6.40NIS per ride). If you need to transfer to another line the ticket is good for 90 minutes. A pass for 10 rides costs 55NIS, while a one-month pass is 216NIS. For the latest route information, call ☎*2800.

Light Rail

Inaugurated in 2011, **Jerusalem Light Rail** (JLR; ☎*2800; www.citypass.co.il, in Hebrew) consists of a single line that runs from Mt Herzl in the west of the city to Cheyl HaAvir in Pisgat Ze'ev, in the city's far northeast. It has 23 stops along a 13.9km route and passes a handful of landmarks including Central Bus Station, Mahane Yehuda Market, Zion Sq and Damascus Gate. It runs from 5.30am to midnight daily except on Shabbat. Tickets cost 6.40NIS. A JLR ticket is good on any Egged bus for 90 minutes from the time of purchase.

Taxi

Plan on spending 20NIS to 25NIS for trips anywhere within the central area of town. Always ask to use the meter. To order a taxi, call **Hapalmach taxi** (☎02-679 2333).

MEDITERRANEAN COAST

Stretching for 273km from Gaza to the Lebanese border, Israel's Mediterranean coastline has some fine beaches, first-rate archaeological sites and dynamic cities and towns.

Tel Aviv

تل أبيب תל אביב

☎03 / POP 404,400

While the State of Israel hits the headlines, the state of Tel Aviv sits back with a cappuccino. Nicknamed 'the Bubble', Tel Aviv (or TLV) is a city of outdoor cafes, boutiques, bistros, leafy boulevards and long sandy beaches – and a favourite with Europeans looking for some year-round sun. All over the city, classic Bauhaus buildings are getting a well-needed facelift, while nearby skyscrapers rise towards the heavens. Yet the real Tel Aviv is best sought out in humble hummus joints, wine bars hidden down alleyways, fresh fruit-shake stalls, quiet pocket parks and chaotic marketplaces.

Tel Aviv is very easy to get around, as its bustling central area focuses on five parallel north–south streets that follow 6km of seafront. Nearest the sand is Herbert Samuel Esplanade, while the hotel-lined HaYarkon St lies a block inland. East of HaYarkon St is Ben Yehuda St, home to backpackers and souvenir shops and the fourth parallel street is the trendy Dizengoff St, which marks the geographic centre of the city. Ibn Gabirol St forms the eastern boundary of the city centre. The Neve Tzedek and Florentine districts mark the southernmost reaches of the city centre before Jaffa, while Park HaYarkon and the Old Port (Namal) mark the northernmost.

Sights

Tel Aviv has a number of superb museums and a selection of neighbourhoods that are well worth a wander. Most sights of interest are within walking distance of the city centre, though you'll need a short hop by bike, bus or taxi to venture out to Ramat Aviv, home to Tel Aviv University and its excellent museums. Jaffa, to the south, is linked to Tel Aviv by a seafront promenade.

CITY CENTRE

Carmel Market MARKET
(Map p208) This frenetic market, Tel Aviv's answer to Jerusalem's Mahane Yehuda, is one of the few places in the city that will remind you that you're in the Middle East. Push past the first few metres of knock-off brand-name clothing and trainers to reach the more aromatic and enticing stalls of fresh fruits and vegetables, hot breads and spices.

Tel Aviv Museum of Art MUSEUM
(Map p208; ☎03-607 7020; www.tamuseum.com; 27 Shaul HaMelech Ave; adult/child 42/34NIS; ⏲10am-4pm Mon-Wed & Sat, to 10pm Tue & Thu, to 2pm Fri) Puts on outstanding temporary exhibitions of Israeli art. Also home to a great permanent collection of Impressionist and post-Impressionist art, including works by Picasso, Matisse, Gauguin, Degas and Van Gogh.

NEVE TZEDEK

Founded in 1887, Jaffa's first Jewish suburb – its old houses are now the most expensive real estate in town – is well worth a wander. The district's cute boutiques, cafes, wine bars and restaurants are centred on Shabazi St (named after a 17th-century Yemenite poet).

Suzanne Dellal Centre DANCE
(Map p208) This former school now serves as a venue for festivals, exhibits and cultural

TEL AVIV'S BAUHAUS HERITAGE

Tel Aviv has more sleek, clean-lined Bauhaus (International Style) buildings than any other city in the world, which is why it was declared a Unesco World Heritage Site in 2003. The ideas and ideals of Bauhaus were brought from Germany to Palestine by Jewish architects fleeing Nazi persecution.

Tel Aviv's **White City heritage** (www.white-city.co.il) is easy to spot, even through the modifications and dilapidation of the past 70 years. Look for structures characterised by horizontal lines, curved corners (eg of balconies), 'thermometer stairwells' (stairwells with a row of vertical windows to provide light), and a complete absence of ornamentation.

The **Bauhaus Center** (Map p208; ☎03-522 0249; www.bauhaus-center.com; 99 Dizengoff St; ⏰10am-7.30pm Sun-Thu, to 2.30pm Fri) sells a variety of architecture-related books and plans of the city, along with postcards of Tel Aviv in its Bauhaus heyday, and runs a **walking tour** starting at its shop every Friday at 10am. A free English-language guided **Bauhaus tour** departs from 46 Rothschild Blvd every Saturday at 11am.

events, and is home to the world-famous Bat Sheva dance troupe. The square outside is a relaxing place for a break.

Nachum Gutman Museum of Art MUSEUM
(Map p208; ☎03-516 1970; www.gutmanmuseum.co.il; 21 Rokach St; adult/child 24/12NIS; ⏰10am-4pm Sun-Thu, to 2pm Fri, to 3pm Sat) This museum displays 200 lively and fanciful works by the eponymous 20th-century Israeli artist.

Home of Shimon Rokach GALLERY
(Map p208; ☎03-516 8042; www.rokach-house.co.il; 36 Rokach St; admission 10NIS; ⏰10am-4pm Sun-Thu, to 2pm Fri & Sat) Built in 1887 by the man who founded Neve Tzedek, this house displays a small collection of strange antiques and sculptures in its courtyard and rooms.

NORTHERN TEL AVIV

TOP CHOICE **Beit Hatefutsoth** MUSEUM
(off Map p213; ☎03-745 7800; www.bh.org.il; 2 Klausner St, Matiyahu Gate, Ramat Aviv; adult/child 40/30NIS; ⏰10am-7pm Sun-Thu, 9am-2pm Fri) Located on the leafy campus of Tel Aviv University in the wealthy suburb of Ramat Aviv, this museum tells the epic story of the Jewish exile and global Diaspora. To get here take bus 25 from the Dizengoff Center, or take bus 127 from the central bus station. Get off at the university, either Matatia Gate No 2 or Frenkel Gate No 7.

Eretz Israel Museum MUSEUM
(Land of Israel Museum; off Map p213; ☎03-641 5244; 2 Chaim Levanon St; www.eretzmuseum.org.il; adult/child 42/28NIS, incl planetarium 74/32NIS; ⏰10am-4pm Sun-Wed, to 8pm Thu, to 2pm Fri & Sat) The Eretz Israel Museum consists of 11 small themed collections (glass, ceramics, folklore, etc) constructed around the Tel Qasile archaeological site. To get here, take Dan bus 25 or Egged bus 86.

Beaches

When the weather is warm, Tel Avivians (or Tel Avivim) flock en masse to the beachfront, a long golden stretch of sand divided into sections, each with its own character. All are clean, safe and well-equipped with umbrellas, beach bars and vocal lifeguards.

Here's a rundown of Tel Aviv's beaches, from north to south:

Metzitzim Beach FAMILY BEACH
(Map p213) A family-friendly bay with a small kids' play area.

Nordau Beach RELIGIOUS BEACH
(Map p213) The city's religious beach, open to women on Sunday, Tuesday and Thursday, and to men on Monday, Wednesday and Friday. It's open to everyone on Saturday, when observant Jews don't go to the beach.

Hilton Beach GAY BEACH
(Map p213) The city's unofficial gay beach, named after the nearby hotel.

Gordon & Frishman Beaches CENTRAL BEACH
(Map p208) Popular with Tel Aviv teens, tourists and toddlers; the place to play beach volleyball.

Jerusalem Beach PARTY BEACH
(Map p208) Loud teenagers characterise this nice, but plain, stretch of sand.

Banana Beach CHILL-OUT BEACH
(Map p208) Has a laid-back, mellow vibe that attracts a 20- and 30-something crowd.

Central Tel Aviv

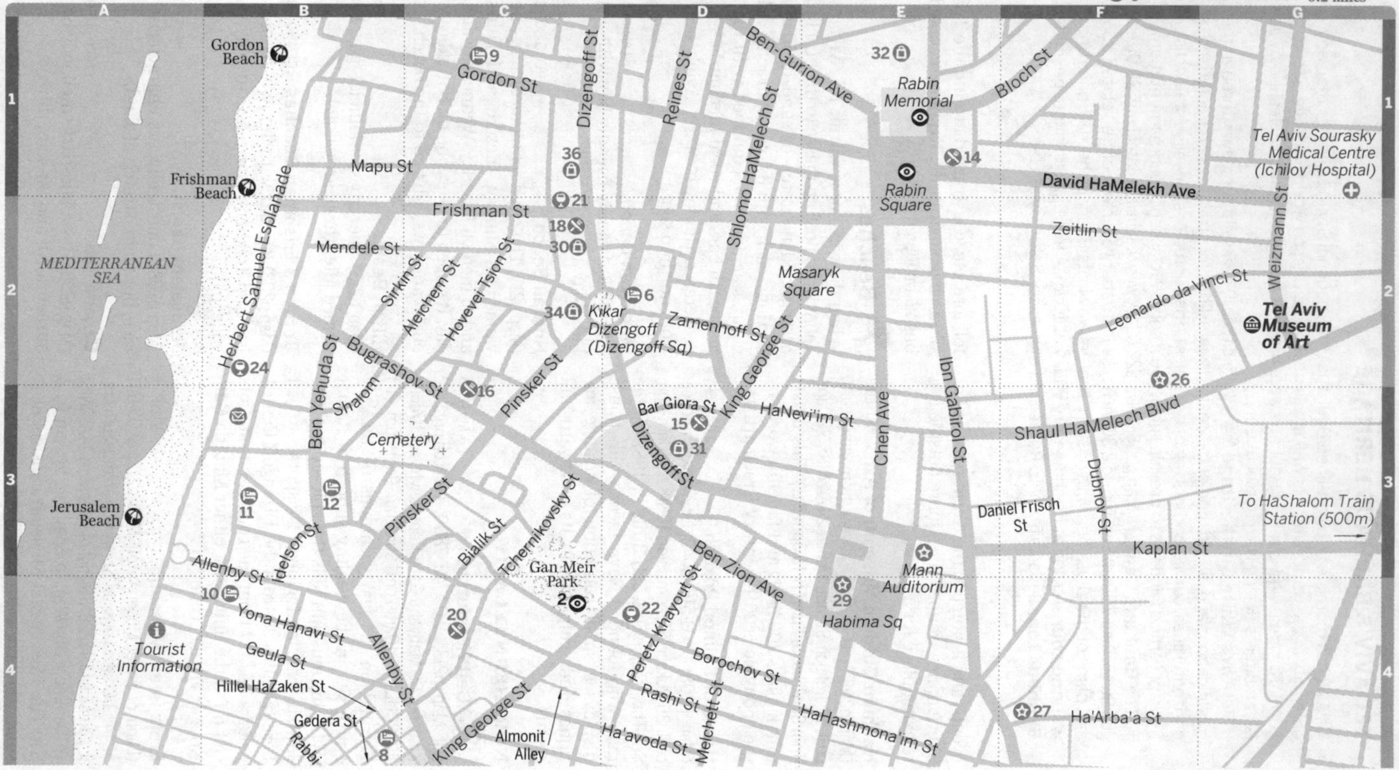

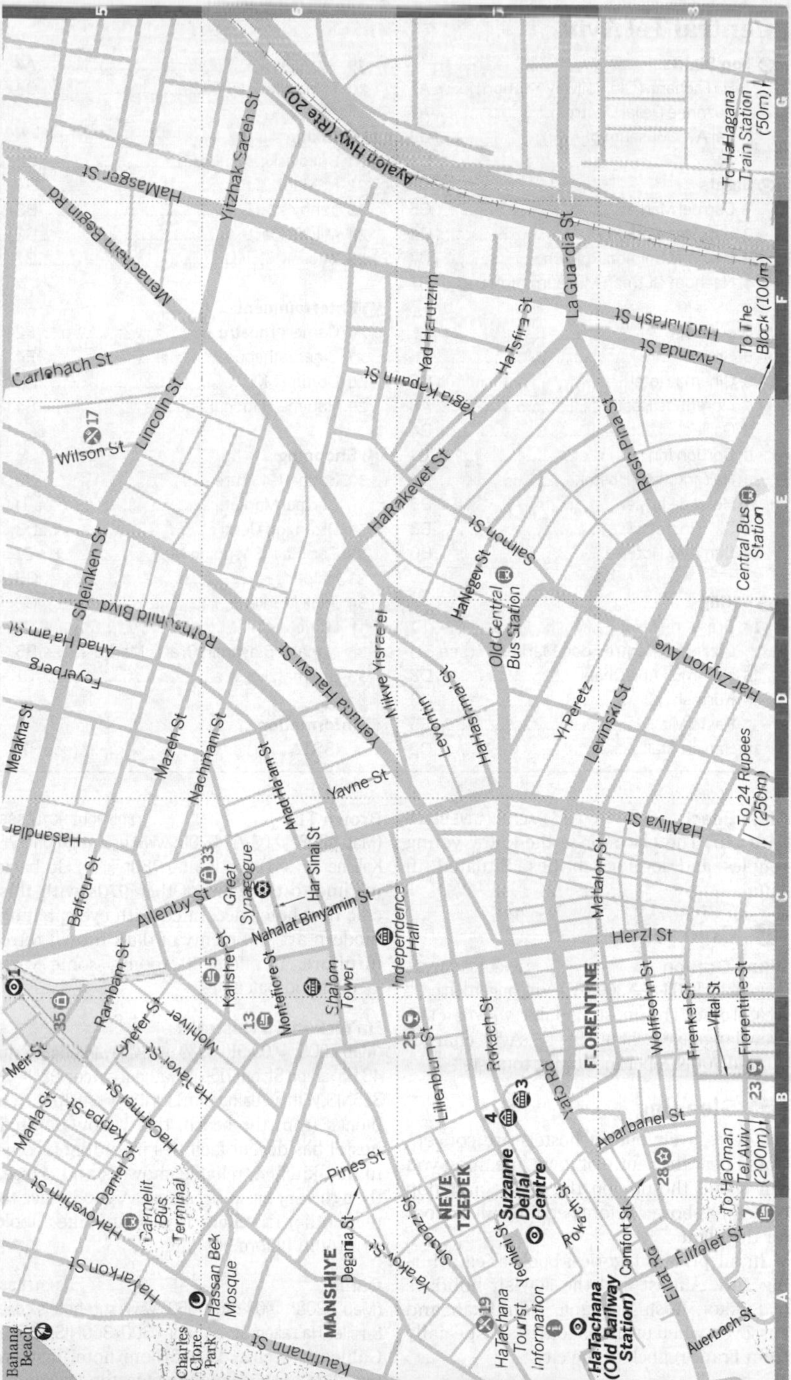
Ayalon Hwy (Rte 20)
HaMasger St
Menachem Begin Rd
Yitzhak Sadeh St
Carlebach St
Lincoln St
Wilson St
17
Sheinken St
Rothschild Blvd
Ahad Ha'am St
Foyerberg
Melakha St
Hasandlar
Balfour St
Allenby St
Mazeh St
Nachmani St
33
Great Synagogue
Ahad Ha'am St
Har Sinai St
Nahalat Binyamin St
Yavne St
Yehuda HaLevi St
HaRakevet St
Yad Harutzim
Yagia Kapaim St
HaTsfira St
La Guardia St
HaCharash St
Lavanda St
To The Block (100m)
To HaHagana Train Station (50m)
Rosh Pina St
Salmon St
HaNegev St
Old Central Bus Station
Central Bus Station
Har Ziyyon Ave
Mikve Yisra'el
Levontin St
HaHashmal St
Yl Peretz
Levinski St
HaAliya St
To 24 Rupees (250m)
Matalon St
Herzl St
Independence Hall
Shalom Tower
Montefiore St
Kalisher St
5
13
Rambam St
Shefer St
Mohliver St
1
35
Meir St
Ha'Tavor St
HaCarmel St
Kappa St
Mania St
Daniel St
Hakovshim St
Carmelit Bus Terminal
Hassan Bek Mosque
Charles Clore Park
Banana Beach
HaYarkon St
Kaufmann St
MANSHIYE
Degania St
Pines St
Lilienblum St
25
Rokach St
NEVE TZEDEK
4
3
Suzanne Dellal Centre
Yechiel St
Shabazi St
Ya'akov St
19
HaTachana Tourist Information
HaTachana (Old Railway Station)
Rokach St
Yafo Rd
FLORENTINE
Wolffsohn St
Frenkel St
Vital St
Florentine St
23
Abarbanel St
28
Comfort St
To HaOman Tel Aviv (200m)
7
Elifelet St
Eilat Rd
Auerbach St
A
B
C
D
E
F
G
5
6
7
8

Central Tel Aviv

Top Sights

	HaTachana (Old Railway Station)	A7
	Suzanne Dellal Centre	A7
	Tel Aviv Museum of Art	G2

Sights

1	Carmel Market	C5
2	Gan Meir Park	C4
3	Home of Shimon Rokach	B7
4	Nachum Gutman Museum of Art	B7

Sleeping

5	Brown TLV	C6
6	Cinema Hotel	D2
7	Florentine Hostel	A8
8	Galileo	B4
9	Gordon Inn	C1
10	HaYarkon 48 Hostel	B4
11	Hotel de la Mer	B3
12	Sky Hostel	B3
13	Sun Aviv Hotel	B6

Eating

14	Brasserie M&R	E1
	Dizengoff Centre Food Market	(see 31)
15	Hummus Abu Dhabi	D3
16	Kurtosh	C3
17	Pasta Mia	E5
18	Sabich Stall	C2
19	Suzanna	A7
20	Tchernikovsky 6	C4

Drinking

21	Bukowski	C2
22	HaMaoz	D4
23	Lenny's	B8
24	Mike's Place	B2
25	Shesek	B7

Entertainment

26	Cameri Theatre	F2
27	Cinematheque	F4
28	Comfort 13	B8
29	Habima National Theatre	E4

Shopping

30	Bauhaus Centre	C2
	Carmel Market	(see 1)
31	Dizengoff Centre	D3
32	Gan Ha'ir Shopping Mall	E1
33	Halper's	C6
34	Junk Market	C2
	Lametayel	(see 31)
35	Nahalat Binyamin Crafts Market	B5
36	Steimatzky	C1

Information

	ISSTA	(see 31)

Alma Beach ALTERNATIVE BEACH

(Map p217) The place for in-the-know young couples and local celebrities. Situated in Jaffa.

Courses

Ulpan Gordon LANGUAGE COURSE

(Map p213; ☎03-522 3095; www.ulpangordon.co.il; 7 LaSalle St) The most popular *ulpan* (Hebrew-language school) in Tel Aviv charges around 700NIS per month for tourists.

Sleeping

Tel Aviv's lively budget hostels are concentrated near the centre of town, meaning you can spend the day on the beach and pop back for a shower before heading out on foot for the night.

In all price categories, book ahead during July, August and the Jewish holidays of Sukkot, Rosh Hashana, Hanukkah and Passover, when overseas tourists (especially from France) flock to the city.

Brown TLV BOUTIQUE HOTEL $$$

(Map p208; ☎03-717 0200; www.browntlv.com; 25 Kalisher St; s/d from US$160/180; ❄📶) Go back in time to the glam of the 1970s with this chic new hotel, decorated with eye-catching modern art and plenty of dark brown retro furniture. It offers 30 rooms, some with jacuzzi and balconies.

HaYarkon 48 Hostel HOSTEL $

(Map p208; ☎03-516 8989; www.hayarkon48.com; 48 HaYarkon St; dm 115NIS, without air-con 98NIS, r 385NIS, without bathroom 330NIS; ❄📶) Just two blocks from the beach, this yellow-painted hostel has decent facilities including a communal kitchen, reliable showers and a free, though very basic, breakfast. A good place to meet other travellers. If you can, take a look at a room before booking.

Galileo HOTEL $$

(Map p208; ☎03-516 0050; www.sun-hotels.co.il; 8 Hillel Ha'zaken St; s/d from 300/360NIS; ❄📶) Galileo is a cute, 12-bedroom hotel just on the edge of the Yemenite Quarter. Its rooms might be on the small side but they're comfortable and tastefully decorated.

Sky Hostel HOSTEL $

(Map p208; ☎03-620 0044; www.sky1hostel.com; 34 Ben Yehuda St; dm 80NIS, s/d 240/320NIS, without bathroom 160/270NIS; 📶) One of the better budget options in the centre of town, Sky has simple rooms, some with air-conditioning and others with fans.

Hotel De La Mer HOTEL $$$

(Map p208; ☎03-510 0011; www.delamer.co.il; 2 Ness Ziona St, cnr HaYarkon; s/d US$159/179; ❄📶) Fancifully branding itself a 'Feng Shui Hotel', the De La Mer gets top marks for its airy pastel-shaded rooms, great spa, personal attention and sea views. The big breakfast comes highly recommended, too.

Sun Aviv Hotel HOTEL $$

(Map p208; ☎03-517 4847; www.sun-aviv.co.il; 9a Montefiore St; s/d 350/380NIS; ❄📶) Sun Aviv is well placed for the cafes and bars on Rothschild Blvd. The rooms may be small, but each is individually styled with colourful wallpaper, artworks and simple furnishings.

Florentine Hostel HOSTEL $

(Map p208; ☎03-518 7551; www.florentinehostel.com; 10 Elifelet St; dm 77NIS, r 200NIS; ❄📶) One for young hipsters, this small hostel has one dorm and a few private rooms. It has a funky Sinai-style roof garden, but due to its 'saba' laid-back alternative vibe, the hostel imposes an age restriction of 18 to 40 years old.

Cinema Hotel HOTEL $$$

(Map p208; ☎03-520 7100; www.atlas.co.il; 2 Zamenhoff St; s/d from 700/750NIS; ❄📶) In a classic Bauhaus building on super-central Kikar Dizengoff, the Cinema – though part of a chain – manages to be charming and individual, complete with old bits of projectors, cinema posters and vintage stage lighting.

Gordon Inn HOSTEL $

(Map p208; ☎03-523 8239; www.hostelstelaviv.com; 17 Gordon St; dm 90NIS, s/d 380/410NIS, without bathroom 380/280NIS; ❄📶) This hostel has a great location, bang in the centre, close to the beach and the lively Ben Yehuda St. Rooms are basic, small and without any creature comforts.

HI Tel Aviv Youth Hostel HOSTEL $$

(Map p213; ☎02-594 5655; www.iyha.org.il; 36 B'nei Dan St; dm/d 162.50/410NIS; ❄📶) With less of an international party vibe than the other hostels, this is a clean and well-kept place with all the necessary amenities, situated close to the buzzing Old Port.

Eating

It's hard to recommend just a handful of Tel Aviv restaurants since there are so many excellent options of all types. Below is a small selection of our favourites.

TEL AVIV FOR CHILDREN

Most children will be entertained for hours on Tel Aviv's many kilometres of soft-sand **beaches**, which are well life-guarded and equipped with ice-cream vendors and beach cafes. But if it's a grassy expanse you're after, try **HaYarkon Park** (Map p213), equipped with a small zoo, pedal boats and playgrounds. Nearby, there are plenty of rides at the **Luna Park** (off Map p213; ☎03-642 7080; www.lunapark.co.il; admission 98NIS, under 2yr free); opening hours change by the month, so call ahead. Calmer rides are to be had at the good playground at **Gan Meir Park** (Map p208) on King George St. The wide wooden boardwalk at the **Old Port** (Map p213) is perfect for a child-friendly wander.

A haven for smaller people and their parents, **Dyada** (Map p213; ☎1 700 700 815; www.dyada.co.il; 75 Ben Gurion Ave) is a children's centre hosting all kinds of regular activities, with a cafe downstairs and a well stocked mother and baby shop. Call or drop in to reserve a place for some toddler tumbling. Many shopping malls, including **Gan Ha'ir** (Map p208) on Ibn Gabirol St, just north of City Hall, and **Dizengoff Center** (Map p208) at the corner of Dizengoff and King George Sts, have hugely popular play areas *(mischakiyot)* for toddlers and young children.

Just outside town, commune with the natural world at the **Ramat Gan Safari** (☎03-630 5328; www.safari.co.il, in Hebrew; Ramat Gan; per person 49NIS), part of which is a conventional zoo and the other a drive-through safari. Check the website for opening hours and a driving map.

Fast food joints are never more than a few steps away in the city, with a particularly good selection along Ben Yehuda, Allenby and Ibn Gabirol Sts. On Thursday afternoon and Friday morning, Dizengoff Center (at the corner of Dizengoff & King George Sts) fills with food stalls.

Brasserie M&R FRENCH $$

(Map p208; ☎03-696 7111; 70 Ibn Gabirol St; mains from 60NIS; ⏲8am-5am) Facing Rabin Sq, this bustling, Parisian-style eatery serves up mouth-watering steak, chicken and seafood dishes, as well as classic breakfasts and cocktails from its Hebrew and French menu.

Tchernikovsky 6 BISTRO $$

(Map p208; ☎03-620 8729; 5 Tchernichovsky St; mains from 68NIS; ⏲noon-midnight Mon-Fri, noon-6pm Sat & Sun; 📶) This lovely local bistro has a delicious menu that changes almost daily and a good wine list; carnivores will melt at the 'butcher's cuts', while vegetarians will delight in gorgonzola salad, homemade gnocchi or polenta with grilled asparagus.

Kurtosh BAKERY $

(Map p208; 39 Bograshov St & 178 Dizengoff St; cakes from 25NIS; ⏲7am-9pm Sun-Thu, until 4pm Fri; 6pm-10pm Sat; 🖉) This Hungarian bakery specialises in long, spiral pastries that look like the hollowed-out cooling tower of a miniature nuclear power plant.

Hummus Abu Dhabi HUMMUS $

(Map p208; 81 King George St; portion 20NIS; ⏲11am-midnight Sat-Thu, to 4pm Fri; 🖉) A classic combo of reggae music and warm plates of hummus, this place certainly 'stirs it up', Bob Marley–style.

Suzanna FUSION $$

(Map p208; 9 Shabazi St; meals 45-65NIS; ⏲10am-midnight) A long-standing Neve Tzedek favourite, Suzanna offers a mix of Mediterranean-inspired dishes, including stuffed vegetables and mezze. During the warm months you can dine under an enormous ficus tree.

24 Rupees INDIAN $$

(off Map p208; 14-16 Shocken St; thalis from 30NIS; ⏲noon-midnight Sat-Thu, to 5pm Fri; 📶🖉) Head straight to Varanasi at this Indian thali hang-out, which is hidden on the 1st floor of what looks like a residential building. Slip off your shoes, slide onto a floor cushion, and munch on vegetarian food served on tin thali platters. The door downstairs is hard to spot and looks locked – don't worry, it's not.

Sabich Stall ISRAELI $

(Map p208; 42 Frishman St; per sabich 15NIS; ⏲9am-11.30pm Sun-Thu, to 4pm Fri; 🖉) This hole-in-the-wall shop specialises in *sabich*, an Iraqi-derived snack, consisting of roast aubergine, boiled egg and potato, salad, hummus, pickles and spicy amba (mango) sauce, all stuffed into a pita.

Pasta Mia ITALIAN $$

(Map p208; ☎03-561 0189; 10 Wilson St; pasta from 54NIS; ⏲noon-midnight daily; 🖉) The big Italian flag outside this little neighbourhood trattoria gives it away. Pasta Mia produces its own fresh pasta daily and is a tiny slice of Tuscany in a grubby Tel Aviv backstreet.

Drinking

All over the city, drinking joints are constantly opening up or changing name. As a general rule, the hottest bars are usually found in the south, particularly around Lillenblum St; most are open seven days a week. Expect to pay between 22NIS to 28NIS for half a litre of beer, while cocktails and wines by the glass begin at 26NIS.

HaMaoz BAR

(Map p208; 32 King George St; ⏲8pm-late Sun-Thu, from 2pm Fri, from 6pm Sat; 📶) Locals and tourists love HaMaoz, which has three main areas – an outdoor garden, an indoor bar and a backroom that looks like someone's apartment.

Bukowski BAR

(Map p208; 39 Frishman St; ⏲10pm-late) Completely enclosed with sound-proof walls and no sign outside, you could walk past Bukowski a dozen times and never know there was a party going on behind that closed door. This local bar, on the corner of Dizengoff St, is a dress-down place with a vociferous following, a long list of drinks, and a cool soundtrack.

Lenny's BAR

(Map p208; 7 Vittal St; ⏲8am-1am Sun-Fri, 10am-late Sat) Young and hip, Lenny's is a great little neighbourhood bar in Florentine. Other bars such as Chaser and Mate Florentine are also on this street so you can crawl easily from here.

Shesek BAR

(Map p208; 17b Lillenblum St; ⏲9pm-late) Shesek is a rough-around-the-edges bar and bohemian haunt well known for pumping out a variety of music (mash-ups and punk to trance and avant-garde hip-hop), nightly

DJs and quality beer (including Taybeh, a microbrew manufactured in Ramallah).

Mike's Place BAR

(Map p208; www.mikesplacebars.com; 86 Herbert Samuel Esplanade & 312 Dizengoff St; ⏲11am-late; 📶) Both the newer bar on Dizengoff St and the original on the beach next to the US Embassy offer burgers, frothy pints, sports and live rock music. The sizable menu has grill-style meals, cocktails and beer. Happy hour is 3pm to 8pm daily (11am to 8pm on Saturday).

☆ Entertainment

Tel Aviv has the best nightlife in Israel, possibly the whole Middle East, but you need to be prepared for some late nights. In some places doors don't open until midnight and the party really doesn't get going until around 2am.

Most of the big commercial clubs are at the Old Port (HaNamal), in the renovated hangars, or along the seafront, and cater for young tourists and soldiers. For more alternative nights out, head south towards Florentine and Salameh/Schlomo Rd.

Nightclubs

Tel Aviv has a number of world-class, party-till-dawn clubs, most without any of the dress codes imposed, for example, in London.

TOP CHOICE **Block** DJ

(off Map p208; www.block-club.com; 157 Shelomo Rd; admission 80NIS; ⏲11pm-late Thu-Sat) The Block hosts big-name DJs playing anything from funk, hip-hop and Afrobeat to drum 'n' bass, house and trance.

Comfort 13 DJ

(Map p208; 13 Comfort St; admission 60NIS; ⏲11pm-late) One of Florentine's trendiest clubs, nights span from trashy pop to electronica, as well as occasional live rock bands.

HaOman Tel Aviv CLUB

(off Map p208; 88 Abarbanel St; admission 100NIS; ⏲1am-late) One of the biggest, brashest clubs in the city, this place hosts international DJs and has plenty of swank, including an on-site sushi bar, a sunken dance floor and five bars. Come dressed to impress.

Cinemas

Cinematheque CINEMA

(Map p208; ☎03-606 0800; 1 Ha'Arba'a St; admission 37NIS) Features classic, retro, foreign, avant-garde, new wave and off-beat films.

Theatre & Dance

Cameri Theatre THEATRE

(Map p208; ☎03-606 0960; www.cameri.co.il; 30 Leonardo da Vinci St) Hosts first-rate theatre performances in Hebrew, on some nights

Northern Tel Aviv

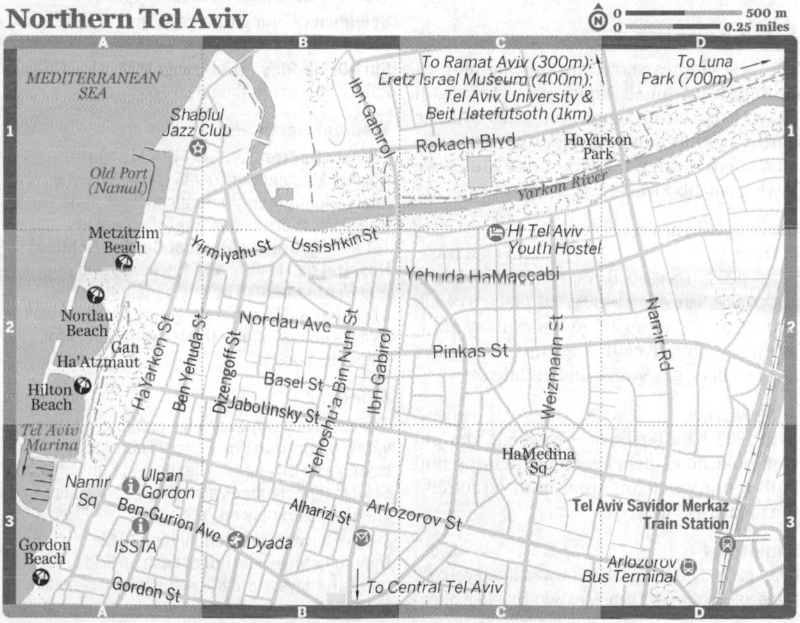

with simultaneous English translation or English-language subtitles.

Habima National Theatre THEATRE
(Map p208; ☎03-629 5555; www.habima.co.il; 2 Tarsat St, Habima Sq) Recently rebuilt, Habima is home to Israel's national theatre company and stages weekly performances with English translations.

Suzanne Dellal Centre DANCE
(Map p208; ☎03-510 5656; www.suzannedellal.org.il; 5 Yechieli St) Venue for dance, music and ballet, and plays home to the world famous Bat Sheva dance company, founded by Martha Graham.

Live Music

Goldstar Zappa Club LIVE MUSIC
(☎03-762 6666; 24 Raul Wallenberg St, Ramat HaChayal) Local and international music luminaries play at this intimate club, 8km northeast of the city centre.

Barby LIVE MUSIC
(☎03-518 8123; 52 Kibbutz Galuyot St) Veteran venue for reggae, rock and random alternative bands. Situated 5km south of the centre.

Shablul Jazz Club JAZZ
(Map p213; ☎03-546 1891; Hangar 13; Old Port) Cool jazz, salsa and world music to keep you finger-wagging, wiggling or jiggling well on into the night.

Shopping

The best clothes shops are on Sheinkin St (with lots of small boutiques), Dizengoff St (with Israeli designer stores toward the northern end), and at the tiny one-of-a-kind shops dotting the Florentine and Neve Tsedek neighbourhoods.

Nahalat Binyamin Crafts Market ARTS & CRAFTS
(Map p208; Nahalat Binyamin St; ⊙9.30am-5.30pm Tue, 9am-4pm Fri) A great place to walk around and soak up Tel Aviv's exuberant atmosphere. Creative offerings include ceramics, jewellery, glasswork and Judaica.

Junk Market ANTIQUES
(Map p208; Kikar Dizengoff; ⊙Tue & Fri) The old stuff sold here includes coins, stamps and 20th-century detritus from both Israel and the former USSR.

Lametayel BOOKS
(Map p208; ☎077 333 4502; www.lametayel.co.il; Dizengoff Centre; ⊙10am-9pm Sun-Thu, to 2.30pm Fri) Specialist in travel books, Lonely Planet titles and maps. Also sells backpacks, hiking gear and tents.

Halper's BOOKS
(Map p208; ☎03-629 9710; 87 Allenby St; ⊙9am-6pm Sun-Thu, to 4pm Fri) Specialist in used English-language titles.

Steimatzky BOOKS
(Map p208; ☎03-522 1513; 109 Dizengoff St; ⊙9am-8pm Sun-Thu, to 4pm Fri) Chain bookstore; this branch has a decent array of English-language titles.

Information

Emergency

Ambulance (☎101)
Fire department (☎102)
Police (☎100)
Tourist police (☎03-516 5832; cnr Herbert Samuel Esplanade & Geula St)

Internet Access

An increasing numbers of cafes, bars and hotels offer wi-fi, as do all Metropoline buses.

Beit Ariela Library (25 Shaul HaMelech St; ⊙10am-6.45pm Sun-Thu, 9-11.45am Fri; wi-fi) The main city library has free wi-fi, plus books in English, French and Russian.

Cyberlink (20 Allenby St; per hr 15NIS; ⊙24hr)

Log-In (21 Ben Yehuda St; per hr 20NIS; ⊙9am-midnight Sun-Fri, from 4pm Sat)

Spielman (77 King George St; per hr 17NIS; ⊙24hr)

Surf-Drink-Play (112 Dizengoff St; per 90min 20NIS; ⊙11am-midnight)

Medical Services

Tel Aviv Doctor (☎054 941 4243; Basel Heights Medical Centre, 35 Basel St; www.telaviv-doctor.com) A medical clinic aimed at travellers, tourists and English-speakers.

Tel Aviv Sourasky Medical Centre (Ichilov) Hospital (☎03-697 4444; www.tasmc.org.il; 6 Weizmann St) The city's main hospital, which has a 24-hour emergency room, as well as a travellers' clinic (the Malram Clinic) for immunisations.

Money

The best currency exchange deals are at the private bureaus that don't charge commission, for example on Dizengoff, Allenby and Ben Yehuda Sts. Most post offices also change travellers cheques, commission-free.

You'll have no problem finding ATMs, though they sometimes run out of cash on Friday nights and Saturdays. Here are some handy central branches:

Bank Discount (66, 103 & 104 Ibn Gabirol St, 55 & 191 Dizengoff St, 71 Ben Yehuda St, 66 Sheinken St)

Bank Leumi (19 Herzl St, 43 Allenby St, 50 Dizengoff St)

Post

Post office (www.israelpost.co.il; ⏰8am-6pm Sun-Thu, to noon Fri) Northern Tel Aviv (Map p213; 170 Ibn Gabirol St); Central Tel Aviv (Map p208; 61 HaYarkon St)

Tourist Information

HaTachana Tourist Information (Map p208; Hangar 5, HaTachana; ⏰10am-8pm Sun-Thu, to 1pm Fri) Small office in the Old Railway Station complex.

Tourist information office (Map p208; ☎03-516 6188; www.visit-tlv.com; 46 Herbert Samuel Esplanade; ⏰9.30am-5pm Sun-Thu, to 1pm Fri) A very helpful office offering maps, tips and tours.

Travel Agencies

ISSTA (Map p208; ☎03-521 0555; www.issta.co.il; 109 Ben Yehuda St) Student travel agency that can sometimes come up with very well-priced airline tickets. It's on the corner of Ben-Gurion Ave.

Websites

Tel Aviv Insider (www.tel-aviv-insider.com) Excellent tips on activities, dining and nightlife.

Tel Aviv Municipality (www.tel-aviv.gov.il/english) Official municipality website.

Visit TLV (www.visit-tlv.com) Tourist information.

ℹ Getting There & Away

During Shabbat, sheruts (share taxis) provide the only public transport.

Air

For details on air links, see p273.

Bus

From Tel Aviv's enormous, confusing and grotty **central bus station** (Map p208; ☎03-638 3945), **Egged** (☎03-694 8888; www.egged.co.il) buses leave for Jerusalem (bus 405, 20NIS, one hour, every 15 minutes); Haifa (bus 910, 26.50NIS, 1½ hours, every 20 minutes); Tiberias (bus 830, 835 and 841, 42NIS, 2½ hours) once or twice hourly from 6am to 9pm; Eilat (bus 390 & 395, 78NIS, five hours), more or less hourly from 6.30am to 5pm (an overnight service departs at 12.30am); and Be'er Sheva (bus 370, 17NIS, 1½ hours, two or three hourly). Tickets can be bought from the driver or from ticket booths.

If staying in the centre or north of the city, Egged bus 480 (20NIS, one hour, every 15 minutes) from the **Arlosorov Bus Terminal** (Map p213; cnr Arlozorov St & Namir Rd) is by far the quickest way to Jerusalem.

Car

Finding street parking in downtown Tel Aviv ranges from difficult to impossible. Most of the main car-rental agencies have offices on HaYarkon St.

Sherut (Shared Taxi)

The sheruts (yellow minibus services) outside the central bus station run to Jerusalem (20NIS) and Haifa (25NIS). On Saturday, they leave from HaHashmal St just east of Allenby St and charge about 20% more than the weekday fare.

Train

Tel Aviv has three **train stations** (☎03-611 7000; www.rail.co.il).

From all three, you can travel to Haifa (30.50NIS, one hour) via Netanya (15.50NIS, 25 minutes), every 20 minutes from 6am to 8pm Sunday to Friday, and on to Akko (39NIS, 1½ hours) and Nahariya (44.50NIS, 1¾ hours). Heading south, you can travel down the coast to Ashkelon (25.50NIS, one hour) and as far as Be'er Sheva (30NIS, 1¼ hours), both services departing hourly. To reach Tel Aviv Merkaz from the centre, take bus 61 north from Dizengoff St to the Arlosorov bus terminal, which is a two-minute walk from the station.

HaHaganna (off Map p208) A five-minute walk from the central bus station.

HaShalom (off Map p208) Next to the Azrieli Center.

Tel Aviv Merkaz (Map p213) Sometimes called Tel Aviv Savidor, at the eastern end of Arlosorov St.

ℹ Getting Around

Getting around the compact centre is easiest on foot or by bicycle, avoiding traffic snarls, packed buses and unscrupulous taxi drivers.

To/From the Airport

Ben-Gurion Airport is 21km southeast of central Tel Aviv. Except very late at night, the airport is served by at least two trains per hour (www.rail.co.il; 14.50NIS, from 3.30am to 11pm daily). At the airport, metered taxis leave from an orderly taxi rank; the ride into central Tel Aviv takes about 20 minutes (if there's not traffic) and costs around 130NIS (day rate) and 152NIS (night rate).

Bicycle

The best way to get around Tel Aviv and Jaffa is on two wheels. In addition to more than 100km of dedicated bicycle paths, running along many of the major thoroughfares, the city now has **Tel-O-Fun** (☎*6070; www.tel-o-fun.co.il), a bicycle-rental scheme similar to Paris' Vélib'. Subscriptions cost 14NIS (daily) and 60NIS (weekly); pay with your credit card at any Tel-O-Fun station. Pick up and drop off the green bicycles at any of over 75 docking stations; the first half-hour is free.

Bus

Tel Aviv city buses are operated by **Dan** (☎03-639 4444; www.dan.co.il; single fare 6.60NIS) and follow an efficient network of routes, from 5.30am to midnight, except Shabbat. A one-day pass *(hofshi yomi),* which allows unlimited bus travel around Tel Aviv and its suburbs (valid from 9am until the end of the day) costs 14NIS. To buy one, you'll need a *Rav Kav* travel card, which can be obtained from a Dan information counter at the central bus station or the Arlozorov Terminal (in a hut near the train station entrance) from 8am to 6pm Sunday to Thursday or until 1pm on Friday.

Taxi

By law, all taxis must use their meter. Plan on 30NIS for trips anywhere within the central city (if you have a group of four people it becomes more cost-effective than the bus).

Jaffa

يافا יפו

☎03 / POP 46,000

It is said that after Noah and all those animals survived the Flood, one of his sons, Japheth, headed for the coast and founded a city that he named Jaffa (Yafo in Hebrew) after himself. During Solomon's time, the city came to prominence as a port and, according to the Bible, it was from here that Jonah set sail to his encounter with the whale. A group of rocks just offshore is said to be where Andromeda, one of Greek mythology's most beautiful princesses, was saved by Perseus.

For thousands of years, while Tel Aviv was nothing more than a collection of sand dunes, Jaffa was one of the great cities of the Mediterranean. The small port doesn't get much seafaring traffic these days, but its hangars are being transformed into cafes, shops and art galleries. The town itself, whose residents are a mixture of Jews, Muslims and Christians, centres on a bustling flea market, and while it can come across as a little shabby, that's all part of Jaffa's unpretentious charm.

Sights

HaTachana HISTORIC SITE

(Old Railway Station; Map p208; www.hatachana.co.il; Neve Tzedek; ⊙10am-10pm Sat-Thu, to 5pm Fri) The one-time terminus of the rail line to Jerusalem, opened in 1892, was recently transformed into a lively hangout, with cafes, restaurants and a host of fashionable boutique shops. The main entrance is on the seafront road off Kaufman St and can easily be reached from Neve Tzedek and the Carmelit bus terminal. Dan buses 10, 18, 25 and 100 all stop close by.

Old City HISTORIC SITE

Jaffa's Old City, on and around a small hill, is centred on **Kikar Kedumim** (Kedumim Sq), which is ringed with restaurants and galleries and dominated by the pastel-shaded, Franciscan **St Peter's Church** (⊙8-11.45am & 3-5pm Oct-Feb, to 6pm Mar-Sep).

In an underground chamber at the centre of the square, a small **visitors centre** (admission free; ⊙10am-6pm Sun-Thu, to 5pm Fri & Sat) has partially excavated remains from the Hellenistic and Roman eras and screens a short film on Jaffa and Andromeda. To the east of the square, on Jaffa's highest point, **HaPisgah Gardens** offer nice views north up the coast to Tel Aviv.

Ilana Goor Museum GALLERY

(☎03-683 7676; www.ilanagoor.com; 4 Mazal Dagim St; adult/child 24/14NIS; ⊙10am-4pm Sun-Fri, to 6pm Sat) This eclectic gallery, in the private home of artist Ilana Goor, is set in a labyrinth of gallery-lined alleyways named after zodiac signs. Built in the 18th century, the building once served as a hostel for Jewish pilgrims arriving in Jaffa.

Flea Market MARKET

(Shuk HaPishpeshim; ⊙10am-6pm Sun-Thu, to 4pm Fri) If you are looking for a Persian rug, Moroccan tea set, beautiful painting or just an old TV, this lively, ramshackle market, a bit southeast of the Ottoman clock tower, is the place to come. Bartering is expected. Located between Olei Zion St and Beit Eshul St.

Ajami NEIGHBOURHOOD

Head south along Yefet St from the clock tower to get to the mostly Arab neighbourhood of Ajami, where gentrified Ottoman-era homes stand next to tiny fishermen's shacks. Notorious for crime and drugs (especially the further south you go), the area featured in the Oscar-nominated 2010 film *Ajami.*

Ajami's seafront now opens out into a large green park (a garbage dump until a few years ago) that makes a great place for a picnic, a game of frisbee or a bicycle ride.

Jaffa

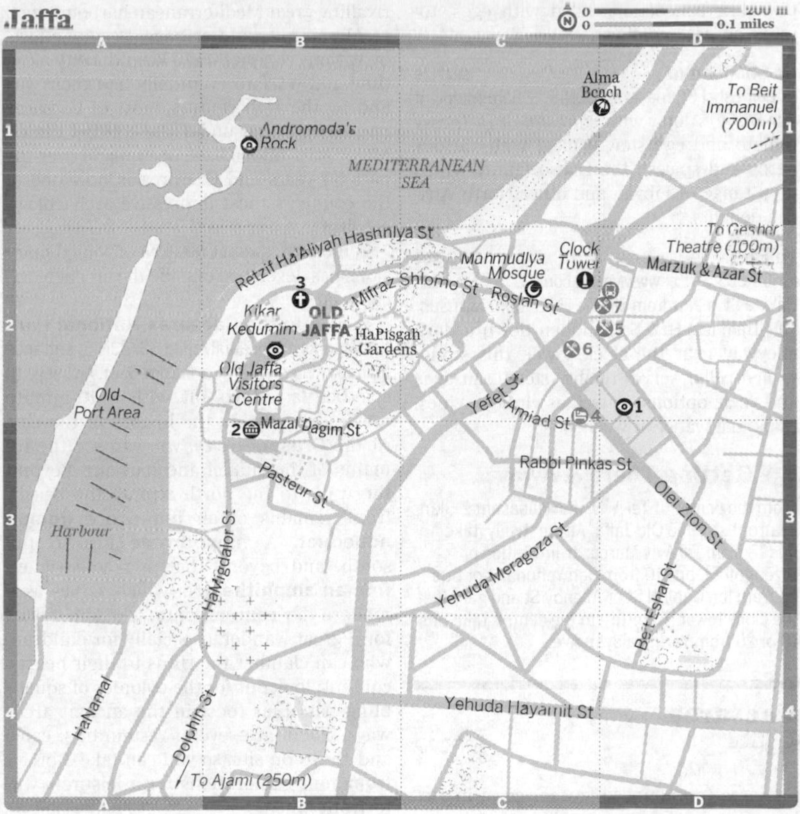

Jaffa

Sights

1 Flea Market D2
2 Ilana Goor Museum B3
3 St Peter's Church B2

Sleeping

4 Old Jaffa Hostel C2

Eating

5 Dr Shakshuka D2
6 Said Abu Elafia & Sons C2
7 Yo'Ezer D2

Sleeping

TOP CHOICE Old Jaffa Hostel HOSTEL $

(☎03-682 2370; www.telaviv-hostel.com; 13 Amiad St; dm/s/d 80/210/250NIS; 📶) In a beautiful old Turkish home, decorated with sepia family photographs, the Jaffa is undoubtedly the most atmospheric option in its price range. The rooms range from tiny singles with low ceilings to large air-conditioned double bedrooms with small balconies.

Beit Immanuel HOSTEL $

(☎03-682 1459; www.beitimmanuel.org; 8 Auerbach St; dm/s/d 110/220/340NIS; 📶) This guesthouse and hostel, attached to a Messianic community centre, is a great alternative to Tel Aviv's party-vibe hostels – perfect if you're seeking a little tranquillity. Opposite an old German church, it was built in 1884 by Baron Ustinov, Peter Ustinov's father.

Eating

Said Abu Elafia & Sons BAKERY $

(7 Yefet St; snacks from 8NIS; ⏲24hr) This legendary family bakery, established in 1880, is famous for its sesame breads (great dipped in zaatar spice), savoury Arab pastries and

pizza-like concoctions filled with eggs, tomato, cheese and olives.

Dr Shakshuka ISRAELI **$**
(3 Beit Eshal St; meals 40-50NIS; ⌚8am-midnight Sun-Fri; ✎) Along with *shakshuka* (a messy tomato and egg stew cooked with various herbs and spices), the Gabso family whips up a range of Libyan and other North African delights.

Yo'Ezer STEAKHOUSE **$$$**
(☎03-683 9115; www.yoezer.com; 2 Yoezer Aish Ha'bira St; mains from 88NIS; ⌚12.30pm-1am Sun-Thu, 11am-1am Fri & Sat) Hidden down a dark alleyway near the clock tower, this stone-walled cellar serves quality steak, sausages and vegie options, as well as vintage wines. Book in advance at weekends.

ℹ Getting There & Away

From the centre of Tel Aviv, it's a pleasant 2.5km seafront stroll to Old Jaffa. Alternatively, take bus 18 from Tel Aviv Mercaz train station or Dizengoff St, bus 10 from Ben Yehuda St or bus 25 from Ibn Gabirol St or Allenby St and get off at the clock tower. To return to the centre, take bus 10 or 25 from Yerushalayim Ave.

Caesarea

قيسارية קיסריה

☎04 / POP 3400

Caesarea (pronounced kay-*sar*-ee-ya in Hebrew) was one of the great cities of antiquity, rivalling great Mediterranean harbours such as Alexandria and Carthage. Despite efforts by various conquerors to keep the city alive, time and warfare eventually had their way and by the 14th century most of Caesarea had disappeared under the shifting dunes. Major excavations have been made over the past 60 years and Caesarea is now one of the country's most impressive archaeological sites.

A modern, gated Caesarea of walled mansions has developed outside the archaeological area.

A visit to the **Caesarea National Park** (www.parks.org.il; adult/child 38/23NIS, entrance to harbour only 13NIS; ⌚8am-6pm Apr-Sep, to 4pm Oct-Mar) starts off with a 10-minute movie dramatising the history of the city. At the **Crusader city**, you can see the remains of the citadel and harbour. Beyond the walls to the north stretch the beachfront remains of an impressive **Roman aqueduct**. A **hippodrome** lies to the south, and beyond that, a reconstructed **Roman amphitheatre**, which serves as a modern-day concert venue. The site makes for a great wander, especially for children, who can clamber the ruins to their hearts' content; look out for the colonies of squabbling bats that roost in the ancient archways. There are several restaurants, cafes and shops on site, so you can take a break from your explorations for a leisurely waterfront lunch.

BAHA'I

Founded in the middle of the 19th century, the Baha'i faith (www.bahai.org) believes that many prophets have appeared throughout history, including Abraham, Moses, Buddha, Krishna, Zoroaster, Jesus and Mohammad. Its central beliefs include the existence of one God, the equality and unity of all human beings, and the unity of all religion.

The origins of the Baha'i faith go back to Ali Muhammad (1819–50), a native of Shiraz, Iran. In 1844 he declared that he was 'the Bab' (Gate) through which prophecies would be revealed. The charismatic Ali was soon surrounded by followers, called Babis, but was eventually arrested for heresy against Islam and executed by firing squad in Tabriz.

One of the Bab's prophecies concerned the coming of 'one whom God would make manifest'. In 1866, a Babi named Mizra Hussein Ali proclaimed that he was this messianic figure and assumed the title of Baha'ullah. His declarations were unwelcome in Persia and he was expelled first to Baghdad, then to Constantinople, Adrianople and finally the Ottoman penal colony of Akko. In his cell in Akko he dedicated himself to laying down the tenets of a new faith, the Baha'i, whose name is derived from the Arabic word *baha* (glory).

The Baha'i faith now has an estimated five million followers worldwide. Only a handful reside permanently in Israel, site of the Baha'i World Centre (the religion's global headquarters), whose gardens and institutions are staffed by volunteers from around the world. Tradition dictates that a Baha'i who is able should make a pilgrimage (https://bahai.bwc.org/pilgrimage) to Akko and Haifa.

Getting There & Away

Caesarea is on the coast 55km north of Tel Aviv and 40km south of Haifa. The best way to get there is by hired car. Taking public transport is a pain, but possible. From Tel Aviv or Haifa, board any bus to Hadera and then switch to bus 76, which departs Hadera at 8.20am, 11.25am, 1.10pm and 2.45pm Sunday to Thursday, and 9.05am, 11.05am, 12.40pm and 3.05pm on Friday.

Haifa

حيفا חיפה

☎04 / POP 264,900

One of the most picturesque cities in the Middle East, the mixed Jewish-Arab port of Haifa offers sweeping views of the sea and one of the most beautiful gardens in the world. Israel's third-largest metropolis can feel a bit staid compared to Jerusalem and Tel Aviv, but its neighbourhoods and the spectacular Baha'i Gardens, which spill down the steep slopes of Mt Carmel, are a nice place to wander for a couple of days.

The bus and train stations and the trendy German Colony are on the flats near the port. Head up the hill a bit and you come to the predominantly Russian Hadar district and the Arab commercial precinct of Wadi Nisnas. High atop Mt Carmel is the stylish Carmel Centre district, home to the university, exclusive residences, and trendy bars and eateries.

Sights

FREE Baha'i Gardens GARDENS

(☎04-835 8358; www.ganbahai.org.il; ⏲9am-5pm Thu-Tue) The stunning, immaculately kept multiple terraces of the dizzily sloped gardens are themselves alone a reason to visit Haifa. Apart from the top two tiers, the gardens – declared a Unesco World Heritage Site in 2008 – are accessible to the general public only on hour-long guided tours. There is one tour per day (except Wednesday) departing at noon; be sure to arrive at 11.30am as it's first come first served and only 60 people are allowed in daily. Meet at the appointed time at Yefe Nof St at the top of the garden (look for the sign). Rain usually causes cancellation.

Amid the perfectly manicured gardens, fountains and walkways rises the golden-domed **Shrine of the Bab** (⏲9am-noon). Completed in 1953, this tomb of the Baha'i prophet Al-Bab integrates both European and oriental design, and is considered one of the two most sacred sites for the world's five million Baha'is (the other is the tomb of Mizra Hussein Ali in Akko). Visitors must remove their shoes and dress modestly (no shorts or bare shoulders).

The best way to get here is by taking the Carmelit subway to the top stop and then walking to the top of the gardens. From the German Colony you can take bus 23.

Gan Ha'Em PARK

On the crest of Carmel, across from the upper Carmelit subway station, is Gan Ha'em (Mother's Park), a cool swath of greenery with cafes, an amphitheatre that hosts summer evening concerts and a hillside **zoo** (admission 30NIS; ⏲9am-6pm Sat-Thu, to 2pm Fri).

Madatech MUSEUM

(www.madatech.org.il; Technion Bldg, 25 Shemaryahu Levin St, Hadar; adult/child 75/65NIS; ⏲10am-4pm Mon & Wed, to 7pm Thu, to 2pm Fri, to 6pm Sat, noon-4pm Sun) Specialising in interactive science exhibits, this museum is housed in the first home of the Technion – Israel Institute of Technology, built in 1913. Admission fees are steep, but the exhibits are impressive – a must-see if you have kids.

Tikotin Museum of Japanese Art MUSEUM

(www.hms.org.il; 89 HaNassi Ave; adult/child 30/20NIS; ⏲10am-4pm Mon-Wed, 4-9pm Thu, 10am-1pm Fri, 10am-4pm Sat) Puts on excellent exhibits of artwork from Japan.

Stella Maris Carmelite Monastery CHURCH

(⏲6am-noon & 3-6pm) This neo-Gothic Carmelite church and monastery, with its wonderful painted ceiling, was originally established as a 12th-century Crusader stronghold. A hospital for the troops of Napoleon in 1799, it was subsequently destroyed by the Turks. In 1836 it was replaced by the present structure.

To reach the monastery, take bus 115 from Hadar, bus 99 from Carmel Centre, or head to Bat Galim and hop on the **cable car** (one-way/return 19/28NIS; ⏲10am-6pm), which whisks you right up to the monastery in a few minutes.

FREE Elijah's Cave RELIGIOUS

(⏲8am-5pm Sun-Thu, to 12.45pm Fri) Considered holy by Christians, Jews and Muslims alike, this grotto is where the prophet Elijah is believed to have hidden from King Ahab and Queen Jezebel after he slew the 450 priests of Ba'al (Kings 1:17-19). There is also

Haifa

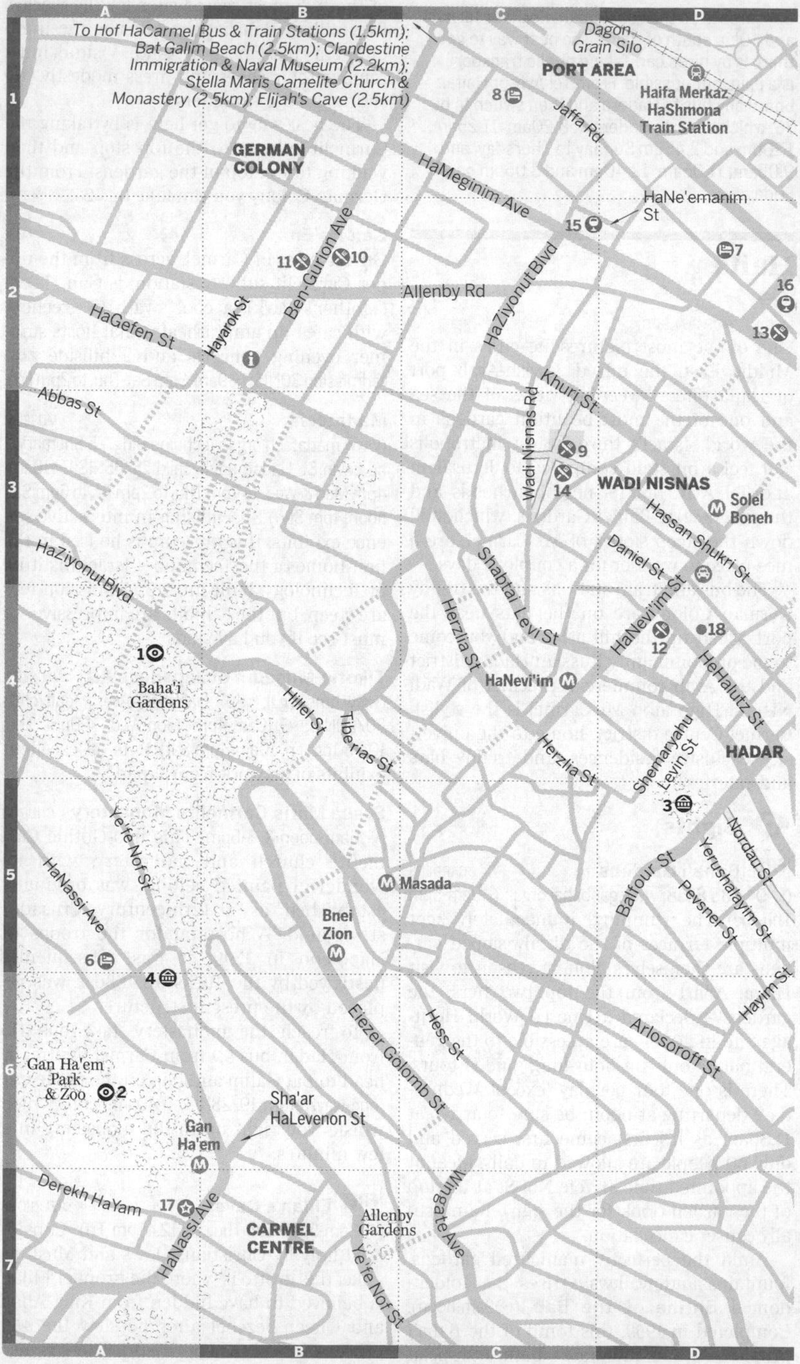
A
B
C
D
1
2
3
4
5
6
7
To Hof HaCarmel Bus & Train Stations (1.5km); Bat Galim Beach (2.5km); Clandestine Immigration & Naval Museum (2.2km); Stella Maris Camelite Church & Monastery (2.5km); Elijah's Cave (2.5km)
Dagon Grain Silo
PORT AREA
Haifa Merkaz HaShmona Train Station
8
Jaffa Rd
GERMAN COLONY
HaMeginim Ave
HaNe'emanim St
15
7
16
13
11
10
Ben-Gurion Ave
Allenby Rd
HaZiyonut Blvd
HaGefen St
Hayarok St
Abbas St
Khuri St
Wadi Nisnas Rd
9
14
WADI NISNAS
Solel Boneh
Hassan Shukri St
Daniel St
Shabtai Levi St
HaZiyonut Blvd
Herzlia St
HaNevi'im St
12
18
HeHalutz St
1
Baha'i Gardens
HaNevi'im
Hillel St
Tiberias St
Herzlia St
Shemaryahu Levin St
HADAR
3
Yefe Nof St
Nordau St
Yerushalayim St
Balfour St
Pevsner St
Masada
HaNassi Ave
Bnei Zion
Hayim St
6
4
Hess St
Eliezer Golomb St
Arlosoroff St
Gan Ha'em Park & Zoo
2
Sha'ar HaLevenon St
Gan Ha'em
Derekh HaYam
17
HaNassi Ave
CARMEL CENTRE
Allenby Gardens
Wingate Ave
Yefe Nof St

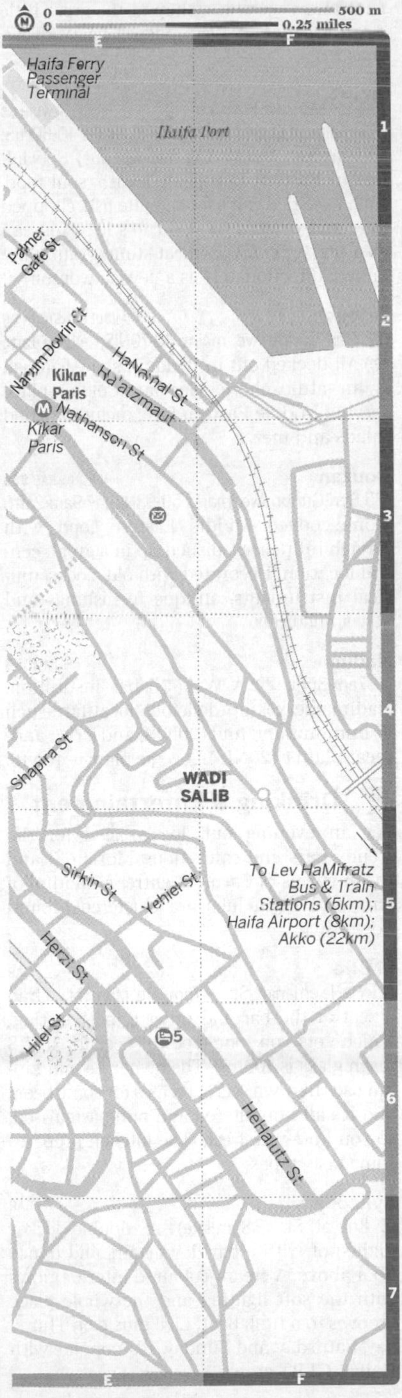

Haifa

Sights
1 Baha'i Gardens A4
2 Gan Ha'em Park & Zoo A6
3 Madatech D5
4 Tikotin Museum of Japanese Art A6

Sleeping
5 Hotel Theodor E6
6 Molada Guest House A5
7 Port Inn D2
8 St Charles Hospice C1

Eating
9 Arab Market C3
10 Douzan B2
11 Fatoush B2
12 Felafel Stores D4
13 Mayan Habira D2
14 Nadima C3

Drinking
15 Li Bira C2
16 Syncopa D2

Entertainment
17 Beat A7

Transport
18 Sherut to Tel Aviv D4

a Christian tradition that the Holy Family sheltered here on their return from Egypt, hence the Christian name, Cave of the Madonna. Outside, the garden is a favourite picnic spot for local Christian Arabs. Modest dress is required. Accessible from Stella Maris by a steep downhill path.

Clandestine Immigration & Naval Museum MUSEUM
(204 Allenby Rd; adult/child 15/10NIS; ⏲8.30am-4pm Sun-Thu) A surprisingly interesting place to brush up on Israel's naval history and the Zionists' 1930s and '40s attempts to sneak European Jews into British-blockaded Palestine. The centrepiece is the *Af-Al-Pi-Chen*, a boat that smuggled 434 Jewish refugees to Palestine in 1947.

Bat Galim Beach BEACH
(www.batgalim.org.il) It's not Pipeline, but surfers can surely catch some waves at Bat Galim Beach. The westernmost break, called Galshanim Beach, is popular with windsurfers and kiteboarders. It's near the bottom of

the Stella Maris Cable Car. To get here, take bus 108, which runs past Paris Sq.

Sleeping

Haifa has plenty of high-end accommodation in the Carmel Centre, but budget options are a little spread out and not too plentiful. Call ahead and reserve a room, especially in July and August.

TOP CHOICE Port Inn GUESTHOUSE $$
(04-852 4401; www.portinn.co.il; 34 Jaffa Rd; dm without/with breakfast 90/130NIS, s/d/tr/q 290/375/495/615NIS;) Bright, clean, simply furnished dorms and rooms, and a lounge, kitchen facilities and a laundry service, make this the most comfortable central budget stay. The dining room is a great place to meet other travellers. Situated about 300m west of Paris Square.

Hotel Theodor HOTEL $$
(04-867 7111; www.theodorhotel.co.il; 63 Herzl St; s/d/tr US$94/110/154;) Newly renovated in 2011, the Theodor is a local landmark, rising 17 stories above Hadar. Rooms are small and tidy with great views from every angle.

St Charles Hospice HOSPICE $
(04-855 3705; www.pat-rosary.com; 105 Jaffa Rd; s/d/q 180/300/390NIS;) Owned by the Latin Patriarchate and run by the Catholic Rosary Sisters, this place has a lovely garden out back and rooms that are simple but comfortably furnished. The gate is often locked so you'll need to ring the bell to enter. Curfew is at 11pm so send an email if you plan a late check-in.

Molada Guest House GUESTHOUSE $
(04-838 7958; www.rutenberg.org.il; 82 HaNassi Ave; s/d/tr 250/350/520NIS;) Run by the Rutenberg Institute for Youth Education, this bare-bones guesthouse has clean rooms, some with sea-view balconies. Reception (open 9am to 3pm Sunday to Thursday) is at the Beth Rutenberg building (77 HaNassi Ave), just down the street. After hours, ring the doorbell and somebody will let you in. It's best to call (or email) ahead to make a reservation.

Eating

In Hadar, around the HaNevi'im St end of HeHalutz St, you'll find excellent felafel and shwarma, as well as bakeries selling sweet pastries, sticky buns and other delights. For fruit and vegetables, shop at the great little **Arab Market** in Wadi Nisnas on Wadi Nisnas Rd.

TOP CHOICE Mayan Habira JEWISH $$
(Fountains of Beer; 4 Nathanson St; mains 40-60NIS; 10am-5pm Wed-Mon, to midnight Tue) Specialises in Eastern European Jewish 'soul food' such as jellied calf's foot, gefilte fish, chopped liver and *petshai* (boiled calf's leg). You can also try *kreplach*, a meat-stuffed dumpling known affectionately as a 'Jewish wonton'.

Fatoush MIDDLE EASTERN $$
(38 Ben-Gurion Ave; mains 40-70NIS; 8am-1am;) All decked out in Bedouin style, Fatoush is an atmospheric German Colony place serving Middle Eastern fare, including good salads and mezze.

Douzan FRENCH, ARAB $$$
(35 Ben-Gurion Ave; mains 50-98NIS; 9am-2am) Home-cooked Middle Eastern food with French influences, dished up in a great, central location. Decorated with old clocks, musical instruments, antique furnishings and velvet cushions.

Nadima HUMMUS $
(7am-3pm;) A Wadi Nisnas institution, Nadima serves up delicious local fare such as hummus and fuul (20NIS) and a rice-and-meat platter (20NIS). A vegie plate is 40NIS.

Drinking & Entertainment

For an evening out, locals head for the trendy bars and cafes along Moriah St and the environs of Carmel Centre. A handful of bars and nightclubs are clustered around downtown.

Li Bira BAR
(21 HaNe'emanim St; 7pm-late Mon-Sat) Grab a seat at the bar and order a 'beer tasting', which gets you four types of beer for 18NIS (each glass is 100ml). The owner Leonid Lipkin uses his own secret recipes for some beers and it's all non-filtered and non-pasteurised, so you know it's fresh. The kitchen prepares some tasty tapas.

Syncopa BAR
(5 Khayat St; 8pm-late) A double-decker nightspot with a bar downstairs and dance floor above. A cream-coloured interior glows with the soft lighting and the whole place grooves to a funk beat. Live music on Thursday, Saturday and Sunday. It's popular with Haifa's GLBT crowd.

Beat LIVE MUSIC
(www.beat.co.il; 124 HaNassi Ave; admission 50-120NIS; ⌚9pm-late Thu, Sat) The best place to hear live music.

Information

The main branch of Bank Leumi is on Jaffa Rd. Exchange bureaux are likewise common; in the Carmel Centre there is one at the corner of Wedgewood and HaNassi. The post office marked on our map will change travellers cheques.

Halfa Tourism Development Association (www.tour-haifa.co.il; 48 Ben-Gurion Ave; ⌚9am-4.30pm Sun-Thu, 8am-1pm Fri, 10am-3pm Sat) Has several useful publications, including *A Guide to Haifa Tourism* and a city map (4NIS) that outlines four themed walking tours.

Rambam Medical Centre (☎1 700 505 150; Bat Galim) One of the largest hospitals in the country.

Getting There & Away

Air

Arkia (☎5758; www.arkia.com) connects Haifa with Eilat three or four times a week (US$84 to US$113). **Haifa airport** (HFA; ☎04-847 6170) is in the industrial zone east of Haifa.

Bus

Arriving from the south, passengers are dropped off at the Hof HaCarmel bus station (adjacent to the train station of the same name), from where you can take bus 103 downtown to the port area. For details, see www.bus.co.il.

During the day, buses depart from both locations every 20 minutes for Tel Aviv (bus 910, 26.50NIS, 90 minutes), while there's an hourly service to Jerusalem (bus 940 or 960, 40NIS, two hours). The 940 leaves from Hof HaCarmel and the 960 departs from Lev HaMifratz.

Heading north, bus 272 (express) goes to Nahariya (17.20NIS, 45 to 70 minutes) via Akko, and bus 251 stops at Akko (13.50NIS, 30 to 50 minutes). Eastbound, bus 430 goes to Tiberias (26.50NIS, 90 minutes).

For Nazareth, take bus 331 (17.20NIS, 45 minutes), from outside the Haifa Merkaz HaShmona train station.

Sherut (Shared Taxi)

Most sheruts (service or shared taxis) depart from different spots in Hadar. The sherut to Akko (weekday/Shabbat 12/15NIS) and Nahariya (weekday/Shabbat 15/18NIS) leaves from the corner of Herzl and Balfour Sts. In addition you can take a sherut to Akko and Nahariya from downtown Sunday to Thursday from near the post office.

The sherut to Tel Aviv (weekday/Shabbat 28/40NIS) departs from 10 HeHalutz St. A sherut to the airport (87NIS) requires a one-day advanced booking, call ☎04-866 2324.

Train

Haifa has three train stations: Hof HaCarmel (good for getting to the beach from the city centre), Haifa Merkaz HaShmona (near the port and downtown, most useful for tourists), and Lev HaMifratz (in the eastern part of the city, close to the Lev HaMifratz bus station).

From Haifa Merkaz HaShmona, trains depart roughly hourly for Tel Aviv (29.50NIS, 90 minutes) via Netanya (26NIS, one hour), and north to Nahariya (19NIS, 45 minutes) via Akko (15NIS, 30 minutes). There are also direct trains to Ben Gurion Airport (38.50NIS, 90 minutes).

Getting Around

Israel's only metro (subway), the **Carmelit** (single trip 6.40NIS; ⌚6am-midnight Sun-Thu, to 3pm Fri, 8pm-midnight Sat) connects Kikar Paris with Carmel Centre, via the Hadar district. Visitors can ride to the top and see the city sights on a leisurely downhill stroll.

Akko (Acre)

عكا עכו

☎04 / POP 52,000

Marco Polo passed through Akko around 800 years ago and, quite frankly, the place hasn't changed much since then. It seduces visitors with narrow alleys, slender minarets, secret passageways, subterranean vaults and impressive ramparts. While other historic towns in Israel are busy packaging their heritage for the benefit of tourists, Akko has taken a more modest approach, leaving its homes for families, not artists, and its souq (market) for fishers, not souvenir hawkers. The city was awarded Unesco World Heritage status in 2002.

The bus and train stations are roughly 2km – an easy walk – from Old Akko.

Sights

A visit to Old Akko begins by stepping through city walls – built by Ahmed Pasha al-Jazzar in 1799, right after Napoleon's retreat – and into another century.

Al-Jazzar Mosque MOSQUE
(admission 10NIS; ⌚8am-5pm Sat-Thu, 8-11am & 1-5pm Fri) This mosque was built in 1781 in typical Ottoman Turkish style, with a little local improvisation in parts – the columns

in the courtyard, for example, were 'adopted' from Roman Caesarea. Around by the base of the minaret, the small twin-domed building contains the sarcophagi of al-Jazzar and his adopted son and successor, Süleyman.

Museum of Underground Prisoners MUSEUM
(adult/child 15/10NIS; ⌚8.30am-4.30pm Sun-Thu, to 1.30pm Fri) Inside the **Akko Citadel**, a rambling structure built by the Turks in the

Akko (Acre)

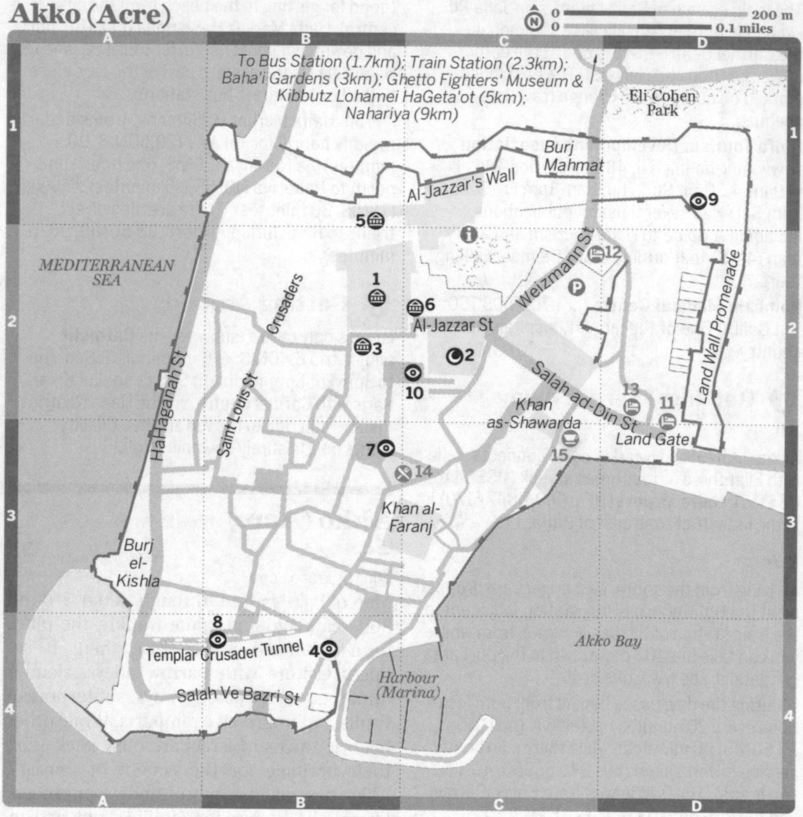

Akko (Acre)

Sights

1 Akko Citadel B2
2 Al-Jazzar Mosque C2
3 Hammam al-Pasha B2
4 Khan al-Umdan B4
5 Museum of Underground Prisoners B1
6 Okashi Art Museum C2
7 Souq B3
Subterranean Crusader City (Knights' Halls & Refetorium) .... (see 1)
8 Templar Crusader Tunnel B4
9 Treasures in the Wall Museum D1
10 Turkish Bazaar C2

Sleeping

11 Akkotel D2
12 HI – Knights Hostel & Guest House C2
13 Walied's Akko Gate Hostel D2

Eating

14 Hummus Said C3

Drinking

15 Leale al-Sultan C3

late 18th century on 13th-century Crusader foundations, this museum is dedicated to Jewish armed resistance during the British Mandate. The Ministry of Defence runs the museum so if you want to enter you'll need to show your passport.

Subterranean Crusader City HISTORIC SITE
(adult/child 25/22NIS) The **Knights' Halls**, a haunting series of vaulted halls that lie 8m below street level, served as the headquarters of the crusading Knights Hospitallers. It's possible that Marco Polo dined in the **Refectorium** (Dining Hall) when he visited Acre. Opposite the entrance you can see a fleur-de-lys, an emblem of the kings of France. The way out of the subterranean depths is through a conspicuously placed souvenir shop that leads into the **Turkish bazaar.**

Treasures in the Wall Museum MUSEUM
(adult/child 15/12NIS) This new museum displays a wealth of ethnographic items from the 19th century, most of them used by early Zionist farmers.

Hammam al-Pasha MUSEUM
Housed in the 1780 bathhouse built by al-Jazzar, this place has a creatively designed 30-minute **multimedia show** (adult/child 25/21NIS) called 'The Story of the Last Bath Attendant'.

Okashi Art Museum MUSEUM
(adult/child 10/7NIS) A gallery devoted to the works of Avshalom Okashi (1916–80), an influential Israeli painter and a resident of Akko.

Souq MARKET
Fresh hummus is boiled in giant vats while nearby fresh-caught fish flop off the tables. As carts trundle past, children shuck corn and vendors hawk fresh fruit, all to the soundtrack of tinny Arabic music playing from battered radios. Visit **Kurdi & Berit** (⌚9.30am-6pm), a tourist-friendly shop that ships herbs and spices worldwide.

Khan al-Umdan & the Harbour HISTORIC BUILDINGS
Old Akko has several large khans (an inn enclosing a courtyard, used by caravans for accommodation), which once served the camel caravans bringing in grain from the hinterland. The grandest is the Khan al-Umdan (Inn of the Pillars), built by al-Jazzar in 1785 (the pillars were appropriated from Caesarea). The ground floor housed the animals, while their merchant owners slept upstairs.

The harbour's marina is still very much in service and if you are around early enough, you can watch the fishing boats come in and unload the day's catch.

Templar Crusader Tunnel UNDERGROUND TUNNEL
(adult/child 15/12NIS) Near the lighthouse car park at the southern tip of Akko, look out for this amazing underground passageway, which connected the port to a Templar palace. You can enter at either end of the tunnel (near the lighthouse or the Khan al-Umdan).

Baha'i Gardens GARDENS
(admission free; https://bahai.bwc.org/pilgrimage; ⌚9am-4pm) These gardens, as well as a shrine called the **Bahje House** constitute the holiest site of the Baha'i faith. This is where Baha'ullah, a follower of the Bab and the founder of the faith (see p218), lived after his release from prison in Akko, and where he died in 1892. It's situated about a kilometre north of the town centre on the main Akko–Nahariya road and served by bus 271; alight when you see the gardens' main gate on the right. Unless you're a Baha'i pilgrim, use the entrance about 500m north, up the side road.

Ghetto Fighters' Museum MUSEUM
(www.gfh.org.il; admission adult/child 20/18NIS; ⌚9am-4pm Sun-Thu) An interesting museum

COMBO TICKETS

You can purchase mix-and-match combination tickets to Akko's attractions from a kiosk in the Festival Garden (outside the tourist office, which screens a short film). The best ticket gets you into the Subterranean Crusader City, the Hammam al-Pasha (Turkish Bath) Exhibit, the Okashi Art Museum, the Templar Crusader Tunnel, the Treasures in the Wall Museum and the grottoes of Rosh HaNikra for 75/65NIS per adult/child. A separate kiosk passes out audio headsets (free with admission) that lead you through the subterranean city. The exhibits are open 9am to 5.15pm Saturday to Thursday and 9am to 2.15pm Friday; from November to March the sites close one hour earlier.

commemorating the ghetto uprisings and Jewish partisans of the Holocaust era. The adjacent **Yad Layeled** (⊘9am-4pm Sun-Thu) is a moving memorial to the 1.5 million children who perished in the Holocaust. It's on the main road between Akko and Nahariya (take bus 271) on the grounds of **Kibbutz Lohamei HaGeta'ot**. The kibbutz was established in 1949 by Jews who spent WWII fighting the Nazis in the forests and ghettos of Poland and Lithuania, and somehow survived.

🛏 Sleeping

HI – Knights Hostel &
Guest House   HOSTEL $
(☑1 599 510 511; www.iyha.org.il; 2 Weizman St; dm/ s/d US$32/48.50/97; @🛜) This gorgeous new IYHA building has 76 rooms spread over three floors, with an ancient aqueduct running through it and ruins in the courtyard.

Akkotel   HOTEL $$$
(☑04-987 7100; www.akkotel.com; Salah ad-Din St; s/d US$145/180; @🛜) Embedded inside the walls of the Old City, the 16 rooms in this hotel all have arched ceilings, flat-screen TVs and modern bathrooms, but not much sunlight.

Walied's Akko Gate Hostel   HOSTEL $
(☑04-991 0410; www.akkogate.com; Salah ad-Din St; dm/s/d 75/200/250NIS; @🛜) This long-running hostel has a friendly owner and good location. Rooms are simply furnished and a little dated and dark, but fine for travellers with low expectations. The kitchen is too basic to do any serious cooking. Call for a free pick-up from the station.

✕ Eating & Drinking

For cheap eating, there are several felafel places around the junction of Salah ad-Din and Al-Jazzar Sts.

TOP CHOICE **Hummus Said**   HUMMUS $
(snacks 15NIS; ⊘6am-2.30pm; 🖉) Deeply entrenched in the souq, this place has become something of an institution, doling up that much-loved Middle Eastern dip to throngs of visitors from around the country. For 15NIS, you'll get salads, pickles, pita and a big glob of hummus with fuul (fava bean paste) or garlic.

Leale al-Sultan   COFFEEHOUSE $
(Khan as-Shawarda; snacks 20NIS; ⊘24hrs) Traditional Middle Eastern coffeehouse sporting sequined cushions, colourful wall hangings and backgammon tables. A Turkish coffee costs 5NIS while a nargileh is 15NIS.

ℹ Information

Emergency (☑04-987 6736; Weizmann St) The police are in the car park near the tourist office.

Tourist information (www.akko.org.il; 1 Weizmann St; ⊘8.30am-6.30pm Apr-Oct, to 4.30pm Nov-Mar; @) North of the Festival Garden, inside the Crusader citadel. Free internet access is available.

ℹ Getting There & Away

Akko's bus terminal and train station are about 2km (an easy walk) from the Old City. The most pleasant way to travel between Akko and Haifa (15NIS, 25 minutes) or Nahariya (8NIS, 15 minutes) is by train along the scenic beachfront railway. Trains pass in both directions three times an hour.

From Haifa (13NIS, 30 to 50 minutes), the fastest buses are 272 and 252 (avoid any and all local buses, which are horribly slow). Bus 272 goes north to Nahariya (8.80NIS, 15 to 25 minutes).

Sheruts (shared taxis) wait outside the Akko bus station and depart when full to Haifa (weekday/Shabbat 12/15NIS) and Nahariya (weekday/Shabbat 9/12NIS).

LOWER GALILEE & SEA OF GALILEE

الجليل الاسفل وبحيرة طبريا

הגליל התחתון והכינרת

Blessed with ancient stone synagogues, archaeological sites associated with Jesus' ministry, and rugged hills cloaked in wildflowers in spring, the Lower Galilee – the part of northern Israel south of Rte 85 (linking Akko with the Sea of Galilee) – is hugely popular with hikers, cyclists, Israeli holidaymakers and, of course, Christian pilgrims. But these days even Nazareth is much more than a place of Christian pilgrimage – it now boasts one of Israel's most sophisticated dining scenes. The shimmering Sea of Galilee (in Hebrew, the Kinneret), too, juxtaposes holiday pleasures with archaeological excavations linked to Jesus' life.

Nazareth

الناصرة   נצרת

☑04 / POP 73,000

Site of the Annunciation and Jesus' childhood home, Nazareth (al-Naasira in Arabic, Natzrat or Natzeret in Hebrew), site

Lower Galilee & Sea of Galilee

0 — 10 km
0 — 6 miles

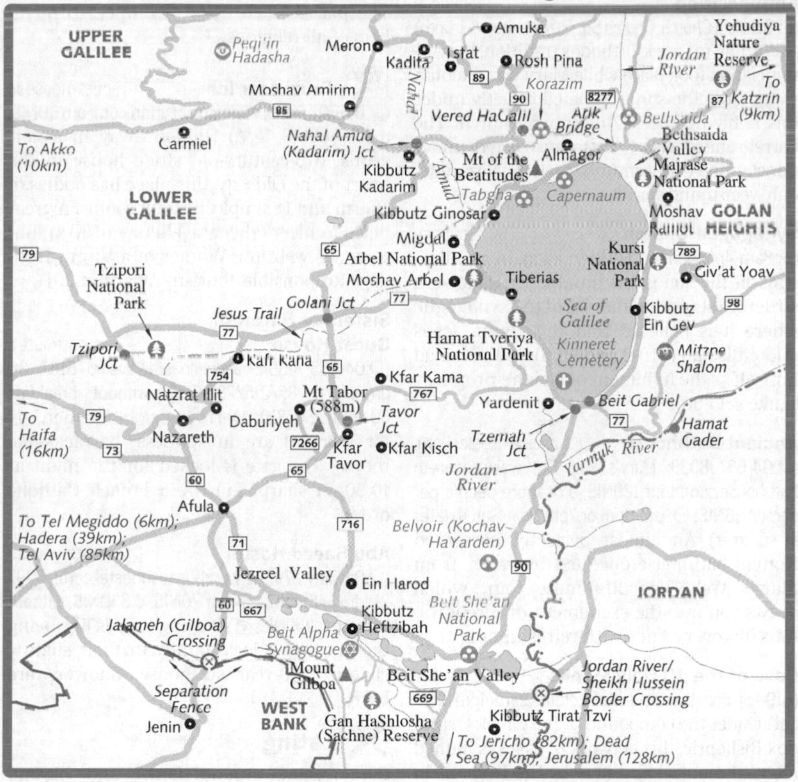

of the Annunciation and Jesus' childhood home, has come a long way since its days as a quiet Jewish village in Roman-ruled Galilee, so if you're expecting bucolic rusticity be prepared for a surprise. These days, Israel's largest Arab city is a bustling mini-metropolis with shop-lined thoroughfares and traffic jams. The Old City, its stone-paved alleys lined with crumbling Ottoman-era mansions, is currently reinventing itself as a sophisticated cultural and culinary destination.

Sights

Basilica of the Annunciation CHURCH
(www.basilicanazareth.org; Al-Bishara St; admission free; ⌚8am-6pm) Dominating the Old City's skyline is the lantern-topped cupola of this Roman Catholic basilica, an audacious modernist structure that's unlike any building you've ever seen. Built from 1960 to 1969, it's believed by many Christians to stand on the site of Mary's home, where many churches (but not the Greek Orthodox) believe the Annunciation took place. The walls of the courtyard and the **upper church** are decorated with a series of vivid **mosaic panels**.

In the dimly lit **lower church**, a sunken enclosure shelters the **Grotto of the Annunciation** (⌚5.30am-6pm, for silent prayer 6-9pm), the traditional site of Mary's house, and remnants of churches from the Byzantine (4th century) and Crusader (12th century) eras.

St Joseph's Church CHURCH
(Al-Bishara St; ⌚7am-6pm) Across the courtyard from the upper level of the Basilica of the Annunciation, this neo-Romanesque church, built in 1914, occupies a site believed by popular tradition to be that of Joseph's carpentry workshop. Down in the crypt, signs explain in situ archaeological discoveries.

Greek Orthodox Church of the Annunciation CHURCH
(St Gabriel's Church; Church Sq; ⏲7am-noon & 1-6pm) According to Greek Orthodox tradition, the Annunciation took place while Mary was fetching water from the spring situated directly under this richly frescoed, 17th-century church. The barrel-vaulted **crypt**, first constructed under Constantine (4th century), shelters Nazareth's only year-round spring.

Synagogue-Church CHURCH
(⏲8am-4pm or 5pm) Hidden away in an alleyway off the souq, this humble Crusader-era structure stands on the site of the synagogue where it is believed that the young Jesus quoted Isaiah (61:1-2 and 58:6) and revealed himself as the fulfilment of Isaiah's prophesy (Luke 4:15-30).

Ancient Bathhouse ARCHAEOLOGICAL SITE
(☎04-657 8539; Mary's Well Sq; www.nazarethbathhouse.com; tour 120NIS, 5 or more people per person 28NIS; ⏲9am-6pm or 7pm Mon-Sat, to later in summer) An almost perfectly preserved Roman bathhouse once fed by water from Mary's Well. The 30-minute tour, which draws you into the excitement of serendipitous discovery, ends with refreshments.

Cave of the 40 Holy Monks CAVE
(6198 St; donation requested; ⏲tours 9am-4pm Mon-Sat) Under the compound of the Greek Orthodox Bishopric, this network of caves is named after 40 monks killed here by the Romans in the 1st century. Opened to the public in 2011.

Mary of Nazareth International Centre RELIGIOUS
(www.cimdn.org; Al-Bishara St; recommended donation 50NIS; ⏲9am-6pm Mon-Sat, last entry 5pm) A multimedia presentation illustrates highlights of the biblical period, ie from Creation through the Resurrection, with an emphasis on the lives of Mary and Jesus. The peaceful rooftop gardens are landscaped with plants mentioned in the Bible. Films in about 20 languages are shown.

Nazareth Village FARM
(☎04-645 6042; www.nazarethvillage.com; Al-Wadi Al-Jawani St/5050 St; adult/child 50/22NIS; ⏲9am-5pm, last tour 3pm Mon-Sat) This recreation of a 1st-century Galilean farmstead is great at helping visitors imagine Nazareth and its economic life in the time of Jesus. Call ahead to find out when guided tours (1¼ hours), available in nine languages, are scheduled to depart.

Sleeping

The places listed below are open to members of all religions.

TOP CHOICE **Fauzi Azar Inn** GUESTHOUSE $$
(☎04-602 0469; www.fauziazarinn.com; dm 90NIS, d 350-500NIS; @☜) Hidden away in a gorgeous, two-century-old stone house in the heart of the Old City, this place has oodles of charm and 14 simple, tasteful rooms. A great place to meet other travellers – or to volunteer (see website). Winner of a Virgin Holidays Responsible Tourism Award in 2011.

Sisters of Nazareth Guest House GUESTHOUSE $
(☎04-655 4304; accueilnasra@live.fr; 6167 St; dm/s/d/tr 85/215/280/385, without breakfast 60/190/230/310) Dorm beds (18 for men, six for women) are in spotless, barracks-like rooms. The gate is locked for the night at 10.30pm sharp. Run by a French Catholic order.

Abu Saeed Hostel GUESTHOUSE $
(☎04-646 2799; www.abusaeedhostel.com; 6097 St; dm without breakfast 70NIS, d 350NIS, without bathroom 250NIS; ☜) Staying here is like being the guest of a local family in their slightly chaotic, 350-year-old house. Showers are basic.

Eating

Connoisseurs around Israel and beyond know that Nazareth's dining scene has recently become so drop-dead delicious that it's worth staying the night (or weekend) for. The buzzword is 'fusion', with European-inspired dishes pimped with local seasonings and then served – with an extra helping of Arab hospitality – in atmospheric Old City mansions. Reservations are recommended on Friday and Saturday.

Méjana LEVANTINE $$
(☎04-602 1067; Al-Bishara Bldg, St Gabriel's Church Sq; mains 47-110NIS; ⏲11am-11pm or later Mon-Sat) Serves superb 'fusion'-style meat, fish and seafood, seasonal salads, and a rotating roster of Levantine dishes such as *shushbarak* (meat dumplings cooked with yoghurt, garlic and mint leaves; 55NIS).

Abu Ashraf HUMMUS $
(Diwan al-Saraya; 6134 St; mains 20NIS; ⏲8am-8pm Mon-Sat, noon-3pm or 4pm Sun; ✎) This old-time hummus joint and coffeehouse (the beans are roasted on the premises) is

famous all over town for its *katayof* (sweet pancakes folded over Umm Ashraf's goat's cheese or cinnamon walnuts and doused with geranium syrup; three for 12NIS).

Felafel Abu Haani Jabali FELAFEL $
(St Gabriel's Church Sq; felafel 13NIS; ⏲10am-midnight Mon-Sat, 5pm-midnight Sun; ☑) Super-fresh felafel since 1968.

Mahroum Sweets PASTRIES $
(www.mahroum-baklawa.com; cnr Paulus VI & Al-Bishara Sts; ⏲8.30am-11pm) Run by the same family since 1890, this is one of the best places in Israel for baklava and other syrup-soaked Arab pastries, as well as *kunafa* (a syrupy, cheese-based pastry) and Turkish delight.

Shopping

TOP CHOICE **Elbabour** FOOD
(Galilee Mill; www.elbabour.com; Al-Bishara St; ⏲8.30am-7pm or 7.30pm Mon-Sat) The other-worldly aroma inside this basement spice emporium has to be inhaled to be believed.

Shababik CRAFT
(6198 St; ⏲10am-4pm Mon-Wed, to 8pm Thu-Sat, to later Jul, Aug & Christmas) Sells one-of-a-kind handmade crafts from Nazareth and nearby villages.

Information

Ministry of Tourism Information (www.goisrael.com; Casanova St; ⏲8.30am-5pm Mon-Fri, 9am-1pm Sat) Has brochures in seven languages.

Police (☎emergency 100; 6089 St) In the Moskubiya, a Russian pilgrims' hostel built in 1904.

Getting There & Away

Bus

Most intercity **buses** (www.bus.co.il) can be picked up along Paulus VI St, at stops on either the northbound or the southbound side. Some destinations:

Akko (Egged bus 343, 29NIS, two hours, eight daily except Saturday)

Haifa's Palmer Sq (Nazareth Tourism & Transport bus 331, 17.20NIS, twice an hour seven days a week)

Tiberias (Nazareth Tourism & Transport bus 431, 19NIS, 40 minutes, hourly except Friday evening and Saturday) via Kafr Kana

For details on buses to Amman run by **Nazarene Tours** (☎04-601 0458, Paulus VI St), see p275.

Tzipori

صفورية ציפורי

☎04

Today one of Israel's most impressive archaeological sites, **Tzipori National Park** (Zippori, Sepphoris; www.parks.org.il; adult/child 27/14NIS; ⏲8am-5pm Apr-Sep, to 4pm Oct-Mar, to 3pm Fri, last entry 1hr before closing) was in ancient times a prosperous and well-endowed city with stone-paved roadways (rutted over time by wagons and chariots), an amazing water-supply system, synagogues, churches and a 4500-seat theatre. The star attraction is a mosaic portrait of a contemplative young woman nicknamed the **Mona Lisa of the Galilee**.

The village of Tzipori and Tzipori National Park are 11km northwest of Nazareth via Rte 79. There's no public transport.

Tiberias

طبريا טבריה

☎04 / POP 42,000

Tiberias is one of the tackiest resorts in Israel, its lakeside strip crammed with 1970s monstrosities. But it's also one of the four holy cities of Judaism, burial place of venerated sages, and a very popular base for Christians visiting nearby holy sites. So, not for the first time, the sacred and the kitsch – plus beaches and hot springs – coexist side by side in a whirl of hawkers, hedonism and holiness.

If you've got a car, the Golan, the Galilee Panhandle, Beit She'an, Nazareth and even Akko are an hour or less away.

Sights & Activities

Hamat Tveriya National Park PARK
(Eliezer Kaplan Ave/Rte 90; adult/child 14/7NIS; ⏲8am-5pm during daylight savings, to 4pm rest of year, closes 1hr earlier Fri) The star attraction here is a 4th-century synagogue with a beautiful zodiac mosaic. Situated 2.5km south of the centre; served by buses 5 and 28 and sheruts.

Yigal Allon Promenade BOARDWALK
Most of Tiberias' sights are along the boardwalk (of sorts) that runs along the lakefront. Parts are kitschy and faded, and the area can feel forlorn in winter, but the views of the Sea of Galilee and the Golan never get old. The following sights are listed from north to south.

Tiberias

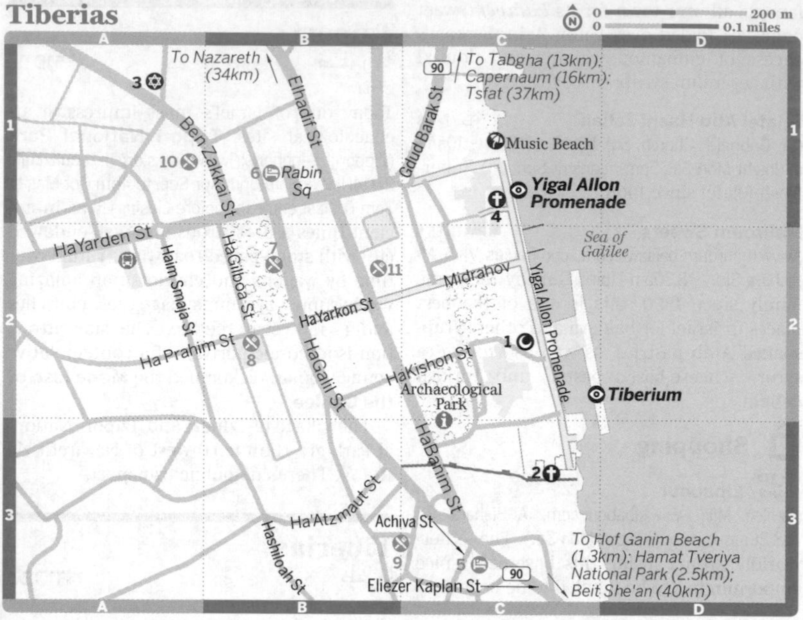

St Peter's Parish Church
(Yigal Allon Promenade; ⌚8.30am-noon & 2.30-5.30pm Mon-Sat, Mass in English 6.30pm Mon-Sat, 8.30am Sun) The roof of this church, originally built by the Crusaders, is shaped like an upturned boat – a nod to Peter, a Sea of Galilee fisher.

Al-Bahr Mosque
(Sea Mosque) When this basalt mosque was built in the 18th century, it had a special entrance for the faithful who arrived by boat.

Tiberium
(admission free; ⌚after dark daily) This jumbo-sized light, laser and music show projected onto a wall of water jets, brings a bit of Las Vegas–style razzmatazz to these sedate shores.

Church & Monastery of the Apostles
(⌚8am-4pm Mon-Sat) At the southern terminus of the promenade is the Greek Orthodox Church and Monastery of the Apostles. From the peaceful, flowery courtyard, steps lead down to the church, its air of mystery enhanced by gilded icons, brass lamps and elaborately carved wood. The three chapels are dedicated to the 12 disciples, Saints Peter and Paul, and Mary Magdalene. To see if a monk is available to show you around, ring the bell high up on the right side of the red door 10m west of the overhead pedestrian bridge.

Jewish Sages' Tombs CEMETERY
Many of Tiberias' Jewish visitors are drawn to the city at least partly by the desire to pray – and ask for divine intercession – at graves believed to be those of some of Judaism's most eminent sages.

The **Tomb of Rabbi Meir Ba'al Hanes** (⌚6am-10pm or later Sun-Thu, 6am-1½hr before sundown Fri), a 2nd-century sage often cited in the Mishnah, is inside a hillside complex 300m up an asphalt road from Hamat Tveriya National Park.

The **Tomb of Rambam** (Ben Zakkai St; ⌚24hr), a Cordova-born polymath also known as Maimonides (1135–1204), is two blocks northeast of the central bus station. Nearby, the **Maimonides Heritage Centre** (⌚10am-3pm Sun-Thu) has exhibits on the sage's life and works.

A few metres away from the Rambam's grave is the **Tomb of Rabbi Yohanan ben Zakkai** (Ben Zakkai St; ⌚24hr), Judaism's most eminent 1st-century sage.

Cycling

The Sea of Galilee is great cycling territory. Completely circumnavigating the lake

Tiberias

Top Sights

Tiberium C2
Yigal Allon Promenade C1

Sights

1 Al-Bahr Mosque C2
2 Church & Monastery of the Apostles C3
3 Jewish Sages' Tombs & Maimonides Heritage Centre A1
4 St Peter's Parish Church C1

Sleeping

5 Aviv Hotel & Hostel C3
6 Tiberias Hostel B1

Eating

7 Felafel Stalls B2
8 Fruit & Veggie Market B2
9 Guy B3
10 Hummus Issa A1
11 Supersol Sheli B2

(60km) takes about six hours; for much of the distance you can follow the Kinneret Trail. For a half-day ride, you can head to Yardenit, 8km south of Tiberias, from where an 8km circuit follows the Jordan River. **Aviv Hotel & Hostel** (☎04-672 0007; 66 HaGalil St; per day 70NIS; ⏰8am-6pm) rents bicycles.

Beaches

Tiberias' only free beach is **Music Beach**, at the northern end of the Yigal Allon Promenade. Another good bet is **Hof Ganim**, 1.5km south of the centre, which is run by the municipality. Pay beaches in or very near Tiberias include **Hof HaTchelet** (admission 28NIS), a bit north of the centre, and **South Beach**.

Sleeping

YMCA Peniel-by-Galilee GUESTHOUSE $$
(☎04-672 0685; www.ymca-galilee.co.il; Rte 90; s/d 250/450NIS; ❄🏊) Set on a secluded section of shady lakeshore, this gem has a clean pebbly beach, a natural pool fed by a warm spring and a lobby with a distinct Mandate-era vibe. The 13 rooms are forgivably simple, but some have kitchenettes. Excellent value. Situated on the east side of Rte 90 about 3km north of Tiberias; served by all buses heading north from Tiberias.

Aviv Hotel & Hostel HOSTEL $
(☎04 672 0007; www.aviv-hotel.co.il; 66 HaGalil St; dm 70NIS, d without breakfast 200-350NIS; ❄@📶) This welcoming hostel has 30 clean, slightly scuffed rooms with practical furnishings, proper spring mattresses, make-'em-yourself beds, fridges and balconies. Dorm beds are all non-bunk; women-only dorm rooms are available.

Tiberias Hostel HOSTEL $
(☎04-679 2611; www.tiberiashostel.com; Rabin Sq; dm 75-85NIS, s/d 250/350NIS; ❄@📶) An easy walk from the bus station, this place has 110 dorm beds – all of them double-decker bunks – in rooms for four to 10 people. The seven doubles are smallish and a bit scuffed. Breakfast is toast and jam.

Eating

For good-value, quick sit-down dining options, try the cafes at the top end of the Midrahov (a pedestrian mall).

Guy ISRAELI $$
(☎04-672 3036; HaGalil St; mains 38-70NIS; ⏰noon-9pm or 10pm Sun-Thu, 11.30am-1hr before sundown Fri; 🥗) The menu here features home-style grilled meats, soups and a delicious array of stuffed vegetables and Iraqi-style *kibbeh* – a pocket of *burghul* (cracked wheat) dough stuffed with chopped meat and fried.

Felafel stalls FELAFEL $
(HaGalil St; mains 17NIS; ⏰8am-10.30pm Sun-Thu, 8am-1hr before sundown Fri) Four stalls occupy temporary digs while Gan Shimon Park – now a huge hole – is turned into an underground parking garage (this is likely to take a while).

Hummus Issa HUMMUS $
(7 Ben Zakkai St; mains 20-30NIS; ⏰8am-7pm Sun-Thu, 8am-4pm Fri; 📶🥗) Very popular.

Fruit & Vegie Market MARKET $
(⏰5am-9pm Sun-Thu, to 1hr before sundown Fri) Cheap, top-quality produce.

Supersol Sheli SUPERMARKET $
(HaBanim St; ⏰7.30am-9pm Sun-Thu, to 2pm Fri) For picnic supplies.

Information

Tiberias' main commercial thoroughfare is HaGalil St. ATMs can be found on HaYarden and HaBanim Sts.

Magen David Adom (☎04-671 7611; cnr HaBanim & HaKishon Sts; ⏰ambulance 24hr;

first aid 7pm-midnight Sun-Thu, 2pm-midnight Fri, 10am-midnight Sat) Provides after-hours first aid and can arrange house (and hotel) calls by doctors.

Poriya Hospital (Baruch Padeh Medical Center; ☎emergency ward 665 2540; www.poria.health.gov.il; Rte 768) Tiberias' government hospital is 8km southwest of the city centre. Served by hourly bus 39.

Solan Express (3 Midrahov; internet per hr 20NIS; ⏲9am-10pm Sun-Thu, to 3pm Fri, opens after Shabbat Sat) Cybercafe and international phone office. Also changes foreign currency.

Tourist office (Archaeological Garden, HaBanim St; ⏲8.30am-3.45pm Sun-Thu, to 11.30am Fri) Has free brochures and maps.

Getting There & Away

Bus

Most intercity buses pass by the rather forlorn **central bus station** (www.bus.co.il; HaYarden St). Destinations served at least hourly (unless otherwise indicated):

Haifa's Merkazit (Lev) HaMifratz bus station (Egged bus 430, 26.50NIS, 1½ hours)

Jerusalem (Egged buses 961, 962 and 963; 40NIS, three hours) via Beit She'an

Kiryat Shmona (mainly Egged bus 841, 29NIS, 1¼ hours) via Rosh Pina

Nazareth via Kafr Kana (Nazareth Tourism & Transport bus 431, 19NIS, 40 minutes)

Tel Aviv (mainly Egged bus 835, 40NIS, twice an hour, 3½ hours)

Tsfat (Veolia bus 450, 14.90NIS, one hour)

Katzrin-based Rama has services to Katzrin (bus 52, five a day Sunday to Friday, one Saturday night) and Hamat Gader (bus 24, 6NIS, one daily Sunday to Friday).

Car

Tiberias is the best place in the Galilee to hire a car.

Avis (www.avis.co.il; cnr HaYarden St & HaAmakim St)

Eldan (www.eldan.co.il; HaBanim St)

Sea of Galilee

بحيرة طبريا ים כנרת

The shores of the Sea of Galilee (in Hebrew, Yam Kinneret or HaKinneret), by far Israel's largest freshwater lake, are lined with great places to relax: beaches, camping grounds, cycling trails and walking tracks.

Jesus spent most of his ministry around the Sea of Galilee. This is where he is believed to have performed some of his best-known miracles (the multiplication of the loaves and fishes, walking on water), and it was overlooking the Kinneret that he delivered the Sermon on the Mount.

Sights

TOP CHOICE **Ancient Boat** HISTORIC SITE

(www.bet-alon.co.il; Kibbutz Ginosar, Rte 90; adult/child 20/15NIS; ⏲8.30am-5pm Sun-Thu, to 4pm Fri, to 5pm Sat) In 1986, at a time when the level of the Sea of Galilee was particularly low, a local fisherman made an extraordinary discovery: the remains of a wooden boat later determined to have plied these waters in the time of Jesus' ministry. The 8.2m fishing vessel, made of 12 different kinds of (apparently recycled) wood, can be seen inside Kibbutz Ginosar's **Yigal Alon Center**, 8km north of Tiberias.

Tabgha CHURCHES

Two churches a few hundred metres apart occupy the stretch of Sea of Galilee lakefront known as Tabgha (an Arabic corruption of the Greek *hepta pega*, meaning 'seven springs'). An attractive walkway links Tabgha with Capernaum, a distance of about 3km.

The austere, German Benedictine **Church of the Multiplication of the Loaves & Fishes** (⏲8am-4.45pm Mon-Fri, to 2.45pm Sat), built in 1982, stands on the site of a 5th-century Byzantine church with a beautiful mosaic floor. Excellent brochures (1NIS) are available along one wall.

A bit to the east, a shady, fragrant garden leads down to the water's edge and the Franciscan **Church of the Primacy of St Peter** (⏲8am-4.50pm) – a chapel lit by the vivid colours of abstract stained glass, built in 1933. The flat rock in front of the altar was known to Byzantine pilgrims as Mensa Christi (Christ's Table) because it was believed that Jesus and his disciples breakfasted on fish here (John 21:9).

TOP CHOICE **Mount of the Beatitudes** CHURCH

(admission per car 10NIS; ⏲8-11.45am & 2-4.45pm, Mass hourly 8am-3pm except noon & 1pm) This hillside Roman Catholic church, with breathtaking views of the Sea of Galilee, stands on a site believed since at least the 4th century to be where Jesus delivered his Sermon on the Mount (Matthew 5-7), whose opening lines – the eight Beatitudes – begin with the phrase 'Blessed are...' Situated 3km (by road) from Tabgha, to which it's linked by a 1km footpath.

Capernaum ARCHAEOLOGICAL SITE
(Kfar Nachum/Kfar Nahum; admission 3NIS; 8am-4.50pm, last entry 4.30pm) Christians believe that this Franciscan-run site was Jesus' home base during the most influential period of his Galilean ministry (Matthew 4:13, Mark 2:1, John 6:59), when he recruited some of his best-known apostles. The renowned **synagogue** consists of two superimposed structures: one made of dark basalt, the other of light-coloured limestone. Both date from after the time of Jesus.

A modern, glass-walled **church** (1991) is dramatically suspended over the ruins of an octagonal 5th-century church that partly obscure **St Peter's House**, where Jesus is believed to have stayed. An explanatory sheet is available at the ticket window. Capernaum is 16km northeast of Tiberias and 3km northeast of Tabgha.

Kursi National Park ARCHAEOLOGICAL SITE
(www.parks.org.il; Rte 92; adult/child 14/7NIS; 8am-4pm Oct-Mar, to 5pm Apr-Sep, to 4pm Fri, last entry 1hr before closing) This Roman-era Jewish fishing village is where Jesus is believed to have cast a contingent of demon spirits out of two men and into a herd of swine (Mark 5:1-13, Luke 8:26-39). Situated across the lake from Tiberias (33km by road).

Sleeping

Camping is possible at public beaches.

Pilgerhaus Tabgha GUESTHOUSE $$$
(04-670 0100; www.heilig-land-verein.de; s/d €98/136;) Opened in 1889, this 70-room German Catholic guesthouse – geared towards Christian pilgrims but open to all – is a tranquil place with glorious gardens, right on the shores of the Sea of Galilee. Situated about 500m from Capernaum Junction.

TOP CHOICE **Genghis Khan in the Golan** HOSTEL $
(052 371 5687; www.gkhan.co.il; Giv'at Yoav, Golan; dm/6-person tent 100/590NIS, linen & towel 30NIS;) Inspired by the *gers* (yurts) used by the nomads of Mongolia, owner Sara Zafrir designed and hand-made five colour-coded yurts, each of which sleeps 10 on comfortable foam mattresses. Situated on Rte 789, 13km southeast of Rte 92's Kursi (Kursy) Junction. Bus 51 links Giv'at Yoav with Tiberias (eight daily Sunday to Thursday, six on Friday, one on Saturday night).

HI – Karei Deshe Guest House & Youth Hostel HOSTEL $$
(02 594 5633; www.iyha.org.il; dm/d US$32/120;) A sparkling-white facility, right on the lake, with 82 double, family and dorm rooms (with four or six beds), a sandy beach, and lots of trees and grass. The nearest bus stop (1.2km from the hostel) is served by all buses heading north from Tiberias.

HI – Porlya Guest House & Youth Hostel HOSTEL $
(Poriya Taiber Youth Hostel; 02-594 5720; www.iyha.org.il; dm/s/d US$33/90/110, additional adult/child US$29/23;) Perched on a hillside high above the Sea of Galilee, the gorgeous new Poriya (Poria) campus, opened in 2011, has rather spartan rooms. Dorm rooms have six beds. Situated 9km south of Tiberias, a steep 4km up Rte 7877 from Rte 90. No public transport.

Getting There & Around

The easiest way to explore this region is by car.

All the buses that link Tiberias with Tsfat, Rosh Pina and Kiryat Shmona – ie take Rte 90 north – pass by Migdal, Ginosar, Capernaum Junction (Tzomet Kfar Nahum, which is a short walk from Tabgha but about 4km west of Capernaum) and the access road (1km long) to Mount of the Beatitudes.

Rama bus 52 (seven daily except mid-afternoon Friday to sundown Saturday), which links Tiberias with the Golan town of Katzrin (1¼ hours), continues from Capernaum Junction east along the northern edge of the lake (Rte 87), passing by Capernaum.

Beit She'an

بيت شيان בית שאן

04

Founded sometime in the 5th millennium BC, Beit She'an – today a struggling modern town – has the most extensive Roman-era ruins in Israel. The extraordinary ruins in **Beit She'an National Park** (Rte 90; adult/child 38/23NIS; 8am-4pm mid-Oct–Mar, to 5pm Apr–mid-Oct, closes 1hr earlier Fri) are the best place in Israel to get a sense of what it might have been like to live, work and shop in the Roman Empire. Colonnaded streets, a 7000-seat theatre, two bathhouses and piles of rubble from the AD 749 earthquake evoke the aesthetics, grandeur, self-confidence and decadence of Roman provincial life in the centuries after Jesus.

Within easy walking distance of the Beit She'an's antiquities, the 62-room **Beit She'an Guest House** (☎02-594 5644; www.iyha.org.il; 129 Menahem Begin Ave/Rte 90; s/d 345/460NIS, additional adult/child 145/113NIS; @📶❄) has very attractive public areas, a great rooftop patio and practical rooms with five beds. Individual dorm beds are not available. Situated across the street and 100m south from the central bus station.

Getting There & Away

Egged bus 961 (at least seven daily Sunday to Thursday, six on Friday) goes north to Tiberias (20NIS, one hour) and south via the Jordan Valley to Jerusalem (40NIS, two hours).

Travellers headed to Jordan can make use of the Jordan River/Sheikh Hussein border crossing (see p38), 10km east of town.

Beit Alpha Synagogue

بيت الفا　בית הכנסת בית אלפא

☎04

The extraordinarily well-preserved mosaics (including a 12-panel zodiac circle) at the **Beit Alpha Synagogue** (Kibbutz Heftzibah; adult/child 21/9NIS; ⏲8am-5pm during daylight savings, 8am-4pm rest of year, closes 1hr earlier Fri) are among the most dazzling ever found in Israel.

Located at Kibbutz Heftzibah, 8km west of Beit She'an along Rte 669. Kavim bus 412 (at least hourly except Friday night and Saturday) goes both to Afula and to Beit She'an.

UPPER GALILEE & GOLAN HEIGHTS

الجليل الاعلى والجولان

הגליל העליון והגולן

The rolling, green hills of the Upper Galilee (the area north of Rte 85) and the wild plateau and peaks of the Golan Heights offer an incredible variety of activities to challenge the body and the soul – and nourish the stomach and the mind. Domestic tourists flock to the area – some come looking for luxurious *tzimmerim* (B&Bs), boutique wineries and gourmet country restaurants, others in search of superb hiking, cycling and horse riding through dazzling carpets of spring wildflowers, white-water rafting, and even skiing. Yet other visitors are attracted by some of the world's best birdwatching and the spiritual charms of Tsfat, the most important centre of Kabbalah (Jewish mysticism) for over five centuries.

This is the most difficult part of the country to explore by public transport, so rent a car if possible. Travelling this way can be very economical if you can share with other travellers and combine your travel with camping on the eastern side of the Galilee.

Tsfat (Safed)

صفد　צפת

☎04 / POP 30,300

The mountaintop city of Tsfat is an ethereal place to get lost for a day or two. A centre of Kabbalah (Jewish mysticism) since the 16th century, it's home to an otherworldly mixture of Hasidic Jews and devout-but-mellow former hippies, many of them American immigrants.

On Shabbat (Friday night and Saturday until sundown), commerce completely shuts down. While this may be inconvenient if you're looking for a bite to eat, the lack of traffic creates a meditative, spiritual Sabbath atmosphere through which joyful Hasidic tunes waft from hidden synagogues and unseen dining rooms.

Sights

Just to the south of the city, the pleasant breeze-cooled park and viewpoint **Gan HaMetsuda** (Citadel Park) was once the site of a Crusader citadel. Central Tsfat's atmospheric old quarters slither down from Yerushalayim St, divided by the broad, stiff stairway that makes up Ma'alot Olei HaGardom St, which was built by the British after the 1929 riots, to divide the warring Arab and Jewish factions. The Arabs were then largely confined to what's now the Artists' Quarter, and the Jews to the easterly Synagogue Quarter.

Synagogue Quarter NEIGHBOURHOOD

Tsfat's long-time Jewish neighbourhood spills down the hillside from HaMaginim Sq (Kikar HaMaginim; Defenders' Sq), which dates from 1777. All of Tsfat's historic Kabbalist synagogues are a quick (if often confusing) walk from here.

Synagogue hours tend to be irregular and unannounced closings are common. Visitors should wear modest clothing (no shorts or bare shoulders); yarmulkes are provided for

Upper Galilee & the Golan Heights

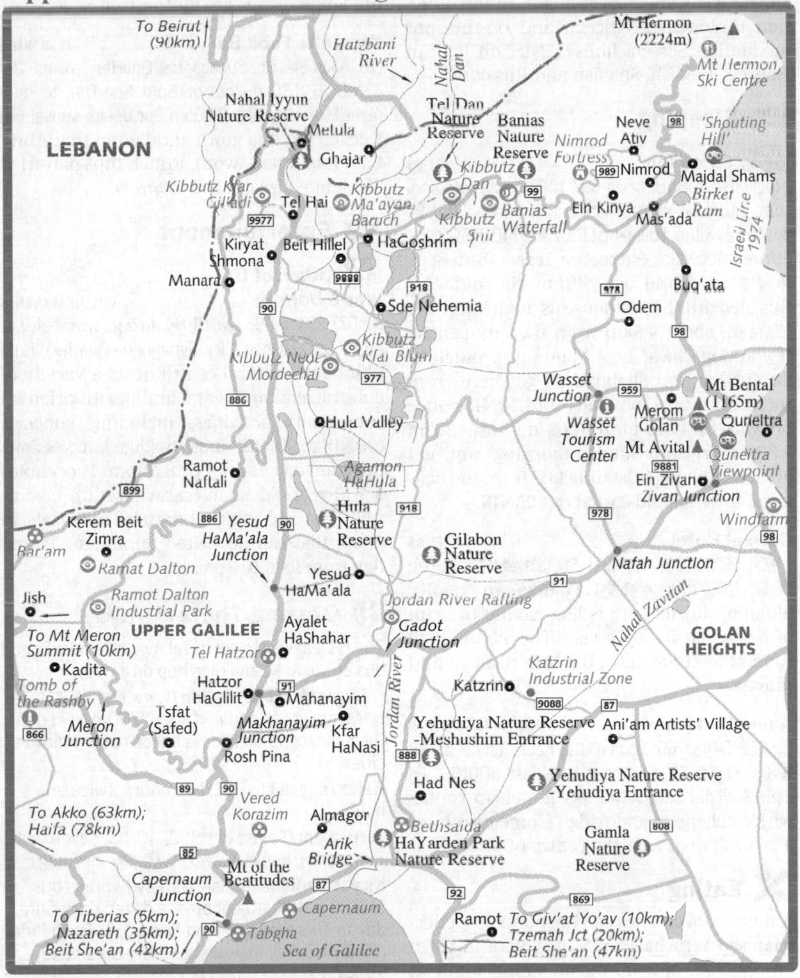

men. Caretakers expect a small donation. Synagogues are closed to tourists on Shabbat and Jewish holidays.

If you're short on time, visit the **Ashkenazi Ari Synagogue** (Najara St; ⏲9.30am-afternoon prayers Sun-Thu, to 12.30pm Fri) and the **Caro Synagogue** (Beit Yosef St; ⏲8.30 or 9am-4 or 5pm Sun-Thu, closes earlier Fri).

The **HaMeiri Museum** (www.bhm.org.il; 158 Keren HaYesod St; adult/child 20/13NIS; ⏲8.30am-2.30pm Sun-Thu, 9.30am-1.30pm Fri) illustrates Jewish life in Tsfat during the 19th and early 20th centuries.

Artists' Quarter NEIGHBOURHOOD

The neighbourhood south of the Ma'alot Olei HaGardom stairway used to be Tsfat's Arab quarter, but after the 1948 war the area was developed as an artists' colony. Most of the galleries and studios are open to visitors, with many artists happy to talk about their work.

Courses

Tzfat Kabbalah Center KABBALAH

(International Center for Tzfat Kabbalah; www.tzfat-kabbalah.org; 1st fl, Fig Tree Courtyard, 18 Alkabetz St, Synagogue Quarter; ⏲9am-6pm Sun-Thu, to

1pm Fri) Adherents of all religions, or none at all, are welcome to drop by for an introduction to Jewish mysticism and on-the-spot meditation. Screens films (15NIS) on Tsfat in Hebrew, English, Spanish and Russian.

Sleeping

TOP CHOICE Safed Inn GUESTHOUSE $$
(Ruckenstein B&B; ☎04-697 1007; www.safedinn.com; cnr HaGdud HaShlishi & Merom Kna'an Sts; dm/s/d/q without breakfast 100/300/400/500NIS, deluxe 400NIS; ⏲reception open 8am-8pm; ❄@📶) A world away from the old city, this delightful guesthouse is high atop Mt Canaan, about 4.5km from the city centre. If you don't have a car, there's not much to do out here on Shabbat. To get here from the centre, take local bus 3 (4.40NIS, once or twice an hour until 9pm, no buses from 2.30pm Fri until Sunday morning) and get off at 'HaPikud'. A daytime taxi from the centre of town should cost about 25NIS.

Carmel Hotel HOTEL $$
(☎04-692 0053; 8 Ha'Ari St/Ya'avetz St; s/d/q US$75/100/150; ❄@📶) Thanks to owner Shlomo, staying here is like having the run of a big, old family house. The 12 smallish rooms aren't romantic, but they're clean and practical.

Adler Apartments STUDIO APARTMENTS $
(☎052 344 7766; badler@013.net.il; office at 88 Yerushalayim St; d without breakfast 300NIS, Fri night & all day Sat 350NIS; ❄) Ten clean rooms with kitchenette and fridge (some also have a jacuzzi) in or near the centre of town.

Eating

A number of eateries can be found on pedestrianised Yerushalayim St. If you're in town on Shabbat, pick up picnic supplies ahead of time.

Maximilian CAFE $$
(2 Arlozoroff St, Artists' Quarter; mains 39-80NIS; ⏲7am-7pm Sun-Thu Oct-Mar, to midnight Apr-Sep, 7am–half-hour before sundown Fri; 📶) Serves a range of tasty pastas, quiches (48NIS), salads and freshly squeezed juices. Situated right next to the General Exhibition.

Tree of Life Vegetarian Cafe VEGETARIAN $$
(HaMaginim Sq, Synagogue Quarter; mains 38-48NIS; ⏲9am-10pm Sun-Thu, to midnight or later in summer, 9am-2hr before sundown Fri; 🖉) Specialities here include portobello mushroom quiche, quinoa pilaf and whole grain desserts sweetened with organic date syrup. Some dishes are gluten-free.

Yemenite Food Bar YEMENITE $
(18 Alkabetz St, Synagogue Quarter; mains 25-33NIS; ⏲8.30am-7pm or 8pm Sun-Thu, to midnight May-early Sep, 8.30am-2hr before sunset Fri) Decked out in a gown and kaftan that Abraham might have worn, Ronen flips pan-fried 'Yemenite pizza' called *lachuch*.

Entertainment

TOP CHOICE Khan of the White Donkey CULTURAL EVENTS
(☎077-234 5719; www.thekhan.org, www.halevav.org; 5 Tzvi Levanon Alley, Synagogue Quarter) This pluralistic cultural centre hosts a variety of cultural, environmental and health-oriented community activities, including concerts (30NIS to 90NIS) or open-stage jam sessions on Thursday at 8pm or 8.30pm. It occupies a 700-year-old khan (caravanserai), beautifully restored with all-natural materials in 2009, that can be visited Sunday to Thursday from 9am to 4pm.

Getting There & Away

The fastest way to get to Tel Aviv is to take Egged bus 361 to Akko and then hop on a train.

The **central bus station** (www.bus.co.il; HaAtzma'ut St), situated about 700m west of the Synagogue Quarter, is linked to the following cities:

Haifa (Egged bus 361, two hours, twice an hour)

Jerusalem (Egged bus 982, 40NIS, seven daily Sunday to Thursday, two on Friday morning)

Kiryat Shmona (mainly Nateev Express bus 511, 20.70NIS, 40 minutes, a dozen daily Sunday to Thursday, eight on Friday) via Rosh Pina (10.20NIS, five minutes) and the Hula Valley.

Tiberias (Veolia bus 450, 14.90NIS, one hour)

Rosh Pina

روش بينا ראש פינה

☎04 / POP 2700

Rosh Pina's 19th-century stone houses, oozing with charm, were discovered years ago by Tel Aviv chic-sters. The town now plays host to artists' studios and some of the most upscale sleeping and dining in the Upper Galilee.

Settled in the 1870s by Jews from Tsfat and from 1882 by immigrants from Romania, Rosh Pina's old town – just three short cobblestone streets – has been turned into a pedestrian zone. At the **Rosh Pina Pioneers Restoration Site**, visitors can explore the quiet lanes, lined with pretty, restored (and unrestored) stone houses, visit the old synagogue and pop into about 15 **galleries** (⏲10am-5pm, later in Jul & Aug) selling jewellery, ceramics and paintings. It's situated about 1.5km up the hill from the roundabout on Old Rte 90.

Rosh Pina's 500 B&B rooms, easy to find online, have created a market glut so prices have dropped a bit in recent years. About 150m down the hill from the Restoration Site, the **Villa Tehila** (☎04-693 7788; www.villa-tehila.co.il, in Hebrew; HaHalutzim St; d from 630NIS; ❄@📶🏊) is a fabulous B&B, whose shaded, 19th-century stone courtyards shelter bubbling fountains, glittering fairy lights, and a veritable menagerie.

Getting There & Away

All long-haul buses to/from the Hula Valley and Kiryat Shmona (eg from Tiberias) pass by the entrance to Rosh Pina on Rte 90, from where it's 1.5km up the hill to the Pioneers Restoration Site.

Nateev Express bus 511 (a dozen daily Sunday to Thursday, eight on Friday), which takes Rte 8900 and thus passes near the outskirts of the Pioneers Restoration Site, goes up the hill to Tsfat (10.20NIS, five minutes), and north to Kiryat Shmona via the Hula Valley.

Hula Valley

وادي الحوله עמק החולה

☎04

The swamps of the Hula Valley were once notorious for malaria, but a massive drainage program completed in 1958 got rid of the malarial Anopheles mosquitoes – and destroyed one of the country's most important wetlands, a crucial stopping point for many of the estimated 500 million birds that pass through Israel on their way from Europe to Africa and vice versa. In recent years about 10% of the old lake has been restored.

The area is served by almost all buses to/from Kiryat Shmona.

Sights & Activities

TOP CHOICE **Hula Nature Reserve** PARK
(www.parks.org.il; adult/child 32/20NIS; ⏲8am-5pm Sun-Thu, to 4pm Fri, last entry 1hr before closing) Migrating birds flock to the wetlands of Israel's first nature reserve, founded in 1964. The visitors centre offers an excellent 3D film on bird migration. Situated 15km north of Rosh Pina, 2km west off Rte 90.

Agamon HaHula PARK
(www.agamon-hula.co.il; admission 3NIS; ⏲9am-dusk Sun-Thu, from 6.30am Fri & Sat, last entry 1hr before closing) To cover the 8.5km path around the restored wetlands, you can either walk or rent a bicycle (52NIS). From late September to April you can see flocks of cranes up close, thanks to the 50-seat **Safari Wagon** (Aglat Mistor; 53NIS; ⏲hourly 9am-1hr before dark, often also at 6am). By road, Agamon HaHula is 7.5km north of the Hula Nature Reserve, and 1.2km off Rte 90.

Tel Dan

تل دان תל דן

☎04

The half-square-kilometre **Tel Dan Nature Reserve** (adult/child 27/14NIS; ⏲8am-5pm during daylight savings, to 4pm rest of year, closes 1hr earlier Fri, last entry 1hr before closing) on the Lebanese border, 1.6km north of Rte 99, boasts two major attractions. The first

RAFTING THE JORDAN

First-time visitors may be surprised at the Jordan's creek-sized proportions, but first-time rafters are often bowled over – sometimes into the soup – by how powerful its flow can be. Several excellent outfits offer rafting and kayaking down the Jordan (from 80NIS) – competition is as fierce as the current, which means standards of service and safety are high.

Kfar Blum Kayaks (☎04-690 2616; www.kayaks.co.il; ⏲10am-3pm or 4pm, to 5pm or 6pm in summer, open Passover-Sukkot or first rains) To get there from Rte 99, take the turn off to Beit Hillel (Rte 9888).

HaGoshrim-Ma'ayan Kayaks (☎04-681 6034/5; www.kayak.co.il; Kibbutz Ma'ayan Baruch; ⏲Apr-Oct) Based up near the Lebanese border at the entrance to Kibbutz Ma'ayan Baruch (a bit north of Rte 99).

is a lush, forested area fed by year-round **springs** gushing eight cubic metres of water per second into the Dan River, the most important tributary of the Jordan. The second is the remains of a **grand city** inhabited by the Canaanites in the 18th century BC and the Israelites during the First Temple period (12th century BC).

Because the reserve is a meeting place of three ecosystems, it supports a surprisingly varied selection of flora and fauna.

Close to the park entrance you'll find the **Galil Nature Center** (Beit Ussishkin; adult/child 20/15NIS; 8am-4.30pm Sun-Thu, to 3pm Fri, 9.30am-4.30pm Sat), which has an old-fashioned but informative natural history room and an archaeology section focusing on Tel Dan. This is where the 940km **Israel National Trail**, which goes all the way to the Red Sea, begins.

Golan Heights

الجولان הגולן

Offering commanding views of the Sea of Galilee and the Hula Valley, the volcanic Golan plateau is a favourite destination for holidaying Israelis. Its fields of basalt boulders – and, on its western edge, deep canyons – are mixed with cattle ranches, orchards, vineyards and small, friendly communities.

Israel captured the Golan Heights from Syria during the 1967 Six Day War, when 90% of the inhabitants fled or were expelled. In the bitterly fought 1973 Yom Kippur War, Syrian forces briefly took over much of the Golan before being pushed back to the current lines.

KATZRIN

قسرين קצרין

04 / POP 6700

The 'capital of the Golan', founded in 1977, is the region's only real town. The lively little commercial centre, a classic 1970s complex, has a bank, some eateries and a first-rate museum.

MINEFIELDS

Some parts of the Golan Heights – particularly those near the pre-1967 border and the 1974 armistice lines – are still sown with anti-personnel mines, so don't stray off marked trails. For more on mines see p271.

Sights & Activities

TOP CHOICE **Golan Archaeological Museum** MUSEUM

(www.mpkatzrin.org.il, in Hebrew; Katzrin town centre; adult/child 17/14NIS, incl Ancient Katzrin Park 26/18NIS; 9am-4pm Sun-Thu, to 2pm Fri) This small museum has a superb collection of carvings and inscriptions from Byzantine-era Golan synagogues.

Ancient Katzrin Park ARCHAEOLOGICAL SITE

(http://parkqatzrin.org.il, in Hebrew; adult/child 24/16NIS, incl Golan Archaeological Museum 26/18NIS; 8am-4pm Sun-Thu, 9am-2pm Fri, 10am-4pm Sat) Excavated ruins of a Byzantine-era Jewish village. Situated 1.6km east of the centre.

Golan Heights Winery WINERY

(www.golanwines.co.il; Katzrin Industrial Park; tasting 10NIS, incl tour 20NIS; 8.30am-6pm Sun-Thu, to 1.30pm Fri, last tour 4.30pm or 5pm Sun-Thu, noon or 12.30pm Fri) This renowned winery, one of many on the Golan and in the Upper Galilee, is 2km east of the centre.

Sleeping & Eating

All places to eat or buy food close on Shabbat, except for two excellent restaurants in the Industrial Zone

SPNI Golan Field School HOSTEL $$

(04-696 1234; www.teva.org.il; Zavitan St; d 405-490NIS, additional adult 131-167NIS, child 87-112NIS;) This place has 33 simple rooms, all with fridge, that can each sleep up to seven. Situated 1km from the main entrance to Katzrin – head down Daliyot St and then turn left on Zavitan St.

Getting There & Away

Rama buses (*8787, *3254; www.bus.co.il, www.golanbus.co.il, in Hebrew) Go to virtually every part of the Golan, as well as to Tiberias, Hatzor HaGlilit (near Rosh Pina) and Kiryat Shmona. To get to Majdal Shams, change in Kiryat Shmona.

GAMLA & YEHUDIYA NATURE RESERVES

جملا & يهودية منتزه

שמורות הטבע גמלא ויהודיה

South of Katzrin, the wilderness presents some terrific hiking along deep canyons and past gushing waterfalls and freshwater pools. Overlooking the Sea of Galilee, **Gamla Nature Reserve** (www.parks.org.il; Rte 808; adult/child 27/14NIS; 8am-5pm Sat-Thu, to 4pm Oct-Mar, to 3pm Fri, last entry 1hr before closing) includes the excavated ruins of an ancient Jewish stronghold whose inhabitants leapt to their deaths rather than fall into the hands of the Romans in AD 67. The reserve is also known for its colonies of griffon vultures. There are several easy hikes here, as well as a wheelchair-friendly walkway to the vultures. Situated 30km south of Katzrin.

Between Gamla and Katzrin lies the star of Israel's northern national parks, the 66-sq-km **Yehudiya Nature Reserve** (adult/child 21/9NIS; ⌚8am-5pm during daylight savingS, to 4pm rest of year), where there's a great **camping ground** (Orchan Laila; ☎04-696 2817; www.campingil.org.il; Yehudiya Parking Lot; per person incl next-day reserve admission 50NIS; ⌚24hr) and some challenging trails. An excellent hiking map is included in the admission fee, and rangers are happy to give tips. Rama bus 51 (seven or eight daily Sunday to Thursday, six on Friday), which connects Katzrin with Tiberias, stops at the Yehudiya parking lot.

BANIAS NATURE RESERVE

بنياس منتزه שמורת הבניאס

The gushing springs, waterfalls and lushly shaded streams of **Banias Nature Reserve** (www.parks.org.il; Rte 99; adult/child 27/14NIS, incl Nimrod Fortress 38/25NIS; ⌚8am-5pm during daylight savings, to 4pm rest of year, last entry 1hr before closing), in the northwestern corner of the Golan, form one of the most beautiful – and popular – nature spots in the whole of Israel. The park's two entrances are about 2.5km apart on Rte 99. Served by Rama bus 58 from Kiryat Shmona to Majdal Shams.

NIMROD FORTRESS & NIMROD

قلعة الصبيبة מבצר נמרוד ונמרוד

Sights

Nimrod Fortress FORTRESS

(www.parks.org.il; Rte 989; adult/child 21/9NIS; ⌚8am-5pm Apr-Sep, to 4pm Oct-Mar, last entry 1hr before closing) Built by the Muslims in the 13th century to protect the road from Tyre to Damascus, Nimrod Fortress towers fairy tale like on a long, narrow ridge (altitude 815m) on the southwestern slopes of Mt Hermon. If you're going to visit just one Crusader-era fortress during your trip, this should be it.

Sleeping

This isolated hilltop hamlet off Rte 98, 9km up the hill (towards Majdal Shams) from Nimrod Fortress, has some interesting places to stay.

TOP CHOICE **Golan Heights Hostel** GUESTHOUSE $$

(Chalet Nimrod Castle Hostel; ☎04-698 4218; www.bikta.net; camping per person 45NIS, dm 110NIS, cabins 600-1000NIS) Has 10 rustic rooms built of recycled wood surrounded by an organic cherry orchard. Call ahead for a dorm bed. Camping is possible.

Ohel Avraham TEPEES $

(Abraham's Tent; ☎04-698 3215, 052 282 1141; camping per person 50NIS, tepee 100NIS plus per person 60NIS; ⌚Passover-Sukkot) Hippyish hillside accommodation in three tepees, a Mongolian-style tent and some shacks. Bring a sleeping bag or blankets. It may be open in the off-season – call to find out.

Getting There & Away

Both Nimrod Fortress and Nimrod are served by Rama bus 58 from Kiryat Shmona to Majdal Shams.

MAJDAL SHAMS

مجدل شمس מג'דל שמס

☎04 / POP 9800

The largest of the Golan's four Druze towns – big enough, in fact, to have traffic jams – Majdal Shams serves as the commercial and cultural centre of the Golan Druze community. Druze flags, which sport five horizontal stripes (blue, white, red, yellow and green), flutter in the wind.

In recent years Skype and mobile phones have pretty much replaced the **Shouting Hill**, across which local Druze families used to communicate by megaphone and which featured prominently in the award-winning 2004 film *The Syrian Bride*.

Around 15km south of Mas'ada, at the **Mitzpe Quneitra** (Rte 98) viewpoint, take a look across the border to the eerie Syrian ghost town of **Quneitra**, destroyed by Israel in the 1967 war and in the UN buffer zone since 1974.

Opened in 2009, the stylish, locally owned **Narjis Hotel** (Malon Butik Narkis; ☎04-698 2961; www.narjishotel.com; Rte 98, d 500-600NIS; @📶) has 21 huge, romantic rooms with modern decor, jacuzzis and balconies. Situated on the road up to Mt Hermon.

Getting There & Away

Majdal Shams is 30km east of Kiryat Shmona. It's served by Rama bus 58 (30 minutes, five daily Sunday to Thursday, three on Friday, one Saturday afternoon) from Kiryat Shmona, which passes by Banias Nature Reserve, Nimrod Fortress and Nimrod.

MT HERMON

خيل الشيخ הר חרמון

Israel's only **ski centre** (☎24hr 1 599 550 560, 03-606 0640; www.skihermon.co.il; Rte 98; adult/child winter 49/44NIS, summer free; ⏰8am-4pm, last entry 3.30pm, may open 7am in winter) is situated at the far northern tip of the Golan, high atop Mt Hermon, known for its crisp mountain air, delicate alpine plants and unpredictable snowfall. The mountain's 2814m summit is in Syrian territory; the highest point controlled by Israel is 2236m.

DEAD SEA

البحر الميت ים המלח

The lowest place on the face of earth, the Dead Sea (elevation -425m) brings together breathtaking natural beauty and compellingly ancient history. In addition to floating in the super-saline waters, don't miss the ruins atop Masada, taken by the Romans in AD 73, and the oases of Ein Gedi, which nourish vegetation so lush it's often compared to the Garden of Eden.

Dead Sea

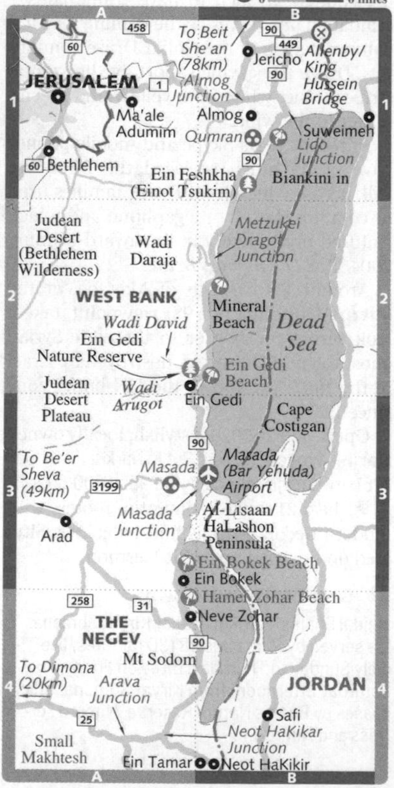

ℹ Getting There & Around

It's possible, though a bit fiddly, to explore the Dead Sea by public bus. To avoid hanging around wilting under the sun, it's a good idea to plan your itinerary in advance.

Egged buses (www.bus.co.il) link sites along Rte 90 (including, from north to south, Qumran, Ein Feshkha, Metzukei Dragot junction, Mineral Beach, Ein Gedi Nature Reserve, Ein Gedi Beach, Kibbutz Ein Gedi, Ein Gedi Spa, Masada, Ein Bokek, Neve Zohar and, for some lines, Neot HaKikar) with:

Jerusalem (buses 421, 444 and 486, 40NIS to 45NIS, 11 daily Sunday to Thursday, seven on Friday until mid-afternoon, three on Saturday evening)

Eilat (bus 444, 75NIS, about three hours, four daily Sunday to Thursday, three on Friday, one or two on Saturday evening)

Tel Aviv (bus 421, 45NIS, 3½ hours, departs Tel Aviv at 8.40am and Neve Zohar at 2pm Sunday to Friday) Departs from the Central (Arlozoroff/Savidor) train station.

Be'er Sheva (bus 384, 40NIS, 2¼ hours, four daily Sunday to Thursday, two on Friday).

All of these lines can be used for travel north and south along Rte 90 (which runs along the Dead Sea's western shore), eg from Masada to Ein Gedi Beach.

Ein Gedi

عين غدي עין גדי

☎08 / POP 520

Nestled in two dramatic canyons that plunge from the arid moonscape of the Judean Desert to the shores of the Dead Sea, Ein Gedi is one of Israel's most magical desert oases.

The area stretches for 6km along Rte 90, with separate turn-offs (and bus stops) for the following places, from north to south: Ein Gedi Nature Reserve (this is the turn-off to use for the oases of Wadi David and Wadi Arugot, the Ein Gedi Youth Hostel and the Ein Gedi Field School), Ein Gedi Beach (1km south of the reserve), Kibbutz Ein Gedi (3km south of the reserve) and Ein Gedi Spa (6km south of the reserve).

👁 Sights & Activities

Ein Gedi Nature Reserve RESERVE

(www.parks.org.il; adult/child incl Ein Gedi Antiquities 27/14NIS) A paradise of dramatic canyons, freshwater springs, waterfalls and lush tropical vegetation (come wearing your swimming costume) that consists of two roughly parallel canyons, **Wadi David** and **Wadi Arugot**, each of which has its own entrance complex and ticket office. The key to a successful hike in the reserve is the excellent colour-coded map brochure given out when you buy your tickets. Food is not allowed in the reserve.

Ancient Synagogue ARCHAEOLOGICAL SITE
(Ein Gedi Antiquities National Park; adult/child with nature reserve 27/14NIS, without nature reserve 14/7NIS; ⌚8am-5pm during daylight savings, to 4pm rest of year, to 3pm Fri) Situated about midway between the Wadi David and Wadi Arugot ticket offices, this 5th-century AD synagogue sports a superb mosaic floor decorated with the 12 signs of the zodiac.

Ein Gedi Beach BEACH
(Rte 90; ⌚24hr) This hugely popular but unpleasantly stony public beach (bring plastic flip-flops) fulfils the bare requirements of those seeking a Dead Sea float in that it has **toilets and changing rooms** (per entry 2NIS; ⌚8am-3.25pm) and a 24-hour snack bar. Renting a towel costs 10NIS (plus a 10NIS deposit). Situated 1km south (a 20-minute walk) along Rte 90 from the Ein Gedi Nature Reserve turn-off.

Sleeping & Eating

The hostels fill up quickly, especially on Thursday and Friday nights, so book early. There are very few dining options in the Ein Gedi area so arrive with picnic supplies and consider having dinner at your hotel or hostel.

SPNI Field School HOSTEL $$
(☎08-658 4288; www.teva.org.il; near Ein Gedi Nature Reserve; dm/s/d 115/345/385NIS, additional adult/child 129/89NIS; ❄📶) The 50 rooms, each with five to seven beds, are not as swish as at the youth hostel, but this is an excellent launching point for early hikes. Dinner (53NIS, on Friday 63NIS) is served almost daily. Reception sells hiking maps. Situated 800m up the hill from the Rte 90 turn-off to Ein Gedi Nature Reserve and the bus stop.

Ein Gedi Youth Hostel HOSTEL $
(Beit Sarah; ☎02-594 5681; www.iyha.org.il; Rte 90, near Ein Gedi Nature Reserve; dm/s/d 118/276/352NIS, additional adult/child 103/81NIS; ❄@📶) The sensational setting and the clean, contemporary rooms, with up to six beds, make this 68-room hostel madly popular. Dinner is 54NIS (64NIS on Friday). Situated 200m up the slope from the Rte 90 turn-off to Ein Gedi Nature Reserve and the bus stop.

Ein Gedi Beach CAMPGROUND $
(Rte 90; toilet & changing rooms per entry 2NIS; ⌚beach & toilet 24hr, changing rooms 8am-3.25pm) There's a 24-hour snack bar in the car park. Bring flip-flops and a flashlight. Situated 1km south of the Ein Gedi Nature Reserve turn-off from Rte 90.

Masada

مصادة מצדה

☎08

After the Romans conquered Jerusalem in AD 70, almost a thousand Jews – men, women and children – made a desperate last stand atop **Masada** (adult/child 27/14NIS), a desert mesa surrounded by sheer cliffs and, from AD 72, the might of the Roman Empire's 10th Legion. As a Roman battering ram was about to breach the walls of their fastness, Masada's defenders chose suicide over enslavement. When Roman soldiers swarmed onto the top of the flat-topped mountain, they were met with silence.

These days, Masada is guarded by the massive visitors centre, home to the superb Masada Museum and a food court.

Sights & Activities

TOP CHOICE **Masada Museum** MUSEUM
(Visitors Centre; admission incl audio guide atop Masada 20NIS; ⌚8.30am-4pm, last entry 3.30pm) A really excellent introduction to Masada's archaeology and history.

Snake Path HIKING
This famously serpentine footpath winds its way up Masada's eastern flank, starting from near the visitors centre.

Ramp Trail HIKING
(adult/child/student 27/14/22NIS) Ascend Masada from the west side via this Roman-built trail, accessible only from Arad (it's a 68km drive from the visitors centre via Rte 31 and then Rte 3199).

Cable Car AERIAL TRAMWAY
(adult return/up only/down only incl admission fee 72/54/27NIS, child 41/28/14/NIS; ⌚every 10 min 8am-5pm during daylight savings, to 4pm rest of year, closes 1hr earlier on Fri, last trip up 1hr before

WORTH A TRIP

QUMRAN قمران קומראן

World-famous for having hidden the **Dead Sea Scrolls** (documents written from 200 BC to AD 68 that include the oldest known manuscripts of the Hebrew Bible) for almost 2000 years, **Qumran** (Rte 90; adult/child 21/9NIS, incl entry to Ein Feshkha 39/19NIS; 8am-5pm during daylight savings, to 4pm rest of year, to 3pm Fri, last entry 1hr before closing) was the site of a small Essene settlement around the time of Jesus, ie from the late 1st century BC until AD 68, when it was destroyed by the Romans. Situated 35km east of Jerusalem and 35km north of Ein Gedi. All Jerusalem–Dead Sea buses pass by here.

closing) Whisks you from the visitors centre to the top in Swiss comfort in just three minutes.

Sleeping

TOP CHOICE **Masada Guest House** HOSTEL $
(08-594 5622; www.iyha.org.il; dm/s/d 138/285/388NIS;) This 280-bed hostel is ideal if you'd like to see sunrise from atop Masada. The swimming pool is open from Passover to Sukkot. Dinner (54NIS, on Friday 64NIS) is served most nights until 8pm. Frequently full, especially on Friday, so reserving is a must. Situated a few hundred metres below the visitors centre.

Camping Zones CAMPGROUND $
If you'd like to camp near Masada, ask the guards at **Chenyon HaDekalim** (the bus parking area next to the Masada Guest House) for permission to pitch your tent. If they're not in the mood, head to the sign-posted **parking area** situated on the Masada access road at a point 1km west of the junction with Rte 90. There are no amenities; bring a flashlight.

Getting There & Away

Masada's visitors centre, on the eastern side of the mountain, is 21km south of the Ein Gedi Nature Reserve; the access road from Rte 90 is 3km long. For details on bus services, see p240. Bus times are posted at the visitors centre's ticket windows.

Neot HaKikar

نأوت هاكيكار נאות הכיכר

08 / POP 410

Snuggled up against the Jordanian border in one of Israel's remotest corners, this agricultural moshav (population 75 families) is the perfect base for exploring the wadis, plateau and bluffs of the southern Dead Sea. Tranquil and laid-back, Neot HaKikar and its sister moshav, Ein Tamar, have some excellent sleeping options and all sorts of options for mountain biking, hiking, birdwatching and exploring the desert by jeep.

Tooling along wadis, up hills and around cliffs on a jeep tour, in the company of a knowledgeable local guide, is a great way to get acquainted with the desert, its flora and – if you're lucky – its fauna. Operators include **Gil Shkedi** (052 231 7371; www.shkedig.com; per person 150NIS, minimum 4; year-round), owner of Shkedi's Camplodge, who has been running excellent desert tours – in an air-con Land Rover – since 1996; one-time camel maven **Barak Horwitz** (052 866 6062; barakhorwitz@gmail.com); and B&B-owner **Ya'akov Belfer** (08-655 5104, 052 545 0970).

Neot HaKikar has about 40 B&B units, none of which offer breakfast unless you special-order it (100NIS per couple).

Shkedi's Camplodge (Khan Shkedi; 052 231 7371; www.shkedig.com; dm/d/q with shared bathroom & without breakfast 90/300/400NIS; closed Jul–mid-Sep;) is a wonderful place to linger for a couple of days. This desert retreat is especially enchanting at night, when guests hang out around the campfire or sip beers in the chill-out tent before heading to one of the cosy dorm tents.

Getting There & Away

Neot HaKikar is 8km southeast of Rte 90's Neot HaKikar junction. For details on bus services, see p240.

NEGEV

النقب הנגב

The Negev Desert, often bypassed by travellers hurrying to Eilat, is much more than just sand. Look closely between the rocks of the wadis (valleys) and you will find water and even wine. The Negev Highlands region is home to so many vineyards it now has its own wine route. Today, ecologists from all over the world come to the kibbutzim of Sde Boker and the Arava to study solar energy and water treatment. But this isn't new. Two thousand years earlier, the Nabataeans cultivated grapes and practically invented desert irrigation, which can still be seen at the ancient ruins of Shivta, Mamshit and Avdat.

This region, comprising 62% of Israel's land mass, may seem sparse, but it offers a world of adventure including mountain hikes, camel treks, 4WD desert drives and Red Sea diving. Yet perhaps the biggest secret of the Negev is Makhtesh Ramon, a crater-like wilderness, which feels like another planet.

Be'er Sheva

بئر السبع באר שבע

☎08 / POP 194,300

Be'er Sheva *(Bear Share-Vah)*, Israel's fourth-largest city and dusty 'capital of the Negev', is home to the pioneering Ben-Gurion University, with over 20,000 students.

Sights

The area's most interesting attractions are not actually in the town itself.

Tel Be'er Sheva ARCHAEOLOGICAL SITE
(adult/child 14/7NIS; ⏲8am-5pm Apr-Sep, to 4pm Oct-Mar) Dating from the early Israelite period (10th century BC), this tel (hilltop ruin) was declared a Unesco World Heritage Site in 2005. The best-preserved parts are the well-engineered cisterns and a 70m well, the deepest in Israel. It's 5km east of Be'er Sheva.

TOP CHOICE **Israeli Air Force Museum** MUSEUM
(www.iaf-museum.org.il, in Hebrew; admission 30NIS; ⏲8am-5pm Sun-Thu, to 1pm Fri) Offers a gripping account of Israel's aeronautical history, displaying about 100 airplanes ranging from Spitfires to Phantoms. Situated 6km west of Be'er Sheva on the Hatzerim (Khatserim) air force base. From the central bus station take bus 31 (8.80NIS, 16 minutes, every hour) to the last stop.

Museum of Bedouin Culture MUSEUM
(www.joealon.org.il; admission 25NIS; ⏲9am-4pm Sat-Thu, to 2pm Fri) This museum contains displays and demonstrations about the Bedouin's rich culture and heritage. It's situated 20km north of Be'er Sheva behind Kibbutz Lahav, near Kibbutz Dvir. The best way to get here is by car.

Sleeping & Eating

TOP CHOICE **HI – Beit Yatziv Hostel** HOSTEL $$
(☎08-627 7444; www.beityatziv.co.il; 79 Ha'Atzmaut St; s/d/ste 250/350/400NIS; ❄📶🏊) Popular with visiting university academics, this place is clean and welcoming, with a swimming pool that's open June to August. Take bus 12 or 13 from the bus station and look for the three large radio antennae.

Beit Ha-Ful ISRAELI $
(cnr Herzl & Ha'Atzmaut Sts; mains from 15NIS; ⏲8am-8pm Sun-Thu, to 2pm Fri; 🖉) For a quick bite in the Old Town you can't beat what locals say is the best fuul (fava bean paste) joint in town.

Getting There & Away

BUS On business days Egged buses run every 30 minutes to Tel Aviv (bus 370, 17NIS, 1½ hours), at least half-hourly to Jerusalem (buses 470 and 446, 32.50NIS, two hours) and every 30 minutes for Dimona (bus 48, 11.80NIS, 30 minutes). Egged services for Eilat (bus 392 or 397, 55NIS, 3½ hours) depart more or less every 90 minutes and run via Mitzpe Ramon (30NIS, 1½ hours). Buses to Masada and Ein Gedi (bus 384, 42NIS, 2¼ hours, four daily Sunday to Thursday, two on Friday) pass through Arad (18NIS, 45 minutes). Metropoline also operates bus services to Tel Aviv (bus 380) and Mitzpe Ramon (bus 60) for the same fares as Egged.

TRAIN The best way to get to Tel Aviv (29NIS, 1½ hours, hourly) is by train from the central **train station** (www.rail.co.il).

Sde Boker & Avdat

سده بوكير وعبدات

שדה בוקר ועבדת

☎08

Kibbutz Sde Boker was established in 1952 by young pioneers who at first planned to breed cattle in the desert. About 3km south by road, **Midreshet Ben Gurion** (www.boker.org.il), a satellite campus of Be'er Sheva's Ben-Gurion University of the Negev, is renowned for its environmental research and education.

Sights

Ben-Gurion Desert Home HOUSE
(adult/child 12/9NIS; ⌚8.30am-4pm Sun-Thu, to 2pm Fri, 10am-4pm Sat) The home of Israel's first Prime Minister is preserved as it was at the time of his death in 1973.

Ben-Gurion Graves MEMORIAL
The graves of David (1886–1973) and Paula Ben-Gurion (1892–1968) lie in a spectacular clifftop setting overlooking the stunning Wadi Zin and the Avdat plain.

Ein Avdat National Park PARK
(adult/child 27/14NIS; ⌚8am-5pm Apr-Sep, to 4pm Oct-Mar) The Ben-Gurion Graves are near the northern entrance of this beautiful, canyon-filled park, where day-hikers can amble through the **Wilderness of Zin**, spotting ibex along the way. Dominated by a steep, winding ravine of soft white chalk and poplar trees, the surprisingly chilly desert pools of **Ein Avdat** are reached via an easy hike through incredible scenery. To get back to Sde Boker, you'll need to wait for a bus (one every 1½ hours).

Avdat National Park PARK
(adult/child 27/14NIS; ⌚8am-5pm Apr-Sep, to 4pm Oct-Mar) Constructed by Nabataeans in the 3rd century BC – and recognised as a Unesco World Heritage Site in 2005 – this city-upon-a-hill served as a caravan stop along the trade route between Petra and the Mediterranean coast. More excitingly for some, parts of *Jesus Christ Superstar* were shot here. Situated 10km south of Sde Boker.

Sleeping

Sde Boker Field School HOSTEL $
(☎08-653 2016; www.boker.org.il; s/d 240/290NIS; ❄) This hostel is often filled with noisy school groups but is available for travellers. Also has a guest house (single/double 300/390NIS).

Mitzpe Ramon

ميتسبي رامون מצפה רמון

☎08 / POP 5500

This small but surprisingly engaging high desert town sits on the edge of Makhtesh Ramon, a dramatic 'erosion cirque' (crater) 300m deep, 8km wide and 40km long. Despite being in the heart of the desert, Mitzpe Ramon (elevation 900m) is also one of the coldest places in Israel – snow falls here more often than in Jerusalem.

Sights

Mitzpe Ramon's old industrial zone is now a fully fledged tourist zone, where once-abandoned hangars have been turned into alternative art galleries, shops and studios.

Makhtesh Ramon LANDMARK, LOOKOUT
Although Israel is a little country, the *makhtesh* is one place where it feels vast. Here the desert landscape opens up and you would be forgiven for thinking you were in Arizona. Unless you suffer from vertigo, the **lookout**, which juts out over the edge of the crater, is a must. Detailed hiking maps are available from the SPNI Field School.

Visitors Centre MUSEUM
(adult/child 25/13NIS; ⌚8am-4pm Sat-Thu, to 3pm Fri) Perched on the crater rim, the visitors centre was undergoing some major renovations at the time of writing but is set to become a new museum, featuring different exhibits on desert, geology, archaeology and astronomy.

Bio Ramon WILDLIFE RESERVE
(adult/child 21/9NIS; ⌚8am-5pm Sat-Thu, to 4pm Fri) This tiny desert wildlife park shows how nature can find a way to survive even in the harshest desert conditions. Just down the hill from the visitors centre.

TOP CHOICE **Alpaca Farm** FARM
(www.alpaca.co.il; admission 25NIS; ⌚8.30am-6.30pm summer, to 4.30pm winter) This farm has over 400 llamas and alpacas, raised for their delicate wool, as well as donkeys, goats and ponies. It also offers horse rides in the desert (150NIS, 1½ hours). In a hidden valley about 3km from Mitzpe Ramon down the dirt track at the end of Ben-Gurion Blvd.

Sleeping

TOP CHOICE **Green Backpackers** HOSTEL $
(☎08-653 2319; www.thegreenbackpackers.com; 10 Nahal Sirpad St; dm 75NIS, d without bathroom 255NIS; ❄@📶) Opened in 2011, this cute, homely hostel has clean rooms, a travellers' message board, shared recipes in the communal kitchen, laundry services, hiking gear and free wi-fi. Located in a quiet cul-de-sac at the end of Nahal Zia St.

Adama HOSTEL $$
(☎08-659 5190; www.adama.org.il; Har Boker St; campsites & dm 80NIS, tepees 175NIS, s/d 275/395NIS, r for 4 people 595NIS) A kind of spiritual and dance retreat set in a large industrial

hangar – if you dig dreadlocks and have a secret love of all things psychedelic, then this could be for you. For a bit of privacy crawl into one of the tepee-like structures. Those with tents can pitch them in the garden.

Desert Shade LODGE $
(☎08-658 6229; www.desert-nomads.com; dm/s/d 70/100/200NIS; @☜) An ecotourism centre with incredible views of the *makhtesh* and accommodation in Bedouin tents or mud huts.

Succah in the Desert HUT $$
(Succah BaMidbar; ☎08-658 6280; www.succah.co.il; half board s/d 300/550, weekends 700NIS) Set 7km from town on a dusty track, this eco-retreat is the place to get away from it all. Has solar electricity, natural building materials and yummy vegetarian food, but few creature comforts. Advance bookings are essential and will avail you of free transport from Mitzpe Ramon.

HI – Mitzpe Ramon Youth Hostel HOSTEL $
(☎08-658 8443; mitzpe@iyha.org.il; dm/s/d 152/320/450NIS; ❄☜) A short downhill walk from the visitors centre, this large hostel is right on the edge of the crater.

Eating

Chez Eugene EUROPEAN $$$
(www.mitzperamonhotel.co.il; 8 Har Ardon St; mains from 78NIS; ⏱7pm-midnight Sun-Thu, noon-4pm Fri, noon-11pm Sat) Using only local ingredients, recently opened Chez Eugene serves succulent steaks, salmon and other delights from Israeli gastro-chef Shahar Dabah.

TOP CHOICE **Haksa** ISRAELI $
(2 Har Ardon St; dishes from 28NIS; ⏱noon-8.30pm Sat-Thu, 1-8.30pm Fri) Haksa offers real home cooking, such as meatballs with aubergine and couscous, and beef goulash. Situated in the owner's home in the industrial area.

Information

The **SPNI Har HaNegev Field School** (har@spni.org.il; ⏱8am-4pm Sun-Thu, to noon Fri) on the edge of the crater is worth visiting if you plan any serious hiking. At the entrance to Ben-Gurion Blvd there is a small commercial concourse with a **Bank Hapoalim** and a **post office** (⏱8am-6pm Sun-Thu, to noon Fri).

Getting There & Away

Mitzpe Ramon lies 23km south of Avdat and 136km north of Eilat. Metropoline bus 60 shuttles hourly to and from Be'er Sheva (16.50NIS, 1¼ hours) from 8am to 9.30pm via Sde Boker and Ein Avdat. From Sunday to Thursday Egged buses 392 or 397 travel to Eilat (44NIS, three hours) at 9.53am, 10.53am, 1.38pm and 5.23pm. The only bus to Eilat on Friday is at 9.38am. Catch the bus to Eilat from the petrol station.

Eilat
ايلات אילת

☎08 / POP 47,500

A thin wedge between Jordan and Egypt at the southern tip of Israel, the glitzy Red Sea resort of Eilat – separated from the Israel of international headlines by 200km of

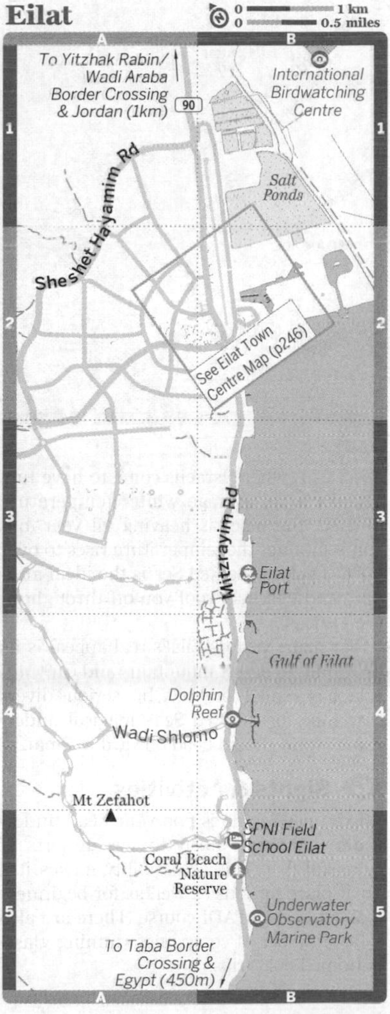

Eilat Town Centre

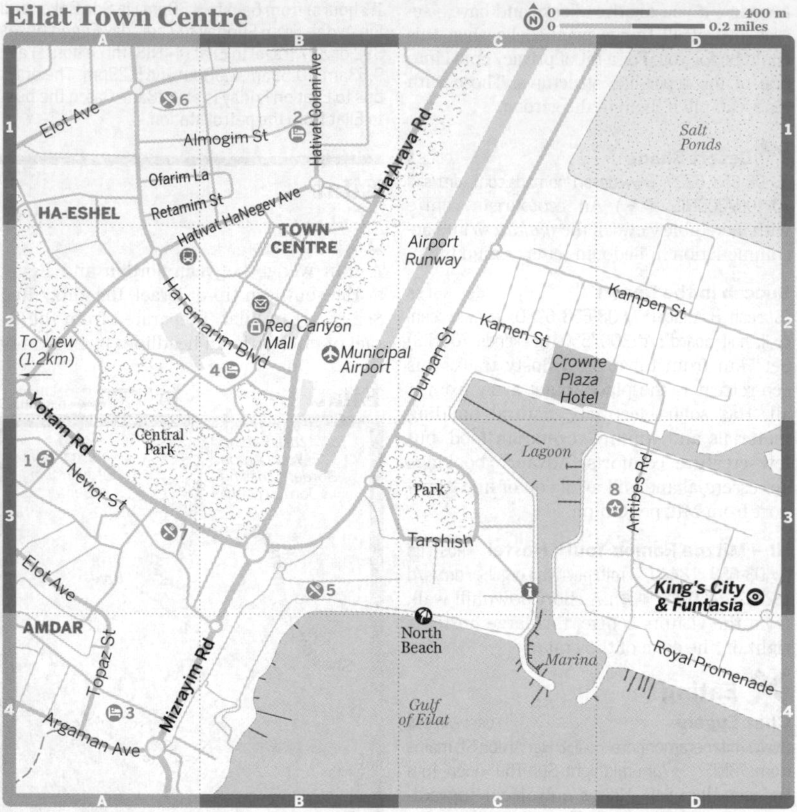

desert – is where Israelis come to have fun. Thanks to an average winter temperature of 21°C, the place is heaving all year, but come summer the temperature rises to over 40°C. Luckily, the Red Sea is the ideal antidote and will help cool you off throughout the year.

For many visitors Eilat's real appeal is its proximity to desert mountains and canyons. Eilat has a small coral reef, but serious divers searching for the Red Sea's magical underwater world should head onward to Sinai.

Sights & Activities

All you need to do is pop your head underwater and you're likely to see all sorts of colourful fish. This accessibility makes it a great place for kids as well as for beginners looking to do a PADI course. There are also a fair number of companies running glass-bottomed boat trips.

Underwater Observatory Marine Park AQUARIUM
(Map p245; www.coralworld.com/eilat; Coral Beach, Mitzrayim Rd; adult/child 89/69NIS; ⌚8.30am-5pm Sat-Thu, to 4pm Fri) Features a magical glassed-in underwater viewing centre – like snorkelling without getting wet – as well as the Oceanarium mock submarine ride and tanks with sharks and rare green and hawksbill turtles, which live for 150 to 200 years. The aquarium displays tropical species you may have missed on the reef and has a pitch-black room for viewing phosphorescent fish. Kids will get a thrill out of the petting pool and the regular feedings that take place between 11am and 3pm.

Dolphin Reef WATER PARK
(Map p245; ☎08-630 0111; www.dolphinreef.co.il; South Beach; adult/child 64/44NIS; ⌚9am-5pm Sun-Thu) Dolphin Reef is home to a group of bottlenose dolphins, which you can observe as they hunt, play and socialise in their

Eilat Town Centre

Top Sights

Activities, Courses & Tours

Sleeping

Eating

Entertainment

'natural habitat'. You can also snorkel with the dolphins (280NIS) or do an introductory dive (320NIS), for which advance booking is advised.

King's City & Funtasia AMUSEMENT PARK
(Map p246; www.kingscity.co.il; East Lagoon; adult/child 125/99NIS; 9am-1am Sun-Thu, to 5pm Fri, 6pm-1am Sat) Housed inside a giant fake castle, this biblical theme park has mazes, kaleidoscopes, 3D films and a heart-thumping water ride through King Solomon's life. Funtasia, a more conventional outdoor amusement park, offers bumper cars, a small roller coaster and a carousel.

TOP CHOICE **Coral Beach Nature Reserve** DIVE SITE
(Map p245; adult/child 33/20NIS; 9am-5pm Sat-Thu, 9am-3pm Fri) For snorkelling, your best option is the beautiful reserve, which has several underwater trails marked by buoys. Snorkelling equipment can be hired for 16NIS.

FREE **International Birdwatching Centre** WILDLIFE RESERVE
(Map p245; 7am-4pm) Tens of millions of migrating birds pass through the Arava and Eilat en route from Africa to Europe and vice versa. Situated directly opposite the Arava border crossing.

Tours

Desert Eco Tours ADVENTURE TOUR
(Map p245 ; 08-637 4259; www.desertecotours.com; Neviot St) Runs reputable 4WD, camel and hiking tours in the Negev, Sinai and southwest Jordan.

Sleeping

Eilat's accommodation ranges from the good to the bad to the downright ugly. Occasionally touts offering cheap private rooms wait at the central bus station. It is advisable to view a place before agreeing to stay.

As a resort town, the cost of hotel rooms in Eilat rises by about 25% on weekends and 50% (or more) from June to August. Reserve ahead, particularly during the holiday season.

Camping is illegal on most of Eilat's beaches. Exceptions are the areas towards the Jordanian border and north of the port and the SPNI Field School on Coral Beach.

If you enjoy outlandish luxury hotels, then Eilat has plenty to choose from. There are more than 40 complexes along North Beach and on the road to Taba.

Arava Hostel HOSTEL $
(Map p246; 08 637 4687; www.a55.co.il; 106 Almogim St; dm/s/d 75/170/185NIS;) This is one of the best budget options in Eilat. The rooms are small, with old-fashioned decor, but this is a good place to meet other backpackers. Laundry facilities available.

Rio BOUTIQUE HOTEL $$
(Map p246; 08-630 1111; 9 Ha Temarim Blvd; s/d from 250/400NIS;) A bargain boutique hotel with tastefully designed rooms and a small swimming pool that can be crowded in summer. Located on a busy road.

Eilat Guesthouse & Youth Hostel HOSTEL $$
(Map p246; 02-594 5611; www.iyha.org.il; Mitzrayim Rd; dm/s/d 160/330/426NIS;) Undergoing renovations at the time of writing, this big, grey concrete building facing the sea will soon have top-quality facilities. Often hosts huge groups of school kids.

SPNI Field School Eilat GUESTHOUSE, CAMPGROUND $
(Map p245; 08-637 1127/2021; www.teva.org.il/english; Coral Beach; campsites per person 50NIS, s/d 220/295NIS) Bring your own tent to camp, or enjoy the spacious and well-equipped rooms (if they're not taken by groups).

Eating & Drinking

Many of Eilat's eating options are spread along the hotel-packed promenade, with cheap eats in the New Tourist Centre.

Cafe Optimi CAFE $$
(Map p245 ; 10 Pninat Centre; mains 52NIS; ⊙9am-2am; ☑) This is the place to come for omelettes, bowls of muesli and huge salads. Vegetarian options include a sandwich of goat's cheese, eggplant and peppers.

TOP CHOICE **Ginger Asian Kitchen & Bar** ASIAN $$
(Map p246; www.gingereilat.com; New Tourist Centre, Yotam St; mains from 59NIS; ⊙noon-midnight; ☑) Seekers of sushi and spicy Asian dishes will love this slick restaurant, with black leather banquettes and a wraparound bar.

Eddie's Hide-A-Way STEAKHOUSE $$
(Map p246; 68 Almogim St; mains from 60NIS; ⊙6-11pm Mon-Fri, from 2pm Sat) Succulent steaks are served at this Eilat institution, as well as good fish dishes, no fewer than seven kinds of shrimp dishes, eight spaghetti delicacies and a nice line of vegetarian mains.

☆ Entertainment

Much of Eilat's nightlife is bar-based, with the action focussed on the Promenade and New Tourist Centre.

HaMoadon CLUB
(Map p245 ; 3 Antibes Rd; admission 60-100NIS; ⊙11pm-6am) The most popular club in Eilat – expect laser beams, cocktails and lots of beautiful young people. Located in the King Solomon Hotel.

View CLUB
(1 HaMelacha St; admission 60-100NIS; ⊙11.30pm-late) It's worth the taxi ride out here for the rooftop bar and dance floor. Packed with locals, it hosts various Israeli and international DJs. Situated 1.5km north of the airport terminal.

ℹ Information

To change money, head for the many change bureaus in the town centre.

Post office (Red Canyon Mall; ⊙8am-6pm Sun-Thu, to noon Fri)

SPNI Field School (eilat@spni.org.il) Has information on hiking and birdwatching in the area.

Tourist information office (eilatinfo@tourism.gov.il; Bridge House, North Beach Promenade; ⊙8.30am-5pm Sun-Thu, 8am-1pm Fri) A helpful place with a plethora of maps and brochures.

Tourist police (⊙10am-3am Sun-Wed, 10am-6am Thu-Sat) Near the tourist information office at North Beach.

Yoseftal Hospital (☎08-635 8011; cnr Yotam Rd & Argaman Ave)

ℹ Getting There & Away

The Yitzhak Rabin/Wadi Araba border crossing between Israel and Jordan is about 3km northeast of Eilat. For details on crossing over to Aqaba and getting to Petra, see p275. For information on travel via the Taba border crossing to Egypt, see p274.

Air

Municipal airport (☎1 700 705 022) Situated slap bang in the middle of the city. Both **Arkia** (☎08-638 4888; www.arkia.com; Red Canyon Mall) and **Israir** (☎1 700 505 777; www.israirairlines.com; Shalom Centre) fly several times daily to Sde Dov and Ben-Gurion airports in Tel Aviv. Book online for the best rates.

Ovda Airport (☎1 700 705 022) About 67km north of the centre of Eilat; serves seasonal charter flights from Europe.

Bus

From the **central bus station** (☎08-636 5120; HaTemarim St) there are services to the following destinations:

Tel Aviv (65NIS, five hours) Buses depart every hour from 5am to 10pm, with an additional overnight service at 1am. The last Friday bus is at 3pm and the first Saturday bus at 11.30am. This line also stops in Be'er Sheva (55NIS, three hours).

Mitzpe Ramon (45NIS, 2½ hours) Buses run more or less hourly on weekdays and at least twice on Saturday.

Jerusalem (65NIS, 4½ hours) Bus 444 runs six services daily. On Saturdays, the first Jerusalem bus departs at 4.30pm.

Masada (55NIS, four hours) Four daily buses.

ℹ Getting Around

Hourly Egged bus 15 goes from the central bus station to the Dolphin Reef, the Underwater Observatory, Coral Beach and the Taba border crossing.

Around Eilat

☎08

Eilat is surrounded by jagged, red-rock mountains created by the tectonic movements of the Great Rift Valley (Syrian–African Rift). The desert environment, blazing with glorious colours (especially at sunrise and sunset), is home to a huge variety of flora and fauna.

Hikers will want to head for the Eilat Mountains, but be sure to pick up a copy of the 1:50,000 SPNI *Eilat Mountains* topographical hiking map (80NIS), available in bookshops and at the SPNI Field School in Eilat.

North of Eilat towards the Dead Sea, on both sides of the border with Jordan, is the beautiful Arava Valley.

Sights & Activities

Timna Park PARK

(www.timna-park.co.il; adult/child 44/39NIS; ⏲8am-4pm Sat-Thu, to 1pm Fri & Sun) About 25km north of Eilat, Timna Park, source of copper for Egypt's pharaohs in the 5th century BC, has some stunning desert landscapes, enlivened with multicoloured rock formations. The most intriguing are the **Natural Arch**, the eroded monolith known as the **Mushroom** and the photogenic **Solomon's Pillars**. There is also a range of excellent day hikes through one of Israel's wildest desert landscapes.

Buses between Eilat and points north pass the park turn-off, 2.5km from the park entrance.

Yotvata Hai-Bar Nature Reserve WILDLIFE RESERVE

(www.parks.org.il; adult/child 43/22NIS; ⏲8.30am-5pm Sun-Thu, to 3.30pm Fri & Sat) Located 35km north of Eilat, this wildlife reserve was created to establish breeding groups of wild animals that are mentioned in the Bible, as well as other threatened species. In addition to savannah areas that can be visited only by car, you can see reptiles, small desert animals and large predators such as wolves and leopards in the **Predator Centre**, and nocturnal animals such as pygmy gerbils in the **Night Life** exhibition hall. Visitors can pitch tents near the entrance for 50NIS a night.

All buses to/from Eilat stop nearby on Rte 90.

Kibbutz Lotan KIBBUTZ

(www.kibbutzlotan.com; Rte 90) Known for its funky geodesic dome houses, Lotan is one of only two kibbutzim in Israel affiliated with the Judaism Reform Movement. Lotan runs regular workshops in alternative building methods, as well as half- and full-day tours that show visitors how to put environmental theory into practice. Its **Bird Reserve** is set on a sandy plain very near the Jordanian border. Check the website for details of courses, activities and the pleasant guesthouse. Lotan is around 45km north of Eilat; all buses to/from Eilat stop nearby on Rte 90.

JUST ACROSS THE BORDER: PETRA, JORDAN

For details on getting from Eilat to the stunning Nabataean city of Petra (p313), which is an easy (day) trip through the Yitzhak Rabin/Wadi Araba border crossing, see p275.

Hiking

About 20km north of Eilat on the Arava Rd (Rte 90) hikers can follow the Israel National Trail to the spectacular **Shehoret Canyon**, which takes around three to four hours to hike. Near the mouth of Shehoret (or 'Black') Canyon lie the impressive **Amram Pillars**, also along the Israel National Trail, where there's an official camping ground (but no water).

An excellent six- to seven-hour hike will take you through the spectacular **Nakhal Gishron** (part of the Israel National Trail) from Har Yoash to the Egyptian border. Get an early start and carry at least 3L of water per person.

Further north, the 600m-long **Red Canyon** can be reached off the highway to Ovda (Rte 12). The canyon, which is just 1m to 3m wide, and 10m to 20m deep, is accessible on foot by way of a 1.5km walking track from the car park. It makes a great 1½-hour hike and involves some climbing.

WEST BANK & GAZA STRIP

الضفة الغربية وقطاع غزة
הגדה המערבית ורצועת עזה

Pocket-sized West Bank is jam-packed with history, biblical sites, bustling souqs and some of the friendliest people you'll ever meet. Sadly, it's also the Middle East poster child for strife, violence and failed peace agreements.

Despite the West Bank's troubled past and uncertain present, its doors are open to tourists. Amid the rolling hills, olive groves and chalky desertscapes you can visit traditional villages and biblical sites galore, from the birthplace of Jesus to the last resting place of Abraham. Palestinian capital Ramallah is a surprisingly vibrant place, with gourmet restaurants and a lively cultural scene. Offbeat sites include Jenin's Freedom Theatre and a cable car strung over Jericho.

Perhaps the most appealing thing about visiting this area is the chance to meet strong, determined and hopeful Palestinians. The West Bank is not the easiest place in which to travel, but the effort is richly rewarded.

At the time of writing, the Gaza Strip was almost completely closed to tourists.

Ramallah & Al-Bireh

رام الله רמאללה ואל-בירה

☎02 / POP 73,000

Ramallah (the name means God's Mountain) and Al-Bireh comprises a bustling, almost-cosmopolitan city, largely free from dense politics and religious fervour, a mere 10km north of Jerusalem. Wander the arteries running from central Al-Manara Sq to find snacks, perfumeries and jewellery shops galore, or head down to the more sedate Al-Muntazah neighbourhood to rub shoulders with Pekingese-toting ladies and local notables.

With polite policemen manning the city's zebra crossings, roaming fez-capped coffee vendors, shoppers, hawkers, and busy, besuited businessmen, Ramallah revels in an air of gleeful sophistication, and makes a terrific place to spend a day.

Sights & Activities

Ramallah makes a good base if you're planning on exploring the local cultural scene.

Yasser Arafat's Tomb TOMB
(Al-Itha'a St; ⌚9am-9pm) The Muqata'a, Yasser Arafat's presidential compound, where he spent his sunset years, is also the site of his tomb, guarded by soldiers and adorned with wreaths. Situated 1km from Al-Manara Sq, on the road to Birzeit and Nablus.

Khalil Sakakini Centre CULTURAL CENTRE
(www.sakakini.org; Al-Muntazah) Hosts art exhibitions by the locally and internationally renowned, along with a whole host of other cultural pursuits. Check the website for upcoming events.

Sleeping

Most foreign visitors come here for the day, basing themselves in Jerusalem. But if you do want to stay in town, there's a reasonable selection of digs for all pockets.

Royal Court Suites Hotel HOTEL $$
(☎296 4040; www.rcshotel.com; Al-Muntazah; s 255-310NIS, d 370-450NIS; @) Rooms are tastefully designed, have excellent bathrooms, and some come with balconies and kitchenettes. There is no wi-fi, but the rooms do come with a cable that you can hook up to a laptop.

Al-Wihdeh Hotel HOTEL $
(☎298 0412; Al-Nahda St, Al-Manara; s/d/tr 100/120/130NIS; wi-fi) Dirt-cheap rooms, free wi-fi and a central location – but it's pretty beat up.

Eating

TOP CHOICE **Pronto Resto-Café** ITALIAN $$
(Al-Muntazah; mains 45-75NIS; ⌚7am-11pm) This dark and cosy little trattoria is a popular spot for musicians, filmmakers, professionals and peacemakers. The carbonara is full of smoky bacon and garlic, and the blue-cheese sandwich is a cheese lover's pungent delight. Top it all off with a glass or two of Palestinian-produced wine.

Zamn CAFE $
(Al-Tireh; coffees from 10NIS, mains 35-60NIS; ⌚7am-11pm; wi-fi) The hippest spot in Ramallah and a meeting ground for reporters and NGO workers, Zamn is a fun place for a morning croissant and cuppa or a lunchtime sandwich. Walk down Dar Ibrahim and bear right at the roundabout.

Sangria's BAR
(Jaffa Rd, Al-Muntazah; ⌚noon-midnight) Ramallah's favourite summer bar, with a glamour-garden ambience.

Entertainment

The entertainment listing *This Week in Palestine* will help you navigate cultural offerings.

Al-Kasaba Theater & Cinematheque CINEMA
(www.alkasaba.org; Al-Manara) A well-known centre for arts, music, film and theatre, right in the city centre.

Khalil Sakakini Centre CULTURAL CENTRE
(www.sakakini.org; Al-Muntazah) The website has details on concerts and films.

Getting There & Around

BUS From the old Arab bus station in East Jerusalem take bus 18 (7NIS, 30 minutes) all the way to Ramallah (non-stop service). Some buses will go to Qalandia checkpoint

Around Bethlehem, Ramallah & Jericho

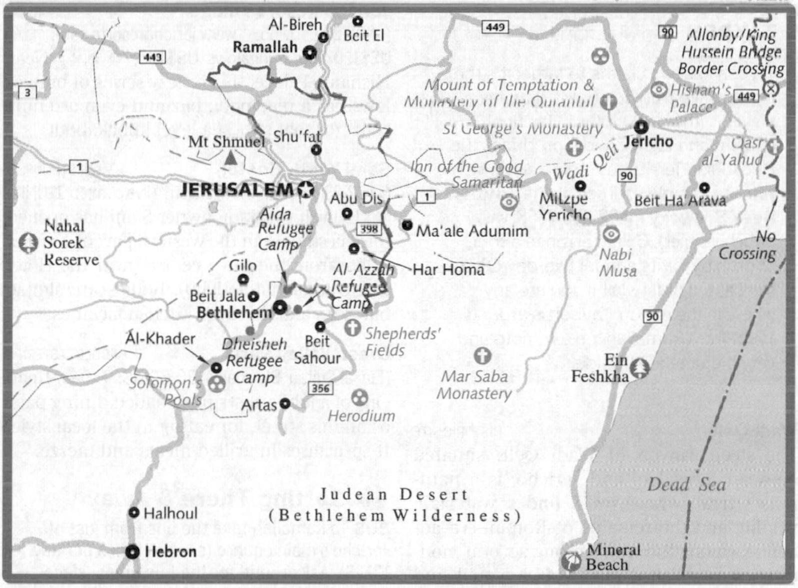

(4NIS), from where you can take a shared taxi another 5.5km to Al-Manara (3NIS per person) – you're there when you see the stone lions. Going the other way you'll need to pass through the Qalandia checkpoint: have your passport ready.

SHERUT From Ramallah to Bethlehem, a private taxi should cost around 70NIS; though it's not very far, the journey takes around 1½ hours, to avoid checkpoints.

Jericho & Around

اريحا יריחו

☎02 / POP 20,300

Jericho is said to be one of the oldest continuously inhabited cities on earth. (This is no idle boast – archaeological evidence traces the city's history back over 10,000 years.) At 260m below sea level, it's also the lowest. The city is famous for Joshua's trumpet blasts, which in tradition caused the walls to come a-tumblin' down. According to the Bible, Jericho was also the first place conquered by the Israelites after their 40 years of desert wandering.

Today, the town is rather scruffy and unkempt, but it retains a raffish charm and a smiley demeanour and has some impressive archaeological sites.

Sights

Ancient Jericho's main sites are best accessed on the 6km anticlockwise loop formed by Ein as-Sultan St and Qasr Hisham St.

Tel al-Sultan (Ancient Jericho) RUIN

(adult/child 10/5NIS; ⌚8am-5pm) The term 'old city' takes on a whole new meaning at this site, first settled some 10,000 years ago. The remains of a round tower, thought to date from 8000 BC, indicates that Jericho was possibly the world's first fortified city. A 20-minute movie at the entrance helps explain the site.

Mount of Temptation & Monastery of the Qurantul RELIGIOUS

(round trip 55NIS; ⌚8am-9pm) If your heart can handle the height better than the hike, take a swingy Swiss-made cable car from near the ancient city ruins of Tel al-Sultan, up to the place where the devil is said to have tested Jesus, by suggesting that after a 40-day fast the Son of God should make a loaf of bread out of a stone (Matthew 4:1-11). The 12th century Greek Orthodox Monastery of the Qurantul (Monastery of the Forty) clings to a cliff side overlooking orange and banana trees in the river valley, the Dead Sea to the south and the Jordan Mountains to the east.

WORTH A TRIP

TAYBEH الطيبة טייבה

Taybeh has two claims to fame: it's the place where tradition holds that Jesus stayed with his disciples in his final hours (John 11:54); and it produces the Palestinian Territories' only beer, which you can sample yourself at the **Taybeh Beer Brewery** (02-289 8868; www.taybehbeer.net). Call to arrange a tour, or drop by for its annual two-day **Oktoberfest**, a must-visit if you are anywhere in the region. Taybeh is around 15km from Ramallah, on a remote and very picturesque hillside.

Wadi Qelt HISTORIC SITE
The steep canyon of Wadi Qelt, situated between Jerusalem and Jericho, is a naturalist's treat, where you'll find a waterfall, wildlife and the remains of Roman-era aqueducts along the way. Among several monasteries established in this area, you'll find the spectacular 5th-century **St George's Monastery** (8am-noon & 3-7pm Sun-Thu, 8am-noon Sat) blending into a rock face. Signs to the Israeli settlement of Mitzpe Yericho, off Hwy 1, will put you on the path, though it's advisable to go with a local guide.

Nabi Musa HISTORIC SITE
(Prophet Moses; 8am-sunset) About 10km northeast of the northern end of the Dead Sea, Nabi Musa is where Muslims believe Moses (Musa in Arabic, Moshe in Hebrew) was buried. A mosque was built on the site in 1269, under Mamluk Sultan Baybar (it was expanded two centuries later).

Hisham's Palace RUIN
(Khirbet al-Mafjar; admission 10NIS; 8am-5pm) The sprawling winter hunting retreat of Caliph Hisham Ibn Abd al-Malik must have been magnificent on its creation in the 8th century, with its baths, mosaic floors and pillars – so much so that archaeologists have labelled it the 'Versailles of the Middle East'. Nearby is a beautiful 5th- or 6th-century **synagogue**.

Zacchaeus Tree RELIGIOUS
(Ein as-Sultan St) This is said to be the very same sycamore that Zacchaeus, a wealthy publican, climbed 2000 years ago for a better view of the preaching Jesus (Luke 19:1-10).

Sleeping & Eating

Jericho Resort Village RESORT $$
(02-232 1255; www.jerichoresorts.com; s/d US$120/140, bungalows US$180;) Near Hisham's Palace, this breezy series of bungalows has a nice pool, bar and even a tennis court for that sub-sea level knockabout.

Sami Youth Hostel GUESTHOUSE $
(02-232 4220; eyad_alalem@live.com; r 120NIS;) English-speaking owner Sami has opened this guesthouse in the western part of Jericho, 3.2km from the town centre (near the Hotel Intercontinental Jericho). Rooms are simple but clean and there are kitchen facilities.

Green Valley Park MIDDLE EASTERN $
(Ein al-Sultan St; mains 30-60NIS; 9am-11pm) One of a jubilant strip of shaded dining patios on this street, for eating in the local style. It specialises in grilled meats and mezze.

Getting There & Away

BUS To Ramallah take the bus from just off Jericho's main square (several times per day, 12NIS). Ask around for the bus times, since they vary; they generally take about 90 minutes via a circuitous route to avoid the Qalandia checkpoint.

SHERUT There are no direct service taxis from Jerusalem to Jericho. If you're not travelling under your own steam, take a service taxi from Al-Musrasa in Jerusalem to Abu Dis (6.50NIS) and then another service taxi from Abu Dis to Jericho (12NIS).

Bethlehem

بيت لحم בית לחם

02 / POP 27,800

Most visitors come to Bethlehem with a preconceived image – a small stone village, a manger and shepherds in their fields – thanks to a childhood crèche, perhaps, or a drawer full of fading Christmas cards. The reality is quite different. Bethlehem positively hums with activity, its winding streets congested with traffic and its main square filled with snap-happy tourists scrambling to keep up with their guides. Christians now make up about 15% of the population (down from 85% in 1948).

Churches now cover many of the holy sites – the most famed is the Church of the Nativity on Manger Sq – but there is also plenty to see and do for the non-religious. There's a lively Old City and bazaar, and numerous cultural centres where you can critique local art, watch performances and talk politics.

Most travellers come on a day trip but to get the most out of your visit it's best to stay overnight – accommodation and food are both cheaper here than in Jerusalem.

Sights

Bethlehem is a relatively small town, sandwiched between the two smaller Christian villages of Beit Sahour and Beit Jala. The old city spreads out on either side of a steep hill, which makes for some leg-aching climbs up and down cobbled streets and seemingly hundreds of steps.

The centre of town is the pretty Manger Sq, on which stands the Church of the Nativity, the police station, post office, municipality buildings, a scattering of souvenir shops and the Peace Center info desk.

Church of the Nativity CHURCH
(5am-8pm, to 6pm winter) Commissioned in AD 326 by Emperor Constantine, this is one of the world's oldest functioning churches. Inside you'll find the underground **Grotto of the Nativity**, where Jesus is said to have been born, and the **Chapel of the Manger**, with its year-round nativity scene. Adjoining the church is the pinkish **St Catherine's Church**, from which Bethlehem's famous Catholic Midnight Mass is broadcast on Christmas Eve. The tour guides (around 50NIS for an hour) hanging around outside the church are usually highly knowledgeable and well worth taking along for the tour.

Milk Grotto Chapel CHURCH
(Milk Grotto St; 8-11am & 2-6pm) Legend has it that when Mary and Joseph stopped here to feed the baby during their flight to Egypt, a drop of milk touched the red rock, turning it white.

Old Bethlehem Museum MUSEUM
(www.arabwomenunion.org; Star St; admission 8NIS; 8am-noon & 2-5pm Mon-Wed, Fri & Sat, 8am-noon Thu) Located in the dusty basement of a typical Palestinian home of the 19th century. See native costumes, peruse the collection of early-20th-century photos of Palestine, and purchase embroidery.

International Center of Bethlehem (Dar Annadwa) CULTURAL CENTRE
(www.annadwa.org; Pope Paul VI St, Madbasseh Sq;) A Lutheran-run cultural centre, with regular exhibitions of Palestinian artists, events, classes, and a quiet cafe.

Green Market MARKET
(off Pope Paul VI St; 8am-6pm Mon-Sat) This souq was established in 1929.

Sleeping

The only time you'll have to worry about finding a room is at Christmas, when prices may rise by up to 50%.

TOP CHOICE **Dar Annadwa** GUESTHOUSE $$
(Abu Gubran; 02-277 0047; www.diyar.ps; 109 Pope Paul VI St, Old City; s/d US$65/90;) This very comfortable, Lutheran-sponsored boutique guesthouse has 13 tasteful rooms equipped with all the amenities.

Arab Women's Union GUESTHOUSE $$
(02-277 5857; www.elbeit.org; Beit Sahour; s/d/tr US$45/60/80; @) The women who run this guesthouse in beautiful Beit Sahour recycle paper, run community programs and produce olive-wood artefacts. The guesthouse has clean and modern rooms and there's a nice balcony where you can relax with a cup of tea.

Casanova Orient Palace HOTEL $$
(02-274 3980; www.casanovapalace.com; s/d/tr from US$45/60/90; @) This perennially popular, Franciscan-run place offers reasonable rooms and a buzzing atmosphere. In a stunning location right beside the Church of the Nativity.

Bethlehem Youth Hostel HOSTEL $
(02-74 8466, 059 964 6146; byh@ejepal.org; 66 Anatreh St; dm 60NIS; @) This brand-new hostel has three spacious dorm rooms, hot showers and a balcony with distant views of the Herodium. It's one street below the Milk Grotto.

Eating

The souq area has some mighty tasty street eats on offer, but anywhere you wander is likely to bring you within biting distance of a tasty, hole-in-the-wall restaurant treat.

TOP CHOICE **Afteem** MIDDLE EASTERN $
(Manger Sq; felafels 6NIS, hummus from 15NIS) A Bethlehem institution for decades, with top-notch hummus and *masabacha* (warm hummus with whole chickpeas).

Square MIDDLE EASTERN, WESTERN $
(Manger Sq; mains from 35NIS; 9am-midnight;) A swish, new lounge-style place that makes a great respite from walking around the city.

Sip a cappuccino or sup a light lunch (salads and pastas) in the basement dining room.

Peace Center Restaurant SANDWICHES, ITALIAN $
(Manger Sq; mains 20-45NIS; ⌚9am-6pm Mon-Sat) Great for a light snack or something more refined, such as Mediterranean salmon or *shish tawooq* (chicken skewers).

Information

Peace Center (www.bpcenter.org; ⌚8am-3pm Mon-Thu & Sat) This information desk offers tourist information and free maps, organises cultural events, and hosts a bookshop and public toilets.

Getting There & Away

Most visitors from Jerusalem enter Bethlehem via the ominous, prison-like checkpoint on the Jerusalem-Bethlehem road. Don't be discouraged – despite intimidating appearances, it's easy for travellers to cross.

BUS Bus 21 from Jerusalem to Bethlehem (7NIS, 30 minutes) departs every 15 minutes between 6am and 9pm (until 6.30pm in winter) from the Damascus Gate bus station. Alternatively, take bus 24 (5NIS) from Jerusalem to the main Bethlehem checkpoint, from where there are taxis into Bethlehem.

SHERUT It's possible to get shared taxis from the main bus station to Jericho (18NIS) and Hebron (9NIS). Share taxis to Hebron also leave from Bab iz-Qaq.

Around Bethlehem

The easiest way to visit the sights around Bethlehem is to hire a taxi for a half or whole day.

Sights

Shepherds' Fields RELIGIOUS
Situated at Beit Sahour, around 1km east of Bethlehem, this is where the shepherds who visited Jesus in his manger are said to have tended their flocks. It's a pleasant stroll up here to a little old church, a favourite photo-op destination for local brides. Accessible by private taxi from Bethlehem (15NIS), or catch Beit Sahour–bound bus 47 (2NIS) from Shepherd's St, just below Manger Sq.

Herodium ARCHAEOLOGICAL SITE
(adult/child 27/14NIS; ⌚8am-5pm Apr-Sep, to 4pm Oct-Mar) About 9km south of Beit Sahour stands Herodium, the amazing volcano-shaped remains of a palace complex built by Herod between 24 and 15 BC.

Mar Saba Monastery RELIGIOUS
(⌚8am-4pm Sun-Thu) This phenomenal cliff-clinging copper-domed hermitage, founded in AD 439, is best seen from the opposite slope. Men can go inside; women can get a bird's-eye view from the Women's Tower. Situated a bleak and beautiful 20km drive east of Bethlehem (beyond Beit Sahour).

Hebron

الخليل חברון

☎02 / POP 183,000

For Jews, Christians and Muslims alike, Hebron (Al-Khalil in Arabic) is considered the cradle of organised religion. For thousands of years the major holy site has been the Tomb of the Patriarchs – the collective tomb of Abraham, Isaac and Jacob, along with their wives (except Rachel). In addition, Islamic tradition states that Adam and Eve lived here after being exiled from the Garden of Eden. Sadly, the common thread of beliefs has done little to improve relations between the major monotheistic religions, as Hebron has long been a flashpoint for religious violence.

What distinguishes Hebron from other Palestinian towns is the presence of Jewish settlers within the city centre itself. There are five microsettlements in the city centre, with other, larger ones on the outskirts, effectively dividing the city into two pieces. For the traveller, this causes some inconveniences, as many streets are barricaded and/or off limits.

Despite its woes, Hebron continues to flourish as a business leader among Palestinian communities. Situated on a former trade route to the Arabian Peninsula, Hebron is still celebrated for its grapes, it skilled traders and its artisans' production of blown glass, leather and hand-painted pottery, just as it has been since antiquity.

Sights

Ibrahimi Mosque/ Tomb of the Patriarchs MOSQUE, SYNAGOGUE
(⌚8am-4pm Sun-Thu, except during prayers) For both Jews and Muslims, this massive stone structure is second in importance only to Jerusalem's Al-Haram ash-Sharif/Temple Mount. Built by Herod (notice the Herodian stones at the base of the walls), the complex was altered by the Byzantines in the 6th century – they added a church, beside which a synagogue was built. In February 1994 an

American-born Jewish settler stopped into the Ibrahimi Mosque and opened fire on Muslims at prayer, killing 29. The building is now segregated into Muslim and Jewish sections, and security is tight.

Sleeping & Eating

Hebron Hotel HOTEL $
(☎02-225 4201; hebron_hotel@hotmail.com; King Faisal St, Ein Sarah; s/d/tr US$35/45/55) An airy lobby gives way to adequate rooms mixing shabby with new.

TOP CHOICE **Abu Mazen** MIDDLE EASTERN $
(Nimra St; mains 25-35NIS; ⏲7am-9pm) Offers great value and tasty home cooking, including *mensaf* (lamb on rice served beside a salted broth of lamb stock and yoghurt) and *kidreh* (a baked casserole of meat, nuts and rice).

Getting There & Away

BUS From Jerusalem take Arab bus 21 (7NIS) from Al-Musrara (near Damascus Gate) to Husan intersection and change to a service taxi (9NIS). For a very different perspective – that of Hebron's Jewish settlers – take Egged bus 160 (9.60NIS, every 30 minutes) from Jerusalem's Central Bus Station. It stops right by the Ibrahimi Mosque/Tomb of the Patriarchs.

SHERUT From the bus station in Hebron, it's possible to catch service taxis to Jericho (30NIS), Bethlehem (9NIS) and Ramallah (27NIS) between 5am and 6pm. Vehicles move when full.

Nablus

نابلس שכם

☎09 / POP 136,000

Scenically situated between the Gerizim and Ebal peaks, this quite attractive, bustling town is the largest West Bank population centre, and is well known for its production of soap, olive wood and olive oil. In the central Palestine/Al-Hussein Sq, you'll find the bus stops, the service taxi ranks and a small market. Immediately to the south, the Old Town stretches eastward along Nasir St. It's generally safe to visit but, as with everywhere in the West Bank, keep your ears open for current updates.

Sights & Activities

Al-Qasaba NEIGHBOURHOOD
In Al-Qasaba (Casbah or Old City), you'll find an Ottoman-era rabbit warren of shops, stalls and pastry stands, spice sacks and vegetable mounds, as well as dozens of ancient mosques, including the **Al-Kebir Mosque** (Great Mosque), which was built on the site of an earlier Crusader church and Byzantine and Roman basilicas.

Jacob's Well CHURCH
(donations appreciated; ⏲8am-noon & 2-4pm) Near the entrance to Balata (population 20,000), the largest UN Relief and Works Agency (UNRWA) refugee camp in the West Bank, you'll find the remains of a Crusader church, marking the spot where Christians believe a Samaritan woman offered Jesus a drink of water.

Hammam Al-Hana BATHHOUSE
(Hammam es Sumara; bath 35NIS, massage 10NIS; ⏲men 6am-11pm Wed-Mon, women 8am-5pm Tue) This tourist-friendly hammam, deep inside the souq, offers a bath, steam room and massage.

Sleeping & Eating

The Nablus speciality is sweets, including Arabic pastries, halva, Turkish delight and especially *kunafa* (vermicelli-like pastry over a cheese base soaked in syrup).

TOP CHOICE **Al-Yasmeen Hotel** HOTEL $$
(☎09-233 3555; www.alyasmeen.com; s/d/tr 180/220/260NIS; ❄📶) Nablus' best hotel and favourite lodging of aid workers and politicos puts you in the middle of it all, at the centre of the Old City. Rooms are clean and well appointed and the staff are extremely helpful and knowledgeable about the West Bank.

Getting There & Away

There is no direct bus service to Nablus from Jerusalem. You will need to change at either Qalandia checkpoint or Ramallah, where a service taxi will cost 17NIS.

Gaza City

غزة עזה

☎08 / POP 450,000

Just 45km long and 10km wide, the Gaza Strip is not on the 'to-do' list for most travellers – and for good reason. Since Hamas took full control of the seaside territory in June 2007 after a bloody showdown with the rival Fatah movement, Gaza has been blockaded by land, sea and sky by neighbouring Israel (Gaza's land border with Egypt was sealed by the Mubarak regime until its fall in 2011). If getting into Gaza is difficult, then getting out can be even harder – crossing the border can take several hours, and travellers can be detained on both sides for questioning.

So why go to Gaza at all? Well, in times of safety and peace, a visit to Gaza could be one you won't quickly forget. Beyond the poverty and rubble, you might find traces of an illustrious Mediterranean trading history spanning three millennia.

Today's Gaza is a paradox of extreme poverty and privilege. While the vast majority of Gazans rely on international aid, you'll also see spacious villas, the odd Mercedes and a few luxury hotels.

Sights

Though it's not exactly tourist central, Gaza City has a fair amount to see. The area around central Palestine Sq holds most of the city's sites of historical interest.

Great Mosque MOSQUE
(Omar al-Mukhtar St; closed to non-Muslims Fri) This converted Crusader-era church is the most distinguished structure in the city. Along its southern wall runs the short, vaulted **Gold Market**, which has served prospective bridegrooms since the Mamluk era.

Napoleon's Citadel FORTRESS
(Daraj Quarter, Old City) In 1799, during his Egyptian campaign, Napoleon Bonaparte camped in Gaza and established his base in this attractive Mamluk-era (13th-century) structure. Parts house an archaeological museum with Hellenistic, Roman and Byzantine artefacts.

Mosque of Said Hashim MOSQUE
(Yafa St; closed to non-Muslims Fri) Built in 1850, this mosque houses the grave of the Prophet Mohammed's great-grandfather, Hashim – a prominent merchant who died as he was passing through Gaza.

TRAVEL WARNING: GAZA

Following Hamas' armed takeover in 2007, Gaza has remained an unstable place and a source of rocket attacks, bombings and kidnappings. Most countries' foreign ministries advise against all nonessential travel to the Gaza Strip while the political situation remains volatile.

St Porphyrius Church CHURCH
(Zaytun Quarter, Old City) This Greek Orthodox Church, built in the 5th century and rebuilt in the Crusader period and the 19th century, still serves Gaza's small (and dwindling) Christian community. You can get the key from the priest who lives above the school opposite the church.

Sleeping

TOP CHOICE **Al-Deira Hotel** HOTEL $$
(08-283 8100; www.aldeira.ps; Al-Rasheed St; s/d US$120/150;) Undoubtedly the best hotel in town, Al-Deira is a swish, stylish and tightly run place with comfy beds, hot showers and a good sea view from its balconies.

Getting There & Away

At the time of writing, access to the Gaza Strip was extremely limited. The Erez Crossing is the only potential way for foreigners (almost exclusively international aid workers) to enter Gaza from Israel. In May 2011 the Rafah border crossing with Egypt was reopened (see p274).

UNDERSTAND ISRAEL & THE PALESTINIAN TERRITORIES

Israel & the Palestinian Territories Today

Optimism about peace was widespread among both Israelis and Palestinians in the heyday of the Oslo peace process, in the mid-1990s. But following years of suicide bombings, rocket attacks from Gaza and calls by Palestinian Islamists for Israel's destruction, many Israelis have become pessimistic. Continuing Israel Defence Force (IDF) roadblocks, settlement construction and settler violence have had a similar impact on the assessment of many Palestinians.

Israeli Prime Minister Binyamin Netanyahu has declared his support for a two-state solution to the Israeli–Palestinian conflict, but since his right-wing coalition government came to power in 2009, it has repeatedly expanded Jewish settlements and offered only vague answers to Palestinian questions about eventual borders, calling into question Netanyahu's commitment to the eventual establishment of a viable Palestinian state next to Israel.

The leadership of the Palestinian Authority (PA) also appears hamstrung. Although PA President Mahmoud Abbas and his prime minister, Salam Fayad, have a long record of support for a two-state solution, they too have seemed reluctant to make any bold moves. Instead, Abbas has been putting great effort into having Palestine admitted to the UN General Assembly as a full member state.

History

Ancient Times

Around 1800 BC, Abraham is believed to have led his nomadic tribe from Mesopotamia to what is now Israel and the Palestinian Territories, then known as Canaan. His descendants were forced to relocate to Egypt because of drought and crop failure but, according to the Bible, Moses led them back in about 1250 BC. Conflicts with the Canaanites and Philistines pushed the Israelites to abandon their loose tribal system and unify under King Saul (1050–1010 BC) and his successors, King David, and King Solomon, builder of the First Temple in Jerusalem.

After Solomon's reign (965–928 BC), two rival entities came into being: the Kingdom of Israel in what is now the northern West Bank and the Galilee; and the southern Kingdom of Judah, with its capital at Jerusalem. After Sargon II of Assyria (r 722–705 BC) destroyed the Kingdom of Israel in 720 BC, the 10 tribes who made up the northern Kingdom of Israel disappeared from the historical record.

The Babylonians captured Jerusalem in 586 BC, destroying the First Temple and exiling the people of Judah to Babylonia (now Iraq). Fifty years later Cyrus II, king of Persia, defeated Babylon and allowed the Jews to return to the Land of Israel. The returning Jews immediately set about constructing the Second Temple, consecrated in 516 BC.

Greeks & Maccabees, Romans & Christians

Greek rule over the Land of Israel began in the late 4th century BC. When the Seleucid king Antiochus IV Epiphanes banned Temple sacrifices, Shabbat and circumcision, the Jews, led by Judah Maccabee, revolted. Using guerrilla tactics, they captured Jerusalem and rededicated the Temple – an event celebrated by the Jewish holiday of Hanukkah.

The Maccabees also established the Hasmonean dynasty, but infighting made it easy for Rome to take over in 63 BC. At times the Romans ruled the Roman province of Judaea directly through a procurator – the most famous of whom was Pontius Pilate – but they preferred a strong client ruler like Herod the Great (r 37–4 BC), whose major construction projects included expanding the Temple.

The 1st century AD was a time of tremendous upheaval in Judea, not least between about 28 and 30 AD, when it's believed Jesus of Nazareth carried out his ministry. In the years following Jesus' crucifixion, which some experts believe took place in AD 33, Jews who believed him to be the Messiah and those who didn't often worshipped side by side. But around the time the Gospels were written (late 1st century CE), theological and political disagreements emerged and the two communities diverged.

Long-simmering tensions in Judaea exploded in AD 66, when the Jews launched the Great Jewish Revolt (the First Jewish–Roman War) against the Romans. Four years later, Titus, the future emperor, crushed the rebels and laid waste to the Second Temple. The mountaintop Jewish stronghold of Masada fell in AD 73, putting an end to even nominal Jewish sovereignty for almost 2000 years.

With the Temple destroyed and the elaborate animal sacrifices prescribed in the Torah suspended, Jewish religious life was thrown into a state of limbo. In an effort to adapt to the new circumstances, Jewish sages set about reorienting Judaism towards prayer and synagogue worship.

After another failed Jewish revolt, the Bar Kochba Rebellion (AD 132–35), the triumphant Romans – in an attempt to erase Jews' connection to the country – renamed Jerusalem 'Aelia Capitolina' and the province of Judaea 'Syria Palaestina'.

Muslims & Crusaders

Islam and the Arabs arrived in Palestine in AD 638 – just six years after the death of the Prophet Mohammed – when Caliph Omar (Umar), the second of the Prophet Mohammed's successors, accepted the surrender of Jerusalem. Jews were again permitted to settle in Jerusalem and Christian shrines, including those established by Helena (Constantine the Great's mother) were preserved.

Omar's successors built Al-Aqsa Mosque and the Dome of the Rock on the Temple

Mount (known to Muslims as Al-Haram ash-Sharif), believed to be the site of Mohammed's Night Journey (Mi'raj) to behold the celestial glories of heaven.

Christian pilgrimage to the holy sites in Jerusalem was blocked in 1071 by the Seljuk Turks. In response, in 1095 Pope Urban II issued a call for a crusade to restore the site of Jesus' Passion to Christianity. By the time the Crusades began, the Seljuks had been displaced by the Fatimid dynasty, which was quite happy to allow the old pilgrimage routes to reopen. But it was too late. In 1099 the Crusaders overwhelmed Jerusalem's defences and massacred its Muslims and Jews.

In 1187 the celebrated Kurdish-Muslim general Saladin (Salah ad-Din) defeated a Crusader army at the Horns of Hattin in Galilee (near Arbel) and took Jerusalem.

The final Crusaders left the Middle East with the fall of Acre in 1291.

Ottomans, Zionists & British

The Ottoman Turks captured Palestine in 1516, and two decades later Sultan Süleyman the Magnificent (r 1520–66) built the present massive walls around Jerusalem's Old City. For most of the 400 years of Ottoman rule, Palestine was a backwater run by pashas more concerned with capricious tax collection than good governance.

While a small numbers of Jews had remained in Palestine continuously since Roman times, and pious Jews had been immigrating whenever political conditions permitted, organised Zionist immigration to agricultural settlements didn't begin until 1882, sparked by pogroms in Russia. For slightly different reasons, Jews from Yemen began arriving the same year. But until after WWI, the vast majority of Palestine's Jews belonged to the old-line Orthodox community, most of it uninterested in Zionism, and lived in Judaism's four holy cities: Hebron, Tsfat (Safed), Tiberias and Jerusalem, which has had a Jewish majority since about 1850.

In November 1917 the British government issued the Balfour Declaration, which stated that 'His Majesty's Government view with favour the establishment in Palestine of a National Home for the Jewish People'. The next month, British forces under General Edmund Allenby captured Jerusalem.

After the end of WWI Jews resumed immigration to Palestine, this time to territory controlled by a British mandate – approved by the League of Nations – that was friendly, modernising and competent. Among the Jewish immigrants were young, idealistic socialists, many of whom established kibbutzim (communal settlements) on marginal land purchased from absentee Arab landlords, sometimes displacing Arab peasant farmers. In the 1930s they were joined by refugees from Nazi Germany.

The anti-Zionist Arab Revolt (1936–39), aimed both at Jews and British forces, was suppressed by the Mandatory government with considerable violence. However, it convinced the British – who, in case of war with Germany, would surely need Arab oil and political goodwill – to severely limit Jewish immigration to Palestine. Just as the Jews of Europe were becoming increasingly desperate to flee Hitler (Jews were allowed to leave Germany until late 1941, provided they could find a country to take them), the doors of Palestine slammed shut.

Independence & Catastrophe

By 1947 the British government, exhausted by WWII and tired of both Arab and Jewish violence in Palestine, turned the problem over to the two-year-old UN. In a moment of rare agreement between the United States and the Soviet Union in 1947, the UN General Assembly voted in favour of partitioning Palestine into two independent states – one Jewish, the other Arab – with Jerusalem under a 'special international regime'. Palestinian Jews accepted the plan in principle, but Palestinian Arabs, and nearby Arab countries, rejected it. Arab bands immediately began attacking Jewish targets, beginning the 1948 Arab–Israeli War.

As soon as the British left, at midnight on 14 May 1948, two thing happened: the Jews proclaimed the establishment of an independent Jewish state, and the armies of Egypt, Syria, Jordan, Lebanon and Iraq invaded Palestine. But to the Arab states' – and the world's surprise – the 650,000 Palestinian Jews were not 'thrown into the sea' but rather took control of 77% of Mandatory Palestine (the Partition Plan had offered them 56%), though without Jerusalem's Old City. Jordan occupied (and annexed) the West Bank and East Jerusalem, expelling the residents of the Old City's Jewish quarter; Egypt took control of the Gaza Strip.

As a result of the 1948 Arab–Israeli War, Israel achieved independence, quickly becoming a place of refuge for Holocaust survivors and Jewish refugees from Arab countries. The establishment of a sovereign Jewish state guaranteed that Jews fleeing persecution would always have a country that would take them in.

But for the Palestinian Arabs, the war is remembered as Al-Naqba, the Catastrophe. At the start of the conflict, at least 800,000 Arabs lived in what was to become Israel. By the end, 160,000 remained in areas under Israeli control. While many fled their homes to escape fighting, others were forced out of their towns and villages by Israeli military units.

After Israel became independent, impoverished Jewish refugees began flooding in, including Holocaust survivors and Jews from Arab countries whose ancient Jewish communities had been targets of anti-Jewish violence. Within three years, Israel's Jewish population had more than doubled.

War, Terrorism & a Peace Treaty

In the spring of 1967 Arab capitals – especially Cairo – were seething with calls to liberate all of historic Palestine from what they saw as an illegitimate occupation by Jewish Israelis. Egyptian President Gamal Abdel Nasser ordered UN peacekeeping forces to withdraw from Sinai and closed the Straits of Tiran to Israeli shipping.

On 6 June Israel launched a pre-emptive attack on its Arab neighbours, devastating their air forces and, in less than a week – the reason why the conflict came to be known as the 'Six Day War' (www.sixdaywar.co.uk) – captured Sinai and Gaza from Egypt, the West Bank and East Jerusalem from Jordan, and the Golan from Syria.

In 1973 Egypt and Syria launched a surprise, two-front attack on Yom Kippur, the holiest day of the Jewish calendar. Unprepared because of intelligence failures, Israel was initially pushed back. Although in tactical and strategic terms Israel eventually achieved victory on the battlefield, it came away from the war feeling defeated, in part because the early Egyptian and Syrian advances, coming just six years after the stunning victory of 1967, were so bloody and traumatic.

In 1977 Egyptian President Anwar Sadat stunned the world by travelling to Jerusalem. He offered to make peace with Israel in return for an Israeli withdrawal from Sinai and promises (never fulfilled) of progress towards a Palestinian state. The Camp David Accords, the first peace treaty between Israel and an Arab state, were signed in 1978.

In 1987 a popular uprising against Israeli rule broke out in the West Bank and Gaza. Known as the Intifada (Arabic for 'shaking off'), this spontaneous eruption of strikes, stones and Molotov cocktails gave Palestinians a renewed sense of hope and purpose.

In 1988 Yasser Arafat, then president of the PA, publicly renounced terrorism. Five years later, Israel and the Palestinian Liberation Organization (PLO) signed the Oslo Accords, under which Israel handed over control of territory to the Palestinians in stages, beginning with the major towns of the West Bank and Gaza. The toughest issues – the future of Jerusalem and Palestinian refugees' 'Right of Return' – were to be negotiated at the end of a five-year interim period.

Renewed Violence & Stalemate

But the Oslo Accords didn't bring real peace. Rather, they drove those on both sides who opposed compromise to greater acts of violence. Hamas and Islamic Jihad launched suicide bombings against Israeli civilians, and in November 1995 a right-wing Orthodox Israeli assassinated Prime Minister Yitzhak Rabin at a peace rally in Tel Aviv.

The Second Intifada (2000–05) brought an unprecedented wave of Palestinian suicide bombings against Israeli civilian targets, including buses, supermarkets, cafes and discos.

Prime Minister Ariel Sharon, a tough-talking former general, sent tanks to occupy West Bank towns previously ceded to the Palestinian Authority.

Depressed and sick, Arafat's command of events and – according to some aides – reality weakened until his death in November 2004.

Over the course of the Second Intifada, over 1000 Israelis, 70% of them civilians, were killed by Palestinians and some 4700 Palestinians, many of them civilians, were killed by Israelis, according to the Israeli human rights group B'Tselem (www.btselem.org).

In 2005 Sharon – completely contradicting his reputation as an incorrigible hardliner – evacuated all 8600 Israeli settlers from the Gaza Strip and four settlements in the northern West Bank. Like many other hawkish Israeli leaders before and after, he had come to the conclusion that Israel's continued occupation of the territories captured in 1967 was against Israeli interests and, in the long run, geopolitically and demographically untenable.

In the 2006 Palestinian legislative elections, Hamas – an Islamic political and militant group classified as a terrorist organisation by the United States, Canada, the European Union, the UK, Japan and Israel – won a landslide victory. The following year Hamas gunmen ran their Fatah counterparts out of the Gaza Strip after several days of bloody fighting, leaving the West Bank and Gaza under rival administrations.

In summer 2006, Israel and the Shiite Lebanese militia Hezbollah, backed by Iran, fought a brief war. Thousands of rockets rained down on Israeli cities, towns and villages, bringing northern Israel to a terrified halt. The scale of Israel's bombing attacks on Lebanese towns was widely condemned, but in mid-2012 a tenuous ceasefire was still holding.

In very late 2008, in response to years of rocket fire from Gaza, Israel launched a major offensive, dubbed Operation Cast Lead, aimed at halting the attacks. After three weeks of fighting, much of Gaza's infrastructure lay in ruins and more than 1000 Palestinians were dead; Israel claimed most were militants. Despite this, a tenuous ceasefire between Hamas and Israel was still holding (more or less) in mid-2012.

People

Israel

As the only Jewish state, Israel and its society are unique in the Middle East – and the world. Over three-quarters of Israelis are Jewish, but Israeli society is surprisingly diverse, encompassing communities of Muslim and Christian Arabs, Bedouins, Druze, Circassians and recently arrived refugees from Africa (especially Eritrea and Sudan).

The ancestors of about half of Israeli Jews immigrated from Europe (especially Russia, Romania, Poland, Germany and Hungary) and the Americas, the other half from Africa (eg Morocco and Ethiopia) and Asia (especially Iraq, Iran, Yemen and India). Despite their diversity of background, Israeli Jews are bound together by a collective memory of exile and persecution.

The army, to which Jewish, Druze and Circassian men and non-Orthodox Jewish women are drafted at the age of 18 (men for three years, women for two), also creates strong bonds, although burdens are not equally shared – most ultra-Orthodox Jews do not serve at all, and these days only a minority do reserve duty. The country is always in a state of security vigilance, in recent times as a result of rocket attacks and attempted infiltrations from Gaza, Hezbollah's huge Iranian-supplied arsenal in Lebanon, instability in Sinai and Syria, and anti-Israel proclamations from Iran.

Despite being very much at the heart of the Middle East, Israel leans toward Europe, and increasingly to America, in its lifestyle, culture and business proclivities. For Israel, inclusion in European events, especially the Eurovision Song Contest (a country-wide favourite) and the Euroleague basketball and EUFA Champions League football championships, are a chance to commune with 'fellow Westerners' on the opposite side of the Mediterranean.

In the business world, too, Israel has forged strong and successful links to Europe, the USA and East Asia. It has one of the world's highest GDPs, fuelled by a keen sense of entrepreneurism and world-class capacity in fields such as computers, chemistry and medical research.

Palestinian Territories

The perspectives and dreams of the residents of the Palestinian Territories have been forged by a century of loss, deprivation and violence. While Islam plays a major role in Palestinians' worldview (only 8% of West Bankers and 0.3% of Gazans are Christians), the defining characteristic is the desire for an independent homeland. For many Palestinians, years of unemployment, poverty and shortages have led to a collective sense of desperation and powerlessness. For others, these factors have inspired them to stand up against their 'oppressors', in some cases joining militant organisations whose tactics include attacks against civilians.

Government & Politics

Israel

Israel is a parliamentary democracy headed by a prime minister. Government decisions are made by the cabinet, presided over by the prime minister; its members (ministers) have executive responsibility for government ministries. The 120-member unicameral legislature, the Knesset, is elected by national proportional representation every four years (although elections are almost always called early). Israel also has a president, whose role is largely ceremonial, except that they must

WRITING ON THE WALL

Most images of Israel's contentious Separation Fence show blank grey stretches of dismal concrete panelling. But like the Berlin Wall of the 1980s, its surfaces – especially those on the Palestinian side – have been appropriated as a blank canvas for artistic outpourings.

Some of the myriad messages painted on its smooth surface speak of hope, others are angry, still more are defiant or ironic, while some enterprising locals have added their restaurant menus to the mix. There are graffiti projects by international professionals, simple painted murals created by schoolchildren, and visitors' spray-canned protests in a spectrum of languages. Some Palestinians think the 'writing on the wall' is an important form of communication with the outside world; others feel that painting on it legitimises its existence and shouldn't be done at all. The most heavily decorated section of wall is to the right of the Bethlehem checkpoint as you enter from Israel, and further on, towards Aida Refugee Camp. British graffiti artist Banksy is one of the most well known to add his mark, along with Pink Floyd's Roger Waters, who appropriately added his lyrics from 'The Wall' to the real thing.

consent to the dissolution of parliament and, after elections, decide which party leader will be given the first shot at forming a coalition. The parliament elects the president for a term of seven years.

Since 2009 Israel's prime minister has been Binyamin Netanyahu, head of the right-wing Likud Party. His coalition, one of the most ideologically right-wing in Israeli history, is made up of parties representing ultra-Orthodox Jews, Jewish settlers and a fragment of the Labour party.

Palestinian Territories

The Palestinian Authority (Palestinian National Authority; PA or PNA) was established in 1994 as an interim body to rule for five years while a bona fide Palestinian government was established (this has yet to happen). According to the Oslo Accords, the PA assumed civil and security control of urban areas (Area A) and civil control of many rural areas (Area B); Israeli settlements, uninhabited areas and main roads (Area C) remain under Israeli civil and security control.

The PA is headed by a president who is supposed to be elected once every four years. In 2005, Mahmoud Abbas (also known as Abu Mazen) won the presidency with 62% of the vote. When his term ran out in 2009, it was extended without new elections; as of early 2012, Abbas remains in power.

The Palestinian Legislative Council (PLC), the PA's parliament, is a unicameral body with 132 members. The majority party (or coalition) confirms the prime minister, who is nominated by the president, and the cabinet ministers selected by the prime minister. In January 2006, the Islamist Hamas party won a 74-seat landslide, but the resultant 'national unity' government collapsed when Hamas staged a violent takeover of Gaza in 2007.

Religion

The largest religious groups in Israel are Jews (75.6%), Muslims (16.9%), Christians (2%) and Druze (1.7%).

Judaism

One of the oldest religions still practised, Judaism is based on a covenantal relationship between the Jewish people and God. The most succinct summary of Jewish theology and Judaism's strict monotheism is to be found in the Shema prayer, which reads, 'Hear O Israel, the Lord is your God, the Lord is One'.

Judaism is based on the Torah (the first five books of the Hebrew Bible, ie the Old Testament) and the Oral Law, as interpreted by rabbis and sages in works such as the Mishna (edited in the 2nd and 3rd centuries AD) and the Talmud (edited from the 4th to 6th centuries AD).

Orthodox Judaism (the most conservative of the religion's streams) – including modern Orthodoxy, whose male adherents usually wear crocheted kippot (skullcaps), and ultra-Orthodoxy (Haredim), whose menfolk wear black hats and suits – holds that the Oral Law, in its entirety, was given at Mt Sinai.

The Reform, Conservative and Reconstructionist Movements believe that Judaism has always been dynamic and proactive, changing and developing over the generations as it dealt with new ideas and circumstances.

Christianity

Christianity is based on the life and teachings of Jesus of Nazareth, a Jew who lived in Judea and Galilee during the 1st century AD; on his crucifixion by the Romans; and on his resurrection three days later, as related in the New Testament. Christianity started out as a movement within Judaism, and most of Jesus' followers, known as the Apostles, were Jews. But after his death, the insistence of Jesus' followers that he was the Messiah caused Christianity to become increasingly distinct from Judaism.

The ownership of holy sites in Israel and the Palestinian Territories has long been a subject of contention among the country's various Christian denominations, which include Armenians, Assyrians, Copts and Ethiopians. At a number of sites in Jerusalem and Bethlehem, relations are still governed by a 'status quo' agreement drawn up in Ottoman times.

The Holy Land's largest denomination, the Greek Orthodox Church – almost all of whose local members are Arabic-speaking Palestinians – has jurisdiction over more than half of Jerusalem's Church of the Holy Sepulchre, and a large portion of Bethlehem's Church of the Nativity.

Islam

Islam was founded by the Prophet Mohammed (AD 570–632), who lived in what is now Saudi Arabia. It is based on belief in the absolute oneness of God (Allah) and in the revelations of His final prophet, Mohammed. The Arabic word *islam* means 'absolute submission' to God and His word. Islam's sacred scripture is the Quran (Koran), which was revealed to Mohammed and is believed to be God's infallible word.

Islam and Judaism share common roots, and Muslims consider Adam, Noah, Abraham, Isaac, Jacob, Joseph and Moses to be prophets. As a result, Jews and Muslims share a number of holy sites, including Al-Haram ash-Sharif/Temple Mount in Jerusalem and the Ibrahimi Mosque/Cave of Machpelah (Tomb of the Patriarchs) in Hebron. Because of their close scriptural links, Muslims consider both Jews and Christians to be an *ahl al-Kitab*, a 'people of the Book'. Judaism has always seen Islam as a fellow monotheistic faith (because of the Trinity, Jewish sages weren't always so sure about Christianity).

Other Belief Systems

Adherents of the Druze, an 11th-century off-shoot of Islam, live in northern Israel (including Mt Carmel) as well as Lebanon and Syria.

Haifa is the world centre of the Baha'i faith, founded in Persia in 1844.

Arts

Israel and the Palestinian Territories may be small in size, but they're big in artistic output – be it literature, the visual arts, music, or, increasingly, film.

Literature

Israelis are enormously proud of the revival of the Hebrew language and the creation of modern Hebrew literature, seeing them as the crowning cultural achievements of the Zionist movement. Some classic names to keep an eye out for (their major works are available in English translation) include Shmuel Yosef Agnon (1888–1970), Israel's only winner of the Nobel Prize for Literature; Yehuda Amichai (1924–2000); Aharon Appelfeld (b 1932); AB Yehoshua (b 1936); Amos Oz (b 1939) and David Grossman (b 1954).

Until recent years, poetry remained the most common form of literary expression in Palestinian circles, and the politically oriented poet Mahmoud Darwish (1941–2008) remains its leading light. Emile Habibi (1922–96) and Tawfiq Zayad (1929–94), Israeli Arabs who long served as members of the Knesset, both wrote highly regarded works of fiction. Habibi's *The Secret Life of Saeed the Pesoptimist* (1974) is a brilliant, tragicomic tale dealing with the difficulties facing Palestinians who became Israeli citizens after 1948. The stunning debut work of Ghassan Kanafani (1936–72), *Men in the Sun* (1963), delves into the lives, hopes and shattered dreams of its Palestinian characters.

Cinema

In recent years, Israeli films – many of which take a highly critical look at Israeli society and policies – have been garnering prizes at major film festivals, including Cannes, Berlin, Toronto and Sundance. Four have made the shortlist of Oscar nominees for Best Foreign Language Film: *Beaufort* (2007), *Waltz with Bashir* (2008), *Ajami* (2009) and *Footnote* (2011). Other feature films to keep an eye out for include *Sallah Shabbati* (Ephraim Kishon, 1964), a satire about life in a 1950s transit camp; *Waltz with Bashir* (2008), a haunting, personal look at the 1982 Lebanon War; and *Yossi & Jagger* (2002), about the secret love between two IDF infantry officers. For a database of made-in-Israel movies, see the website of the Manhattan-based Israel Film Center (www.israelfilmcenter.org).

Most feature-length Palestinian movies are international productions shot, but not completely produced, in the region. The first Palestinian film nominated for an Oscar was the controversial *Paradise Now* (2005), directed by Nazareth-born Hany Abu-Assad, which puts a human face on Palestinian suicide bombers.

The West Bank has two movie venues, the Al-Kasaba Theatre & Cinematheque (www.alkasaba.org) in Ramallah and the internationally supported Cinema Jenin (www.cinemajenin.org). Cinema has not done as well in Gaza, where all films must be approved by Hamas censors; a brief shot of a woman's uncovered hair is enough to get a movie banned.

The Israeli–Palestinian conflict provides the backdrop for a host of powerful, award-winning documentaries by Palestinians and Israelis (or both working together), including Juliano Mer-Khamis' *Arna's Children* (2003), about a children's theatre group in Jenin; the hard-hitting *Death in Gaza* (2004), whose director, James Miller, was killed during production; Yoav Shamir's *5 Days* (2005), which looks at the Israeli pullout from Gaza; Shlomi Eldar's *Precious Life* (2010), about the relationships formed during a Gaza baby's medical treatment in Israel; Ra'anan Alexandrowicz's *The Law in These Parts* (2011), about Israel's military legal system in the West Bank; and *5 Broken Cameras* (2011) by Emad Burnat on the anti–Separation Fence protests at Bil'in. To take the edge off these tension-filled flicks, check out Ari Sandel's zany *West Bank Story* (2005), a spoof on the musical *West Side Story*.

Music

Israeli music is rich tapestry of modes, scales and vocal styles that cross back and forth between East and West. The country was producing 'world music' before the phrase even existed.

In the realms of Israeli pop and rock, names to listen for include Shlomo Artzi, Arik Einstein, Matti Caspi, Shalom Hanoch, Yehudit Ravitz, Assaf Amdursky and, more recently, Aviv Getten. Idan Raichel introduced Ethiopian melodies to a mainstream audience.

Among the Israeli hip-hop artists and groups you may come across are Shabak Samech, HaDag Nachash, Subliminal, The Shadow and the Israeli-Palestinian group DAM.

One of the most exuberant performers of dance music has been Dana International (www.danainternational.co.il), a half-Yemenite transsexual who won the Eurovision Song Contest in 1998.

Mizrahi (Oriental or Eastern) music, with its Middle Eastern and Mediterranean scales and rhythms, has its roots in the melodies of North Africa (especially Umm Kulthum–era Egypt and mid-century Morocco), Iraq and Yemen.

Over the last few years, performers such as Etti Ankri, Ehud Banai, David D'Or, Kobi Oz, Berry Sakharof and Gilad Segev have turned towards traditional – mainly Sephardic and Mizrahi – liturgical poetry and melodies, producing works with massive mainstream popularity.

Born in the shtetls of Eastern Europe, Jewish 'soul' can take you swiftly from ecstasy to the depths of despair – you can check it out at the Tsfat Klezmer Festival

Israel also has a strong Western classical tradition thanks to Jewish refugees from Nazism and post-Soviet immigrants from Russia. The Israel Philharmonic Orchestra (www.ipo.co.il) – whose first concert, in 1936, was conducted by Arturo Toscanini – is world renowned.

In the Palestinian Territories, music lessons have become increasingly important to children in recent years, as a therapeutic escape from the rigours of everyday life. Teenagers and 20-somethings have expanded into hip-hop and rap; two of the most popular groups are Gaza-based PR (Palestinian Rappers) and Israeli Arabs Dam Rap (www.damrap.com), who rap in a heady mixture of Arabic, Hebrew and English.

In addition to catchy Arabic pop from Beirut and Cairo, visitors to the West Bank might also come across traditional classical and folk music, created on the oud (a stringed instrument whose resonator is shaped like a pear), the *daf* (tambourine) and the *ney* (flute).

Theatre & Dance

Per capita, Israelis attend the theatre more frequently than almost any other people. Most performances are in Hebrew, with a few in Arabic, Russian and Yiddish. Some troupes offer English supertitle translations once or more a week – attending is a great way to immerse yourself in the local culture. Tel Aviv and Jaffa have a profusion of companies and venues, and in Jerusalem there are frequent festivals, both large and small. Festival Acco (www.accofestival.co.il) puts on fringe productions each fall.

Palestinian theatre has long been an important expression of Palestinian national aspirations. Two of the main centres are the Palestinian National Theatre (www.pnt-pal.org) in East Jerusalem and Al-Kasaba Theatre & Cinematheque (www.alkasaba.org) in Ramallah.

Israelis and Palestinians alike love dance, albeit of different kinds. Israel has several renowned contemporary dance troupes. Tel Aviv's Bat Sheva Dance Company (www.batsheva.co.il), founded by Martha Graham in 1964, is probably the best known; it is now led by celebrated choreographer Ohad Naharin (b 1952). Israel's folk dance of choice is the hora, with its origins in Romania; a great place to see it is at the Karmiel Dance Festival (www.karmielfestival.co.il). Palestinians, meanwhile, go in for a line dance called the dabke. One of the best Palestinian dance groups is El-Funoun (www.el-funoun.org), based in Al-Bireh.

Food & Drink

Food is a national passion in both Israel and the Palestinian Territories, and the humble dish that probably unites the two nations more than any other is hummus. Ask any Israeli or Palestinian where to find the best hummus and you're likely to find yourself in the midst of a long, animated debate. Ask how they like it, and you'll be lectured on the pros and cons of hummus with fuul (fava bean paste), tahina (sesame seed paste) and the version containing soft whole chickpeas, known as *masabacha*.

Dining out is common among both Israelis and Palestinians. Tel Aviv, Jerusalem, Nazareth and Ramallah are filled with top-end restaurants covering every conceivable cuisine, while even the smallest village will usually have a place or two dispensing the ubiquitous felafel, shwarma, or local specialities.

Vegetarians will find it remarkably easy to maintain a varied and tasty diet, particularly in Israel where many restaurants do not serve meat because of the laws of keeping kosher. Some dishes to watch out for include: falafel (fried chickpea balls served with salad and hummus in a pita pocket), *shakshuka* (a rich egg-and-tomato breakfast dish served in a frying pan), *jachnun* (Yemenite weekend speciality made of rolled pastry served with a slow-boiled egg, strained tomatoes and fiery *schug*, a Yemenite hot pepper and garlic relish), and *sabich* (fried aubergine, boiled egg, potato, salads and spicy amba – Iraqi mango chutney – stuffed into a pita).

A real treat is the variety of juices, which are freshly squeezed and sold at streetside stands. Try pomegranate juice for a vitamin kick – but watch out for resultant blue-stained teeth. Coffee in all its permutations – instant (*nes* in Hebrew), cappuccino (*hafuch* in Hebrew) and Turkish with cardamom (*qahwa bi-hel* in Arabic, *kafeh turki im hel* in Hebrew) – is popular throughout. Tea prepared with fresh mint leaves and lots of sugar (*shai bi-naana* in Arabic, *tey im nana* in Hebrew) is a favourite among Palestinians and Jews from North Africa and the Middle East.

Alcohol is widely available, but observant Muslims don't drink at all and most Jews drink very little. The main Israeli beer brands are Maccabee and Goldstar; the Palestinian Territories' only brewery, Taybeh (boxed text, p252), produces some excellent brews.

Note that in both Israel and the Palestinian Territories, tipping 10% or 12% of the bill is as much of an established practice as it is in the West.

Daily Life

Though Israel and the Palestinian Territories are, in many ways, like chalk and cheese, there are a number of elements of daily life that are remarkably similar on either side of the Separation Fence. For both populations, family life is of prime importance; many Israeli families eat dinner together each Friday night, before the younger generation head off to nightclubs. Similarly, extended families are highly valued in the Palestinian Territories, and grandparents frequently live with or close by their younger family members. For both Israelis and Palestinians, religious holidays – be it Christmas, Eid or Passover – are the perfect excuse for big family celebrations, with meals, parties and barbeques stretching out for up to a week at a time.

Israel society was founded on socialist principles, exemplified by the shared community life of the kibbutz. But the vast majority of contemporary Israelis have shifted to a decidedly bourgeois, consumer-driven existence. Increased wealth and a love of the outdoors have made them an active lot: hiking, cycling, windsurfing, backpacking, camping and other leisure activities are hugely popular. Hebrew culture and the arts are immensely important, so reading literature and going out to concerts, the theatre and films is woven into the fabric of Israeli-Jewish life.

Gaza is largely controlled by Muslim fundamentalists, but much of the West Bank retains a moderate outlook, and Ramallah in particular exhibits the trappings of modern, Western living, including fast cars, health clubs and late-night bars.

Israeli women enjoy a freedom, opportunity and status on a par with their European counterparts and have historically played significant roles in the economy, politics and even the military. (Israel was one of the first countries to elect a female prime minister, Golda Meir, in 1969.) Though Palestinian women have traditionally assumed the role of home-based caregiver, recent years have seen more women encouraged to enter higher education and to work outside the home. However, as in Ottoman times, marriage and divorce in both Israel and the Palestinian Territories remain in the hands of a very conservative religious establishment, which tends to favour male prerogatives over women's rights. As there is no civil marriage in Israel, couples of mixed religious background wishing to wed must do so outside of Israel (eg in Cyprus).

Palestinians earn far less than the average Israeli (the annual per-capita income in the West Bank is just US$2900, compared with Israel's US$29,800), a factor that has done much to keep Palestinians frustrated with their lot.

Language

Israel's two official languages are Hebrew and Arabic; the first language of most of the Arab population is the Palestinian dialect of Arabic. Most Israelis and many Palestinians speak at least some English. On the streets of Israel you'll also hear a lot of Russian, French and Amharic. Some ultra-Orthodox Jews and older Ashkenazim still speak Yiddish (medieval German mixed with Hebrew), and a small number of Sephardic Jews still use Ladino (Judeo-Español), a blend of Hebrew and Spanish written – like Yiddish – with the Hebrew alphabet.

Most road signs appear in English, Hebrew and Arabic, but often with baffling transliterations. Caesarea, for example, may be rendered Qesariyya, Kesarya, Qasarya, and so on; and Tsfat may appear as Zefat, Zfat, or Safed.

Environment

With an area of nearly 28,000 sq km, Israel and the Palestinian Territories are geographically dominated by the 6000km-long Great Rift Valley (also known as the Syrian-African Rift), to which the Sea of Galilee, the Dead Sea and the Red Sea all belong.

Between this mountain-fringed valley and the Mediterranean Sea lie the Judean Hills (up to 1000m high), which include Jerusalem and Hebron, and the fertile coastal plain, where the bulk of Israel's population and agriculture is concentrated. The arid, lightly populated Negev, the country's southern wedge, consists of plains, mountains, wadis and makhteshes (erosion craters).

The country's strategic location at the meeting point of three continents has created a unique ecological mix. African tropical mammals such as the hyrax live alongside Asian mammals such as the Indian porcupine and the relatively rare European marten. In the arid Negev, for instance, travellers can feel an African influence in the isolated acacia stands, the nimble antelopes and the towering horns of the ibex, while in the Galilee there are Mediterranean forests, with gnarled oaks, almonds and sycamores.

ALL THINGS ECO

To get yourself acquainted with the Israeli and Palestinian eco-scene, dip into some of the following internet resources.

Arava Institute for Environmental Studies (www.arava.org) A research and teaching centre that brings together Israelis, Palestinians and Jordanians.

Blaustein Institutes for Desert Research (http://cmsprod.bgu.ac.il/Eng/Units/bidr) Your first stop for information on desertification and sustainable desert living.

Eco-Tourism Israel (www.ecotourism-israel.com) A good guide to Israel's ecotourism options.

Friends of the Earth Middle East (www.foeme.org) Promotes cooperation between Israeli, Palestinian and Jordanian environmentalists.

Israel Nature and Parks Authority (www.parks.org.il) Runs Israel's nature reserves and archaeological sites.

Society for the Protection of Nature in Israel (SPNI; www.teva.org.il, in Hebrew, www.aspni.org, in English) Israel's oldest and largest environmental organisation.

Some 500 million birds from an incredible 283 species migrate through Israel and the Palestinian Territories each year; check out www.birds.org.il, www.birds-eilat.com or www.birdingisrael.com to find out more.

National parks comprise around 25% of Israel's total area, creating sanctuaries safe from urban sprawl and industry. Israel is increasingly concerned with environmental issues, including the protection of beaches from development, and recycling.

Environmental Issues

Israel is the only country in the world that ended the 20th century with more trees than it had at the end of the 19th century. But while afforestation programs recreated forest habitats and innovative desert agriculture – using technologies such as drip irrigation, which was invented here – 'made the desert bloom', demands on the land from urbanisation have resulted in the same problems found in many parts of the world: air and water pollution, overuse of natural resources and poor waste management. Things are even worse on the coast of Gaza, where the problem of surface pollution is accompanied by seawater seepage into the aquifers.

Israel and the West Bank's most publicised environmental threat is the drying up of the Dead Sea, which has continued unabated for 30 years, the result of the intensive use of the water of the Jordan River. There have long been proposals to refill the Dead Sea with seawater either from the Mediterranean, through a 'Med-Dead Canal', or from the Red Sea, via a 'Red-Dead Canal' (and to use the difference in altitude to generate hydroelectricity). For details, visit the Friends of the Earth Middle East website (www.foeme.org) and click on 'Projects'.

SURVIVAL GUIDE

Directory A–Z

Accommodation

Though Israel ranks as one of the most expensive destinations in the Middle East, its accommodation manages to cater to all budgets, with a good selection of hostels, midrange guesthouses and top-end luxury hotels. In the summer (especially July and August) and around Jewish and Israeli holidays (especially Sukkot and Passover), prices can rise significantly and room availability plummets.

The Palestinian Territories offers more limited, but less expensive, accommodation. Room prices remain fairly constant year-round, the only exception being in Bethlehem, where rates rise around Christmas and Easter. Be sure to book well ahead if you're planning on travel at these times.

Prices in this book are for double rooms in high season and include bathrooms, breakfast and taxes unless otherwise indicated.

For Israel, the following price ranges apply:

$ less than 350NIS (US$93)

$$ 350NIS to 600NIS (US$93 to US$160)

$$$ more than 600NIS (US$160)

For the Palestinian Territories, the following price ranges apply:

$ less than 260NIS (US$70)

$$ 260NIS to 400NIS (US$70 to US$106)

$$$ more than 400NIS (US$106)

B&BS (TZIMMERS)

The most popular form of accommodation in the Galilee and Golan is the *tzimmer* (or *zimmer*). Facilities vary from simple rooms with shared facilities to romantic studio apartments with jacuzzis; for a double, count on paying 400NIS at the very least. To find a *tzimmer* (which we translate as B&B, though not all serve breakfast), check out www.zimmeril.com or www.israel-tours-hotel.com.

CAMPING

The cheapest way to overnight is in a tent (or at least a sleeping bag). Particularly mellow are some of the sites around the northeastern shore of the Sea of Galilee, many of which charge per car (they're free if you arrive on foot). Paying a fee for admission or parking gets you security, a decent shower block and toilet facilities.

Camping is forbidden inside nature reserves. Fortunately, various public and private bodies run inexpensive **camping sites** (www.campingil.org.il) at about 100 places around the country, including 22 operated by the **Israel Nature and Parks Authority** (☎3639, 02-500 6261; www.parks.org.il, search for 'overnight campgrounds'). Some are equipped with shade roofs (so you don't need a tent), lighting, toilets, showers and barbecue pits. In Hebrew, ask for a *chenyon laila* or an *orchan laila*.

In the Palestinian Territories, camping should be avoided due to general security concerns.

HOSTELS

Almost three dozen independent hostels and guesthouses in all parts of the country, including some of the country's best accommodation deals (dorm beds for 100NIS), are members of **Israel Hostels** (ILH; www.hostels-israel.com). If you're interested in meeting other travellers, these places are usually your best bet.

Israel's 19 official Hostelling International (HI) hostels and guesthouses offer clean, well-appointed rooms, often with four or more beds; doubles go for about 350NIS. Some also offer dorm beds. For details, check out the website of the **Israel Youth Hostels Association** (☎1 599 510 511; www.iyha.org.il/eng).

The **Society for the Protection of Nature in Israel** (☎03-638 8688, 057 200 3030; www.teva.org.il/english) runs nine field schools *(bet sefer sadeh)* in areas of high ecological value. They offer basic but serviceable rooms (also about 350NIS for a double), often with four or more beds, but most are accessible only by car.

HOTELS & GUESTHOUSES

Israel's hotels and guesthouses range from grim to gorgeous. Generally speaking, hotel prices are highest in Tel Aviv, Eilat and Jerusalem. Most serve generous smorgasbord breakfasts.

In the Palestinian Territories, most decent hotels, as well as some guesthouses, are in Ramallah and Bethlehem. Elsewhere in the West Bank, new hotels are being built, but most places tend to be basic and prices, due to low occupancy, unchanged for years. **Palestine Hotels** (www.palestinehotels.com) is an excellent hotel booking website.

KIBBUTZ GUESTHOUSES

Capitalising on their beautiful, usually rural locations, quite a few kibbutzim offer midrange guesthouse accommodation. Often constructed in the socialist era, but significantly upgraded since, these establishments allow access to kibbutz facilities, including the swimming pool, and serve delicious kibbutz-style breakfasts. For details and reservations, check out the **Kibbutz Hotels Chain** (☎03-560 8118; www.kibbutz.co.il).

Activities

CYCLING

Mountain biking has become hugely popular in Israel in recent years. Many cycling trails go through forests managed by the **Jewish National Fund** (www.kkl.org.il); for details, click 'Cycling Routes' on its website. **Shvil Net** (www.shvil.net) publishes Hebrew-language cycling guides that include detailed topographical maps.

HIKING

With its unbelievably diverse terrain – ranging from the alpine slopes of Mt Hermon to the parched wadis of the Negev – and almost 10,000km of marked trails, Israel offers some truly superb hiking. Don't forget to bring a hat and plenty of water, and plan your day so you can make it back before dark. The website **Tiuli** (www.tiuli.com), run by Lametayel, Israel's largest camping equipment store, has details in English on hiking options around the country.

At national parks and nature reserves run by the **Israel Nature and Parks Authority** (www.parks.org.il), walking maps with English text are usually handed out when you pay your admission fee. In other areas, the best maps to have – in part because they indicate minefields and live-fire zones used for IDF training – are the 1:50,000-scale topographical maps produced by the Society for the Protection of Nature in Israel.

In the West Bank, it's generally not a good idea to wander around the countryside unaccompanied. Consult local organisations for up-to-date information on areas considered safe; Jericho and environs are usually a good bet.

WATERSPORTS

The Red Sea has some of the world's most spectacular and species-rich coral reefs. Good value scuba courses – and dive packages – are available in Eilat, but the underwater life is a lot more dazzling across the border in the Sinai.

Israel's Mediterranean beaches, including those in Tel Aviv, are generally excellent, offering ample opportunities to swim, windsurf and sail. For freshwater swimming head to the Sea of Galilee; the super-saline Dead Sea offers that quintessential 'floating' experience.

Business Hours

In predominantly Muslim areas – East Jerusalem, Nazareth, Akko's Old City, the West Bank and Gaza – businesses may be closed all day Friday but remain open on Saturday.

Christian-owned businesses (eg in Nazareth, Bethlehem and the Armenian and Christian Quarters of Jerusalem's Old City) are closed on Sunday.

Opening hours in Israel:

Banks Most are open from 8.30am to sometime between 12.30pm and 2pm Monday to Thursday, and in addition a couple of afternoons a week. Many branches are open on Sunday, and some also open on Friday morning.

Bars & Pubs Hours are highly variable, but many – especially in Tel Aviv – are open until the wee hours. Thursday and Friday are the biggest nights out.

Clubs & Discos The trendiest boogie joints don't open their doors until after midnight, closing around dawn. In Tel Aviv and Eilat most operate seven days a week, while in Haifa and Jerusalem they only open on weekends (ie Thursday and Friday nights).

Post offices Generally open from 8am to 12.30pm or 1pm Sunday to Thursday, with many reopening from 3.30pm to 6pm on certain days. Friday hours are 8am to noon.

Restaurants Hours are highly variable, though only a few upmarket places take siestas. Most kosher restaurants are closed on Shabbat (Friday night and Saturday).

Shopping malls Generally open from 9.30am or 10am to 9.30pm or 10pm Sunday to Thursday and until 2pm or 3pm on Friday and the eves of Jewish holidays.

Shops Usually open from 9am to 6pm or later Sunday to Thursday and until 2pm or 3pm on Friday and the eves of Jewish holidays.

Children

Israel and the Palestinian Territories are extremely family-oriented, so children are welcome pretty much everywhere.

Beaches are usually clean, well equipped with cafes and even playgrounds, and great for a paddle, a sandcastle or a swim. As wheelchair access to nature reserves has improved in recent years, so has the ease of getting around with a pram (stroller).

In the vast majority of hotels, guesthouses and B&Bs, babies and toddlers can sleep in their parents' room for free; older children (often from age 3) are welcome for an extra charge. In hostels and SPNI field schools, rooms generally have at least four beds, making them ideal for families.

In the West Bank, pushing a pram (stroller) around chaotic towns like Ramallah, Nablus and Bethlehem can be laborious – and then there's the matter of getting through checkpoints.

Customs Regulations

Israel allows travellers aged 18 and over to import duty-free up to 1L of spirits and 2L of wine, 250ml of perfume, 250g of tobacco products, and gifts worth no more than US$200. Live animals can be brought into Israel but require lots of advance paperwork. Fresh meat, pornography and 900MHz cordless phones are prohibited.

PRACTICALITIES

» For daily news in English, try the English edition of left-of-centre Haaretz (www.haaretz.com), or the right-of-centre Jerusalem Post (www.jpost.com).

» Fifteen-minute English news bulletins can be heard on IBA World (Reshet Reka; www.iba.org.il/world) daily at 6.30am, 12.30pm and 8.30pm; the BBC World Service can be picked up on 1323 kHz AM/MW.

» Israeli law bans smoking in all enclosed public spaces.

» Israel TV's Channel 1 broadcasts nine minutes of English news at 4.50pm from Sunday to Thursday. Cable and satellite packages generally include news stations such as BBC, CNN, Sky, Fox and MSNBC.

» Like the rest of the Middle East, Israel uses the metric system.

Discount Cards

A Hostelling International (HI) card is useful for obtaining discounts at official HI hostels. An International Student Identity Card (ISIC) doesn't get you anywhere near as many discounts as it once did (none, for instance, are available on public transport).

If you'll be visiting lots of the national parks and historical sites run by the **Israel Nature and Parks Authority** (INPA; www.parks.org.il), you can save some serious cash by purchasing a 14-day Green Card, which gets you into all 65 INPA sites for just 145NIS (a six-park version costs 105NIS).

Embassies & Consulates

Jerusalem may be Israel's capital, but most diplomatic missions are located in or near Tel Aviv. A few countries maintain consulates in Jerusalem, Haifa and/or Eilat.

Most diplomatic missions are open in the morning from Monday to Thursday or Friday, and some for longer hours. The following are in Tel Aviv unless specified otherwise:

Australia (☎03-693 5000; www.israel.embassy.gov.au; 28th fl, Discount Bank Tower, 23 Yehuda HaLevi St, 65136)

Canada (☎03-636 3300; www.canadainternational.gc.ca/israel; 3 Nirim St, 67060)

Egypt (www.egyptembassy.net, for Egyptian embassy in Washington) Eilat (☎08-637 6882; 68 Afrouni St, 88119 Eilat; ⊙9-11am Sun-Thu); Tel Aviv (☎03-546 4151; 54 Basel St, 64239; ⊙9-11am Sun-Tue) In Eilat, deliver your passport, application and one passport-sized photo in the morning and pick up the visa around 2pm the same day. In Tel Aviv the process may take a few days.

France Jerusalem (☎02-625 9481; www.consulfrance-jerusalem.org; 5 Paul Émile Botta St, 91076); Tel Aviv (☎03 520 8500; www.ambafrance-il.org; 112 Herbert Samuel Esplanade, 63572)

Germany (☎03-693 1313; www.tel-aviv.diplo.de, in German & Hebrew; 19th fl, 3 Daniel Frisch St, 64731)

Ireland (☎03-696 4166; www.embassyofireland.co.il; 17th fl, 3 Daniel Frisch St, 64731)

Jordan (☎03-751 7722; www.jordanembassytelaviv.gov.jo; 10th fl, 14 Abba Hillel St, Ramat Gan) You can apply in the morning and pick your visa up around 2pm the same day; bring one passport-sized photo. Linked to adjacent Tel Aviv by Dan bus 66.

Netherlands (☎03-754 0777; http://israel.nlambassade.org; 14 Abba Hillel St, Ramat Gan, 52506)

New Zealand (☎03-695 1869; www.mfat.govt.nz; 3 Daniel Frisch St, 64731)

Turkey (☎03-524 1101; 202 HaYarkon St, 63405)

UK Jerusalem (☎02-541 4100; www.ukinjerusalem.fco.gov.uk; 19 Nashashibi St, Sheikh Jarrah, 97200); Tel Aviv Consular Section (☎03-725 1222; www.ukinisrael.fco.gov.uk; 6th fl, Migdalor Bldg, 1 Ben Yehuda St, 63801)

USA Haifa (☎04-853 1470; 26 Ben-Gurion Ave, 35023); Jerusalem (☎02-622 7230; http://jerusalem.usconsulate.gov; 18 Agron Rd, 94190); Tel Aviv (☎03-519 7475; http://israel.usembassy.gov; 71 HaYarkon St, 63903)

Food

Prices in this book represent the cost of a standard main-course dish. For Israel, the following price ranges apply:

$ less than 30NIS (US$8)

$$ 30NIS to 70NIS (US$8 to US$18.50)

$$$ more than 70NIS (US$18.50)

For the Palestinian Territories, the following price ranges apply:

$ less than 35NIS (US$9)

$$ 35NIS to 55NIS (US$9 to US$14.50)

$$$ more than 55NIS (US$14.50)

Gay & Lesbian Travellers

Tel Aviv is the gay capital of Israel, if not the Middle East, and nearly all bars and nightspots that don't specifically cater to gays are gay-friendly. Other cities – even Jerusalem – have smaller, but active gay scenes; see individual destination listings.

Gay culture is virtually nonexistent in the Palestinian Territories. In fact, many gay Palestinians have taken refuge in Israel. To better understand the difficult plight of gay and lesbian Palestinians, click on www.globalgayz.com/middle-east/palestine and www.aswatgroup.org.

Internet Access

There are wi-fi hotspots all over Israel (eg in all McDonald's branches) and in quite a few places in the Palestinian Territories. Wi-fi is also available on some intra-city buses (though it's rather slow). HI youth hostels and many fancy hotels charge for wi-fi and the use of internet computers; at other hostels and in midrange hotels wi-fi is often free. Internet cafes are becoming scarce but, where available, appear in city listings under Information.

Language Courses

Several Israeli universities operate overseas programs for students of Hebrew, Arabic and Middle Eastern studies. Participants don't necessarily need to speak Hebrew, but may be required to study it as part of their curriculum. **Birzeit University** (http://home.birzeit.edu/pas/courses.html), near Ramallah, runs both beginners and advanced courses in Arabic language.

Travellers wishing to learn Hebrew will probably want to look for an *ulpan* – a language school catering mainly to new immigrants to Israel. Prices are very reasonable; tourist information offices can provide details.

Money

ATMS

ATMs are widespread throughout Israel, but are less common in the Palestinian Territories so take cash along with you. Visa, MasterCard and, increasingly, American Express and Diners cards are accepted almost everywhere. Most, but not all, ATMs do Visa and MasterCard cash advances.

CASH

The official currency in Israel, and the most widely used currency in the Palestinian Territories, is the new Israeli shekel (NIS or ILS), which is divided into 100 agorot. Coins come in denominations of 10 and 50 agorot (marked ½ shekel) and one, two and five NIS; notes come in denominations of 10, 20, 50, 100 and 200NIS.

TRAVELLERS CHEQUES & WIRE TRANSFERS

Travellers cheques can be changed at most banks, but charges can be as high as 20NIS per cheque; instead use a no-commission exchange bureau or the post office. Post offices offer Western Union international-money-transfer services.

Post

Sent with **Israel Post** (www.israelpost.co.il), letters and postcards to North America and Australasia take seven to 10 days to arrive; to Europe it's a bit less. Incoming mail takes three or four days from Europe and around a week from other places. A domestic letter weighing up to 50gm costs 1.70NIS. Internationally, postcards and airmail letters cost 4NIS to Europe and 5.80NIS to North America or Australia.

Public Holidays

In addition to the main Islamic holidays (see p624), the following are observed in Israel and the Palestinian Territories:

New Year's Day Official holiday in the Palestinian Territories but not in Israel (1 January).

Christmas (Orthodox) Celebrated by Eastern Orthodox churches 6 to 7 January and by Armenians in the Holy Land on 18 to 19 January.

Passover (Pesach) Weeklong celebration of the liberation of the Israelites from slavery in Egypt (25 March to 1 April 2013, 14 to 21 April 2014, 3 to 10 April 2015).

Easter Sunday (Western) For Catholics and Protestants (31 March 2013, 20 April 2014, 5 April 2015).

Easter Sunday (Orthodox) For Eastern Orthodox and Armenians (5 May 2013, 20 April 2014, 12 April 2015.

Holocaust Memorial Day (Yom HaSho'ah) Places of entertainment closed. At 10am sirens sound and Israelis stand silently at attention (7 to 8 April 2013, 27 to 28 April 2014, 15 to 16 April 2015).

Memorial Day (Yom HaZikaron) Commemorates soldiers who fell defending Israel. Places of entertainment closed. At 8pm and 11am sirens sound and Israelis stand silently at attention (14 to 15 April 2013, 4 to 5 May 2014, 22 to 23 April 2015).

Israel Independence Day (Yom Ha'Atzma'ut) Celebrated on 16 Apr 2013, 6 May 2014, 23 Apr 2015.

International Labour Day Official holiday in both Israel and the Palestinian Territories (1 May).

Nakba Day Palestinian commemoration of the *nakba* (catastrophe) of 1948 (15 May).

Shavuot (Pentecost) Jews celebrate the giving of the Torah at Mt Sinai (14 to 15 May 2013, 3 to 4 June 2014, 23 to 24 May 2015).

Tish'a B'Av (Ninth of Av) Jews commemorate the destruction of the Temples in Jerusalem. Restaurants and places of entertainment closed (15 to 16 July 2013, 2 to 3 August 2014, 25 to 26 July 2015).

Rosh HaShanah (Jewish New Year) Celebrated 16 to 18 September 2012, 4 to 6 September 2013, 24 to 26 September 2014.

Yom Kippur (Jewish Day of Atonement) Solemn day of reflection and fasting. Israel's airports and land borders close, all transport ceases (25 to 26 September 2012, 13 to 14 September 2013, 3 to 4 October 2014).

Sukkot (Feast of the Tabernacles) Week-long holiday that recollects the Israelites' 40 years of wandering in the desert (30 September to 7 October 2012, 18 to 25 September 2013, 8 to 15 October 2014).

Hanukkah (Festival of Lights) Jews celebrate the rededication of the Temple after the Maccabean revolt (8 to 15 December 2012, 27 November to 5 December 2013, 16 to 24 December 2014).

Christmas (Western) Public holiday in the West Bank, but not in Israel or Gaza. Celebrated by Catholics and Protestants on 24 to 25 December.

Safe Travel

AIRPORT & BORDER SECURITY

If border officials suspect that you're coming to take part in pro-Palestinian political activities, or even to visit the West Bank for reasons other than Christian pilgrimage, they may ask a lot of questions. Having a Muslim name and passport stamps from places like Syria, Lebanon or Iran may also result in some pointed enquiries. The one sure way to get grilled is to sound evasive or to contradict yourself – the security screeners are trained to try to trip you up.

MINEFIELDS

Some parts of Israel and the Palestinian Territories – particularly along the Jordanian border and around the periphery of the Golan Heights – are still sown with anti-personnel mines. Known mined areas are fenced with barbed wire sporting dangling red (or rust) triangles and/or yellow and red 'Danger Mines!' signs. Flash floods sometimes wash away old mines, depositing them outside of known minefields. Wherever you are, never, ever, touch anything that looks like it might be an old artillery shell, grenade or mine!

Telephone

MOBILE PHONES

Overseas mobile phones work in Israel (so long as your gadget can handle 900/1800 MHz), but roaming charges can be ruinous. Israel's three main mobile phone companies, **Orange** (Big Talk; www.orange.co.il, in Hebrew), **Pelefon** (Talk & Go; www.pelephone.co.il, in Hebrew) and **Cellcom** (www.cellcom.co.il, in Hebrew), all offer pay-as-you-go SIM cards at their many outlets.

PHONE CODES

Israel's country code is ☎972; the Palestinian Territories use both ☎972 and ☎970. Local area codes are given at the start of each city or town section in this chapter. To call abroad from Israel, available international access codes include ☎012 (012 Smile), ☎013 (013 Netvision), ☎014 (Bezeq) and ☎018 (018). All offer remarkably cheap rates to most countries, though it pays to find out what their latest offers are.

PHONECARDS

Prepaid local and international calls can be made using a variety of phonecards, sold at post offices, lottery kiosks and newsstands.

SECURITY SITUATION

Israel has some of the most stringent security policies in the world. In recent years the number of annual terrorist attacks inside Israel has dropped to the single digits (by comparison, in March 2002 alone over 130 Israelis were killed in Palestinian attacks), but it pays to remain vigilant about suspicious people (or packages), especially when travelling by public bus. Keep an eye on the news and heed local travel advice while on the road.

When entering bus or rail terminals, shopping malls, many supermarkets, and all sorts of other public venues, your bags are likely to be searched and in some cases X-rayed. You may also be wanded. Abandoned shopping bags, backpacks and parcels are picked up by bomb squad robots and blown up.

Road passage between many Palestinian West Bank towns and Israel is regulated by Israeli army roadblocks, where you'll need to show a passport and may have to answer questions about your reason for travel. The situation in the West Bank and Gaza (which is effectively off-limits) remains unpredictable, so monitor the news closely before travelling in the area. Some good rules of thumb:

» Always carry your passport.

» Don't wander into the refugee camps on your own.

» Travel during daylight hours.

» Dress modestly. Cover up bare shoulders and legs – you'll blend in with the crowd a bit better and won't cause inadvertent offence. This applies to both men and women (but especially women).

» Avoid political demonstrations, which often get out of hand and can turn into violent confrontations.

» Use caution when approaching road blocks and checkpoints. Remember: soldiers may have no idea that you're just a curious visitor.

Travellers with Disabilities

In Israel, access for people in wheelchairs and with other disabilities has improved significantly in recent years. Hotels, hostels and other accommodation are required to have at least one room available for wheelchair users, and many tourist sites such as museums and historic sites can accommodate people with disabilities. Many nature reserves have trails that are wheelchair accessible (see www.parks.org.il). Restaurants are a mixed bag, with few claiming to be fully accessible (ie including bathrooms). Some information is also available from **Access Israel** (www.aisrael.org).

The Palestinian Territories are less well equipped and getting around is made more difficult by road checkpoints, which are usually crossed on foot; lines for these can be long and crowded and sometimes require moving over and around barriers.

Visas

In general, Western visitors to Israel and the Palestinian Territories are issued free tourist (B-2) visas. You need a passport that's valid for at least six months from the date of entry. (For specifics on who qualifies, visit www.mfa.gov.il and click on 'About the Ministry' and then 'Consular Service'.)

Most visas issued at an entry point are valid for 90 days. But travellers, eg those entering by land from Egypt or Jordan, may be given just 30 days or even two weeks – it's up to the discretion of the border control official.

Kibbutz volunteers must secure a volunteer's visa.

You'll probably be subjected to extra questioning if you have certain stamps in your passport (eg from Lebanon, Syria, Pakistan or Sudan), though after a long wait you'll probably be allowed in. You may be asked to provide evidence of sufficient funds for your intended length of stay.

If there is any indication that you are coming to participate in pro-Palestinian protests or are seeking illegal employment, you may find yourself on the next flight home.

For information on the implications of an Israeli stamp in your passport, see p36.

EXTENSIONS

To extend a tourist (B-2) visa beyond the time given you upon entry, you can either apply to extend your visa (170NIS) or do a 'visa run' to Egypt (Sinai) or Jordan. This might get you an additional three months – or just one. Ask other travellers for the latest low-down.

Visas are extended by the **Population Immigration and Border Authority** (☎1 700 551 111; www.piba.gov.il, in Hebrew; ⏲generally 8am-noon Sun-Tue & Thu), part of the **Ministry of the Interior** (☎for information 3450 or 1222 3450), which has offices in most cities and large towns. Join the queue by 8am or you could be waiting all day. Bring a passport-sized photo and evidence of sufficient funds for the extended stay.

Travellers who overstay by just a few days report no hassles or fines.

Volunteering

For a list of Israeli organisations interested in foreign volunteers, go to the websites of **Ruach Tova** (www.ruachtova.org) or the **National Council on Volunteering** (www.ivolunteer.org.il); for the latter, click on 'Volunteer Opportunities' and then 'Visitors'.

For details on volunteering on a kibbutz (communal farm), contact the **Kibbutz Program Centre** Citizens of the US & Canada (☎001-212 462 2764, fax 001-212-462-2765; www.kibbutzprogramcenter.org; Ste 1004, 114 W 26th St, New York, NY 10001) Candidates from everywhere else (☎03-524 6154/6, fax 03-523 9966; www.kibbutz.org.il/volunteers; 6 Frishman St, Tel Aviv; ⏲8.30am-2.30pm Sun-Thu).

For details on paid volunteering on an archaeological site, see p41.

Women Travellers

Female travellers can expect the same sort of treatment they'd receive in most European countries, though it's important to follow sensible travel advice, such as not hitchhiking alone, and other precautions one generally adheres to back home. Dress modestly in religious areas such as the Old City and Mea She'arim in Jerusalem, the churches of Nazareth and around the Sea of Galilee, and in the West Bank and Gaza (where you'll be more of a novelty, but treated generally as a 'sister'). Note that the more religious male Jews and Muslims may not wish to shake a woman's hand. On some beaches on both sides of the Green Line, foreign women may attract unwanted attention.

Work

Travellers used to be able to turn up in Tel Aviv and find plenty of casual work in bars and restaurants, but authorities have been cracking down on businesses hiring illegal workers and opportunities are now slim. Your best chances for gainful employment are through Tel Aviv guesthouses and restaurants near the beach.

Working legally requires a permit from the Ministry of the Interior and, as in North America or Western Europe, these aren't easy to get – with one exception. If you would qualify for an *oleh* (new immigrant) visa – ie if you have at least one Jewish parent or grandparent – you can get a working visa with relative ease.

Getting There & Away

Entering Israel & the Palestinian Territories

A frequent topic of conversation among travellers is the entrance procedure for Israel and the Palestinian Territories. It's rigorous, and you can expect a barrage of questions about your recent travels, occupation, any acquaintances in Israel or the West Bank and possibly your religious or family background. Expect extra enquiries if your passport has stamps from places like Syria or Lebanon, or you're headed to less touristed parts of the West Bank. If you are meeting friends in Israel, have their phone number handy.

For details on the ramifications of having an Israeli stamp in your passport when you visit Arab and Muslim countries, see p36.

Air

Except with some European budget carriers, fares into Israel aren't especially cheap. The best deals are normally available on the Internet, frequently direct from the airlines' websites themselves. Tel Aviv is only rarely an allowable stop on round-the-world itineraries.

AIRPORTS

Israel's main gateway is **Ben-Gurion International Airport** (TLV; ☎arrivals & departures 03-972 3333; www.iaa.gov.il), situated 50km northwest of Jerusalem and 18km southeast of central Tel Aviv. Its ultramodern international terminal, finished in 2004 at a cost of US$1 billion, handles about 11 million passengers a year. For details on arrivals and departures, go to the website and click 'Ben Gurion Airport', then 'Passenger Services' and finally 'On Line Flights'. Airport security is tight, so international travellers should check in at least three hours prior to their flight – when flying both to and from Israel.

AIRLINES

The following airlines fly to/from Israel:

Arkia (☎03-690 3712; www.arkia.com; 74 HaYarkon St) Has daily flights to Eilat (one-way from 200NIS) from Sde Dov airport and also offers flights to Europe.

easyJet (www.easyjet.com) From Tel Aviv to London, Basel and Geneva.

El Al (☎03-977 1111; www.elal.co.il; 32 Ben Yehuda St)

Israir (☎03-795 4038; www.israirairlines.com; 23 Ben Yehuda St) Domestic airline.

Airline offices in Tel Aviv:

Air Canada (☎03-607 2104; www.aircanada.com; Azrieli Center, 132 Menachem Begin Rd)

Air France (☎03-755 5010; www.airfrance.com; 7 Jabotinsky St, Ramat Gan)

Alitalia (☎03-971 1047; www.alitalia.com; Terminal 3, Ben-Gurion airport)

American Airlines (☎03-795 2122; www.aa.com; 29 Ben Yehuda St)

Cathay Pacific (☎03-795 2111; www.cathaypacific.com; 29 Ben Yehuda St)

Lufthansa (☎03-975 4050; www.lufthansa.com; Terminal 3, Ben-Gurion airport) E-ticket counter only at airport.

Qantas (☎03-795 2144; www.qantas.com; 29 Ben Yehuda St)

Royal Jordanian Airlines (☎03-516 5566; www.rj.com; 5 Shalom Aleichem St)

Land

BORDER CROSSINGS

Frontiers with Syria and Lebanon are sealed tight, but there are open land borders with Egypt and Jordan; cross on foot or by private vehicle, but not in a taxi or rental car. Drivers and motorcyclists will need the vehicle's registration papers, proof of liability insurance and a driving licence from home (but not necessarily an international driving licence).

Egypt

TABA CROSSING

The only border post between Israel and Egypt that's open to tourists is at **Taba** (☎08-637 2104, 08-636 0999; www.iaa.gov.il; ⏲24hr), on the Red Sea near Eilat. Israel charges a 103NIS departure fee; Egypt has a E£30 entrance fee. There's an exchange bureau on the Egyptian side. At the time of writing, it was not possible to take a car across.

Local bus 15 links Eilat's central bus station with the Taba crossing (7.50NIS, 20 minutes), or you can take a taxi (30NIS). For details on buses and shared taxis for onward travel on the Egyptian side, see p152.

You can get a 14-day Sinai-only entry permit at the border, allowing you to visit Red Sea resorts stretching from Taba to Sharm el-Sheikh, plus St Katherine's. If you're planning on going further into Egypt, you'll need to arrange an Egyptian visa in advance, eg at the Egyptian consulate in Eilat or the embassy in Tel Aviv.

Mazada Tours (www.mazada.co.il) runs overnight buses from Tel Aviv (☎03-544 4454; 141 Ibn Gabirol St) and Jerusalem (☎02-623 5777; 6 Yanai St, Jerusalem) to Cairo (one-way/return US$146/165, 12 hours) via Taba, and vice versa.

RAFAH CROSSING

As a result of the Arab Spring, this crossing is now officially open between 10am and 6pm Saturday to Thursday (excluding public holidays), but is often closed for days at a time. Foreign nationals wishing to cross must first seek special permission from the Egyptian Ministry of Foreign Affairs' **Palestinian Affairs Division** (☎02-2574 9682, call noon-3pm) in Cairo.

If you enter Gaza through Rafah, you cannot continue on to Israel – you must also exit through Rafah. Be prepared to wait for an extended period (possibly weeks) for the crossing to open, or while you wait for approval from Egyptian authorities to let you back into Egypt.

Jordan

There are three border crossing points with Jordan. Israel charges a departure tax of 103NIS (167NIS at Allenby/King Hussein Bridge); Jordan charges JD5 to enter and JD8 to exit. None of the crossings have ATMs, though all theoretically have exchange services.

Nearly all nationalities require a visa to enter Jordan. Conveniently, single-entry, extendable, two-week visas are issued with a minimum of fuss at the Jordan River/Sheikh Hussein Crossing (visa JD20) and the Yitzhak Rabin/Wadi Araba crossing (visa is free).

However, visas are *not* available at the Allenby Bridge/King Hussein Bridge crossing – if you want to enter Jordan here or need a multiple-entry visa (single/multiple-entry JD20/60 or 88/168NIS), contact the Jordanian embassy in Ramat Gan, near Tel Aviv (see p269).

ALLENBY BRIDGE (KING HUSSEIN BRIDGE)

This often-crowded **crossing** (www.iaa.gov.il; 8am-early afternoon Sun-Thu, 8am-about noon Fri & Sat, closed Yom Kippur & Eid al-Adha, hours subject to change), between the West Bank and Jordan, is 8km east of Jericho, 46km east of Jerusalem and 60km west of Amman. Controlled by Israel, it is the only point at which West Bank Palestinians can enter Jordan, so traffic can be heavy, especially between 11am and 3pm. Try to get to the border as early in the day as possible – times when tourists can cross may be limited and delays are common. Bring plenty of cash (Jordanian dinars are the most useful) and make sure you have small change.

Jordanian visas are *not* available at the crossing – you can get one at the Jordanian embassy in Tel Aviv (see p269).

From opposite Jerusalem's Damascus Gate, shared taxis run by **Abdo** (02-628-3281) leave for the border (40NIS per person, twice per hour until around 11am). After 11am they offer private taxis (150NIS to 180NIS), with hotel pick-up as an option. Egged buses 961, 948 and 966 from West Jerusalem's central bus station to Beit She'an (and points north) stop on Rte 90 at the turn-off to Allenby Bridge (12NIS, 45 minutes, hourly). Walking the last few kilometres to the crossing is forbidden, so you'll have to take a taxi (up to 50NIS).

From Amman, you can take a *servees* (shared taxi) or minibus (JD8, 45 minutes). **JETT** (962-6-566 4146; www.jett.com.jo) runs a daily bus from Abdali (JD7.250, departure at 7am).

YITZHAK RABIN (WADI ARABA)

Located just 3km northeast of Eilat, this **crossing** (08-630 0530/555; www.iaa.gov.il; 6.30am-8pm Sun-Thu, 8am-8pm Fri & Sat) is handy for trips to Aqaba, Petra and Wadi Rum.

A taxi from Eilat costs 35NIS. If you're coming by bus from Be'er Sheva, the Dead Sea or Jerusalem, you don't have to go all the way into Eilat – ask the driver to let you out at the border turn-off.

Once you are in Jordan, you can take a cab to Aqaba (JD8), from where you can catch a minibus for the 120km ride to Petra (JD5, 2½ hours); the latter leave when full between 6.30am and 8.30am, with an occasional afternoon service.

JORDAN RIVER BRIDGE (SHEIKH HUSSEIN BRIDGE)

The least used of the three, this **crossing** (04-609 3400; www.iaa.gov.il; 6.30am-9pm Sun-Thu, 8am-8pm Fri & Sat, closed Yom Kippur & Al-Hijra/Muslim New Year) is 8km east of Beit She'an and 30km south of the Sea of Galilee.

The Israeli side is connected with Beit She'an (17 minutes, three daily Sunday to Thursday, two on Friday) by Kavim bus 16 and **taxis** (04-658 5834; one-way 50NIS). On the Jordanian side, frequent service taxis travel to/from Irbid's West bus station (JD1, 45 minutes), and to Amman.

Nazarene Tours (04-601 0458; Paulus VI St, Nazareth) links Nazareth with Amman (75NIS, five hours) on Sunday, Tuesday, Thursday and Saturday. Departures are from the company's Nazareth office (near the Nazareth Hotel) at 8.30am; and from Amman's **Maraya Hotel** (www.marayahotel.com; University St) at 2pm. Reserve by phone at least two days ahead.

Getting Around

Air

Flights to Eilat from Tel Aviv's Sde Dov airport, Ben-Gurion airport's domestic terminal and Haifa are handled by **Arkia** (www.arkia.com), **El Al** (www.elal.co.il) and **Israir** (www.israirairlines.com).

Deals are often available online, with one-ways going for as little as 79NIS.

Bicycle

If you cycle between cities, bear in mind the hot climate, winter rainfall, steep hills and erratic drivers; bicycles are not allowed on certain major highways. One of the best places for leisure cycling is around the Sea of Galilee; bicycles can be hired in Tiberias.

Bus

Almost every town and village has bus service at least a few times a day, though from mid-afternoon on Friday until Saturday after dark, most intercity buses don't run at all.

Sample one-way fares include: Jerusalem to Tel Aviv (18NIS), Tel Aviv to Kiryat Shmona (47NIS) and Tel Aviv to Eilat (75NIS).

Return tickets – also good for two one-ways or for two passengers travelling together –

HITCHING

Although hitching was once a common way of getting around Israel (it's still common in the Upper Galilee and Golan), increasing reports of violent crime make this a risky business and we do not recommend it. Women should not hitch without male companions and all travellers should be circumspect about the cars they get into. The local method of soliciting a lift is simply to point an index finger at the road.

cost 15% less than two single tickets. On some lines, a *kartisiya* (kar-tees-ee-*yah*), a punch card valid for six or eight trips, can also save you money. Students no longer qualify for discounts.

Israel no longer has two bus monopolies, but rather about 20 private companies that compete for routes in Ministry of Transport tenders. The **Public Transportation Info Center** (☎1 900 72 1111; www.bus.co.il), easy to use once you figure it out, provides details in English on all bus companies' routes, times and prices.

The West Bank is served by local buses that travel between cities and to/from East Jerusalem.

Car & Motorcycle

To drive a vehicle in Israel and the Palestinian Territories, all you need is your regular driving licence (an international driving license is not required).

Having your own wheels doesn't make much sense in Jerusalem or Tel Aviv – parking can be a huge hassle – but it's a great idea in the Galilee, Golan and Negev, where buses can be scarce. A car will also let you take advantage of cheap accommodation options, including hostels and (almost) free camping.

Car hire with insurance and unlimited kilometres costs as little as US$200 per week or US$600 per month. Local companies with good rates include **Cal Auto** (www.calauto.co.il) and **Eldan** (www.eldan.co.il).

Note that most Israeli rental agencies forbid you to take their cars into the Palestinian Territories; a notable exception is Green Peace (see p205).

Local Transport

BICYCLE

Bicycle paths have been going up in cities all over Israel, but the most developed network is in Tel Aviv.

TAXI

Insist that Israeli taxi drivers use the meter (Palestinian yellow taxis rarely have a meter installed), and watch your progress on a map to ensure that the shortest route is followed. A trip across town in Jerusalem or Tel Aviv shouldn't cost more than 30NIS to 35NIS. Taxi tariffs rise 25% between 9pm and 5.30am.

Sherut

To Israelis it's a sherut (sheh-*root*) while the Palestinians call it a *servees* (ser-*vees*), but whatever name you use, shared taxis are a useful way to get around. These vehicles, often 13-seat minivans, operate on a fixed route for a fixed price, like a bus except that they don't have fixed stops and depart only when full. Some sheruts operate 24/7 and are the only means of public transport in Israel during Shabbat, when prices rise slightly.

Train

Israel Railways (☎5770 or 03-611 7000; www.rail.co.il) runs a comfortable and generally convenient network of passenger rail services that link Tel Aviv with destinations such as Ben-Gurion Airport, Haifa, Akko, Nahariya, Jerusalem and Be'er Sheva. Details on services are also available from the **Public Transportation Info Center** (☎1-900-721 111; www.bus.co.il). Return tickets are 10% cheaper than two on-ways. Children under 10 get a 20% discount. Trains do not run from mid-afternoon Friday until Saturday night.

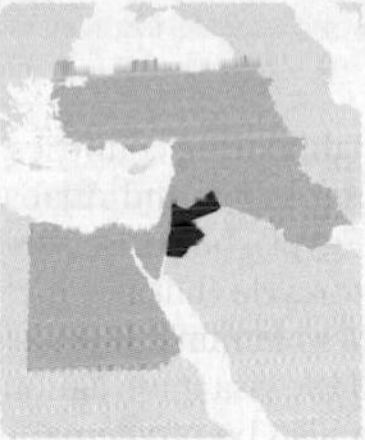

Jordan

Includes »

Best for Nature

- » Ajloun Forest Reserve (p297)
- » Dana Biosphere Reserve (p311)
- » Mujib Biosphere Reserve (p301)
- » Wadi Rum (p322)

Best for Culture

- » Petra (p313)
- » Jerash (p293)
- » Umm Qais (p298)
- » Karak (p309)

Why Go?

Ahlan wa sahlan! – 'Welcome to Jordan!' From the Bedouin of Wadi Rum to the taxi drivers of Amman, you'll be on the receiving end of this open-armed welcome every day. It's this, and a sense of stability amid a problematic neighbourhood, that makes travel in Jordan such a delight.

With heavyweight neighbours pulling big historical punches, Jordan easily holds its own. Amman, Jerash and Umm Qais were cities of the Roman Decapolis, while biblical sites include Bethany-Beyond-the-Jordan, where Jesus was baptised, and Mt Nebo, where Moses reputedly surveyed the Promised Land. Grandest of all is the sublime Nabataean capital of Petra, carved from vertical cliffs.

But Jordan is not just about antiquities – it also offers the great outdoors. Whether diving in Aqaba, trekking in the camel-prints of Lawrence of Arabia or hiking through stunning canyons, Jordan's eco-savvy nature reserves offer the best of adventures in the Middle East.

When to Go

Amman

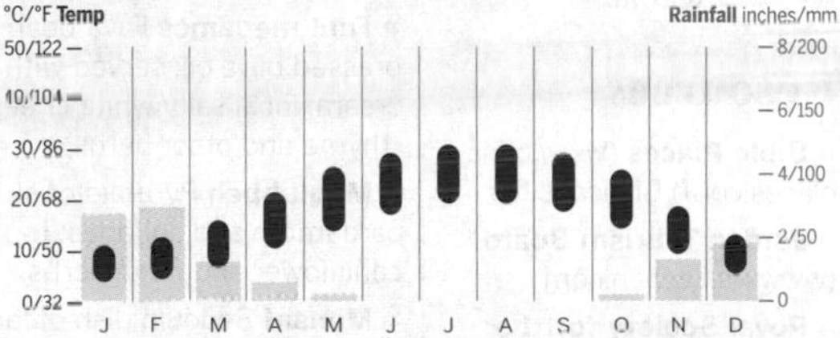

Mar–May The weather is perfect, with warm days, cool nights and spectacular wildflowers.

Sep–Nov A good time to go hiking, with less visitors and relief after intense summer heat.

Dec–Feb The Red and Dead Seas offer balmy dips, while upland Jordan shivers with winter chills.

AT A GLANCE

» **Currency** Jordanian dinar (JD)

» **Mobile Phones** Sim cards widely available

» **Money** ATMs widespread; credit cards (except Amex) widely accepted

» **Visas** Available on arrival

Fast Facts

» **Capital** Amman

» **Country code** ☎962

» **Language** Arabic (English widely spoken)

» **Official name** Hashemite Kingdom of Jordan

» **Population** 6.5 million

Exchange Rates

Australia	A$1	JD0.73
Egypt	E£1	JD0.18
Euro Zone	€1	JD0.94
Israel & the Palestinian Territories	1NIS	JD0.19
Syria	S£10	JD0.12
UK	£1	JD1.15
US	US$1	JD0.71

For current exchange rates see www.xe.com.

Resources

» **Bible Places** (www.bibleplaces.com) Biblical sites

» **Jordan Tourism Board** (www.visitjordan.com)

» **Royal Society for the Conservation of Nature** (www.rscn.org.jo) Nature reserves

» **Ruth's Jordan Jubilee** (www.jordanjubilee.com) Petra information

Connections

Jordan is easily visited overland from neighbouring countries, with visas available on arrival at border crossings and Aqaba port. Arrival in Jordan is by boat (from Egypt), bus or service taxi; you can bring your own car or motorcycle (but not hire car). Leaving Jordan by land requires more planning: if you're intending to visit Syria, in particular, read the visa information on p37. Onward travel in the region can also be problematic after visiting Israel and the Palestinian Territories (see p36).

ITINERARIES

One Week

Arrive in **Aqaba** from Egypt, and party in Jordan's holiday town. On day two, take the early-morning bus to **Wadi Rum**, of Lawrence of Arabia fame. Hike or share the cost of a 4WD desert tour and return to Aqaba. On day three, take the early-morning bus to Wadi Musa and explore the rock-hewn wonders of **Petra**, a world-class site. On day four, catch the evening bus to **Amman** and spend day five exploring the capital. On day six, watch a chariot race in the Roman ruins of **Jerash** and leave the next day on a direct bus from Amman – either north to Damascus or west to Jerusalem via the King Hussein crossing, taking note of visa restrictions.

Two Weeks

Amplify the above by travelling the **King's Highway** between Petra and Amman, either by taxi or a minibus-hitching combo, visiting the Crusader castles of **Shobak** and **Karak**, the escarpment village of **Dana**, and dramatic **Wadi Mujib** en route. Chill out in the travel-friendly town of **Madaba** from where you can tour the **Dead Sea** and **Bethany**, or romp round the **Eastern Desert** castles.

Essential Food & Drink

» **Fuul medames** Fava-bean dish drizzled with fresh-pressed olive oil; served with unleavened Arabic bread, sour cream, local salty white cheese and a sprinkling of *zaatar* (thyme and other herbs).

» **Maqlubbeh** Pyramid of steaming rice garnished with cardamom and sultanas; topped with slivers of onion, meat, cauliflower and fresh herbs.

» **Mensaf** Bedouin dish of lamb, rice and pine nuts, combined with yogurt and the liquid fat from the cooked meat.

» **Kunafa** Addictive dessert of shredded dough and cream cheese, smothered in syrup.

» **Marrameeya** Sage-based herbal tea, especially delicious at Dana.

» **Petra Kitchen** Cook your own Jordanian speciality in Wadi Musa.

AMMAN عمان

☎06 / POP 2.8 MILLION

Jordan's capital city, Amman, is one of the easiest cities in the region to enjoy the Middle East experience. The city has two distinct parts: urbane Western Amman, with leafy residential districts, cafes, bars, modern malls and art galleries; and earthy Eastern Amman where it's easier to sense the more traditional, conservative and Islamic pulse of the capital.

At the heart of the city is the chaotic, labyrinthine 'downtown', the must-see of a capital visit. At the bottom of the city's many hills, and overlooked by the magisterial Citadel, it features spectacular Roman ruins and the hubbub of Jordanian life – best understood by joining the locals in the nightly promenade between mosque, souq and coffeehouse.

History

Despite its ancient lineage, Amman as it appears today is largely a mid-20th century creation and visitors looking for the quintessential vestiges of a Byzantine Middle East will have to look quite hard. What they will see instead is a homogeneous, mostly low-rise, cream-coloured city of weathered concrete buildings, some sparklingly clad in white marble, others in need of a facelift.

That's not to say that Amman is without history. In fact, impressive remnants of a Neolithic settlement from 8500 BC were found in the 1970s at Ain Ghazal in Eastern Amman. They illustrate a sophisticated culture that produced the world's earliest statues – some of which are displayed at the archaeological museum.

Then there is Jebel al-Qala'a, the present site of the Citadel, and one of the oldest and most continuously inhabited parts of the city, established around 1800 BC. Referred to subsequently in the Old Testament as Rabbath, the city was besieged by King David who burnt many inhabitants alive in a brick kiln.

Visitors bump into Amman's Egyptian heritage each time they see a company or restaurant called Philadelphia, after the Ptolemy ruler Philadelphius (283–246 BC). He rebuilt the city during his reign and it was named Philadelphia after him. It was one of the cities of the Roman Decapolis before being assumed into the Roman Empire under Herod in around 30 BC. Philadelphia, meaning 'City of Brotherly Love', was redesigned in typically grand Roman style, with a theatre, forum and Temple to Hercules, the striking remains of which are a highlight of downtown.

From about the 10th century little more is heard of Amman until the 19th century when a colony of Circassians settled there in 1878. In 1900 it was estimated to have just 2000 residents. In 1921 it became the centre of Transjordan when King Abdullah made it his headquarters. Following the formation of the state of Israel in 1948, Amman absorbed a flood of Palestinian refugees, and doubled its population in a mere two weeks. It continues to grow, swelled by Iraqi refugees escaping the chaos across the border.

Sights

Built originally on seven hills (like Rome), Amman now spreads across 19 hills and is therefore not a city to explore on foot. That said, the downtown area – known locally as *il-balad* – with its budget hotels and restaurants, banks, post offices and Amman's ancient sites, is compacted into a relatively small area in the heart of the great metropolis. All other areas of the city fan out from there.

DOWNTOWN

Citadel RUINS

(Map p284; Jebel al-Qala'a; admission JD2; ⏲8am-4pm Sat-Thu Oct-Mar, to 7pm Sat-Thu Apr-Sep,

NATIONAL MUSEUM

Amman's congested downtown is midway through a major redevelopment project and already the outline of public gardens, panoramic vantage points and pedestrian trails linking the Citadel and the Roman Theatre are beginning to take shape. The highlight of this project is the new international-standard **National Museum** (Map p288; Omar Matar St), which is located next to the City Hall. While the museum is reportedly complete, and key items such as Jordan's share of the Dead Sea Scrolls, have been relocated, the museum was still closed at the time of writing. Rumour has it that the authorities are awaiting a suitable occasion to give fanfare to the museum's inauguration. Come what may, the first visitors are expected in 2012 (*in sha' Allah!*).

Jordan Highlights

1. Admire the engineering precision of the **Roman Theatre** (p282) in Amman
2. Wander the colonnaded streets of **Jerash** (p293), a well-preserved Roman provincial city
3. Hike and splash along the trails of Jordan's spectacular **nature reserves** (p333)
4. Descend to the depths for a bob in the **Dead Sea** (p300), the lowest point on earth
5. Piece together early Christian history in the mosaics of **Madaba** (p305)
6. Listen to the thunder of ghostly hooves at **Karak Castle** (p310) and **Shobak Castle** (p312), Jordan's most impressive Crusader castles
7. Tread the path of history through Petra's **Siq** (p313), the sheer-sided chasm leading to an ancient world
8. Don mask and flippers and hover with the pipe fish over spectacular coral gardens in the **Red Sea** (p325)
9. Live a 'Lawrence moment' by riding through **Wadi Rum** (p322) on a camel
10. Admire the risqué frescoes in the bathhouse of **Qusayr Amra** (p304), a Unesco World Heritage site

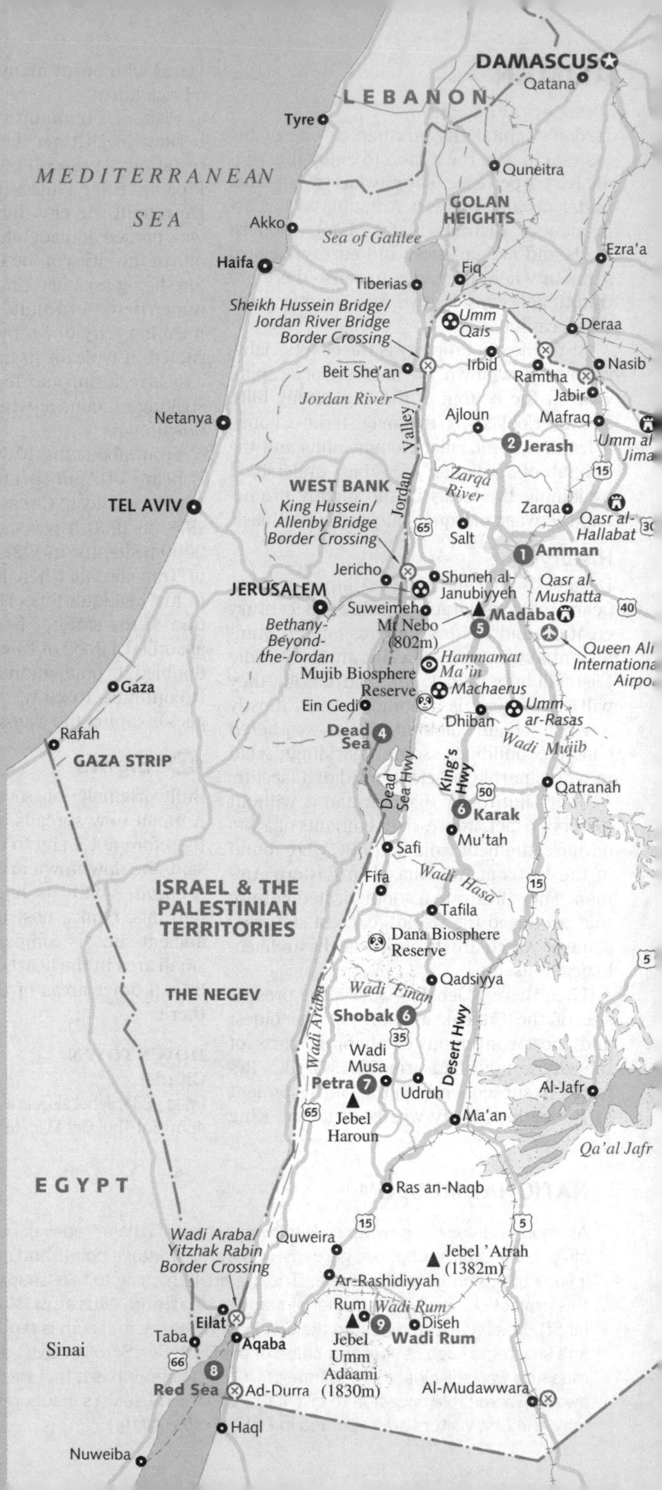

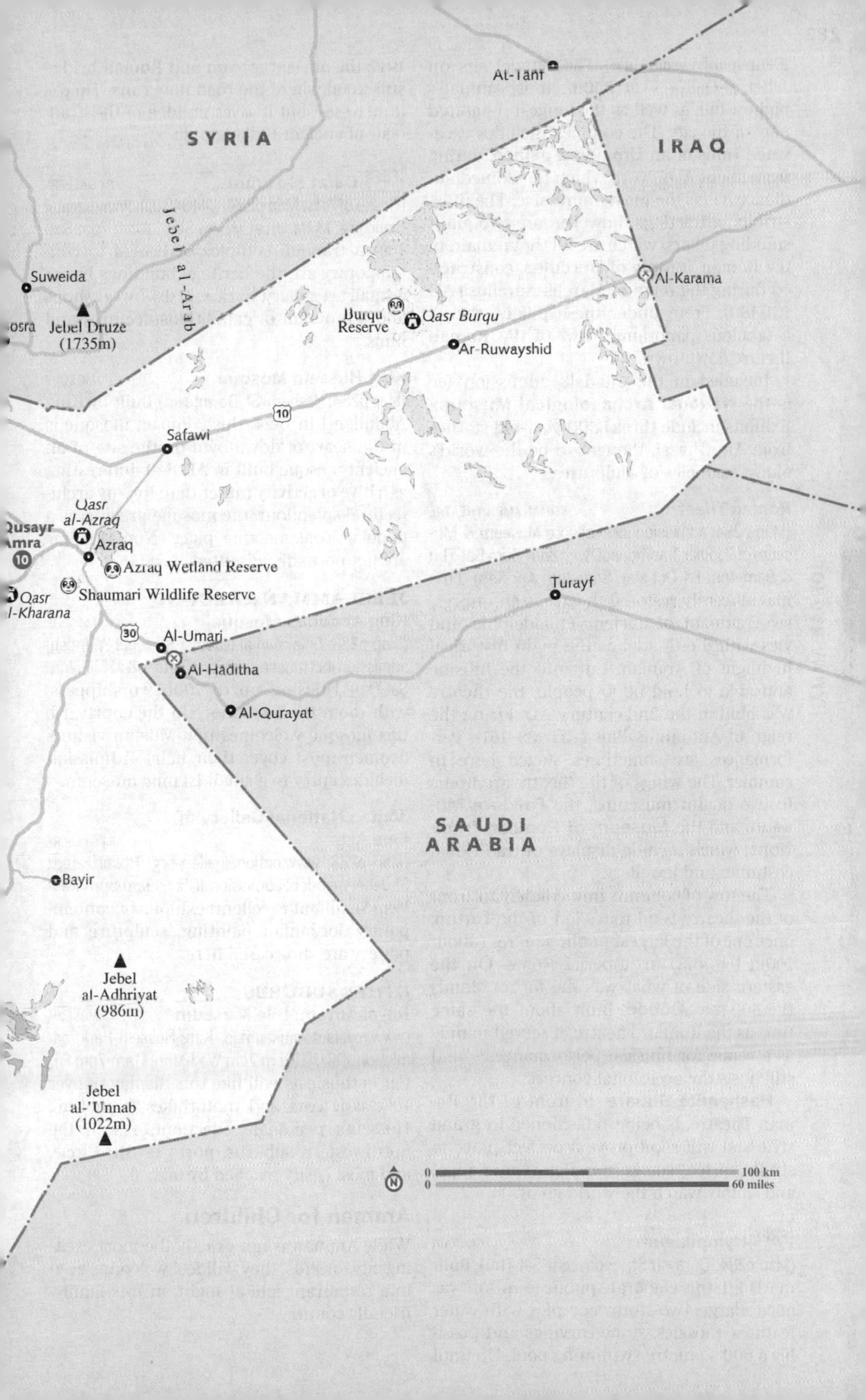
SYRIA
IRAQ
SAUDI ARABIA
Al-Tanf
Al-Karama
Jebel al-Arab
Suweida
Jebel Druze (1735m)
osra
Burqu Reserve
Qasr Burqu
Ar-Ruwayshid
10
Safawi
Qasr al-Azraq
Qusayr Amra
Azraq
Azraq Wetland Reserve
Shaumari Wildlife Reserve
Qasr al-Kharana
30
Al-Umari
Al-Haditha
Al-Qurayat
Turayf
Bayir
Jebel al-Adhriyat (986m)
Jebel al-'Unnab (1022m)
N
0
100 km
60 miles

10am-4pm Fri year-round) The Citadel sits on Jebel al-Qala'a – at 850m, it is Amman's highest hill, as well as the longest inhabited part of the city. The complex includes excavated ruins of an **Umayyad palace**, dating from about AD 720, of which the domed audience hall is the most impressive. The most striking attractions, however, are two giant standing pillars, which are all that remain of the Roman **Temple of Hercules**, constructed during the reign of Marcus Aurelius (AD 161–180). From under these pillars, there's a fabulous panoramic view of the Roman theatre downtown.

Included in the Citadel's admission fee is the **National Archaeological Museum**. Exhibits include three 8500-year-old statues from Ain Ghazal, thought to be the world's oldest examples of sculpture.

Roman Theatre ROMAN AMPHITHEATRE
(Map p284; admission incl Folklore Museum & Museum of Popular Traditions JD1; ⏲8am-4pm Sat-Thu & 9am-4pm Fri Oct-Mar, 8am-7pm Apr-Sep) This magnificently restored theatre is an impressive remnant of ancient Philadelphia and vies with the Citadel as the main historical highlight of Amman. Cut into the hillside and able to hold 6000 people, the theatre was built in the 2nd century AD during the reign of Antoninus Pius (AD 138–161). Performances are sometimes staged here in summer. The wings of the theatre are home to two quaint museums, the **Folklore Museum** and the **Museum of Popular Traditions**, which include displays of traditional costumes and jewellery.

The row of columns immediately in front of the theatre is all that's left of the **forum**, once one of the largest public squares (about 100m by 50m) in imperial Rome. On the eastern side of what was the forum stands the 500-seat **Odeon**. Built about the same time as the Roman Theatre, it served mainly as a venue for musical performances – and still hosts the occasional concert.

Hashemite Square, in front of the Roman Theatre, is being refashioned in grand style and will soon prove a perfect place to stroll, sip tea, smoke nargileh (water pipe) and simply watch the world go by.

FREE **Nymphaeum** FOUNTAIN
(Map p284; Quraysh St; ⏲daylight Sat-Thu) Built in AD 191, this elaborate public fountain was once a large, two-storey complex with water features, mosaics, stone carvings and possibly a 600 sq metre swimming pool. Up until 1947, the ancient stream and Roman bridge still stood where the road now runs. There's little to see, but it gives an idea of the grandeur of ancient Philadelphia.

FREE **Darat al-Funun** ART GALLERY
(House of Arts; Map p284; ☎4643251; www.daratalfunun.org; 13 Nadim al Mallah St; ⏲10am-7pm Sat-Thu) A tranquil complex dedicated to contemporary art, the heritage buildings house a small art gallery, library, artists' workshops and a program of exhibitions, lectures and films.

King Hussein Mosque MOSQUE
(Map p284; Hashemi St, Downtown) Built by King Abdullah I in 1924, this compact mosque is in the heart of downtown on the site of an ancient mosque built in AD 640. Interesting as a hive of activity rather than for any architectural splendour, the mosque precinct is a popular local meeting place. Non-Muslims are not normally admitted.

JEBEL AMMAN & AROUND

King Abdullah Mosque MOSQUE
(Map p288; Suleiman al-Nabulsi St, Jebel Weibdeh; admission incl museum JD2; ⏲8-11am & 12.30-2pm Sat-Thu) Housing up to 7000 worshippers, with room for 3000 more in the courtyard, this mosque welcomes non-Muslim visitors (women must cover their hair). Admission includes entry to a small Islamic museum.

Jordan National Gallery of Fine Arts ART GALLERY
(Map p288; www.nationalgallery.org; Hosni Fareez St, Jebel Weibdeh; admission JD5; ⏲9am-5pm Wed-Mon) Small but excellent; exhibits of contemporary Jordanian painting, sculpture and pottery are showcased here.

OTHER SUBURBS

Royal Automobile Museum MUSEUM
(www.royalautomuseum.jo; King Hussein Park; admission JD3; ⏲10am-7pm Wed-Mon, 11am-7pm Fri) Car enthusiasts will like this display of over 70 classic cars and motorbikes from King Hussein's personal collectiont. It's in the northwestern suburbs, north of 8th Circle, and most easily reached by taxi.

Amman for Children

While Amman is not exactly the most exciting city for kids, they will feel welcome, even in a restaurant late at night, in this family-friendly country.

DON'T MISS

BATHING WITH BRUISERS

If you thought you felt sore after walking up and down Amman's multiple hills, then just wait until you see what they do with you at the local hammam (Turkish bath). The large, muscular attendants (male or female, depending on your sex) could easily retrain as Sumo wrestlers and you can rely on them to find parts of the body you didn't know you had. In fact, they'll remove parts of the body you didn't know you had, as the art of extreme exfoliation counts as one of their many talents.

A largely Ottoman creation, based no doubt on a Roman obsession with communal bathing, Turkish baths have existed as places of social gathering and ritual cleansing across the Middle East for centuries. Amman's bathhouses, despite being largely modern affairs, belong to this decidedly masochistic tradition. Think we're exaggerating? Then pay a visit to the **Al-Pasha Turkish Bath** (Map p284; ☎4633002; www.pashaturkishbath.com; Al-Mahmoud Taha St; ⏲9am-2am, last booking midnight) and you can make up your own mind.

The full service of pummelling, scrubbing and nose-hair plucking costs around JD28. Generally speaking, women are welcome during the day, while evenings are men only. Book ahead as, believe it or not, this is a very popular pastime. Also, be sure to bring a modest swimming costume. Al-Pasha is easiest to find if you're coming along Abu Bakr as-Siddiq St (Rainbow St) from the 1st Circle; it's the fifth street on the right. Taxis know it as near Ahliya School for Girls.

Amman Waves WATERPARK
(www.ammanwaves.com; Airport Rd; adult/child JD14/8; ⏲10am-7pm) This Western-style waterpark is about 15km south of town, along the highway to the airport. Note that adults should respect local sensibilities and wear appropriate swimwear (no Speedos or bikinis).

FREE **Haya Cultural Centre** CULTURAL CENTRE
(Ilya Abu Madhi St, Shmeisani; ⏲9am-6pm Sat-Thu) Designed especially for children, this centre has a library, playground, an interactive eco-museum and an inflatable castle. It also organises regular activities and performances for kids. Easiest accessed by taxi.

Tours

For information on organised day trips from Amman, see p342.

Sleeping

Downtown Amman has many budget hotels. Places listed below all promise hot water and some even deliver. Unless otherwise stated, all of the midrange hotels are located in the Jebel Amman area. Top-end hotels are located in Jebel Amman and Shmeisani.

DOWNTOWN

TOP CHOICE **Jordan Tower Hotel** HOTEL $
(Map p284; ☎4614161; www.jordantoweramman.com; 48 Hashemi St; male & female dm JD9, s/d/tr JD20/32/38; ❄@📶) This inviting establishment (probably the only no-smoking hotel in Amman) is run by a Jordanian-British couple. Rooms are bright and snug with flat-screen TVs, though the bathrooms are small. The location is a winner: you couldn't be closer to the key sights without offering beds in the Forum! Popular daytrips and transport options start from around JD15.

Palace Hotel HOTEL $
(Map p284; ☎4624326; www.palacehotel.com.jo; Al-Malek Faisal St; s/d/tr JD25/30/40, without bathroom JD14/20/25; @❄📶) With many years of experience in offering good-value budget accommodation, the Palace's location in the heart of King Faisal St can't be bettered. Daytrips and onward transport options available.

Farah Hotel HOTEL $
(Map p284; ☎4651443; www.farahhotel.com.jo; Cinema al-Hussein St; 4- to 6-bed dm JD6, s/d/tr JD22/30/39, without bathroom JD14/20/27; @📶) A firm favourite with travellers, this is the only hotel downtown to have a shady garden. The hotel's security will be a comfort to women travelling solo. Wi-fi (JD2) is free after a stay of three days.

Cliff Hotel HOTEL $
(Map p284; ☎4624273; Al-Amir Mohammed St; s/d/tr/q without bathroom JD8/10/12/15, breakfast JD1.500; 📶) This long-standing shoestring favourite has basic if dark rooms, but there's a big bright and sociable lounge area.

Downtown Amman

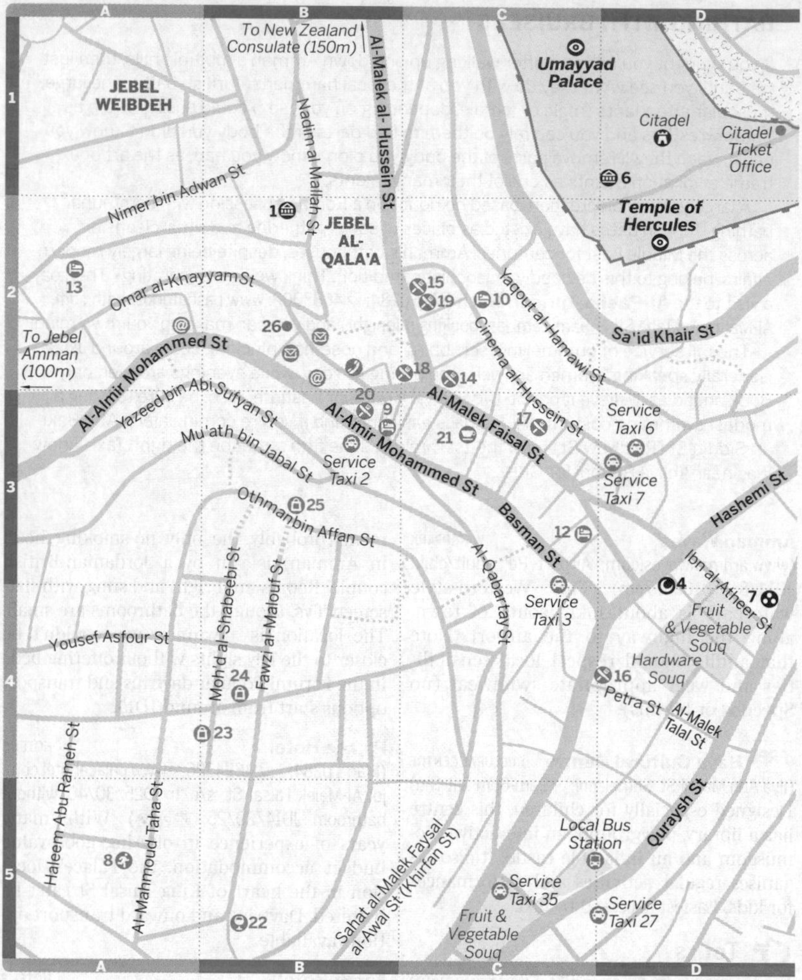

Sydney Hostel HOTEL $
(off Map p284; ☎4641122; sydney_hostel@yahoo.com; 9 Sha'ban St; dm/s/d/tr without bathroom JD7/15/25/33; ❄@📶) Not as conveniently located as other downtown options and lacking the social atmosphere of other travellers' haunts, this hotel nonetheless boasts big rooms – a novelty for the price.

JEBEL AMMAN

TOP CHOICE Jordan Inter Continental Hotel HOTEL $$$
(Map p288; ☎4641361; www.intercontinental.com; Al-Kulliyah al-Islamiyah St; r from JD140; ❄@📶🏊) The granddaddy of luxury hotels in Amman, the much-loved InterCon has been hosting foreign dignitaries since the early days of Jordan's founding. Today it continues to attract an interesting mix of distinguished guests, including top brass on R&R from Iraq and visiting royalty from the Gulf.

Caravan Hotel HOTEL $
(Map p288; ☎5661195; caravan@go.com.jo; Al-Ma'moun St; s/d/tr/q JD22/28/33/38; @) Almost opposite the King Abdullah Mosque, the Caravan Hotel is something of a travellers' institution with a quiet side street location

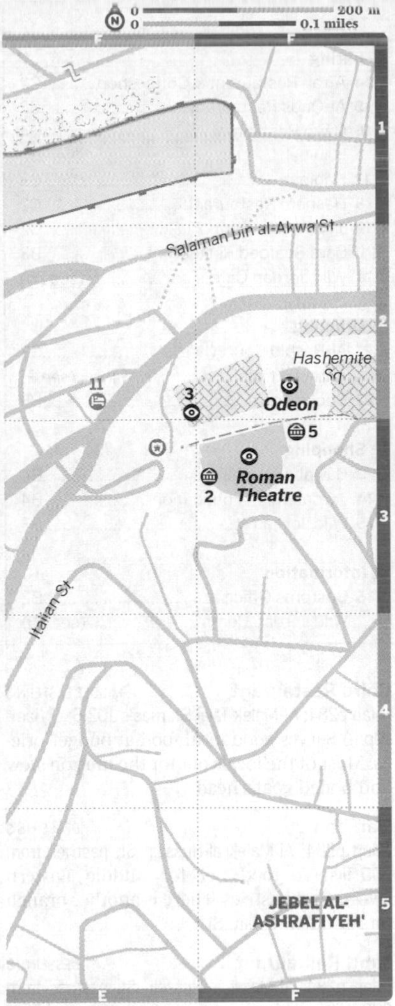

near downtown. With 45 years of experience helping travellers, the Caravan offers a comprehensive transport service.

Hisham Hotel HOTEL $$
(Map p288; ☎4644028; www.hishamhotel.com.jo; Mithqal al-Fayez St; s/d from JD65/76; ❄@📶) An excellent choice if you're looking for a hotel removed from city congestion while still within easy reach of downtown.

Toledo Hotel HOTEL $$
(Map p288; ☎4657777; www.toledohotel.jo; Umayyah bin Abd Shams St; s/d/tr from JD70/80/90; ❄@📶🏊) The Moorish-style Toledo offers a quality experience on the cusp of the top-end sector. The ornate foyer, with its Moroccan-style tiles, key-hole arches and free wi-fi access, is a winner.

OTHER SUBURBS

AlQasr Metropole Hotel HOTEL $$$
(☎5689671; www.alqasrmetropole.com; 3 Arroub St, Shmeisani; s/d JD100/110; ❄@📶) Straddling the boundary between midrange and top-end in terms of facilities if not price, this hotel is the closest thing to a boutique establishment in Amman, with large contemporary paintings in the foyer. The easiest way to reach this place, in the heart of Shmeisani, is by taxi.

Canary Hotel HOTEL $
(Map p288; ☎4638353; canary_h@hotmail.com; 17 Al-Karmali St; s/d JD24/32; @) In the leafy Jebel Weibdeh area, the cosy B&B-style Canary feels a million miles from the chaos of downtown.

Ocean Hotel HOTEL $$$
(☎5517280; www.oceanhotel.com.jo; Shatt al Arab St, Umm Ultheima; s/d from JD77/100; ❄@📶) Offering peace and quiet on the wealthy side of town, and encompassing the cavernous Diwan al-Sultan Ibrahim Restaurant. Most casily reached by taxi.

Le Meridien HOTEL $$$
(☎5696511; www.lemeridien.com; Al-Malekah Noor St, Shmeisani; r from JD120; @❄🏊) Considerably more affordable than the competition, with flawless rooms and world-class service. Located near King Abdullah Mosque, it's most easily reached by taxi.

Eating

Budget eateries are concentrated downtown. Take a local approach to choosing a dinner venue: promenade Rainbow St in Jebel Amman, Culture St in Shmeisani or Waqalat St around the 7th Circle in Swafei, and pick the most appealing of the many restaurants.

DOWNTOWN

TOP CHOICE **Hashem Restaurant** FELAFEL $
(Map p284; Al-Amir Mohammed St; the works JD3; ⏲24hr) You haven't tried falafel until you've eaten here. Pop in a handful of mint leaves first, park a wedge of raw onion between your teeth and don't touch the scalding copper vats of beans (harder than you'd imagine given the space available). This legendary eatery, run for half a century by a Turkish family, is so popular that there's

Downtown Amman

Top Sights

	Odeon	F2
	Roman Theatre	F3
	Temple of Hercules	D2
	Umayyad Palace	C1

Sights

1	Darat al-Funun	B2
2	Folklore Museum	F3
3	Forum	E2
4	King Hussein Mosque	D3
5	Museum of Popular Traditions	F3
6	National Archaeological Museum	D1
7	Nymphaeum	D4

Activities, Courses & Tours

8	Al-Pasha Turkish Bath	A5

Sleeping

9	Cliff Hotel	B3
10	Farah Hotel	C2
11	Jordan Tower Hotel	E2
12	Palace Hotel	C3
13	Sydney Hostel	A2

Eating

14	Afrah Restaurant & Coffeeshop	C2
15	Al-Quds Restaurant	C2
16	Cairo Restaurant	D4
	Habibah	(see 15)
17	Habibah	C3
18	Hashem Restaurant	C2
19	Jabri Restaurant	C2
20	Sara Seafood Restaurant	B3
	Wild Jordan Café	(see 25)

Drinking

21	Al-Rashid Court Café	C3
	Auberge Café	(see 9)
22	Books@café	B5

Shopping

23	Bawabet al-Sharq	B4
24	Jordan River Foundation	B4
25	Wild Jordan	B3

Information

26	Customs Office	B2
	Wild Jordan Centre	(see 25)

stiff competition for tables, many of which overflow into the alleyway.

Afrah Restaurant & Coffeeshop MIDDLE EASTERN $$
(Map p284; Al-Malek Faisal St; mains from JD5; ⌚9am-1am) Old coffeepots, brass trays and other Oriental bric-a-brac are suspended from the ceiling of this popular new restaurant, recalling days of yore. Live Arab pop entertainment is offered nightly after around 9pm. Access is via a steep staircase up an alleyway, next to the Farah Hotel.

Sara Seafood Restaurant SEAFOOD $
(Map p284; Al-Malek al-Hussein St; fish dish from JD5; ⌚10am-1am) A hit with locals, this new restaurant doesn't look much from the outside and looks positively uninviting from the street entrance (next to Cliff Hotel), but it turns out some of downtown's best seafood.

Al-Quds Restaurant BEDOUIN $
(Jerusalem Restaurant; Map p284; Al-Malek al-Hussein St; pastries from 800 fils, mains from JD6; ⌚7am-10pm) Specialises in sweets and pastries, but has a good value restaurant at the back. The house speciality is *mensaf,* a Bedouin dish of lamb and rice.

Cairo Restaurant MIDDLE EASTERN $
(Map p284; Al-Malek Talal St; meals JD2-5; ⌚6am-10pm) Serves good local food at budget prices. Most of the locals opt for the mutton stew and boiled goat's head.

Habibah DESSERTS $
(Map p284; Al-Malek al-Hussein St; pastries from 500 fils) A good bet for Middle Eastern sweets and pastries. There is another branch on Al-Malek Faisal St.

Jabri Restaurant DESSERTS $
(Map p284; Al-Malek al-Hussein St; pastries from 800 fils, mains JD4-6; ⌚8am-8pm Sat-Thu) Famed for its baklava and other local sweet delicacies.

JEBEL AMMAN

TOP CHOICE **Romero Restaurant** ITALIAN $$$
(Map p288; ☎4644227; www.romero-jordan.com; Mohammed Hussein Haikal St; mains JD10-18) This exceptional restaurant is no pizza parlour. A revered local favourite, it was established by Italian immigrants half a century ago in an elegant traditional townhouse and comes complete with period furniture, Venetian chandeliers and a roaring fire in winter.

Fakhr El-Din Restaurant MIDDLE EASTERN $$$
(Map p288; ☎4652399; Taha Hussein St; mains JD8-15) Tastefully decorated and with crisp white linen cloths, this fine dining restaurant is located in a 1950s house with a beautiful little garden. Over 10 years, a million guests have visited this establishment in search of what the proprietor terms 'genuine Arabic cuisine and hospitality'.

Blue Fig Café FUSION $$
(off Map p288; Al-Emir Hashem bin al-Hussein St; mains JD4-8; ⊙8.30am-1am) If you're wondering where Amman's fashionable set go to escape their own cuisine, look no further than this supercool, glass-and-steel restaurant near Abdoun Circle.

Abu Ahmad Orient Restaurant MIDDLE EASTERN $$
(Map p288; 3rd Circle; mains JD5-11; ⊙noon-midnight) This excellent Lebanese place has a leafy outdoor terrace that bustles with life during the summer months.

Haboob Grand Stores SUPERMARKET $
(Map p288; Al Kulliyah al Islamiyah St; ⊙7am-midnight) Between 1st and 2nd circles, this is a handy place to stock up with picnic material. It sometimes closes on Friday.

OTHER SUBURBS

Reaching venues in suburbs beyond Downtown and Jebel Amman is difficult by public transport. The best way to locate them is by taxi. If you're driving, leave the car at the hotel and hail a cab!

Diwan al-Sultan Ibrahim Restaurant MIDDLE EASTERN $$
(☎5517383; Ocean Hotel, Shatt al-Arab St, Umm Utheina; mains JD10-15; ⊙noon-midnight) Highly recommended by locals and expats for its high-quality Lebanese food. The fresh fish is the speciality with options arrayed on ice. Located off the 6th Circle, near the Umm Utheina shopping centre.

La Terrasse JORDANIAN $$$
(☎5601675; 11 August St, Shmeisani; mains JD10-25; ⊙1pm-1am) Delicious local dishes and soups in a cosy, relaxed upper storey dining area. Most nights, after 10.30pm, the tiny stage is given over to live Arab singers. Ask locally, as this place is hard to find without the help of a taxi driver.

Safeway outlet SUPERMARKET $$
(Nasser bin Jameel St, Shmeisani; ⊙24hr) Located around 500m southwest of the Sports City junction.

C-Town Shopping Centre SUPERMARKET $$
(Zahran St, Sweifieh & Abdul Hameed Sharaf St, Shmeisani; ⊙7am-midnight) Branches close to 7th Circle and in Shmeisani.

Drinking

Some of the cafes in downtown are perfect retreats from which to watch the world go by, write up your journal, tweet a friend, meet locals and play backgammon. A dozen or more cafes can be found around Hashemite Sq – a great place for people-watching in summer.

The place to be seen in Amman at night is Abdoun Circle, where there are dozens of popular cafes.

DOWNTOWN

Auberge Café COFFEEHOUSE
(Map p284; Al-Amir Mohammed St, downtown; ⊙10am-midnight) One floor below the Cliff Hotel, this gritty Jordanian spot is popular with local men. You'll have to make your way through the tobacco haze to reach the balcony, which overlooks the main street. You'll have to fight with the regulars to sit there, mind.

DON'T MISS

WILD JORDAN CAFÉ

Don't visit the RSCN booking office without sparing time for a bite at the wonderful, ecofriendly **Wild Jordan Café** (Map p284; Othman Bin Affan St; ⊙11am-midnight; mains JD7-12; ☑). The emphasis is on locally sourced produce, healthy wraps, organic salads, fresh herbs and delicious smoothies. The glass walls and open-air terrace offer vistas of the Citadel and downtown Amman. While you're there, pop into the **Wild Jordan nature shop** where you can buy olive oil soaps and hand-crafted silver earrings; profits are returned to the local communities that made them. Before you leave, pick up a downtown walking trail brochure for some backstreet revelations.

Jebel Amman

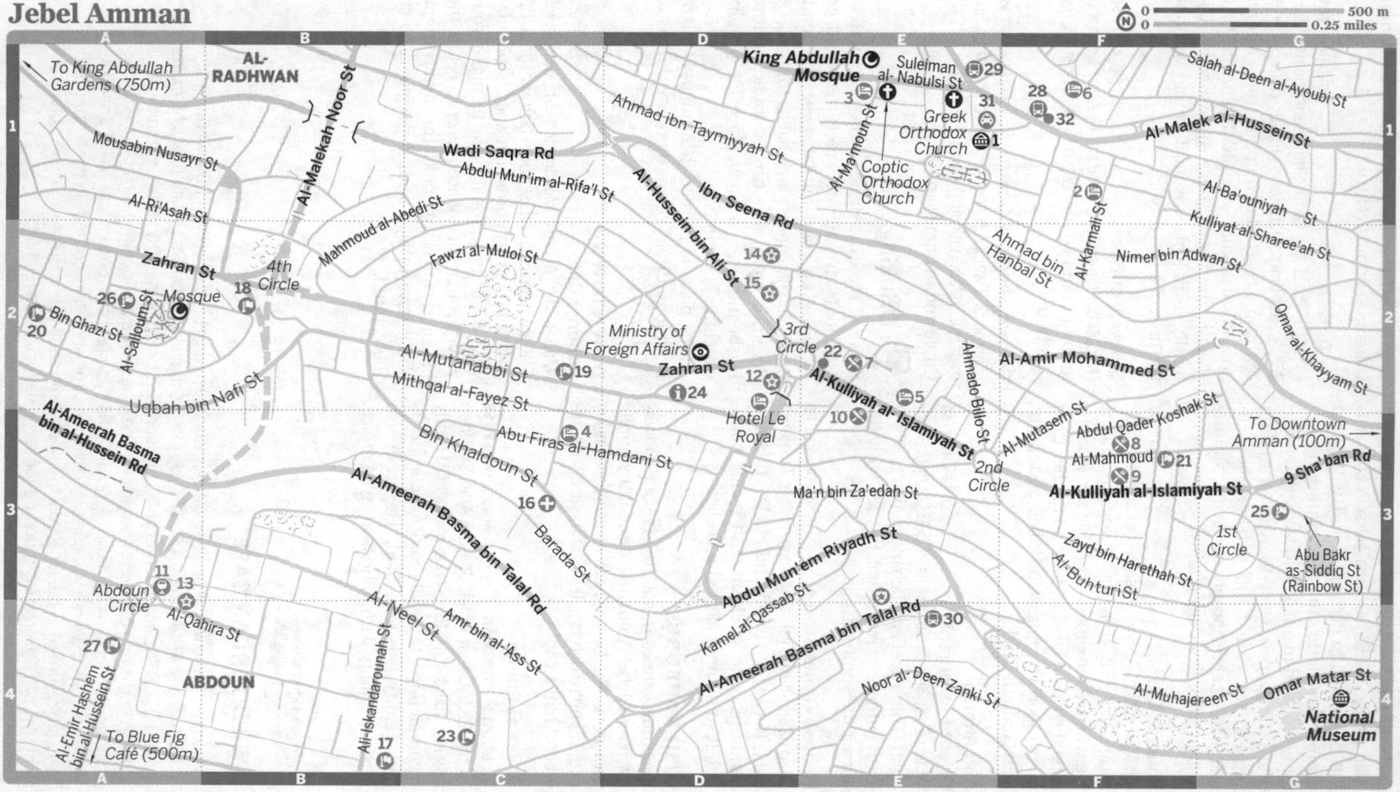
0 500 m
0 0.25 miles
N
A
B
C
D
E
F
G
1
2
3
4
To King Abdullah Gardens (750m)
AL-RADHWAN
Al-Malekah Noor St
Wadi Saqra Rd
Abdul Mun'im al-Rifa'I St
Mousabin Nusayr St
Al-Ri'Asah St
Mahmoud al-Abedi St
Fawzi al-Muloi St
Zahran St
4th Circle
18
26
Mosque
Al-Salloum St
20
Bin Ghazi St
Ahmad ibn Taymiyyah St
Al-Hussein bin Ali St
Ibn Seena Rd
King Abdullah Mosque
3
Al-Ma'moun St
Coptic Orthodox Church
Suleiman al- Nabulsi St
Greek Orthodox Church
29
31
1
28
32
6
Salah al-Deen al-Ayoubi St
Al-Malek al-Hussein St
2
Al-Karmali St
Al-Ba'ouniyah St
Kulliyat al-Sharee'ah St
Ahmad bin Hanbal St
Nimer bin Adwan St
14
15
Omar al-Khayyam St
3rd Circle
22
7
Ministry of Foreign Affairs
Zahran St
Al-Mutanabbi St
19
Mithqal al-Fayez St
24
12
Hotel Le Royal
Al-Kulliyah al- Islamiyah St
5
10
Ahmado Billo St
Al-Amir Mohammed St
Uqbah bin Nafi St
Al-Ameerah Basma bin al-Hussein Rd
Abu Firas al-Hamdani St
4
Bin Khaldoun St
16
Barada St
Al-Ameerah Basma bin Talal Rd
Ma'n bin Za'edah St
2nd Circle
Al-Mutasem St
Abdul Qader Koshak St
8
Al-Mahmoud
21
9
Al-Kulliyah al-Islamiyah St
To Downtown Amman (100m)
9 Sha'ban Rd
25
1st Circle
Abu Bakr as-Siddiq St (Rainbow St)
Zayd bin Harethah St
Al-Buhturi St
Abdul Mun'em Riyadh St
Kamel al-Qassab St
Al-Ameerah Basma bin Talal Rd
30
Noor al-Deen Zanki St
Al-Muhajereen St
Omar Matar St
National Museum
11
Abdoun Circle
13
Al-Qahira St
Al-Neel St
Amr bin al-'Ass St
27
ABDOUN
Al-Emir Hashem bin al-Hussein St
To Blue Fig Café (500m)
Ali-Iskandarounah St
17
23

Jebel Amman

Top Sights

King Abdullah Mosque E1
National Museum G4

Sights

1 Jordan National Gallery of Fine Arts E1

Sleeping

2 Canary Hotel F1
3 Caravan Hotel E1
4 Hisham Hotel C3
5 Jordan InterContinental Hotel E2
6 Toledo Hotel F1

Eating

7 Abu Ahmad Orient Restaurant E2
8 Fakhr el-Din Restaurant F3
9 Haboob Grand Stores F3
10 Romero Restaurant E3

Drinking

Living Room .... (see 10)
11 Tche Tche Café A3

Entertainment

12 Cine Le Royal D2
13 Galleria A4
14 Grand Zara Cinema D2
15 JJ's D2

Information

16 Al-Khalidi Medical Centre C3
17 British Embassy B4
18 Dutch Embassy B2
19 French Embassy C2
20 German Embassy A2
21 Iraqi Embassy F3
22 Jacob's Pharmacy E2
23 Lebanese Embassy C4
24 Ministry of Tourism & Antiquities D2
25 Saudi Arabian Consulate G3
26 Syrian Embassy A2
27 Yemeni Embassy A4

Transport

28 Abdali Bus Station F1
29 Airport Express Bus E1
30 Muhajireen Bus Station (Minibuses to Dead Sea & Wadi as-Seer) E4
31 Service Taxis to Damascus, Beirut & Baghdad E1
32 Trust International Transport Booking Office F1

Books@café CAFE

(Map p284; Omar bin al-Khattab; ⌚10am-midnight) You may need to keep your sunglasses on when you enter this establishment – the retro floral walls and beaded curtains in psychedelic colours are a fun if dazzling throwback to the '70s. This is typical modern Jordanian coffeehouse chic and the tasty global food (mains JD5 to JD12) is far less interesting than the hip young Jordanians lounging on sofas in corners or with their noses in a new book. The on-site bookshop stocks Lonely Planet titles.

Al-Rashid Court Café CAFE

(Map p284; Al-Malek Faisal St, downtown; tea or coffee from JD3; ⌚10am-midnight Sat-Thu, 1-11pm Fri) The 1st-floor balcony here is *the* place to pass an afternoon and survey the chaos of the downtown area below, though competition for seats is fierce. Also known as the Eco-Tourism Café, this is one of the best places for the uninitiated to try a nargileh (JD2). Although you won't see any local women here, it's well accustomed to foreign tourists. To find it, look for the flags of the world on the main facade; the entrance is down the side alley.

JEBEL AMMAN

Tche Tche Café CAFE

(Map p288; Abdoun Circle, Jebel Amman; snacks JD1-3; ⌚10am-11pm) You'll have to arrive early to get a seat in this bright and buzzing cafe, one of a chain that stretches across the Middle East. Far from a traditional coffeehouse, it's a hit with Jordanian women who come to smoke nargileh and enjoy the Arabic pop.

Living Room COCKTAIL BAR

(Map p288; Mohammed Hussein Haikal St, Jebel Amman; ⌚1pm-1am) Part lounge, part sushi bar and part study (think high-backed chairs, a fireplace and the daily newspaper), the Living Room is so understated that it's easily missed. It offers quality bar meals (JD6 to JD10), fine music and delicious iced tea with lemon grass and mint. Non-teetotallers can enjoy the full complement of expertly crafted cocktails on offer, which are served up deliciously strong.

OTHER SUBURBS

Rovers Return PUB
(Ali Nasouh al-Taher St, Sweifieh; ⌚1pm-late) A godsend for homesick *Coronation St* fans, this popular, cosy English pub near the 7th Circle has wood panelling and a lively atmosphere. The comfort food (meals JD5 to JD8) includes authentic fish and chips, and roast beef with gravy. The entrance is round the back of the building and can be hard to find – look for the red 'Comfort Suites' sign. Located off 7th Circle, opposite Standard Chartered Bank.

Entertainment

Nightclubs

JJ's NIGHTCLUB
(Map p288; Grand Hyatt Amman, Al-Hussein bin Ali St, Jebel Amman; ⌚8.30pm-late Mon-Sat) The Grand Hyatt's disco is where Amman's glamorous set enjoy an evening out. The music varies greatly depending on the whims of the DJ, though it's always fresh and innovative.

Cinemas

Programs for these modern cinemas are advertised in the two English-language newspapers, the *Jordan Times* and the *Star*. Tickets cost JD5.

Cine Le Royal CINEMA
(Map p288; 3rd Circle, Jebel Amman) Part of Le Royal Hotel.

Galleria CINEMA
(Map p288; Abdoun Circle, Jebel Amman)

Grand Zara Cinema CINEMA
(Map p288; 3rd Circle, Jebel Amman) In the Zara Centre behind the Grand Hyatt.

Shopping

Amman is a good place to shop for souvenirs in Jordan, with everything from tourist kitsch to high-quality handicraft boutiques,

LOCAL KNOWLEDGE

HIS EXCELLENCY NAYEF HMEIDI AL-FAYEZ: MINISTER OF TOURISM & ANTIQUITIES

In the following interview, His Excellency Nayef Al-Fayez identifies the key elements that make Jordan a special and unique destination.

With so much heritage, how do you persuade tourists that Jordan is not all about ruins? Jordan is a very modern country, as you can see from Amman, but there is always a link between past and present. That link is the people. In fact, the people are the most wonderful part of our country. Jordanian hospitality is legendary and we welcome visitors as 'guests of God'.

With limited public transport to key destinations, and with high entry fees to national parks and Petra, is it fair to say that Jordan is actively targeting the wealthier tourist? Jordan is open for everyone. We do have plans for scheduled tourist transportation, and we already operate JETT buses to the main destinations, but as with any government our main task is to move the population around at affordable prices. This is why we subsidise public transport.

This year, 2011, has obviously been a tough one with problems in neighbouring countries impacting on tourism to Jordan. What measures have been taken to reassure tourists that Jordan is safe? The Middle East comprises 22 countries and each country is different. Jordan is what we call the 'Switzerland of the Middle East' because of its stability. Jordan shouldn't be made guilty by geography!

Is it difficult convincing foreign tourists that Jordan is a destination in its own right, as opposed to a stopover between Egypt and Syria? There is plenty of interest for a two-week visit because Jordan is so much more than just Petra. Wadi Rum is a Unesco World Heritage Site, for example, and of course the Bible is your guidebook for the sites of the Holy Land in Jordan.

How can visitors play their part in a sustainable future for tourism in Jordan? Integrating with local communities is key – if people feel the value of tourism, they will work hard to preserve and protect sites for the future.

many of which are run to benefit local communities.

The following are among the better places, and are generally open 9am to 6pm Saturday to Thursday. Prices are fixed. Rainbow St is good for a browse.

Jordan River Foundation HANDICRAFTS
(Map p284; www.jordanriver.jo; Bani Hamida House, Fawzi al-Malouf St, Jebel Amman; ⌚8.30am-7pm Sat-Thu, 10am-5pm Fri) Supporting top-notch worthy causes through selling equally top-notch crafted items, this shop has become something of an institution in Amman. Only the highest-quality pieces make it into the showroom.

Wild Jordan HANDICRAFTS
(Map p284; Othman bin Affan St, downtown; ⌚10am-10pm) Beautiful products made in Jordan's nature reserves. All profits are returned to the craftspeople and to the nature-reserve projects.

Bawabet al-Sharq HANDICRAFTS
(Map p284; Abu Bakr as Siddiq St, downtown; ⌚9am-7pm) The 'Gate of the Orient' has locally made (some on site) home decor items tending towards the kitsch. Sales benefit several Jordanian women's groups.

Information

Emergency

Ambulance (☎911)

Fire department (☎911)

Ministry of Tourism & Antiquities (Map p288; ☎4603360, ext 254; ground fl, Al-Mutanabbi St, Jebel Amman; ⌚8am-9pm) The centre for the tourist police

Police (☎911)

Tourist Police (Map p284; Hashemi St) Small booth near the Roman Theatre.

Internet Access

Amman has plenty of internet cafes, particularly in downtown.

Books@café (Map p284; Omar bin al-Khattab, downtown; per hr JD2; ⌚10am-midnight) A professional set-up with fast connections.

Internet Yard (Map p284; dweib@joinnet.com.jo; Al-Amir Mohammed St, downtown; per hr JD1; ⌚9.30am-midnight)

Welcome Internet (Map p284; Al-Amir Mohammed St, downtown; per hr JD1; ⌚10.30am-1am)

Media

The *Jordan Times* and the *Star* are the two English-language newspapers and both are worth a read.

Jordan Today (www.jordantoday.com.jo) is a free monthly booklet that includes a yellow pages listing of embassies, airlines and the like. *Where to Go* is similar and includes a useful collection of Amman restaurant menus. Pick them up in the better hotels and restaurants.

Medical Services

The English-language *Jordan Times* and *Star* list the current telephone numbers of doctors and pharmacies on night duty throughout the capital.

Al-Khalidi Medical Centre (Map p288; ☎4644281; www.kmc.jo; Bin Khaldoun St, Jebel Amman)

Italian Hospital (☎4777101; Italian St, downtown) Located a short walk southeast of Quraysh St. Service taxis 25 and 26 stop nearby.

Jacob's Pharmacy (Map p288; 3rd Circle, Jebel Amman; ⌚9am-3am) One of the more conveniently located pharmacies.

University Hospital (☎5353666; University of Jordan complex, northern Amman) Located about 10km northwest of downtown. Take any minibus or service taxi to Salt from Raghadan bus station or charter a taxi.

Money

Changing money is easy, and the downtown area especially has many banks, ATMs and moneychangers.

Post

Central Post Office (Map p284; Al-Amir Mohammed St, downtown; ⌚7.30am-5pm Sat-Thu, 8am-1.30pm Fri)

Customs Office (Map p284; ⌚8am-2pm Thu-Sat) Diagonally opposite the Parcel Post Office.

Parcel Post Office (Map p284; Omar al-Khayyam St, downtown; ⌚8am-3pm Mon-Thu & Sun, to 2pm Sat)

Telephone

The private telephone agencies around downtown are the cheapest places for international and domestic calls.

Communication International (Map p284; Nimer Bin Adwan St, downtown)

Tourist Information

Ministry of Tourism & Antiquities (Map p288; ☎4603360, ext 254; ground fl, Al-Mutanabbi St, Jebel Amman; ⌚8am-9pm) The most useful place for information is this office, southwest of the 3rd Circle. The staff is friendly, and speaks good English.

Wild Jordan Centre (Map p284; ☎4616523; www.rscn.org.jo; Othman Bin Affan St, downtown) Provides information and bookings for activities and accommodation in Jordan's nature reserves. The centre is run by the Royal

Society for the Conservation of Nature (RSCN). There's also a small crafts shop and organic cafe here.

Getting There & Away

Air

The only domestic air route is between Amman and Aqaba. For details, see p341. For a list of airlines serving Amman, see p339.

Bus, Minibus & Service Taxis

There are two main bus and minibus stations in Amman. In addition, there are smaller bus stations serving specific destinations such as the Dead Sea, as well as private coaches from the JETT and Trust offices.

Service taxis are generally faster, but they don't always follow fixed schedules. They depart from the same stations as the minibuses.

All departures are more frequent in the morning and most dry up completely after sunset.

MAIN PUBLIC BUS STATIONS

North Bus Station (Tabarbour) Located in the northern suburbs, this station offers services to the north. A taxi to this station from downtown costs from JD3. Fairly regular minibuses and service taxis leave between 7am and 6.30pm for the following destinations: Ajloun (900 fils, two hours, every 30 minutes), Jerash (800 fils, 1¼ hours, hourly) and Madaba (750 fils, 45 minutes, every 10 minutes from 6am to 8pm). Services are also available for Deir Alla (for Pella, one hour), Fuheis (45 minutes), Irbid (two hours), Ramtha (two hours), Salt (45 minutes) and Zarqa (for Azraq, 30 minutes); all these services cost under JD1. There's also a daily airport bus (JD3, 45 minutes, every 30 minutes from 6.15am to midnight).

South Bus Station (Wahadat) Almost all buses and service taxis heading south leave from this station in the southern suburbs by Middle East Circle (Duwaar Sharq al-Awsat). A taxi to this station from downtown costs from JD2.500. For Petra, minibuses and service taxis (JD5, four hours) depart for Wadi Musa when full from the far corner of the lot between around 7am and 4pm. Buses to Aqaba (JD5.500, five hours) leave every two hours or so until 9pm. There are regular buses to Karak (JD1.650, two hours) until 5pm, Shobak (JD4, 2½ hours) and Ma'an (JD2.750, three hours); most services stop running around 4pm. For Dana there are three buses a day from 11am for Qadsiyya (JD3, three hours); otherwise take a bus to Tafila (JD2.550, 2½ hours) and change. There are semiregular service taxis to Karak (JD3, 2½ hours), Ma'an (JD6, three hours) and also infrequently to Aqaba (JD10, five hours).

OTHER PUBLIC BUS STATIONS

Abdali Bus Station (Map p288; Al-Malek al-Hussein St, Jebel Amman) This station is a 20-minute walk (2km uphill) from downtown; service taxi 6 or 7 from Cinema al-Hussein St goes right by. This is the station to use for air-conditioned buses and service taxis for international destinations, especially Syria (see p339).

Muhajireen Bus Station (Map p288) This small station is opposite the Muhajireen police station. Minibuses to Wadi as-Seer leave frequently from here during daylight hours (300 fils, 30 minutes). There are also services to Madaba and Mt Nebo (500 fils, 45 minutes) between 6am and 5pm.

PRIVATE COACH STATIONS

JETT (☎5664146; www.jett.com.jo; Al-Malek al-Hussein St, Shmeisani) The domestic JETT office is about 500m northwest of the Abdali bus station. Passengers board the bus outside the office. There are six buses daily to Aqaba (JD7.5, five hours, 7am, 9am, 11am, 2pm, 4pm and 6pm), and one bus to King Hussein Bridge (JD7.250, one hour, 7am), for entry into Israel and the Palestinian Territories. There are daily services to Irbid (JD1.900, two hours, every 30 minutes from 6am to 7.30pm). A daily JETT bus connects Amman with Petra, largely designed for those wanting to visit on a day trip. The service leaves at 6.30am (single/return JD8/16) and drops passengers off at Petra Visitor Centre in Wadi Musa at 9.30am. The return bus leaves at 4pm so bear in mind this option leaves very little time for visiting the sites of Petra. A weekly JETT bus departs for Amman Beach at the Dead Sea (single/return JD8) on Fridays at 8am and returns at 4pm. If there are insufficient passengers, however, the service is cancelled.

Trust International Transport (☎5813427) Has daily buses to Aqaba (JD7, four hours, four daily) between 7.30am and 7pm. All buses leave from the office inconveniently located at 7th Circle, near the Safeway shopping centre. A taxi to/from downtown costs JD2.500 to JD3. Trust also has a **booking office** (Map p288; ☎4644627) at Abdali bus station. Other services, such as to Irbid and to Damascus in Syria, are sometimes on offer. Check with the office for current timings.

Hijazi Travel & Tours (☎02-7240721) Runs daily buses to Irbid (JD1.900, 1½ hours, every 15 to 20 minutes from 6am to 7pm). The buses leave from the North Bus Station.

Car

All the major hotels have car rental offices. The largest selection of rental companies is at King Abdullah Gardens. See p341 for details.

Train

At the time of writing, due to the unrest in Syria, the train service to Damascus had been suspended.

Getting Around

To/From the Airport

Queen Alia International Airport is 35km south of the city. The **Airport Express Bus** (Map p288; ☎0880 022006, 4451531) runs between the airport and the North Bus Station (Tabarbour), passing through the 4th, 5th, 6th and 7th Circles en route. This service (JD3, 45 minutes) runs hourly between 7am and 11pm, and at 1am and 3am, from the airport daily. From Amman, it starts at 6am to 10pm hourly and also runs at 2am and 4am.

A taxi costs JD20 to JD25 from the airport to Amman, slightly less in the opposite direction.

Taxi

PRIVATE TAXI

Private taxis are painted yellow. They are abundant, can be flagged from the side of the road and fares are cheap. A taxi from downtown to Shmeisani, for example, costs JD2.500 and it's JD3 to Tabarbour. For longer journeys around town, you're best off agreeing a price per hour (JD10 was the current going rate at the time of writing).

SERVICE TAXI

Most fares cost from 350 fils per seat, and you usually pay the full amount regardless of where you get off. After 8pm, the price for all service taxis goes up by 25%. Some of the more useful routes (see map p284):

No 2 From Basman St, for 1st and 2nd Circles

No 3 From Basman St, for 3rd and 4th Circles

No 6 From Cinema al-Hussein St, for Abdali station and JETT offices

No 7 From Cinema al-Hussein St, past Abdali station and King Abdullah Mosque to Shmeisani

No 27 From Italian St for South Bus Station

No 35 From Quraysh St for Al Muhajiroon Police Station

JERASH & THE NORTH

You might expect that the far north of Jordan, with its exceptional Roman ruins, biblical associations, lively cities and complex terrain, would feature as a standard part of any visitor's trip to the country. This, however, is not the case and the region receives relatively few visitors compared with Petra and the South. For those in the know, this is excellent news as it means that it is quite possible to enjoy epic sites like Jerash without the epic crowds normally associated with a world-class destination.

Although many of the sites can be covered in a day trip from Amman, this ancient and populous region, dotted with olive groves and pine forests and liberally strewn with the ruins of Rome's great Decapolis cities, repays a longer visit. The availability of public transport and friendly accommodation facilitate this, and if the springtime flowers happen to be blooming, it will prove to be a hard region to leave.

Jerash جرش

☎02 / POP 123,190

These beautifully preserved Roman ruins, located 51km north of Amman, are deservedly one of Jordan's major attractions. Excavations have been ongoing for 85 years but it is estimated that 90% of the city is still unexcavated. In its heyday the ancient city, known in Roman times as Gerasa, had a population of around 15,000.

Allow at least three hours to do Jerash justice. The best times to visit are before 10am or after 4pm, but this is tricky if you are relying on public transport.

In July and August, Jerash hosts the **Jerash Festival** (www.jerashfestival.com.jo), featuring local and overseas artists, music and drama performances inside the ancient city, and displays of traditional handicrafts.

History

Although inhabited from Neolithic times, and settled as a town during the reign of Alexander the Great (333 BC), Jerash was largely a Roman creation and well-preserved remains of all the classic Roman structures – forum, cardo maximus, hippodrome, nymphaeum – are easily distinguishable among the ruins.

In the wake of Roman general Pompey's conquest of the region in 64 BC, Gerasa (as Jerash was then known) became part of the Roman province of Syria and, soon after, a city of the Decapolis. The city reached its peak at the beginning of the 3rd century AD, when it was bestowed with the rank of Colony, after which time it went into a slow decline as trade routes shifted.

By the middle of the 5th century AD, Christianity was the region's major religion and the construction of churches proceeded at a startling rate. With the Sassanian invasion from Persia in 614, the Muslim conquest

Jerash

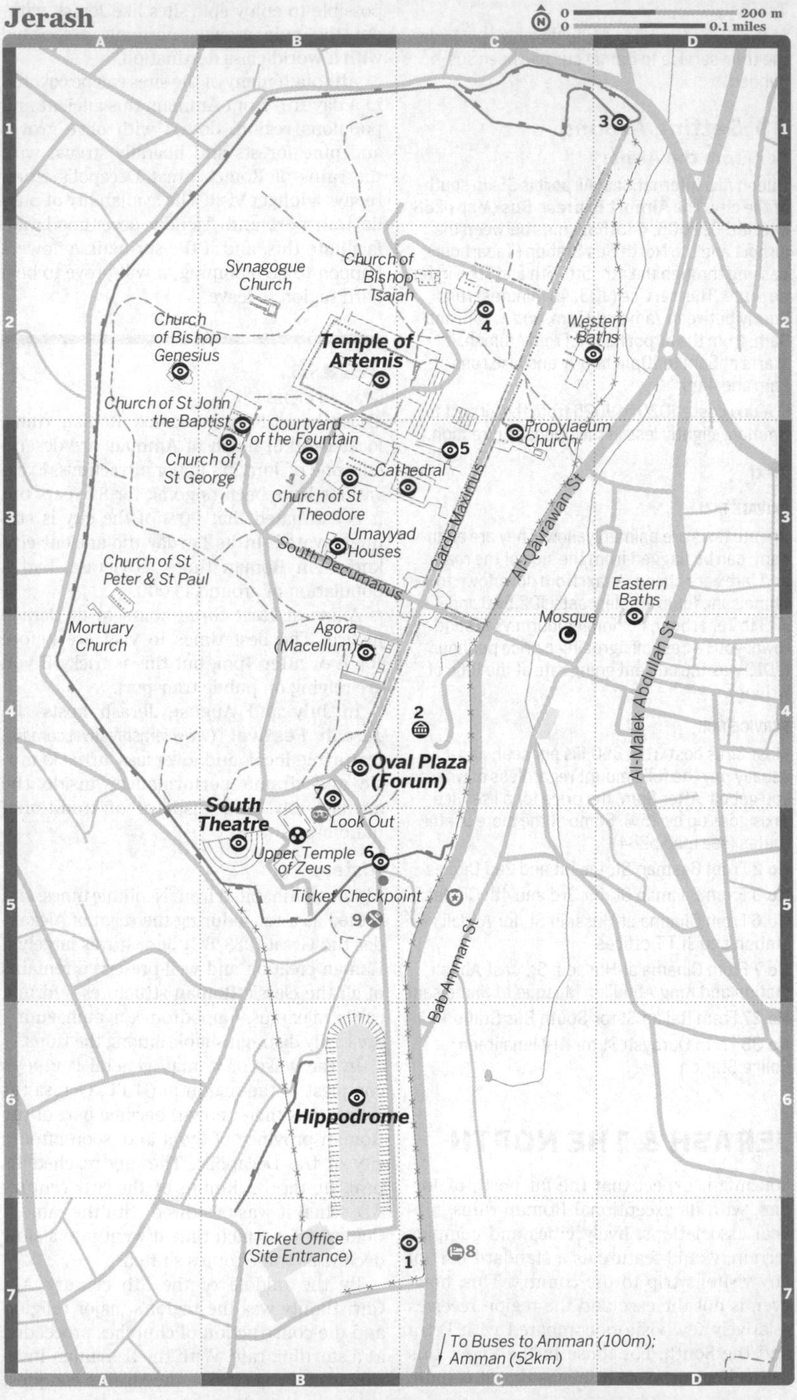

0 200 m
0 0.1 miles
A
B
C
D
1
2
3
4
5
6
7
Synagogue Church
Church of Bishop Isaiah
Church of Bishop Genesius
Temple of Artemis
Western Baths
Church of St John the Baptist
Courtyard of the Fountain
Propylaeum Church
Church of St George
Cathedral
Church of St Theodore
Umayyad Houses
South Decumanus
Cardo Maximus
Al-Qayrawan St
Church of St Peter & St Paul
Eastern Baths
Mosque
Mortuary Church
Agora (Macellum)
Al-Malek Abdullah St
Oval Plaza (Forum)
South Theatre
Look Out
Upper Temple of Zeus
Ticket Checkpoint
Bab Amman St
Hippodrome
Ticket Office (Site Entrance)
To Buses to Amman (100m); Amman (52km)
1
2
3
4
5
6
7
8
9

Jerash

Top Sights

in 636 and a devastating earthquake in 747, Jerash's heyday passed and its population shrank to about a quarter of its former size.

Sights

Roman ruins ARCHAEOLOGICAL SITE
(admission JD8; 8am-4.30pm Oct-Apr, to 7pm May-Sep) The ruins at Jerash cover a huge area and can seem daunting at first, especially as there is virtually no signage. To help the ruins come alive, engage one of the knowledgeable guides (JD20) at the ticket checkpoint to help you navigate the main complex. Alternatively, visit the main structures in the sequence in which they're presented below. The whole route, walking at a leisurely pace and allowing time for sitting on a fallen column and enjoying the spectacular views, takes a minimum of three to four hours.

At the extreme south of the site is the striking **Hadrian's Arch**, also known as the Triumphal Arch, which was built in AD 129 to honour the visit of Emperor Hadrian. Behind the arch is the **hippodrome**, which hosted chariot races watched by up to 15,000 spectators.

The **South Gate**, originally one of four along the city wall and built in AD 130, leads into the city proper. The **Oval Plaza** (forum) is one of the most distinctive sites of Jerash, unusual because of its shape and huge size (90m long and 80m at its widest point). Fifty-six Ionic columns surround the paved limestone plaza, linking the *cardo maximus* with the Temple of Zeus.

The elegant remains of the **Temple of Zeus**, built around AD 162, can be reached from the forum – a worthwhile climb if just for the view. Next door, the **South Theatre** was built in the 1st century AD with a capacity of 5000 spectators. From the upper stalls, the acoustics are still wonderful as demonstrated by the occasional roving minstrel or drummer.

To the northeast of the forum lies the **cardo maximus**, the city's main thoroughfare, also known as the colonnaded street. Stretching for 800m to the **North Gate**, the street is still paved with the original stones, rutted by the thousands of chariots that once jostled along its length.

The colonnaded street is punctuated by the **nymphaeum**, the main fountain of the city, before giving rise to a superb propylaeum or monumental gateway, and a staircase. The **Temple of Artemis**, towering over Jerash at the top of the stairs, was dedicated to the patron goddess of the city, but alas was dismantled to provide masonry for new churches under Theodorius in AD 386.

Further to the north is the **North Theatre**, built originally in AD 165 and now restored to former glory.

The small **museum** (admission free; 8.30am-6pm Oct-Apr, to 5pm May-Sep) contains a good collection of artefacts from the site.

Sleeping & Eating

An overnight stop is more rewarding: the modern town of Jerash, which encompasses the ruins of the Eastern Baths, comes to life after sunset and is a pleasant place to explore in the early evening. It's important to book ahead.

TOP CHOICE **Hadrian Gate Hotel** HOTEL $$
(077 7793907; s/d/tr/penthouse from JD25/40/50/70;) Run by the always friendly Ismail Khasim and his son Walid, Jerash's only hotel boasts a spectacular location overlooking the ruins and within walking distance of Hadrian's Gate. Breakfast is served on the rooftop terraces with a panoramic view. The hotel closes by 11pm, but you can call the proprietors for a late admission.

Olive Branch Resort HOTEL $$
(6340555; www.olivebranch.com.jo; campsite own tent/hired tent JD11/14, s/d/tr from JD35/50/60;

) Around 7km from Jerash on the road to Ajloun, this hilltop hotel in attractive grounds has comfortable rooms with satellite TV, balconies with great views and a restaurant. A taxi from Jerash costs JD3 one way.

TOP CHOICE **Lebanese House** LEBANESE $$
(mains JD4-9; noon-11pm;) Overlooking orchards, and a 10-minute walk from central Jerash, this is a local favourite, with top-notch Lebanese dishes and an attractive terrace seating. Culinary delicacies include buttery cow testicles...or you could just stick to the excellent vegetarian dishes.

Jerash Rest House BUFFET $
(6351437; buffet JD5; noon-5pm) The only restaurant inside the ruins, this is a welcome stop for weary visitors. Located near the South Gate, it attracts large volumes of tourists, but service is quick and efficient, and the buffet is tasty.

Getting There & Away

BUS & MINIBUS Buses and minibuses run frequently between Amman's north bus station and Jerash (800 fils, 1¼ hours), though they can take an hour to fill with enough passengers to warrant departure. From Jerash, minibuses travel regularly to Irbid (JD1, 45 minutes) and Ajloun (600 fils, 30 minutes) until mid-afternoon. Jerash's bus station is a 15-minute walk west of the site, at the second set of traffic lights. If you don't fancy the walk, you can often jump on buses headed to Amman from the junction southeast of the main ticket office. Transport drops off significantly after 5pm.

TAXI Service taxis sometimes leave up to around 8pm (later during Jerash Festival) from the bus station, but it's not guaranteed. A private taxi between Amman and Jerash should cost around JD18 to JD25 each way, with a bit of determined bargaining. From Jerash, a taxi to Irbid costs around JD14 to JD20.

Ajloun عجلون

02 / POP 94,458

Ajloun (or Ajlun) is another popular and easy day trip from Amman, and can be combined with a trip to Jerash if you leave early.

Sights

Qala'at ar-Rabad (Ajloun Castle) CASTLE
(admission JD1; 8am-4pm Oct-Apr, to 7pm May-Sep) Three kilometres west of town, Qala'at ar-Rabad is the main attraction in Ajloun and a fine example of Islamic military architecture. Built in AD 1184–88 by the Arabs as protection against the Crusaders, it was enlarged in 1214 with the addition of a new gate in the southeastern corner, and once boasted seven towers as well as a surrounding dry moat that dropped to more than 15m deep.

The castle commands fine views of the Jordan Valley and was one in a chain of beacons and pigeon posts that allowed messages to be transmitted from Damascus to Cairo

SALUTE THE TROOPS AT JERASH'S CHARIOT RACE

Have you ever considered how and why Rome managed to conquer the lands of the Middle East so easily? Pay a visit to the spectacular ruins at Jerash, and you may just find the answer.

The answer doesn't lie in the ruins of empire scattered around the site, but in the novel re-enactment, held twice daily at the hippodrome. Bringing entertainment back to the playing field for the first time in 1500 years, the **Roman Army and Chariot Experience** (www.jerashchariots.com; admission JD12; shows 11am & 2pm Sat-Wed, 11am Fri) is faithful to history, right down to the Latin commands.

Visitors will have a chuckle at the lively repartee of the master of ceremonies, one Adam Al-Samadi, otherwise known as Gaius Victor. Dressed as a Roman legionnaire with a feather pluming from his helmet, he stands erect like a true centurion. 'Salute the troops,' he demands in a cockney English accent as he hitches his tunic and raises a spear to the amassed veterans of the Jordan army – in their new uniform of the Sixth Roman Legion.

'So Gaius Victor,' I ask after the show. 'What is it that makes such an erudite fellow like you do a job like this?' 'Call it bread and circuses,' he says. 'That's what kept people happy under the Romans and I guess that's what keeps us happy today.'

Forget the disciplined armies; forget the orderly organisation of labour and provisions – local people fell under the magic of Rome. As a spare soldier blasts the horn from atop Jerash's triumphal arch, his scarlet cloak furling behind him and the flag of Jordan blowing in the wind, it's easy to see how.

in a single day. Largely destroyed by Mongol invaders in 1260, it was almost immediately rebuilt by the Mamluks. In the 17th century, an Ottoman garrison was stationed here, after which it was used by local villagers. Qala'at ar-Rabad was 'rediscovered' by the well-travelled JL Burckhardt, who also stumbled across Petra. Earthquakes in 1837 and 1927 badly damaged the castle, though slow and steady restoration is continuing.

The castle is an uphill walk (3km) from the town centre. Occasional minibuses (100 fils) go there, but a return trip by taxi from Ajloun (JD7 to JD10), with 30 minutes to look around, is money well spent.

Sleeping & Eating

There are a few places for a snack and a drink inside Ajloun Castle. For something more substantial, both **Abu-Alezz Restaurant** (meals JD2-3) and **Al-Raseed** (meals JD2-3) near the main roundabout in Ajloun offer standard Jordanian fare. Alternatively, head into the surrounding hills for a picnic.

Qalet al-Jabal Hotel HOTEL $
(☎6420202; www.jabal-hotel.com; s/d/tr from JD28/38/48) About 1km downhill from Ajloun Castle, this busy little hotel boasts a gorgeous garden of flowering jasmine, grapevines and roses. The proprietors even make their own wine. The decor is a tad tired, but there are expansive views from many of the rooms. The highlight of the hotel is the outdoor terrace (open to non-residents) where slow-cooked meals are served.

Ajloun Hotel HOTEL $
(☎6420524; s/d from JD25/35) Located just 500m down the road from the castle, this is a handy option for an early-morning visit to the castle. There's a comfortable lounge area in the foyer, but most of the rooms are very basic.

Getting There & Away

From the centre of town, minibuses travel regularly to Jerash (600 fils, 30 minutes along a scenic road) and Irbid (JD1, 45 minutes). From Amman (900 fils, two hours), minibuses leave half hourly from the north bus station.

Ajloun Forest Reserve

محمية عجلون الطبيعية

Located in the Ajloun Highlands, this small (13 sq km) but vitally important **nature reserve** (⏲year-round) was established by the RSCN in 1988 to protect forests of oak, carob, pistachio and strawberry trees (look for the peeling, bright orange bark) and provide sanctuary for the endangered roe deer.

To reach the reserve, charter a taxi for the 9km from Ajloun (around JD5 to JD7, one-way).

Sights & Activities

Several marked trails, some self-guided, weave through the hilly landscape of wooded valleys. Particularly worthwhile is the **Soap Trail**, a guided trail (7km, four hours, year round) that combines panoramic viewpoints with visits to a soap workshop. The products of this cooperative can be bought, along with other fair-trade products in the reserve's craft shop, the **Soap House** (⏲9am-4pm).

Sleeping & Eating

The Ajloun Forest Reserve operates **tented bungalows** (☎6475673; s/d/tr/q JD60/70/80/90). The ablution block contains composting toilets and solar-heated showers. There are also rustic **cabins** (s/d from JD91/103) available, equipped with private bathroom and terrace. Bring mosquito repellent in the summer.

In the tented **rooftop restaurant** (meals JD13; ✎), there are lunchtime buffets with a good vegetarian selection. Outside, barbecue grills are available for public use.

Irbid

إربد

☎02 / POP 751,634

Jordan's second largest city is a university town, and one of its more lively and progressive. Irbid is also a good base for exploring the historic sites of Umm Qais, Pella and even Jerash. The town comes alive at night, especially in the energetic area around the university, where the streets are lined with restaurants and internet cafes.

Sights

FREE **Dar As Saraya Museum** MUSEUM
(Al Baladia St; ⏲8am-6pm) Located in a stunning old villa of basaltic rock, just behind the town hall, this new museum is a real gem. Built in 1886 by the Ottomans, the building is typical of the caravanserai established along the Syrian pilgrimage route, with rooms arranged around a paved internal courtyard. It was used as a prison until 1994 and now houses a delightful collection

of local artefacts that illustrate Irbid's long history.

FREE **Museum of Archaeology & Anthropology** MUSEUM
(10am-1.45pm & 3-4.30pm Sun-Thu) This highly recommended museum features exhibits from all eras of Jordanian history arranged in chronological order.

Sleeping & Eating

It has to be said that the standard of hotels in Irbid is not great. The redeeming feature, especially among the budget options, is the great friendliness of the welcome.

Al-Joude Hotel HOTEL $
(7275515; off University St; s/d/tr from JD30/35/60;) Irbid's only midrange hotel has seen better days – which, to be fair, is reflected in the budget price. Of an evening, half of Irbid pours into the hotel's popular News Cafe, or the Al-Joude Garden Restaurant.

Omayah Hotel HOTEL $
(7245955; omayahhotel@yahoo.com; King Hussein St; s/d JD20/30;) Good value for money, this recently renovated budget hotel has a friendly, helpful proprietor, and solo women will feel comfortable here.

Al-Ameen al-Kabeer Hotel HOTEL $
(7242384; Al-Jaish St; dm/s/d without bathroom from JD8/12/15) The friendly management gives personal and attentive service at this city centre hotel, but it's very much a budget option with basic rooms and shared bathrooms.

Al-Joude Garden Restaurant JORDANIAN $$
(off University St; mixed grill meals JD6-10) Students, visiting parents and local families crowd into the courtyard outside Al-Joude Hotel to sip fresh fruit juices and smoke a strawberry nargileh.

Clock Tower Restaurant JORDANIAN $
(Al Jaish St; meals JD3-5; 8.30am-9.30pm) The name of this popular local is written in Arabic but, as it's right next to the clock tower and has a huge spit of shwarma roasting in the window, it's hard to miss.

Getting There & Away

Approximately 85km north of Amman, Irbid is home to three main minibus/taxi stations.

North bus station From here, there are minibuses to Umm Qais (45 minutes), Mukheiba (for Al-Himma; one hour) and Quwayliba (for the ruins of Abila; 25 minutes) for between 400 fils and JD1.

South bus station (New Amman bus station) Air-conditioned Hijazi buses (JD1.900, 90 minutes) leave every 15 to 20 minutes between 6am and 7pm for Amman's north bus station. There are also less comfortable buses and minibuses from Amman's north bus station (less than JD1, about two hours) and plenty of service taxis (JD1). Minibuses also leave the South bus station for Ajloun (45 minutes), Jerash (45 minutes) and the Syrian border, for around 800 fils.

West bus station (Mujamma al-Gharb al-Jadid) About 1.5km west of the centre, minibuses go from here to Al-Mashari'a (45 minutes) for the ruins at Pella, Sheikh Hussein Bridge for Israel and the Palestinian Territories (45 minutes), and Shuneh ash-Shamaliyyeh (North Shuna; one hour) for between 800 fils and JD1.200.

For transport to Syria contact **Trust International Transport** (7251878; Al-Jaish St) near Yarmouk University.

Getting Around

Service taxis (200 fils) and minibuses (100 fils) going to the South bus station can be picked up on Radna al-Hindawi St, three blocks east of the Al-Ameen al-Kabir Hotel. For the North station head to Prince Nayef St. For the West station take a bus from Palestine St, just west of the roundabout.

A standard taxi fare from *al-Bilad* (the town) to *al-Jammiya* (the university) is 500 fils. A minibus from University St to the university gate costs 200 fils. Otherwise it's a 25-minute walk.

Umm Qais (Gadara) أم قيس

02/ POP >5000

Tucked in the far northwest corner of Jordan, and about 25km from Irbid, are the ruins of Umm Qais, site of both the ancient Roman city of Gadara and an Ottoman-era village. The hilltop site offers spectacular views over the Golan Heights in Syria, the Sea of Galilee (Lake Tiberias) to the north, and the Jordan Valley to the south.

Sights

Ruins ARCHAEOLOGICAL SITE
(Gadara; admission JD3; 24hr) Entering the site from the south, the first structure of interest is the well-restored and brooding **West Theatre**. Constructed from black basalt, it once seated about 3000 people. This is one of two such theatres – the **North Theatre** is overgrown and missing the original black basalt rocks, which were recycled by villagers in

other constructions. Nearby is a colonnaded courtyard and the remains of a 6th-century **Byzantine church**. Beyond this is the **decumanus maximus**, Gadara's main road. A set of overgrown **baths** are to the west.

Leave some time for Beit Russan, a former residence of an Ottoman governor and now a **museum** (admission free; ⏲8am-5pm Oct-Apr, to 6pm May-Sep). It is set around an elegant and tranquil courtyard. The main mosaic on display (dating from the 4th century and found in one of the tombs) contains the names of early Christian notables and is a highlight, as is the headless, white marble statue of the Hellenic goddess Tyche, which was found sitting in the front row of the west theatre.

Surrounding the museum are the ruins of the **Ottoman village** dating from the 18th and 19th centuries and also known as the acropolis.

Sleeping & Eating

Umm Qais Hotel HOTEL $

(☎7500080; www.umqaishotel.com; s/d/tr from JD15/30/40) With modest rooms above a bakery (guess where bread for breakfast comes from), and a stone's throw from the ruins, this family-run hotel makes up for the lack of attractions with hearty hospitality.

TOP CHOICE **Umm Qais Resthouse** JORDANIAN $$

(☎7500555; meals JD5-10; ⏲10am-7pm, to 10pm Jun-Sep; 🖉) Without doubt, one of the best parts of the Umm Qais site is pausing to have a mint and lemon at the Umm Qais Resthouse, perched atop a small hill in the heart of the ruins, inside a converted Ottoman house. The restaurant is part of a famed consortium of top-notch restaurants in Jordan and offers an impressive seasonal menu highlighting fresh produce, local wines and locally raised meats.

Getting There & Away

Minibuses leave Irbid's North bus station for Umm Qais (800 fils; 45 minutes) on a regular basis. There's no direct transport from Amman. To continue to Pella on public transport, you'll have to backtrack to Irbid.

DEAD SEA & THE WEST

There are several excellent reasons to visit the Dead Sea region, not least for a float in the sea itself. Bethany-Beyond-the-Jordan is an important archaeological site that pinpoints a major event in the life of Jesus to a remarkably specific location on the banks of the Jordan River.

For something completely different, beautiful Mujib Biosphere Nature Reserve offers some of Jordan's wettest and wildest adventure opportunities.

Public transport is unreliable on the Dead Sea Hwy and this is one place to consider renting a car or taxi for the day. Most budget travellers visit the Dead Sea as part of an organised day trip from Amman or Madaba.

Bethany-Beyond-the-Jordan (Al-Maghtas)

المغطس

This important site is claimed by Christians to be the place where Jesus was baptised by John the Baptist, where the first five apostles met, and where the prophet Elijah ascended to heaven in a chariot. It wasn't until the

DEAD SEA FAST FACTS

» The Dead Sea is part of the Great Rift Valley; it is the lowest spot on earth at 425m below sea level and more than 390m deep.

» It is not actually a sea, but a lake filled with incoming water with no outlet.

» It is the second-saltiest body of water on earth (after Lake Aral in Djibouti) with a salt content of 31%.

» Egyptians used Dead Sea mud (bitumen) in their mummification process; the last lump of floating bitumen surfaced in 1936.

» The majority of Dead Sea minerals (including calcium and magnesium) occur naturally in our bodies and have health-giving properties.

» The Dead Sea is 3 million years old, but has shrunk by 30% in recent years (half a metre per year) due to evaporation and the demands of the potash industry, one of Jordan's most valuable commodities.

1994 peace treaty with Israel that the remains of churches, caves and baptism pools were unearthed. Pope John Paul II authenticated the site in March 2000.

Entry to **Al-Maghtas (Baptism Site)** (adult/child under 10 JD12/free; 8am-4pm Nov-Mar, to 6pm Apr-Oct) includes a mandatory guided tour. The shuttle bus makes a brief stop at Tell Elias, where the prophet Elias is said to have ascended to heaven after his death, and then normally continues to the **Spring of John the Baptist**, one of several places where John is believed to have baptised. The main archaeological site is the church complex next to the likely **site of Jesus's baptism**. The trail continues to the muddy **Jordan River**, where you too could be baptised if you had the foresight to bring your own priest.

Tours often return via the **House of Mary the Egyptian** and a two-room **hermit cave**. On the way back, ask to be dropped at the archaeological site of **Tell Elias** (Elijah's Hill), which includes a 3rd-century church, the cave of John the Baptist, baptism pools and the Byzantine **Rhotorius Monastery**.

Getting There & Away

Take any minibus to Suweimeh, en route to the Dead Sea. About 5km before the town, the road forks; the baptism site is signposted to the right. From here, you'll need to walk or hitch the 5km to the visitor centre.

A taxi from Madaba to the site, taking in the Dead Sea and Mt Nebo en route, costs around JD25. Bethany is included in good value tours of the Dead Sea through hotels in Madaba.

Dead Sea البحر الميت

05 / POP >5000

The Dead Sea is at the lowest point on earth and has such high salinity (due to evaporation) that nothing but the most microscopic of life forms can survive in it. Indeed, the only things you're likely to see in the Dead Sea are a few over-buoyant tourists. A dip in the sea is one of those must-do experiences, but be warned: you'll discover cuts you didn't know you had, so don't shave before bathing! Sadly, the Dead Sea is under threat from shrinking water levels (see p610).

Sights & Activities

The most luxurious way to swim on the Jordanian side of the Dead Sea is at one of the upmarket resorts, which cost from JD25 (weekday at the Holiday Inn) to JD40 (at the Mövenpick Resort & Spa) for day access to their sumptuous grounds, private beaches and swimming pools.

The resorts and public areas are very busy on Fridays – useful for finding a ride back to Amman if you missed the last bus. Take lots of water, as the humidity and heat is intense (over 40°C in summer) and there's little shade.

Dead Sea Panorama Complex VIEWPOINT
(admission JD3; 8am-10pm) If you've had enough of a splash for one day and feel like gaining the high ground, hop in a taxi (JD8) from Amman Beach and visit this lookout. The **museum** (9am-4pm) and restaurant complex is a great way to contextualise the Dead Sea and admire the panoramic view.

Beaches

Amman Beach PUBLIC BEACH
(adult/child JD15/10; 9am-8pm) Most budget visitors head here, about 2km south of the resorts. The landscaped grounds include a clean beach, sun umbrellas and freshwater showers. The vibrant local atmosphere makes it a great place to strike up a conversation with a Jordanian family. Locals generally swim fully clothed, though foreigners shouldn't feel uncomfortable here in a modest swimming costume. Women on their own may prefer shorts and a T-shirt.

Al-Wadi Resort FAMILY BEACH
(adult/child JD25/18; 9am-6pm Sat-Thu, to 7pm Fri) This privately run resort has a variety of water games, including a wave machine and slides. There are two restaurants (open 10am to 5pm), one selling snacks and the other offering an Arabic menu. Children are measured on entry: those under 95cm are admitted free! The resort is about 500m north of the Convention Centre at the head of the resort strip.

O Beach PRIVATE BEACH
(www.obeach.net; adult/child JD20/17; 9am-6pm) This luxury private beach, stepped down the hillside in a series of landscaped terraces and infinity pools, is a great way to enjoy the Dead Sea in comfort without having to pay for a night in the neighbouring hotels. Various packages are available with discounts on weekdays (adult/child JD15/12). There are several restaurants and bars, and a buffet at the weekend.

Sleeping & Eating

About 5km south of Suweimeh is a strip of opulent pleasure palaces that offer the latest in spa luxury. There are no budget or midrange options.

TOP CHOICE **Holiday Inn Resort Dead Sea** RESORT $$$
(☎3495555; www.ichotelsgroup.com; s/d from JD100/120; ❄@≋✈) One of the newest hotels in the area, this excellent resort will appeal to families, with its easier access to the Dead Sea. It is located at the far northern end of the hotel strip, well away from the current construction boom.

Mövenpick Resort & Spa RESORT $$$
(☎3561111; www.moevenpick-hotels.com; r from JD215; ❄@✈) The resort to beat, with Moroccan kasbah-style luxury accommodation, tennis courts, the gorgeous Zara spa, a fantastic assortment of bars and restaurants ,and a poolside bar.

Dead Sea Spa Hotel RESORT $$$
(☎3561000; www.deadseaspahotel.com; r from JD120; ❄≋) Has a medical emphasis in a spa offering dermatological treatments.

Kempinski Hotel Ishtar RESORT $$$
(☎3568888; www.kempinski.com; s/d from JD200/220; ❄@≋✈) The Sumerian-style Kempinski is a palace among hotels.

Getting There & Away

Buses from Amman direct to Amman Beach leave on a demand-only basis from Muhajireen bus station between 7am and 9am; the journey takes an hour and a half, and the last bus returns to Amman around 5pm (4pm in winter).

JETT buses offer a Friday-only service from Amman (JD8 return) at 8am, returning at 4pm if there are sufficient passengers. The bus leaves from the JETT office near Abdali bus station. Check with the JETT office in Amman (p292) for the latest timetable.

Unreliable minibuses from Amman usually run only as far as Suweimeh, from where you must take a taxi – if you can find one.

The best way to reach the area without a car is to go on a daytrip. The budget hotels in Amman and Madaba organise taxi tours, taking in Bethany-Beyond-the-Jordan, Amman Beach and Hammamat Ma'in for around JD55, with an hour's stop at each site.

Mujib Biosphere Reserve

محمية الموجب

The Mujib Biosphere Reserve (215 sq km) was established by the RSCN for the captive breeding of the Nubian ibex, but it also forms the heart of an ambitious ecotourism project.

There's no public transport to the reserve so you need to rent a car or take a taxi from Amman, Madaba or Karak.

BRAVING LUXURY IN A DEAD SEA SPA

Even if you're a die-hard, old-school traveller who feels that sleeping on a bed with a soft mattress is a sign of weakness, there's a certain gratification in succumbing to the spa experience. You'll be in good company: Herod the Great and Cleopatra, neither noted as wimpish types, both dipped a toe in spa waters. So ditch the hiking boots for a day, step into a fluffy bathrobe and brave the clinically white, marble entrance hall of a Dead Sea pleasure dome.

The spa experience (from around JD30) usually begins with a mint tea and a spa bag to stow your worldly goods – this isn't going to be a chlorinated swim in the municipal pool back home. You'll then be shown to the mirrored changing rooms, with Dead Sea soaps and shampoos and more towels than you'll have body to towel down. This marks the point of no-return: the silent-padding assistants waft you from here along marble corridors to the opulent bathhouses.

All the spas offer a range of cradling Dead Sea waters with different levels of salinity. There's usually a foot spa and a float in a Damascene-tiled Jacuzzi. Outside pools assault visitors with a variety of bullying jet sprays. Best of all are the little pots that bubble when you sit in them and ought to be X-rated.

Luxury of this kind is an extreme sport and by the time you reach the spa's private infinity pool, you'll be so seduced by the ambience you won't have the energy to try the saunas, steam rooms or tropical sprays, let alone the gym. Lie instead under an oleander by the pool, sip a chilled carrot juice and wonder why you resisted the spa experience for so long.

Sights & Activities

First stop is the **visitor centre** (☎07-97203888), by the Dead Sea Hwy. The easiest hike on offer is the wet **Siq Trail** (per person JD15.500); described by the guides as 'Petra with Water', this is an exciting 2km wade and scramble into the gorge, ending at a dramatic waterfall. Bring a swimming costume, towel and shoes that can get wet, and a watertight bag for valuables.

The most exciting option is the **Malaqi Trail** (per person JD64; ⏲1 Apr-31 Oct), a guided half-day trip that involves a hike up into the wadi, a visit to some lovely swimming pools and then a descent (often swimming) through the siq, finally rappelling down the 18m waterfall (not appropriate for non-swimmers or those with a fear of heights). You need a minimum of five people for this exhilarating trip.

Guides are compulsory for all but the Siq trail and should be booked in advance through the RSCN in Amman (see p291).

Sleeping & Eating

The reserve operates 15 **chalets** (☎07-97203888; s/d/tr without bathroom JD60/71/81; ❄) on the windy shores of the Dead Sea. They are very popular, so book in advance. Each chalet has twin beds, and freshwater showers are available in the communal shower block. The small restaurant serves early breakfast (7am to 8.30am) for hikers. For JD13, chalet guests can also order a lunch or dinner of chicken, salad and mezze. A share of the profits is returned to the running of the reserve.

AZRAQ & THE EAST

The landscape east of Amman quickly turns into a featureless stone desert, known as the *badia,* cut by twin highways running to Iraq and Saudi Arabia. It has its own haunting, if barren, beauty, partly because it seems so limitless: indeed this is what 80% of Jordan looks like, while supporting only 5% of its population. If you stray into this territory, you'll be surprised to find you're not the first to do so. A whole assortment of ruined hunting lodges, bathhouses and pleasure palaces, known collectively as 'desert castles', have lured people into the wilderness for centuries. Most of these isolated outposts were built or adapted by the Damascus-based Umayyad rulers in the late 7th and early 8th centuries.

Accommodation and public transport is almost non-existent out here so most travellers visit the region on a tour from budget hotels in Amman. Alternatively, hire a car and make a thorough job of it by staying overnight in Azraq.

Qasr al-Hallabat & Hammam as-Sarah

حمام الصرح & قصر الحلابات

Crumbling Qasr al-Hallabat was originally a Roman fort built as a defence against raiding desert tribes. During the 7th century it was converted into a monastery and then the Umayyads fortified it into a country estate. The site consists of the square Umayyad fort and a partially restored mosque.

Some 2km down the road heading east is the Hammam as-Sarah, an Umayyad bathhouse and hunting lodge. It has been well restored and you can see the underground channels for the hot, cool and tepid bathrooms.

From Amman's north bus station, take a minibus to Zarqa (20 minutes), where you can get another to Hallabat (30 minutes) and ask to be dropped off outside either site.

Azraq الأزرق

☎05 / POP 8000

The oasis town of Azraq (meaning 'blue' in Arabic) lies 80km east of Amman. For centuries an important meeting of trade routes, the town is still a junction of truck roads heading northeast to Iraq and southeast to Saudi Arabia. South Azraq was founded early last century by Chechens fleeing Russian persecution, while North Azraq is home to a minority of Druze, who fled French Syria in the 1920s.

Sights & Activities

Azraq Wetland Reserve WILDLIFE RESERVE
(☎3835017; admission JD8.120; ⏲9am-6pm)
Azraq is home to the Azraq Wetland Reserve, which is administered by the RSCN and good for bird-watching. The Azraq Basin was originally 12,710 sq km (an area larger than Lebanon), but over-pumping of ground water sucked the wetlands dry in the 1970s and '80s. Salt was added to the wound, quite literally, when over-pumping destroyed the natural balance between the freshwater aquifer and the underground brine.

DON'T MISS

DESERT CASTLES

There are dozens of ruins belonging to the Umayyad dynasty scattered across the gravel plains of the Eastern Desert, so how do you choose which ones to visit?

Below is a list of the main castles and a guide to their accessibility. The castles fall into two convenient sets. The most famous ones lie on the so-called 'Desert Castle loop'. These are accessible on a day trip from Amman via Azraq, by tour or by car. Individual castles can be reached with more difficulty by a combination of minibus and taxi.

The other set lies on the so-called 'Eastern Desert Highway', or Hwy 10, which leads from the town of Mafraq to the Iraqi border. These are much more time-consuming to visit.

Each of the two sets takes a long, full day to cover. You can combine the two sets by staying the night in Azraq and using Hwy 5 to cut between the two.

Set 1: Desert Castle Loop

CASTLE NAME	PUBLIC TRANSPORT?	4WD?	BY TOUR?	WORTHWHILE?
Qasr al-Hallabat (p302)	Yes	No	Sometimes	✓✓
Qasr al-Azraq (p303)	Yes	No	Yes	✓✓✓
Qasr 'Uweinid	No	Yes	No	✓
Qusayr Amra (p304)	Taxi from Azraq	No	Yes	✓✓✓
Qasr al-Kharana (p304)	Taxi from Azraq	No	Yes	✓✓✓
Qasr Al-Mushatta	Taxi from Amman	No	No	✓

Set 2: Castles of the Eastern Desert Highway

CASTLE NAME	PUBLIC TRANSPORT?	4WD?	BY TOUR?	WORTHWHILE?
Umm al-Jimal (p305)	Yes	No	Sometimes	✓✓
Qasr Deir al-Kahf	No	No	No	✓
Qasr Aseikhin	No	No	No	✓
Qasr Burqu	No	Yes	No	✓✓

Fortunately, there is hope that this once-great oasis can be restored to its former glory. Since 1994, with serious funding and a commitment from the UN Development Program (UNDP), the Jordanian government and the RSCN have successfully halted the pumping of water from the wetlands to urban centres. A brand new pipeline between Diseh (near Wadi Rum) and Amman has also helped ease pressure on the wetland springs.

Around 1.5 million cubic metres of fresh water is now being pumped back into the wetlands every year by the Jordanian Ministry of Water, an ongoing process aimed at restoring about 10% of the wetlands to their previous capacity. The RSCN has rehabilitated a small section (12 sq km) of the wetlands and the on-site visitor centre has well documented (if somewhat tragic) exhibits detailing the history of the basin's demise and hoped-for restoration.

Qasr al-Azraq CASTLE
(admission JD1, ticket also valid for Qusayr Amra & Qasr al-Kharana; ⏲8am-6pm, to 4pm Oct-Mar)
This brooding black basalt castle dates back to the Roman emperor Diocletian (300 AD), but owes its current form to the beginning of the 13th century. It was originally three storeys high, but much of it crumbled in an earthquake in 1927. The Umayyads maintained it as a military base, as did the Ayyubids in the 12th and 13th centuries. In the 16th century the Ottoman Turks stationed a garrison here.

After the 16th century, the only other recorded use of the castle was during WWI when Sherif Hussein (father of King Hussein) and TE Lawrence made it their desert headquarters in the winter of 1917, during the Arab Revolt against the Ottomans. Lawrence, who famously wrote in the *Seven Pillars of Wisdom* of the 'Roman legionaries who languished here', stayed in the room directly above the southern entrance. Unfortunately, the ancient fort was almost destroyed in 1927, following a violent earthquake, and it now requires some imagination.

Shaumari Wildlife Reserve WILDLIFE RESERVE
(Mahmiyyat ash-Shaumari; www.rscn.org.jo; ⌚8am-4pm) This reserve, 10km south of Azraq, was established in 1975 to reintroduce endemic wildlife, particularly the endangered Arabian oryx (white antelope with long, straight horns). Despite intense funding hurdles, the continuous threat of poaching and natural predators, species such as oryx, Persian onagers (wild ass), goitered gazelle and ostrich have flourished here, a testament to RSCN efforts. At the time of writing, the reserve was undergoing extensive redevelopment and was temporarily closed to visitors.

Sleeping & Eating

A string of truck-stop restaurants lines the 1km stretch of road south of the main T-junction.

TOP CHOICE **Azraq Lodge** HOTEL $$
(☎3835017; s/d from JD62/73; ❄✍) Sensitively renovated by the RSCN, this former 1940s British military hospital is run by a delightful family of Chechen descent, who serve their outstanding traditional cuisine in the on-site restaurant. There is a **handicraft workshop** (⌚9am-5pm) on site where local women craft (and sell) painted ostrich eggs and traditional textiles.

Al-Azraq Resthouse HOTEL $$
(☎3834006; s/d/tr incl breakfast from JD40/52/65; ❄≋) This poorly maintained hotel features unkempt rooms in need of maintenance, but is a port in a storm if needed. Located about 2km north of the Azraq T-junction and 1.5km along a local track.

Zoubi Hotel HOTEL $
(☎3835012; r from JD10) This utterly no-frills, family-run budget option has seen better days, but in the absence of other accommodation it at least provides a convenient place to kip for a night. Located behind the Refa'i Restaurant in South Azraq, about 800m south of the T-junction.

Azraq Palace Restaurant JORDANIAN BUFFET $
(buffet with/without salad JD10/7, plates JD2-5; ⌚11am-4pm & 6-11pm) This is probably the best place to eat in town and where most groups stop for lunch. For a light lunch, choose the salad-only buffet.

Getting There & Away

Minibuses run up and down the road along northern and southern Azraq in search of passengers before joining the highway to Zarqa (JD1.200, 1½ hours). If you are driving, Azraq is a long and straight drive along Rte 30 from Zarqa.

Qusayr Amra قصر عمرا

One of the best-preserved desert buildings of the Umayyads, the Unesco World Heritage Site of **Qusayr Amra** (admission JD1, ticket also valid for Qsar al-Azraq & Qasr al-Kharana; ⌚8am-6pm May-Sep, to 4pm Oct-Apr) is the highlight of a trip into the Eastern Desert. Part of a much greater complex that served as a caravanserai, bathhouse and hunting lodge, the *qusayr* (little castle) is famous for its rather risqué 8th-century frescoes of wine, women and wild times. That said, the information boards in the visitor centre at Qusayr Amra delightfully assure the visitor that 'none of the paintings of Qusayr Amra portray scenes of unbridled loose-living or carryings-on'.

Qusayr Amra is on the main road, 26km from Azraq, southwest of the junctions of Hwys 30 and 40. From Azraq, take a minibus towards Zarqa as far as the junction, then you'll have to hitch as buses won't stop on the main road. Alternatively, charter a taxi from Azraq on a combined visit with Qasr al-Kharana, which is along the same road, closer to Amman.

Qasr al-Kharana قصر الضرانه

Located in the middle of a vast treeless plain, this mighty **fortress** (admission JD1, ticket also valid for Qusayr Amra & Qasr Al-Azraq; ⌚8am-6pm May-Sep, to 4pm Oct-Apr) was most likely the inspiration for the 'desert castles' moniker. The intimidating two-storey structure is marked by round, defensive towers and narrow windows that appear to be arrow slits. If you take a closer look, however, you'll soon realise that the towers are completely solid, which means that they couldn't be manned by armed soldiers. Furthermore, it would be impossible to fire bows from the bizarrely shaped 'arrow slits', meaning that they most likely served as air and light ducts.

The origins of the building are something of a mystery: it was built either by the Romans or Byzantines, although what you see today is the result of renovations carried out by the Umayyads in AD 710. Around 60 labyrinthine rooms surround the central courtyard, suggesting that the building may have been used as a meeting place for the Damascus elite and local Bedouin.

You'll need a taxi to reach this site. The complex is only signposted coming from Amman, so if you're coming from Azraq, keep an eye out for the nearby communication masts that disappointingly blight the site.

Umm al-Jimal أم الجمال

The atmospheric, ruined basalt city of **Umm al-Jimal** (Mother of Camels; admission free; ⏲daylight hr), only 10km from the Syrian border, is known by archaeologists as the 'Black Gem of the Desert'. It is thought to have been founded around the 2nd century AD and to have formed part of the defensive line of Rome's Arab possessions. It continued to flourish into Umayyad times as a city of 3000 inhabitants, but was destroyed by an earthquake in AD 747. Much of what remains is urban (as opposed to monumental) architecture, including houses, reservoirs, various churches, a Roman barracks and the impressive **Western Church**.

It's possible to see Umm al-Jimal on a day trip from Amman. Take a local minibus from Raghadan station to Zarqa (20 minutes), a minibus from there to Mafraq (45 minutes) and then another minibus 20km on to the ruins (20 minutes).

MADABA & THE KING'S HIGHWAY

الطريق الملوكي & مادبا

Of Jordan's three highways (only one of which is a dual carriageway) running from north to south, the King's Highway is by far the most interesting and picturesque, with a host of attractions lying on the road or nearby. The highway connects the mosaic town of Madaba to the pink city of Petra via Crusader castles, Roman forts, biblical sites, a windswept Nabataean temple and some epic landscapes – including the majestic Wadi Mujib and a gem of a nature reserve at Dana.

Unfortunately, public transport along the King's Highway is patchy and stops altogether at Wadi Mujib, between Dhiban and Ariha; you can either take a private vehicle for part of the way or try to hitch. Alternatively, the Palace Hotel (p283) in Amman and budget hotels in Madaba can organise transport along the highway.

Madaba مادبا

☎05 / POP 152,900

The relaxed market town of Madaba is best known for a collection of superb, Byzantine-era mosaics. The most famous of these is the mosaic map on the floor of St George's Church, but there are many others carpeting different parts of the town, many of which are even more complete and vibrant in colour. Look for the chicken – there's one in most mosaics, and trying to spot it may save 'mosaic-fatigue' syndrome.

One third of Madaba's population is Christian (the other two-thirds are Muslim), making it one of the largest Christian communities in Jordan. The town's long tradition of religious tolerance is joyfully – and loudly – expressed on Fridays. This is one day when you shouldn't expect a lie-in: the imam summons the faithful before dawn, then the carillon bells get the Orthodox

TOURING THE DESERT CASTLES

Jumping on an organised tour of the desert castles from Amman makes a lot of sense, especially if you're short of time or on a tight budget. Tours can be arranged at the Palace, Farah and Cliff hotels in Amman (see p283), which charge about JD15 to JD20 per person for a full-day trip. You're unlikely to get a better deal by negotiating directly with the driver of a service taxi or private taxi in Amman, and regular taxi drivers are rarely keen on leaving the city. Tours, which can also be arranged from the Black Iris and Mariam hotels in Madaba, usually encompass the big three – Al-Azraq, Amra and al-Kharana.

Christians out of bed, and finally Mammon gets a look-in with the honks and groans of traffic.

Madaba is worth considering as an alternative place to stay to Amman: Madaba is far more compact, has excellent hotels and restaurants, and is less than an hour by regular public transport from the capital. Madaba is also a good base for exploring the Dead Sea, Bethany and other sites such as Mt Nebo, Mukawir and Hammamat Ma'in.

Sights

Admission for the Archaeological Park, the Church of the Apostles and Madaba Museum is a combination ticket (JD2) covering all three sites.

Mosaic Map MOSAIC
(Talal St; admission JD1; ⏲8am-5pm Sat-Thu Nov-Mar, 8am-6pm Sat-Thu Apr-Oct, 9.30am-5pm Fri year-round) Madaba's most famous site is the Mosaic Map, located in the 19th-century Greek Orthodox St George's Church. In 1884 Christian builders came across the remnants of an old Byzantine church on the site of their new construction. Among the rubble, having survived wilful destruction, fire and neglect, the mosaic they discovered had extraordinary significance: to this day, it represents the oldest map of Palestine in existence and provides many historical insights into the region.

The mosaic was crafted in AD 560 and has 157 captions (in Greek) depicting all the major biblical sites of the Middle East from Egypt to Palestine. It was originally around 15m to 25m long and 6m wide, and once contained more than two million pieces. Although much of the mosaic has been lost, enough remains to sense the majesty of the whole.

FREE **Shrine of the Beheading of John the Baptist (Latin Church)** CHURCH
(Talal St; ⏲9am-5pm) This operational early 20th-century Roman Catholic Church has recently been transformed by the restoration of the ancient sites upon which the church sits. The real gem of the complex is the **Acropolis Museum**, housed in the ancient, vaulted underbelly of the church. Here, an ancient well dating to the Moabite era, 3000 years ago, is still operational. Spare some time and energy to scale the **belfry** for the best panorama in Madaba.

Archaeological Park ARCHAELOGICAL SITE
(Abu Bakr as-Seddiq St; combined ticket JD2; ⏲8am-4pm Oct-Apr, to 5pm May-Sep) This park includes exceptional mosaics from all around the Madaba area. The large roofed structure in front as you enter contains the **Hippolytus Hall**, a former Byzantine villa with some superb classical mosaics (the upper image shows a topless Aphrodite sitting next to Adonis and spanking a naughty winged Eros). The other half of the structure is the 6th-century **Church of the Virgin Mary**. There are also remains of a Roman road.

Church of the Apostles ARCHAELOGICAL SITE
(King's Highway; combined ticket JD2; ⏲9am-4pm Oct-Apr, 8am-5pm May-Sep) Has a remarkable mosaic dedicated to the 12 apostles. The central portion shows a vivid representation of the sea, surrounded by fish and a comical little octopus.

Madaba Museum MUSEUM
(Haya Bint Al-Hussin St; combined ticket JD2; ⏲8am-5pm Oct-Apr, to 7pm May-Sep) Housed in several old Madaba residences, this museum contains a number of ethnographic exhibits and some more good mosaics.

Sleeping

TOP CHOICE **Black Iris Hotel** GUESTHOUSE $
(☎3241959; www.blackirishotel.com; near Al-Mouhafada Circle; s/d/tr JD22/30/40; 📶) For a 'home away from home' feeling, it's hard to beat this popular hotel run by one of Madaba's Christian families. The rooms are cosy and there's a spacious sitting area. It's a good bet for women travelling alone. The hotel is easy to spot from Al-Mouhafada Circle.

Mariam Hotel HOTEL $$
(☎3251529; www.mariamhotel.com; Aisha Umm al-Mumeneen St; s/d/tr/q JD30/40/48/60; ❄@📶🏊) Excellent facilities include a bar and a cheerful communal lobby. Ask Charl, the owner, about a trip to see the local dolmens – neolithic structures with a stone slab supported by two stone uprights, most probably used as burial chambers – a subject he is knowledgeable and passionate about.

Queen Ayola Hotel HOTEL $
(☎3244087; www.queenayolahotel.com; Talal St; s/d/tr JD20/25/30, s/d without bathroom JD10/18; 📶) A cosmopolitan Russian-speaking owner has transformed this former dive into one of the most happening places in town. With a bar offering happy hour and serving excel-

lent food, the hotel looks set to become a favourite with travellers.

Mosaic City Hotel HOTEL $$
(☎3251313; www.mosaiccityhotel.com; Yarmouk St; s/d JD32/44, extra bed JD15; ❄) This attractive, 21-room hotel is a welcome new addition to Madaba's midrange accommodation. Some of the bright and spacious rooms have balconies overlooking lively Yarmouk St.

St George's Church Pilgrim House GUESTHOUSE $
(☎/fax 3253701; pilgrimshousemadaba@gmail.com; Talal St; s/d/tr JD25/35/45, 📶) For a charactreful place to stay, consider this pilgrim house, attached to St George's Church. Rooms are ascetically simple.

Moab Land Hotel GUESTHOUSE $
(☎/fax 3251318; moabland_hotel@orange.jo; Talal St; s/d/tr JD30/35/40) With grand views of St George's Church and beyond, this family-run hotel couldn't be more central. The reception is on the upper floor.

Madaba Inn Hotel HOTEL $$
(☎3259003; www.madaba-inn.com; Talal St; s/d/tr JD45/70/80; ❄@📶) Though needing refurbishment, this 33-room hotel is in a good central position and has car parking. Wi-fi is restricted to the lobby.

Madaba Hotel GUESTHOUSE $
(☎/fax 3240643; Al-Jame St; s/d/tr from JD18/25/35, without bathroom JD15/20/30) This central, eight-room family-run guesthouse has had a recent makeover but is still on the spartan side with dorm-style beds.

Eating

For freshly baked Arabic bread, head for the ovens opposite the Church of the Apostles. There are several grocery stores in town.

TOP CHOICE **Haret Jdoudna Complex** JORDANIAN $$
(Talal St; mains JD8-15; ⏰noon-midnight; 🖉) Popular with locals and discerning diners from Amman, and set in one of Madaba's restored old houses, this restaurant is a Madaba favourite. Sit indoors by a roaring fire in winter or in the shaded courtyard in summer and sample the traditional Jordanian dishes. Buy a souvenir of a good night out from the handicraft shop within the complex and you'll have the added satisfaction of contributing to a good cause.

Adonis Restaurant & Cafe JORDANIAN $$
(jehadalamat@yahoo.com; Ishac Al Shuweihat St; mixed grill JD6; ⏰11am-2am) Housed in a beautifully restored typical Madaba residence, and run by one of the town's returning sons, this excellent restaurant has quickly become established as the place to be on weekends.

Ayola Coffeeshop & Bar CAFE $
(ayola@hotmail.com; Talal St; snacks around JD2; ⏰8am-11pm; 📶🖉) If you want a toasted sandwich (JD2), Turkish coffee (JD1), glass of arak with locals, or a comfortable perch on which to while away some time with fellow travellers, this is the place to come.

Bowabit Restaurant CAFE $$
(www.bowabitmadaba.com; Talal St; mains JD7.500; ⏰10am-midnight) With two tables overhanging the road opposite St George's Church, photographs of old Madaba on the wall and excellent Italian-style coffee (cappuccino JD3), this is a number-one place to relax after strolling round town.

Dardasheh Restaurant & Bar CAFE $
(Al-Hassan bin Ali St; snacks JD2.500; 📶) A cosy and cosmopolitan atmosphere and wi-fi help make this central venue a popular meeting point for travellers.

Information

All the town's half-dozen banks can change money and have ATMs.

Tour.Dot Internet (Talal St, per hr 500 fils; ⏰9am-2am) Among Madaba's better internet cafes.

VOLUNTARY WORK

For those who like Madaba well enough to stay, there's an opportunity to teach English at the **New Orthodox School** (☎3250636; diodoros@orange.jo) that makes for an excellent gap-year experience. Run by Father Innocent (self-confessedly 'Innocent by name, Guilty by every other means') and attached to St George's Church, the not-for-profit school promotes 'mutual respect and peaceful coexistence' among youngsters of different religious communities. Volunteers receive free accommodation, pocket money and private Arabic lessons.

Visitor centre (Abu Bakr as-Seddiq St; ⌚8am-5.30pm Oct-Apr, to 6pm May-Sep) A good place to begin a visit to Madaba. The well-run centre has a wide selection of free brochures, various displays, culturally revealing exhibits, helpful staff and clean toilets.

Getting There & Away

The bus station is about 15 minutes' walk east of the town centre, on the King's Highway.

Amman From Muhajireen, the south (Wahadat) and the north (Tabarbour) bus stations in Amman, there are regular buses and minibuses (between 500 fils and 750 fils, one hour) throughout the day for Madaba. Minibuses return to Amman until around 8pm (earlier on Friday). Taxis cost JD12 during the day, JD15 at night.

Petra The Black Iris and the Mariam Hotel can arrange transport to Petra via the King's Highway (from around JD18 per person, minimum three people) and to the Dead Sea (JD28).

There is no public transport to Karak along the King's Highway.

Around Madaba

MT NEBO جبل نيبو

Mt Nebo, on the edge of the East Bank plateau and 9km from Madaba, is where Moses is said to have seen the Promised Land. He then died (aged 120!) and was buried in the area, although the exact location of the burial site is the subject of conjecture.

The entrance to the **complex** (admission JD1; ⌚8am-4pm Oct-Apr, to 6pm May-Sep) is clearly visible on the Madaba–Dead Sea road. The first church was built on the site in the 4th century AD, but most of the **Moses Memorial Church** you'll see today was built in the 6th century. The impressive main-floor mosaic measures about 9m by 3m, and is magnificently preserved. It depicts hunting and herding scenes interspersed with an assortment of African fauna, including a zebu (humped ox), lions, tigers, bears, boars, zebras, an ostrich on a leash, and a camel-shaped giraffe. The inscription below names the artist. Even to the untrained eye, it's clear that this is a masterpiece.

The church is likely to be closed until 2014 for refurbishment, but it's worth coming to the **lookout**: the views across the valleys to the Dead Sea, Jericho, the Jordan Valley and the spires of Jerusalem are superb, especially on a cold day in winter when it is crystal clear.

Alternatively, come for lunch at **Nebo Restaurant & Terrace** (buffet JD10; ⌚11.30am-6pm Sat-Thu, till late Fri). This stylish new venture, with panoramic windows and a roof terrace, has its own ovens for fresh Arabic bread.

From Madaba, shared taxis run to the village of Fasiliyeh, 3km before Mt Nebo (JD1.500). For an extra JD1 or so the driver will drop you at Mt Nebo. A return taxi, with about 30 minutes to look around, shouldn't cost more than JD8 per vehicle.

HAMMAMAT MA'IN (ZARQA MA'IN)

حمامات ماعين (زرقاء ماعين)

Drive anywhere in the hills above the Dead Sea and you'll notice occasional livid green belts of vegetation, a curtain of ferns across a disintegrating landscape of sulphurous rock, a puff of steam and the hiss of underground water. In fact, the hills are alive with the sound of thermal springs – there are about 60 of them suppurating below the surface and breaking ground with various degrees of violence.

The most famous of these is **Hammamat Ma'in** (admission per person JD15; ⌚9am-9pm) in Wadi Zarqa Ma'in. Developed into a hot-springs resort, the water at the bottom of the wadi ranges from a pleasant 45°C to a blistering 60°C and contains potassium, magnesium and calcium, among other minerals. The water tumbles off the hillside in a series of waterfalls and less assuming trickles, and is collected in a variety of pools for public bathing.

The entrance fee permits use of the Roman baths, the family pool at the base of the waterfall closest to the entrance, and the swimming pool. It also includes a sandwich and a cold drink from the complex shop. The valley is overrun with people on Fridays during the spring and autumn seasons.

The exquisite little **Six Senses Spa** (www.sixsenses.com; ⌚9am-8pm) offers a range of different treatments and experiences. There are two thermal pools naturally hovering at 42°C and a natural sauna cave (65°C to 70°C) buried discreetly in the heart of the wadi. Stay at the adjacent **Evason Ma'In Hotsprings Six Senses Spa Resort** (☎3245500; www.sixsenses.com/evason-ma-in; s/d JD150/170 ❄@≋✓), shaded with mature trees and made characterful with extravagant Arabesque features, and you can make a weekend of it.

A taxi from Madaba costs about JD15/25 (one-way/return) including about an hour's waiting time at the springs.

Machaerus (Mukawir)

مكاريوس (مكاور)

05 / POP >5000

Just beyond the village of Mukawir is the spectacular 700m-high hilltop perch of **Machaerus** (JD1.500; daylight hr), the castle of Herod the Great. The ruins themselves are only of moderate interest, but the setting is breathtaking and commands great views out over the surrounding hills and the Dead Sea.

Machaerus is known to the locals as Qala'at al-Meshneq (Gallows Castle). The ruins consist of the palace of Herod Antipas, a huge cistern, the low-lying remains of the baths, and defensive walls. Machaerus is renowned as the place where John the Baptist was beheaded by Herod Antipas, the successor to Herod the Great, at the request of the seductive dancer Salome. The castle is about 2km past the village and easy to spot.

In Mukawir village, by the side of the road leading to the castle, is a weaving centre and gallery. This women's cooperative is run from the **Bani Hamida Centre** (www.jordanriver.jo; 8am-3pm Sun-Thu), where some of the gorgeous, colourful woven rugs and cushions are on sale. Profits are returned to the cooperative and make a substantial difference to local Bedouin lives.

From Madaba, minibuses (600 fils, one hour) go to the village of Mukawir four or five times a day (the last around 5pm). Unless you have chartered a taxi from Madaba, you'll probably need to walk the remaining 2km (downhill most of the way). However, your minibus driver may, if you ask nicely and sweeten the request with a tip, take you the extra distance.

Wadi Mujib

وادي الموجيب

Stretching across Jordan from the Desert Highway to the Dead Sea is the vast Wadi Mujib, proudly known as the 'Grand Canyon of Jordan'. This spectacular valley is about 1km deep and over 4km from one edge to the other. The canyon forms the upper portion of the Mujib Biosphere Reserve (see p301), which is normally accessed from the Dead Sea Highway.

Even if you are not intending to make the crossing, it's worth travelling to the canyon rim. Just after Dhiban, the road descends after 3km to an awesome **lookout**. Some enterprising traders have set up a tea stall here, and fossils and minerals from the canyon walls are for sale. This is the easiest point on the road to stop to absorb the view, take a photograph and turn round if you're heading back to Madaba.

Dhiban is where almost all transport south of Madaba stops. The only way to cross the mighty Mujib from Dhiban to Ariha (about 30km) is to charter a taxi for JD12 each way. Hitching is possible, but expect a long wait.

Karak

الكرك

03 / POP 28,000

The evocative ancient Crusader castle of Karak (or Kerak) became a place of legend during the 12th-century battles between the Crusaders and the Muslim armies of Saladin (Salah ad-Din). Although among the most famous, the castle at Karak was just one in a long line built by the Crusaders, stretching from Aqaba in the south to Turkey in the north. The fortifications still dominate the modern walled town of Karak.

At one point in its chequered history, the castle belonged to a particularly unsavoury knight of the cross, Renaud de Chatillon.

SLEEPING & EATING IN WADI MUJIB

There's nowhere between Madaba and Karak to stay or eat, except one outpost, high on the southern wall of Wadi Mujib. The strategically placed **Trajan Rest House and Restaurant** (079 5903302; trajan_resthouse@yahoo.com; bed in shared room JD10, without breakfast JD5) is perched like an eyrie on the canyon rim, and is mainly visited for its restaurant – a cavernous grotto of Bedouin artefacts. Every day the hospitable owner, Mr Awad, and his family prepare an **open buffet** (JD10; 11.30am-4.30pm) of local fare.

The 'emergency' accommodation here is intended for those who get stuck and is basic, with curtains for doors. The Trajan is your best bet for hitching a ride across Wadi Mujib.

Hated by Saladin for his treachery, de Chatillon arrived from France in 1148 to take part in the Crusades. He was renowned for his sadistic delight in torturing prisoners and throwing them off the walls into the valley 450m below; he even went to the trouble of having a wooden box fastened over their heads so they wouldn't lose consciousness before hitting the ground.

Sights

Karak Castle CASTLE
(☎2351216; admission JD1; ⌚8am-4pm Oct-Mar, to 7pm Apr-Sep) The castle is entered through the **Ottoman Gate**, at the end of a short bridge over the dry moat. The path leading up to the left from inside the entrance leads to the **Crusader Gallery** (stables). At the end of the gallery, a long passageway leads southwest past the **soldiers' barracks** and **kitchen**. Emerging from the covered area, you will see the overgrown **upper court** on your right, and going straight ahead you will go past the castle's main **Crusader church**. At the far southern end of the castle is the impressive **Mamluk keep**, in front of which some stairs lead down to the **Mamluk palace**, built in 1311 using earlier Crusader materials. More stairs lead down to the delightful underground **marketplace**, which leads back to the entrance.

Sleeping

TOP CHOICE **Karak Rest House** HOTEL $$
(☎2351148; moaweyaf@gmail.com; Al-Qala'a St; s/d JD28/47) You won't find a more convenient bed for the night than in this characterful hotel, right next door to the castle. With fantastic sweeping views of Wadi Karak from many of the rooms, elaborate Middle Eastern–style fixtures and fittings, and an elegant if somewhat faded lobby, this hotel is a great place to enjoy a cup of Egyptian tea under the pergola.

Al-Mujeb Hotel HOTEL $$
(☎2386090; almujeb_hotel@yahoo.com; King's Hwy; s/d/tr JD30/45/55; ❄) This sprawling, three-storey hotel has recently had a makeover with all rooms refurbished. The hotel is around 5km from Karak, by the junction on the road to Ar-Rabba.

Towers Castle Hotel HOTEL $
(☎/fax 2354293; Al-Qala'a St; s/d/tr JD15/25/35) Close to the castle, this friendly budget hotel is a good meeting place for younger travellers. Don't be put off by the dingy reception area: the rooms, with their floral motifs, are clean and many open onto balconies with views across Wadi Karak.

Eating

Most restaurants are near the castle on Al-Mujamma St or near the statue of Saladin. Shwarma stands are clustered around Al-Jami St.

TOP CHOICE **Kir Heres Restaurant** JORDANIAN $$
(Al-Qala'a St; mains JD5-7; ⌚9am-10pm; 🍷) A cut above the rest, this award-winning restaurant is a surprise find in Karak. The chef (and owner), Saddam, is from Karak and he has a passion for food, reflected in the inventive menu. There are ostrich steaks (JD10) and chicken dishes prepared with local herbs (JD7). This is also the only restaurant in town selling alcohol.

King's Restaurant JORDANIAN $
(Al-Mujamma St; mezze JD2.500, mains JD5; ⌚8am-10pm) Opposite an open area called Castle Plaza, this boulevard restaurant with tables on the pavement attracts travellers at all times of the day and night.

King's Castle Restaurant BUFFET $
(lunch buffet JD10; ⌚noon-4pm) The daily buffet here is popular with tour groups.

Shehab Restaurant JORDANIAN $$
(Al-Qala'a St; mains JD6; @) This restaurant offers free internet and a free drink if ordering a meal.

Al-Fid'a Restaurant JORDANIAN $
(Al-Mujamma St; mains JD5; ⌚8am-10pm) Another popular place selling standard local fare of chicken, dips and salads.

Al-Motaz Sweets SWEETS $
(An-Nuzha St; ⌚8am-10pm) This Arabic pastry shop is a must for those with a sweet tooth.

Getting There & Away

From the bus/minibus station at the bottom of the hill just south of town, reasonably regular minibuses go to Amman's south bus station (JD1.650, two hours) via the Desert Highway. Minibuses also run fairly frequently to Tafila (950 fils, one hour) – the best place for connections to Qadsiyya (for Dana Biosphere Reserve) and Shobak. To Wadi Musa (for Petra), take a minibus to Ma'an (JD2.200, two hours) and change there. Minibuses to Aqaba (JD2.700, three hours) run about four times a day, mostly in the morning.

Tafila الطفيلة

☎03 / POP 85,600

Tafila is a busy transport junction and you may have to change transport here. Minibuses run frequently from Karak (JD1, one hour) across the dramatic gorge of **Wadi Hasa**. There are also direct minibuses to/from the south bus station in Amman (JD2.500, 2½ hours) via the Desert Highway; Aqaba (JD1.800, 2½ hours) via the Dead Sea Highway; Ma'an (JD1.300, one hour) via the Desert Highway; and Qadsiyya (for Dana Biosphere Reserve; JD1, 30 minutes) down the King's Highway.

Dana Biosphere Reserve محمية دانا الطبيعية

☎03

The RSCN-run **Dana Biosphere Reserve** (adult/student JD8.120/4.060, guests staying in RSCN accommodation free) is one of Jordan's hidden gems and is its most impressive ecotourism project. The gateway to the reserve is the charming 15th-century stone village of **Dana**, which clings to a precipice overlooking the valley and commands exceptional views. It's a great place to spend a few days hiking and relaxing. Most of the reserve is accessible only on foot.

Sights & Activities

The reserve is the largest in Jordan and includes a variety of terrain – from sandstone cliffs over 1500m high near Dana to a low point of 50m below sea level in Wadi Araba. Sheltered within the red-rock escarpments are protected valleys that are home to a surprisingly diverse ecosystem. About 600 species of plants (ranging from citrus trees and juniper, to desert acacias and date palms), 180 species of birds, and over 45 species of mammals (of which 25 are endangered) – including ibexes, mountain gazelles, sand cats, red foxes and wolves – thrive in the reserve. Dana is also home to almost 100 archaeological sites, including the 6000-year-old copper mines of **Khirbet Feynan**.

The **visitor centre** (www.rscn.org.jo; ⌚8am-3pm) in the Dana Guest House complex includes a museum, an RSCN craft shop, nature exhibits, craft workshops (closed by 3.30pm) and a food-drying centre for making organic food. This is also the place to obtain further information about the reserve and its hiking trails and to arrange a guide. Most trails require a guide costing (for a minimum of four people): JD10 per person for up to two hours, JD13 for three to four hours, JD16 for five to six hours. For a full day (minimum of 10 people), it costs JD16 per person.

Hiking routes include the unguided **Wadi Dana Trail** (14km) to Feynan Lodge, which switchbacks steeply down into the gorge (coming back is a real killer!).

Sleeping & Eating

TOP CHOICE **Dana Guest House** ECOLODGE $$
(☎2270497; dhana@rscn.org.jo; d JD80, s/d/tr/q without bathroom JD55/70/85/100) With panoramic views across the reserve and a roaring fire in winter, enthusiastic park rangers and a collection of like-minded fellow travellers, this is one ecolodge that lives up to its reputation. Run by the RSCN, the lodge is cut into the hillside with the balcony and dining-room on the ground floor and minimalist, stone-walled rooms on the floor below. Meals are shared around long trestle tables.

Rummana Campground CAMPGROUND $$
(s/d/tr/q tent incl park entry fee JD44/54/64/74; ⌚15 Mar-31 Oct) Location, location, location is what this wonderful RSCN campsite is all about. The price may seem steep given the minimal facilities, but it's worth it to wake up to the sound of Dana's copious wildlife singing in your ears. Dinner (JD11) and breakfast (included in the camp fee) are lavish affairs of freshly prepared Jordanian specialities. There's a 20% discount for students.

Feynan Ecolodge ECOLODGE $$
(☎2270497; www.feynan.com; Wadi Feynan; s/d incl park entry fee JD85/95, ⌚1 Sep-30 Jun) This one-of-a-kind ecolodge is privately run in partnership with the RSCN and only accessible on foot from Dana or by 4WD from the Dead Sea Highway. The lodge offers various activities such as encounters with local Bedouin and star-gazing.

Dana Tower Hotel GUESTHOUSE $
(☎079 5688853; dana_tower2@hotmail.com; s/d/tr without bathroom JD5/10/12, summer rooftop campsite JD2) With names like 'Flying Carpet' and 'Sunset Royal', the small, unheated rooms, some of which are decorated with

LOCAL KNOWLEDGE

MALIK AL-NANAH: ECO GUIDE AT DANA

Graduated in biology from Ma'an University, Malik Al-Nanah knows and loves the reserve's residents – like the rockmartin whose nest is attached to the lodge, a fitting metaphor for the relationship nurtured between people and nature here.

What's your favourite time of year here? All year! In summer, there's the bird migration, skies are cloudy and the sunsets are fantastic. You may see up to 40 griffin vultures and even short-eared owls.

And your most exciting wildlife encounter? I've seen wolf, wild cat and horned viper – all rare animals. But the best was probably seeing, at 5am one morning, a family of ibex.

What role does the community play? The whole philosophy of the RSCN is to protect nature by supporting local people – through employment, use of supplies and children's workshops.

Any famous visitors? Yes, the royal family have stayed here – in Room 9 – and the king sends guests here, too.

Why should people visit? Clean air, waking up early, seeing animals and hearing bird song – in short, you can learn the meaning of nature here.

What if they can't make it to Dana? Go to the RSCN's Wild Jordan Centre in Amman – we've taken nature to the city there and it's inspiring!

travellers' graffiti, are a winner with younger backpackers. Lunch and dinner of 22 dishes including chicken, salad and dips (JD5) can be provided on request.

Al-Nawatef Camp CAMPGROUND $
(☎2270413, 079 6392079; nawatefcamp@hotmail.com; half-board per person JD15) Perched on the edge of a neighbouring wadi, this camp with fabulous views comprises goat-hair chalets with comfortable beds (and balconies) and a shared shower block. Many hiking options are possible. Set your own tent up in the grounds for JD5 and order dinner (JD5) or breakfast (JD2) to suit. The camp is signposted 2km off the King's Highway, 5km south of the Dana turning in Qadsiyya.

Dana Hotel HOTEL $
(☎2270537, 079 5597307; www.danavillage.piczo.com; s/d JD12/20) This 17-room, no-frills hotel in Dana Village is run by the Sons of Dana, a cooperative that provides social programs to around 150 local residents. Meals, in a commodious dining room with en-suite *majlis* on the 1st floor, cost JD5.

Getting There & Away

Minibuses run every hour or so between Tafila and Qadsiyya (JD1, 30 minutes). The turn-off to Dana village is 1km north of Qadsiyya – ask to be dropped off at the crossroads. From here it's a 2.8km steep downhill walk to Dana village (the budget hotels may collect you). There are three daily buses to Amman (JD3, three hours); the first bus leaves Qadsiyya between 6am and 7am.

A taxi to Petra or Karak costs around JD30 to JD40.

Shobak شوبك

☎03

Sights

FREE **Shobak Castle** CASTLE
(daylight hr) Perched in a wild, remote landscape, Shobak Castle wins over even the most castle-weary, despite being less complete than its sister fortification at Karak. Formerly called Mons Realis (Mont Real, or Montreal – the Royal Mountain), it was built by the Crusader king Baldwin I in AD 1115. It withstood numerous attacks from the armies of Saladin before succumbing in 1189 (a year after Karak), after an 18-month siege. Rising above the surrounding plateau, it is an impressive sight from a distance.

Excavation on the castle's interior is ongoing and has revealed a market, two Crusader churches and, at the northern end of the castle, a semicircular keep whose exterior is adorned with Quranic inscriptions, possibly dating from the time of Saladin. The court of Baldwin I is also worth a look. The real highlight is the underground **escape tunnel** that winds down seemingly forever into the bowels of the earth, finally resurfacing way outside the castle at the base of the hill. Bring a torch and nerves of steel.

Sleeping & Eating

Most people visit Shobak en route to or from Petra but if you fancy staying over, try **Montréal Hotel** (☎077 6951714; www.jhrc.jo; r/ste JD20/38;), a comfortable hotel with a spectacular view of the castle. Alternatively, **Jaya Tourist Camp** (☎079 5958958; jayatouristcamp.yolasite.com; per person JD20) has 15 tents in a tranquil spot on high ground opposite Shobak Castle. For an interesting experience, consider staying at the refurbished caves at **Showbak Camp & Caves Zaman Motel** (☎077 7996834; showbakcavehotel@yahoo.com; per person JD12) at the foot of the castle. The caves have been in the owner's family for generations.

Getting There & Away

Occasional buses link Shobak village with Amman's south station (JD4, 2½ hours), and there are irregular minibuses to Karak from Aqaba via the Shobak turn-off (ask the driver before setting out). Either way you'll still need a taxi for the last 3km or so to the fort.

PETRA & THE SOUTH

Travel along the King's Highway and you'll notice that somewhere after Dana the character of the countryside changes. As the fertile hilltop pastures of the north give way to the more arid landscapes of the south, you suddenly find you're in epic country – the country that formed the backdrop for *Lawrence of Arabia* and *Indiana Jones and the Last Crusade*. To make the most of this exciting part of Jordan, with its unmissable world wonders at Petra and Wadi Rum, you need to spend a day or two more than the map might suggest. Find some time to hike and stay with the Bedouin, and the experience is sure to become a highlight of your entire Middle Eastern trip.

Before catching the ferry to Egypt or crossing into Israel and the Palestinian Territories, spare an evening for Aqaba, a popular night out with travellers.

Petra & Wadi Musa

بترا & ادي موسى

☎03 / POP 20,000

If you can go to only one place in Jordan, make it Petra, the ancient rose-red city of the Nabataeans – Arabs who controlled the frankincense trade routes of the region in pre-Roman times. It was rediscovered by accident in 1812 by a Swiss explorer called Burckhardt (the same chap who stumbled on the temple at Abu Simbel in Egypt). Until his momentous journey, disguised as an Arab, the neglected city, hidden deep in the rocky valleys of Wadi Musa, had escaped the attention of the Western world for hundreds of years.

For the modern visitor, as for Burckhardt, the sublime experience of emerging from the Siq (a canyon-like cleft in the rock, marking the entrance to Petra) is a hard act to follow, although there are other spectacles waiting in the wings, not least the Theatre and the imposing facades of the Royal Tombs. Magnificent as they are, these dramatic gestures of immortality may prove to be less memorable than a quiet amble through forgotten tombs, the illumination of a candy swirl of rock at sunset, the aroma from a chain of cloves, bought from a Bedouin stall holder, or the sense of sheer satisfaction, perched on top of the High Place, of energy well spent. Give it a couple of days to do this wonderful site justice!

The village that has sprung up around Petra is Wadi Musa (Moses' Valley) – a string of hotels, restaurants and shops stretching about 5km from Ain Musa, the head of the valley, down to the entrance to Petra. The village centre is at Shaheed roundabout, with shops, restaurants and budget hotels, while midrange hotels are strung out along the main road for the remaining 2km towards the entrance to Petra.

Sights

Petra ARCHAEOLOGICAL SITE

The spectacular sandstone city of Petra was built in the 3rd century BC by the

PETRA TICKETS

» The ticket office is in the Petra visitor centre (currently under reconstruction – due for completion by early 2013).

» Entry fees are JD50/55/60 for one-/two-/three-day passes (payable only in Jordanian currency). Multiday tickets are non-transferable.

» Children under 15 are admitted free.

» If you are visiting Petra as a day trip from Israel the entry fee is JD90.

Petra

WALKING TOUR

Splendid though it is, the Treasury is not the full stop of a visit to Petra that many people may imagine. In some ways, it's just the semicolon – a place to pause after the exertions of the Siq, before exploring the other remarkable sights and wonders just around the corner.

Even if you're on a tight schedule or worried the bus won't wait, try to find another two hours in your itinerary to complete this walking tour. Our illustration shows the key highlights of the route, as you wind through Wadi Musa from the **Siq 1**, pause at the **Treasury 2** and pass the tombs of the broader **Outer Siq 3**. With energy and a stout pair of shoes, climb to the **High Place of Sacrifice 4** for a magnificent eagle's-eye view of Petra. Return to the **Street of Facades 5** and the **Theatre 6**. Climb the steps opposite to the **Urn Tomb 7** and neighbouring **Silk Tomb 8**: these Royal Tombs are particularly magnificent in the golden light of sunset.

Is the thought of all that walking putting you off? Don't let it! There are donkeys to help you with the steep ascents and Bedouin stalls for a reviving herb tea. If you run out of steam, camels are on standby for a ride back to the Treasury.

TOP TIPS

» **Morning Glory** From around 7am in summer and 8am in winter, watch the early morning sun slide down the Treasury facade.

» **Pink City** Stand opposite the Royal Tombs at sunset (around 4pm in winter and 5pm in summer) to learn how Petra earned its nickname.

» **Floral Tribute** Petra's oleanders flower in May.

SAM OWEN

Treasury

As you watch the sun cut across the facade, notice how it lights up the ladders on either side of Petra's most iconic building. These stone indents were most probably used for scaffolding.

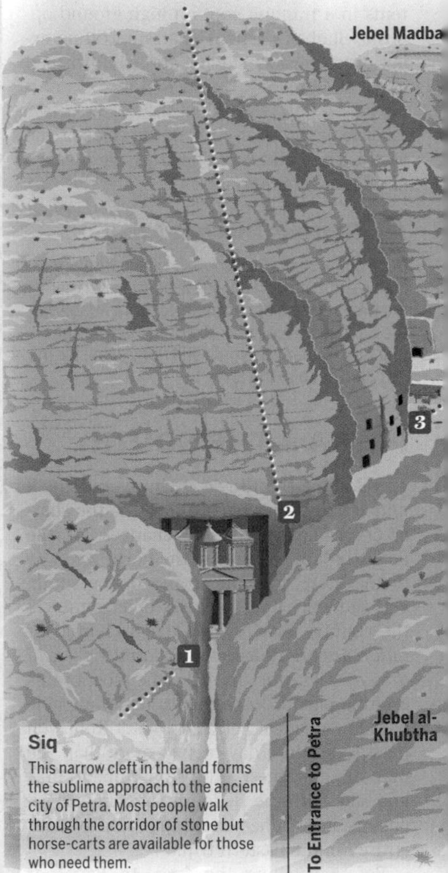

Siq

This narrow cleft in the land forms the sublime approach to the ancient city of Petra. Most people walk through the corridor of stone but horse-carts are available for those who need them.

SAM OWEN

Down Differently

A superb walk leads from the High Place of Sacrifice, past the Garden Tomb to Petra City Centre.

High Place of Sacrifice

Imagine the ancients treading the stone steps and it'll take your mind off the steep ascent. The hilltop platform was used for incense-burning and libation-pouring in honour of forgotten gods.

SAM OWEN

JENNY WALKER

Outer Siq

Take time to inspect the tombs just past the Treasury. Some appear to have a basement but, in fact, they show how the floor of the wadi has risen over the centuries.

Street of Facades

Cast an eye at the upper storeys of some of these tombs and you'll see a small aperture. Burying the dead in attics was meant to deter robbers – the plan didn't work.

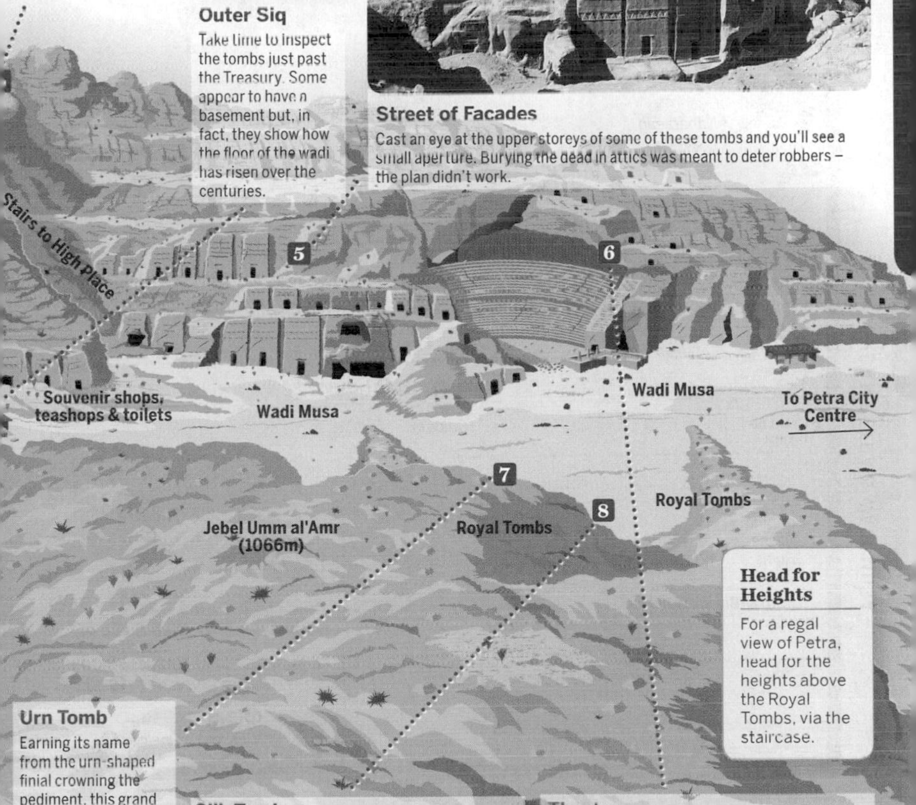

Head for Heights

For a regal view of Petra, head for the heights above the Royal Tombs, via the staircase.

Urn Tomb

Earning its name from the urn-shaped finial crowning the pediment, this grand edifice with supporting arched vaults was perhaps built for the man represented by the toga-wearing bust in the central aperture.

Silk Tomb

Perhaps Nabataean builders were attracted to Wadi Musa because of the colourful beauty of the raw materials. Nowhere is this more apparent than in the weather-eroded, striated sandstone of the Silk Tomb.

Theatre

Most stone amphitheatres are freestanding, but this one is carved almost entirely from the solid rock. Above the back row are the remains of earlier tombs, their facades sacrificed in the name of entertainment.

SAM OWEN

SAM OWEN

JENNY WALKER

Petra

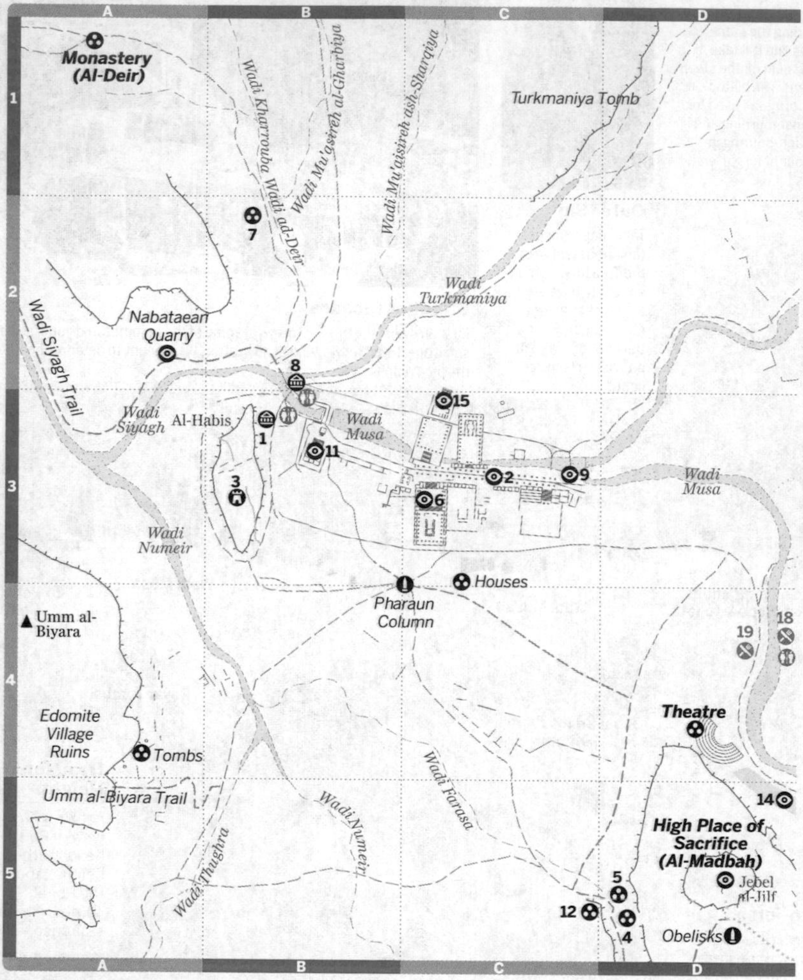

Nabataeans, who carved palaces, temples, tombs, storerooms and stables from the sandstone cliffs. From here, they commanded the trade routes from Damascus to Arabia, and great spice, silk and slave caravans passed through, paying taxes and protection money. In a short time, the Nabataeans made great advances – they mastered hydraulic engineering, iron production, copper refining, sculpture and stone carving. Archaeologists believe that several earthquakes, including a massive one in AD 555, forced the inhabitants to abandon the city.

You approach Petra through the legendary 1.2km-long, high-sided **Siq**. This is not a canyon, but rather a rock landmass that has been rent apart by tectonic forces. Just as you start to think there's no end to the Siq, you catch breathtaking glimpses ahead of the most impressive of Petra's sights, the **Treasury**, known locally as Al-Khazneh. Carved out of iron-laden sandstone to serve as a tomb, the Treasury gets its name from the misguided local belief that an Egyptian pharaoh hid his treasure in the top urn. The Greek-style pillars, alcoves and plinths are truly masterpieces of masonry work.

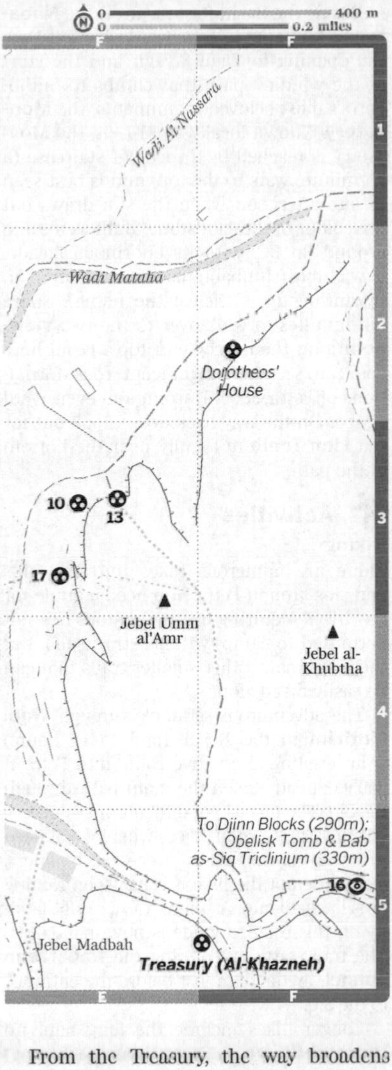

Petra

Top Sights

High Place of Sacrifice (Al-Madbah) D5
Monastery (Al-Deir) A1
Theatre D4
Treasury (Al-Khazneh) F5

Sights

1 Al-Habis Museum B3
2 Colonnaded Street C3
3 Crusader Fort B3
4 Garden Tomb D5
5 Garden Triclinium D5
6 Great Temple C3
7 Lion Tomb (Lion Triclinium) B2
8 Nabataean Museum B2
9 Nymphaeum C3
10 Palace Tomb E3
11 Qasr al-Bint B3
12 Roman Soldier's Tomb C5
13 Royal Tombs E3
14 Street of Facades D5
15 Temple of the Winged Lions C3
16 The Siq F5
17 Urn Tomb E3

Eating

18 Basin Restaurant D4
19 Nabataean Tent Restaurant D4

From the Treasury, the way broadens into the **Outer Siq**, riddled by over 40 tombs known collectively as the **Street of Facades**. Just before you reach the weatherworn 7000-seat **Theatre**, notice a set of steps on the left. These ascend to the **High Place of Sacrifice**, a hill-top altar, an easy but steep 45-minute climb. Descend on the other side of the mountain via the **Garden Tomb**, **Roman Soldier's Tomb** and **Garden Triclinium** and follow your nose back to the Street of Facades, not far after the Theatre.

Almost opposite the Theatre, you'll notice another set of steps that lead to a fine set of tomb facades cut into the cliffs above. These belong to the **Royal Tombs** and are worth a visit not just as they illustrate some of the best carving in Petra, but also because they give access to another of the city's mystic high places. To climb to the plateau above the Royal Tombs (one hour round trip), pass the **Urn Tomb**, with its arched portico, and look for stairs just after the three-storey **Palace Tomb**. If the tea vendor at the top is available, ask him to show you an aerial view of the Treasury. Return the way you came or search out a set of worn steps leading down a gully to the Urn Tomb.

Returning to the Theatre, the main path turns west along the **colonnaded street**, which was once lined with shops, passing the rubble of the **nymphaeum** en route to the elevated **Great Temple** and the **Temple of the Winged Lions** on the opposite side of the wadi. At the end of the colonnaded street, on the left, is the imposing Nabataean temple known locally as **Qasr al-Bint** – one of the few free-standing structures in Petra.

From Qasr al-Bint, the path leads towards two restaurants, on either side of the wadi. The one on the left is the **Nabataean Tent Restaurant** (lunch buffet JD10, drinks JD2; ⌚11.00am-3pm); the one on the right is the more up-market **Basin Restaurant** (lunch buffet JD17, fresh orange juice JD4; ⌚11.00am-4pm), run by the Crown Plaza Resort. Both offer a good range of salads and hot dishes. If these don't appeal, there are plenty of stalls dotted around the site where you can buy water, herb tea and minimal snacks.

Behind the Nabataean Tent Restaurant is the small hill of Al-Habis (the prison). A set of steps winds up to **Al-Habis Museum** (⌚8am-4pm), the smaller of Petra's two museums. From here you can take a path anticlockwise around the hill with fine views overlooking fertile **Wadi Siyagh**. Eventually you will come to another set of steps to the top of a hill, the site of a ruined **Crusader fort**, built in AD 1116. The views across Petra are spectacular. Allow an hour to circumnavigate the hill and reach the fort.

WALKING TIMES TO KEY SIGHTS IN PETRA

The following table indicates one-way walking times at a leisurely pace. At a faster pace without stopping, you can hike from Petra Visitor Centre to the Treasury in 20 minutes and the museum in 40 minutes along the main thoroughfare. Don't forget to double the time for the uphill return journey.

DIRECT ROUTE	TIME (MINS)	DIFFICULTY
Visitor Centre to Siq entrance	15	Easy
Siq entrance to Treasury	20	Easy
Treasury to Royal Tombs	20	Easy
Treasury to Obelisk at High Place of Sacrifice	45	Moderate
Obelisk to Museum (via main thoroughfare)	45	Easy
Treasury to Museum	30	Easy
Museum to Monastery	40	Moderate

Beside the Basin Restaurant is the **Nabataean Museum** (⌚9am-5pm, to 4pm Oct-Mar), the opening to Wadi Siyagh and the start of the winding path that climbs to one of Petra's most beloved monuments, the **Monastery**. Known locally as Al-Deir, the Monastery is reached by a rock-cut staircase (a 45-minute walk to the top) and is best seen in late afternoon when the sun draws out the colour of the sandstone. Built as a tomb around 86 BC, with its enormous facade, it was most probably used as a church in Byzantine times (hence the name). Spare ten minutes to walk over to the two **viewpoints** on the nearby cliff tops. From here you can see the magnificent rock formations of Petra, Jebel Haroun and even Wadi Araba. On the way back down, look out for the **Lion Tomb** in a gully near the bottom of the path.

Activities

Hiking

There are numerous hikes into the hills and siqs around Petra. You need a guide for any hikes requiring overnight stops (it's not permitted to camp within Petra itself), but there are many other smaller trails that can be easily hiked alone.

The adventurous scramble through **Wadi Muthlim** to the Royal Tombs (1½ hours) is an exciting alternative route into Petra if you've already taken the main path through the Siq. The hike is not difficult or strenuous, but there are several places where you'll need to lower yourself down over-sized boulders. Don't attempt the hike if it has been raining or is likely to rain. As there was a recent fatality on this route, a guide is now mandatory. The trail starts by entering the **Nabataean Tunnel**, by the dam just before the entrance to the Siq.

Longer hikes include the long haul up **Umm al-Biyara** (a steep hour each way) and the day return hike to **Jebel Haroun**, crowned with the tomb of the biblical prophet Aaron (known to Muslims as Prophet Haroun). For each of these trails, walk to the Snake Monument and ask local Bedouin for the trailhead, or follow a network of paths towards the obvious high points.

Courses

Petra Kitchen COOKING COURSE
(☎2155700; www.petrakitchen.com; cookery course per person JD35; ✉) If you've always wanted to know how to whip up heavenly

FINDING YOUR OWN PACE IN PETRA

Instead of trying to 'see it all' (the quickest way to monument-fatigue), make Petra your own by sparing time to amble among unnamed tombs or sip tea at a Bedouin stall.

» **Half Day** (five hours) Stroll through the Siq, savouring the moment of revelation at the Treasury. Climb the steps to the High Place of Sacrifice and take the path through Wadi Farasa, passing a paintbox of rock formations.

» **One Day** (eight hours) Complete the half-day itinerary, but pack a picnic. Visit the Royal Tombs, walk along to Qasr al-Bint and hike the wadi that leads to Jebel Haroun as far as Snake Monument – an ideal perch for a snack and a snooze. Save some energy for the climb to the Monastery, a fitting finale for any Petra visit.

» **Two Days** Spend a second day scrambling through exciting Wadi Muthlim and restore your energies over a barbecue at the Basin Restaurant. Sit near the Theatre to watch the Royal Tombs at sunset – the best spectacle in Petra. Reward your efforts with a Turkish bath and a drink in the Cave Bar – the oldest pub in the world.

hummus or bake the perfect baklava, Petra Kitchen is for you. Offering nightly cookery courses, a local chef is on hand to make sure you don't make a camel's ear of the authentic Jordanian dishes. The experience starts at 6.30pm (7.30pm in summer) and the price includes printed recipes. Located on the main road in lower Wadi Musa.

Sleeping

You can't overnight in Petra itself.

LOWER WADI MUSA

The following hotels are located at the bottom end of town, within walking distance to the entrance to Petra.

Mövenpick Hotel HOTEL $$$
(☎2157111; www.moevenpick-hotels.com; s/d JD155/170; ❄@📶🏊✈) This beautifully crafted Arabian-style hotel, 100m from the entrance to Petra, is worth a visit simply to admire the inlaid furniture, marble fountains, wooden screens and brass salvers. Petals are floated daily in the jardinière, while a roaring fire welcomes winter residents to the Burckhardt Library (a lounge on the upper floor).

Petra Moon Hotel HOTEL $$
(☎2156220; www.petramoonhotel.com; s/d/tr JD60/70/90; ❄@📶🏊) This newly renovated hotel is a luxurious complex with modern rooms, sumptuous bathrooms, and a rooftop swimming pool with splendid sunset views. Located on the hill behind the Mövenpick Hotel.

Petra Palace Hotel HOTEL $$$
(☎2156723; www.petrapalace.com.jo; s/d/tr JD90/120/165; ❄@📶🏊) An attractive, well-established hotel, with palm-tree entrance, big bright foyer and helpful management. The lively bar and restaurant are further drawcards. On the main road in lower Wadi Musa.

Petra Guest House HOTEL $$$
(☎2156266; www.crowneplaza.com; s/d/tr JD97/105/130; ❄@🏊) You can't get closer to the entrance to Petra without sleeping in a cave – and indeed the hotel's bar (the famous Cave Bar) is located in one. Choose from motel-like chalets or sunny (if cramped) rooms in the main building.

La Maison HOTEL $$
(☎2156401; www.lamaisonhotel.com.jo; s/d/tr JD70/80/90; ❄) The brass jardinières decorating the foyer set the tone for this good-value hotel with stylish rooms, just uphill from the entrance to Petra.

Silk Road Hotel HOTEL $$
(☎2157222; www.petrasilkroad.com; s/d/tr JD60/70/90; ❄) Hand-painted panels of Bedouin camps stretch across the foyer and restaurant walls of this old favourite, 300m from the entrance to Petra. Ask for a room with a view.

WADI MUSA TOWN CENTRE

The following hotels are near the bus station. Free transport to and from the entrance to Petra is usually offered once a day.

TOP CHOICE **Amra Palace Hotel** HOTEL $$
(☎2157070; www.amrapalace.com; s/d/tr JD44/72/84; ❄@📶🏊) This lovely hotel lives up to its name with a magnificent lobby, marble pillars, giant brass coffeepots and

Wadi Musa

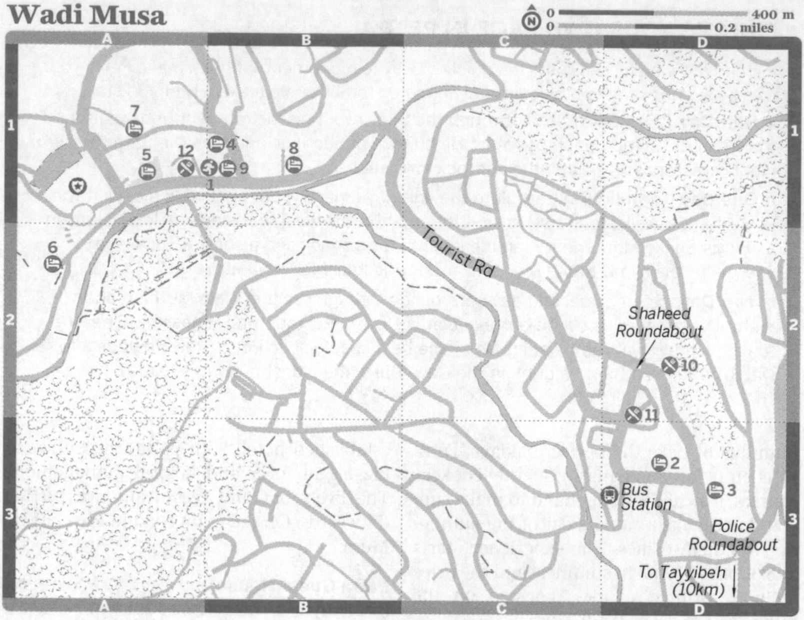

Wadi Musa

Activities, Courses & Tours
1 Petra By Night Tours.......B1
Petra Kitchen.......(see 9)

Sleeping
2 Amra Palace Hotel.......D3
3 Cleopetra Hotel.......D3
4 La Maison.......B1
5 Mövenpick Hotel.......A1
6 Petra Guest House.......A2
7 Petra Moon Hotel.......A1
8 Petra Palace Hotel.......B1
9 Silk Road Hotel.......B1

Eating
Al-Saraya Restaurant.......(see 5)
10 Al-Wadi Restaurant.......D2
11 Cleopatra Restaurant & Coffee Shop.......D2
Oriental Restaurant.......(see 12)
12 Red Cave Restaurant.......A1

Drinking
Al-Maqa'ad Bar.......(see 5)
Cave Bar.......(see 6)
Wranglers Pub.......(see 8)

Shopping
Made in Jordan.......(see 9)

Damascene-style furniture. Most rooms have views across the valley. Services include a heated pool, jacuzzi, summer terrace and excellent Turkish bath (JD13 per person). Located downhill from the bus station, with pretty gardens of roses and jasmine, this is undoubtedly one of the best hotels in Wadi Musa.

Cleopetra Hotel HOTEL $
(☎2157090; www.cleopetrahotel.com; s/d/tr JD20/30/40;) One of the friendliest budget hotels in town, with bright, fresh rooms and a communal sitting area. Located uphill from Shaheed Roundabout.

UPPER WADI MUSA

Al-Anbat Hotel II HOTEL $
(☎2156265; www.alanbat.com; s/d/tr JD20/35/45, buffet lunch/dinner JD8;) Located some way out of town, on the road between 'Ain Musa and Wadi Musa, this three-storey resort with great views offers midrange quality for budget prices. The

same friendly family run the central Al-Anbat III and the budget option next door, Al-Anbat I.

Eating

Al Saraya Restaurant INTERNATIONAL $$$
(6.30am-11pm JD18/22;) Serving a top-notch international buffet in an elegant banquet hall, this fine-dining restaurant offers quality dishes that match the general opulence of the Mövenpick Hotel in which it is located.

Red Cave Restaurant JORDANIAN $$
(starters JD1, mains from JD5; 9am-10pm) Cavernous, cool and friendly, this restaurant specialises in local Bedouin specialities including *mensaf* and *maqlubbeh* (steamed rice with meat). On the main road in lower Wadi Musa, it's deservedly a popular travellers' meeting point.

Oriental Restaurant JORDANIAN $$
(mains JD6; 11am-9.30pm) Together with the neighbouring **Sandstone Restaurant** (entrees/mains JD2/8), this main-street favourite offers simple fare of tasty mixed grills, salad and mezze with pleasant outdoor seating. Located next to Red Cave Restuarant.

Al-Wadi Restaurant JORDANIAN $
(salads JD1, mains JD4-5; 7am-late) A lively spot on Shaheed Roundabout offering local Bedouin specialities such as *gallaya* and *mensaf*.

Cleopatra Restaurant & Coffee Shop JORDANIAN $
(buffet JD6; 6am-11pm) Open buffets, with a range of Bedouin specialities. Off Shaheed Roundabout.

Drinking

TOP CHOICE **Cave Bar** BAR
(4pm-11pm;) Occupying a 2000-year-old Nabataean rock tomb next to the Petra Guest House, the Cave Bar is arguably the oldest bar in the world and invites a drink among the spirits, alcoholic or otherwise.

Al-Maqa'ad Bar BAR
(4-11pm) If you prefer your spirits *on* rather than *in* the rocks, try Al-Maqa'ad Bar. The Mövenpick hotel bar has a superb Moroccan-style interior with carved wooden grills: it's worth having a cocktail just to enjoy the ambience.

Wranglers Pub BAR
(2pm-midnight) A simple beer is at its most sociable at this pub located inside Petra Palace Hotel and decorated with assorted local memorabilia.

Shopping

Made in Jordan CRAFT
(www.madeinjordan.com) This excellent shop sells quality crafts from various local enterprises. Products include olive oil, soap, paper, ceramics, embroidery, nature products, jewellery and camel hair shawls. The fixed prices reflect the quality and uniqueness of each piece.

Information

The Housing Bank and Jordan Islamic, up from the Shaheed roundabout, are good places to change money and both have ATMs. There are a couple of banks (but no ATMs) at the lower end of town near Petra.

Petra visitor centre (Map p316; 6am-9pm) Just before the entrance to Petra, has a helpful information counter, several souvenir shops and toilets.

Rum Internet (per hr JD1; 10am-midnight) Located downhill from the Shaheed Roundabout in Wadi Musa.

Seven Wonders Restaurant (per hr JD3.50; 9am-11pm) Internet cafe near the entrance to Petra, a few doors up from the Mövenpick. Serves a luxury hot chocolate.

Wadi Musa Pharmacy Has a wide range of medications and toiletries and is located near the Shaheed Roundabout.

Getting There & Around

Minibuses to and from other cities generally leave from the Wadi Musa bus station. The station is located in the town centre, a 10-minute walk uphill from the entrance to Petra. Private (yellow) unmetered taxis shuttle between the two (around JD3).

The easiest way to find information about transport is to ask at your hotel or log on to **Jordan Jubilee** (www.jordanjubilee.com).

Amman A daily JETT bus connects Amman with Petra, largely designed for those wanting to visit on a day trip. The service leaves at 6.30am from the JETT office, near Abdali Bus Station (single/return JD8/16, four hours) and drops off passengers at the Petra visitor centre in Wadi Musa. The return bus leaves at 4pm. Regular minibuses travel every day between Amman's south bus station (Wahadat) and Wadi Musa (JD5, four hours) via the Desert Highway. These buses leave Amman and Wadi

DON'T MISS

PETRA BY NIGHT

Like a grumbling camel caravan of snorting, coughing, laughing and farting miscreants, 200 people and one jubilantly crying baby make their way down the Siq 'in silence'. Asked to walk in single file behind the leader, breakaway contingents surge ahead to make sure they enjoy the experience 'on their own'. And eventually, sitting in 'reverential awe' outside the Treasury, the collected company show its appreciation of Arabic classical music by lighting cigarettes from the paper bag lanterns, chatting energetically, flashing their cameras and audibly farting some more.

Welcome to public entertainment in the Middle East! If you really want the Siq to yourself, come in the winter, go at 2pm or take a virtual tour on the internet.

But despite the promotional literature to the contrary, silence and solitude is not what the **Petra by Night Tour** (adult/child under 10 JD12/free; ⌚8.30pm Mon, Wed & Thu) is all about. What this exceptional and highly memorable tour does give you is the fantastic opportunity to experience one of the most sublime spectacles on earth in the fever of other people's excitement. Huddles of whispering devotees stare up at the candlelit god blocks, elderly participants are helped over polished lozenges of paving stones, the sound of a flute wafts along the neck-hairs of fellow celebrants – this is surely much closer to the original experience of the ancient city of Petra than walking through the icy stone corridor alone.

Musa when full every hour or so between 7am and 4pm.

Aqaba Minibuses leave Wadi Musa for Aqaba (JD5, 2½ hours) at about 6am, 8.30am and 3pm – ask around the day before to confirm or check through your hotel.

Karak A minibus sometimes leaves at around 7am (JD3), but demand is low so it doesn't leave every day. Alternatively, travel via Ma'an.

Ma'an Minibuses leave Wadi Musa for Ma'an (JD1.500, 45 minutes) fairly frequently throughout the day (more often in the morning), stopping briefly at the university, about 10km from Ma'an. From Ma'an there are connections to Amman, Aqaba and (indirectly) Wadi Rum.

Wadi Rum There is a daily minibus (JD5, two hours) around 6am. It's a good idea to reserve a seat the day before – your hotel should be able to contact the driver. You may well be charged extra for 'luggage' (around JD3), especially if it takes up a seat that could be used for a paying customer. If you miss this bus, or the service isn't operating, take the minibus to Aqaba, get off at the Ar-Rashidiyyah junction and catch another minibus or hitch the remainder of the journey to Wadi Rum.

Wadi Rum وادي رم

☎03

Western visitors have been fascinated by the magnificent landscape of Wadi Rum ever since TE Lawrence wrote so evocatively about its sculpted rocks, dunes and Bedouin encampments in *Seven Pillars of Wisdom* in the early 20th century. David Lean's *Lawrence of Arabia,* which was party filmed here, not only contributed to the myth of the man who took part in the Arab Revolt, but also gave epic status to Wadi Rum itself.

Wadi Rum is everything you'd expect of a quintessential desert: extreme in summer heat and winter cold; violent and moody as the sun slices through chiselled siqs at dawn or melts the division between rock and sand at dusk; exacting on the Bedouin who live in it; and vengeful on those who ignore its dangers. For most visitors, on half- or full-day trips from Aqaba or Petra, Wadi Rum offers one of the easiest and safest glimpses of the desert afforded in the region. For the lucky few who can afford a day or two in their itinerary to sleep over at one of the desert camps, it can be an unforgettable way of stripping the soul to basics.

Sights

Named in honour of Lawrence's book, the **Seven Pillars of Wisdom** is a large rock formation, with seven fluted turrets, easy to spot from the visitor centre. Farther along Wadi Rum, the enormous, dramatic **Jebel Rum** (1754m) towers above Rum Village. Of the sites closest to Rum Village (distances from the Rest House in brackets), there's a 1st-century BC **Nabataean temple** (400m) and good views from **Lawrence's Spring** (3km), named after Lawrence because he wrote so invitingly of it in *Seven Pillars of Wisdom*.

Activities

There are several rewarding hikes in the area, though bear in mind that many of them require walking through soft sand – a tiring activity at the best of times and dangerously exhausting in the summer. Ask at the visitor centre for information on the three-hour loop **hike** from the visitor centre to the Seven Pillars of Wisdom and up Makharas Canyon (take the left branch of the wadi), curving around the northern tip of Jebel Umm al-Ishrin back to the visitor centre.

With a guide, you can make the excellent rock scramble through **Rakhabat Canyon**, crossing through Jebel Umm al-Ishrin.

A **camel ride** offers one of the best ways to understand the rhythms of the desert. A one-hour trip costs JD10. Full-day camel hire costs JD60 per day – see the rates posted at the visitor centre. Beware that after one hour of camel riding, most people choose to get off and walk!

For ideas on more adventurous trips, see www.bedouinroads.com.

Sleeping

There are no hotels in Wadi Rum, but camping can range from a goat-hair blanket under the stars at an isolated Bedouin camp to a mattress under partitioned canvas in a 'party tent'. Mattress, blankets and food are provided, but bring your own linen.

Some desert camps are located near the village of Diseh – clearly signposted off the Wadi Rum approach road, 16km from the Desert Highway. Hitch a ride near the police checkpoint to the village (8km – be prepared for a wait), or request someone from the camp come to meet you.

RUM VILLAGE & AROUND

TOP CHOICE **Rum Stars Camp** BEDOUIN CAMP $

(☎079 5127025; www.rumstars.com; half board in tent per person JD25) Situated deepest in the desert, this camp takes about 20 minutes by 4WD to reach. In a magnificent spot, tucked into the side of a mountain and overlooking a quintessential Wadi Rum landscape, the camp is simple but well run by Bedouin brothers who are passionate about their Bedouin heritage.

Bait Ali Lodge ECO-CAMP $$

(☎079 5548133; www.baitali.com; half board in tent per person JD35, in small/medium/large cabin 45/48/53; ❄) Tucked behind a hill, with a sublime view of the desert, this ecofriendly camp is signposted 15km from the Desert Highway. Accommodation is either in army tents or twin-bed cabins and hot water is available. Facilities include an extensive nightly barbecue and a bar.

Mohammed Mutlak Camp BEDOUIN CAMP $

(☎077 7424837; www.wadirum.org; half board in tent per person JD30) This camp is in a beautiful spot overlooking Jebel Qattar. Dinner often includes delicious lamb cooked in a *zarb* (ground-oven).

Rest House CAMPING $

(☎2018867; mattress & blankets in 2-person tent per person JD3) Only recommended if you arrive in Wadi Rum too late to head into the desert. Pitch your own tent for JD2 (includes use of toilets and showers).

DISEH

Diseh camps include the secluded, upmarket **Rahayeb Camp** (☎079 6909030; www.rahayebcamp.com; half-/full-board per person JD32/38); **Zawaideh Desert Camp** (☎079 5840664; zawaideh_camp@yahoo.com; half-board per person JD20), close to the road and accessible by car; and **Captain's Camp** (☎2016905, 079 5510432; captains@jo.com.jo; half-board per person JD35), a well-run midrange camp with hot showers, snug seating areas and good buffets.

Eating

Rum Gate Restaurant BUFFET $$

(Wadi Rum visitor centre; buffet lunch JD10; ⏰8am-5pm; ❄✓) A fine selection of dishes is offered in the buffet between noon and 4pm (popular with tour groups); outside this time, the restaurant is a buzzing meeting place for guides, weary hikers and independent travellers who congregate over a non-alcoholic beer (JD2) and a chicken sandwich (JD5).

Rest House BUFFET $$

(breakfast JD3, lunch JD10, dinner buffet JD10; ⏰7am-8.30pm) Dining here is open-air and buffet-style.

Ali's Place CAFE $

(snacks JD4; ⏰6am-1am) Tea and snacks.

Information

Admission to **Wadi Rum Protected Area** (per person JD5; children under 12 free) is strictly controlled and all vehicles, camels and guides must be arranged either through or with the approval of the **visitor centre** (☎fax 2090600;

HIGHLIGHTS OF WADI RUM

The main highlights of Wadi Rum are shown below (distances from the visitor centre in brackets):

Barrah Siq (14km) A long, picturesque canyon accessible on foot or by camel.

Burdah Rock Bridge (19km) This impressive 80m-high bridge can be viewed from the desert floor or, better still, you can scramble up to it with a guide (one hour).

Jebel Khazali (7km) Narrow siq with rock inscriptions.

Lawrence's House/Al-Qsair (9km) Legend has it that Lawrence stayed here during the Desert Revolt. The remote location and supreme views of the red sands are the main attractions.

Sand Dunes/Red Sands (6km) Superb red sand dunes on the slopes of Jebel Umm Ulaydiyya that seem to catch alight at sunset.

Sunset and Sunrise Points (11km) The places to be at dawn and dusk if you want to see the desert at its most colourful.

Umm Fruth Rock Bridge (13km) Smaller and more visited than Burdah, this bridge is tucked into an intimate corner of the desert.

Wadak Rock Bridge (9km) Easy to climb, this little rock bridge offers magnificent views across the valley.

www.wadirum.jo; ⌚7am-7pm), 7km north of Rum village.

Most people visit the desert as part of a 4WD trip arranged on arrival at the visitor centre; half-/full-day excursions cost around JD67/80. Prices are regulated, but do not include overnight stays in a Bedouin camp (around JD30 extra).

Baggy trousers or skirts and modest shirts or blouses, besides preventing serious sunburn, will earn you more respect from the conservative Bedouin, especially out in the desert.

Getting There & Away

Minibus

Aqaba At the time of writing, there was at least one minibus a day to Aqaba (JD2, one hour) at around 7am. A second one may run at 8.30am.

Wadi Musa There is a fairly reliable daily minibus (JD5, 1½ hours) at 8.30am. Check current departure times at the visitor centre or the Rest House when you arrive in Wadi Rum.

Ma'an, Karak or Amman The minibuses to either Aqaba or Wadi Musa can drop you off at the Ar-Rashidiyya crossroads with the Desert Highway (JD1.500, 20 minutes), where it is easy to hail onward transport.

Taxi

Occasionally taxis wait at the visitor centre (and sometimes the Rest House) for a fare back to wherever they came from – normally Aqaba, Wadi Musa or Ma'an. It costs about JD25 to JD30 to Aqaba, and JD45 to Wadi Musa (Petra). A taxi jeep from Rum village to the Ar-Rashidiyya crossroads with the Desert Highway costs around JD10.

Aqaba العقبة

☎03 / POP 133,200

Aqaba is the most important city in southern Jordan and, with feverish development underway, is being groomed as the country's second city, if not in size at least in terms of status, revenue and tourism potential. Perched on the edge of the Gulf of Aqaba, ringed by high desert mountains and enjoying a pleasant climate for most of the year, Aqaba has what it takes to make a major resort. That's a fact not lost on hotel chains, which continue to expand along the coast.

Surprisingly, given this radical makeover, Aqaba retains the relaxed small-town atmosphere of a popular local holiday destination. For the visitor, although there's not much to 'do' as such, the town offers a sociable stopover en route to the diving and snorkelling clubs to the south, and the big destinations of Wadi Rum and Petra to the northeast. It's also an obvious place to break a journey to/from Israel and the Palestinian Territories or Egypt.

Sights

FREE **Ayla** RUIN

(Corniche; ⌚24hr) Located along the Corniche, and incongruously squeezed between the marina and the Mövenpick Resort, Ayla is the site of the ancient port of Aqaba.

Aqaba Fort FORT
(off King Hussein St; incl Aqaba Museum JD1; 8am-4pm Sat-Thu, 10am-4pm Fri) This squat fortification, at the other end of the Corniche near to the giant flag, measures around 50m by 50m, and is unusual in having sides of slightly uneven length. The castle was built between 1510 and 1517, as attested by the Arabic inscriptions inside the monumental gateway, and was used as a khan (travellers' inn) for pilgrims on their way to Mecca.

Aqaba Museum MUSEUM
(Museum of Aqaba Antiquities; west of King Hussein St; admission JD1; 8am-4pm Sat-Thu, 10am-4pm Fri) The museum, part of the Aqaba Fort complex, was previously the home of the great-great-grandfather of the present king, Abdullah II. The collection of artefacts includes coins, ceramics and 8th-century Islamic stone tablets.

Activities

Diving & Snorkelling

According to the **Jordan Royal Ecological Society** (06-5676173; www.jreds.org), the Gulf of Aqaba has over 110 species of hard coral, 120 species of soft coral and about 1000 species of fish, with some superb sites for diving and snorkelling. Access is south of the town centre and ferry passenger terminal.

Aqaba's dive agencies are very professional. A one-/two-tank shore dive costs around JD20/40 and an additional JD12 for full equipment rental. Night dives and PADI courses (from JD300 including certification) are available.

For snorkelling, all the places listed below rent out flippers, mask and snorkel for JD8 per day. Some offer snorkelling boat trips for around JD25 per person.

Arab Divers DIVING, SNORKELLING
(03 2031808; www.aqaba-divevillage.com) Highly recommended year after year by Lonely Planet readers.

Dive Aqaba DIVING, SNORKELLING
(03-2108883; www.diveaqaba.com) A highly professional training centre known for its high-quality teaching staff.

Royal Diving Club DIVING, SNORKELLING
(03-2017035; www.rdc.jo) Around 12km south of the city, this is one of Aqaba's most famous institutions.

Aqaba International Dive Center DIVING, SNORKELLING
(079 7774211; www.aqabadivingcenter.com) Popular, well-equipped and one of Aqaba's best.

Red Sea Diving Centre DIVING, SNORKELLING
(03 2022323; www.aqabascubadiving.com) One of the most established dive centres in Aqaba.

Aqaba Adventure Divers DIVING, SNORKELLING
(079 5843721; www.aqaba-diving.com) Operates dives in conjunction with Bedouin Garden Village.

Swimming & Hammans

The cafe-lined public beaches of Aqaba are aimed at sunset strollers rather than swimmers. The Tala Bay complex, south of Aqaba features a huge sandy bay in attractively landscaped gardens, surrounded by upmarket hotels.

Aqaba Turkish Baths BATHHOUSE
(2031605; King Hussein St; 10am-10pm) Offers the full works – massage, steam bath and scrubbing – for a very reasonable JD12. Women and couples must book a couple of hours ahead.

Mövenpick Resort Hotel SWIMMING
(www.movenpick-aqaba.com; King Hussein St; day use JD40; 8am until sunset) Day use of a clean beach, three pools, health club, sauna and jacuzzi; includes a JD10 drink voucher.

InterContinental Hotel SWIMMING
(www.intercontinental.com; King Hussein St; day use JD50; 8am until sunset) Day use of beautiful gardens, pools and beach; includes a JD25 food and drink voucher.

Boat Trips

If you don't have time to go diving or snorkelling, the next best thing is a **glass-bottom boat**. Hire a boat for at least two to three hours to see the best fish.

Boats, which operate between 6am and sunset, congregate along the central public beach or at a jetty in front of Aqaba Castle. The rate for a boat (holding about 10 people) is JD15 per 20 minutes, JD25 for 40 minutes and JD35 for an hour. A three-hour trip costs JD100 and a half-day trip is around JD150. Bring a swim suit and snorkelling equipment.

Sindbad CRUISE
(2050077; www.sindbadjo.com; Marina) Operates popular cruises around the Gulf of Aqaba. Prices range from JD15 per person

Aqaba

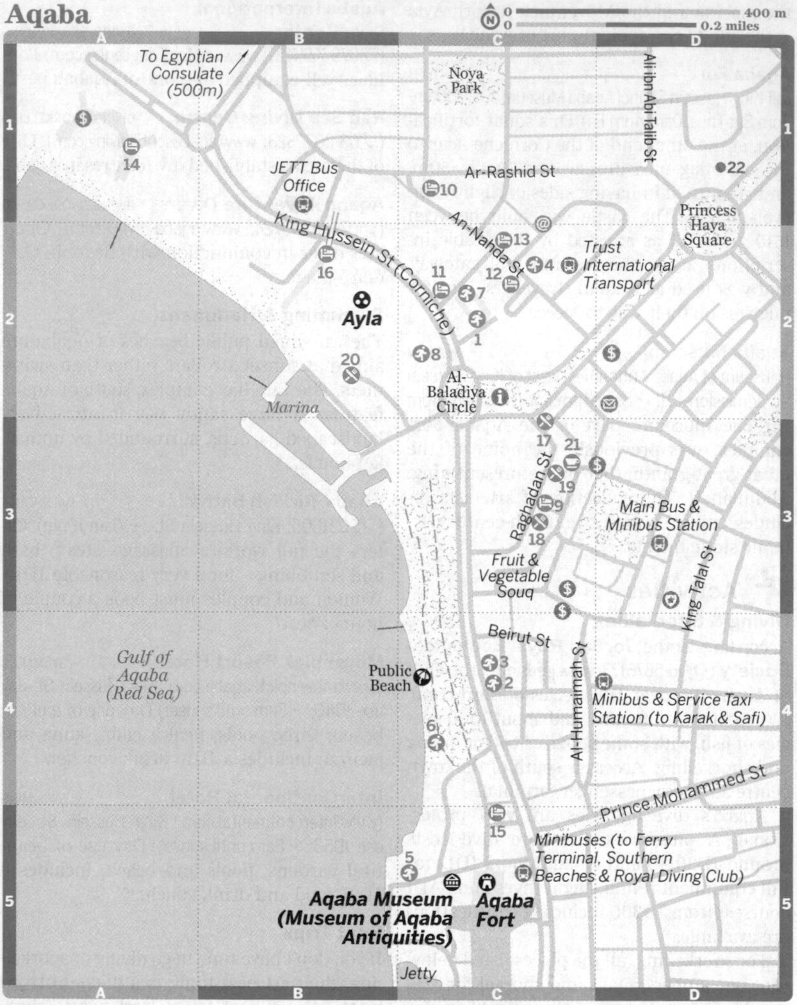

for a two-hour sunset cruise, to JD29 for a half-day trip with snorkelling (equipment included) and barbecue. The cruises operate on a daily basis and depart from the end of the pier. Make sure that you buy your ticket half an hour before departure (1pm for the barbeque trip; 6pm for a sunset cruise).

Sleeping

Unless otherwise stated, budget places listed here offer (nonsatellite) TV, air-conditioning and private bathroom with hot water (not always reliable); they don't include breakfast. Midrange places have a fridge, satellite TV, telephone and hot water, and prices include breakfast.

TOP CHOICE InterContinental Hotel RESORT **$$$**
(☎2092222; www.intercontinental.com; King Hussein St; r from US$120; ❄@≋☞) An imposing full stop at the end of the bay, the InterCon boasts less of an infinity pool than an 'infinity sea': on a calm day, the Gulf of Aqaba stretches in one seamless ripple all the way to Egypt. With exceptional landscape gardening, pools, a lazy river and a terracotta army of fully grown palm trees, the InterCon

Aqaba

Top Sights

	Aqaba Fort	C5
	Aqaba Museum (Museum of Aqaba Antiquities)	C5
	Ayla	B2

Activities, Courses & Tours

	Aqaba Adventure Divers	(see 7)
1	Aqaba International Dive Centre	C2
2	Aqaba Turkish Baths	C4
3	Arab Divers	C4
4	Dive Aqaba	C2
5	Glass-Bottom Boat Dock	C5
6	Glass-Bottom Boats	C4
	InterContinental Hotel	(see 14)
	Mövenpick Resort Hotel	(see 16)
7	Red Sea Diving Centre	C2
8	Sindbad	C2

Sleeping

9	Al-Amer Hotel	C3
10	Al-Cazar Hotel	C1
	Al-Kholil Hotel	(see 9)
	Al-Shula Hotel	(see 9)
11	Aqaba Gulf Hotel	C2
12	Captain's Hotel	C2
13	Golden Tulip	C2
14	InterContinental Hotel	A1
15	Moon Beach Hotel	C6
16	Mövenpick Resort Hotel	B2

Eating

17	Ali Baba Restaurant	C3
18	Al-Mabrouk Beach Touristic Restaurant	C3
19	Al-Tarboosh Restaurant	C3
	Captain's Restaurant	(see 12)
20	Royal Yacht Club Restaurant	B2
	Syrian Palace Restaurant	(see 9)

Drinking

21	Al Fardos Coffee Shop	C3
	Friends	(see 8)

Transport

22	Royal Jordanian	D1

has stolen the top spot in Aqaba's luxury accommodation.

Captain's Hotel BOUTIQUE HOTEL **$$**
(☎2060710; www.captains-jo.com; An-Nahda St; s/d JD75/85;) Aqaba's version of a boutique hotel, with Arabian-style furniture and massage showers.

Aqaba Gulf Hotel HOTEL **$$$**
(☎2016636; www.aqabagulf.com; King Hussein St; r JD130;) This excellent hotel was the first to be built in Aqaba and it has quite an honour roll of guests.

Mövenpick Resort Hotel RESORT **$$$**
(☎2034020; www.moevenpick-aqaba.com; King Hussein St; r from US$125;) Spread-eagled across the main road, this resort has a palatial interior decorated with mosaics and Moroccan lamps.

Moon Beach Hotel HOTEL **$**
(☎2013316; ashrafsaad77@yahoo.com; King Hussein St; s/d/tr with sea view JD18/30/35;) The best of the budget options. Most rooms have sea views and the delightful family-run management makes up for the dodgy decor.

Golden Tulip HOTEL **$$**
(☎2051234; www.goldentulipaqaba.com; As-Sadah St; s/d JD65/80, low season weekdays JD35/50;) Recommended hotel in the town centre, but beware knees and elbows in the surprisingly mean-sized bathrooms.

Al-Cazar Hotel HOTEL **$$**
(☎2014131; www.alcazarhotel.orange.jo; An-Nahda St; s/d/tr from JD35/40/50;) Faded old grand dame of Aqaba, the Al-Cazar has two dozen overgrown Washington palms in its front garden.

Al-Amer Hotel HOTEL **$**
(☎/fax 2014821; Raghadan St; s/d/tr JD20/25/30;) A quality budget option, though rooms need a repaint. If you get peckish, the Syrian Palace Restaurant is right next door.

Al-Shula Hotel HOTEL **$**
(☎2015153; alshulahotel@yahoo.com; Raghadan St; s/d/tr JD22/27/34;) Most rooms have views to the sea across the new mosque complex – good for a 4.30am wake-up call!

Al-Kholil Hotel HOTEL **$**
(☎/fax 2030152; Zahran St; s/d JD15/20, d with balcony JD25;) This very basic hotel is at least central. The low ceilings are a serious inconvenience to tall people.

Eating

Aqaba's speciality is fish, particularly *sayadieh*: it's the catch of the day, delicately spiced, served with rice in an onion and tomato (or tahina) sauce.

TOP CHOICE **Ali Baba Restaurant** JORDANIAN $$
(Raghadan St; mains JD5-12 ⏲8am-midnight; ❄✍) With its wooden awning, leafy cannas and potted palm trees, this favourite still draws the crowds. It has a large outdoor seating area wrapped around the corner facade and offers a large menu of mezze, grilled meats and fish, including *sayadieh* (JD8.500).

Captain's Restaurant SEAFOOD $$$
(An-Nahda St; mains JD8-15; ⏲8am-midnight; ❄) Serving consistently good quality seafood, including *sayadieh* and seafood salad, this is a perennially popular choice for locals with something to celebrate.

Royal Yacht Club Restaurant ITALIAN $$$
(www.romero-jordan.com; Royal Yacht Club; mains JD8-15; ⏲noon-4.30pm & 6-11pm; ❄✍) With views of the marina, this elegant, wood-panelled restaurant is the place to savour a romantic sunset and mingle with Aqaba's nouveau riche.

Al-Mabrouk Beach Touristic Restaurant SEAFOOD $$
(Raghadan St; mains JD10; ⏲9am-11.30pm; ❄) This attractive restaurant is a friendly and popular place for a large fish supper.

Syrian Palace Restaurant SYRIAN $
(Raghadan St; mains JD3-10; ⏲10am-midnight) As the name implies, this is a good option for Syrian and Jordanian food, including fish dishes. It's next to the Al-Amer Hotel.

Al-Tarboosh Restaurant PASTRY $
(Raghadan St; pastries around 200 fils; ⏲7.30am-midnight) This is one of two neighbouring pastry shops that offer a great range of meat, cheese and vegetable sambusas. Order a bag for takeaway or sit and eat them straight from the oven at the tables outside.

Drinking

Al-Fardos Coffee Shop COFFEEHOUSE
(coffee 500 fils) Just off Zahran St, this is a traditional coffeehouse where local men sip coffee, play backgammon and watch Arabic music videos. Foreign women are welcome.

Friends BAR
(upper storey, Aqaba Gateway; beer JD2.500-3; ⏲3.30pm-3am) This relaxed and friendly place, with sensible prices, is on a terrace that captures the sea breezes. Try the Dizzy Buddah (JD7); have two, and you may as well sleep over.

Information

Aqaba has a good sprinkling of internet cafes, particularly along As-Sadah St, most of which charge around JD1 to JD2 per hour. There are plenty of banks with ATMS and moneychangers around town.

10zll Internet Cafe (As-Sadah St; per hr JD1, ⏲24hr) Next to Days Inn, this large establishment has coffee and soft drinks.

General post office (⏲7.30am-7pm Sat-Thu, to 1.30pm Fri) Opposite Zahran St in the centre of town.

Tourist office (Baladiya Circle; ⏲8am-2.30pm Sun-Thu) Located in a kiosk in the middle of a new park between carriageways, the tourist office has lots of leaflets and precious little else, despite friendly staff. There's another branch inside Aqaba Museum.

Getting There & Away

For information about crossing the border to/from Israel and the Palestinian Territories, see p340.

Air

Royal Jordanian (☎2016555; www.rj.com; Ash-Sherif al-Hussein bin Ali St; ⏲9am-5pm Sun-Thu) Tickets to Amman cost JD37 one-way.

Boat

For details of boat services between Aqaba and Nuweiba in Egypt, see p340.

Bus

Ordinary public buses travel between the main bus/minibus station in Aqaba and Amman's south (Wahadat) station (JD5.500, five hours) about every hour between 7am and 3pm, sometimes later.

JETT bus office (☎2015222; King Hussein St) Next to the Mövenpick Resort Hotel. Has buses six times daily to Amman (JD7.500, four hours), between 7am and 6pm. The office is a 10-minute walk from the centre.

Trust International Transport (☎2032200; just off An-Nahda St) Has four daily buses to Amman (JD7, four hours) at 7.30am, 11.30am, 2.30pm and 8.30pm. There are also buses to Irbid (JD9, 5½ hours) at 8.30am and 3.30pm.

Minibus

With the exception of those to Karak, minibuses leave from the main bus/minibus station on Ar-Reem St.

Wadi Musa (for Petra, JD5, 2½ hours) Leave when full between 7am and 2pm; you may have to wait up to an hour. Otherwise, get a connection in Ma'an (JD3, 80 minutes).

Wadi Rum (JD1.500, one hour) Leave at around 6.30am and, more reliably, 11am. At other times, catch a minibus towards Ma'an, get off at the turn-off to Wadi Rum at Ar-Rashidiyya and then hitch a ride to Rum Village.

Karak (JD2.500, three hours) Via Safi and the Dead Sea Highway. Minibuses leave from the small station next to the mosque on Al-Humaimah St.

Taxi

Taxis can be chartered to Petra (one-way JD50, 1½ hours) and Wadi Rum (one-way JD30, one hour).

Getting Around

Minibuses (JD1) leave from near the entrance to Aqaba Fort, on King Hussein St, for the Royal Diving Club via the southern beach camps, dive sites, and the ferry terminal (for boats to Egypt).

UNDERSTAND JORDAN

Jordan Today

In the spring of 2011, Jordanians joined fellow protestors in Egypt, Tunisia, Libya and Syria in demonstrations popularly dubbed as the 'Arab Spring'. Comprised largely of young students, and peaceful in their approach, Jordanian protestors argued on the streets of Amman for higher wages and a fuller embracing of democracy. At the time of writing, the demonstrations had whittled down to a weekly gathering of die-hards after Friday prayers. Most Jordanians, in contrast, had returned to the more important task of making a living in difficult economic times.

Democratic reforms have long been in place in Jordan. In November 1989 the first full parliamentary elections since 1967 were held, and women were allowed the vote. Four years later most political parties were legalised and able to participate in parliamentary and municipal elections.

Despite these concessions, democracy in Jordan is still something of an alien concept. Perceived as promoting the interests of the individual over those of the community, it runs against the grain of tribal traditions where respect for elders is paramount. In common with other parts of the Middle East, Jordan traditionally favours strong, centralised government under an autocratic leader – what might be called 'benign dictatorship'.

Of course, benign dictatorship is only as good as the leader. King Abdullah is widely regarded both at home and abroad as both wise and diplomatic in his role – a modernising monarch in touch with the sensibilities of a globalised world, supportive of social and economic reform and committed to stamping out corruption.

History

In Jordan history is not something that happened 'before'. It's a living, breathing part of everyday life, witnessed not just in the pragmatic treatment of ancient artefacts but also in the way people live. Jordanians value their heritage and are in no hurry to eschew ways of life that have proved successful for centuries. Each period of history thus features in the experiences of a visitor, not only through a pile of fallen columns, but in the taking of tea with old custodians of the desert or the bargaining for a kilim with designs inherited from the Byzantine era.

Early Settlements

Just step foot in Jordan and you begin your encounter with history. Visit the dolmens near Madaba, for example, and you'll be entering the cradle of civilisation; dating from 4000 BC, the dolmens embody the sophistication of the world's first villages.

The copper and bronze ages helped bring wealth to the region (1200 BC). You can find forgings from Jordan's ancient copper mines in the Dana Biosphere Reserve. Trading in these metals had a cohesive impact – travel

ONE OF THE WORLD'S SEVEN WONDERS

It's official: Petra is one of the new Seven Wonders of the World. At least, that's according to a popularity poll organised by the privately run New7Wonders Foundation in Switzerland. The winners, which include Chichen Itza in Mexico, Christ the Redeemer in Brazil, the Colosseum in Italy, the Great Wall of China, Machu Picchu in Peru and the Taj Mahal in India, were selected in 2007 through a staggering 100 million votes cast by internet or telephone – the largest such poll on record.

the King's Highway and not only will you walk on the path of royalty, but you'll also see how this route helped unify city-states into a recognisable Jordan between 1200 BC and 333 BC.

Great Empires

The Greeks, Nabataeans and Romans dominated Jordan's most illustrious historical period (333 BC to AD 333), leaving the magnificent legacies of Petra and Jerash. Located at the centre of the land bridge between Africa and Asia, the cities surrounding the King's Highway profited from the caravan routes that crossed the deserts from Arabia to the Euphrates, bringing shipments of African gold and South Arabian frankincense via the Red Sea ports in present-day Aqaba and Eilat.

By the 4th century BC, the growing wealth of Arab lands attracted the attention of Alexander the Great. The precocious 21-year-old stormed through the region in 334 BC, winning territories from Turkey to Palestine and bringing access to the great intellectual treasures of the classical era.

Trade was the key to Jordan's golden era (8 BC to AD 40), thanks to the growing importance of a nomadic Arab tribe from the south, known as the Nabataeans. The Nabataeans produced only copper and bitumen (for waterproofing boat hulls), but they knew how to trade in the commodities of neighbouring nations. They never possessed an 'empire' in the common military and administrative sense of the word; instead, from about 200 BC, they established a 'zone of influence' that stretched from Syria to Rome – one that inevitably attracted the conquering tendencies of the Roman Empire.

You only have to visit Jerash for five minutes, trip over a fallen column and notice the legions of other columns beside, to gain an immediate understanding of the importance of the Romans in Jordan. This magnificent set of ruins indicates the amount of wealth the Romans invested in this outpost of their empire. It's perhaps a fitting legacy of their rule that the Jordanian currency, the dinar, derives its name from the Latin *denarius* (ancient Roman silver coin).

Spirit of the Age

Under the influence of Rome, Christianity replaced the local gods of the Nabataeans, and several hundred years later Islam took its place. The arrival of Islamic dynasties is evident from the 7th century onwards, literally strewn over the deserts of eastern Jordan in the form of the intriguing Umayyad structures that dot the stark landscape. The conflict between Islam and Christianity, evident at Jordan's crusader castles in Ajloun, Karak and Shobak, is a defining feature of the next thousand years.

British imperialism dominates Jordan's history prior to the Arab Revolt of 1914; ride a camel through Wadi Rum and cries of 'To Aqaba!' hang in the wind. And so does the name of Lawrence, the British officer whose desert adventures have captured the imagination of visitors to such an extent that whole mountains are named after him. The Arab Revolt may not have immediately achieved its goal during peace negotiations, but it did lead directly to the birth of the modern state of Jordan. A series of treaties after 1928 led to full independence in 1946, when Abdullah was proclaimed king.

Modern State of Jordan

Jordan's modern history is about independence, modernisation (under the much beloved King Hussein and his son and heir, the current King Abdullah). It's also marked by cohabitation with difficult neighbours. Much of the conflict stems from the creation of a Jewish national homeland in Palestine, where Arab Muslims accounted for about 90% of the population. Their resentment informed the dialogue of Arab-Israeli relations for the rest of the 20th century. Today, after the settlement of successive waves of refugees, the majority of the population of Jordan is made up of Palestinians.

On 26 October 1994, Jordan and Israel and the Palestinian Territories signed a momentous peace treaty, and for the past two decades Jordan has been preoccupied with its neighbours to the east rather the west – a shift in focus necessitated firstly by the Gulf War and subsequently by the US-led invasion of Iraq, which led to a further influx of refugees, this time from Iraq. Ironically, the refugees brought their relative prosperity with them – a windfall that has stimulated the economy throughout the past decade and helped turn Amman, in particular, into a cosmopolitan, modern city.

People & Society

Bedouin Roots

A strong tradition of hospitality and lively sense of humour make Jordanians easy to connect with. These are traits that belong

BOOKS ON JORDAN

Lonely Planet offers a detailed *Jordan* guide. Other key reading includes:

» *Seven Pillars of Wisdom* (TE Lawrence; 1935) Describes Lawrence's epic adventures in Jordan and the part he played in the Arab Revolt (he wrote some of it in Amman).

» *Kingdom of the Film Stars: Journey into Jordan* (Annie Caulfield; 1997) Entertaining, personal account of the author's relationship with a Bedouin man in Jordan.

» *Petra: Lost City of the Ancient World* (Christian Augé and Jean-Marie Dentzer; 2000) An excellent, portable background introduction to Petra.

» *Married to a Bedouin* (Marguerite van Geldermalsen; 2006) An idea of life with the Bedouin at Petra.

» *Walking in Jordan* (2001) and *Walks & Scrambles in Rum* (Tony Howard and Di Taylor; 1993) Describe dozens of hikes in Jordan, from wadi walks to climbing routes.

to the Bedouin tradition. In fact, over 98% of Jordanians are Arab, descended from the original desert dwellers of Arabia. Living a traditional life of livestock rearing, the few remaining nomadic Bedouin are concentrated mainly in the Badia – the great desert plains of eastern Jordan. The majority of Jordan's indigenous population, however, now enjoy the benefits of settlement and education. While many are wistful about the stories of their grandparents, they are not nostalgic about the hardships they faced.

The most easily identifiable aspect of the Bedouin inheritance is an ingrained tribal respect for local elders, or sheikhs. This characteristic is extended to the ultimate leaders of the country. Claiming unbroken descent from Prophet Mohammed, Jordan's Hashemite royal family is a nationally beloved and regionally respected institution associated with benign and diplomatic governance and a history of charitable works. Despite protests against the government in the 2011 Arab Spring, there was no popular demand for a republic.

Importance of Family

Family ties are all-important to both modern and traditional Jordanians and paying respect to parents is where the sense of obeisance to elders is engendered. Socialising generally entails some kind of get-together with the extended family, with lines drawn loosely between the genders. This is reflected in terms of physical divisions within the house, where separate seating areas are reserved for men and women.

In Jordan, a woman's 'honour' is still valued in traditional society, and sex before marriage or adultery is often dealt with harshly by other members of the woman's family. Traditional concepts of *ird* (honour) run deep but sit uneasily with the freedoms many affluent Jordanian women have come to expect, largely thanks to universal access to one of the region's best education systems. A minimum of six women MPs is guaranteed by royal decree and while only 14% of the labour force was made up of women in 1991, by 2010 (according to UN data) this had risen to over one quarter.

Urbanisation

There is an increasing polarisation in Jordanian society between town and country. In Amman, modern Western-leaning middle- and upper-class youths enjoy the fruits of a good education, shop in malls, drink lattes in mixed-sex Starbucks and obsess over the latest fashions. In rural areas, meanwhile, unemployment is high and many populations struggle with making ends meet. For this reason, economic migration is common in Jordan, and many working-class families have at least one male who is temporarily working away from home – whether in Amman, the Gulf States, or further abroad.

Religion

Over 92% of the population are Sunni Muslims. A further 6% are Christians living mainly in Amman, Salt, Madaba and Karak. There are tiny Shiite and Druze groups.

Most Christians belong to the Greek Orthodox Church, but there are also some Greek Catholics, a small Roman Catholic community, and Syrian, Coptic and Armenian Orthodox communities.

Arts & Crafts

Walk the streets of Madaba, with bright coloured kilims flapping in the wind, hike to the soap-making villages of Ajloun, or watch elderly Bedouin women threading beads at Petra, and it will become immediately apparent that the country has a strong handicraft tradition. The authorities have been quick to support this aspect of Jordan's heritage and now craft cooperatives are widespread, resulting in benefits for local communities and ensuring that Jordan's rich legacy endures for future generations. Taking an interest in Jordanian crafts, then, is not a remote aesthetic exercise – it represents sustainable tourism at its best.

Kilims

Jordan has a long-established rug-making industry dating back to the country's pre-Islamic, Christian communities. *Mafrash* (rugs) are usually of the flat, woven kind, compared with carpets that have a pile. To this day, especially in Madaba and Mukawir, it's possible to watch kilims based on early Byzantine designs being made.

Embroidery

This is an important skill among Jordanian women and most learn the craft at a young age. Teenagers traditionally embroider the clothes they will need as married women. Embroidery provides an occasion for women to socialise, often with a pot of tea spiced up with a pinch of local gossip.

Mosaic

With a noble and distinguished lineage in Jordan, mosaics are made from tiny squares of naturally coloured rock called tesserae – the more tesserae per centimetre, the finer and more valuable the mosaic. Portable pieces are available.

Copper

Some of the oldest copper mines in the world are traceable to the hillsides of southern Jordan (especially near Feynan, in the Dana Biosphere Reserve). Copper is used in everyday utensils, as well as for heirlooms such as the family serving dish or coffee pot.

Jewellery

A bride traditionally receives a gift of jewellery on her wedding day as her dowry, and this remains her personal property. The most common designs are protective silver amulets, such as the 'hand of Fatima' (daughter-in-law of the Prophet Mohammed). These are used as protection from evil spirits known as *djinn* (from which we get the word 'genie').

Food & Drink

While not as famous as the cuisine in Egypt or Turkey, Jordan nonetheless has a distinc-

A GOOD BUY

Several shops around Jordan sell high-quality handicrafts made by Jordanian women. Profits from the sale of all items go to local NGOs that campaign to raise rural living standards, improve the status of rural women, provide income generation for marginalised families, nurture young artists, and protect the local environment.

If you want to spend your money where it counts, then you may like to buy from the outlets of the following community-based income-generating programs:

Jordan River Foundation (www.jordanriver.jo) The showroom in Jebel Amman displays works from three major projects, including Bani Hamida Women's Weaving Project.

Made in Jordan (www.madeinjordan.com) Products include olive oil, soap, paper and ceramics.

Nature shops (www.rscn.org.jo) These figure prominently at the Wild Jordan Centre in Amman and RSCN visitor centres.

Noor Al-Hussein Foundation (www.nooralhusseinfoundation.org) Maintains a showroom in Aqaba, Iraq Al-Amir and Wadi Musa.

Souk Jara street market (www.jara-jordan.com; Fawiz al-Malouf St; ⏲10am-10pm Fri May-Aug) Village initiative in Amman, selling traditional handicrafts.

tive culinary tradition, largely thanks to the Bedouin influence.

The Bedouin speciality is *mensaf* – delicious spit-roasted lamb, basted with spices until it takes on a yellow appearance. It's served on a platter of rice and pine nuts, flavoured with the cooking fat, and often centrally garnished with the head of the lamb. Honoured guests are served the eyes (which have a slightly almond flavour); less honoured guests are offered the tongue (a rich-flavoured, succulent meat). The dish is served with a sauce of yogurt, combined with the cooking fat.

In Wadi Rum you might be lucky enough to be offered a Bedouin barbecue from the *zarb,* a pit oven buried in the desert sand. Another Jordanian favourite is *maqlubbeh* (sometimes called 'upside down') – steamed rice pressed into a pudding basin, topped with meat, eggplant, tomato and pine nuts.

Dessert here, as in many parts of the Middle East, may be *kunafa* or *muhalabiyya* (a milk custard containing pistachio nuts).

If you fancy learning how to make your own mezze when you get home, try an evening course at Petra Kitchen (p318).

The universal drink of choice is sweet black tea (coffee comes a close second); most social exchanges, including haggling over a kilim, are punctuated with copious glasses that are usually too hot to handle. Other options include *yansoon* (aniseed herbal tea) and *zaatar* (thyme-flavoured tea).

Bottled mineral water (JD1 for a 1.5L bottle) is widely available, as are the usual soft drinks, Amstel beer and locally produced wines.

Environment

The Land

Jordan can be divided into three major geographic regions: the Jordan Valley, the East Bank plateau and the desert. The fertile valley of the Jordan River is the dominant physical feature of the country's western region, running from the Syrian border in the north, along the border with Israel and the Palestinian Territories and into the Dead Sea. Part of the larger African Rift Valley, the Jordan Valley continues under the name Wadi Araba and extends to the Gulf of Aqaba, where Jordan claims a sneeze-sized stretch of the Red Sea. The majority of the population lives in a hilly 70km-wide strip running the length of the country, known as the East Bank plateau. The remaining 80% of the country is desert, stretching into Syria, Iraq and Saudi Arabia.

Wildlife

Spring is the best time to see some of Jordan's two thousand flowers and plants, including the black iris, Jordan's redolent national flower.

Two of Jordan's most impressive wild animals are the Arabian oryx and Nubian ibex, resident at the Shaumari Wildlife Reserve and Mujib Biosphere Reserve respectively. Jordan is an important corridor for migratory birds en route to Africa and southern Arabia.

Nature Reserves

The Royal Society for the Conservation of Nature (RSCN; www.rscn.org.jo) operates six reserves in Jordan, of which Mujib and Dana Biosphere Reserves are the undoubted highlights. The Azraq Wetland Reserve, located in eastern Jordan, is a good place for bird-watching, and the Ajloun Forest Reserve protects a beautiful area of woodland, perfect for hiking.

Environmental Issues

The RSCN has pioneered models for sustainable development and tourism by working closely with local communities and making them stakeholders in conserving local reserves. The society has also been responsible for reintroducing several endemic animals in Jordan, including the endangered oryx.

Despite these welcome initiatives, there are still major problems, including a chronic lack of water, the pressure of tourism on fragile sites such as at Petra and in Wadi Rum, and increasing desertification through overgrazing.

Solutions to these problems are constantly under review and there are ambitious plans to build a pipeline, known as the 'Peace Conduit', connecting the Red and Dead Seas to provide desalinated water and to raise the diminishing level of the Dead Sea (see p610).

SURVIVAL GUIDE

Directory A–Z

Accommodation

Jordan has accommodation to suit most budgets. Prices in this book are for double rooms in high season (September to October, and from March to early May) and include private bathroom and breakfast unless otherwise indicated.

$ less than JD40 (US$56)

$$ JD40 to JD90 (US$56 to US$127)

$$$ more than JD90 (US$127)

The **Royal Society for the Conservation of Nature** (RSCN; www.rscn.org.jo) offers some of the country's most interesting accommodation options in nature reserves. These need to be booked in advance during peak seasons (seethe Wild Jordan Centre, p291).

Holiday weekends are extremely busy in Aqaba and the Dead Sea. Outside these periods, in nonpeak seasons, you can often negotiate discounts on published rates.

Activities

Diving and snorkelling are popular pastimes in the Gulf of Aqaba – see p325 for details.

Hiking is well organised in the Dana Biosphere Reserve, Wadi Rum Protected Area and Mujib Biosphere Reserve. Mujib in particular offers some great canyoning and rappelling. Wadi Rum is the Middle East's premier climbing destination.

For details of outdoor activities in Jordan's nature reserves, contact the RSCN.

Business Hours

Everything closes Friday lunchtime for weekly prayers. During Ramadan, business hours are reduced. Few businesses or institutions work exactly the hours they advertise!

Government offices 8am-3pm Sun-Thu

Banks 8.30am-3pm Sun-Thu

Private businesses 9am-8pm Sat-Thu

Children

Children are instant ice breakers in Jordan and you'll find people go out of their way to make families feel welcome.

Avoid summer visit because the extreme heat is hard for children to tolerate. Stick to bottled mineral water, and if travelling with infants, remember that disposable nappies are not readily available outside Amman and Aqaba.

Customs Regulations

» Up to 1L of alcohol and 200 cigarettes can be imported, duty free.

» Drugs, weapons and pornography are strictly prohibited.

» No restrictions on the import and export of Jordanian or foreign currencies.

Embassies & Consulates

The following embassies and consulates are in Amman. Egypt also has a consulate in Aqaba. See p35 for an overview of visas for neighbouring countries. In general, offices are open 9am to 11am Sunday to Thursday for visa applications and 1pm to 3pm for collecting visas.

Australia (☎06-5807000; www.jordan.embassy.gov.au; 3 Youssef Abu Shahhout, Deir Ghbar)

Canada (☎06-5203300; www.canadainternational.gc.ca/jordan; Abdul Hameed Shoman St, Shmeisani)

Egypt Consulate (off Map p326; ☎03-2016171; cnr Al-Isteglal & Al-Akhatal Sts, Aqaba; ⊙8am-3pm Sun-Thu) Embassy (☎06-5605175; fax 5604082; 22 Qortubah St, Jebel Amman; ⊙9am-noon Sun-Thu) Between 4th and 5th circles.

France (Map p288; ☎06-4604630; www.ambafrance-jo.org; Al-Mutanabbi St, Jebel Amman)

PRACTICALITIES

» For a newspaper, try the *Jordan Times* (www.jordantimes.com).

» For radio, try Radio Jordan (96.3 FM) or the BBC World Service (1323 AM).

» International Student Identity Card (ISIC) allows discounts at some tourist sites; university ID cards are not accepted.

» Jordan's electricity supply is 220V, 50 AC. Sockets are mostly of a local two-pronged variety, although some places use European two-pronged and British three-pronged sockets.

» Laws banning smoking in public places are rarely enforced. Top-end hotels reserve a few non-smoking rooms, but in all other public places, including buses and taxis, smoking is commonplace.

» Jordan uses the metric system.

Germany (Map p288; ☎06 5930367; www.amman.diplo.de; 31 Bin Ghazi St, Jebel Amman) Between 4th and 5th circles.

Iraq (Map p288; ☎06-4623175; fax 4619172; Al-Kulliyah al-Islamiyah St, Jebel Amman) Near the 1st circle.

Ireland Honorary Consulate (☎06-625632; King Hussein St, Jebel Amman)

Israel Consulate (☎06-5503529; Maysaloon St, Shmeisani)

Lebanon (Map p288; ☎06-5929111; fax 5929113; Al-Neel St, Abdoun) Near the UK embassy.

Netherlands (Map p288; ☎06-5902200; www.netherlandsembassy.com.jo; 22 Ibrahim Ayoub St) Near the 4th circle.

New Zealand Consulate (off Map p284; ☎06-4636720; fax 4634349; 99 Al-Malek al-Hussein St, Downtown) On the 4th floor of the Khalaf Building.

Saudi Arabia Consulate (Map p288; ☎06-5924154; fax 5921154; 1st Circle, Jebel Amman)

Syria (Map p288; ☎06-5920684; Abdoun Prince Hashem bin Al-Hussein St, Jebel Amman) Near the 4th circle.

UK (Map p288; ☎06-5909200; www.britain.org.jo; Dimashq St, Wadi Abdoun, Abdoun)

USA (☎06-5906000; http://usembassy-amman.org.jo; 20 Al-Umawiyeen St, Abdoun) Near Abdoun Circle, 10 minutes' walking distance from the Blue Fig Café.

Yemen (Map p284; ☎06-5923771; Al-Ameer Hashem bin al-Hussein St, Abdoun Circle)

Food

Prices in this book represent the cost of a standard main-course dish, unless stated otherwise. A main dish is often accompanied by salad and various pickles, dips (such as hummus) and garnishes. These are offered free of charge and are invariably served with flat Arabic bread. This means that a main dish often doubles as a meal.

$ less than JD5 (US$7)

$$ JD5 to JD10 (US$7 to US$14)

$$$ more than JD10 (US$14)

Gay & Lesbian Travellers

Most sources state that gay sex is not illegal in Jordan (though some dispute this).

There is a subdued underground gay scene in Amman, but public displays of affection are frowned upon. Two men or women holding hands, however, is a normal sign of friendship.

There are a few places in Amman that are discreetly gay friendly, such as the multipurpose Books@café and the Blue Fig Café, which attract a young gay and straight crowd.

Internet Access

There are internet cafes in almost every town in Jordan, with costs averaging JD1.500 per hour. Connecting to the internet from your hotel room is increasingly feasible from even the most budget of hotels.

Jordan boasts numerous internet service providers, including **Cyberia** (www.cyberia.jo).

Language Courses

Jordan isn't a bad place to study Arabic, though living costs are a little higher than in Egypt or Syria. The following are in Amman:

British Council (☎06-46033420; www.britishcouncil.org/jordan.htm) Can put individuals in touch with a private tutor.

University of Jordan Language Center (☎06-5355000, ext 2370; www.ju.edu.jo; University of Amman) Offers tailormade courses with private instruction for individuals and small groups, geared to students' special interests.

Maps

» The Jordan Tourism Board's free *Map of Jordan* will suffice for most people.

» The Royal Geographic Centre of Jordan's 2005 *Map of Petra* (JD3) is worth buying if you intend to do any hiking.

» *Jordan*, by Kümmerly & Frey, is good, and probably the best if you're driving.

» GEO Project's *Jordan* (1:730,000) includes an excellent map of Amman.

Money

The currency in Jordan is the dinar (JD) – known as the *jay-dee* among hip young locals – and is made up of 1000 fils. A pi astre refers to 10 fils. Often when a price is quoted, the ending will be omitted, so if you're told that something is 25, it's a matter of working out whether it's 25 fils, 25 piastre or 25 dinars! Although it sounds confusing, most Jordanians wouldn't dream of ripping off a foreigner, with the possible exception of taxi drivers.

ATMS

ATMs abound in all but the smallest towns. Banks that accept both Visa and MasterCard include the Arab Bank and Jordan Gulf Bank, while the Housing Bank for Trade & Finance,

WARNING – PRICE RISES

If there is one bone of contention between our readers and those involved with tourism in Jordan, it is the issue of prices. Many travellers expect to find prices exactly as quoted in the book and become suspicious of landlords and taxi drivers who charge more. By the same token, many service providers in Jordan feel frustrated when travellers insist on prices that may be unrealistic even a relatively short time after printing.

There are many reasons why prices in Jordan rise quickly. For the past five years, for example, volatile oil prices, instability among neighbouring countries and continued immigration have all contributed to high inflation.

In summary, while every effort is made to ensure that our published prices for entrance fees, tours, accommodation, restaurants, food items and private transport is accurate at the time of writing, this book is only a *guide* to pricing, not a definitive statement of costs.

One piece of good news: public bus prices, which are heavily subsidised by the government, remain stable.

Cairo-Amman Bank and Jordan Islamic Bank have numerous ATMs for Visa. The Jordan National Bank and HSBC ATMs allow you to extract dinars from your MasterCard and are Cirrus compatible. If an ATM swallows your card, call ☎06-5669123 (Amman).

CREDIT CARDS

Credit cards are widely accepted in midrange and top-end hotels and restaurants, and a few top-end shops. A commission (up to 5%) is often added.

MONEYCHANGERS

There are plenty of moneychangers in Amman, Aqaba and Irbid, keeping longer hours than the banks. Many only deal in cash, but some take travellers cheques, usually for a commission. Check the rates at banks or in the English-language newspapers.

It's not difficult to change money in Jordan; most hard currencies are accepted. Syrian, Lebanese, Egyptian, Israeli and Iraqi currency can all be changed in Amman, usually at reasonable rates, though you may have to shop around. Egyptian and Israeli currency is also easily changed in Aqaba.

TIPPING

Tips of 10% are generally expected in better restaurants. A service charge of 10% is automatically added at most midrange and top-end restaurants.

TRAVELLERS CHEQUES

Travellers cheques are easily cashed by banks and some moneychangers, though commissions vary considerably, so shop around.

Photography

Digital accessories and memory cards are widely available for competitive prices. Many camera shops can burn photos onto a CD and print digital pictures.

Post

Postal rates from Jordan:

	LETTER/ POSTCARD	1KG PARCEL
Middle East	600 fils	JD9
UK/Europe	800 fils	JD18.600
USA/Canada	JD1	JD15.300
Australia	JD1	JD14.700

Public Holidays

In addition to the main Islamic holidays (p624), Jordan observes:

New Year's Day 1 January

Good Friday March/April

Labour Day 1 May

Independence Day 25 May

Army Day & Anniversary of the Great Arab Revolt 10 June

Christmas Day 25 December

Safe Travel

Jordan is very safe to visit and travel around – remarkably so considering the political turmoil surrounding it. There is little crime or anti-Western sentiment. The police keep a sharp eye on security, so carry your passport with you at all times, and expect to show it at checkpoints near the border with Israel and the Palestinian Territories and roads that approach the Dead Sea

Telephone

The telephone system in Jordan is privatised, so visitors can make a call from a private telephone agency, call from a hotel or shop, or buy a telephone card from one of the 1000 or more payphones throughout Jordan.

Local calls cost around 150 fils for three minutes. The easiest place to make a call is at your hotel, where local calls are often free. The cost of overseas calls from Jordan varies widely: check with your service provider.

Overseas calls can be made at any card payphone or from hotels, but are substantially more expensive. Reverse-charge telephone calls are not normally possible.

MOBILE PHONES

Mobile phones in Jordan use the GSM system. Two main service providers are **Zain** (www.zain.com) and **Orange** (www.orange.jo), both of which offer a full range of plans and prepaid SIM cards.

PHONE CODES

☎962	Jordan country code
☎00	International access code

The following area codes precede six- or seven-digit landline, mobile and info numbers:

☎02	Northern Jordan
☎03	Southern Jordan
☎05	Jordan Valley, central and eastern districts
☎06	Amman district
☎07	Prefix for eight-digit mobile phone numbers
☎0800	Prefix for toll-free numbers
☎1212	Local directory assistance (Amman)
☎131	Local directory assistance (elsewhere)
☎132 or ☎133	International directory assistance

Time

Jordan is two hours ahead of GMT/UTC in winter and three hours ahead between 1 April and 1 October.

Toilets

Most hotels and restaurants, except those in the budget category, now have Western-style toilets. Squat toilets come with either a hose or water bucket provided for cleaning and flushing. Toilet paper should be thrown in the bin provided, as the sewerage system is not designed for paper. Public toilets are generally best avoided except at Petra.

Tourist Information

Jordan runs a good network of visitor centres inside the country, and the **Jordan Tourism Board** (www.visitjordan.com) has a comprehensive website. Contact the following offices for a package of brochures and maps:

France (☎01-55609446; hala@visitjordan.com; 122 rue Paris, 92100 Boulogne-Billancourt, Paris)

Germany (☎069-9231880; germany@visitjordan.com; Weser Strasse 4, 60329, Frankfurt)

UK (☎02072231878; uk@visitjordan.com; 115 Hammersmith Rd, London, W14 0QH)

USA (☎1877 7335673, 703 2437404; contactus@visitjordan.com; Suite 102, 6867 Elm St, McLean, VA 22101)

Travellers with Disabilities

Jordanians are quick to help those with disabilities, but cities are crowded and traffic is chaotic, and visiting most attractions, such as the vast archaeological sites of Petra and Jerash, involves long traverses over uneven ground. Horse and carriages are provided at Petra to help elderly travellers or those with disabilities.

The Royal Diving Club (p325), south of Aqaba, is a member of the **Access to Marine Conservation for All** (AMCA; www.amca-international.org), an initiative to enable people with disabilities to enjoy scuba diving and snorkelling.

Visas

Visas are required by all foreigners entering Jordan (JD20). Single-entry tourist visas (valid for up to a month from date of entry) are issued at land borders and airports on arrival; multi-entry visas are obtainable from Jordanian embassies or consulates.

For details of visas for other Middle Eastern countries, see p35.

EXCEPTIONS

King Hussein Bridge (Allenby Bridge)

This is the only border where visas are not

issued; you must obtain them from Jordanian embassies or consulates outside the country (they are generally issued within 24 hours). If you want to re-enter Jordan here, you do not need to reapply for a Jordanian visa, providing you return through King Hussein Bridge within the validity of your Jordanian visa or extension. Keep the stamped exit slip and present it on returning. This option does not apply at any of Jordan's other border crossings.

Aqaba If you arrive in Jordan's southern city of Aqaba, you are entitled to a free visa as part of the free-trade agreement with the Aqaba Special Economic Zone Area (Aseza). If you stay in Jordan for more than 15 days, you must register with the **Aqaba Special Economic Zone Authority** (Aseza; ☎2091000; www.aqabazone.com; Ash-Sherif al-Hussein bin Ali St-Amman Hwy) in Aqaba, opposite Safeway.

TRANSIT VISAS

For stays of less than 24 hours en route to a third country, you can request a free-of-charge transit visa, which also exempts you from the JD4 departure tax.

EXTENSIONS

Extensions for a stay of up to three months are available for free on registration with the police in Amman or Aqaba.

The process is simple but involves a little running around. Request your hotel to write a short letter confirming where you are staying. Your hotel will also need to fill out two copies of a small card, which states all their details (you fill in the details on the back). Take the form, the letter, a photocopy of the page in your passport with your personal details, your Jordanian visa page and your passport to the relevant police station. Plan to arrive between 10am and 3pm Saturday to Thursday (it's best to go early). Extensions are usually granted on the spot.

Amman Start the process of lodging your paperwork at the **Al-Madeenah Police Station** (Map p284; ☎4657788; 1st fl, Al-Malek Faisal St, downtown), opposite the Arab Bank. Complete the process at **Muhajireen Police Station** (Markaz Amn Muhajireen; Map p288; Al-Ameerah Basma bin Talal Rd), west of the downtown area (from downtown, take a taxi or service taxi No 35 from along Quraysh St).

Aqaba The **police station** (☎2012411; Ar-Reem St; ⏲7am-9pm Sat-Thu) is opposite the bus station.

BEWARE THE TRICKS OF THE TRADE

Taken for a ride The taxi fare quoted on the meter is in fils, not in dinars, and visitors often misunderstand this when paying. Perhaps understandably, it is rare for a taxi driver to point out this mistake.

Crafty business Shop owners often claim something is genuinely locally crafted as part of a profit-share scheme, when in fact it is imported from abroad.

Money for old rope So-called 'antiques' are often merely last year's stock that has gathered an authentic-looking layer of dust. Similarly, 'ancient' oil lamps and coins are seldom what they are purported to be.

Women Travellers

Most women who travel around Jordan experience no problems, and find they are welcomed with a mixture of warmth and friendly concern for their safety. That said, varying levels of sexual harassment do occur, especially in tourist areas where local men assume that 'anything goes'. Harassment can be somewhat mitigated by dressing modestly in baggy trousers or skirts, with loose shirts or blouses that cover the cleavage, shoulders and upper arms. It's not necessary to cover your head.

Women may feel uncomfortable on public beaches in Aqaba and may prefer to wear shorts and a loose T-shirt over swimwear at Dead Sea public beaches. Many restaurants usher female customers into their family areas, where single men are not permitted.

Attitudes towards women vary greatly throughout the country. In the upmarket districts of Amman, women are treated the same as they would be in any Western country, whereas in rural areas more traditional attitudes prevail.

Work

Work is not really an option for most foreigners passing through Jordan. Those hoping to work with Palestinian refugees might have luck with the public information office of the **UN Relief & Works Agency** (UNRWA; ☎06-5609100, ext 165; jorpio@unrwa.org; Al-Zubeid Bldg,

Mustapha bin Abdullah St, Shmeisani, Amman); contact them at least three months in advance.

Occasional vacancies for qualified English teachers occur at the **British Council** (☎06-4636147; www.britishcouncil.org.jo) or the **American Language Center** (☎06 5523901; www.alc.edu.jo), but you need to have solid teaching experience.

DEPARTURE TAX

Jordan's departure tax for foreigners is JD4 by land, JD6 by sea and JD15 by air. If you are leaving by air, the departure tax is generally included in the ticket price.

Getting There & Away

Entering the Country

For information on Jordanian visas and entry requirements, see Visas (p337).

Air

The main international airport is **Queen Alia International Airport** (☎06-4452700), 35km south of Amman.

Royal Jordanian (☎06-5100000; www.rj.com; 9th fl, Housing Bank Centre, Shmeisani, Amman) is the excellent national carrier, but from the main European capitals you can generally get cheaper deals with other airlines. In Amman there are convenient offices in the Jordan InterContinental Hotel on Al-Kulliyah al-Isalamiyah St (☎06-4644267) and along Al-Malek al-Hussein St (☎06-5663525), uphill from the Abdali bus station.

Royal Wings (www.royalwings.com.jo – website under construction), a subsidiary of Royal Jordanian, has smaller planes for short flights from Amman to Aqaba (twice daily).

The following other airlines fly to/from Jordan and have offices in Amman:

Air France (☎06-5100777; www.airfrance.com)

British Airways (☎06-5828801; www.ba.com)

Emirates (☎06-4615222; www.emirates.com)

Gulf Air (☎06-653613; www.gulfair.com)

KLM (☎06-655267; www.klm.com)

Kuwait Airways (☎06-5690144; www.kuwait-airways.com)

Lufthansa Airlines (☎06-5200180; www.lufthansa.com)

Qatar Airways (☎06-5679444; www.qatarairways.com)

Turkish Airlines (☎06-5548100; www.turkishairlines.com)

Land

BORDER CROSSINGS

In addition to the crossings below, Jordan has three borders with Saudi Arabia (at Al-Umari, Al-Mudawwara and Ad-Durra), but as visas for Saudi are not given for casual travel, it's off-limits for most people.

Iraq

Travel to Iraq is not recommended at present. Minibuses and service taxis leave from Amman's Abdali bus station for Baghdad, but the lack of security along the highway (via Fallujah) made this an extremely dangerous option at the time of writing.

If the situation improves, the easiest way to reach the capital is by air-conditioned **Jordan Express Tourist Transport** (JETT; ☎06-5854679; www.jett.com.jo; Al-Malek al-Hussein St, Shmeisani) bus service to Baghdad on Saturdays and Wednesdays at 2.30pm (JD28.400).

Israel & the Palestinian Territories

Three border crossings are open to foreigners: Sheikh Hussein Bridge in the north, King Hussein Bridge near Amman, and Wadi Araba in the south. These border crossings are known respectively as Jordan River Bridge, Allenby Bridge, and Yitzhak Rabin in Israel and the Palestinian Territories; you should refer to them as such only when travelling on the Israeli side of the border.

From Amman, **Trust International Transport** (☎06-5813427) has buses from its office at 7th Circle (p292) to Tel Aviv (six hours), Haifa (seven hours) and Nazareth (seven hours), departing daily except Saturday at 8.30am. Buses cross the border at Sheikh Hussein Bridge. Bus schedules change frequently, so check departure times and book (and collect) tickets in advance from the bus station. There is one **Jordan Express Tourist Transport** (JETT; ☎06-5854679; www.jett.com.jo) bus to King Hussein Bridge (JD7.250, one hour, 7am).

SHEIKH HUSSEIN BRIDGE (JORDAN RIVER BRIDGE)

» This **border crossing** (⏲6.30am-10pm Sun-Thu, 8am-8pm Fri & Sat) links northern Jordan with Beit She'an in Galilee.

» Regular service taxis travel between the West bus station at Irbid and the border (JD1, 45 minutes).
» From the bridge it's a 2km walk to the Israeli side.
» Taxis go to the Beit She'an bus station (10 minutes) for onward connections.
» Travelling in the other direction, take a bus to Tiberias, and change at Beit She'an (6km from the border). From there, take another bus to the Israeli border (arrive early because there are few buses).
» Israeli exit tax is 96NIS at this border.

KING HUSSEIN BRIDGE (ALLENBY BRIDGE)

» This **border crossing** (⌚8am-2.30pm Sun-Thu, to 11.45pm Fri & Sat) offers travellers the most direct route between Amman and Jerusalem or Tel Aviv.
» Take a service taxi from Amman's Abdali or south bus station to King Hussein Bridge (JD8, 45 minutes) or there's a single daily JETT bus (JD7.250, one hour, 7am).
» Buses (JD2) shuttle between the two borders (expect long delays). It's not possible to walk, hitch or take a private vehicle across this border.
» To get to Jerusalem from the border, take a sherut (Israeli shared taxi; around US$50 for the car, 30 minutes) to Jerusalem's Damascus Gate.
» Travelling in the other direction, an Israeli exit tax of 167NIS (compared to around 96NIS at other borders) is payable. If you intend to return to Israel, keep the Jordanian entrance form safe – you will have to present it on exiting the border.
» You cannot take your own car or motorcycle through this border.
» At the Israeli border post, request officials to stamp the Jordanian exit slip rather than your passport if you intend to visit Syria and/or Lebanon. For entry to those countries, there must be no evidence in your passport of your trip to Israel, including use of any of Jordan's border crossings with Israel and the Palestinian Territories. For more information, see p36.

WADI ARABA (YITZHAK RABIN)

» This handy **border crossing** (⌚6.30am-10pm Sun-Thu, 8am-8pm Fri & Sat) in the south of the country links Aqaba to Eilat.
» Taxis run between Aqaba and the border (JD8, 15 minutes).
» You can walk the short distance across the border in a matter of minutes.
» Buses run to central Eilat, 2km away (five minutes).
» Travelling in the other direction, buses from Jerusalem to Eilat will stop at the turn-off for the border (five minutes), a short walk away.
» Israeli exit tax is 96NIS at this border.

Syria

The border crossings between Jordan and Syria are at Ramtha/Der'a and Jabir/Nasib. Note that most people need a visa from the Syrian Embassy in their home country: they are not available at the border, nor from the Syrian Embassy in Amman.

Travel to Syria is not recommended at present. If conditions in Syria improve, it's quicker and cheaper to take a direct bus or *servees* (service taxi) between Amman and Damascus rather than negotiate local transport and border crossing formalities on your own.

The air-conditioned **Jordan Express Tourist Transport** (JETT; ☎06-5854679; www.jett.com.jo; Al-Malek al-Hussein St, Shmeisani) bus travels between Amman and Damascus (JD8, seven hours, twice daily). JETT's international terminal is close to the Abdali bus station in Amman. The bus schedule changes frequently; buy your ticket in advance.

If you want to explore Jerash and Umm Qais in Jordan or Ezra'a and Bosra ash-Sham in Syria, it's also possible to take a bus from Irbid's south bus station to Ramtha (JD1), another minibus or service taxi to the border and then transport to Der'a and Damascus beyond.

The enormous yellow *servees* leave regularly throughout the day from the lower (eastern) end of the Abdali bus station for Damascus (JD10). They generally cross at Jabir. From Irbid's south bus station, service taxis go to Damascus (JD5).

Sea

There are two main boat services to Nuweiba in Egypt. Departure times are often subject to change, so call the **passenger terminal** (☎03-2013236; www.abmaritime.com.jo/english) before travelling and arrive at least 90 minutes before departure. Buy your tickets at the ferry port on the morning of departure (you'll need your passport). Fares must be paid for in US dollars.

The fast boat (US$75, one hour) leaves daily at 1pm except Saturday. Fares for children under eight are US$60.

There is also a slower car ferry service (US$65, three hours or more) that officially leaves at 11pm. Some days it doesn't leave at all. Fares for children under eight are US$55.

There are money-exchange facilities at the terminals at Nuweiba and Aqaba. The Jordanian side offers a decent exchange rate, but avoid travellers cheques, which attract a huge commission. You can get a free Sinai permit on arrival at Nuweiba. If you want a full Egyptian visa, enquire at the Egyptian consulate in Aqaba in advance (p334). Passports are collected on the boat in both directions and handed back on arrival at immigration.

Getting Around

Public transport is designed primarily for the locals and as it is notoriously difficult to reach many of the sights of interest (especially the Dead Sea, desert castles and King's Highway) consider hiring a car or using tours organised by hotels in Amman and Madaba.

Air

There is only one domestic air route, between Amman and Aqaba. You can buy tickets at any travel agency or Royal Jordanian office.

Royal Jordanian (☎06-5100000; www.rj.com) Flights twice daily (JD37 one-way, one hour).

Royal Wings (www.royalwings.com.jo, website under construction) A subsidiary of Royal Jordanian, it has daily flights.

Bicycle

Cycling is not necessarily fun in Jordan. In summer, it's prohibitively hot, and cyclists on the King's Highway have reported stone throwing by groups of young children. Cycling north or south can be hard work, as there is a strong prevailing western wind. Anywhere from the East Bank plateau down to the Dead Sea or Jordan Valley makes for exhilarating descents, but coming the other way will really test your calf muscles. Bring plenty of spare parts and contact **Cycling Association** (www.cycling-jordan.com) for tips before departure (see p630 for more information).

Bus & Minibus

The national bus company **JETT** (☎06-5854679; www.jett.com.jo; Al-Malek al-Hussein St, Shmeisani, Amman) operates the most comfortable bus service from Amman to Aqaba. It also has limited services to King Hussein Bridge border crossing, Petra and the Dead Sea.

Other reliable companies with regular services from Amman include **Trust International Transport** (☎06-5813427) to Aqaba, and **Hijazi** (☎06-638110, 02-7240721) to Irbid.

Just about all towns in Jordan are connected by 20-seat minibuses, although the King's Highway, Dead Sea area and eastern Jordan are less well served. Minibuses leave when full and it can take an hour or more for the seats to fill up. They may leave earlier if you're ready to pay extra for the empty seats.

Car & Motorcycle

Hiring a car is an ideal way to get the most out of Jordan. Distances are generally short and many prime destinations are difficult to get to by public transport. Road conditions are generally good outside Amman.

DRIVING LICENCE

International Driving Permits (IDPs) are not needed. If you're driving, keep your driving licence, rental or ownership papers and car registration in an easily accessible place.

FUEL & SPARE PARTS

Petrol is available along the Desert and King's Highways and in most sizeable towns. There are precious few mechanics in Jordan able to deal with the average modern motorcycle and its problems.

HIRE

Charges, conditions, drop-off fees, insurance costs and waiver fees in case of accident vary considerably, so it's worth shopping around. Daily rates are JD40 to JD50; weekly rates JD140 to JD200. You can normally drop off the rental car in another city (eg Aqaba). Many hire companies require a minimum three-days hire, and all require a deposit of up to JD400, payable upon pick up and refunded upon return of the car.

The following hire companies are reliable:

Avis (☎06-5699420, 24hr 777-397405; www.avis.com.jo; King Abdullah Gardens, Amman) Offices at King Hussein Bridge and Aqaba; branches at the airport, Le Royal Hotel and Jordan InterContinental Hotel. The biggest car-hire company in Jordan.

JORDAN IN A HURRY? TAKE A TOUR!

Usually shy away from tours? Well Jordan is one place to make an exception, especially if you're short of time or on a tight budget. Tours run by budget hotels in Amman and Madaba have filled the public transport gaps to destinations like the Eastern Desert, the Dead Sea and the King's Highway. The 'tours' are really just transport, so don't expect much from the guide-cum-driver. They do, however, offer a chance to meet fellow travellers and share costs.

The Cliff, Jordan Tower, Farah and Palace hotels in Amman (see p283) offer popular daytrips to the Eastern desert castles; another top trip is to Jerash, Ajloun and Umm Qais. Good value trips along the King's Highway leave Amman at 8.30am and travel to Petra (9½ hours) via Madaba, Wadi Mujib, Karak, Shobak and Dana. The Black Iris Hotel and the Mariam Hotel in Madaba (see p306) can arrange similar itineraries. A seat in a four-seater taxi or minibus costs from around JD15 to JD50, depending on the number of fellow passengers, stops, time and distance.

There are a few tour companies with a good reputation for comprehensive (but more expensive) tours around Jordan; try **Petra Moon** (☎03-2156665; www.petramoon.com) in Wadi Musa to get an idea of what's on offer.

Budget (☎06-5698131; www.budget.com; 125 Abdul Hameed Sharaf St, Amman)

Europcar (☎06-5655581; www.europcar.middleeast.com; Isam Al-Ajlouni St, Amman) Branches at Radisson SAS, King Abdullah Gardens and in Aqaba.

Hertz (☎06-5920926; www.hertz.com; King Abdullah Gardens, Amman) Offices at the airport, Grand Hyatt Amman, Sheraton and in Aqaba.

Reliable Rent-a-Car (☎06-5929676; www.rentareliablecar.com; 19 Fawzi al-Qawegli St, Amman) Contact Mohammed Hallak.

INSURANCE

All car rentals come with some kind of insurance, but you should find out how much your excess is (ie the maximum you will have to pay in case of an accident) – it may be as high as JD400. For JD7 to JD10 extra per day, you can buy Collision Damage Waiver (CDW), which takes your deductible down to JD100 or even zero.

ROAD RULES

Vehicles drive on the right-hand side of the road in Jordan – at least in theory. More often, they loiter in the middle. The general speed limit inside built-up areas is 50km/h or 70km/h on multilane highways in Amman, and 90km/h to 110km/h on the highways. Note that indicators are seldom used, rules are only occasionally obeyed, the ubiquitous horn is a useful warning signal and pedestrians must take their chances. Wearing a seat belt is now compulsory.

Keep your passport, driving licence, rental agreement and registration papers handy, especially along the Dead Sea Highway where there are quite a few police check posts.

Hitching

In Wadi Rum and along the King's and Dead Sea Highways, you may need to wave down a ride; it's customary to give a few dinars to the driver. For general information on hitching, see p633.

Local Transport

BUS

Local city buses are generally packed, routes are confusing and the chances of being pickpocketed are higher. Take a service taxi instead.

TAXI

Private taxis are good value in the cities. Note that metered fares are displayed in fils not dinars, and if you proffer the fare in dinars by mistake, the driver is unlikely to correct you.

White service taxis are a little more expensive than minibuses and don't cover as many routes, but they are generally faster and take less time to fill up (there are generally only four seats). Inside cities like Amman, service taxis offer extensive coverage and are a good alternative to walking or taking private taxis. For more details on taxis in Jordan, see p293.

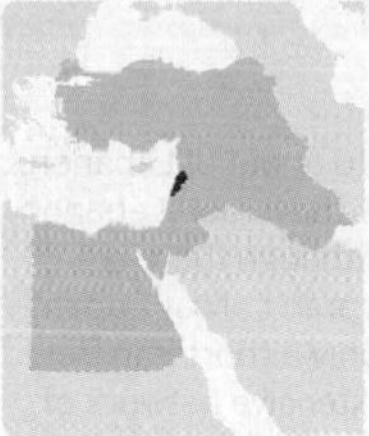

Lebanon

Includes »

Best for Nature

» Jeita Grotto (p360)
» Qadisha Valley (p368)
» Chouf Mountains (p375)

Best for Culture

» Baalbek ruins (p377)
» Tripoli Old City (p364)
» Sidon Old City (p370)
» National Museum of Beirut (p346)

Why Go?

Its name is a byword for conflict but Lebanon, the original land of milk and honey, is a friendly, welcoming and culturally rich country with one slipper in the Arab world and one Jimmy Choo planted firmly in the West. It's home to a bubbling-hot nightlife in Beirut, a notorious Hezbollah (Party of God) headquarters in backwater Baalbek, a fistful of flash ski resorts, and a dozen cramped and poverty-stricken Palestinian refugee camps.

Hike the Qadisha Valley and it's hard to imagine that a conflict has ever existed here; wander past the pockmarked shell of Beirut's Holiday Inn and you'll wonder if there will ever be lasting peace. Lebanon is chaotic and fascinating – scarred by decades of civil war, invasions and terrorist attacks, yet blessed with serene mountain vistas, majestic ancient ruins and a people who are resilient, indomitable and renowned for their hospitality. Heed travel warnings but don't miss the compelling and confusing wonders of Lebanon.

When to Go

Beirut

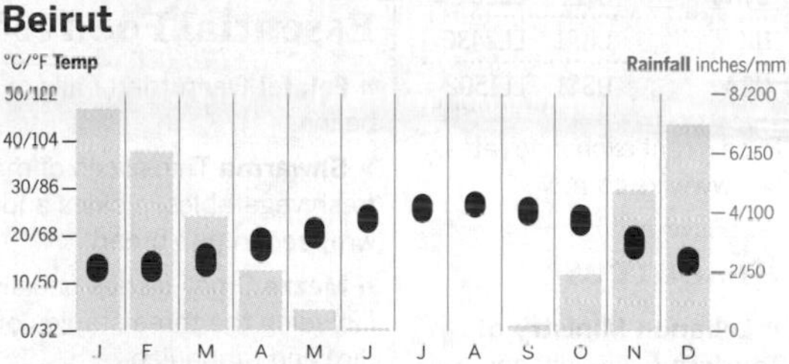

Dec–Apr Skiing – and après-ski parties – in the mountains.

May–Sep The perfect time to go hiking along wild trails and through cedar forests.

Jul–Aug Baalbek's famous arts festival brings the ancient Roman ruins to life.

AT A GLANCE

» **Currency** Lebanese lira (also known as the Lebanese pound; LL)

» **Mobile Phones** Good coverage; local SIM cards are widely available

» **Money** ATMs widely available; credit cards accepted in larger establishments

» **Visas** Available at the airport for many nationalities

Fast Facts

» **Capital** Beirut

» **Country code** ☎961

» **Language** Arabic (English and French widely spoken)

» **Official name** Republic of Lebanon

» **Population** 4 million

Exchange Rates

Australia	A$1	LL1552
Euro Zone	€1	LL1988
Israel & the Palestinian Territories	1N1S	LL397
Syria	S£1	LL26.24
UK	UK£1	LL2436
USA	US$1	LL1502

For current exchange rates, see www.xe.com.

Resources

» **Lebanon Ministry of Tourism** (www.lebanon-tourism.gov.lb)

» **Lebanon Tourism** (www.lebanontourism.org)

» **LebanonTourism.com** (www.lebanontourism.com)

Connections

There aren't many choices for getting into or out of Lebanon. The only land crossings are into Syria, as the Israel–Lebanon land border has been closed for years. Although there are several border crossings into Syria, they aren't always open (see p395 for more details). Lebanon's only airport is in Beirut. It's small but efficient, handling an extensive network of international flights to and from Europe and the Arab world.

ITINERARIES

One Week

Begin your trip in **Beirut**, indulging in the capital's funky bars and cooler-than-cool cafe scene. After two days of hedonism, visit the fairy-tale cave of **Jeita Grotto** before continuing north to pretty **Byblos**, where ancient ruins are sprinkled beside an azure sea. Spend a relaxing day in Byblos or drive up to the **Qadisha Valley** for a long nature hike. Next, move on to **Tripoli**, explore its medieval souqs and munch on its famous sweets. If the road is open, cross the mountains to **Baalbek** – the fabled 'Sun City'. If the road is closed, you'll have to go through Beirut to get to Baalbek. On day seven, detour to **Aanjar's** Umayyad city ruins on the return to Beirut.

Two Weeks

If it's winter, spend two days skiing at **the Cedars**, with a visit to the Gibran Museum in **Bcharré**. If it's summer, spend an extra day hiking in the **Qadisha Valley**. Set aside two days to explore **Sidon** and **Tyre**, southern cities with tumultuous pasts and a wealth of ancient remains, then head over to **Deir al-Qamar** to soak up the small-town atmosphere and the wonders of the **Beiteddine Palace**. Backtracking to Beirut, spend your final days relaxing poolside at one of its chi-chi beach clubs.

Essential Food & Drink

» **Felafel** Deep-fried balls of chickpea paste and/or fava beans.

» **Shwarma** Thin slices of marinated meat garnished with fresh vegetables, pickles and tahina (sesame-seed paste), wrapped in pita bread.

» **Mezze** Small dishes usually served as starters, often including the three staples of hummus, *muttabal* (aubergine dip) and tabbouleh.

» **Zaatar** A blend of Middle Eastern herbs, sesame seeds and salt, used as a condiment on meats, vegetables, rice and bread.

» **Arak** Aniseed-flavoured liquor, best served with water and ice.

Lebanon Highlights

1. Marvel at **Jeita Grotto** (p360) and its glittering forest of stalactites and stalagmites
2. Explore the haunting ruins of the ancient 'Sun City' of **Baalbek** (p377)
3. Wander through seaside ruins and celebrate a Mediterranean sunset in pretty **Byblos** (p360)
4. Delve into the traditional, atmospheric souqs of **Old Sidon** (p370)
5. Drink and be merry in the cooler-than-cool cafes and dive bars of Beirut's **Hamra** and **Gemmayzeh** (p355) districts
6. Hike past rock-cut monasteries and gushing waterfalls in the scenic **Qadisha Valley** (p368)
7. Ski Lebanon's pristine mountain slopes at **the Cedars** (p369)

BEIRUT بيروت

☎01 / POP 1.3 MILLION

Beirut, the nation's capital, is a fabulous place of glitz, glamour, restaurants and beach clubs – if, that is, you're one of the lucky ones. While the city centre is filled with suave sophistication, the outskirts of town comprise some of the most deprived Palestinian refugee camps of all, and its crowded slums provide a breeding ground for Hezbollah fighters. If you're looking for the real East-meets-West so talked about in the Middle East, this is precisely where it's at. Crowded and ancient, beautiful and blighted, hot and heady, home to Prada and Palestinians, Beirut is many things at once, but all, without doubt, compelling.

History

Though there's evidence of a city on the site of modern Beirut dating back at least to ancient Egyptian times, it wasn't until the Roman era that the city really came into its own, both as a commercial port and military base and, by the 3rd century AD, as the location of a world-renowned school of law, one of the first three in the world. The city's fame continued until AD 551, when a devastating earthquake and resultant tsunami brought massive death, destruction and decline. The law school was moved to Sidon, and Beirut didn't regain its importance as a trading centre and gateway to the Middle East until the 16th century, under local emir Fakhreddine.

In the 19th century Beirut enjoyed a commercial boom, but also experienced the first of much meddling by European powers as French troops arrived at the city's port. The early years of the 20th century saw citywide devastation, the combined result of a WWI Allied blockade, famine, revolt and plague, which killed a quarter of its population. Following WWII, however, Beirut slowly became a major business, banking and publishing centre, and remained so until the bloody, brutal civil war that ravaged the city's streets and citizens put paid to its supremacy.

Following the end of the war in 1990, rehabilitation of the city's infrastructure became the major focus of both the local and national governments, to restore its Paris of the East reputation. Beirut's battle scars, however, remain visible throughout the city.

Sights & Activities

Beirut doesn't have many sights as such. The student district of Hamra is alive with cafes, restaurants and bars, and is a good place for people-watching. Directly north of Hamra runs the seafront Corniche, or Ave de Paris, along which are stringed Beirut's beach clubs and most of its top hotels. To the south is affluent Verdun, home to designer clothes shops that line the Rue Verdun. East from Hamra, you'll reach the beautifully restored Beirut Central District (BCD), at the centre of which is the landmark Place d'Étoile, also known as Nejmeh Sq, lined with pavement cafes. Just east again is the Place des Martyrs, where the huge Mohammed Al-Amin Mosque (reminiscent of İstanbul's Blue Mosque) is another useful landmark.

Edging the Place des Martyrs is the Rue de Damas, which was once the Green Line separating warring East and West Beirut, and further west you'll find the funky Gemmayzeh district, centred on Rue Gouraud. A little south from here, you'll reach Achrafiye, another super-cool district, famous for its restaurants, bars and clubs on Rue Monot.

National Museum of Beirut MUSEUM

(Map p347; ☎426 703/4; www.beirutnationalmuseum.com; cnr Rue de Damas & Ave Abdallah Yafi; adult/student/child LL5000/1000/1000, guide US$30; ⌚9am-5pm Tue-Sun) This must-see museum situated on the former Green Line has an impressive, but not overwhelming, collection of archaeological artefacts, and offers a great overview of Lebanon's history and the civilisations that made their home here.

Highlights include some beautifully observed Phoenician marble statues of baby boys (from Echmoun, 5th century BC), lovely 3rd- and 4th-century AD mosaics, Byzantine gold jewellery (found in a jar under the floor of a villa in Beirut) and the famous, much-photographed Phoenician gilded bronze figurines from Byblos. A floor plan is distributed free with tickets, or you can opt for a more informative written guide (LL10,000) from the gift shop.

The museum screens a fascinating 12-minute documentary in its **theatrette** (ground fl; ⌚9am-4pm) in English hourly or French on demand, detailing how curators saved the collection during the civil war and subsequently restored it to its former glory.

To get to the museum, walk 15 minutes south from Sodeco Sq along Rue de Damas, or hail a service taxi and ask for the Musée or the Hippodrome.

Beirut Art Center GALLERY

(☎397 018; http://beirutartcenter.org; Jisr el-Wafi, Adlieh; ⌚noon-8pm Mon-Sat) Dedicated to

Greater Beirut

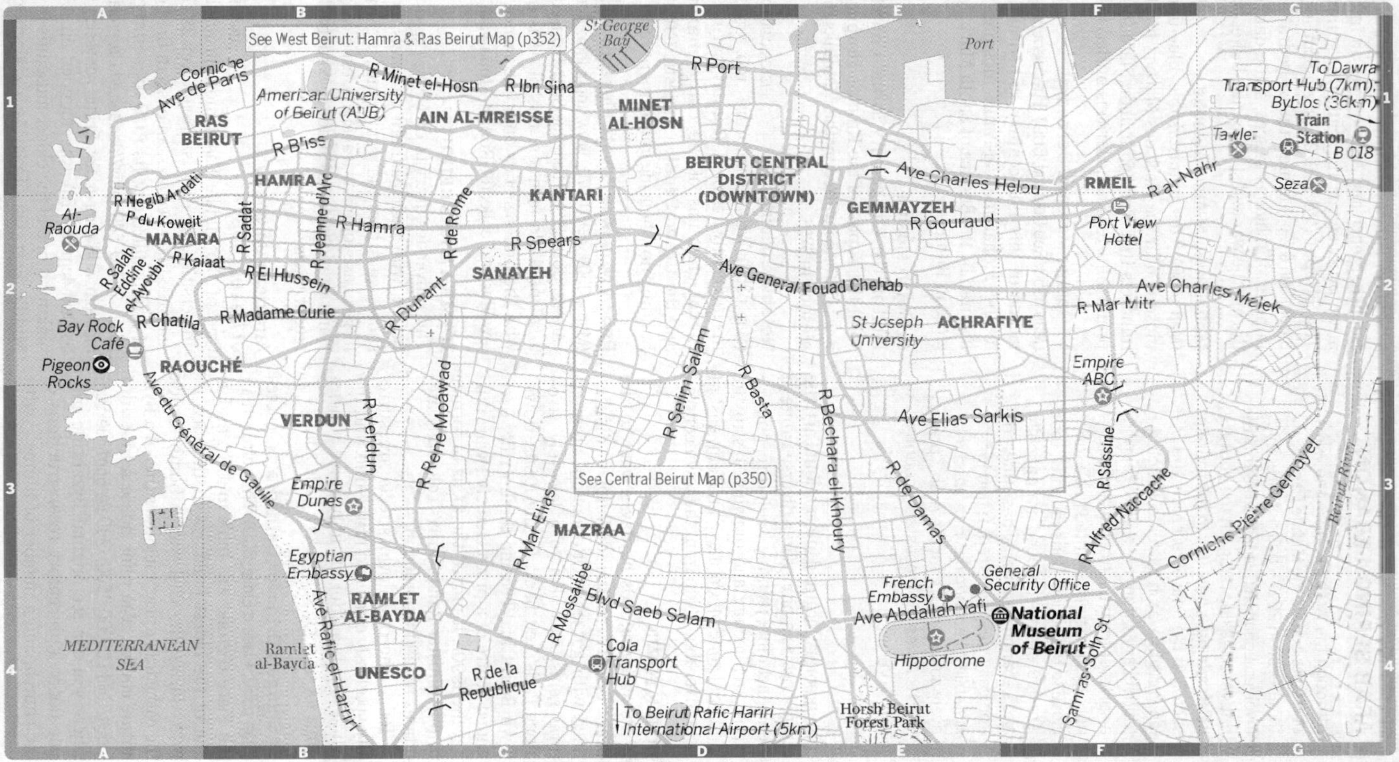

ARAB SPRING: LEBANON

Although the 'Arab Spring' – the wave of revolts across the Middle East that began in 2011 – has not directly involved Lebanon (aside from Syrian refugees seeking refuge in the country), its effects have been felt in the tourism sector. At the time of research, the Syrian uprising was in full force, keeping tourists away from the region. Fearing a spillover from the troubles in Syria, nobody, it seemed, wanted to be too close to the action. Consequently, tourism figures have dropped dramatically and Lebanon's economy has suffered. Ironically, despite its reputation for instability, Lebanon has remained relatively calm throughout the Arab Spring; in 2011 it was the most stable country in the region.

contemporary local and international art, the centre hosts exhibitions in a diverse range of media including painting, sculpture, photography, architecture and drawing. It's in the industrial zone off Corniche an Nahr, east of Achrafiye, about 3km from the town centre.

DOWNTOWN

In its swinging '60s heyday, a visit to the BCD, Beirut's central downtown district, filled with gorgeous Ottoman-era architectural gems, was akin to a leisurely stroll along Paris' Left Bank. By the 1980s, downtown Beirut had become the horrific, decimated centre of a protracted civil war; during the 1990s, it proved the focus of former prime minister Rafiq Hariri's colossally ambitious rebuilding program.

Today, the downtown streets are surreally, spotlessly clean and traffic-free, and the whole area beautiful and impressive, though some locals suggest it lacks a little soul.

St George's Orthodox Cathedral CHURCH
(Map p350; Place d'Étoile, BCD) This church in the Place d'Étoile was built in 1767, and is one of the oldest buildings in the city. In 1975, during the civil war, a bomb struck the cathedral, unearthing the ruins of a Byzantine church. The ruins house a **museum** (adult/child LL5000/1000; ⌚10am-6pm Tue-Sun) where you can see original Byzantine mosaic floors, 12th-century reconstructions of the church, and a number of tombs – with skeletons. A seven-minute documentary in English, French and Arabic gives an informative overview of the cathedral's history. The **chapel** (☎980 920; ⌚9am-8pm Tue-Sat, 3-8pm Sun & Mon) behind the cathedral has a number of religious frescos, some damaged during the war and still bearing bullet holes.

Mohammed al-Amin Mosque MOSQUE
(Map p350) This unmistakable blue-domed mosque near the Place des Martyrs has four minarets that stand 65m high. Slain former prime minister Rafiq Hariri is buried here.

St George Maronite Cathedral CHURCH
(Map p350; Rue Gouraud, BCD) The neoclassical facade of this 19th-century cathedral, next to the Mohammed al-Amin mosque, was inspired by the Basilica of Santa Maria Maggiore in Rome.

Al-Omari Mosque MOSQUE
Built in the 12th century as the Church of John the Baptist of the Knights Hospitaller, it was later converted by the Mamluks into a mosque in 1291.

Notable Buildings HISTORIC BUILDINGS
(Map p350) Worth exploring, too, are the magnificently restored **Roman baths**, the Roman-era ruins of the **cardo maximus** and the **Grand Serail**, a majestic Ottoman building now housing government offices.

Robert Mouawad Private Museum MUSEUM
(Map p350; ☎980 970; www.rmpm.info; Rue de L'Armee, BCD; ⌚9am-5pm Tue-Sun) Housed in a splendid old mansion, this place is filled with the findings of its one-time owner, the jeweller and collector Robert Mouawad.

HAMRA & RAS BEIRUT

The university districts of Hamra and Ras Beirut, with their plethora of hotels, bookshops, cafes, bars and restaurants, is the preferred base for many travellers, especially as Hamra's nightlife has made a comeback in recent years.

American University of Beirut (AUB) UNIVERSITY
One of the Middle East's most prestigious universities, the AUB is spread over 28 calm and tree-filled hectares, an oasis in the heart of a fume-filled city. Its **AUB museum** (Map p352; ☎340 549; http://ddc.aub.edu.lb/projects/museum; AUB campus, Ras Beirut; admission free; ⌚10am-4pm Mon-Fri) was founded in 1868, making it one of the oldest museums in the Middle East. On display is a collection of

Lebanese and Middle Eastern artefacts dating back to the early Stone Age; a fine collection of Phoenician glass and Arab coins from as early as the 5th century BC; and a large collection of pottery dating back to 3000 BC. Closed during university and public holidays.

CORNICHE

Stretching roughly from Pigeon Rocks in the south to the St George Yacht Club, the seafront Corniche is every Beiruti's favourite promenade spot, especially in the early evening around sunset, and then on – aided by backgammon, nargilehs and barbecues – late into the night. Here, you'll find old-timers discussing the way things used to be, and young hopefuls debating how they will be one day. Grab a piece of sea wall and a strong coffee, and delight in some people-watching par excellence amid pole fishermen, families, courting couples and cavorting children. And if it's something more serene you're looking for, walk on down to **Pigeon Rocks** (Map p347), Beirut's famous natural offshore arches.

If you fancy a dip, several of Beirut's chic, beach clubs are situated along this stretch (note that the word 'beach' is used loosely, since there's barely a grain of sand to be found in any of them and you'll most likely be swimming in a pool).

La Plage SWIMMING
(Map p352; ☎366 222; Ain al-Mreisse; admission weekday/weekend US$25/35; ⏰9am-7pm May-Oct) Filled with beautiful, bronzed bodies.

St George Yacht Motor Club SWIMMING
(Map p350; ☎356 065; www.stgeorges-hotel.com; Ain al-Mreisse; admission weekday/weekend US$25/30) Extensive facilities and upscale crowd.

AUB Beach SWIMMING
(Map p352; Ain al-Mreisse; AUB students/guests LL3500/15,000) Slightly scruffy but with a great student vibe.

ACHRAFIYE

Built on the site of the Roman City of the Dead, Achrafiye is an attractive and largely sedate area, historically one of the preserves of Beirut's Christian population and today dotted with galleries, antiques shops and churches. Though eclipsed by neighbouring area Gemmayzeh in terms of cool, and vying with Hamra's resurging popularity, Achrafiye's once legendary nightclubbing street, Rue Monot, is still a lively place for a drink or three.

FREE **Sursock Museum** MUSEUM
(Map p350; ☎334 133; Rue Sursock, Achrafiye) With its stained glass dramatically illuminated at night, you won't miss this museum, which opens only when there are exhibitions scheduled. Although closed for restoration at the time of research, it is due to reopen soon.

GEMMAYZEH

Gemmayzeh, centring on pretty Rue Gouraud, is for many locals Beirut at its best. Here's where hole-in-the-wall bars fill with revellers and the strains of live music as night sets in, and where, during the day, you can peruse some cute and arty boutiques. There's also a scattering of art galleries for those interested in Beirut's contemporary arts scene.

Beirut for Children

Beirutis go gaga for children, and you'll have no problem finding family-friendly activities, restaurants and hotels throughout town. Good brands of baby supplies – nappies, powdered milk and the like – are widely available at pharmacies.

Planet Discovery MUSEUM
(Map p350; ☎980 650; www.solidere.com.lb; Beirut Souks, Saad Zaghloul St, BCD; admission LL7500; ⏰8.30am-6pm Mon-Fri, 10.30am-7pm Sat & Sun) For something slightly cerebral, head to this fun and interactive science museum for ages three to 15.

St George Yacht Motor Club SWIMMING
(Map p350; ☎356 065; www.stgeorges-hotel.com; Ain al-Mreisse; admission weekday/weekend US$25/30) The yacht club has a nice children's pool, a playground and grassy lawns to dash about on.

Sanayeh Public Garden PARK
(Map p352; Rue Spears, Sanayeh) Though Beirut's hardly blessed with an abundance of open spaces, kids can let off steam somewhere green at the Sanayeh Public Garden, with bike and skate hire available.

Tours

TOP CHOICE **Walk Beirut** WALKING TOUR
(www.bebeirut.org; tour LL30,000) This excellent walking tour, led by AUB history graduates, covers Beirut's historical centre. It's informative and entertaining and brings Beirut's troubled past to life. The 3½-hour tour includes Place d'Étoile, Martyr's Square, the Jewish quarter, the bullet-riddled Holiday

Central Beirut

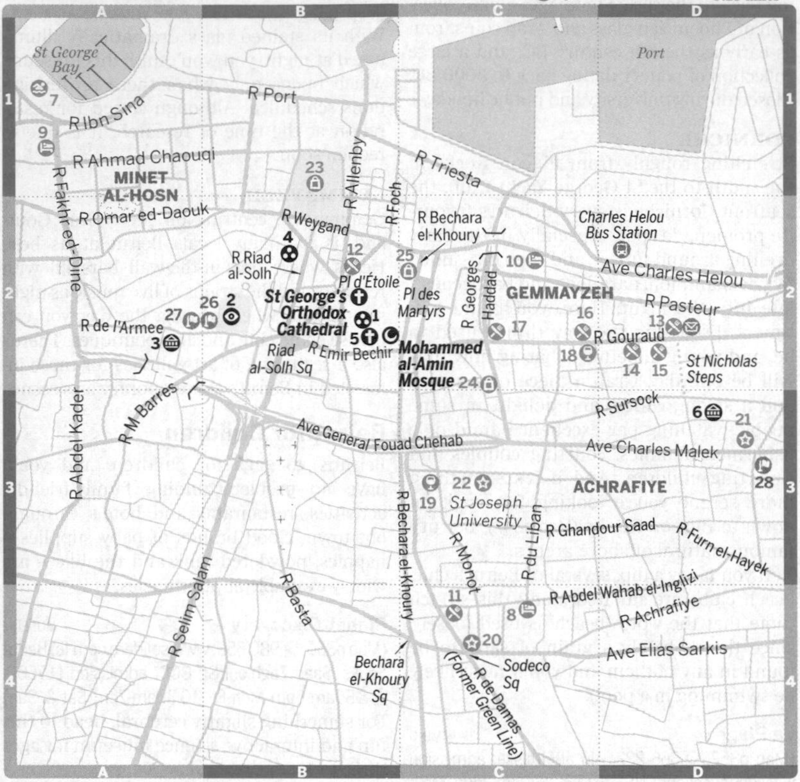

Inn, the Roman baths, Beirut's unique architectural styles and more. Book online.

Festivals & Events

Beirut Jazz Festival MUSIC
(www.beirutsouks.com.lb) Held in September, the Beirut Souks come alive with music.

Beirut International Film Festival FILM
(www.beirutfilmfoundation.org) Held in October, this festival showcases films from Lebanon and the Middle East.

Beirut International Marathon MARATHON
(www.beirutmarathon.org) Held each autumn, usually in November, and popular with international athletes.

Docudays FILM
(www.docudays.net) Beirut's International Documentary Festival, held every November or December, sees international audiences flock to the city.

Sleeping

Decent budget accommodation is thin on the ground in Beirut, and Lonely Planet regularly receives traveller emails from those who booked a room – or an airport taxi – only to find none awaiting them. To try to guard against this, reconfirm your booking 24 hours before your arrival, and take along any email or fax correspondence as proof of dates, times or prices.

Most of Beirut's midrange options are located in and around Hamra. It's well worth asking about discounts (sometimes as much as 40%) if you're visiting out of season.

35 Rooms HOTEL $$$
(Map p352; ☎345 676; www.35rooms.com; Rue Baalbek, Hamra; s/d/ste from US$140/155/250; ❄📶) Living up to its claim as the 'trendiest hotel in town', the 35 rooms here are large, comfortable and fashionably minimalist. In a

Central Beirut

Top Sights	
Mohammed al-Amin Mosque	B2
St George's Orthodox Cathedral	B2
Sights	
1 Cardo Maximus	B2
2 Grand Serail	B2
Planet Discovery	(see 23)
3 Robert Mouawad Private Museum	A2
4 Roman Baths	B2
5 St George Maronite Cathedral	B2
6 Sursock Museum	D3
Activities, Courses & Tours	
7 St George Yacht Motor Club	A1
Sleeping	
8 Hotel Albergo	C4
9 InterContinental Phoenicia Hotel	A1
Pension al-Nazih	(see 10)
10 Talal's New Hotel	C2
Eating	
11 Abdel Wahab el-Inglezi	C4
Al Dente	(see 8)
12 Al-Balad	B2
13 Aliacci	D2
14 La Tabkha	D2
15 Le Chef	D2
16 Olio	C2
17 Paul	C2
Drinking	
18 Bar Louie	C2
19 Pacífico	C3
Torino Express	(see 18)
Entertainment	
20 Cassino	C4
21 Empire Sofil Center	D3
22 Monnot Theatre	C3
Shopping	
23 Beirut Souks	B1
24 Saifi Village	C2
25 Virgin Megastore	C2
Information	
26 Australian Embassy	B2
27 British Embassy	A2
28 Dutch Embassy	D3

great location in bustling Hamra, with super-friendly staff and a full buffet breakfast, this place is hard to beat. Suites and apartments have kitchenettes.

L'Hote Libanais HOMESTAY **$$**
(☎03-513 766; www.hotelibanais.com; s US$60-80, d US$78-110) If you really want to get under the skin of the country, stay with the people, an option made possible by L'Hote Libanais, which arranges B&B homestays in Beirut and beyond. Discounts for multiple-night stays and a range of accommodation are on offer. Email the helpful staff for the full list of excellent homestay options.

Hotel Albergo HOTEL **$$$**
(Map p350; ☎339 797; www.albergobeirut.com; 137 Rue Abdel Wahab el-Inglezi, Achrafiye; d US$310-2700;) If it's unequivocal luxury you're after in that most perfect of boutique settings, look beyond the hefty price tag. Attentive staff, divine Italian food at the Al Dente restaurant and a cute rooftop pool complete the plush picture in this delicious, antique-embellished old place.

InterContinental Phoenicia Hotel HOTEL **$$$**
(Map p350; ☎369 100; www.ichotelsgroup.com; Rue Fakhr ed-Dine, Minet al-Hosn; d/ste from US$315/600;) Beirut's most prestigious pre–civil war address is now back on the luxury scene, with miles of marble and all the whistles and bells you could hope for. Heavy security is usually in place since this is the favourite haunt of Lebanese politicians and elite.

Casa d'Or HOTEL **$$**
(Map p352; ☎746 400; www.casadorhotel.com; Rue Jeanne d'Arc, Hamra; s/d/ste US$90/100/140;) One of Beirut's best midrange hotels, the Casa d'Or has bright, cheery and well-equipped rooms; equally appealing are its substantial off-season discounts.

Mayflower Hotel HOTEL **$$**
(Map p352; ☎340 680; www.mayflowerbeirut.com; Rue Neamé Yafet, Hamra; s/d US$90/120;) An old-fashioned Beirut institution, the Mayflower's rooms are looking a little weary but they're comfortable enough. The rooftop pool is a definite bonus, and a

West Beirut: Hamra & Ras Beirut

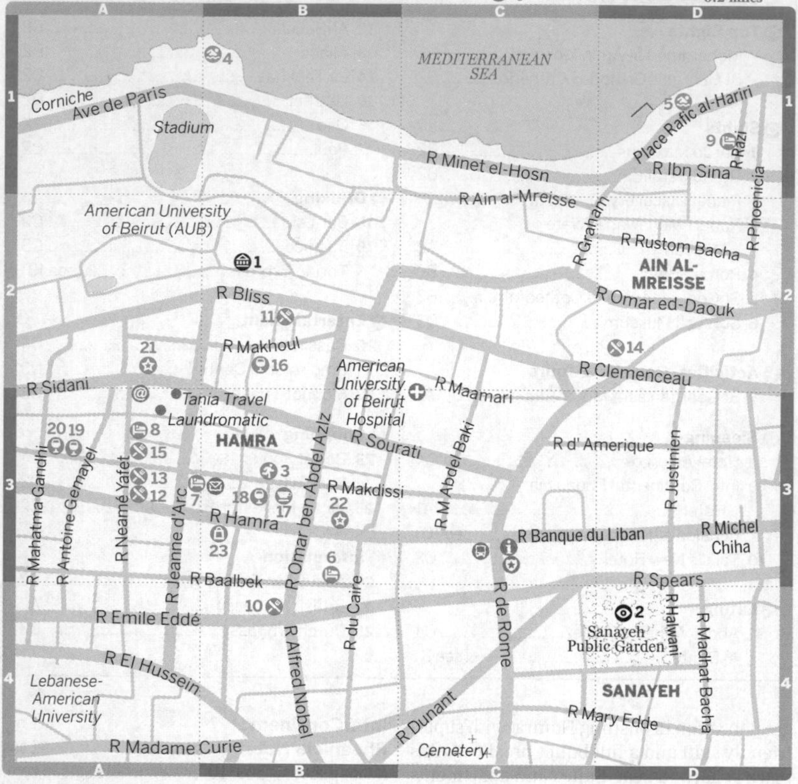

drink or two at the venerable Duke of Wellington bar a must.

Port View Hotel HOTEL $$
(Map p347; ☎567 500; www.portviewhotel.com; Rue Gouraud, Gemmayzeh; s/d US$59/89; ❄@📶) A notch or two above the budget options in terms of comfort, the Port View is small, friendly and comfortable, and within easy walking distance of Rue Gouraud's bars and restaurants.

Talal's New Hotel HOTEL $
(Map p350; ☎562 567; www.talalhotel.com; Ave Charles Helou, Gemmayzeh; dm US$12-15, d US$40; ❄📶) A friendly owner and a livelier vibe than nearby al-Nazih make this place probably the best budget bet in town. Rooms are small and simple but clean (but not all have a bathroom), and the owner will strive to squeeze you in on the roof in summer if the place is full. There's a communal kitchen and laundry facilities.

Pension al-Nazih HOTEL $
(Map p350; ☎564 868; www.pension-alnazih.8m.com; Rue Chanty, Gemmayzeh; dm/s/d US$17/25/45; ❄📶) A decent, plain option located just a few steps away from Talal's, the hotel's 10 rooms are ever popular with travellers and are clean, basic and quiet. Breakfast costs US$3 extra, and airport pick-up can be arranged for US$25. Only double rooms come with bathroom.

Regis Hotel HOTEL $
(Map p352; ☎361 845; www.regishotel-lb.com; Rue Razi, Ain al-Mreisse; s/d/tr US$40/50/60; ❄@) It might look bleak and barren from the outside, but this basic place – while in no sense cosy – offers large rooms, and regularly receives good feedback from travellers.

Eating

Beirutis love to eat out, whether at chic top-end brasseries or at tiny hole-in-the-wall

West Beirut: Hamra & Ras Beirut

Sights
1 AUB Museum ... B2
2 Sanayeh Public Garden ... D4

Activities, Courses & Tours
3 American Language Center ... B3
4 AUB Beach ... B1
5 La Plage ... D1

Sleeping
6 35 Rooms ... B3
7 Casa d'Or ... A3
8 Mayflower Hotel ... A3
9 Regis Hotel ... D1

Eating
10 Barbar ... B4
11 Bliss House ... B2
12 Bread Republic ... A3
13 Consumers Co-op ... A3
14 Pasta di Casa ... D2
15 Walimat Wardoh ... A3

Drinking
16 Blue Note ... B2
17 Cafe de Prague ... B3
18 Dany's ... B3
19 Li Beirut ... A3
20 Rabbit Hole ... A3

Entertainment
21 Democratic Republic of Music ... A2
22 Mojo Jazz Club ... B3

Shopping
23 Librairie Antoine ... B3

shwarma joints; and the city stays open late for its diners, with few arriving for dinner before 9pm or 10pm. The best thing about Beirut is the breadth of choice, with things changing fast on the culinary scene: by all means sample our own personal highlights, but don't miss the opportunity to branch out to seek your own.

Every sector of Beirut is blessed with its own complement of felafel, kebab, fruit juice and shwarma stands, and a good rule of thumb, as ever, is to go where the locals seem to be going. A popular chain is **Barbar** (Map p352; Rue Spears, Hamra) for quick and cheap mezze and shwarmas. For a decent cappuccino and croissant, you can't beat **Paul** (Map p350; Rue Gouraud, Gemmayzeh).

TOP CHOICE Seza ARMENIAN $$
(Map p347; ☎570 711; Rue Patriarch Arida, Mar Mikhael; mains LL25,000; ⊙lunch & dinner Tue-Sat) Set in a converted house, this intimate restaurant dishes up an interesting and delicious fusion of Armenian and Lebanese cuisine, cooked by local women rather than by professional chefs. Try the *kofta* – meatballs served with wild cherry sauce, cashew nuts and fried bread. It's in a backstreet off Rue al-Nahr.

Aliacci ITALIAN $$
(Map p350; ☎566 199; www.aliacci.com; Rue Gouraud, Gemmayzeh; mains LL20,000, pizza from LL15,000; ⊙lunch & dinner) He may be Lebanese but Aliacci's inspiration comes from the other side of the Med. With Italian music and decor, this charming restaurant channels the essence of a simple trattoria – great food and a decent wine selection.

Al Dente ITALIAN $$$
(Map p350; ☎202 440; Hotel Albergo, 137 Rue Abdel Wahab el-Inglizi, Achrafiye; mains US$50; ⊙lunch & dinner, closed Sat lunch) Suitably grand and resplendent as the Hotel Albergo's significant other, this restaurant's Italian dining is indulgent and divine. Bookings are essential.

Walimat Wardeh LEBANESE $
(Map p352; ☎343 128; Rue Neamé Yafet, Hamra; mains LL15,000; ⊙9am-1am Mon-Sat) Simple, stylish and well hidden – look for the blue sign down the road from the Mayflower Hotel – this place offers great music and a daily changing chalked-up menu, veering from Lebanese towards wider Mediterranean.

Pasta di Casa ITALIAN $$
(Map p352; ☎366 909; Rue Clemenceau, Ras Beirut; mains around LL17,000; ⊙lunch & dinner) With its rafters, chequered curtains and tablecloths, you'd be forgiven for thinking you'd stumbled into a tiny Italian backstreet eatery. The pasta portions are huge and delicious, and the prices are very reasonable. Bring cash, since credit cards aren't accepted.

Tawlet LEBANESE $$
(Map p347; ☎448 129; www.tawlet.com; 12 Rue al-Nahr, ground fl, Chalhoub Bldg, Achrafiye; dishes LL15,000; ⊙lunch Mon-Sat) To really experience the various cuisines of Lebanon, Tawlet hosts an 'open kitchen where every day a different

MEZZE ON THE MENU: LEBANESE CUISINE

The equivalent of Italian antipasto or Spanish tapas, Lebanese mezze is the perfect way to start a meal… or, with enough little dishes, to be a meal. The following form the nucleus of the Lebanese mezze, and are usually accompanied by a plate of whatever vegetables are in season – tomatoes, cucumbers, radishes and local greens – as well as the all-important pita bread.

» **Hummus** Chickpea and tahina dip

» **Muttabal** Eggplant and tahina dip

» **Tabbouleh** Parsley, tomato and bulgur wheat salad

But don't limit yourself to these three staples – indulge your palate as you explore Lebanon's tantalising menu.

» **Warak arish** Stuffed vine leaves (also known as *wara anaib*)

» **Fattoush** Salad of toasted bread and tomatoes

» **Sambusas** Fried cheese or meat pastries, similar to samosas

» **Kibbeh** Finely ground meat croquettes with cracked wheat

» **Labneh** Thick yoghurt seasoned with olive oil and garlic

» **Kofta** Mincemeat with parsley and spices grilled on a skewer

» **Kibbeh labaniyye** Kibbeh balls cooked in a warm yoghurt sauce

» **Moujaddara** Lentils cooked with rice and onions

» **Sayadieh** Fish and rice topped with onion sauce

» Fast food options are just as tasty:

» **Mankouche** Thyme and olive oil pizza

» **Lahma bi-ajeen** Spiced ground meat and tomato pizza

» **Felafel** Deep-fried balls of chickpea paste and/or fava beans

» **Shwarma** Thin slices of marinated meat garnished with fresh vegetables, pickles and tahina, wrapped in pita bread

Don't forget to wash it all down with the local drink, arak, made from distilled grape juice and flavoured with anise. And to finish off the meal in style, relax with a nargileh, a water pipe used for smoking flavoured tobacco.

producer or cook prepares typical dishes from his or her region'. The menu is set, and bookings are recommended. It's off Rue al-Nahr, behind the Anthurium flower shop.

Olio ITALIAN $$

(Map p350; ☎563 939; Rue Gouraud, Gemmayzeh; mains from LL20,000, pizzas from LL12,000; ⏲lunch & dinner) Fill up on wood-fired pizza and delicious bruschettas (big enough to be a meal) washed down with stout red wines at this little Italian joint amid Rue Gouraud's manifold dining options.

Abdel Wahab el-Inglezi LEBANESE $$

(Map p350; ☎200 550; Rue Abdel Wahab el-Inglizi, Achrafiye; mains from LL16,000; ⏲lunch & dinner) Set in a pretty, old Ottoman house, this choice is renowned for its sumptuous buffets and high-quality hummus, of which it has more varieties than you can shake a chickpea at.

Al-Balad LEBANESE $$

(Map p350; ☎985 375, Rue Ahdab, BCD; mezze LL15,000; ⏲lunch & dinner) Situated downtown, Al-Balad remains ever-popular. With traditional Lebanese cooking prepared to its own special recipes, this is one of the best places for a tableful of mezze.

Le Chef LEBANESE $

(Map p350; ☎445 373; Rue Gouraud, Gemmayzeh; mains LL9000; ⏲breakfast, lunch & dinner Mon-Sat) A beloved Beiruti institution; don't miss a lunch or two at this little Lebanese time warp, where waiters dish up vast platefuls of 'workers' food' to all and sundry. There's no atmosphere but the food is good value.

La Tabkha LEBANESE $
(Map p350; ☎579 000; Rue Gouraud, Gemmayzeh; mains LL8000; ⏲lunch & dinner) A great bet for vegetarians, who'll love the lunchtime mezze buffet. This minimalist place offers good French and Lebanese dishes, with a menu that changes daily.

Bliss House FAST FOOD $
(Map p352; Rue Bliss, Ras Beirut; shwarma LL3000; ⏲24hr) Always packed with AUB students grabbing a late-night snack or two, Bliss's three shopfronts offer decent-quality fast food at good prices.

Bread Republic CAFE $
(Map p352; off Rue Hamra, Hamra; ⏲7.30am-11pm) After a night of bar-hopping, this small cafe near Rue Neamé Yafet (next to Radio Shack) will purify your blood with healthy organic fare such as chunky lentil soup and monk bean salad.

Self-Catering

Beirut is packed with small neighbourhood grocery shops, usually with a good greengrocer alongside. The **Consumers Co-op** (Map p352; Rue Makdissi, Hamra; ⏲7am-11pm) is the best supermarket that Hamra has to offer, with lots of local and imported goodies, and a great charcuterie a few doors down.

Drinking

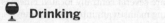

For a drink in the afternoon, the coffee stops of the Corniche and Hamra are your best, and liveliest, bets. Hamra's nightlife has seen an upsurge in recent years, but in Gemmayzeh and, to a lesser extent, Achrafiye, you can bar-hop merrily into the wee hours.

Bars

Dictateur BAR
(30 Bedawi St, Mar Mikhael; ⏲5pm-late) Set in a building scheduled to be demolished at some future date, this venue's semi-industrial decor is quirky yet decidedly cool. The three levels include a funky bar, lounge, restaurant and rooftop terrace. To get here, ask a taxi to take you to Mandaloun; it's behind this, on Bedawi St.

Torino Express BAR
(Map p350; Rue Gouraud, Gemmayzeh; ⏲10am-2am) One of Beirut's coolest small bars, this place is a cafe by day, transforming into a happy, friendly bar by night, aided by some delicious cocktails.

Rabbit Hole BAR
(Map p352; Rue Makdissi, Hamra; ⏲3pm-late) This unpretentious hole-in-the-wall bar is known for its herb-infused, fresh-fruit cocktails. Settle down at the wooden bar for happy hour (5pm to 8pm). There's a different DJ every night.

Li Beirut BAR
(Map p352; Rue Makdissi, Hamra; ⏲6pm-late) A couple of doors down from Rabbit Hole, listen to oriental jazz and traditional Lebanese music in this atmospheric venue. There's mood lighting and cushioned benches upstairs, a traditional dive bar downstairs

Dany's BAR
(Map p352; off Rue Makdissi, Hamra; www.danyslb.com; ⏲9am-2am) This laid-back, cosy bar gets happening later in the evening. There's a small basement stage, and music encompasses jazz, funk, soul, indie and electro.

Pacífico BAR
(Map p350; Rue Monot, Achrafiye; ⏲7pm-late) Styling itself on 1920s Havana, this club prides itself on its food (Cuban-Mexican) and lengthy cocktail list.

Blue Note BAR
(Map p352; www.bluenotecafe.com; Rue Makhoul, Hamra; ⏲11am-2am) This is one of the very best places to hear jazz and blues in Lebanon. Local – and sometimes international – bands perform at least every Thursday, Friday and Saturday.

Bar Louie BAR
(Map p350; Rue Gouraud, Gemmayzeh; ⏲11am-late) Laid-back and lively, this little bar hosts live music almost nightly.

Cafes

Cafe de Prague CAFE
(Map p352; Rue Makdissi, Hamra; ⏲9am-late) Popular with AUB students, intellectuals and artists, this cafe has comfy chairs and low-set tables, and feels like a large lounge room. Bring your laptop or you'll look out of place.

Bay Rock Café CAFE
(Map p347; www.bayrockcafe-lb.com; Ave du Général de Gaulle, Raouché; ⏲24hr) Grab a cold beer and watch the sun go down at this cafe spectacularly situated overlooking Pigeon Rocks – or wiggle with the belly dancers

LISTEN TO THE BAND

When tracking down live music in Beirut, your best first point of reference is the newspaper and magazine listings, along with flyers and posters, which you'll find largely on the streets of Hamra and at the **Virgin Megastore** (Map p350; Place des Martyrs, BCD). Along with one-off concerts, several Beirut venues offer reliable live music options almost every night of the week. The **Democratic Republic of Music** (Map p352; www.drmlebanon.com; Rue Sidani, Hamra), otherwise known as DRM, is one of the best venues for live music. For jazz, check out **Blue Note** (Map p352; www.bluenotecafe.com; Rue Makhoul, Hamra; ⏰11am-2am) or **Mojo Jazz Club** (Map p352; www.mojo-beirut.com; Rue Hamra, Hamra); **Li Beirut** (Map p352; Rue Makdissi, Hamra; ⏰6pm-late) for traditional Lebanese sounds; and **Bar Louie** (Map p350; Rue Gouraud, Gemmayzeh; ⏰11am-late) for funky small live outfits.

Outside the capital, it may be more difficult to track down live music, though during the summer months you're likely to stumble across small local festivals with great music performances in a variety of shapes and sizes. Across the country, there are also a few notable places to head to for evening drinks and tunes. The **Cafés du Bardouni** (p377) in Zahlé usually have live performances going on in the summer months. Down south, the **Al-Midane Café** (p376) at Deir al-Qamar has great live music in the atmospheric town square at summer weekends. And finally, if you see a wedding in swing anywhere, see if you can wangle yourself an invitation to step inside (usually not difficult, due to the Lebanese love of guests): the music's almost always live and the dance floor heaving with generations of Lebanese at their partying best.

who usually perform around midnight at weekends.

Al-Raouda CAFE
(Map p347; Corniche, Manara; ⏰7.30am-midnight Jun-Sep, 8am-8pm Oct-May) Stop in for a hit of strong coffee or a languid nargileh at Al-Raouda, a waterfront favourite with local families. It's a little tricky to find: walk down the lane right next to the Luna Park entrance, then look for the misspelt 'El Rawda' sign.

☆ Entertainment

Beirut's nightlife, along with Tel Aviv's in Israel, is justifiably considered among the best in the Middle East. Things don't usually get going until well after midnight (not surprising, considering the habitual dining hour is some time around 11pm), and continue till dawn and long beyond.

Nightclubs

B 018 CLUB
(Map p347; www.b018.com; Lot 317, La Quarantine; ⏰9pm-7am) Easily the most famous club in town, this equally gay-friendly underground place, a couple of kilometres east of downtown, is known for its mock-horror interior and sliding roof, which always opens at some point during the night. To get here, ask a cab driver to take you to the Forum de Beyrouth and follow the clubbers from there.

Cassino CLUB
(Map p350; www.cassinobeirut.com; cnr Sodeco Sq & Rue de Damas; ⏰9pm-5am Sun-Thu) If you're tired of techno, head on over to chic Cassino for Arabic pop, champagne and cigars galore, but remember to dress the part.

Cinemas

There are several centrally located cinemas screening mainstream international movies.

Empire ABC CINEMA
(Map p347; ABC Mall, Achrafiye)

Empire Dunes CINEMA
(Map p347; Dunes Centre, Verdun)

Empire Sofil Centre CINEMA
(Map p350; Sofil Centre, Ave Charles Malek, Achrafiye)

Theatre

Monnot Theatre THEATRE
(Map p350; ☎202 422; Rue St Joseph University, Achrafiye) Next to St Joseph's Church, the Monnot Theatre hosts a regular program of live music and theatre performances.

Sport

Hippodrome HORSE RACING
(Map p347; ☎632 515; Ave Abdallah Yafi; admission LL5000-15,000; ⏰11am-4pm Sun) This racing venue, just behind the National Museum of Beirut, is one of the few places in the Middle East where you can legally place a bet.

Shopping

You'll find good-value shopping opportunities strung along Rue Hamra.

Beirut Souks SHOPPING MALL
(Map p350; www.beirutsouks.com.lb; Saad Zaghloul St, BCD) You can find anything you want at this modern shopping complex.

Librairie Antoine BOOKS
(Map 352; Rue Hamra, Hamra) If you're out of holiday reading, this place stocks literature (including Lebanese) in English, French and Spanish, and has a good children's section.

Saifi Village SHOPPING MALL
(Map p350; BCD; ⏰10am-7pm Mon-Sat, late night shopping Thu) Saifi Village is a cute, restored residential district filled with arts, crafts and clothing boutiques.

Virgin Megastore MUSIC, BOOKS
(Map p350; Opera Bldg, Place des Martyrs) A huge collection of books and maps, local and regional music, and the place to pick up tickets for Lebanon's summer festivals.

Information

Though there are lots of useful landmarks by which to navigate around town (the towering, derelict former Holiday Inn being the most obvious), navigating Beirut can still be a little tricky. The blue signs on street corners don't usually give the name of the street itself; instead, only the sector (suburb) name and rue (street) number. On top of this, numbered buildings are rare, and many streets don't have names at all, or are locally known by a different name from the one given on a map. That said, armed with a good street map, getting familiar with this compact city is actually rather easy.

Dangers & Annoyances

The biggest danger – and annoyance – in Beirut is the traffic. Rules both on and off the road are nonexistent, and pedestrians should take particular care when crossing the road. As with everywhere in Lebanon, it makes sense to keep abreast of the news and to avoid political demonstrations and unaccompanied travel to Beirut's Palestinian refugee camps.

Emergency

Ambulance (☎140)
Fire (☎175)
Police (☎112)
Tourist police (☎350 901)

Internet Access

Wi-fi is widely available in nearly every accommodation range, as well as in most cafes – all you need is your laptop. Otherwise, there's no shortage of internet cafes all across Beirut; the highest concentration is in the vicinity of the AUB campus. Opening hours are very flexible, though most open around 9am and stay open until well after midnight. Prices are generally around the LL3000 per hour mark.

Skynet (Map 352; Rue Sidani, Hamra) One of the best places with fast connections.

Maps

Zawarib Beirut (LL8000), a large-scale A–Z-style street map of the entire city (in English), and *Lebanon Tourist Map* (US$8), published by **Paravision** (www.paravision.org), are widely available in bookshops.

Media

Beirut's two foreign-language newspaper dailies are the French *L'Orient Le Jour* (www.lorientlejour.com; LL2000) and the English *Daily Star* (www.dailystar.com; LL2000). Online, the very best source of independent news is **Ya Libnan** (www.yalibnan.com).

Though its production is often beset by problems, *Time Out Beirut* (www.timeoutbeirut.com; LL7000), when it does appear, is an invaluable source of local information.

Medical Services

American University of Beirut Hospital
(Map p352; ☎350 000, 354 911; Rue Sourati, Hamra) Considered one of the best hospitals in the Middle East, with English and French spoken.

Money

There are ATMs all over the city, most of which dispense both US dollars and Lebanese lira. Moneychangers are dotted plentifully along Rue Hamra. Note that at the time of research there was nowhere to change travellers cheques.

Post

Libanpost, the national post office, has plenty of branches scattered through town. Standard opening hours are 8am to 5pm Monday to Friday and 8am to 1.30pm Saturday. Two convenient branches:

Hamra (Map p352; Malla Bldg, Rue Makdissi, Hamra)

Gemmayzeh (Map p350; Zighbi Bldg, Rue Gouraud, Gemmayzeh)

Tourist Information

Tourist information office (Map p352; ☎343 073; www.destinationlebanon.gov.lb; Ground fl, Ministry of Tourism Bldg, 550 Rue Banque du Liban, Hamra; ⏰8am-1.30pm & 2-5pm Mon-Thu, 8am-3pm Fri, 8am-1pm Sat) Enter by the back door, through a covered car park, to find helpful staff, informative brochures and LCC bus route maps.

Tourist police (Map p352; ☎752 428; ⏲24hr) For complaints or problems (including robbery), contact this office opposite the tourist information office.

Getting There & Away

For information on transport between Syria and Beirut, see p395.

Buses, minibuses and service taxis to destinations north of Beirut leave from Gemmayzeh's **Charles Helou bus station** (Map p350) and the **Dawra transport hub** (Dora; off Map p347), 7km northeast of town. To destinations south and southeast, they leave from the **Cola transport hub** (Map p347), about 2km south of the BCD.

Getting Around

To/From the Airport

Beirut Rafic Hariri International Airport (off Map p347; ☎628 000; www.beirutairport.gov.lb) is approximately 5km south of Beirut's city centre. There are no scheduled buses servicing the airport but you can catch a minivan (LL1000) to get into the city. Go to the Departures entrance (upstairs from Arrivals) and wait for a minivan with an aeroplane sticker on the windscreen. One comes by every five to 10 minutes. Take this to the Charles Helou bus station in Gemmayzeh. (For downtown, hop off at Place des Martyrs; for Hamra, disembark at Bechara el-Khoury square).

To get to the airport from Hamra, take a minivan (No 4; LL1000) from outside the tourist information office to Bechara el-Khoury Sq. From here you can catch another minivan (the minivan has no number – look for the aeroplane sticker on the windscreen; LL1000) directly to the airport entrance. These airport buses pass by every five minutes. From Achrafiye, take LCC bus (No 2, 5 or 8; LL1000) to Bechara el-Khoury Sq and change here for the airport bus. If you have excess luggage, expect to pay extra.

If you can stretch your budget, the most hassle-free way to get to town is to prearrange a taxi with your hotel. Even budget hostels offer this service, charging around US$20 to US$25 for the ride; this is probably cheaper than you'll be offered at the airport itself without a fair amount of bargaining. If you do opt for a normal yellow cab, agree to the price before climbing inside.

TRAVEL WARNING: STAYING SAFE

Though its recent history has included several lengthy periods of relative calm, Lebanon's chequered religious, political and social fabric has frequently caused tensions to flare suddenly and violently.

Many countries, including the UK, Australia and the USA, currently include Lebanon on their list of countries to which all but essential travel should be avoided. Most specifically, foreign offices advise against travel south of Nahr al-Litani (the Litani River) or into Palestinian refugee camps, and suggest avoiding all public demonstrations.

Despite the bleak warnings, you'll find warm, welcoming people in Lebanon, eager to help travellers, and you'll quickly feel safe and at home.

Nevertheless, it's important to remember that circumstances can change extremely rapidly: in summer 2006, for example, many travellers suddenly found themselves stranded after Israel's attacks on the country shut down the international airport and rendered the main highway to the Syrian border impassable. Most crucially when in Lebanon, keep your eye on the news. **Ya Libnan** (www.yalibnan.com) and the **Daily Star** (www.dailystar.com.lb) are both good sources of up-to-the-minute online news.

More general suggestions include trying to avoid driving at night (largely due to Lebanon's hair-raising, headlight-free driving) and taking local advice when travelling in the south. If you're planning on visiting any Palestinian refugee camps, make sure you take a reliable local companion. Recent threats against UN Interim Forces in Lebanon (UNIFIL) troops have led some to warn against visiting restaurants or other establishments frequented by UNIFIL staff in Tyre. It may pay to talk with your embassy in Lebanon if you're in any doubt as to your safety.

Moreover, due to the Syrian crisis, there have been reports of violent conflicts in Tripoli between opponents and supporters of the Syrian government. Seek advice before travelling to Tripoli and to the north of the country.

Finally, theft is a minor problem, but random crime is far lower than in most Western cities. There are occasional spates of motor-scooter bag snatchings, particularly in Beirut, but as in any large city, you only need to exercise normal precautions.

Buses

Beirut is well serviced by its network of slow, crowded, but good-value buses. The red-and-white **Lebanese Commuting Company** (LCC; www.lccworld.com) buses operate on a 'hail-and-ride' system: just wave at the driver and, in theory at least, the bus will stop. There are no timetables, but buses generally run from around 5.30am to 9pm daily at intervals of 15 minutes or so.

The LCC bus routes most useful to travellers are listed below. A short trip will almost always cost LL1000, a longer ride LL2000.

No 1 Hamra–Khaldé Rue Sadat (Hamra), Rue Emile Eddé, Hotel Bristol, Rue Verdun, Cola roundabout, Airport roundabout, Kafaat, Khaldé.

No 2 Hamra–Antelias Rue Sadat (Hamra), Rue Emile Eddé, Radio Lebanon, Sassine Sq, Dawra transport hub, Antelias.

No 5 Charles Helou–Hay as-Saloum Manara, Verdun, Yessoueiye, Airport roundabout, Hay as-Saloum.

No 6 Cola–Byblos Antelias, Jounieh, Byblos (Jbail).

No 7 National Museum–Bharssaf National Museum, Beit Mery, Brummana, Baabdat, Bharssaf.

Car & Motorcycle

If you have nerves of steel and a penchant for *Grand Theft Auto*, you may well enjoy driving in and around Beirut. The best local car rental company is **Advanced Car Rental** (☎999 884/5; www.advancedcarrent.com), which offers great discounts on its published rates, and is highly recommended. And hey, they even throw in their very own CD, a sort of Arabic easy-listening compilation, for the ride.

Taxi & Service Taxi

Private taxi companies usually have meters; make sure your driver turns the meter on or agrees to a fare in advance. Within Beirut, taxis charge anywhere from LL5000 to LL10,000, depending on your destination.

Service (shared) taxis cover the major routes in Beirut. The fare is LL2000 on established routes within the city and LL5000 to LL10,000 to outlying suburbs.

AROUND BEIRUT

Beit Mery & Brummana

بيت مرعي & برومانا

☎04

Set in pine forests some 800m above and 17km east of Beirut, Beit Mery – its name means 'House of the Master' in Aramaic – is a lazy weekend getaway for Beirutis seeking respite from city pollution, and offers sweeping panoramic views over the capital. The town dates back to Phoenician times and is home to Roman and Byzantine ruins, including some fine **floor mosaics** in a nearby 5th-century Byzantine church (ask locally for directions). Also worth a visit is the 18th-century Maronite monastery of **Deir al-Qalaa**, built over the remains of a Roman temple.

Beit Mery's **al-Bustan Festival** (www.albustanfestival.com) is held in mid-February, with a varied program of chamber, choral and orchestral music. Many of the festival's performances take place at the Hotel al-Bustan.

About 4km northeast of Beit Mery is Brummana, a more bustling resort town connected to Beit Mery by a continuous strip of hotels, eateries, cafes, shops and nightclubs. In summer it's equally popular with Beirutis escaping the city heat and has a carnival-like atmosphere, especially on weekends. There's nothing particular to do here except to eat, drink and be merry (Beit Merry, perhaps); be aware that it's extremely quiet outside summer season and weekends.

Sleeping & Eating

There are dozens of places to stay and eat in both Beit Mery and Brummana, but unless you're in Lebanon for an extended stay, there's not much reason to favour them over Beirut itself.

Hotel al-Bustan HOTEL $$$
(☎972 980/82; www.albustanhotel.com; Beit Mery; s/d/ste from US$280/320/345; ❄@📶🏊) One of the smartest hotels in the two towns, this is a good choice during the popular al-Bustan Festival, since many concerts are performed in the hotel itself.

Restaurant Mounir LEBANESE $$$
(☎873 900; Main St, Brummana; mains US$30; ⏱lunch & dinner, closed Mon) A good place for a long lunch, this restaurant has a pleasant terrace (equipped with a children's playground) with spectacular views over Beirut and the Mediterranean. Book in advance and request a table with a view.

Getting There & Away

Service taxis from the National Museum or Dawra usually charge LL5000 to either Beit Mery or Brummana. LCC bus 7 (LL1000, 40 minutes) departs from Beirut opposite the National Museum.

Jeita Grotto مغارة جعيتا

☎09

Undoubtedly one of Lebanon's greatest natural wonders and biggest tourist attractions, this stunning **cave system** (☎220 840; www.jeitagrotto.com; adult/child under 12yr LL18,150/10,175; ⏰9am-6pm Tue-Sun Jun-Sep, 9am-5pm Tue-Sun Oct-May, closed late Jan-early Feb) is not to be missed, and is open every day in July and August. Extending around 6km back into the mountains, the caves were used as an ammunition store during the civil war, and their lower strata are flooded each winter due to the rising levels of the Nahr-el-Kalb (or Dog River) for which they form the source.

The incredible upper cavern, however, stays open all year, and can be explored on foot even when boat rides into the lower cavern are suspended due to flooding. Strategic lighting showcases the stalactites and stalagmites in all their crystalline glory. And despite all kinds of tatty side attractions – including a toy train ride – the site remains a spectacular day trip from Beirut. Bear in mind that there's no photography allowed: you can stow your camera in lockers at the mouth of the caverns.

To get to the grotto, which lies about 18km northeast of Beirut, take a minibus (LL1500) or LCC bus 6 (LL1500) from Dawra and ask the driver to drop you at the Jeita turn-off on the Beirut–Jounieh Hwy. From here, negotiate a return price with a waiting taxi for the 5km journey (around US$12 to US$15), and make sure to figure in waiting time. One-way taxis from the grotto back to the highway or Dawra charge a premium. Alternatively, a return taxi trip from Beirut should cost around US$25.

Jounieh جونيه

☎09 / POP 103,227

Once a sleepy fishing village, Jounieh, 21km north of Beirut, is now a high-rise strip mall hemmed in by the sea on one side and the mountains on the other. Famous as the home of noisy bars, camp restaurants catering to Saudi sheikhs and lurid 'super' nightclubs filled with bored exotic dancers, it's not somewhere you might want to spend too much time. But it does have two worthwhile distractions, both reachable on a day trip from Beirut: the soaring heights of the Teleferique, and the equally dizzying gaming tables of the venerable Casino du Liban.

Sights & Activities

Jounieh Teleferique CABLE CAR
(☎936 075; adult/child return LL9000/5000; ⏰10am-11pm Jun-Oct, to 7pm Nov-May, closed Mon) Dubbed the Terrorifique by some, this attraction runs cable cars up from Jounieh to the mountaintop Basilica of Our Lady of Lebanon at Harissa. The views from the summit are spectacular.

Casino du Liban CASINO
(☎855 888; www.cdl.com.lb; Rue Maameltein; ⏰slot-machines 10am-6am, gaming rooms 4pm-4am) The historic casino, once host to celebrities such as Liz Taylor and David Niven, still has a kitsch charm for those longing for a taste of days gone by. Guests must be over 21 and wear smart casual gear (no jeans or sports shoes); a suit and tie are required (for men, of course) if you want to play the roulette wheels.

Eating

Jounieh has plenty of chain restaurants and glitzy, overpriced steak places.

Chez Sami SEAFOOD $$$
(☎910 520; www.chezsamirestaurant.com; Rue Maameltein; mains US$40; ⏰noon-midnight) A standout from the crowd, and considered one of the best seafood restaurants in Lebanon, Chez Sami is simple but stylish and offers great seaside views and a lovely summer terrace. There's no menu, so take your pick from the catch of the day and come early – the crowds think it's the catfish's pyjamas.

Getting There & Away

From Beirut's Dawra transport hub, catch LCC bus 6 (LL3000, 40 minutes) to Jounieh. Service taxis (LL5000) also depart from the transport hub; ask the driver to drop you on the highway near the footbridge. A private taxi from Beirut to Jounieh costs around US$20 to US$25.

NORTH OF BEIRUT

Byblos (Jbail) بيبلوس

☎09 / POP 21,600

A pretty fishing port with a plethora of ancient remains and some interesting fishy fossils, Byblos is one of the highlights of the entire Middle Eastern Mediterranean coast. The medieval town has a charming souq near the ruins, and the harbour is lined with a string of good restaurants.

History

Excavations have shown that Byblos (the biblical Gebal) was probably inhabited as early as 7000 years ago; by the middle of the 3rd millennium BC it had become the busiest trading port on the eastern Mediterranean and an important religious centre, all under the direction of the maritime Phoenicians. Close links to Egypt fostered its cultural and religious development, and as the city flourished it developed its own distinct art and architecture, part Egyptian, part Mesopotamian. It was in Byblos, too, that our modern alphabet is said to have had its roots, developed by the Phoenicians as a way of accurately recording its healthy trade transactions.

The city was renamed Byblos by the Greeks, who ruled here from 333 BC; it was named after the Greek word *bublos*, meaning papyrus, which was shipped from Egypt to Greece via Byblos' port. As the Greek empire fell into decline, the Romans, under Pompey, arrived in town, constructing temples, baths, colonnaded streets and public buildings galore. Later allied to Constantinople and conquered in the 7th century by the Islamic invasion, in 1104 the city fell to the Crusaders, who set about building a castle and moat with stone and columns taken from the earlier Roman temples.

Subsequent centuries under Ottoman and Mamluk rule saw Byblos' international reputation as a trading port decline, just as Beirut's star was in the ascendancy. Byblos soon settled into a new incarnation as a sleepy fishing port, which it remains to this day. Excavations of its former glories began in 1860 and continue, at a snail's pace, today.

Sights & Activities

Ruins HISTORIC SITE

(☎540 001; adult/child/student LL6000/2000/2000; ⏲8.30am-sunset) This ancient site is entered through the restored 12th-century **Crusader castle** that dominates the sturdy 25m-thick **city ramparts** (which date from the 3rd and 2nd millennia BC). It's well worth taking a guide from here (LL30,000 to LL40,000 depending on the size of your group) to show you around the expansive site in detail. There are great views from the top of the ramparts, offering a good overview of the layout of the ancient city.

From the Crusader castle, turn left past the remains of the city gate and follow the path until you reach the L-shaped **Temple of Resheph** dating from the 3rd millennium BC. From here, move on to check out the intriguing **Obelisk Temple** from the early 2nd century BC; bronze votive offerings in the shape of human figures discovered here

DON'T MISS

SOMETHING FISHY

Tucked away in an alleyway in the Byblos souq is the workshop of young local palaeontologist Pierre Abi-Saad and his fascinating hundred-million-year-old haul of fishy history. Discovered in a quarry owned by his family for generations, almost 1km above sea level, his glimpses into a prehistoric underwater world are today represented in almost every major international natural history museum, though he keeps his favourites for the long-awaited day when he, too, will open a museum of his own findings to the world.

More than 80% of the fossils Pierre has found represent species now extinct, and many haven't yet been studied or named. Adorning the walls of his workshop and adjoining shop are eels, stingrays, octopi, jellyfish, eels, shrimp and coelacanths, one of the earliest fish ever to exist. His collection even includes such oddities as a fossil of a fish that had swallowed another fish before its ancient demise, and a 4m-long complete shark, the largest in the world. Fossils for sale come with a certificate of authentication.

Mémoire du Temps (☎540 555; www.memoryoftime.com; Byblos souq; ⏲9am-7.30pm) provides a fascinating glimpse into a distant fishy past and is where you'll usually find Pierre, chipping away enthusiastically at a hunk of limestone. His enthusiasm is infectious, his friendliness disarming, and you might even be invited up to the quarry yourself, to fish for your own ancient catch – without getting even your little toe wet.

Byblos (Jbail)

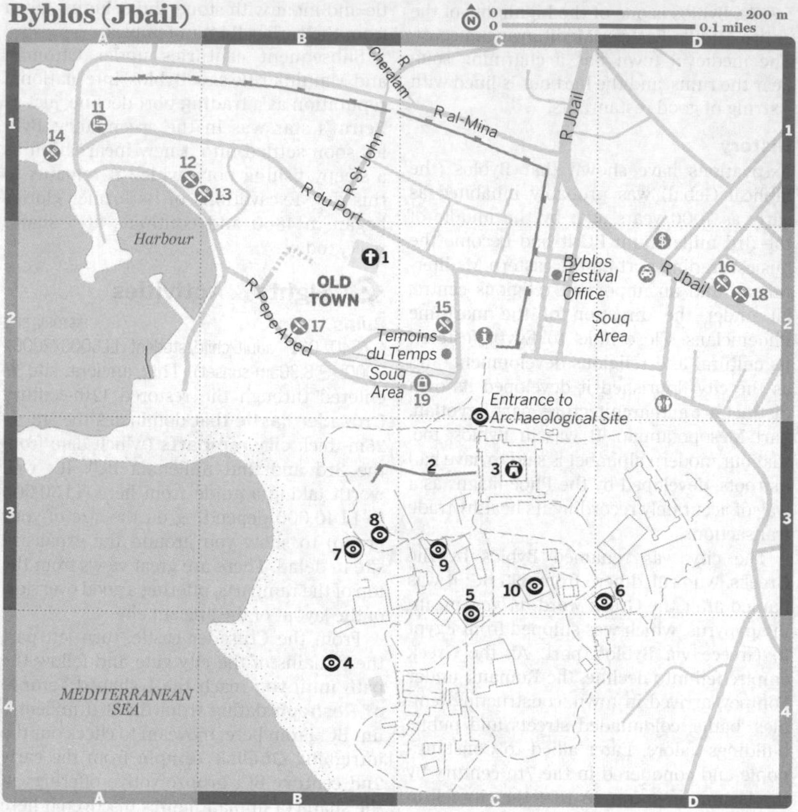

are now famously displayed at Beirut's National Museum.

Following the path southwest, head past the **King's Well**, a spring that supplied the city with water until the end of the Hellenistic era (and where, according to legend, Isis sat weeping on her search for Osiris), to some of the earliest remains on the site. These **early settlements** comprise the remnants of Neolithic (5th century BC) and Chalcolithic (4th century BC) enclosures, houses and huts. Throughout this area, large burial jars were found containing preserved bodies curled up in the foetal position.

Nearby, Byblos' old temple, the **Temple of Baalat Gebal** (the Mistress of Byblos), dates back to the 4th century BC. This was the largest and most important temple constructed at Byblos, dedicated to Aphrodite during the Roman period, and was rebuilt a number of times in the two millennia that it survived. Many temple findings, including alabaster vase fragments inscribed with the names of Old Kingdom pharaohs, are today also housed in the capital's National Museum. The six standing columns approaching the temple are the vestiges of a Roman colonnaded street, built as the temple approach around 300 AD.

To the northwest of the temple, towards the sea, is the **Roman theatre**, a reconstruction that's one-third the size of the original, situated near the cliff edge with great views across the sea. Behind this are nine **royal tombs**, cut in vertical shafts deep into the rock in the 2nd millennium BC; some of the sarcophagi found here are now housed in the National Museum, including that of King Hiram, whose sarcophagus has one of the earliest Phoenician alphabet inscriptions in the world. His grave shaft also is inscribed, this time with the eerie phrase, 'Warning here. Thy death is below.'

Byblos (Jbail)

Sights

Church of St John the Baptist CHURCH
(Eglise St Jean Marc) This Romanesque-style church, at the centre of the Crusader town, was begun in 1115, and was slowly added to in subsequent centuries. It's thus an interesting mixture of Arab and Italian designs, with remains of Byzantine mosaics scattered about the area. It also features an unusual open-air baptistery, which sits against the north wall, its arches and four supporting pillars topped by a dome.

Festivals & Events

Byblos International Festival MUSIC
(www.byblosfestival.org) Gets the town going each summer with a host of local and international performers. Check the website for up-to-date festival and ticket details, and events listings.

Sleeping

Byblos Sur Mer HOTEL $$$
(548 000; Rue du Port; s/d US$240/260;) A class act, with great harbour views from the rooms, a seafront pool and a central location, this hotel is a very stylish base from which to explore Byblos – and areas further north. The glass-panelled floor of the hotel's main restaurant, **Dar L'Azrak** (mains US$50; lunch & dinner Apr-Sep), provides views of the ruins below.

Hotel Ahiram HOTEL $$
(540 440; www.ahiramhotel.com; s/d US$110/120;) A cracking little three-star, the Ahiram makes for a comfortable sleep. All rooms have balconies with sea views, and the hotel has direct access to a small, pebbly beach. Ask about substantial off-season discounts.

Eating & Drinking

For cheap eats, head to the many felafel and shwarma joints along Rue Jbail; local favourites include **Restaurant Rock** and the **Kaddoum Centre**.

Feniqia LEBANESE $
(540 444; Byblos souq; mains from LL10,000; 9am-midnight) On the corner of the square opposite the tourist office, this is a fab place for a filling breakfast, lazy lunch or evening tipple. As well as serving Lebanese fare, you can get tasty burgers and pizzas. It's a great people-watching place, especially on summer weekend evenings.

Byblos Fishing Club LEBANESE $$
(Pepe's; 540 213; Old Port; mains LL28,000; 11am-midnight) A Lebanese institution, the Fishing Club was founded by the legendary Pepe (who features on the photograph-covered wall dandling many a '60s film star on his knee). There's a little museum devoted to Pepe's memory. However, meals are overpriced and overhyped, so come for a sunset drink instead. In summer, the Fishing Club runs an alfresco Italian restaurant, **Pepe Hacienda**, in a lovely garden around the corner.

Bab el-Mina SEAFOOD $$
(540 475; www.babelmina.com; Old Port; mains LL25,000; noon-midnight) Boasting a lovely location overlooking the port, the restaurant specialises in fish and traditional Lebanese mezze, at competitive prices. Some say it's better value than Pepe's.

Information

Banque Libanaise pour le Commerce (Rue Jbail)

Post office (Rahban St) Look for the Coral Petrol Station on Rue Jbail, 30m east of the station on a side street. Around 20m up the hill on your right, the post office is on the 2nd floor.

Temoins du Temps (Byblos souq) If you don't want to traipse to the post office, this souvenir shop opposite the tourist office sells stamps. There's a post box next to the shop.

Tourist office (☎540 325; Byblos souq; ⌚9am-5pm Mar-Nov, closed Sun) Located in the souq near the entrance to the archaeological site, it has maps of the site.

Getting There & Away

The **service taxi stand** (Rue Jbail) in Byblos is across the road from the Banque Libanaise pour le Commerce. A service taxi to/from Dawra transport hub in Beirut costs LL6000 (about eight services depart between 7am and 6pm). LCC bus 6 (LL1500, around one hour) and minibuses (LL1500) also leave from Dawra transport hub and travel regularly along the coast road between Beirut and Byblos, stopping on Rue Jbail.

Tripoli (Trablous) طرابلس

☎06 / POP 237,909

Tripoli, 85km north of Beirut, is Lebanon's second largest city and the north's main port and trading centre. Famous for its medieval Mamluk architecture, including a large souq area considered the best in Lebanon, it might nevertheless seem a little run-down and provincial if you've come direct from Beirut. However, the city certainly warrants a day or so of souq-wandering and sweets-sampling, Tripoli's main speciality being *haliwat al-jibn,* a teeth-jarringly sweet confection made from curd cheese and served with syrup.

Be warned, you won't have much luck finding a drink in town. For a beer on a hot day, head to Al-Mina, the port area 3km west of town.

History

As early as the 8th century BC, Tripoli was already a thriving trading post, thanks to the constant comings and goings of traders from Tyre, Sidon and Arwad (the latter in present-day Syria). Each community settled in its own area, a fact reflected in the city's name, which derives from the Greek word *tripolis,* meaning 'three cities'.

Conquered in turn by the Seleucids, Romans, Umayyads, Byzantines and Fatimids, Tripoli was invaded by the Crusaders in AD 1102, who held on to it for 180 years and built its imposing, and still-standing, hilltop fortress, the Citadel of Raymond de Saint-Gilles. In 1289 the Mamluk Sultan Qalaun took control of the city, and embarked upon an ambitious building program; many of the mosques, souqs, madrassas and khans that remain in the old city today date from either the Crusader period or subsequent Sultan Qalaun era. The Turkish Ottomans took over the city in 1516 and ruled, in relative peace, until 1920, when it became part of the French mandate of Greater Lebanon.

With a large influx of Palestinian refugees from 1948 onward, the city became the site of ferocious fighting during the civil war. Huge UN-administered refugee camps still hug Tripoli's outskirts, including the Nahr el-Bared camp, now infamous for its protracted Palestinian/Lebanese army deadlock in 2007.

Sights & Activities

Citadel of Raymond de Saint-Gilles CASTLE

(admission LL7500; ⌚8am-6pm) Towering above Tripoli, this Crusader fortress was originally built during the period from 1103 to 1104. It was burnt down in 1297 and partly rebuilt the following century by a Mamluk emir.

The most impressive part of the citadel is the imposing entrance, with its moat and three gateways (one Ottoman, one Mamluk, one Crusader). Guided tours are available and prices depend on group size: it's generally LL5000/15,000/20,000 for one person/small group/large group. Since there's an architecturally muddled rabbit warren of parts inside, and very little labelling, it makes sense to employ their services if you want to learn more about the citadel's history.

OLD CITY

Dating from the Mamluk era (14th and 15th centuries), the compact Old City is a maze of narrow alleys, colourful souqs, hammams, khans, mosques and madrassas. It's a lively and fascinating place where craftspeople, including tailors, jewellers, soap makers and coppersmiths, continue to work as they have done for centuries. The **Souq al-Sayyaghin** (the gold souq), **Souq al-Attarin** (for perfumes and spices), the medieval **Souq al-Haraj** and **Souq an-Nahhassin** (the brass souq) are all well worth a wander.

Great Mosque MOSQUE

The Great Mosque, built on the site of a 12th-century Crusader cathedral and incorporating some of its features, has a magnificent entrance and an unusual minaret that was probably once the cathedral bell tower.

Madrassas HISTORIC BUILDINGS

Opposite the mosque's northern entrance is the **Madrassa al-Nouriyat**, which has distinctive black-and-white stonework and a beautiful inlaid mihrab, and is still in use today. Attached to the east side of the Grand Mosque is the **Madrassa al-Qartawiyya**, converted between 1316 and 1326 from the former St Mary's church. Its elegant black-and-white facade and honeycomb patterned half-dome above the portal are well worth a look.

Al-Muallaq Mosque MOSQUE

(Hanging Mosque) You have to glance up to see Al-Muallaq Mosque, a small and unusual 14th-century mosque on the 2nd floor of a building. Located just opposite is the **Hammam al-Jadid**, the city's best-preserved bathhouse, in use from around 1740 well into the 1970s. It has some lovely coloured glass windows.

Khan as-Saboun KHAN

(⌚10am-5pm Mon-Sat, to 4pm Sun) At the souq's centre, the Khan as-Saboun was built in the 16th century and first used as an army barracks; since then, it has for generations functioned as a point of sale for Tripoli's famous soaps. Today you can still stop in to pick up any of its 400 types of soap; check out the huge one carved into the shape of an open volume of the Quran.

Hammam al-Abd BATHHOUSE

(basic bath LL15,000; ⌚8.30am-midnight) To the west of the Khan as-Saboun is the 300-year-old Hammam al-Abd, the city's only functioning bathhouse. Unfortunately, it's only open to men, unless you are travelling with a group of women and can rent out the whole place.

Khan al-Khayyatin KHAN

One of the most beautiful buildings in the old city is the Khan al-Khayyatin, formerly a Crusader hospital and today a beautifully restored 14th-century tailors' souq lined with small workshops.

Khan al-Misriyyin KHAN

To the northwest of the khan is Khan al-Misriyyin, believed to date from the 14th century when it was used by Egyptian merchants. On the 1st floor of the dilapidated khan, you can find **Sharkass** (⌚10am-7pm Jun-Sep, to 5pm Oct-May). Making soap since 1803, the family produces good-quality, authentic Tripoli soap; you're welcome to buy a bar of natural or perfumed soap, or simply to look around. Note that the shop is on the 1st floor (not the one with the same name on the ground).

Taynal Mosque MOSQUE

Standing on its own to the south of the souqs on the outskirts of the Old City, but well worth the walk, is the restored Taynal Mosque. It dates from 1336 and represents probably the most outstanding example of Islamic religious architecture in Tripoli. As with all the Old City mosques, dress demurely (women should cover their legs, arms and head), take off your shoes outside, and check first that it's OK to enter. Some Old City mosques offer full cloaks for women to don, not particularly comfortable at the height of summer.

Al-Burtasiya Mosque & Madrassa MOSQUE

Close to the souq, the mosque has a particularly fine mihrab decorated with stone and glass mosaics overlaid with gold leaf.

Sleeping

Unfortunately, there are no decent midrange options in Tripoli.

TOP CHOICE **Chateau des Oliviers** BOUTIQUE HOTEL $$$

(☎411 170/90; www.chateau-des-oliviers.com; off Haykalieh Rd, Haykalieh; s US$110-300, d US$135-300; ❄📶🏊) Known locally as Villa Nadia, this boutique hotel set on a hilltop only a few kilometres south of Tripoli is decorated with antiques and exotic furnishings collected by eccentric host Nadia Dibo, on her many travels around the world. There are 17 rooms, an extensive and lush garden, a restaurant, bar and even a nightclub. It's worth the trip to Tripoli just to spend a night in the villa. To get here, turn into Haykalieh Rd at the Hypermarket approximately 3km south of Tripoli. Turn right about 500m after Haykal Hospital and follow the signs.

Hotel Koura HOTEL $

(☎03-371 041; off Rue Tall; dm/r from US$15/50; ❄📶) Recently renovated, this friendly, family-run place is without doubt the best of Tripoli's budget bunch. The bright, simple rooms with stone walls are arranged around a central shared lounge. The extremely accommodating owners can arrange day trips.

Eating & Drinking

Tripoli's eating options aren't especially exciting, but if you're looking for cheap eats,

Tripoli (Trablous): Old City

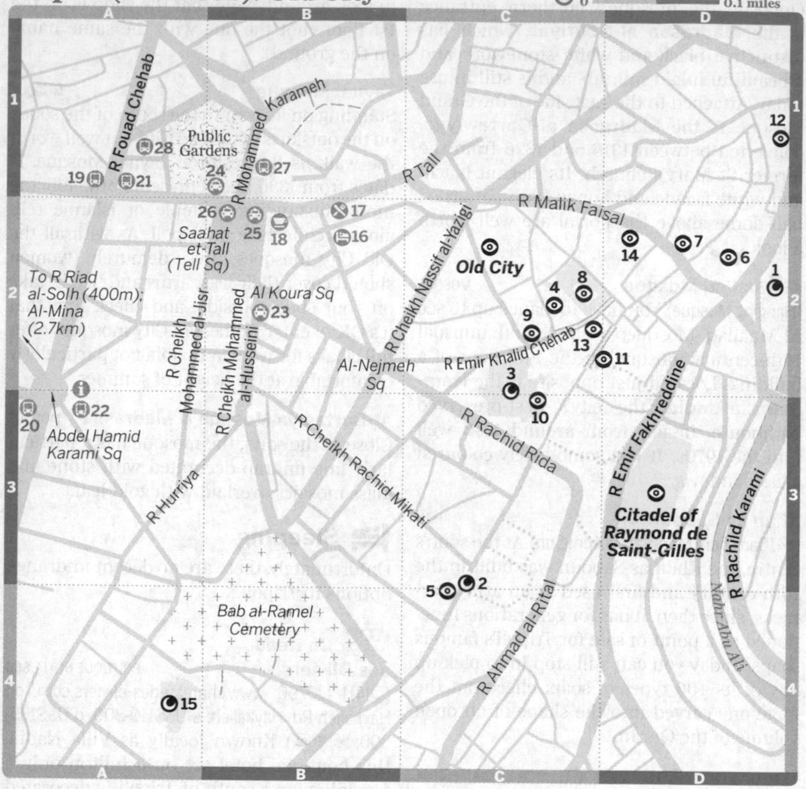

it's best to either wander the area around the Old City (where you'll find street vendors selling sweet corn and felafel) or Rue Riad al-Solh, which has a plethora of budget fast-food joints.

If you want to drink alcohol with your meal, head to the restaurants in Al-Mina, the port area.

Silver Shore SEAFOOD **$$$**
(☎601 384; Corniche, Al-Mina; meals US$35; ⏰11am-8pm) Considered the best seafood restaurant in northern Lebanon, this place is locally known for its hot sauce, made to a secret recipe. Be aware that it closes very early in the evening.

'46 INTERNATIONAL **$$**
(☎212 223; Corniche, Al-Mina; mains LL25,000; ⏰7am-1am) Named after the year it first opened, this place dispenses perfectly satisfactory pastas, steaks and salads, making it a cut above Tripoli's other dining options. The entrance is around the back of the restaurant.

Rafaat Hallab & Sons BAKERY **$**
(Rue Tall; ⏰5am-midnight) Founded in 1881, this is a popular central branch of what is probably the best Halab patisserie in Lebanon and certainly the best place to sample Tripoli's famous sticky baklava-type sweets (from LL1500 per portion).

Café Fahim CAFE **$**
(Rue Tall; ⏰6am-10pm) A cavernous old cafe with an echoing, vaulted interior filled with local men, young and old, smoking nargileh and playing backgammon. It's not cosy but the terrace is a good place for sipping tea and people-watching.

Information

Tripoli comprises two main areas: the city proper, which includes modern Tripoli and the Old City; and Al-Mina, the rather down-and-out

Tripoli (Trablous): Old City

Top Sights

- Citadel of Raymond de Saint-Gilles ... D3
- Old City ... C2

Sights

1. Al-Burtasiya Mosque & Madrassa ... D2
2. Al-Muallaq Mosque ... C3
3. Great Mosque ... C2
4. Hammam al-Abd ... C2
5. Hammam al-Jadid ... C4
6. Khan al-Khayyatin ... D2
7. Khan al-Misriyyin ... D2
8. Khan as-Sabouri ... C2
9. Madrassa al-Nouriyat ... C2
10. Madrassa al-Qartawiyya ... C3
    Sharkass ... (see 7)
11. Souq al-Attarin ... D2
12. Souq al-Haraj ... D1
13. Souq al-Sayyaghin ... C2
14. Souq an-Nahhassin ... D2
15. Taynal Mosque ... A4

Sleeping

16. Hotel Koura ... B2

Eating

17. Rafaat Hallab & Sons ... B2

Drinking

18. Café Fahim ... B2

Transport

19. Ahdab Minibuses ... A1
20. Connex Buses to Beirut ... A3
21. Kotob Buses ... A1
22. Minibuses to Bcharré ... A3
23. Service Taxis to Bcharré & The Cedars ... B2
24. Service Taxis to Beirut ... B1
25. Service Taxis to Syria ... B2
26. Taxis to Al-Mina ... B2
27. Transtour buses to Syria & Turkey ... B1
28. Tripoli Express buses ... A1

port area, 3km west along the seafront. The geographical centre of town is Saahat et-Tall (pronounced 'at-tahl'), a large square by the clock tower, where you'll find the service taxi and bus stands, and most of Tripoli's cheap hotels.

The old city sprawls east of Saahet et-Tall, while the modern centre is west of the square, along Rue Fouad Chehab. In Al-Mina you'll find the Corniche – shabby by day but alive with milling locals by night – and some nice, relaxed pavement cafes and bars.

Money

There are ATMs all over town, and lots on Rue Riad al-Solh.

Post

Al-Mina post office (Rue ibn Sina)

Main post office (Rue Fouad Chehab) Around 400m south of Abdel Hamid Karami Sq.

Tourist Information

Tourist office (☎433 590; www.lebanon-tourism.gov.lb; Abdel Hamid Karami Sq; ⏰8am-5pm Mon-Sat) Not very helpful but staff members speak English and French. Opening hours can be erratic.

Getting There & Away

At the time of research, bus services from Tripoli to Syria were disrupted by the political situation in Syria. When services resume, it is anticipated there will be changes in the timetables. It's best to check with bus drivers in Tripoli's main square.

To/From Beirut

Three companies – Connex, Kotob and Tripoli Express – run bus services from Beirut to Tripoli. All leave from Zone C of Charles Helou bus station in Beirut; there's no need to book ahead.

Connex has 20 buses daily in either direction (LL5000, 90 minutes via Jounieh and Byblos, every 30 minutes from around 7am to 8.30pm). Tripoli Express runs smaller buses daily (LL3000, 90 minutes, every 10 to 15 minutes from 5am to 6pm). Kotob, which runs older buses daily, is the cheapest option but takes longer (LL2000, up to two hours, every 15 minutes from 6am to 6.30pm).

Ahdab also runs minibuses from Tripoli to Beirut (LL3000, around two hours, every 15 minutes from 6am to 8pm). All bus and minibus services depart from Rue Fouad Chehab and Rue Tall in Tripoli.

Service taxis leave about every half-hour to Beirut (LL6000, 1½ hours) from near the service taxi booth, just in front of the clock tower.

To Bcharré, the Cedars & Baalbek

Daily minibuses to Bcharré (LL4000, 80 minutes, three to four services between 9am and 5pm) leave from outside the Marco Polo travel agency, which is about 25m from the tourist office on Abdel Hamid Karami Sq. For the Cedars, organise a taxi at Bcharré (around LL20,000).

A service taxi from Tripoli to Bcharré costs LL6000 (from 6am to 5pm) and to the Cedars it's LL10,000; both leave from Al-Koura Sq.

During summer, it's possible to take a taxi from Bcharré or the Cedars to Baalbek (around US$80 to US$100, 1½ hours). Note that the road is closed from November to March.

Getting Around

Service taxis travel within the old and new parts of Tripoli (LL1000) and to Al-Mina (LL1000).

Bcharré & the Qadisha Valley بشرى & وادي قاديشا

06

The trip up to the pretty town of Bcharré takes you through some of the most beautiful scenery in Lebanon. The road winds along mountainous slopes, continuously gaining in altitude and offering spectacular views of the Qadisha Valley, a Unesco World Heritage site home to rock-cut monasteries and hermits' dwellings, and teeming with wildlife. Red-roofed villages perch atop hills or cling precariously to the mountainsides; the Qadisha River, with its source just below the Cedars ski resort, runs along the valley bottom, while Lebanon's highest peak, Qornet as-Sawda (3090m), soars overhead. With plentiful opportunities for hiking quiet valley trails or scaling bleak mountain landscapes, this is the perfect antidote to all that's fiery, fraught or frivolous down the coast in Beirut.

Bcharré is the only town of any size in the area, and is particularly famous as the birthplace of Lebanese poet Khalil Gibran. If you're not here in skiing season (when the Cedars resort, further up the mountain road, should be your winter sports base), it's a nice place to relax for a few days and is especially recommended as a launching point for hikes down into the stunning Qadisha Valley.

Sights & Activities

Bcharré's little town centre is dominated by the St Saba Church in the main square, Place Mar Sea.

Gibran Museum MUSEUM
(671 137; www.gibrankhalilgibran.org; adult/student LL5000/3000; 10am-6pm Mar-Nov, to 5pm Nov-Mar, closed Mon) According to his wishes, the famous poet and artist Khalil Gibran (1883–1931), author of the much-loved *The Prophet* (1923), was buried in a 19th-century monastery built into the rocky slopes of a hill overlooking Bcharré. The museum here houses a large collection of Gibran's paintings, drawings and gouaches, and also some of his manuscripts. His coffin is in the monastery's former chapel, which is cut straight into the rock. Those unfamiliar with the poet's work will be able to stock up at the gift shop. If you have time, climb the stairs behind the museum to visit the site of Phoenician tombs. The museum is on the eastern outskirts of the town.

Qadisha Grotto CAVE
(admission LL4000; 8am-5pm, closed mid-Dec–mid-May) This small grotto extends around

HIKING IN THE QADISHA VALLEY

There are plentiful options for hiking in both the gorgeous Qadisha Valley and the surrounding mountains, and a number of groups offer guided walks in the area. Don't miss your chance to explore this little Garden of Eden in a turbulent Middle East.

The **Lebanon Mountain Trail** (www.lebanontrail.org) is a long-distance hiking path, running the whole length of Lebanon, which also passes through the area; its website offers useful information on walking in the valley. Below are three highly recommended organisations that offer regular treks here.

Esprit-Nomade (03-223 552; www.esprit-nomade.com) Arranges weekly hikes, treks and snowshoeing, with an emphasis on responsible ecotourism.

Lebanese Adventure (03-234 178, 03-214 989; www.lebanese-adventure.com) Runs outdoor evenings on weekends, including some great moonlight hikes with overnight camping.

Liban Trek (01-329 975; www.libantrek.com) A trekking club running day and weekend hikes throughout Lebanon, as well as mountain biking, caving and stargazing.

To learn more about the Qadisha Valley itself, go to www.qadishavalley.com.

500m into the mountain and has some great limestone formations. Though not as extraordinary as Jeita Grotto, its spectacular setting nevertheless makes it well worth a visit.

The grotto is a 7km walk from Bcharré; follow the signs to L'Aiglon Hotel and then take the footpath opposite. It's then a 1.5km walk to the grotto.

Sleeping & Eating

Hotel Chbat HOTEL **$$**
(☎671270; www.hotelchbat.net; Rue Gibran, Bcharré; d US$115; ❄@📶) More Swiss-looking than Lebanese, this friendly, chalet-style hotel has comfortable rooms with balconies, many of which have sitting rooms attached and lovely views across the valley. There are two restaurants and the lounge/bar usually has a roaring log fire in winter.

Hotel Tiger House HOSTEL **$**
(☎672 480; tigerhousepension@hotmail.com; Rue Cedre; dm/s/d US$10/20/40; 📶) On the high road out towards the Cedars ski resort, this is a basic option without much privacy but the owners are welcoming. Outside the high summer or ski seasons, you'll likely have the bonus of a whole dorm room to yourself. Breakfast costs LL5000.

La Montagnard INTERNATIONAL **$**
(☎672 222; Main St, Bcharré; mains LL5000-15,000; ⏲11am-10pm) Situated on the street directly below the Hotel Chbat, this cosy bar and restaurant succeeds in channeling a rustic mountain theme (with wooden furniture and a fireplace) and has good views of the valley. It offers sandwiches, burgers and simple meals.

Information

L'Intime Internet Café (per hr LL1000; ⏲10am-midnight) is about 20m from the St Saba Church in the main square.

Getting There & Away

The bus and service taxi stop are outside the St Saba Church. See p367 for details of services between Tripoli, Bcharré and the Cedars.

There's also a minibus to Beirut's Dawra transport hub, which leaves every morning at 7am (LL6000). When the road is open (between March and November), you can take a taxi from Bcharré all the way to Baalbek (1½ hours) across the beautiful, bleak mountains for around US$80 to US$100.

The Cedars الأرز

☎06

One of Lebanon's most attractive ski resorts, the Cedars is also its oldest and most European in feel. The village takes its name from one of the country's few remaining groves of cedar trees, which stands on the right-hand side of the road as you head up towards the ski lifts. A few of these slow-growing trees are thought to be approaching 1500 years old, and fall under the protection of the Patriarch of Lebanon, who holds a festival here each August.

Since the trees are protected, you can usually walk through the forest on marked trails (the area is reliably open 9am to 6pm between May and October; check at other times), except when the ground is soft and tree roots might be unwittingly damaged by visitors.

The ski season takes place here from around December to April, depending on snow conditions, and there are currently six lifts in operation. Equipment can be rented from a number of small ski shops at the base of the lifts, coming in at around US$5 to US$12 per day. An adult day pass to the slopes costs US$23 Monday to Friday and US$30 at weekends; the price drops to US$17 and US$23 if it's just for the afternoon. For more on skiing in Lebanon, contact **Ski Lebanon** (☎09-231 611; www.skileb.com) for information, packages, trips and accommodation bookings.

Sleeping & Eating

There's a good sweep of accommodation for all budgets at the Cedars, with great off-season discounts if you're here in summer for the hiking. Check, too, about midweek rates during the winter, which are usually substantially cheaper than weekend prices. There aren't many dedicated restaurants in town, as most people eat at their hotels after a day on the slopes.

Hotel Cedrus HOTEL **$$$**
(☎678 777; www.cedrushotel.com; d from US$170; ❄📶) This comfortable option on the main street has large rooms, a cosy bar and a popular restaurant serving French and Lebanese cuisine. It's a good base for skiing, hiking and tours into the Qadisha Valley.

L'Auberge des Cedres RESORT **$$$**
(☎678 888; www.smresorts.net; r from US$200, chalets for 6 from US$435; ❄@🏊) Popular with well-heeled Beirutis, this place offers stylish,

LEBANON'S CEDARS

The most famous of the world's several species of cedar tree are the cedars of Lebanon, mentioned in the Old Testament, and once covering great swathes of the Mt Lebanon Range.

Jerusalem's original Temple of Solomon was made from this sort of cedar wood, and the ancient Phoenicians, also, found it appealing for its fragrance and durability. Such a long history of deforestation, however, has meant that today just a few pockets of cedars remain in Lebanon – despite the tree appearing proudly on the nation's flag.

Of these remnants of a once-abundant arboreal past, the best places to view the remaining cedars of Lebanon are either at the Chouf Cedar Reserve, or at the small grove at the Cedars ski resort in the north of the country. Still, with plenty of reforestation projects going on, there are hopes that Lebanon will one day be forested by its beautiful, long-living national emblem once more.

comfortable accommodation in its cosy mountain lodge and its serviced chalets. In summer you can camp in style in a luxury tent (for two people US$200) and go mountain biking, hiking or ballooning. Breakfast costs US$10.

Hotel Mon Refuge HOTEL **$$**
(☎671 397; s/d/apt US$41/82/164; ❄) This simple place has pleasant rooms and apartments sleeping up to 12 people, all with open fires. There's a nice, cosy restaurant downstairs. Breakfast costs extra.

Getting There & Away

During the winter months, a daily minibus usually operates between Beirut's Dawra transport hub and the Cedars: check locally for details.

SOUTH OF BEIRUT

Sidon (Saida) صيدا

☎07 / POP 170,516

A small, workaday but attractive port town lying 40km south of Beirut amid thick citrus and banana groves, Sidon is most famous in modern times as the birthplace of assassinated former prime minister Rafiq Hariri. Delving back rather further into history, though, it was once a rich and flourishing Phoenician city, with tight trade links to ancient Egypt and a globally renowned glass-making industry.

Traces of Sidon's rich history can still be found all over town, with many ancient remnants tucked away in its intriguing medieval souqs. Unlike pretty Byblos to the north, Sidon makes few concessions to tourists: here, the history is very much part of everyday life, and while this means that options for accommodation and eating out are fairly limited, it also offers a stronger sense of DIY exploration than some of Lebanon's busier destinations.

Sights & Activities

With the exception of the Sea Castle, all Sidon's sights are free to visit. However, opening hours can be a little erratic: if a place is closed, it pays to ask around since someone will probably be able to tell you where the keyholder is to be found.

Sea Castle CASTLE
(Qasr al-Bahr; admission LL4000; ⏲9am-6pm Jun-Sep, to 4pm Oct-May) Erected in 1228 by the Crusaders, the Sea Castle sits on a small island that was formerly the site of a temple dedicated to Melkart, the Phoenician version of Hercules, and is connected to the mainland by a fortified stone causeway. Like many other coastal castles, it was largely destroyed by the Mamluks to prevent the Crusaders returning to the region, but was renovated by Fakhreddine in the 17th century. On calm days, you can see numerous broken rose granite columns lying on the sea floor beneath the castle; archaeologists think there's plenty more of this sort of history to be discovered further off Sidon's coast.

OLD CITY

Old Sidon, a fascinating labyrinth of vaulted souqs, tiny alleyways and medieval remnants, stretches out behind the buildings fronting the harbour. Officially, there are 60 listed historic sights here, many in ruins, although renovation work is ongoing.

In the **souqs** you'll find craftspeople plying the same trades their ancestors did for centuries. There are plenty of opportunities to pick up the local fragrant orange-blossom water (good in both sweet and savoury cooking, or as a cordial for summer drinks) and *sanioura*, a crumbly, shortcake-like biscuit.

FREE Khan al-Franj KHAN

(⏲10am-6pm) A highlight of the souq area is the Khan al-Franj (Inn of the Foreigners), the most beautiful and best preserved of all the limestone khans built by Fakhreddine (Fakhr ad-Din al-Maan II) in the 17th century. Wonderfully restored, it consists of vaulted arcades surrounding a large rectangular courtyard with a central fountain. Today it houses the Hariri Foundation, founded by assassinated former PM Rafiq Hariri, which works on various restoration projects throughout the city and beyond.

FREE Palace Debbané HISTORIC BUILDING

(Al-Moutran St, Sidon souq; ⏲9am-6pm Sat-Thu) Another gem, entered from the souq via a tall staircase marked with a sign. Built in 1721, this former Ottoman aristocrat's building has intricate Mamluk decoration, including tile work and cedar wood ceilings, and various historical exhibits.

Great (Omari) Mosque MOSQUE

(Port Rd) Facing the northern tip of the harbour, the Great (Omari) Mosque is said to be one of the finest examples of Islamic religious architecture of the 13th century, and was originally converted from a fortified Knights Hospitaller structure. Severely damaged by the Israeli bombings of 1982, it underwent a long restoration and now looks spectacular once again. It's open to non-Muslims outside prayer times; as always, remember to dress appropriately.

FREE Musée du Savon MUSEUM

(Soap Museum; ☎733 353; Rue al-Moutran; ⏲9am-6pm Sat-Thu) Located in an old soap factory dating from the 17th century, this surprisingly interesting museum is Lebanon's only museum of that most humble yet indispensable of products. Well laid-out, with trilingual explanations (Arabic, English, French) on the art of 'saponification' (which we nonsaponifiers might simply call 'soap-making'), the museum also has a stylish cafe and a boutique with some lovely illustrated history and cookery books, as well as the foaming white stuff itself.

Bab as-Saray Mosque MOSQUE

Just behind the Khan al-Franj, the Bab as-Saray Mosque is the oldest in Sidon, dating from 1201, and filled with beautiful stonework. It may not always be open to non Muslims, so check before entering.

Sleeping & Eating

Along the Corniche, the strip beneath the Al-Qualaa Hotel is filled with felafel, seafood and mezze joints, one of the most popular being **Abou Ramy** (⏲8am-7pm). Otherwise, delve into the souq and follow your nose to find yourself dining on fresh food with ancient men in equally ancient surroundings.

Al-Qualaa Hotel HOTEL $$

(☎734 777; www.alqualaa.com; Port Rd; d US$100; ❄) Sidon's nicest accommodation lies on the main road in front of the town port, in a beautifully restored building. Ask for a room with a sea view to make the most of a stay in

TRAVEL WARNING: THE SOUTH

With a tragic history marred by frequent Israeli incursions, along with regular Palestinian and Hezbollah offensives, southern Lebanon has suffered unlike any other region since the early days of the civil war right up to the present day. In 2006, the Israel-Hezbollah war saw civilian casualties and widespread destruction in the countryside south of Sidon and Tyre, and thousands of UNIFIL troops remain stationed throughout the area.

While travelling here, don't venture too far off the main roads between Sidon and Tyre. Some foreign offices advise staying away from bars and restaurants popular with off-duty UN troops in Tyre. The land itself is still littered with unexploded mines and cluster bombs, so it's definitely not the place to set off on any kind of hike.

If you do wish to explore outside Sidon and Tyre, heed local advice: you can check with locals, embassy staff, UNIFIL or Lebanese soldiers and, as always, stay informed on the news front. For more information on UNIFIL itself, go to www.un.org/Depts/dpko/missions/unifil.

this light- and antique-filled place. There is also a couple of lovely rooftop cafes.

Yacoub Hotel HOTEL **$$**
(☎737 733; www.yacoubhotel.com; Rue al-Moutrah; d US$90; ❄) This clean, quiet choice is in a converted 200-year-old building and offers spotless, comfortable and attractive rooms. You'll see it signposted off to the left on your way up from the harbour to the soap museum.

Rest House LEBANESE **$$**
(☎722 469; mains from LL18,000; ⏱11am-11pm) On the seafront overlooking the Sea Castle and the lapping waves, this upscale government-owned restaurant in an old Ottoman khan has a pleasant, shaded garden terrace and a long menu of tasty mezze.

Information

Almost everything of interest to visitors is along or just off the seafront. Saahat an-Nejmeh, a huge roundabout, marks the centre of town, and is where you'll also find the bus and service taxi stands, along with the police station.

On Rue Riad as-Solh, which runs south off Saahat an-Nejmeh, there are dozens of banks, ATMs, travel agencies and moneychangers.

Post office (Rue Rafiq al-Hariri)

Tourist office (☎727 344; ⏱8.30am-2pm Mon-Sat) A small office, with maps of Sidon's historic sites, operating inside the Khan al-Franj.

Getting There & Away

To/From Beirut

Buses and service taxis from Beirut to Sidon leave from the Cola transport hub. To Sidon, **Zantout** (☎03-223 414) runs regular bus services, roughly hourly from 6am to 9pm (LL2500, 30 minutes). Minibuses (LL1500) to/from Sidon leave every 10 to 15 minutes from 6.30am to 8.30pm, and service taxis cost LL6000. In Sidon, buses depart from the Lebanese Transport Office at Saahat an-Nejmeh, and service taxis from the service taxi stand just across from the roundabout.

To Tyre

The Zantout bus from Sidon to Tyre (LL1250, 45 minutes to one hour, roughly hourly from 6am to 7.30pm) leaves from the Lebanese Transport Office at the southern end of the town on Rue Fakhreddine, the continuation of Rue Riad as-Solh, near the Castle of St Louis. A service taxi from Sidon to Tyre costs LL3500 and a minibus costs LL1500 (both leaving from Saahat an-Nejmeh).

Temple of Echmoun معبد أشمون

About 2km northeast of Sidon, this **temple** (admission free; ⏱8am-dusk) is Lebanon's only Phoenician site boasting more than mere foundations. Today it contains the remains of temples and shops, as well as some interesting mosaics (although most are damaged).

Begun in the 7th century BC, the temple complex was devoted to Echmoun, god of the city of Sidon, and other buildings were later added by the Persians, Romans and Byzantines. Today the highlight of the site is undoubtedly the throne of Astarte, flanked by two winged sphinxes.

From Sidon you can take a taxi (LL10,000), service taxi (LL2000) or minibus (LL1000) to the turn-off on the highway at the fun fair, then walk a pleasant, orchard-lined 1.5km to the ruins.

Tyre (Sour) صور

☎07 / POP 142,755

Notoriously famous for its local hero Hassan Nasrallah and best-known scenically for its extraordinary Roman ruins, Tyre is an oft-troubled town with an abundance of both UN soldiers and Unesco World Heritage sites.

Tyre's origins date back to its foundation in approximately 2750 BC, after which it was ruled by the Egyptians and then the famous King Hiram (who sent cedar wood and skilled workers to Jerusalem so that the Hebrew King Solomon could build the Temple of Jerusalem), under whom it prospered. Later colonised variously by the Assyrians, Neo-Babylonians, Greeks, Seleucids, Romans, Byzantines, Arabs, Crusaders, Mamluks and Ottomans, Tyre began to languish from the 13th century onwards and, despite many attempts, never quite recovered its former glory.

Every time the city attempts to get to its feet following disaster, it seems to be struck down by a new catastrophe. Though it has generally proved safe to visit in recent times, be sure to heed local travel warnings, and it makes sense to avoid Palestinian refugee camps unless you're with a trusted local. Nevertheless, Tyre remains a picturesque and intriguing destination whenever times are quieter down south, and if you can visit, you really should.

Tyre (Sour)

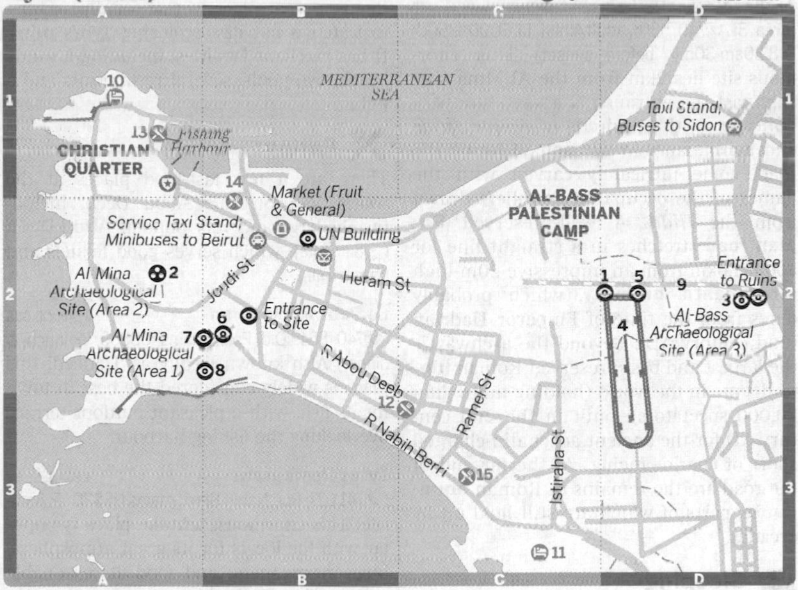

Tyre (Sour)

Sights

1 Aqueducts ... D2
2 Crusader Cathedral ... A2
3 Funerary Complex ... D2
4 Hippodrome ... D2
5 Monumental Archway ... D2
6 Mosaic Street ... B2
7 Rectangular Arena ... B2
8 Roman Bathhouse ... B2
9 Roman Road ... D2

Sleeping

10 Hotel-Restaurant al-Fanar ... A1
11 Rest House ... C3

Eating

12 Abou Deeb ... C3
13 Le Petit Phoenicien ... A1
14 Tanit Restaurant ... B2
15 Tyros Restaurant ... C3

Sights

The old part of Tyre lies on the peninsula jutting out into the sea. The modern town is on the left-hand side as you arrive from Beirut. Behind the port is the Christian quarter, with its tiny alleys and old houses with shaded courtyards.

In 1984 Tyre was declared a Unesco World Heritage site, and its archaeological remains are divided into three parts: Al-Mina (Areas 1 and 2) on the south side of the city, Al-Bass (Area 3) on the original mainland section, and a medieval site in the centre of town. Taking a guide is highly recommended here: expect to pay LL30,000 for one or two people, or LL45,000 for a group.

Al-Mina Archaeological Site ARCHAEOLOGICAL SITE
(Areas 1 & 2; ☎740 115; adult/child LL6000/3500; ⊙8.30am-30min before sunset) The ruins, dating to the third millennium BC, cover a large area leading down to the ancient Egyptian **submerged harbour**. It features a **mosaic street** paved with impressive geometrical Roman and Byzantine mosaics, on each side of which are rows of large columns, made of green marble imported from Greece. Look out also for the unusually large public **Roman bathhouse** from the 2nd or 3rd century AD and a 4th-century **rectangular arena**, which would have held up to 2000 spectators, perhaps to watch some sort of ancient water sport.

A five-minute walk north of the main Al-Mina site brings you to the ruins of a 12th-century **Crusader cathedral**, along with a network of Roman and Byzantine roads.

Al-Bass Archaeological Site ARCHAEOLOGICAL SITE
(Area 3; ☎740 530; adult/child LL6000/3500; ⏲8.30am-30min before sunset) This enormous site lies 2km from the Al-Mina site. Just past the entrance is a vast **funerary complex**, with hundreds of ornate stone and marble ancient sarcophagi lining the road, some intricately carved with the names of the occupants or reliefs drawn from the *Iliad*. A well-preserved **Roman road** stretches in a straight line for about 1.6km from an impressive 20m-high **monumental archway**, which probably dates from the time of Emperor Hadrian (2nd century AD). Beyond the archway is the largest and best preserved Roman **hippodrome** in the world (holding more than 20,000 spectators), built in the 2nd century AD for the ancient adrenalin-charged sport of chariot racing. At the far end of the road are the remains of Roman **aqueducts**, parts of which are still held up by arcades.

Sleeping

TOP CHOICE **Hotel/Restaurant al-Fanar** HOTEL **$$**
(☎741 111; www.alfanarresort.com; Rachid Nakle St; s/d US$70/90; ❄📶) With its toes almost in the water, this hotel's location is the principal plus here. Run by a charming family, it's also homely, peaceful and welcoming, with rooms that are simple but clean. There are two little terraces, a pub in the cellar and, outside, a tiny beach. The restaurant overlooks the lighthouse and serves homemade meals.

Rest House HOTEL **$$$**
(☎742 000; www.resthouse-tyr.com.lb; Istiraha St; garden view d US$140-170, ste US$140-400; ❄@📶🏊) Large, bright, airy and tranquil, this is a great place to rest (or dip) aching feet after a hot day exploring Tyre's ruins. It has excellent facilities, including a sandy beach, two pools, several restaurants and a pub.

Eating

There are a few fast-food places at the roundabout on Rue Abou Deeb, including the large and very popular **Abou Deeb** (⏲8am-late), which serves good felafels and shwarmas.

Le Petit Phoenicien SEAFOOD **$$$**
(☎740 564; Old Port; mains US$35; ⏲lunch & dinner) Also known locally as 'Hadeed', this place is widely considered the best in town for its fish, with a pleasant outdoor terrace overlooking the fishing harbour.

Tyros Restaurant LEBANESE **$$**
(☎741 027; Rue Nabih Berri; mains US$20; ⏲8am-late) This enormous, tentlike place is popular with the locals for its great atmosphere, huge mezze menu and food at reasonable prices. There's live music most Saturday nights.

Tanit Restaurant INTERNATIONAL **$$**
(☎347 539; mains LL20,000; ⏲10am-late) The atmospheric Tanit is popular with locals and UNIFIL troops for its bar as well as its food, an eclectic mix of mezze to stir-fries and steaks. The restaurant is around the corner from the fishing harbour.

Information

The post office and banks with ATMS can be found near the service taxi stand in the town centre. Many cafes have wi-fi.

WORTH A TRIP

CAVES, CASTLES & THE MIRACLE AT CANA

According to the Gospel of St John, Jesus Christ is said to have performed his first great miracle of changing water into wine at the wedding feast of Qanah. The location of the biblical Qanah is disputed but the Lebanese believe Qana, 10km southeast of Tyre, is the true site and that the **Grotto of Cana** (adult/child LL4000/2000; ⏲8am-sunset) is the cave where Jesus Christ is believed to have slept the night. A series of ancient sculptures depicting the life of Jesus are etched into the rock lining the path to the cave.

At Tibneen, 28km southeast of Tyre, stand the ruins of a **crusader castle** (admission free) built in 1105. The massive fortification wall is hard to miss, as is its commanding position on a hilltop in the centre of town. On a clear day, the views from the castle are spectacular – sweeping across the fertile landscape, the mountains and the coast – and are reason enough to visit.

Getting There & Away

For Beirut, microbuses (LL3000, one to 1½ hours, every 15 minutes from around 5am to 9pm) go direct from Tyre. Minibuses also travel from Tyre to Beirut (LL2000 to LL3000, one to two hours, 6am to 8pm depending on passenger demand).

The first bus from Tyre to Sidon (LL1500, 30 to 45 minutes) leaves at 6am from the roundabout north of the entrance to the Al-Bass site. The last leaves at 8pm, and they come about twice per hour in between.

A service taxi from Beirut's Cola transport hub costs around LL10,000 to LL15,000; from Sidon to Tyre, a service taxi will cost LL3500.

Chouf Mountains

جبال الشوف

These spectacular mountains, southeast of Beirut, are the southernmost part of the Mt Lebanon Range. In places they're wild and beautiful; in others they're dotted with small villages and terraced for easy cultivation. Throughout, they're a beautiful place for a day or two's exploration.

BEITEDDINE PALACE (BEIT AD-DIN)

بيت الدين

Located in otherwise unexceptional Beiteddine village, one of the highlights of the Chouf mountains is undoubtedly the early 19th-century **Beiteddine Palace** (Beit ad-Din; adult/child/student LL7500/2000/5000; ⏲9am-5.15pm Tue-Sun Apr-Oct, to 3.15pm Nov-May), around 50km southeast of Beirut.

Sitting majestically on a hill, surrounded by terraced gardens and orchards, the palace was built over a period of 30 years by Emir Bashir, Ottoman-appointed governor of the region, starting in 1788. Meaning 'House of Faith', the Beiteddine Palace was built over and around an older Druze hermitage. During the French mandate the palace was used for local administration, and after 1930 it was declared a historic monument. In 1943 Lebanon's first president after independence declared it his summer residence. The palace was extensively damaged during the Israeli invasion; it's estimated that up to 90% of the original contents were lost during this time. When fighting ended in 1984, the palace was taken over by the Druze militia, and Walid Jumblatt, their leader, ordered its restoration and declared it a 'Palace of the People'. In 1999 the Druze returned it to the government.

Although conceived by Italian architects, the palace incorporates many traditional forms of Arab architecture. The main gate opens onto a 60m-wide **outer courtyard** (Dar al-Baraniyyeh) that's walled on three sides only; the fourth side has great views out over valleys and hills.

A double staircase on the outer courtyard's western side leads into a smaller **central courtyard** (Dar al-Wousta) with a central fountain. Beyond this courtyard is the third – and last – **inner courtyard** (Dar al-Harim). This was the centre of the family quarters, which also included a beautiful **hammam** and huge kitchens.

Underneath the Dar al-Wousta and Dar al-Harim are the former stables, now home to an outstanding collection of 5th- and 6th-century **Byzantine mosaics**. Found at Jiyyeh, 30km south of Beirut, they were brought by Walid Jumblatt to Beiteddine in 1982. Whatever you do, don't miss them: they're truly stunning.

The palace hosts a wonderful annual **music festival** (www.beiteddine.org) during July and August. Check the festival website for full details.

Sleeping & Eating

Beiteddine Palace is really best experienced on a day trip from Beirut or from the lovely nearby Deir al-Qamar.

Aside from a few snack bars, Beiteddine doesn't really have any other food options: pack yourself a picnic from Beirut or Deir al-Qamar, and eat it in the palace garden beside the beautiful open-air mosaics.

Mir Amin Palace HOTEL **$$$**
(☎05-501 315; www.miraminpalace.com; s/d US$280/300; ❄@📶🏊) The only sleeping option nearby is this ultra-luxurious place, originally built by Emir Bashir for his eldest son. There are 24 beautifully decorated rooms here, and a lovely bar/restaurant worth a visit for the views alone.

Getting There & Away

Service taxis from Beirut's Cola transport hub run from Beirut to Beiteddine (LL10,000, two hours, roughly hourly). The service taxi stand in Beiteddine is close to the palace on the main square; bear in mind that there are few service taxis after dark.

DEIR AL-QAMAR دير القمر

☎05

One of the prettiest mountain villages, a few kilometres from Beiteddine, Deir al-Qamar was the seat of Lebanon's emirates during the 17th and 18th centuries, and today is a sleepy, enchanting place for a lazy stroll and a sunset drink.

Sights

Main Square SQUARE

The main square has some fine examples of Arab architecture, including the **Mosque of Emir Fakhreddine Maan** built in 1493; a **silk khan** built in 1595 and now housing the French Cultural Centre; and the 18th-century **Serail of Youssef Chehab**, which saw a bloody factional massacre in its central courtyard in 1860.

Castle Moussa CASTLE

(☎500 106; www.moussacastle.com; adult/child LL10,000/5000; ⊙8am-8pm Jun-Sep, to 6pm Oct-May) Just outside town, 2km down the road towards Beiteddine, is the kitschy 'outsider art' masterpiece of Castle Moussa, a modern castle built by an eccentric businessman that houses an eclectic collection of moving dioramas, mechanical tableaux, and thousands upon thousands of guns. Prepare to be amused, but not everyone will be impressed.

Sleeping & Eating

La Bastide HOTEL $$

(☎505 320, 03-643 010; s/d US$60/80) More like a cosy B&B than a hotel, this lovely place on the road towards Beiteddine, around 1km from Deir al-Qamar, makes a great base for exploring the Chouf. Ask for a room with a view over the valley, or a family-sized room with three beds and a kitchenette.

Al-Midane Café CAFE $

(salads from LL14,000; ⊙10am-late) A lovely choice for light meals and lingering on Deir al-Qamar's central square, this place has live music on summer weekends until midnight and beyond.

Getting There & Away

Service taxis from Beirut to Beiteddine can drop you at Deir al-Qamar en route.

CHOUF CEDAR RESERVE محمية ارز الشوف

The largest of Lebanon's three natural protectorates, the **Chouf Cedar Reserve** (☎05-502 230; www.shoufcedar.org; admission LL5000; ⊙10am-6pm Jun-Sep, to 3.30pm Oct-May) comprises an incredible 5% of Lebanon's total land area and has over 250km of hiking trails. Within it are ancient rock-cut fortress remains as well as six of the country's last remaining cedar forests, some with trees thought to be around 2000 years old. More than 200 species of birds and mammals (including wolves, gazelles and wild boar) inhabit or regularly pass through the area.

There are four main entrances (Ain Zhalta Bmohray, Barouk, Maasser and Niha), where you will find ranger huts with information on hikes and guides (LL60,000) if you don't want to hike alone. If you want to stay overnight, the Chouf Cedar Reserve operates seven **guesthouses** (per person US$30) or you can contact the **Association for Forests, Development & Conservation** (☎05-280 430; www.afdc.org.lb; dm US$30), which operates a forest ecolodge around 7km from the reserve.

If you're not coming here by your own car, negotiate a taxi fare (around US$20) from Beiteddine, some 10km away.

BEKAA VALLEY وادي البقاع

The fertile, pastoral Bekaa Valley is famous for its magnificent archaeological sites at Baalbek and Aanjar, and infamous for being the homeland of Hezbollah (Party of God), along with crops of 'Red Leb', high-quality cannabis. Heavily cultivated over millennia (the valley was one of Rome's 'breadbaskets'), it's actually a high plateau between the Mt Lebanon and Jebel Libnan ash-Sharqiyya (Anti-Lebanon) ranges. Though less agriculturally productive than in centuries past, due to a combination of deforestation and poor crop planning, its plentiful vineyards are slowly gaining an international reputation for their wines. Though you'll see Hezbollah's yellow flag fluttering around Baalbek, you'll find the locals (a mixture of Christians and Shiites) a welcoming lot and the attractions of the valley as intoxicating as its vintages.

Zahlé زحله

☎08 / POP 79,803

A cheerful and bustling town with some nice riverside restaurants and a holiday feel in the summer months, Zahlé makes a great lunchtime or evening stop on the way between Beirut and Baalbek, or even an alternative base for exploring the Bekaa Valley if you find its happy atmosphere and

WORTH A TRIP

FRUITS OF THE EARTH: THE BEKAA'S VINEYARDS

It would be a shame to come to the Bekaa Valley and not have a quick tipple at one or two of its vineyards, which are fast becoming international names in the world of wine. It's best to call in advance to make an appointment, and to ask for specific directions to the vineyards.

Lebanon's oldest and most famous winery, **Ksara Winery** (☎08-813 495; www.ksara.com-lb; Ksara; ⏲9am-6pm Jun-Sep, to 4pm Oct-May) had its first vines planted here in the 18th century and has unique underground caves for maturing the wine. Take a 45-minute tour of the caves, and munch on cheese and cold cuts along with your wine tastings. To get here, take a southbound service taxi (LL1500) from Zahlé to Ksara Village, a five-minute walk from the winery.

Chateau Kefraya (☎08-645 333/444; www.chateaukefraya.com; Zahlé; ⏲10am-5pm) is Lebanon's largest wine producer. If you're here between 25 August and 1 September, you'll witness the annual grape harvest. At other times, don't miss lunch at the stylish Dionysus restaurant, with French cuisine to complement the winery's best vintages.

Call in advance to experience a feast at the trendy **Massaya & Co** (☎03-735 795, 08-510 135; www.massaya.com; Tanail) vineyard's Le Relais restaurant, then stroll through the vines overseen by Sami Ghosn, an LA architect-turned-winemaker.

cool climate (at 945m) particularly enticing. There are no tourist attractions as such: a visit to Zahlé is really all about hanging out at the Cafés du Bardouni, the open-air cafes that crowd along the water's edge and serve copious quantities of the local arak (aniseed liquor).

Sleeping & Eating

Hotel Monte Alberto HOTEL $$
(☎810 912; www.montealberto.com; s/d US$77/88; ❄) Located high above town, the hotel commands amazing views from its simple rooms. If you're a fan of all things kitsch, you'll be able to choose between the vaguely cowboy funicular railway leading up the hill to the hotel and the revolving restaurant at the top.

Cafés du Bardouni CAFES $$
In the summer months, head down to the riverside, where the Cafés du Bardouni all offer mezze, grills and ice cream galore. Most open between 11am and noon, and stay open late into the night, for live music, a spot of gambling and lots of whirring, flashing fairground attractions for the kids.

Getting There & Away

Minibuses run from Beirut to Zahlé (LL6000, around one hour, approximately every 15 minutes from 4am to 1am), leaving from the southwest side of the roundabout at the Cola transport hub. Service taxis (LL10,000) leave from the same spot. Both will drop you off at the highway roundabout turn-off, which is just over 1km from the centre of town. You can walk or negotiate a private taxi from there.

To get to Baalbek from Zahlé, take a service taxi (LL10,000, 30 minutes) from the main taxi stand on a square off Rue Brazil, or walk to the highway roundabout at the southern end of town, where you can hail a passing microbus (LL3000, 45 minutes).

Baalbek بعلبك

☎08 / POP 31,962

Known as the Heliopolis or 'Sun City' of the ancient world, Baalbek's ruins, without doubt, comprise the most impressive ancient site in Lebanon and are arguably the best preserved in the Middle East. Their temples, built on an extravagant scale that outshone anything in Rome, have enjoyed a stellar reputation throughout the centuries, yet still manage to maintain the appealing air of an undiscovered wonder, due to their position in the middle of quiet, bucolic Baalbek. The town itself, 86km northeast of Beirut and administrative headquarters for both the Bekaa Valley and the Hezbollah party, is small, quiet and friendly, only really coming to life each July with the arrival of the famous annual **Baalbek Festival** (www.baalbek.org.lb), which runs whenever the political situation allows.

Baalbek

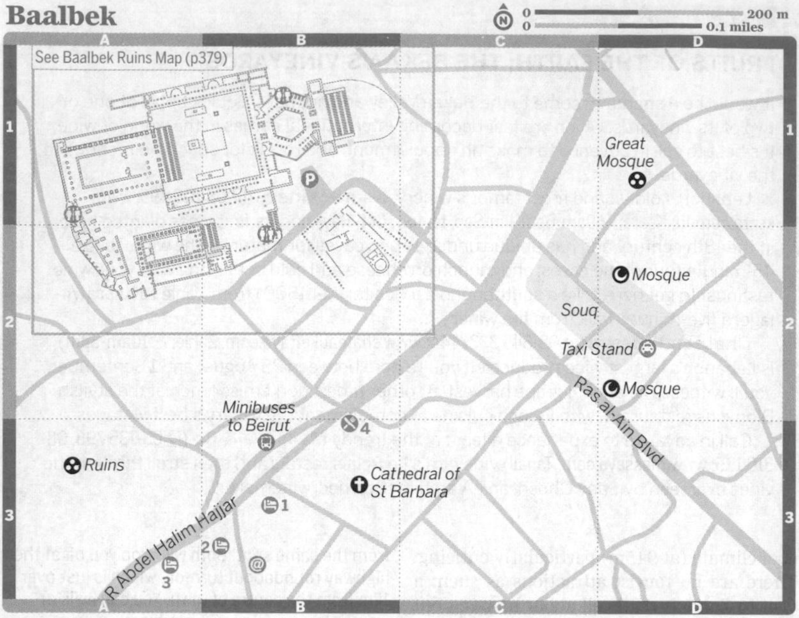

Baalbek

Sleeping
1 Hotel Jupiter B3
2 Palmyra Hotel B3
3 Palmyra Hotel Annexe A3

Eating
4 Castello Resto Café B3

Sights

TOP CHOICE Baalbek Ruins ARCHAEOLOGICAL SITE

(Map p379; ☎370 645; admission LL12,000, under 8yr free; ⊙8.30am-30min before sunset) The ruins are simply stupendous. The first of the two greatest temples at the main site is the **Temple of Jupiter**, completed around AD 60. Built on a massive substructure around 90m long, and incorporating some of the largest building blocks ever used, it was originally approached by a monumental staircase that rose high above the surrounding buildings. Today its remaining **six standing columns** (themselves some of the largest in the world) are a massive and spectacular reminder of the size and majesty of the original ancient structure.

Adjacent to the Temple of Jupiter is the second of Baalbek's great temples, the **Temple of Bacchus**, known in Roman times as the 'small temple' and dedicated to Venus/Astarte rather than to Bacchus. Completed around AD 150, it's amazingly well preserved and still stunningly ornate, displaying tablatures decorated with images of the gods, from Mars and Victory to Diana, Vulcan and Ceres. Near the main ruins, look in on the exquisite **Temple of Venus**, a circular building with fluted columns. And if it looks vaguely familiar to any National Trust–going Brits, here's why: there's an exact 18th-century copy of the temple in the grounds of Stourhead, in Wiltshire.

The very best time to visit the site is during the early morning or – even better – late in the afternoon, when the light's great, the crowds are thinnest and the temperatures cooler. It's highly recommended to take an accredited guide at the entrance to the site (around US$20 for an hour), who will really bring the stones to life.

Sleeping

Palmyra Hotel HOTEL $$

(Map p378; ☎376 011; Rue Abdel Halim Hajjar; r US$70) As unmissable as the ruins themselves, the Palmyra is a little preserved piece of 19th-century Middle Eastern history, with guests as diverse as Jean Cocteau, General de Gaulle and the Shah of Iran having graced its portals. Comfortable, creaky rooms might be showing their age, and the rattle of elderly plumbing might disturb a sound sleep, but a night here is atmospheric, spooky and unforgettable. There's a snug little bar, a restaurant and – to bypass the creaks and groans – a more luxurious annexe (doubles US$100).

Hotel Jupiter HOTEL **$**
(opposite page; ☎376 715; Rue Abdel Halim Hajjar; s/d US$20/50) Entered via an arcade northeast of the Palmyra Hotel, Jupiter has large but basic rooms equipped with fans off a central courtyard. It can be noisy. Breakfast costs US$5.

Eating

Castello Resto Café CAFE **$$**
(opposite page; Rue Abdel Halim Hajjar; mains LL18,000; ⏲9am-late) This modern cafe just down the street from the Palmyra Hotel has mood lighting, comfy couches and a terrace for summer dining. After all that sightseeing, sit back with a coffee, fresh juice or a good Lebanese mezze.

Information

The main road, Rue Abdel Halim Hajjar, is where you'll find the town's two banks, a number of ATMs, the ruins and the Palmyra Hotel. Note that neither of the banks cashes travellers cheques, and no hotels appear willing to accept credit cards.

Post office Heading along Ras al-Ain Blvd, it's up a side street before the Riviera Restaurant.

Network Center (opposite page; off Rue Abdel Halim Hajjar; per hr LL1500; ⏲9am-1am) Up a side street between the Palmyra and Jupiter hotels.

Getting There & Away

The only public transport options from Beirut to Baalbek are minibuses and service taxis. From the Cola transport hub, a minibus to Baalbek costs LL8000 (1½ hours); a service taxi costs LL15,000. The bus stop in Baalbek is just up the road from the Palmyra Hotel, and the service taxi stand is in the souq area.

For information about how to get to Baalbek from Zahlé, see p377. In summer, you can negotiate a private taxi to take you across the barren, beautiful mountains to the Cedars or Bcharré (1½ hours) for around US$80 to US$100.

Aanjar عنجر

☎08 / POP 2400

The best-preserved Islamic archaeological site in Lebanon, Aanjar's 1300-year-old **Umayyad city** (admission LL6000; ⏲8am-

Baalbek Ruins

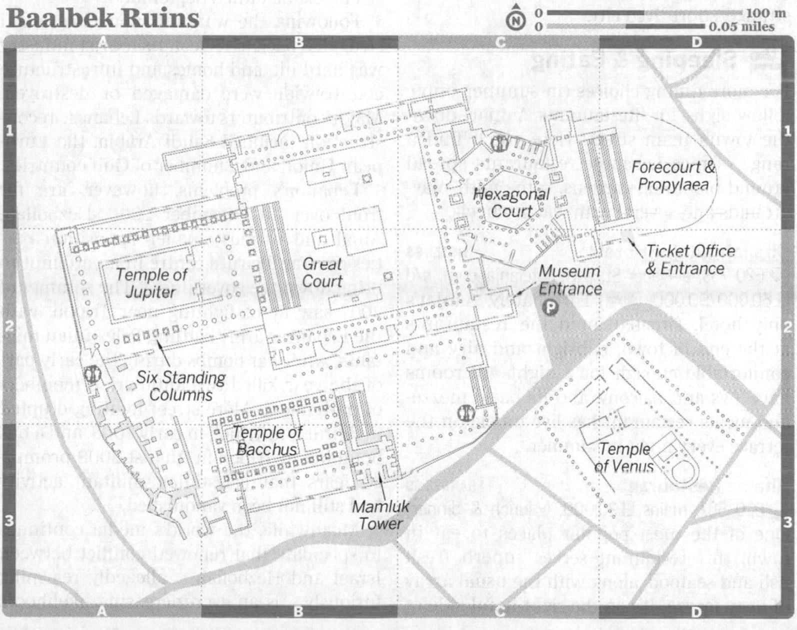

sunset) comprises the remains of a walled city, discovered by accident in the 1940s by archaeologists who were digging down for something else entirely.

The Umayyads ruled briefly but energetically from AD 660 to 750, and Aanjar is thought to have been built as a commercial centre or strategic outpost by their sixth Umayyad caliph, Walid I (r 705–15), meaning that the whole site might only have been inhabited for as little as 50 years. The walled and fortified city was built along symmetrical Roman lines; the layout is in four equal quarters, separated by two 20m-wide avenues, the **cardo maximus** and the **decumanus maximus**. There is a **tetrapylon**, a four-column structure, where the two streets intersect, built in alternating layers of large blocks and narrow bricks, a Roman-type structure built in a typically Byzantine style.

In the city's heyday, its main streets were flanked by palaces, baths, mosques, shops (600 have been uncovered) and dwellings. Perhaps the most striking of all the remains today are those of the **great palace**, one wall and several arcades of which have been reconstructed.

Guides can be found sitting sipping strong coffee at the cafe in front of the entrance to the site, and engaging one is highly advised, to get the most out of a trip to this strange, short-lived city.

Sleeping & Eating

For more dining choices (in summer only), follow signs for 'Restaurants Aanjar' down the town's main street. Here you'll find a range of nice Lebanese restaurants spread around blooming gardens, some with playgrounds and several with water wheels.

Challalat Anjar Hotel HOTEL **$$**
(☎620 753; al-Naber St; www.hotelanjar.com; s/d LL60,000/90,000; ❄@) Fortunately, Aanjar's only hotel, situated amid the restaurants at the end of town, is bright and airy and comfortable enough for a night. All rooms have TVs and balcony, and its basic mezze-and-meats restaurant has live music on the terrace every night in summer.

Shams Restaurant LEBANESE **$$**
(☎620 567; mains LL20,000; ⏰lunch & dinner) One of the most popular places to eat in town, this restaurant serves superb fresh fish and seafood, along with the usual array of tasty mezze. It's on the right-hand side of the road into Aanjar, about 500m from the main Damascus highway.

Getting There & Away

It's a bit tricky to get to Aanjar without your own car. From the Cola transport hub, catch a minivan to Chtaura (a town approximately 6km before Zahlé). From Chtaura, or from Zahlé, take a service taxi heading south or to the Syrian border; you can ask to be dropped off at Aanjar town (LL2000), a 2km walk from the highway to the archaeological site, or be dropped off at the site (LL5000).

Alternatively, negotiate a private taxi trip from Zahlé: a return trip, including a one-hour wait at the site, should cost around US$30.

UNDERSTAND LEBANON

Lebanon Today

On 12 July 2006, days after a Hezbollah incursion resulted in the deaths and kidnappings of several Israeli soldiers, Israel invaded Lebanon with the aim of destroying Hezbollah. For the following 33 days, Israeli warplanes pounded the country, resulting in the deaths of over 1000 Lebanese civilians. On 14 August fighting finally came to an end, though Israel maintained an air and sea blockade until 8 September.

Following the war, Lebanon once again struggled back to its feet. Its tourist industry was hard hit, and homes and infrastructure countrywide were damaged or destroyed. Major contributors towards Lebanese reconstruction included Saudi Arabia, the European Union and a number of Gulf countries.

Lebanon's problems, however, are far from over. In December 2006, Hezbollah, Amal and various smaller opposition parties overran Beirut's centre in an attempt to bring down the government. The summer of 2007 saw fierce fighting near Tripoli, with the Lebanese army battling Palestinian militants, while car bombs during the early part of the year killed two anti-Syrian members of parliament. More street fighting erupted in Beirut and Tripoli in early 2008, and a bus bombing in Tripoli in August 2008 prompted fears that Palestinian militant activity had still not been vanquished.

Meanwhile, the world's media continues to speculate that renewed conflict between Israel and Hezbollah – allegedly rearming furiously – is an ever-increasing likelihood.

Though the Lebanese continue to live in hope, it seems fair to assume that the dark days are not over yet. The impact of Syria's internal conflict which began in 2011 (and is still going in 2012) has yet to be fully felt in Lebanon. Syrian refugees have taken shelter in Tripoli and the north of Lebanon. Although there has been some violence in Tripoli between opponents and supporters of Syria's President Bashar al-Assad, the rest of the country has remained relatively calm.

History

Prior to its independence, Lebanon formed a part of Greater Syria. See p442 for information on the country before independence.

Early Years of Independence

Lebanon was officially declared independent in 1943, when, on 22 November, France – which had held its mandate since the end of WWI – gave in to the country's demands for independent rule. In 1946 the last French troops withdrew and a jubilant Lebanon was left to fend for itself.

Prior to full independence, the government (also known as the National Assembly) had already been uniquely divided along religious lines: Christians and Muslims held parliamentary seats at a ratio of 6:5, broadly representing the religious make-up of the country established by a 1932 census. The president, the constitution stated, must be a Maronite Christian and the prime minister a Sunni Muslim. The speaker was to be a Shiite Muslim and the chief of staff a Druze. Though probably done with lofty aims, dividing the country along sectarian lines from the very start was to be a major source of strife for years to come.

The early years of independence for the fledgling government weren't easy. First came economic strife and next, on 14 May 1948, the declaration of Israeli independence in former Palestine. Immediately, Lebanese soldiers joined pan-Arab armies and Palestinian fighters in the struggle against Israel. During 1948 and 1949, while war raged, Palestinian refugees flooded north into Lebanon; Amnesty International claims that the tiny nation absorbed more Palestinians than any other country, over 100,000 by the end of 1949 alone. Though initially welcomed into Lebanon, the Maronite majority soon became uneasy about the refugees, mostly Sunni Muslims, who threatened to tilt their precarious balance of power. In 1949 Lebanon accepted an armistice with

PARTY OF GOD

You'll probably hear far more in the world media about Baalbek's local Hezbollah party than you'll ever hear about its temples. From its roots as one of dozens of militia groups fighting during Lebanon's civil war, following a Shiite doctrine propagated by the Ayatollah Khomeini, Hezbollah has risen to become what many consider to be a legitimate resistance party, with its own radio station, TV network, countrywide network of social services and 14 democratically elected seats in the Lebanese parliament.

Upon its foundation, the party initially aimed to bring to justice those accused of war crimes during the civil war (particularly Phalangist Christians), to create an Islamic government in Lebanon, and to eradicate 'Western colonialist' influences within the country. Since then, however, Hezbollah has given up on the second of these aims, replacing it with the desire to destroy the 'unlawful entity' that is present-day Israel. Regular vicious attacks on Israel's northern border attest to its attempts to carry this out.

Often represented to the outside world as a bloodthirsty and brutal organisation only interested in bombings, kidnappings and mayhem, Hezbollah nevertheless does far more than simply amassing arms and planning raids against Israel and potential aggressors. Its network of schools, hospitals, garbage disposal plants, training institutes for farmers, fresh water distribution points and childcare facilities are unsurpassed in Lebanon, bringing crucial aid to thousands of Lebanon's poor and needy. The money for all this, says the group, comes from 'donations', though many believe it's actually directly from deep Iranian high-profile pockets.

However the aid gets there, though, get there it does – to many impoverished communities in southern Lebanon and southern Beirut who would, if Hezbollah did not exist, almost certainly go without.

DISPLACED & DISPOSSESSED

Most Palestinians who ended up as refugees in Lebanon were relegated to UN Relief and Works Agency (UNRWA)-administered refugee camps, 12 of whose original 16 still house most of Lebanon's Palestinian population today.

According to UNRWA, there are now about 455,000 registered Palestinian refugees in Lebanon, and Amnesty International estimates that there are another 3000 to 5000 second-generation unregistered refugees living illegally and without rights.

Palestinian refugees in Lebanon still suffer from a lack of opportunities, prohibited from joining professions such as engineering and medicine, largely barred from owning property and with only limited access to public health care, education and welfare programs. Most are still provided for by UNRWA, which runs the camps' schools, hospitals, women's centres and vocational training programs.

They are not, however, Lebanon's only disadvantaged group. The Geneva-based Internal Displacement Monitoring Centre (IDMC) estimates there are up to 600,000 Internally Displaced Persons in Lebanon, defined as individuals forced out of their homes due to war, persecution or natural disaster. Many are still displaced following Lebanon's civil war, and Israeli invasions and occupation of southern Lebanon.

For more information, visit the IDMC website at www.internal-displacement.org or UNRWA at www.un.org/unrwa/english.

Israel, but though 1948's UN Resolution 194 stated that refugees should be allowed to return home if they wanted to, this was mainly not to be. The Palestinian refugees, largely against their own and locals' will, were in Lebanon to stay.

By the 1950s the National Assembly was once again struggling against economic crisis, along with growing support for pan-Arabism, which advocated the creation of a united Arab entity in the Middle East. In 1952 staunchly pro-Western president Camille Chamoun quickly garnered Muslim enemies by refusing all notions of pan-Arabism, and in 1958, when his term was about to end, the unpopular president tried to extend his presidency to a second term. Lebanon's first civil war soon erupted, with pro-Western Maronites pitted against largely Muslim, pro-pan-Arabism opponents. Chamoun panicked, turning to the US for help, and on 15 July 1958, 15,000 US troops landed in Beirut.

The presence of US troops quelled trouble and Chamoun was finally persuaded to resign, to be replaced by a new president, Fouad Chehab. With Chehab's talent for smoothing ruffled feathers, Lebanon soon prospered, Beirut rapidly developing as the banking capital of the Arab world. Civil war, believed the optimistic Lebanese, was a thing of the past.

Swinging '60s?

By the mid-'60s, Beirut, the newly crowned 'Paris of the East', was booming, but Palestinian refugees and the Shiites of the south remained in poverty. As Beirut basked in newfound riches, the less fortunate grew bitter and restive, and the good times were already numbered.

The collapse of the country's largest bank in 1966 and, after that, soon the 1967 Arab-Israeli Six Day War brought yet more Palestinian refugees into Lebanon. Refugee camps soon became centres of guerrilla resistance, and the government watched impotently as Palestinian attacks on Israel from Lebanese soil rapidly increased.

In May 1968, Israeli forces retaliated across the border. Meanwhile, with sectarian tensions growing, the Lebanese army clashed violently with Palestinian guerrillas. Palestinian forces proved too strong an opponent for the army, and in November 1969 Lebanon signed the Cairo Agreement with the Palestinian Liberation Organisation (PLO), agreeing to large-scale autonomy of its refugee camps and refugees' freedom 'to participate in the Palestinian revolution'.

Maronite opposition to the agreement was immediate. Many Muslims, on the other hand, felt an innate sympathy for their fellow Palestinians. In response, a group of Christians known as Phalangists began to arm and train young men, and by March 1970 fighting between Phalangists and Palestinians had erupted on Beirut's streets as southern Lebanon suffered under Israeli reprisals against relentless guerrilla attacks. Rapidly, the country factionalised and took up arms.

Civil War

It's widely agreed that Lebanon's civil war began on 13 April 1975 when Phalangist gunmen attacked a Beirut bus, killing 27 Palestinian passengers. Soon, it was outright chaos. In December, Phalangists stopped Beirut traffic and killed Muslim travellers. Muslims retaliated, prompting 'Black Saturday' during which around 300 people died.

The slaughter rapidly reached horrific proportions. In January 1976, Phalangists led a massacre of some 1000 Palestinians in Karantina, a Beirut slum. Two days later, Palestinians attacked the southern coastal town of Damour, and killed over 500 Christians. In August, Phalangists set their sights on the Tel al-Zaatar refugee camp, killing between 2000 and 3000 Palestinian civilians.

Soon Beirut was divided along the infamous Green Line, which split the city in two, with Christian enclaves to the east and Muslims to the west. Though allegiances and alliances along its border would shift many times in the coming strife, the Green Line would remain in place for 15 years.

Syria & Israel Intervene

In 1976 the civil war gave Syria a reason to send tens of thousands of troops into Lebanon, initially sympathetic to the Palestinians and the pan-Arab cause. It wasn't long, though, before Syria switched allegiance to the Maronite side, occupying all but the far south and angering other Arab countries.

In October 1976 the Arab League nevertheless brokered a deal with Syria, allowing it to keep 40,000 troops in Lebanon as part of a peace-keeping 'Arab Deterrent Force'. Syria was left in primary control of Lebanon, and the first of the civil war's 150 short-lived ceasefires was declared.

But Palestinian attacks on Israel continued, prompting Israel to launch 'Operation Litani' in 1978, swiftly occupying most of southern Lebanon. Immediately, the UN demanded Israel's withdrawal and formed the UN Interim Force in Lebanon (UNIFIL) to 'restore international peace'. Though Israel withdrew to a 19km 'Security Zone', it simultaneously installed a puppet South Lebanon Army (SLA) and proclaimed an 1800 sq km region south of Nahr al-Litani (the Litani River) 'Free Lebanon'. For the coming years, this area too would be knee-deep in war.

In 1982 Israeli 'Operation Peace for Galilee' troops marched into Lebanon, heading to Beirut, supported tacitly by Maronite and Phalangist leaders. By 15 June, Israeli forces had surrounded and besieged West Beirut, bombarding 16,000 PLO fighters entrenched there. Heavy fighting, unsurprisingly, ensued, and in just two months the city was in ruins and 20,000, from both sides of the Green Line, were dead. On 21 August the PLO left Beirut, guaranteed safe passage by multinational forces. By now, however, battle was also raging in the Chouf Mountains, the historic preserve of Druze and Christians, and an area until now free from the ravages of war. The Lebanese army joined the Phalangists and Israelis against the Druze, who themselves were aided by the Shiite militia Amal, until the US intervened and another ceasefire was called.

The US, however, was becoming increasingly entrenched in the war, appearing to favour Israel and Lebanon's beleaguered government. In 1983 came the reprisals. In April, an Islamic jihad suicide attack on the US embassy in Beirut left 63 dead. In October, suicide bombers hit the US and French military headquarters in Beirut, killing over 300. In 1984 abductions and the torture of foreigners – whose involvement in Lebanese affairs the abductors deeply resented – began. The following year, international forces hastily left Lebanon.

Battle of the Camps

In early 1985, the last Israeli troops finally withdrew to their self-proclaimed 'security zone', leaving their interests in the hands of the SLA and Christian militias, who immediately clashed with Druze and Shiite opponents around Sidon. In West Beirut fighting continued between Shiite, Sunni and Druze militias, all battling for the upper hand.

In the midst of the chaos, PLO forces began to return to Lebanon. Concerned, however, that this would lead to a renewed Israeli invasion of the south, the Shiite Amal fought to remove them. Heavy fighting battered the Palestinian refugee camps during 1986, causing many more thousands of casualties.

To add to the confusion, in 1987 the National Assembly government finally fell

WHO IS HASSAN NASRALLAH?

Born in 1960 in a poor Beirut suburb, Hassan Nasrallah has gained international notoriety in recent years for being the public face and voice of Hezbollah.

His career began in 1975 during the civil warwhen he joined the Amal movement, a Shiite militia. In 1982, following a period of religious study in Iraq and after Israel's invasion of Lebanon, he joined Hezbollah, and soon became known for his charismatic brand of fierce and fiery rhetoric. In 1992, after Hezbollah's former leader was killed in an Israeli helicopter attack he took on the role of Hezbollah's Secretary-General. Nasrallah's own eldest son, Muhammed, was later killed in combat with Israel in 1997.

Often branded a terrorist by the West, Nasrallah has publicly criticised both the Taliban and Al-Qaeda, but he remains set on the destruction of Israel.

His leadership has seen Hezbollah responsible for kidnappings and bombings, as well as for far-reaching social, medical and educational programs throughout the impoverished south and beyond.

apart and split in two, with a Muslim government to the west of Beirut and a Christian administration to the east. Fighting along the Green Line continued to rage as Christian leaders attempted to drive Syria from Lebanon, angering Syria still more by accepting arms from Iraq, Syria's gravest enemy. It wasn't until 1989 that a road to peace finally seemed viable, with the drafting of the Taif Accord.

Road to Peace

The Taif Accord, the product of a committee consisting of the Saudi and Moroccan kings and the Algerian president, proposed a comprehensive ceasefire and a meeting of Lebanon's fractured parliament to discuss a new government charter, which would redress the Christian–Muslim balance of power. The accord was formally ratified on 5 November 1989, and constitutional amendments included the expansion of the National Assembly from 99 to 128 seats, equally divided between Christians and Muslims.

Despite some resultant in-fighting, in August 1990 the National Assembly voted to accept the terms of the Taif Accord. With the exception of the still-occupied south, the country saw peace for the first time in 15 years, and the civil war officially ended on 13 October 1990.

Syria's continued presence in Lebanon beyond the civil war was justified with reference to Lebanon's weak national army and the government's inability to carry out Taif Accord reforms, including dismantling militias, alone. In 1990 Syria formalised its dominance over Lebanon with the Treaty of Brotherhood, Co-operation and Coordination, followed in 1992 by a defence pact. In May 1991, most militias – except Hezbollah – were officially dissolved. In line with Taif Accord conditions, Syria began its military pullout in March 1992, taking another 13 years to complete the job. The last Westerners kidnapped by Hezbollah were released in 1992.

Postwar Reconstruction

From 1993 onward, the Lebanese army and life were slowly rebuilt and Rafiq Hariri, a Lebanese-born multimillionaire and entrepreneur, became prime minister.

Meanwhile, however, the south remained impoverished and the base for Israeli–Hezbollah offensives. In 1993 Israel launched 'Operation Accountability' and in 1996 'Operation Grapes of Wrath' in response to Hezbollah and Palestinian attacks, the latter a land-sea-air offensive that devastated newly rebuilt structures, destroyed Beirut's power station, and killed around 106 civilians in the beleaguered southern village of Qana.

In 1999 Israel launched further attacks, targeting Beirut's power stations, while Hezbollah continued its offensives. Sustained losses, however, led to calls within Israel for military withdrawal, and its army finally withdrew from southern Lebanon on 24 May 2000. Hezbollah stated, however, that Israel would remain its target until Israeli troops were also withdrawn from Shebaa Farms, a 31 sq km area southeast of Lebanon, captured by Israel in the 1967 Six Day War. In the years since the civil war, this bone of contention has frequently been the alleged reason for Hezbollah violence and Israeli retaliation.

In Lebanon, discontent rumbled on. Maronite groups opposed Syria's refusal to withdraw from Lebanon while Shiites and Hezbollah continued to support its presence. On 2 September 2004, the UN issued Security Council Resolution 1559, which called 'upon all remaining foreign forces to withdraw from Lebanon'. Syria still did not comply, and on 20 October 2004, Prime Minister Hariri tendered his resignation, announcing that he would not be a candidate to head the next government.

Killing of Rafiq Hariri

On 14 February 2005, a massive Beirut car bomb killed the former prime minister, Rafiq Hariri. The event triggered a series of demonstrations, with protesters placing blame firmly on Syria. Tens of thousands of protestors called for Syrian withdrawal from Lebanon, for an independent commission to investigate the murder of Hariri, and for the organisation of free parliamentary elections. Together, these events became known as the Cedar Revolution. On 14 March, Lebanon's largest-ever public demonstration was held in Martyrs' Sq, Beirut, with between 800,000 and one million attendees spanning sectarian divisions. The result was the March 14 Alliance, an anti-Syrian governmental alliance led by Saad Hariri, son of the murdered ex-prime minister, Samir Geagea and Walid Jumblatt.

With the UN, the USA, Russia and Germany all backing Lebanese calls for withdrawal, Syria finally bowed to pressure, withdrawing its 14,000 remaining troops from Lebanon on 27 April 2005 after almost 30 years of occupation. For the first time in more than two decades, Lebanon was completely free from military forces other than its own. This situation, however, was destined not to last.

The months after Syria's withdrawal were characterised by a spate of car bombs and targeted assassinations of anti-Syrian politicians and journalists, with growing calls for the expedition of a UN probe into Hariri's murder.

The 2005 parliamentary elections, the first after Syria's withdrawal, saw a majority win for the March 14 Alliance led by Saad Hariri, with Fouad Siniora elected Lebanon's new prime minister. The elections also saw Hezbollah become a legitimate governmental force, winning 14 seats in parliament, while in the south its fighters continued to launch attacks on Israeli troops and towns. Though Siniora publicly denounced the attacks, it seemed that once again Lebanese authorities were powerless to stop them.

Meanwhile, the investigation into Hariri's death continued. The UN Security Council, along with the Lebanese cabinet, approved a special tribunal to prosecute those responsible for the crime. In 2011, four Hezbollah members were indicted for Hariri's assassination.

People

National Psyche

Though Lebanon's 18 official religions have fought quite consistently since the country's creation in 1943, one of the central paradoxes of the Lebanese psyche is the country's

WHO IS HEZBOLLAH?

The vicious 1983 suicide attacks on international forces in Lebanon heralded the first public appearance of Islamic Jihad, the armed wing of the radical, Iran-backed Shiite Hezbollah. Though relatively new, the group would soon prove a key figure in the civil war.

Historically, the Shiites had always been Lebanon's poor, concentrated in the south and having borne the brunt of Israeli retaliation against Palestinian guerrillas. As a minority group, they had little say in the country's government and had been displaced in vast numbers without adequate central aid.

With Syrian approval, Iranian revolutionary guards began to preach to the disaffected, who proved fertile ground for its message of overthrowing Western imperialism and the anti-Muslim Phalange. Alongside suicide bombings, its ruthless armed wing also resorted to taking hostages, including CIA bureau chief William Buckley, who was tortured and killed; Associated Press bureau chief Terry Anderson; and UK envoy Terry Waite, who were held for almost seven and five years, respectively.

Today, Hezbollah's armed tactics revolve around rocket attacks on Israel and kidnap missions against its soldiers. Tthe group also concentrates on welfare projects in the still-stricken south, and holds 14 seats in the Lebanese parliament.

collective and overriding national pride in its tolerance of others. You're sure to hear this repeated throughout your trip, even when there's sectarian fighting going on just up the road.

You'll likely also experience the strange collective amnesia that seems to descend on the population if the country's civil war is brought up in conversation. A painful memory for most, reticence to talk about it (despite the physical scars that still pepper the landscape) is common. You usually won't encounter the same problem, however, if you mention current politics: everyone is keen to share an opinion on the political issue of the day. Another common feature among the Lebanese is the overriding optimism that 'everything's going to be all right', in the end.

While each of these three things may seem strange to a first-time visitor, you'll soon realise that all are essential to keeping the troubled country soldiering on, no matter how bad life gets.

However, the element of national identity that will most profoundly affect visitors to the country is the justifiably legendary hospitality of the Lebanese towards their guests who, as the Lebanese saying goes, are a 'gift from God'. You'll be assured a warm welcome every step of the way, and will barely have to pause on a street corner for someone to offer you assistance, refreshingly free of strings. This makes Lebanon a reassuringly comfortable place to spend time, despite the country's reputation for frequent violence, and it won't take long for you to start reciprocating the Lebanese affection for their visitors ten-fold.

Daily Life

Though it's hard to generalise about such a traditionally factionalised country, family life, as in most Middle Eastern destinations, is central to all in Lebanon. Extended families often live close together, and many children live at home until married, either to save money for their own home or simply because they prefer it that way. Social life, too, is both close-knit and gregarious: everyone within a small community tends to know everything there is to know about everyone else.

Marriage is a second crucial factor throughout Lebanon, and members of all religions tend to marry young. An unmarried woman in her thirties will raise eyebrows, though a man still single at 30, as in most parts of the Middle East, is usually thought to be simply waiting for the right girl. And though there has traditionally been an expectation that people will marry within their religion, this barrier is slowly being broken down: many mixed-religion couples opt for marriage in Cyprus or Greece, if

BRAIN DRAIN

A favourite topic of Lebanese conversation is the country's 'brain drain'. Current unofficial estimates suggest that one in three educated Lebanese citizens would like to live abroad, while a recent study by the Beirut Research and Development Centre (BRDC) found that 22% of the Lebanese population is actively working on an exit strategy. Another survey of university students showed that as many as 60% are hoping to leave Lebanon following graduation.

There are a number of reasons why so many of Lebanon's bright young things are disappearing elsewhere, not the least the climate of fear that has lingered after the Israel-Hezbollah war of summer 2006. Terrorist attacks on Lebanese politicians, in which civilians are sometimes caught up, have also sent young Lebanese in pursuit of jobs overseas. Most popular tend to be the burgeoning Gulf States, which have the advantage of high salaries and being fairly close to home, with the USA, Canada and Europe all close seconds.

The second principal reason for the mass exit is that salaries in Lebanon are often too low to provide a comfortable, viable living. Those who manage to acquire good jobs – often through family connections – hold tight to them and are reluctant to relinquish the security and move on.

Although Lebanon was largely spared the impact of the Global Financial Crisis, and many people returned to Lebanon after losing their jobs abroad, the influx is temporary. Most intend to leave as soon as jobs and salaries overseas become available.

one half of the couple (usually the woman) doesn't choose to convert.

Alongside the importance of family and marriage, a university education is highly valued in Lebanon. Financial constraints aren't too much of an issue: those whose parents can't afford to subsidise them usually take part-time jobs alongside their classes. This is true for both men and women, since women of all religions are now readily accepted into all areas of the workplace, including the government. Many young people study with a view to emigrating overseas, lured by higher salaries and the promise of a safer, calmer lifestyle away from the unrest.

As you'll notice from the pace of Beirut nightlife, young Christians – both male and female – usually have far greater social freedom than Muslims or members of other religions. But while these freedoms may at first appear similar to their Western counterparts, there are definite limits to acceptable behaviour. Drinking heavily, sleeping around and taking drugs are frowned upon in Lebanese society – not that you'd necessarily know it on a night out at Beirut's nightclubs. And while party-central Beirut seems, on the surface, no different from any European capital city, venture just a few dozen kilometres north or south and you'll find people in traditional villages living and farming almost exactly as they did a century or more ago. Add to this a substantial Palestinian population almost entirely cut off from the mainstream – and rarely referred to in conversation by the Lebanese themselves – and you'll find that daily life in this tiny country is incredibly complex, and often wildly contrasting.

Population

Lebanon's official population of just over four million people is boosted by its Palestinian refugees, whom the UN Relief and Works Agency (UNRWA) puts officially at around 455,000.

It's a largely urban population, with around 90% of people living in cities, of which Beirut is the most highly populated, followed by Tripoli, Sidon and Tyre. According to the CIA World Factbook, the population growth rate currently stands at around 0.24%, which is very low for the Middle East. Lebanon has a youthful population: nearly a quarter is under 14 years of age.

Religion

Lebanon hosts 18 'official' religious sects, which are Muslim (Shiite, Alawite, Ismaili and Sunni), Christian (Maronite, Greek Orthodox and Catholic, Armenian Catholic, Gregorian, Syrian Orthodox, Jacobite, Nestorian, Chaldean, Copt, Evangelical and Roman Catholic), Druze and Jewish. There are also small populations of Baha'is, Mormons, Buddhists and Hindus.

Muslims are today estimated to comprise around 60% of the population, though before the civil war unofficial statistics put the Muslim to Christian ratio closer to 50:50. The shift is attributed to the mass emigration of Christians during and since the civil war, and to higher birth rates among Muslims.

Traditionally, Muslim Shiites have largely inhabited the south of the country, the Bekaa Valley and southern suburbs of Beirut. Sunnis, meanwhile, have been concentrated in Beirut, Tripoli and Sidon; the Druze in the Chouf Mountains; and Maronite Christians (the largest Christian group) in the Mt Lebanon region. Though recent years have seen population shifts, particularly in Beirut, this still largely holds true today.

Arts

In summer, many towns and villages hold fabulous dance and music festivals, which are well worth looking out for. Baalbek's international festival is a particular highlight on the calendar. The nation's capital hosts its own lively arts scene and is well equipped with theatres, cinemas and venues for the visual and performing arts.

Literature

Though for much of the 20th century Beirut was the publishing powerhouse of the Middle East, it suffered during the civil war and much of its recent literary output has been shaped by this long drawn-out and horrific event. Even today, a great deal of Lebanon's literary output remains concerned with themes drawn from these 15 years of hardship.

Of the writers who remained in Lebanon during the civil war, Emily Nasrallah is a leading figure, and her novel *Flight Against Time* is highly regarded. Those who work overseas include London-based Tony Hanania, born in 1964 and author of the 1997

TOP LEBANESE READS

Here's some fact and some fiction to accompany any journey through Lebanon.

» *Sitt Marie Rose: A Novel* (1982), by Etel Adnan

» *The Stone of Laughter* (1998), by Hoda Barakat

» *The Rock of Tanios* (1994), by Amin Maalouf

» *Memory for Forgetfulness: August, Beirut 1982* (1982), by Mahmoud Darwish

» *Death in Beirut* (1976), by Tawfiq Yusuf Awwad

» *Pity the Nation: Lebanon at War* (2001), by Robert Fisk

» *Beirut* (2010), by Samir Kassir

» *The Ghost of Martyr's Square* (2010), by Michael Young

» *The Prophet* (1923), by Khalil Gibran

» *Lebanon: A House Divided* (2006), by Sandra Mackey

» *From Beirut to Jerusalem* (1998), by Thomas Friedman

» *Lebanon: Beware of Small States* (2010), by David Hirst

» *The Hills of Adonis: A Journey in Lebanon* (1990), by Colin Thurbon

Homesick and 2000 *Eros Island*, and Amin Maalouf, whose most enchanting book, *The Rock of Tanios*, is set in a Lebanese village where the Sheikh's son disappears after rebelling against the system.

Of those authors most widely available in translation, Lebanon's two major figures are Elias Khoury and feminist author Hanan al-Shaykh. Al-Shayk's *Story of Zahra* is a harrowing account of the civil war, while her *Beirut Blues* is a series of long letters that contrast Beirut's cosmopolitan past with the book's war-torn present. Elias Khoury has published 10 novels, many available in translation: his 1998 novel *Gate of the Sun* has achieved particular international acclaim.

Poet Khalil Gibran (1883–1931) remains the celestial light in Lebanon's poetry scene. Interestingly, today poetry is once again flourishing in the largely Shiite south, partly due to a movement known as Shu'ara al-Janub (Poets from the South), for whom poetry has become a means of expressing the frustrations and despair of life in that most war-ravaged of regions.

Cinema & TV

Lebanese cinema managed to survive the raw civil war years and is today reappearing with vigour and verve, despite frequently difficult circumstances. **Docudays** (www.docudays.com), Beirut's annual documentary festival, is highly regarded internationally and attracts a global crowd, while several film academies in the city churn out young hopefuls. A cinematic highlight occurred in 2007, when two Lebanese directors, Nadine Labaki and Danielle Arbid, made it to the prestigious Cannes Film Festival for their respective films *Caramel* and *Un Homme Perdu*, the former dealing daringly with inter-religious marriage and lesbianism.

The greatest of the cinematic lates was undoubtedly Georges Nasser, whose tragic 1958 *Ila Ayn?* (Whither?) is a classic of Lebanese cinema, and who became the first to represent Lebanon in the Cannes festival. Later, the civil war temporarily brought Lebanon's film industry to a virtual halt, and most filmmakers were forced to work outside the country, seldom having their films shown within its boundaries. Ironically, though, many critics believe Lebanese cinema actually produced some of its best work under the highly restricted circumstances of the tragic war.

Modern classics to look out for are *West Beirut* (1998), directed by LA-based Ziad Duweyri (a former Tarantino cameraman), which tells the semi-autobiographical story of a teenager living in West Beirut during the first year of the civil war, and the award-winning documentary *Children of Shatila*, of the same year, which looks at the history of the notorious refugee camp through children's eyes. On the lighter side of things, look out for Michel Kammoun's *Falafel*, a romantic comedy involving a young man on his perilous way to a Beirut party, and also Nadine Labaki's *Where Do We Go Now?* (2011), a comedic look at how a group of

Lebanese women ease tensions between Christians and Muslims in their village.

Music

Lebanon's two most famous female vocalists are the living legend Fairouz and the younger Najwa Karam, known as the 'Sun of Lebanese song'. Fairouz has enjoyed star status since her first recordings in Damascus in the 1950s, and later became an icon for Lebanon during the civil war (which she sat out in Paris). Now in her seventies, she still performs several concerts annually, composing new songs with her son Ziad, a renowned experimental jazz performer.

Najwa Karam, meanwhile, has managed to create an international audience for traditional Lebanese music, rising to stardom during the 1990s. With more than 16 albums under her belt, including the 2001 *Nedmaneh* with over four million copies sold worldwide, she remains a driving force on the Lebanese music scene.

Current hot names in mainstream pop include Nancy Ajram, Haifa and the 4 Cats, all producing catchy tunes and raunchy videos. More good, solid pop is presented by Fadl Shakir. Another popular male musician, who marries classical Arabic music with contemporary sounds, is Marcel Khalife, hailing from Amchit, near Byblos. An oud (lute) player with a cult following, many of his songs have a controversial political side, such as his composition for the dead of the Sabra and Shatila refugee camps.

In the bars and clubs of Beirut's Hamra and Gemmayzeh districts, contemporary fusions of oriental trip-hop, lounge, drum and bass and traditional Arabic music, for both the dance floor and chilling out, have for the last few years dominated sound systems. Groups such as the Beirut based REC Project specialise in Arab deep house and lounge. Soap Kills and Mashrou3 Leila are also popular. You'll hear these sounds, along with traditional belly-dancing tunes remixed to electronic music, almost anywhere you stop off for a strong drink and a good dance or two.

Architecture

Ancient architecture in Lebanon can be found at Baalbek's spectacular remains, in the traces of the Romans in Beirut and at the Umayyad ruins at Aanjar.

Much of Lebanon's more recent heritage architecture has been damaged over the last century by the combined effects of war and redevelopment, though there remain a substantial number of examples of the country's traditional architecture dotted about the country. To the north, Tripoli's old city souqs contain a wealth of medieval and Islamic architecture, while Deir al-Qamar, in the southern Chouf Mountains, is a well-preserved village with some beautiful 18th- and 19th-century villas and palaces. Beiteddine Palace, also in the Chouf Mountains, is a melange of Italian and traditional Arab architecture, more remarkable for its lavish interiors than any architectural innovation.

Interior designers are doing wonderful work in Lebanon these days, and Beirut's B 018 nightclub, designed by Bernard Khoury, is a top-notch example. Situated on the former Green Line, the club pays homage to the past at a site that was formerly a quarantine zone, a refugee camp and the site of an appalling massacre during the war – and is

MUSTN'T-MISS MOVIES

If you get the chance, don't fail to look up some of these cinematic treasures.

- *Where Do We Go Now?* (2011), directed by Nadine Labaki
- *Towards the Unknown* (1957), directed by Georges Nasser
- *West Beirut* (1998), directed by Ziad Duweyri
- *The Little Wars* (1982), directed by Maroun Baghdadi
- *The Broken Wings* (1962), directed by Yousef Malouf
- *In the Shadows of the City* (2000), directed by Jean Chamoun
- *Caramel* (2007), directed by Nadine Labaki
- *Bosta* (2005), directed by Philippe Aractingi
- *Giallo* (2005), directed by Antoine Waked
- *Bint el-Haress* (1967), directed by Henry Barakat
- *Harab Libnan* (2001), directed by Omar al-Issawi

worth a visit as much for its appearance as its sizzling-hot DJs and crowd.

Painting

Lebanon's first art school was established in 1937, and by the 1950s and '60s a number of galleries opened to showcase the country's art, while the private Sursock Museum, in Achrafiye, began to show new artists.

Though, like most of Lebanon's cultural output, the visual arts suffered during the civil war, the scene re-established itself with vigour soon afterwards. Apart from the earlier William Blake–style paintings of poet Khalil Gibran, famous 20th-century artists include the painters Hassan Jouni, Moustafa Farroukh and Mohammed Rawas. Better-known contemporary painters include Marwan Rechmawi, Bassam Kahwaji, Amin al-Basha, Helen Khal, Salwa Zeidan and Etel Adnan (who, like Gibran, is also a writer). Salwa Raodash Shkheir is a current Lebanese star of the sculpture world.

The photography and visual arts scene is the most vibrant and cutting-edge of all the arts in the region. The best places to experience the current Lebanese visual arts scene are the numerous small galleries around Hamra and Gemmayzeh, in the studios of Saifi Village and in the Beirut Art Centre.

Theatre & Dance

Most theatre in Lebanon is based in Beirut, where prominent and established Lebanese playwrights such as Roger Assaf, Jalal Khoury and Issam Mahfouz are trying to encourage younger artists – though lack of funding remains a perennial problem – and a revitalised Lebanese theatre scene is gradually emerging.

As in other parts of the Middle East, both *dabke*, the traditional Levantine folk dance, and *raks sharki* (belly dancing) are very popular. **Caracalla** (www.caracalla.org) is the closest thing Lebanon has to a national dance troupe. Founded by Ahmed Caracalla, the choreographer of the Baalbek Festival in the 1960s, the group's performances are inspired by oriental dance, but also combine opera, dance and theatre. With colourful costumes and musicals based on diverse sources, from Shakespeare to modern Lebanese literature, they can be seen at some of Lebanon's summer festivals, and at the Monnot Theatre in Achrafiye.

TRAVELLING SUSTAINABLY IN LEBANON

There are many simple but effective ways to have a positive impact while visiting oft-troubled Lebanon.

» Engage the services of a park guide at nature reserves, whose fee goes towards preserving and enhancing the area.

» Share the wealth among the lesser-known businesses: limiting your use of international chains will ensure a better distribution of tourist income.

» Don't stick solely to our Eating recommendations: you'll be evenly distributing the tourist dollar, and embarking on your own adventure of the senses, if you go where your taste buds take you.

» Consider hiking with one of Lebanon's many trekking groups (see p368) who have valuable insights into low-impact tourism.

» If you're renting a car, try to team up with other travellers to split the cost: you're reducing the environmental impact substantially if you can cram four travellers into a Fiat Punto.

» Look for recycling points for your plastic water bottles, which bob with the tide in alarming numbers along the Beirut seashore.

» Take a registered guide to show you around ancient historic sites. In recent years, work has been sporadic for these invaluable sources of local knowledge.

Take a look at the **Lebanese Greenpeace** (www.greenpeace.org.lb) site, the **Ministry of the Environment** (www.moe.gov.lb), the **Society for the Protection of Nature in Lebanon** (www.spnlb.org) or the **UN** (www.unep.org/Lebanon) for more information on Lebanon's environment.

Food & Drink

Lebanese cuisine has a reputation as being one of the very best in the Middle East. The proof of the pudding, as they say, is in the eating, so sample as much of it as you possibly can.

Fresh ingredients, including numerous types of fruit, vegetables and pulses, are plentiful in Lebanon. Mezze, small dishes often served as starters, are a godsend for vegetarians even in the most far-flung parts of the country, with hummus, tabbouleh and salads galore, while seafood and grilled meats are staunch favourites of carnivores. In Beirut, the diversity and quality of food on offer matches any international city: want tapas at two in the morning, or sushi at six? You'll find it all here.

Arabic or 'Turkish' coffee is particularly popular in Lebanon – look out for the men dispensing tiny, strong cups of it from the back of battered old Volkswagen vans – while delicious freshly squeezed vegetable and fruit juices are on offer almost everywhere throughout the summer. Alcohol, too, is widely available in Lebanon; Beirut's awash with cocktails, but the most popular alcoholic old-timer is the potent aniseed-flavoured arak, mixed liberally with water and ice, and sipped alongside meals or a long game of backgammon. The best local beer is Almaza, which lives up to its name ('diamond' in Arabic) when served ice-cold.

For more on Lebanese cuisine, see p354.

Environment

The Land

Though Lebanon is one of the smallest countries in the world, its terrain is surprisingly diverse. Four main geographical areas run almost parallel to each other from north to south. They are (from west to east): the coastal plain, the Mt Lebanon Range, the Bekaa Valley and the Jebel Libnan ash-Sharqiyya (Anti-Lebanon) range.

The Mt Lebanon Range includes Lebanon's highest summit, Qornet as-Sawda (3090m), and an example of the famous cedars of Lebanon at the Cedars. Jebel Libnan ash-Sharqiyya marks the border between Lebanon and Syria. Its highest summit is Jebel ash-Sheikh (Mt Hermon), at 2814m.

Environmental Issues

Ravaged by more than two decades of war, anarchy, unfettered construction and weak state control, Lebanon's environment remains very fragile, and some of the only areas to have escaped destruction are, ironically, the heavily landmined or cluster-bombed areas, still filled with unexploded ordnance.

The complete lack of basic service industries or infrastructure during the civil war meant that solid waste was dumped throughout the country, and many water sources are still polluted. Air pollution is another serious, ongoing problem, particularly in Beirut, with a couple of million cars (many of them ancient, spluttering wrecks or petrol-guzzling SUVs) plying its crowded roads. Add to this catastrophic oil spills caused by the 2006 Israel-Hezbollah war, and it's not a pretty picture that emerges.

All is not lost for Lebanon, however. A host of local and international NGOs are working to secure a better future for Lebanon's environment, while the government itself seems, in theory at least, committed to change. Huge national parks such as Chouf Cedar Reserve (which makes up an incredible 5% of Lebanon's landmass) are, though underfunded and overstretched, working hard on protecting its wildlife. With time, money and persistence, there's still hope for the country to prove that, as the saying goes, great things come in small packages.

SURVIVAL GUIDE

Directory A–Z

Accommodation

Accommodation prices quoted are for double rooms (unless otherwise indicated) with a bathroom, and with breakfast and taxes included. Generally, budget options are under US$80 per double room, midrange between US$80 and US$120, and top-end over US$120. Prices are quoted for a room in high season (June to September) except for the Cedars, which is for a room between December and March. Prices are either in US dollars or in Lebanese lira (LL), depending on which is quoted by the establishment itself.

Note that in low season large discounts are often available, sometimes 50% or even more, so it's always worth checking. Some smaller places, however, may shut up shop if there seems to be no likelihood of travellers, so it might pay to call in advance if you have any doubts.

As an alternative to the places listed in this chapter, the **Lebanese Youth Hostel Federation** (www.lyhf.org) lists nine hostels serving the country, though no hostel in Beirut itself. Most are in small, rural villages, offering a taste of real local life, and have beds for around US$10 to US$20 per person per night. For upscale homestays across the country, look no further than **L'Hote Libanais** (☎03-513 766; www.hotelibanais.com), which can organise a single stay or an entire itinerary for very reasonable prices.

Prices in this book are for rooms in high season and include bathrooms, breakfast and taxes unless otherwise indicated.

$ less than LL60,000 (US$80)

$$ LL60,000 to LL135,000 (US$80 to US$120)

$$$ more than LL135,000 (US$120)

Activities

The Lebanese passion for adventure translates into a wide variety of options for adventure activities, including trekking (see p368).

Association Libanaise d'Etudes Speleologique CAVING
(ALES; ☎03-666 469; www.alesliban.org) Caving trips for all levels of experience.

Atlantis Diving College DIVING
(www.atlantisdivingcollege.com) Takes care of underwater outings.

Beirut by Bike CYCLING
(www.beirutbybike.com) Has bike rental from various points around Beirut. Check online for current locations.

Blue Carrot Adventure Club ADVENTURE SPORTS
(☎03-553 007; www.blue-carrot.com) Mountain-biking expeditions as well as a host of other adventure activities.

Ski Lebanon SKIING
(09-231 611; www.skileb.com) The best site for information on where and when to ski, and where to stay.

Business Hours

Shops 9am-6pm Mon-Fri, to midafternoon Sat

Banks 8.30am-2pm Mon-Fri, to noon Sat

Post offices and government offices 8am-5pm Mon-Fri, to 1.30pm Sat

Restaurants Nonstandard opening hours; in Beirut they may stay open all night

Embassies & Consulates

Nationals of New Zealand should contact the UK embassy for assistance.

Australia (Map p350; ☎01-960 600; Serail Hill, BCD, Beirut)

Canada (☎04-713 900; Coolrite Bldg, Autostrade, Jal ad-Dib, Beirut)

Egypt (Map p347; ☎01-825 566; Dr Muhammed El-Bethri St, Watta Moseitbeh, Beirut)

France (Map p347; ☎01-420 000; Rue de Damas, Beirut) Near the National Museum.

Germany (☎04-914 444; Mtaileb, Rabieh, Beirut) Near the Jesus and Mary School.

Italy (☎05-954 955; PO Box 57, Baabda, Beirut)

Jordan (☎05-922 500; Rue Elias Helou, Baabda, Beirut)

Netherlands (Map p350; ☎01-211 150; Netherlands Tower, Achrafiye, Beirut)

Syria (☎05-922 580; Hazmieh)

UK (Map p350; ☎01-960 800; Serail Hill, BCD, Beirut)

US (☎04-542 600; Awkar, PO Box 70-840, Antelias) Opposite the Municipality.

Food

Prices in this book represent the cost of a standard main-course dish.

$ less than LL15,000 (US$10)

$$ LL15,000 to LL45,000 (US$10 to US$30)

$$$ more than LL45,000 (US$30)

Gay & Lesbian Travellers

Homosexuality is illegal in Lebanon, but there's a thriving – if clandestine – gay scene in Beirut. **B 018** (www.b018.com) nightclub is a gay-friendly establishment, while Beirut's hammams and cafes provide plenty of opportunities to meet and greet.

Your first point of contact, though, should be **Helem** (☎01-745 092; www.helem.net; 1st fl, Yamout Bldg, 174 Rue Spears, Beirut), whose name derives from the Arabic acronym for the Lebanese Protection for Lebanese Gays, Bisexuals and Transgenders. The organisation's website and its offshoot, www.beirut.helem.net, offer plenty of information, listings and news.

Other useful gay and lesbian resources:

Bint el Nas (www.bintelnas.org)

Gay Middle East (www.gaymiddleeast.com)

Travel and Transcendence (wwww.travelandtranscendence.com)

Language Courses

The following centres in Beirut provide courses in Arabic for foreigners:

AMBergh Education (www.arabic-studies.com) Offers group and individual courses, and can help find accommodation.

American Language Center (Map p352; ☎01-741 262; www.alc.edu.lb; Rue Hamra, Hamra, Beirut; ⏰9am-6pm Mon-Sat)

American University of Beirut (Map p352; ☎01-374 444; www.aub.edu/lb)

Money

Lebanon's currency is the Lebanese lira (LL), also known locally as the Lebanese pound. Banknotes are of the following denominations: 1000, 5000, 10,000, 20,000, 50,000 and 100,000; there are also LL250 and LL500 coins.

US dollars are widely accepted countrywide, and higher-end establishments rarely quote prices in anything else.

ATMs are reliable and available, and dispense cash in both Lebanese lira and US dollars.

Budget hotels and restaurants generally do not accept credit cards. Tipping is widespread in Lebanon. For professional guides, hotel porters and parking valets, tipping somewhere around LL2000 or more, depending on the level of service, will be appreciated. Waiters are usually tipped around 10%, but check your bill before doing so, since some places automatically add a 15% service charge.

Photography

There are plenty of shops selling memory cards and batteries for digital cameras all around Beirut, but especially along Rue Hamra. Outside Beirut, you may have problems finding memory cards, though batteries (rarely rechargeable) are widely on sale. An 8GB memory card goes for around US$12; a pack of four AA batteries costs around US$5.

Public Holidays

New Year's Day 1 January

Feast of Saint Maroun 9 February – feast of the patron saint of the Maronites

Easter March/April Good Friday to Easter Monday inclusive

Labour Day 1 May

Martyrs' Day 6 May

Assumption 15 August

All Saints' Day 1 November

Independence Day 22 November

Christmas Day 25 December

Also observed are Muslim holidays; see p624 for dates.

Safe Travel

See 'Travel Warning: Staying Safe' (p358) for information on safety in Lebanon.

Telephone

MOBILE PHONES

Mobile-phone coverage extends throughout most of the country (bar a few remote, mountainous areas). Your mobile phone from home will probably work on a local network, though of course you'll pay heavily for the privilege of making calls or sending text messages. MTC and Alfa SIM cards are widely available from phone stores, newsagents,

PRACTICALITIES

» The *Daily Star* provides good coverage of local news in English, the daily *L'Orient Le Jour* in French. The monthly magazine *Time Out Beirut* is useful for upcoming events, openings and exhibitions in Beirut.

» The BBC World Service can be received on 1323kHz; popular locally are Radio One, Light FM and Nostalgie. The major local TV channels are the government-run broadcaster Tele-Liban and five commercial channels: New TV, MTV, Future TV, NBN and LBC.

» European two-round-pin plugs are needed to connect to Lebanon's electricity supply (220VAC, 50Hz).

» Lebanon uses the metric system for weights and measures.

ISRAELI PASSPORT STAMPS

Lebanon denies entry to travellers with evidence of a visit to Israel in their passport (see p36 for more details). If asked at a border crossing or at the airport if you've ever been to Israel, bear in mind that saying 'yes' (if you have) will mean you won't be allowed into the country.

post offices, kiosks or anywhere the MTC or Alfa symbols are displayed. A SIM card costs about LL50,000 to LL60,000. Prepaid recharge cards cost LL12,000 and LL39,000.

You can buy a mobile phone from US$30.

PHONE CODES

The country code for Lebanon is ☎961, followed by the local area code (minus the zero), then the subscriber number. Local area codes are given at the start of each city or town section in this chapter. The area code when dialling a mobile phone is ☎03 or ☎70. The international access code (to call abroad from Lebanon) is ☎00.

Visas

All nationalities need a visa to enter Lebanon, though costs and visa requirements are constantly changing. For the most up-to-date information, visit the website of Lebanon's **General Security Office** (www.general-security.gov.lb).

PLACES OF ISSUE

Citizens of Jordan and Gulf Cooperation Countries (Kuwait, Saudi Arabia, United Arab Emirates, Qatar, Bahrain and Oman) are entitled to a free three-month visa at the airport. At the time of writing, tourist visas were free of charge.

Citizens of most other countries are entitled to a free one-month visa at the airport. Check with your local embassy/the website above if unsure.

The same visa policy applies, in principle, at all Syrian-Lebanese border crossings, but be aware that visas may not always be issued free of charge (some travellers have reported being charged LL50,000 to obtain their one-month entry visa).

For other nationalities, visas must be obtained in advance at any Lebanese embassy or consulate: you'll need two passport photos, and possibly a letter from your employers stating that you'll be returning to your job. Visas are usually issued the next day, but may take longer.

EXTENSIONS

To extend your one-month visa to a three-month visa, go to the **General Security Office** (Map p347; ☎1717, 01-429 060/061; Rue de Damas, Beirut; ⏲8am-1pm Mon-Thu, to 10am Fri, to noon Sat) in Beirut, a few days before your first month ends. Take a passport photo, your passport, and photocopies of your passport ID page and the page where your entry visa was stamped.

SYRIAN VISAS

Since the opening of the Syrian Embassy in Beirut in December 2008, you can now get a Syrian visa in Lebanon. Officially, only passport holders from countries that have no Syrian consulate (excluding, of course, Israel) can obtain visas at the Syrian border.

Women Travellers

Lebanon, in general, is an easy destination for solo female travellers, more akin in attitudes to neighbouring Israel than, for example, to next-door Syria. Revealing, Western-style clothes are common in Beirut and Jounieh, and in the beach clubs that line the sands from Sidon up to Byblos, but outside the main centres, long-sleeved, loose clothing is still preferable. This is particularly the case in the south, the north around Tripoli and in the Bekaa Valley, all predominantly Muslim areas, and, of course, when entering holy places. For further advice for female travellers, see p618.

Getting There & Away

You can travel to Lebanon by air, or by land from Syria. Note, though, that political tensions have often been known to close land borders between Lebanon and Syria, so check locally at your time of travel that the borders are open.

Air

Beirut Rafic Hariri International Airport (BEY; ☎01-628 000; www.beirutairport.gov.lb) is Lebanon's only airport. The national carrier, **Middle East Airlines** (MEA; ☎01-622 000; www.mea.com.lb; Beirut), has an extensive network including flights to and from Europe and to the Arab world. It's reliable and has a decent safety record.

The following international airlines, among others, currently service Beirut:

Air France (AF; ☎01-977 977; www.airfrance.com; Beirut)

Cyprus Airways (CY; ☎01-371 136; www.cyprusairways.com; Beirut)

EgyptAir (MS; ☎01-980 166; www.egyptair.com.eg; Beirut)

Emirates (EK; ☎01-734 500; www.emirates.com; Beirut)

Gulf Air (GF; ☎01-323 332; www.gulfairco.com; Beirut)

Lufthansa (LH; ☎01-347 007; www.lufthansa.com; Beirut)

Malaysia Airlines (MH; ☎01-741 344; www.mas.com.my; Beirut)

Royal Jordanian Airline (RJ; ☎01-379 990; www.rja.com.jo; Beirut)

Turkish Airlines (TK; ☎01-999 849; www.turkishairlines.com; Beirut)

Land

BORDER CROSSINGS

The only land crossings from Lebanon are into Syria (the Israel-Lebanon land border has not been open for some years). Note, though, that these are often closed at short notice, so check in advance that they're open before travel. There are four in total, but the most reliably open crossing is at Masnaa, on the Beirut-Damascus highway. The other three are at Al-Qaa, at the northern end of the Bekaa Valley; Aarida, on the coastal road from Tripoli to Lattakia; and Aabouyide on the Tripoli to Homs route.

So long as the borders are open, citizens of most countries can obtain a Lebanese visa at the border. Some travellers occasionally manage to obtain their Syrian visa at the Lebanese border, but this is a decidedly hit-and-miss affair, and could end up being frustrating if you're denied entry. It's far better to arrange your Syrian visa in Beirut or in advance of travel to Lebanon.

BUS

Buses to Syria from Beirut leave from the **Charles Helou bus station** (Map p350). You must go there in person to book your ticket; while buses are rarely full, it's still worth booking a seat the day before you travel and to check that services are actually running.

Due to civil unrest in Syria at the time of writing, bus services to Syria were limited, with no services to Lattakia or Homs. Check again as the situation changes. Buses for Damascus (LL20,000, three hours) depart at 7.30am every morning except Friday. Buses for Aleppo (ask for Halab; LL15,000, seven hours) leave every two hours starting from 7.30am.

TTS (☎01-399 777) buses from Beirut to Amman in Jordan (US$30, seven hours) leave from the Tayyouneh roundabout every Tuesday, Thursday, Saturday and Sunday at 7.30am. It is advisable to book a seat in advance.

From Tripoli – border openings and security situation allowing – there are services running to Syria. At the time of research, a number of services were suspended due to the civil unrest in Syria. It is best to check with the companies on Tripoli's main square for details of times and prices.

CAR & MOTORCYCLE

Since Lebanon levies a steep charge at the border for bringing in your car (calculated on a sliding scale, depending on the vehicle's value), it's not really advisable to try bringing your own vehicle into the country. If you're touring the Middle East in your own car, your best bet is to park it securely in Damascus, and take the bus into Lebanon from there.

Getting Around

There are no air services or trains operating within Lebanon, but the country is so small (you can drive from one end to the other in half a day) that you don't really need them. In and around Beirut and the coastal strip, the bus, minibus and taxi network is extensive, cheap and fairly reliable. To fully explore the hinterland of the country (especially around the Qadisha Valley, Bekaa Valley and the south) it's well worth hiring a car or negotiating a private taxi to avoid waiting for hours for a bus that eventually decides not to arrive at all.

Bicycle

Lebanon's steep terrain and the state of many urban roads demand a rugged, all-terrain bicycle. There are few designated bike lanes or routes, however, and drivers – whose driving style could politely be described as 'loose' or 'creative' – aren't exactly used to giving space to cyclists plying the country's roads. If you have thighs and nerves of steel, however,

JUST ACROSS THE BORDER: CRAC DES CHEVALIERS & DAMASCUS, SYRIA

If all's quiet on Lebanon's eastern front and the Beirut-Damascus land border is open, don't miss the incredible Crac des Chevaliers castle (Qala'at al-Hosn). And, while in Syria, how could you miss historic Damascus?

Secure your Syrian visa (see Border Crossings p395) before leaving home or at the Syrian embassy in Beirut (p392), to allow you to make the easy 4½-hour drive from Beirut to Damascus by bus or service taxi. Once in Damascus (p400), meander through the Ottoman lanes of the Old City, haggle for spices in Souq al-Hamidiyya and marvel at its stately Umayyad Mosque, before settling down for a single Thousand and One night at the delightful Dar al-Yasmin.

The next morning, take a bus to Homs (p417) and another on to Crac des Chevaliers (p419), to transport yourself into a Crusader castle fantasy, with towers fit for a bevy of Rapunzels. Then it's back to Damascus, via Homs (staying the night, if you've time, to imbibe its laid-back, friendly air), to hop aboard a bus that will whisk you back from the thrum of life in ancient Damascene lanes to the pace of the Beirut fast lane, a few hours – and a century or two – away.

cycling the countryside is certainly stunningly scenic and the fresh mountain air a joy.

Bus & Microbus

Buses travel between Beirut and all of Lebanon's major towns. There are three main bus pick-up and drop-off points in Beirut:

Charles Helou bus station (Map p350) Just east of downtown, for destinations north of Beirut (including Syria).

Cola transport hub (Map p347) This is in fact a confused bustling intersection (often known as Mazraa), generally serving the south and the Bekaa Valley.

Dawra transport hub (off Map p347) Northeast of Beirut, and covering the same destinations as Charles Helou bus station, it's usually a port of call on the way in and out of the city.

Charles Helou is the only formal station and is divided into three signposted zones:

Zone A For buses to Syria.

Zone B For buses servicing Beirut (where the route starts or finishes at Charles Helou bus station).

Zone C For express buses to Jounieh, Byblos and Tripoli.

Zones A and C have ticket offices where you can buy tickets for your journey. In the other stations (Cola and Dawra transport hubs), ask any driver for your bus (if someone doesn't find you first). Buses usually have the destination displayed in the front window, but largely in Arabic only.

There is a growing number of independently owned microbuses that cover the same routes. The advantages are that they're comfortable, frequent and often quicker than regular buses. The disadvantages are that they're more expensive and, since they're privately owned, you're taking a chance on the driver's motoring skills. You pay for your ticket on board, either at the start or end of the journey.

See individual town and city listings for detailed information on bus services.

Car

You need to be a competent driver with very steady nerves to contemplate driving in Lebanon, since there are few rules of the road. A three-lane road, for example, can frequently become seven lanes. Hairpin bends and potholed roads are frequent in the mountains, and few roads are gritted after a snow fall. Beirut's traffic is often heavy, and road signs (where there are any at all) can be cryptic or misleading.

Having said all that, renting a car is a fantastic way to get to some of the most out-of-the-way parts of the country, especially if time is tight. With a car, you've got the freedom to explore the small villages peppering the Qadisha Valley, and make your own unexpected discoveries en route. In addition to being generally cautious, remember to stop at military checkpoints and have your passport and car rental papers ready for inspection.

As well as the usual gamut of international operators (Avis, Budget, Thrifty and Sixt all have offices in Beirut), local outfit

Advanced Car Rental (☎01 999 884/5; www.advancedcarrent.com) comes highly recommended.

Local Transport

BUS

Some towns, including Beirut, have privately owned buses that operate a hail-and-ride system. Fares are generally LL1000 for all except the most distant destinations; see individual town or city information for details.

TAXI & SERVICE TAXI

Most routes around Lebanese towns and cities are covered by service, or shared, taxis (see p633), which are usually elderly Mercedes with red licence plates and a taxi sign on the roof. You can hail them at any point on their route and also get out wherever you wish by saying *'anzil huun'* (drop me off here). Be sure to ask *'servees?'* before getting in (if it's an empty car), to ensure the driver doesn't try to charge you a private taxi fare. Going rates are generally LL1500 to LL2000 for trips within a town, and LL5000 to LL10,000 for trips to outlying areas.

If you want to engage a private taxi, make sure the driver understands exactly where you want to go and negotiate the fare clearly before you get in (fares are suggested in relevant sections). Bear in mind that it might actually be cheaper, especially if you're planning on taking several day trips, to rent a car.

Tours

Several Lebanese operators organise reliable tours within Lebanon, and to Syria and Jordan. They cover most of Lebanon's highlights, are reasonably priced and usually include lunch, guide (in English or French), entrance fees and pick-up/drop-off at your hotel, and transport is usually in air-con coaches or minibuses. Half-day trips cost from US$30 per person, full-day trips around US$60 to US$80.

Tour operators:

Adonis Travel (☎09-949 599; www.adonistravel.com/lebanon) Offers trips within Lebanon and multicountry itineraries.

Cynthia Tours (☎03-636 162; www.cynthia-tours.com) Offers customised small and large group tours within Lebanon, Syria and Jordan. Multilingual guides.

Nakhal & Co (01-389 389; www.nakhal.com; Sami el-Solh Ave, Ghorayeb Bldg, Beirut) One of the largest tour operators, with tours within Lebanon and abroad.

Tania Travel (Map p352; ☎01-739 682; www.taniatravel.com; Rue Sidani, Hamra, Beirut; ⏲8am-6pm Mon-Sat)

Syria

Includes »

Prices

Throughout this chapter we have not cited prices for sleeping and eating listings, as most hotels and restaurants were closed at the time of writing. Instead of specific prices, we have indicated price categories, from budget to top end (see p446 and p447 for more detail). The price ranges for these categories were applicable before hostilities began, and should be used as a rough guide only.

Why Go?

At the time of writing, you can't go: if you can, you shouldn't. Peaceful protests that began in early 2011 have grown into an armed uprising against the Assad regime. A year later, and despite the UN and Arab League calling for an end to violence, the Syrian army continues to shell and shoot its citizens. Homs has become the most widely reported battleground, but there is violent conflict across the country.

How long this will continue is impossible to guess. When it ends, the wealth of historic sites, from Palmyra in the desert to the Crac des Chevaliers, within sight of the Mediterranean, will lure us back and the gracious hospitality of Syrians will warm us to their country.

As we have been unable to visit Syria, we have updated this chapter by phone and email, and by asking advice and information from Syrians still in the country.

When to Go

Damascus

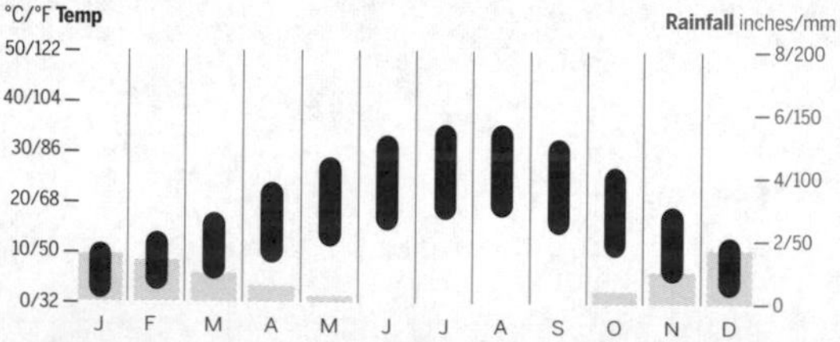

Mar–Apr Spring along the coast and then in the hills, which are carpeted with flowers.

Jun–Jul Scorching in the desert but magical on the Mediterranean.

Sep–Oct Autumn brings rich light and lower temperatures. Perfect.

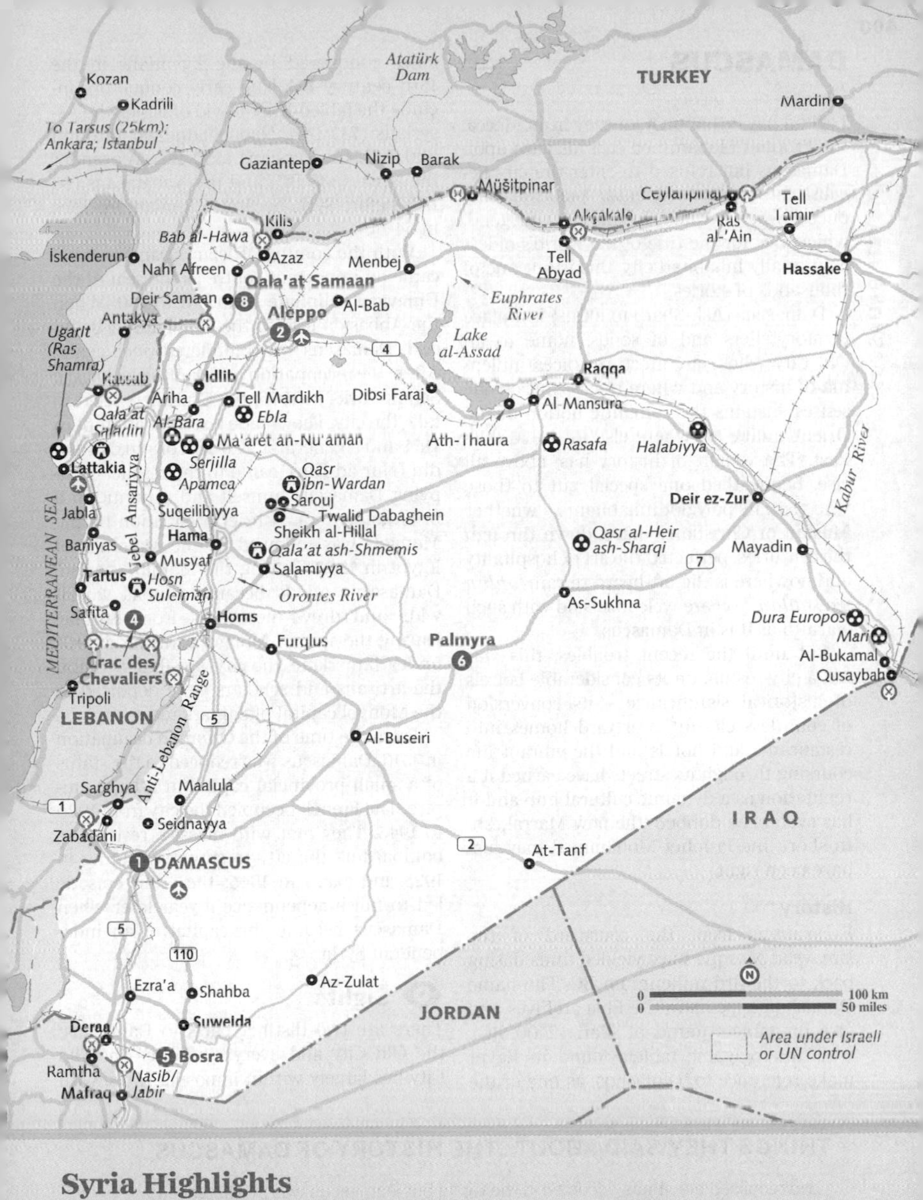

Syria Highlights

1. Walk **Damascus Old City** (p401) and step into the past
2. Shop in **Aleppo's souqs** (p430) for silks as well as sheep's heads
3. Be scrubbed down in a medieval **hammam** (bath), to be found all across the country
4. Storm the **Crac des Chevaliers** (p419), the finest castle in the world
5. Spend a day in **Bosra** (p415) to appreciate its brooding ruins
6. Cross the desert to the majestic ruins of **Palmyra** (p436), one of the most picturesque
7. **Sit in a cafe** anywhere to appreciate the charm and friendliness of Syrians
8. Visit the place where **St Simeon** stood on his pillar (p432) to understand the passion of early Christianity

DAMASCUS دمشق

☎011 / POP 2.5 MILLION

Legend has it that on a journey from Mecca, the Prophet Mohammed cast his gaze upon Damascus but refused to enter the city because he wanted to enter paradise only once – when he died. In this city of legend, which vies for the title of the world's oldest continually inhabited city, this is but one of thousands of stories.

Damascus (Ash-Sham to locals) is a place of storytellers and of souqs, home to an Old City whose architecture traces millennia of history and where the assault on the senses sustains the romantic notion of the Orient unlike anywhere else in the Middle East. The weight of history has, above all else, bequeathed one special gift to those who visit: its polyglot inhabitants – whether Muslim or Christian – have, down through the centuries, perfected the art of hospitality and nowhere is the oft-heard refrain '*ahlan wa sahlan*, you are welcome', said with such warmth as it is in Damascus.

But until the recent troubles, this was not a city resting on its considerable laurels of historical significance – its conversion of countless elegant courtyard homes into restaurants and hotels and the vibrant life coursing through its streets have earned it a reputation as a dynamic cultural hub and it has even been dubbed 'the new Marrakesh'. In short, the Prophet Mohammed may just have been right.

History

Excavations from the courtyard of the Umayyad Mosque have yielded finds dating back to the 3rd millennium BC. The name Dimashqa appears in the Ebla archives and also on tablets found at Mari (2500 BC), while hieroglyphic tablets found in Egypt make reference to 'Dimashqa' as one of the cities conquered by the Egyptians in the 15th century BC. The early conquerors include the fabled King David of Israel, the Assyrians (732 BC), Nebuchadnezzar (around 600 BC), the Persians (530 BC), Alexander the Great (333 BC) and the Nabataeans (85 BC), before Syria became a Roman province in 64 BC.

With the coming of Islam, Damascus became an important centre as the seat of the Umayyad caliphate from 661 to 750. When the Abbasids moved the caliphate to Baghdad, Damascus was plundered once again. After the occupation of Damascus by the Seljuk Turks in 1076, the Crusaders tried to take the city. They made a second attempt in 1154 and a general of Kurdish origin, Nureddin (Nur ad-Din), came to the rescue, occupying Damascus himself and ushering in a brief golden era. A brief occupation by the Mongols was followed by the Mamluks of Egypt in 1260. During the Mamluk period, Damascene goods became famous worldwide and drew merchants from Europe. During the second Mongol invasion of 1401 under Tamerlane, the city was flattened and the artisans and scholars were deported to the Mongol capital of Samarkand.

From the time of the Ottoman occupation in 1516, Damascus was reduced to the status of a small provincial capital in a large empire. The French occupied the city from 1920 to 1945. They met with massive resistance, bombarding the city to suppress rioting in 1925 and again in 1945; the latter episode led to full independence a year later when Damascus became the capital of an independent Syria.

Sights

There are two distinct parts to Damascus: the Old City and everything else. The Old City lies largely within imposing walls, with

THINGS THEY SAID ABOUT...THE HISTORY OF DAMASCUS

'...no recorded event has occurred in the world but Damascus was in existence to receive news of it. Go back as far as you will into the vague past, there was always a Damascus...She has looked upon the dry bones of a thousand empires and will see the tombs of a thousand more before she dies...To Damascus, years are only moments, decades are only flitting trifles of time. She measures time, not by days and months and years, but by the empires she has seen rise, and prosper and crumble to ruin. She is a type of immortality.'

Mark Twain, The Innocents Abroad, 1869

'Some cities oust or smother their past. Damascus lives in hers.'

Colin Thubron, Mirror to Damascus, 1967

most visitors entering via Souq al-Hamidiyya (the eastern end of which begins immediately south of the citadel), which runs into the Umayyad Mosque. Another major thoroughfare through the Old City is Straight St (also known as Sharia Medhat Pasha and Sharia Bab Sharqi). The Christian Quarter, home to the Old City's boutique hotels, lies at the eastern end of the Old City, between Bab Sharqi and Bab Touma.

West and northwest of the Old City, the city centre is compact and finding your way around on foot is no problem. The main street, Sharia Said al-Jabri, begins at the Hejaz train station and runs northeast, changing its name to Sharia Bur Said. It finishes in Saahat Yousef al-Azmeh, the square that is at the heart of the modern city. The streets off this square are home to most of the airline offices, the main tourist office, the central branch of the Commercial Bank of Syria (CBS) and a host of hotels and restaurants. Souq al-Saroujah, the home of the city's backpacker hotels, is southeast of the square. South of Souq Saroujah is Martyrs' Sq (known to locals as Al-Merjeh), the city's 'downtown' district.

IN OR OUT

Should you go to Syria? At the time of writing, the US, UK and many other governments have recalled their ambassadors and advise against all travel in Syria, urging any foreigners in the country to leave while they can. When the situation changes – and no one knows when that will be – the country will still present risks to travellers. You are advised to exercise caution and be sure to check the local as well as the national security situation.

OLD CITY

Most of Damascus' significant sights are in the Old City, which is surrounded by what was initially a **Roman wall**. The wall itself has been flattened and rebuilt several times over the past 2000 years. Its best-preserved section is between Bab as-Salaama (Gate of Safety) and Bab Touma (Thomas' Gate, named for a son-in-law of Emperor Heraclius).

Next to the **citadel** (closed to the public, but a visitor centre is planned) is the entrance to the main covered market, the **Souq al-Hamidiyya**, constructed in the late 19th century. The souq is Damascus' busiest and it's a place to stroll amid black-cowled Iranian pilgrims, Bedouin nomads just in from the desert and people from all walks of Syrian life. At the far end of this wide shop-lined pedestrian avenue is an arrangement of Corinthian columns supporting a decorated lintel – the remains of the **western temple gate** of the 3rd-century Roman Temple of Jupiter.

Umayyad Mosque MOSQUE

(Map p404; admission S£50; ⏲dawn until after sundown prayers, closed 12.30-2pm Fri for noon prayers) Welcome to the most beautiful mosque in Syria and one of the holiest in the world for Muslims. Converted from a Byzantine cathedral (which in turn had occupied the site of the Temple of Jupiter), Damascus' crowning glory was built in AD 705. At the time, under Umayyad rule, Damascus had become the capital of the Islamic world and the caliph, Khaled ibn al-Walid, built what he called 'a mosque the equal of which was never designed by anyone before me or anyone after me'. It is Islam's first truly imperial building.

The mosque's outstanding feature is its golden **mosaics**, which adorn the facade of the prayer hall on the southern side of the courtyard, and a 37m stretch along the western arcade wall, which Damascenes believe represents the Barada Valley and the paradise that the Prophet Mohammed saw in Damascus. Traces remain elsewhere around the courtyard, leaving you to imagine the sublime aspect of the mosque in its heyday.

The expansive courtyard is flanked on three sides by a two-storey arched arcade and is occupied by an unusual **ablutions fountain** topped by a wooden canopy, and, on the western side, a small octagonal structure, the **Dome of the Treasury**, adorned with exquisite 14th-century mosaics and perched atop eight recycled Roman columns. The three minarets all date from different periods: the one on the northern side, the **Minaret of the Bride**, is the oldest; the one in the southwestern corner, the Mamluk-styled **Al-Gharbiyya minaret**, is the most beautiful; while the one on the southeastern corner, the **Minaret of Jesus**, is the tallest, and so named because local tradition has it that this is where Christ will appear on earth on Judgment Day.

The cavernous, rectangular **prayer hall** on the southern side of the courtyard is an Ottoman reconstruction that took place

DAMASCUS IN...

Two Days

Spend the morning at the **National Museum**. After lunch, walk along the **Souk el Hamidiya** to the Roman colonnade and the **Umayyad Mosque**. Allow plenty of time for the mosque, as much to soak up the atmosphere as to see the interior. Step into the **tomb of Saladin**, beside the mosque and then shop in the **Souq al-Bzouiyya**, the Spice Souq, before taking a taxi to **Mt Qassiun** in time for sunset. The following day, start at **Bab Sharki** and walk down the **street called Straight**, stopping to visit the early Christian sites. In the afternoon, visit the **Khan Asad Pasha** and the nearby **Azem Palace**, ending with tea at **Nowfara Café.**

Four Days

With another couple of days to look around the city, you could dig deeper into the Old City – visit some of the medieval buildings, including the **Madrassa az-Zahiriyya** and the **Bimaristan Nureddin**, then tour some of the old mansions before returning to the souks. To get out of town, think of heading to the Christian enclave at **Seidnayya** and **Maalula**, or south to **Bosra**.

after a devastating fire in 1893. At the centre of the hall, resting on four great pillars above the transept, is the **Dome of the Eagle**, while looking somewhat out of place in the sanctuary is the green-domed, marble-clad **shrine of John the Baptist** (Prophet Yehia to Muslims), which supposedly holds the head of the man himself; other places around the Middle East make a similar claim. On the eastern side of the courtyard is the entrance to the **shrine of Hussein**, son of Ali and grandson of the Prophet. The shrine attracts large numbers of Shiite (mostly Iranian) pilgrims.

Such are the major landmarks of the Umayyad Mosque, but our favourite experience of a visit here is to find a quiet corner under the arches and watch as the devout explore one of Islam's foremost places of worship, mullahs rub shoulders with curious Western tourists and children gambol around the courtyard oblivious to the need for reverence. Mosques in the Islamic world are centres of community life and nowhere is this more true than here, especially close to sunset.

The tourist entrance to the Umayyad mosque is on the north side, but first you'll need to buy a ticket outside the northwestern corner of the mosque; look for the 'Putting on Special Clothes Room' sign. Women are required to don the grey robes supplied, which will cover the head (obligatory).

Next to the ticket office in the small garden north of the mosque's walls is the modest, red-domed **Mausoleum of Saladin**, the resting place of one of the great heroes of Arab history. The mausoleum was originally built in 1193, and admission is included in the price of the Umayyad Mosque ticket.

NORTH OF THE MOSQUE

Madrassa az-Zahiriyya TOMB

(Map p404; ⏲9am-5pm) Northwest of Saladin's mausoleum is the restored 13th-century madrassa, within which is buried Sultan Beybars – another Islamic warrior hero, this time of the Mamluk dynasty. It was Beybars who won several decisive victories over the Crusaders, driving them from the region.

Sayyida Ruqayya Mosque MOSQUE

Also near the Umayyad Mosque is the modern, Iranian-built Shiite Sayyida Ruqayya Mosque, dedicated to the daughter of the martyr Hussein, son of Ali. Powerful in the passion it inspires in the (mostly Iranian) pilgrims, breathtaking in the extravagance of its decoration, this mosque is one of the most fascinating sights in Damascus and its presence ripples out through the surrounding streets.

This is one of the major pilgrimage sites for Shiite pilgrims to Damascus and although it has long been thus, the current mosque dates back only to the late 1980s. While the portico, courtyard and main 'onion' dome are relatively restrained and quite beautiful, the interior of the prayer hall is a riot of mirror mosaics given added power by the weeping and chanting pilgrims. It can all be a little overwhelming if you've become accustomed to subtle Damascene interiors, but should on no account be missed.

Non-Muslims may enter, except during Friday noon prayers.

SOUTH & EAST OF THE MOSQUE

Azem Palace MUSEUM

(Map p404; adult/student S£150/10; 9am-3.30pm Wed-Mon winter, to 5.30pm Wed-Mon rest of year, closed Fri noon-2pm summer & 11am-1pm winter) The largest and arguably the most beautiful of the Damascene courtyard homes, this was built in 1749 by the governor of Damascus, As'ad Pasha al-Azem. It's fashioned in the typical Damascene style of striped stonework, which is achieved by alternating layers of black basalt and limestone. The rooms of the palace are magnificent, decorated with inlaid tile work and exquisite painted ceilings. The expansive courtyard, too, is lovely and often filled with local families seeking refuge from the Damascus heat.

Souq al-Bzouriyya MARKET

Just around the corner from the palace is Souq al-Bzouriyya (literally the Seed Bazaar, but in reality the Spice Souq), heavily scented with cumin, coffee and perfumes. Halfway along, on the left, is Hammam Nureddin, the most elegant of Damascus' old bathhouses.

Khan As'ad Pasha HISTORIC BUILDING

(admission S£75; 9am-3pm Sat-Thu) Just beyond the hammam is the towering entrance to Khan As'ad Pasha, arguably the finest and most ambitious piece of civic architecture in the Old City – a cathedral among khans. Built in 1752 under the patronage of As'ad Pasha al-Azem, it's a supremely elegant arrangement of eight small domes around a larger circular aperture, allowing light to stream in above a circular pool. The domes are supported on four colossal grey-and-white piers that splay into graceful arches, with a backdrop of more horizontal grey-and-white magnificence. Don't fail to climb up to the 1st floor, where the cell-like rooms of the old khan surround the balconies that look down into the main courtyard with some marvellous interplays of light and shadow. It's a special place.

Madrassa an-Nuri HISTORIC BUILDING

Swinging back to the west, the Madrassa an-Nuri is the mausoleum of Saladin's predecessor, Nureddin.

Bimarstan Nureddin HISTORIC BUILDING

Just south of the Souq al-Hamidiyya, the Bimarstan Nureddin was built in the 12th century as a mental hospital and was for centuries renowned in the Arab world as an enlightened medical-treatment centre.

Arab Medical & Science Museum MUSEUM

(Map p404; adult/student S£150/10; 9am-3pm Sat-Thu) Inside, the hodgepodge exhibits are displayed around a cool, peaceful courtyard.

Roman Arch MONUMENT

Heading east, about two-thirds of the way along Sharia Medhat Pasha – **Straight St** (Via Recta) – are the remains of a Roman arch. The arch roughly marks the starting point of what's referred to as the Christian Quarter, although it's by no means exclusive.

FREE **St Paul's Chapel** CHURCH

(Bab Kisan; 8am-6pm) Marks the spot where, according to the biblical tale, the disciples lowered St Paul out of a window in a basket one night so that he could flee the Jews. The simple stone chapel occupies the gate itself; to get here, you have to leave the Old City via Bab Sharqi and follow the walls around to the southwest.

Chapel of Ananias CHURCH

(Sharia Hanania; admission S£25; 9am-7pm) The old cellar is reputedly the house of Ananias, an early Christian disciple who baptised St Paul. The crypt church has multilingual translations of the story of the two disciples, although scholars dispute whether this is Ananias' actual house.

NATIONAL MUSEUM & AROUND

National Museum MUSEUM

(Map p408; 221 9938; adult/student S£150/10; 9am-4pm Wed-Mon Oct-Jan, to 6pm Wed-Mon Apr-Sep, closed for Fri prayers) Located off Sharia Shoukri al-Quwatli, this is Syria's most important museum and well worth a visit. After passing the shady garden strewn with unlabelled antiquities, for which no room could be found within the museum's walls, you enter the museum proper through the imposing facade (the relocated entrance of Qasr al-Heir al-Gharbi, a desert fortress near Palmyra that dates to AD 688).

The exhibits are presented thematically and grouped into preclassical, classical and Islamic sections; labelling (in Arabic and English) is improving thanks to a joint Syrian–Italian overhaul. Highlights include the finely wrought stone friezes from the *qasr*, which you'll see immediately upon entering; tablets from the ruins of Ugarit showing one of the world's first

Damascus Old City

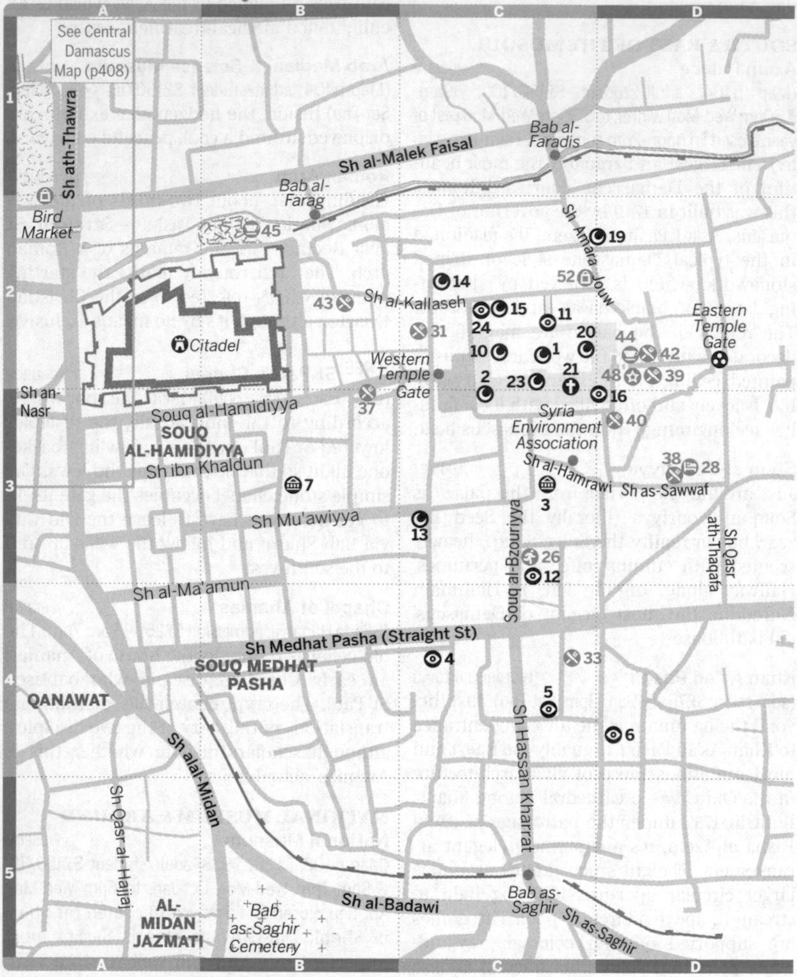

alphabets; the downstairs Hypogeum of Yarhai, an extraordinary reconstruction of an underground burial chamber from Palmyra's Valley of the Tombs; and the astonishing frescoed, 2nd-century synagogue from Dura Europos in eastern Syria, our favourite room in the whole museum.

Takiyya as-Süleimaniyya MONASTERY

(Map p408) Immediately east of the National Museum is the black-and-white-striped Takiyya as-Süleimaniyya, built in 1554 to the design of the Ottoman Empire's most brilliant architect, Mirmar Sinan. It's currently closed to the public, but the pencil-thin Ottoman-style minarets tower above the rooftops.

Hejaz Train Station NOTABLE BUILDING

(Map p408) The grand Hejaz train station, completed in 1917, was the northern terminus of the Hejaz Railway, built to ferry pilgrims to Medina. Compared with the transport palaces of Europe, the station is a provincial affair, but the interior has a beautifully decorated ceiling. The actual platforms of the station are closed and the block behind, where the tracks used to run, is the

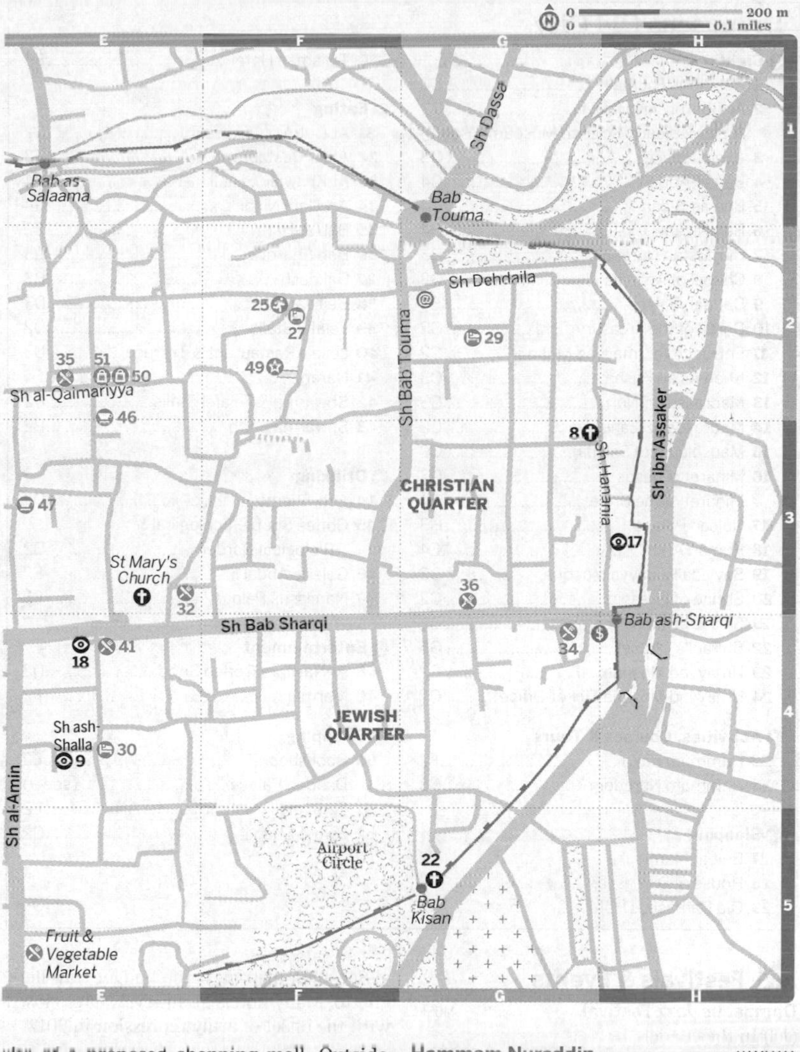

site of a proposed shopping mall. Outside there's a steam locomotive dating from 1908.

Activities

There are a few hammams in the Old City, all of which offer a full service of massage, bath, exfoliation and sauna with towel, soap and tea.

Hammam Bakri HAMMAM
(Map p404; ☎542 6606; Sharia Qanayet al-Hattab; ⏰women 10am-5pm Sat-Thu, men 5pm-midnight Sat-Thu, 10am-midnight Fri) A local bath in the Christian quarter, near Bab Touma.

Hammam Nureddin HAMMAM
(Map p404; ☎222 9513; Souq al-Bzouriyya, ⏰9am-midnight Sat-Thu) One of the oldest hammams in the city and strictly men only.

Tours

Many agencies and hotels will organise day trips. **Al-Rabie** (☎231 8374) and **Al-Haramain Hotels** (☎231 9489) usually offer them to Bosra, Suweida and the Sayyida Zeinab Mosque; Crac des Chevaliers; Apamea; and Maalula, Seidnayya and Jebel Qassioun.

Damascus Old City

Sights

1 Ablutions Fountain C2
2 Al-Gharbiyya Minaret C3
Arab Medical & Science Museum . (see 7)
3 Azem Palace C3
4 Beit al-Aqqad C4
5 Beit as-Sibai C4
6 Beit Nizam D4
7 Bimarstan Nureddin B3
8 Chapel of Ananais G3
9 Dahdah Palace E4
10 Dome of the Treasury C2
11 Entrance to Umayyad Mosque C2
12 Khan As'ad Pasha C3
13 Madrassa an-Nuri C3
14 Madrassa az-Zahiriyya C2
15 Mausoleum of Saladin C2
16 Minaret of Jesus D3
Minaret of the Bride .... (see 11)
17 Na'san Palace H3
18 Roman Arch E4
19 Sayyida Ruqayya Mosque D2
20 Shrine of Hussein C2
21 Shrine of John the Baptist C2
22 St Paul's Chapel G5
23 Umayyad Mosque C2
24 Umayyad Mosque Ticket Office C2

Activities, Courses & Tours

25 Hammam Bakri F2
26 Hammam Nureddin C3

Sleeping

27 Beit al-Mamlouka F2
28 House of Damascus D3
29 Old Damascus Hotel G2
30 Talisman Hotel E4

Eating

31 Abu al-Azz C2
32 Aldar Restaurant E3
33 Al-Khawali C4
34 Art Café Ninar G4
35 Bab al-Hara E2
36 Bab Sharqi G3
37 Bakdash B3
38 Beit Jabri D3
39 Felafel Stalls D2
40 Leila's Restaurant & Terrace D3
41 Naranj E4
42 Shwarma & Felafel Stalls D2
43 Shwarma Shop B2

Drinking

44 Ash-Shams D2
45 Coffee Shop – Ecological & Biological Garden B2
46 Galerie Abdal E2
47 Narcissus Palace E3

Entertainment

48 Al-Nawfara Coffee Shop D2
49 Marmar F2

Shopping

50 Bookshop E2
Dahdah Palace .... (see 9)
51 Ezrat al-Harastani E2
52 Sweet Shop C2

Festivals & Events

Damascus Jazz Festival MUSIC
(Jul) In the citadel.

Silk Road Festival PERFORMING ARTS
(late Sep) Celebrates Syria's long cultural history with events in Damascus, Aleppo, Palmyra and Bosra.

Damascus International Film Festival FILM
(Nov-Dec) Local and international films (you can see most of the films in Syria at other times too).

Sleeping

The Damascus hotel scene has been improving for several years, particularly the top and bottom end. Sharia Bahsa, in the Souq al-Saroujah district, is the budget travellers' ghetto. Many hotels at all levels have closed with the onset of army repression in 2012.

TOP CHOICE **Al-Rabie Hotel** HOTEL $
(Map p408; ☎231 8374; alrabiehotel@hotmail.com; Sharia Bahsa) One of the best backpacker choices in all the Middle East, this enchanting 600-year-old house has a gorgeous courtyard featuring trailing vines, an orange tree and a fountain. Modern additions include a satellite TV and comfortable seating. Some rooms look onto the courtyard and some feature ornate high ceilings, large windows and exposed stonework; all are clean and have heating and fans. The staff is friendly and traveller-savvy.

TOP CHOICE **Talisman** BOUTIQUE HOTEL $$$
(Map p404; ☎541 5379; www.talismanhotels.com; near Straight St; ❄@≋) One of the first boutique hotels in the Old City, it has since spawned two others, each with its own character (the one near Bab as-Salaama being the most intimate). Rooms are individually decorated with local antiques, there's wireless internet throughout and the service is gracious and discreet. Drinks are served and dinner can be provided if advance notice is given.

Afamia Hotel HOTEL $$
(Map p408; ☎222 8963; www.afamiahotel.com; ❄) The Afamia wins our vote for Damascus' best midrange hotel. Traveller friendly, well located close to the Hejaz train station and a 10-minute walk from the Old City, the hotel has a mix of rooms that were renovated recently (executive) and older rooms (classic). There are plans for all the rooms to be renovated which will make it a fine choice whichever room you get. The newer rooms aren't large but have plump doonas, comfortable beds, hairdryers, clean bathrooms and satellite TV; there are also plans for in-room ADSL internet access. Some rooms also have balconies.

House of Damascus GUESTHOUSE $
(Map p404; ☎094 431 8068; www.houseofdamascus.com; @) For student accommodation. Set in a lovely old Damascus house not far from the Umayyad Mosque, the rooms have shared bathrooms and there's dial-up internet connection, a fridge, satellite TV and two shared kitchens.

Ghazal Hotel HOTEL $
(Map p408; ☎231 3736; www.ghazalhotel.com; Sharia Bahsa) This friendly, clean hotel gets rave reviews from travellers. Its ample public areas don't quite have the character of the others further west, but the overall package is outstanding.

Sultan Hotel HOTEL $$
(Map p408; ☎222 5768; sultan.hotel@mail.sy; Sharia Mousalam al-Baroudi; ❄) Just west of the Hejaz station and a short walk to the Old City, this is the accommodation of choice for most archaeological missions to the country. Although the 31 rooms are basic but clean, what really makes this place is the level of service: the staff is exceptionally friendly and helpful. There's a library of novels to borrow and a lounge/breakfast area with satellite TV.

Old Damascus Hotel BOUTIQUE HOTEL $$
(Map p404; ☎541 4042; www.old-damas.com; near Bab Touma; ❄@) With an intimate courtyard, lovely spacious rooms and an attention to detail that has few rivals in the Old City, Old Damascus Hotel is outstanding. We also love the fact that it's run, at least in part, by women.

Beit al-Mamlouka BOUTIQUE HOTEL $$$
(Map p404; ☎543 0445/6; www.almamlouka.com; ❄@) This courtyard house, which dates from 1650, has been converted into a sumptuous boutique hotel. Staying in the Süleyman the Magnificent room, with its painted ceiling and marble fountain, is a once-in-a-lifetime experience, made even better by the hotel's high level of service and great position within the walls of the Old City. There are only eight rooms, all of which are individually and beautifully decorated. The marmalade on your breakfast table comes from the trees in the courtyard and the rooftop terrace is a fine place to wile away an afternoon.

Eating

The most atmospheric places to eat are the historic courtyard restaurants in the Old City, where prices are generally reasonable, at least by Western standards. If you want alcohol with your meal, you'll need to venture into the Christian Quarter rather than the area around the Umayyad Mosque, although some places in the latter area will whisper in your ear that alcohol is available. In central Damascus, the best restaurants are found in the area around Saahat Yousef al-Azmeh.

CENTRAL DAMASCUS

The side streets off Martyrs' Sq are crammed with cheap eateries, which mostly offer shwarma and felafel, but the southern perimeter of the square and the surrounding streets are more famous for their **sweet shops**, with windows dominated by great pyramids of baklava and other glorious Damascene sweets.

Another popular spot for cheap restaurants is just up the hill from Al-Rabie and Al-Haramain Hotels, in the Souq al-Saroujah district, where all the budget hotels are concentrated. There are places offering roast chicken, shwarma and some of the best *fatta* (an oven-baked dish of chickpeas, minced meat or chicken, and bread soaked in tahina) we tasted in Syria, as well as **bakeries** where the locals buy their bread.

Central Damascus

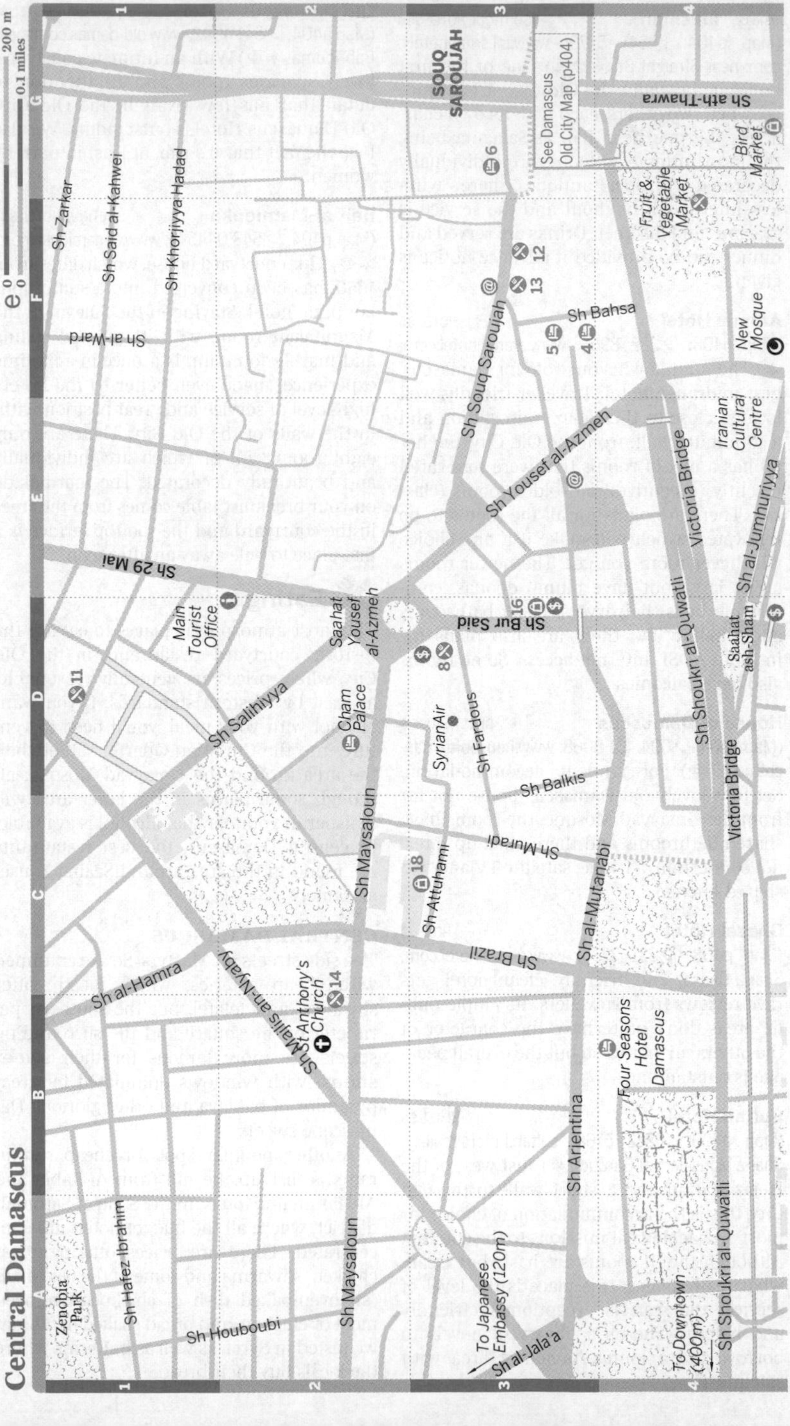

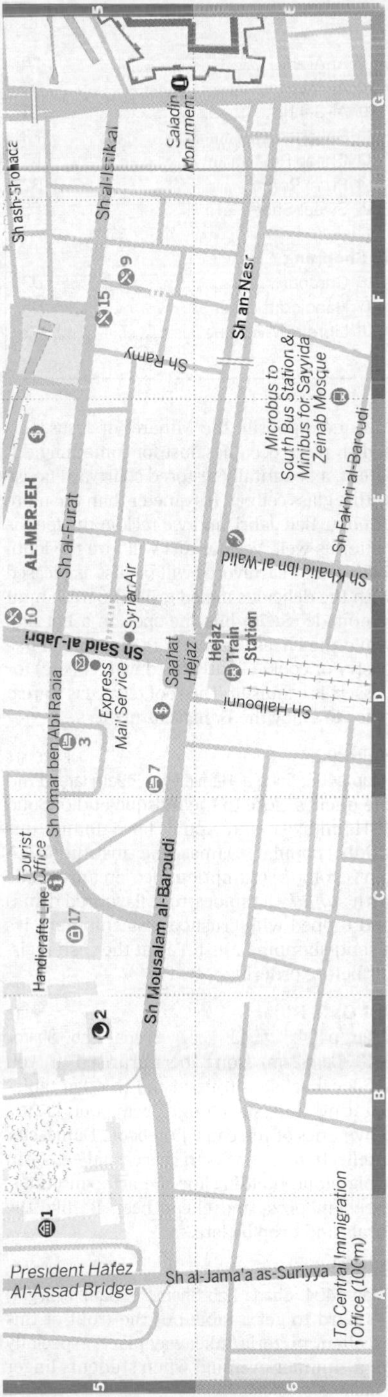

Abu Kamal SYRIAN **$**

(Map p408; ☎221 1159; Sharia Bur Said; ⏰11am-10pm) Simple, solid and uncomplicated are the qualities that make this place stand out. Both the food, with its emphasis on grilled meat and mezze, and the service can be counted on, although waiters tend to put extra dishes on your table in the hope you will want them. Send back the ones you don't want. No alcohol.

Al-Masri EGYPTIAN **$**

(Map p408; ☎333 7095; Sharia Said al-Jabri; ⏰7.30am-5pm) 'The Egyptian' is popular with local office workers, with a menu featuring the kind of home-cooked fare you'd find in Cairo's backstreets, along with local favourites such as *shakshuka* (fried egg and mince meat) and *shish tawooq* (grilled chicken kebab, often served with garlic and lemon sauce).

Downtown INTERNATIONAL **$$**

(☎332 2321; Sharia al-Amar Izzedin al-Jazzari; ⏰10am-1am) This hip, contemporary cafe has Scandinavian-style decor (think chocolate-coloured wood and clean lines) and the most decadently delicious sandwiches, salads and fresh juices in Damascus. Try the caviar en croute sandwich with cucumber, dill, caviar, cream cheese and a boiled egg (S£500), and the strawberry and blackberry juice. Downtown is ideal if you've been on the road a while and crave tastes from home.

Al-Arabi SYRIAN **$**

(Map p408) On a pedestrianised street off the southeastern corner of Al-Merjeh, Al-Arabi consists of two adjacent, cheap restaurants, one more casual, the other a little fancier with a separate family section. For the culinary adventurous, specialities include sheep testicles and sheep-brain salad with potatoes, but there are plenty of less challenging dishes including stuffed grape leaves, borek and *kibbeh* (cracked-wheat croquettes) with yogurt.

Al-Sehhi SYRIAN **$**

(Map p408; ☎221 1555; Sharia al-Abed; ⏰11am-midnight) This modest family restaurant, off Sharia 29 Mai, confines itself to the basics – mezze, grilled meats, and very good *fatta;* they eat every part of the sheep here (brains, testicles, tongue...). There's a separate 'family area' for women diners.

Pizza Roma PIZZA **$**

(Map p408; ☎331 6434; 3 Sharia Odai bin ar-Roqa; ❄) If you're keen on American-style (pan,

Central Damascus

Sights

rather than thinner Italian) pizzas, this is the most popular place in town. You'll find it west of the Cham Palace Hotel.

OLD CITY

In the small alley east of the Umayyad Mosque, just past the Al-Nawfara Coffee Shop, are a couple of very good shwarma places and a stall that does great felafel. There's another collection of felafel and shwarma hole-in-the-wall eateries in the covered market lane that runs north off Souq al-Hamidiyya.

TOP CHOICE Naranj SYRIAN $$$

(Map p404; ☎541 3600; Straight St; ❄) By the Roman arch on Straight St, this is the finest restaurant in the Old City and one of the best in the country. The huge dining room is separated from the kitchen by a glass screen. Food is delicious, whether the specials such as kebab with cherry sauce, or the standard mezze, bread is fresh baked and everything served with style. The roof terrace is perfect for dining on a warm evening. Book ahead.

TOP CHOICE Bab al-Hara SYRIAN $$

(Map p404; ☎541 8644; Sharia al-Qaimariyya; ⏲9.30am-midnight) West of the Umayyad Mosque, Bab al-Hara is one of our favourite Old City restaurants. The grills have that reassuring taste of charcoal, the *kibbeh* is some of the tastiest we've tried and the *fatta* is hearty and very good. The service is casual and obliging. Highly recommended.

TOP CHOICE Leila's Restaurant & Terrace SYRIAN $$

(Map p404; ☎544 5900; Souq al-Abbabiyya; ⏲11am-2am) In the shadow of the Umayyad Mosque, opposite the Minaret of Jesus, this stylish place occupies, just for something different, a beautifully restored courtyard house with a glass ceiling. It's quieter than the more popular Beit Jabri, and we reckon the food is better as well. Vegetarians will love the lentil *kibbeh* and carnivores will be just as pleased with the delicious mixed grill. The fresh mint lemonade (S£75) hits the spot on a hot day, while the cheese *mamoul* (a shortbread-like pastry or cookie lightly filled with cheese) for dessert is exquisite. The roof terrace is a great place to enjoy the Damascus night.

Bakdash ICE CREAM $

(Map p404; Souq al-Hamidiyya; ⏲9am-late) Find the queues close to the mosque-end of Souq al-Hamidiyya and you'll have found this wildly popular Damascene institution. A purveyor of scrumptious ice creams made with *sahlab* (a tapioca-root flavoured drink) and topped with crushed pistachio nuts, it's a souq-shopping must. Pay at the cash register before ordering.

Art Café Ninar PUB $

(Map p404; ☎542 2257; Sharia Bab Sharqi; ⏲10.30am-2am) Don't be surprised if you see local artists sitting at the wooden tables painting and sketching, or a poet jotting down lines of verse in a notebook. Damascus' intellectual set flocks to this casual eatery in a big stone building for the art exhibitions, excellent pizza and cheap beer. Be like the locals and drop by late.

Bab Sharqi PIZZA $

(Map p404; Sharia Bab Sharqi; ⏲11am-midnight) It's hard to get a table out the front of this excellent pizzeria/takeaway place, especially on a summer evening, when students linger over cold beers, bottles of Syrian wine, Italian-style pizzas and delicious *toshka* (Armenian toasted meat and cheese sandwiches).

Abu al-Azz SYRIAN **$$**
(Map p404; ☎221 8174; Souq al-Hamidiyya; ⏲9am-late) This place is popular with locals as much as tourists. Arab families pack the place over summer. Look for the sign 'Rest. Al Ezz Al Shamieh Hall', then pass through the bustling ground-floor bakery and up a narrow staircase to two floors of dining; the upper level is the most atmospheric. Expect mezze, salads and kebabs, live oriental music all day and whirling dervishes in the evening from around 10.30pm. No alcohol served.

Beit Jabri SYRIAN **$$**
(Jabri House; Map p404; ☎541 6254; 14 Sharia as-Sawwaf; ⏲9.30am-12.30am) This informal and phenomenally popular cafe is set in the partially restored courtyard of a stunning 18th-century Damascene house. The menu runs from breakfasts and omelettes to oriental mezze and mains. The quality of the food and service is OK, but doesn't always live up to the surrounds.

Al-Khawali SYRIAN **$$**
(Map p404; ☎222 5808; cnr Maazanet al-Shahim; ⏲noon-2am) A touch of class pervades this place, off Straight St, unlike the more casual atmosphere that you find elsewhere, and the food is first rate. Try the aubergine and see what great mezze is all about, or the *jedy bzeit* (lamb with lemon sauce), but everything on the menu is subtly flavoured and delicious. Best of all, bread baked on the premises arrives on your table still warm from the oven. No alcohol or credit cards.

OLD DAMASCUS HOUSES: A TOUR

Old Damascus is divided into two distinct and often mutually exclusive realms: the public and the private. The former is full of clamorous souqs and an ever-changing world of traders, transients and tourists; the latter is an oasis of calm, sophistication and graceful architecture. From the outside, these old Damascus homes are invisible, with no hint of what lies behind the high stone walls; courtyards such as these were often home to as many as a dozen families.

Starting from the northeastern corner of the Old City, **Dar al-Yasmin**, **Old Damascus Hotel** and **Beit al-Mamlouka** are three old homes converted into hotels, where the beautiful courtyards are wonderful places to peek into and even better places to stay. South of here, close to Bab Sharqi, is **Na'san Palace** (Map p404; Sharia Hanania; ⏲8am-2pm Sun-Thu), which has a narrow courtyard in sombre tones offset by the extravagantly decorated *iwan* (arched alcove serving as a summer retreat).

West along Straight St, turn south from the Roman arch and follow the signs to **Dahdah Palace** (Map p404; 9 Sharia ash-Shalla; admission free; ⏲9am-1pm & 4-6pm Mon-Sat), a 17th-century residence owned by the Dahdah family. Ring the bell for an informal guided tour by the charming Mrs Dahdah and her daughter of the lovely courtyard, fragrant with jasmine and lemon trees, the *iwan*, and the reception room with its exquisite niche. They also sell antiques (see p413).

Further west, **Beit Nizam** (Map p404; Sharia Nasif Pasha; ⏲8am-2pm Sun-Thu) is another breathtakingly beautiful 18th-century house, executed on a grand scale with two large courtyards; the one to the rear is adorned with orange trees and rose bushes. In the mid-19th century, it served as the French consulate and it's often used these days as a set for film and TV productions. Just around the corner, **Beit as-Sibai** (Map p404; Sharia al-Qabbani; ⏲8am-2pm Sun-Thu), built between 1769 and 1774, was being restored at the time of research.

Head north towards Straight St, pausing en route at **Al-Khawali**, one of Damascus' best restaurants, then head west to **Beit al-Aqqad** (Map p404; ⏲223 8038; 8-10 Souq as-Souf; ⏲9am-3pm Sun-Wed, to 1pm Thu). Formerly the home of a wealthy family of textile merchants, it now houses the Danish Institute in Damascus. Visitors are welcome to wander in and look at the courtyard, which lies beyond the entrance patio and is graced by an expanse of gorgeous inlaid-stone decoration and one of the highest *iwans* in the city.

After visiting the grandest old Damascus home of all, the **Azem Palace**, a number of courtyard restaurants are fine places to finish, among them **Beit Jabri** – don't miss the beautifully restored *qa'a* (reception room) up the stairs at the far end of the courtyard – **Bab al-Hara**, and **Narcissus Palace**.

BOOKS ABOUT DAMASCUS

» *Mirror to Damascus*, Colin Thubron (1967) An engaging journey through the history of Damascus before the tourists arrived.

» *Hidden Damascus: Treasures of the Old City*, Brigid Keenan (2001) Lavishly illustrated study of old Damascus that you'll want on your coffee table back home.

» *Damascus Nights*, Rafik Schami (1997) This wonderful novel about a Damascus storyteller losing his voice takes you into the heart of the Old City. Schami's subsequent books, *The Dark Side of Love* (2009), *The Calligrapher's Secret* (2010) and *Damascus: Taste of a City* are also excellent.

» *Damascus: Taste of a City*, Marie Fadel & Rafik Schami (2002) A beautifully presented and wonderfully entertaining extended walk through the lanes and home kitchens of Old Damascus, complete with recipes.

» *Syria Through Writers' Eyes*, Marius Kociejowski (ed) (2006) A collection of writing about Syria down through the centuries, with a good section on the capital.

Aldar Restaurant SYRIAN **$$$**
(Map p404; ☎544 5900; ⊙11am-2am) In a chic conversion of an old Damascene building off Sharia Bab Sharqi, beside the Assieh School, and stylishly blending old and new, Aldar dishes up some of the tastiest Syrian cuisine in the city, with creative touches added to classics.

Drinking

There are loads of places in the Souq al-Saroujah backpacker district, with the low outdoor stools a great place to discuss regional politics and local popular culture over a tea.

The finest places to relax in Damascus are the two historic coffeehouses, Al-Nawfara Coffee Shop, which has a storyteller some evenings, and **Ash-Shams** (Map p404; Sharia al-Qaimariyya; ⊙9am-midnight), nestled in the shadow of the Umayyad Mosque's eastern wall. Lingering over a tea here should be on every visitor's itinerary.

A number of restaurants double as coffeehouses in Old City buildings. The better ones include Leila's Restaurant & Terrace and Beit Jabri.

Coffee Shop – Ecological & Biological Garden CAFE
(Map p404; ⊙9am-11pm) Just outside the northeastern corner of the citadel, near Bab al-Farag and overlooking the trickle that is the Barada River, this agreeable modern coffee shop has outdoor and indoor tables alongside a garden set up by the Syria Environment Association. Although the plants need time to mature, it's an initiative worth supporting, quite apart from being a pleasant place to rest from the clamour of the Old City.

Galerie Albal CAFE
(Map p404; ☎544 5794; Sharia Shaweesh) For something a bit different, Galerie Albal, about a five-minute walk from the coffeehouses east along Sharia al-Qaimariyya, is a loud, Western-style cafe with an art gallery above. It's where the city's bohemian types congregate, and there is a handful of similar places alongside.

Narcissus Palace CAFE
(Map p404; ☎541 6785; ⊙noon-1am) Packed to its very attractive rafters with young people catching up over a nargileh and tea, Narcissus Palace features music clips blaring from the satellite TV, backgammon pieces clinking, the fountain gently playing and extremely friendly staff to make sure everyone is happy. Great stuff.

Entertainment

TOP CHOICE **Al-Nawfara Coffee Shop** CAFE
(The Fountain Coffee Shop; Map p404; Sharia al-Qaimariyya; ⊙9am-midnight) Not only is this lovely old cafe an institution for imbibing tea and a nargileh, it's the home of Syria's last professional *hakawati* (storyteller). Every night after sunset prayers, Abu Shady takes to the stage to tell an epic tale of glorious days long past. Depending on the crowd, it can either be filled with banter or a little quiet as people come and go, often talking over the top of him. Either way, this is a Damascus must-see, not least because this is a dying art form. A collection is taken near the end of the show.

For more information on Abu Shady and his storytelling tradition, see the boxed text p445.

Marmar CLUB

(Map p404; ☎544 6425; Sharia ad-Dawanneh; ❄) The most popular nightclub in town, a bar/restaurant at Bab Touma that morphs into a club on Thursday and Friday nights and occasionally hosts live gigs on Sundays.

Shopping

The Old City is awash with souqs. Apart from the bustling **Souq al-Hamidiyya** (Map p404), the main souq in the city and with a wonderful atmosphere, the tributary souqs are roughly demarcated into specialities, one handling clothes, another sweets and spices, another jewellery, yet another stationery items and so on.

For handicrafts, some of the better shops are those along Sharia Hanania in the far east of the Old City, or along Sharia Medhat Pasha (Straight St), east of the Roman arch.

If you're looking for the famous Damascene sweets to take back home, you could try the stalls selling individually wrapped nougat-and-pistachio items in **Souq al-Bzouriyya** (Map p404), the **sweet shop** (Map p404) on the corner of Sharia al-Kallaseh and Sharia Amara Jouw, or the **sweet shops** (Map p404) on Martyrs' Sq, with great pyramids of baklava to choose from.

Ghraoui SWEETS

(Map p408; ☎231 1323; www.ghraouichocolate.com; Sharia Bur Said) Sells the finest candied fruits and chocolates – the apricot half-coated with chocolate is a classic, as are the fresh cocoa truffles. There's a second branch in the departures lounge at Damascus International Airport.

Handicrafts Lane HANDICRAFTS

In the new part of town, the place to head for all manner of locally crafted souvenirs is this small shaded alleyway adjoining the Takiyya as-Süleimaniyya Mosque, just south of Sharia Shoukri al-Quwatli. Traders have now also filled some of the student cells of the attached madrassa.

Dahdah Palace ANTIQUES

(Map p404; 9 Sharia ash-Shalla; ⏲9am-1pm & 4-6pm Mon-Sat) One excellent place for antiques, with a range of artefacts recovered from demolished Damascene houses.

Ezrat al-Harastani HANDICRAFTS

(Map p404; ☎541 2602; Sharia al-Qaimariyya) For a range of beautiful and highly original handcrafted boxes, just east of the Eastern Temple Gate.

Bookshop BOOKS

(Map p404; Sharia al-Qaimariyya; ⏲11am-7pm) A small bookshop selling a handful of four-day-old international newspapers and an excellent selection of novels and some books about Syria. You can also leave your books here.

Librairie Avicenne BOOKS

(Map p408; ☎221 2911; avicenne@net.sy; 4 Sharia Attuhami; ⏲9am-8pm Sat-Thu) The best English-language bookshop in Syria.

Information

Emergency

Ambulance (☎110)

Fire (☎113)

Police (☎112)

Internet Access

The internet situation is changing fast. When it works, the following are among some of the better places to get connected.

Central post office (Map p408; Sharia Said al-Jabri; ⏲8am-7pm Sat-Thu, 8am-1pm Fri & holidays) Reasonable connections upstairs in the main post office building.

Ci@o Net (Map p408; ⏲7.30am-midnight) Off Sharia Yousef al-Azmeh, with fast connections and good for internet-connected phone calls.

E1 Café Net (Map p404; Sharia Dehdaila; ⏲10am-midnight) Close to Bab Touma and one of the better options in the Old City.

Internet Café Smile (Map p408; Sharia Souq Saroujah; ⏲11am-midnight Sat-Thu, 2pm-midnight Fri) Convenient for Souq al-Saroujah's budget hotels.

Internet Corner (Map p408; 1st fl, Abdin Bldg, Sharia Hammam al-Ward; ⏲10am-2am) Fast connections and good work stations in the backpacker quarter. It's still signposted as 'Fast Link'.

Medical Services

Cham Clinic (Map p408; ☎333 8742; ⏲24hr) Behind the Meridien Hotel. Doctors speak English.

Shami Hospital (Map p408; ☎373 4925; Sharia Jawaher an-Nehru) Northwest of the main centre of town. Accepts credit cards.

Money

There are numerous branches of the Commercial Bank of Syria (CBS; Map p408) around town and most have Visa- and Visa Electron–enabled ATMs. Most branches have exchange booths where you can change money easily; the branch on Saahat Yousef al-Azmeh will change travellers cheques. There's also an ATM and an exchange booth at Damascus International Airport. If you need to use MasterCard, there's a branch of Banque Bemo Saudi Fransi (Map p404) with an ATM just outside Bab Touma.

Post

Central post office (Map p408; Sharia Said al-Jabri; ⌚8am-7pm Sat-Thu, 8am-1pm Fri & holidays)

Telephone

City telephone office (Map p408; Sharia an-Nasr; ⌚8am-7pm Sat-Thu, to 1pm Fri & holidays) A block east of the Hejaz train station. Card phones are on the street around the corner (buy cards from the telephone office or any street vendor). You can send faxes from inside the telephone office (bring your passport).

Tourist Information

Main tourist office (Map p408; ☎232 3953; www.syriatourism.org; Sharia 29 Mai; ⌚9.30am-8pm Sat-Thu) Just up from Saahat Yousef al-Azmeh in the centre of town. Staff don't always speak English.

Tourist office (Map p408; ☎221 0122; Handicrafts Lane; ⌚9.30am-8pm Sat-Thu) A second, smaller office near the National Museum.

Getting There & Away

Air

Several SyrianAir offices are scattered about the city centre; one convenient **office** (Map p408; ☎245 0097/8) is on Saahat Hejaz, just opposite the train station.

Most of the other airline offices are grouped across from the Cham Palace Hotel on Sharia Maysaloun, or one block south on Sharia Fardous.

Bus & Microbus

There are two main bus stations in Damascus: Harasta Garage (Karajat Harasta, also known as Pullman Garage), offering Pullman bus services to the north and international services to Turkey; and Al-Samariyeh Garage (Karajat al-Samariyeh), which has services to the south (eg Bosra) and departures for Jordan and Lebanon. In addition there are several other minibus and microbus stations serving regional destinations.

Harasta/Pullman Garage Harasta/Pullman Garage is about 6km northeast of the city centre. All the big private bus companies have their offices here. Al-Kadmous runs a 24-hour service to Aleppo every hour on the hour (five hours); to Deir ez-Zur (six hours, hourly from 6am to 2.30am); 14 buses to Homs (two hours, from 6.15am to 8.15pm); to Hama (2½ hours, four daily); to Tartus (3½ hours, hourly from 5.30am to 11pm); and to Palmyra (four hours, hourly from 6am to 2.30am). Al-Ahliah has services to Aleppo (hourly between 6am and 8pm), and to Lattakia (4½ hours, five daily). If you're travelling to Turkey, Hatay has Pullman services to Antakya (eight hours) and İstanbul (36 hours), leaving at 10pm daily. JETT buses also travel to Antakya and İstanbul at 10pm daily. To get to Harasta, you can take a microbus from outside the fruit and vegetable market on Sharia al-Ittihad, just near Al-Haramain and Al-Rabie Hotels.

Al-Samariyeh Garage For services to the south (ie Bosra) and international destinations like Amman and Beirut (but not Turkey), head to the new Al-Samariyeh Garage (Mezzeh West); on the western outskirts of the city. For Bosra (two hours), we recommend Damas Tours, with new air-con buses heading south every two hours from 8am to 10pm. Al-Muhib also runs buses south at exactly the same times and prices as Damas Tours. Private bus companies have frequent services from Al-Samariyeh Garage to Beirut (4½ hours), departing every hour or so between 7.30am and 6.30pm, plus several buses daily to Amman (four to seven hours depending on border formalities). There's no bus service from Damascus to Baalbek.

Other bus stations Microbuses to Deraa (for the Jordanian border) leave from the Deraa Garage (Karajat Deraa) in the south of the city. You're much better off getting a Pullman bus from Al-Samariyeh Garage. For Maalula (one hour) and Seidnayya (40 minutes), head to Maalula Garage (Karajat Maalula), just east of Saahat Abbasseen.

Service Taxi

The main service-taxi station is at Al-Samariyeh Garage. Taxis leave throughout the day and night for Amman (four to seven hours, depending on border formalities) and Irbid (3½ to five hours) in Jordan, and Baalbek (2½ hours) and Beirut (from four hours, depending on border formalities) in Lebanon.

Train

All trains depart from the **Khaddam train station** (☎888 8678), about 5km southwest of the centre. There are three daily express services to Aleppo at 6.50am, 3.10pm and 4.50pm (4½ hours) and a slower service at midnight (six hours). Most trains on this line are new and comfortable.

Getting Around

To/From the Airport

Damascus International Airport is 32km southeast of Damascus. In the arrivals hall, there's an ATM next to the Commercial Bank of Syria ex-

WORTH A TRIP

BOSRA بصرى

The black-basalt town of Bosra, 137km from Damascus, is an easy day trip from the capital. Once the capital of the Roman province of Arabia, it's now something of a backwater. But what a weird and wonderful backwater it is. Bosra's gigantic Roman theatre is alone worth the trip here and the surrounding ruins are brooding and atmospheric.

The **Citadel** (adult/student S£150/10; ⊙9am-6pm Mar-Nov, to 4pm Dec-Feb) is a unique construction – it began life as a massive Roman theatre and later had its fortifications grafted on. The theatre was built early in the 2nd century AD, when Bosra was the capital of the Roman province of Arabia. The first walls were built during the Umayyad and Abbasid periods, with further additions being made in the 11th century by the Fatimids.

The magnificent 15,000-seat **theatre** is a rarity among Roman theatres in that it is completely freestanding rather than built into the side of a hill. It's a wonderful experience to be lost in the dark, oppressive fortress halls and dimly lit vaulted corridors and then to emerge through a sunlit opening to find yourself suddenly looking down on a vast, steeply terraced hillside of stone seating.

Other sites located in the Old Town north of the citadel include the old **Roman baths**, a 4th-century **monastery**, a **cathedral** (c 512) with an unfortunate concrete roof in one corner, various monumental gates, partially reconstructed **colonnades** of basalt corridors, the **Roman market** in lighter sandstone with mosaic-floor remnants off its northwestern side, vast cisterns and the **Mosque of Omar**, which dates to the 12th century.

There is a cluster of restaurants in the open square facing the Citadel. All of them serve similar, inexpensive set menus of Syrian staples. **Restaurant 1001 Nights** (☎795 331) is a long-standing traveller favourite, with a 25% discount for students. Budget travellers may be able to unfurl a sleeping bag to stay overnight; there's a shower and toilet but you'll need your own sleeping bag. Single women may not feel comfortable doing this. There are no fixed prices for overnight stays; ask when you arrive. At the other end of the scale, the **Bosra Cham Palace** (☎790 881; www.chamhotels.com; ❄🏊), a few hundred metres south from the Citadel entrance, is a top-end hotel with well-presented if dull rooms, a large swimming pool and a licensed coffeehouse and restaurant popular with tour groups.

If you need to change cash, the **exchange booth** (⊙8am-2pm & 4-6pm Sat-Thu) just southeast of the Citadel is usually working. If closed, you might be able to change at the Basra Cham Palace, which *may* even take travellers cheques. Staff at the **tourist office** (⊙9am-7pm), southeast of the Citadel, are willing but their resources (and English) are limited.

To get to Bosra from Damascus, you could drive yourself, rent a car and driver or take a bus or tour. Damas Tours runs new air-con buses between Bosra and Damascus (two hours, every two hours from 8am to 10pm). Al-Muhib runs similar services at the same times. Both leave from Damascus's Al-Samariyeh Garage. Minibuses run between Bosra and Deraa between 4.30am and 4pm. These leave when full from the front of the tourist information office.

change booth, enabled for Cirrus, Maestro, Visa and MasterCard. The booth exchanges cash, but not travellers cheques. There's a 24-hour tourist info office, supplying free city maps, but don't expect the staff to be either there or awake in the wee small hours.

The airport bus service (30 minutes, half-hourly between 6am and midnight) runs between the airport forecourt and the southwest corner of the otherwise-empty Baramke Garage. Look for the orange-and-white bus to the right as you exit the arrivals hall.

Taxis into the city centre can be organised at the desk just outside the arrivals hall.

Car-rental companies like Hertz and Europcar have booths in the arrivals hall, but it's rare that we've seen anyone behind the desk.

Bus & Taxi

Damascus is well served with a local bus and microbus network, but as the centre is so compact, you'll rarely have to use it.

All taxis are yellow and have meters. There are thousands of them.

AROUND DAMASCUS

The major attractions within an easy day trip from the capital include the outstanding Roman ruins at Bosra and the important Christian sites of Seidnayya and Maalula.

Seidnayya صيدنايا

Perched spectacularly on an enormous rocky outcrop, the Greek Orthodox **Convent of Our Lady of Seidnayya** is one of the most important places of Christian pilgrimage in the Middle East, due to the presence of a portrait of the Virgin Mary purportedly painted by St Luke. All manner of miracles have been attributed to this icon; at the time of the Crusades, the Christians considered Seidnayya second in importance only to Jerusalem. Veneration of the icon is fervent, and it's fascinating to witness Muslim pilgrims as well as Christians. Most of the structure dates from the 19th century.

Ascend the four flights of stairs (or take the lift), duck through the low wooden doorway, then pass to the courtyard on the right. Just off the courtyard is the pilgrimage shrine containing the famed relic, in a small dark room lit by candles amid the murmuring of the prayers of the devout and an aura of the sacred. Before entering, remove your shoes and ensure you're modestly dressed. The Feast of Our Lady of Seidnayya is held on 8 September each year, and the spectacle is worth attending if you're in the area. The main celebrations begin on the night of the 7th.

Travellers generally visit Seidnayya on a day trip from Damascus. There are regular microbuses to Seidnayya (40 minutes) from Maalula Garage in northeastern Damascus. It's possible to combine Seidnayya with a visit to Maalula, although public transport between the two is infrequent.

Maalula معلولا

☎011 / POP 5000

In a narrow valley in the foothills of Jebel Libnan ash-Sharqiyya, Maalula is a picturesque village huddled beneath a sheer cliff. If arriving by minibus, alight at the main village intersection, where there's a traffic island and the road splits. Head right up the hill, and at the top head right again; the road switches back, climbing steeply to the small **Convent of St Thecla** (Deir Mar Teqla), tucked snugly against the cliff. From here there are pretty views of the village.

Thecla was a pupil of St Paul and one of the earliest Christian martyrs. As one legend has it, after being cornered against the cliff at Maalula by soldiers sent to execute her, Thecla prayed to God, lightning stuck the cliff and a cleft appeared in the rock face, facilitating her flight. The shrine, beneath a rocky overhang at the top of the convent, is the highlight of any visit here. Otherwise, the convent, a sanctuary for nuns and orphans, is of minor interest, but ahead lies the legendary escape route, **St Thecla Gap**. Cut through the rock by run-off from the plateau above the village, this narrow, steep-sided ravine resembles a modest version of the famed Siq at Petra.

LANGUAGE OF CHRIST

The mainly Greek Catholic village of Maalula is one of just three villages where Aramaic, the language of Jesus Christ, is still spoken – the other two, Jabadeen and Sarkha, are nearby although they're now predominantly Muslim. Aramaic was once widely spoken in the Middle East and is one of the oldest continually spoken languages in the world, reaching its zenith around 500 BC. It bears similarities to both Arabic and Hebrew. The number of speakers has been steadily dwindling and remains under threat, but interest in keeping the language alive has increased dramatically.

Pilgrims from all over the world can study religion in Aramaic at St Ephrem's Clerical Seminary, in Seidnayya, while the Syrian government recently established an Institute for Aramaic, and new texts and language-learning materials are being written in the ancient language which was, until recently, an oral language only; many of Maalula's Aramaic speakers cannot write it. In Maalula's Monastery and Church of St Sergius, Aramaic is proudly alive and well. Local worshippers all speak Aramaic (although the 7.30am liturgy is conducted in Arabic because the service has a written base), accounting for around half of the world's Aramaic speakers.

At the end of the canyon, head to the left and follow the road for picturesque views of the village and valley, and the Byzantine **Monastery and Church of St Sergius** (Deir Mar Sarkis or Convent of Sts Serge & Bacchus). Built in AD 325, this is one of the oldest churches in the world. According to legend, Sergius (Sarkis) was a Roman legionary who, after converting to Christianity and refusing to make sacrifices to the god Jupiter, was executed. The low wooden doorway leading into the monastery is over 2000 years old; however, the highlight is the small church itself, which still incorporates features of the pagan temple that previously stood here. The splendid collection of icons includes some rare 17th-century gems.

The hillside south of the church is riddled with small caverns that archaeologists believe were inhabited by prehistoric man some 50,000 to 60,000 years ago. This road loops back to the village, where it's possible to catch a minibus back to Damascus.

Sleeping & Eating

As Maalula is an easy half-day trip from Damascus, there's no need to stay overnight unless you want to attend the Festival of the Cross (13 September) or the St Thecla Festival (24 September). It's possible to stay overnight in simple rooms at the Convent of St Thecla, where there are no fixed rates; make a generous donation instead. Otherwise try the **Maaloula Hotel** (777 0250; maaloula@scs-net.org;). **La Grotta** (777 0909), adjacent to the Monastery and Church of St Sergius, is the best eating option.

Getting There & Away

From Damascus, minibuses (one hour) depart from Maalula Garage. In Maalula, buses stop at the main intersection in the village centre, just downhill from the Convent of St Thecla.

HOMS حمص

031 / POP 1.3 MILLION

Even before it became the scene of the government's all-out attack on its people, there was little of interest in Homs. In March 2012, parts of the city were described by the UN as having been 'devastated'. But it's one of those crossroads towns that you might have to pass through at some stage.

Sleeping & Eating

An-Nasr al-Jedid Hotel HOTEL
(5227 423; Sharia Shoukri al-Quwatli) If you need to sleep in Homs this hotel, in a beautiful 100-year-old building, was about the best of the budget places in town, but that wasn't saying much.

Lord Suites Hotel HOTEL
(5247 4008; www.lordsuiteshotel.com; Saahat Al Saa al-Jadida;) This is a spotlessly clean midrange alternative.

Blue Stone CAFE
(5245 9999; 9am-late) On the corner of Sharias al-Jibawi and Qasr ash-Sheikh, this was the most happening bar/cafe/restaurant in the Christian Quarter and served pizzas, pastas and big bowls of salad.

Information

There's no shortage of ATMs in Homs. For internet, **Messenger** (Sharia Tarablus; per hr S£50; 24hr) is excellent. The **post office** (Sharia Abdel Moniem Riad) is about 200m north of the clock-tower roundabout, while the **telephone office** (Sharia Shoukri al-Quwatli; 8am-8pm Sat-Thu, to 1pm Fri) is just east of the clock-tower roundabout.

Getting There & Away

From the Pullman Garage, about 2.5km north-east of the city on the Hama road, Al-Ahliah and Al-Kadmous have the most frequent departures, including at least hourly to Damascus (two hours) and Aleppo (2½ hours). Other, less-regular departures include Tartus (one hour), Lattakia (3½ hours) and Palmyra (two hours). Buses go to Hama (30 minutes, half hourly).

Bright, new minibuses flit in and out of the 'hob-hob' bus station, about 8km south of the city centre on the Damascus road. Most of them go to Hama (45 minutes). They depart when full and you can generally turn up at any time, climb straight in, and expect to be away in less than 10 minutes.

HAMA حماه

033 / POP 850,000

Two sounds have defined Hama. One is the sound of army shells and gunfire: the city was decimated in 1982 during President Hafez al-Assad's brutal repression of an Islamist insurgency. The other, the serenade of Hama's creaking ancient wooden *norias* (water wheels) is famous throughout the Middle East, and made this attractive, though conservative, town one of the country's tourism hotspots. Hama was also an excellent base for visiting Crac des Chevaliers, Apamea and other sights in the area. Now there is also the sound of protests against Bashar al-Assad and of reprisals by the regime.

Sights

Norias HISTORIC SIGHT

Hama's main attraction is the *norias* (water wheels up to 20m in diameter) that have graced the town for millennia. Because both the water wheels and the blocks on which they are mounted are wooden, the friction when they turn produces a mournful groaning.

There have been *norias* in Hama since at least the 4th century AD, but the wheels seen today were designed by the 13th-century Ayyubids, who built around 30 of the things. Of these, 17 *norias* survive, although all have been reconditioned and/or rebuilt.

The most accessible *norias* are right in the middle of town, but the most impressive wheels lie about 1km upstream, and are collectively known as the **Four Norias of Bechriyyat**. In the opposite direction, about 1km west of the centre, is the largest of the *norias,* known as **Al-Mohammediyya**. It dates from the 14th century.

OLD TOWN

Most of the old town was destroyed during the 1982 bombardment, leaving only a small remnant edging the west bank of the river, between the new town centre and the citadel and some of this was shelled in 2012. Highlights included the **Al-Mamuriyya Noria**, the historic **Hammam al-Uthmaniyya** (men 8am-noon & 7pm-midnight, women noon-6pm) and, virtually next door, the so-called **Artists' Palace** (Ateliers des Peintures; 8am-3pm), occupying a former khan; the old storerooms are now used as studio and exhibition space for local artists.

Azem Palace Museum MUSEUM

(adult/student S£75/5; 8am-3pm Wed-Mon) This small but lovely museum was once the residence of the governor, As'ad Pasha al-Azem (r 1700–42). The *haramlek* (women's quarters), behind the ticket office, and the upstairs courtyard are particularly beautiful, leading Ross Burns, historian and author of the sage *Monuments of Syria,* to describe this place as 'one of the loveliest Ottoman residential buildings in Syria'.

An-Nuri Mosque MOSQUE

A short distance north of Azem Palace is the splendid riverside An-Nuri Mosque, built by the Muslim commander Nureddin, uncle of Saladin, in the late 12th century. If you cross the bridge beside the mosque, you have a very picturesque view of the river and three *norias,* which are, from east to west, **Al-Kaylaniyya**, **As-Sahuniyya** and **Al-Jabariyya**.

Hama Museum MUSEUM

(Sharia Ziqar; adult/student S£150/10; 9am-4pm Wed-Sun Nov-Mar, to 6pm Wed-Sun Apr-Oct) A 4th-century-AD mosaic depicting a *noria* is one of the artefacts displayed in the museum, 1.5km north of the centre. Other exhibits cover the region in the Iron Age, Roman and Islamic periods. All are well presented and have informative labelling in English.

Sleeping

Hama had some of the best accommodation in Syria outside of Damascus and Aleppo, but at the time of writing, all hotels were closed.

TOP CHOICE **Riad Hotel** HOTEL $

(239 512; www.syriaphotoguide.com/riadhotel; Sharia Shoukri al-Quwatli; @) Large and extremely clean rooms have satellite TV and good beds; most have private bathrooms and those with shared bathrooms have one bathroom per two rooms. Some rooms have balconies onto the street and comfortable seating; others have queen-sized beds. Abdullah, your host, is friendly, knowledgeable and even has a decent Aussie accent. With a kitchen and ADSL internet for guests at reception, it all adds up to one of Syria's best budget hotels.

Noria Hotel HOTEL $$

(512 414; www.noria-hotel.com;) Head for the rooms in the new section of this two-star, 4th-floor hotel, many of which are of a standard better than many four-star Syrian hotels. The stunning corner suite has a hydromassage bath, pleasing decor and views of the old town. Service is excellent and credit cards are accepted. Situated in the small streets between Sharia Shoukri al-Quwatli and the river.

Orient House Hotel BOUTIQUE HOTEL $$

(225 599; Sharia al-Jalaa;) In a splendid, restored 18th-century building, with beautifully decorated ceilings, oriental lamps and

a big, central, light-filled courtyard, this is Hama's most atmospheric accommodation. There's a new extension, so ask for one of the rooms in the Ottoman-era building. Rooms are well equipped with TV and fridge, and there's a good restaurant on site. The only downside is the location, at least a 20-minute walk from the centre; take a taxi.

Cairo Hotel HOTEL $
(☎222 280; cairohot@aloola.sy; Sharia Shoukri al-Quwatli; ❄@) The rooms here all come with private bathrooms, satellite TV and comfortable beds. There's internet at reception and staff are friendly and knowledgeable.

Apamee Cham Palace LUXURY HOTEL $$$
(☎525 335; www.chamhotels.com; ❄≋) A luxury hotel in a winning location just across the river from the old town, with tennis courts and a large swimming-pool area.

Eating

In the couple of blocks along Sharia Shoukri al-Quwatli and its side streets, there were a number of cheap felafel, shwarma, kebab and chicken restaurants. Among our favourites: **Ali Baba Restaurant** (Sharia Shoukri al-Quwatli; ⏲10am-late) for excellent felafels; and **Broasted Fawwaz** (☎223 884; ⏲8am-late) off Sharia al-Buhturi, known for delicious hot chicken. **Le Jardin** (☎525 335; Sharia abi Nawas; ⏲4pm-late), overlooking the splendid An-Nuri Mosque, river and water wheels, serves good mezze, alcohol and nargileh.

TOP CHOICE **Aspasia Restaurant** SYRIAN $$
(☎522 288; www.aspasia-hama.com; ⏲noon-midnight) Hama's best restaurant occupies a splendid, open-stone courtyard in the old town, but it's not just about atmosphere here. The food is delicious with an extensive menu that encompasses the usual range of mezze, as well as Western and local mains. The service is impeccable and there's an upstairs terrace that opens 6pm nightly for the tea-and-nargileh crowd, although the views are limited. No alcohol.

Four Norias SYRIAN $$
(Sharia al-Buhturi; ⏲9am-late) On the banks of the river beside the *norias*, around 500m east of the centre, this large open-air terrace restaurant is popular with families and gets lively on summer evenings. There's a long list of mezze and kebabs, and costumed boys serving nargileh. No alcohol.

Information

Internet was supplied by **Happy Net** (☎216 057; ⏲24hr) at the back of the Noria Hotel, off Sharia Shoukri al-Quwatli, and **Space Net** (Sharia Abu al-Feda; ⏲24hr).

There were ATMs all over Hama, with at least three along Sharia Shoukri al-Quwatli. The **Commercial Bank of Syria** (Sharia ibn Rushd & on Sharia Shoukri al-Quwatli) changed cash and (sometimes) travellers cheques.

The **post office** (⏲8am-2pm Sat-Thu) is on the north side of the river. From the clock tower, walk north and cross the bridge. Turn right at the first major road and continue walking until you see the post office on the left-hand side of the road, near the Syrian Telecom Office.

The **phone office** (⏲8am-7pm Sat-Thu) is off Sharia Shoukri al-Quwatli, at the side of the former post office building.

The **tourist office** (☎511 033; www.syriatourism.org; Sharia Said al-A'as; ⏲8am-8pm Sat-Thu) is in a small building in the gardens just north of the river.

Getting There & Away

The Pullman Garage is a 20-minute walk southwest of the town centre, just beyond the minibus station. The microbus station is on the same road, slightly closer to town. Minibuses from the town centre to the bus station leave from the clock tower and run between 7.30am and 10pm.

Al-Ahliah and Al-Kadmous have the most frequent departures from Pullman Garage, with regular services to Damascus (2½ hours) via Homs (30 minutes), and Aleppo (2½ hours). Al-Ahliah has four daily services to Lattakia (3½ hours) via Homs and Tartus. Al-Kadmous also has four daily buses to Deir ez-Zur via Homs and Palmyra.

Microbuses travel to Homs every 10 minutes from 7am to 10pm, but you're much better off paying the little bit extra to travel with one of the luxury bus companies. Microbuses also travel to Suqeilibiyya (for Apamea) when full.

CRAC DES CHEVALIERS

قلعة الحصن

☎031

Author Paul Theroux described Crac des Chevaliers as the epitome of the dream castle of childhood fantasies. TE Lawrence simply called it 'the finest castle in the world'. Impervious to the onslaught of time, Crac des Chevaliers (in Arabic Qala'at al-Hosn) is one of Syria's must-see sights. It was added to Unesco's World Heritage list in 2006.

Crac des Chevaliers

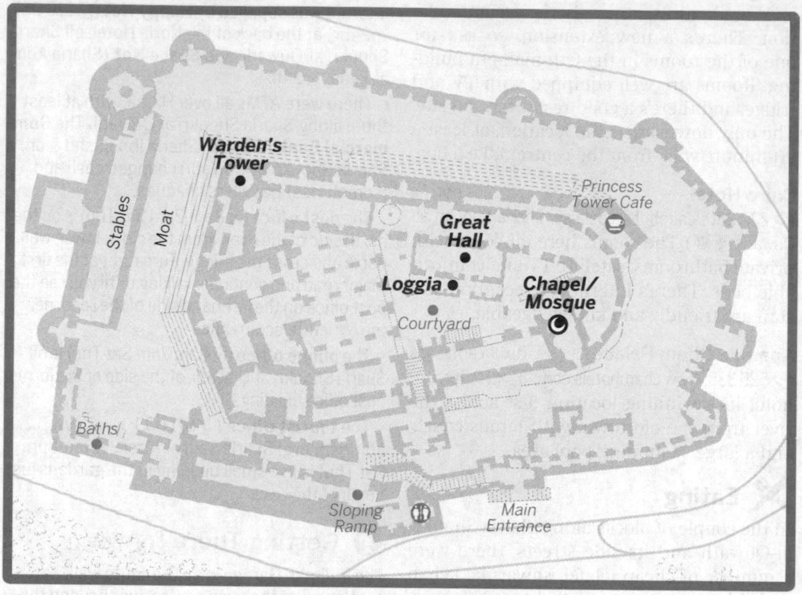

History

The castle watches over the only significant break in the Jebel Ansariyya. Anyone who held this breach, known as the Homs Gap, between the southern end of the range and the northern outreaches of the Jebel Libnan ash-Sharqiyya (Anti-Lebanon Range), was virtually assured authority over inland Syria.

The first fortress known to have existed on this site was built by the emir of Homs in 1031, but it was the Crusader knights who, around the middle of the 12th century, largely built and expanded Crac into its existing form. Despite repeated attacks and sieges, including one led by Saladin, the castle held firm. In fact, it was never truly breached; the Crusaders just gave it up.

When the Mamluk sultan Beybars marched on the castle in 1271, the knights at Crac des Chevaliers were a last outpost. Jerusalem had been lost and the Christians were retreating. Numbers inside the castle, built to hold a garrison of 2000, were depleted to around 200. Even though they had supplies to last for five years, Crac des Chevaliers must have seemed more like a prison than a stronghold. Surrounded by the armies of Islam and with no hope of reprieve, the Crusaders departed after a month, having negotiated safe conduct to head to Tripoli.

Sights

Castle CASTLE

(adult/student S£150/10; 9am-6pm Apr-Oct, to 4pm Nov-Mar) The remarkably well-preserved castle comprises two distinct parts: the outside wall, with its 13 towers and main entrance; and the inside wall and central construction, built on a rocky platform. A **moat** dug out of the rock separates the two walls.

A suggested route for exploration is to walk from the main entrance up the sloping ramp and out to the moat. Visit the **baths**, which you can get down to by a couple of dogleg staircases over in the corner on your left, then move on to the **stables**, from where you gain access to the three towers that punctuate the southern wall.

Continue around the wall and enter the **inner fortress** through the tower at the top of the access ramp into an open **courtyard**. The **loggia**, with its Gothic facade, on the western side of the yard, is the single most impressive structure in the castle, its delicate ceiling offering relief from the otherwise formidable aesthetic elsewhere. Behind the loggia is the **Great Hall**.

Opposite the loggia is a **chapel** that was converted to a mosque after the Muslim conquest (the minbar, or pulpit, still remains). The staircase that obstructs the main door is a later addition and leads to the upper floors of the fortress. From here, you can climb to the round tower in the southwest corner, which is known as the **Warden's Tower** – on a clear day there are magnificent views from the roof.

Sleeping & Eating

Crac des Chevaliers is just an hour or so from Tartus, Homs or even Hama, so most people visit on a day trip. Then again, a view of the Crac when you wake up is one the most romantic hotel views in Syria and possible if you stay at the Beibars Hotel.

Beibars Hotel HOTEL $$
(/fax 734 1201; akrambibars@mail.sy; Sharia Okbah Ben Nafee;) This comfortable hotel has stunning, sweeping views of the castle just across the valley. All rooms have views, although in the cheaper rooms you need to go onto the balcony to see the castle; those on the top floor (reception level) are the best. The rooms are clean, light and extremely good for the price. The same owners also run **La Table Ronde**, 150m southwest of the castle. This run-down, mediocre place serves meals and it's here that you'll be directed if staying at Beibars Hotel.

TOP CHOICE **Restaurant al-Qalaa** SYRIAN $
(734 1435, 0933 874 692; 8.30am-10pm Apr-Oct, to 6pm Nov-Mar) The best restaurant at the Crac is al-Qalaa which has good food and stunning views of the castle and surrounding valleys. A lone, white, two-storey building immediately west of the castle, on the next hilltop, its all-you-can-eat menu comprises a wide range of mezze as well as grilled chicken or meat. Out of season, call ahead to be sure it has food. Alcohol is served.

Princess Tower Cafe SYRIAN $
In the castle's northwestern corner, serves mezze, grills and drinks. The setting is better than the food, although the latter is better than it used to be after a change of management. Not always open when you want it to be.

Getting There & Away

Crac des Chevaliers lies approximately 12km north of the Homs–Tartus highway. The castle is on the crest of the hill, perched above the village of Hosn.

Coming from Damascus or Hama, it's necessary to change buses in Homs. Buses from Homs to Crac des Chevaliers (1½ hours) leave every hour on the hour; the last bus returning to Homs departs from the castle at 5.30pm in summer or 2.30pm in winter.

From Tartus, catch a Homs microbus. You'll be dropped off on the main highway at the turn-off for the castle, from where you shouldn't have to wait too long for a microbus to take you up the hill. To return, catch the microbus back down to the junction on the Homs–Tartus highway and flag down a passing microbus to Tartus.

> **DON'T MISS**
>
> **WALK THE CASTLE**
>
> After visiting the castle, drive or walk north from the entrance and follow the paved road that circles the castle perimeter and then climbs up to Restaurant al-Qalaa, from where you'll have the iconic, panoramic views of the castle that drew you here in the first place. It's about a 15-minute walk from the castle entrance.

APAMEA أفاميا

Don't miss Apamea (note that Arabic speakers do not use the sound 'p', so they pronounce it 'Afamia'). If it weren't for Palmyra's unsurpassable magnificence, the ruins of **Apamea** (adult/student S£150/10) would be famous as one of the great ancient sites of the Middle East. As it is, Apamea is like a condensed version of the pink-sandstone desert city, but executed in grey granite and transposed to a high, wild grassy moor overlooking the Al-Ghab Plain. Although little remains of the city's temples and other public buildings, its grand colonnade is one of the most extensive and beautiful in the region.

The main feature of the ruins of Apamea is the north–south **cardo** (main street), marked out along much of its length by parallel colonnades. At 2km, Apamea's cardo is longer than the one at Palmyra. Many of its columns, originally erected in the 2nd century AD, bear unusual carved designs and some have twisted fluting, a feature unique to Apamea.

Microbuses (40 minutes) and minibuses (40 minutes) regularly run the 45km from Hama to the village of Suqeilibiyya, where it's necessary to change to a microbus for Qala'at al-Mudiq (10 minutes), the hilltop village adjacent to Apamea. The whole trip takes about an hour, except on Friday, when you can wait ages for a connection.

From Aleppo, a day trip could be combined with a trip to the Dead Cities and even Qala'at Samaan.

ALEPPO حلب

021 / POP 3 MILLION

The Old City of Aleppo (Haleb in Arabic) can seem like an evocation of *The Thousand and One Nights,* and once lost in Aleppo's magical and labyrinthine souqs, you won't want to be found. But Aleppo has so much more, with the lovely and predominantly Christian district of Al-Jdeida, and it's here and in the Old City that you find some of Syria's best restaurants and boutique hotels. The city is outwardly more conservative than many of Syria's other cities (you'll see more women wearing the chador than elsewhere), but beneath the surface there are plenty of friendly, fun-loving locals keen to introduce travellers to the city's many charms.

History

Written archives from the ancient kingdom of Mari indicate that Aleppo was already the centre of a powerful state as long ago as the 18th century BC, and the site may have been continuously inhabited for the past 8000 years. Its pre-eminent role in Syria came to an end with the Hittite invasions of the 17th and 16th centuries BC, and the city appears to have fallen into obscurity thereafter.

With the fall of Palmyra to the Romans, Aleppo became the major commercial link between the Mediterranean Sea and Asia. The town was destroyed by the Persians in AD 611 and fell easily to the Muslims later during their invasion in 637. The Byzantines overwhelmed the town in 961 and again in 968, but they could not take the citadel.

Three disastrous earthquakes also shook the town in the 10th century and Nureddin (Nur ad-Din) subsequently rebuilt the town and fortress. In 1124 the Crusaders under Baldwin laid siege to the town. After raids by the Mongols in 1260 and 1401, in which Aleppo was all but emptied of its population, the city finally came into the Ottoman Turkish orbit in 1516.

It prospered greatly until an earthquake in 1822 killed over 60% of the inhabitants and wrecked many buildings, including the citadel. The flood of cheap goods from Europe in the wake of the Industrial Revolution, and the increasing use of alternative trading routes, slowly killed off a lot of Aleppo's trade and manufacturing industry.

Sights

There are three main areas of Aleppo where you'll spend most of your time, and all are within a short walk of each other. Most of Aleppo's cheap hotels are clustered in the new city, a compact zone centred on Sharias al-Quwatli and al-Baron; restaurants, the National Museum and moneychangers are also here.

To the southeast are the citadel and the Old City with its souqs and two hotels, while northeast of the centre are the main Christian quarters, including the charming cobbled Al-Jdeida district, where you'll find the best restaurants and numerous midrange hotels.

OLD CITY

Souqs MARKET

Aleppo's souq, which runs for 1.5km from the 13th-century **Bab Antakya** (Map p428) in the west to the citadel in the east, makes the Old City one of the Middle East's main attractions. This partially covered network of bustling passageways extends over several hectares, and once under the vaulted stone ceiling you're swallowed up into another world, transported back in time to the medieval bazaars of our imaginings with clamour, commerce and smells that you'll never forget. Parts of these dimly lit and atmospheric markets date to the 13th century, but the bulk of the area is an Ottoman-era creation. The best way to explore is to simply lose yourself in the labyrinth.

At one time walled and entered only by one of eight gates, the Old City has long since burst its seams and now has few definable boundaries. Exploring its seemingly infinite number of alleys and cul-de-sacs could occupy the better part of a week, depending on how inquisitive you are. We recommend visiting at least twice: once on a busy weekday to experience the all-out, five-senses assault of the souq, and a second time on a Friday when, with all the shops closed, the lanes are silent and empty. Relieved of the need to keep flattening yourself against the wall to let the overladen donkeys and minivans squeeze by, you're free to appreciate architectural details.

Great Mosque MOSQUE
(Al-Jamaa al-Kebir; Map p428; admission S£25; ⊙sunrise to just after sunset) On the northern edge of the souqs, this is the younger sibling (by 10 years) of the Umayyad Mosque in Damascus. Its most impressive feature is its freestanding minaret dating from 1090.

Inside the mosque is a fine carved wooden minbar, and behind the railing to the left of it is supposed to be the head of Zacharias, the father of John the Baptist. More, perhaps, than the architecture, the mosque's appeal lies in its life and it is often filled with young and old men who wander in, pick a Quran off the shelves and settle down against a pillar to read, while some chant beautifully at the western end of the prayer hall.

Madrassa Halawiyya HISTORIC BUILDING
(Map p428) Opposite the western entrance of the mosque, the Madrassa Halawiyya was built in 1245 as a theological college on the site of what was the 6th-century Cathedral of St Helen. The prayer hall incorporates all that remains of the cathedral, a semicircular row of six columns with intricately decorated, acanthus-leaved capitals. The cathedral was seized by the Muslims in 1124 in response to atrocities committed by the Crusaders. The madrassa was undergoing restoration work at the time of writing, but remained open.

FREE **Al-Shibani School** HISTORIC BUILDING
(Map p428; ☎331 9270; Al Jaloum quarter; ⊙9am-4pm Wed-Mon) South of the main souq, the splendid 16th-century Al-Shibani School houses a permanent exhibition, which details the work underway to make the city more liveable.

Al-Adliyya Mosque MOSQUE
(Map p428) Towards the bottom of Souq al-Nahaseen, just before it becomes Sharia Bab Qinnesrin, a short passageway leads to Al-Adliyya Mosque, built in 1555 and one of the city's major Ottoman-era mosques. It's worth a quick look inside for the fine tiling.

Al-Joubaili Soap Factory HISTORIC BUILDING
(Map p428) Heading south, follow your nose to Al-Joubaili Soap Factory, ages old and still producing soaps the traditional way using olive oil and bay laurel. At the time of research it was closed to the public.

Bimaristan Arghan HISTORIC BUILDING
(Map p428) Directly across the street, behind railings, is the splendid Bimaristan Arghan, one of the most enchanting buildings in Aleppo. Dating from the 14th century, it was converted from a house into an asylum. The main entrance gives access to a beautifully kept courtyard with a central pool overhung by greenery.

Citadel CASTLE
(Map p428; adult/student S£150/10; ⊙9am-6pm Wed-Mon Apr-Sep, to 4pm Wed-Mon Oct-Mar) Sitting atop a huge, man-made, earthen mound east of the Old City, the citadel dominates the city skyline. The first fortifications were built by the Seleucids (364–333 BC), but everything seen today dates from much later. The citadel served as a power base for the Muslims during the 12th-century Crusades, when the moat, 20m deep and 30m wide, was dug. Much rebuilding and strengthening occurred during Mamluk rule from 1250 to 1517 and it's largely their work that survives.

On the southern side, its moat is spanned by a step-bridge that then climbs at a 45-degree angle to the imposing 12th-century **fortified gate**. As you climb up, it's easy to imagine just how the citadel's defenders were able to hold out against invaders; attacking armies would have been dangerously exposed on the bridge, as they confronted the massive fortifications of the gate, and the twisting entrance of five right-angled turns inside the gate made storming the structure a complicated task.

Once inside, the castle is largely in ruins, although the **throne room**, above the entrance, has been lavishly restored. On

DON'T MISS

AL-ATTARINE

The main souq, **Souq al-Attarin** (Map p428), runs east-west between the citadel and Bab Antakya. Until the development of the New City in the 19th century, this was Aleppo's main street. In amongst the souqs are numerous khans; the most impressive is the **Khan al-Jumruk** (Map p428). Completed in 1574, at one time it housed the consulates and trade missions of the English, Dutch and French, as well as 344 shops. The khan now serves as a cloth market.

Aleppo: New City

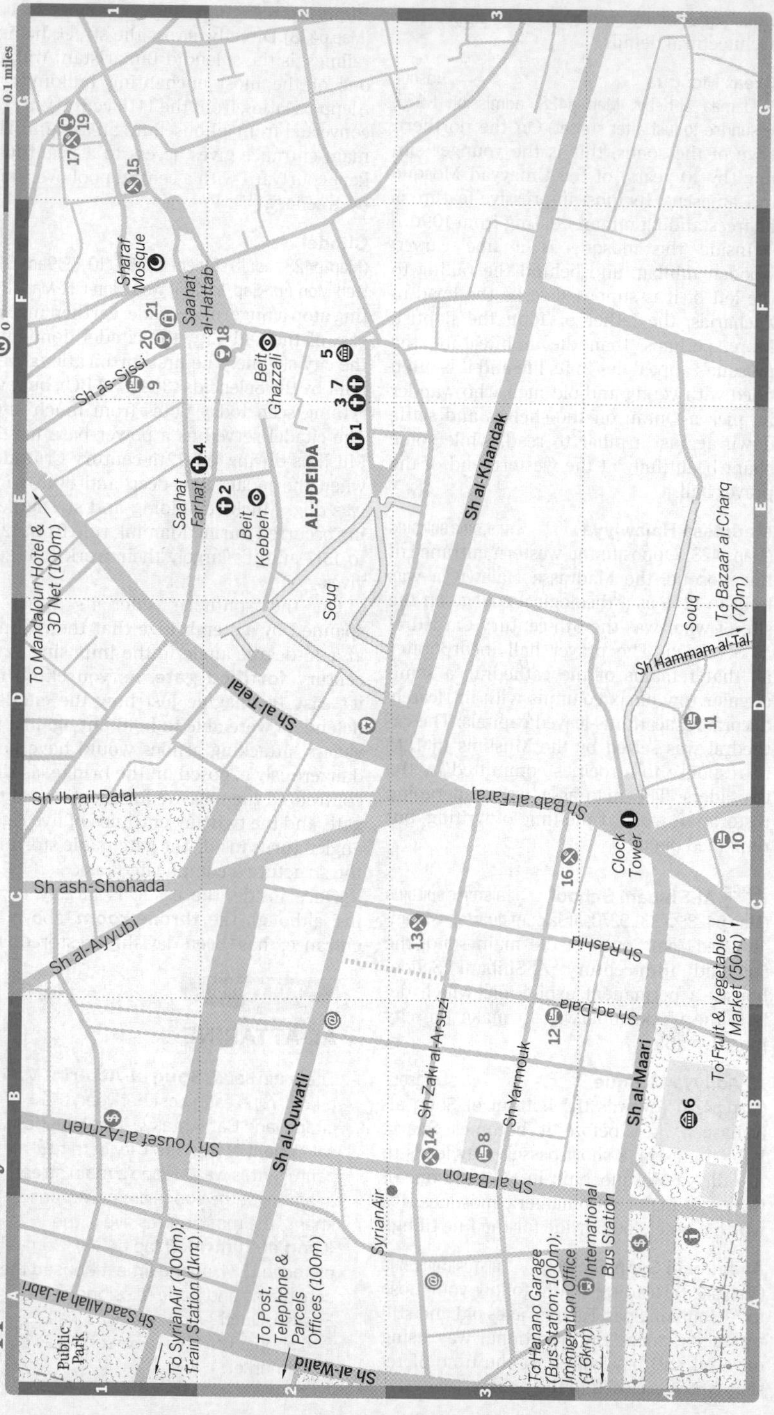

Aleppo: New City

Sights

1 Armenian Cathedral of the 40 Martyrs ... E2
2 Greek Catholic Church ... E2
3 Greek Orthodox Church ... E2
4 Maronite Cathedral ... E1
5 Museum of Popular Tradition ... F2
6 National Museum ... B4
7 Syrian Catholic Church ... F2

Sleeping

8 Baron Hotel ... B3
9 Beit Wakil ... F1
10 Hanadi Hotel ... C4
11 Hotel al-Gawaher ... D4
12 Tourist Hotel ... B3

Eating

13 Abou al-Nawas ... C3
14 Al-Andalib ... B3
15 Haj Abdo Al-Fawwa ... G1
16 Juice Bars & Liquor Stores ... C3
17 Kaser al Wali ... G1

Drinking

18 Al-Mashrabia Pub & Restaurant ... F2
19 Ciao ... G1
20 Sissi House ... F1

Shopping

21 Orient House Antiques ... F1

your right as you climb up through the ruins, note the **Ayyubid Palace** dating from the 13th century – it has a soaring entrance portal with stalactite stone decoration. To the rear of the palace is a recently renovated **Mamluk-era hammam**.

Back on the main path, off to the left is the small 12th-century **Mosque of Abraham**, attributed to Nureddin and one of several legendary burial places for the head of John the Baptist. Atop the hill, at the citadel's northern end, there's a sparsely endowed **museum** (admission S£75) in an Ottoman-era barracks, which is next to the **cafe** and **Great Mosque**.

Although the ruins themselves are interesting to pick your way through, the main attraction is the views from the battlements over the patchwork of roofs, domes and minarets. To find out more about the ongoing restoration of the citadel, visit the website of the Citadel Friends (www.aleppocitadelfriends.org).

CHRISTIAN QUARTER

The Christian quarter of **Al-Jdeida** is a charming, beautifully maintained warren of long, narrow stone-flagged alleyways. The quarter is undergoing something of a rebirth, with age-old townhouses being converted into hotels, restaurants and bars.

Museum of Popular Tradition MUSEUM

(Le Musee des Traditions; Map p424; ☎333 6111; Sharia Haret al-Yasmin; adult/student S£75/5; ⊙8am-2pm Wed-Mon) One of the main attractions here, housed in the lovely Beit Ajiqbash (1757). The artefacts showcasing everyday life in centuries past are interesting enough, but it's the splendid architecture and intricate interior decoration that will live in the memory, especially the guest room, with its amazing silver ceiling and snake-entwined light fitting, and the courtyard decoration. This is how many homes in Al-Jdeida once looked.

Churches CHURCH

Close to the museum you'll find five major churches, each aligned to a different denomination.

Immediately west of the museum is the **Syrian Catholic Church** (Mar Assia al-Hakim; Map p424), built in 1625 and happy to admit visitors who come knocking.

Next stop is the 19th-century **Greek Orthodox Church** (Map p424) and further beyond that, on Haret al-Yasmin, is the entrance to the 17th-century **Armenian Cathedral of the 40 Martyrs** (Map p424); if possible, it's worth visiting on a Sunday to observe the Armenian Mass performed here, which is still pervaded with a sensuous aura of ritual. It starts at 10am and lasts two hours.

North of these three, on Saahat Farhat, are the **Maronite Cathedral** (Map p424) and a smaller **Greek Catholic Church** (Map p424), which date to the 19th century.

National Museum MUSEUM

(Map p424; ☎221 2400; Sharia al-Baron; adult/student S£150/10; ⊙9am-5.30pm Wed-Mon Apr-Sep, to 3.30pm Wed-Mon Oct-Mar) Aleppo's main museum could be mistaken for a sports hall if it weren't for the extraordinary colonnade of giant granite figures that fronts the entrance. The wide-eyed characters are replicas of pillars that once supported the ceiling of an 8th- or 9th-century-BC temple-palace complex unearthed in Tell Halaf in northeastern Syria.

Inside, the collection is made up of other finds from northern Syria – there are some beautiful pieces, including some from Mari, Ugarit and around Hama, with some fascinating cuneiform tablets from Ebla. But the labelling is abysmal and the presentation is otherwise poor.

Activities

Hammam Yalbougha an-Nasry HAMMAM
(Map p428; Sharia al-Qala'a) At the foot of the citadel, on the southeast side, was one of Syria's finest working bathhouses. Originally constructed in 1491, it has a splendid sun clock inside the dome above reception. Closed for renovation for some years, if it's operational again, don't leave Aleppo without having a massage and scrub here.

Hammam al-Sallhia HAMMAM
(☎333 3572; Sharia Bab al-Makkam) If Hammam Yalbougha an-Nasry is still closed, women should try this place, around 300m south of the citadel entrance. It's open for women from 11am to 5pm but not necessarily every day.

Hammam al-Nahaseen HAMMAM
(Map p428; ⏲7am-8pm) This renovated, men-only place, in the heart of the souq just south of the Great Mosque, is open long hours and is still a local favourite, despite increasingly attracting tourists.

Sleeping

Aleppo has terrific accommodation across a range of budgets. All are well located, with the bulk of the budget hotels in the new part of town. The midrange and top-end places are clustered around the lovely Al-Jdeida district, with two midrange choices in the Old City near Bab Antakya.

Aleppo's midrange and top-end accommodation is outstanding and largely occupies restored courtyard houses in Al-Jdeida and just off the lanes of the souq in the Old City. Unless indicated otherwise, all of these hotels provide comfortable rooms with heating and satellite TV. All except the Baron accept credit-card payment.

TOP CHOICE **Dar Halabia** BOUTIQUE HOTEL $$
(Map p428; ☎332 3344; www.halabia-travel.com; ❄@📶) One of only two hotels in the souq, its courtyard may not be as polished as the boutique hotels in Al-Jdeida, but it's an outstanding place to stay. It occupies three old houses and has 19 rooms, the most attractive of which are on the ground floor around the courtyard of the main building, although all rooms are comfortable. The area's quite lonely at night when the whole quarter is deathly silent, but the hotel is lovely, spotlessly clean and great value. There are no TVs, but there's free wi-fi.

TOP CHOICE **Mansouriya Palace Hotel** LUXURY HOTEL $$$
(off Map p428; ☎363 2000; www.mansouriya.com; ❄@🏊) One of the most beautiful and romantic hotels in Syria, you need a significant amount of money to stay here, but in return you get to stay in a beautifully reimagined palace in the heart of the Old City. The same owners also run the top-end but less expensive **Beit Salahieh** (www.beitsalahieh.com) with fabulous views of the citadel.

Hanadi Hotel HOTEL $
(Map p424; ☎223 8113; Sharia ad-Dala; ❄) This could just be the best place for budget travellers in town, with friendly, multilingual staff, an enormous sun terrace high above the Aleppo clamour and spotless, freshly painted rooms (what's with so much pink?). Some travellers may not like the squat toilets and the entrance staircase could be Aleppo's steepest, but these are small drawbacks in a place with so much going for it.

Baron Hotel HISTORIC HOTEL $$
(Map p424; ☎211 0880/1; www.the-baron-hotel.com; Sharia al-Baron; ❄) Welcome to one of the most famous hotels in the Middle East, and while it may have lost most of its polish, it still retains plenty of ramshackle charm. Public areas (including the famous bar and the sitting room with a signed bill from TE Lawrence) are looking worse for wear, and rooms (even those that have been recently renovated) have peeling paintwork. Although it's overpriced, it's all about atmosphere and history here.

Tourist Hotel HOTEL $
(Map p424; ☎211 6583; Sharia ad-Dala; ❄) Run by the formidable Madam Olga and her family, this small hotel is one of our budget favourites in Aleppo. It's famous throughout

the country for its standards of cleanliness (it's immaculate), and rooms are well sized, light and comfortable. Some even have balconies and there's 24-hour hot water and fresh linen daily.

Hotel al-Gawaher HOTEL $

(Map p424; ☎/fax 223 9554; gawaherh@aloola.sy; Bab al-Faraj) The simple rooms come complete with clean linen, private bathroom, toilet paper and soap, fans and electric heaters. Some have balconies onto the street, others have windows onto the interior salons, and some even have satellite TV. The 2nd-floor lounge is a pleasant place to hang out. Rooms on the top floor require a stiff climb.

Dar al-Kanadil BOUTIQUE HOTEL $$

(Map p428; ☎332 4908; www.halabia-travel.com; ❄) Opened in mid-2008, this fine old house has tastefully decorated, large rooms arrayed around two open courtyards. The bathrooms here are lovely, and one of the upstairs terraces has partial views over the Old City rooftops to the citadel.

Mandaloun Hotel BOUTIQUE HOTEL $$

(off Map p424; ☎228 3008; www.mandalounhotel.com; ❄@) It's difficult to imagine what lies behind the plain facade of this hotel. Gorgeous is the first word that comes to mind when describing the courtyard, complete with fountain and antique furniture, as well as a cosy restaurant and bar. The downstairs

SAVING THE OLD CITY

To the untrained eye, the Old City of Aleppo is one of the best preserved of its kind in the Middle East, but looks can be deceptive. Misguided planning in the 1950s saw major roads ploughed through the Old City, causing considerable damage, compounded by new building construction, greater pollution and growing property speculation into the 1970s. During this period the number of residents halved (120,000 people now inhabit the Old City), and its geographical area (around 355 hectares) is now around one-third of its late-19th-century extent.

The long and complicated process of restoring the Old City began in 1986, when Unesco inscribed it on the list of World Heritage sites. In 1994, Aleppo municipality joined with the German government (via the offices of the German Agency for Technical Cooperation or GTZ, now known as GIZ) to undertake a long-term program of rehabilitation. The aim is to improve living conditions within the Old City, by nurturing local communities and businesses to ensure that it survives, not as a museum piece, but as a historic, living entity.

More specifically, according to Rana Nakhal, public relations officer for the project, these goals are to be achieved by overhauling the Old City's ageing infrastructure, providing interest-free micro-credit to residents to enable them to renovate their homes, promoting economic development within the Old City, developing health and educational facilities and increasing awareness of the city's heritage values and needs.

The scorecard thus far has been impressive. The provision of small loans to residents has seen around 1000 homes renovated and 240 buildings classified as protected historical monuments within the Old City, while GTZ itself completely rehabilitated a number of buildings. Traffic management and renewal of the water supply and sewer networks are also underway. The exodus from the Old City has also ceased, with population numbers now rising. Much remains to be done, however, both in urgent structural repairs and in maintenance or rehabilitation.

Tourism is certainly part of the plan, but many buildings have been designated off-limits to hotels and restaurants in a bid to preserve their original functions and to slow the exodus of residents from the Old City. At the same time, according to Ms Nakhal, 'tourism is helping in the restoration process (which costs a lot of money) as well as creating new job opportunities, which reflect positively on the local economic development and on the residents. Many investments have taken place in Al-Jdeida and the impact on the neighbourhood has been very positive'.

If you're eager to learn more, we highly recommend a visit to Al-Shibani School, one of the buildings reinvigorated by the project, and which hosts an exhibition entitled 'The Rehabilitation of the Old City of Aleppo'.

Aleppo: Old City

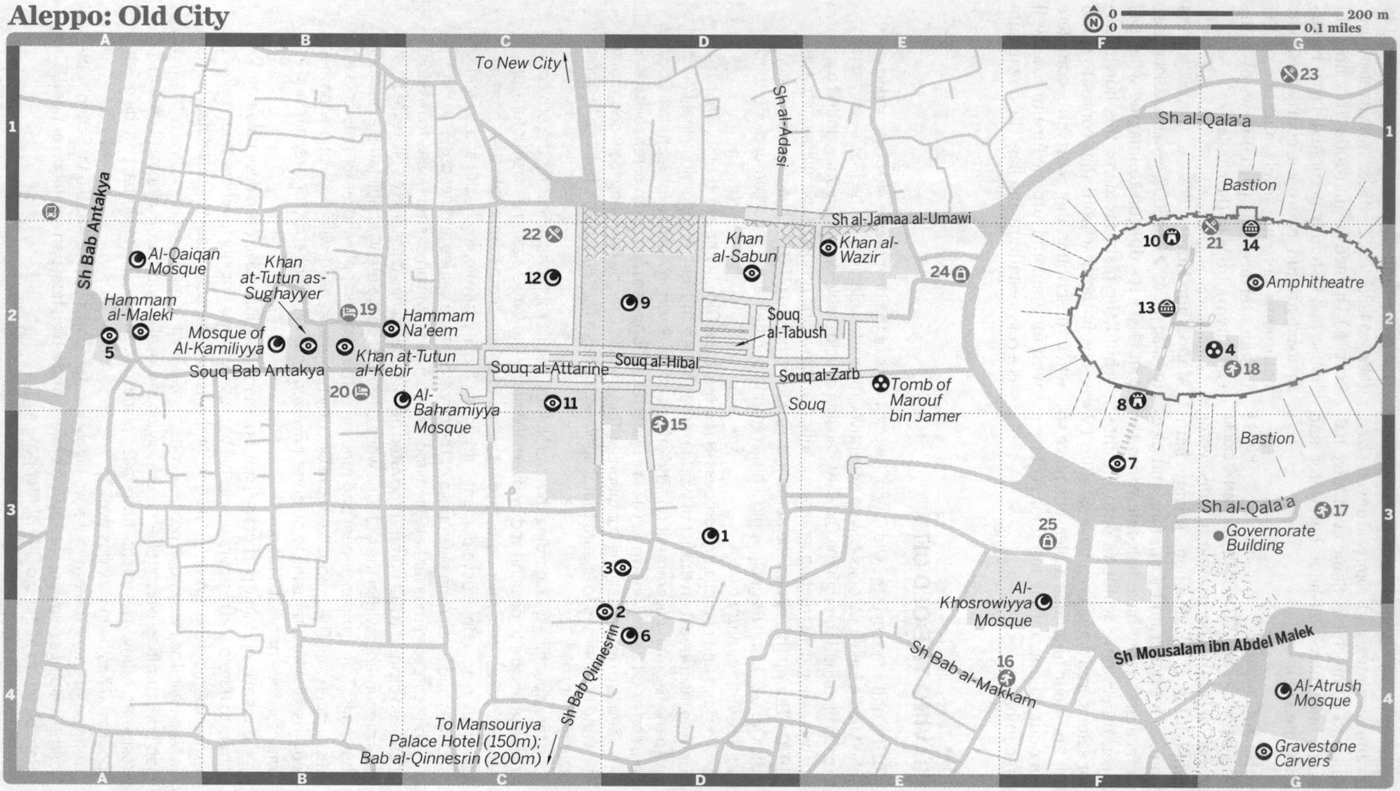

Aleppo: Old City

Sights

1	Al-Adliyya Mosque	D3
2	Al-Joubaili Soap Factory	D4
3	Al-Shibani School	D3
4	Ayyubid Palace	G2
5	Bab Antakya	A2
6	Bimaristan Arghan	D4
7	Entrance Gateway to Citadel	F3
8	Fortified Keep	F2
9	Great Mosque	D2
10	Great Mosque (Citadel)	F2
11	Khan al-Jumruk	C2
12	Madrassa Halawiyya	C2
13	Mosque of Abraham	F2
14	Museum	G2

Activities, Courses & Tours

15	Hammam al-Nahaseen	D3
16	Hammam al-Sallhia	F4
17	Hammam Yalbougha an-Nasry	G3
18	Mamluk-era Hammam	G2

Sleeping

19	Dar al-Kanadil	B2
20	Dar Halabia	B2

Eating

21	Cafes	G2
22	Restaurant-Coffee Shop Ahlildar	C2
23	Roof Top Garden	G1

Shopping

24	Sebastian	E2
25	Souq al-Shouna	F3

rooms are knockouts, but rooms on the top floor are cramped.

Beit Wakil BOUTIQUE HOTEL $$$
(Map p424; ☎221 7169; www.beitwakil.com; Sharia as-Sissi; ❄) In the Al-Jdeida quarter, this romantic hotel has 19 small rooms with an understated, sometimes quite simple aesthetic. The public areas have enormous charm, while one of the suites is stunning, located in the house's former reception room.

Eating

Known for its richness and use of spices, Aleppine cuisine is distinctive within Syria and, in turn, the Middle East. Dining here is a real pleasure. Although street-food joints are ubiquitous, the good restaurants are mostly concentrated in Al-Jdeida.

The block bounded by Sharias al-Maari, Bab al-Faraj, al-Quwatli and al-Baron is full of cheap eateries offering the usual array of roast chicken, shwarma and felafel. A row of excellent juice stands lines up at the Bab al-Faraj end of Sharia Yarmouk. There are tiny stalls along the length of Souq Bab Antakya/az-Zarb/al-Attarine selling cheap felafel, kebabs, hummus, pastries and fuul.

TOP CHOICE **Haj Abdo al-Fawwal** VEGETARIAN $
(Map p424; ⏲7am-4pm) Opening early every morning, this is the best place to get Aleppine-style fuul, delicately seasoned with cumin, paprika, garlic, lemon juice and fresh parsley. Crowds start gathering around the tiny shop from 7am, bearing empty containers of every size and description, pushing and shoving their way to the front for their share of this aromatic dish. Don't leave Aleppo without trying some for yourself. It's off Saahat al-Hatab.

Roof Top Garden SYRIAN $$
(Map p428; ☎331 9999; Al-Mustadamiyah Quarter) The most spectacular of all settings, on a roof looking up at the citadel, the Roof Top of the wonderful Beit Salahieh Hotel serves exquisite Syrian cuisine with frills and backed (literally) by a serious bar.

Al-Andalib SYRIAN $
(Map p424; ☎222 4030; Sharia al-Baron; ⏲noon-1am) The atmosphere at this rooftop restaurant one block north of the Baron Hotel is boisterous, and the place is packed most evenings. It serves a huge set meal of kebabs, salads, dips and fries, and a limited alcohol list. Come prepared to have a good time.

Kaser al-Wali SYRIAN $$
(Map p424; ☎446 1389; ⏲9am-1.30am; ❄) In the northwestern corner of Al-Jdeida, off Sharia al-Arba'aeen, Kaser al-Wali has fast become the restaurant of choice of many locals and travellers in Damascus. The expansive covered courtyard is rather lovely, and the food contains all the usual suspects but they're especially good here, and there's live traditional music from 10.30pm Wednesday to Monday.

Abou al-Nawas SYRIAN $
(Map p424; ☎211 5100; Sharia Rashid) This long-standing favourite has a menu that stretches way beyond the basics to include the kind of dishes that are usually only ever served up at home (patrons are often invited into the kitchen to choose from the daily pots). There's an excellent-value set meal, which gives you a daily dish of your choice with rice or fries, pickles, tea or coffee, and a sweet. Be clear that this is what you're ordering, because the waiters inevitably encourage you to order a more expensive main dish instead. No alcohol.

Restaurant-Coffee Shop Ahlildar INTERNATIONAL $
(Map p428; ☎333 0841; Souq ibn al-Khashab; ⏰8.30am-10pm) Overlooking the entrance to the Great Mosque, this fine restaurant means you can eat and then return to the souqs without having to traipse all the way back to Al-Jdeida for lunch. The food is fresh and tasty (we especially enjoyed the grilled cheese and well-priced *shish tawooq*), and there's a huge range of mezze, salads, soups, grills and a few Western dishes such as pizza. The inside tables are pleasant, but the upstairs terrace is the best.

Bazaar al-Charq SYRIAN $$
(off Map p424; ☎224 9120; ❄) Set in a reconstructed underground bazaar with vaulted ceilings, there is an extensive menu of mezze, grills, salads, soups and a few plats du jour; our lentil soup and mixed grill went down a treat. The live traditional music at 10.30pm Wednesday to Sunday rounds out a nice package. Our only complaint? When it came time to pay, 'service is not included' was whispered in our ears and they were disinclined to return our change.

Beit Wakil SYRIAN $$
(Map p424; ☎221 7169; Sharia as-Sissi; ❄) This hotel-restaurant has a lovely setting in one of Al-Jdeida's most beautiful buildings. Guests sit in an atmospheric courtyard and can choose from an array of mezze and local specialities. The food is good though not spectacular, and service can be stuffy. It's licensed and accepts credit cards.

Drinking

The outdoor cafes on Sharia al-Qala'a, opposite the entrance to the citadel, are great places to enjoy a coffee, fresh juice or nargileh and watch the world go by.

Sissi House BAR
(Map p424; ☎212 4362; Sharia as-Sissi) The food isn't what it used to be at Sissi House but the upstairs bar is a sophisticated place for a drink with a jazz pianist every night of the week and a singer on Saturdays.

Mashrabia Pub & Restaurant PUB
(Map p424; ☎211 5249; ⏰4pm-1.30am) Nostalgia buffs may want to pop into the pricey, small bar at the venerable Baron Hotel, but most visitors prefer this laid-back joint in Al-Jdeida, where the drinks are cheaper and the decor more atmospheric. There's also an extensive snack menu here.

Ciao BAR
(Map p424; Sharia al-Arba'aeen; ⏰4pm-1.30am) This is another cool place for a drink.

Shopping

Aleppo Souq MARKET
The best place to shop in Aleppo is without a doubt the souqs (Map p428) of the Old City and great buys include textiles, brocade, gold, silver, carpets and olive soap. Although the pressure to buy has grown in recent years, the souq remains overwhelmingly targeted at a local market – apart from the architecture, that's what gives it its charm.

Like any Middle Eastern souq, Aleppo's bazaar is broken down into the usual demarcations: gold in one alley, spices in another, carpets in one spot, scarves across the way. The exception to this is bustling Souq al-Attarine (Map p428), which sells everything: hardware, clothing, spices, perfumes and even meat. South of Souq al-Attarine, the laneways almost exclusively give way to fabrics, clothing and shoes. North of al-Attarine, the souq is at its most dense.

Souq al-Hibal MARKET
Squeezed around the Great Mosque are veins of parallel narrow alleys that in places are barely wide enough for people to pass each other. Here, Souq al-Hibal is devoted to shops selling cord, braid and rope, while Souq al-Tabush is crammed with stalls selling buttons, ribbons and all manner of things necessary for a woman to run up her family's clothes.

Souq az-Zarb MARKET
(Map p428) A good place to head for *jalabiyyas* (robes) or a keffiyeh. Shops in the souq open from early in the morning until around 6pm Saturday to Thursday, while on

Friday virtually the whole souq closes and is eerily deserted.

Sebastian ARTS & CRAFTS
(Map p428; ☎332 3672; Sharia al-Qala'a; ⏰8am-8pm Sat-Thu) On the fringes of the souq, this place stocks a small but superb range of high-quality textiles, tablecloths, inlaid backgammon boards and boxes. However, the speciality is rustic kilims, silk rugs and antique carpets costing anything from US$50 to US$15,000. The multilingual owner, Mohammed, is highly knowledgeable, accepts credit cards and provides certificates.

Orient House Antiques ANTIQUES
(Map p424; 1st fl, Saahat al-Hatab; ⏰8am-8pm) Over in Al-Jdeida, the Beit Sissi store is a wonderful place to browse for antiques and bric-a-brac.

Souq al-Shouna HANDICRAFTS
(Map p428) A handicrafts market behind the sheesha cafes on the southwestern side of the citadel. While there are price tags, bargaining is still possible, although not required, and it's a good place to get an idea of prices before plunging into the souqs.

Information

Emergency

Ambulance (☎110)
Fire (☎113)
Police (☎362 4300)

Internet Access

Internet cafes are annoyingly thin on the ground but among the reliable ones are **3D Net** (Map p424; ⏰10am-10pm) in front of the Mandaloun Hotel, **Adam Internet** (Map p424; Sharia Zaki al-Arsuzi; ⏰24hr) around the corner from the Baron Hotel and **Concord Internet Cafe** (Map p424; ☎270 060; Sharia al-Quwatli; ⏰9.30am-3am).

Money

CBS Exchange al-Kattab (Map p424; ⏰8am-7pm), outside the tourist office, changes money and has an ATM.

Otherwise, try one of the two branches of the **Commercial Bank of Syria** (Map p424; Sharia Yousef al-Azmeh) that are north of Sharia al-Quwatli; they may change travellers cheques with a commission but don't count on it.

ATMs are dotted around town, but there are few in the old town.

Post & Telephone

Main post & telephone office (Map p424; ☎362 4010; ⏰8am-5pm) In the enormous building on the far side of Saahat Saad Allah al-Jabri. For international calls, use the card phones dotted around town, including in front of the post office and the National Museum.

Tourist Information

Tourist office (Map p424; ☎212 1228; www.syriatourism.org; Sharia al-Baron; ⏰8.30am-7pm Sat-Thu) In the gardens opposite the National Museum, it occasionally stocks maps and is generally more willing than especially useful.

Getting There & Away

Air

Aleppo's airport offers semi-regular connections to Turkey, Europe and other cities in the Middle East. Domestic services also run to Damascus (one hour).

Bus

All luxury, long-distance buses to destinations within Syria leave from the Al-Ramuseh Garage, some 7km south of the city centre. Although no services operate from the old Hanano Garage, buses connect the old bus station with the new.

From Al-Ramuseh, **Al-Kadmous** (☎224 8837; www.alkadmous.com) runs 24-hour services to Damascus on the hour (four hours) as well as regular services to Hama (2½ hours), Homs (three hours) and Deir ez-Zur (five hours). Dozens of other private companies run similar services for the same prices, while a handful of companies cover the Aleppo–Lattakia route (3½ hours). There are no direct services to Tartus or Palmyra – change at Homs for these.

Seven or eight companies offer daily services from Al-Ramuseh to Beirut (six hours) via Tripoli (five hours).

You'll find the International Bus Station north of the tourist office. Little more than a car park, it's the place for buses to Antakya, İstanbul and Amman, with a handful of early-morning and late-night departures to each; travel times vary widely, depending on how long the border crossing takes. If you can't wait around for a bus to Antakya, service taxis leave when full from the International Bus Station.

Microbuses covering local routes around Aleppo leave from the sprawling City Bus Station outside Bab Antakya.

Train

The **train station** (☎221 3900) is housed in an attractive old building about a 25-minute walk from the central hotel area, north of the big public park. Please note that all departure times listed are subject to change, so check at the station for the latest departure times.

At the time of writing, there were three daily express services to Damascus at 3.50am,

WORTH A TRIP

QALA'AT SAMAAN قلعة سمعان

Also known as the Basilica of St Simeon, the ruins of **Qala'at Samaan** (adult/student S£150/10; ⊙9am-6pm Apr-Sep, to 4pm Oct-Mar) are among the most atmospheric of Syria's archaeological sites. The basilica commemorates St Simeon Stylites, one of Syria's most eccentric early Christians.

Simeon was the son of a shepherd who opted at a young age for life in a monastery. Finding monastic life insufficiently ascetic, he retreated to a cave in the barren hills, where he lived under a regimen of self-imposed severity. Word spread and people began to visit to seek his blessing. Simeon apparently resented this invasion of his solitude so intensely that he was driven, in AD 423, to erect a 3m-high pillar upon which he took up residence so that people couldn't touch him. Legend goes that as his tolerance of people decreased he erected ever-higher pillars. In all he's said to have spent close to 40 years on top of his pillars, the last of which was 18m in height. There was a railing around the top, and an iron chain attached to the stone to stop him toppling off in the middle of the night. Simeon would preach daily from his perch and shout answers to his audiences' questions; however, he refused to talk to women and even his mother was not allowed near the column. After his death in 459, an enormous church was built around the most famous pillar, and pilgrims from all parts of Christendom came to pay their respects.

The site today is remarkably well preserved, with the quite lovely Romanesque facade still standing and the arches of the octagonal yard still reasonably complete. There's plenty of ornamental carved stonework to admire, although Simeon's pillar is in a sad state and is nothing more than a boulder, reduced centuries ago by pilgrims chipping away at it for holy souvenirs.

The church had a unique design with four basilicas arranged in the shape of a cross, each opening onto a central octagonal yard covered by a dome. Beneath the dome stood the pillar. Completed in around 491 after about 14 years of building, it was the largest church in the world at the time. With the arrival of Islam in Syria, the Byzantine Christians were put on the defensive and the church complex was fortified, hence the name Qala'at (fortress). It eventually fell to the Islamic Fatimid dynasty in 1017.

Views of the surrounding countryside are simply stunning, especially towards the west and to Turkey in the north.

Eating options are limited at Qala'at Samaan and the surrounding villages. You might be lucky and get invited to share lunch with some farmers. But more certain is to take some food with you for a picnic with an unforgettable view.

Qala'at Samaan is a 40-minute drive from Aleppo. Microbuses to the village of Daret' Azze (one hour) leave Aleppo every hour or so from the microbus bays, and this is as close to the site as you can get by public transport. From here, there are no local buses or taxis to take you the remaining 6km, so the only options are to hitch or walk, or convince the minibus driver to take you the extra distance.

5.40am and 4.45pm (4½ hours) and one slow service at midnight (6½ hours). The services go via Hama and Homs. The middle-of-the-night express services are considerably cheaper on the Damascus line.

To Lattakia, there are two daily express trains (2½ hours) at 6am and 5.30pm, and two slow trains (3½ hours) at 6.45am and 3.50pm. A daily train travels to Deir ez-Zur (4½ hours) at 4.10pm.

For long-haul travellers, there are services to Tehran on Sundays at 3pm, and to Gaziantep (Friday, 6am) and Mersin (Friday, 3am) in Turkey.

DEAD CITIES

These eerie and ancient ghost towns are dotted along the limestone hills that lie between the Aleppo–Hama highway in the east and the Orontes River in the west. By some estimates, there are hundreds, if not thousands, of such cities in northern Syria, ranging from single monuments to whole villages complete with houses, churches, mills, hammams and even wine presses. They date from the time when this area was part of the hinterland of the great Byzantine city of Antioch; the great mystery is why these towns and villages were abandoned. The latest theory is that they were emptied by demographic shifts – trade routes changed and the people moved with them.

Al-Bara is the most extensive of the Dead Cities, dotted over a wide area of olive groves and intensively farmed land where vegetables, olives, grapes and apricots are grown alongside. The highlights are the striking pyramid tombs, 200m apart, decorated with Corinthian pilasters and carved acanthus leaves, a very visible testament to the one-time wealth of the settlement. The larger of the two still holds five sealed, decorated sarcophagi, although the interior (viewed through a metal grill) is strewn with graffiti.

The most evocative of the Dead Cities is undoubtedly **Serjilla** (adult/student S£75/5), especially in winter when the ruins might be shrouded in mist. It has the most semi-complete buildings, all sitting in a natural basin in windswept and hilly moorland. Although Serjilla has been deserted for about 15 centuries, the buildings' stone facades are remarkably well preserved and it's easy to get a feel for what the town would have looked like in its heyday. At Serjilla's centre is a small plaza flanked by a two-storey tavern and a large hammam. Next door lies an *andron* (men's meeting place), and further east, a small church along with substantial remnants of private houses and villas. It's a spooky place and the red hue of the building materials provides some quite beautiful interplays of light.

You're best off visiting the Dead Cities on a combined Qala'at Samaan/Dead Cities tour from Aleppo or in your own car, as they're extremely difficult to reach on public transport and are scattered over a large area.

LATTAKIA اللاذقية

041 / POP 1.05 MILLION

A busy port since Roman times, Lattakia has a Mediterranean feel, an outward-looking inclination and true joie de vivre. Sustained assaults by the Syrian army have damaged parts of the city, but you may still need to come here to reach Qala'at Saladin and Ugarit.

Sights & Activities

National Museum of Lattakia MUSEUM
(Sharia Jamal Abdel Nasser; adult/student S£150/10; 9am-6pm Wed-Mon Apr-Sep, 8am-4pm Wed-Mon Oct-Mar) This small museum is housed in a charming old khan near the waterfront. The best of the museum's displays are inscribed tablets from Ugarit, beautiful jewellery, coins and figurines, ceramics and pottery and a Crusader-era chain-mail suit and swords.

Sleeping

In a normal year, prices at some midrange hotels drop by as much as 15% in winter and rise by up to 20% in summer.

Safwan Hotel & Hostel HOTEL $
(453 801, 093 337 6900; safwanhotel@go.com; Sharia Mousa bin Nosier) This could be our favourite backpackers' hotel in Lattakia. It's not that the rooms are anything special – they're basic and sometimes run-down, but clean (it pays to ask to see a few before choosing). Rather, the place is run by *Tintin* fan Mohammad Ziadeh and his family, and Mohammad is switched on to travellers' needs.

Hotel al-Atlal HOTEL $
(476 121; Sharia Yousef al-Azmeh) This simple, quiet establishment has immaculate rooms with snug beds and freshly laundered sheets; the bathrooms have squat toilets. There's a pleasant common area with free tea and satellite TV. The family who run the place add much warmth to your stay.

Al-Cazino Hotel HOTEL $$
(/fax 461 140/142; Al-Corniche;) In an imposing and well-located French Mandate–era building, this hotel has large, comfortable rooms with satellite TV, although some are starting to show their age. The hotel is home to the city's most popular reception venue, so it can be noisy. If you're choosing between here and the other midrange option, the Riviera, we'd stay here.

Eating

For something a cut above the rest, Sharia al-Mutanabi (known locally as the 'American quarter' because an American school used to be based here, but it could also be because of the proliferation of Western-style eateries) is a fascinating insight into modern Syria with loads of cool restaurants. We suggest just wandering along this street and you're sure to find something that appeals.

Snack stalls are around the Saahat al-Sheikh Daher area, where you'll find fast-food places specialising in felafel, kebabs and shwarma. There's a good spit-rotisserie **chicken take-away** (whole chicken, salad, hummus & bread S£150) next door to the Hotel Riyad.

Express Cafe AMERICAN $
(☎456 200; 22 Sharia al-Mutanabi; ⏲9am-midnight; ❄) An American diner in the Hard Rock Cafe style, this bright and noisy place offers burgers, steaks, pizzas and hot and cold sandwiches. It also does great milkshakes, and there's a bar downstairs.

Stop 5 AMERICAN $$
(☎477 919; 27 Sharia al-Mutanabi; ⏲11am-midnight; ❄) Resembles a New York bar, with shelves of spirits, posters advertising happy hours and wood-panelled walls. The food is good, ranging across pizzas, burgers and steaks, and management doesn't mind if you sit for a while nursing a drink and a snack.

Last Station SYRIAN $$
(☎468 871; 20 Sharia al-Mutanabi; ⏲11am-11pm) Popular with local families, this old-fashioned place does tasty food at very reasonable prices. Expect everything from Syrian mezze to pizza. Alcohol is served.

Spiros FISH $$
(☎478 238; Al-Corniche; ⏲noon-midnight) Just back from the docks, Spiros is unpretentious but probably Lattakia's best place for fish, with a small range of mezze, meat mains and calamari on the menu. But here you'll be invited into the kitchen to choose from the day's fish catch. Not surprisingly, it's hugely popular with locals.

Allegro INTERNATIONAL $$
(☎458 000; Sharia al-Mutanabi; ⏲11am-midnight) Lattakia's hippest restaurant is in a sleek contemporary space, with lots of chocolate wood and concealed lighting, that wouldn't be out of place in Beirut or even Madrid. It's a great spot for lunch, when it buzzes with noisy groups of locals enjoying the delicious food – a mix of Asian, Mexican, Italian and French that's served up on big white plates. Alcohol is served.

Zekrayat Restaurant INTERNATIONAL $$
(☎459 979; ⏲9am-midnight; ❄) This place would be right at home in Damascus or Aleppo with its blend of modern and traditional, stone-walled decor (think Bedouin cushions and wrought-iron chairs), although the slick young clientele could only come from Lattakia. The food is outstanding with a blend of Western and local dishes, as well as ice-cream sundaes, fresh-fruit cocktails and nargilehs.

Mandaloun LEBANESE $$
(☎454 400; Sharia al-Merkan; ⏲1-11.30pm) Dress up for this elegant restaurant with stone walls and vaulted ceilings, where you'll be dining with Lattakia's affluent cigar-smoking set. The French and oriental cuisine is superb – try the tasty pink lentil soup or hearty traditional French onion soup for starters, and the melt-in-your-mouth filet mignon. There are excellent Lebanese wines on the menu and the service is faultless.

Drinking

There's a real coffee culture in Lattakia, and many places serve up espresso that could stand up and be counted in Italy.

There are loads of good places around Sharia al-Mutanabi, including Lacasta Café, and off Sharia Baghdad, including Prose Poem and Olabi cafes.

Information

The **tourist office** (☎416 926; www.syriatourism.org; Sharia 14 Ramadan; ⏲8am-8pm Sat-Thu), opposite the Riviera Hotel, can supply maps. There are Syriabank ATMs all over Lattakia. One of the more central ones is at the **Commercial Bank of Syria No.2 Branch** (Sharia Baghdad); it may also change travellers cheques for a fee. The main **post office** (⏲8am-2pm Sun-Thu) is just north of the train station, in a little alley off Sharia Suria.

There were good connections at **Center Net** (Sharia al-Mutanabi; ⏲11am-11pm) and **Virus Internet Café** (☎465 540; Sharia Baghdad; ⏲24hr). **Fire Net** (Sharia al-Maghreb al-Arabi; ⏲24hr) also had a wireless room for people travelling with laptops.

Getting There & Away

Air

Basil al-Assad International Airport lies about 25km southeast of Lattakia. There are three weekly flights to Damascus, but services increase considerably in summer. There's also one weekly flight to Cairo.

There's a local office of **SyrianAir** (☎476 863/4; 8 Sharia Baghdad; ⏲8am-8pm).

Bus

The Pullman Garage is on Sharia Abdel Qader al-Husseiny about 200m east of the train station. Numerous private companies have their offices here.

Al-Kadmous has a 24-hour service to Damascus (four hours) leaving on the hour; its regular minibus service to Tartus (one hour) runs between 6am and 9pm, stopping at Baniyas en route.

There are also four services daily to Homs (two hours), while Al-Ahliah has four daily buses to Hama. One or two companies also run services to Aleppo (3½ hours), although we recommend you take the train.

Microbus

The main microbus station is on Al-Jalaa St near Al Fursan Park, 1km north of the train station.

Microbuses for Ugarit (Ras Shamra) go from a back alley down the side of the big white school on Saahat al-Sheikh Daher.

Microbuses to Baniyas (45 minutes), Tartus (one hour), Homs (two hours) and Hama (three hours) leave from Beirut Garage, near the train station. From the same station, Izreq runs a daily minibus service to Antakya in Turkey. If you call it will collect you at your hotel.

Taxi

Part of the service taxi station next to the train station is known locally as **Beirut Garage** (☎353 077), and it's from here that services run down the coast and across the border into Lebanon. They leave when full for Tripoli and Beirut. If you call ☎353 077, they may collect you from your hotel.

Train

If you're travelling to Aleppo, we recommend you take a train rather than the bus, as they're extremely comfortable and the scenery is stunning, especially for the first 1½ hours from Lattakia.

The train station is about 1½km east of the city centre on Saahat al-Yaman. There are four daily departures for Aleppo: two express services (2½ hours) at 6.25am and 5.25pm, and two slow services (3½ hours) at 7.10am and 3.40pm.

AROUND LATTAKIA

Ugarit

رأس شمرا

The low-lying ruins at **Ugarit** (Ras Shamra; adult/student S£150/10; ⏰9am-4pm Nov-May, to 6pm Jun-Oct) are all that remains of a city that was once the most important on the Mediterranean coast. From about the 16th to the 13th century BC, it was a centre for trade with Egypt, Cyprus, Mesopotamia and the rest of Syria. The writing on tablets found here is widely accepted as the earliest-known alphabet, and the tablets are on display in the museums in Lattakia, Aleppo and Damascus, as well as the Louvre in Paris. Today, the masonry left behind shows you the layout of the streets and gives you some vague idea of where the most important buildings were. Come here for the sense of history, not for the visual effect.

Regular microbuses make the trip from Lattakia to Ugarit. They leave from a back alley down the side of the big white school on Saahat al-Sheikh Daher.

Qala'at Saladin

قلعة صلاح الدين

Although Qala'at Saladin is less celebrated than Crac des Chevaliers, TE Lawrence was moved to write: 'It was I think the most sensational thing in castle building I have seen'. The sensational aspect is largely due to the site – the castle is perched on top of a heavily wooded ridge with precipitous sides dropping away to surrounding ravines. It's pretty amazing, a fact recognised by Unesco, which inscribed it on its World Heritage list in 2006.

The **castle** (adult/student S£150/10; ⏰9am-4pm Wed-Mon Nov-Mar, to 6pm Wed-Mon Apr-Oct) is 24km east of Lattakia and is a very easy

GOLDEN AGE OF UGARIT

Until a worker ploughing a farm near the coast adjacent to Lattakia struck an ancient tomb, the site of Ugarit was unknown. This exciting and important discovery in 1928 led to the excavation of the site the next year by a French team led by Claude FA Schaeffer. What he found was astonishing.

The oldest finds at Ugarit date back to 6000 BC. Findings that date from around 1450 BC to 1200 BC reveal a sophisticated and cosmopolitan metropolis with palaces, temples and libraries with clay tablets bearing inscriptions. These clay tablets, representing a Semitic language – it is still thought by many to be the earliest-known alphabet in the world – became a celebrated finding. The site also revealed vast Mycenaean, Cypriot, Egyptian and Mesopotamian influences in the artefacts, a result of trade both by sea and by land.

half-day trip. Begun by the Byzantines in the 10th century, it was taken over by the Crusaders in the early 12th century and the construction of the castle as you see it today was carried out some time before 1188, the year in which the Crusaders' building efforts were shown to be in vain. After a siege of only two days, the armies of Saladin breached the walls and the Western knights were squeezed out of yet another of their strongholds.

After climbing up through the gate tower, the inner courtyard is watched over by two relatively intact **towers**; it is possible to climb the internal staircase in each tower up to the 1st floor and roof for fine views of the surrounding countryside. Other highlights include the **stables**, the **Ayyubid Palace** (1169–1260) and the **sunken cistern**.

To get here, take a microbus from Lattakia to the small town of Al-Haffa (30 minutes). These leave from the minibus station near the stadium. Taxis and local cars wait at the bus stop at Al-Haffa and will take you the further 6km to the castle.

PALMYRA تدمر

☎031

The rose-gold ancient ruins of Palmyra (known in Arabic as Tadmor) are one of the premier ancient sites in the Middle East, and for many travellers, the standout highlight of any visit to Syria. Rising out of the desert of central Syria, flanked by an expansive oasis, and just three hours from Damascus, Palmyra must rank high on your list of must-sees. Some travellers come on a day trip from Damascus, but sunrise and sunset are the most beautiful times here and we recommend an overnight stay as a minimum, preferably two.

Modern Palmyra is a typical tourist town along well-worn Middle Eastern trails. Expect camera shops selling memory cards, carpet shops, souvenir shops selling Crusader helmets and restaurants with faux-Bedouin decor. And as it is entirely reliant on tourism, expect fierce competition and some hassle from hotels, restaurants, guides and hawkers when it reopens.

History

Tadmor is mentioned in texts discovered at Mari dating back to the 2nd millennium BC. Early rulers included the Assyrians, Persians and Seleucids, for whom it served as an indispensable staging post for caravans travelling between the Mediterranean, Mesopotamia and Arabia. It was also an important link on the old Silk Route from China and India to Europe, with the city prospering greatly by levying heavy tolls on the caravans.

But it was the Romans who made Tadmor their own. As they expanded their frontiers during the 1st and early 2nd centuries AD to occupy the eastern Mediterranean shores, Tadmor became stranded between the Latin realms to the west and those of the Parthians to the east. The oasis used this situation to its advantage, taking on the role of middleman between the two clashing superpowers. The influence of Rome grew, and the city they dubbed Palmyra (City of Palms) became a tributary of the empire and a buffer against rivals to the east.

The emperor Hadrian visited in AD 129 and declared Palmyra a 'free city', allowing it to set and collect its own taxes. In 212, under the emperor Caracalla (himself born of a Syrian mother), Palmyra became a Roman colony. Further wealth followed and Palmyra spent lavishly, enlarging its great colonnaded avenue and building more and larger temples.

After the interlude of Zenobia, a further rebellion in 273, in which the Palmyrenes massacred a garrison of 600 Roman archers, elicited a brutal response and Aurelian's legionaries slaughtered large numbers and put the city to the torch. Palmyra never recovered.

The emperor Diocletian (r 254–305) later fortified the broken city as one in a line of fortresses marking the eastern boundary of the Roman Empire, and Justinian further rebuilt the city's defences in the 6th century. The city survived primarily as a military outpost and the caravan traffic all but dropped away.

In 634 the city fell to a Muslim army led by Khaled ibn al-Walid, and from this time Palmyra all but fades from history. It was finally and completely destroyed by an earthquake in 1089.

Sights

Ruins ARCHAEOLOGICAL SITE

There's no entry fee and no opening hours for the ruins, although three sites (the Temple of Bel, the Theatre and Elahbel, one of the funerary towers) do have set hours and require you to pay. Allow at least a day to explore the ruins, possibly with a break in

Palmyra

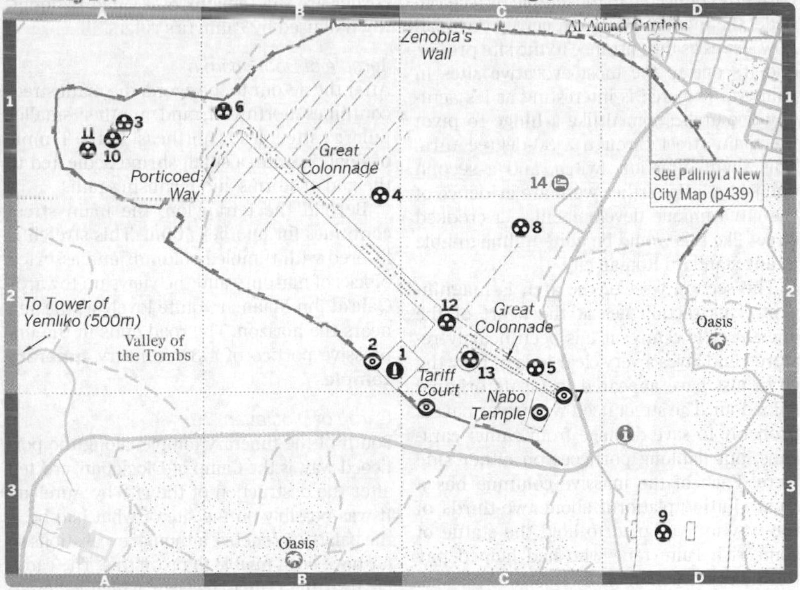

the heat of the day and with a sunset trip up to Qala'at ibn Maan. Although Palmyra is Syria's single-most popular attraction and tour groups spill from buses and into the ruins at regular intervals, the site is large enough to find a quiet corner and imagine you have the place to yourself. If you can do this at sunrise or sunset, when the columns and temple walls turn golden or rose pink, this is when you'll really understand the magic of Palmyra.

Temple of Bel
(adult/student S£150/10; 9am-6pm Apr-Sep, 8am-4pm Oct-Mar) Bel was the most important of the gods in the Palmyrene pantheon, and the Temple of Bel is the most complete structure left in Palmyra. Once inside, you'll see that the complex consists of two parts: a huge walled *temenos* (courtyard), and at its centre, the *cella* (the temple proper), which dates from AD 32.

Just to the left of the entrance into the *temenos* is a sunken passage that enters the temple from the outside wall and gradually slopes up to the level of the courtyard. This was probably used to bring sacrificial animals to the precincts. The podium of the sacrificial altar is on the left, and beside it are the foundations of a banqueting hall. Inside the *cella* is a single chamber with *adytons* (large niches) at either end. To see how the temple once stood, visit room two of the Palmyra Museum.

The earth-coloured building by the Temple of Bel was originally the residence of the Ottoman governor of Palmyra. It later became a prison, and at the time of research was going to open as a visitors centre.

Palmyra

Sights

1	Agora	B2
2	Banqueting Hall	B2
3	Camp of Diocletian	A1
4	Church	B1
5	Diocletian's Baths	C2
6	Funerary Temple	B1
7	Monumental Arch	C3
8	Temple of Baal Shamin	C2
9	Temple of Bel	D3
10	Temple of Standards	A1
11	Temple of the Camp of Diocletian	A1
12	Tetrapylon	C2
13	Theatre	C2

Sleeping

14	Zenobia Cham Palace	C1

Monumental Arch

Formerly connected to the temple by a colonnade, the monumental arch across the road now serves as the entrance to the site proper, and it's one of the most evocative sites in Palmyra. The arch is interesting as it's actually two arches joined like a hinge to pivot the main street through a 30-degree turn. This slight direction switch, and a second one just a little further west, are evidence of the city's unique development – a crooked street like this would be quite unimaginable in any standard Roman city.

The section west of the arch is magnificent. This section lies at the heart of the ancient civic centre; it has been heavily restored and gives a very clear idea of how the city must have appeared in all its original splendour. The street itself was never paved, probably to save damage from camel caravans, but flanking porticoes on either side were. Each of the massive columns has a small, jutting platform about two-thirds of the way up, designed to hold the statue of some rich Palmyrene who had helped pay for the construction of the street.

Theatre

South of the main colonnaded street is the city's **theatre** (admission S£75; ⏲9am-6pm Apr-Sep, 8am-4pm Oct-Mar), which was buried by sand until the 1950s. Since its discovery it has been extensively restored.

Tetrapylon

About one-third of the way along the colonnaded street is the beautiful, reconstructed tetrapylon, a monumental structure that marked a junction of thoroughfares and marks the second pivot in the route of the colonnaded street. Its square platform bears at each corner a tight grouping of four columns. Each of the four groups of pillars supports 150,000kg of solid cornice. A pedestal at the centre of each quartet originally carried a statue. Only one of the 16 pillars is of the original pink granite (probably brought from Aswan in Egypt).

Agora

The agora was the hub of Palmyrene life, the city's most important meeting space, used for public discussion and as a market where caravans unloaded their wares and engaged in the trade that brought the desert oasis its wealth. What remains today is a clearly defined courtyard measuring 84m by 71m. The central area was once enclosed by porticoes on all four sides and the pillars carried statues. Adjoining the agora in the northwest corner are the remains of a small banqueting hall used by Palmyra's rulers.

Temple of Baal Shamin

After the detour to the agora, the main street continues northwest, and another smaller pillared street leads northeast to the Temple of Baal Shamin, a small shrine dedicated to the god of storms and fertilising rains.

Beyond the tetrapylon, the main street continues for another 500m. This stretch is littered with tumbled columns and assorted blocks of masonry and the views up towards Qala'at ibn Maan are quite lovely as the sun nears the horizon. The road ends in the impressive portico of a 3rd-century **funerary temple**.

Camp of Diocletian

South of the funerary temple, along the porticoed way, is the Camp of Diocletian, erected after the destruction of the city by Aurelian. It was possibly on the site of what had been the palace of Zenobia, although excavations so far have been unable to prove this. The camp lay near the Damascus Gate, which led on to a 2nd-century colonnaded street that supposedly linked Emesa (Homs) and the Euphrates.

Towers

To the south, at the foot of some low hills, is a series of tall, freestanding square-based towers known as the **Towers of Yemliko**. These were constructed as multistorey burial chambers, stacked with coffins posted in pigeonhole-like niches. The niches were sealed with stone panels carved with a head-and-shoulder portrait of the deceased; you can see many of these in the special displays at the National Museum in Damascus.

It's possible to visit one of these towers, **Elahbel**, on a tour organised by the Palmyra Museum. Tours leave from the museum at 8.30am, 10am, 11.30am and 4.30pm (no 11.30am tour on Fridays, no 4.30pm tour October to March) and include a visit to the impressive **Hypogeum of the Three Brothers**, an underground burial chamber with beautiful frescos.

Qala'at ibn Maan CASTLE

(adult/student S£75/5; ⏲noon-sunset Wed-Mon)

Perched high on a hilltop to the west of the ruins is Qala'at ibn Maan, also known as the Arab Castle or citadel. From here, there are spectacular sunset views over the ruins. Though it's possible to walk here, many travellers choose to take one of the many tours

Palmyra New City

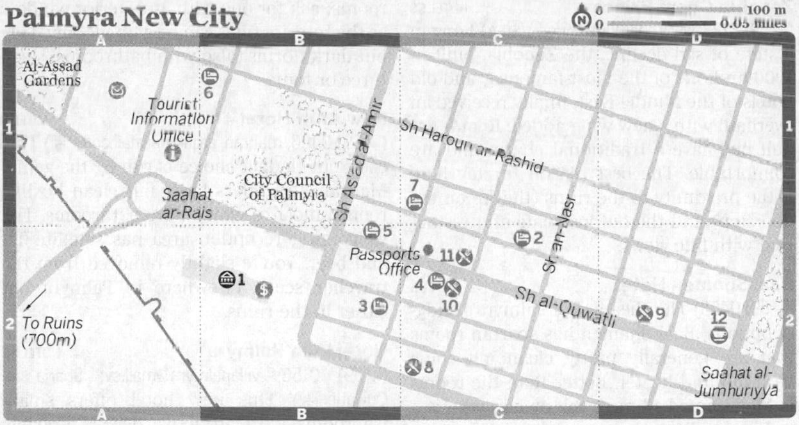

Palmyra New City

Sights

1 Palmyra Museum B2

Sleeping

2 Al-Nakheel Hotel C2
3 Baal Shamen Hotel B2
4 Hotel Villa Palmyra C2
5 Ishtar Hotel B2
6 New Afqa Hotel B1
7 Sun Hotel C1

Eating

8 Casa Mia C2
9 Cheap Restaurants D2
10 Spring Restaurant C2
11 Traditional Palmyra Restaurant & Pancake House C2

Drinking

12 Cave Cafeteria D2

sold by hotels in town (approximately S£150 per person).

Palmyra Museum MUSEUM
(adult/student S£150/10; ⌚8am-1pm & 4-6pm Wed-Mon Apr-Sep, 8am-4pm Wed-Mon Oct-Mar) With improving but still patchy labelling in English and Arabic, Palmyra Museum is worth a quick visit to add some context to the ruins. There's a good, large-scale model of the Temple of Bel in its original state and some fine mosaics found in what are presumed to be nobles' houses, just east of the temple.

Other highlights include a collection of coins depicting Zenobia and her son, countless busts and reliefs that formed part of the panels used to seal the loculi in Palmyra's many funerary towers and *hypogea* (underground burial chambers), and an outstanding, 3m-high statue of the goddess Allat, associated with the Greek Athena.

Upstairs are newer exhibits that add a little depth to this otherwise modest collection: four mummies discovered in 2004 (note the shoes and children's bones arrayed in front of the four adult bodies) and a room exhibiting local Bedouin clothes and jewellery.

Tours

Most hotels organise trips to surrounding sights, and those that don't can suggest a taxi driver who can.

Sleeping

At the time of writing, all hotels in Palmyra are closed. Before the unrest, Palmyra had a good selection of budget and midrange hotels as well as one of Syria's oldest hotels at the top end.

TOP CHOICE **Al-Nakheel Hotel** HOTEL $
(☎591 0744; www.alnakheelhotel.net; ❄) Arguably the best value accommodation in any price range in Palmyra, Al-Nakheel has traditional Bedouin styling in the public areas with some of it overflowing into the rooms; one has a balcony with views over the distant ruins. Best of all, it's all presided over by Mohamed, a local Bedouin who's an engaging host.

Zenobia Cham Palace HOTEL $$
(☎591 8123; www.chamhotels.com; ❄@) Long in a state of sad decline, the Zenobia, built in 1900 and one of the most famous grand old hotels of the Middle East, finally received an overhaul with a new wing added. Rooms are dull but have a traditional charm and are comfortable. The best reason to stay here is the proximity to the ruins (they're on the doorstep) and the outdoor cafe and restaurant with fine views.

Baal Shamen Hotel HOTEL $
(☎591 0453) The cheapest of Palmyra's budget options, Baal Shamen has spartan rooms that are generally pretty clean; all come with fan and heater. Better than the rooms is Mohammed Ahmed, the owner, who is a welcoming host.

Ishtar Hotel HOTEL $$
(☎591 3073/4; www.ishtarhotel.net; Sharia al-Quwatli; ❄@) It's not that the rooms here are anything special – as the management freely admits, they're 'simple and clean'. But this is one of the friendliest places in town, the rooms are comfortable, there's free internet for half an hour for guests, a reasonable restaurant and cave-themed basement bar. A good package all round.

Sun Hotel HOTEL $
(☎591 1133; sunhotel-sy@hotmail.com; @) This recommended small hotel is a mixed bag, although all rooms have fans and clean bathrooms; ask for one with an exterior window as the interior ones can be a bit gloomy. Tidy but dark dorms (also with bathrooms) sleep three or four.

New Afqa Hotel HOTEL $
(☎591 0386; mahran_afqa@hotmail.com; ❄) This excellent budget choice is run by the genial Mahran and offers basic but clean boxlike rooms, most of which have bathrooms. The welcoming reception area has satellite TV and beer. You're slightly removed from the traveller scene elsewhere in Palmyra but closer to the ruins.

Hotel Villa Palmyra HOTEL $$
(☎591 0156; villapalmyra@mail.sy; Sharia al-Quwatli; ❄) This new hotel offers smallish rooms with attractive decor; probably the most comfortable midrange rooms in Palmyra and it's also the best-run hotel in the category. Ask for a room that faces the street unless you want to look out onto a wall… There's a rooftop restaurant, as well as a downstairs bar and pub.

Eating & Drinking

Most places to eat are on or around the main drag, Sharia al-Quwatli. Most places serve alcohol.

Of the hotel restaurants, the Ishtar Hotel serves a good set menu of mezze, soup, *mensaf* (lamb on a bed of rice) and dessert, while the upstairs roof restaurant at the Hotel

QUEEN OF THE DESERT

The most picaresque character in Palmyra's history was responsible for the city's most glorious historical moment, and also its subsequent rapid downfall. Palmyra's ruler, Odainat (also called Odenathus), was assassinated in AD 267. His second wife, Zenobia, took over in the name of their young son, Vabalathus. Rome refused to recognise this arrangement, not least because Zenobia was suspected of involvement in her husband's death. The emperor dispatched an army to deal with the rebel queen. Zenobia met the Roman force in battle and defeated it. She then led her army against the garrison at Bosra, then the capital of the Province of Arabia, and successfully invaded Egypt. With all of Syria and Palestine and part of Egypt under her control, Zenobia, who claimed to be descended from Cleopatra, declared her independence from Rome and had coins minted in Alexandria bearing her image and that of her son, who assumed the title of Augustus, or emperor.

The Roman emperor Aurelian, who had been prepared to negotiate, was not amused. After defeating Zenobia's forces at Antioch and Emesa (Homs) in 271, he besieged Palmyra itself. Zenobia was defiant to the last and instead of accepting the generous surrender terms offered by Aurelian, made a dash on a camel through the encircling Roman forces. She headed for Persia to appeal for military aid, only to be captured by Roman cavalry at the Euphrates. Zenobia was carted off to Rome in 272 as Aurelian's trophy and reputedly paraded in the streets, bound in gold chains. Later freed, she married a Roman senator and lived out her days in Tibur (now Tivoli), close to Rome.

Villa Palmyra serves reasonable buffet-style meals. The Zenobia Hotel gets mixed reviews, although the setting is lovely and the terrace is a great place to nurse a beer while ruminating on the passing of ages. Other good hotel bars include the cave-basement at Ishtar Hotel and the downstairs bar of the Hotel Villa Palmyra. Most restaurants also serve alcohol. One of the best local cafes is the Cave Cafeteria near Saahat al-Jumhuriyya. Women won't feel comfortable here.

Spring Restaurant SYRIAN $
(☎591 0307; Sharia al-Quwatli) The friendly Spring has a ground-floor dining area and a Bedouin tent on the roof where you can enjoy a meal and nargileh (S£100) in summer. The set *mensaf* meal is S£250, mezze cost around S£50 and grills start at S£150. Students get a 20% discount.

Traditional Palmyra Restaurant & Pancake House SYRIAN $
(☎591 0878; Sharia al-Quwatli) The most popular restaurant in town, this long-standing place serves decent *mensaf*, lamb or chicken casseroles and a few other local specialities; all meals come with soup and complimentary tea. There are also delicious sweet and savoury pancakes (around S£200) if you don't want the full set meal.

Casa Mia SYRIAN $
(☎591 6222) Casa Mia is popular partly for its classy, if understated, traditional decor and partly for its local specialities such as *quaj* (oven-baked vegetables), *mjadarah* (burghul and lentils) and *kusa mahshi* (rice, meat and zucchini). The *mensaf* we had here was especially tasty. The menu doesn't list prices. It's off Sharia al-Omar.

ℹ Information

Palmyra's helpful **tourist information office** (☎591 0574; www.syriatourism.org; Saahat ar-Rais; ⌚8am-6pm Sat-Thu) is situated across from the museum. There is a **Commercial Bank of Syria exchange booth** (⌚8am-8pm Sun-Thu, 10am-8pm Fri & Sat) in front of the museum; it doesn't change travellers cheques. The **post office** (⌚8am-2pm Sat-Thu) is in front of the Al-Assad Gardens, just west of the tourist office. There is internet at the Traditional Palmyra Restaurant and elsewhere.

ℹ Getting There & Away

Palmyra doesn't have a bus station. The most popular (and regular) buses are those of Al-Kadmous. They stop at the Sahara Café on the edge of town (2km from the museum). The ticket office is in front of the cafe. Buses to Damascus leave hourly from 6am to 7pm, at 9.30pm and hourly from 12.30am to 6am. Buses to Deir ez-Zur (two hours) leave hourly from 8am to 8pm. Services run less often to Homs and Hama. Other private companies offer a similar service and leave from a spot 200m north of the Sahara Café.

Microbuses and minibus service taxis travel to Homs between 6am and sunset. They leave from outside the Osman Mosque.

EUPHRATES

One of the most historically significant rivers on earth, the Euphrates cuts a swathe through northeastern Syria, and arrayed along its banks, and in its hinterland, are a number of little-visited but rewarding sites, including the ancient Mesopotamian city of Mari, the Graeco-Roman city of Dura Europos, where the synagogue on show at the National Museum in Damascus was found. The later Roman fort of Resafa is also here, but travel in this part of Syria is currently impossible.

UNDERSTAND SYRIA

Syria Today

Protests against the regime of President Bashar al-Assad began in January 2011 and escalated dramatically in the following year. By March 2012, the UN reckoned that at least 9000 people had been killed in the government's violent crackdown, the majority of them civilians. Parts of Deraa, Hama, Lattakia, Deir ez-Zur and many other cities and towns have been badly damaged, and the Baba Amr district of Homs became a bloodbath, with civilians, fighters of the Free Syrian Army and foreign journalists among an estimated 700 casualties. Most places in the country have continued to see regular protests in spite of violent reprisals.

On 8 March 2012, a Syrian minister, Abdo Hussameddin, resigned his post and his membership of the ruling Baath Party. In his resignation speech, posted on YouTube, the minister said that he was 'joining the revolution of the people who reject injustice and the brutal campaign of the regime'. Whether others follow and the regime crumbles remains to be seen.

The Arab League put forward a peace plan in January 2012 that was rejected by the Assad government. A joint Arab League/United Nations plan, put forward by the former UN Secretary-General Kofi Annan in April, has called for a ceasefire on both sides, as well as the right to protest, the release of detainees and a reformed, inclusive political process. At the same time, the US and other countries have continued to call for President Assad to hand over power.

For news of what's happening in Syria, albeit with restrictions, check out the BBC (www.bbc.co.uk) or Syria News Wire (www.newsfromsyria.com), a blog from Damascus and London.

History

Historically, Syria included the territories that now make up modern Jordan, Israel and the Palestinian Territories, Lebanon and Syria itself. Due to its strategic position, its coastal towns were important Phoenician trading posts. Later, the area became a pivotal part of the Egyptian, Persian and Roman Empires, and many others in the empire-building business.

Syria finally ended up as part of the Ottoman domains ruled from İstanbul, and was dished out to France (along with Lebanon) when the Ottoman Empire broke up after WWI. This caused considerable local resentment, as the region had been briefly independent from the end of WWI until the French took over in 1920.

France never had much luck with its Syria–Lebanon mandate. Local opposition to its policy of carving up the country into mini-states (Grand Liban, Lebanon, Aleppo and Damascus) and minority enclaves (for the Druze and Alawites) led to revolts against French rule. Elections were held in 1928 and 1932, but moves to establish a constitution were stymied by the occupying power, which compounded its unpopularity in 1939 when it ceded the northern cities of Antioch (Antakya) and Alexandretta (Iskenderun) to encourage Turkey's neutrality in WWII.

A nationalist government was formed under Shoukri al-Quwatli in August 1943, but the French continued to be in denial about the waning of its influence in the region, bombing Damascus after locals had demonstrated in support of a final handover of administrative and military services to the new government. The situation was only resolved after the British intervened and oversaw the final departure of all French troops and administrators at the end of the war.

Post WWII

A period of political instability followed and by 1954, after several military coups, the nationalist Ba'ath Party ('Ba'ath' means 'renaissance') took power virtually unopposed. A brief flirtation with the Pan-Arabist idea of a United Arab Republic (with Egypt) in 1958 proved unpopular and coups in 1960, 1961 and 1963 saw the leadership change hands yet again. By 1966 the Ba'ath Party was back in power, but it was severely weakened by losses in two conflicts: the Six Day War with Israel in 1967 and the Black September hostilities in Jordan in 1970. At this point, Defence Minister Hafez al-Assad seized power.

Assad maintained control longer than any other post-independence Syrian government, with a mixture of ruthless suppression and guile. The most widely condemned example of the former came on 2 February 1982, when Assad ordered the shelling of the old city in Hama in response to a growing campaign by the Muslim Brotherhood. He followed this with a warning that anyone left in the city would be declared a rebel. In the fighting that followed, between 10,000 and 25,000 people were killed out of a total population of 350,000, and mosques, churches and archaeological sites were damaged and destroyed.

In 1998, Assad was elected to a fifth seven-year term with a predictable 99.9% of the vote. It took failing health to finally remove the man from power; his death was announced on 10 June 2000.

Disappointment

Following the death of Assad senior, his son Bashar acceded to power, continuing the minority Alawites' hold on power. A new government was formed in December 2001 with a mandate to push forward political, economic and administrative reforms. For a while, a wave of change swept Syria, the so-called 'Damascus Spring' buzzing with a proliferation of private newspapers, internet bloggers, and public debate not seen in the country in decades. Foreign goods flooded into Syria, private banks were allowed to open and mobile phones made a belated but wildly popular appearance.

But 'not so fast' was the message that came from the old guard that had surrounded Bashar's father – anything perceived as opposing the government was quickly shut down. Reforming the country's unwieldy bureaucracy, whose membership depends more on political patronage and nepotism than on merit, also proved a road too far, as did any hope of curbing the state's far-reaching powers under the emergency laws brought in in 1963, after the coup that brought the Ba'ath party to power.

As a result, while many of the economic reforms were left untouched, political reforms stalled. There was more freedom and less fear than during the rule of Assad senior, but Syrians suffered low wages and rising prices. The country appeared to be going through a boom – certainly a tourism boom – as a result of an improving international standing (even the US reopened its embassy in Damascus) and there was an influx of investment and hope, in some places. But life for the majority of Syrians continued to be difficult, with around a quarter of young people out of work. This tense situation was finally ignited by the 'Arab spring' uprisings that swept across North Africa from late 2010.

Uprising

Small-scale public protests that began in Deraa in March 2011 may not have escalated had the security forces not killed four unarmed protestors and then killed one of the mourners at the funeral. President Assad's brother, Maher Assad, then led an armoured division to suppress any further dissent. The death of dozens of unarmed people in the assault led to protests around the country. By mid-May, the UN reported that at least 1000 had been killed by the security forces and by *shabiha* – pro-Assad armed gangs. *Shabiha* have also been involved in torture, which Amnesty International says is now widespread, with more than half of the cases coming from Deraa.

President Assad did make some concessions, ending the emergency laws and promising electoral reform, but armed resistance to the regime grew along with the security forces' use of heavy weapons, including tanks and the air force. Defecting soldiers from the Syrian Army formed the basis for the creation of the Free Syrian Army. In October 2011, the Syrian National Council (www.syriancouncil.org) – an organisation of dissidents and defected politicians made up predominantly of Sunni Muslims, including the Islamist Muslim Brotherhood party – announced its mission to replace the Assad government. Based outside Syria and promising to uphold democratic rights and abide by the rule of law, it soon won support from Western governments, while Russia, which maintains a naval base along the Syrian coast, and China continued to support Assad.

People

Daily Life

In the public realm, when the fighting stops, Syrians will have to face a number of challenges common to the region. On one level, Syrians are well educated with an overall literacy rate of around 80% (86% for men, 74% for women). School attendance is compulsory for children aged between six and 12, and there are four national public universities, which have combined enrolments of almost 200,000. At the same time, unemployment is far higher than the official rate of 10% suggests (before the uprising, it was assumed that at least 20% of under-24s were unemployed). Inflation (officially around 10% before the uprising) is threatening to run out of control. Compounding the problem, wages are low – average government salaries are just US$300 per month and university graduates such as doctors rarely earn more than US$700. One result of this has been a serious and ongoing 'brain drain', with many graduates heading overseas to find better-paying work. The obligatory 30-months military service for all 18 year-old males has also played its part.

In the private sphere, family ties remain extremely close, families are large, and extended families often live together. Rural-urban migration over recent years now means that more than half of the country's population lives in the cities.

Population

Syria has a population of around 22.5 million, about 90% of which is Arab. Minorities such as the Bedouin Arabs (about 100,000) and smaller groupings of Armenians, Circassians and Turks are among the population. There are also around one million Kurds.

The country's annual population growth has declined from 3.6% during the 1990s to a shrinking of -0.8%. Over one-third of Syrians are under 14 years old, with the average age of the population just 21.9 years of age.

Religion

Islam is practised by about 90% of the population. Between 15% and 20% of this is made up of minorities such as Shiite, Druze and Alawite, but the vast majority are Sunni Muslims. Christians account for most of the remaining 10% of the population and belong to various churches including Greek Orthodox, Greek Catholic, Syrian Orthodox, Armenian Orthodox, Maronite, Roman Catholic and Protestant. There is a tiny Jewish population.

Arts

Syria has contributed some of the Arab world's best-loved cultural figures, but cultural life fell into decline during the reign of Hafez al-Assad, thanks largely to government repression and a critical lack of government funding. Now writers, musicians and cinematographers are starting to make waves again.

Literature

Most Syrian writers to have made their name beyond Syria's borders have done so from exile. The most famous contemporary example is Rafik Schami (b 1946), who left Syria in 1971. His *A Hand Full of Stars* is an outstanding work for teenagers, but *The Dark Side of Love* is his best-known (and most widely available) work.

Zakariya Tamir (b 1931), Syria's master of the children's story, deals with everyday city life marked by frustration and despair born of social oppression. Having been virtually forced to leave Syria in 1980, he was awarded the Syrian Order of Merit in 2002. His *Tigers on the Tenth Day and Other Stories* is wonderful.

But not everyone was forced to leave. The Damascene Nizar Qabbani (1923–98) became one of the Arab world's most beloved poets, credited with transforming formal Arabic poetry with the use of everyday language. He was adored in the 1950s for his love poems, and later for his expressions of the Arabs' collective feelings of humiliation and outrage after the wars with Israel.

Of the noted writers who remained in Syria, the most celebrated and outspoken was Ulfat Idilbi (1912–2007), who wrote about the late Ottoman Empire and French Mandate and the drive for liberation and independence. *Sabriya: Damascus Bitter Sweet* is critical of the mistreatment of women by their families, much of its anger stemming from Idilbi's own experience of being married off at 16 to a man twice her age. *Grandfather's Tale* is also worth tracking down.

In 2007, the release of *A Story Called Syria,* a collection of pieces by 40 writers, was celebrated and quickly followed by calls from Syria's writers and intellectuals to reinvigorate the literature scene, something that is now more likely to happen, if the revolutionary renaissance in Egypt and Tunisia is anything to go by.

Music

Syria's most famous musical star, Farid al-Atrache (1915–74), spent most of his career in Cairo and remains Syria's most beloved musical export across the region. Sometimes called the 'Arab Sinatra', he was a highly accomplished oud player and composer, who succeeded in updating Arabic music by blending it with Western scales and rhythms and the orchestration of the tango and waltz. His melodic improvisations on the oud (he's still known as 'King of the Oud') and his *mawal* (a vocal improvisation) were the highlights of his live performances, and recordings of these are treasured. By the time of his death, he was considered – and still is by many – to be the premier male Arabic music performer.

After a quiet period on the Syrian music scene, there were signs of a revival, thanks to the local success of albums by Kulna Sawa (*All Together*), Lena Chamamian, Itar Shameh, Anas and Friends, Gene and InsaniT, and by the charismatic Lena Chamamian (*Shamat*). A sold-out Woodstock-type concert that toured the country in 2007 featuring many of these bands. One of the biggest voices to have emerged from Syria in recent years is the singer Omar Souleyman. Coming from deep up-country, near the Turkish border, his fast-paced renditions of local folk songs have morphed, thanks to a collaboration with Icelandic singer Björk, into a global sound.

Cinema

Cairo has long been regarded as the home of Arab cinema, a status now being challenged by Gulf States. Syrian film-makers have long resented this, none more so that the country's leading director, Nabil Maleh. Maleh's *The Extras* (1993) captured the stifling repression of the Assad

END OF STORY?

In one of the tales in *The Thousand and One Nights*, a king commissions a merchant to seek out the most marvellous story ever. The merchant sends out his slaves on the quest and at last success is achieved – a slave hears a wondrous story told in Damascus by an old man who tells stories every day, seated on his storyteller's throne. Jump forward several centuries, and in Damascus today there's still an old man who tells stories every day, seated on just such a throne. His name is Abu Shady and he's the last of the Syrian *hakawati* (professional storytellers). *Hakawati* were a common feature of Middle Eastern city street life as far back as the 12th century. With the spread of coffee drinking during Ottoman times, the storytellers moved off the street and into the coffeehouses. As with many Arab traditions, the art of public storytelling has largely failed to survive the 20th century, supplanted in the coffeehouses first by radio, then by TV.

According to Abu Shady, the last professional storyteller before him in Syria went into retirement in the 1970s. As a boy, Abu Shady went with his father to watch the *hakawati* perform at the coffeehouses, and fell in love with stories. 'It was my habit to read too much,' he told us. 'When I was young I would run away from my job at the library to read books.' Abu Shady trained as a tailor but he would read every moment he could: Jean Paul Sartre, Victor Hugo, Ernest Hemingway, Khalil Gibran…

When the previous *hakawati* decided to retire and stop performing at Al-Nawfara Coffee Shop (see p412), its owner, Ahmed al-Rabat, persuaded Abu Shady to take over, and in the early 1990s, he revived the profession. Since then, Abu Shady has been appearing nightly at Al-Nawfara in the shadows of the Umayyad Mosque. Costumed in baggy trousers and waistcoat with a tarboosh on his head, he recounts nightly from his volumes of handwritten tales. These include the legendary exploits of Sultan Beybars and Antar ibn Shadad, both Islamic heroes and – as Abu Shady tells it – regular doers of fantastic feats, sorcery and cunning roguery. He also invents his own stories, incorporating current events. The assembled listeners know the stories, but it's Abu Shady's delivery they come for: he interjects with jokes and comments, works the audience, punctuates the words with waves of his sword, and smashes it down on a copper-top table for startling emphasis. The audience responds with oohs and aahs, cheering and interjecting comments of their own.

Sadly, the audience is dwindling. Abu Shady says that nobody has the time to listen to stories anymore, although ever the optimist, he told us that the new generation 'are starting to get bored with satellite TV and internet and they are returning to stories'. We asked Abu Shady what the future is for the *hakawati*: 'It will die not because of a lack of interest, but because no one wants to take such a low-paying job.' Even so, he hopes that his son, Shady, who already deputises when Abu Shady travels overseas for international festivals, will follow in his footsteps. Shady told us he stands ready to ensure that the era of the Arab storyteller doesn't end when his father hangs up his tarboosh.

regime in its tale of an unmarried couple looking for a space to have an affair. In April 2011, Maleh and many other Syrian film-makers issued a call for solidarity from film-makers everywhere in protest at the fact that 'peaceful Syrian citizens are being killed today for their demands of basic rights and liberties'. An outpouring of new work is anticipated.

Environment

Syria is one of the worst countries in the Middle East when it comes to both environmental awareness and government programs to protect the environment, despite facing the pressing issues of water scarcity, desertification and pollution. While Jordan, Lebanon and Israel are fast catching on to the benefits of ecotourism, Syria had, at the time of writing, just one lonely member of their ranks: **Eco Tourism Syria** (www.ecotourismsyria.com). Although the company is something of a work in progress, its website is the best of its kind in Syria and tours can be organised to key biodiversity areas in the country. It's deserving of your support.

The only other environmental organisation of note in the country is the **Syria Environment Association** (Map p404; ☎011-4467 7800; www.sea-sy.org, in Arabic; Beit Jumaa, Sharia al-Hamrawi, Old City, Damascus), which has an office in Damascus. This NGO has initiated a number of tree-planting programs and is heavily involved in trying to save Damascus' Barada River. It also has an 'ecological garden' with a cafe (p412) just outside Bab al-Farag in Damascus.

SURVIVAL GUIDE

Directory A–Z

Accommodation

Syria has some outstanding budget accommodation, with the best choices in Damascus, Aleppo and Palmyra, and some good choices in Hama and Lattakia if they reopen. In some cases, the rooms are terrific – simple, yet clean and sometimes with bathrooms and satellite TV. But best of all, these are places switched on to the travellers' network, great for meeting fellow travellers and arranging tours to nearby sites.

There's at least one good midrange hotel in most major tourist hotspots – expect comfortable rooms with good bathrooms, satellite TV and good service. But the real highlight is the plethora of boutique hotels that usually straddle the upper midrange and top-end categories. These are to be found in the old cities of Damascus and Aleppo. These places invariably occupy traditional Syrian homes arrayed around an interior courtyard, making an art form of traditional decoration detail in the public areas and usually in the rooms themselves. While in Syria, you should stay in at least one, whatever your budget.

We have not cited prices as most hotels were closed at the time of writing. Some hoteliers indicated that when they reopen, hotels might charge half of their pre-uprising rates. Syrian hotels were already used to seasonal adjustments – Mediterranean prices jumped in summer and fell in winter, just as Damascus and the desert prices rose.

Instead of room rates, we have indicated price category, from budget to top end.

$ less than S£1450 (US$25)

$$ S£1450 to S£5800 (US$25 to US$100)

$$$ more than S£5800 (US$100)

STUDENT ACCOMMODATION

Although you'll find flyers advertising shared student accommodation all over the Old City in Damascus, one place we recommend is House of Damascus (p407).

BEST HOTELS

Budget

- Al-Rabie Hotel (Damascus; p406)
- Ghazal Hotel (Damascus; p407)
- Hanadi Hotel (Aleppo; p426)
- Tourist Hotel (Aleppo; p426)

Boutique

- Talisman (Damascus; p407)
- Beit al-Mamlouka (Damascus; p407)
- Old Damascus Hotel (Damascus; p407)
- Dar Halabia (Aleppo; p426)

Business Hours

The official weekend is Friday and Saturday. Most museums and sites are closed on Tuesday.

Banks Generally follow the government office hours but there are exceptions. Some branches keep their doors open for only three hours from 9am, while some exchange booths are open as late as 7pm.

Government offices and post offices Government offices open 8am to 2pm daily except Friday and holidays. Post offices are open later in the large cities.

Restaurants Between noon and midnight daily. Cafes tend to open earlier and close later.

Shops 9am to 1.30pm and 4pm to 9pm summer, 9am to 1.30pm and 4pm to 8pm winter. Usually closed on Fridays and holidays. In Damascus souq, shops usually don't close at lunchtime and some stay open on Fridays. Aleppo souq shuts down on Friday, but doesn't close for lunch on other days.

Children

On the one hand, travelling in Syria with children can be a delight, as Syrians are extraordinarily welcoming to children; having children with you will quickly break down the barriers with locals and add a whole new dimension to your trip. Formula is readily available in pharmacies, and disposable nappies are stocked in supermarkets. Restaurants usually have high-chairs and are extremely welcoming to families.

At the same time, very few Syrian hotels have child-friendly facilities and child-friendly sights are next to nonexistent (castles like Crac des Chevaliers and Qala'at Saladin may be exceptions for kids of a certain age). Few towns have easily accessible public gardens with playground equipment or shopping malls with amusement centres. As a result, you'd do well to come prepared with your own entertainment for the little ones.

Discount Cards

Students get massive discounts on site admissions on presentation of an internationally recognised card such as the ISIC.

Embassies & Consulates

Most embassies and consulates are open from around 8am to 2pm and are closed on Friday, Saturday and public holidays. The following are in Damascus. Note: the Canadian embassy currently provides emergency consular services to Australians; Irish and New Zealand interests are looked after by the UK embassy.

Canada (☎011-611 6692; www.damascus.gc.ca; Block 12 Autostrad al-Mezze)

Egypt (☎011-333 3561; fax 011 333 7961; Sharia al-Jala'a, Abu Roumana)

France (☎011-339 0200; www.ambafrance-sy.org; Sharia Ata Ayyubi, Salihiyya)

Germany (☎011-332 3800/1; www.damaskus.diplo.de; 53 Sharia Ibrahim Hanano)

Iran (☎011-222 6459; fax 011-222 0997; Autostrad al-Mezzeh)

Italy (☎011-333 8338; www.amb damasco.esteri.it; Sharia al-Ayyubi)

Japan (☎011-333 8273; Sharia Shark Asiya al-Jala, Abu Roumana)

Jordan (☎011-613 6261; damascus@fm.gov.jo; Miza Eastern Villas, Western Tarablus St, Bldg 27) Close to Al-Akram Mosque.

Lebanon (☎011-333-8606; Atta Al-Ayoubi Street, Rawda)

Netherlands (☎011-333 6871; fax 011-333 9369; Sharia al-Jala'a, Abu Roumana)

Spain (☎011-613 2900/1; emb.damasco@mae.es; Sharia Shafi, east Mezze) Behind Hotel Al-Hayat.

Turkey (☎011-333 1411; dakkabe@citechco.net; 58 Sharia Ziad bin Abi Soufian, Al Rawda)

UK (☎0932 004 424; www.ukinsyria.fco.gov.uk; Kotob Bldg, 11 Sharia Mohammed Kurd Ali, Malki)

USA (☎011-3391 4444; http://damascus.usembassy.gov; 2 Sharia al-Mansour, Abu Roumana)

Food

Prices in this book represent the cost of a standard main-course dish. We have not cited prices for meals or dishes because of the difficulty of researching accurate and up-to-date information during the uprising. We have instead indicated price category, from budget to top end.

$ less than S£200 (US$3.50)

$$ S£200 to S£500 (US$3.50 to US$9)

$$$ more than S£500 (US$9)

Gay & Lesbian Travellers

Homosexuality is prohibited in Syria and conviction can result in imprisonment.

Cleopatra's Wedding Present by Robert Tewdwr Moss is an entertaining account of a gay American's travels through Syria.

Language Courses

If you're a would-be student of the Arabic language, there are a number of options in Damascus.

British Council (☎331 0631; www.britishcouncil.org/syria; Sharia Karim al-Khalil) Offers intensive courses in Modern Standard or Syrian Colloquial Arabic at three levels. You'll find it off Sharia Maysaloun. It was closed at the time of writing.

Damascus University (Map p408; ☎212 9494; www.damascusuniversity.edu.sy; Language Institute, Faculty of Human Arts, University of Damascus, Sharia Filasteen) Offers courses in Syrian Arabic.

Money

The official currency is the Syrian pound (S£), also called the lira. There are 100 piastres (also known as *qirsh*) to a pound but this is redundant as the smallest coin is one pound. Other coins come in denominations of two, five, 10 and 25. Notes come in denominations of 50, 100, 200, 500 and 1000.

There's at least one branch of the Commercial Bank of Syria in every major town and most will change US dollars or euros. There's also a small number of officially sanctioned private exchange offices, which change cash at official bank rates. The advantage is that whereas banks usually close for the day at 12.30pm or 2pm, the exchange offices are often open until 7pm.

ATMS

There are now ATMs everywhere in Syria in most tourist centres and medium-sized towns. Most ATMs accept Visa and are Cirrus or Maestro enabled. Some will take MasterCard. Displays on each ATM announce which cards are accepted. One drawback for those hoping to survive on ATM cash withdrawals while in Syria is that most ATMs set a daily withdrawal limit, usually around S£3000, and often run out of cash.

CREDIT CARDS

Major credit cards are increasingly being accepted by travel agencies, hotels and shops, but they're not yet accepted in many restaurants. This situation will change as soon as Visa and MasterCard are given permission to set up shop in Syria; at present all transactions must be processed through Lebanon, and a surcharge of around 10% is levied on the customer to cover this.

TIPPING & BARGAINING

Tipping is expected in the better restaurants and by all tour guides. Whatever you buy, remember that bargaining is an integral part of the process and listed prices are always inflated to allow for it. If you're shopping in the souqs, bargain hard – even a minimum amount of effort will almost always result in outrageous asking prices being halved.

TRAVELLERS CHEQUES

It's becoming increasingly difficult to cash travellers cheques in Syria. If you do find a bank that will change your cheques, you must have the bank receipt with the cheque numbers detailed on it. Exchange offices never change them.

Post

The Syrian postal service is slow but trustworthy. Letters mailed from the main cities take about a week to get to Europe and up to a month to get to Australia or the USA.

Public Holidays

In addition to the main Islamic holidays (p624), Syria celebrates the following public holidays:

New Year's Day 1 January
Revolution Day 8 March
Al-Adha Day 15 March
Mother's Day 21 March
Easter March/April
Hijra New Year's Day 6 April
National Day 17 April
May Day 1 May
Martyrs' Day 6 May
Liberation War of October Day 6 October
Christmas Day 25 December

Telephone

MOBILE PHONES

You can purchase an inexpensive Syriatel or MTN SIM card to use in your mobile phone while you're in the country. Cards are available at mobile-phone shops throughout the country (these are ubiquitous) and at the arrivals hall at Damascus International Airport. Non-Syrian mobile phones work fine in Syria (usually through Syriatel), but roaming charges can be prohibitive.

PRACTICALITIES

» As well as the three state-run Arabic daily newspapers, there's one English-language daily, the *Syria Times* (S£5). This is published under direct government control and is big on propaganda and short on news.

» You can pick up the BBC World Service on a range of radio frequencies, including AM 1323 in Damascus and the Europe short-wave schedule in Aleppo. See www.bbc.co.uk/worldservice for details.

» CNN, BBC World and a handful of European satellite channels can be accessed in many hotel rooms.

» The country's electrical current is 220V AC, 50Hz. Wall sockets are the round, two-pin European type.

» Syria uses the metric system.

PHONE CODES

The country code for Syria is ☎963, followed by the local area code (minus the zero), then the subscriber number. The international access code (to call abroad from Syria) is ☎00. The numbers for directory assistance are ☎141 142 (national calls) and ☎143 144 (International calls).

PHONECARDS

Syrian Telecom cards are available from mobile-phone shops and kiosks and you'll find phones on the streets in most cities, especially outside the government telephone office. You'll need a S£200 card to make calls within Syria (S£20 per minute), and a S£350 card to phone Europe and other Western destinations (around S£50 per minute).

Visas

PLACES OF ISSUE

Everyone, except citizens of Arab countries, requires a visa to enter Syria. The basic rule is that you should obtain a visa at the Syrian embassy or consulate in your home country. Avoid applying in a country that's not your own or that you don't hold residency for, as the Syrian authorities don't like this: at best, they'll ask you for a letter of recommendation from your own embassy (often an expensive and time-consuming proposition); at worst, they'll turn you down flat. US citizens should be aware that many US embassies abroad have a policy of not issuing letters of recommendation – leading to the ridiculous situation where they issue letters stating that they don't issue letters of recommendation. If your home country doesn't have a Syrian embassy or consulate, there's no problem with you applying in another country; alternatively, you can obtain a visa on arrival.

Officially, the Syrian embassy in Amman issues visas only to nationals and residents of Jordan and to nationals of countries that have no Syrian representation. That said, we receive occasional reports that citizens without Jordanian residence were obtaining single-entry Syrian visas in Amman for JD90.

In Turkey, you can get Syrian visas in both Ankara and İstanbul, but you'll need a letter of recommendation from your embassy. The Syrian embassy in Beirut, Lebanon, may issue visas to non-Lebanese.

If there's no Syrian representation in your country, you might be able to obtain a visa on arrival at borders, airports or ports, but we don't recommend that you count on this. We have heard many stories of people being turned back.

TYPES

There are three types of visa: transit, single entry and multiple entry. Transit visas are only good for airport stays. Both single- or multiple-entry visas are valid for 30 days inside Syria, although the embassy's visa stamp may say 15 days, and must be used within three months of the date of issue. Don't be misled by the line on the visa stating a validity of three months – this simply means the visa is valid *for presentation* for three months. You'll usually require two photographs and have to fill out two forms, sometimes online.

COST

The cost of visas varies according to the reciprocal agreement Syria has made with your home country. For example, UK citizens pay UK£30 for a single-entry visa, US citizens US$131 and Australian citizens A$100. If you book travel arrangements through a foreign tour operator that has a working relationship with a Syrian operator, you are entitled to a free visa, collectable at the point of entry.

ISRAELI PASSPORT STAMPS

Remember also that *any* evidence of a visit to Israel – most visa application forms ask if you've been to 'Occupied Palestine' – will see your application turned down flat. Later, if Syrian border officials see that you have an Israeli visa or stamp in your passport, or if a scan of recent stamps suggests that you have recently travelled through Israel and the Palestinian Territories, you will be refused entry to Syria.

EXTENSIONS

In one of the most welcome changes for travellers in Syria in recent years, you're no longer required to seek a visa extension if you wish to stay in the country longer than 15 days; at the time of writing, this requirement was still being stamped on visas by Syrian embassies around the world even though it no longer applies. The rule change means that you must instead seek a visa extension after 30 days, which takes the need for extensions beyond the concern of most travellers.

If you're staying in Syria for more than 30 days you'll have to visit an immigration office, which you'll find in all main cities. Unless you ask for a longer extension, the usual length of the extension is a further 15 days, although up to one-and-a-half months is routinely granted upon request. They are usually only granted on the 29th or 30th day of your stay, so if you apply earlier expect to be knocked back. The specifics vary from place to place but there are always a couple of forms to complete and you need two to six passport photos. The cost is never more than S£50.

Aleppo **Immigration office** (Map p424; ☎225 5330; ⏲8am-1.30pm Sat-Thu) In the square near the Chabha Cham Palace Hotel, west of the Old City. A taxi should cost no more than S£50.

Damascus **Central immigration office** (Map p408; Sharia Filasteen; ⏲8am-2pm Sat-Thu) One block west of Baramke Garage. Go to the 2nd floor, fill in three forms, present four photos (the Kodak Express just west of the Hejaz train station can do them in 10 minutes; S£200 for eight photos), pay S£50 and return 24 hours later to pick it up.

Hama **Passport office** (Sharia Ziqar; ⏲8am-2pm Sun-Thu) On the northern edge of town, near the museum; a modern building with 'Passport' written in English above the main entrance.

Lattakia **Immigration office** (⏲8am-2pm Sun-Thu) Beyond the tourist office, near Saahat Jumhuriyya.

Palmyra **Passports office** (Sharia al-Quwatli; ⏲8am-1.30pm Sat-Thu) Come with three photos and pick up your passport the next day.

Women Travellers

Until the recent uprising, Syria was an extraordinarily safe country in which to travel, and foreign women were generally treated with courtesy and respect. But as the regime's grip weakens, so there will be a greater risk of unwanted predatory male attention. To minimise the chance of any unpleasant encounters, follow the advice given on clothing and behaviour on p618 and try to sit next to women on public transport. Clothing guidelines are particularly important in rural areas, which tend to be more conservative. We do not recommend hitching a ride in Syria, whatever the circumstances.

DEPARTURE TAX

There's a departure tax of S£550 payable for all foreigners leaving the country, whether by air or land. The tax is now usually included in airline tickets, but be prepared to pay in Syrian currency at land borders.

Getting There & Away

Entering Syria

For information on Syrian visas and entry requirements, see p449.

Air

Syria's main **international airport** (☎544 5983-9) is 32km southeast of Damascus and has regular connections to other cities in the Middle East, Europe, Africa and Asia on a variety of European- and Middle East–based airlines. There are also reasonable regional and occasionally European connections from **Aleppo** (☎421 1200). Lattakia has just one weekly SyrianAir flight to Cairo.

Syrian Arab Airlines (SyrianAir; www.syriaair.com) is the national airline. It has a small fleet, which includes some recently purchased Airbuses. From Damascus, SyrianAir flies to destinations across Europe and the Middle East.

Land

Syria has borders with Lebanon, Turkey, Jordan and Iraq. It also shares a border with Israel, the hotly disputed Golan Heights, but it's a definite no-go zone that's mined and is patrolled by UN peacekeepers.

BORDER CROSSINGS

Iraq

The only open border crossing with Iraq is just south of Al-Bukamal in the extreme east of the country, although whether it's open to foreign travellers depends on the prevailing political and security winds.

Jordan

There are two border crossings between Syria and Jordan: at Nasib/Jabir and Deraa/Ramtha. These crossings are 3km apart. If crossing by car, service taxi or bus you'll cross through the main Nasib/Jabir post, on the Amman–Damascus highway. If you're travelling by train or local transport, you'll use Deraa/Ramtha. Microbuses from the bus station at Deraa charge S£250 per person to take you across the border to Ramtha.

The best way to get to Deraa from Damascus is to catch a bus from Baramke Garage.

From Damascus, there are daily buses to Amman (p451), for which you need to book in advance as demand for seats is high, or you can catch a service taxi. The famous Hejaz railway trip is also a possibility

Jordanian visas are issued at the border, or can be obtained in advance from the embassy in Damascus. It's cheaper to get it at the border.

Lebanon

There are plenty of buses from Damascus to Beirut (p451), although to travel direct to Baalbek the only option is a service taxi (see p414 for details). You can also travel by bus or service taxi to Beirut via Tripoli from Aleppo (p451) and Lattakia (p451).

See p394 for information on obtaining Lebanese visas.

Turkey

There are several border crossings between Syria and Turkey. The busiest and most convenient links Antakya in Turkey with Aleppo, via the Bab al-Hawa border station. This is the route taken by all cross-border buses, including those from Damascus and Aleppo (p451) bound for Antakya and onward Turkish destinations.

An interesting alternative to the bus might be the weekly train from Aleppo to İstanbul (p452).

You can also make your way by microbus from Lattakia, on the Syrian coast, to the border post on the outskirts of the village of Kassab and on to Antakya via Yayladağı.

While Turkish visas are issued at the border (p541), you must already be in possession of a valid visa to enter Syria – see p449.

Getting Around

Air

SyrianAir has a monopoly on domestic flights in the country, and operates flights from Damascus to Aleppo, Deir ez-Zur, Lattakia and Qamishle. Students and under 26s can usually get discounted tickets.

Bus

Syria has a well-developed road network, and bus transport is frequent and cheap. Distances are short, so journeys rarely take more than a few hours. Carry your passport at all times as you'll need it to buy tickets.

Several kinds of buses ply the same routes, but the most safe and comfortable way to travel is by 'luxury' Pullman bus.

MINIBUS & MICROBUS

Minibuses operate on many of the shorter routes, eg Hama–Homs, Tartus–Lattakia and Homs–Lattakia. They take about 20 people, are often luridly decorated and have no schedule, departing when full. This means that on less-popular routes, you may have to wait quite some time until one fills up. Journey times are generally longer than with the other buses, as they set people down and pick them up at any and all points along the route – hence their common name of 'hob-hob' (stop-stop) – and often detour from the main road.

The term 'microbus' is blurred, but in general refers to the little white vans (mostly Japanese) with a sliding door. These are used principally to connect the major cities and towns with surrounding small towns and villages. They are replacing the lumbering old minibuses with which they compete, and are faster and slightly more expensive. They follow set routes but along that route passengers can be picked up or set down anywhere. The fare is the same whatever distance you travel.

PULLMAN BUS

Dozens of private bus companies operate excellent services between the major cities. Routes are few and operators are in fierce competition for passengers. Every city bus station (known locally as *karajats,* or garages) has a row of prefab huts serving as booking offices for the various companies. There's no central information source for departure times or prices, so it's a case of walking around and finding out which company has the next bus to your destination, although chances are that the touts will find you before you get too far.

Fares vary little and buses are pretty much the same (large, newish, air-con). Seats are assigned at booking. A rigid no-smoking rule is imposed on most buses (although some drivers seem to be exempt), and during the journey a steward will distribute cups of water. A few companies do have the edge when it comes to the cleanliness and roadworthiness of their vehicles; particularly recommended are Al-Kadmous (sometimes signed 'KT') and Al-Ahliah.

Car & Motorcycle

You'll need an International Driving Permit (IDP) if you decide to drive in Syria. Traffic runs on the right-hand side of the road. The speed limit is 60km/h in built-up areas, 70km/h on the open road and 110km/h on major highways. The roads are generally quite reasonable, but when heading off into the backblocks you'll find that most signposting is in Arabic only.

Europcar (☎011-212 0624/5; www.europcar.com) has been joined by **Hertz** (☎011-221 6615; www.hertz.com), a number of other international firms and a gaggle of sometimes dodgy local companies. The international firms will be expensive, local companies cheaper, but be sure the car is safe and keep your eye on insurance arrangements.

Most firms have desks at the airport, and offices on or around the Cham Palace Hotel on Sharia Maysaloun in central Damascus. You'll need an IDP and a sizeable cash or credit-card deposit; the minimum hire is usually three days.

Local Transport

Service taxis (shared taxis; ser-*vees*) only operate on the major routes and can cost twice the microbus fare – sometimes more.

Tours

Tours of some of the country's highlights can be organised by hotels and agencies in Damascus, Hama, Aleppo and some other places.

Train

The once-neglected Syrian railway system has seen significant improvements over the past decade, including the purchase of French-made locomotives. The main line connects Damascus, Aleppo, Deir ez-Zur, Hassake and Qamishle. A secondary line runs from Aleppo to Lattakia, along the coast to Tartus and again inland to Homs and Damascus.

Departures are often in the middle of the night, meaning that the only route where we recommend the train over the bus is between Lattakia and Aleppo; this goes through spectacular countryside, starts and terminates in centrally located stations, has at least one reasonable departure time and is very comfortable. At least one midmorning departure time makes the service a viable alternative to the bus between Damascus and Aleppo, although the scenery is uninspiring.

First class is air-con with aircraft-type seats; 2nd class is the same without air-con – it's probably not worth it except in summer. Student discounts are only given on 2nd-class tickets.

Turkey

Includes »

Best for Nature

» Cappadocia (p454)
» Mt Nemrut (p530)
» Blue Voyage (p499)
» Doğubayazıt (p524)
» Birecik (p531)

Best for Culture

» İstanbul (p455)
» Konya (p512)
» Ephesus (p488)
» Mardin (p527)
» Bursa (p476)

Why Go?

Hoş geldiniz (welcome) to the perfect introduction to the Middle East. Although most Turks see their country as European, the nation packs in as many wailing minarets and spice-trading bazaars as its southeastern neighbours, Iran, Iraq and Syria. This bridge between continents has absorbed Europe's modernism and sophistication, and Asia's culture and tradition. Travellers can enjoy historical hot spots, mountain outposts, expansive steppe and one of the world's finest cuisines, without having to forgo comfy beds and punctual buses.

Such potent mixtures of natural splendour and ancient remains result from millennia of eventful history, during which the greatest Middle Eastern empires established capitals in Anatolia (Asian Turkey). Travelling Turkey's beaches and plains is like turning the pages of a historical thriller, with mosques and *medreses*, hamams and *hans* (caravanserais) never far from view.

When to Go

Istanbul

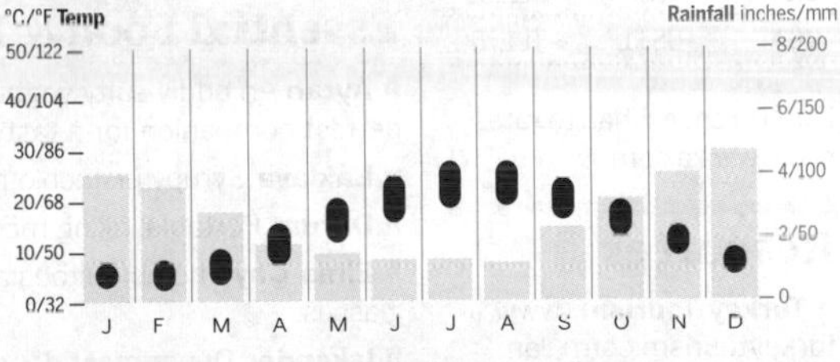

Apr Beat the summer crowds and avoid the summer sun, a perfect time for hiking.

Jul–Sep Time for sun-worshippers to hit the beaches of the Med.

Dec–Jan It's ski season in the icy mountains of eastern Anatolia.

AT A GLANCE

» **Currency** Turkish lira (TL). One Turkish lira is worth 100 kuruş.

» **Mobile Phones** Buying a local phone and chip is less complicated than registering your phone with a Turkish provider.

» **Money** ATMs widespread; credit cards accepted.

» **Visas** Apply to most nationalities; pay in cash at the border.

Fast Facts

» **Capital** Ankara
» **Country code** ☎90
» **Language** Turkish
» **Official name** Türkiye Cumhuriyeti (Turkish Republic)
» **Population** 79 million

Exchange Rates

Australia	A$1	TL1.81
Euro Zone	€1	TL2.32
Iran	IRR\ £10,0000	TL0.14
Iraq	IQD$100	TL0.15
Syria	SYP£10	TL0.30
UK	UK£1	TL2.85
USA	US$1	TL1.75

For current exchange rates see www.xe.com.

Resources

» **Turkey Tourism** (www.turkeytourism.com) Jam-packed with information.

» **Go Turkey** (www.goturkey.com) Official portal.

» **Hello Turkey** (www.helloturkey.net) Jumbled but useful.

Connections

Straddling Europe and Asia, Turkey occupies the same important position on the travellers trail today that it once occupied on the trade routes. Land borders with Bulgaria and Greece funnel visitors through to Asia via the country's exciting capital of İstanbul, while ferry services link the vibrant coastal resorts with nearby Greek islands and further afield to Italy and Cyprus. Though you could spend a lifetime just getting to know this fascinating country, the pull of the exotic Arabic nations to the south is hard to resist. There are major border crossing points with Syria (especially Reyhanli, Yayladaği and Akçakale), and road (Gurbulak) and rail (Kapikoi) routes to Iran. Increasingly Iraq (Silopi) is being seen as a viable option by adventurous tourists. The land border with Armenia has been closed for many years.

ITINERARIES

Two Weeks

Party at night, sightsee by day in atmospheric **İstanbul**, before heading to the sobering **Gallipoli battlefields**. Sail through **Troy** en route to classical **Ephesus**. Don't miss a quick inland trip to the unique travertines of **Pamukkale**, then hit the coast again staying in an **Olympos** tree house. From here meander along the Med coast, stopping at the walled city of **Antalya** and biblical **Antakya** before moving on to Syria.

Three Weeks

Follow the three-week itinerary as far as Antalya, then whirl northeast to **Konya** with your fellow dervishes. From there, it's just a few hours to **Cappadocia**, otherworldly home of fairy chimneys. Next, drag yourself east towards **Malatya**, from where you can visit ethereally beautiful **Mt Nemrut** strewn with stone heads. Before crossing to Iraq, leave Turkey with fond memories by strolling along the gorgeous Cumhuriyet Caddesi in picture-postcard **Mardin**.

Essential Food & Drink

» **Ayran** An oddly salty yoghurt drink that Turks swear is the perfect companion for a tasty kebap.

» **Baklava** Syrupy pistachio pastries sent to tempt the weak.

» **Durum** Portable, filling meaty treats wrapped in pide.

» **Elma Çay** The ubiquitous apple tea, served in curvy glasses.

» **İskender** Döner meat doused in tomato sauce with a dollop of yoghurt.

» **Rakı** This aniseed-flavoured, clear spirit that turns white when mixed is not for the faint of heart.

» **Simit** Delicious rings of sesame bread, wholesome street food.

İSTANBUL

☎ASIAN SIDE 0216 / ☎EUROPEAN SIDE 0212 / POP 13 MILLION

İstanbul's populous neighbourhoods – dating from the Byzantine era, from the golden age of the Ottoman sultans and from recent, less-affluent times – form a dilapidated but ultimately cohesive mosaic. Here, you can retrace the steps of the Byzantine emperors when visiting Sultanahmet's monuments and museums; marvel at the magnificent Ottoman mosques on the city's seven hills; and wander the cobbled streets of the ancient Jewish, Greek and Armenian neighbourhoods in the city's western districts. Centuries of urban sprawl unfurl before your eyes on ferry trips up the Bosphorus or Golden Horn.

The city's feeling of *hüzün* (melancholy) is being relegated to the past, replaced with a sense of energy, innovation and optimism not seen since the days of Süleyman the Magnificent. Stunning contemporary art galleries are opening around the city, and the possibility of a European-flavoured future is being embraced in the rooftop bars of Beyoğlu and the boardrooms of Levent. İstanbul is fast converting itself into one of Europe's must-see cities and there has never been a better time to visit.

History

Late in the 2nd century, the Roman Empire conquered the small city-state of Byzantium – renamed Constantinople after Emperor Constantine moved his capital there in AD 330.

The city walls kept out barbarians for centuries while the western part of the Roman Empire collapsed. When Constantinople fell for the first time, it was to the misguided Fourth Crusade (1202–04).

In 1453, after a long, bitter siege, Mehmet the Conqueror marched to Aya Sofya (also known as Haghia Sofia or Sancta Sophia) and converted the church into a mosque.

As capital of the Ottoman Empire, the city experienced a new golden age. During the reign of Süleyman the Magnificent (1520–66), it was graced with many beautiful new buildings. Occupied by Allied forces after WWI, İstanbul came to be thought of as the decadent capital of the sultans, just as Atatürk's armies were shaping a new republican state.

When the Turkish Republic was proclaimed in 1923, Ankara became the new capital. Nevertheless, İstanbul remains the centre for business, finance, journalism and the arts.

Sights

Straddling the Bosphorus strait, İstanbul is broadly split into Asian and European 'sides'. European İstanbul is further divided by the Golden Horn (Haliç) into Old İstanbul in the south and Beyoğlu in the north.

OLD İSTANBUL

Sultanahmet is the heart of Old İstanbul and boasts many of the city's famous sites. The adjoining area, with hotels to suit all budgets, is called Cankurtaran (*jan*-kur-tar-an), although if you say 'Sultanahmet' most people will understand where you mean.

Topkapı Palace PALACE

(Topkapı Sarayı; Map p464; www.topkapisarayi.gov.tr; Babıhümayun Caddesi; admission palace TL20, harem TL15; ⌚9am-7pm Wed-Mon summer, 9am-5pm winter) Possibly the most iconic monument in İstanbul, opulent Topkapı Palace is a highlight of any trip. The palace was begun by Mehmet shortly after the Conquest of 1453 and Ottoman sultans lived in this impressive environment until the 19th century. It consists of four massive courtyards and a series of imperial buildings, including pavilions, barracks, audience chambers and sleeping quarters. Make sure you visit the mind-blowing **harem**, the palace's most famous sight, and the **Treasury**, which features an incredible collection of precious objects.

Aya Sofya MOSQUE

(Church of Holy Wisdom; Map p464; Aya Sofya Meydanı, Sultanahmet; adult/child under 6yr TL20/free, audio guide TL10; ⌚9am-5pm Tue-Sun Nov-Apr, until 7.30pm May-Oct, upper gallery closes 15-30min earlier) No doubt you will gasp at the overblown splendour of Aya Sofya, one of the world's most glorious buildings. Built as part of Emperor Justinian's (AD 527–65) effort to restore the greatness of the Roman Empire, it was completed in AD 537 and reigned as the grandest church in Christendom until the Conquest in 1453. The exterior does impress, but the interior, with its sublime domed ceiling soaring heavenward, is truly awe-inspiring.

Supported by 40 massive ribs, the dome was constructed of special hollow bricks made in Rhodes from a unique light and porous clay; these rest on huge pillars

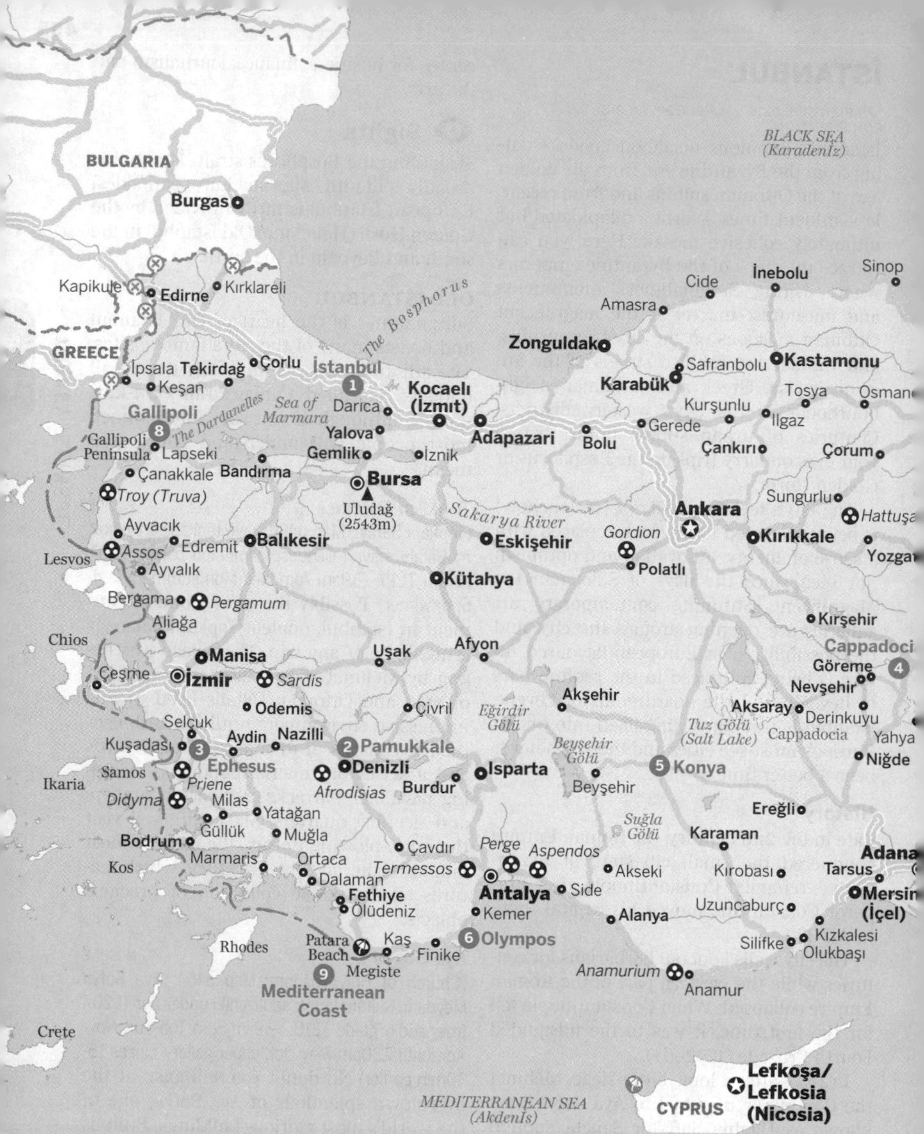

Turkey Highlights

1 Incredible architecture, fantastic food, happening nightlife: historic **İstanbul** (p455) surprises first-time visitors, and second-time visitors too

2 Scale the snow-white hillside and dip your toes in the thermal travertines at picturesque **Pamukkale** (p491)

3 Try to visit the ancient ruined city of **Ephesus** (p488) without once uttering the word 'wow!'

4 Take a balloon flight over the fairy-chimney studded landcape of **Cappadocia** (p454) and imagine you've been cast in *Star Wars*

5 Save your whirling for an evening at the home of the dervishes in **Konya** (p512)

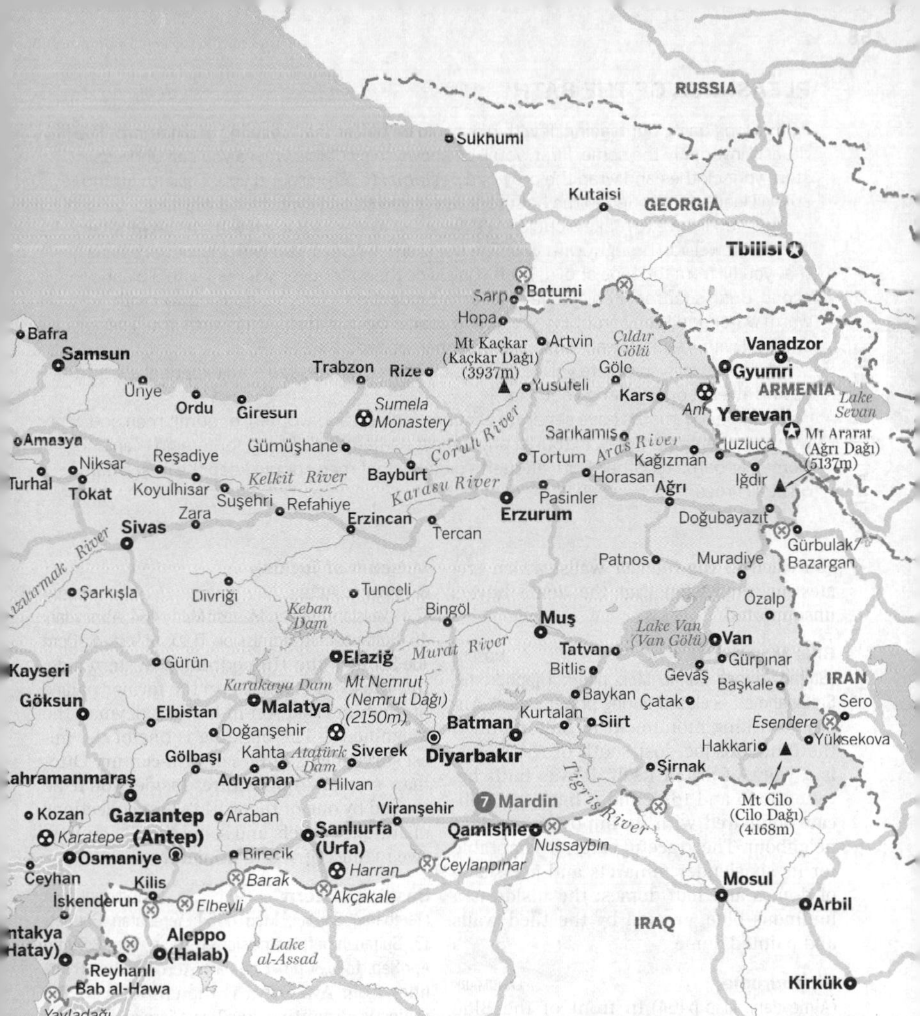

6 You won't be out of your tree at hippy hangout **Olympos** (p503)

7 Explore architectural treasures in the Kurdish heartland of **Mardin** (p527)

8 Let the facts of **Gallipoli** (p480) horrify you, then pay your respects and vow to make sure it never happens again

9 Sun, sea, sand – it's all there on the **Mediterranean Coast** (p496)

10 Leaving Turkey without visiting a **hamam** is as crazy as leaving without trying an *İskender kebap*!

PLEASURES OF THE BATH

After a long day's sightseeing, few things could be better than relaxing in a hamam. The ritual is invariably the same. First, you'll be shown to a cubicle where you can undress, store your clothes and wrap the provided *peştamal* (cloth) around you. Then an attendant will lead you through to the hot room where you sit and sweat for a while.

Next you'll have to make a choice. It's cheapest to wash yourself with the soap, shampoo and towel you brought with you. The hot room will be ringed with individual basins that you fill from the taps above. Then you sluice the water over yourself with a plastic scoop. But it's far more enjoyable to let an attendant do it for you, dousing you with warm water and then scrubbing you with a coarse cloth mitten. Afterwards you'll be lathered with a sudsy swab, rinsed off and shampooed.

When all this is complete you're likely to be offered a massage – an experience worth having at least once during your trip.

Traditional hamams have separate sections for men and women, or admit men and women at separate times. In tourist areas most hamams are happy for foreign men and women to bathe together. Bath etiquette dictates that men should keep the *peştamal* on at all times.

concealed in the interior walls, which creates an impression that the dome hovers unsupported.

Blue Mosque MOSQUE

(Sultan Ahmet Camii; Map p464; Hippodrome, Sultanahmet; ⏲closed during prayer times) Another striking monument in Sultanahmet, the Blue Mosque, just south of Aya Sofya, is a work of art in itself. It was built between 1606 and 1616, and is light and delicate compared with its imposing, ancient neighbour. The graceful exterior is notable for its six slender minarets and a cascade of domes and half domes; the inside is a luminous blue, created by the tiled walls and painted dome.

Hippodrome LANDMARK

(Atmeydanı; Map p464) In front of the Blue Mosque is the Hippodrome, where chariot races were once held. It was also the scene of a series of riots during Justinian's rule. While construction started in AD 203, the Hippodrome was later added to and enlarged by Constantine.

The **Obelisk of Theodosius** (Map p464) is an Egyptian column from the temple of Karnak. It features 3500-year-old hieroglyphics and rests on a Byzantine base. South of the obelisk are the remains of a **spiral column** (Map p464) of intertwined snakes. Erected at Delphi by the Greeks to celebrate their victory over the Persians, it was later transported to the Hippodrome, where the snakes' heads were stolen during the Fourth Crusade.

Museum of Turkish & Islamic Arts MUSEUM

(Türk ve İslam Eserleri Müzesi; Map p464; Atmeydanı 46, Sultanahmet; admission TL10; ⏲9am-4.30pm Tue-Sun) On the Hippodrome's western side, this museum is housed in the former palace of İbrahim Paşa, son-in-law of Süleyman the Magnificent. The building is one of the finest surviving examples of 16th-century Ottoman secular architecture. Inside, you'll be wowed by one of the world's best collections of antique carpets and some equally impressive manuscripts and miniatures.

Basilica Cistern HISTORIC BUILDING

(Yerebatan Sarnıçı; Map p464; Yerebatan Caddesi 13, Sultanahmet; admission TL10; ⏲9am-6.30pm Apr-Sep, to 5.30pm Oct-Mar) Across the tram lines from Aya Sofya is the entrance to the majestic Byzantine Basilica Cistern, built by Justinian in AD 532. This vast, atmospheric, column-filled cistern stored up to 80,000 cubic metres of water for regular summer use in the Great Palace, as well as for times of siege.

İstanbul Archaeology Museum MUSEUM

(Arkeoloji Müzeleri; Map p464; Osman Hamdi Bey Yokuşu, Gülhane; admission TL10; ⏲9am-6pm Tue-Sun May-Sep, to 4pm Oct-Apr) Downhill from the Topkapı Palace, this superb museum complex is a must-see for anyone interested in the Middle East's ancient past. The main building houses an outstanding collection of Greek and Roman statuary, including the magnificent sarcophagi from the royal necropolis at Sidon in Lebanon. A separate building on the same site, the **Museum of the Ancient Orient** (Map p464), houses

Hittite relics and other older archaeological finds.

Divan Yolu Caddesi LANDMARK

Walk or take a tram westward along Divan Yolu from Sultanahmet, looking out on your right for a complex of **sultan's tombs** (Map p468) that was constructed for 19th-century sultans, including Mahmut II (1808–39), Abdülaziz (1861–76) and Abdülhamid II (1876–1909).

A bit further along, on the right, you can't miss the **Çemberlitaş** (Map p468), also known as the Banded Stone or Burnt Column. Constantine the Great erected the monumental column in AD 330 to celebrate the dedication of Constantinople as capital of the Roman Empire.

Grand Bazaar BAZAAR

(Kapalı Çarşı; Map p468; ⏲8.30am-7pm Mon-Sat) Hone your haggling skills before dipping into the mind-boggling Grand Bazaar. Just north of Divan Yolu, this labyrinthine medieval shopping mall consists of some 4000 shops selling everything from carpets to clothing, including silverware, jewellery, antiques and belly-dancing costumes. It's probably the most confusing and manic shopping precinct you could hope to experience. Sure, the touts are ubiquitous, but come with the right frame of mind and you'll realise it's part of the fun. With several kilometres of lanes, it's also a great place to ramble and get lost – which you will certainly do at least once.

Starting from a small masonry *bedesten* (covered market) built during the time of Mehmet the Conqueror, the bazaar grew to cover a vast area as shopkeepers put up roofs and porches so that commerce could be conducted comfortably in all weathers.

Beyazıt NEIGHBOURHOOD

Right beside the Grand Bazaar, the Beyazıt area takes its name from the graceful **Beyazıt Camii** (Map p468), built between 1501 and 1506 on the orders of Sultan Beyazıt II. The **Sahaflar Çarşısı** (Old Book Bazaar; Map p468) is nearby and the great gateway on the north side of the square belongs to **İstanbul University** (Map p468).

Süleymaniye Camii MOSQUE

(Mosque of Sultan Süleyman the Magnificent; Map p468; Prof Sıddık Sami Onar Caddesi; donation requested) Behind the university, to the northwest, is one of the city's most prominent landmarks and İstanbul's grandest mosque complex, the Süleymaniye Camii. It was commissioned in the 16th century by the most powerful of Ottoman sultans, Süleyman the Magnificent, and was designed by Mimar Sinan, the most famous of all imperial architects.

EMINÖNÜ

Eminönü is the gateway to Old İstanbul at the southern end of the Galata Bridge that is invariably lined with fisherman. At sunset there are glorious views of the Galata Tower across the Golden Horn in Beyoğlu.

Yeni Cami MOSQUE

(New Mosque; Map p468; Yenicami Meydanı Sokak, Eminönü; donation requested) Looming large at the southern end of Galata Bridge, the building of Yeni Cami was started in 1597 and completed, six sultans later, in 1663.

Spice Bazaar BAZAAR

(Mısır Çarşısı; Map p468; ⏲8.30am-6.30pm Mon-Sat) Beside Yeni Cami is the atmospheric Spice Bazaar, awash with spice and food vendors; it's a great place for last-minute gift shopping.

Rüstem Paşa Camii MOSQUE

(Mosque of Rüstem Paşa; Map p468; Hasırcılar Caddesi; donation requested) To the west, on a platform above the fragrant market streets, is the 16th-century Rüstem Paşa Camii, a small, richly tiled mosque designed by the great Ottoman architect Sinan.

BEYOĞLU

Beyoğlu, on the northern side of the Golden Horn, was once the 'new', or 'European', city. Today trendy Beyoğlu continues that tradition of modernity as the business centre of İstanbul, as well as playing host to the city's best nightlife and dining. The Tünel funicular railway runs uphill from Karaköy to the southern end of Beyoğlu's pedestrianised main street, İstiklal Caddesi. A tram runs from there to Taksim Square, at the north end of the street, and the heart of 'modern' İstanbul; it's home to many luxury hotels and airline offices.

Galata Tower LANDMARK

(Galata Kulesi; Map p472; Galata Meydanı, Karaköy; admission TL11; ⏲9am-8pm) Cross the Galata Bridge and cut uphill from Karaköy towards the cylindrical Galata Tower. Its claims to be the oldest tower in the world are on slightly dodgy ground, though a wooden lighthouse built by Byzantine emperor Anastasius Oilozus did stand on this spot in AD 528. The

İstanbul

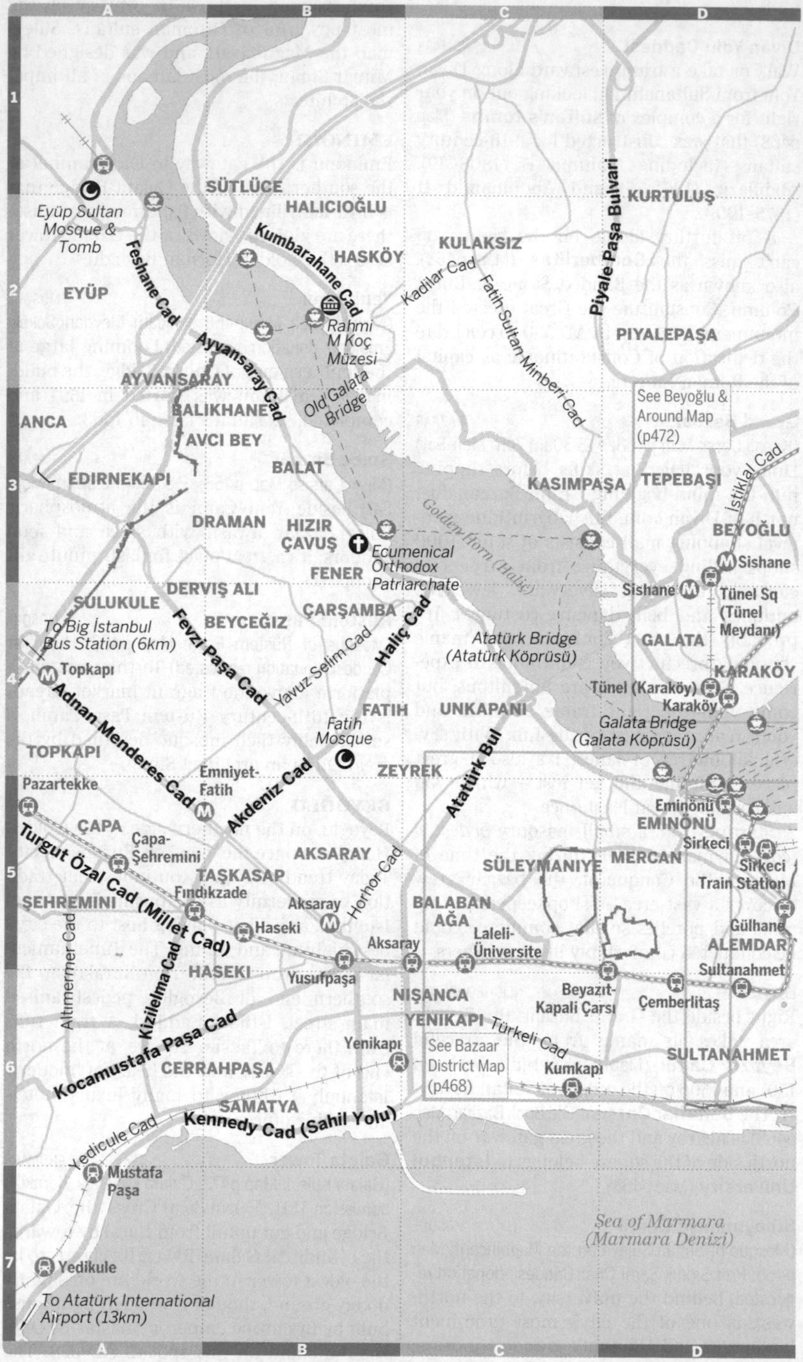
A
B
C
D
1
2
3
4
5
6
7
SÜTLÜCE
HALICIOĞLU
KURTULUŞ
Eyüp Sultan Mosque & Tomb
Kumbarahane Cad
HASKÖY
KULAKSIZ
Feshane Cad
Kadılar Cad
Fatih Sultan Minberi Cad
Piyale Paşa Bulvari
EYÜP
Rahmi M Koç Müzesi
PIYALEPAŞA
Ayvansaray Cad
AYVANSARAY
Old Galata Bridge
See Beyoğlu & Around Map (p472)
BALIKHANE
ANCA
AVCI BEY
EDIRNEKAPI
BALAT
KASIMPAŞA
TEPEBAŞI
İstiklal Cad
DRAMAN
HIZIR ÇAVUŞ
Golden Horn (Haliç)
BEYOĞLU
Ecumenical Orthodox Patriarchate
Sishane
FENER
DERVIŞ ALI
Sishane
Tünel Sq (Tünel Meydanı)
SULUKULE
ÇARŞAMBA
Haliç Cad
BEYCEĞIZ
To Big İstanbul Bus Station (6km)
Fevzi Paşa Cad
Yavuz Selim Cad
Atatürk Bridge (Atatürk Köprüsü)
GALATA
KARAKÖY
Topkapı
Tünel (Karaköy)
Karaköy
Adnan Menderes Cad
FATIH
UNKAPANI
Galata Bridge (Galata Köprüsü)
Fatih Mosque
TOPKAPI
ZEYREK
Akdeniz Cad
Atatürk Bul
Pazartekke
Emniyet-Fatih
Eminönü
EMINÖNÜ
ÇAPA
Çapa-Şehremini
AKSARAY
Horhor Cad
Sirkeci
Turgut Özal Cad (Millet Cad)
TAŞKASAP
SÜLEYMANIYE
MERCAN
Sirkeci Train Station
Fındıkzade
ŞEHREMINI
Aksaray
BALABAN AĞA
Gülhane
Haseki
ALEMDAR
Altımermer Cad
Aksaray
Laleli-Üniversite
Kızılelma Cad
HASEKI
Yusufpaşa
Sultanahmet
Beyazıt-Kapali Çarsı
Çemberlitaş
NIŞANCA
Kocamustafa Paşa Cad
YENIKAPI
Türkeli Cad
Yenikapı
See Bazaar District Map (p468)
SULTANAHMET
CERRAHPAŞA
Kumkapı
SAMATYA
Kennedy Cad (Sahil Yolu)
Yedicule Cad
Mustafa Paşa
Sea of Marmara (Marmara Denizi)
Yedikule
To Atatürk International Airport (13km)

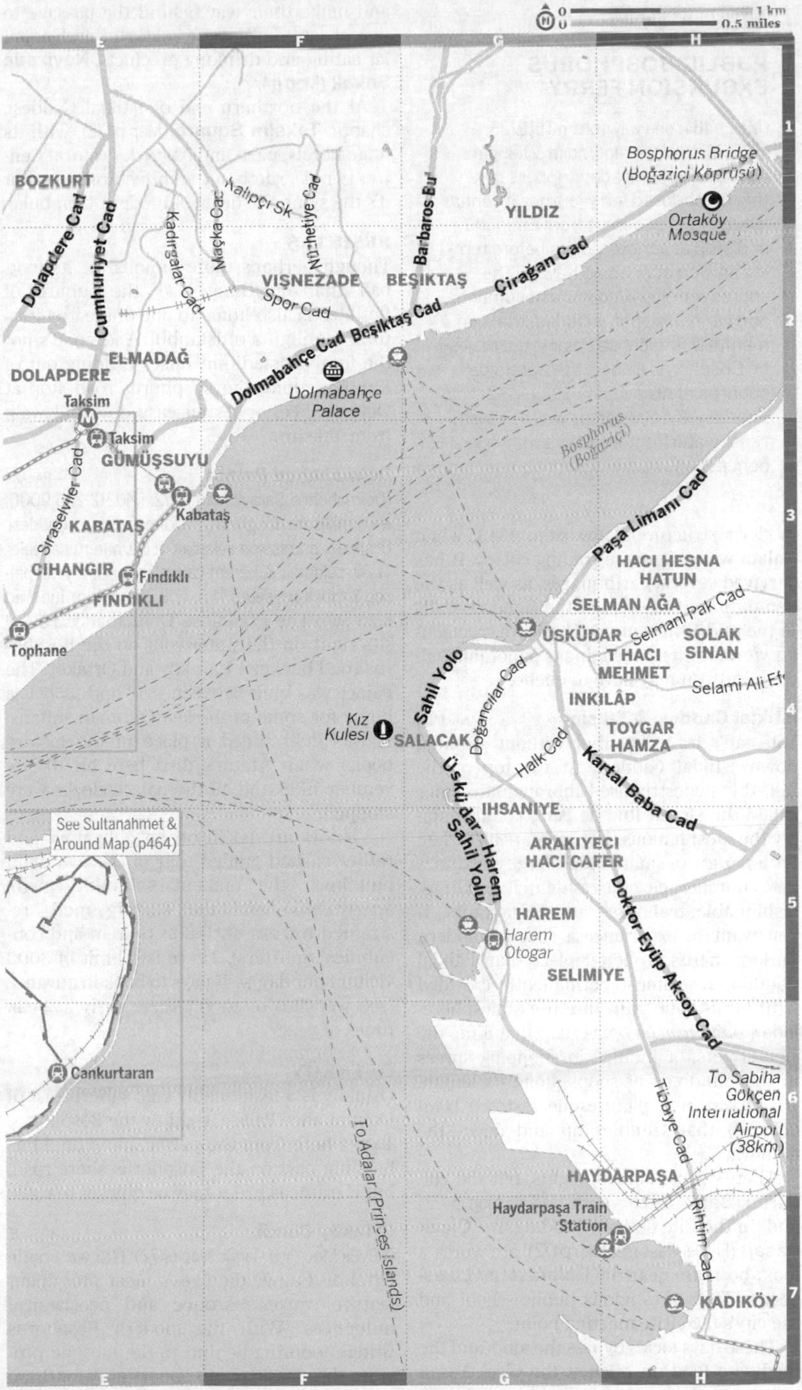
0 1 km
0 0.5 miles
E
F
G
H
1
2
3
4
5
6
7
BOZKURT
Dolapdere Cad
Cumhuriyet Cad
Kadirgalar Cad
Maçka Cad
Kalıpçı Sk
Nüzhetiye Cad
Barbaros Bul
YILDIZ
Bosphorus Bridge
(Boğaziçi Köprüsü)
Ortaköy Mosque
VIŞNEZADE
BEŞIKTAŞ
Spor Cad
Çırağan Cad
Beşiktaş Cad
Dolmabahçe Cad
ELMADAĞ
DOLAPDERE
Dolmabahçe Palace
Taksim
Taksim
GÜMÜŞSUYU
Bosphorus
(Boğaziçi)
Sıraselviler Cad
Kabataş
KABATAŞ
Paşa Limanı Cad
CIHANGIR
Fındıklı
FINDIKLI
HACI HESNA HATUN
SELMAN AĞA
Selmani Pak Cad
Tophane
ÜSKÜDAR
SOLAK SINAN
T HACI MEHMET
Selami Ali Efe
Sahil Yolo
Doğancılar Cad
INKILÂP
Kız Kulesi
SALACAK
TOYGAR HAMZA
Halk Cad
Kartal Baba Cad
Üsküdar - Harem Sahil Yolu
IHSANIYE
See Sultanahmet & Around Map (p464)
ARAKIYECI HACI CAFER
Doktor Eyüp Aksoy Cad
HAREM
Harem Otogar
SELIMIYE
Cankurtaran
To Sabiha Gökçen International Airport (38km)
Tibbye Cad
To Adalar (Princes Islands)
HAYDARPAŞA
Haydarpaşa Train Station
Rihtim Cad
KADIKÖY

DON'T MISS

PUBLIC BOSPHORUS EXCURSION FERRY

(Map p464; one way/return TL15/25; ⏲10.35am year-round, noon & 1.35pm mid-Apr–Oct) Most day trippers take this much-loved ferry journey its entire length. Ferries depart from Eminönü and stop at various points before turning around at Anadolu Kavağı. The shores are sprinkled with monuments and various sights, including the monumental Dolmabahçe Palace, the majestic Bosphorus Bridge, the waterside suburbs of Arnavutköy, Bebek, Kanlıca, Emirgan and Sarıyer, as well as lavish *yalı*s (waterfront wooden summer residences) and numerous mosques.

modern structure dates from 1348, when Galata was a Genoese trading colony. It has survived several earthquakes, as well as the demolition of the rest of the Genoese walls in the mid-19th century. There are spectacular views from its vertiginous panorama balcony, but you may have to queue.

İstiklal Caddesi & Taksim LANDMARK

You can't leave İstanbul without strolling down İstiklal Caddesi. At the top of the hill, this pedestrianised thoroughfare, once called the Grand Rue de Péra, is indisputably the most famous thoroughfare in Turkey. It's a parade of smart shops, large embassies and churches, elegant residential buildings, fashionable teahouses and restaurants. If you want to experience a slice of modern Turkey, there's no better place than İstiklal Caddesi. It's almost permanently crowded with locals, who patronise the atmosphere-laden *meyhaneler* (taverns) that line the side streets, or indulge in shopping sprees in the hundreds of shops along its length. It's served by a picturesque restored tram (TL1.50) that trundles up and down the boulevard.

There's a plethora of sights, but the colourful **Balık Pazar** (Fish Market; Map p472) and, in the Cité de Pera building, the **Çiçek Pasajı** (Flower Passage; Map p472), are worth a look; both are near the **Galatasaray Lisesi** (Map p472), a prestigious public school and the city's favourite meeting point.

These days locals bypass the touts and the mediocre food on offer at the Çiçek Pasajı and make their way behind the passage to one of İstanbul's most colourful and popular eating and drinking precincts, **Nevizade Sokak** (Map p472).

At the northern end of İstiklal Caddesi, chaotic **Taksim Square** (Map p472), with its huge hotels, park and Atatürk Cultural Centre, is not exactly an architectural gem but it's the symbolic heart of modern İstanbul.

BEŞIKTAŞ

Though perhaps more famous for its football than anything else, the suburb of Beşiktaş is also home to one of the architectural highlights of İstanbul. And no, it's not the football stadium! Buses heading out of Karaköy along the Bosphorus road stop at Dolmabahçe, or it's an easy downhill walk from Taksim.

Dolmabahçe Palace PALACE

(Dolmabahçe Sarayı; Map p472; ☎0212-236 9000; www.millisaraylar.gov.tr; Dolmabahçe Caddesi, Beşiktaş; admission selamlık TL30, harem-cariyeler TL20, selamlık & harem-cariyeler TL40, crystal palace & clock museum TL6; ⏲8.30am-4pm Tue-Wed & Fri-Sun) The grandiose Dolmabahçe Palace sits right on the waterfront on the Bosphorus road between Karaköy and Ortaköy. The palace was built between 1843 and 1856 as a home for some of the last Ottoman sultans. It was guaranteed a place in the history books when Atatürk died here on 10 November 1938 and all the palace clocks were stopped.

Visitors are taken on an obligatory and rather rushed guided tour of the two main buildings: the opulent **selamlık** (men's apartments) and the slightly more restrained **harem-cariyeler** (harem and concubines' quarters). There is a limit of 3000 visitors per day, so it pays to book in advance (see website) or to get there early at peak times of year.

ORTAKÖY

Ortaköy is a fashionably chic suburb east of Dolmabahçe Palace, right by the Bosphorus. To get here from the palace, jump on a bus heading east on the Bosphorus shore road, but if traffic is bad it may be quicker to walk.

Ortaköy Camii MOSQUE

(Büyük Mecidiye Camii; Map p472) The waterside Ortaköy Camii, the area's most prominent feature, mixes baroque and neoclassical influences. With the modern Bosphorus Bridge looming behind it, the mosque provides the classic photo opportunity for those wanting to illustrate İstanbul's 'old meets new' character, though it was undergoing refurbishments at the time of research.

Try to time your visit for Sunday, when a bustling street market fills the area's cobbled lanes.

PRINCES' ISLANDS (ADALAR)

With good beaches, open woodland, a couple of monasteries, Victorian villas and transport by horse-drawn carriages, this string of nine spotless islands, especially **Büyükada** (Map p460), which is the biggest, make an ideal escape from the noise and hustle of İstanbul. Ferries (TL3) to the islands leave from the Adalar İskelesi dock at Kabataş opposite the tram stop. Try to go midweek to avoid the crowds.

Activities

Ağa Hamamı BATHHOUSE

(Map p472; ☎0212-249 5027; Turnacibaşı Sokak 48; bath services TL40-70; ⏲24hrs) No frills, traditional hamam near Taksim. It's considerably cheaper and less impressive to look at than the options below, but it's the authentic experience and popular with budget travellers. Note that men and women share the same bath.

Cağaloğlu Hamamı BATHHOUSE

(Map p464; ☎0212-522 2424; www.cagaloglu hamami.com.tr; Yerebatan Caddesi 34; bath services TL78-98; ⏲8am-10pm men, 8am-8pm women) The city's most beautiful hamam. It's pricey and pretty touristy, but the surroundings are simply exquisite. Separate baths each have a large *camekan* (reception area) with private, lockable cubicles.

Çemberlitaş Hamamı BATHHOUSE

(Map p468; ☎0212-522 7974; www.cemberlita shamami.com; Vezir Hanı Caddesi 8, Çemberlitaş; bath services TL69-117; ⏲6am-midnight) The building was designed by the great Ottoman architect Mimar Sinan in 1584, and it is one of İstanbul's most atmospheric hamams.

Hodja Pasha Cultural Centre TRADITIONAL DANCE

(Map p464; ☎0212-511 4626; www.hodjapasha.com; Ankara Caddesi 3B; dance night TL60; ⏲8pm-10pm Tue & Thu, 9pm-11pm Sat, museum noon-6pm daily) Located in a converted bathhouse dating from the 1470s, this cultural centre is an increasingly popular stop on the tourist trail not only for its small dance museum but also for its Turkish Dance Night featuring traditional dances from across the country. It's a great opportunity to see the whirling dervishes in action if you won't be visiting Konya.

Tours

İstanbul's CouchSurfing community (www.couchsurfing.org) is extraordinarily active and organises a varied range of events on an almost daily basis. Everybody is welcome, but you are expected to cover your own costs.

City Sightseeing İstanbul BUS TOUR

(Maps p464, p472; ☎0212-234 7777; www.plantours.com; one-day ticket adult/student/child €20/15/free) Convenient 'hop-on hop-off' bus tour of the city visiting all the major attractions with offices on Taksim Square and in front of Aya Sofya.

İstanbul Walks WALKING TOUR

(Map p464; ☎0212-516 6300; www.istanbulwalks.net; Küçük Ayasofya Mah. Sifahamami Sokak No 1, Sultanahment; walks €25-60) City walks with professional English-speaking guides.

Festivals & Events

İstanbul International Music Festival MUSIC

(www.iksv.org/muzik) From early June to early July, this festival attracts big-name artists from around the world who perform in venues that are not always open to the public (such as Aya İrini Kilisesi).

Sleeping

İstanbul's accommodation is becoming quite pricey, but discounts are sometimes offered for cash payment. The most convenient place to stay for visiting the attractions is Cankurtaran, where a variety of options for all budgets is crammed into a small area. Night owls and foodies will probably prefer to stay in the area around Taksim Square, which is better located for the city's best restaurants and nightlife. Unless otherwise stated, rates include breakfast and private bathrooms; the exception is hostel dorms, which have shared bathrooms.

SULTANAHMET & AROUND

TOP CHOICE **Neorion Hotel** BOUTIQUE HOTEL $$$

(Map p464; ☎0212-527 9090, www.neorionhotel.com; Orhaniye Caddesi 14, Sirkeci; s/d €145/180; ❄@☒) Luxury and attention to detail are what make the Neorion one of the city's best choices for couples, families or business travellers. The hotel takes the standard

Sultanahmet & Around

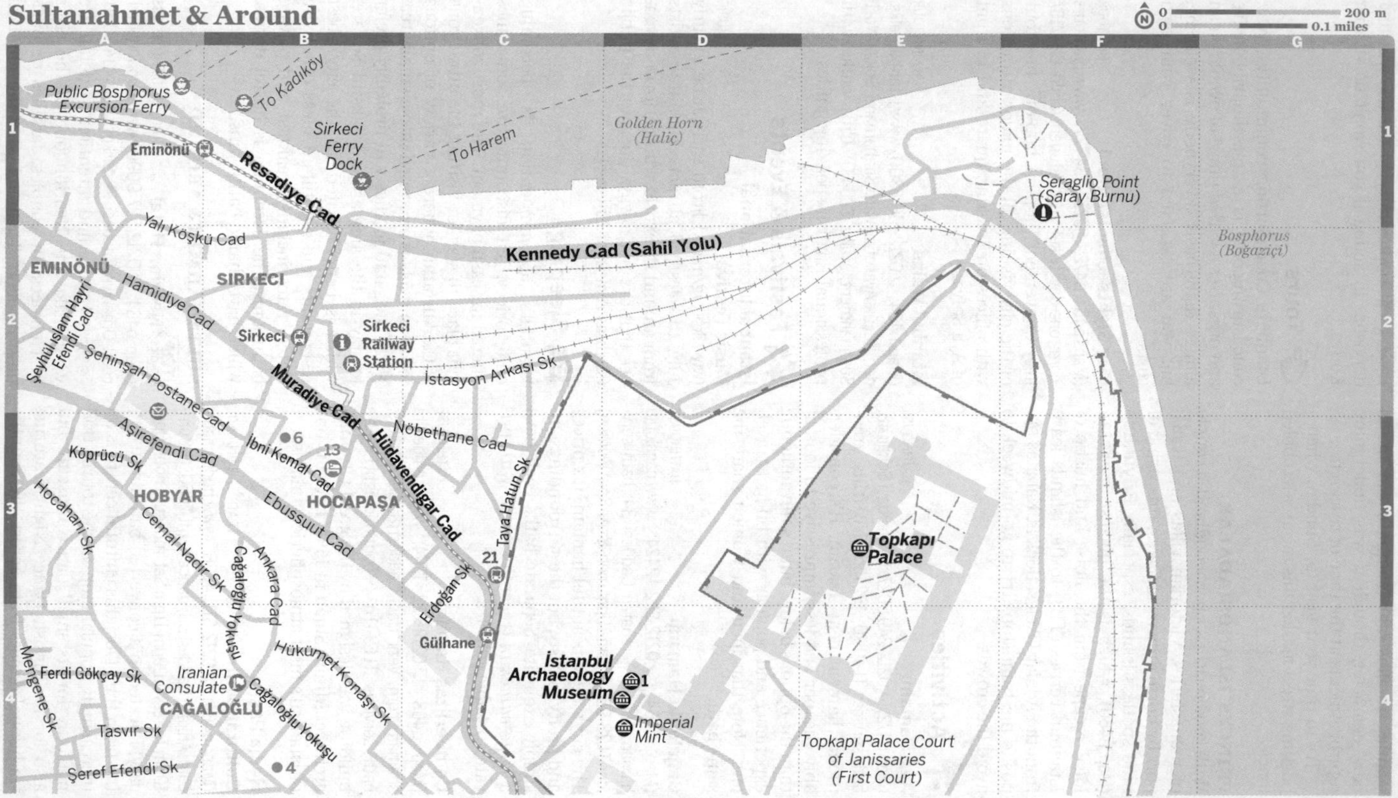

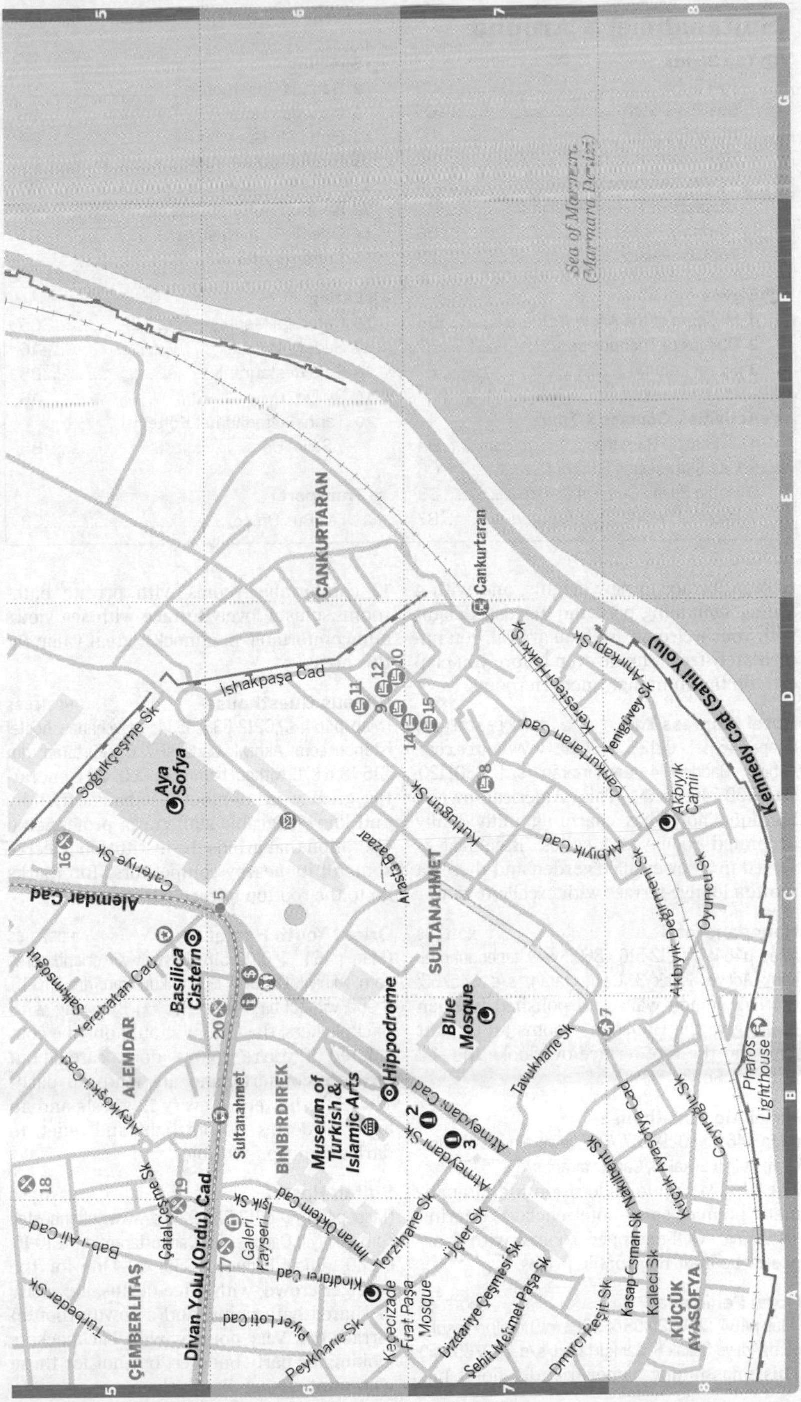
Sea of Marmara
(Marmara Denizi)
CANKURTARAN
Cankurtaran
İshakpaşa Cad
Soğukçeşme Sk
Aya Sofya
Alemdar Cad
Caferiye Sk
Basilica Cistern
Yerebatan Cad
Salkımsöğüt
ALEMDAR
Alayköşkü Cad
Sultanahmet
BINBIRDIREK
Museum of Turkish & Islamic Arts
Hippodrome
Blue Mosque
SULTANAHMET
Arasta Bazaar
Kutlugün Sk
Tavukhane Sk
Kerestecі Hakkı Sk
Cankurtaran Cad
Akbıyık Cad
Akbıyık Camii
Akbıyık Değirmeni Sk
Oyuncu Sk
Yeni̇güvey Sk
Ahırkapı Sk
Kennedy Cad (Sahil Yolu)
Pharos Lighthouse
Cayıroğlu Sk
Küçük Ayasofya Cad
Nakilbent Sk
Atmeydanı Cad
Atmeydanı Sk
Terzihane Sk
İmran Öktem Cad
Işık Sk
Galeri Kayseri
Çatalçeşme Sk
Divan Yolu (Ordu) Cad
ÇEMBERLITAŞ
Bab-ı Ali Cad
Türbedar Sk
Piyer Loti Cad
Peykhane Sk
Klodfarer Cad
Kaçecizade Fuat Paşa Mosque
Üçler Sk
Dizdariye Çeşmesi Sk
Şehit Mehmet Paşa Sk
Dmirci Reşit Sk
Kasap Osman Sk
Kaleci Sk
KÜÇÜK AYASOFYA
A
B
C
D
E
F
G
5
6
7
8
1
2
3
5
7
8
9
10
11
12
14
15
16
17
18
19
20

Sultanahmet & Around

rooftop terrace to new heights, and with a sauna, swimming pool and Turkish delight with your welcome drink on arrival, you immediately feel at home even before you clap eyes on the stunningly modern rooms.

Hotel Empress Zoe BOUTIQUE HOTEL **$$$**
(Map p464; ☎0212-518 2504; www.emzoe.com; Akbıyık Caddesi 4, Cankurtaran; s/d €80/120, ste €160-240; ❄@) This American-owned boutique hotel has charming individually decorated rooms and suites. Breakfast is served in a flower-filled garden and there's a rooftop lounge-terrace with excellent views.

Hanedan Hotel HOTEL **$$**
(Map p464; ☎0212-516 4869; www.hanedanhotel.com; Adliye Sokak 3, Cankurtaran; s/d €45/65; ❄) Pale lemon walls and polished wooden floors give the Hanedan's rooms an elegant feel, and the roof terrace overlooks the sea and Aya Sofya.

Hotel Alp Guesthouse HOTEL **$$**
(Map p464; ☎0212-517 7067; www.alpguesthouse.com; Adliye Sokak 4, Cankurtaran; s/d €75/70; ❄) The Alp lives up to its location in Sultanahmet's premier small-hotel enclave, offering attractive, well-equipped rooms, with four-poster beds, at reasonable prices.

Hotel Peninsula HOTEL **$$**
(Map p464; ☎0212-458 6850; www.hotelpeninsula.com; Adliye Sokak 6, Cankurtaran; s/d €50/65; ❄) This unassuming, super-friendly hotel has 12 comfortable rooms with private bathrooms, plus a lovely terrace with sea views and comfortable hammocks; great value for this area.

Bahaus Guesthouse HOSTEL **$$**
(Map p464; ☎0212-638 6534; www.bahaushostelistanbul.com; Akbıyık Caddesi 7, Cankurtaran; dm €15-18, d €70, without bathroom €60; @) Generating great word-of-mouth, Bahaus's friendly and knowledgeable staff run a professional operation that avoids the institutional feel of some of its nearby competitors. Top marks go to the rooftop terrace bar.

Orient Youth Hostel HOSTEL **$$**
(Map p464; ☎0212-518 0789; www.orienthostel.com; Akbıyık Caddesi 13, Cankurtaran; dm €10-15, d €50, without bathroom €40; @) Bursting with backpackers, the Orient should only be considered if you're young, don't care about creature comforts, and are ready to party. There's a shower for every 12 guests and an array of dorms – from light and quiet, to dark and uncomfortable.

Sultan Hostel HOSTEL **$$**
(Map p464; ☎0212-516 9260; www.sultanhostel.com; Akbıyık Caddesi 21, Cankurtaran; dm €10-16, d €60, without bathroom €50; @) One for the younger crowd, with huge dorms, a paucity of shared bathrooms, and a rowdy rooftop terrace bar. Very popular with backpackers looking for party buddies, but not for those who want a quiet night's sleep.

BEYOĞLU & AROUND

TOP CHOICE 5 Oda BOUTIQUE HOTEL $$$
(Map p472; ☎0212-252 7501; www.5oda.com; Şahkulu Bostan Sokak 16, Beyoğlu; d €145; ❄@) The name means 'five rooms' and that is exactly what is on offer at this stylish little hotel. You get everything here from a kitchenette to a DVD player, and even a king-sized bed with hypoallergenic covers!

World House Hostel HOSTEL $$
(Map p472; ☎0212-293 5520; www.worldhouseistanbul.com; Galipdede Caddesi 85, Beyoğlu; dm €12-17, d €50; @) A well-established and perennial favourite close to the Galata Tower, this place has everything that you would expect from a professionally run hostel with four-, six-, eight- and 14 bed dorms. The only drawback is the hill!

Taksim Sofa HOSTEL $$
(Map p472; ☎0212-245 1053; www.taksimsofahostel.com; Kuloğlu Sokak 5, Beyoğlu; dm TL21-30, d without bathroom TL75) One of the few hostels in the vicinity of Taksim Square, this and its sister hostel Taksim Lounge (below) boast great locations and price for budget travelers who value their nocturnal experiences as highly as their diurnal ones.

Taksim Lounge HOSTEL $$
(Map p472; ☎0212-252 7759; Billurcu, Beyoğlu; dm TL30, d without bathroom TL90) A new hostel hidden away on a side street a few blocks from Taksim Square, it is surprisingly quiet despite being just a short stagger from the city's main nightlife. Still a bit rough around the edges, but the dorms are not overloaded with beds and it has plenty of potential.

Eating

Teeming with affordable fast-food joints, cafes and restaurants, İstanbul is a food-lover's paradise. Sultanahmet has the least impressive range of eating options in the city, so if food is your passion cross the Galata Bridge and join the locals in Beyoğlu, or check out the possibilities online at İstanbul Eats (http://istanbuleats.com).

SULTANAHMET & AROUND

Nominating Sultanahmet's best döner kebap is a hard ask, but many locals are keen on the döner at **Sedef** (Map p464; Divan Yolu 21; TL6-11), which is only open during the day.

Caferağa Medresesi TURKISH $
(Map p464; Caferiye Sokak; soup TL5, köfte TL10; ⌚8.30am-6pm) This teensy lokanta in the gorgeous courtyard of a Sinan-designed medrese near Topkapı Palace is a rare treat in Sultanahmet, allowing you to nosh in stylish surrounds without paying through the nose.

Tarihi Sultanahmet Köftecisi Selim Usta TURKISH $$
(Map p464; www.sultanahmetkoftesi.com, in Turkish, Divan Yolu Caddesi 12; TL11-15; ⌚11am-11pm) Beware the other *köfte* places along this strip purporting to be the *meşhur* (famous) *köfte* restaurant – Number 12 is the real McCoy.

Sir Evi INTERNATIONAL $$$
(Map p464; www.sirevirestaurant.com, in Turkish; Hoca Rüstem Sokak 9; mains TL18-29; ⌚10.30am-2.30am) Meals score for their size and price rather than their quality, but the biggest draw is the entertainment. Waiters serenade guests with everything from disco anthems to Arabesk numbers, and everyone joins in.

Sefa Restaurant TURKISH $$
(Map p464; Nuruosmaniye Caddesi 17, Cağaloğlu; mains TL8-16; ⌚7am-5pm) Locals rate this place, which is on the way to the Grand Bazaar. You can order from an English-language menu or choose from the bain-marie. Try to arrive early-ish for lunch; many dishes run out by 1.30pm.

BEYOĞLU & AROUND

Head here for the city's best and cheapest eats.

TOP CHOICE Sofyalı 9 TURKISH $$
(Map p472; ☎0212-245 0362; Sofyalı Sokak 9, Tünel; meze TL4-10, mains TL13-25; ⌚11am-1am Mon-Sat) Tables at this gem are hot property at weekends. It serves some of the city's best *meyhane* (tavern) food – notably the *Arnavut ciğeri* (Albanian fried liver), fried fish and meze – in surroundings as welcoming as they are attractive.

Gani Gani Naum Paşa TURKISH $$
(Map p472; www.naumpasakonagi.com; Taksim Kuyu Sokak 11; pides TL7-9.50, kebaps TL12-15; ⌚10am-11pm) Kebap in a cave? It's a possibility at this quirky place where every dining room has a different theme. Young Turkish couples love lolling on the traditional Anatolian seating at this cheap and friendly eatery.

Zencefil VEGETARIAN $$
(Map p472; Kurabiye Sokak 8; mains TL7-15; ⌚11am-11pm Tue-Sun; ✎) Comfortable and quietly stylish, this popular vegetarian cafe offers

Bazaar District

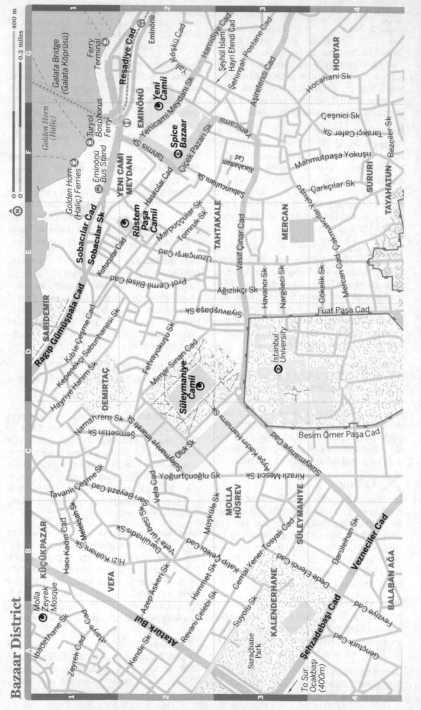

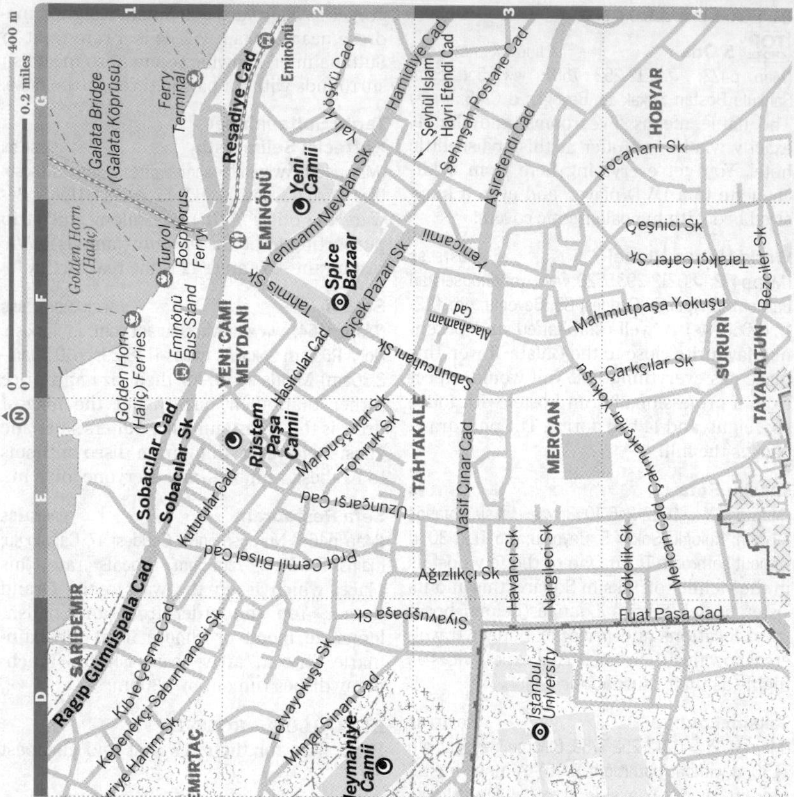

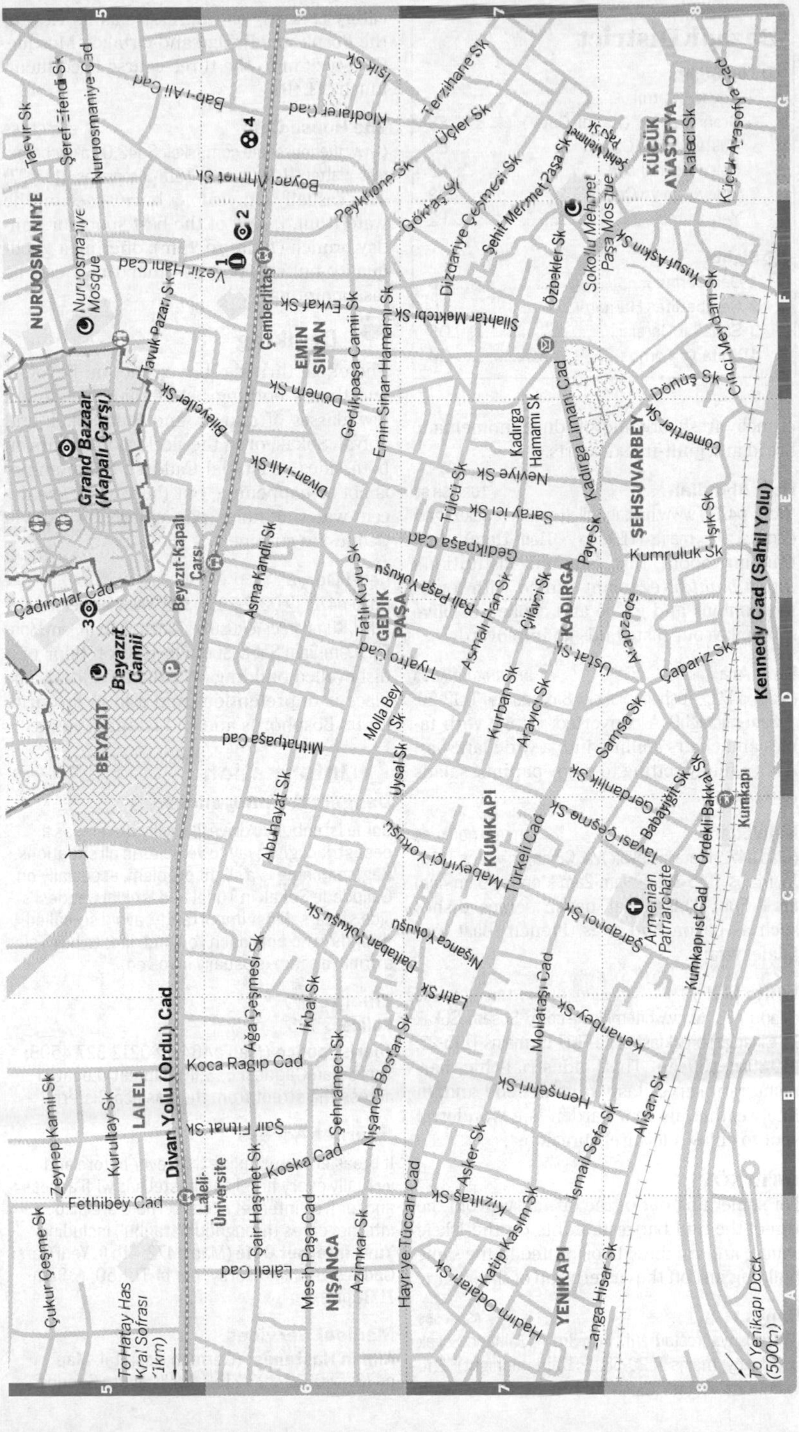

NURUOSMANIYE
Nuruosmaniye Mosque
Grand Bazaar (Kapalı Çarşı)
BEYAZIT
Beyazıt Camii
Beyazıt-Kapalı Çarşı
Çemberlitaş
EMIN SINAN
GEDIK PAŞA
KADIRGA
KUMKAPI
ŞEHSUVARBEY
KÜÇÜK AYASOFYA
Sokollu Mehmet Paşa Mosque
Armenian Patriarchate
LALELI
Laleli-Üniversite
NIŞANCA
YENIKAPI
Kumkapı
Kennedy Cad (Sahil Yolu)
Divan Yolu (Ordu) Cad
To Hatay Has Kral Sofrası (1km)
To Yenikapı Dock (500m)
Tasvir Sk
Şeref Efendi Sk
Nuruosmaniye Cad
Bab-ı Ali Cad
Işık Sk
Klodfarer Cad
Boyacı Ahmet Sk
Vezir Hanı Cad
Tavuk Pazarı Sk
Bileyciler Sk
Çadırcılar Cad
Terzihane Sk
Üçler Sk
Peykhane Sk
Gökdaş Sk
Dizdariye Çeşmesi Sk
Şehit Mehmet Paşa Sk
Şehit Mehmet Paşa Yokuşu
Özbekler Sk
Yusuf Aşkın Sk
Kaleci Sk
Küçük Ayasofya Cad
Cinci Meydanı Sk
Dönüş Sk
Comerler Sk
Evkaf Sk
Gedikpaşa Camii Sk
Emin Sinan Hamamı Sk
Silahtar Mektebi Sk
Dönem Sk
Divan-ı Ali Sk
Tülcü Sk
Neviye Sk
Kadırga Hamamı Sk
Kadırga Limanı Cad
Saray İçi Sk
Gedikpaşa Cad
Paye Sk
Kumruluk Sk
Işık Sk
Asma Kandil Sk
Tatlı Kuyu Sk
Ali Paşa Yokuşu
Asmalı Han Sk
Çilavcı Sk
Üstat Sk
Arapzade
Çapariz Sk
Tiyatro Cad
Molla Bey Sk
Kurban Sk
Arayıcı Sk
Samsa Sk
Mithatpaşa Cad
Uysal Sk
Gerdanlık Sk
Babayiğit Sk
Ördekli Bakkal Sk
Abuhayat Sk
Mabeyinci Yokuşu
Türkeli Cad
Tavaşi Çeşme Sk
Kumkapı İst Cad
Daltaban Yokuşu Sk
Nişanca Yokuşu
Şarapnel Sk
Ağa Çeşmesi Sk
İkbal Sk
Latif Sk
Mollataşı Cad
Kenanbey Sk
Koca Ragıp Cad
Şehnameci Sk
Nişanca Bostan Sk
Hemşehri Sk
Alişan Sk
Zeynep Kamil Sk
Kurultay Sk
Şair Fitnat Sk
Şair Haşmet Sk
Koska Cad
Asker Sk
İsmail Sefa Sk
Fethibey Cad
Çukur Çeşme Sk
Mesih Paşa Cad
Azimkar Sk
Hayriye Tüccarı Cad
Kızıltaş Sk
Katip Kasım Sk
Langa Hisar Sk
Hadım Odaları Sk
Laleli Cad

Bazaar District

Top Sights

Sights

crunchy-fresh organic produce, homemade bread and guilt-free desserts.

Hacı Abdullah TURKISH $$
(Map p472; www.haciabdullah.com.tr; Sakızağacı Caddesi 9a; mains TL9-18; ⏲11am-11pm) Just thinking about this İstanbul institution's *imam bayıldı* (eggplant stuffed with tomatoes, onions and garlic and cooked in olive oil) makes our taste buds go into overdrive.

Kafe Ara INTERNATIONAL $$
(Map p472; Tosbağ Sokak 8a; mains TL13-26; ⏲8am-midnight) A converted garage with tables and chairs spilling into a wide laneway, Ara's a funky setting to enjoy paninis, salads and pastas.

Kahvedan INTERNATIONAL $$
(Map p472; Matara Sokak 1/A, Cihangir; wraps TL10-15, mains TL15-30; ⏲9am-2am Mon-Fri, 9am-4am Sat & Sun) This expat haven serves dishes such as bacon and eggs, French toast and falafel wraps.

White Mill INTERNATIONAL $$
(Map p472; www.whitemillcafe.com; Susam Sokak 13, Cihangir; breakfast plate TL17-19, mains TL15-23; ⏲9.30am-1.30am) This industrial-chic bar-restaurant serves tasty organic food and, in fine weather, its rear garden is a wonderful spot to enjoy a leisurely breakfast.

ORTAKÖY

For something out of the ordinary, avoid the run-of-the-mill bar-restaurants on the İskele square and try these two, located in the same building just off the eastern end of the square.

Banyan ASIAN $$$
(www.banyanrestaurant.com; 3rd fl, Salhane Sokak 3, Ortaköy; mains TL29-58; ⏲11am-midnight) The excellent Asian food served at this stylish eatery is nearly as impressive as its view of the Bosphorus Bridge and Ortaköy Mosque. Get stuck in to the three-course fixed menu lunch (TL40).

The House Café BUFFET $$$
(www.thehousecafe.com; İskele Sq 42, Ortaköy; breakfast platter TL28, mains TL18-39, pizzas TL18-27) This casually chic cafe, a huge space on the waterfront, is one of the best spots for Sunday brunch (10am to 2pm), offering a good-quality buffet. Food at other times can be disappointing.

Drinking

There's a thriving bar scene in Beyoğlu, and there's nothing better than swigging a few glasses of rakı around Balo Sokak and Sofyalı Sokak, or in the sleek rooftop bars on both sides of İstiklal Caddesi. Sultanahmet is not as happening, but there are a few decent watering holes, particularly on Akbıyık Caddesi in summer.

Leb-i Derya BAR
(Map p472; ☎0212-293 4389; www.lebiderya.com; 6th fl, Kumbaracı Yokuşu 57, Tünel; ⏲4pm-3am Mon-Fri, 10am-3am Sat & Sun) On the top floor of a dishevelled building off İstiklal Caddesi, this place is unpretentious and a local favourite for its Bosphorus and Old İstanbul views.

Information

Dangers & Annoyances

Some İstanbullus drive like rally drivers; as a pedestrian, give way to vehicles in all situations. Bag-snatching is a slight problem, especially on Galipdede Sokak in Tünel and İstiklal Caddesi's side streets. Most importantly, avoid so-called 'friends' who approach you and offer to buy you a drink; a scam is usually involved.

Emergency

Police ☎155

Tourist police (Map p464; ☎0212-527 4503; Yerebatan Caddesi 6, Sultanahmet) Located across the street from the Basilica Cistern.

Internet Access

It is easier to get online than ever before and virtually every hotel and hostel has wi-fi access and/or free internet access. There are also internet cafes throughout İstanbul, including **Yuva Internet Café** (Map p472; 4th fl, Yeni Çarşı Caddesi 8, Galatasaray; per hr TL1.50; ⏲9am-11.30pm).

Medical Services

Alman Hastanesi (German Hospital; Map p472; ☎0212-293 2150; Sıraselviler Caddesi

119, Taksim; ⌚8.30am-6pm Mon-Fri, 8.30am-5pm Sat)

Amerikan Hastanesi (American Hospital; Off Map p472; ☎0212-444 3777; Güzelbahçe Sokak 20, Nişantaşı; ⌚24hr emergency department)

Money

Banks with ATMs are widespread, including in Sultanahmet's Aya Sofya Meydanı (Map p464) and all along İstiklal Caddesi in Beyoğlu. The exchange rates offered at the airport are usually as good as those offered in town, but count your money carefully.

Post

İstanbul's central post office (Map p464) is a few blocks southwest of Sirkeci Railway Station and in Sultanahmet there's a handy PTT (post office) booth on Aya Sofya Meydanı (Map p464).

Tourist Information

There are some great websites providing online tourist information for the ever-increasing hordes of visitors to the city, such as www.istanbulcityguide.com and www.greatistanbul.com. For a calendar of events see www.theguideistanbul.com.

Atatürk International Airport (IST; Atatürk Hava Limanı; ☎0212-663 0793; www.ataturkairport.com; ⌚24hr) Office in international arrivals area, though often closed out of season.

Sultanahmet (Map p464; ☎0212-518 1802; ⌚9am-5.30pm) At the northeast end of the Hippodrome.

Taksim Sq (Off Map p472; ☎0212-245 6876; ⌚9am-5.30pm Mon-Sun)

Getting There & Away

Air

İstanbul's **Atatürk International Airport** (IST; Atatürk Hava Limanı; ☎0212-463 3000; www.ataturkairport.com) is 23km west of Sultanahmet. **Sabiha Gökçen International Airport** (☎0216-585 5000; www.sgairport.com), some 50km east of Sultanahmet, on the Asian side of the city, is increasingly popular for cheap flights from Europe.

Many foreign airlines have their offices north of Taksim, along Cumhuriyet Caddesi in Elmadağ. Travel agencies can also sell tickets and make reservations; though in most cases it is just as easy to buy online via the airline websites. For more details regarding flying to and from Turkey see p542; for details on flying around the country see p543.

Boat

Yenikapı (Map p468), south of Aksaray Sq, is the dock for fast ferries across the Sea of Marmara to Yalova, Bursa and Bandırma (from where you can catch a train to İzmir). These carry both passengers and cars.

Bus

The huge **International İstanbul Bus Station** (İstanbul Otogarı; ☎0212-658 0505; www.otogaristanbul.com, in Turkish) is the city's main otogar (bus station) for intercity and international routes. It's in Esenler, about 10km northwest of Sultanahmet. Buses leave from here for virtually everywhere in Turkey, as well as for international destinations including Azerbaijan, Armenia, Bulgaria, Georgia, Greece, Iran, Romania and Syria.

The Light Rail Transit (LRT) service stops here en route to/from the airport. If you're coming from Taksim Square, bus No 830 (TL1.50, one hour) leaves about every 20 minutes from around 6.30am to 8.40pm. A taxi from Sultanahmet to the otogar costs around TL30 (20 minutes); from Taksim Square (TL40, 30 minutes). Many bus companies offer a free *servis* (shuttle bus) to or from the otogar.

If you're heading east to Anatolia, you might want to board at the smaller **Harem Bus Station** (☎216-333 3763), north of Haydarpaşa Railway Station on the Asian shore, but the choice of service there is more limited. When arriving in İstanbul by bus from anywhere in Anatolia it's considerably quicker to get out at Harem and take the car ferry to Sirkeci/Eminönü (TL1.50, 20 minutes, every 30 minutes 7am to 9.30pm), than stay on the bus until you reach the international station.

Car & Motorcyle

It makes no sense to drive around İstanbul itself and have to deal with the traffic and parking problems. However, if you're heading out of the city, all the main car-hire agencies have desks at Atatürk International Airport, and some at Sabiha Gökçen International Airport.

Train

For services to Edirne and Europe go to **Sirkeci Railway Station** (Map p464; ☎0212-520 6575) on the Golden Horn. Daily international services from Sirkeci include the Bosfor/Balakan Ekspresi, stopping in Sofia, Bulgaria (from TL45, 12½ hours), Bucharest, Romania (from TL84, 19 hours) and Belgrade, Serbia (from TL112, 19½ hours). The Dostluk/Filia Ekspresi to Thessaloniki, Greece, had been cancelled at the time of research. European trains will terminate at Yenikapı after the completion of Marmaray, an ambitious public transport project aimed at relieving İstanbul's woeful traffic congestion, due for completion in late 2013.

Trains from Anatolia and from countries to the east and south terminate at **Haydarpaşa Railway Station** (☎0216-336 4470), on the Asian

Beyoğlu & Around

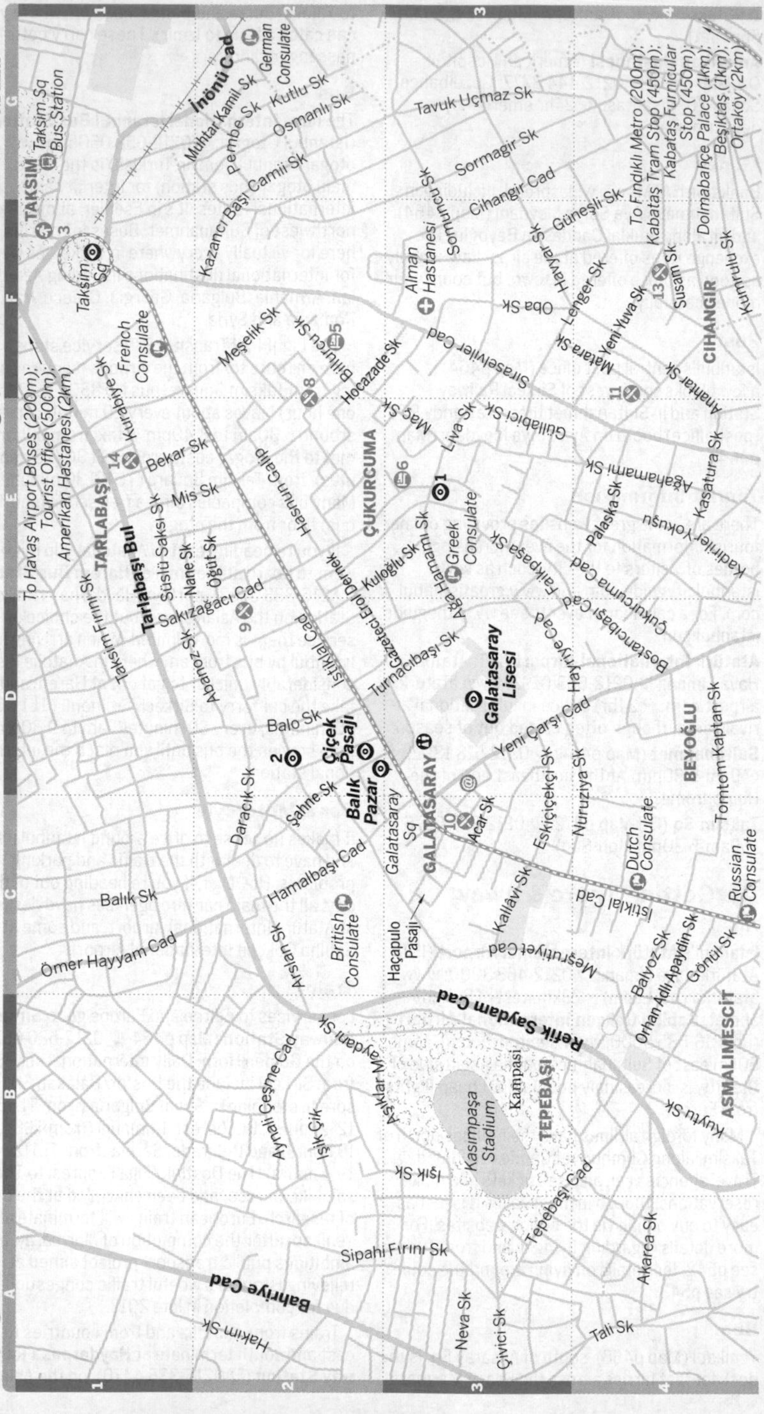

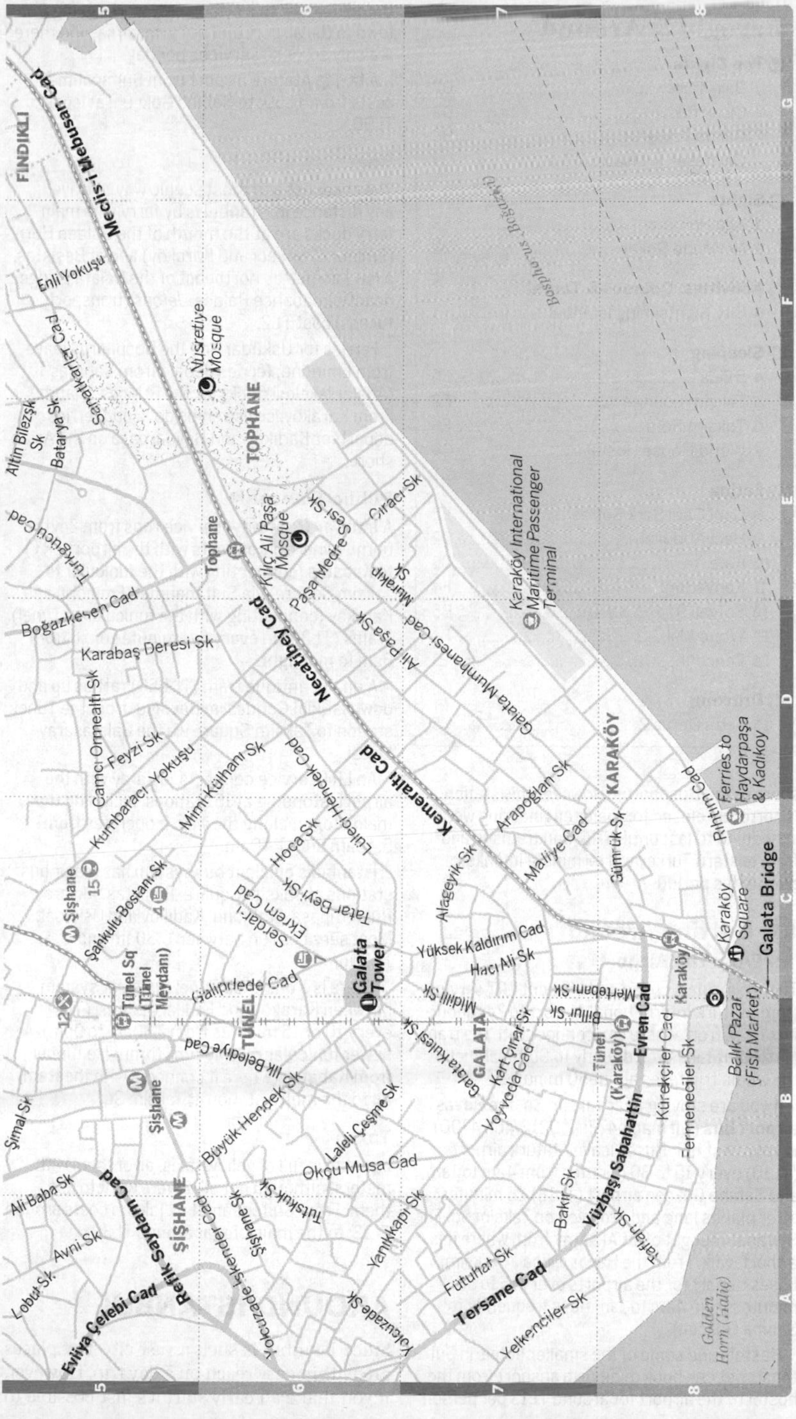
FINDIKLI
TOPHANE
KARAKÖY
GALATA
TÜNEL
ŞIŞHANE
Meclis-i Mebusan Cad
Enli Yokuşu
Sanatkarlar Cad
Altin Bilezşk Sk
Batarya Sk
Türkgücü Cad
Boğazkesen Cad
Karabaş Deresi Sk
Gamcı Ormealtı Sk
Feyzi Sk
Kumbaracı Yokuşu
Şahkulu Bostanı Sk
Nusretiye Mosque
Tophane
Kılıç Ali Paşa Mosque
Paşa Medre Sesi Sk
Cıracı Sk
Murakıp Sk
Ali Paşa Sk
Necatibey Cad
Kemeraltı Cad
Galata Mumhanesi Cad
Karaköy International Maritime Passenger Terminal
Bosphorus (Boğaziçi)
Mimi Külhanı Sk
Lüleci Hendek Cad
Hoca Sk
Tatar Beyi Sk
Serdar-i Ekrem Cad
Alageyik Sk
Arapoğlan Sk
Maliye Cad
Gümrük Sk
Rıhtım Cad
Ferries to Haydarpaşa & Kadıköy
Galata Bridge
Karaköy Square
Karaköy
Yüksek Kaldırım Cad
Hacı Ali Sk
Mertebani Sk
Billur Sk
Midilli Sk
Galata Tower
Galipdede Cad
Tünel Sq (Tünel Meydanı)
Şişhane
İlk Belediye Cad
Galata Kulesi Sk
Kart Çınar Sk
Voyvoda Cad
Tünel (Karaköy)
Evren Cad
Kürekçiler Cad
Fermeneciler Sk
Balık Pazar (Fish Market)
Yüzbaşı Sabahattin
Büyük Hendek Sk
Laleli Çeşme Sk
Okçu Musa Cad
Tütsüküş Sk
Şişhane Sk
İskender Cad
Yanıkkapı Sk
Bakır Sk
Fütuhat Sk
Tersane Cad
Yelkenciler Sk
Fafan Sk
Yolcuzade Sk
Yolcuzade İskender Cad
Şimal Sk
Ali Baba Sk
Avni Sk
Lobut Sk
Refik Saydam Cad
Evliya Çelebi Cad
Golden Horn (Haliç)
12
15
4
7
5
6
7
8
A
B
C
D
E
F
G

Beyoğlu & Around

Top Sights

	Balık Pazar	D2
	Çiçek Pasajı	D2
	Galata Tower	B6
	Galatasaray Lisesi	D3
Sights		
1	Ağa Hamamı	E3
2	Nevizade Sokak	D2
Activities, Courses & Tours		
3	City Sightseeing İstanbul	F1
Sleeping		
4	5 Oda	C5
5	Taksim Lounge	F2
6	Taksim Sofa	E3
7	World House Hostel	C6
Eating		
8	Gani Gani Şark Sofrası	E2
9	Hacî Abdullah	D2
10	Kafe Ara	C3
11	Kahvedan	F4
12	Sofyalı 9	B5
13	White Mill	F4
14	Zencefil	E1
Drinking		
15	Leb-i Derya	C5

shore of the Bosphorus. However this station is currently closed for major engineering work scheduled to last until 2015, and trains to and from eastern Turkey will terminate in Ankara during this period.

Getting Around

To/From the Airport

There's a quick, cheap and efficient LRT service from Atatürk International Airport to Zeytinburnu (TL2), from where you connect with the tram (TL2) that takes you directly to Sultanahmet – the whole trip takes about 50 minutes.

If you are staying near Taksim Sq, the **Havaş airport bus** (Off map p472; ☎0212-465 4700) is your best bet. Buses leave Atatürk airport (TL10) every 15 to 30 minutes from 4am to 1am, and Sabiha Gökçen airport (TL18) 25 minutes after planes land and drop you on Taksim Sq. For Sultanahmet get off at Aksaray from where it is a short walk. From the Havaş office at Taksim, buses depart for the airports every 15 to 30 minutes from 4am to 1am (less frequently to Sabiha Gökçen).

Hostels and some of the smaller hotels in Sultanahmet can book minibus transport from the hostel to the airport for around TL13 per person. Unfortunately, this option only works going *from* town to the airport and not vice versa, and there are only six or so services per day.

A taxi to Atatürk airport from Sultanahmet costs from TL50; to Sabiha Gökçen, at least TL90.

Boat

The cheapest and most scenic way to travel any distance in İstanbul is by ferry. The main ferry docks are at the mouth of the Golden Horn (Eminönü, Sirkeci and Karaköy) and at Beşiktaş, a few kilometres northeast of the Galata Bridge, near Dolmabahçe Palace. *Jetons* (transport tokens) cost TL2.

Ferries for Üsküdar and the Bosphorus leave from Eminönü; ferries depart from Kabataş (Adalar İskelesi dock) for the Princes' Islands. From Karaköy, cruise ships dock and ferries depart for Kadıköy and Haydarpaşa on the Asian shore.

Public Transport

A *tramvay* (tramway) service runs from Zeytinburnu (where it connects with the airport LRT) to Kabataş (connecting with the funicular to Taksim Square) via Sultanahmet, Eminönü and Karaköy (connecting with the funicular to Tünel). Trams (TL2) run every five minutes or so from 6am to midnight.

A quaint antique tram (TL1.50) rattles up and down İstiklal Caddesi in Beyoğlu, from the Tünel station to Taksim Square via the Galatasaray Lisesi.

An LRT service connects Aksaray with the airport, stopping at 15 stations, including the main otogar, along the way. It operates from 5.40am until 1.40am.

İstanbul's efficient bus system has major bus stations at Taksim Square, Beşiktaş, Aksaray, Rüstempaşa-Eminönü, Kadıköy and Üsküdar. Most services run between 6.30am and 11.30pm.

There is a one-stop Tünel funicular system between Karaköy and İstiklal Caddesi (TL2, every 10 or 15 minutes from 7.30am to 9pm). A newer funicular railway runs through a tunnel from Kabataş (where it connects with the tram) up to the metro station at Taksim Sq.

Taxi

İstanbul is full of yellow taxis, all of them with meters, although not all drivers want to use them. From Sultanahmet to Taksim costs around TL13; to the main otogar around TL30.

AROUND İSTANBUL

Since İstanbul is such a vast city, few places are within easy reach on a day trip. However, if you make an early start it's just possible to see the sights of Edirne in Thrace (Trakya), the only bit of Turkey that is geographically within Europe. The fast ferry link means that you can also just make it to Bursa and back in a day, although it's much better to plan to stay overnight there. Also worth a detour is İznik, a historic walled town on the shores of a peaceful lake, easily accessible from İstanbul.

Edirne

0284 / POP 139,000

European Turkey's largest settlement outside İstanbul, it was briefly the capital of the Ottoman Empire. You'll find none of the razzmatazz or crowds of the Aegean or Mediterranean coasts here, but Edirne is hardly a backwater. With the Greek and Bulgarian frontiers half an hour's drive away, the streets are crowded with foreigners, locals and off-duty soldiers. At the end of June is the oily **Kırpınar Wrestling Festival**.

Sights

Edirne is disregarded by all but a handful of travellers who come to enjoy the stunning architecture, particularly the mosques.

Mosques MOSQUE

Dominating Edirne's skyline like a massive battleship is the **Selimiye Cami** (1569–75), the finest work of the great Ottoman architect Mimar Sinan. Its lofty dome and four tall (71m), slender minarets create a dramatic perspective. Smack-bang in the centre of town and dating from 1414, the **Eski Cami** (Old Mosque) has rows of arches and pillars supporting a series of small domes. The **Üç Şerefeli Cami** (Three-Balcony Mosque) is notable for its four strikingly different minarets, which were all built at different times and cast a shadow over **Hürriyet Meydani** (Freedom Square). In splendid isolation to the north of the town, the great imperial mosque **Sultan II Beyazıd Külliyesi** was built by the Ottoman architect Hayreddin (1484–1512).

Edirne Archaeology & Ethnography Museum MUSEUM

(Edirne Arkeoloji ve Etnografya Müzesi; admission TL3; 9am 5pm Tue-Sun) Situated behind the Selimiye Cami, this interesting little museum focuses on local crafts and customs. The city is home to the Ottoman lacquering technique and there are several examples on show here, as well as reconstructed Ottoman houses that feature a circumcision room!

Sleeping & Eating

The best-value accommodation is along Maarif Caddesi and the best eating is along Saraçlar Caddesi. The riverside restaurants south of the centre are more atmospheric, but most open only in summer and are booked solid at weekends. The city's speciality dish is *Edirne ciğeri*, deep-fried calf liver with chili and yoghurt.

Edirne Selimiye Taş Odalar BOUTIQUE HOTEL $$$

(212 3529; www.tasodolar.com; Selimiye Camii Arkasi; s/d €80/110;) A historic stone mansion overlooking the Selimiye Cami with pleasing rooms filled with antiques.

Efe Hotel BOUTIQUE HOTEL $$

(213 6166; www.efehotel.com; Maarif Caddesi 13; s/d TL90/130;) The Efe is a stylish place, especially the lobby, which is filled with antiques and curios. The rooms, particularly the 2nd-floor doubles, are big and bright, with fridges and electric kettles.

Tuna Hotel HOTEL $$

(/fax 214 3340; Maarif Caddesi 17; s/d TL60/85;) An excellent choice for the price, the Tuna is at the quieter southern end of Maarif Caddesi.

Getting There & Away

The otogar is 9km east of the city centre. There are regular bus services for İstanbul (TL10, 2½ hours, 235km) but it is worth booking ahead at peak times of year. The nearest border crossing to Bulgaria is at Kapıkule, but border guards occasionally prevent pedestrians from crossing, so your best bet is to buy a bus ticket that will take you over the border.

İznik

0224 / POP 23,200

A walled town situated by a lake and regionally famous for its tile-making, İznik is popular with weekending İstanbullus but largely ignored by foreigners, helping to preserve its Turkish character. If you are interested in tiles, it's worth seeking out the **İznik Foundation** (757 6025; www.iznik.com; Vakif Sokak 12) and arranging a visit to its tile-making compound.

Sights

Most of the attractions sit within the town's walls, but a stroll along the lakefront is time well spent.

Aya Sofya RUINS

(Church of Holy Wisdom; admission TL7; ⊙9am-7pm Tue-Sun) The ruins of the Aya Sofya feature a mosaic floor from its Christian origins, but it was converted into a mosque during the Ottoman conquest. Though destroyed by fire in the 16th century, a modern reconstruction incorporated İznik tiles into the design.

Yeşil Cami MOSQUE

(Green Mosque) Built between 1378 and 1387, the minaret, decorated with green-and-blue glazed zigzag tiles, is a wonder.

İznik Museum MUSEUM

(İznik Müzesi; Müze Sokak; admission TL3; ⊙9am-7pm Tue-Sun) Spare an hour to visit this museum to see some nice examples of İznik tiles.

Sleeping & Eating

İznik is proud of its lake fish, and the waterside bars and cafes are the best place to try it.

Çamlık Motel HOTEL $$

(☎757 1362; www.iznik-camlikmotel.com; Göl Sahil Yolu; r TL100; ❄) At the southern end of the lakefront, this modern motel has spacious rooms and a restaurant with water views. It's a favourite with tour groups, so book ahead on summer weekends. The restaurant is recommended by locals as İznik's best spot to enjoy fish.

Kaynarca Pansiyon PENSION $

(☎757 1753; www.kaynarca.net; Kılıçaslan Caddesi, Gündem Sokak 1; s/d/tr TL40/70/90, dm without bathroom TL25; @) Cheap and central, the dorm rooms share a squat toilet, so you might want to consider whether your budget stretches to a private room. Internet is available in the cybercafe next door.

Köfteci Yusuf TURKISH $

(Atatürk Caddesi 75; köfte TL6) A favourite lunchtime spot for juicy *köfte* and other grills with chunky bread and hot green peppers. Make sure you leave room for the gorgeous desserts.

Getting There & Away

There are hourly buses from İstanbul's main otogar to Bursa (TL7.50, 1½ hours) and frequent buses to Yalova (TL7.50, one hour), where you can catch a fast ferry to İstanbul (TL3, 30 minutes).

Bursa

☎0224 / POP 1.9 MILLION

Sprawling at the base of Uludağ, Bursa was the first capital of the Ottoman Empire. Today, Turkey's biggest winter-sports centre is a modern, prosperous city with lots of vitality and personality. Allow at least a day to take in the ancient mosques, medreses, hamams and their enthralling designs. If you feel in need of some pampering, the **thermal springs** in the village-like suburb of Çekirge are the perfect salve after exploring the city or Uludağ's tree-clad slopes.

Sights & Activities

Ulu Cami MOSQUE

(Grand Mosque; Atatürk Caddesi) Right in the city centre, the largest of Bursa's mosques is the Seljuk Ulu Cami, built in 1396. Behind it, the sprawling **Bazaar** is proudly local, especially if you find İstanbul's Grand Bazaar too touristy.

Bursa Citadel CASTLE

Uphill from the Ulu Cami along Orhan Gazi Caddesi are the ruined remains of the Bursa Citadel walls. The main reason for the walk, though, is to visit the 14th-century tombs of Osman and Orhan, the first Ottoman sultans, which sit in a pleasant park at the summit.

Muradiye Complex PARK

A kilometre beyond the tombs lies the delightful Muradiye Complex, with a mosque and 12 decorated tombs dating from the 15th and 16th centuries. With a shady park in front, it's a peaceful oasis in a busy city.

Yeşil Cami MOSQUE

(Green Mosque; 1424) About 1km east of Heykel is the supremely beautiful Yeşil Cami and its stunningly tiled **Yeşil Türbe** (Green Tomb; ⊙8am-noon & 1-5pm).

Uludağ PARK

Whether visiting in winter or summer, it's worth taking a cable-car ride up the 2543m Uludağ (Great Mountain) to take advantage of the view and the cool, clear air of Uludağ National Park. To get to the **teleferik** (cable car; return trip TL10) from Bursa, take a city bus from stop 1 or a Teleferik dolmuş from behind the City Museum (Kent Müzesi). Bear in mind that the skiing facilities, while some of Turkey's best, are not up to the standard of European resorts.

Sleeping

Bursa caters mainly for business visitors and budget options are limited, though there are some decent midrange options in the centre. Also consider Çekirge, which is quieter and though the suburb's hotels are generally more expensive, the price includes the use of their mineral baths.

Kitap Evi Otel BOUTIQUE HOTEL $$$
(☎225 4160; www.kitapevi.com.tr; Kavaklı Mahallesi & Burç Üstü 21; s €90-160, d €120-190, ste €220; ❄@) In a sea of faceless business hotels this gorgeous boutique hotel and former bookstore stands alone. It's not cheap, but in Bursa you get what you pay for and two of the rooms even have an en-suite hamam. The courtyard restaurant is worth a look as well.

Mutlu Hotel HOTEL $$
(☎233 2829; Murat Caddesi 19, Çekirge; s/d TL60/90; ❄) A reliable choice, the Mutlu combines a rustic wooden exterior with spacious marble thermal baths. The decor sometimes struggles to get past 1973, but the cafe outside is more modern.

Hotel Artıç HOTEL $$$
(☎224 5505; www.artichotel.com; Ulu Camii Karşısı 95, Bursa; s/d/tr TL90/160/220; ❄) A decent option with light, spacious rooms and good views of Ulu Cami from the breakfast salon. Ask for a discount on the posted rates.

Hotel Güneş HOSTEL $
(☎222 1404; İnebey Caddesi 75, Bursa; s/d/tr/q without bathroom TL30/50/60/70) The family-run Güneş is Bursa's best budget pension, with small, neat rooms in a restored but rickety Ottoman house next to the Inabey Hamam.

Eating & Drinking

Bursa is the home of the well-known *İskender kebap* and the rather less well-known *kestene şekeri* (candied chestnuts). Don't leave town without trying both.

Make sure you spend an evening at one of the fish restaurants on Sakarya Caddesi, Bursa's most atmospheric eating precinct. Almost everywhere along this strip is of a high standard and whichever restaurant you pick you really can't go wrong. After eating there, you'll find some lively bars nearby along Sakarya Caddesi and Altıparmak Caddesi.

Kebapçi İskender TURKISH $$
(Ünlü Caddesi 7; İskender TL20; ⏰lunch & dinner) Official inventors of the *İskender kebap* (it's patented!), they have been churning out this national obsession since 1867. Trying a piece of history here isn't cheap, though.

Iskender TURKISH $$
(Atatürk Caddesi 60; İskender TL16; ⏰lunch & dinner) They may not have the patent to prove it, but they also claim to be the geniuses behind the invention of the famous meat feast. If you're an *İskender* addict, try both and tell us which one is best.

Gren Café Restaurant BAR CAFE $
(www.grencafe.com, in Turkish; Sakarya Caddesi 46; mains TL6-14; ⏰noon-late) Sick of the ubiquitous *İskender* and looking for something different? Enjoy the photography and art exhibitions while munching on a snacky menu of sandwiches, burgers and pasta.

Information

The city centre, with its banks and shops, is along Atatürk Caddesi, between the Ulu Cami (Grand Mosque) to the west and the main square, Cumhuriyet Alanı, commonly called Heykel (Statue), to the east.

Çekirge is a 10-minute bus or dolmuş ride from Heykel via Atatürk Caddesi. Bursa's otogar is an inconvenient 10km north of the centre; take bus No 38 (TL2, 45 minutes) and get off at stop 4.

Getting There & Away

The fastest way to get to İstanbul (TL24, 2½ to three hours) is to take a bus to Yalova, then a catamaran to İstanbul's Yenikapı docks. Get a bus that departs Bursa's bus terminal at least 90 minutes before the scheduled boat departure.

Karayolu ile (by road) buses to İstanbul take four to five hours and drag you around the Bay of İzmit. Those designated *feribot ile* (by ferry) or *express* go to Topçular, east of Yalova, and take the ferry to Eskihisar, a much quicker and more pleasant way to go.

AEGEAN COAST

While the Aegean coast may not be as scenic as the Mediterranean, its beaches define the western edge of the Anatolian landmass formerly known as Asia Minor, and the area is studded with fantastic historic sites. Come here to see Troy, Ephesus and Pergamum, and more recent history at the battlefield sites on the Gallipoli Peninsula.

Çanakkale

☎0286 / POP 86,600

The liveliest settlement on the Dardanelles, this sprawling harbour town would be worth a visit for its sights, nightlife and overall vibe even if it didn't lie opposite the Gallipoli Peninsula. The other major reason for coming here is as a base for visiting the ruined city of Troy. The actual wooden horse from the 2004 *Troy* movie is at the northern end of the waterfront and a scale model of the ancient city accompanies it.

The sweeping promenade heaves during the summer months and Çanakkale has become a popular destination for weekending Turks; if possible, plan your visit for midweek.

Sleeping

Rooms are expensive around Anzac Day (25 April) and are usually booked solid months before that date.

TOP CHOICE **Kervansaray Hotel** BOUTIQUE HOTEL $$
(☎217 8192; www.otelkervansaray.com; Fetvane Sokak 13; s/d/tr TL100/150/170; ❄@) Çanakkale's only boutique hotel is as lovely as you could hope for, laying on Ottoman touches in keeping with the restored house it occupies. The 19 rooms have a dash of character, without being overdone, and there is a lovely courtyard.

Çanak Hotel HOTEL $$
(☎214 1582; www.canakhotel.com, in Turkish; Dibek Sokak 3; s/d €40/60; ❄@) This excellent midrange option is just off Cumhuriyet Meydanı, with a stunning rooftop bar and games room, and a skylit atrium.

Efes Hotel HOTEL $
(☎217 3256; www.efeshotelcanakkale.com; Aralık Sokak 5; s/d TL40/60; ❄) A short hop from the clock tower and with cheery decor and a welcoming owner, Efes Hotel is the top budget choice for couples or singles looking for private rooms. The breakfasts are great, and there's a little garden with a fountain.

Yellow Rose Pension HOSTEL $
(☎217 3343; www.yellowrose.4mg.com; Aslan Abla Sokak 5; dm/s/d TL20/35/60, s/d without bathroom TL30/50; @) This bright but spartan guesthouse has a central yet quiet location plus extras including a laundry service (TL15) and fully equipped kitchen.

Anzac House Hostel HOSTEL $
(☎213 5969; www.anzachouse.com; Cumhuriyet Meydanı 59; dm/s/d/tr without bathroom TL25/45/70/90) Not to be confused with the three-star Anzac Hotel, central Anzac House is a haunt for dorm-seeking budget backpackers. Ask to see the rooms before you pay; some of the private rooms are tiny, windowless boxes.

Eating & Drinking

Çanakkale's restaurants disappoint, but its nightlife doesn't. There is a lively bar and music scene along Matbaa and Fetvane Sokaks, and on the waterfront along Kayserili Ahmet Paşa Caddesi, where rock-music joints rule. To eat on the hoof, browse the stalls along the *kordon* (waterfront promenade) offering corn on the cob, mussels and other simple items. A local speciality is *peynir helvası,* made with soft white village cheese, flour, butter and sugar.

Doyum KEBAB $$
(Cumhuriyet Meydanı 13; mains TL5-15) With its stone-fired pide oven, Doyum is acknowledged by some to be the best kebap and pide joint in town.

Gülen KEBAB $$
(Cumhuriyet Meydanı 27; mains TL5-15) Gülen knocks out a mighty fine pide, as well as some mouthwateringly juicy flame-grilled kebaps.

Getting There & Away

There are regular buses to Ayvalık (TL25, 3½ hours), İstanbul (TL35, six hours) and İzmir (TL35, 5½ hours), and 24-hour ferry services to Eceabat (from TL2, 25 minutes). The new otogar is 8km outside the town and some companies drop off here, but a local bus runs between the terminal and the pier every half an hour.

Troy (Truva)

☎0286

'The wind brought wealth to Troy', said the ancient inhabitants of this legendary city. These days the wind is still there, but there is not much left of the city and the ruins of Troy are among Turkey's least impressive historical sites. However, it's an important stop for history buffs, and for those who have read Homer's *Iliad,* the ruins have a romance few places on earth can match.

The ticket booth for the ruins of **Troy** (☎283 0536; admission per person/car TL15/5; ⌚8.30am-7pm May–mid-Sep, to 5pm mid-Sep–Apr)

Aegean Coast

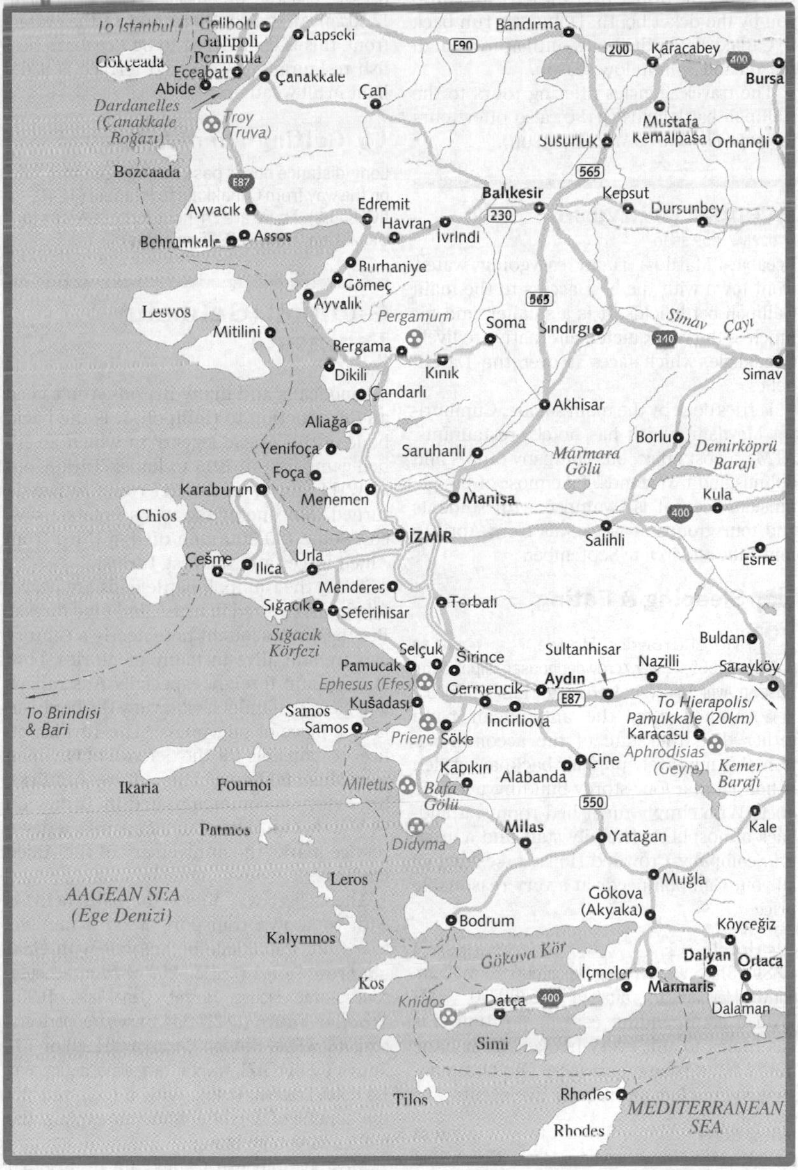

is 500m before the site. The site is rather confusing for nonexpert eyes (guides are available), but the most conspicuous features, apart from the reconstruction of the Trojan Horse, include the **walls** from various periods; the Graeco-Roman **Temple of Athena**, of which traces of the altar remain; the Roman **Odeon**, where concerts were held; the **Bouleuterion** (Council Chamber), built around Homer's time (c 800 BC).

From Çanakkale, dolmuşes to Troy (TL5, 35 minutes, 30km) leave every hour on the half hour from 9.30am to 5.30pm from a station under the bridge over the Sarı, and drop you by the ticket booth. Dolmuşes run back to Çanakkale on the hour, until 5pm in high season and 3pm in low season.

The travel agencies offering tours to the Gallipoli battlefields (p480) also offer tours to Troy (TL60 to TL75 per person).

Eceabat (Maydos)

0286 / POP 5500

Eceabat (Maydos) is an easygoing waterfront town with the best access to the main Gallipoli battlefields. It is a smaller, and for much of the year quieter, alternative to lively Çanakkale, which faces it over the Dardanelles.

Ferries dock by the main square, Cumhuriyet Meydanı, which has hotels, restaurants, ATMs, a post office, bus company offices and dolmuş and taxi stands. Like most of the peninsula, Eceabat is swamped with students and tour groups at weekends from April to mid-June and in late September.

Sleeping & Eating

TOP CHOICE Hotel Crowded House HOSTEL $$
(814 1565; www.crowdedhousegallipoli.com; Huseyin Avni Sokak 4; dm/s/d/tr TL18/55/75/95;) Named after the antipodean band rather than the state of the accommodation, this massively popular backpacker den is housed in a four-storey building near the dock. With simply furnished rooms, a laid-back atmosphere, friendly staff and a great tour company, Crowded House takes care of all your Gallipoli needs at a very reasonable price.

TJs Hotel HOSTEL $
(814 3121; www.anzacgallipolitours.com; Cumhuriyet Meydanı 5/A; dm/s/d TL15/50/70;) With a commanding central position, TJs has rooms to suit every budget, from basic hostel bunk-rooms upwards. The Ottoman-style rooftop bar has regular live events.

Hotel Boss HOTEL $$
(814 1464; www.heyboss.com; Cumhuriyet Meydanı 14; s/d TL50/75;) Behind its clapboard facade, this weirdly narrow place is a pleasant enough option. Opt for a corner room or one facing the water (eg No 1) to get more space. The same management run the similar **Hotel Boss II** (Mehmet Akif Sokak) and the pricier **Aqua Boss Hotel** (İstiklal Caddesi).

Liman Restaurant SEAFOOD $$
(İstiklal Caddesi 67; mains TL8-20; 10am-12.30am) At the southern end of the waterfront, this is considered to be Eceabat's best fish restaurant; its covered terrace is a delight in all weathers.

Getting There & Away

Long-distance buses pass through Eceabat on the way from Çanakkale to İstanbul (TL40, five hours). There are 24-hour ferry services to Çanakkale (from TL2, 25 minutes).

Gallipoli (Gelıbolu) Peninsula

0286

Antipodeans and many Britons won't need an introduction to Gallipoli; it is the backbone of the 'Anzac legend' in which an Allied campaign in 1915 to knock Turkey out of WWI and open a relief route to Russia turned into one of the war's greatest fiascos. Some 130,000 men died, a third from Allied forces and the rest Turkish.

Today the Gallipoli battlefields are peaceful places, covered in brush and pine forests. But the battles fought here nearly a century ago are still alive in many memories, both Turkish and foreign, especially Australians and New Zealanders, who view the peninsula as a place of pilgrimage. The Turkish officer responsible for the defence of Gallipoli was Mustafa Kemal (the future Atatürk); his victory is commemorated in Turkey on 18 March. On Anzac Day (25 April), a dawn service marks the anniversary of the Allied landings.

The easiest way to see the battlefields is with your own transport or on a minibus tour from Çanakkale or Eceabat with **Hassle Free Tours** (213 5969; www.anzachouse.com; Anzac House Hostel, Çanakkale; TL90), **Trooper Tours** (217 3343; www.troopertours.com; Yellow Rose Pension, Çanakkale; TL99) or **TJs Tours** (814 3121; www.anzacgallipolitours.com; TJs Hotel, Eceabat; TL45). With a tour you get the benefit of a guide who can explain the battles as you go along.

Most people use Çanakkale or Eceabat as a base for exploring Gallipoli. Car ferries frequently cross the straits from Çanakkale to Eceabat (from TL2, 20 minutes). From Eceabat, take a dolmuş or a taxi to the Kabatepe Information Centre & Museum on the western shore of the peninsula.

Some travellers prefer to join an organised tour from İstanbul.

Ayvalık

0266 / POP 34,650

Back from the palm trees and touristy restaurants on Ayvalık's waterfront, the tumbledown old Greek village becomes a wonderful outdoor museum. Horses and carts clatter down the village's narrow streets, past headscarf-wearing women holding court outside picturesque shuttered houses.

Activities

The town is best known as a gateway to the offshore Alibey Island (Cunda) and the Greek isle of Lesvos. In summer, **cruises** (per person incl meal around TL10-12) around the bay's islands leave Ayvalık at about 11am,

Gallipoli (Galibolu) Peninsula

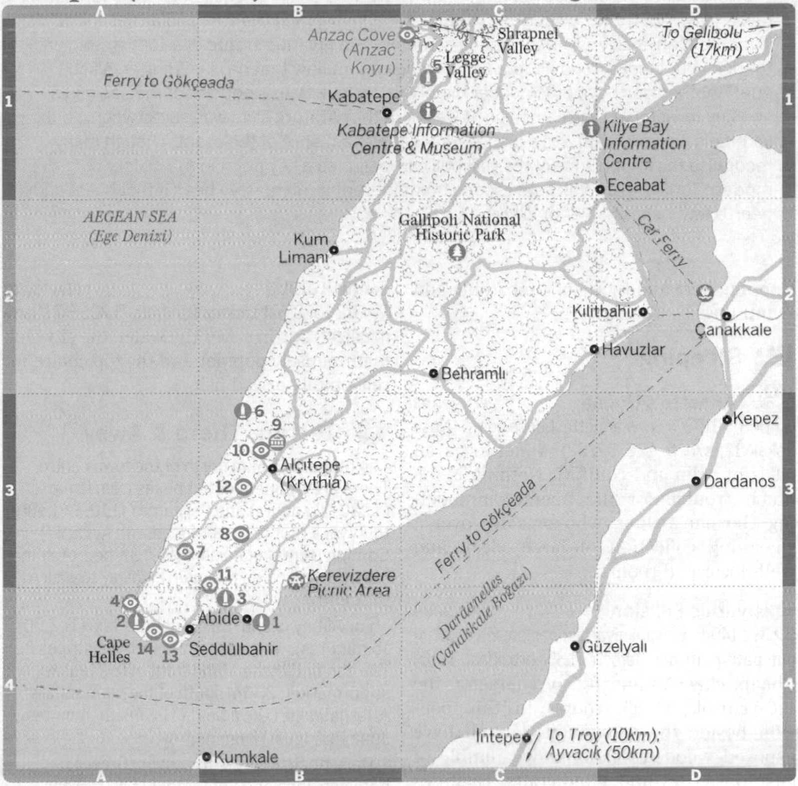

Gallipoli (Galibolu) Peninsula

Sights

1 Çanakkale Şehitleri Anıtı B4
2 Cape Helles British Memorial A4
3 French War Memorial & Cemetery B4
Gallery of the Gallipoli Campaign .... (see 9)
4 Lancashire Landing Cemetery A4
5 Mehmetçiğe Derin Saygı Anıtı C1
6 Nuri Yamut Monument B3
7 Pink Farm Cemetery A3
8 Redoubt Cemetery B3
9 Salim Mutlu War Museum B3
10 Sargı Yeri Cemetery B3
11 Skew Bridge Cemetery B3
12 Twelve Tree Copse Cemetery B3
13 'V' Beach Cemetery A4
14 Yahya Çavuş Şehitliği A4

GALLIPOLI BATTLEFIELDS

The weight of Gallipoli's military history makes touring the battlefields a moving experience, and the statistics are horrifying. Allied casualties included at least 21,200 British, 10,000 French, 8700 Australians, 2700 New Zealanders and 1350 Indians, as well as more than 97,000 wounded. Amongst the casualties were 14-year-old James Martin, officially the youngest victim of the campaign, whose name adorns the Lone Pine Memorial, and John Simpson Kirkpatrick, aka the 'Donkey Guy', a medic who achieved legendary status for countless death-defying acts of bravery in using his donkey to retrieve wounded soldiers from the front line. He finally 'stopped one' (a bullet) on 19 May 1915 and is buried at Hell's Spit.

However, we should also not forget that two-thirds of all the casualties were Turkish (around 87,000), and you can pay your respects to them at the vast and atmospheric **Turkish Cemetery**. Overlooking the cemetery is a gigantic statue of a Turkish soldier, though your guide will no doubt point out the design flaw that he is holding an Allied gun! Another worthy spot to ponder history is Chunuk Bair, highpoint of the peninsula and key to victory in the campaign. It was here that Atatürk's life was saved when a bullet hit his pocket watch and a plaque marks the exact spot of the event. Though many recognise the importance of the Gallipoli campaign as a key point in the history of modern Turkey, just think for a second how different it might have been if that bullet had been a few inches higher or lower!

stopping here and there for sunbathing and swimming.

Sleeping

TOP CHOICE **Annette's House** PENSION **$$**
(☎663 3193; www.annetteshouse.com; Neşe Sokak 12; s/d/tr €26/52/62) Annette's is an oasis of calm and comfort. Nothing is too much trouble for the uberaccommodating German owner, who presides over a charming collection of large, clean and well-decorated rooms.

Taksiyarhis Pension PENSION **$**
(☎312 1494; www.taksiyarhispension.com; r without bathroom per person TL35, breakfast TL10) Cheap, cheerful and full of character, the 120-year-old Greek rooms in this pension beside the eponymous church have exposed wooden beams and a jumble of cushions, rugs and handicrafts. Facilities include a communal kitchen, book exchange and bicycles for hire.

Eating

Balıkcı SEAFOOD **$$**
(Balıkhane Sokak 7; mains TL17; ⊙dinner) Make yourself the fisherman's friend by dining on the tiled terrace at this seafood restaurant run by a cooperative of marine environmentalists and fishermen.

Sehir Kulübü SEAFOOD **$$**
(☎312 1088; Yat Limanı; fish from TL20; ⊙7.30am-midnight) Jutting over the water, the city club is immensely popular and the top choice for reasonably priced fish.

Getting There & Away

The otogar is 1.5km north of the town centre. There are frequent direct buses from İzmir (TL20, 2½ hours) and Bergama (TL10, 1½ hours) to Ayvalık (not to be confused with Ayvacık!). Coming from Çanakkale (TL17, 3¼ hours), some buses drop you on the main highway to walk to the centre.

For Alibey Island, take a dolmuş taxi (TL2.50, 15 minutes), which are white with red stripes. You can find these at the front of the Tansas supermarket, 200m south of the main square. Alternatively, take a boat (TL2.50, 20 minutes, June to August) from nearby.

Daily boats operate to Lesvos (Greece) between June and September (€40/50 one way/return, 1½ hours). There are three boats a week from October to May. Schedules change frequently and reservation is essential. For information and tickets, contact **Jale Tours** (☎331 3170; www.jaletur.com; Yeni Liman Karşısı 150).

Bergama & Pergamum

☎0232 / POP 58,210

As Selçuk is to Ephesus, so Bergama is to Pergamum: a workaday market town that's become a major stop on the tourist trail because of its proximity to the remarkable ruins of Pergamum. During Pergamum's heyday (between Alexander the Great and the Roman domination of Asia Minor) it was one of the Middle East's richest and most powerful small kingdoms and the site of the pre-eminent medical centre of ancient Rome.

Sights

Asclepion RUINS

(Temple of Asclepios; admission/parking TL15/3; 8am-5pm) One of the highlights of the Aegean coast, the well-proportioned Asclepion, an easy 3km walk from the city centre, was a famous medical school with a library that rivalled that of Alexandria in Egypt.

Acropolis RUINS

(admission TL20; 8am-5pm) The ruins of the Acropolis, 6km from the city, are striking. The hilltop setting is absolutely magical, and the well-preserved ruins are magnificent, especially the vertigo-inducing 10,000-seat **theatre** and the marble-columned **Temple of Trajan**, built during the reigns of emperors Trajan and Hadrian and used to worship them as well as Zeus. Take the cable car (TL8) up the hill, otherwise it's a long, hard hike.

Red Basilica RUINS

(Temple of Serapis) These battered red stone ruins are the most eyecatching structure in the town itself. The Basilica is a vast cathedral-like edifice that was originally a 2nd-century temple dedicated to Egyptian gods and was described by St John as one of the seven churches of the Apocalypse.

Archaeology Museum MUSEUM

(Arkeoloji Müzesi; İzmir Caddesi; admission TL5; 8am-noon & 1-5pm Tue-Sun) This excellent museum has a small but important collection of artefacts from the Asclepion and the Acropolis, including a collection of 4th-century statues from the so-called 'Pergamum School'.

Sleeping

TOP CHOICE **Akropolis Guest House** BOUTIQUE HOTEL $$

(631 2621; www.akropolisguesthouse.com; Kayalik Sokak 3; s €40-75, d €60-75;) This 150-year-old stone house is the closest Bergama gets to boutique, with attractively and individually decorated rooms surrounding a pool and garden. It also has a restaurant set in a barn and a terrace with Acropolis views.

Odyssey Guest house PENSION $$

(631 3501; www.odysseyguesthouse.com; Abacıhan Sokak 13; s/d TL65/75, s/d without bathroom TL40/55;) Slip off your shoes and slip on the slippers in this 180-year old Ottoman house. Clean, simple rooms are furnished with copies of Homer's *Odyssey*, there's a book exchange and breakfast is served on the rooftop terrace.

Gobi Pension PENSION $

(633 2518; www.gobipension.com; Atatürk Bulvarı 18; s/d €20/32, without bathroom €15/24; @) On the main road behind a greenery-draped terrace, this is a great family run place with bright, cheery rooms, most with new private bathrooms.

Eating

Bergama Ticaret Odası TURKISH $$

(Ulucamii Mahallesi; meze TL5, mains TL10-20; 10.30am-11pm) Run by Bergama municipality, this restaurant occupies a beautifully restored 200-year-old Greek house.

Balik Evi SEAFOOD $$

(Atatürk Bulvari 45; mains TL10-15) Bergama's only fish restaurant, and one of the very few eating houses in town that is licensed to sell you a beer with your meal.

Pala Kebap Salonu KEBAB $

(Kasapoğlu Caddesi 4; kebap TL6.50; 8am-11pm Mon-Sat) Nothing more than a hole in the wall, but terrifically popular for the spicy Bergama *köfte*.

Information

İzmir Caddesi (the main street) is where you'll find ATMs, the PTT and pretty much everything else you are likely to need.

Getting There & Around

Bergama's new otogar lies 7km from the centre on the main highway, but it is useful only for long-distance buses. From the bus station a free service shuttles into town until 7pm, but some companies continuing to destinations such as İzmir will drop you on the highway at the bottom end of the town's main thoroughfare rather than entering the otogar; the centre is walkable from here. Nearby destinations are served from the old otogar near the Red Basilica from where you can catch frequent dolmuşes to/from İzmir (TL10, two hours, 110km) and Ayvalık (TL7.50, one hour, 60km).

İzmır

0232 / POP 3.4 MILLION

Though you may eventually fall for it, İzmir can take some getting used to. Certainly nowhere else in the region can prepare you for the sheer size, sprawl and intensity of the place.

Though the heart of the city is the architecturally impressive Konak Meydani, it's at the seafront, along the *kordon* where İzmir's traffic has been beaten back, that the city really comes into its own. Inland, things are more hectic, but you'll find a buzzing bazaar, some interesting ruins and a newly restored Jewish quarter.

Sights

Since most of old İzmir was destroyed after WWI, there's little in the way of historical sights compared with other Turkish cities.

FREE Ethnography Museum MUSEUM
(Ethnografya Müzesi; Bahra Baba Park; 8.30am-6.30pm Tue-Sun) An interesting little arts and crafts museum, on a hill overlooking Turgutreis Parkı, at the southern end of Konak Meydani. It will teach you the secrets of local traditions from camel-wrestling to evil-eye making.

Archaeology Museum MUSEUM
(Arkeoloji Müzesi; admission TL8; 8.30am-5pm Tue-Sun) Adjacent to the Ethnography museum, the Archaeology Museum is overpriced but contains some nice pieces for those interested in the history of the region.

Agora RUINS
(admission TL3; 8.30am-7pm, to 5pm Sat) The remains of an extensive 2nd-century Roman marketplace, just southeast of the sprawling modern bazaar.

Kadifekale FORTRESS
Take Bus 33 to this hilltop fortress, where women still weave *kilims* on horizontal looms and the views are breathtaking. It is not safe to walk there.

Sleeping

İzmir's waterfront is dominated by high-end business hotels, which fill up quickly during the summer; inland are budget and midrange places, particularly around the train station, though pick carefully as many also rent by the hour. The best options are along 1368 Sokak.

TOP CHOICE Konak Saray Hotel BOUTIQUE HOTEL $$
(483 6946; www.konaksarayhotel.com; Anafartalar Caddesi 635; s/d €35/50;) This beautiful Ottoman house has been transformed into a superior boutique hotel. Rooms are a touch small, but stylish and modern, and soundproofed to keep bazaar noise out.

Otel İzmir Palas HOTEL $$$
(465 0030; www.izmirpalas.com.tr; Atatürk Caddesi; s/d TL130/170) Okay, so palace is stretching it, but this is one of the more affordable places to stay on the waterfront. A decent restaurant and fantastic views of the bay make up for the lack of character.

Güzel İzmir Oteli HOTEL $
(483 5069; www.guzelizmirhotel.com; 1368 Sokak 8; s/d €24/39;) A decent choice for budget travellers, it's a safe bet in the otherwise ropey station area, but the uninspiring and sometimes small rooms are a bit of a disappointment after the nice reception.

Eating

The place to be seen on a romantic summer's evening is the sea-facing *kordon,* though you pay for the location. In Alsancak, you lose the sunset views but gain atmosphere; try 1453 Sokak (Gazi Kadinlar Sokağı). For fresh fruit, veg or freshly baked bread and delicious savoury pastries, head for the canopied market, just off Anafartalar Caddesi.

Sakız TURKISH $$
(Şehit Nevresbey Bulvarı 9/A; mains TL12-25; noon-2pm & 7.30-10pm Mon-Sat;) Inventive mains and an extensive lunch menu of vegetarian dishes mean that this is still one of our favourite places to dine in the city.

Balık Pişirisci SEAFOOD $$
(Atatürk Caddesi 212; mains TL15-20; noon-10.30pm) Simple, yet hugely popular with the locals who wait patiently for tables at this reasonably priced fish restaurant.

Information

İzmir's two main avenues run parallel to the waterfront. Atatürk Caddesi (Birinci Kordon or First Cordon), known locally as the *kordon*, is on the waterfront; a block inland is Cumhuriyet Bulvarı, the İkinci Kordon (Second Cordon). Main squares Konak Meydanı (Government House Square) and Cumhuriyet Meydanı are on these avenues.

Konak opens on to the bazaar and Anafartalar Caddesi, the bazaar's main street, leads to the train station, Basmane Garı. The Basmane-Çankaya area, near the station, has medium-priced hotels, restaurants and bus ticket offices. İzmir's shopping, restaurant and nightclub district of Alsancak is to the north.

The **Tourist office** (☎483 5117; Akdeniz Mahallesi 1344 Sokak 2) is on the seafront.

Getting There & Away

Air

Turkish Airlines flies to all major national destinations and some international ones from İzmir. Other airlines serving the city include Onur Air, Atlasjet, Pegasus and Sun Express Airlines. The airport is 18km south of the city and a shuttle bus (TL10, 30 minutes) runs from Gazi Osman Paşa Bulvarı to both terminals between 3.30am and midnight.

Bus

İzmir is a major transport hub and it pays to buy your tickets in advance. From the otogar 6.5km northeast of the centre, frequent buses leave for Bergama (TL10, two hours), Kuşadası (TL10.50, 1¼ hours), Selçuk (TL8, one hour) and other destinations nationwide. Buses to Çeşme (TL12, two hours) leave from a local bus terminal in Üçkuyular, 6.5km southwest of Konak but usually pass through the otogar as well.

Train

Most intercity trains arrive at the Basmane Garı. Four daily trains go to Bandırma (TL17, 6½ hours) and coordinate with the ferry across to İstanbul. Express trains run to Selçuk/Ephesus (TL4.75, 1½ hours) and Ankara (sleeper TL27, 15 hours), where you'll need to change for destinations in eastern Turkey.

Çeşme

☎0232 / POP 21,300

The Çeşme Peninsula is İzmir's summer playground, which means it can get busy with Turkish tourists at weekends and during the school holidays. Çeşme itself is a family-orientated resort and transit point for the Greek island of Chios, 8km west. It has a tangle of narrow backstreets and a dramatic Genoese fortress, and makes a good base for visiting the town of Alaçatı with its old Greek stone houses and windsurfing beach.

Sleeping

There's a wealth of good-value, homey pensions in Çeşme. Local pensions are usually open from May to October and bookings are essential in summer and at weekends. Big reductions are available in low season at the places that stay open.

Ridvan Otel HOTEL $$
(☎712 6336; www.ridvanotel.com; Cumhuriyet Meydani 11; s/d TL60/100; ❄) Though by no means a good-looking hotel from the outside, the restaurant is reasonable, the staff helpful and the functional, minimalist rooms have balconies.

Barınak Pansiyon PENSION $
(☎712 6670; 3052 Sokak 58; s/d TL35/55) One of a clutch of good cheapies on this street, this place scores for cleanliness, friendliness and value for money.

Suntree Motel BUNGALOW $
(☎722 2010; www.suntreemotel.com, in Turkish; Altinkum; bungalow per person TL70, camping TL10) Located 4km south of town, this vaguely hippy hangout offers simple bungalows, hammocks and camping with basic shared bathrooms. Next to a pretty beach, it's a good place to escape the crowds. Take an Altinkum dolmuş (TL3.50) from near the tourist office.

DON'T FORGET YOUR NAZAR BONCUK

Nazar Boncuk is a ubiquitous Turkish 'evil-eye' charm. As in many cultures, Turks believe the 'evil eye' can bring you bad luck, and use Nazar Boncuks (literally 'evil-eye beads') to ward off malicious forces associated with envious eyes. Nazar Boncuks of various shapes and sizes are pinned to the clothes of babies, guard the doorways of restaurants and hang on walls and doors.

The bead reflects evil intent back to the onlooker. With its concentric dots of colours, it resembles an eye, its blue colour is said to help protect the user.

This tradition goes back to the Arabian craftsmen who settled in İzmir during the Ottoman Empire's decline. Today the genuine eye beads are produced by a handful of glass masters in nearby Görece and Kurudere. Their methods and techniques have changed very little over the centuries.

Eating

On the front are touristy restaurants specialising in seafood – and multilingual menus. For cheaper, more locally orientated places, head to İnkilap Caddesi.

Tokmak Hasan'in Yeri TURKISH $
(Çarsı Caddesi 11; mains TL4-8; ⏰7am-8pm Mon-Sat) Rather hidden away, this simple place serves terrific home cooking at low prices.

Patika Restaurant & Café-Bar BAR-RESTAURANT $$
(Cumhuriyet Meydanı; mains TL12-16; ⏰3pm-midnight) This is the place for fish and meat at affordable prices. Between 9pm and 4am there's live Turkish music and sometimes belly dancing, but no alcohol.

Pasifik Otel Restaurant SEAFOOD $$
(Tekke Plajı Mevkii 16; mains TL10-15; ⏰noon-midnight) If you fancy a walk and some fish, head to the Pasifik, at the northern end of the seafront, where you can enjoy a great fish casserole.

Information

The **tourist office** (☎/fax 712 6653; İskele Meydanı 6; ⏰8.30am-noon & 1pm-5.30pm Mon-Fri), ferry and bus ticket offices, banks with ATMs, restaurants and hotels are all within two blocks of the main square.

Getting There & Away

Buses from Çeşme's otogar run every 45 minutes to İzmir's otogar (TL12, two hours) and also go to Üçkuyular terminal (TL10, 1¼ hours).

In summer, there are daily ferries to the Greek island of Chios, and two weekly ferries in winter. Buy your ticket in advance (passenger return €40, car return €120) at the harbour. See p629 for more information.

There are also weekly ferry services to Ancona (Italy) from May to September, with tickets available through Marmara Lines (www.marmaralines.com).

Selçuk

☎0232 / POP 27,280

Selçuk boasts one of the Seven Wonders of the Ancient World, an excellent museum, a fine basilica and mosque, a stork nest-studded aqueduct and, right on the town's doorstep, Ephesus. However, compared to the vast tourism factory of nearby Kuşadası, Selçuk's tourism industry is a small-scale, workshop-sized affair.

Sights

Selçuk is not only close to Ephesus, it's also blessed with superb monuments scattered around the centre.

Basilica of St John HISTORIC BUILDING
(St Jean Caddesi; admission TL5; ⏰8am-4.50pm, to 6.30pm May-Sep) Don't miss the conspicuous Basilica of St John, atop Ayasuluk Hill. It was built in the 6th century on the site where it was believed St John the Evangelist had been buried.

FREE **Temple of Artemis** RUINS
(Artemis Tapınağı; ⏰8am-5pm, to 7pm May-Sep) The Temple of Artemis, between Ephesus and Selçuk, was once one of the Seven Wonders of the Ancient World. In its prime, it was larger than the Parthenon at Athens. Unfortunately, only one of the original 127 pillars now remains.

Ephesus Museum MUSEUM
(Uğur Mumcu Sevgi Yolu Caddesi; admission TL5; ⏰8am-4.30pm, to 7pm May-Sep) Houses a striking collection of artefacts, including the headless effigy of Priapus, the Phallic God, as seen on every postcard from İstanbul to Antakya.

Sleeping

There is plenty of competition here and while prices are low, standards are high. Get ready to resist the touts trying to woo you as soon as you step off the bus.

Selçuk

Top Sights

Basilica of St John	C1
Ephesus Museum	C3
Temple of Artemis	A3

Sleeping

1 Australia & New Zealand Guesthouse	C3
2 Boomerang	C3
3 Homeros Pension	C2
4 Jimmy's Place	E3
5 Naz Han	D2

Eating

6 Ejder Restaurant	E2
7 Mehmet & Alibaba Kebab House	C3
8 Old House	E2
9 Pinar Pide Salonu	D2

Selçuk

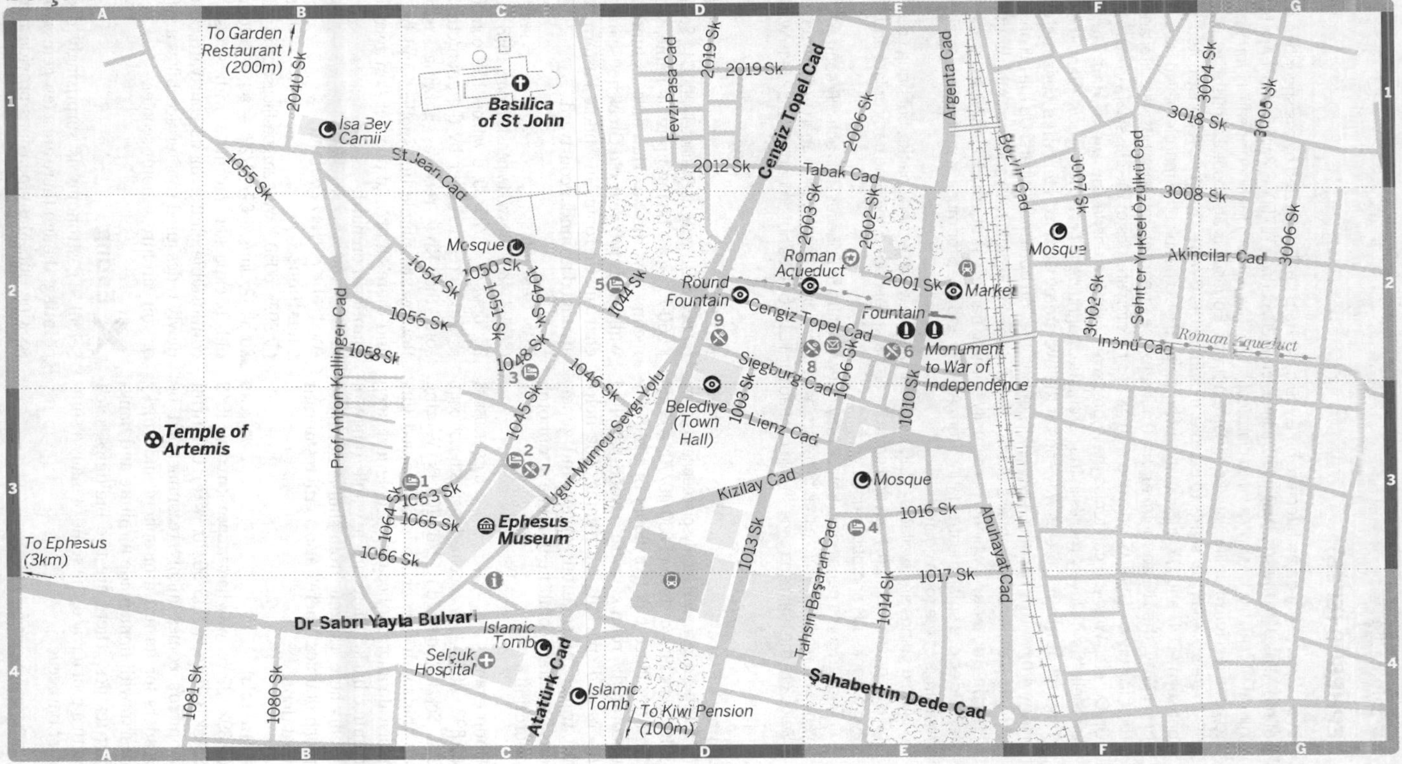
0 200 m
0 0.1 miles
A
B
C
D
E
F
G
1
2
3
4
To Garden Restaurant (200m)
2040 Sk
Basilica of St John
İsa Bey Camii
St Jean Cad
1055 Sk
Mosque
1050 Sk
1054 Sk
1051 Sk
1049 Sk
1056 Sk
1058 Sk
Prof Anton Kallinger Cad
1048 Sk
1046 Sk
1045 Sk
1044 Sk
Temple of Artemis
1063 Sk
1064 Sk
1065 Sk
1066 Sk
Ephesus Museum
Ugur Mumcu Sevgi Yolu
To Ephesus (3km)
Dr Sabri Yayla Bulvari
Islamic Tomb
Selçuk Hospital
Atatürk Cad
Islamic Tomb
To Kiwi Pension (100m)
1081 Sk
1080 Sk
Fevzi Pasa Cad
2019 Sk
2012 Sk
Cengiz Topel Cad
Tabak Cad
2006 Sk
2003 Sk
2002 Sk
Roman Aqueduct
Round Fountain
2001 Sk
Market
Fountain
Monument to War of Independence
Siegburg Cad
1006 Sk
1010 Sk
1003 Sk
Lienz Cad
Belediye (Town Hall)
Kizilay Cad
Mosque
1016 Sk
1013 Sk
Tahsin Başaran Cad
1014 Sk
1017 Sk
Abuhayat Cad
Şahabettin Dede Cad
Argenta Cad
Bozvir Cad
3007 Sk
Mosque
3002 Sk
Sehit er Yuksel Özülkü Cad
İnönü Cad
Roman Aqueduct
Akincilar Cad
3008 Sk
3018 Sk
3004 Sk
3005 Sk
3006 Sk
1
2
3
4
5
6
7
8
9

DON'T MISS

EPHESUS (EFES)

Even if you're not an architecture buff, you can't help but be dazzled by the sheer beauty of the ruins of **Ephesus** (Map p490; admission TL20, parking TL7.50; ⏰8am-5pm Oct-Apr, to 7pm May-Sep), the best-preserved classical city in the eastern Mediterranean. If you want to get a feel for what life was like in Roman times, Ephesus is an absolute must-see.

There's a wealth of sights to explore, including the **Great Theatre**, reconstructed between AD 41 and 117, and capable of holding 25,000 people; the marble-paved **Sacred Way**; the 110-sq-metre **agora** (marketplace), heart of Ephesus' business life; and the **Library of Celsus**, adorned with niches holding statues of the classical Virtues. On Curetes Way, you can't miss the impressive Corinthian-style **Temple of Hadrian**, on the left, with lovely friezes in the porch; the magnificent **Terraced Houses** and the **Trajan Fountain**. Curetes Way ends at the two-storey **Gate of Hercules**, constructed in the 4th century AD, which has reliefs of Hercules on both main pillars. Up the hill on the left are the ruined remains of the **Prytaneum** (municipal hall) and the **Temple of Hestia Boulaea**, in which a perpetually burning flame was guarded. Finally, you reach the **Odeon**, a small theatre dating from AD 150 and used for musical performances and meetings of the town council.

Audio guides are available (TL10). You can also buy water and snacks, but bring your own as prices are high. Heat and crowds can be problematic so come early or late and avoid weekends and public holidays.

Though some pensions in Selçuk may offer free lifts to Ephesus, this actually contravenes municipal law. Note that there are two entry points, roughly 3km apart. A taxi from Selçuk to the main entrance should cost about TL15, but it's not an unpleasant 2.5km walk.

Jimmy's Place HOTEL **$$**
(☎892 1982; www.jimmysplaceephesus.com; 1016 Sokak 19; s/d/ste from €30/40/70; ❄@≋) Jimmy's Place has five floors of tastefully decorated rooms with wood-panelled floors and spacious bathrooms. The helpful travel information service and generous breakfast combine to make a topnotch operation.

Boomerang GUESTHOUSE **$$**
(☎892 4879; www.boomerangguesthouse.com; 1047 Sokak 10; dm/s/d TL12/65/100; ❄) Verging on the swish, owner Abdullah named this place Boomerang because people just keep coming back. There are a whole range of rooms here, ranging from simple dorms to plush doubles. There's also a grill restaurant next door.

Homero's PENSION **$**
(☎892 3995; www.homerospension.com; 1048 Sokak 3; dm/s/d TL15/50/70; ❄@) Colourful Homero's comes highly recommended by readers for its fun atmosphere and quirky design with homemade furniture and hanging textiles. There are two buildings, each with a roof terrace, the scene of many a summer barbecue.

Naz Han HOTEL **$$**
(☎892 8731; www.nazhanhotel.net; 1044 Sokak 2; r €60-70; ⊖❄) Living up to its name, which means 'coy', the Naz Han hides behind high walls. This 100-year-old Greek house has five charismatic rooms in Middle Eastern style, arranged around a courtyard.

Kiwi Pension PENSION **$**
(☎892 4892; www.kiwipension.com; 1038 Sokak 26; dm/s/d €8/25/35, d without bathroom €25; ❄@≋) Presided over by the energetic Alison, the Kiwi receives glowing reports. Rooms are simple but spotless and bright, and there's a private pool set 1km away in a mandarin orchard.

Australia & New Zealand Guesthouse HOSTEL **$**
(☎892 6050; www.anzguesthouse.com; 1064 Sokak 12; dm/s/d €9/22/28; ⊖❄) A colourful old backpacker favourite with sofas and comfortable clutter in its courtyard, and a newly redesigned roof terrace. Bikes are free or you can hire a motor scooter.

Eating

Selçuk's gastronomy is surprisingly disappointing, though there are a few gems worth seeking out. Many pensions provide home-cooked meals or barbecues for guests, especially in summer.

TOP CHOICE **Mehmet & Alibaba Kebab House** KEBAB $$
(1047 Sokak 4; mains TL8-16; ⏲7am-11pm) If you find a better value, better tasting kebap anywhere else on your travels around Turkey then we want to hear about it. The food here is gobsmackingly good, as the testimonials plastered all over the walls attest.

Ejder Restaurant TURKISH $$
(Cengiz Toppel Caddesi 9; mains TL7-17; ⏲breakfast, lunch & dinner) Nestled under the arches of the Roman aqueduct this is an atmospheric Anatolian diner that is hugely popular with travellers. Everybody who eats here signs the guestbook and leaves a memento of their visit; even the late Steve Irwin left his autograph.

Old House TURKISH $$
(Eski Ev; 1005 Sokak 1/A; mains TL9-18; ⏲8am-midnight) Set in a courtyard among fruit trees, this cool, intimate place serves tasty Turkish dishes. Try the speciality Old House kebap.

Garden Restaurant RESTAURANT $
(Garden Motel, Kale Altı 5; mains TL7-11; ⏲Apr-Sep) About as organic as it gets in Selçuk, this restaurant enjoys a bucolic setting amid plots where the majority of the produce on your plate is grown. The selection of mezes is particularly good.

Pinar Pide Salonu TURKISH $
(Siegburg Caddesi 3; pide TL4-7; ⏲9am-midnight) Some travellers claim that this little place serves the best pide anywhere. It also does some good kebaps and salads.

Information

On the western side of Atatürk Caddesi, the main road, a park spreads out in front of one wing of the Ephesus Museum. Many pensions can be found in the quiet, hilly streets between the museum and Ayasuluk Hill, northwest of the centre. The town centre is east of Atatürk Caddesi.

The **tourist office** (☎892 6945; Agora Caddesi 35; ⏲8am-noon & 1-5pm Mon-Fri Oct-Apr, daily May-Sep) is opposite the museum.

Getting There & Away

Selçuk's otogar is directly across Atatürk Caddesi from the tourist office. These days it's easy enough to get to Selçuk direct from İzmir (TL10, 1½ hours) and to continue to Pamukkale (TL25, 3 hours) or Bodrum (TL25, 3¼ hours). Tickets to destinations on the Mediterranean coast usually require a change of buses at Denizli (4½ hours).

Frequent minibuses head for Kuşadası (TL5, 30 minutes) and over to the beach at Pamucak.

Kuşadasi

☎0256 / POP 50,000

It's easy to sneer at Kuşadası's package hotels, fast-food restaurants, in-your-face bazaar, karaoke bars, tattoo parlours and holiday crowds. But many locals are very proud of the place, seeing it as exemplifying a can-do, make-the-best-of-yourself spirit, and those who revile it as snobs.

Kuşadası itself is short on specific sights, although there's a minor stone **fortress** once used by pirates on an island in the harbour, and an old **caravanserai** near the harbour. Kuşadası's most famous beach is **Kadınlar Denizi** (Ladies Beach), 2.5km south of town and served by dolmuşes (TL5, 30 minutes) running along the coastal road.

Sleeping

Beware the touts at the otogar and harbour; it's best to decide where you're heading before arrival and stick with the choice. Book ahead in summer.

TOP CHOICE **Sezgin Hotel Guesthouse** HOTEL $
(☎614 4225; www.sezginhotel.com; Aslanlar Caddesi 68; s/d €25/35; ❄@≋) Perhaps the top budget choice for style, with large, almost Swiss-style wood-panelled rooms, comfortable beds, armchairs, TVs, fridges and balconies overlooking a garden.

WORTH A TRIP

PRIENE, MILETUS & DIDYMA

Kuşadası makes a good base for visits to the superb ancient cities of **Priene, Miletus and Didyma** (all 3 sites admission TL15; ⏲8.30am-6.30pm May-Sep, 9am-5.30pm Oct-Apr), all to its south. If you're pushed for time, a 'PMD' tour from Kuşadası tour operators costs around €35. Perched high on the craggy slopes of Mt Mykale, Priene has a beautiful, windswept setting; Miletus boasts a spectacular theatre; and in Didyma is the stupendous Temple of Apollo.

Ephesus (Efes)

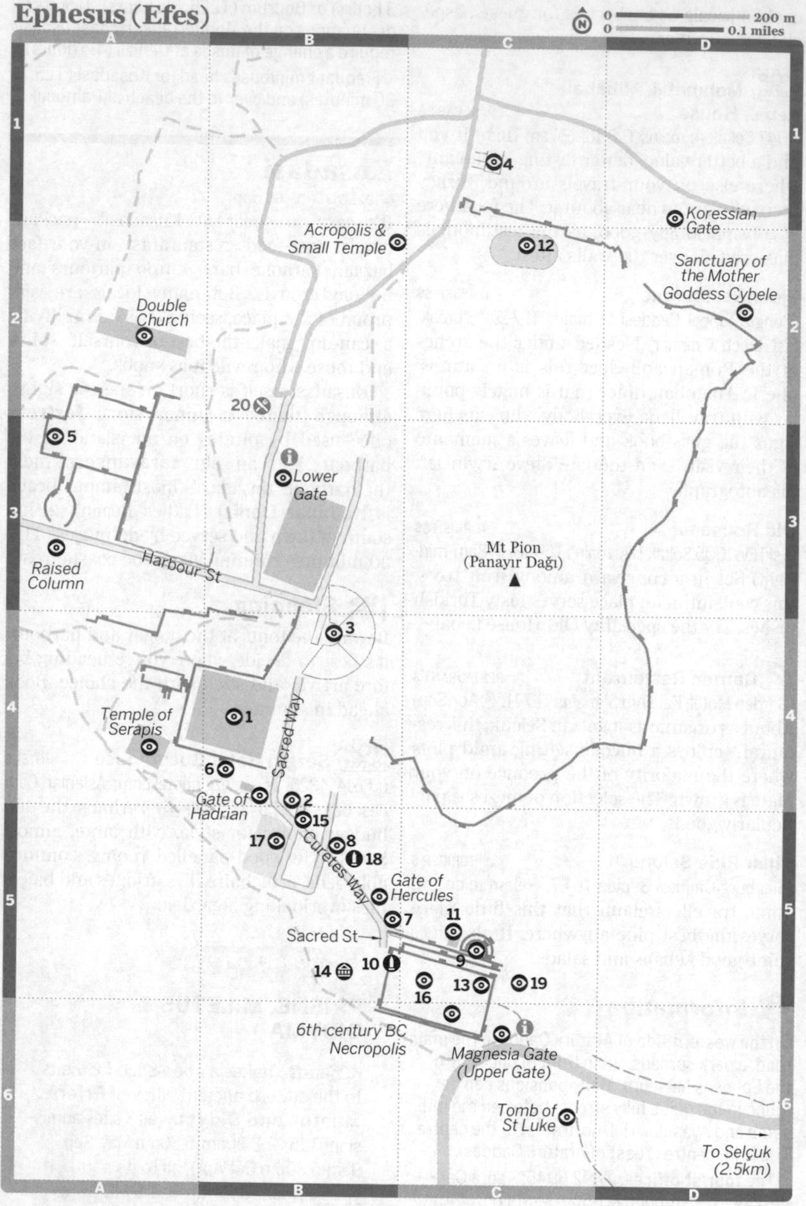

Hotel Istanköy HOTEL $$

(☎614 1328; www.hotelistankoy.com.tr; Unlu Sokak 4; s/d €40/60; ❄@≋) The Istanköy gets rave reviews from the package holiday crowds, not so much for the rooms, which are much as you would expect for a hotel in this category, but for the barrage of activities for all ages that they organise throughout the summer months. There's karaoke for your sister, barbecue night for your dad and even bingo night for your granny, but that's what you come to a place like Kuşadası for, right?

Ephesus (Efes)

Sights

Eating

Liman Hotel PENSION $

(☎614 7770; www.limanhotel.com; Kıbrıs Caddesi, Buyral Sokak 4; s/d €33/42; ❄☒) Mr Happy's, as it prefers to be known, is a budget favourite with an enviable position near the seafront. Catering for a young crowd, there is everything from a book exchange and a barbecue terrace to belly-dancing performances (and a chance to join in) on offer.

Eating & Drinking

Just beyond the PTT, a passage leads to the old Kaleiçi neighbourhood, which has narrow streets packed with restaurants and bars. For a drink, Barlar Sokak (Bar St) is chock-a-block with Irish-theme pubs and rowdy drinking dens. It's a scruffy-around-the-edges kind of place, but after a few drinks it can be lots of fun.

Saray INTERNATIONAL $$$

(Bozkurt Sokak 25; mains TL18-34; ⏲9am-2am) Enjoying a following among both locals and expats, the Saray has a refined courtyard and, inside, an unpretentious dining room that often rocks with happy-hour sing-a-longs. The menu, a typical Kuşadası calling-all-ports affair, includes some decent Turkish and vegetarian choices, and even Peking duck!

Planet Yucca INTERNATIONAL $$

(Sağlick Caddesi 56; mains TL15-28; ⏲lunch & dinner) Bizarrely billed as a Mexican-Chinese-Turkish restaurant, this place has a gigantic menu of options from across the globe. Free taxi pick-ups encourage you to splurge.

Toros SEAFOOD $$$

(Balikci Limam 5; mains TL20-45; ⏲lunch & dinner) At the southern end of the waterfront near the tourist office, this place claims to be the oldest restaurant in town. Let's face it, to be in business since 1894 they must be doing something right.

Getting There & Away

Boat

All Kuşadası travel agencies sell tickets to the Greek island of Samos. There's at least one daily boat to/from Samos (€30 one way, €35 same-day return, one hour 15 minutes) between April and October, but the ferries do not operate in the winter.

Bus

The most useful dolmuş stop is 1.5km inland at the roundabout on Adnan Menderes Bulvarı, with regular connections to Selçuk (TL5, 30 minutes). From the otogar on the bypass road, direct buses depart for several far-flung parts of the country, or you can change at İzmir. In summer, three buses run daily to Bodrum (TL20, 2½ hours); in winter, take a dolmuş to Söke (TL4, every 30 minutes) and change for Bodrum there.

Pamukkale

☎0258 / POP 2500

Way inland, east of Selçuk, Pamukkale is renowned for gleaming white ledges (travertines) with pools that flow down over the plateau edge. It used to be one of the most familiar images of Turkey, but these days it has lost a bit of its gloss. Sadly, in recent years the water supply has dried up and only a small number of pools are open to bathers. Above and behind this fragile natural wonder lie the magnificent ruins of the Roman city of Hierapolis, an ancient spa resort.

Pamukkale is also a good base from which to explore the ruined city of Afrodisias (Geyre).

Sights

Travertines LANDMARK

(admission incl Hierapolis Ruins TL20; ⏲daylight) A network of saucer-shaped thermal pools cascading down a white calcite hillside, this

WORTH A TRIP

AFRODISIAS (GEYRE)

Ephesus may be the crème de la crème of western Anatolia's archaeological sites, but the ruined city of **Afrodisias** (admission TL8; ⏲9am-7pm May-Sep, to 5pm Oct-Apr), near Karacasu southeast of Nazilli, is thought by many to rival it. Because of its isolation, it is less overrun with coach parties. Most of what you see dates back to at least the 2nd century AD. If it's not too busy, the site exudes an eerie ambience that is unique and unforgettable. The 270m-long **stadium**, one of the biggest in the classical world, is a startling vision, as are the **Temple of Aphrodite** and the white-marble **theatre**.

The only downside is that access by public transport is not easy. It's more sensible to arrange a tour (TL60 per person) from Pamukkale, or if you can fill a car try to negotiate a price with a local taxi driver. Tours leave with a minimum of four people, it's best to book in advance as groups don't always fill, even in high season.

unique geological feature is quite unlike anything else on earth. You need to take your shoes off to scale the hillside, so bring a thick pair of old socks. Bathing is strictly controlled these days and only certain pools are open for bathers.

Hierapolis Ruins RUINS
(admission incl Travertines TL20) The hilltop ruins of Hierapolis include a huge theatre, a colonnaded street, a latrine building and a vast necropolis. They are spread over a wide area; allow at least half a day to do them justice.

Antique Pool SPA
(adult/child TL25/10; ⏲9am-7pm) Take some time to swim amid sunken Roman columns in the health-giving waters of the Hierapolis' Antique Pool.

Hierapolis Archaeology Museum MUSEUM
(admission TL3; ⏲9am-12.30pm & 1.30-7.15pm Tue-Sun) This excellent museum contains some spectacular sarcophagi and friezes from Hierapolis and nearby Afrodisias. As you return to the village, keep looking back for great views of the glittering travertines.

Sleeping & Eating

Intense competition in Pamukkale leads to high quality and good value accommodation. Most places provide good, cheap home-cooked meals and serve wine and beer. Several welcoming, family-run pensions are clustered at the junction of İnönü and Menderes Caddesis.

Melrose Hotel PENSION $
(☎272 2250; www.melrosehousehotel.com; Valli Vefti Ertürk Caddesi 8; s/d TL50/60; ❄@≋) Clean-as-a-whistle rooms, two swimming pools and a warm welcome. The nicer rooms have bijou balconies and kitschly romantic circular beds.

Beyaz Kale Pension PENSION $
(☎272 2064; www.beyazkalepension.com; Oguzkaan Caddesi 4; s/d €20/25; ❄@≋) Despite not actually being white, the 'White Castle' is handy for the centre of the village and has spotless rooms arranged around a pool. Welcoming family hostess Haçer is a whiz in the kitchen, especially when it comes to vegetarian food. Larger rooms are also available.

Aspawa Pension PENSION $
(☎272 2094; www.aspawapension.com; Turgut Özal Caddesi 28; s/d/tr €20/26/33; ❄@≋) Another centrally located pension, the Aspawa ticks all the value boxes with good food in a family atmosphere.

Sinter Teras Hotel PENSION $
(☎708 8116; Hasan Tahsin Caddesi; s/d/tr TL45/60/75; ❄) If you get a homely feeling at this new hotel, it is probably because it is actually a home. In the high season the family retreats to a corner of the edifice and the guests get the run of the place. You eat with your hosts and the clean, spacious rooms with huge bathrooms are lovingly tended.

Artemis Yoruk Hotel HOTEL $
(☎272 2073; www.artemisyorukhotel.com; Atatürk Caddesi; dm/s/d/tr/q TL20/35/60/90/120; ❄@≋) With a supercentral location, this sprawling building has a wide range of rooms, from four-bed dorms to private and family rooms. The bar offering 'bloody cold beer' can get pleasingly raucous.

Getting There & Away

Pamukkale has no proper otogar; buses drop you at Denizli where the better bus companies throw in the connecting dolmuş (TL2, 30 minutes) for free. There are several direct buses to Selçuk (TL25, three hours) and Bodrum (TL27, 3½ hours) from Denizli, and you can buy your ticket at the bus offices in Pamukkale.

Bodrum

0252 / POP 31,600

Some people will tell you Bodrum is an unsophisticated, low-end resort town. In fact, Bodrum manages to welcome the summer hordes without diluting its character and charm. With laws in place restricting the height of buildings, the town has a neat architectural uniformity. Out of season, the whitewashed houses and subtropical gardens can appear almost idyllic.

Sights & Activities

Castle of St Peter MUSEUM

Bodrum's star attraction is the conspicuous Castle of St Peter. Built in 1437 by the Crusaders, the castle houses the **Museum of Underwater Archaeology** (admission TL10; 8am-4.30pm Oct-Apr, 9am-7pm Tue-Sun May-Sep), containing finds from shipwrecks dating back to 1025. It also holds a model of a Carian princess's tomb, which can be found inside the **French Tower** (admission TL5; 8am-4pm Tue-Fri).

Mausoleum of Halicarnassus RUINS

(Turgutreis Caddesi; admission TL8; 8am-5pm Tue-Sun), There is little left of the monumental tomb of King Mausolus, once among the Seven Wonders of the Ancient World.

Blue Cruises BOAT TOUR

(cruise €10) Yachts moored along Neyzen Tevfik Caddesi on the Western Bay run day trips around the bay and to nearby islets, with opportunities for swimming and sunbathing along the way.

Sleeping

There are plenty of budget hotels and pensions in the centre and along the Eastern Bay, but the closer you are to the front the less chance you'll have of getting a good night's sleep. A number of upmarket boutique hotels line the coast just east of the Eastern Bay. Many options close in winter when prices may be heavily reduced, but you should book ahead in summer.

TOP CHOICE **Su Otel** BOUTIQUE HOTEL $$$

(316 6906; www.suhotel.net; Tugurtreis Caddesi, 1201 Sokak; s/d/ste €60/75/110;) Hidden away on a quiet street, this is a peaceful refuge with a porticoed courtyard, decorated in refreshing Aegean blue and white.

El Vino Hotel BOUTIQUE HOTEL $$$

(313 8770; www.elvinobodrum.com; Pamili Sokak; r €120;) The dark backstreet location doesn't look that promising, but behind the stone wall is one of the town's loveliest hotels. The El Vino's rooms are spacious and well-appointed, with wooden floors, large beds, TVs and writing desks.

Mars Otel HOTEL $$

(316 6559; www.marsotel.com; Tugurtreis Caddesi, İmbit Çikmazi 29; s/d €45/50;) More like a mini-resort than a hotel, this is arguably the top value choice at the upper end of the budget spectrum.

Kilavuz Otel HOTEL $$

(316 3892; www.kilavuzotel.com; Atatürk Caddesi, Adliye Sokak 17; s/d TL70/100;) This place strikes a good balance between proximity to the front and the need for peace and quiet, offering 15 simply furnished, clean rooms. Try to avoid falling into the pool on arrival.

Baç Pansiyon PENSION $

(316 1602; bacpansiyon@turk.net; Cumhuriyet Caddesi 16; s TL55-80, d TL65-90;) Small but stylish and all in marble, wood and wrought iron, this central hotel boasts great views of the bay. It sits right above the water and four of its 10 comfortable rooms have delightful balconies over the waves.

Hotel Güleç Pansiyon PENSION $

(316 5222; Üşkuyular Caddesi 22; s/d €25/37;) Popular with backpackers for its accessible price, location near the bus station and tasty breakfasts served in the lovely garden. Some of the mattresses are a little hard.

Sevin Pension PENSION $

(316 7682; www.sevinpension.com; Türkkuyusu Caddesi 5; s/d/ste €28/40/50;) A prime (albeit noisy) location and helpful staff feature at this basic budget choice. Cheaper rooms are rather bare, but bright and airy and good value at this price.

Eating

Bodrum's finest and most expensive restaurants are all located along the Western Bay;

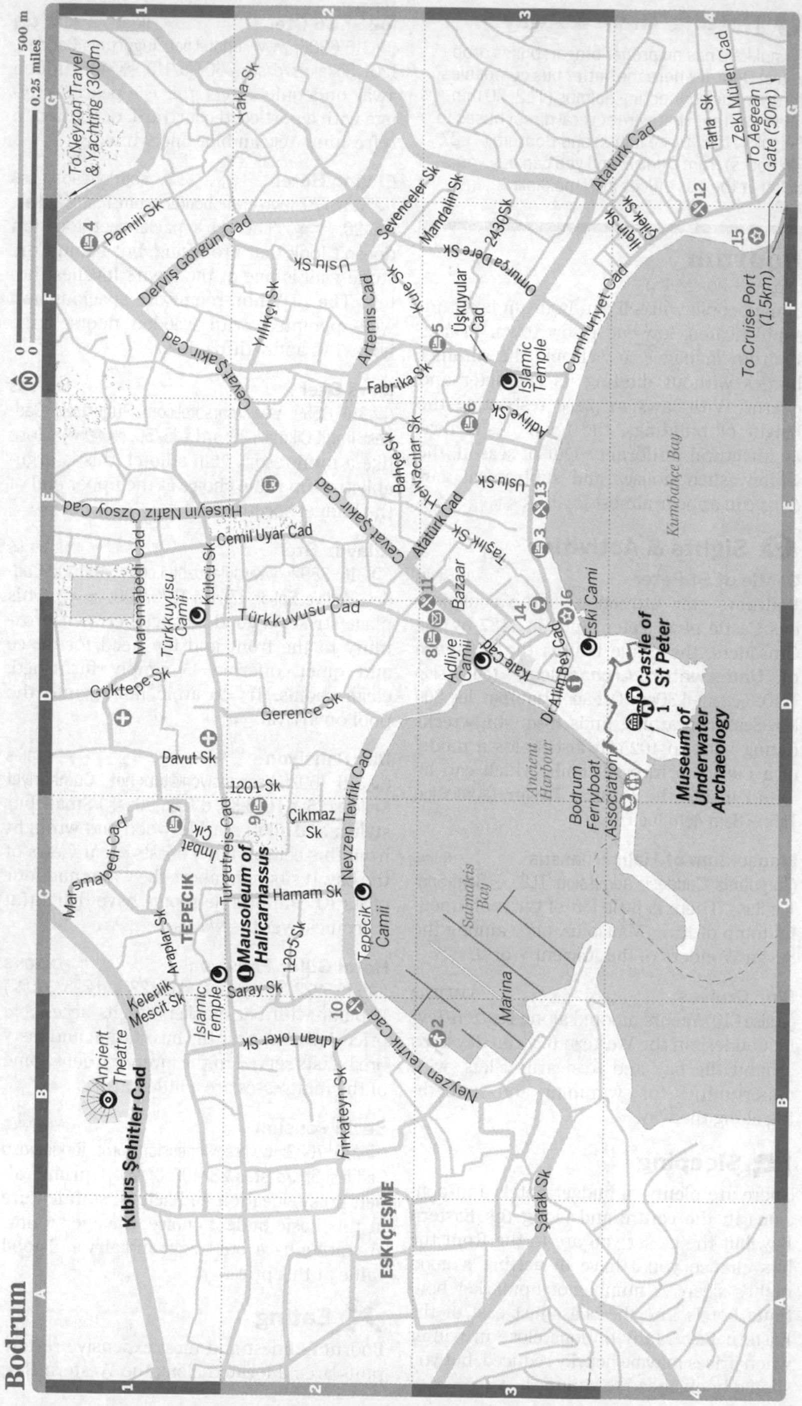
Bodrum
0 500 m
0 0.25 miles
To Neyzon Travel & Yachting (300m)
To Cruise Port (1.5km)
To Aegean Gate (50m)
Kıbrıs Şehitler Cad
Ancient Theatre
Kelerlik Mescit Sk
Islamic Temple
Saray Sk
Mausoleum of Halicarnassus
TEPECIK
Araplar Sk
Marsmabedi Cad
İmbat Çık
Turgutreis Cad
Hamam Sk
1205 Sk
Çikmaz Sk
1201 Sk
Davut Sk
Gerence Sk
Göktepe Sk
Türkkuyusu Camii
Külcü Sk
Türkkuyusu Cad
Cemil Uyar Cad
Hüseyin Nafiz Özsoy Cad
Cevat Şakir Cad
Yıllıkçı Sk
Dervis Görgün Cad
Pamili Sk
Yaka Sk
Uslu Sk
Artemis Cad
Sevenceler Sk
Mandalin Sk
Kule Sk
Fabrika Sk
Bahçe Sk
Helvacılar Sk
Atatürk Cad
Taşlık Sk
Bazaar
Adliye Camii
Kale Cad
Dr Alim Bey Cad
Eski Cami
Castle of St Peter
Museum of Underwater Archaeology
Bodrum Ferryboat Association
Ancient Harbour
Kumbahçe Bay
Adliye Sk
Islamic Temple
Üşkuyular Cad
Onurga Dere Sk
2430Sk
Cumhuriyet Cad
Ilgın Sk
Çiçek Sk
Tarla Sk
Zeki Müren Cad
Neyzen Tevfik Cad
Tepecik Camii
Salmakis Bay
Marina
Adnan Toker Sk
Firkateyn Sk
ESKIÇEŞME
Şafak Sk
1
2
3
4
5
6
7
8
9
10
11
12
13
14
15
16

Bodrum

it's worst on the Eastern Bay. In between, on Cevat Şakir Caddesi and in the bazaar are the best value options, where you can pick up a döner wrapped in pide for TL5.

Nazik Ana TURKISH $
(Eski Hukumel Sokak 7; meat mains TL5-9, veg mains TL2-3; 9am-10pm, closed Sun Oct-Apr) Hidden away down a narrow alley and definitely worth hunting out, this simple but atmospheric place is a huge hit locally. With its point-and-pick counter, it's a great place to sample different Turkish dishes.

Liman Köftecisi TURKISH $$
(Neyzen Tevfik Caddesi 172; mains TL9-20; 8am-midnight) Despite the barnlike interior, the famous Liman serves delicious food at decent prices. *Köfte* is the speciality. Of the six types, the *Liman köfte* (think *İskender* made with *köfte*) is the top dish.

Orfoz SEAFOOD $$$
(Cumhuriyet Caddesi 177; mains from TL22; dinner) Ask around for the best seafood restaurant in town and it won't be long before somebody directs you here, but quality comes at a price. The portions are smallish and if you get carried away you can easily end up with a frightening bill.

Tranca TURKISH $$$
(Cumhuriyet Caddesi 36; meze TL6-18, mains TL16-32; 11am-midnight) Jutting out into the bay, the family-run Tranca boasts just about the best views of anywhere in Bodrum. Its speciality is *tuzda balık* (fish baked in salt) costing TL70 for a minimum of two people.

Drinking

There is no boredom in Bodrum for party people, but the town also has its share of quieter options. For cheap and cheerful head to the Eastern Bay, for expensive and classy, think Western Bay.

Halıkarnas DISCO
(admission TL50; Cumhuriyet Caddesi 178; 10pm-5am) Bodrum's oldest and most famous nightclub, with a capacity for 5000 revellers. They claim that if you haven't been to Halıkarnas then you haven't been Bodrum, and they might just be right.

Marine Club Catamaran DISCO
(admission TL40; www.clubcatamaran.com; Dr Alim Bey Caddesi; 10pm-4.30am) Setting sail at 1.30am, this floating favourite can fit 1500 party animals on to its transparent dancefloor.

Campanella Bar BAR
(Cumhuriyet Caddesi; noon-4am) Ring out the bells! This charming, oriental-style bar above a shop on a narrow alley usually has live music playing.

Information

The otogar (Cevat Şakir Caddesi) is 500m inland from the Adliye (Yeni) Camii, a small mosque at the centre of the town. The PTT and several banks with ATMs are nearby.

Bodrum is famous for its scuba diving. Look for the dive centres on the boats moored near the **tourist office** (316 1091; Kale Meydanı; 8am-noon & 1-5pm Mon-Fri Oct-Apr, daily May-Sep) beside the Castle of St Peter. For online information see www.bodrumturkeytravel.com.

Getting There & Away

Airlines including Turkish Airlines fly from İstanbul and elsewhere to Bodrum International Airport, 60km away and connected to Bodrum by Havaş shuttle bus.

By bus, there are services to more or less anywhere you could wish to go. Useful services include those to İstanbul (TL75, 12 hours), Kuşadası (TL25, 2½ hours) and Marmaris (TL18, three hours).

Daily ferries link Bodrum with Kos, Greece (€20 same-day return, one hour); hydrofoils (€25 same-day return, 40 minutes) operate from Monday to Saturday between May and October. From about May to September there are also two weekly hydrofoils to Rhodes (Rhodos; €47 same-day return, two hours 15 minutes); check with the **Bodrum Ferryboat Association** (☎316 0882; www.bodrumferryboat.com; Kale Caddesi Cümrük Alanı 22), on the dock past the western entrance to the castle.

MEDITERRANEAN COAST

The western Mediterranean Turkish coast, known as the 'Turquoise Coast', is a glistening stretch of clear blue sea where gods once played in sublime pebble coves, and spectacular ruins abound. In villages too pretty to do justice with mere words, sun-kissed locals yawn and smile at travellers' never-ending quest for the 'Med Life'.

The region's seamless mix of history and holiday inspires and enchants. At places such as Patara and Olympos, your hand-packed sandcastles are humbled by vine-covered ruins and Lycian tombs. If you prefer to interact with your surroundings, plunge into activities such as scuba diving at Kaş and kayaking atop the underwater city in Kekova.

The eastern Mediterranean coast, meanwhile, has long lived in its more fashionable western neighbour's shadow. But the Arab-spiced area has at least as many pristine beaches as the Turquoise Coast.

Marmaris

☎0252 / POP 40,000

An unashamedly brash harbour town that swells to more than 200,000 people during summer, Marmaris is heaven or hell depending which way your boat floats. It sports one of Turkey's swankiest marinas, and a stunning natural harbour where Lord Nelson organised his fleet for the attack on the French at Abukir in 1798. Not far away, the deeply indented Reşadiye and Hisarönü Peninsulas hide bays of azure backed by pine-covered mountains and gorgeous fishing villages.

Sights & Activities

Sunworship by day and hedonism by night, Marmaris caters to a beach and party crowd but is short on sights.

Castle CASTLE
(admission TL3; ⌚8am-noon & 1-5pm Tue-Sun) The small castle houses a modest archaeological museum. Walk the castle walls for lovely views of Marmaris.

Boat Trips BOAT TOUR
Numerous boat trips around Marmaris Bay are on offer along the waterfront, visiting beaches and islands. On a day tour (around TL30 per person) you'll usually visit Paradise Island, Aquarium, Phosphoros Cave, Kumlubuku, Amos, Turunç, Green Sea and İçmeler. Two- and three-day trips (from around €90 person per day) often go to Dalyan and Kaunos.

Beaches & Diving BEACH, DIVING
The best beach is İçmeler 10km south of town, though you can also swim at the pebbly beach near the centre. Marmaris is also a popular place to **scuba dive** (day excursion around €30), and there are several dive centres on the waterfront.

Armutalan Hamamı BATHHOUSE
(136 Sokak 1; massage TL40; ⌚9am-10pm Apr-Oct) Armutalan Hamamı is reputedly the second biggest in Turkey and lies a few kilometres west of the centre, behind the government hospital.

Sleeping

Marmaris has hundreds of good-value sleeping options, especially for self-caterers. Many places close in low season, but those that stay open offer serious discounts.

Royal Maris Hotel HOTEL $$$
(☎412 8383; www.royalmarishotel.com; Atatürk Caddesi 34; s/d TL170/210; ❄≋@) It offers two pools, a private beach, a hamam, fitness centre and spacious balconies with stunning views – remarkably affordable.

Orkide Hotel HOTEL $$
(☎417 8006; www.orkidehotel.com; Kemal Elgin Bulvari; s/d TL190/140; ≋@) Though it is 2km

south of the marina, this award-winning, family-run hotel has a great location near the beach. Readers laud the personal treatment afforded to guests, which is a rare commodity in mega-resorts such as Marmaris. Transfers from nearby airports can be arranged.

Maltepe Pansiyon PENSION $
(☎412 1629; www.maltepepansiyon.com; 66 Sokak 9; s/d TL50/80; ❄@) A longstanding budget choice, with small but spotless rooms, this is one of a cluster of very similar cheap options on this street. Don't forget to look for Nuriye, Memo the owner's ridiculously obese cat, which is famous throughout Turkey.

Eating

For something cheap and cheerful, try the bazaar area between the post office and the mosque, or the old town area around the castle, where there's a host of small Turkish restaurants. There is a cluster of 24-hour kebap joints at the marina end of Ulusal Egemenlik Bulvari, some with extensive menus.

Meryem Ana TURKISH $
(35 Sokak 5/B; mains TL5-6; ✎) Simple and understated, this place serves terrific traditional home cooking, including several vegetarian options. A firm family affair, you can see the mother and aunt hard at work in the kitchen.

Fellini ITALIAN $$$
(Barboras Caddesi 71; meals TL19-45; ⊙9am-midnight) Perennially popular with both locals and visitors in the know, this attractive waterfront restaurant does great thin-crust pizzas and pasta.

Aquarium Restaurant INTERNATIONAL $$$
(Barboras Caddesi 37; meals TL18-38; ⊙9am-midnight) Run by a Turkish-Kiwi couple, this loud and proud port-side restaurant serves grills and steaks to a jovial crowd. Slightly overpriced, but it's got the location covered.

Drinking

Marmaris is a party town, so drinkers and hedonists should stagger straight to **Barlar Sokak** (also called 39 Sokak or Bar St) where there is no shortage of bars and discos to choose from. Action here keeps going until the early hours.

Information

İskele Meydanı (the main square) and the **tourist office** (☎412 1035; İskele Meydanı 2; ⊙8am-noon & 1-5pm Mon-Fri mid-Sep–May, daily Jun-mid-Sep) are by the harbour, north of the castle. The post office is on 51 Sokak. Barlar Sokak runs parallel to the harbour behind the castle.

Getting There & Away

The nearest airports to Marmaris are at Dalaman (92km) and Bodrum (74km). The otogar is 3km north of town, near the turnoff to Fethiye.

There are frequent buses and dolmuşes to Bodrum (TL18, four hours), İzmir (TL27, 4½ hours), Antalya (TL45, 6½ hours) and Fethiye (TL17, three hours). The bigger bus companies pick up from their offices along Gral Mustafa Muğliali Caddesi.

Catamarans to Rhodes sail daily in summer (one way/same-day return/open return €43/45/65, 50 minutes). They do not operate from November to mid-April. Buy your ticket in any Marmaris travel agency.

Köyceğiz

☎0252 / POP 4000

The star attraction here is the brackishly-beautiful and serene Lake Köyceğiz Gölü. As it's so tough to rival the Med, this farming town attracts only modest tourism, and still depends mostly on citrus fruits, olives, honey and cotton for its livelihood. This region is also famous for its liquidambar trees, the source of precious amber gum. Despite its sleepiness, the surrounding Köyceğiz-Dalyan Nature Reserve has a growing reputation among outdoor types for its excellent hiking and cycling.

Sleeping

Most of the accommodation is either on or just off the lakeside Kordon Boyu.

Flora Hotel HOTEL $
(☎262 4976; Cengiz Topi 110; s/d/apt TL40/70/80; ❄@) The foyer is filled with flags in tribute to the foreign guests who often come for arranged walks in the nearby Gölgeli Mountains with owner/guide Alp.

Alila Hotel HOTEL $$
(☎262 1150; www.hotelalila.com; Emeksiz Caddesi 13; s/d TL50/80; ❄≋) By far the most character-filled hotel in town. Twelve of the rooms boast direct views of the water and friendly owner Ömar attends to every detail (right down to the swan-folded towels).

Tango Pansiyon PENSION $
(☎262 2501; www.tangopension.com; Ali İhsan Kalmaz Caddesi 112; dm/s/d per person TL20/30/50; ❄@) Managed by the local school's sports teacher, this place is big on activities. Rooms are bright, cheerful and well maintained, and there's a pleasant garden.

Fulya Pension PENSION $
(☎262 2301; Ali İhsan Kalamaz Caddesi 100; s/d TL25/50; ❄@) A decent but basic budget option. Rooms are clean and cheap, all have balconies and there's a large roof terrace. Bikes are available for free, and the TL20 boat trips are a bargain.

Eating

Seafood restaurants gather near the lake, cheap and cheerful establishments near the square. Try the local delicacy *köyceğiz lokması*, a round, syrupy fritter.

Colıba TURKISH $$
(Cengiz Topel Caddesi 64; mains TL6-15; ⏲10am-1am) Cool-headed staff serve meze, grills and house speciality *alabalık* (trout) to young couples and businessmen. Whitewashed and wooden, Colıba has a shaded terrace with views of the lake front.

Pembe Restaurant SEAFOOD $$
(Cengiz Topel Caddesi 70; meals around TL8-15) Next to Colıba, this pink-and-purple restaurant does reasonably priced seafood and meat dishes.

Mutlu Kardeşler KEBAB $
(Fevzipaşa Caddesi; kebap TL6, pide TL3-5; ⏲7am-10pm) Funky in a rural kind of way, this simple place is much-loved locally and has tables on a little terrace out the back.

Getting There & Away

There are frequent buses and dolmuşes to Fethiye (TL10, 1¾ hours), Marmaris (TL8, one hour) and Dalyan (TL8, 30 minutes), a sleepy little town across the lake, which can also be reached by an easy boat trip (TL30).

Fethiye

☎0252 / POP 75,000

In 1958 an earthquake levelled the old harbour city of Fethiye, sparing only the ancient remains of Telmessos (400 BC) from its wrath. Today Fethiye is once again a prosperous and proud hub of the western Mediterranean coast. Its natural harbour, tucked away in the southern reaches of a broad bay scattered with pretty islands, is perhaps the region's finest.

Sights & Activities

Telmessos RUINS
Telmessos is in fact a whole bunch of ruins that includes a **Roman Amphitheatre** and some **Lycian Sarcophogi**, which are dotted around the town. Perhaps the most eyecatching member of the Telmessos ruins club, though, is the Ionic **Tomb of Amyntas** (admission TL10; ⏲8am-7pm May to Oct, to 5pm Nov-Apr), a temple facade carved into a rock face and dating from 350 BC.

Fethiye Museum MUSEUM
(505 Sokak; admission TL5; ⏲8.30am-5pm) An interesting collection of Lycian finds from Telmessos and other nearby ancient settlements. Of particular interest is the Trilingual Stele, dating from 358 BC and a key tool in the decoding of the Lycian language.

12-Island Tour BOAT TOUR
(per person TL25; ⏲Apr-Oct) Be sure to sign up for this tour, which mixes swimming, cruising and sightseeing around Fethiye Bay. Hotels and agencies sell tickets or you can negotiate a price with the boat companies at the marina. The boats usually stop at six islands and cruise by the rest.

Sleeping

Fethiye has some good-value midrange digs, but not much at the deluxe end. Most accommodation is west of the marina or up the hill behind it. Some places will organise a lift from the otogar.

Yildirim Guesthouse PENSION $
(☎614 4627; www.yildirimguesthouse.com; Fevzi Çakmak Caddesi 21; dm/s/d/tr TL20/60/80/120; ❄) Facing the harbour, this super little guesthouse has three dorms (one mixed) and top-notch private rooms for all tastes. At the budget end of the scale, it is as good as anywhere else you'll find in town.

Villa Daffodil HOTLEL $$
(☎614 9595; www.villadaffodil.com; Fevzi Çakmak Caddesi 115; s/d TL70/100; ❄≋) This large Ottoman-designed guesthouse is one of the few older buildings to survive. The rooms have slanted ceilings and a homely feel; the best have sea views and ante-rooms. Hussein, a retired colonel, is a genial manager.

Tan Pansiyon PENSION $
(☎614 1584; 30 Sokak 43; s/d TL40/55) This traditional Turkish pension is run by a charming

DON'T MISS

BLUE VOYAGES

For many travellers a four-day, three-night cruise on a gület (traditional wooden yacht) between Fethiye and Kale (Demre) is the highlight of their trip to Turkey. Usually advertised as a Fethiye–Olympos voyage, the boats actually start or stop at Kale and the trip to/from Olympos (1¼ hours) is by bus. From Fethiye, boats call in at Ölüdeniz and Butterfly Valley and stop at Kaş, Kalkan and Üçağız (Kekova), with the final night at Gökkaya Bay. A less common route is between Marmaris and Fethiye, also taking four days and three nights.

Food and water are usually included in the price, but you have to buy your booze on the boat. All boats are equipped with showers, toilets and smallish but comfortable double cabins (usually six to eight of them). In practice, most people sleep on mattresses on deck.

Depending on the season the price is €150 to €180 per person (don't buy your ticket in İstanbul!), but while it's OK to bargain, note that cheaper companies may skimp on food and/or the crew may not speak English. Extras such as free watersports, often prove to be empty promises and during summer some larger companies may farm out unknowing tourists to lazy captains with suspect boats.

We recommend owner-operated outfits, as they run a much tighter ship! Boats come and go just about every day of the week between late-April and October. Competition is stiff between the following companies:

Almila Boat Cruise (☎0535-636 0076; www.beforelunch.com)

Big Backpackers (☎0252-614 1981; www.bluecruisefethiye.com)

Olympos Yachting (☎0242-892 1145; www.olymposyachting.com)

elderly couple. Rooms are small (the bathrooms smaller), but it's sparkling clean and quiet, and there is a kitchen for guest use.

Eating

One way to taste Fethiye's fabulous fish without losing too many Turkish lire is to bring your own! Pick your fish at the local market, ferry it to one of the restaurants nearby and ask them to cook it. For around TL5 they will even throw in a sauce, green salad, garlic bread, fruit and coffee.

Meğri Lokantasi TURKISH $$
(www.megrirestaurant.com; Çarşı Caddesi 26; mains TL14-25; ⏰8am-2am low season, to 4am high season) Packed with locals who spill on to the streets, the Meğri does excellent and hearty home-style cooking. The *güveç* (casseroles) are a speciality.

Paşa Kebab KEBAB $$
(Çarşı Caddesi 42; meze TL4-5, pide TL5-9, kebap TL9-15; ⏰9am-midnight) Considered locally to offer the best kebaps in town, this honest and unpretentious place has a well-priced menu. Try the Paşa special, an oven-baked beef, tomato and cheese concoction.

Deniz SEAFOOD $$$
(Uğuur Mumcu Parkı Yanı 10; TL15-30) This place has a big reputation locally for its fresh fish. Pick your meal from the aquarium in front of you, and look away while the deed is done.

Drinking

Fethiye's bars and nightclubs are mostly cheek-by-jowl along one little street, Hamam Sokak, which is just off İskele Meydanı. Alternatively, you may want to check out the options along Dispanser Caddesi. Hardcore ravers head 12km southeast to the suburb of Hisarönü.

Val's Cocktail Bar BAR
(Müge Sokak; beer TL5; ⏰9am-1am) A cute little bar run by Englishwoman Val and located near the new Cultural Centre. It stocks a mean selection of drinks, a book exchange and suitably strong coffee.

Club Bananas CLUB
(Hamam Sokak; beer TL7; ⏰10pm-5am) Any venue where staff set fire to the bar and then dance on it is hard to overlook when enjoying a big night out.

Information

Atatürk Caddesi, the main street, has banks with ATMs. The **tourist office** (☎614 1527; İskele Meydanı; ⏰8.30am-7.30pm Mon-Fri, 10am-5pm Sat & Sun) is opposite the marina, just past the Roman theatre.

Getting There & Away

Fethiye's otogar is 2.5km east of the centre. For northbound buses, you must change at Antalya or Muğla. Buses from the otogar to Antalya (TL20, 4½ hours) head east via Kalkan (TL10, 1½ hours) and Kaş (TL13, three hours). For Ölüdeniz (TL4, 25 minutes), dolmuşes leave from near the mosque.

Ölüdeniz

☎0252 / POP 2000

Over the mountains to the south of Fethiye, lovely Ölüdeniz's sheltered bluish lagoon beside lush national park and a long spit of sandy beach have been a curse as much as a blessing. Ölüdeniz (Dead Sea) is now one of the most famous beach spots on the Mediterranean, with far too many package-holiday hotels backed up behind the sands.

Sights & Activities

The **lagoon** (admission TL4; ⏰8am-8pm) is tranquillity incarnate and is a gorgeous place to sun yourself. Ölüdeniz is also a mecca for **tandem paragliding** (and parasailing). Companies here offer tandem paragliding flights off 1960m Baba Dağ (Mt Baba) for TL100 to TL160, but check that your company has all the right credentials.

Sleeping & Eating

Sugar Beach Club RESORT $
(☎617 0048; www.thesugarbeachclub.com; Ölüdeniz Caddesi 20; campsite per person/car/caravan TL10/10/10, bungalow r TL50-100; ⏰Apr-Oct; ❄@) About 600m to the right of the main drag, this is a well-run theme park for beach-party backpackers. It has a private strip of beach shaded by palms, shaded lounging areas, a beach cafe-bar and spotless bungalows. Bikes can be hired and there are small shops onsite.

Oba Restaurant INTERNATIONAL $$
(Mimar Sınan Caddesi; mains TL15-25; ⏰8am-midnight) Built like a log cabin, the Oba Hostel's restaurant has a great reputation for home-style food at a palatable price. It also does great Turkish/European breakfasts, including homemade muesli with mountain yoghurt and local pine honey.

Getting There & Away

Frequent minibuses run between Ölüdeniz and Fethiye (TL4, 25 minutes).

Patara

☎0242/ POP 1000

Scruffy little Patara, outside Gelemiş, is the perfect spot to mix your ruin-rambling with some dedicated sand-shuffling on 20-odd kilometres of wide, golden **beach** (admission to beach & ruins TL2). With its rural setting and unhurried pace of life, it's a great place to chill out for a few days. The extensive **ruins** include a triple-arched triumphal gate at the entrance to the site, with a necropolis containing several Lycian tombs nearby. All in all, it's a good combination of nature and culture.

Sleeping & Eating

All the places to stay and most of the places to eat are in Gelemiş village, 1.5km inland from the ruins and 2.5km from the beach. Most hotels also serve food.

Patara View Point Hotel PENSION $$
(☎843 5184; www.pataraviewpoint.com; s/d €35/45; ❄@≋) A generous piece of luxury at this hotel, and that is just the view. The rooms themselves are wonderfully rustic with an understated but elegant style, and the garden is adorned with traditional farm implements.

Akay Pension PENSION $
(☎843 5055; www.pataraakaypension.com; s/d/tr €18/25/29; ❄) Run by super-keen-to-please Kazım and family, the pension has well-maintained little rooms and comfortable beds with balconies overlooking orange trees. The cooking here is legendary, and worth trying even if you stay elsewhere.

Golden Pension PENSION $
(☎843 5162; www.pataragoldenpension.com; s/d €25/30; ❄) Offering homely rooms with balconies, a pretty shaded terrace and run by a friendly family that offers attentive service without being overbearing. It's a peaceful and private spot with a roof terrace restaurant.

Getting There & Away

Buses on the Fethiye–Kaş route drop you on the highway 4km from Gelemiş village. From here, dolmuşes run to the village approximately hourly.

Minibuses run from the beach through the village to Fethiye (TL10, 1½ hours, six daily), and just as regularly to Kalkan (TL5, 25 minutes) and Kaş (TL9.50, 45 minutes).

Kalkan

0242 / POP 4000

Kalkan is a stylish hillside harbour town that slides steeply into a sparkling blue bay. It's as rightly famous for its restaurants as its sublimely pretty beach and makes a smart alternative to the better-known, neighbouring Kaş.

Once an Ottoman-Greek fishing village called Kalamaki, Kalkan is now devoted to upmarket tourism. Development continues unchecked on the outskirts of town, but thankfully Kalkan's charms are found right in its centre.

Sleeping

TOP CHOICE The Elixir BOUTIQUE HOTEL $$$
(843 5032; Kalamar Yolu 81; d €120-160;) It's always exciting to see a hotel attempt something new, especially when they pull it off. Part body-focused retreat, part designer hotel, The Elixir features two swimmingly handsome pools (one on the roof), and a smooth-edged Turkish bath.

Türk Evi PENSION $$
(844 3129; www.kalkanturkevi.com; Şehitler Caddesi 19; d TL80-110;) Multilingual and multi-talented Önder and Selma Elitez run one of the more endearing places to stay on the western Mediterranean coast. The beautifully restored stone house has eight rooms filled with rare antique furniture, including some original bathtubs.

Holiday Pension PENSION $
(844 3154; Süleyman Yılmaz Caddesi 2; d TL70, without breakfast TL50) The rooms are simple but charming, some with old wooden beams, antique lace curtains and delightful balconies offering good views.

Çelik Pansiyon PENSION $
(844 2126; Süleyman Yılmaz Caddesi 9; s/d TL40/50;) One of the few cheap guesthouses open year-round, the Çelik Pansiyon has a roof terrace but rather spartan rooms, though they're quite spacious and spotless.

Eating & Drinking

Eating here is top notch but often pricey, so follow the crowds. For drinking there are good choices on Hassan Altan Caddesi, while a strip of rowdier bars aimed at a younger crowd can be found near the municipal parking lot.

Korsan Meze TURKISH $$
(Yat Limanı; meze TL10-15) Opposite the town beach this traditional meze restaurant has been consistently churning out great food for the last 30 years. The same owners also run a seafood joint **Korsan Fish Terrace** (mains TL25-35) and a kebap house **Korsan Kebab** (mains TL12-20), both of which are on Atatürk Caddesi.

Belgin's TURKISH $$
(Nolu Sokak; mains TL15-25; 10am-midnight) In a 150-year-old former olive-oil press, Belgin's serves traditional Turkish food at tempting prices on roof-terrace tables.

Aubergine INTERNATIONAL $$$
(www.kalkanaubergine.com; İskele Sokak, mains TL25-35; 8am-3am) With tables right on the yacht marina, as well as cosy seats inside, the restaurant is famous for its slow-roasted wild boar, as well as its swordfish fillet served in a creamy vegetable sauce.

Moonlight Bar BAR
(Süleyman Yılmaz Caddesi 17; beer €5; 9am-4am) Kalkan's oldest bar is still one of its most 'happening', though the majority of the people at the tables outside, and on the small dance floor, are tourists.

Getting There & Away

In high season, minibuses connect Kalkan with Fethiye (TL10, 1½ hours, 81km) and Kaş (TL5, 30 minutes, 29km). Eight minibuses run daily to Patara (TL5, 25 minutes, 15km).

Kaş

0242 / POP 6000

The mountain known as 'Sleeping Man' (Yatan Adam, 500m) has watched Kaş evolve from a beautiful place of exile for political dissidents, to a funky boutique shopping and cafe strip, to a seaside adventure playground. While Kaş proper may not sport the finest beach culture in the region, it's a yachties' haven and the atmosphere of the town is wonderfully mellow.

Sights

Antiphellos RUINS

In addition to enjoying the town's mellow atmosphere and small pebble beaches, you can walk west a few hundred metres to see the well-preserved **Hellenic amphitheatre**. It's well worth going up the hill along Uzun Çarşı Sokak to reach the **Lion Tomb**, a Lycian sarcophagus mounted on a high base. There are also several Lycian **rock tombs** cut into the cliffs above the town – go at a cool time of day.

Activities

The surrounding areas are ideal for day trips by sea or scooter and many adventure sports are on offer, including some world-class diving.

Boat Trip BOAT TOUR

The most popular boat trip (TL25 to TL30) is to Kekova Island and Üçağız, a three-hour excursion that includes time to see several interesting ruins as well as stops for swimming. Other standard excursions go to the Mavi Mağara (Blue Cave), Patara and Kalkan, or to Liman Ağzı, Longos and several nearby islands. There are overland excursions to the wonderful 18km-long Saklıkent Gorge.

Bougainville Travel OUTDOORS

(☎836 3737; www.bougainville-turkey.com; İbrahim Selin Caddesi 10) If you want to do anything active while you are in Kaş, this long-established English-Turkish tour operator offers scuba diving, trekking, mountain-biking and canyoning trips in the area. The sea-kayaking day trips over the Kekova sunken city (€30), suitable for all fitness levels, will be the highlight of your stay in Kaş.

Sleeping

Cheap pensions are mostly uphill, to the west of Atatürk Bulvarı, and just around the corner from the otogar. More expensive hotels and restaurants are to the east. Places that stay open out of season offer sizeable price reductions.

Hideaway Hotel HOTEL $$

(☎836 1887; www.hotelhideaway.com; Amfi Tiyatro Sokak; s/d TL90/120; ❄@≋) Aptly named, the quiet Hideaway is located at the far end of town. Rooms are simple but in good order and all have a balcony. There's a roof terrace with views over the sea and the adjacent amphitheatre.

Santosa Pension PENSION $$

(☎836 1714; Recep Bilgin Sokak 4; s/d TL65/80; ❄) Clean, quiet and cheap is how best to describe this backpacker hangout. The rooms are simple and tasteful, excellent for the price.

Ateş Pension PENSION $$

(☎836 1393; www.atespension.com; Amfi Tiyatro Sokak; s/d TL65/80; ❄@) Well run by Ahmed and family, this is a friendly place with a pleasant roof terrace where barbecues are held. Guests also have use of the kitchen.

Hilal Pansiyon PENSION $

(☎836 1207; www.korsan-kas.com; Süleyman Yildirim Caddesi 8; s/d €23/38; ❄) The friendly but otherwise run-of-the-mill Hilal has barbecues and a terrace featuring potplants. The travel agency underneath offers guests 10% discounts on activities including kayaking, diving and trips to Saklıkent.

Kaş Kamping CAMPGROUND $

(☎836 1050; www.kaskamping.com; Hastane Caddesi 3; campsites TL20, standard/deluxe bungalow TL60/150) Situated on an attractive rocky site 800m west of town, this has long been the most popular place for camping. There's a lovely swimming area and bar.

Eating

Wander through the narrow streets behind the Cumhuriyet Meydani in search of some pleasant gastronomic surprises.

Kösk TURKISH $$

(Gürsöy Sokak; meze TL6, mains TL15-25) Though it's relatively new on the scene, Kösk already has a faithful band of local followers who are keen to recommend it for its friendly staff, great prices and mouthwatering meze.

İkbal TURKISH $$$

(Sandikci Sokak; meals TL20-35; 9am-midnight) Pricey, but serves delicious fish dishes and the house special, slow-roasted leg of lamb, is to die for.

Bi Lokma TURKISH $$

(Hukumet Caddesi 2; mains TL12-20; 9am-midnight) The Bi Lokma has tables meandering around a terraced garden overlooking the harbour. Sabo (Mama) turns out great traditional dishes, including famous *mantı* (Turkish ravioli) and Mama's pastries. The wine list is also reasonably priced.

Natur-el TURKISH $$

(Gürsöy Sokak 6; meals TL15-20) With its dishes cooked to old Ottoman recipes passed down from generation to generation, Natur-el provides a chance to sample Turkish cuisine at its brilliant best. If you haven't yet tried *mantı*, choose from one of the three varieties here.

Sultan Garden Restaurant TURKISH $$$
(Hükümet Caddesi; mains TL18-30; ⏰10am-midnight) This is a very pretty place on the harbour, complete with original Lycian tombs and a functional cistern. The vegie burger is awesome and the *hünkar beğendı* (spiced lamb pieces on aubergine puree) is soft and flavoursome.

Çinarlar PIZZERIA $$
(Mütfü Efendi Sokak 4; pide TL8-10, pizza TL12-18; ⏰8am-1am) Perennially popular among Kaş' young, who come for the affordable pide and pop music, it also has a pleasant courtyard tucked away off the street. The same owners run the **Meydan** on the square which has the same menu but less of a party vibe.

Drinking

Rejoice! There are a couple of buzzing bars in Kaş. Not the kind of boisterous places you would find in Marmaris or Kuşadası, but more civilised venues heavy on atmosphere. The following are all recommended.

Red Point Bar BAR
(Topçu Sokak) Lively rock bar with dancing and drinking until well into the early hours.

Echo Bar BAR
(Limanı Sokak) Chic jazz bar with a distinctly upmarket clientele.

Hideaway Café & Bar BAR
(Cumhuriyet Caddesi 16a) Cute garden cafe-bar hidden away on a side street.

Getting There & Away

There are half-hourly dolmuşes to Kalkan (TL5, 30 minutes), Olympos (TL6, 2½ hours) and Patara (TL9.50, 45 minutes), and daily buses to İstanbul (TL75, 15 hours), Ankara (TL60, 11 hours) and İzmir (TL42, 8½ hours). For other destinations, connect at Fethiye (TL13, three hours) or Antalya (TL20, 3½ hours).

Olympos & Çiralı

☎0242

Olympos has long had an ethereal hold over its visitors. It was an important Lycian city in the 2nd century BC, but along with the other Lycian coastal cities it went into decline in the 1st century BC. Its fortunes twisted and turned through Roman rule, 3rd-century-AD pirate attacks and fortress-building during the Middle Ages by the Venetians, Genoese and Rhodians (you can still see remains hanging from the clifftops). By the 15th century the site had been abandoned.

Çıralı, 1km to the east, has less of a party reputation than Olympos and is the perfect place to experience the fine art of *keyif* (quiet relaxation). Çıralı boasts a fine stretch of clear sand. The area is an important nesting ground for sea turtles.

> WORTH A TRIP
>
> **CHIMAERA**
>
> The **Chimaera** (admission TL3.50) is a cluster of flames that blaze from crevices on the rocky slopes of Mt Olympos. The Olympians devoutly worshipped Hephaestus (Vulcan), the god of fire, the veneration no doubt springing at least in part from reverence for this mysterious eternal flame. It's located about 7km from Olympos but most pensions in Olympos and Çıralı can set you up with tours to see it (they cost around TL15).

Sights

Ancient Olympos BEACH, RUINS
You have to walk through the ramshackle ruins of ancient Olympos (admission per day/week TL3/7.50) to get to the beach. It's a wild, abandoned place where the remains of ancient buildings peek out from forested coppices, rock outcrops and riverbanks.

Sleeping & Eating

OLYMPOS

Staying in an Olympos tree house has long been the stuff of travel legend, and the natural setting is stunning. The tree-house dream is fading in the face of modern conveniences, but all camps include breakfast and dinner in the price, although drinks are extra. Bathrooms are generally shared, but many bungalows (offered as an alternative to tree houses) have private bathrooms and some have air-con. In general the level of accommodation is pretty similar wherever you stay and prices are also fairly standard.

Not all tree houses have reliable locks, so store valuables at reception. It's also worth being extra attentive with personal hygiene while staying here – every year some travellers get ill. The huge influx of visitors, over the summer in particular, can overwhelm the camps' capacity for waste disposal. Be vigilant when it comes to eating and don't swim around the point area.

Turkmen Tree Houses CAMPGROUND, PENSION **$$**
(892 1249; www.olymposturkmentreehouses.com; tree house TL30, bungalow TL65-80, luxury bungalow TL110; ❄) The luxury bungalows on offer here are a step up in quality from most other places, with en-suite jacuzzi and TV, but for those who prefer the simple life, the treehouses are amongst the most well maintained in town.

Şaban CAMPGROUND, PENSION **$**
(892 1265; www.sabanpansion.com; dm/tree house TL25/35, bungalow TL40-50; ❄) The sight of travellers laid out in hammocks snoozing in the shade soon confirms the local lore: you come here to chill. Şaban is not a party place; instead it sells itself on tranquillity, space, a family feel and great home cooking. It's a good choice for women travelling alone.

Kadir's Yörük Top Treehouse CAMPGROUND, PENSION **$**
(892 1250; www.kadirstreehouses.com; dm/bungalow TL35/65; ❄) Kadir's started the tree-living trend. There are three bars (including the time-honoured Bull Bar), a rock-climbing wall and a range of other activities on offer.

Orange Pension CAMPGROUND, PENSION **$**
(892 1317; www.olymposorangepension.com; bungalow TL60, without bathroom TL50; ❄) The wooden en-suite rooms upstairs have a futuristic Swiss Family Robinson feel, while the concrete rooms downstairs are perhaps the future of Olympos. It's got a great communal dining area and the same guys run a nightclub hidden in the valley.

Varuna TURKISH **$**
(mains TL10-15; 8am-2.30am) Close to the beach, this popular spot serves snacks and mains including fresh trout, *gözleme* (pancake) and *şiş kebaps* (roast skewered meat) in attractive open cabins, or you can just grab a beer (TL6).

ÇIRALI

Çıralı, to put it crudely, is just two dirt roads lined with pensions. To put it another way, it's a delightful beach community for nature lovers and post-backpackers. There are about 60 pensions here, some near the path up to the Chimaera and others close to the beach and the Olympos ruins.

Myland Nature Hotel HOTEL **$$$**
(825 7044; s/d TL167/225; ❄@) This artsy, holistic and ecologically minded hotel is an ideal destination for those in search of soul cleansing, peace of mind or yoga classes and massage.

Hotel Canada HOTEL **$$**
(825 7233; www.canadahotel.net; d €60, bungalow €90; ❄@) This is a beautiful place to stay, offering pretty much the quintessential Çıralı experience – warmth, friendliness and steady relaxation among hammocks and citrus trees. It's ideal for families and children. Carrie and Saban are impeccable hosts.

Arcadia Hotel HOTEL **$$$**
(825 7340; www.arcadiaholiday.com; s/d with half board €100/125; ❄) The Canadian-Turkish owners of these four luxury bungalows have established a lovely escape amid verdant gardens at the northern end of the beach, across the road from Myland Nature. The place is well laid out and well managed, and the restaurant is of a high standard.

Orange Motel PENSION **$$**
(825 7327; www.orangemotel.net; s/d €45/55, bungalow €85; ❄) A smart and affordable choice right on the beach. The garden is hung with hammocks and the stairs leading to the agreeable rooms are wrought in iron. The evening meal (TL20) is about as wild as it gets in Çıralı; nonguests often drop by for a taste of what's cooking.

Getting There & Away

Buses and minibuses plying the Fethiye-Antalya road will drop you at a roadside restaurant from where hourly minibuses go on to Çıralı and Olympos (TL3, 20 minutes). From October to April there are five a day, with the last in each direction around 4pm.

Antalya

0242 / POP 960,000

Once seen by travellers as the gateway to the 'Turkish Riviera', Antalya is now generating a buzz among culture-vultures. Situated directly on the Gulf of Antalya (Antalya Körfezi), the largest Turkish city on the Mediterranean is stylishly modern and classically beautiful. It boasts the creatively preserved Roman-Ottoman quarter of

Kaleiçi, a pristine Roman harbour, plus stirring ruins in the surrounding Bey Mountains (Beydağları). The archaeological museum is world class, there are a number of chic Med-carpet clubs, and the opera and ballet season at the Aspendos amphitheatre draws considerable attention.

Sights

Kaleiçi NEIGHBOURHOOD
Around the harbour is the lovely historic district called Kaleiçi, whose walls once repelled raiders. It's a charming hill full of twisting alleys, atmosphere-laden courtyards, souvenir shops and lavishly restored mansions, while cliffside vantage points on either side of the harbour provide stunning views over a beautiful marina and the soaring Bey Mountains.

Heading down from the **clock tower** you will pass the **Yivli Minare** (Grooved Minaret), which rises above an old church that was converted into a mosque. In the southern reaches of Kaleiçi, the quirky **Kesik Minare** (Cut Minaret) is built on the site of a ruined Roman temple.

Just off Atatürk Caddesi, the monumental **Hadrian's Gate** was erected during the Roman emperor Hadrian's reign (AD 117–38).

Suna & İnan Kıraç Kaleiçi Museum MUSUEM
(Kocatepe Sokak 25; admission TL3; 9am-noon & 1-6pm Thu-Tue) Don't miss this excellent museum in the heart of Kaleiçi. It houses a fine collection of Turkish ceramics, together with rooms set up to show important events in Ottoman family life.

Karaalioğlu Parkı PARK
Need some hush and a cool place to rest your sightseeing-abused feet? Nothing beats Karaalioğlu Parkı, a large, attractive and flower-filled park that's good for a stroll.

Activities

Excursion yachts BOAT TOURS
(TL30 to TL90) Yachts tie up in the Roman Harbour in Kaleiçi, offering boat trips that visit the Gulf of Antalya islands and some beaches for a swim.

Association for the Unity of Mankind HEALTH & FITNESS
(244 5807; Hesapçı Sokak 7) Morning and evening classes in yoga, meditation, aerobics and arts and crafts. A weekly schedule is posted outside the front door.

Sleeping

There are boutique hotels and pensions aplenty in Kaleiçi and most are housed in renovated historic buildings.

Hotel Alp Paşa BOUTIQUE HOTEL $$
(247 5676; www.alppasa.com; Hesapçı Sokak 30-32; s/d €60/80, with Jacuzzi €80/100;) The most effectively signposted hotel in the Kaleiçi labyrinth has 60 individually designed rooms that are fitted with tasteful Ottoman detail. The outdoor courtyard displays Roman columns and other artefacts unearthed during the hotel's construction. There's an onsite hamam and an atmospheric stone-walled restaurant.

White Garden Pansiyon PENSION $
(248 9115; www.whitegardenpansion.com; Hesapçı Geçidi 9; s/d €30/40;) The White Garden combines tidiness, discretion and class beyond its price, not to mention impeccable service from Metin and co. The building and courtyard have been beguilingly restored.

Mediterra Art Hotel BOUTIQUE HOTEL $$$
(244 8624; www.mediterraart.com; Zafer Sokak 5; d/ste TL170/220;) The sign of things to come in Antalya, perhaps, is this upscale masterpiece of wood and stone, offering sanctuary by a cutting-edge pool, and a marvellous winter dining room. The small though modestly luxurious rooms have LCD TVs.

Kaleiçi Lodge BOUTIQUE HOTEL $$
(243 2270; www.kaleicilodge.com; Hesapçı Sokak 37; s/d €32/45;) This stylish small hotel is very affordable. The antique-adorned lobby and hallways lead to red-draped, sharp-lined rooms.

Sabah Pansiyon PENSION $
(247 5345; www.sabahpansiyon.com; Hesapçı Sokak 60; s/d TL40/60, villas from TL200;) A sprawling place with a huge variety of rooms, from simple budget options to luxury villas set around a pool, and all at affordable prices. There is a tour agency on site and breakfast is served at the Yemeli Restaurant, opposite.

Eating

A nearly endless assortment of cafes and eateries are tucked in and around the harbour area; those perched over the bay command the highest prices. For cheap eating, cross Atatürk Caddesi and poke around deep in the commercial district.

Antalya (Kaleiçi)

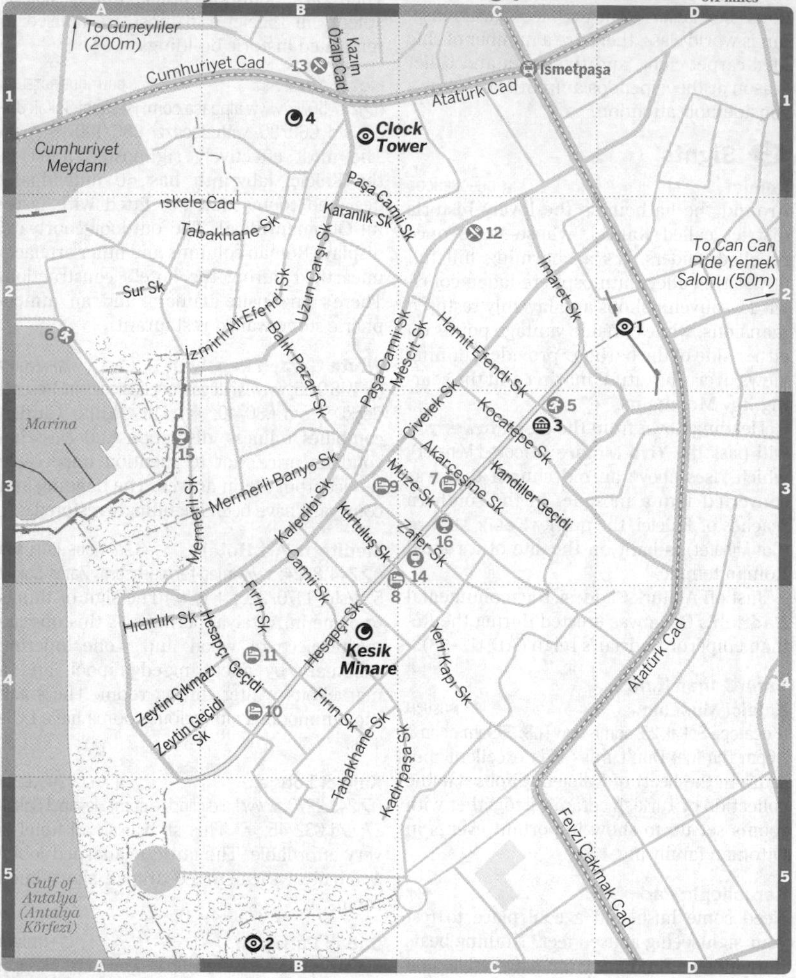

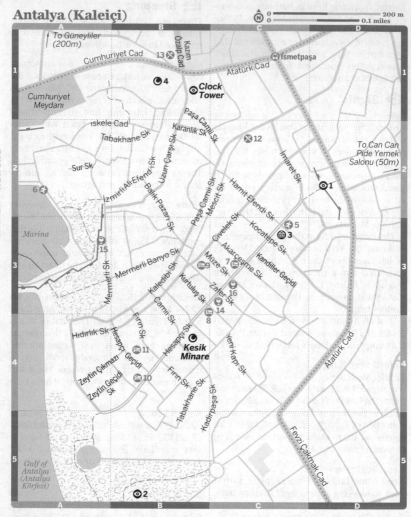

Hasanağa Restaurant TURKISH **$$**
(Mescit Sokak 15; meals TL9-25) Packed on Friday and Saturday nights, when traditional Turkish musicians and folk dancers entertain. Entrées are predictable, but the chefs produce some wonderful dishes, such as the sizzling Ottoman Plate.

Parlak Restaurant TURKISH **$$**
(Kazım Özlap Qvenue Zincirlihan 7; meals TL13-24) This sprawling, open-air patio is a local legend for its slow-roasted chicken cooked on open charcoal grills. The service is theatrical and exact, as waiters shuffle meze and seafood off white tablecloths. A good choice if you're looking to relax for a while.

Güneyliler KEBAB **$$**
(Elmali Mahallesi 4 No 12; meals TL7-25) With its bare, cafeteria-style interior, this *very* reasonably priced local favourite isn't much to look at. But the wood-fired *lahmacun* and grilled kebaps are served with so many complimentary extras, you're likely to return again and again.

Can Can Pide Yemek Salonu TURKISH **$**
(Hasim Iscan Mahallesi, Arik Caddesi 4a; Adana durum TL7; ⌚9am-11pm Mon-Sat) Looking for

Antalya (Kaleiçi)

Top Sights	**Sleeping**
Clock Tower ... B1	7 Hotel Alp Paşa ... C3
Kesik Minare ... B4	8 Kaleiçi Lodge ... B3
	9 Mediterra Art Hotel ... B3
Sights	10 Sabah Pansiyon ... B4
1 Hadrian's Gate ... D2	11 White Garden Pansiyon ... D4
2 Karaalioğlu Parkı ... B5	
3 Suna & İnan Kiraç Kaleiçi Museum ... C3	**Eating**
4 Yivli Minare ... B1	12 Hasanağa Restaurant ... C2
	13 Parlak Restaurant ... B1
Activities, Courses & Tours	
5 Association for the Unity of Mankind ... C3	**Drinking**
6 Excursion Boats ... A2	14 Dem-Lik ... C3
	15 Kale Bar ... A3
	16 Lounge ... C3

something cheap and cheerful? The Can Can most certainly can, offering fantastically prepared *çorba* (soup), pide and Adana *durum*. It's elbow room only, so nudge right in.

Drinking

There are many bars in Kaleiçi and around the yacht harbour. Try the following.

Kale Bar BAR

(Mermerli Sokak 2) Artfully constructed around the old city wall, Kale Bar has spectacular harbour views that are reflected in the drinks prices.

Dem-Lik BAR

(Zafer Sokak 16) A lively venue, filled with Turkish students who crowd into the garden setting and rock out to banging blues tunes.

Lounge BAR

(Hesapçı Sokak 33) For those who prefer their laid-back, this is a comfy bar with sofa seats and mood music, ideal for a chilled night sipping cocktails.

Information

The otogar is 4km north of the centre on the D650 highway to Burdur. A convenient tram (TL2.50) runs from here to the city centre, marked by a clock tower. Get off at Ismetpaşa in front of the PTT, from where it is a short walk downhill to Kaleiçi, entered via Hadrian's Gate (Hadriyanüs Kapısı), just off Atatürk Caddesi. Atatürk Caddesi is lined with banks and ATMs. The **tourist office** (☎/fax 241 1747; Yavuz Ozcan Parkı; ⌚8am-7pm) is west of Cumhuriyet Meydanı.

Getting There & Away

Antalya's airport is 10km east of the city centre on the Alanya highway. Turkish Airlines offers frequent flights to/from İstanbul and Ankara. Atlasjet also has flights to/from İstanbul.

From the vast otogar, buses head for a thousand destinations, including Göreme (TL40, 10 hours) and Konya (TL35, six hours). Dolmuşes run every 15 minutes from the adjacent Mini Garaj for Olympos (TL10, 1½ hours) and Manavgat/Side (TL15, 1½ hours).

Side

☎0242 / POP 20,000

The seasonal village of Side (*see*-duh) is the Turkish version of a carnival by the sea. With its souvenir-peddlers, quaint sandy beaches, family-friendliness and peculiar slapstick charm, this once-docile fishing town is now a firmly established playground. Glorious Roman and Hellenistic ruins mark out the road and the evening performance at the ancient amphitheatre is spectacularly showbiz. The touts are a tedious downside, but visitors to Side often return, happy to be fleeced now and then by the same 2000 year-old tricks, happy to swim in the sea, happy to bask on the rocks, happy to unwind in Side.

Sights

Side's impressive ancient structures include a huge **theatre** (admission TL10; ⌚9am-7.30pm) with 15,000 seats, one of the largest in Anatolia; a Roman bath, now a **museum** (admission TL10; ⌚9am-7.30pm Tue-Sun) with an excellent small collection of statues and sarcophagi; and seaside

Temples of Apollo & Athena, dating from the 2nd century AD.

Sleeping & Eating

While the number of restaurants increases every season, the menus can be a bit predictable. For drinking, Barbaros Caddesi has plenty of choices.

Beach House Hotel HOTEL $$
(☎753 1607; www.beachhouse-hotel.com; Barbaros Caddesi; r €20; ❄@) Run by a long-term Australian expat, this justifiably popular spot has a prime beachside locale, yet still promotes restfulness. Most rooms face the sea and all have spacious balconies. The neighbouring Soundwaves Restaurant, run by the same crew, is also recommended.

Hotel Sevil HOTEL $
(☎753 2041; www.chilloutside.com; Zambak Sokak 32; s/d TL50/70; ❄≋) Set around a pretty garden of mulberry trees, palms and roses, this budget choice features a smart little bar and a genuine travel vibe.

Moonlight Restaurant SEAFOOD $$
(Barbaros Caddesi 49; meals TL15-25) The classiest joint in town, with an extensive Turkish wine list and unfussy service. The mostly seafood offerings are well presented and very fresh. The biggest drawcard, however, is the romantic back patio.

Getting There & Away

In summer, Side has direct bus services to Ankara (TL35, 10 hours), İzmir (TL40, 8½ hours) and İstanbul (TL57, 13 hours). Otherwise, frequent minibuses connect Side with Manavgat otogar (TL2, 4km), from where buses go to Antalya (TL15, 1¼ hours), Alanya (TL15, 1¼ hours) and Konya (TL30, 5½ hours).

Alanya

☎0242 / POP 88,000

Alanya has mushroomed from a sparsely populated highway town on a silky sand beach to a densely populated tourist haven. Unless they do the odd boat cruise or beach stroll, many visitors to Alanya just shuffle between the airport shuttle and the hotel pool, perhaps venturing to a restaurant and banging nightclub after dark. But Alanya has something special up its dusty sleeve. Looming high above the modern centre is a brilliant fortress district, with trappings of a fine Seljuk castle, a wonderful mess of ruins, active remnants of village life and a touch of revamped 'Ottomania'.

Sights

Alanya Fortress CASTLE
(Alanya Kalesi; admission TL10; ⊙9am-7pm) Alanya's crowning glory is the Seljuk fortress on top of the promontory, overlooking the city as well as the Pamphylian plain and the Cilician mountains.

Kızıl Kule HISTORIC BUILDING
(Red Tower; admission TL3; ⊙9am-7pm) This octagonal tower down by the harbour was built in 1226. It houses a small ethnographical

WORTH A TRIP

PERGE, ASPENDOS & TERMESSOS

Between Antalya and Alanya there are several magnificent Graeco-Roman ruins to explore. Breath-taking **Perge** (admission TL15; ⊙9am-7.30pm), 15km east of Antalya and 2km north of Aksu, has a 12,000-seat stadium and a 15,000-seat theatre. Another stunning place is **Aspendos** (admission TL15, parking TL4; ⊙8am-7pm), 47km east of Antalya. Here you'll see the world's best-preserved Roman theatre, dating from the 2nd century AD and still used for performances during the Aspendos Opera & Ballet Festival every June or July. The former capital of the fierce Termessians, who fought off Alexander the Great, **Termessos** (admission TL5; ⊙8am-5.30pm) is high in the mountains, 34km inland from Antalya. The ruins have a spectacular setting but demand some vigorous walking and climbing. Unless a coach party turns up, these places are all eerily deserted.

The only gripe is that it's not convenient to get to these sites by public transport. The easiest way to see them is with your own transport or on a tour from Antalya. A full-day tour to Perge and Aspendos, with side trips to spots such as Side, costs €40 per person; a half-day tour taking in Termessos costs around TL100 per car load. Ask at your pension or hotel in Antalya. Plenty of agencies in Antalya hire out cars from €30 per day.

museum and there are fine views of the harbour from the roof terrace.

Activities

Boat Trips BOAT TOUR
(per person incl lunch TL35; 10.30am) Boats leave from near Gazipaşa Caddesi every day for a six-hour voyage around the promontory, visiting several caves and **Cleopatra's Beach**.

Tours TOUR
Many operators organise tours to local sights. A typical tour including **Aspendos** and **Side** costs around TL70 per person, while a 4WD safari to visit villages in the **Taurus Mountains** costs about TL50.

Sleeping

Alanya is low on budget accommodation, as pensions have been superseded by a million faceless concrete lumps targeting tour groups or self-caterers. İskele Caddesi is your best bet if you are on a budget.

Temiz Otel HOTEL $
(513 1016; http://temizotel.com.tr; İskele Caddesi 12; s/d TL60/110;) Hotel 'Clean' is just that. Plus the rooms are spacious and the balconies offer a bird's-eye view of the thumping club and bar action below.

Baba Hotel HOTEL $
(513 0095; İskele Caddesi 6; s/d TL30/50) Baba is about the cheapest pad in town, but you pay for what you get (which is not much). The front entrance is located on the left side of a cement stairway just off the street.

Eating

The cheap restaurant scene is being swallowed by rising rents, so if you're tired of tourist traps, look for a *köfte* joint or any lokanta popular with workers.

Ottoman House SEAFOOD $$$
(www.ottomanhousealanya.com; Damlataş Caddesi 31; meals 20-30) In an old stone Ottoman house this is probably the most atmospheric place to eat in Alanya. There is live music every night, but come on a Thursday or Sunday for the all-you-can-eat fish barbecue.

Köyüm Gaziantep Başpınar TURKISH $$$
(Hükümet Caddesi; meals TL18-30) For something more adventurous than standard grills and seafood, this is one of central Alanya's best options. Traditional food from Gaziantep is on offer.

Köfte D'Köfte TURKISH
(Kale Caddesi; meals TL15-25) A flashy yellow-and-red sign greets diners at this 'boutique' fast-food joint at the bottom of castle hill. Attentive service and generous meat, rice and salad combinations are all part of the deal.

Drinking

Alanya has a bouncing but bawdy nightclub scene that can keep you up all night whether it is for the right reasons or the wrong reasons. Head for Gazipaşa Caddesi if you like your music loud.

Red Tower Brewery Restaurant BAR, RESTAURANT
(www.redtowerbrewery.com; İskele Caddesi 80) If EU membership were dependent on a good brewpub, then the Red Tower would be Turkey's sole delegate. Not only is this place rare, it also makes staggeringly good Pilsen. The varied menu is great, too; they even serve up sushi.

Robin Hood Bar BAR, CLUB
(Gazipaşa Caddesi) Sherwood Forest comes to Turkey at this neon madhouse where they rob the rich to pay for drinks. The **Latin Club** above also gets pretty noisy.

Getting There & Away

The otogar is on the coastal highway (Atatürk Caddesi), 3km west of the centre. There are frequent buses to Antalya (TL15, two hours) and to Adana (TL35, 10 hours), stopping in a number of towns (including Anamur) en route.

Fergün Denizcilik (511 5565; www.fergun.net; İskele Caddesi 84) runs ferries to Girne (Cyprus) twice a week on Monday and Thursday (TL170 return, including taxes, two hours).

Antakya (Hatay)

0326 / POP 215,000

The biblical town of Antioch, Antakya (confusingly, also called Hatay) was a major Roman settlement and, until 1938, part of the French protectorate of Syria. Both St Paul and St Peter dropped by to preach here, and you can visit the ancient **Church of St Peter** (St Pierre Kilisesi; admission TL8; 9am-noon & 1-6pm), 3km northeast of town. The magnificent Roman mosaics in the **Antakya Archaeology Museum** (Gündüz Caddesi; admission TL8; 9am-6.30pm Tue-Sun) more than justify an overnight stop on the way to Syria.

Sleeping & Eating

There is a large number of restaurants on and around Hürriyet Caddesi.

TOP CHOICE **Liwan Hotel** BOUTIQUE HOTEL $$$
(☎215 7777; www.theliwanhotel.com; Sihlalı Kuvetler Caddesi 5; s/d TL150/200; ❄) In a building formerly owned by the President of Syria, this is arguably the best boutique hotel in the region.

Antakya Catholic Church Guesthouse HOTEL $
(☎215 6703; www.anadolukatolikkilisesi.org/antakya; Kutlu Sokak 6; r TL30) Run by the local Catholic church, this is an acceptable budget option. As it has only eight rooms it's a good idea to book in advance.

Getting There & Away

The otogar is 7km northwest of the centre and has direct buses to most western and northern points. There are also frequent services to Gaziantep (TL20, four hours) and Şanlıurfa (TL30, seven hours).

The Jet bus company (www.jetturizim.com.tr) has direct daily buses across the Syrian border to Aleppo (TL10, three hours) and Damascus (TL15, seven hours) though services were suspended at the time of writing. Alternatively, for Aleppo catch a local bus to Reyhanlı (TL5, 45 minutes) from the petrol station at the top end of İstiklal Caddesi, and then a dolmuş to the Turkish border, where you have to walk a few kilometres to the Syrian post. See also p543.

CENTRAL ANATOLIA

On central Turkey's hazy plains, the sense of history is so pervasive that even the average kebap chef can remind you that the Romans preceded the Seljuks. This is, after all, the region where the whirling dervishes first whirled, Atatürk began his revolution, Alexander the Great cut the Gordian knot and King Midas turned everything to gold. Julius Caesar came here to utter his famous line, *'Veni, vidi, vici'* ('I came, I saw, I conquered').

In Safranbolu and Amasya, drinking in the history involves sipping *çay* and gazing at the half-timbered Ottoman houses. While these are two of Turkey's most beautiful towns, offering Ottoman digs with cupboard-bathrooms, other spots are so little visited that foreigners may find themselves entered as just *turist* (tourist) in hotel guest books. This offers the opportunity to get to grips with everyday Anatolian life in a coach-party free environment – where historical heavyweights from the Hittites to Atatürk established major capitals.

Ankara

☎0312 / POP 4.2 MILLION

İstanbullus may quip that the best view in Ankara is the ride home, but the Turkish capital has more substance than its reputation as a staid administrative centre suggests. The capital established by Atatürk offers a mellower, more manageable vignette of urban Turkey than İstanbul, and two of the country's most important sights: the Anıt Kabir, Atatürk's hilltop mausoleum; and the Museum of Anatolian Civilisations, which will help you solve clues at sites left on the Anatolian plains by Hittites, Phrygians and other ancient folk. It can be a disjointed place, but two or three neighbourhoods have some charm: the historic streets in the hilltop citadel, the chic Kavaklıdere district and Kızılay, one of Turkey's hippest urban quarters.

Sights

When it comes to sights Ankara can't compete with İstanbul, but that's not to say that what there is isn't impressive.

Anıt Kabir MONUMENT
(Mausoleum of Atatürk; ⏱9am-5pm mid-May–Oct, to 4pm Nov-Jan, to 4.30pm Feb–mid-May) If you're an Atatürk devotee, you can't leave the city without having paid your respects to the founder of modern Turkey at the Anıt Kabir, 2km northwest of Kızılay Meydanı.

Museum of Anatolian Civilisations MUSEUM
(Anadolu Medeniyetleri Müzesi; admission TL15; ⏱8.30am-5.15pm) With the world's richest collection of Hittite artefacts, the state-of-the-art Museum of Anatolian Civilisations, housed in a beautifully restored 15th-century *bedesten,* is Turkey's best museum outside İstanbul.

Citadel FORTRESS
Just up the hill, it's also well worth exploring the side streets of the citadel, the most scenic part of Ankara. Inside it, local people still live as if in a traditional Turkish village.

Roman baths RUINS
(Roma Hamaları; admission TL3; ⏱8.30am-12.30pm & 1.30-5.30pm) About 400m north of Ulus Meydanı, take a look at the surprisingly

well-preserved remains of the Roman baths, dating back to the 3rd century. Southeast of the baths, you'll find more Roman ruins, including the **Column of Julian** (AD 363) in a square ringed by government buildings, and the **Temple of Augustus & Rome**.

Sleeping

The first three listings are in the citadel or on the hill leading to it from Ulus Meydanı. However, locals advise against wandering Ulus' streets after about 9pm, so you may prefer to stay in Kızılay, which is pricier but has better restaurants and bars. Book ahead to beat the business travellers and bureaucrats to a room.

TOP CHOICE Angora House Hotel BOUTIQUE HOTEL **$$**
(☎309 8380; angora house@gmail.com; Kalekapısı Sokak 16 18, Ulus; s/d/tr €70/120/150; ⊙Mar Oct; @) Ankara's original boutique hotel is in a great location inside the citadel and offers beautiful, individually decorated rooms in a restored house, benefiting from some fine half-timbering and a walled courtyard.

Hotel Metropol HOTEL **$$**
(☎417 3060; www.hotelmetropol.com.tr; Olgunlar Sokak 5, Kızılay; s/d TL85/140; ❄) Quite a snip at these prices, the three-star Metropol provides quality and character across the board. The breakfast is excellent, but laundry rates are high.

Hitit Oteli HOTEL **$**
(☎310 8617; Hisarparkı Caddesi 12, Ulus; s/d TL50/70) A noticeable step up in quality compared to the nearby budget places. The rooms are not as smart as the reception, with its fish tank and arches, but it is a reasonable option near the museum.

Kale Otel HOTEL **$**
(☎311 3393; Şan Sokak 13, Ulus; s/d TL40/60) Though the carpets could do with a scrub, this is one of the closest hotels to the museum. The Kale's yellow-and-red facade is rather off-putting, but its pink-and-red interior is more palatable. This is one of Ulus' more pleasant budget options.

Eating

Head to Ulus Meydanı for cheap eats.

TOP CHOICE Le Man Kültür INTERNATIONAL **$$**
(Konur Sokak 8a-b, Kızılay; mains TL9-27; ⊙10am-11pm) One of Kızılay's coolest hangouts, this restaurant packs in the ripped denim and beehives (of the Amy Winehouse variety) between walls decorated with subversive cartoons. The menu ranges from kebaps to Mexican and even Argentinean dishes.

Zenger Paşa Konağı TURKISH **$$**
(www.zengerpasa.com, in Turkish; Doyran Sokak 13, Ulus; mains TL12-27; ⊙noon-12.30am) Built in 1721 for governor Mehmet Fuat Paşa, the Zenger Paşa is crammed with Ottoman ephemera. It looks at first like a deserted ethnographic museum, but the pide, meze and grills, still cooked in the original oven, plus the perfect citadel views, attract wealthy Ankaralıs.

Mutlu Kebap KEBAB **$**
(Ruzgarli Caddesi 3, Ulus; mains TL3-12; ⊙9am-midnight) Monster-size pides and the usual array of kebaps on offer here, along with a few surprises such as the refreshingly tasty *yayli çorbasi* (yoghurt soup). A worthwhile spot for cheap eats in the budget hotel district.

Information

Ankara's citadel crowns a hill 1km east of Ulus Meydanı (Ulus Sq), the heart of Old Ankara, and near most of the inexpensive hotels. The newer Ankara lies further south, with better hotels, restaurants and nightlife in Kızılay and Kavaklıdere. There are internet cafes and banks with ATMs around Ulus Meydanı, and Karanfıl Sokak in Kızılay.

Atatürk Bulvarı is the main north–south axis. Ankara's mammoth otogar is 5.5km southwest of Ulus and 4.5km west of Kızılay. A free bus service to Ulus runs from behind the taxi rank to the corner of Cumhuriyet Bulvarı.

PTT (Atatürk Bulvarı) Just south of Ulus Meydanı.

Tourist office (☎310 8789; Mustafa Kemal Bulvarı 67, Ulus; ⊙9am-5pm Mon-Fri, 10am-5pm Sat) Opposite the train station.

Getting There & Away

Air

Ankara's Esenboğa airport, 33km north of the city centre, is the hub for Turkish Airlines' domestic-flight network; there are daily nonstop flights to most Turkish cities with Turkish Airlines or Atlasjet. International flights are generally cheaper using one of İstanbul's airports.

Bus

Ankara's huge otogar (Ankara Şehirlerarası Terminali İşletmesi; AŞTİ) is the vehicular heart of the nation, with coaches going everywhere all day and night. They depart for İstanbul (TL27 to TL40, six hours) at least every 30 minutes.

Train

The train station is just over 1km southwest of Ulus Meydanı along Cumhuriyet Bulvarı. A fast express service runs to Konya, but some of the long-haul services can be excruciatingly slow.

Sivas

0346 / POP 295,000

Sivas lies at the heart of Turkey geographically as well as politically, thanks to its role in the run-up to the War of Independence. The Congress building resounded with plans, strategies and principles as Atatürk and his adherents discussed their great goal of liberation. With a colourful, sometimes tragic history and some of the finest Seljuk buildings ever erected, Sivas is a good stopover en route to the wild east.

Sights

Don't miss the buildings in the adjoining park: the **Çifte Minare Medrese** (Seminary of the Twin Minarets) with a grand Seljuk-style gateway; the fabulous **Şifaiye Medresesi**, a former medical school that's one of the city's oldest buildings; and the 13th-century **Bürüciye Medresesi**. Southeast of the park are the 1197 **Ulu Cami** (Great Mosque) and the glorious **Gök Medrese** (Blue Seminary); west of it is the **Atatürk Congress & Ethnography Museum** (Atatürk Kongre ve Etnografya Müzesi; Inonü Bulvarı; admission TL3; 8.30am-noon & 1.30-5pm Tue-Sun), in the imposing Ottoman school building that hosted the Sivas Congress in September 1919.

Sleeping

Hotels line Eski Belediye Sokak, just east of the main square, and include the following:

Sultan Otel HOTEL $$
(221 2986; Eski Belediye Sokak 18; s/d/tr TL90/140/170;) Difficult to beat for value for money, and a favourite with midweek business travellers.

Otel Madımak HOTEL $$
(221 8027; Eski Belediye Sokak 2; s/d/tr TL60/90/120;) Comfortable burgundy digs, but be aware that this hotel carries sad memories of a hate crime that took place here in 1993 when 37 Alevi intellectuals and artists were burned alive in a religiously motivated mob arson attack.

Eating

Cheap eats can be found at the street stalls along İnönü Bulvarı and Atatürk Caddesi.

Sema Hanımın Yeri TURKISH $
(İstasyon Caddesi Öncü Market; mains TL5-7; 8am-midnight) The welcoming Madame Sema serves home-cooked food at this rustic, wood-panelled joint.

Information

The **tourist office** (222 2252; 9am-5pm Mon-Fri) is in the *valılık* (provincial government headquarters) building on the main square.

Getting There & Away

Buses go to destinations including Amasya (TL20, 3½ hours), Ankara (TL30, six hours) and Erzurum (TL30, seven hours). Services are not that frequent, so you might want to book ahead at one of the ticket offices just east of Hükümet Meydanı, along Atatürk Caddesi.

Sivas is a main rail junction. The *Doğu Ekspresi* and *Erzurum Ekspresi* go through Sivas to Erzurum and Kars daily; the *Güney Ekspresi* (from İstanbul to Kurtalan) runs four times a week in each direction, though the final leg to İstanbul was temporarily suspended at time of research.

Konya

0332 / POP 1.1 MILLION

Turkey's equivalent of the 'Bible Belt', conservative Konya is the home town of the whirling dervish orders and a bastion of Seljuk culture. It also has modern significance as an economic boom town. Luckily, the city derives considerable charm from this juxtaposition of old and new, and boasts one of Turkey's finest and most characteristic sights, the Mevlâna shrine.

Sights & Activities

The town centre stretches from Alaaddin Tepesi, the hill topped by the Alaaddin Camii mosque (1221), along Mevlâna Caddesi to the Mevlâna Müzesi.

Karatay Müzesi MUSEUM
(Alaaddin Meydanı; admission TL3; 9am-5pm) Once a Muslim theological seminary, this is now a museum housing a superb ceramic collection.

İnceminare Medresesi MUSEUM
(Seminary of the Slender Minaret; Adliye Bulvarı; admission TL3; 9am-noon & 1-5.30pm) Now the Museum of Wooden Artefacts and Stone Carving.

Sleeping

Hotel Balıkçılar HOTEL $$
(☎350 9470; www.balikcilar.com, in Turkish; Mevlâna Karşısı 2; s/d/tr/ste €65/85/105/120, breakfast €12; ❄) Easily the best reception area in town, styled as a cobbled Ottoman street. Facilities include a large lobby bar, restaurant, sauna, hamam and occasional *sema* (dervish ceremony) performances.

Hotel Rumi HOTEL $$
(☎353 1121; www.rumihotel.com; Durakfakih Sokak 3; s/d/tr/ste US$70/100/125/150; ❄@) Boasting a killer position near the Mevlâna Museum, the stylish Rumi has 33 rooms and suites with curvy chairs, slender lamps and mirrors. There's a hamam in the basement and unmatched views from the terrace restaurant.

Ulusuan Otel PENSION $
(☎351 5004; Çarşi PTT Arkasi 4; s/d TL40/70; ❄) Shared bathrooms have never looked so good in this spick and span budget option where the management positively falls over itsef to make sure you enjoy your stay.

Otel Mevlâna PENSION $
(☎352 0029; Cengaver Sokak 2; s/d/tr from TL45/70/ 90; ❄) On a side street across Mevlâna Caddesi from Otel Bera Mevlâna, this friendly central option is a good choice for backpackers of both sexes and represents superb value for the standard of accommodation.

Eating & Drinking

Hungry travellers will be disappointed by Konya's paucity of good restaurants, and you should choose where you eat carefully – if you suspect hygiene practices are not what they should be, give the place a miss. The local speciality is *fırın,* greasy oven-roasted mutton served on puffy bread.

Gülbahçesı Konya Mutfağı TURKISH $
(☎351 0768; Gülbahçe Sokak 3; mains TL3-14; ⏲8am-10pm) One of Konya's best restaurants, mostly because of its upstairs terrace with excellent views. Dishes include *yaprak sarma* (stuffed grapevines leaves), spicy Adana kebap and *etli ekmek* (bread with meat). No alcohol is served.

Osmanlı Çarşısı BAR
(☎353 3257; İnce Minare Sokak) Looking like an apple smoke–spewing pirate ship, this early-20th-century house behind the İnceminare Medresesi has terraces and seats on the street. Nargilehs are being lit or bubbling away everywhere you look.

DON'T MISS

MEVLÂNA MUSEUM

Join the pilgrims and head straight to the wonderful **Mevlâna Museum** (Mevlâna Müzesi; admission TL3; ⏲9am-6.30pm Tue-Sun, 10am-6pm Mon), at the eastern end of Mevlâna Caddesi. The former lodge of the whirling dervishes, it is topped by a brilliant turquoise-tiled dome – one of the most inspiring images of Turkey. Although it's virtually under siege from devout crowds, there's a palpable mystique here. To see the modern-day dervishes whirl, there is a free performance every Saturday at 8pm at the **Mevlâna Cultural Centre**, and you should book your attendance in advance through your hotel.

Information

You'll find numerous banks with ATMs and internet cafes around Alaaddin Tepesi, and the PTT just south of Mevlâna Caddesi near Hükümet Meydanı. The **tourist office** (☎353 4021; Aslanlı Kişla Caddesi 5; ⏲8.30am-5.30pm Mon-Sat) is hidden away in a courtyard around the corner from the Mevlâna Müzesi.

Getting There & Away

There are three daily flights to and from İstanbul with Turkish Airlines. Express trains link Konya with Ankara, though connections to İstanbul are suspended until the completion of building works in the capital in 2015.

The otogar is 14km north of the centre; free *servis* take half an hour for the trip into town. There are frequent buses to all major destinations, including Ankara (TL20, four hours), İstanbul (TL45, 11½ hours), Kayseri (TL25, four hours) and Sivas (TL30, seven hours). There are lots of ticket offices in the centre.

CAPPADOCIA (KAPADOKYA)

Between Kayseri and Nevşehir, Central Anatolia's mountain-fringed plains give way to a land of fairy chimneys and underground cities. The fairy chimneys – rock columns, pyramids, mushrooms and a few camels – were formed, alongside the valleys of cascading white cliffs, when Erciyes Dağı (Mt Erciyes) erupted. The intervening millennia added to the remarkable Cappadocian canvas, with Byzantines carving cave churches and subterranean complexes to house thousands of people.

The region's towns are small and geared towards tourism to varying degrees, with excellent value accommodation, top-notch eating and a plethora of tour companies keen for your business. Göreme is the most popular base, especially for budget travellers; Ürgüp is rather more refined; while Avanos and Mustafapaşa retain a tranquil, small village feel. There literally is something for everybody here.

Information

The following Cappadocia-based agencies offer varied programs of cycling, horse-riding, hiking, ballooning (see the box, p515) and even quad-biking in the surrounding countryside. All companies also offer essentially the same standard, colour-coded day tours to local attractions with slight variations. The Green Tour, visiting the underground cities and Ihlara Valley, is the most difficult to do on public transport. The Red Tour takes in one of the open-air museums, Pigeon and Rose Valleys, Avanos and Ürgüp but is easy enough to do on your own. The Blue Tour is the only one that visits Mustafapaşa, with hiking in the Soğanli valley and birdwatching at Sultansazliği Bird Sanctuary thrown in.

Neşe Tour (☎271 2525; www.nesetour.com; Terminal Karsisi 3, Göreme)

Nomad Travel (☎271 2767; www.nomadtravel.com.tr; Belediye Caddesi 9, Göreme)

Argeus Tours (☎341 4688; www.argeus.com.tr; İstiklal Caddesi 7,Ürgüp)

Getting There & Away

The main access town for Cappadocia is Göreme, and though intercity bus companies will happily sell you a ticket for 'Göreme', only very few services really terminate there and most will drop you at the otogar in nearby Nevşehir. Though in theory a free *servis* should be thrown in, very often that is not the case and your requests for assistance will be met with offers of 'help' or 'advice' that come with a price tag. Instead take a local blue bus (TL3, 15 minutes) to the Göreme turn off in the town centre where you can await one of the half-hourly connecting services (7.45am-5.30pm) to Göreme (TL2, 15 minutes). Ignore the touts and taxi drivers at the Nevşehir otogar who will tell you a long walk is involved and offer to cut you a special deal. There is no walk and the deal isn't special.

Getting away from Göreme and Ürgüp however is much less stressful than arriving. Regular intercity buses pick up from the town otogars serving nationwide destinations.

The closest airports are at Kayseri and Nevşehir and good value flights are offered by Turkish Airlines and Sun Express.

Getting Around

The Cappadocia towns are linked via a circuitous two-way minibus route. Buses leave from Ürgüp to Avanos (TL2, 20 minutes) via Ortahisar, Göreme Open-Air Museum, Göreme village, Çavuşin and (on request) Paşabağları and Zelve every two hours from 8am to 4pm. There's also an hourly municipal bus running between Göreme and Avanos from 8.15am to 7.15pm, a half hourly one from Avanos to Nevşehir via Göreme, and seven daily buses between Ürgüp and Mustafapaşa.

Central Cappadocia

Göreme

☎0384 / POP 6500

Göreme is the archetypal travellers' utopia: a beatific village where the surreal surroundings spread a fat smile on everyone's face. Beneath the honeycomb cliffs, the locals live in fairy chimneys – or, increasingly, run hotels in them. The wavy white valleys in the distance, with their hiking trails, panoramic

DON'T MISS

CAPPADOCIA FROM ABOVE

At any given moment, chances are there are more hot-air balloons airborne over Cappadocia than anywhere else on the planet. This is *the* place to get your balloon wings if you haven't yet done so. Flight conditions are especially favourable here and the views across the valleys and fairy chimneys are simply unforgettable – it's a magical experience. Though fairly pricey, it's worth every euro, and if you shop around you can get a decent deal. Surprisingly it often works out considerably cheaper to book with your hotel than directly with the balloon companies, who will charge around €170 per person for a one-hour flight in a 20-passenger balloon. Operators offer different packages (and safety standards) but the following have good credentials:

Butterfly Balloons (☎271 3010; www.butterflyballoons.com; Uzundere Caddesi 29, Göreme)

Ürgüp Balloons (☎341 5636; www.urgupballoons.com; İstiklal Caddesi 52, Ürgüp)

viewpoints and rock-cut churches, look like giant tubs of vanilla ice cream.

Tourism is having an impact on this destination and these days a visitor can start the day in a hot-air balloon, before touring a valley of rock-cut Byzantine churches at Göreme Open-Air Museum. Nonetheless, rural life is still apparent around Göreme, where once upon a time, if a man couldn't lay claim to one of the rock-hewn pigeon houses, he would struggle to woo a wife.

Sights

Göreme Open-Air Museum MUSEUM
(Göreme Açık Hava Müzesi; admission TL15; ⏰8am-5pm) Cappadocia's top attraction is Göreme Open-Air Museum. Medieval frescos can be seen in the rocky monastic settlement, where some 20 monks lived. The best-preserved churches are from the 10th to 13th centuries, although some are even older than that. The stunning **Karanlık Kilise** (Dark Church; admission TL8) is one of the most famous and fresco-filled of the churches, and it is worth paying the extra admission fee. Across the road from the main entrance, the **Tokalı Kilise** (Buckle Church) is also impressive, with an underground chapel and fabulous frescos.

Sleeping

Intense competition keeps prices low and standards high. Pack warm clothes between October and May as it gets very cold at night.

Fairy Chimney Inn BOUTIQUE HOTEL $$
(☎271 2655; www.fairychimney.com; Güvercinlik Sokak 5/7; s/d/tr from €44/55/66, students €22; @) This fairy chimney high on Aydınlı Hill is a former Byzantine monastery, wonderfully converted by its owner, a German anthropologist. Rooms are beautifully decorated, with simple furniture, cushions and carpets, and a refreshing lack of TVs and Jacuzzis. Other treats include the cave hamam, communal lounge, home-cooked meals, volunteer opportunities and glorious garden terrace.

Elysee Pension PENSION $$
(☎271 2244; www.elyseegoreme.com; Mizraz Sokak 18; s/d/tr/q €30/55/75/85) Expect a warm welcome at this beautiful pension, which is really a boutique hotel with an overly modest owner. You get far more than what you pay for here.

Kookaburra Pension PENSION $
(☎271 2549; www.kookaburramotel.com; Konak Sokak 10; s/d TL30/50, dm without breakfast TL15; @) This quirky pension, with agricultural tools and pot plants decorating its stone passages, has tidy, spacious rooms with private bathrooms. The roof terrace is a knockout and there's a bar-restaurant up top.

Backpacker's Cave Hotel HOSTEL $$
(☎271 2555; www.cappadociabackpackers.com; Cevizler Sokak 13; dm TL20, s/d TL50/80; @) Yasin's place is a cozy little backpacker hangout offering cave rooms, Ottoman rooms and all the assistance you can possibly need for exploring Cappadocia.

Kemal's Guest House GUESTHOUSE $$
(☎271 2234; www.kemalsguesthouse.com; Karşıbucak Sokak; dm/s/d/tr/ste €13/27/ 40/57/80) Entered via a flowery garden and reception with big bookshelves and battered sofas, popular Kemal's is run by a genial Turkish-Dutch couple. Barbara offers guided hikes and her beau, for whom the guesthouse is named, teaches cooking and rustles up Turkish feasts. There are

cave, Ottoman and modern rooms, and single-sex cave dorms with private bathrooms.

Köse Pension HOSTEL $$
(☎271 2294; www.kosepension.com; Ragıp Üner Caddesi; dm/d/tr TL15/80/90, tw hut TL50, s/tr without bathroom TL25/75;) Köse Pension has some rough edges but, unlike most hostels, it has a swimming pool in the garden and a terrace where communal meals are served. Run by Edinburgh-born Dawn Köse and family, this backpacker institution is cheerily painted with grinning spiders and winding creepers. On the roof are wooden huts and a 20-bed dorm.

Kaya Camping Caravaning CAMPGROUND $
(☎343 3100; campsites per adult/child TL15/10; @) This impressive camping ground is 2.5km from the centre of town, uphill from the Göreme Open-Air Museum. Set among fields of vines and a good sprinkling of trees, it has magnificent views and top-notch facilities.

Eating

Most of Göreme's pensions provide good, cheap meals but you could also take advantage of some fine eateries in town.

TOP CHOICE **Seten** ANATOLIAN $$$
(www.setenrestaurant.com; Aydınlı Sokak 14; mains TL16-40) Named after a traditional wheat grinder (there is one in the courtyard) this original restaurant is an annex of the Sultan Cave Suites Hotel. Serving only Cappadocian dishes prepared in traditional style and using only local produce, the results are spectacular. They even have their own wine, made from the uniquely local *Emir* grape.

Nazar Börek ANATOLIAN $
(Müze Caddesi 30; mains TL5-10) If you're after a cheap and filling meal, sample the börek, *gözleme* and *sosyete böregi* (stuffed spiral pastries with yoghurt and tomato sauce) served at this simple place. Friendly staff and a pleasant outdoor eating area on the canal make this place a perennially popular option.

Dibek TURKISH $$
(Hakkı Paşa Meydanı 1; mains TL15-25; ⏲9am-11pm) Dibek is one of Göreme's most original restaurants, and the best place to try a *testi kebap* (meat and vegetable dish cooked in a sealed pot, which is broken to serve). You must give three hours' notice before eating, so the dish can be slow-cooked in an oven in the stone floor.

Fırın Express TURKISH $$
(Eski Belediye Yanı Sokak; pide & pizza TL5-9, mains TL9-18; ⏲11am-11pm) Set slightly back from the main strip, this wood cabin–like eatery is praised by carnivores and vegetarians for its pide and pizza. More substantial claypot dishes are also available.

Meeting Point Café INTERNATIONAL $$
(Müze Caddesi 34; mains TL10-17) Missing your favourite comfort foods? A Turkish–South African couple dishes up curries, burgers, fruit smoothies, filter coffee and homemade cakes.

Around Göreme

The easy 3km walk (or even easier drive) from Göreme to laid-back **Üçhisar** passes the breathtaking viewpoint **Göreme Panorama** along the way. The views from the town itself, built around a **rock citadel** (admission TL3; ⏲8am-8.15pm) are pretty awesome too with **Pigeon Valley** and the rest of the rocky gang splayed out before you. **Rose Valley** particularly lives up to its name; watching its pink rock slowly change colour at sunset is best accompanied by meze in one of the local eateries.

Off the road from Göreme to Avanos is the excellent **Zelve Open-Air Museum** (admission TL5; ⏲8am-5pm, last admission 4.15pm). It is less visited than the Göreme Valley (though the monastic seclusion once offered here is long gone) and has rock-cut churches, a rock-cut mosque and some opportunities for serious scrambling. In the same area, some of the finest fairy chimneys can be seen at **Devrent Valley**, also known as Imagination Valley for its chimneys' anthropomorphic forms; and **Paşabağları**, where you can climb inside one formation to a monk's quarters, decorated with Hellenic crosses. These places are typically included in the Red Tour.

Southwest of Göreme is a series of 6th- and 7th-century **underground cities** once occupied by Byzantine Christians taking refuge from the Persian and Arabic armies that sought to eliminate them. The largest of these is at **Derinkuyu** (admission TL15; ⏲8am-5pm), arranged on seven levels and which, unbelievably, was once home to 10,000 people and their livestock. Another city at **Kaymaklı** (admission TL15; ⏲8am-5pm) is located 10km to the north and is the most popular with tour groups. Visitors should be aware that there is little in the way of information at the sites, and some of the pushy guides at the entrance barely speak English.

Continuing southwest you reach a beautiful canyon full of rock-cut churches dating back to Byzantine times, **Ihlara Valley** (Ihlara Vadısı; admission TL5; ⊙8am-6.30pm). Footpaths follow the course of the river, Melendiz Suyu, which flows for 13km between the narrow gorge at Ihlara village and the wide valley around **Selime Monastery** (⊙dawn-dusk). To get there by bus, you must change in Nevşehir and Aksaray, making it tricky to do a day return from Göreme and have time to walk the valley. The Green Tour is by far the best way to see Ihlara Valley and the underground cities in a day.

Avanos

☎0384 / POP 11,800

Avanos is famous for pottery made with red clay from the Kızılırmak (Red River), which runs through its centre, and white clay from the mountains. The old town is rundown and its riverside setting does not match the other Cappadocian centres. However, it boasts some superb views of Zelve and, when the pottery-purchasing tour groups have moved on, it's an appealingly mellow country town.

Sleeping & Eating

Kirkit Pension PENSION **$$**
(☎511 3148; www.kirkitpension.com; Atatürk Caddesi; s/d/tr €40/50/70; @) Set in converted old stone houses, this long-running pension is known throughout Cappadocia for its congenial, laid-back atmosphere. The simple rooms are decorated with kilims, historical photographs of the region and Uzbek bedspreads.

Sofa Hotel HOTEL **$$**
(☎511 4478; www.sofa-hotel.com; Orta Mahalle Gedik Sokak 9; s/d TL60/100; ⊖) Lots of Cappadocian cave establishments have their idiosyncrasies, but this hotel is downright bonkers. Staircases, bridges and terraces lead you up the hill, past eyes suddenly staring out from a mosaic fragment or a pottery face, to 33 rooms crammed with knick-knacks.

Dayının Yeri TURKISH **$$**
(www.dayininyeri.com.tr; Atatürk Caddesi; mains TL10-15) Down by the bridge, this shiny, modern *ocakbaşıs* (grill restaurant) is one of Cappadocia's best, and is an essential stop on any visit to Avanos. The kebaps and pide are equally sensational.

Ürgüp

☎0384 / POP 18,600

If you have a soft spot for upmarket hotels and fine dining, you need look no further – Ürgüp is the place you're after. With a spectacular natural setting and a wonderful location at the very heart of central Cappadocia, this is one of the most seductive holiday spots in the whole of Turkey.

Sleeping

The ever-growing battalion of boutique hotels in the town's honey-coloured stone buildings (from pre-1923 when the town had a large Greek population) are proving very popular with travellers.

TOP CHOICE **Esbelli Evi** BOUTIQUE HOTEL **$$$**
(☎341 3395; www.esbelli.com; Esbelli Mahallesi Sokak 8; s/d/ste €90/120/200; ❄@) Consummate host Süha Ersöz opened Cappadocia's first boutique hotel. Having bought surrounding properties to preserve Esbelli's atmosphere of hilltop serenity, his complex now has 10 rooms and five suites in nine houses. However, it still feels small and intimate, thanks to the welcoming atmosphere and the communal areas where guests are encouraged to congregate.

Serinn House BOUTIQUE HOTEL **$$$**
(☎341 6076; www.serinnhouse.com; Esbelli Mahallesi Sokak 8; s/d €100/140; @≋) The five exquisitely tasteful rooms at this jaw-droppingly gorgeous boutique hotel have managed to push the bar on style even in a town that prides itself on its high-class accommodation. With a magical courtyard and gourmet chef on hand in the restaurant, this place is a treat.

Cappadocia Palace BOUTIQUE HOTEL **$$**
(☎341 2510; www.hotel-cappadocia.com; Dar Sokak 3; s/d/tr standard €30/44/55, cave €60/88/95; @) This large, comfortable hotel is housed in a converted Greek mansion near Cumhuriyet Meydanı. There's a lovely arched restaurant-lounge and an attractive foyer area. It's crazy good value and everybody seems to know it, so book ahead.

Hotel Elvan PENSION $$
(☎341 4191; www.hotelelvan.com; Barbaros Hayrettin Sokak 11; s/d/tr TL50/75/95; @) A friendly welcome and homely atmosphere await you at this unpretentious but immaculate guesthouse. There's a small roof terrace and comfortable dining room. It's excellent value, but unfortunately closed in the low season.

Büyük Otel HOTEL $$
(☎341 2525; www.buyukotelurgup.com; Atatürk Bulvarı; s/d TL50/100) A faceless reception gives way to faceless rooms at this massive yellowstone block. However it is central, big enough to have rooms when others are full and is one of the few acceptable options at the cheaper end of the scale.

Eating & Drinking

Down by the square, *pastanes* and cafes vie for attention with their sweet eats and shiny window displays.

TOP CHOICE **Ziggy's** BAR, RESTAURANT $$
(www.ziggycafe.com; Yunak Mahallesi, Teyfik Fikret Caddesi 24; mains TL10-33, set menu TL40) Cool Ziggy's, named after the owner's dog, in turn named after the David Bowie song, has a series of terraces. The 12-course set menu features 10 meze plates, including the distinctive smoked aubergine. Hosts Selim and Nuray add some İstanbul sophistication to the Cappadocian views.

Dimrit INTERNATIONAL $$$
(www.dimrit.com; Yunak Mahallesi, Teyfik Fikret Caddesi 40; mains TL20-35) With meze served in curvy dishes and three types of rakı, Dimrit's hillside terraces are top spots to spend a sunset. The extensive menu features salads, fish, classic grills and house specials.

Ehlikeyf TURKISH $$
(Cumhuriyet Meydanı; mains TL12-24) Competing with nearby Şömine in the sophistication stakes, Ehlikeyf occupies a sleek dining room with a wavy ceiling. Dishes such as the fabulous *Ehlikeyf kebap* (steak served on slivered fried potatoes, garlic yogurt and a demiglace sauce) arrive on glass plates.

Şömine Cafe & Restaurant TURKISH $$
(www.sominerestaurant.com; Cumhuriyet Meydanı; meze TL7, salads TL6-8, mains TL13-29) This popular restaurant on the plaza has a roof terrace and an attractive indoor dining room. Start with a salad or a meze choice such as *sosyete mantısı* (one large ravioli), then attack a *kiremit* (clay-baked meat or vegetable dish).

Mustafapaşa

☎0384 / POP 1600

Until WWI, it was called Sinasos and was predominantly an Ottoman-Greek settlement. Today Mustafapaşa is the sleeping beauty of Cappadocia, a peaceful village with pretty, old stone-carved houses, some minor rock-cut churches and a few good places to stay. If you want to get away from it all, this is the place to base yourself.

Sleeping & Eating

Hotel Pacha PENSION $$
(☎353 5331; www.pachahotel.com; Sinasos Meydanı; s/d €30/45) This is the real thing: a family-run business that offers a warm welcome and home-cooking by the lady of the house, Demra. The restored Ottoman-Greek pile has a great feel about it from the moment you enter its pretty, vine-trellised courtyard.

Old Greek House HOTEL, RESTAURANT $$
(☎353 5141; www.oldgreekhouse.com; Şahin Caddesi; s TL70, d TL90-120) Inhabited by the same family since 1938, this historic hotel houses a **restaurant** (mains TL32-45; ⏲11.30am-9.30pm) that is about the best place to try Ottoman cuisine in Cappadocia. Prepared by half a dozen village women, the dishes include unusual choices and some of the best baklava we've tasted. The hotel is an excellent place to stay thanks to its historic aura.

Kayseri

☎0352 / POP 1.2 MILLION

Mixing Seljuk tombs, mosques and modern developments, Kayseri is Turkey's most Islamic city after Konya. It is one of the country's economic powerhouses, a group of regional capitals together nicknamed the 'Anatolian tigers'. Colourful silk headscarves are piled in the bazaar (one of the country's biggest) and businesses shut down at noon on Friday when many Muslims go to the mosque for prayers. If you are passing through this transport hub, it's worth taking a look at a Turkish boomtown with a strong sense of its own history.

Sights

Citadel CASTLE
South of the main square at the centre of the old town, the fabulous basalt-walled citadel was built in the early 13th century during the reign of the Seljuk sultan Alaattin

Keykubat. It has been restored several times over the years (twice in the 15th century).

FREE Güpgüpoğlu Konağı MUSEUM
(8am-5pm Tue-Sun) Just southeast of the citadel is the wonderful Güpgüpoğlu Konağı, a fine stone mansion dating from the 18th century, which now houses an interesting ethnographic museum.

Notable buildings ARCHITECTURE
Among Kayseri's distinctive features are important building complexes founded by Seljuk queens and princesses, such as the impressive **Mahperi Hunat Hatun Complex**, east of the citadel, and the striking **Çifte Medrese** (Twin Seminaries) to the northwest. On the other side of the bazaar is the **Ulu Cami** (Great Mosque), a good example of early Seljuk style. The adjoining religious schools of Çifte Medrese, in Mimar Sinan Parkı north of Park Caddesi, date back to the 12th century.

Scattered about Kayseri are several conical **Seljuk tombs**.

Sleeping & Eating

Smoky business hotels are the norm here and accommodation should be booked in advance. The western end of Sivas Caddesi has a strip of fast-food joints that still seem to be pumping when everything else in town is quiet.

Hotel Çapari HOTEL $$
(222 5278; www.hotelcapari.com, in Turkish; Donanma Caddesi 12; s/d/tr TL90/140/175;) With thick red carpets and friendly staff, this three-star hotel on a quiet street off Atatürk Bulvarı is one of the best deals in town.

Hotel Sur HOTEL $$
(222 4367; Talas Caddesi 12; s/d/tr TL40/75/90) Beyond the dark reception and institutional corridors, the Sur's rooms are bright, comfortable and some overlook the city walls.

Bent Hotel HOTEL $$
(221 2400; www.benthotel.com; Atatürk Bulvarı 40; s/d/tr TL75/100/120) The name may not inspire confidence, but the Bent is a good midrange choice overlooking the pedal boats in Mimar Sinan Parkı.

Lider Teras TURKISH $
(Sivas Caddesi 6; mains TL7-13) Stylish yet affordable with a rooftop terrace and views of the citadel and Erciyes Dağı. The menu consists of fresh salads and juicy meats, and don't forget to sample a selection of the delicious sticky desserts on offer.

Elmacioğlu İskender et Lokantası KEBAB $$
(1st & 2nd fl, Millet Caddesi 5; mains TL8-25; 9am-10.30pm) *Iskender kebaps* are the house speciality, available with *köfte* or in 'double' form. Mmmm...

Information

You'll find banks with ATMs and a helpful **tourist office** (222 3903; Cumhuriyet Meydanı; 8am-5pm Mon-Fri) in the centre.

Getting There & Away

Turkish Airlines and Onur Air have daily flights to/from İstanbul. Sun Express serves İzmir twice a week.

The futuristic otogar is about 3km northwest of the centre. On an important north-south and east-west crossroads, Kayseri has many bus services, including to Sivas (TL20, three hours) and Göreme (TL10, 1½ hours). Dolmuşes for Ürgüp (TL5, 1¼ hours) run from the west garage.

The train station is at the northern end of Atatürk Bulvarı, 500m north of the old town. There are useful services to Adana, Ankara, Diyarbakır, Kars and Sivas, mostly daily, and the international train to Tehran also stops here.

BLACK SEA & NORTHEASTERN ANATOLIA

Travel no further: you've found what you're looking for. A place where resorts are nonexistent, where you can really feel a sense of wilderness and adventure, and where superb archaeological sites and hidden treasures are set among eerie landscapes – welcome to the Black Sea coast and eastern Turkey.

The craggy and spectacular coastline of the Black Sea is scattered with the legacy of the civilisations and empires that have ebbed and flowed in this historic region. Often empty of other travellers, the local castles, churches and monasteries – which are often as important as the must-see sights in other parts of Turkey – remember the kings of Pontus, the Genoese and the Ottomans.

From the Black Sea coast it's reasonably straightforward to get to northeastern Anatolia. This far-flung outpost is almost a void on the tourist radar due to its remoteness,

WORTH A TRIP

DRIVING THE BLACK SEA COAST

To see some of the Black Sea region's best views, looking north out to sea, travel the glorious, vertigo-inducing curves on the coastal road from **Amasra**, with its Roman and Byzantine ruins, to beachy **Sinop**.

Continuing east, **Samsun** has little of interest for tourists, but there are excellent beaches around the cheerful resort town of **Ünye**, on a wide bay 95km east of Samsun. About 80km further to the east, **Ordu** is a bustling city with a palm-lined seafront boulevard. **Giresun** is famous for its hazelnuts and cherries, having introduced the latter to Italy, and from there to the rest of the world.

making it a red rag to those hungry for the unknown. Here the flavours of the neighbouring Caucasus, Central Asia and Iran are already palpable. The *saklı cennet* (secret paradise) is a perfect blend of nature and culture, with many palaces, castles, mosques and churches dotted around the steppe.

If you're overlanding to Iran, Iraq or Syria, you will certainly need to transit parts of these fascinating areas; bear in mind that the weather can be bitterly cold and snowy in winter, especially in eastern Turkey.

Trabzon

☎0462 / POP 800,000

Trabzon is one of those 'love it or hate it' kind of places. The slightly seedy port-town character puts off some people, while others appreciate the city's cosmopolitan buzz and sprawling, authentic bazaar. Life in Trabzon centres upon the whirl of activity on its main square, Meydan Parkı. Beeping dolmuşes hurtle anticlockwise like a modern chariot race, while local students team headscarves with Converse All Stars, beneath a giant screen showcasing the city's beloved Trabzonspor football team.

Sights

Aya Sofya MOSQUE
(Church of Divine Wisdom; admission TL3; ⏲9am-6pm Tue-Sun Apr-Oct, 9am-5pm Tue-Sun Nov-Mar) Without doubt, Trabzon's star attraction is the 13th-century Aya Sofya, 4km west of town and reachable by dolmuş from Atatürk Alanı. Marvel at the vividly coloured frescos and mosaic floors.

Atatürk Köşkü MUSEUM
(Atatürk Villa; admission TL2; ⏲8am-7pm May-Sep, 8am-5pm Oct-Apr) This beautiful 19th-century mansion is set high above the town and houses a museum of Atatürk antiquities. It is accessible by bus from the northern side of Atatürk Alanı.

Sumela Monastery MONASTERY
(admission per person/car TL8/10; ⏲9am-6pm) Of all the dreamy spots in eastern Turkey that make you feel like you're floating through another time and space, Sumela, 46km south of Trabzon, wins the time-travel prize by a long shot. Carved out of a sheer cliff like a swallow's nest, this Byzantine monastery features superb frescos (partially damaged by vandals), some dating from the 9th century.

The monastery is in the Altındere Vadısı Milli Parkı (Altındere Valley National Park). If you're visiting by public transport, try to catch a dolmuş from Trabzon at around 8am to avoid the midmorning flow of tour groups. You can also visit on a tour (TL20) departing at 10am daily from Trabzon with **Eyce Tours** (☎326 7174; www.eycetours.com, in Turkish).

Sleeping

Many of the cheapies off the northeastern corner of Atatürk Alanı and along the coastal road double as brothels.

Nazar Otel HOTEL $$
(☎323 0081; www.nazarotel.com.tr, in Turkish; Güzelhisar Caddesi 5; s/d TL70/100; ❄) A smart lobby gives way to somewhat dated rooms, but the Nazar is a decent business-class option that frequently offers deals.

Otel Horon HOTEL $$
(☎326 6455; www.hotelhoron.com; Sıramağazalar Caddesi 125; s/d TL100/130; ❄📶) Inside the aubergine-coloured walls, any shortcomings in design are overcome by wi-fi, well-stocked minibars and city views from the rooftop bar-restaurant.

Hotel Nur HOTEL $$
(☎323 0445; Camii Sokak 15; s/d TL45/80; ❄) A long-standing, but often overly popular, travellers' favourite, the Nur has amiable

English-speaking staff and small, brightly painted rooms. The lounge is good for getting the travellers' lowdown on going to Georgia.

Hotel Anıl HOTEL $
(☎326 7282; Güzelhisar Caddesi 12; s/d TL40/70; ❄) The flash reception lures travellers in, and the rooms in pink and yellow are actually good value; even the downstairs rooms have views.

Eating

Trabzon is not the Black Sea's gastronomic highlight, but scores of decent eateries line Atatürk Alanı and two streets to the west, Uzun Sokak (Long Lane) and Kahramanmaraş Caddesi (Maraş Caddesi for short).

Bordo Mavi INTERNATIONAL $$
(Halkevi Caddesi 12; meals TL12-18; ⊙11am-10pm) This cosmopolitan garden cafe adjoins the clubhouse of Trabzonspor, the local football team. It's not at all boozy or noisy, though, and the excellent pizzas and pasta have an authentic tinge of Italy.

Reis'in Yeri TURKISH $$
(Liman Mukli İdare; meals TL10-20; ⊙11am-11pm) It can be easy to forget Trabzon is a coastal city, until you head downhill, away from the traffic and over the pedestrian overbridge, to this sprawling fish/chicken/*köfte* grill place. It doubles as a beer garden and you can hire rowboats to steer around the tiny cove.

Üstad TURKISH $
(Atatürk Alanı 18b; meals TL6-9) Locals squeeze into this compact lokanta right on Trabzon's main square. We can thoroughly recommend the *biber dolması* (stuffed peppers) that come with a robust pinch of chilli.

Drinking

Stress Café CAFE, BAR
(☎321 3044; Uzun Sokak) Stress? You must be joking! One of Trabzon's best live music and nargileh spots, the Stress Café is laaaaaaaid-back.

Kalender BAR
(Zeytinlik Caddesi 10) Low tables and mood lighting give this place near the Trabzon Museum a cosmopolitan vibe. It's perfect for a coffee and brunch.

Information

Modern Trabzon is centred on Atatürk Alanı (also known as Meydan Parkı), uphill from the port. Banks with ATMs, exchange offices and the PTT are on Maraş Caddesi.

Tourist office (☎/fax 326 4760, Camii Sokak, ⊙8am-5pm Mon-Sat Oct-May) is south of Atatürk Alanı.

Georgian consulate (☎326 2226; trabzon.con@mfa.gov.ge; Perlevpaşa Sokak 10)

Russian consulate (☎326 2600; trabzon@yandex.ru; Şh Refik Cesur 6, Ortahisar)

Getting There & Away

Turkish Airlines, Pegasus Airlines, Onur Air and Sun Express fly to/from Turkish locations including İstanbul.

Two shipping offices down by the harbour sell tickets for ferries going to Sochi in Russia (about US$70-150), but you need to have your Russian visa sorted in advance. There is no regular timetable but you can usually count on at least two weekly services.

From Trabzon's otogar, about 3km from the centre, you can reach numerous destinations in Turkey as well as Tbilisi (Tiflis) in Georgia and Erivan in Armenia (via Georgia). There are regular services to Erzurum (TL25, five hours), Kars (TL50, 10 hours) and Kayseri (TL50, 12 hours).

Erzurum

☎0442 / POP 368,000

Erzurum is a contradictory place: it's Islamic to its core, with deep roots in tradition, but has adapted to Western consumerism. A gregarious student population adds a liberal buzz to the air. Here you can shop till you drop and quaff rakı – all while the muezzins call the faithful to prayer.

Sights

The city promotes itself as the architectural capital of eastern Anatolia and an impressive array of Seljuk monuments make this tag well deserved. If oohing and aahing over the wonderful medreses and mosques on the main drag isn't your thing, come in winter and enjoy the nearby Palandöken ski resort.

Citadel CASTLE
(admission TL3; ⊙8am-5pm) The well-preserved walls of the 5th-century citadel loom over a maze of narrow streets, offering good views of the town and the surrounding steppe.

Çifte Minareli Medrese TOWER, RELIGIOUS
(Twin Minaret Seminary; Cumhuriyet Caddesi) Another must-see is the beautifully symmetrical minaret, a famous example of Seljuk architecture dating from the 1200s.

Erzurum

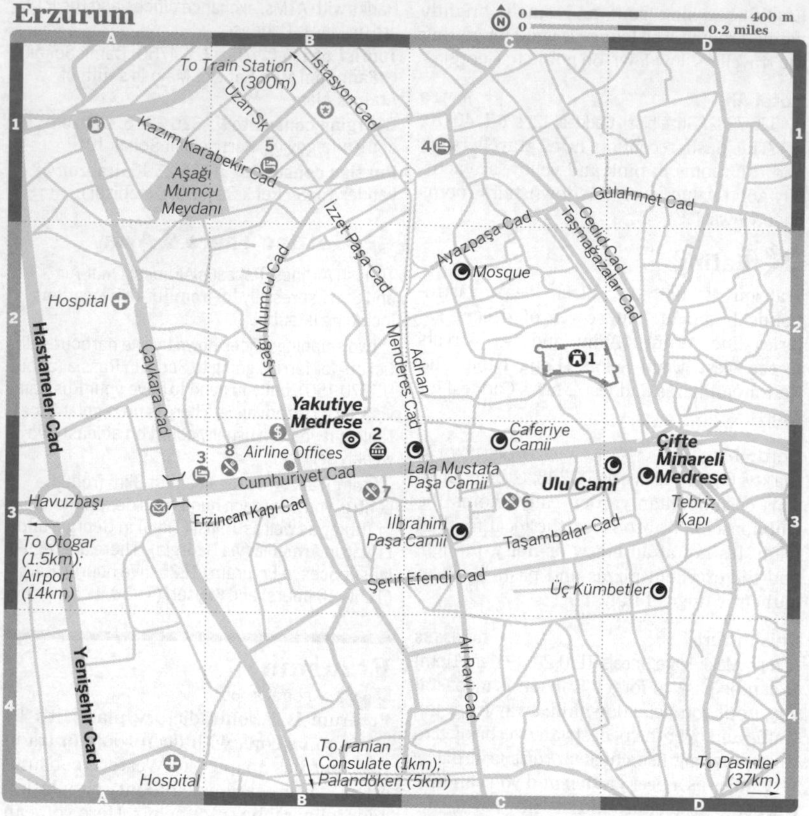

Erzurum

Top Sights
- Çifte Minareli Medrese D3
- Ulu Cami D3
- Yakutiye Medrese B3

Sights
- 1 Citadel C2
- 2 Turkish-Islamic Arts & Ethnography Museum B3

Sleeping
- 3 Esadaş Otel A3
- Grand Hotel Hitit .... (see 5)
- 4 Yeni Çınar Oteli C1
- 5 Yeni Ornek B1

Eating
- 6 Erzurum Evleri C3
- 7 Güzelyurt Restorant B3
- 8 Kılıcoğlu B3

The eye-catching carved portal is flanked by twin brick minarets decorated with small blue tiles.

Ulu Cami MOSQUE
(Great Mosque; Cumhuriyet Caddesi) Built in 1179, unlike the adjacent Çifte Minareli, the Ulu Cami is restrained but elegant.

Yakutiye Medrese TOWER, RELIGIOUS
(admission TL3; Yakutiye Seminary; Cumhuriyet Caddesi; ⌚8am-noon & 1-5pm Tue & Thu-Sun) On a square in the centre of the main street, this seminary with its wonderfully ornate doorway and colourful minaret was built by the local Mongol emir in 1310. It is now home to the **Turkish-Islamic Arts and Ethnography Museum**.

Sleeping

Esadaş Otel HOTEL $$$
(☎235 2201; www.erzurumesadas.com.tr, in Turkish; Cumhuriyet Caddesi 7; s/d TL110/160; ❄)

Right on the main thoroughfare and close to everything, including our beloved Kılıçoğlu pastry shop. It offers terrific breakfast, with three varieties of olives, local cheeses, sausages and yogurt. Haggle for a better price if business is slack.

Grand Hotel Hitit HOTEL $
(☎233 5001; www.grandhitithotel.com.tr, in Turkish; Kazım Karabekir Caddesi 26; s/d TL40/70) A good lair in this price bracket, with rooms that seemingly get plenty of TLC. Convenient location and good views from the rooftop breakfast room.

Yeni Ornek HOTEL $
(☎233 0053; Kazım Karabekir Caddesi 25; s/d/ste TL40/70/105) Style? Erm, no. The red-and-gold trimmed Yeni Ornek is as no-frills as it gets but the rooms are well-kept and the staff pleasant. After a long day's turf-pounding, sink into the comfy leather armchairs in the lobby and try to figure out what that old telephone switchboard is doing there.

Yeni Çınar Oteli HOTEL $
(☎213 6690; Bakırçılar Çarşisi 18; s/d TL30/50) This place may not look like much, but has plenty of virtues for true budget-seekers. It's clean, safe, quiet and within walking distance of everything you might need. The only flaw is that the street is deserted and dimly lit at night; it is home to a few similar places in this price range.

Eating

You'll find plenty of eateries sprinkled around Cumhuriyet Caddesi.

TOP CHOICE **Erzurum Evleri** TURKISH $$
(Cumhuriyet Caddesi, Yüzbaşı Sokak 5; mains TL8-20) It feels like half the paraphernalia from six centuries of the Ottoman Empire has ended up in this log cabin, with an onslaught of collectibles from floor to ceiling. Surrender to the languor of the private alcoves with cushions and low tables, and treat yourself to soup, börek or *tandır kebap* (stewed lamb).

Güzelyurt Restaurant TURKISH $$
(www.guzelyurtrestaurant.com.tr, in Turkish; Cumhuriyet Caddesi 42; mains TL9-20) This iconic restaurant, in business since 1928, is so adorable because it feels so anachronistic, with shrouded windows and thick carpets. The meze are a headliner, but the menu also features mains such as 'Bof Straganof' (*sic*), all served by old-school, bow-tied waiters.

Kılıçoğlu BAKERY $
(Cumhuriyet Caddesi 13; snacks & pastries from TL3) A smart pastry shop that turns out snacks, 27 kinds of baklava and 23 ice-cream flavours.

Information

The otogar is 2km from the centre along the airport road. The centre is compact and you'll find everything you need on or around Cumhuriyet Caddesi, the main drag.

The **Iranian consulate** (☎/fax 315 9983/316 1182; Alparslan Bulvarı; ⊙8.30am-5pm Mon-Fri) is about 2km from the centre, towards Palandöken.

Getting There & Away

Turkish Airlines has daily flights to İstanbul and Ankara from the airport, 14km from the centre. Onur Air operates a daily flight to Istanbul and Sun Express has weekly flights to Antalya, Bursa, İstanbul and İzmir.

Erzurum has frequent buses to most big towns in eastern Turkey, including Doğubayazıt (TL20, 4½ hours), Trabzon (TL25, five hours) and Kars (TL15, three hours).

Erzurum has rail connections with Ankara (TL42, 24 hours) via Kayseri and Sivas, and a daily train to Kars (TL10, 4½ hours).

Kars

☎0474 / POP 80,000

What a quirky city. 'Where am I?' is probably what you'll find yourself wondering on arrival. With its stately, pastel-coloured stone buildings dating from the Russian occupation, spooky castle and well-organised grid plan, Kars looks like a slice of Russia in northeastern Anatolia. And the mix of influences – Azeri, Turkmen, Kurdish, Turkish and Russian – adds to the feeling of surprise.

Kars is a great base for visiting the dramatic ruins at Ani (see p524), and you can ski in winter at the low-key resort town of Sarıkamış.

Sleeping

TOP CHOICE **Kar's Otel** BOUTIQUE HOTEL $$$
(☎212 1616; www.karsotel.com; Halitpaşa Caddesi 79; s/d TL220/290; ❄) Seeking a luxurious cocoon with homely qualities, efficient hosts and a big dollop of atmosphere? Look no further than this savvy boutique hotel, housed

in an old Russian mansion. It breathes an air of repose, though some might find the white colour scheme a bit too clinical. Its Ani Restaurant is recommended.

Grand Ani Otel HOTEL $$$
(☎223 7500; Ordu Caddesi; s/d/ste €70/100/125; ❄☒) Sauna, restaurant, hamam, fitness centre – with the facilities on offer here you'll have to drag yourself away from the hotel to go and see the original grand Ani!

Güngören Hotel HOTEL $
(☎212 5630; fax 223 4821; Millet Sokak; s/d TL30/50) Attentive staff, good-sized rooms with modern furniture, and a handy location. Perks include a satisfying breakfast, a restaurant and a men-only hamam.

Hotel Temel HOTEL $
(☎223 1376; fax 223 1323; Yenipazar Caddesi; s/d TL35/60) Unlike the Güngören, the Temel offers a lift, as well as neat rooms with immaculate sheets and a soothing blue-and-yellow colour scheme. The management gets mixed reviews.

Eating

Kars is noted for its excellent *bal* (honey) and the local *kaşar peyniri* (mild yellow cheese).

TOP CHOICE **Ocakbaşı Restoran** ANATOLIAN $
(Atatürk Caddesi; mains TL5-8) This well-established restaurant is the pinnacle of Kars' eating scene. Sample its signature dishes, *ali nazık* (eggplant puree with yogurt and meat) and *Anteplim pide* (sesame bread stuffed with meat, cheese, parsley, nuts and eggs), and you'll understand why.

> WORTH A TRIP
>
> **ANI**
>
> Set amid spectacular scenery 45km east of Kars, **Ani** (admission TL7; ⏲8.30am-5pm) exudes an eerie ambience. The site was completely deserted in 1239 after a Mongol invasion, but before that it was a stately Armenian capital, rivalling Constantinople in power and glory. Fronted by a hefty wall, the ghost city now lies in fields overlooking the Arpa Çayi gorge, which forms the border with Armenia. The ruins include several notable churches and a cathedral built between AD 987 and 1010.

It has two rooms, including a mock troglodytic one (wow!), but it's not licensed (boo!).

Information

Atatürk Caddesi, the main street, is where you will find most of what you need.

Azerbaijani consulate (☎223 6475/1361; fax 223 8741; Eski Erzurum Caddesi; ⏲9am-6pm Mon-Fri) Northwest of the centre.

Celil Ersoğlu (☎212 6543; celilani@hotmail.com) Acts as a private guide and speaks good English. His mobile: 0532-226 3966.

Tourist office (☎212 6817; Lise Caddesi; ⏲8am-noon & 1-5pm Mon-Fri) Organises dolmuşes to Ani (around TL40 per person).

Getting There & Away

The otogar is 2km southeast of the centre. There are frequent services to Erzurum (TL15, three hours) and one morning bus to Van (TL30, six hours). If you're heading to Doğubayazıt, you'll have to change in Iğdır (TL15, three hours).

Daily flights to Ankara and İstanbul with Turkish Airlines leave from the airport 6km outside of town.

Doğubayazıt

☎0472 / POP 36,000

What an awesome backdrop: on one side, Mt Ararat (Ağrı Dağı, 5137m), Turkey's highest mountain; on the other, İshak Paşa Palace, a breathtakingly beautiful palace-mosque-fortress complex. Not bad for a charmless frontier town high on testosterone (read: lots of soldiers, policemen, moustached men and the occasional tout, but, alas, very few women on the streets).

A lack of charm doesn't, however, mean a lack of character. This is a quintessentially Kurdish town that prides itself on its strong Kurdish heritage, which it celebrates during the **Kültür Sanat ve Turizm Festival** (Culture and Arts Festival) in late June. Doğubayazıt is also the main kicking-off point for the overland trail through Iran (the border is 35km away).

Sights & Activities

Doğubayazıt is small and easily negotiated on foot.

İshak Paşa Palace PALACE
(İshak Paşa Sarayı; admission TL3; ⏲9am-5.30pm Apr-Oct, to 5pm Nov-Mar) Your jaw will drop in amazement the minute you see this palace. Perched romantically among rocky crags, 6km southeast of town, this fortress-palace-

WORTH A TRIP

MT ARARAT

Hikers with a sense of adventure will surely be itching to climb the country's highest peak Mt Ararat (5137m) – but you need a permit, a guide and a healthy bank balance to do so. Various tour companies based in Doğubayazıt offer similar four- to seven-day treks, but usually require a group of at least six (4-day climb around €650). You can apply for a permit through any reputable travel agency in Turkey but should do so well in advance. Permit regulations have changed several times over the last few years, so we recommend you seek current advice when planning your trip. At the time of writing you were required to send a scan of your passport and confirmed trekking dates at least a month in advance.

mosque is the epitome of the *Thousand and One Nights* castle fantasy. Built between 1685 and 1784, it blends elements of Seljuk, Ottoman, Georgian, Persian and Armenian architecture.

Minibuses (TL2, 15 minutes) rattle between the otogar and the palace, leaving when full, or a taxi will cost around TL30 for a return trip, waiting time included.

Sleeping & Eating

Accommodation is hit-and-miss here, and the two camping ground–cum-pensions near İshak Paşa Palace are definitely not recommended for women. For eating try along Dr İsmail Beşikçi Caddesi.

Hotel Grand Derya HOTEL $$
(☎312 7531; Abdullah Baydar Caddesi 203; s TL60-80, d TL100-120; ❄) An ideal retreat after a few days' clambering in knee breeches and hiking boots, this excellent venue offers comfortable rooms with all the mod cons. For Ararat views, request a room ending with 01 or 12 (avoid those ending in 02). Bring earplugs for the 5am call to prayer emanating from the nearby mosque.

Hotel Tahran HOTEL $
(☎312 0195; www.hoteltahran.com; Büyük Ağrı Caddesi 124; s/d TL30/56; @) The Tahran's recipe for success is to keep prices low, standards high and employ attentive (in a good way) staff. Although on the small side, the rooms come equipped with crisp sheets and views of Mt Ararat. Bilal, the affable manager, is well clued-up on Iran. A safe bet for solo women travellers, too.

TOP CHOICE **Yöresel Yemek Evi** KURDISH $
(Dr İsmail Beşikçi Caddesi; mains TL5-7) Yay! Some feminine touches in this male-dominated city! This place is run by an association of Kurdish women whose husbands are imprisoned. They slap up lip-smacking *yöresel* (traditional) meals from steel trays at bargain-basement prices.

Information

Nişantaş Döviz (Dr İsmail Beşikçi Caddesi; ⌚7am-7pm Mon-Sat, 7am-noon Sun) A moneychanger that often has Iranian rials.

Getting There & Away

There are five daily minibuses to Van (TL15, three hours). To get to Kars, change minibus at Iğdır (TL5, 45 minutes); the journey should cost about TL20. Long-distance buses usually involve a change in Erzurum (TL20, 4½ hours).

Minibuses (TL5) to the Iranian border (Gürbulak) leave hourly until 5pm from near the junction of Ağrı and Rıfkı Başkaya Caddesis, just past the petrol station.

SOUTHEASTERN ANATOLIA

Turkey's wild child, southeastern Anatolia feels different from the rest of the country, and that's part of its appeal. Apart from a few Arabic and Christian pockets, this huge chunk of territory is predominantly Kurdish.

What does it have on its menu? For starters, you can choose from a wealth of historical cities, such as Mardin, the region's trophy piece, perched on a hill dominating Mesopotamia; Şanlıurfa, swathed in historical mystique; and the old city of Diyarbakır, ensnared in mighty basalt walls.

For the main course, how about natural wonders? Adjust your camera to 'panoramic' and shoot life-enhancing images of Mt Nemrut (Nemrut Dağı), topped with colossal ancient statues, or shimmering Van Gölü (Lake Van).

Best of all, you can savour these sights without any tourist hustle and bustle. Oh, and southeastern Anatolia has its fair share of gastronomic pleasures (mmm, pistachio baklava...).

Van

☎0432 / POP 367,400

Liberal, vibrant Van with its casual, urban vibe and gorgeous lakeside location, was always something of an anomaly in conservative southeastern Anatolia. Live bands knocking out Kurdish tunes, and bareheaded girls making eye contact with foreigners, were reflections of a refreshing frontier town bursting with positive energy.

Unfortunately that all changed just prior to our research, when the city was rocked by two massive earthquakes that claimed the lives of an estimated 4000 people and left an additional 40,000 homeless. At the time of writing the town is slowly rebuilding, hampered by inclement weather conditions and aftershocks. Many buildings around the town remain uninhabitable and the costs of the disaster are still being assessed.

Sights

Van Castle CASTLE
(admission TL3; ⏲9am-dusk) Van's main claim to fame is its castle, about 3km west of the city centre, where you'll also find the foundations of **Eski Van** (the old city).

Akdamar Kiliseli CHURCH
(Church of the Holy Cross; admission TL3) Van's 8th-century Armenian rulers took refuge on **Akdamar Island** in Van Gölü (Lake Van) when the Arab armies flooded through from the south. The church here is one of the wonders of Armenian architecture.

Sleeping

The earthquake put the brakes on Van's tourist industry, and one of the city's top central hotels, the Bayram, collapsed with considerable loss of life. The options below were open at the time of writing.

Büyük Urartu Oteli HOTEL $$
(☎212 0660; www.buyukuraartuotel.com, in Turkish; Hastane 2 Sokak 60; s/d TL100/140; ❄🏊) Despite the professional, English-speaking staff, the rooms at this reliable option are nothing to write home about. Luckily the facilities go some way to compensating you.

Van Ada Palas HOTEL $$
(☎216 2716; www.vanadapalas.tr.gg; Cumhuriyet Caddesi; s/d TL80/120) Pick your floor according to your favourite colour – green, yellow or blue. And if you like red, then try somewhere else.

Eating

Prior to the earthquake, Van had a surprisingly lively bar scene. For eating and drinking, look along the two main streets, Cumhuriyet Caddesi and Kazım Karabekir Caddesi.

Halil İbrahim Sofrası TURKISH $
(Cumhuriyet Caddesi; mains TL6-12) One word describes this downtown hotspot: yum. The eclectic food is well presented and of high quality, with service and sleek surrounds to match.

Safa 3, Çorba 1 Paça Salonu TURKISH $
(Kazım Karabekir Caddesi; soups TL2; ⏲24hr) Gastronomic adventurers should head to this quirky little restaurant. Regulars swear by the *kelle* (sheep's head); we're happy for them to be the judge! The spicy lentil soup takes you into more conservative culinary territory.

Getting There & Away

Flights to/from Ankara and İstanbul with Turkish Airlines and Pegasus Airlines are still coming into Van, but bus services have been heavily disrupted by the earthquake. For services to Iran, see p628.

Dıyarbakir

☎0412 / POP 843,400

Tension, violence? What tension, what violence? Since the 1980s, this animated city has been the centre of the Kurdish resistance movement and violent street demonstrations still occur from time to time. But oh, how things are changing. Filled with soul, heart and character, Diyar has begun to tap into its tourism potential. Behind its basalt walls, the old city is crammed full of historical buildings and Arab-style mosques.

The **Nevruz Festival** (21 March) is a great occasion to immerse yourself in Kurdish culture. However, the festival was banned recently.

Sights

City Walls FORTRESS

Diyarbakır's single most conspicuous feature is the old city's 6km circuit of **walls**, probably dating from Roman times. They make a striking sight whether you're walking along the top or the bottom.

Ulu Cami MOSQUE

(Gazi Caddesi) Of Diyarbakır's many mosques, this is the most impressive, built in 1091 by an early Seljuk sultan.

Nebi Camii MOSQUE

(intersection of Gazi Caddesi and İnönü Caddesi) Note the quirky detached minaret sporting a stunning combination of black-and-white stone.

Sleeping

There are plenty of accommodation options along Kıbrıs Caddesi, but pick a room at the back to avoid traffic noise.

TOP CHOICE **Otel Büyük Kervansaray** HISTORIC HOTEL $$

(☎228 9606; Gazi Caddesi; s/d/ste TL100/140/250; ❄≈) This is your chance to sleep in the 16th-century Deliller Han; a converted caravanserai. It's not the height of luxury, but it scores high on amenities, with a great restaurant in a converted camel stable, a bar, a hamam and a nifty pool.

Hotel Surkent HOTEL $

(☎228 1014; İzzet Paşa Caddesi; s/d without breakfast TL40/60; ❄) Tangerine frames and aluminium plates on the facade, flamingo-pink walls, technicolour bed linen and flashy orange curtains: the owners of the Surkent certainly like your life to be colourful. The top-floor rooms boast good views, it's in a peaceful street and close to everything. Downsides: there's no lift, and breakfast is extra.

Hotel Birkent HOTEL $

(☎228 7131; İnönü Caddesi; s/d €20/30; ❄@) We saw some female travellers at this mostly hassle-free venture, which is a good sign. Expect neat bathrooms, spotless rooms, turquoise bedspreads, a convenient location and copious breakfast.

Aslan Palas HOTEL $

(☎221 1227; Kıbrıs Caddesi 21; s/d TL30/60; ❄) A worthwhile backup for cash-strapped male travellers who don't mind sharing bathrooms. Prices don't include breakfast.

Eating

A stroll along Kıbrıs Caddesi reveals plenty of informal places to eat, and tantalising pastry shops.

TOP CHOICE **Selim Amca'nın Sofra Salonu** TURKISH $$$

(Ali Emiri Caddesi; mains TL10-17, set menu TL25) This bright eatery outside the city walls is famous for its *kaburga dolması* (lamb or chicken stuffed with rice and almonds). Round it off with a devilish *Irmik helvası* (a gooey dessert).

Şafak Kahvaltı & Yemek Salonu TURKISH $

(Kıbrıs Caddesi; mains TL6-10) Nosh on freshly prepared meat dishes and expertly cooked pide in this brisk Diyarbakır institution. It's also a good place for a restorative morning *kahvaltı* (breakfast).

Information

Most services useful to travellers are in Old Diyarbakır, on or around Gazi Caddesi. An informative English language website http://diyarbakirtravel.com is packed with information about the city and surroundings.

The **tourist office** (☎228 1706; Kapısı; ⏰8am-5pm Mon-Fri) is in a tower of the wall.

Getting There & Away

There are numerous daily flights between Diyarbakır and İstanbul and Ankara, and Turkish Airlines flies twice daily to/from İzmir. Minibuses A1, A2 and A3 (TL2, 15 minutes) connect the airport with the city centre.

The otogar is some 14km from the centre, on the Urfa road (about TL20 by taxi), but most companies have offices on İnönü Caddesi or Gazi Caddesi. Frequent buses run to Şanlıurfa (TL15, three hours) among others. Hourly minibuses to Mardin (TL10, 1¼ hours) leave from the minibus terminal, İlçe Garajı, 1.5km southwest of the city.

To get to Iraq, take a bus to Cizre (TL20, four hours) or Silopi (TL22, five hours) from the main otogar. There are about four services per day. See p542 for more details.

Mardin

☎0482 / POP 55,000

Pretty as a picture, Mardin is a highly addictive, unmissable spot with a fabulous setting, a breathtaking layout and a wealth of architectural treasures. With its minarets poking out of a labyrinth of brown lanes, its castle dominating the old city and the honey-coloured stone houses that trip down the hillside, it emerges like a phoenix from the roasted Mesopotamian plains.

Another draw is the mosaic of people. With Kurdish, Yazidi, Christian and Syrian cultures, among others, it has a fascinating social mix.

Sights

Start at the western end of Cumhuriyet Caddesi and make your way leisurely along, enjoying the wonderful architectural treats along the way.

Cumhuriyet Caddesi HISTORIC STREET
A superbly restored mansion dating from the late 19th century, the building housing the **Mardin Museum** (Mardin Müzesi; admission TL3; Cumhuriyet Meydanı; ⏲8am-5pm Tue-Sun) outshines the small collection of Assyrian and Bronze Age artefacts inside. A little further east along Cumhuriyet Caddesi keep your eyes peeled for the three-arched facade of an **ornately carved house**. Continuing, take the steps on the left (north) for the **Sultan İsa Medresesi** (⏲daylight), which dates from 1385 and is the town's prime architectural attraction.

Back on Cumhuriyet Caddesi, and opposite the gorgeous **post office** in a 17th-century caravanserai, you can't miss the minaret of the 14th-century **Şehidiye Camii**. It's superbly carved, with colonnades all around and three small domes superimposed on the summit.

Bazaar MARKET
Strolling through the rambling bazaar, a block downhill from Cumhuriyet Caddesi, be sure to keep your eyes open for the ornate **Ulu Cami**, a 12th-century Iraqi Seljuk structure.

Forty Martyrs Church CHURCH
(Kırklar Kilisesi; Sağlık Sokak) West of town and also worth visiting is this 15th-century church, with the martyrs depicted above the doorway of the church as you enter. If it's closed, bang on the door to alert the caretaker.

Sleeping & Eating

Mardin is packed with boutique hotels, but value for money is hard to come by. If you are on a budget consider visiting on a day trip from Diyarbakır or a homestay booked through **Nomad Tours Turkey** (☎533 747 1850; www.nomadtoursturkey.com).

TOP CHOICE **Erdoba Konakları** BOUTIQUE HOTEL $$$
(☎212 7677; www.erdoba.com.tr; Cumhuriyet Caddesi 135; s/d TL160/220; ❄) Right in the heart of the old town, this serene boutique hotel comprises four finely restored mansions, with lots of period charm. Downside: only five rooms come with a view (but a few terraces look onto the Mesopotamia plain). There's a high-quality onsite restaurant.

Otel Bilem HOTEL $$
(☎212 5568; www.bilemhotel.net, in Turkish; Vali Ozan Caddesi 72, Yenişehir; s/d TL70/100; ❄) A safe albeit unsexy choice in the new part of Mardin (Yenişehir), 2km northwest of Cumhuriyet Meydanı. Although its facade and lobby have been renovated, the high-rise Bilem is no architectural beauty queen, yet it's often full to the brim with tour groups.

TOP CHOICE **Cercis Murat Konağı** SYRIAN $$$
(☎213 6841; Cumhuriyet Caddesi; mains TL20-25) The Cercis occupies a traditional Syrian Christian home with two finely decorated rooms and a terrace affording stunning views. Conjured up by local women (there's a TV screen where you can watch them at work in the kitchen), the dainty dishes include *mekbuss* (eggplant pickles with walnut), *kitel raha* (Syrian-style meatballs) and *dobo* (piece of lamb with garlic, spices and black pepper).

Kamer Vakif KURDISH $
(Cumhuriyet Caddesi; mains TL10-15) Run by a support organisation for female victims of domestic violence, this is a superb place to try local dishes and contribute to a good cause.

Getting There & Away

Mardin airport is 20km south of town and receives daily Turkish Airlines flights from Ankara and İstanbul. There are hourly minibuses to Diyarbakır (TL10, 1¼ hours) and Şanlıurfa (TL20, three hours). For the Iraq border head to Silopli (TL20, three hours) via Cizre, and for the Syrian border to Nusaybin (TL8, one hour). See p542 for more details.

Şanlıurfa (Urfa)

☎0414 / POP 498,100

Mystical and pious, Şanlıurfa (the Prophets' City) is a spiritual centre par excellence and a great pilgrimage town. This is where the prophets Job and Abraham left their marks. As has been the case with centuries of pilgrims before you, the first sight of the Dergah complex of mosques and the holy Gölbaşı area (with the call to prayer as a soundtrack) will be a magical moment that you will remember for a long time to come.

In Urfa you'll feel like you've finally reached the Middle East, courtesy of its proximity to Syria. Women cloaked in black *chadors* elbow their way through the odorous crush of the bazaar streets; moustached gents in *şalvar* (traditional baggy Arabic trousers) swill tea and click-clack backgammon pieces in shady courtyards. Welcome to one of Turkey's most exotic cities.

Sights

It's also worth visiting the numerous **mosques** dotted about the centre.

Kale FORTRESS

(fortress; admission TL3; 8am-8pm) Sitting on Damlacık hill, from which Abraham was supposedly tossed, Kale looks magnificent when floodlit. Come up here for unobstructed views over Urfa. It can be reached via a flight of stairs or a tunnel cut through the rock.

Gölbaşı Park PARK

Surrounded by a complex of **mosques**, the park is a symbolic re-creation of a legend in which the Islamic prophet Abraham (İbrahim) ended up, quite literally, in a bed of roses after a tussle with Nimrod, the Assyrian king. Pilgrims come to pay their respects, then feed fat, sacred carp in a nearby pool. Afterwards explore the wonderful **bazaar**.

Sleeping

TOP CHOICE **Aslan Guest House** PENSION $$

(215 1575; www.aslankonukevi.com; 12 Eylul Caddesi, 1351 Sokak 10; dm/d/ste TL25/90/120;) Located in a heritage building around a cute courtyard, this is a well-thought-out budget choice, with a terrace restaurant and bar. The Harran-Nemrut tour agency is based here, expertly run by English-speaking owner Özcan Aslan, and organising excellent trips to Harran and Mt Nemrut.

Hotel Rabis HOTEL $$

(216 9595; www.hotelrabis.com; Sarayönü Caddesi; s/d TL70/120;) A model of shiny mid-range quality, with thick carpets, flat-screen TVs and double glazing. There are good views from the rooftop terrace, too. One of the better deals in town.

Hotel Arte HOTEL $$

(314 7060; www.otel-arte.com; Ataturk Bulvarı, Sinema Sokak 7; s/d TL70/100;) The designled interior of the Arte features bright, Barbie-esque plastic chairs, laminate floors, contemporary furniture and floor-to-ceiling windows.

Hotel Bakay HOTEL $

(215 8975; Asfalt Yol Caddesi; s/d TL40/60;) A safe bet that won't hurt the pocket, the Bakay is remarkably clean, but be prepared to trip over your backpack in the tiny rooms. Some are brighter than others, so ask to check out a few before settling in.

Eating & Drinking

Head for the *çay bahçesis* in the Gölbaşı park to relax over a cup of tea in leafy surrounds. The city is famed for its atmospheric *konuk evi,* charming 19th-century stone mansions that have been converted into restaurants.

Be careful what you eat in summer, because the heat makes food poisoning more likely.

TOP CHOICE **Çift Mağara** TURKISH $$

(Çift Kubbe Altı Balıklıgöl; mains TL8-15) The dining room is directly carved into the rocky bluff that overlooks the Gölbaşı, but the lovely terrace for dining alfresco beats the cavernous interior. It's famed for its delicious *içli köfte*.

Gülhan Restaurant TURKISH $$

(Atatürk Bulvarı; mains TL8-13) Razor-sharp waiters; well-presented food; the right mood; slick and salubrious surrounds – all good ingredients. The dishes are all pretty tasty, but if you want a recommendation, go for the Bursa *İskender kebap*.

Cevahir Konuk Evi TURKISH $$

(www.cevahirkonukevi.com; Yeni Mahalle Sokak; mains TL10-20;) This *konuk evi* offers excellent tabouleh and faultlessly cooked *tavuk şiş* (chicken kebap). You can also stay the night (single/double TL160/190).

Büyükfırat INTERNATIONAL $

(Sarayönü Caddesi; mains TL5-10) With its fountain and breezy outdoor seating, this restaurant-cafe-fast-food joint is the perfect salve

WORTH A TRIP

HARRAN

About 50km to the southeast of Urfa, Harran is one of the oldest continuously occupied settlements in the world. Its ruined walls, Ulu Cami, crumbling fortress and beehive houses are powerful, evocative sights. Minibuses for Harran (TL4, one hour) leave approximately hourly from the regional terminal below the Urfa otogar, or take a tour with Harran-Nemrut based at the Aslan Guest House (p529).

after a day's sightseeing. Nosh on burgers, pizzas, stews and kebaps or slug down a freshly squeezed orange juice.

Information

The city's main thoroughfare changes its name along its length and is called, at various points: Atatürk, Köprübaşı, Sarayönü and Divan Yolu Caddesis.

Getting There & Away

Turkish Airlines has daily flights to/from Ankara and İstanbul, but the airport is an inconvenient 45km from town. Havas Bus (TL10, 45 minutes) runs between the airport and the centre with departures coordinated with flight arrivals.

The otogar is 5km north of the centre on the road to Diyarbakır some services drop you at the roundabout nearby. Frequent buses connect Şanlıurfa with Gaziantep (TL15, 2½ hours) and Diyarbakır (TL15, three hours).

To get to Syria, take a minibus to Akçakale (TL5, one hour), then catch a taxi over the busy border to Talabiyya.

Mt Nemrut

Mt Nemrut (Nemrut Dağı; 2150m) is one of the great must-see attractions of eastern Turkey. Two thousand years ago, right on top of the mountain and pretty much in the middle of nowhere, an obscure Commagene king chose to erect fabulous temples and a funerary mound. The fallen heads of the gigantic decorative statues of gods and kings that now lie on the mountain, toppled by earthquakes, form one of Turkey's most enduring images.

Access to Nemrut Dağı Milli Parkı (Mt Nemrut National Park) costs TL6.50. There are a few possible bases for visiting Mt Nemrut. To the north is Malatya, where the tourist office organises all-inclusive daily minibus tours (TL100, early May to late September/early October), with a sunset visit to the heads, a night at a hotel below the summit and a second, dawn visit.

Alternatively, visit the mountain from the south via Kahta, where sunrise and sunset tours are available. The Kahta trip is notorious for hassles and rip-offs, but this route is more scenic.

Sleeping

MALATYA

Grand Akkoza Hotel HOTEL $$
(326 2727; www.grandakkozahotel.com; Çevre Yolu Üzeri Adliye Kavşağı 135; s/d TL90/130; ❄@) This glass-fronted three-star venture provides a good level of comfort and service. There's also a hamam, sauna and gym. It's awkwardly placed (if you're not driving) on the busy ring road, but within easy access of the city centre.

Malatya Büyük Otel HOTEL $$
(325 2828; Halep Caddesi, Yeni Cami Karşısı; s/d TL60/90; ❄) This sharp-edged monolith wins no awards for character but sports serviceable (if small) rooms with salubrious bathrooms and dashing views of a huge mosque. The location is handy – the bazaar is one block behind – and the staff are obliging.

Yeni Hotel HOTEL $$
(323 1423; yenihotel@turk.net; Yeni Cami Karşısı Zafer İşhanı; s/d TL50/80; ❄) Quite transparently intended to rival the neighbouring Malatya Büyük, this well-run establishment has rooms in pastel hues, with electric-blue bedspreads.

KAHTA

In summer, and if you have your own car, you may consider staying in some of the camping grounds on the slopes of the mountain rather than in the town itself.

Zeus Hotel HOTEL $$
(725 5694; www.zeushotel.com.tr; Mustafa Kemal Caddesi 20; campsites per person TL20, s/d €60/80; ❄≋) A group-friendly stalwart, this solid three-star option gets an A+ for its swimming pool in the manicured garden. Angle for the renovated rooms, which feature top-notch bathrooms and flat-screen TVs.

Pension Kommagene PENSION $
(☎725 5385; Mustafa Kemal Caddesi; campsites per person TL10, d without breakfast TL50 d without bathroom or breakfast TL36; ❄) The most obvious choice for tight-fisted travellers, primarily because of the lack of competitors in this price bracket. Rooms are not flashy but are clean, secure and well organised. Add TL7 for breakfast.

Gaziantep (Antep)

☎0342 / POP 1.3 MILLION

Gaziantep is a greatly underrated city that proclaims a modern, laissez-faire attitude while thumbing its nose at Urfa's piety. It's one of the most desirable places to live in eastern Anatolia, with the biggest city park this side of the Euphrates and a buzzing cafe culture.

Sights

FREE **Kale** CASTLE
(citadel) The unmissable kale offers superb vistas over the city. Not far south of the citadel is a buzzing bazaar area, which has recently been restored and includes Zincirli Bedesten. Scattered in the centre are numerous old **stone houses** and **caravanserai**, also being restored as part of Gaziantep's ongoing regeneration.

Gaziantep Museum MUSEUM
(İstasyon Caddesi; admission TL2; ⊙8.30am-noon & 1-5pm Tue-Sun) Don't skip this museum, with its display of fabulous mosaics unearthed at the rich Roman site of Belkıs-Zeugma.

Sleeping

Gaziantep is rolling in accommodation, much of it on or near Suburcu, Hürriyet and Atatürk Caddesis.

TOP CHOICE **Anadolu Evleri** BOUTIQUE HOTEL $$
(☎220 9525; www.anadoluevleri.com; Köroğlu Sokak 6; s/d/ste €70/90/110; ❄@) A tastefully restored old stone house in a lovely position, this oasis celebrates local tradition: a beguiling courtyard, beamed or painted ceilings, mosaic floors, secret passageways, and antique furniture and artefacts. It's spitting distance from the bazaar, yet feels quiet and restful.

Yesemek Otel HOTEL $$
(☎220 8888; www.yesemekotel.com; İsmail Sokak 4; s/d TL50/80; P❄) Right in the thick of things, the well-regarded Yesemek Otel offers great service and facilities, including a restaurant and a private *otopark*, although its executive look doesn't really scream 'holidays'.

Yunus Hotel HOTEL $
(☎221 1722; hotelyunus@hotel.com; Kayacık Sokak; s/d TL40/60; ❄) As far as physical beauty goes, this is a real plain Jane, but it's a secure spot to hang your rucksack, the rates are good and it's handily set in the centre of town.

Eating & Drinking

This fast-paced and epicurean city is reckoned to harbour more than 180 pastry shops and to produce the best *fıstık* (pistachio) baklava in the world.

TOP CHOICE **İmam Çağdaş** TURKISH $$
(Kale Civarı Uzun Çarşı; mains TL10-16) This pastry shop and restaurant is run by Imam Çağdaş, our culinary guru, who concocts wicked pistachio baklavas that are delivered daily to customers throughout Turkey. And if there was a kebap Oscar awarded, this place would also be a serious contender.

WORTH A TRIP

BIRECIK'S BALD IBISES

They may be bald and ugly, but the highly managed population of just under 100 critically endangered Northern Bald Ibises at Birecik, 55km east of Gaziantep, represents a fifth of the entire world population! So precious are these birds that they are taken into captivity just prior to their migration and released again when breeding time comes around. Special permission is needed to visit them, contact Turkey's Birdlife International partner **Doğa Derneği** (☎0312-481 2545; www.dogadernegi.org in Turkish; Hürrieyt Caddesi 43, Ankara) for details on how to do so. Take the opportunity to ask about the organisation's 'Conservation Houses', accommodation set-ups in areas of natural beauty, the proceeds from which are used to fund nationwide conservation projects.

Gaziantep (Antep)

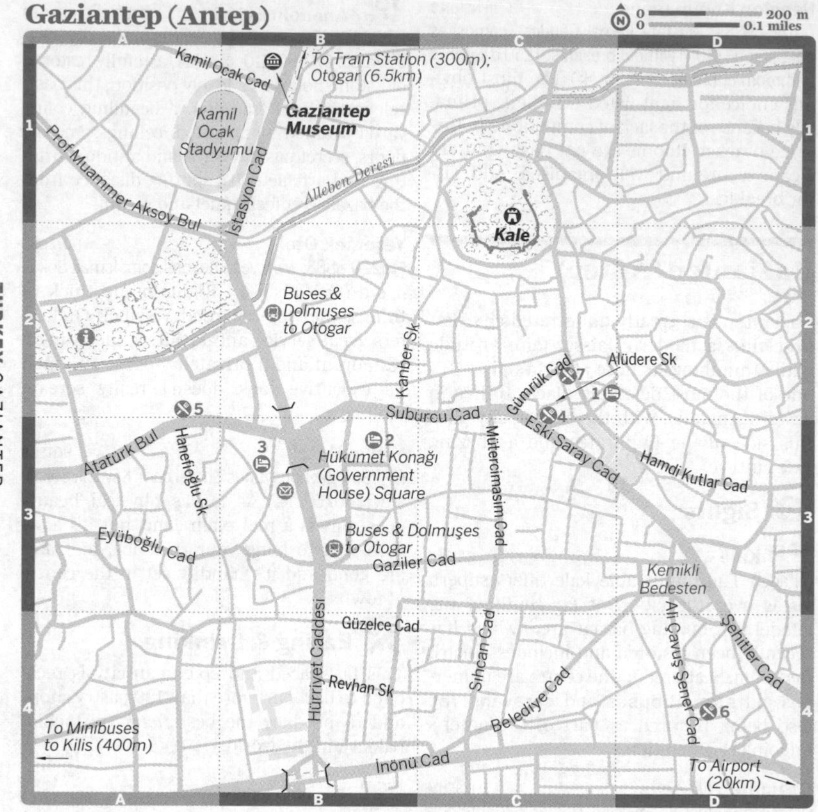

Gaziantep (Antep)

Top Sights
- Gaziantep Museum ... B1
- Kale ... C1

Sleeping
1. Anadolu Evleri ... C2
2. Yesemek Otel ... B3
3. Yunus Hotel ... B3

Eating
4. Çavuşoğulu ... C2
5. Çınarlı ... A2
6. Çulcuoğlu Et Lokantasi ... D4
7. İmam Çağdaş ... C2

Çınarlı KURDISH **$$**
(Çınarlı Sokak; mains TL7-15) The Çınarlı has long enjoyed a great reputation for its *yöresel yemeks* (traditional dishes). Choose between three small rooms, decorated with rugs, weapons and other collectibles, and a bigger dining room, where you can enjoy live music in the afternoon.

Çulcuoğlu Et Lokantasi TURKISH **$**
(Kalender Sokak; mains TL7-12; ⌚11.30am-10pm Mon-Sat) Just surrender helplessly to your inner carnivore at this Gaziantep institution. The yummy kebaps are the way to go, but grilled chicken also puts in menu appearances. Don't be discouraged by the unremarkable entrance.

Çavuşoğlu TURKISH **$**
(Eski Saray Caddesi; mains TL5-10) This sprightly outfit rustles up dishes that will fill your tummy without emptying your wallet. Portions are copious, the meat is perfectly slivered and the salads are fresh.

Information

The throbbing heart of Gaziantep is the intersection of Atatürk Bulvarı/Suburcu Caddesi and

Hürriyet/İstasyon Caddesis, marked by a large statue of Atatürk. Most hotels, banks with ATMs and sights are within walking distance of this intersection.

The **tourist office** (☎230 5969; 100 Yıl Atatürk Kültür Parkı İçi; ⊙8am-noon & 1-5pm Mon-Fri) is in the city park.

Getting There & Away

The airport is 20km from the centre and has several daily flights to/from Ankara and İstanbul. A Havaş bus shuttle (TL9, 35 minutes) runs to town, with departures coordinated with flight arrivals.

The otogar is about 7km from the town centre with services to Şanlıurfa (TL10, 2½ hours) and Antakya (TL15, four hours). Buses and dolmuşes for the otogar stop on Hürriyet Caddesi.

There's no direct bus to Syria; you'll have to go to Kilis first, then taxi to the border or to Aleppo. Minibuses to Kilis (TL8, 65km) leave every 20 minutes or so from a separate *garaj* (minibus terminal) on İnönü Caddesi.

To get to Aleppo and Damascus by train, you'll need to go to İslahiye to catch the twice-weekly train to Syria. The Gaziantep train station is 800m north of the centre.

UNDERSTAND TURKEY

Turkey Today

Secular Turkey has grown in international prominence in recent years, and its cultural and political common ground with its European and Arabic neighbours has succeeded in allowing it to maintain generally good relations with its neighbours. However as political tensions in the region have increased, so has the pressure on Turkey to choose sides. The deteriorating relationship with former close ally Syria is of particular relevance, and is seen by some in the region as an indication that when it comes to the crunch Turkey is likely to 'go west'. On the other hand, Islamic Turkey took a strong stance against Israel in May 2010 when Israeli troops violently stormed the *Mavi Marmara*, a Turkish aid vessel bound for Gaza, which resulted in the deaths of nine aid workers.

In June 2011 the 10-year-old Justice & Development Party (AKP) won its third consecutive national election with an increased majority, taking almost 50% of the votes cast. The party, which is led by Recep Tayyip Erdoğan, bills itself as pro European and as an advocate of social conservativism, but Erdoğan has been accused of seeking to overturn secularism and surreptitiously enforce an Islamic agenda.

The country remains intent on joining the EU and has made several concessions in order to do so, but its failure to recognise EU member Cyprus and a feeling that it is still not doing enough over the Kurdish issue continue to be stumbling blocks for entry. That said, it has answered many of the economic questions, and by 2005 the economy was considered robust enough to introduce the new Turkish lira (YTL; Yeni Türk Lirası), renamed the Turkish lira (TL; Türk Lirası) in 2009.

Domestically, the most pressing problem is Turkey's own 'war on terror'– the Kurdish issue. After decades of clashes between the military and the Kurdistan Workers Party (PKK), the situation simmered down as a series of concessions were made by the government. However the PKK ended its 14-month ceasefire in May 2010, with its chief promising to take the fight out of the mountains of southeastern Anatolia and Kurdish Iraq – to western Turkey, and the situation once again flared up. Another proposed ceasefire until the June 2011 elections, announced in August 2010, was over by February 2011 as the situation became increasingly volatile.

Against this background of violence, the pro-Kurdish Peace and Democracy Party (BDP) surprised everybody by taking 36 seats in the southeast of the country, though 6 of the 36 deputies elected were behind bars at the time of the elections. This did nothing to calm the situation and the Turkish army began a new offensive against the PKK in August 2011. The accidental killing of 35 civilians by army strikes in December 2011 caused mass protests throughout the Kurdish region. In an attempt to prevent tensions from boiling over, the Turkish government announced in January 2012 it would pay compensation to the bereaved families.

History

Few countries can claim to have played such a significant role in the history of human civilisation as Turkey, and the country's location on the major trade routes between Europe and Asia identified it as a major strategic target for many of the greatest empires of modern times. From the Hittites to the Romans, the Byzantines through the Seljuks, the Ottomans and more recently the revolutionary republic of Mustafa Kemal Atatürk, the greatest global powers of their age each recognised the importance of the land we today call Turkey and all left their indelible marks on the varied landscape.

A quick glance across the map will reveal a plethora of names that may sound familiar. Thanks to the travels of St Paul, Turkish localities figure prominently in the Bible and, though the names may have changed, the history remains eternal. Take for example Antioch (now Antakya) the place where the term 'Christian' was first coined; or Ephesus, burial site of St Luke; and, of course, Nicaea (today the tile-producing town of İznık) where the first efforts were made to attain a consensus in Christian thinking. For a complete review we recommend *A Guide to Biblical Sites in Greece and Turkey* by Clyde Fant and Mitchell Reddish.

In Turkey lies the legendary city of Troy, the deceitful conquest of which was romanticised and immortalised in Homer's *Iliad,* and the city of Konya, which gave birth to the wonderful whirling dervishes. And also there is the Gallipoli Peninsula, a place of pilgrimage for many who come to remember the fallen in the ultimately futile campaign to control the Bosphorus during WWI.

Modern Turkey is a country that has been shaped by its past. The result of this fascinating yet frequently turbulent history of conquest and reconquest is a rich cultural heritage drawing from the influence of some of the world's greatest civilisations, and moulding them into a wonderfully unique modern culture of which the Turks are justifiably proud.

Early Anatolian Civilisations

The Hittites, the greatest early civilisation in Anatolia, were a force to be reckoned with from 2000 to 1200 BC. Their capital, Hattuşa, is now an atmospheric site east of Ankara.

After the collapse of the Hittite empire, Anatolia splintered into small states and it wasn't until the Graeco-Roman period that parts of the country were reunited. Christianity later spread through the region, preached by the apostle Paul, who crossed Anatolia on the new Roman roads.

Rome, then Byzantium

In AD 330 the Roman emperor, Constantine, founded a new imperial city at Byzantium (İstanbul). Renamed Constantinople, the strategic city became the capital of the Eastern Roman Empire and was the centre of the Byzantine Empire for 1000 years. During the European Dark Ages, the Byzantine Empire kept alive the flame of Roman culture, although it was intermittently threatened from the east (Persians, Arabs, Turks) and west (European powers such as the Goths and Lombards).

Coming Of The Turks: Seljuks & Ottomans

The Byzantine Empire began to decline from 1071, when the Seljuk Turks defeated its forces at Manzikert, north of Lake Van. The Seljuks overran most of Anatolia, establishing a provincial capital at Konya. Their domains stretched across the Middle East and their distinctive, conical-roofed tombs still dot Turkey.

The Byzantines endeavoured to protect Constantinople and reclaim Anatolia, but during the Fourth Crusade (1202–04), which was supposedly instigated to save Eastern Christendom from the Muslims, an unruly Crusader force sacked Constantinople.

The Seljuks, meanwhile, were defeated by the Mongols at Köse Dağ in 1243. The region fractured into a mosaic of Turkish *beyliks* (principalities) and Mongol fiefdoms, but by 1300, a single Turkish bey, Osman, established the Ottoman dynasty.

Having captured Constantinople in 1453, the Ottoman Empire reached its zenith a century later under Süleyman the Magnificent. It expanded deep into Europe, Asia and North Africa, but when its march westward stalled at Vienna in 1683, the rot set in. By the 19th century, European powers had begun to covet the Ottomans' domains.

Nationalism swept Europe after the French Revolution, and Greece, Romania, Montenegro, Serbia and Bosnia all won independence from the Ottomans. The First Balkan War removed Bulgaria and Macedonia from the Ottoman map, while Bulgarian, Greek and Serbian troops advanced on İstanbul. The empire was now known as the 'sick man of Europe'.

Republic

WWI stripped the Turks of Syria, Palestine, Mesopotamia (Iraq) and Arabia, and the victorious Europeans intended to share most of Anatolia among themselves, leaving the Turks virtually nothing.

Enter Mustafa Kemal Atatürk, the father of modern Turkey. Atatürk made his name by repelling the British and Anzac forces in their attempt to capture Gallipoli. Rallying the tattered Turkish army, he outmanoeuvred the Allied forces in the War of Independence and, in 1923, pushed the invading Greeks into the sea at Smyrna (İzmir).

After renegotiation of the WWI treaties, a new Turkish Republic, reduced to Anatolia and part of Thrace, was born. Atatürk embarked on a modernisation program, introducing a secular democracy, the Latin script, European dress and equal rights for women (at least in theory). The capital shifted from İstanbul to Ankara. Many of the sweeping changes did not come easily and their reverberations can still be felt today. In population exchanges with Greece, around 1.5 million Greeks left Turkey and nearly half a million Turks moved in; deserted 'ghost villages' can still be seen.

Since Atatürk's death in 1938, Turkey has experienced three military coups and, during the 1980s and '90s, had conflict with the Kurdistan Workers Party (PKK), which aimed to create a Kurdish state in Turkey's southeast corner.

People & Society

As a result of Atatürk's reforms, republican Turkey has largely adapted to a modern Western lifestyle, but the Turks' mentality reflects their country's position at the meeting of Europe and Asia. The constant sway between two worlds can be disconcerting. In İstanbul, İzmir, Antalya and coastal resorts, you'd be forgiven for thinking you were in Europe; you will not need to adapt much in order to fit in. In smaller towns and villages, however, you may find people warier and more conservative.

The Turks have an acute sense of pride and honour. They are fiercely proud of their history and heroes, especially Atatürk, whose portrait and statues are ubiquitous – insulting him or his effigy is considered a serious crime. The extended family plays a key role, and formality and politeness are important.

Language

Turkish is the official language. It's been written in the Latin script since Atatürk rejected Arabic in 1928. In southeastern Anatolia, most Kurds speak Turkish. In remote regions of Anatolia you'll hear Kurmancı and Zazakı, the two Kurdish dialects, spoken. South of Gaziantep you'll hear Arabic being spoken alongside Turkish.

Religion

Turkey is about 80% Sunni Muslim and an additional further 19.8% of the population are Alevi Muslims, living mainly in the east of the country. The religious practices of Sunnis and Alevis differ markedly.

The country espouses a more relaxed version of Islam than many Middle Eastern nations. Many men drink alcohol, but almost no one touches pork, and many women wear headscarves.

Of the remaining 0.2%, the two most significant Christian minorities are the Armenians (formerly from Anatolia) and the Greeks (formerly spread throughout the country) though both groups now live mainly in İstanbul. As part of the terms ending the Greco-Turkish war in 1922, Turkey and Greece agreed on the mutual expulsion of almost 2 million citizens based on religious identity. This involved almost 1.5 million Anatolian Greek Orthodox Christians being relocated to Greece in exchange for some 500,000 Muslims sent to Turkey.

A small Jewish community of around 25,000 also lives mostly in İstanbul, while a declining community of Nestorian and Assyrian Orthodox Christians are based in the southeast of the country.

Arts

Cinema

Several Turkish directors have won worldwide recognition, most notably the late Yilmaz Güney, director of *Yol* (The Road), *Duvar* (The Wall) and *Sürü* (The Herd). The Cannes favourite Nuri Bilge Ceylan probes the lives of village migrants in the big city in *Uzak* (Distant), and looks at male-female relationships in *İklimler* (Climates).

Ferzan Özpetek's *Hamam* (Turkish Bath) addresses the previously hidden issue of homosexuality in Turkish society. The new name to watch is Fatih Akin, who ponders the Turkish experience in Germany in *Duvara Karsi* (Head On) and *Edge of Heaven*.

Music

Turkey's successful home-grown pop industry managed to gain European approval

CARPETS

Turkey is famous for its beautiful carpets and *kilims* (woven rugs). It's thought that the Seljuks introduced hand-woven carpet-making techniques to Anatolia in the 12th century. Traditionally, village women wove carpets for their family's use, or for their dowry; today, the dictates of the market rule, but carpets still incorporate traditional symbols and patterns. The Ministry of Culture has sponsored projects to revive age-old weaving and dyeing methods in western Turkey; some shops stock these 'project carpets'. Remember that authentic antique carpets cannot be taken out of the country. They will be taken from you at customs.

While the carpets themselves can be supremely beautiful, the tactics used to sell them to you are sometimes not so pleasing! An apparently helpful new friend on the street may well turn out to be a carpet salesman, and a free cup of tea as you peruse the stock is often a tactic just to keep you listening to the sales pitch. One reader was even locked inside a carpet shop and told they had to buy a carpet because they hadn't paid for their tea!

faster than the country's politicians when Sertab Erener won the Eurovision Song Contest with *Every Way that I Can* in 2003.

The big pop stars include pretty-boy Tarkan, who Holly Valance covered, and chanteuse Sezen Aksu. Burhan Öçal is one of Turkey's finest percussionists; his seminal *New Dream* is a funky take on classical Turkish music. Ceza is the king of İstanbul's thriving hip-hop scene.

With an Arabic spin, Arabesk is also popular. The genre's stars are Orhan Gencebay and the Kurdish former construction worker, Ibrahim Tatlıses. Two Kurdish folk singers to listen out for are Aynur Doğan and Ferhat Tunç.

Architecture

Turkey's architectural history encompasses everything from Hittite stonework and Graeco-Roman temples to modern tower-blocks in İstanbul. The most distinctively Turkish styles, however, are perhaps the Seljuk and Ottoman. The Seljuks left magnificent mosques and medreses, distinguished by their elaborate entrances. The Ottomans also built grand religious structures, as well as fine wood-and-stone houses in towns such as Safranbolu and Amasya.

Environment

The Land

The Dardanelles, the Sea of Marmara and the Bosphorus divide Turkey into Asian and European parts. Eastern Thrace (European Turkey) comprises only 3% of the 779,452-sq-km land area; the remaining 97% is Anatolia, a vast plateau rising eastward towards the Caucasus Mountains. With more than 7000km of coastline, snowcapped mountains, rolling steppes, vast lakes and broad rivers, Turkey is geographically diverse.

Environmental Issues

Turkey's embryonic environmental movement is making slow progress; discarded litter and ugly concrete buildings (some half-finished) disfigure the western in particular. Desertification is a long-term threat for the country.

Big dam projects have caused environmental problems. The 22-dam Güneydoğu Anadolu Projesi (GAP) is changing southeastern Anatolia's landscape as it generates hydroelectricity for industry. Parched valleys have become fish-filled lakes, causing an explosion of diseases. GAP has also generated problems with Syria and Iraq, the countries downriver.

In 2008 dam-builders' plans to drown Hasankeyf saw the historic southeastern town named on the World Monuments Watch list (alongside four other Turkish sites).

İstanbul has a branch of **Greenpeace Mediterranean** (☎/fax 0212-292 7619/7622; Kallavi Sokak 1/2, Beyoğlu) and the Turkish Birdlife International partner is **Doğa Derneği** (☎0312-481 2545; www.dogadernegi.org in Turkish; Hürrieyt Caddesi 43, Ankara).

Wildlife

Turkey has a number of endangered species, including the Mediterranean Monk Seal (450 remain, 100 breeding), the Asia Minor Spiny Mouse (now confined to a small area of the coast), the Northern Bald Ibis (500 remain, 100 breed in Turkey), and the Taurus Frog (world distribution covers just 10 square kilometres).

Food

Turkish food is regarded as one of the world's greatest cuisines. Kebaps are, of course, the mainstay of restaurant meals; ubiquitous lokantas (restaurants) sell a wide range. Try the *durum* döner kebap – compressed meat (usually lamb) cooked on a revolving upright skewer over coals, then thinly sliced. Laid on pide bread, topped with tomato sauce and browned butter and with yoghurt on the side, döner kebap becomes *İskender kebap,* primarily a lunchtime delicacy. Equally common are *köfte* (meatballs).

A quick, cheap fill, Turkish pizza is a freshly cooked pide topped with cheese, egg or meat. Alternatively, *lahmacun* is a paper-thin Arabic pizza with chopped onion, lamb and tomato sauce. Other favourites are *gözleme* (pancake) and *simit* (a ring of bread decorated with sesame seeds).

Fish dishes, although excellent, are often expensive; check the price before ordering.

For vegetarians, meze can be an excellent way to ensure a varied diet. Most restaurants should be able to rustle up *beyaz peynir* (ewe's- or goat's-milk cheese), *sebze çorbası* (vegetable soup), börek (flaky pastry stuffed with white cheese and parsley), *kuru fasulye* (beans) and *patlıcan tava* (fried aubergine).

For dessert, try *fırın sütlaç* (rice pudding), *aşure* ('Noah's Ark' pudding, featuring up to 40 different ingredients), baklava (honey-soaked flaky pastry stuffed with walnuts or pistachios), *kadayıf* (syrup-soaked dough, often topped with cream) and *dondurma* (ice cream).

The famously chewy *lokum* (Turkish delight), widely available throughout Turkey, has been made here since the 18th century. For more information on Turkish cuisine, look out for Lonely Planet's *World Food Turkey* guide. Also see the Middle Eastern Cuisine chapter, p590.

Drink

The national hot drink, *çay,* is served in tulip-shaped glasses with copious amounts of sugar. Tiny cups of traditional Turkish *kahve* (coffee) are served *şekersiz* (with no sugar), *az şekerli* (medium sweet) or *çok şekerli* (very sweet). Unfortunately, Nescafé is fast replacing *kahve* and, in tourist areas, it usually comes *sütlü* (with milk).

The Turkish liquor of choice is *rakı,* a fiery aniseed drink like the Greek ouzo or Arab arak; do as the Turks do and cut it by half with water. Turkish *şarap* (wine), both red *(kırmızı)* and white *(beyaz),* is improving in quality and is worth a try. You can buy Tuborg or Efes Pilsen beers everywhere, although outside the resorts you may need to find a Tekel store (the state-owned alcoholic-beverage and tobacco company) to buy wine. In strongly Islamic towns such as Konya and Şanlıurfa the drinking of alcohol in public is frowned upon. Give your liver a rest and stick to the *çay.*

Ayran is a yoghurt drink, made by whipping up yoghurt with water and salt and if you are brave enough, try *salgam suyu,* a salty, spicy juice made from fermented red carrot.

SURVIVAL GUIDE

Directory A–Z

Accommodation

In smaller tourist towns such as Fethiye, Selcuk and Pamukkale, touts may try to pressure you into choosing their hotel as soon as you step off the bus. Pick your accommodation before you arrive and be polite but firm once the sales pitch begins.

Turkish hotels may quote rates in different currencies, and the currency used by the individual establishment is provided in the text. Establishments are listed in order of preference.

Prices in this book are for rooms in high season and include bathrooms, breakfast and taxes unless otherwise indicated.

$ less than TL70 (€40)

$$ TL70 to TL150 (€40 to €95)

$$$ more than TL150 (€95)

CAMPING

» Camping facilities are dotted about Turkey, although not as frequently as you might hope.

» Facilities vary and bathroom facilities are occasionally unhygienic.

» Some hotels and pensions will also let you camp in their grounds for a small fee, and they sometimes have facilities especially for campers.

HOSTELS

» Given that pensions are so cheap, Turkey has no real hostel network.

» Outside of İstanbul the best places to find hostels are backpacker hangouts such as Göreme or Selçuk.

» Many pensions also offer dormitories and hostel-style facilities, generally with shared bathroom.

PENSIONS & HOTELS

» Pensions are simple, often family-run and offer a good, clean single room from around TL40 a night (and a dorm bed from around TL20).

» Pensions are often cosy and represent better value than full-blown hotels.

» Breakfast is usually included in the price and other meals are frequently offered too.

HOTELS

» In most cities there is a variety of old and new hotels, which range from the depressingly basic to full-on luxury.

» Even in the cheapest places the price usually includes an en-suite bathroom.

» In tourist-dependent areas, particularly at the coast, many hotels close in winter; others offer substantial reductions.

» Budget hotels are mostly used by working Turkish men travelling on business and are not always suitable for lone women. It's not unusual for the decor to be a hangover from another age.

» Midrange hotels usually represent excellent value and offer modern facilities such as cable TV and air-conditioning/heating.

» Among the most charismatic of the top-end hotels are the atmospheric boutique hotels. These are often housed in old Ottoman mansions and other historic buildings, and are dripping with style.

TREE HOUSES

» Olympos, on the coast southwest of Antalya, is famous for its 'tree houses', environmentally unfriendly wooden shacks of minimal comfort in depleted forested settings near the beach.

» Increasingly, these basic shelters are being converted into chalets with more comfort.

Business Hours

The working day gets shortened during the holy month of Ramazan (Ramadan). More Islamic cities such as Konya and Kayseri virtually shut down during noon prayers on Friday. Apart from that, Friday is a normal working day in Turkey. The day of rest, a secular one, is Sunday. Opening hours of tourist attractions and tourist information offices may shorten in the low season in tourist resorts.

Banks, Businesses, Government Offices 8.30am-noon & 1-5pm Mon-Fri

Post Offices 9am-5.30pm Mon-Fri, later in summer in tourist resorts

Restaurants breakfast 8-11am, lunch noon-4pm, dinner 6-11pm

Bars 4pm-2am

Nightclubs 10pm-5am

Shops 9am-6pm Mon-Sat

Customs Regulations

It's strictly illegal to export antiquities. Customs officers spot-check luggage and will want proof that you have permission from a museum before letting you leave with an antique carpet. You can take out the following:

Cigarettes 200

Cigars 50

Tobacco 200g

Alcohol five 1L bottles or seven 700ml bottles

Perfume five 120ml bottles of different perfumes

Embassies & Consulates

Foreign embassies are in Ankara but many countries also have consulates in İstanbul. In general they are open from 9am to noon Monday to Friday, and some open in the afternoon until 5 to 6pm. For more information, visit www.mfa.gov.tr/resident-diplomatic-and-consular-missions.en.mfa.

Australia Ankara (☎0312-459 9500; 7th fl, Uğur Mumcu Caddesi 88, Gaziosmanpaşa); İstanbul (☎0212-393 8542; 2nd fl, Suzer Plaza, Askerocağı Caddesi 15, Elmadağ)

Bulgaria (☎0312-467 2071; Atatürk Bulvarı 124, Kavaklıdere, Ankara)

Canada (☎0312-409 2700; Cinnah Caddesi 58, Çankaya, Ankara)

Egypt Ankara (☎0312-426 1026; fax 427 0099; Atatürk Bulvarı 126, Kavaklıdere); İstanbul (☎0212-324 2180; Akasyalı Sokak 26, 4 Levent)

France Ankara (☎0312-455 4545; Paris Caddesi 70, Kavaklıdere); İstanbul (Map p472; ☎0212-334 8730; İstiklal Caddesi 8, Taksim)

Germany Ankara (☎0312 455 5100; Atatürk Bulvarı 114, Kavaklıdere); İstanbul (Map p472; ☎0212-334 6100; İnönü Caddesi 16-18, Taksim)

Greece Ankara (☎0312-448 0873; gremb.ank@mfa.gr; Zia Ur Rahman Caddesi 9-11, Gaziosmanpaşa); Edirne (☎0284-235 5804; Kocasinan Mahallesi 2 Sokak 12); İstanbul (Map p472; ☎0212-393 8290; Turnacıbaşı Sokak 32, Galatasaray)

Iran Ankara (☎0312-468 2820; Tahran Caddesi 10, Kavaklıdere); Erzurum (☎0442-315 9983; fax 316 1182; Alparslan Bulvarı, 201 Sokak); İstanbul (Map p464; ☎0212-513 8230; 2nd fl, Ankara Caddesi 1, Cağaloğlu)

Iraq Ankara (☎0312-468 7421; fax 468 4832; Turan Emeksiz Sokak 11, Gaziosmanpaşa); İstanbul (☎0212-299 0120; Köybaşi Caddesi 3, Yeniköy)

Ireland (☎0312-459 1000; fax 446 8061; Uğur Mumcu Caddesi 88, MNG Binasi B-Bl 3, Gaziosmanpaşa, Ankara)

Israel Ankara (☎0312-459 7500; fax 459 7555; Mahatma Gandhi Caddesi 85, 06700 Gaziosmanpaşa); İstanbul (☎212-317 6500; Yapı Kredi Plaza, Blok C, Kat 7, Levent)

Jordan (☎0312-440 2054; fax 440 4327; Mesnevi Dede Korkut Sokak 18, Çankaya, Ankara)

Lebanon Ankara (☎0312-446 7485; fax 446 1023; Kızkulesi Sokak 44, Gaziosmanpaşa); İstanbul (☎0212-236 1365; fax 227 3373; Teşvikiye Caddesi 134/1, Teşvikiye)

Netherlands Ankara (☎0312-409 1800; fax 409 1898; Hollanda Caddesi No 3, Yıldız); İstanbul (Map p472; ☎0212-393 2121; fax 292 5031; İstiklal Caddesi 197, Tünel)

New Zealand (☎0312-446 3333; Kızkulesi Sokak 14, Gaziosmanpaşa, Ankara)

Russia Ankara (☎0312-439 2122; www.turkey.mid.ru; Karyağdi Sokak 5, Çankaya); İstanbul (Map p472; ☎0212-292 5101; visavi@rambler.ru; İstiklal Caddesi 219-225A, Beyoğlu)

Switzerland Ankara (☎0312-457 3100; Atatürk Bulvarı 247, Kavaklıdere); İstanbul (☎212-283 1282; Büy ükdere Caddesi 173, Levent)

Syria Ankara (☎0312-440 9657; fax 438 5609; Sedat Simovi Sokak 40, Çankaya); İstanbul (☎0212-232 7100; Maçka Caddesi, Ralli Apt 37 Kat 3, Teşvikiye)

UK Ankara (☎0312-455 3344; fax 455 3352; Şehit Ersan Caddesi 46a, Çankaya); İstanbul (Map p472; ☎0212-334 6400; fax 334 6401; Meşrutiyet Caddesi 34, Tepebaşı, Beyoğlu)

USA Ankara (☎0312-455 5555; fax 467 0019; Atatürk Bulvarı 110, Kavaklıdere); İstanbul (☎0212 335 9000, fax 335 9019; Üçşehitler Sokak 2, İstinye)

Food

Prices in this book represent the cost of a standard main-course dish.

$ less than TL10 (€5.50)

$$ TL10 to TL22 (€5.50 to €12.50)

$$$ more than TL22 (€12.50)

Gay & Lesbian Travellers

» Overt homosexuality is socially acceptable only in a few small pockets in İstanbul, Bodrum and other resorts.
» Prejudice remains strong, be discreet.
» In İstanbul there is an increasing number of openly gay bars and nightclubs, mainly around the Taksim Square end of İstiklal Caddesi.
» Some readers have reported being solicited in unisex hamams.
» **Lambda İstanbul** (www.lambdaistanbul.org, in Turkish) is Turkey's gay and lesbian support group.

Internet Access

» Throughout the country free wi-fi access is standard even in the cheapest hostels, and many restaurants, cafes and even buses offer wi-fi.
» An internet cafe is never far away, and fees are generally TL1.50 to TL2 for an hour.
» In accommodation listings, we have used the @ icon only where the hotel provides a computer with internet access for guest use.

Language Courses

For Turkish language courses try **Dilmer** (www.dilmer.com) in İstanbul.

Money

Turkish lira (TL) comes in notes of five, 10, 20, 50 and 100, and one-lira coins. One Turkish lira is worth 100 kuruş, which is available in one, five, 10, 25 and 50 kuruş coins.

Inflation is less of a problem than previously in Turkey, but many businesses still prefer to quote prices in euros or even US dollars. In listings we have used the currency quoted by the business in question.

ATMS

ATMs readily dispense Turkish lira to Visa, MasterCard, Cirrus, Maestro and Eurocard holders; there's hardly a town without a machine. Some tellers also dispense euros and US dollars.

CASH

US dollars and euros are the easiest currencies to change, although many banks and exchange offices will change other major currencies, such as UK pounds and Japanese yen. You may find it difficult to exchange Australian or Canadian currency except at banks and offices in major cities.

CREDIT CARDS

Visa and MasterCard are widely accepted by hotels, restaurants, carpet shops etc, although many pensions and local restaurants do not accept them outside the main tourist areas. You can also get cash advances on these cards. Amex cards are less often accepted.

MONEYCHANGERS

It's easy to change major currencies in most exchange offices, some PTTs, shops and hotels, although banks may make heavy weather of it. Places that don't charge commission usually offer a worse exchange rate instead.

Foreign currencies are readily accepted in shops, hotels and restaurants in main tourist areas. Taxi drivers accept foreign currencies for big journeys but travellers should agree on a price in advance.

TIPPING

Turkey is fairly European in its approach to tipping and you won't be pestered by demands for baksheesh, as elsewhere in the Middle East. Leave waiters and bath attendants around 10% of the bill; in restaurants, check a tip hasn't been automatically added to the bill. It's normal to round off metered taxi fares.

TRAVELLERS CHEQUES

Banks, shops and hotels often see it as a burden to change travellers cheques and will probably try to get you to go elsewhere or charge a premium. In case you do have to change them, try Akbank.

Post

The English language website of the **PTT** (Posta Telgraf Ve Telefon; www.ptt.gov.tr) is currently being updated to include a convenient branch locator and cost calculator.

Public Holidays

Turkey observes the following national holidays in addition to the traditional Islamic holidays:

New Year's Day 1 January
Children's Day 23 April
Youth & Sports Day 19 May
Victory Day 30 August
Republic Day 29 October
Anniversary of Atatürk's Death 10 November

Safe Travel

Although Turkey is one of the safest countries in the region, you should take all the usual precautions and watch out for the following.

- The TL5 and TL50 are superficially similar to each other so be aware which note you are handing over. Some unscrupulous business owners and taxi drivers are happy to take advantage if you're not paying attention.
- In İstanbul, single men are sometimes approached in areas such as Sultanahmet and Taksim and lured to a bar by new 'friends'. The scammers may be accompanied by the fig leaf of a woman. The victim is then made to pay an outrageous bill, regardless of what he drank. Drugging is sometimes a problem, especially for lone men. It pays to be a tad wary of who you befriend, especially when you're new to the country.
- Hard-sell tactics of carpet sellers can drive you to distraction. 'Free' lifts and other cheap services often lead to near-compulsory visits to carpet showrooms or hotel commission for touts.
- In southern Antolia the PKK (PKK/Kongra-Gel) once again began to step up its campaign for recognition during 2010

PRACTICALITIES

- Turkey uses the metric system for weights and measures.
- The electrical current is 220V AC, 50Hz. Wall sockets are the round, two-pin European type.
- For the news in English, pick up *Today's Zaman* (www.todayszaman.com).
- TRT (Türkiye Radyo ve Televizyon) provides short news broadcasts in English, French and German on the radio and online at www.trt.net.tr.
- Digiturk offers hundreds of Turkish and international TV channels.

and roads in this region are sometimes closed during escalations. Keep your finger on the pulse of the current situation.

Telephone & Fax

» Türk Telekom (www.turktelekom.com.tr) payphones can be found in many major public buildings and facilities, public squares and transportation termini.

» They are operated by pre-paid cards on sale at Türk Telekom centres or (with a small mark-up) in shops and newsagents. The company has a monopoly and as a result calls are pricey.

» For one-off calls look for signs advertising metered phones (*kontörlü telefon*) where you pay according to the clock.

» Türk Telekom centres have faxes, but using them requires lots of paperwork and they may insist on retaining your original! It's easier to use your hotel fax, but check the cost first.

» **Country code** ☎90

» **International access code** ☎00.

MOBILE PHONES

» Calling a *cep* (mobile) costs roughly three times the cost of calling a landline, no matter where you are.

» Mobile phone numbers start with a four-digit code beginning with ☎05.

» If you set up a roaming facility with your home phone provider, you should be able to connect your own mobile to the Turkcell or Telsim network.

» If you buy a local SIM card and use it in your home mobile, the network detects and bars foreign phones within a month.

» Avoid barring by registering your phone at a certified cell phone shop. Take your passport with you!

» Turkcell credit (*kontör*) and SIM cards are readily available at shops displaying the company's blue and yellow logo, found on every street corner, the bigger the card you buy the better the rates.

Toilets

Most hotels and public facilities have toilets that are Western-style, but you'll sometimes see squat toilets. Carry toilet paper and place it in the bin, if one is provided, to avoid inadvertently flooding the premises. Almost all public toilets require a payment of TL1.

Visas

» Nationals of the following countries don't need to obtain a visa when visiting Turkey for up to three months: Denmark, Finland, France, Germany, Israel, Italy, Japan, New Zealand, Sweden and Switzerland.

» Nationals of Australia, Belgium, Canada, Hungary, Ireland, the Netherlands, Norway (one month only), Portugal, Spain, the UK and the USA do need a visa, though this is just a passport stamp that you buy on arrival at the airport or at an overland border, rather than at an embassy in advance.

» Join the queue to buy your visa before joining the one for immigration.

» Citizens of all of the countries that do need a visa pay US$20 (or €15), except Canadians who pay US$60 (or €45).

» The customs officers expect to be paid in one of these currencies and may not accept Turkish lira.

» You *must* pay the exact amount in cash, no change is given.

» The standard visa is valid for three months and, depending on your nationality, usually allows for multiple entries.

» In theory, a Turkish visa can be renewed once after three months, but the bureaucracy and costs involved mean that it's much easier to leave the country and then come back in again on a fresh visa.

» Before entering Turkey make sure that your passport is not due to expire for another six months.

» For details of visas for other Middle Eastern countries, see the Visas sections in the Directories of the other country chapters.

Women Travellers

» Though some women travel around virtually unmolested, others report constant harassment.

» A good rule of thumb is to tailor your behaviour and dress to your surroundings. Except in resorts, you should dress modestly, and cover your hair when visiting mosques or religious buildings.

» To avoid unwanted attention, wear a wedding ring or carry a photo of your 'husband' and 'child'.

» In more conservative areas of the country (eastern and southern Anatolia especially) your contact with men should be polite and formal, not chatty and friendly or they are likely to get the wrong idea about your intentions.

» Men and unrelated women are not expected to sit beside each other in long-distance buses, and lone females are sometimes assigned a seat at the front, near the driver.
» Outside of tourist resorts some restaurants that aim to attract women often set aside a section for families. Look for the term *aile salonu* (family dining room).
» Very cheap hotels are not recommended for single women travellers. If a place has a bad vibe, find somewhere else.

Getting There & Away

Entering Turkey

Before entering Turkey make sure that your passport has at least six months' life in it. Once you get the hang of the visa process (see p541) it should all be plain sailing.

Air

Turkey's most important airport is İstanbul's **Atatürk International Airport** (www.ataturkairport.com), 25km west of the city centre. The cheapest fares are almost always to İstanbul, and to reach other Turkish airports, even **Ankara** (www.esembogaairport.com), you often have to transit in İstanbul. Other international airports:

Antalya (www.aytport.com)
Bodrum (www.bodrum-airport.com)
Dalaman (www.atmairport.aero)
İzmir (www.adnanmenderesairport.com)

Turkey's award-winning national carrier is **Turkish Airlines** (THY; Türk Hava Yollari; ✆0212-444 0849; www.thy.com), which has direct flights from İstanbul to major European cities and regional capitals including Beirut, Cairo, Damascus, Dubai, Jeddah, Kuwait, Riyadh and Tehran and Tripoli. **Armavia Airlines** (www.u8.am) has two weekly departures to Yerevan, Armenia.

Other major airlines flying regular routes to and from Turkey are listed below:

Air Canada (www.aircanada.com)
American Airlines (www.aa.com)
Atlasjet (www.atlasjet.com)
British Airways (www.britishairways.com)
Delta Airlines (www.delta.com)
EasyJet (www.easyjet.com)
Emirates Airlines (www.emirates.com)
Iran Air (www.iranair.com)
Iraqi Airways (www.iraqiairways.co.uk)
Lufthansa (www.lufthansa.com)
Malaysia Airlines (www.malaysiaairlines.com)
Olympic Airways (www.olympicair.com)
Pegasus (www.flypgs.com)
Singapore Airlines (www.singaporeair.com)

Land

BORDER CROSSINGS

Turkey shares borders with Azerbaijan, Bulgaria, Georgia, Greece, Iran, Iraq and Syria. The land border with Armenia remains closed. There are plenty of ways to get into and out of the country by rail or bus, but the process can often be long and frustrating with baggage checks on both sides of the border regardless of the country. For details on getting to Turkey from countries outside the Middle East, see p628.

Iran

For information about travel to Iran, see p628.

Iraq

Iraq is still a dangerous country and you should read our warning – p156 before considering visiting. Crossing the Turkish–Iraqi border at Habur, 15km southeast of Silopi (reached by bus from Mardin or Diyarbakır via Cizre), is straightforward but pricey. At Silopi's otogar, you'll soon realise that the crossing is a well-organised business that's in the hands of the local taxi mafia. For around US$70 (or the equivalent in euros), a taxi driver will handle all formalities up to the Iraqi border post, but don't be afraid to haggle. Some readers have reported taxi drivers stuffing their bags with contraband, so keep your wits about you.

After the Turkish customs post, the taxi drives you to the Ibrahim Khalil border post (the Iraqi side; p182), over the bridge on the Tigris. Here you might be asked where you are staying in Iraq – be honest and clear. It can help if you have an Iraqi contact. The Kurdish Regional Government issues its own tourist visa, which is good for travelling within Iraqi Kurdistan only. Citizens of most countries, including the USA, Australia and New Zealand as well the EU, are automatically issued a free, 10-day tourist visa at the point of entry. Extensions are available; see p181 for more information.

Then you can take one of the Iraqi (well, Kurdish) taxis that wait in a car park just outside customs, and head to nearby Zakho or the provincial capital, Dohuk.

Syria

There are eight border posts between Syria and Turkey, but the border at Reyhanlı/Bab al-Hawa near Antakya is by far the most convenient, and therefore the busiest. At the time of writing, deteriorating political relations between Turkey and Syria had resulted in the closure of one border point (Nusaybin Qamishle 75km east of Mardin) and, with continuing instability in Syria, you should check the situation on the ground prior to travelling.

Also close to Antakya is the border post at Yayladağı, convenient for Lattakia (Syria). Other crossings to Syria include via Kilis, 65km south of Gaziantep and the Akçakale border, 54km south of Şanlıurfa.

All foreigners need a visa to enter Syria (p449). Getting a single-entry visitor visa is a straightforward, same-day process at the embassy in Ankara or İstanbul (p538) but costs vary by nationality; you need two passport photos. We recommend that you do not leave the application process until you get to the border.

Sea

Turkey has passenger-ship connections with Greece, Italy and northern Cyprus. For details see p628.

Getting Around

Air

Internal flights are reasonably priced, and, given the distances involved in traversing the country, are well worth the investment if time is an issue.

Atlasjet (☎0212-663 2000; www.atlasjet.com) A growing network, with flights from Bodrum, İstanbul, İzmir and Antalya to cities throughout the country.

Onur Air (☎0212-468 6687; www.onurair.com.tr) Flights from Antalya, Bodrum, Dalaman, Diyarbakır, Erzurum, Gaziantep, İstanbul, İzmir and Trabzon, among others.

Pegasus Airlines (☎0212 692 7777; www.flypgs.com) Flights between İstanbul and locations from Antalya to Van.

Sun Express Airlines (☎0232-444 0797; www.sunexpress.com.tr) A Turkish Airlines subsidiary.

Turkish Airlines (THY; ☎0212-444 0849; www.thy.com) Connects all the major cities and resorts, via its two main hubs, İstanbul and Ankara.

Bus

Turkish buses go just about everywhere you could possibly want to go and, what's more, they do so cheaply. Long-distance buses usually include a courtesy service of free tea, coffee or water and a snack, and the better companies even have wi-fi access. All Turkish bus services are officially smoke-free.

A town's otogar (bus station) is often on the outskirts, but the bigger bus companies often have free *servis* to ferry you into the centre and back again. Most otogars have an *emanet* (left-luggage room) that will charge a small fee, or you can sometimes leave luggage at the bus company's ticket office. In addition to intercity buses, the otogar often handles dolmuşes that operate local routes, although some locations have a separate station for such services.

Major bus companies with extensive route networks include the following:

Kamıl Koç (☎444 0562; www.kamilkoc.com.tr, in Turkish) Mainly western Turkey.

Metro Turizm (☎444 3455; www.metroturizm.com.tr) Nationwide.

Ulusoy (☎444 1888; www.ulusoy.com.tr, in Turkish) Nationwide.

Younger travellers looking for a wild time with other young travellers might consider the convenience of the **Fez Bus** (Map p464; ☎0212-520 0434; www.feztravel.com; Taya Hatun Sokak 3, Kat 3, Sirkeçi, İstanbul) which offers hop-on hop-off routes to the main tourist resorts of the Aegean and the Mediterranean from İstanbul and Cappadocia.

Car & Motorcycle

In the major cities, plan to leave your car in a parking lot and walk – traffic is terrible.

DRIVING LICENCE

An international driving permit (IDP) may be handy if your driving licence is from a country likely to seem obscure to a Turkish police officer.

FUEL

There are plenty of modern petrol stations in the west, many open 24 hours. In the east they are a bit more scarce but you won't have trouble finding one. Be warned:

petrol prices are high and are not showing any signs of going down.

HIRE

You must be at least 21 years old to hire a car in Turkey and you might be asked to produce a credit card. Hiring a car is expensive, with considerable drop-off fees but reductions for long-term hire. All the main car-hire companies are represented in the main towns and resorts. It's better to stick to the well-established companies (such as Avis, Budget, Europcar, Hertz and Thrifty) as they have bigger fleets and better emergency backup. You can get great discounts through **Economy Car Rentals** (www.economycarrentals.com), which covers most of the country, but you need to book at least 24 hours in advance.

INSURANCE

You must have third-party insurance, valid for the entire country. If you don't have it, you can buy it at the border.

ROAD RULES

Drink-driving is a complete no-no. Maximum speed limits, unless otherwise posted, are 50km/h in towns, 90km/h on highways and 120km/h on an *otoyol* (motorway). Driving is hair-raising during the day because of fast, inappropriate driving and overladen trucks, and dangerous at night, when you won't be able to see potholes, animals, or even vehicles driving with their lights off!

Local Transport

With a few exceptions, you probably won't use public buses in large cities. In İstanbul, the underground metro and the tram are quick and efficient ways of getting around.

Taxis are plentiful. They have meters – just make sure they're switched on.

Train

Turkish State Railways (TCDD; www.tcdd.gov.tr/tcdding) runs services all across the country with the exception of the coastal resorts, but they have a hard time competing with long-distance buses and airlines for speed. That said, if you've got time on your hands, sleeper trains are much more comfortable than the cramped buses for long journeys, and though they can take up to twice as long they can often be much cheaper. Though you usually have to book sleeper carriages in advance, on some services a 'first come first served' system operates, so it pays to get on-board early. InterRail and Balkan Flexipass passes are valid on the services, but Eurail passes are not.

At the time of research, major engineering works in İstanbul were having an effect on the frequency of rail services in and out of the capital. For updates on the current situation, plus comprehensive information on timetables and costs for rail services across Turkey, see www.seat61.com/Turkey2.htm.

Understand the Middle East

population per sq km

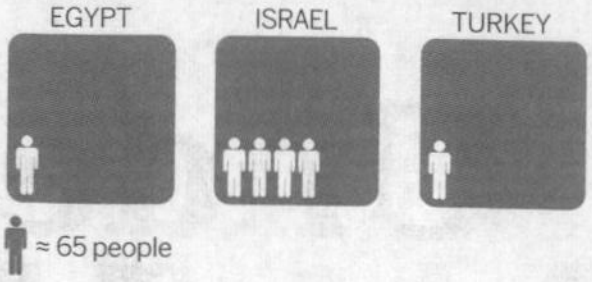

The Middle East Today

Arab Spring

When a young, unemployed man named Mohammed Bouazizi set fire to himself in the central Tunisian town of Sidi Bouzid in December 2010, few imagined the firestorm of change his desperate suicide would ignite across the region. Within months, the 30-year dictatorship of Egyptian president Hosni Mubarak had been overthrown in a popular uprising. A year later, leaders of similarly long standing had been swept from power in Libya and Yemen. And in Syria, a peaceful uprising had become a full-scale armed insurrection when faced with the brutality and intransigence of Bashar al-Assad's regime.

The hope that these changes engendered swept through the Middle East like a cooling breeze. For decades, travellers to the region had encountered locals who grumbled about the governments who ruled over them. But they did so in fear of being overhead and knowing full well that they were powerless to effect change. With the Arab Spring, opposition to governments suddenly took centre stage in political debate. An entire people from Tripoli to Damascus had found their voice and anything seemed possible.

People

» **Population** 236.13 million

» **Highest/lowest life expectancy (years)** 81 (Israel)/73 (Turkey)

» **Highest/lowest adult literacy rate (%)** 97 (Israel)/71 (Egypt)

Arab Winter

And then, reality took over. In Egypt, the heady aspirations of a people for democracy, freedom and prosperity would become mired in complications – the army remained in control as the grand arbiter of Egypt's future while Islamist parties swept the board in parliamentary elections. At the time of writing, ordinary Egyptians were beginning to wonder what had happened to their revolution, and whether their lives would actually be any better as a result.

Top Books

From the Holy Mountain (William Dalrymple) Well-told journey through the region's landscape of sacred and profane

The Innocents Abroad (Mark Twain) Still many people's favourite travel book about the region, 140 years later

The Thousand and One Nights Resonates with all the allure and magic of the Middle East

Nine Parts of Desire (Geraldine Brooks) Fascinating look at the lives of Middle Eastern women

The Great War for Civilisation (Robert Fisk) A recent account

Middle East Myths

» Middle Easterners are hostile to Westerners

» Middle Eastern women are universally oppressed

» Religion divides

belief systems
(% of population)

if Middle East were 100 people

60 would be Arab
25 would be Turkish
9 would be Kurds
3 would be Jewish
3 would be other

In Syria, it was far worse. By early 2012, Syria was experiencing a civil war in all but name. The regime of Bashar al-Assad, who had come to power amid great hopes for reform and generational change a decade earlier, unleashed the full force of its formidable security apparatus on ordinary Syrians. With the regime isolated and a death toll numbering in the thousands and growing daily, Syrians continue to pay an extremely heavy price for demanding freedom from their government.

And some other things don't change: a peace agreement between Israel and the Palestinians seems as far away as ever.

Iraq at Peace

With the Arab Spring having lost its way and descended into conflict, it's unusual that Iraq has come to represent a beacon of hope for the region. In December 2011, the last US troops left Iraq, a symbolic ending, at least, to one of the bloodiest chapters in recent Middle Eastern history. It would be an exaggeration to suggest that Iraq is now at peace – violence may be much-reduced but continues at alarming rates, while the Iraqi government and parliament remains paralysed by infighting and sectarian tensions. But things have nonetheless improved dramatically since the dark days of war. With the Americans gone and Iraqis now running the country, the sting has been taken out of the insurgency, with many Iraqis daring to hope that the worst is well and truly behind them. In Iraqi Kurdistan in particular, life has been transformed into an oasis of peace, prosperity and relative freedom. People elsewhere in the Middle East are now hoping that it won't take more bloody conflict for the Kurdish experience to be replicated across the region.

Land

» **Land area**
2,535,241 sq km

» **Highest point**
Mt Ararat 5137m

» **Lowest point**
Dead Sea -408m

» **Major rivers**
Nile, Tigris, Euphrates, Jordan

Top Films

Lawrence of Arabia (1962) Evokes the complicated, early 20th-century Middle East

Caramel (2007) Women in war-ravaged Beirut

Nina's Tragedies (2005) The angst of modern Israel

Paradise Now (2005) Palestinian suicide bombers in close-up

Do & Don'ts

» **Do** take the time to talk with older Middle Easterners – it's amazing how far this region has come

» **Don't** eat with your left hand

» **Do** learn a few words in Arabic/Hebrew/Turkish – locals really appreciate the gesture

» **Don't** say you're an atheist (better to say 'I'm a seeker' or 'I'm not religious')

» **Do** ask permission, always, before taking photos of people

» **Don't** lose your patience – causing a confrontation won't end well

History

The Middle East *is* history, home to a roll call of some of the most important landmarks in human history. Mesopotamia (now Iraq) was the undisputed cradle of civilisation. Damascus (Syria), Aleppo (Syria), Byblos (Lebanon), Jericho (Israel and the Palestinian Territories) and Erbil (Iraq) all stake compelling claims to be the oldest continuously inhabited cities on earth. And it was here in the Middle East that the three great monotheistic religions – Judaism, Christianity and Islam – were born. Fast forward to the present and the great issues of the day – oil, religious coexistence, terrorism and conflicts over land – find their most compelling expression in the Middle East. It remains as true as it has for thousands of years that what happens here ripples out across the world and will shape what happens next in world history.

This section sketches out the broadest sweeps of Middle Eastern history – for further details see the more-specific history sections in the individual country chapters throughout this book.

The Epic of Gilgamesh, written in 2700 BC and one of the first works of world literature, tells the story of a Sumerian king from the ancient city of Uruk (which gave Iraq its name).

Ancient Middle East

Cradle of Civilisation

The first human beings to walk the earth did just that: they walked. In their endless search for sustenance and shelter, they roamed the earth, hunting, foraging plants for food and erecting makeshift shelters as they went. The world's first nomads, they carried what they needed; most likely they lived in perfect harmony with nature and left next to nothing behind for future generations to write their story.

The first signs of agriculture, arguably the first major signpost along the march of human history, grew from the soils surrounding Jericho in what is now the West Bank, around 8500 BC. Forced by a drying climate and the need to cluster around known water sources, these early Middle Easterners added wild cereals to their diet and learned to farm them. In

TIMELINE

250,000 BC

The earliest traces of human presence appear in the Nile Valley. Little is known about them, but they are thought to be nomadic hunter-gatherers.

5000 BC

Al-Ubaid culture, the forerunner to the great civilisations that would earn Mesopotamia (now Iraq) the sobriquet of the cradle of civilisation, rises between the Tigris and Euphrates rivers.

4000 BC

The Sumerian civilisation takes hold in Mesopotamia. They would rule the region until the 24th century BC and invent cuneiform, the world's first writing.

the centuries that followed, these and other farming communities spread east into Mesopotamia (a name later given by the Greeks, meaning 'Between Two Rivers'), where the fertile soils of the Tigris and Euphrates floodplains were ideally suited to the new endeavour. For some historians, this was a homecoming of sorts for humankind: these two rivers are among the four that, according to the Bible, flowed into the Garden of Eden.

In around the 5th century BC, the Sumerians became the first to build cities and to support them with year-round agriculture and river-borne trade. In the blink of a historical eye, although almost 2000 years later in reality, the Sumerians invented the first known form of writing: cuneiform, which consisted primarily of pictographs and would later evolve into alphabets on which modern writing is based. With agriculture and writing mastered, the world's first civilisation had been born.

Elsewhere across the region, in around 3100 BC, the kingdoms of Upper and Lower Egypt were unified under Menes, ushering in 3000 years of Pharaonic rule in the Nile Valley. For a detailed rundown on the history of ancient Egypt, see p143.

Birth of Empire

The moment in history when civilisations evolved into empires is unclear, but by the 3rd century BC, the kings of what we now know as the Middle East had listened to the fragmented news brought by traders of fabulous riches just beyond the horizon.

The Sumerians, who were no doubt rather pleased with having tamed agriculture and inventing writing, never saw the Akkadians coming. One of many city-states that fell within the Sumerian realm, Akkad, on the banks of the Euphrates southwest of modern Baghdad, had grown in power, and, in the late 24th and early 23rd centuries BC, Sargon of Akkad conquered Mesopotamia and then extended his rule over much of the Levant. The era of empire, which would convulse the region almost until the present day, had begun.

Although the Akkadian Empire would last no more than a century, Sargon's idea caught on. The at-once sophisticated and war-like Assyrians, whose empire would, from their capital at Nineveh (Iraq), later encompass the entire Middle East, were the most enduring power. Along with their perennial Mesopotamian rivals, the Babylonians, the Assyrians would dominate the human history of the region for almost 1000 years.

The 7th century BC saw the conquest of Egypt by Assyria and, far to the east, the rise of the Medes, the first of many great Persian empires. In 550 BC, the Medes were conquered by Cyrus the Great, widely regarded as the first Persian shah (king). Over the next 60 years, Cyrus and his

PYRAMIDS

The Great Pyramid of Khufu (built in 2570 BC) remained the tallest artificial structure in the world until the building of the Eiffel Tower in 1889.

3100 BC

Menes unites the kingdoms of Upper and Lower Egypt. Thus begins one of the great civilisations of antiquity, ancient Egypt of the pharaohs who would rule for almost 3000 years.

1800 BC

According to the Book of Genesis, Abraham, the great patriarch of the Jewish faith and prophet in both Christianity and Islam, is born in Ur of the Chaldees in Mesopotamia.

1750 BC

The Babylonian kingdoms are first united under Hammurabi, creating the capital, the Hanging Gardens of Babylon. They would rule the Tigris–Euphrates region for over 500 years.

1600–609 BC

The Assyrian Empire rules from its capital at Nineveh (present-day Iraq) over a territory that reaches as far as Egypt. Its heyday is around 900 BC.

successors, Cambyses (r 525–522 BC) and Darius I (r 521–486 BC), battled with the Greeks for control over Babylon, Egypt, Asia Minor and parts of Greece.

Egypt won independence from the Persians in 401 BC, only to be reconquered 60 years later. The second Persian occupation of Egypt was brief: little more than a decade after they arrived, the Persians were again driven out of Egypt, this time by the Greeks. Europe had arrived on the scene and would hold sway in some form for almost 1000 years until the birth of Islam.

Five out of the Seven Wonders of the Ancient World were within the boundaries of the modern Middle East: the Temple of Artemis (Turkey), the Mausoleum of Halicarnassus (Turkey), the Hanging Gardens of Babylon (Iraq), Pharos of Alexandria (Egypt) and the Pyramids of Giza (Egypt).

Greeks

The definition of which territories constitute 'the Middle East' has always been a fluid concept. Some cultural geographers claim that the Middle East includes all countries of the Arab world as far west as Morocco. But most historians agree that the Middle East's eastern boundaries were determined by the Greeks in the 4th century BC.

In 336 BC, Philip II of Macedonia, a warlord who had conquered much of mainland Greece, was murdered. His son Alexander assumed the throne and began a series of conquests that would eventually encompass most of Asia Minor, the Middle East, Persia and northern India. Under Alexander, the Greeks were the first to impose any kind of order on the Middle East as a whole.

In 331 BC, just five years after taking control, Alexander the Great's armies swept into what is now Libya. Greek rule extended as far east as what is now the Libyan city of Benghazi, beyond which the Romans would hold sway. Ever since, the unofficial but widely agreed place where the Middle East begins and ends has been held to be Cyrenaica in Libya.

Upon Alexander's death in 323 BC, his empire was promptly carved up among his generals. This resulted in the founding of three new ruling dynasties: the Antigonids in Greece and Asia Minor; the Ptolemaic dynasty in Egypt; and the Seleucids. The Seleucids controlled the swath of land running from modern Israel and Lebanon through Mesopotamia to Persia.

But, this being the Middle East, peace was always elusive. Having finished off a host of lesser competitors, the heirs to Alexander's empire then proceeded to fight each other. It took an army arriving from the west to again reunite the lands of the east – this time in the shape of the legions of Rome.

Pax Romana

Even for a region accustomed to living under occupation, the sight of massed, disciplined ranks of Roman legions marching down across the plains of central Anatolia must have struck fear into the hearts of peo-

1500 BC

The Phoenicians set out to conquer the waters of the Mediterranean from their base in Tyre and Sidon (modern-day Lebanon). They rule the seas for 1200 years.

WERNER FORMAN/CORBIS©

» Phoenician coin, 10th century BC

15th century BC

Hieroglyphic tablets make reference to a city called 'Dimashqa', conquered by the Egyptians. It's the first written record of a city that may date back to 3000 BC.

ple across the region. But this was a region in disarray and the Romans chose their historical moment perfectly.

Rome's legionaries conquered most of Asia Minor (most of Turkey) in 188 BC. Syria and Palestine soon fell, if not without a fight then without too much difficulty. When Cleopatra of Egypt, the last of the Ptolemaic dynasty, was defeated in 31 BC, the Romans controlled the entire Mediterranean world. Only the Sassanids in Persia held Rome at bay.

Foreign occupiers they may have been, but the Romans brought much-needed stability and even a degree of prosperity to the region. Roman goods flooded into Middle Eastern markets, improving living standards in a region that had long ago lost its title as the centre of the world's sophistication. New methods of agriculture increased productivity across the region and the largely peaceful Roman territories allowed the export of local products to the great markets of Rome. Olive

PHOENICIANS

The ancient Phoenician Empire (1500–300 BC), which thrived along the Lebanese coast, may have been the world's first rulers of the sea, for their empire was the Mediterranean Sea and its ports, and their lasting legacy was to spread the early gains of Middle Eastern civilisation to the rest of the world.

An offshoot of the Canaanites in the Levant, the Phoenicians first established themselves in the (now Lebanese) ports of Tyre and Sidon. Quick to realise that there was money to be made across the waters, they cast off in their galleys, launching in the process the first era of true globalisation. From the unlikely success of selling purple dye and sea snails to the Greeks, they expanded their repertoire to include copper from Cyprus, silver from Iberia and even tin from Great Britain.

As their reach expanded, so too did the Phoenicians' need for safe ports around the Mediterranean rim. Thus it was that Carthage, one of the greatest cities of the ancient world, was founded in what is now Tunisia in 814 BC. Long politically dependent on the mother culture in Tyre, Carthage eventually emerged as an independent, commercial empire. By 517 BC, the powerful city-state was the leading city of North Africa, and by the 4th century BC, Carthage controlled the North African coast from Libya to the Atlantic.

But the nascent Roman Empire didn't take kindly to these Lebanese upstarts effectively controlling the waters of the Mediterranean Sea, and challenged them both militarily and with economic blockades. With Tyre and Sidon themselves severely weakened and unable to send help, Carthage took on Rome and lost, badly. The Punic Wars (Phoenician civilisation in North Africa was called 'Punic') between Carthage and Rome (264–241 BC, 218–201 BC and 149–146 BC) reduced Carthage, the last outpost of Phoenician power, to a small, vulnerable African state. It was razed by the Romans in 146 BC, the site symbolically sprinkled with salt and damned forever.

663 BC

After a series of military and diplomatic confrontations, Ashurbanipal, King of the Assyrians, attacks Egypt, sacks Thebes and loots the Temple of Amun.

586 BC

Babylonia's King Nebuchadnezzar marches on Jerusalem, destroys the Jewish temple and carries the Jewish elite and many of their subjects into Mesopotamian exile.

550 BC

Cyrus the Great forms one of the ancient world's most enlightened empires in Persia, known for its tolerance and the freedoms granted to subject peoples.

525 BC

The Persian king Cambyses conquers Egypt, rules as pharaoh, then disappears with his army in the Saharan sands as he marches on Siwa.

trees, with their origins in Turkey and the Levant, were, like the oilfields of today, a lucrative product, with insatiable demand in Rome driving previously unimaginable growth for local Middle Eastern economies.

What the Mesopotamians began with their city-states, the Romans perfected in the extravagant cities that they built to glorify the empire but which also provided new levels of comfort for local inhabitants. Their construction or development of earlier Phoenician and Greek settlements at Ephesus (see the boxed text, p488), Palmyra, Baalbek and Jerash announced that the Romans intended to stay.

The Cyrus Cylinder, which is housed at the British Museum with a replica at the UN, is a clay tablet with cuneiform inscriptions, and is widely considered to be the world's first charter of human rights.

Jewish Revolt

So was the Roman Middle East a utopia? Well, not exactly. As just about any foreign power has failed to learn right up to the 21st century, Middle Easterners don't take kindly to promises of wealth in exchange for sovereignty. The Jews living in Palestine in particular found themselves stripped of political power and operating in an ever-diminishing space of religious and economic freedom. By the middle of the 1st century AD,

ALEXANDER THE GREAT

One of the greatest figures to ever stride the Middle Eastern stage, Alexander (356–323 BC) was born into greatness. His father was King Philip II of Macedonia, who many people believed was a descendant of the god Hercules, and his mother was Princess Olympias of Epirus, who counted the legendary Achilles among her ancestors. For his part, the precocious young Alexander sometimes claimed that Zeus was his real father.

Alexander was the ultimate alpha male, as well versed in poetry as in the ways of war. At the age of 12, the young Alexander tamed Bucephalus, a horse that the most accomplished horsemen of Macedonia dared not ride. By 13, he had Aristotle as his personal tutor. His interests were diverse: he could play the lyre, learned Homer's *Iliad* by heart and admired the Persian ruler Cyrus the Great for the respect he granted to the cultures he conquered.

He rode out of Macedonia in 334 BC to embark on a decade-long campaign of conquest and exploration. His first great victory was against the Persians at Issus in what is now southeast Turkey. He swept south, conquering Phoenician seaports and thence into Egypt where he founded the Mediterranean city that still bears his name. In 331 BC, the armies of Alexander the Great made a triumphant entrance into Cyrenaica. After the Oracle of Ammon in Siwa promised Alexander that he would indeed conquer the world, he returned north, heading for Babylon. Crossing the Tigris and the Euphrates, he defeated another Persian army before driving his troops up into Central Asia and northern India. Eventually fatigue and disease brought the drive to a halt and the Greeks turned around and headed back home. En route, Alexander succumbed to illness (some say he was poisoned) and died at the tender age of 33 in Babylon. The whereabouts of his body and tomb remain unknown.

334 BC

A youthful Alexander the Great of Macedonia marches out of Greece and doesn't stop until a vast empire stretching from Libya to India is within his grasp.

323 BC

Alexander the Great dies aged just 33. His empire is carved up among his generals: the Antigonids (Greece and Asia Minor); the Ptolemaic dynasty (Egypt); and the Seleucids (everywhere else).

3rd century BC

The Nabataeans build their rock-hewn fortress of Petra and hold out against the Romans until AD 106, through entrepreneurial guile, military might and carefully negotiated treaties.

188 BC

The massed ranks of the Roman legionnaires conquer Asia Minor (Turkey), then continue south sweeping all before them. The Romans would rule the Middle East in some form for over six centuries.

Jews across the Roman Empire had had enough. Primary among their grievances were punitive taxes, the Roman decision to appoint Jewish high priests and the not-inconsiderable blasphemy of Emperor Caligula's decision in AD 39 to declare himself a deity. The anti Roman sentiment had been bubbling away for three decades, in part due to one rebellious orator – Jesus of Nazareth (see p582) – and to a Jewish sect called the Zealots, whose creed stated that all means were justified to liberate the Jews.

Led by the Zealots, the Jews of Jerusalem destroyed a small Roman garrison in the Holy City in AD 66. Infighting within the revolt and the burning of food stockpiles in order to force wavering Jews to participate had disastrous consequences. Jerusalem was razed to the ground and up to 100,000 Jews were killed in retaliation; some Jewish historians claim that the number of dead over the four years of the revolt reached a million.

The failed uprising and the brutal Roman response (which came to be known as the First Jewish-Roman War) would have consequences that have rippled down through the centuries. Jerusalem was rebuilt as a Roman city and the Jews were sent into exile (which, for many Jews, ended only with the creation of the State of Israel in 1948). Few people in the Middle East dared to challenge the Romans after that.

In 333 BC, Persian Emperor Darius, facing defeat by Alexander, abandoned his wife, children and mother on the battlefield. His mother was so disgusted she disowned him and adopted Alexander as her son.

Byzantines

In AD 331, the newly converted Emperor Constantine declared Christianity the official religion of the 'Holy Roman Empire', with its capital not jaded, cynical Rome but the newly renamed city of Constantinople (formerly Byzantium, later to become İstanbul). Constantinople reached its apogee during the reign of Justinian (AD 527–65), when the Byzantine Empire consolidated its hold on the eastern Mediterranean.

But the Byzantine (or Eastern Roman) Empire, as it became known, would soon learn a harsh lesson that the Ottomans (ruling from the same city; see p557) would later fail to heed. Spread too thinly by controlling vast reaches of the earth and riven with divisions at home, they were vulnerable to the single most enduring historic power in Middle Eastern history, stirring in the deserts of Arabia: Islam.

Under Ptolemaic patronage and with access to a library of 700,000 written works, scholars in Alexandria calculated the earth's circumference, discovered it circles the sun and wrote the definitive edition of Homer's work.

Islamic Middle East

Arrival & Spread of Islam

No one in sophisticated Constantinople, an opulent city accustomed to the trappings of world power, could have imagined that the greatest threat to their rule would come from a small oasis community in the desert wastes of Arabia. The Byzantines, it is true, were besieged in their coastal forts of

146 BC
The destruction of Carthage (in present-day Tunisia) by the Romans signals the end of more than a millennium of Phoenician/Punic dominance of the Mediterranean.

64 BC
Pompey the Great abolishes the Seleucid kingdom, annexes Syria and transforms it into a province of the Roman Empire. Rome sets its sights on Egypt.

31 BC
The Romans defeat Cleopatra, bringing to an end the era of the pharaohs and drawing Egypt under their control. Unable to bear the ignominy, Cleopatra commits suicide.

AD 0
Jesus of Nazareth, founder of the Christian faith, is born in Bethlehem (in the present-day Palestinian Territories), which was, at the time, fully incorporated into the Roman Empire.

BAGHDAD THE BEAUTIFUL

When Haroun ar-Rashid came to power in AD 786, Baghdad, on the western bank of the Tigris, had only been in existence for 24 years. By the time he died, it had become one of the world's pre-eminent cities. Haroun ar-Rashid tried to rename the city Medinat as-Salaam (City of Peace). Although the name never caught on, everything else that Haroun ar-Rashid and his immediate successors did was an unqualified success. Baghdad was remade into a city of expansive pleasure gardens, vast libraries and distinguished seats of learning, where the arts, medicine, literature and sciences all flourished. It was soon the richest city in the world. The crossroads of important trade routes to the east and west, it rapidly supplanted Damascus as the seat of power in the Islamic world, which stretched from Spain to India. Al-Maamun, Haroun's son and successor, founded the Beit al-Hikmah (House of Wisdom), a Baghdad-based academy dedicated to translating Greek and Roman works of science and philosophy into Arabic. It was only through these translations that most of the classical literature we know today was saved for posterity.

the southern Mediterranean, their power extending scarcely at all into the hinterland. And the Sassanid empire to the east was constantly chipping away at poorly defended Byzantine holdings. But there was little to suggest to these heirs to the Roman domain that these were anything more than minor skirmishes on the outer reaches of their empire.

In the 7th century AD, southern Arabia lay beyond the reach of both the Byzantines and the Sassanids. The cost and difficulty of occupying the Arabian Peninsula simply wasn't worth the effort, home as it was only to troublesome nomads and isolated oases. Thus it was that when, far from the great centres of power, in the nondescript town of Mecca (now in Saudi Arabia), a merchant named Mohammed (b AD 570) began preaching against the pagan religion of his fellow Meccans, no one in Constantinople paid the slightest attention. For full details on the birth of Islam, see p578.

There is no finer work in English on the history of the Arabs, from the Prophet Mohammed to modern times, than *A History of the Arab Peoples* by Albert Hourani – it's definitive, encyclopedic and highly readable.

Mohammed died in 632, but within a few short decades the entire Middle East would be under the control of his followers. Under Mohammed's successors, known as caliphs (from the Arabic word for 'follower'), the new religion spread rapidly, reaching all of Arabia by 634. By 646, Syria, Palestine and Egypt were all in Muslim hands, while most of Iraq, Iran and Afghanistan were wrested from the Sassanids by 656. By 682, Islam had reached the shores of the Atlantic in Morocco.

Umayyads

Having won the battle for supremacy over the Muslim world, Mu'awiyah, the Muslim military governor of Syria and a distant relative of Mohammed who became the fifth caliph, moved the capital from Medina to Da-

AD 33

Jesus is crucified by the Romans in Jerusalem. According to Christian tradition, he rises from the dead three days later, then ascends to heaven. His followers spread out across the world.

AD 39

The Roman emperor Caligula, not content with ruling much of the world, declares himself a deity, adding to the resentment already felt by Jews and Christians living across the Roman Empire.

AD 66–70

The Jews in Jerusalem and elsewhere revolt against oppressive Roman rule. The uprising is brutally put down, the Jewish temple destroyed and, within four years, over 100,000 Jews are killed.

267–71

Queen Zenobia seizes power in Palmyra, defeats the Roman legion sent to dethrone her, briefly occupies Syria, Palestine and Egypt, and declares herself independent of Rome. Rome is not amused.

mascus and established the first great Muslim dynasty – the Umayyads. Thanks to the unrelenting success of his armies, Mu'awiyah and his successors found themselves ruling an empire that held sway over almost a third of the world's population.

The decision to make Damascus the capital meant that, for the first time in the Middle East's turbulent history, the region was ruled from its Levantine heartland. The Umayyads gave the Islamic world some of its greatest architectural treasures, including the Dome of the Rock in Jerusalem and the Umayyad Mosque in Damascus – lavish monuments to the new faith, if a far cry from Islam's simple desert origins.

History, however, has not been kind to the Umayyads. Perhaps seduced by Damascus' charms, they are remembered as a decadent lot, known for the high living, corruption, nepotism and tyranny that eventually proved to be their undoing. News of Umayyad excesses never sat well with the foot soldiers of Islam and even confirmed their long-held suspicions about their adherence to Islamic tenets.

Abbasids

In 750, the Umayyads were toppled in a revolt fuelled, predictably, by accusations of impiety. Their successors, and the strong arm behind the revolt, were the Abbasids. The Abbasid caliphate created a new capital in Baghdad, and the early centuries of its rule constituted what's often regarded as the golden age of Islamic culture in the Middle East. The most famous of the Abbasid caliphs was Haroun ar-Rashid (r 786–809) of *The Thousand and One Nights* fame (see the boxed text, p602). Warrior-king Haroun ar-Rashid led one of the most successful early Muslim invasions of Byzantium, almost reaching Constantinople. But his name will forever be associated with Baghdad, which he transformed into a world centre of learning and sophistication.

After Haroun ar-Rashid's death, the cycle that had already scarred Islam's early years – a strong, enlightened ruler giving way upon his death to anarchy and squandering many of the hard-won territorial and cultural gains of his reign – was repeated.

Seljuks

By the middle of the 10th century, the Abbasid caliphs were the prisoners of their Turkish guards, who spawned a dynasty of their own, known as the Seljuks (1038 1194). The Seljuks extended their reach throughout Persia, Central Asia, Afghanistan and Anatolia, where the Seljuk Sultanate of Rum made its capital at Konya. The resulting pressure on the Byzantine Empire was intense enough to cause the emperor and the Greek Orthodox Church to swallow their pride and appeal to the rival Roman Catholic Church for help.

BAGHDAD

The Court of the Caliphs by Hugh Kennedy is the definitive account of Abbasid Baghdad in its prime, blending careful scholarship and Arab sources with a lively and compelling style.

331

Emperor Constantine declares Christianity the official religion of the Roman Empire and moves his capital to Constantinople (previously known as Byzantium). This event marks the birth of the Byzantine Empire.

527–65

Emperor Justinian reigns over the Byzantine Empire whose realm extends through the Mediterranean, including coastal North Africa and most of the Middle East.

570

The Prophet Mohammed is born in Mecca (present-day Saudi Arabia). Despite his humble origins, he will become the 25th and most revered prophet of the world's second-largest religion.

» Mecca, Saudi Arabia

What happened next would plant the seeds for a clash of civilisations, whose bitterness would reverberate throughout the region long after the swords of Islam and Christianity had been sheathed.

Crusades & Aftermath

Preparing for War

With the Muslim armies gathering at the gates of Europe, and already occupying large swathes of Iberia, Pope Urban II in 1095 called for a Western Christian military expedition – a 'Crusade' – to liberate the holy places of Jerusalem in response to the eastern empire's alarm. Rome's motives were not entirely benevolent: Urban was eager to assert Rome's primacy in the east over Constantinople. The monarchs and clerics of Europe attempted to portray the Crusades as a 'just war'. In the late 11th century, such a battle cry attracted zealous support.

The Crusades Through Arab Eyes by Amin Maalouf is brilliantly written and captures perfectly why the mere mention of the Crusades still arouses the anger of many Arabs today.

Bitterly fought on the battlefield, the Crusades remain one of the region's most divisive historical moments. For the Muslims, the Christian call to arms was a vicious attack on Islam itself, and the tactics used by the Crusaders confirmed the Muslim suspicion that Christianity's primary concern was imperial conquest. So deep does the sense of grievance run in the region that President Bush's invasion of Iraq in 2003 was widely portrayed as the next Christian crusade. In the Christian world view, the Crusades were a necessary defensive strategy, lest Islam sweep across Europe and place Christianity's very existence under threat.

Christian Invasion

Whatever the rights and wrongs, the crusading rabble enjoyed considerable success. After linking up with the Byzantine army in 1097, the Crusaders successfully besieged Antioch (modern Antakya, in Turkey), then marched south along the coast before turning inland, towards Jerusalem, leaving devastation in their wake. A thousand Muslim troops held Jerusalem for six weeks against 15,000 Crusaders before the city fell on 15 July 1099. The victorious Crusaders then massacred the local population – Muslims, Jews and Christians alike – sacked the non-Christian religious sites and turned the Dome of the Rock into a church.

Curiously, even after the gratuitous violence of the Crusades, Christians and Muslims assimilated in the Holy Land. European visitors to Palestine recorded with dismay that the original Crusaders who remained in the Holy Land had abandoned their European ways. They had become Arabised, taking on eastern habits and dress – perhaps it was not an unwise move to abandon chain mail and jerkins for flowing robes in the Levantine heat. Even with their semi-transformation into locals, the Crusaders were never equipped to govern the massive, newly

622

When his message from Allah, imparted to Mohammed by the Archangel Gabriel, is rejected by powerful Meccans, the Prophet flees to Medina. In the Islamic calendar, this flight is known as the Hejira and marks Year Zero.

632

After returning to Mecca at the head of Islam's first army in 630, the Prophet Mohammed dies in Mecca. Despite squabbles over succession, his followers carry the new religion across the world.

642

Islam's battle for succession reaches its critical moment with the death of Hussein, the son of Ali. Ever since this date, the Muslim world has been divided into strains – Sunni and Shiite.

646

Barely a decade after the death of Mohammed, Syria, Palestine and Egypt have all been conquered by the followers of Islam. Modern Israel aside, they have been predominantly Muslim ever since.

SALADIN – THE KURDISH HERO OF ARAB HISTORY

Saladin – or Salah ad-Din (Restorer of the Faith) al-Ayyoub – was born to Kurdish parents in 1138 in what is modern-day Tikrit in Iraq. He joined other members of his family in the service of Nureddin (Nur ad-Din) of the ruling Zangi dynasty. By the time Nureddin died in 1174, Saladin had risen to the rank of general and had already taken possession of Egypt. He quickly took control of Syria and, over the next 10 years, extended his authority into parts of Mesopotamia. In 1187, Saladin crushed the Crusaders at the Battle of Hittin and captured Jerusalem, precipitating the Third Crusade and pitting himself against Richard I (the Lionheart) of England. After countless clashes, the two rival warriors signed a peace treaty in 1192, giving the coastal territories to the Crusaders and the interior to the Muslims. Saladin died three months later in Damascus, where he is buried.

resentful Middle East. A series of Crusader 'statelets' arose through the region during this period.

Muslim Backlash

These statelets aside, the Middle East remained predominantly Muslim, and within 50 years, the tide had begun to turn against the Crusaders. The Muslim leader responsible for removing the Crusaders from Jerusalem (in 1187) was Salah ad-Din al-Ayyoub, better known in the West as Saladin.

Saladin and his successors (a fleeting dynasty known as the Ayyubids) battled the Crusaders for 60 years until they were unceremoniously removed by their own army, a strange soldier-slave caste, the Mamluks, who ran what would today be called a military dictatorship. The only way to join their army was to be press-ganged into it – non-Muslim boys were captured or bought outside the empire, converted to Islam and raised in the service of a single military commander. They were expected to give this commander total loyalty, in exchange for which their fortunes would rise (or fall) with his. Sultans were chosen from among the most senior Mamluk commanders, but it was a system that engendered vicious, bloody rivalries, and rare was the sultan who died of natural causes.

Saladin in his Time by PH Newby reads like a novel with surprising plot twists, epic events and picaresque characters brought to life.

The Mamluks were to rule Egypt, Syria, Palestine and western Arabia for nearly 300 years (1250–1517), and it was they who finally succeeded in ejecting the Crusaders from the Near East, prising them out of their last stronghold of Acre (modern-day Akko in Israel) in 1291.

Ottoman Turks

Rise of the Ottomans

Turkey, saved for now from an Islamic fate by the Crusaders, had remained largely above the fray. But the Byzantine rulers in Constantinople felt anything but secure. The armies of Islam may have been occupied

656
Islam takes hold in Iraq, Persia and Afghanistan, defeating the ruling Sassanids and building on the expansion of Islam, which had been born just a few decades before.

660
Mu'awiyah moves the capital of the Muslim world from Arabia to Damascus, shifting Islam's balance of power. The Umayyad caliphate rules over an empire that encompasses almost the entire Middle East.

711
The armies of Islam cross from North Africa into Europe and the Iberian Peninsula is soon under their control. Al-Andalus, in southern Iberia, becomes a beacon for tolerance and the arts.

750
The first Arab dynasty, the Umayyad caliphate in Damascus, falls amid accusations of impiety, and power shifts to Baghdad, the base for the Abbasids.

fighting the Crusaders (and each other) in the so-called Holy Lands, but the Byzantines looked towards the south nervously, keeping their armies in a state of high readiness. Little did they know that their undoing would come from within.

Süleyman the Magnificent was responsible for achievements as diverse as building the gates of Jerusalem and introducing to Europe, via Constantinople, the joys of coffee.

In 1258, just eight years after the Mamluks seized power in Cairo and began their bloody dynasty, a boy named Osman (Othman) was born to the chief of a Turkish tribe in western Anatolia. He converted to Islam in his youth and later began a military career by hiring out his tribe's army as mercenaries in the civil wars, then besetting what was left of the Byzantine Empire. Payment came in the form of land.

Rather than taking on the Byzantines directly, Osman's successors (the Ottomans) deliberately picked off the bits and pieces of the empire that Constantinople could no longer control. By the end of the 14th century, the Ottomans had conquered Bulgaria, Serbia, Bosnia, Hungary and most of present-day Turkey. They had also moved their capital across the Dardanelles to Adrianople, today the Turkish city of Edirne. In 1453 came their greatest victory, when Sultan Mehmet II took Constantinople, the hitherto unachievable object of innumerable Muslim wars almost since the 7th century.

Sixty-four years later, on a battlefield near Aleppo, an army under the gloriously named sultan Selim the Grim routed the Mamluks and assumed sovereignty over the Hejaz. At a stroke, the whole of the eastern Mediterranean, including Egypt and much of Arabia, was absorbed into

WHO ARE THE ARABS?

The question of who the Arabs are exactly is still widely debated. Fourteen centuries ago, only the nomadic tribes wandering between the Euphrates River and the central Arabian Peninsula were considered Arabs, distinguished by their language. However, with the rapid expansion of Islam, the language of the Quran spread to vast areas. Although the Arabs were relatively few in number in most of the countries they conquered, their culture quickly became established through language, religion and intermarriage. In addition to the original nomads, the settled inhabitants of these newly conquered provinces also became known as Arabs. In the 20th century, rising Arab nationalism legitimised the current blanket usage of the term to apply to all the peoples of the Middle East – except the Persians, Kurds, Israelis and Turks.

The most romanticised group of Arabs is no doubt the Bedouin (Bedu in Arabic). While not an ethnic group, they are the archetypal Arabs – the camel-herding nomads who roam all over the deserts and semideserts in search of food for their cattle. From among their ranks came the warriors who spread Islam to North Africa and Persia 14 centuries ago. Today, the Bedouin are found mainly in Jordan, Iraq, Egypt's Sinai Peninsula and the Gulf States.

786–809

Haroun ar-Rashid rules the Abbasid world from his capital of Baghdad. This was the Abbasid heyday and provides the setting for tales in *The Thousand and One Nights*.

969

The Shiite general Jawhar lays the foundations for a new palace city, Al-Qahira (Cairo). Two years later, a new university and mosque complex, al-Azhar, is founded.

1038–1194

The Seljuks, the former Turkish guards of the Abbasids, seize power, effectively ruling the Abbasid Empire. In addition to Turkey, they take Afghanistan, Persia and much of Central Asia.

1097

In response to a cry for help from the besieged Byzantines in Constantinople, the Christian Crusaders sweep down across the Middle East, trying to end Muslim rule in the Holy Land.

the Ottoman Empire. By capturing Mecca and Medina, Selim the Grim claimed for the Ottomans the coveted title of the guardians of Islam's holiest places. For the first time in centuries, the Middle East was ruled in its entirety by a single Islamic entity.

Golden Age

The Ottoman Empire reached its peak, both politically and culturally, under Süleyman the Magnificent (r 1520–66), who led the Ottoman armies west to the gates of Vienna, east into Persia, and south through the holy cities of Mecca and Medina and into Yemen. His control also extended throughout North Africa. A remarkable figure, Süleyman was noted as much for codifying Ottoman law (he is known in Turkish as Süleyman Kanunı – law bringer) as for his military prowess. Süleyman's legal code was a visionary amalgam of secular and Islamic law, and his patronage of the arts saw the Ottomans reach their cultural zenith.

Another hallmark of Ottoman rule, especially in its early centuries, was its tolerance. In general, Christian and Jewish communities were accorded the respect the Quran outlines for them as 'People of the Book' (see the boxed text, p581) and were given special status. The Ottoman state was a truly multicultural and multilingual one, and Christians and Muslims rose to positions of great power within the Ottoman hierarchy. In a move unthinkable for a Muslim ruler today, Sultan Beyazit II even invited the Jews expelled from Iberia by the Spanish Inquisition to İstanbul in 1492.

But as so often happened in Middle Eastern history upon the death of a charismatic leader, things began to unravel soon after Süleyman died fighting on the Danube. The Ottomans may have held nominal power throughout their empire for centuries to come, but the growing decadence of the Ottoman court and unrest elsewhere in the countries that fell within the Ottoman sphere of influence ensured that, after Süleyman, the empire went into a long, slow period of decline.

Under Attack

Only five years after Süleyman's death, Spain and Venice destroyed virtually the entire Ottoman navy at the Battle of Lepanto (in the Aegean Sea), thereby costing the Ottomans control over the western Mediterranean. North Africa soon fell under the sway of local dynasties. Conflict with the Safavids – Persia's rulers from the early 16th century to the early 18th century – was almost constant.

To make matters worse, within a century of Süleyman's death, the concept of enlightened Ottoman sultans had all but evaporated. Assassinations, mutinies and fratricide were increasingly the norm among Constantinople's royals, and the opulent lifestyle was taking its toll.

OTTOMAN EMPIRE

Ottoman Centuries by Lord Kinross is perhaps the definitive history of the Ottoman Empire, covering everything from the key events of Ottoman rule to the extravagances of its royal court.

1099
After a withering siege, the Crusaders enter Jerusalem, massacre thousands regardless of their religion and claim the city for Christianity. The Dome of the Rock is turned into a church.

1171
The Kurdish-born general Salah ad-Din al-Ayyub (aka Saladin) seizes power from the Fatimid Shiite caliph in Egypt, restores Sunni rule and establishes the Ayyubid dynasty.

1187
Saladin retakes Jerusalem from the Crusaders and forever after becomes a hero to Muslims around the world. Fighting elsewhere between Saladin's forces and the Crusaders continues.

1192
Saladin signs a peace treaty with his long-time enemy, Richard the Lionheart. The Crusaders get the coast, the Muslims get the interior and Saladin dies three months later.

Lords of the Horizons: A History of the Ottoman Empire by Jason Goodwin is anecdotal and picaresque but still manages to illuminate the grand themes of Ottoman history.

Süleyman was the last sultan to lead his army into the field, and those who came after him were generally coddled and sequestered in the fineries of the palace, having minimal experience of everyday life and little inclination to administer or expand the empire. The Ottomans remained moribund, inward looking and generally unaware of the advances that were happening in Europe – the Ottoman clergy did not allow the use of the printing press until the 18th century, a century and a half after it had been introduced into Europe.

Just as it had under the similarly out-of-touch Umayyads in the 8th century, the perceived impiety of the sultans and their representatives gave power to local uprisings. The Ottoman Empire lumbered along until the 20th century, but the empire was in a sorry state and its control over its territories grew more tenuous with each passing year.

European Incursions

Europe had begun to wake from its medieval slumber and the monarchs of France and Great Britain, in particular, were eager to bolster their growing prosperity by expanding their zones of economic influence. More than that, the prestige that would accompany colonial possessions in lands that had held an important place in the European imagination was undeniable. The reflected glory of 'owning' the Holy Lands or becoming the rulers over what was once the cradle of civilisation was too much for these emerging world powers to resist, and fitted perfectly within their blueprint for world domination. They may have talked of a 'civilising mission'. They may even have believed it. But it was prestige and greed that ultimately drove them as they cast their eye towards the Middle East.

In 1798, Napoleon invaded Egypt. It was not by accident that he chose the Middle East's most populous country as his first conquest in the region. By conquering the one-time land of the pharaohs, this ruler with visions of grandeur and an eye on his place in history announced to the world that France was the world power of the day. The French occupation of Egypt lasted only three years, but left a lasting mark – even today, Egypt's legal system is based on a French model.

The British, of course, had other ideas. Under the cover of protecting their own Indian interests, they forced the French out of Egypt in 1801.

Decline

Four years later, Mohammed Ali, an Albanian soldier in the Ottoman army, emerged as the country's strongman and he set about modernising the country. As time passed, it became increasingly obvious that Constantinople was becoming ever more dependent on Egypt for military backing rather than the reverse. Mohammed Ali's ambitions grew. In the

1250
The Mamluks, a military empire forged from the ranks of the Muslim armies, seize power for themselves and begin a 300-year rule over Egypt, Syria and Palestine.

1258
Baghdad is sacked by the Mongol hordes sweeping down out of Central Asia, destroying the city and officially ending the Abbasid Cailphate. Osman (founder of the Ottomans) is born.

1291
With energy drained from the Crusader cause, the Mamluks drive the last Crusaders from their coastal fortress of Acre (now Akko in Israel) and from the Middle East.

1453
After encircling the city during his Eastern European conquests, Sultan Mehmet II of the Ottoman Empire captures Constantinople, which had never before been in Muslim hands.

1830s, he invaded and conquered Syria, and by 1839 he had effective control of most of the Ottoman Empire.

While it might have appeared to have been in Europe's interests to consign the Ottoman Empire to history, they were already stretched by their other colonial conquests and holdings (the British in India, the French in Africa) and had no interest, at least not yet, in administering the entire region. As a consequence, the Europeans prevailed upon Mohammed Ali to withdraw to Egypt. In return, the Ottoman sultan gave long-overdue acknowledgment of Mohammed Ali's status as ruler of a virtually independent Egypt, and bestowed the right of heredity rule on his heirs (who continued to rule Egypt until 1952). In some quarters, the Ottoman move was viewed as a wise strategy in keeping with their loose administration of their empire. In truth, they had little choice.

At the Battle of the Pyramids, Napoleon's forces took just 45 minutes to rout the Mamluk army, killing 1000 for the loss of just 29 of their own men.

The emboldened Europeans were always at the ready to expand their influence in the region. In 1860, the French sent troops to Lebanon after a massacre of Christians by the local Druze. Before withdrawing, the French forced the Ottomans to set up a new administrative system for the area guaranteeing the appointment of Christian governors, over whom the French came to have great influence.

While all of this was happening, another import from the West – nationalism – was making its presence felt. The people of the Middle East watched with growing optimism as Greece and the Ottomans' Balkan possessions wriggled free, marking the final death knell of Ottoman omniscience and prompting Middle Easterners to dream of their own independence. In this, they were encouraged by the European powers,

OTTOMAN CONQUEST OF EUROPE

Just as the forces of Christian Europe were on the verge of expelling Al-Andalus, the Islamic civilisation that ruled southern Spain from Christian soil, the Ottoman Turks, gathering in the east, opened a new front.

Horse-borne, and firing arrows from the saddle, the Ottoman Turks emerged from the Anatolian steppe in the 14th century, eager to gain a foothold on European soil. It was the boldest of moves, considering that the Abbasid advance on Constantinople had prompted the fierce European backlash of the Crusades. But the Ottomans were better equipped to take on war-weary Europe and advanced so swiftly – so seemingly miraculously – into Eastern Europe that Martin Luther openly wondered whether they should be opposed at all. The Ottoman Empire, at its greatest extent, reached from western Libya to the steppes of Hungary.

The end of Ottoman expansion is variously pinpointed as the failed Vienna campaign in 1683 or the treaty of Karlowitz (in which the Ottomans lost the Peloponnese, Transylvania and Hungary) in 1699 when the Ottomans sued for peace for the first time.

1492

Muslim Al-Andalus falls to the Christian armies of the Spanish Reconquista, ending seven centuries of enlightened but increasingly divided rule. Jewish people begin arriving across the Middle East.

1520–66

Süleyman the Magnificent rules over the golden age of the Ottoman Empire, expanding the boundaries of the empire down into Arabia (including the holy cities of Mecca and Medina), Persia and North Africa.

JOHN ELK III / LONELY PLANET IMAGES ©

» Ottoman decoration

1571

Five years after the death of Süleyman the Magnificent, Spain and Venice defeat the Ottomans at the Battle of Lepanto in the Aegean. Ottoman power has peaked and will never be as strong again.

who may have paid lip service to the goals of independence, but were actually laying detailed plans for occupation. Mistaking (or, more likely, deliberately misinterpreting or ignoring) the nationalist movement as a cry for help, the European powers quickly set about filling the vacuum of power left by the Ottomans.

The Ottoman regime, once feared and respected, was now universally known as the 'sick man of Europe'. European diplomats and politicians condescendingly pondered the 'eastern question', which in practice meant deciding how to dismember the empire and cherry-pick its choicest parts. In 1869, Mohammed Ali's grandson Ismail opened the Suez Canal. But within a few years, his government was so deeply in debt that in 1882, the British, who already played a large role in Egyptian affairs, occupied the country. It was a sign of things to come.

ORIENTALISM

Orientalis, by Edward Said is dense and academic but is *the* seminal work on the history of Western misconceptions and stereotypes about the Middle East from colonial times to the present.

Colonial Middle East

Broken Promises

With the exception of Napoleon's stunning march into Egypt, Britain and France had slowly come to occupy the Middle East less by conquest than by stealth. European advisers, backed by armed reinforcements when necessary, were increasingly charting the region's future and it would not be long before their efforts were rewarded.

With the outbreak of WWI in 1914, the Ottoman Empire made its last serious (and ultimately fatal) error by throwing its lot in with Germany. Sultan Mohammed V declared a jihad (holy war), calling on Muslims everywhere to rise up against Britain, France and Russia (who were encroaching on Eastern Anatolia). When the British heard the Ottoman call to jihad, they performed a masterstroke – they negotiated an alliance with Hussein bin Ali, the grand sherif (Islamic custodian and descendant of the Prophet Mohammed) of Mecca, who agreed to lead an Arab revolt against the Turks in return for a British promise to make him 'King of the Arabs' once the conflict was over. This alliance worked well in defeating the Ottomans.

There was just one problem. With the Ottomans out of the way, the British never had any serious intention of keeping their promise. Even as they were negotiating with Sherif Hussein, the British were talking with the French on how to carve up the Ottoman Empire. These talks yielded the 1916 Sykes-Picot Agreement – the secret Anglo-French accord that divided the Ottoman Empire into British and French spheres of influence. With a few adjustments, the Sykes-Picot Agreement determined the post-WWI map of the Middle East. Not surprisingly, this remains one of the most reviled 'peace agreements' in 20th-century Middle Eastern history.

1683
The Ottoman armies march on Vienna, but their defeat marks the end of Ottoman expansion and furthers the centuries-long period of Ottoman decline.

1760s
The Wahhabi movement in central Arabia calls for a return to Islam's roots. Wahhabi Islam still prevails in Saudi Arabia and forms the basis for al-Qaeda thought.

1798
Napoleon invades Egypt, ushering in the period of colonial rivalry between France and Britain (who force the French out in 1801) that would ultimately redraw the map of the Middle East.

1839
Mohammed Ali of Egypt, an Albanian Ottoman soldier, establishes de facto control over declining Ottoman Empire from his base in Egypt. The dynasty he founded would rule Egypt until 1952.

European Occupation

In the closing year of the war, the British occupied Palestine, Transjordan, Damascus and Iraq. After the war, France took control of Syria and Lebanon, while Britain retained Egypt in addition to its holdings elsewhere. The Arabs, who'd done so much to free themselves from Ottoman rule, suddenly found themselves under British or French colonial administration, with the prospect of a Jewish state in their midst not far over the horizon thanks to the 1917 Balfour Declaration (see the boxed text, p565).

When the newly minted League of Nations initiated its system of mandates in 1922, thereby legitimising the French and British occupations, the sense of betrayal across the region was palpable. As was the colonial way, no one had thought to ask the people of the region what they wanted. As the Europeans set about programs of legal and administrative reform, their occupying forces faced almost continual unrest. The Syrians and Lebanese harried the French, while the predominantly Arab population of Palestine battled the British.

A Peace to End All Peace: Creating the Modern Middle East, 1914-1922 by David Fromkin is an intriguing account of how the map of the modern Middle East was drawn arbitrarily by European colonial governments.

WHAT HAPPENED TO THE ARMENIANS?

The final years of the Ottoman Empire saw human misery on an epic scale, but nothing has proved as enduringly controversial as the fate of the Armenians. For millennia, this large but disparate community had lived in eastern Anatolia. In the early 20th century, the Orthodox Christian Armenians made the error of siding with the Russians against the Muslim Turk majority. It was an error for which they paid dearly.

The tale begins with eyewitness accounts, in autumn 1915, of Ottoman army units rounding up Armenian populations and marching them towards the Syrian desert. It ends with an Anatolian hinterland virtually devoid of Armenians. What happened in between remains one of the most controversial episodes in the 20th-century Middle East.

The Armenians maintain, somewhat compellingly it must be said, that they were subject to the 20th century's first orchestrated 'genocide'. They claim that over a million Armenians were summarily executed or killed on death marches and that Ottoman authorities issued a deportation order with the intention of removing the Armenian presence from Anatolia. To this day, Armenians demand an acknowledgement of this 'genocide'. Very few Armenians remain in Turkey, although there are significant Armenian communities in Syria, Iran and Israel and the Palestinian Territories.

Less compellingly, although with equal conviction, Turkey refutes any claims that such 'genocide' occurred. It does admit that thousands of Armenians died, but claims the Ottoman order had been to 'relocate' Armenians with no intention to eradicate them. The deaths, according to Turkish officials, were the result of disease and starvation, direct consequences of the tumultuous state of affairs during a time of war.

1860

The massacre of Christians by the Druze in Lebanon's mountains prompts the French to send troops to restore order. The Ottomans remain nominal sovereigns, but the French never really leave.

1869

Ismail, the grandson of Mohammed Ali and ruler of Egypt, formally opens the landmark engineering feat that is the Suez Canal. Britain is heavily involved in Egyptian affairs.

1882

Weary of the Egyptian government's alleged financial ineptitude, the British formalise their control over the country, making it their first full-blown colonial possession in the Middle East.

1896

Theodor Herzl publishes *Der Judenstaat* (*The Jewish State*), in which he makes a call for a Jewish state in Palestine. This event is often described as the moment when Zionism was born.

The problems in Palestine were particularly acute. Since taking control of Palestine in 1918, the British had been under pressure to allow unrestricted Jewish immigration to the territory. With tension rising between Palestine's Arab and Jewish residents, they refused to do this and, in the late 1930s, placed strict limits on the number of new Jewish immigrants. It was, of course, a crisis of Britain's own making, having promised to 'view with favour' the establishment of a Jewish state in Palestine in the Balfour Declaration of 1917.

When Zionist and British policy makers were looking for a homeland for the Jewish people, sites they considered included Uganda, northeastern Australia and the Jebel Akhdar in the Cyrenaica region of Libya.

Turkish Independence

As Iraq, Syria, Lebanon and Palestine simmered, Turkey was going its own way, mercifully free of both the Ottoman sultans and their European successors. Stripped of its Arab provinces, the Ottoman monarchy was overthrown and a Turkish republic was declared under the leadership of Mustafa Kemal 'Atatürk', a soldier who became Turkey's first president in 1923.

His drive toward secularism (which he saw as synonymous with the modernisation necessary to drag Turkey into the 20th century) found an echo in Persia, where, in 1923, Reza Khan, the commander of a Cossack brigade who had risen to become war minister, overthrew the decrepit Ghajar dynasty. After changing his name from Khan to the more Persian-sounding Pahlavi (the language spoken in pre-Islamic Persia), he moved to set up a secular republic on the Turkish model. Protests from the country's religious establishment caused a change of heart and he had himself crowned shah instead. In 1934, he changed the country's name from Persia to Iran.

Looking back now at the turbulent years between the two world wars, it's easy to discern the seeds of the major conflicts that would come to define the Middle East in the late 20th and early 21st centuries: the Arab-Israeli conflict, Iran's Islamic Revolution and Turkey's struggle to forge an identity as a modernising Muslim country.

Israel's Independence

For the past 60 years, no issue has divided the Middle East quite like Israeli independence. Four major conflicts, numerous skirmishes and an unrelenting war of words and attrition have cast a long shadow over everything that happens in the region. If a way could be found to forge peace between Israel and the Palestinians, the Middle East would be a very different place.

There is very little on which the two sides agree, although the following historical chronology is *probably* among them: in early 1947 the British announced that they were turning the entire problem over to the newly created UN. The UN voted to partition Palestine, but this was

1897
Herzl helps found the World Zionist Organization. He writes: 'At Basel I founded the Jewish State. In five years perhaps, and certainly in 50 years, everyone will perceive it.'

1914
WWI breaks out. The Ottomans side with Germany, while the Allies persuade the Grand Sherif of Mecca to support them in return for promises of post-war independence for the Arabs.

1915
In the last years of the Ottoman Empire, Turkey's Armenian population is driven from the country. More than a million Armenians are killed in what Armenians claim was a genocide.

1916
The French and British conclude the secret Sykes-Picot Agreement, which divides the region between the two European powers in the event of an Allied victory.

rejected by the Arabs. Britain pulled out and the very next day the Jews declared the founding of the State of Israel. War broke out immediately, with Egypt, Jordan and Syria weighing in on the side of the Palestinian Arabs. Israel won.

Beyond that, the issue has become a forum for claim and counter-claim to the extent that for the casual observer, truth has become as elusive as the peace that all sides claim to want. What follows is our summary of the main bodies of opinion about Israeli Independence among Israelis and Palestinians as they stood in 1948.

The Israeli View

For many Israelis in 1948, the founding of the state of Israel represented a homecoming for a persecuted people who had spent almost 2000 years in exile. Coming so soon as it did after the horrors of the Holocaust, in which more than six million Jews were killed, Israel, a state of their own, was the least the world could do after perpetrating the Holocaust or letting it happen. The Holocaust was the culmination

ZIONISM: A PRIMER

Contrary to popular belief, Zionism, the largely secular movement to create a Jewish homeland in Palestine, began decades before the Holocaust. In the late 19th century, pogroms against Jews in the Russian Empire and the 1894 Dreyfus Affair (in which a French Jewish officer was wrongly accused of treason) shone uncomfortable light on racism against the Jews in Europe. Two years later, Theodor Herzl, a Hungarian Jew, published *Der Judenstaat* (*The Jewish State*), which called for the setting up of a Jewish state in Palestine. In 1897, Herzl founded the World Zionist Organization (WZO) at the First Zionist Congress in Basel. At the conclusion of the Congress, Herzl is said to have written in his diary: 'At Basel I founded the Jewish State. If I said this out loud today I would be greeted by universal laughter. In five years perhaps, and certainly in 50 years, everyone will perceive it.' Another leading Zionist, Chaim Weizmann, who would later become the first president of Israel, was instrumental in lobbying the British government for what became the 1917 Balfour Declaration, whose text assured Jews that the British government would 'view with favour' the creation of 'a national home for the Jewish people' in Palestine, provided that 'nothing shall be done which may prejudice the civil and religious rights of existing non-Jewish communities in Palestine'. Over the years that followed, the WZO funded and otherwise supported the emigration of Jews to Palestine under the catch cry 'A land without people for a people without land'. The Jews were indeed a people without land, but the rallying cry ignored the presence in Palestine of hundreds of thousands of Arabs who had lived on the land for generations. The WZO also set up numerous quasi-state institutions that were transplanted to the new Israeli state upon independence.

1917

The British government's Balfour Declaration promises 'a national home for the Jewish people' in Palestine. The declaration gives unstoppable momentum to the Zionist movement.

1922

The League of Nations grants Syria and Lebanon to the French, and Palestine, Iraq and Transjordan to the British. Egypt becomes independent but Britain remains in control.

1923

Kemal Atatürk, becomes the first president of Turkey on a mission to modernise the country and create a secular state. Reza Khan seizes power in Iran.

1920s & 1930s

Jewish immigration to Palestine gathers pace. The arrival of the immigrants prompts anger among Palestinian Arabs and the British impose restrictions on the number of arrivals.

of decades, perhaps even centuries of racism in European countries. In short, the Jewish people had ample reason to believe that their fate should never again be placed in the hands of others.

Although the Jews were offered a range of alternative sites for their state, it could never be anywhere but on the southeastern shores of the Mediterranean. By founding a Jewish state in Palestine, the Jews were returning to a land rich in biblical reference points and promises – one of the most enduring foundations of Judaism is that God promised this land to the Jews. Indeed, it is difficult to overestimate the significance of this land for a people whose traditions and sacred places all lay in Palestine, especially Jerusalem. This may have been the driving force for many observant religious Jews. But the dream of a return had deeper cultural roots, maintained down through the generations during an often difficult exile and shared by many secular Jews. This latter branch of Jewish society hoped to create an enlightened utopia, an egalitarian society in which a strong and just Israel finally took its rightful place among the modern company of nations. It was, according to the popular Zionist song that would become Israel's national anthem, 'the hope of 2000 years'.

ISRAELI INDEPENDENCE

Israel was the last country in the region to achieve independence, following in the wake of Egypt (1922), Iraq (1932), Lebanon (1941), Jordan and Syria (both 1946).

The Palestinian View

For many Palestinians in 1948, the founding of the state of Israel was 'Al-Naqba' – the Catastrophe. Through no fault of their own, and thanks to decisions made in Europe and elsewhere, and on which they were never consulted, the Palestinians were driven from their land. While the British were promising Palestine to the Jews in 1917, the Palestinians were fighting alongside the British to oust the Ottomans. Later, subject to British occupation, Palestinians suffered at the hands of Jewish extremist groups and found themselves confronted by an influx of Jews who had never before set foot in Palestine but who claimed equal rights over the land. Many Palestinians who had lived on the land for generations could do nothing without international assistance. No one came to their aid. In short, when they were offered half of their ancestral homelands by the UN, they had ample reason to reject the plan out of hand.

As with the Israelis, it is difficult to overestimate the significance of this land for Palestinians, many of whose traditions and sacred places lay in Palestine. Jerusalem (Al-Quds) is the third-holiest city for Palestinian Muslims after Mecca and Medina (the Prophet Mohammed is believed to have ascended to heaven from the Al-Aqsa Mosque), and the holiest city on earth for Palestinian Christians. But this was never really about religion. Had they not lived alongside the Jews for centuries, many Palestinians asked, considered them equals and given them the respect that their religion deserved? For the Palestinians forced to flee, it was about

1939–45

After decades of anti-Semitism in Europe, more than six million Jews are killed by the Nazis and their allies during WWII, giving fresh urgency to the call for a Jewish state.

1947

Britain hands the issue over to the newly formed UN, which decides to partition Palestine into two states, one Jewish, the other Palestinian. Arabs reject the plan.

1948

The British withdraw from Palestine, Israel declares independence and the Arab armies of neighbouring countries invade. The new State of Israel wins the war, and increases its territory.

» Israeli flag

the right to the homes in which people had lived and to the fields that they had farmed. As they fled into their own exile, they longed for a Palestinian homeland taking its rightful place among the modern company of nations.

Arab Middle East

Arab (Dis)unity

The Arab countries that waged war against Israel were in disarray, even before they went to war. Newly independent themselves, they were governed for the most part by hereditary rulers whose legitimacy was tenuous at best. They ruled over countries whose boundaries had only recently been established and they did so thanks to centuries of foreign rule, ill prepared to tackle the most pressing problems of poverty,

ISRAELI INDEPENDENCE: A PRIMER

In addition to the books listed below, *The War for Palestine: Rewriting the History of 1948*, edited by Eugene L Rogan and Avi Shlaim, brings together both Israeli and Palestinian scholars.

History by Israelis

» *1948: A History of the First Arab-Israeli War* by Benny Morris – Israel's most prominent historian has drawn criticism from both sides.

» *The Birth of the Palestinian Refugee Problem Revisited* by Benny Morris – an attempt to explain why 700,000 Palestinians ended up in exile.

» *The Arab-Israeli Wars: War and Peace in the Middle East* by Chaim Herzog and Shlomo Gazit – although it covers more recent events, Herzog takes a long look at 1948.

» *The Ethnic Cleansing of Palestine* by Ilan Pappe – a controversial text that challenges many of Israel's founding myths.

» *The Invention of the Jewish People* by Shlomo Sand – a polemical book that revisits the question of Jewish identity.

History by Palestinians

» *The Question of Palestine* by Edward W Said – an eloquent, passionate, but fair-minded study of the issue by the late, leading Palestinian intellectual.

» *Expulsion of the Palestinians: The Concept of 'Transfer' in Zionist Political Thought, 1882-1948* by Nur Masalha – revealing insights from Zionist archives.

» *The Iron Cage: The Story of the Palestinian Struggle for Statehood* by Rashid Khalidi – looks at 1948 and the decades that preceded it.

1951

King Abdullah I, the founder of modern Jordan, is assassinated as recriminations ripple out across the Arab world in the wake of its devastating defeat by Israel.

1952

Gamal Abdel Nasser leads a coup against the monarchy in Egypt and becomes the first Egyptian ruler over Egypt since the days of the pharaohs.

1956

Shortly after becoming Egyptian president, Nasser nationalises the Suez Canal, then stares down Israel, Britain and France who are forced to retreat. Nasser's popularity soars.

1958–61

Egypt and Syria unite to form the United Arab Republic, a short-lived union that Nasser hopes will spark a pan-Arab mega-state that brings together all the Arab countries of the region.

illiteracy and the lack of a clear national vision for the future. Although united in the common cause of opposing Israel, they were divided over just about everything else.

The disastrous performance of the combined Arab armies in the 1948 Arab–Israeli War had far-reaching consequences for the region. People across the region blamed their leaders for the defeat, a mood fuelled by the mass arrival of Palestinian refugees in Lebanon, Syria, Egypt and, most of all, Jordan, whose population doubled almost overnight. Recriminations over the humiliating defeat and the refugee problem it created laid the groundwork for the 1951 assassination of King Abdullah of Jordan. Syria, which had gained its independence from France in 1946, became the field for a seemingly endless series of military coups.

In 1922, there were around 486,000 Palestinian Arabs and 84,000 Jews. By 1946, the Palestinian population had doubled to 1.1 million, whereas Jews had increased 550% to around 610,000.

Rise of Nasser

But it was in Egypt, where the army blamed the loss of the war on the country's corrupt and ineffective politicians, that the most interesting developments were taking shape. In July 1952, a group of young officers toppled the monarchy, with the real power residing with one of the coup plotters: Gamal Abdel Nasser. King Farouk, descendant of the Albanian Mohammed Ali, departed from Alexandria harbour on the royal yacht, and Colonel Nasser – the first Egyptian to rule Egypt since the pharaohs – became president in elections held in 1956. His aim of returning some of Egypt's wealth to its much-exploited peasantry struck a chord with Egypt's masses. He became an instant hero across the Arab world.

Nasser's iconic status reached new heights in the year of his inauguration, when he successfully faced down Britain and France in a confrontation over the Suez Canal, which was mostly owned by British and French investors. On 26 July, the fourth anniversary of King Farouk's departure, Nasser announced that he had nationalised the Suez Canal to finance the building of a great dam that would control the flooding of the Nile and boost Egyptian agriculture. A combined British, French and Israeli invasion force, which intended to take possession of the canal, was, to great diplomatic embarrassment, forced to make an undignified retreat after the UN and US applied pressure. Nasser emerged from the conflict the most popular Arab leader in history.

Attempts at Unity

Such was Nasser's popularity that the Syrians joined Egypt in what would prove to be an ultimately unworkable union, the United Arab Republic. At the time, it seemed as if Nasser's dream of pan-Arab unity was one step closer to reality. But behind the staged photo opportunities in which the region's presidents and monarchs lined up to bask in Nasser's reflected glory, the region was as divided as ever. With the United Arab

1961

Kurds in northern Iraq launch a short-lived military campaign for an independent Kurdistan. The move fails and will become an important justification for later campaigns against the Kurds.

1964

Against the objections of Jordan and, of course, Israel, the Palestine Liberation Organisation (PLO), an umbrella group of Palestinian resistance groups, is formed.

1967

Israel launches a pre-emptive strike and destroys Egypt's air force. Israel emerges from the resulting Six Day War with much of the West Bank, Sinai, the Golan Heights and the Gaza Strip.

1968-69

Saddam Hussein emerges as the key powerbroker in Iraq after a coup brings the Baath Party to power. A year later, Yasser Arafat becomes leader of the PLO.

Republic at Jordan's borders to the north and south, King Hussein feared for his own position and tried a federation of his own with his Hashemite cousins in Iraq; it lasted less than a year before the Iraqi Hashemite monarchy was overthrown, and British troops were sent in to Jordan to protect Hussein. Egypt and Syria went their separate ways in 1961.

Meanwhile, Lebanon was taking an entirely different course, exposing the fault lines that would later tear the country apart. The Western-oriented Maronite Christian government that held sway in Beirut had been, in 1956, the only Arab government to support the US and UK during the Suez Canal crisis.

And yet, for all the division and gathering storm clouds, there was a palpable sense of hope across the Arab world. Driven by Nasser's 'victory' over the European powers in the 1956 Suez crisis, there was a growing belief that the Arab world's time was now. While this manifested itself in the hope that the region had acquired the means and self-belief to finally defeat Israel when the time came, it was also to be found on the streets of cities across the region.

Rise of the PLO

All too often, the Arab-Israeli conflict, as with so many other events in the Middle East, has been explained away as a religious war between Jews and Muslims. There has at times indeed been a religious dimension, especially in recent years with the rise of Hamas in the Palestinian Territories and the religious right in Israel. But this has always been fundamentally a conflict over land, as was shown in the years following Israel's independence. Governments – from the Ba'ath parties of Syria and Iraq to Nasser's Egypt – invariably framed their demands in purely secular terms.

It again became clear after the formation in 1964 of the Palestine Liberation Organisation (PLO). Although opposed by Jordan, which was itself keen to carry the banner of Palestinian leadership, the PLO enjoyed the support of the newly formed Arab League. The Palestine National Council (PNC) was established within the PLO as its executive body – the closest thing to a Palestinian government in exile. The PLO served as an umbrella organisation for an extraordinary roll call of groups that ranged from purely military wings to communist ideologues. Militant Islamic factions were, at the time, small and drew only limited support.

Just as the PLO was at risk of dissolving into an acrimony born from its singular lack of a united policy, an organisation called the Palestine National Liberation Movement (also known as Al-Fatah) was established. One of the stated aims of both the PLO and Al-Fatah was to train guerrillas for raids on Israel. Al-Fatah emerged from a power struggle as the dominant force within the PLO, and its leader, Yasser Arafat, would

Arafat by the Palestinian writer Said K Aburish is a highly critical look at one of the Middle East's most intriguing yet flawed personalities. *Arafat: The Biography* by Tony Walker and Andrew Gowers is also good.

1970

Hafez al-Assad assumes power in Syria after what he called 'The Corrective Revolution'. At the head of the Syrian Ba'ath Party, he ruled Syria until his death in 2000.

1973

Egypt launches a surprise attack on Israel. After initial gains, Israel recovers to seize yet more territory. Despite the defeat, the war is hailed as a victory in the Arab world.

1975

After years of tension, war breaks out in Lebanon between Palestinians and Christian militias. The fighting, which draws in other militant groups, will last until 1990.

1977

Egyptian president Anwar Sadat's landmark visit to Jerusalem reverberates around the region. Egypt is expelled from the Arab League and Sadat is hailed around the world.

become chair of the executive committee of the PLO in 1969 and, later, the PLO's most recognisable face.

At the same time, Islam as a political force *was* starting to stir. Nasser may have been all-powerful, but there was a small group of clerics who saw him, Egyptian or not, as the latest in a long line of godless leaders ruling the country. Sayyid Qutb, an Egyptian radical and intellectual, was the most influential, espousing a return to the purity of grassroots Islam. He also prompted the creation of the Muslim Brotherhood, who would withdraw from society and prepare for violence and martyrdom in pursuit of a universal Muslim society. Qutb was executed by Nasser in 1966, but the genie could not be put back in the bottle, returning to haunt the region, and the rest of the world, decades later.

Arab–Israeli Wars

1967 War

With the Arab world growing in confidence, war seemed inevitable. In May 1967, the Egyptian army moved into key points in Sinai and announced a blockade of the Straits of Tiran, effectively closing the southern Israeli port of Eilat. The Egyptian army was mobilised and the country put on a war footing. On 5 June, Israel responded with a devastating preemptive strike that wiped out virtually the entire Egyptian air force in a single day. The war lasted only six days (hence the 'Six Day War'), and

NATIONS WITHOUT A STATE: PALESTINIANS & KURDS

Everyone seems to agree that there will one day be a Palestinian state, even if no one dares to predict when it might come to pass. The same cannot be said for the Kurds, despite being more numerically significant. Why?

Well, for a start, the major Kurdish cities of Erbil and Sulaymaniyah just don't resonate in geo-political circles in quite the same way as Jerusalem and the Holy Land, with their significance for the world's three largest monotheistic religions. Nor have the Kurds produced anyone with the charisma to capture the world's attention quite like Yasser Arafat – love him or loathe him, the world could never ignore him. Although the Kurds have, from time to time, found favour with one world power or another, their shifting alliances and the short attention spans of world leaders have meant that the Kurds have never had a powerful backer consistently willing to champion their cause; not for nothing did John Bulloch and Harvey Morris call their 1993 history of the Kurds *No Friends but the Mountains*. Perhaps most importantly of all, given the chronic levels of instability already at large in the Middle East, no world leader would ever dare to suggest slicing off large sections of Turkey, Iraq, Iran and Syria to create a Kurdish state.

1978

Anwar Sadat and Israel's Menachem Begin sign the Camp David peace treaty. Egypt gets Sinai and recognises Israel's right to exist.

1979

After brutal repression of opposition protests, the Shah of Iran, Reza Pahlavi, leaves Iran. The Islamic Revolution brings Āyatollāh Ruhollāh Khomeini to power.

1980

Counting on a weakened Iran in the wake of the Islamic Revolution, Saddam Hussein launches a surprise attack on Iran. The war, in which millions died and neither country gained any territory, would last until 1988.

1981

Anwar Sadat is assassinated in Cairo during a military parade, by a member of his armed forces (and also a secret member of an Islamist group) as the parade passes the presidential box.

when it was over, Israel controlled the Sinai Peninsula, the Gaza Strip, the West Bank (including Jerusalem's Old City) and the Golan Heights.

After more than a decade of swaggering between Cairo and Damascus, and empty promises to the Palestinians that they would soon be returning home, the Six Day War was viewed as an unmitigated disaster throughout the Arab world and sent shockwaves across the region. Not only were leaders like Nasser no match for the Israelis, despite the posturing, but also tens of thousands more Palestinian refugees were now in exile. The mood across the region was grim. A humiliated Nasser offered to resign, but in a spontaneous outpouring of support, the Egyptian people wouldn't accept the move and he remained in office. In November 1970 the president died of a heart attack, reportedly a broken man.

1973 War

With Palestinian militancy on the rise, the year 1970 saw the ascension of new leaders in both Egypt (Anwar Sadat) and Syria (Hafez al-Assad). Preparations were also well under way for the next Middle Eastern war, with these radical new leaders under constant pressure from their citizens to reclaim the land lost in 1967. On 6 October 1973, Egyptian troops crossed the Suez Canal, taking Israel (at a standstill, observing the holy day of Yom Kippur) almost entirely by surprise. After advancing a short distance into Sinai, however, the Egyptian army stopped, giving Israel the opportunity to concentrate its forces against the Syrians on the Golan Heights and then turn back towards Egypt. Although the war preserved the military status quo, it was widely portrayed throughout the region as an Arab victory.

Although the 1973 war is painted as a victory and reassertion of Arab pride by many historians, by the time it ended, the Israelis actually occupied more land than when it began.

When the war ended in late 1973, months of shuttle diplomacy by the US secretary of state, Henry Kissinger, followed. Pressure on the USA to broker a deal was fuelled when the Gulf States embargoed oil supplies to the West 10 days after the war began. The embargo's implications were massive, achieving nothing less than a shift in the balance of power in the Middle East. The oil states, rich but underpopulated and militarily weak, gained at the expense of poorer, more populous countries. Huge shifts of population followed the two oil booms of the 1970s, as millions of Egyptians, Syrians, Jordanians, Palestinians and Yemenis went off to seek their fortunes in the oil states.

1973 WAR

Peace & Revolution

The Middle East had reached a temporary stalemate. On one side, Israel knew that it had the wherewithal to hold off the armed forces of its neighbours. But Israel also lived in a state of siege and on maximum alert, all the time facing escalating attacks at home and abroad on its citizens from Palestinian terrorist groups aligned to the PLO. On the

1982
Israel invades Lebanon. In September, Israeli forces surround the Palestinian refugee camps, Sabra and Shatila, while Phalangists massacre thousands. Israel withdraws in 1983.

1983
Turkey returns to democratic rule after a succession of coups. The new constitution that forbids prior political participation suggests that the Turkish military remains the real power in the country.

1984
Abdullah Öcalan forms the Kurdistan Workers Party (PKK) and launches a brutal insurgency that paralyses Turkey's southeast. The 'war' lasts until Öcalan is captured in 1999.

1987
A grassroots uprising known as the intifada breaks out in the Palestinian Territories. Although the PLO later tries to claim credit, the intifada is a spontaneous national rebellion.

other side, Arab governments continued with their rhetoric but knew, although none admitted it, that Israel was here to stay. To the north, Lebanon was sliding into a civil war that was threatening to engulf the region. Something had to give.

Camp David

On 7 November 1977, Egyptian president Anwar Sadat made a dramatic visit to Israel to address the Israeli Knesset with a call for peace. The Arab world was in shock. That the leader of the Arab world's most populous nation, a nation that had produced Gamal Abdel Nasser, could visit Israeli-occupied Jerusalem had hitherto been inconceivable. The shock turned to anger the following year when Sadat and the hardline Israeli prime minister, Menachem Begin, shepherded by US president Jimmy Carter, signed the Camp David Agreement. In return for Egypt's long-coveted recognition of Israel's right to exist, Egypt received back the Sinai Peninsula. Egypt did rather well out of the deal, but was widely accused of breaking ranks and betrayal for one simple reason: the Palestinians received nothing. Arab leaders meeting in Baghdad voted to expel Egypt from the Arab League and moved the group's headquarters out of Cairo in protest. The peace treaty won Sadat (and Begin) a Nobel Peace Prize, but it would ultimately cost the Egyptian leader his life: he was assassinated in Cairo on 6 October 1981.

Iran's Islamic Revolution

Before his death, and with Sadat basking in the acclaim of the international community, one of the few friends he had left in the region was facing troubles of his own. Discontent with the shah of Iran's autocratic rule and his personal disregard for the country's Shiite Muslim religious traditions had been simmering for years. Political violence slowly increased throughout 1978. The turning point came in September of that year, when Iranian police fired on anti-shah demonstrators in Tehran, killing at least 300. The momentum of the protests quickly became unstoppable.

On 16 January 1979, the shah left Iran, never to return (he died in Egypt a year later). The interim government set up after his departure was swept aside the following month when the revolution's leader, the hitherto obscure Āyatollāh Ruhollāh Khomeini, returned to Tehran from his exile in France and was greeted by adoring millions. His fiery brew of nationalism and Muslim fundamentalism had been at the forefront of the revolt, and Khomeini achieved his goal of establishing a clergy-dominated Islamic Republic (the first true Islamic state in modern times) with brutal efficiency. Opposition disappeared, executions took place after meaningless trials and minor officials took the law into their own hands.

1990

Saddam Hussein's Iraq invades Kuwait and remains there until the US-led coalition (operating from its bases in Saudi Arabia) drives him out in early 1991. Saddam turns on Iraqi Shiites and Kurds.

1991

Israel and its Arab neighbours sit down for the first time to discuss a comprehensive peace plan in Madrid. Talks dissolve in recrimination, but the fact that they do so face to face is seen as progress.

1993

After a year and a half of secret negotiations between Israel and the Palestinians, Yasser Arafat and Yitzhak Rabin sign the Oslo Accords setting out a framework for future peace.

1994

Building on the goodwill generated by the Oslo Accords, Jordan under King Hussein becomes the second Arab country (after Egypt in 1979) to sign a peace treaty with Israel.

Bloody Aftermath

The Middle East's reputation for brutal conflict and Islamic extremism owes much to the late 1970s and early 1980s. It was the worst of times in the Middle East, a seemingly relentless succession of bloodletting by all sides. The religious fervour that surrounded Khomeini's Iran and the images of the masses chanting *'Marg bar amrika!'* ('Death to America!')

WHO ARE THE KURDS?

The Kurds, the descendants of the Medes who ruled an empire over much of the Middle East in 600 BC from what is now northwestern Iran, are the Middle East's largest minority group. Kurds (who are predominantly Sunni Muslims) constitute significant minorities in Turkey (20% of the population), Iraq (15%), Iran (10%) and Syria (7% to 8%). The Kurdish homeland is a largely contiguous area split between southeastern Turkey, northeastern Syria, northern Iraq and northwestern Iran.

Turkey

Turkey's sparsely populated eastern and southeastern regions are home to perhaps seven million Kurds, while seven million more live elsewhere in the country, more or less integrated into mainstream Turkish society. Relations between Turks and Kurds soured after the formation of the republic, in which Atatürk's reforms left little room for anything other than Turkishness. Until relatively recently the Turkish government refused to even recognise the existence of the Kurds, insisting they be called 'Mountain Turks'.

Since 1984, when Abdullah Öcalan formed the Kurdistan Workers' Party (PKK), a separatist conflict raged in Turkey's Kurdish areas, prompting Turkey's government to declare a permanent state of emergency. After 15 years and the deaths of some 30,000 people, Öcalan was captured in 1999. The insurgency died out.

In 2002, the Turkish government finally gave some ground on the issue of Kurdish rights, approving broadcasts in Kurdish and giving the go-ahead for Kurdish to be taught in language schools. Emergency rule was lifted in the southeast. Life for Kurds in the southeast has since become considerably easier, although worrying but low-level fighting has recently resumed.

Iraq

Iraq is home to over four million Kurds, who live in the northern provinces of the country. The 1961 Kurdish campaign to secure independence from Iraq laid the foundations for an uneasy relationship between the Kurds and the Iraqi state. After the 1991 Gulf War, when an estimated two million Kurds fled across the mountains to Turkey and Iran, the Kurdish Autonomous Region was set up in northern Iraq under UN protection and Kurdish Iraq became a model for a future federal Iraqi system.

After the fall of Saddam, the Kurds won 17% of the vote in the 2005 elections and Kurdish leaders restated their commitment to a federal but unified Iraq.

RUSSELL MOUNTFORD/LONELY PLANET IMAGES©

» Slogan for peace, Jerusalem

1995

Israeli prime minister Yitzhak Rabin is assassinated by a Jewish extremist who hoped to end the process Rabin had begun with the Oslo Accords. A year later, the right-wing Binyamin Netanyahu is voted into power.

1999

Jordan's King Hussein dies of cancer, having ruled since 1952. He is seen as one of the architects of peace in the region and more than 50 heads of state attend his funeral.

also marked the moment when militant Islam became a political force and announced to the world that the West was in its sights. While this development applied to only a small proportion of the region's Muslims, the reputation has stuck.

A Modern History of the Kurds by David McDowall has been updated to 2004 (although the body of the work finishes in 1996), and it remains an excellent primer on the social and political history of the Kurds, focusing on Turkey and Iraq.

The events that flowed from, or otherwise followed, the Iranian Revolution read like a snapshot of a region sliding out of control. In 1979, militants seized the Grand Mosque in Mecca. They were ejected several weeks later only after bloody gun battles inside the mosque itself, leaving more than 250 people dead inside Islam's holiest shrine. In November of that year, student militants in Tehran overran the US embassy, taking the staff hostage. They would be released only after 444 days in captivity. Away to the north, in 1980, Turkey's government was overthrown in a military coup, capping weeks of violence between left- and right-wing extremists. The same year, Saddam Hussein, supported by the US, invaded Khuzestan in southwestern Iran, on the pretext that the oil-rich province was historically part of Iraq. The resulting war lasted until 1988 and claimed millions of lives as trench warfare and poison gas were used for the first time since WWI.

Lebanon Falls Apart

In June 1982, Israel marched into Lebanon, joining Syria, the PLO and a host of Lebanese militias in a vicious regional conflict from which no side emerged with clean hands. The PLO had long been using the anarchy at large in Lebanon to set up a state within a state, from where they launched hundreds of rocket attacks across the Israeli–Lebanese frontier. Led by Defence Minister Ariel Sharon, Israel entered the war claiming self-defence. But these claims lost considerable credibility when, weeks after the PLO leadership had already left Beirut for Tunis, Israeli soldiers surrounded the Palestinian refugee camps of Sabra and Shatila in Beirut and stood by as their Phalangist allies went on a killing rampage. Hundreds, possibly thousands, of civilians were killed. Israel withdrew from most of Lebanon in 1983, but continued to occupy what it called a self-declared security zone in southern Lebanon.

Covering Islam by Edward Said is a classic, exploring how the Iranian Revolution and Palestinian terrorism changed forever the way we view the Middle East.

The Lebanese Civil War rumbled on until 1990, but even when peace came, Israel controlled the south and Syria's 30,000 troops in Lebanon had become the kingmakers in the fractured Lebanese polity. In the 15 years of war, more than a million Lebanese are believed to have died.

Intifada

Down in the Palestinian Territories, violence flared in 1987 in what became known as the 'First Intifada' (the grass roots Palestinian uprising). Weary of ineffectual Palestinian politicians having achieved nothing of value for their people in the four decades since Israeli independence,

2000
The second Palestinian intifada breaks out in the Palestinian Territories. In Damascus, Hafez al-Assad dies after 30 years in power and his son, Bashar, becomes president.

2003
The US and the UK, with a much smaller coalition and less international support than in 1990–91, invade Iraq, winning the war, but Iraq descends into looting and open insurgency.

2004
Evidence of the torture of Iraqi prisoners emerges from the US-controlled Abu Ghraib prison in Baghdad. The United States' reputation in the region sinks to an all-time low.

2005
Yasser Arafat, chairman of the PLO and leader of the Palestinian Authority, dies in Paris and is later buried in Ramallah, ending four eventful decades at the frontline of Middle Eastern politics.

ordinary Palestinians took matters into their own hands. Campaigns of civil disobedience, general strikes and stone-throwing youths were the hallmarks of the intifada, which ran until 1993.

War & Peace

While all of this was going on, elsewhere in the region there were a few bright spots. Turkey had returned to democratic rule in 1983, albeit with a new constitution barring from public office anyone who had been involved in politics prior to the 1980 coup. In 1988, Iran and Iraq grudgingly agreed to a ceasefire. A year later, Egypt was quietly readmitted to the Arab League and Jordan held its first elections in more than 20 years. But these important landmarks were overshadowed by events in Lebanon, which had led many people to wonder whether the region would ever be at peace.

Iraq, Kuwait & the West

Just as the region was breathing a collective sigh of relief at the end of the Lebanese Civil War and the cessation of hostilities between Iraq and Iran, Iraq invaded Kuwait in August 1990. The 1990s were, it seemed, destined to repeat the cycle of violence that had so scarred the previous decade.

Fearful that Saddam Hussein had Saudi Arabia in his sights, King Fahd requested help from the USA. The result was a US-led coalition whose air and ground offensive drove Iraq out of Kuwait. In the process, Iraqi president Saddam Hussein (previously supported by the West in his war against Iran) became world public enemy number one. When the US-led coalition stopped short of marching on Baghdad, the Iraqi leader used his reprieve to attack the country's Shiite population in the south and the Kurds in the north with levels of brutality remarkable even by his standards. Not willing to wait around for Saddam's response to the Kurds' perceived support for the US-led coalition, hundreds of thousands of Kurds streamed across the border into Turkey in one of the largest refugee exoduses in modern history.

There was another, less immediately obvious consequence of the war. The presence of US troops on Saudi soil enraged many in a country known for its strict (some would say puritanical) adherence to Wahhabi Islamic orthodoxy. To have the uniformed soldiers of what many considered to be Islam's enemy operating freely from the same soil as the holy cities of Mecca and Medina was considered an outrage. From this anger, many respected analysts argue, would come al-Qaeda.

Israeli-Palestinian Peace?

And yet, from the ashes of war came an unlikely movement towards peace. While attempting to solicit Arab support for the anti-Iraq coalition,

Pity the Nation: Lebanon at War by Robert Fisk ranges far beyond Lebanon's borders and is a classic account of the issues that resonate throughout the region. Fisk's polemical style has made him a controversial figure, especially among right-wing Israelis.

2006
After Hezbollah captures two Israeli soldiers, Israel launches a sustained air attack on Lebanon. The resulting war produces a stalemate and is widely portrayed throughout the region as a victory for Hezbollah.

2006
The height of the insurgency against the US military and administrative presence in Iraq. According to the UN, more than 100 civilians die every day, with suicide bombings a near-daily occurrence.

2008
Civil war threatens again in Lebanon after Hezbollah besieges the government. Syria admits to indirect talks with Israel through Turkish mediators.

December 2010
A young Tunisian man sets himself ablaze in the town of Sidi Bouzid, the trigger for a popular uprising that would lead to the demise of leaders in Tunisia, Libya and Egypt.

then-US president George Bush promised to make Arab-Israeli peace a priority once the Iraqis were out of Kuwait. Endless shuttling between Middle Eastern capitals culminated in a US-sponsored peace conference in Madrid in October 1991. It achieved little, but by late summer 1993 it was revealed that Israel and the Palestinians had been holding secret talks in Norway for 18 months. The 'Oslo Accords' were cemented with one of the most famous handshakes in history, between Yasser Arafat and Israeli prime minister Yitzhak Rabin on the White House lawn in September 1993.

An unprecedented era of hope for peace in the Middle East seemed on the horizon. Lebanon had just held its first democratic elections for 20 years and the mutually destructive fighting seemed well and truly at an end. In 1994, Jordan became the second Arab country to sign a formal peace treaty with Israel.

But, sadly, it was not to last. The peace process was derailed by the November 1995 assassination of Rabin and the subsequent election to power of hardline candidate Binyamin Netanyahu. A blip of hope re-emerged when Netanyahu lost office to Ehud Barak, a prime minister who pulled his troops out of occupied south Lebanon and promised to open negotiations with the Syrians and the Palestinians. But critical momentum had been lost. When these talks came to nothing at two high-stakes summits at Camp David and in the Egyptian resort of Sharm el-Sheikh during the last months of the Clinton presidency, everyone knew that an opportunity had been lost.

In September 2000, after Ariel Sharon, by then the leader of the right-wing Likud Party, visited the Al-Aqsa Mosque in Jerusalem, riots broke out among Palestinians. This was the trigger, if not the ultimate cause, for the second Palestinian intifada that has continued in one form or another in the years since. The election of that same Ariel Sharon – a politician as reviled by Palestinians as Yasser Arafat was by Israelis – as Israeli prime minister in 2001 was another nail in the coffin of the already much-buried peace process. Although the death of Yasser Arafat in November 2004 offered some signs for hope, the violent occupation of Palestinian land and bloody suicide bombings targeting Israeli citizens continued. By then, the hope that had spread like a wave across the Middle East in the early 1990s had come to seem like a distant memory.

PALESTINIANS

Of the almost 11 million Palestinians, only five million live in Israel (1.3 million) or the Palestinian Territories (3.7 million). Palestinians comprise around 60% of Jordan's population, with around 400,000 in each of Lebanon and Syria.

Prelude to the Arab Spring

Some things don't change in the Middle East. Israel and the Palestinians still trade accusations of bad faith and no solution has been found to the Arab-Israeli conflict. Hundreds of thousands of Palestinian refugees (including second- and third-generation exiles) languish in refugee camps,

2011

Hosni Mubarak is driven from power after having ruled Egypt since succeeding Anwar Sadat in 1981. He is later put on trial, while Egyptians attempt to build a democracy from scratch.

2011

Syria descends into civil war, a popular and largely peaceful uprising giving way to an armed insurrection in which army defectors battle government loyalists with civilians caught in between.

December 2011

More than eight years after the US-led invasion of Iraq, the last US troops leave the country. Iraqi security forces now responsible for security and the government is by elected parliament.

2012

A UN peace plan for Syria, negotiated by former Secretary General Kofi Annan, brings a fragile ceasefire and a fall in the number of killings, but fighting soon resumes.

many still holding on to the keys of homes they left in 1948 or 1967. And wars great and small continue to flare around the region.

Iraq War

In 2003, US and UK forces, with support from a small band of allies, invaded Iraq. Their military victory was swift, driving Saddam Hussein from power, but the aftermath has proved to be infinitely more complicated. With large communities of Shiites, Kurds and the hitherto all-powerful Sunnis vying for power, the country descended into a sectarian conflict with strong echoes of Lebanon's civil war. Hundreds of thousands, perhaps millions of Iraqis fled the fighting, placing huge pressure on the resources of neighbouring countries. Iraq has since begun to stabilise and the US troops have left, but the Iraqis have paid a terrible price for their freedom.

In 1997, Israeli agents poisoned Hamas activist Khaled Meshaal in Amman. Jordan's King Hussein insisted Israel hand over the antidote. Meshaal, who lives in Syria, later became leader of Hamas.

Seeds of Change

In 2006, Israel and Hezbollah fought a bitter month-long war that shattered the Lebanese peace, while fighting broke out between Hezbollah and the Lebanese government in 2008. The power of Hezbollah, and the shifting of Palestinian power from Al-Fatah to Hamas in the Palestinian Territories, has confirmed a process that had begun with the PLO in the 1960s: the rise of nonstate actors as powerful players in the Middle East.

Governments of Arab countries have singularly failed to meet the aspirations of their people, from bringing about a lasting peace between Israel and the Palestinians to providing the basic services necessary to lift them out of poverty. Little wonder, then, that many Middle Easterners have turned to organisations such as Hezbollah and Hamas who, in the eyes of many Arabs, have matched their words with actions. Both groups have built up extensive networks of social safety nets and, with some success, taken on Israel on the battlefield. That these groups are avowedly Islamic in focus and enjoy the support of arch-enemy Iran has only served to widen the gulf between Israel (and the US) and its neighbours.

By 2010, the region had reached something of an impasse with the issues of the past 60 years frozen into seemingly perpetual division that sometimes spilled over into open warfare, but more often festered like an open wound. The Palestinian still dreaming of returning home. The Israeli still dreaming of a world free from fear. In the meantime, the two sides came no closer to a resolution. These are real issues that make life a daily struggle for ordinary people and the sad fact remains that, for many Middle Easterners, life is no easier than it was 60 years ago. But such a time frame is the mere blink of an historical eye for this part of the world.

2012

The impact of the fighting in Syria ripples across the region with large numbers of Syrian refugees in neighbouring countries, and Turkey accusing Syria of following rebels across the border.

TIM BARKER/LONELY PLANET IMAGES©

» Syrian flag, Crac des Chevaliers, Syria

2012

Egypt's difficult road to democracy sees a number of leading presidential hopefuls banned from office, while clashes increase between the military and protesters, leading to dozens of deaths.

Religion

The Middle East is where it all began for the three big monotheistic world religions: Judaism, Christianity and Islam. Infusing almost every aspect of daily life in the region, from the five-times-daily call to prayer and cultural norms to architecture and disputes over historical claims to land, these three religions provide an important backstory to your travels in the Middle East.

Islam

Birth of Islam

Islam: A Short History by Karen Armstrong is almost like Islam 101, a readable journey through Islam's birth and subsequent growth with easy-to-follow coverage of the schism between Sunnis and Shiites.

Abdul Qasim Mohammed ibn Abdullah ibn Abd al-Muttalib ibn Hashim (the Prophet Mohammed) was born in 570 AD. Mohammed's family belonged to the Quraysh tribe, a trading family with links to Syria and Yemen. By the age of six, Mohammed's parents had both died and he came into the care of his grandfather, the custodian of the Kaaba in Mecca.

At the age of 40, in 610, Mohammed retreated into the desert and it is believed that he began to receive divine revelations from Allah via the voice of the archangel Gabriel; the revelations would continue throughout Mohammed's life. Three years later, Mohammed began imparting Allah's message to Meccans, gathering a significant following in his campaign against idolaters. His movement appealed especially to the poorer, disenfranchised sections of society.

Islam provided a simpler alternative to the established faiths, which had become complicated by hierarchical orders, sects and complex rituals, offering instead a direct relationship with God based only on the believer's submission to God (Islam means 'submission').

By 622, Mecca's powerful ruling families had forced Mohammed and his followers to flee north to Medina where Mohammed's supporters rapidly grew. In 630 Mohammed returned triumphantly to Mecca at the head of a 10,000-strong army to seize control of the city. Many of the surrounding tribes quickly swore allegiance to him and the new faith.

When Mohammed died in 632, the Arab tribes spread quickly across the Middle East, in very little time conquering what now constitutes Jordan, Syria, Iraq, Lebanon and Israel and the Palestinian Territories. To the east, Persia and India soon found themselves confronted by the new army of believers. To the west, the unrelenting conquest swept across North Africa. By the end of the 7th century, the Muslims had reached the Atlantic and marched on Spain in 710, an astonishing achievement given the religion's humble desert roots.

Shiite & Sunni

Despite the Prophet Mohammed's original intentions, Islam did not remain simple. The Prophet died leaving no sons and no instructions as to who should succeed him. Competing for power were Abu Bakr, the father of Mohammed's second wife Aisha, and Ali, Mohammed's cousin and

RELIGIONS IN THE MIDDLE EAST

The following graph shows the approximate distribution of Christians, Sunni and Shiite Muslims across the Middle East. For updates on this information, see www.populstat.info.

Jews make up around 80% of Israel's and around 15% of the Palestinian Territories' populations. Christians make up less than 10% of most Middle Eastern populations, except in Lebanon, where 39% of the population is Christian.

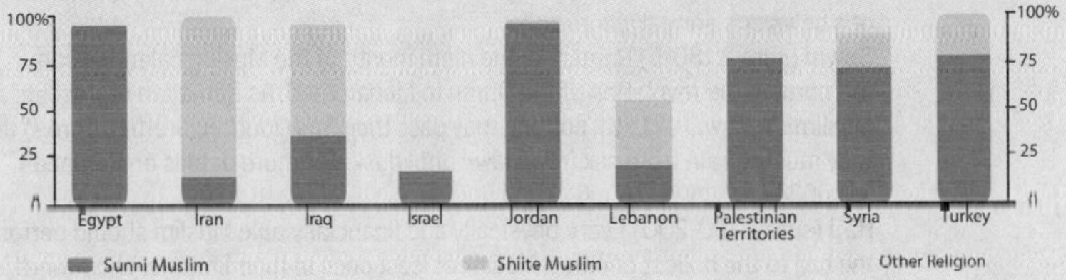

the husband of his daughter Fatima. Initially, the power was transferred to Abu Bakr, who became the first caliph, or ruler, with Ali reluctantly agreeing.

Abu Bakr's lineage came to an abrupt halt when his successor was murdered. Ali reasserted his right to power and emerged victorious in the ensuing power struggle, moving his capital to Kufa (later renamed Najaf, in Iraq), only to be assassinated himself in 661. After defeating Ali's successor, Hussein, in 680 at Karbala, the Umayyad dynasty rose to rule the majority of the Muslim world, marking the start of the Sunni sect. Those who continued to support the claims of the descendants of Ali became known as Shiites.

Beyond this early dynastic rivalry, there's little doctrinal difference between Shiite Islam and Sunni Islam, but the division remains to this day. Sunnis comprise some 90% of the world's Muslims, but Shiites are believed to form a majority of the population in Iraq, Lebanon and Iran. There are also Shiite minorities in almost all Arab countries.

The Story of the Qur'an: Its History and Place in Muslim Life by Ingrid Mattson is a landmark 2007 text that's filled with insights into what it means to be a Muslim in the 21st century.

The Quran

QURAN

For Muslims the Quran is the word of God, directly communicated to Mohammed. It comprises 114 suras, or chapters, which govern all aspects of a Muslim's life.

It's not known whether the revelations were written down during Mohammed's lifetime, although Muslims believe the Quran to be the direct word of Allah as told to Mohammed. The third caliph, Uthman (644–56), gathered together everything written by the scribes (parchments, stone tablets, the memories of Mohammed's followers) and gave them to a panel of editors under the caliph's aegis. A Quran printed today is identical to that agreed upon by Uthman's compilers 14 centuries ago.

Another important aspect of the Quran is the language in which it is written. Some Muslims believe that the Quran must be studied in its original classical Arabic form ('an Arabic Quran, wherein there is no crookedness'; sura 39:25) and that translations dilute the holiness of its sacred texts. For Muslims, the language of the Quran is known as *sihr halal* (lawful magic).

Five Pillars of Islam

In order to live a devout life, Muslims are expected to observe, as a minimum, the five pillars of Islam.

Shahada This is the profession of faith, Islam's basic tenet: 'There is no god but Allah, and Mohammed is the Prophet of Allah'. This phrase forms an integral part of the call to prayer and is used at all important events in a Muslim's life.

Sala (sura 11:115) This is the obligation of prayer, ideally five times a day: at sunrise, noon, mid-afternoon, sunset and night. It's acceptable to pray at home or elsewhere, except for Friday noon prayers, which are performed at a mosque.

Zakat (sura 107) Muslims must give alms to the poor to the value of one-fortieth of a believer's annual income.

Sawm (sura 2:180-5) Ramadan, the ninth month of the Muslim calendar, commemorates the revelation of the Quran to Mohammed. As Ramadan represents a Muslim's renewal of faith, nothing may pass their lips (food, cigarettes, drinks) and they must refrain from sex from dawn until dusk. For more details on Ramadan see p624.

Hajj (sura 2:190-200) Every physically and financially able Muslim should perform the hajj to the holiest of cities, Mecca, at least once in their lifetime. The reward is considerable: the forgiving of all past sins.

Call to Prayer

Five times a day, Muslims are called, if not actually to enter a mosque to pray, at least to take the time to do so where they are; the call to prayer is made by the muezzin. The midday prayers on Friday, when the imam of the mosque delivers his weekly khutba, or sermon, are considered the most important. For Muslims, prayer is less a petition to Allah (in the Christian sense) than a ritual reaffirmation of Allah's power and a reassertion of the brotherhood and equality of all believers.

The act of praying consists of a series of predefined movements of the body and recitals of prayers and passages of the Quran, all designed to express the believer's absolute humility and Allah's sovereignty.

The flight of Mohammed and his followers from Mecca to Medina (the Hejira) marks the birth of Islam and the first year of the Islamic calendar – 1 AH (AD 622).

Islamic Customs

In everyday life, Muslims are prohibited from drinking alcohol (sura 5:90-5) and eating carrion, blood products or pork, which are considered unclean (sura 2:165), the meat of animals not killed in the prescribed manner (sura 5:1-5) and food over which the name of Allah has not been said (sura 6:115). Adultery (sura 18:30-5), theft (sura 5:40-5) and gambling (sura 5:90-5) are also prohibited.

Islam is not just about prohibitions but also marks the important events of a Muslim's life. When a baby is born, the first words uttered to it are the call to prayer. A week later follows a ceremony in which

MUSLIM PRAYER

Allahu akbar, Allahu akbar	God is great, God is great
Ashhadu an la Ilah ila Allah	I testify that there is no God but Allah
Ashhadu an Mohammed rasul Allah	I testify that Mohammed is his Prophet
Haya ala as-sala	Hurry towards prayer
Haya ala af-fala	Hurry towards success
Allahu akbar, Allahu akbar	God is great, God is great
La Ilah ila Allah	There is no God but Allah

THINGS WE SHARE

Despite what you read in the papers, the differences between the three religions are fewer than you might think. As most Muslims will attest, the God invoked in Friday prayers across the Middle East is the same God worshipped in synagogues and churches around the globe. Where they differ is in their understanding of when God's revelations ceased. While Judaism adheres to the Old Testament, Christianity adds the teachings of the New Testament, and Muslims claim that their holy book, the Quran, is the final expression of Allah's will and the ultimate and definitive guide to his intentions for humankind.

The Quran never attempts to deny the debt it owes to the holy books that came before it. Indeed the Quran itself was revealed to Mohammed by the archangel Gabriel. The suras contain many references to the earlier prophets – Adam, Abraham (Ibrahim), Noah, Moses (Moussa) and Jesus (although Muslims strictly deny his divinity) are all recognised as prophets in a line that ends definitively with the greatest of them all, Mohammed. Not surprisingly, given the shared heritage, Muslims traditionally attribute a place of great respect to Christians and Jews as *ahl al-kitab* (the people of the book, sura 2:100-15).

the baby's head is shaved and an animal sacrificed in remembrance of Abraham's willingness to sacrifice his son to Allah. The major event of a boy's childhood is circumcision, which normally takes place between the ages of seven and 12. When a person dies, a burial service is held at the mosque and the body is buried with the feet facing Mecca.

Judaism

Judaism is the first recorded monotheistic faith and one of the oldest religions still practised. Its major tenet is that there is one God who created the universe and remains omnipresent. Judaism's power is held not in a central authority or person, but rather in its teachings and the Holy Scriptures.

Until the foundation of the State of Israel in 1948, Jewish communities lived peacefully alongside their Muslim neighbours in all countries of the Middle East covered by this book; Iraq was home to a particularly large Jewish community. Tiny Jewish communities may remain in some Muslim countries, but most fled or were expelled in the years following 1948.

A Brief Guide to Judaism: Theology, History and Practice by Naftali Brawer is one of the better introductions to what is often a complex faith, focusing on major ideas and historical events rather than the minutiae of Jewish doctrine.

Foundations of Judaism

The patriarch of the faith was Abraham who, according to the calculations of the Hebrew Torah, was born 1948 years after Creation and lived to the ripe old age of 175. According to Jewish belief he preached the existence of one God and in return God promised him the land of Canaan (the Promised Land in Jewish tradition), but only after his descendants would be exiled and redeemed. Accordingly, his grandson Jacob set off for Egypt, where later generations found themselves bound in slavery. Moses led them out of Egypt and received the Ten Commandments on Mt Sinai.

It was Rambam, the 12th-century Jewish rabbi, who laid out the 13 core principles of Jewish belief. These principles include the belief in one unique God to whom prayer must be directed; the belief that God rewards the good and punishes the wicked; and the belief in the coming of the Messiah and the resurrection of the dead. Having said this, Judaism doesn't focus on abstract cosmological beliefs and rather than a strict adherence to dogmatic ideas, actions such as prayer, study and performing mitzvah, which means adherence to the commandments, are of greater importance.

The Torah & Talmud

The basis for the Jewish religion is the Torah, the first five books of the Old Testament. The Torah contains the revelation from God via Moses more than 3000 years ago, including, most importantly, God's commandments (613 commandments in total). The Torah is supplemented by the rest of the books of the Old Testament, of which the most important are the prophetic books.

These books are, in turn, complemented by the Talmud, a collection of another 63 books. The Talmud was written largely in exile after the Romans crushed the Jewish state and destroyed the Temple in Jerusalem in AD 70, and within its pages is most of what separates Judaism from other religions. Included are plenty of rabbinical interpretations of the earlier scriptures, with a wealth of instructions and rulings for Jewish daily life.

Jewish Customs

The most obvious Jewish custom you'll experience in Israel is Shabbat, the day of rest. It begins on Friday night with sundown and ends at nightfall on Saturday. No work of any kind is allowed on Shabbat, unless someone's health is at stake. Tasks such as writing or handling money are forbidden. Starting a fire is also prohibited and in modern terms this means no use of electricity is allowed (lights can be turned on before Shabbat starts but must stay on until it ends). Permitted activities include visiting with friends and family, reading and discussing the Torah, and prayer at a synagogue. Sex is also allowed; in fact, it's a double mitzvah on Shabbat.

God's laws, as recorded in the Torah, govern every facet of an observant Jew's life, including issues like the prohibition of theft, murder and idolatry. There are other commandments to which Jews must adhere, such as eating kosher foods and reciting the shema (affirmation of Judaism) twice daily.

Some Jewish sects are easily recognised by their clothing, although most Jews wear Western street clothes. The most religious Jews, the Hasidim (or *haredim*), are identified by their black hats, long black coats, collared white shirts, beards and *peyot* (side curls). *Haredi* women, like Muslim women, act and dress modestly, covering up exposed hair and skin (except the hands and face).

Many Jews, both secular and orthodox, wear a kippa (skullcap). It's sometimes possible to infer a person's background and religious or even political beliefs by the type of kippa they wear. A large crocheted kippa, often in white, is a sign that the wearer is either a Braslav Hassid or a Messianist, perhaps an extreme right-wing settler. Muted brown or blue kippot (skullcaps) that are crocheted generally indicate strong Zionist beliefs; the Israel Defence Forces (IDF) provides standard-issue olive kippot.

JEWISH PRESENCE

Reeva Simon's *The Jews of the Middle East and North Africa in Modern Times* looks at the Jewish presence in the region during the last two centuries, with half of the book taken up with country-by-country sections that include Turkey, Syria, Iraq, Lebanon, Egypt and Israel and the Palestinian Territories.

Christianity

Jesus preached in what is present-day Israel and the Palestinian Territories, but Christians form only minority groups in all Middle Eastern countries. Lebanon's one million Maronites have followers all over the world, but by far the biggest Christian sect in the region is formed by the Copts of Egypt, who make up most of that country's Christian population. Originally it was the apostle Mark who established Christianity in Egypt, and by the 4th century it was the state religion. The Coptic Church split from the Byzantine Orthodox Church in the 5th century after a dispute about the human nature of Jesus.

Christianity is the world's largest religion, with an estimated 2 billion followers. Islam comes next with at least 1.3 billion adherents. Judaism has an estimated 14 to 18 million people.

THE BIBLE AS HISTORY

For archaeologists in the 'Holy Lands', where the events related in the Bible's Old Testament are said to have taken place, little in the way of written archives has been found and historians cannot say for sure whether characters such as Abraham, Moses or even Solomon existed. The Old Testament was compiled from a variety of sources and probably set down in script no earlier than the 6th century BC.

When it comes to the New Testament and episodes related in the Gospels by Matthew, Mark, Luke and John, this was the Roman era and there are numerous written accounts, inscriptions and works of art that enable us to say with certainty that Herod, Pontius Pilate and a man called Jesus did exist. Even so, many sites commonly held to be of biblical significance were only fixed in the 4th century, some 300 years after the death of Christ.

Otherwise, the Arab Christians of the Middle East belong to many churches in all main branches of the religion – Orthodox, Catholic and Protestant. The number of Christians in the Middle East is, however, in decline thanks largely to falling birth rates and high rates of emigration among the region's Christians.

Foundations of Christianity

Jesus of Nazareth was born in Bethlehem in what is now the Palestinian Territories in the year zero (or AD 1, depending on who you believe) of the Christian calendar. After baptism by John the Baptist, Jesus was said to have been led by God into the desert, where he remained for 40 days and nights, during which time he refuted the temptations of the Devil. It is said that his ministry was marked by numerous miracles, such as healings, walking on water and the resuscitation of the dead (Lazarus). At the age of 33, Jesus was accused of sedition and condemned to death by Jerusalem's Roman governor Pontius Pilate. After being crucified, Christians believe that Jesus was resurrected and ascended to heaven. Although doctrinal differences have tied Christian scholars and adherents in knots for centuries – hence the proliferation of different sects – Christians believe that God's divine nature is expressed in the Trinity: God, Jesus Christ and the Holy Spirit.

From the Holy Mountain: A Journey in the Shadow of Byzantium by William Dalrymple takes the reader through the heart of the Middle East and pays homage to the survival of Eastern Christianity.

The followers of Jesus came to be known as Christians (Christ is a Greek-derived title meaning 'Anointed One'), believing him to be the son of God and the Messiah. Within a few decades of Jesus' death, having interpreted and spread his teachings, his followers had formed a faith distinct from Judaism. A Greek-speaking Christian community emerged in Jerusalem in the mid-2nd century and the Greek Orthodox Church is now the largest denomination in Israel and the Palestinian Territories, having jurisdiction over more than half of Jerusalem's Church of the Holy Sepulchre and a bigger portion of Bethlehem's Church of the Nativity than anybody else. Numerous other denominations claim bits and pieces of other holy sites and ownership is fiercely defended.

Architecture

Middle Eastern architecture ranges from the sublime to the downright ugly. On one hand, the graceful lines of Islamic architecture draw on the rich historical legacy left by the great empires that once ruled the region. On the other, the perennially unfinished cinder-block architecture of grim functionality blights many city outskirts and smaller towns. We prefer to concentrate on the former.

Ancient World

Ancient Egyptian Architecture

Ancient Egyptian Architecture

- » Pyramids of Giza
- » Temple of Karnak
- » Great Temple of Abu Simbel
- » Temple of Hathor
- » Valley of the Kings
- » Temple of Horus
- » Luxor Temple
- » Temple of Philae
- » Egyptian Museum

The tombs and temples of ancient Egypt rank among the Middle East's most impressive architectural forms. Whereas private homes have disappeared – most were built of sun-dried mud-brick and occurred along now-flooded stretches of the Nile Valley – ancient Egypt's public architecture has stood the test of time. In most cases, Pharaonic tombs and temples (including the Pyramids of Giza) were built of locally quarried sandstone and sturdy granite. Another reason they have survived is that most were built on higher ground than residential areas, and thus have remained above the levels reached by the floodwaters of the Nile.

The tombs of ancient Egypt were designed at once to impress with their grandeur and to deter tomb raiders from plundering the treasures contained within. As a result, most were almost fortress-like, with thick sloping walls, very few openings and labyrinthine passageways in the interior. Tomb decoration was often elaborate, adorned with hieroglyphics and frescos, and it is from such imagery that archaeologists have been able to piece together so much of what we know about the period, from religious beliefs and the afterlife to questions of dynastic succession.

Such paintings also adorned the facades of temples, and temple hieroglyphics, once decoded, have also become another rich source of information about historical events and even everyday life. Egyptian temples, each dedicated to one among many Egyptian gods, are most often characterised by the use of flat roofs, massive stone blocks and tightly spaced columns. Most were also aligned with important astronomical occurrences, their measurements and design carefully calculated by royal astronomers and, in some cases, the pharaohs themselves.

Greek & Roman Architecture

Although it is Roman architecture that dominates the ruined cities that are such a feature of travelling in the Middle East, the Romans drew heavily on the architecture of the ancient Greeks. Indeed, it was from the Greeks that the Romans acquired their prototypes for temples, theatres, monumental gateways, public squares (agora to the Greeks, forum to the Romans) and colonnaded thoroughfares.

But in the Middle East at least it was the Romans who perfected these forms and it is the Roman version that endures, at once monumental in scale and extremely intricate in their detail. They also added their own innovations, many of them to do with water – perhaps the most enduring of these are aqueducts and the concept of richly decorated public baths, the forerunner to the hammam.

Most of the buildings that survive played critical roles in public Roman life: the temples were the focus of religious devotion, the theatres and amphitheatres were the centrepieces of public entertainment and the monumental arched gateways reinforced the cult that surrounded the emperors of ancient Rome. Private homes, often belonging to wealthy noble families, often had floors paved in intricate mosaics.

Aside from individual elements of public Roman architecture, the whole was also extremely important and it was in town planning that the Romans really made their mark. In the cities of the ancient Roman Empire, city life revolved around a public square (forum), which was a meeting place (and sometimes a market) and surrounded by imposing temples and administrative buildings. A well-ordered grid of streets, paved with flagstones and sometimes lined with porticoes, surrounded the forum, with two main streets – the north–south cardo and the east–west decumanus, which usually intersected at the forum providing the main thoroughfares. An outer defensive wall, beyond which lay farmland, usually encircled the core of the city.

Greek & Roman Architecture

» Ephesus (Efes), Turkey

» Baalbek, Lebanon

» Palmyra, Syria

» Caesarea, Israel

» Jerash, Jordan

» Temple of Amun, Egypt

Places of Worship

Mosques

Embodying the Islamic faith and representing its most predominant architectural feature throughout the region is the masjid (mosque, also called a *jamaa*). The building, developed in the very early days of the religion, takes its form from the simple private houses where the first believers gathered to worship.

Prayer Hall

The house belonging to the Prophet Mohammed is said to have provided the prototype of the mosque. It had an enclosed oblong courtyard with huts (housing Mohammed's wives) along one wall and a rough portico providing shade. This plan developed with the courtyard becoming the *sahn*, the portico the arcaded *riwaq* and the house the *haram* (prayer hall).

The prayer hall is typically divided into a series of aisles. The central aisle is wider than the rest and leads to a vaulted niche in the wall called the mihrab; this indicates the direction of Mecca, towards which Muslims must face when they pray. Also in the prayer hall is usually a minbar (a wooden pulpit that stands beside the mihrab), from where the imam delivers his khutba (sermon) at the main Friday noon prayers.

Before entering the prayer hall and participating in communal worship, Muslims must perform a ritual washing of the hands, forearms, neck and face (by washing themselves before prayer, the believer indicates a willingness to be purified). For this purpose mosques have traditionally had a large ablutions fountain at the centre of the courtyard, often fashioned from marble and worn by centuries of use. These days, modern mosques just have rows of taps.

Rising above the main mosque structure is at least one (but often numerous) minarets, some of which were adapted from former church steeples. In ancient times, the minaret was where the muezzin climbed to call the faithful to prayer – these days, a loudspeaker performs a similar function.

Stylistic Developments

Within these overarching architectural themes, each region developed its own local flourishes. The Umayyads of Damascus favoured square minarets, the Abbasid dynasty built spiral minarets echoing the ziggurats of the Babylonians, and the Fatimids of Egypt made much use of decorative stucco work. The Mamluks (1250–1517), a military dynasty of former slaves ruling out of Egypt, brought a new level of sophistication to mosque architecture – their buildings are characterised by the banding of different coloured stone (a technique known as *ablaq*) and by the elaborate carvings and patterning around windows and in the recessed portals. The best examples of their patronage are found in Cairo but impressive Mamluk monuments also grace the old cities of Damascus, Tripoli and Jerusalem. Tripoli's Taynal Mosque and Cairo's Mosque of Qaitbey, with its exquisitely carved dome, are perhaps the high points of Mamluk style.

Islam: Art & Architecture, edited by Markus Hattstein and Peter Delius, is comprehensive, lavishly illustrated and one of those coffee-table books that you'll treasure and dip into time and again.

But it was the Ottoman Turks who left the most recognisable (and, given the reach of the Ottoman Empire, widespread) landmarks. Ottoman mosques were designed on the basic principle of a dome on a square, and are instantly recognisable by their slim pencil-shaped minarets. The Süleymaniye Camii in İstanbul and the Selimiye Mosque in Edirne, both the work of the Turkish master architect Sinan, represent the apogee of the style.

Synagogues

Although many synagogues follow a similar style, there is also great variety in their architectural forms. This is partly because Jewish tradition dictates that God can be present wherever there are 10 adults gathered together.

There are, however, some elements common to all synagogues. The first of these is the presence of an ark (in some cases simply a cupboard,

AGA KHAN: ISLAMIC ARCHITECTURE'S SAVIOUR

If there's one figure who has been responsible above all others for reviving Islamic architecture worldwide, it's the Aga Khan. The Aga Khan IV, the current imam (religious teacher) of the largest branch of the Ismaili Shia Muslims, inherited a vast family fortune upon succeeding to this hereditary position in 1957. Ever since, he has set about putting the money to good use.

Through the Aga Khan Development Network (www.akdn.org), one of the largest private development organisations in the world, the Aga Khan funds programs encompassing public health, education, microfinance, rural development and architecture. His interventions in the field of architecture in a region blighted by decades of ill-conceived development and urban decay have been particularly eye-catching.

The main focus of his efforts has been the Historic Cities Program, which aims to rescue, restore and bring back to life public buildings across the Islamic world. Egypt and Syria have been the main beneficiaries in the Middle East. Rather than focusing solely on bricks and mortar, the projects prioritise improvements in social infrastructure and living conditions in surrounding areas, thereby transforming architectural restoration into wider projects for social renewal.

A further pillar in the Aga Khan's master plan has been the triennial Aga Khan Award for Architecture (www.akdn.org/akaa.asp), one of the world's most prestigious architecture awards. The award's primary aim is to promote excellence and creativity in Islamic architecture within a framework of heritage values and contemporary design, with special consideration given to social, historical and environmental issues. Winning projects since the award was announced in 1977 have included the restorations of İstanbul's Topkapı Palace, Cairo's Citadel of Saladin and Aleppo citadel.

or a chest), which contains the scrolls of the Torah. All synagogues also have a table (or in some cases a platform or pulpit) from which the Torah can be read, and from where some services are conducted. In most synagogues, a light is also illuminated at all times to symbolise the menorah (candelabra) in the Temple in Jerusalem. The synagogue, or at the very least its prayer room, should also be aligned to face towards Jerusalem.

There are also a number of Talmudic instructions on the form that synagogues should take – they must have windows and be taller than other buildings in town – although these were often ignored or simply not possible.

Other features of Jewish religious architecture vary from one synagogue to the next – some are simple prayer rooms, others are adorned with inscriptions in Hebrew and otherwise richly decorated. In many cases, there are also separate sections of the synagogue for men and women.

Synagogues

» Hurva Synagogue, Jerusalem

» Western Wall, Jerusalem

» Hamat Tveriya National Park

» Beit Alpha

» Synagogue Quarter, Tsfat

» Tzipori

» Hisham's Palace, Jericho

Churches

As with synagogues, Christian architecture varies greatly, although there are some mainstays amid such diversity. After the first three centuries of Christianity (during which time the faith was illegal and when worshippers most often gathered in private homes), the church evolved from a one-room meeting place to one that contained a space for the congregation and a separate space where the priest could perform the rites of Mass. Over time, church architecture became more sophisticated with aisles (which became necessary as churches grew in size), a steeple (which usually housed the bells), chapels and a baptistery.

Early church architecture, and indeed many of its most enduring forms, owes much to the Romans. It was not the temples that provided the greatest inspiration because these had little space for the congregation. Rather, inspiration (and indeed the name) came from the Roman basilicas which were not places of worship but places for meetings, markets and administrative functions such as courts. More specifically, many Roman basilicas had a semi-circular apse covered with a half-dome roof, which became an essential element in later church architecture. Roman mausoleums, with their square or circular domed structures, also filtered into Christian architecture – Jerusalem's Church of the Holy Sepulchre is one clear example of this trend.

Architecture and Polyphony: Building in the Islamic World Today is an exciting work stemming from the Aga Khan Award for Architecture. It's filled with the innovations of modern Middle Eastern architecture – an antidote to the dominance of mosques in the aesthetics of Middle Eastern cities.

Another crucial and oft-observed element of church architecture is a floor plan in the shape of a cross. Although the exact shape of this cross may vary depending on the region and date of construction, the two main forms mimic the Latin and Greek crosses – the former has a rectangular form and has a long nave crossed by a shorter transept, while the Greek cross design was usually square with the four 'arms' of equal length.

For two fine examples of ancient Christian monasteries, in Iraq and Egypt respectively, see p164 and p137.

Mosaics were also a stunning feature of churches, particularly in Byzantine times. The best examples are in Madaba in Jordan.

Secular Architecture

Urban Buildings

Palaces & Private Homes

It's in the cities of the Middle East that you'll find the region's major architectural landmarks. Beyond the soaring mosques that adorn city skylines at almost every turn, it's the private world of palaces and homes that truly distinguishes urban Middle Eastern architecture. Often hidden behind high walls, these palaces were built on the premise of keeping the outside world at bay, allowing families to retreat into a generous-size refuge.

Usually built around a courtyard, these private homes and palaces were perfectly adapted to the dictates of climate and communal living. The homes often housed up to a dozen families, each with their own space opening onto the shared patio. The palaces worked on the same principle, containing the royal living quarters with separate rooms for women and domestic staff. Most such residences included a cooling central fountain and an iwan (arched alcove that served as a summer retreat), and were adorned with tilework, woodcarved lintels and elegant arches. Comfortable and stylish, private and largely self-contained, these homes were ideally suited to a region with long, hot summers and where complicated rules of engagement existed between the public and private spheres. You'll find such architecture in most Middle Eastern cities, but the most splendid examples are in Damascus.

Urban Spaces

The Middle East's cities are also where the failure of architecture and urban planning to keep pace with burgeoning populations is most distressingly on show. Take Cairo, for example. In 1950, Cairo had a population of around 2.3 million. Now as many as 18 million people live cheek-by-jowl within greater Cairo's ever-expanding boundaries. The result is an undistinguished sprawl of grime-coated, Soviet-style apartment blocks and unplanned shanty towns, often without even the most basic amenities.

A TALE OF THREE CITIES

Aleppo & Damascus

A major issue facing urban Middle Eastern architecture is the decay of the beautiful homes of the old cities that once formed the core of Damascus, Aleppo and other cities. Throughout the 20th century, the trend was for old-city residents to leave homes that had been in their families for generations and move into modern homes in newer parts of town. Emptying old cities with ageing infrastructure were left behind and vulnerable to developers.

Belatedly, but perhaps just in time, something is being done to halt the decline. Since 1994, Unesco, the local Aleppo government and the German Agency for Technical Cooperation have been involved in an ambitious program of rehabilitation to make the remaining areas of Aleppo's old town more liveable. A similar plan was also in its early stages in Damascus until the program was put on hold due to the conflict in Syria. Tourism is playing an important role in bringing Syria's old cities back to life – many courtyard homes in Damascus and Aleppo have been saved from the wrecker's ball, painstakingly restored and converted into boutique hotels.

Cairo

Even more ambitious has been the attempt to impose some order onto Cairo's unsightly sprawl. Funded by the Aga Khan Development Network (see the boxed text, p586), the first stage of the US$30 million project involved creating the 30-hectare Al-Azhar Park on land reclaimed from what had been a rubbish dump for 500 years. The project also involved restoring 1.5km of the 12th-century Ayyubid Wall, rescuing a number of dilapidated mosques and an integrated plan for improving housing, infrastructure and living conditions in the adjacent Darb al-Ahmar, one of Cairo's poorest districts and home to more than 90,000 people; many of the rooftops were fitted with solar heating systems, water cisterns and vegetable gardens. It's one of the most exciting projects for urban renewal seen in the Middle East for decades. Let's hope it encourages other governments to do the same.

Rural Buildings

Architecture in rural areas of the Middle East has always been a highly localised tradition, determined primarily by the dictates of climate. In the oases, particularly the Saharan towns of Egypt's Western Oases, mud-brick was easy to manufacture and ensured cool interiors under the baking desert sun. Although perfectly adapted to ordinary climatic conditions, these homes also proved extremely vulnerable to erosion and rains, which explains why so few examples remain across the region.

Among other natural building forms in the Middle East, the extremely sturdy conical beehive houses of central Syria are among the most distinctive. They owe their endurance to the whitewashing of the unusually thick mud walls, which reflects the sun and slows the ageing of the underlying structural materials.

But the undoubted star when it comes to unique traditional architecture is Cappadocia (Kapadokya), where homes and churches were hewn from the weird and wonderful landscape of caves, rock walls and soft volcanic tuff.

But most forms of vernacular rural architecture face an uncertain future. Unrelenting urbanisation in Middle Eastern cities has stripped rural areas of much of their lifeblood. The result has been the widespread abandonment of traditional forms of architecture. Rural poverty has led to government-housing programs, which have chosen modern concrete constructions rather than the more expensive adaptations of the indigenous forms that coexisted in perfect harmony with the environment for centuries. The simple truth about the future of rural architecture in the Middle East is this: unless places become established as tourist attractions, their traditional architecture will disappear within a generation, if it hasn't done so already.

CAIRO

Per capita, Cairo has one of the lowest ratios of green space to urban population on earth with just one footprint-sized plot of earth per inhabitant.

Middle Eastern Cuisine

For all the religious, political and social issues that divide the region, an emphatic belief in the importance of good food is one thing on which all the people of the Middle East agree. And little wonder given what's on offer.

Remember also that Middle Easterners see eating as a social event to be shared with family and friends, a means of marking the most important moments in life, and a pastime that's worth spending hours over. In short, life revolves around food. Add to this the hospitality that transforms eating into a celebration where everyone's welcome and you'll quickly come to understand that the whole culture of eating here is almost as enjoyable as the food itself.

Staples & Specialities

At times, Middle Eastern cooking draws on a range of influences, from sophisticated Ottoman and Persian sensibilities, or the spare improvisation of the desert cooking pot, to a Mediterranean belief in letting fresh ingredients speak for themselves. At others, the Middle East's gastronomic traditions can be relatively simple when it comes to a meal's constituent elements. Where the excitement really lies is in the astonishing variety at large in its feasts of colour and complementary tastes.

A New Book of Middle Eastern Food by Claudia Roden brought the cuisines of the region to the attention of Western cooks when it was released in 1968. It's still an essential reference, as fascinating for its cultural insights as for its great recipes.

Mezze

Mezze (meze in Turkish) ranks alongside Spanish tapas and Italian antipasto as one of the world's greatest culinary inventions. A collection of appetisers or small plates of food, mezze allows you to sample a variety of often complementary tastes and takes the difficulty out of choosing what to order – choose everything! Mezze mirrors the time-honoured practice of hosts throwing a party, offering up for their guests a banquet of choice. Largely vegetable-based and bursting with colour and flavour, it's the region's most compelling culinary flourish.

Although it's usually perfectly acceptable for diners to construct an entire meal from the mezze list and forgo the mains on offer, there are subtle differences from country to country in just how far you can take this mezze obsession. Mezze is the headline act when it comes to Levantine cuisine, but it's the understudy to kebabs in Turkey and the trusted warm-up to the region's other cuisines. For more on mezze in Lebanon, see p354.

Breads

For all the variety of the Middle Eastern table, bread (*khobz* or *a'aish*, which means 'life') is the guaranteed constant, considered a gift from God and the essential accompaniment to any Middle Eastern meal. In fact, it's considered such a necessity that few Middle Eastern restaurants dare to charge a cent for it. If you're wandering through the streets of an Arab city in the morning and you see a large queue forming at an otherwise innocuous hole in the wall, you've almost certainly stumbled upon the local bakery. Fresh bread is the only way that Middle Easterners will have it.

The staple Middle Eastern bread follows a 2000-year-old recipe. Unleavened and cooked over an open flame, it's used in lieu of cutlery to scoop dips and ripped into pieces to wrap around morsels of meat. Dinner is always served with baskets of bread to mop up mezze, while kebabs are often served with a tasty bread canopy coated in tomato, parsley and spices.

Arabesque: Modern Middle Eastern Food by Greg and Lucy Malouf lists the 42 essential ingredients from the region and offers insights into how they can be used to create authentic dishes.

Salads

It's inconceivable for most people in the region to eat a meal without salad. In summer, it's almost sacrilegious, considering the zest and freshness that Middle Eastern salads bring to a meal, perfectly complementing a piping hot kebab. Middle Easterners are loyal to their basic salads and don't mind eating them meal after meal. Elaborations or creative flourishes are rare and simplicity is the key: crunchy fresh ingredients (including herbs), often caressed by a shake of oil and vinegar at the table. Salads are eaten with relish as a mezze or as an accompaniment to a meat or fish main course. Three salads, found throughout the region, form an integral part of the local diet:

fattoosh – toasted *khobz*, tomatoes, onions and mint leaves, sometimes served with a smattering of tangy pomegranate syrup
shepherd's salad – colourful mix of chopped tomatoes, cucumber, onion and pepper; extremely popular in Turkey, where it's known as *çoban salatası*
tabbouleh – the region's signature salad combines burghul wheat, parsley and tomato, with a tangy sprinkling of sesame seeds, lemon and garlic

POPULAR MEZZE SPECIALITIES

Among the seemingly endless candidates, we've narrowed it down to the following dishes (spellings may differ from country to country).

baba ghanoog – purée of grilled aubergines (eggplants) with tahina and olive oil

basturma – cold, sliced meat cured with fenugreek

borek – pastry stuffed with salty white cheese or spicy minced meat with pine nuts; also known as *sambousek*

fatayer – triangular deep-fried pastries stuffed with spinach, meat or cheese

hummus bi tahina – cooked chickpeas ground into a paste and mixed with tahini, lemon, olive oil and garlic

kibbeh – minced lamb, burghul wheat and pine nuts made into a lemon-shaped patty and deep-fried

labneh – thick yogurt flavoured with garlic and sometimes with mint

loobieh – French bean salad with tomatoes, onions and garlic

mouhamarra – walnut and pomegranate syrup dip

muttabal – purée of aubergine mixed with tahini, yogurt and olive oil; similar to but creamier than baba ghanoog

shanklish – tangy, eye-wateringly strong goat's cheese served with onions, oil and tomatoes

tahina – paste made of sesame seeds and served as a dip

wara ainab – stuffed vine leaves, served both hot and cold; in Egypt also called mahshi

Snack Foods

The regional stars of the snack-food line-up are shwarma and felafel, and they're both things of joy when served and eaten fresh. Shwarma is the Arabic equivalent of the Greek *gyros* sandwich or the Turkish döner kebap – strips are sliced from a vertical spit of compressed lamb or chicken, sizzled on a hot plate with chopped tomatoes and garnish, then stuffed into a pocket of bread. Felafel is mashed chickpeas and spices rolled into balls and deep-fried; a variation known as ta'amiyya, made with dried fava beans, is served in Egypt.

In Egypt look out for shops sporting large metal tureens in the window: these specialise in the vegetarian delight *kushari,* a delicate mix of noodles, rice, black lentils and dried onions, served with an accompanying tomato sauce that's sometimes fiery with chilli. An alternative more often seen at Israeli sandwich stands is *shakshuka,* a Moroccan dish of eggs poached in tangy stewed tomatoes, which makes a good breakfast but is eaten any time.

In Lebanon, nothing beats grabbing a freshly baked *fatayer bi sbanikh* (spinach pastry) from one of the hole-in-the-wall bakeries that dot city streets. In Turkey, visitors inevitably fall deeply in love with melt-in-the-mouth *su böreği,* a noodle-like pastry oozing cheese and butter.

Variations of the pizza abound, one of the most delicious being Egypt's *fiteer,* featuring a base of thin, filo-style pastry. Try it topped with salty haloumi cheese, or even with a mixture of sugar-dusted fruit. In Turkey, the best cheap snack is pide, the Turkish version of pizza, a canoe-shaped dough topped with *peynirli* (cheese), *yumurtalı* (egg) or *kıymalı* (mince). A *karaşık pide* will have a mixture of toppings.

The most unassuming of all Middle Eastern fast foods is also one of the most popular. Fuul is mopped up by bread for breakfast and ladled into a pocket of bread for a snack on the run. You'll find it in Egypt (where it's the national dish), Syria, Jordan, Lebanon and Iraq.

COOKBOOK

The Complete Middle East Cookbook by Tess Mallos is full of easy-to-follow recipes and devotes individual chapters to national cuisines, including those of Turkey, Iraq, Iran, Egypt and Israel.

Kebabs & Other Meats

There are more variations on the kebab in this part of the world than you could poke a skewer at. Every country has its specialities – Syria has the delicious *kebab Halebi* (Aleppine kebab, served with a spicy tomato sauce), Turkey is understandably proud of its luscious *İskender kebap* (döner kebap on a bed of pide bread with a side serving of yogurt) and Lebanon has an unswerving devotion to *shish tawooq* (grilled chicken kebab, often served with a garlic sauce).

The kebab might be king, but when it comes to meat dishes there are courtiers waiting in the wings. Primary among these is *kibbeh,* a strong candidate for the title of Lebanon's national dish. Indeed, these croquettes of ground lamb, cracked wheat, onion and spices are considered the ultimate test of a Lebanese cook's skills. In Damascus *kibbeh* are shaped into mini footballs and stuffed with spiced lamb, pine nuts and walnuts, then shallow-fried until golden brown. In Beirut they're served raw like a steak tartare, accompanied with fresh mint leaves, olive oil and spring onions. Raw *kibbeh (kibbeh nayye)* has many variations. In northern Lebanon you often find mint and fresh chillies mixed through the meat. In Aleppo, a chilli paste is layered on top of the *kibbeh* with walnuts and onions. *Kibbeh saniye* is *kibbeh* flattened out on a tray with a layer of spiced lamb and pine nuts in between.

Another culinary star is *kofta* (spiced ground meat formed into balls; *köfte* in Turkey), which is served in innumerable ways and is the signature element of the Egyptian favourite *daood basha* (meatballs cooked in a *tagen* pot with pine nuts and tomato sauce).

The Turkish dish *imam bayıldı* ('the imam fainted') is aubergine stuffed with onion and garlic, slow-cooked in olive oil and served cold. Legend has it that an imam fainted with pleasure on first tasting it.

VEGETARIANS & VEGANS

Though it's quite normal for the people of the Middle East to eat a vegetarian meal, the concept of vegetarianism is quite foreign. Say you're a vegan and they will either look mystified or assume that you're 'fessing up to some strain of socially aberrant behaviour.

Fortunately, it's not that difficult to find vegetable-based dishes. You'll find yourself eating loads of mezze and salads, fuul, tasty cheese and spinach pastries, the occasional omelette or oven-baked vegetable *tagens* (stews baked in a terracotta pot) featuring okra and aubergine.

Watch out also for those vegetables that are particular to Middle Eastern cuisine, including *molokhiyya* (aka *moolookhiye* or *melokhia*), a slimy but surprisingly sexy green leafy vegetable known in the West as mallow. In Egypt it's made into an earthy garlic-flavoured soup that has a glutinous texture and inspires an almost religious devotion among the locals. In Syria and Lebanon *molokhiyya* is used to make strongly spiced lamb and chicken stews.

The main source of inadvertent meat eating is meat stock, which is often used to make otherwise vegetarian pilafs, soups and vegetable dishes. Your hosts may not even consider such stock to be meat, so may assure you that the dish is vegetarian. Chicken and mutton are the biggest hide-and-seekers in the region's food, often lurking in vegetable dishes and mezze.

The best country for vegetarians is Israel, where kosher laws don't permit the mixing of meat and dairy products, resulting in a lot of 'dairy' restaurants where no meat in any form is served.

Rice Dishes

Although not native to the Middle East, rice is a region-wide staple that's ever-present in home cooking but far less common on restaurant menus. Usually cooked with lamb or chicken, a subtle blend of spices and sometimes saffron, its arrival as the centrepiece of an already groaning table is often a high point of the meal. It's also the point at which you wish you hadn't eaten so much mezze.

If your average Middle Easterner loves rice, it's the Bedouins who revere it. Easy to store, transport and cook, rice was perfectly suited to the once-nomadic lifestyle of many Bedouin. For this hardy desert people, *mensaf* (lamb served on a bed of rice and pine nuts and accompanied by a tangy yogurt sauce) is what it's all about. Such is *mensaf's* popularity that you'll find it on menus in the Palestinian Territories, Jordan and Syria (especially around Palmyra).

Another regional rice specialty that won't disappoint is *makhlooba* (literally 'upside-down') rice, which Damascenes adore. It's cooked in stock and spices with chickpeas, onions and off-the-bone lamb shanks, then pressed in a deep bowl and turned upside down to reveal a delicious work of art. The vegetarian version incorporates eggplants with almonds and pine nuts.

To ask, 'Do you have any vegetarian dishes?' in Egypt say, '*Andak akla nabateeyya?*' In Turkey ask, '*Etsiz yemekler var mı?*' (Is there something to eat that has no meat?) In other countries ask for dishes that are '*bidoon lahem*' (without meat).

Desserts & Sweets

All Middle Easterners love their sweets but they come closest to worshipping them in Syria and Turkey. The prince of the regional desserts is undoubtedly *muhalabiyya* (also known as *mahallabiye*), a blancmange-like concoction made of ground rice, milk, sugar, and rose or orange water, topped with chopped pistachios and almonds. Almost as popular is *ruz bi laban* (rice pudding, known as *fırın sütlaç* in Turkey).

But best of all are the pastries. Although these are sometimes served in restaurants for dessert, they're just as often enjoyed as an any-time-of-the-day snack. Old favourites include *kunafa,* a vermicelli-like pastry over a vanilla base soaked in syrup; and the famous baklava, made from delicate filo drenched in honey or syrup. Variations on baklava are flavoured with fresh nuts or stuffed with wickedly rich clotted cream (called *kaymak* in Turkey, *eishta* elsewhere).

Drinks

Tea & Coffee

Drinking tea *(shai, chai* or *çay)* is the signature pastime of the region and it is seen as strange and decidedly antisocial not to swig the tannin-laden beverage at regular intervals throughout the day. The tea will either come in the form of a tea bag plonked in a cup or glass of hot water (Lipton is the usual brand) or a strong brew of the local leaves. Sometimes it's served with *na'ana* (mint) and it always comes with sugar. Be warned that you'll risk severe embarrassment if you ask for milk, unless you're in a tourist hotel or restaurant.

Damascus: Tastes of a City by Rafik Schami is one of the most engaging books written about Middle Eastern food, introducing you to the kitchens and characters of Old Damascus.

Surprisingly, Turkish or Arabic coffee *(qahwa)* is not widely consumed in the region, with instant coffee (always called Nescafé) being far more common. If you do find the real stuff, it's likely to be a thick and powerful Turkish-style brew that's served in small cups and drunk in a couple of short sips. In private homes, a good guest will accept a minimum of three cups but when you've had enough, gently tilt the cup from side to side (in Arabic, 'dancing' the cup).

Alcoholic Drinks

Though the region is predominantly Muslim and hence abstemious, most countries have a local beer. The best are Turkey's Efes, Egypt's Stella and Sakkara, Lebanon's famous Almaza and Jordan's Amstel, a light brew made under licence from the popular Dutch brewer Amstel. Less impressive are Syria's Barada (Damascus) and Al-Charq (Aleppo), and Israel's Maccabee, the dark-draught Gold Star and light Nesher. The most interesting ale is the preservative-free Taybeh. The product of the Arab

THE CAFE & COFFEEHOUSE EXPERIENCE

There's nothing more authentically Middle Eastern than spending an hour (or an afternoon) soaking up the ambience and fragrant nargileh smoke at a *qahwa* (coffeehouse; *ahwa* in Egypt); in Turkey they're called *çay bahçesis* (tea gardens). Most serve up more tea than coffee and all have loyal, predominantly male, clients who enjoy nothing more than a daily natter and a game of dominoes or *towla* (backgammon). Adding to the atmosphere is the smoke from countless water pipes, a fragrant cloud of lightly scented tobacco that's one of the Middle East's most distinctive sensory experiences.

Called a nargileh in Turkey, Lebanon, Jordan and Syria and a sheesha in Egypt, the water pipe is a tradition, an indulgence and a slightly naughty habit all wrapped into the one gloriously relaxing package. A feature of coffeehouses from Ankara to Aswan, it's as addictive as it is magical. Consider yourselves warned.

When you order a water pipe you'll need to specify the type of tobacco and molasses mix you'd like. Most people opt for tobacco soaked in apple juice (known as *elma* in Turkey and *tufah* in Egypt), but it's also possible to order strawberry, melon, cherry or mixed-fruit flavours. Some purists order their tobacco unadulterated, but in doing this they miss out on the wonderfully sweet aroma that makes the experience so memorable. Once you've specified your flavour, a decorated bulbous glass pipe filled with water will be brought to your table, hot coals will be placed in it to get it started and you'll be given a disposable plastic mouthpiece to slip over the pipe's stem. Just draw back and you're off. The only secret to a good smoke is to take a puff every now and again to keep the coals hot; when they start to lose their heat the waiter (or dedicated water-pipe minder) will replace them. Bliss!

world's first microbrewery (in Ramallah), it comes in light and malt-heavy dark varieties.

Wine is growing in popularity in the Middle East, thanks largely to the wines being produced in Lebanon. Lebanon's winemaking, which is based on the 'old-world' style, began with the French winemaker Gaston Hochar who took over an 18th-century castle, Château Musar in Ghazir, 24km north of Beirut, in 1930. Together with his sons, Hochar created a wine that, despite the civil war, was able to win important awards in France, including the prestigious Winemaker's Award for Excellence. Ninety per cent of their produce is exported. The main wine-growing areas are Kefraya and Ksara in the Bekaa Valley and we particularly recommend the products of Château Musar and Ksara's Reserve du Couvent. For more information on some of Lebanon's wines see the boxed text, p377. Turkey and Israel also have small wine-producing areas with growing reputations.

If there is a regional drink, it would have to be the grape-and-aniseed firewater known as raki in Turkey and as arak (lion's milk) in the rest of the region. The aniseed taste of these two powerful tipples perfectly complements mezze. You'll find many Middle Easterners for whom mezze without arak (combined with water and served in small glasses) is just not taking your mezze seriously.

Nonalcoholic Drinks

Juice stalls selling cheap and delicious freshly squeezed *asiir* (juices) are common throughout the region. Popular juices include lemon (which is often blended with sugar syrup and ice, and sometimes with mint), orange, pomegranate, mango, carrot and sugar cane, and you can order combinations of any or all of these. For health reasons, steer clear of stalls that add milk to their drinks.

Other traditional drinks include *aryan*, a refreshing yogurt drink made by whipping yogurt with water and salt to the consistency of pouring cream. Another favourite is the delicious and unusual *sahlab* (*sahlep* in Turkey), a drink made from crushed tapioca-root extract and served with milk, coconut, sugar, raisins, chopped nuts and rosewater. Famed for its aphrodisiacal properties, it is served hot in winter and cold in summer.

In the baking heat of an Egyptian summer, coffee and tea drinkers forgo their regular fix for cooler drinks such as the crimson-hued, iced *karkadai,* a wonderfully refreshing drink boiled up from hibiscus leaves, or *zabaady* (yogurt beaten with cold water and salt).

Celebrations

Food plays an important part in the religious calendar of the region and holy days usually involve a flurry of baking and hours of preparation in the kitchen.

Ramadan & Other Islamic Celebrations

The region's most important religious feasts occur during Ramadan (Ramazan in Turkish), the Muslim holy month. There are two substantial meals a day during this period. The first, *imsak* (or *sahur*), is a breakfast eaten before daylight. Tea, bread, dates, olives and pastries are scoffed to give energy for the day ahead. *Iftar,* the evening meal prepared to break the fast, is a special feast calling for substantial soups, rice dishes topped with almond-scattered grilled meats and other delicacies. *Iftar* is often enjoyed communally in the street or in large, specially erected tents. In Turkey, a special round flat pide is baked in the afternoon and collected in time for the evening feast.

COOKING COURSE

Cooking courses are few and far between in the Middle East, but Petra Kitchen (p318; www.petrakitchen.com) in Wadi Musa, near Petra in Jordan, is worth the wait, with local Bedouin teachers and plenty to learn and sample.

FOOD & RITES OF PASSAGE

In the Middle East, food is always associated with different milestones in an individual's and a family's life. When a baby is born, Egyptians mark the birth of a son by serving an aromatic rice pudding with aniseed called *meghlie;* in Syria and Lebanon it's called *mighlay* and is made of rice flour and cinnamon. The same dish is called *mughly* in the Palestinian Territories, where it is believed to aid lactation.

In Syria and Lebanon, chickpeas and tooth-destroying sugar-coated almonds are the celebratory treats when the baby's first tooth pushes through. In Egypt, *ataïf* (pancakes dipped in syrup) are eaten on the day of a betrothal and biscuits known as *kahk bi loz* (almond bracelets) are favourites at wedding parties. Turkish guests at engagement parties and weddings are invariably served baklava.

Mourning carries with it a whole different set of eating rituals. A loved one is always remembered with a banquet. This takes place after the burial in Christian communities, and one week later in Muslim communities. The only beverages offered are water and bitter, unsweetened coffee. In Israel and the Palestinian Territories, Muslims may serve dates as well, while Christians bake *rahmeh,* a type of bun commemorating the soul of the departed. Muted varieties of much-loved sweets, such as *helva* and *lokum* (Turkish delight), are commonly part of the mourning period in Turkey; a bereaved family will make *irmik helvası* (semolina *helva*) for visiting friends and relatives.

When observant Jews mourn the dead, religious dictates urge them to sit around the deceased for seven days and then have a solemn meal of bread, to signify sustenance, and boiled eggs and lentils, whose circular forms invoke the continuation of life.

The end of Ramadan (Eid al-Fitr) is also celebrated in great culinary style. In Turkey, locals mark this important time with Şeker Bayramı (Sugar Festival), a three-day feast in which sweet foods (especially baklava) occupy centre stage.

The Arab Table: Recipes and Culinary Traditions by May Bsisu takes a holistic approach that blends practical recipes with discursive sections on Arab culinary philosophy, with a special focus on celebratory meals.

Jewish Celebrations

The Shabbat (Sabbath) meal is an article of faith for most Jews and central to that weekly celebration is the bread known as *challah* (Sabbath bread), which is baked each week by Jewish householders in Israel and the Palestinian Territories. A slowly cooked heavy stew called *cholent* is another Sabbath tradition widely enjoyed in Israel. Fatty meat, beans, grains, potatoes, herbs and spices stewed for hours in a big pot will heartily serve the family as well as their guests.

The Pesah (Jewish Passover) is celebrated even by the nondevout, which comprises the majority of Israelis. Unleavened bread is the best-known ingredient. During Hanukkah, potato pancakes and special jam doughnuts *(soofganiot)* are traditional dishes, while Rosh HaShanah means eating sweet foods like apples, carrots or braided *challah* bread dipped in honey.

Easter

Easter heralds another round of feasting, with Good Friday's abstinence from meat bringing out dishes such as *m'jaddara* (spiced lentils and rice) or *shoraba zingool* (sour soup with small balls of cracked wheat, flour and split peas) in Lebanon and Syria. *Selak,* rolls of silver beet (Swiss chard) stuffed with rice, tomato, chickpeas and spices, are also served. The fast is broken on Easter Sunday with round semolina cakes called *maamoul* (which also appear as desserts on some Damascus restaurant menus) stuffed with either walnuts or dates. The Armenian Christmas, the Epiphany (6 January), has the women busy making *owamaut* (small, deep-fried honey balls).

The Arts

The Middle East's artistic heritage is an extremely rich one, from the modern genre of film-making to the ancient arts of literature and music. Under often extremely difficult circumstances, and often from exile, the Middle East's film-makers, writers and musicians of the modern era continue to produce some remarkable work. But there is a sense that the artistic world in the Middle East is currently on hold, waiting for the fallout from the Arab Spring before charting its new course.

For information on Jordan's booming crafts industry, see p332, while Egyptian crafts are covered in the boxed text, p78.

Cinema

Perhaps even more so than wider Middle Eastern society, the region's film industries stand at a crossroads. On one level, a small, elite company of directors is gaining critical acclaim, picking up awards at international festivals and inching its way into the consciousness of audiences around the world. But the industry as a whole has spent much of the last two decades in crisis, plagued by a critical lack of government funding, straining under the taboos maintained by repressive governments or fundamentalist religious movements, and facing unprecedented competition from Middle Easterners' unfettered access to satellite TV channels. Amid the upheaval of the Arab Spring, film-makers have at times been prominent voices for reform, but funding for film-making is likely to remain a marginal priority for years to come.

Arab Film Distribution (www.arabfilm.com) is the Amazon.com of Arab cinema, with a large portfolio of DVDs that you just won't find on the shelves of your local rental store.

A few brave directors are gently trying to expand the frontiers of acceptable political and social dialogue but, unless they go into exile, they're forced to do so on budgets that would make Hollywood directors weep. Syrian film-maker Meyar al-Roumi, who lives in France, summed up the difficulties in a 2007 interview with the BBC: 'The establishment is the only source of funding films. Producers are much more interested in TV as its revenues are higher,' and then there's the issue of political boundaries: 'My work relies on self-criticism,' said al-Roumi, 'of my life, my friends and my country because I love it. But this made my films unwelcome here'.

And the dangers faced by directors and actors who transgress conservative social mores were demonstrated by the three-month jail sentence handed down to Egypt's leading comic actor, Adel Imam, in February 2012 for insulting Islam and mocking politicians in his films and plays.

The way most Middle Eastern directors survive under such conditions is to produce films that either overtly support the government line and stray dangerously close to propaganda, or to focus on the microscopic details of daily life, using individual stories to make veiled commentaries on wider social and political issues. It is in this latter body of work, schooled in subtlety and nuanced references to the daily struggles faced by many in the region, that Middle Eastern film truly shines.

For a detailed rundown on Lebanese cinema see p388.

Egypt: Coming of Age

Israeli films have received more Oscar nominations (10) for Best Foreign Language Film than films from any other Middle Eastern country (including in 2007, 2008, 2009 and 2011), although they've yet to win the prize.

In its halcyon years of the 1970s, Cairo's film studios turned out more than 100 movies a year, filling cinemas throughout the Arab world. These days the annual figure is closer to 20 and most are soap-opera-style genre movies that rely on slapstick humour, usually with a little belly dancing thrown in for (rather mild) spice.

For all the gloom that has hung over the local film industry in recent years, Egypt's creative talents have set about reclaiming the country's once-undisputed title as the Middle East's cinematic powerhouse. The revival relies on a bold, ground-breaking willingness to confront social taboos in a way that few Egyptian film-makers have dared for decades.

Despite signs that the Egyptian government censors are lightening up, directors in the country must still be wary of a conservative backlash. The portrayal of a lesbian kiss in *Until Things Get Better* saw the director Khaled Youssef threatened with arrest on moral grounds.

The new trend towards controversial subject matter must have come as music to the ears of Youssef Chahine, Egypt's premier director for more than half a century. This Alexandria-born stalwart of international film festivals, who died in Cairo aged 82 in June 2008, directed over 40 films in an illustrious career that saw him given the lifetime achievement award at the Cannes Film Festival in 1997. Known for championing free speech and for his willingness to take on authoritarian Egyptian governments, Western meddling in the Middle East and religious fundamentalism, Chahine, more than any other figure, laid the foundations for the brave new world of Egyptian cinema. His final film *Heya Fawda* (*Chaos*; 2007), which confronted police brutality and corruption, was a fitting epitaph to a stirring career.

Israel & the Palestinian Territories: Worlds Apart

Israel

Film directors from elsewhere in the Middle East must look with envy at the level of government funding and freedom of speech enjoyed by Israeli film-makers. It's a freedom that Israeli directors have used to produce high-quality films that have been praised for their even-handedness by juries and audiences alike at international film festivals.

A readiness to confront uncomfortable truths about Israel's recent history has long been a hallmark of Amos Gitai (b 1950) who has won

MUST-SEE MOVIES

» *Lawrence of Arabia* (1962) David Lean's masterpiece captures all the hopes and subsequent frustrations for Arabs in the aftermath of WWI.

» *Yol* (The Way; 1982) By Yilmaz Güney and epic in scale, it follows five finely rendered Turkish prisoners on parole around their country. It won the coveted Palme d'Or in Cannes.

» *West Beirut* (1998) Begins on 13 April 1975, the first day of the Lebanese Civil War, and is Ziad Doueiri's powerful meditation on Lebanon's scars and hopes.

» *Paradise Now* (2005) Palestinian director Hany Abu-Assad's disturbing but finely rendered study of the last hours of two suicide bombers. It was nominated for the Best Foreign Language Film Oscar in 2005.

» *Caramel* (2007) A stunning debut for Lebanese director Nadine Labaki. It follows the lives of five Lebanese women struggling against social taboos in war-ravaged Beirut.

» *Once Upon a Time in Anatolia* (2011) Runner-up at the 2011 Cannes Film Festival, this Nuri Bilge Ceylan film broods across the Anatolian steppe.

YILMAZ GÜNEY: MIRROR TO TURKISH HISTORY

The life of Yilmaz Güney (1937–84) provides a fascinating window onto late 20th-century Turkey. In particular, the life story and films of this Turkish Kurdish director speak volumes for the often fraught relationship between Turkey's governments and the country's creative talents.

Güney began his professional life as a writer, before becoming a hugely popular young actor who appeared in dozens of films (up to 20 a year according to some reports), before again changing tack to become the country's most successful film director. But behind that seemingly steady rise lies a life that reads like a scarcely believable film plot. Güney was first arrested in 1961 for writing what was condemned as a communist novel, then again in 1972 for sheltering anarchist students. In 1974, he was convicted of killing a public prosecutor. He wrote many of his screenplays behind bars – including the internationally acclaimed *The Herd* (1978). In 1981, he escaped from prison and fled to France.

It was from exile that Güney produced his masterpiece, the Palme d'Or-winning *Yol* (*The Way;* 1982), which was not initially shown in Turkish cinemas: its portrait of what happens to five prisoners on a week's release was too grim for the authorities to take. His following within Turkey was also never as widespread as his talents deserved, not least because his portrayal of the difficulties faced by Turkey's Kurds alienated many in mainstream Turkish society.

plaudits for his sensitive and balanced portrayal of half a century of conflict. He became a superstar almost overnight with *Kadosh* (1998), which seriously questioned the role of religion in Israeli society and politics. He followed it up with *Kippur* (1999), a wholly unsentimental portrayal of the 1973 war, and *Kedma* (2001), which caused a stir by questioning many of the country's founding myths through the lens of the Israeli War of Independence. If Israeli cinema is entering a period of international acclaim, as many believe, Gitai is more responsible than anyone else for the renaissance.

But Gitai has not been the only director to produce the works of national self-criticism that set Israel apart from other Middle Eastern film industries. Avi Mograbi goes a step further than Gitai with no-holds-barred depictions of the difficulties of life for the Palestinians under Israeli occupation.

Beyond the politically charged films that are causing a stir, there's also a feeling within Israel that the country's film industry is entering something of a golden age. Highlighting the sense of excitement, Shira Geffen and Etgar Keret won the Caméra d'Or for best film by debut directors at the 2007 Cannes Film Festival for *Meduzot (Jellyfish)*. At the same festival, Eran Kolirin's *The Band's Visit* won the Jury Prize of the International Federation of Film Critics. Joseph Cedar (b 1968) has been nominated twice for an Academy Award for Best Foreign Language Film with *Beaufort* (2007) and *Footnote* (2011).

Young Lebanese director Ziad Doueiri, whose slick debut *West Beyrouth* (1998) is considered one of the best films about the Lebanese Civil War, was Quentin Tarantino's lead cameraman for *Pulp Fiction* and *Reservoir Dogs*.

Palestinian Territories

The picture for Palestinian directors could not be more different. Starved of funding, faced with the barriers erected by Israeli censors and living in occupation or exile, Palestinian film-makers have done it tough, but have nonetheless turned out some extraordinary movies.

One Palestinian director who has made an international impact is the Hebron-born Michael Khaleifi, whose excellent *Images from Rich Memories, The Anthem of the Stone* and *Wedding in Galilee* were all shot covertly inside the Palestinian Territories. Rasheed Masharawi has been rejected in some Palestinian circles for working with Israeli production companies, but the quality of his work is undeniable. Elie Suleiman's work – which includes *Cyber Palestine, Divine Intervention* and the notable *Chronicle of a Disappearance* – is a wonderful corpus of quietly angry and intensely powerful films.

Decorative Arts

The serpentine swirl of a calligrapher's pen. The exquisite intricacy of exotic arabesques, geometric patterning and illuminated manuscripts. The microscopic detail of thousands of mosaic pieces combined to create large-scale masterpieces. These are the images that rank among the greatest signifiers of the Middle East's artistic and aesthetic richness.

Islam's restriction on the portrayal of living figures could have sounded the death knell for Middle Eastern artists. Instead, the exploration of the artistic possibilities of the Arabic script and the application of geometric principles to the world of decorative arts produced a distinctive and highly original artistic tradition very much rooted in the region's cultural and religious history. Wedded to these post-Islamic forms were adaptations from the long-standing figurative art traditions of Asia Minor, Persia and areas further east. Granted special dispensation to glorify the sacred, the illuminated manuscripts from Turkey and Iraq, and miniature paintings from Iran, provided a bridge to earlier art forms and depth to a decorative arts tradition of extraordinary diversity.

ARABIAN NIGHTS

To learn more about how the stories of *The Thousand and One Nights* came together, read the excellent introduction by Husain Haddawy in *The Arabian Nights*.

In the areas of calligraphy, metalwork, ceramics, glass, carpets and textiles, Middle Eastern artisans and craftspeople (Armenians, Christians, Jews and Muslims) have for more than 1200 years applied complex and sumptuous decorations to often very practical objects to create items of extraordinary beauty. Plenty of such items are on view in the region's museums, including the Topkapı Palace in İstanbul. However, to appreciate the achievements of Islamic art, visit one of the older mosques in which tiling, woodcarving, inlaid panelling and calligraphy are often combined in exaltation of Allah.

Decorative Islamic art is, for a Muslim, foremost an expression of faith, and nowhere is this more important than in the most sophisticated of these arts – calligraphy. Early calligraphers used an angular script called Kufic that was perfect for stone carving. Modern calligraphy uses a flowing cursive style, more suited to working with pen and ink.

Another of the region's signature art forms is the mosaic, traditionally made from tiny squares called tesserae, chipped from larger rocks. The tesserae are naturally coloured, and carefully laid on a thick coating of wet lime. Mosaics depicting hunting, deities and scenes from daily life once adorned the floors and palaces of the Byzantine Middle East and, before them, the extravagant public and private buildings of the Romans. The art of mosaic making continues in such places as Madaba in Jordan, but is absent from most other Islamic countries.

Literature

The Middle East is the cradle of storytelling. The telling of tales that are both mischievous and reveal the social and political times from which they arise has always occupied centre stage in Middle Eastern life, from the epic tales from the 8th-century Baghdad court of Haroun ar-Rashid, so wonderfully brought to life in *The Thousand and One Nights,* to the wandering storytellers who once entertained crowds in the coffeehouses and theatres of the region. It's a heritage with two tightly interwoven strands: entertainment through suspense and comedy, and thinly veiled commentaries on the issues of the day. The region's literary talents are worthy heirs to this ancient tradition and it's these storytellers – the poets and novelists – far more than government-controlled newspapers and 'information' ministries, who serve as the great chroniclers of Middle Eastern life.

BEST MIDDLE EASTERN LITERATURE

» *The Prophet* by Khalil Gibran somehow expounds in poetic form on the great philosophical questions while speaking to the dilemmas of everyday life.

» Choose anything by Orhan Pamuk and you won't be disappointed, but it was with *The Black Book* that he leapt onto the international stage.

» Naguib Mahfouz rarely sounds a wrong note. Choose anything from *The Cairo Trilogy*, but if you have to choose just one Mahfouz title, *The Harafish* would be our desert-island choice.

» *The Map of Love* by Ahdaf Soueif is the Booker-nominated historical novel by this Anglo-Egyptian writer. *In the Eye of the Sun* is simply marvellous.

» *Memed My Hawk* by Yaşar Kemal deals with near-feudal life in the villages of eastern Turkey and is considered perhaps the greatest Turkish novel of the 20th century.

» *The Stone of Laughter* by Hoda Barakat is a lyrical work by a young Lebanese writer that beautifully charts Lebanon's civil war.

» *The Dark Side of Love* by Syria's Rafik Schami could just be the first 'Great Arab Novel' of the 21st century, with its follow-up *The Calligrapher's Secret* also brilliant.

Like Middle Eastern film-makers, the writers of the region face many challenges, from government repression and a lack of funding to the stellar rise of satellite TV. But perhaps of far greater importance is the lack of a book-buying culture in Arabic-speaking countries. Storytelling in the Middle East, including poetry, was always a predominantly oral tradition and it was not until the 20th century that the first Arabic-language novels appeared. The audiences never really made the transition from the public performance to the printed page.

But performing the last rites for Arabic literature (note that Israeli writers face few such challenges) would be premature. Unable to sell many books at home, many writers in the region have learned to survive from international sales. The Palestinian poet Mahmoud Darwish, for example, combined a devoted local audience, which he cultivated through hugely popular public readings, with an equally devoted international following, so much so that he is the bestselling poet in France.

According to one UN estimate, Spain translates more books each year than have been translated into Arabic in the past 1000 years.

Poetry

The Lebanese-born poet Khalil Gibran (1883–1931) is, by some estimates, the third biggest-selling poet in history behind Shakespeare and Lao Tse. Born in Bcharré in Lebanon, he spent most of his working life in the US, but it didn't stop him from becoming a flag bearer for Arabic poetry. His masterpiece, *The Prophet* (1923), which consists of 26 poetic essays, became, after the Bible, America's second biggest selling book of the 20th century.

Mahmoud Darwish (1941–2008) has become one of the most eloquent spokesmen for Palestinian rights, his more than 30 volumes of poetry reading like a beautifully composed love letter to the lost land of his childhood. At his funeral in August 2008, one mourner told the BBC that he 'symbolises the Palestinian memory'. Another leading Arab poet and one of the great celebrities of the Arab literary scene is Syria's Nizar Qabbani (1923–98), who was unusual in that he was able to balance closeness to successive Syrian regimes with subject matter (love, eroticism and feminism) that challenged many prevailing opinions within conservative Syrian society. His funeral in Damascus – a city that he described in his will as 'the womb that taught me poetry, taught me creativity and granted me the alphabet of jasmine' – was broadcast live around the Arab world.

Novels

The novel as a literary form may have come late to the Middle East, but that didn't stop the region producing three winners of the Nobel Prize for Literature: Shmuel Yosef Agnon (1966), a Zionist Israeli writer whose works are published in English under the name SY Agnon; Naguib Mahfouz (1988); and Orhan Pamuk (2006).

Naguib Mahfouz: His Life & Times by Rasheed El-Elnany is the first (and, it must be said, long-overdue) English-language biography of the Arab world's most accomplished and prolific novelist.

Much of the credit for the maturing of Arabic literature can be given to Naguib Mahfouz (1911–2006), who was unquestionably the single most important writer of fiction in Arabic in the 20th century. A life-long native of Cairo, Mahfouz began writing in the 1930s. From Western-copyist origins he went on to develop a voice that is uniquely of the Arab world and draws its inspiration from storytelling in the coffeehouses and the dialect and slang of the streets. He repeatedly fell foul of Egypt's fundamentalist Islamists, first for his 1959 novel *Children of Gebelawi* (which was banned for blasphemy in Egypt) and later for defending Salman Rushdie; Mahfouz was seriously injured in an assassination attempt in 1994. His best-known works are collectively known as *The Cairo Trilogy,* consisting of *Palace Walk, Palace of Desire* and *Sugar Street.*

Orhan Pamuk (b 1952) is Turkey's latest literary celebrity. His works include an impressive corpus of novels and an acclaimed memoir of İstanbul, *Istanbul – Memories of a City.* His work has been translated into more than 50 languages and, like Mahfouz, Pamuk has never shirked from the difficult issues; in *Snow* (2004), Pamuk unflinchingly explores the fraught relationship between two of the great themes of modern Turkish life: Islamic extremism and the pull of the West. Also like Mahfouz, Pamuk is known as a staunch defender of freedom of speech.

Among the region's other best-known writers are Turkey's Yaşar Kemal (b 1923) and the Israeli writer Amos Oz; Oz's name regularly appears as a candidate for the Nobel Prize for Literature and his work includes essays and award-winning novels with themes that speak to the pride and angst at the centre of modern Israeli life. Of the native Lebanese writers, the most famous is Hanan al-Shaykh (b 1945), who writes poignant but humorous novels that resonate beyond the bounds of the Middle East. Also worth tracking down are the works of

THE THOUSAND & ONE NIGHTS

After the Bible, *The Thousand and One Nights* (in Arabic, *Alf Layla w'Layla,* also known as *The Arabian Nights*) must be one of the best-known, least-read books in the English language.

That few people have read the actual text is unsurprising considering that its most famous English-language edition (translated by the Victorian adventurer Sir Richard Burton) runs to 16 volumes. The appeal of reading the volumes is further reduced by the old Middle Eastern superstition that nobody can read the entire text of *The Thousand and One Nights* without dying.

With origins that range from pre-Islamic Persia, India and Arabia, the stories as we now know them were first gathered together in written form in the 14th century. *The Thousand and One Nights* is a portmanteau title for a mixed bag of colourful and fantastic tales (there are 271 core stories). The stories are mainly set in the semi-fabled Baghdad of Haroun ar-Rashid (r AD 786–809), and in Mamluk-era (1250–1517) Cairo and Damascus.

All versions of *The Thousand and One Nights* begin with the same premise: the misogynist King Shahriyar discovers that his wife has been unfaithful, whereafter he murders her and takes a new wife every night before killing each in turn before sunrise. The wily Sheherezade, the daughter of the king's vizier, insists that she will be next, only to nightly postpone her death with a string of stories that leaves the king in such suspense that he spares her life so as to hear the next instalment.

Jordan's Abdelrahman Munif (1933–2004), Egypt's prolific Nawal el-Saadawi (b 1931) and Lebanese-born Amin Maalouf (b 1949).

Of the new wave of Middle Eastern writers, the names to watch include Alaa al-Aswany (Egypt), Ahdaf Soueif (Egypt), Khalid al-Khamisi (Egypt), Laila Halaby (Lebanon) and Dorit Rabinyan (Israel).

Music

If you're a music lover, you'll adore the Middle East, which has home-grown music as diverse as the region itself. Yes you'll hear Bob Marley and other Western icons in traveller hang-outs such as Dahab, but this is one part of the world where local artists dominate air time and you're far more likely to hear Umm Kolthum, soulful Iraqi oud (Middle Eastern lute) or the latest Lebanese pop sensation.

Arab

Classical

If one instrument has come to represent the enduring appeal of classical Arabic music, it's the oud, an instrument that has made the transition from backing instrument to musical superstar in its own right. The oud is a pear-shaped, stringed instrument and is distinguished from its successor, the Western lute, by its lack of frets, 11 strings (five pairs and a single string) and a neck bent at a 45- to 90-degree angle. Oud players are to be found throughout the region, but its undisputed masters are in Iraq, where the sound of the oud is revered as a reflection of the Iraqi soul.

Even so, Syria produced the Arab world's so-called 'King of the Oud', Farid al-Atrache (1915–74). Sometimes called the 'Arab Sinatra', he was a highly accomplished oud player and composer, who succeeded in updating Arabic music by blending it with Western scales and rhythms and the orchestration of the tango and waltz. His melodic improvisations on the oud and his *mawal* (a vocal improvisation) were the highlights of his live performances, and recordings of these are treasured. By the time of his death, he was considered – and still is by many – to be the premier male Arabic music performer of the 20th century.

The other defining feature of classical Arabic music is the highly complicated melodic system known as *maqam*. The foundation for most traditional music in the Arab world, *maqam* is based on a tonal system of scales and intervals and is wholly different from Western musical traditions. Master *maqam* and you've mastered the centuries-old sound of the region.

Arab Gateway – Music (www.al-bab.com/arab/music/music.htm) has everything from clear explanations of the basics for the uninitiated to links and downloads of contemporary Arab music, while Al-Mashriq – Music (http://almashriq.hiof.no/base/music.html) offers more links to Arabic music than you can poke a stick at.

ARAB MUSIC

Contemporary Arab Music

Seemingly a world away from classical Arabic music, and characterised by a clattering, hand-clapping rhythm overlaid with synthesised twirlings and a catchy, repetitive vocal, the first true Arabic pop came out of Cairo in the 1970s. As Arab nations experienced a population boom and the mean age decreased, a gap in popular culture had developed that the memory of the greats couldn't fill. Enter Arabic pop. The blueprint for the new youth sound (which became known as *al-jeel,* from the word for generation) was set by Egyptian Ahmed Adawiyya, the Arab world's first 'pop star'.

During the 1990s there was a calculated attempt to create a more upmarket sound, with many musicians mimicking Western dance music. Tacky electronics were replaced with moody pianos, Spanish guitars and thunderous drums. Check out the Egyptian singer Amr Diab, whose heavily produced songs have made him the best-selling artist ever in the Arab world (achieved with his 1996 album *Nour al-Ain).*

Heading the current crop of megastar singers (the Arabic music scene is totally dominated by solo vocalists, there are no groups) are Majida al-Rumi of Lebanon, Iraqi-born Kazem (Kadim) al-Saher and the enduring legend of Iraq's Ilham al-Madfai, who founded the Middle East's first rock band back in the 1960s. Syria's prolific Omar Suleyman, who emerged from that quintessential Middle Eastern genre of wedding performances, has produced over 500 albums, appeared at the 2011 Glastonbury Festival and has collaborated with everyone from Björk to Damon Albarn.

Your could buy your music from Amazon.com, but Maqam (www.maqam.com) claims to be the world's largest distributor and online retailer of Arab music, with a sideline in cinema and musical instruments.

Otherwise, in the fickle world of Arab pop, regional influences are minimised and Arab pop music is like its Western counterpart in that fashions change almost as regularly as the stars change hairstyles. Watch Arab MTV and you'll soon learn what's hot, although that doesn't necessarily mean that they'll be around tomorrow.

Turkish

Traditional Turkish music is enjoying something of a revival with Sufi music, dominated by traditional instrumentation, leading the way. Sufi music's spiritual home is Konya and the sound is bewitchingly hypnotic – a simple repeated melody usually played on the *nai* (reed pipe), accompanied by recitations of Sufi poetry.

Sufi music's growing popularity beyond Turkey's borders owes much to the work of artists like Mercan Dede (www.mercandede.com), whose blend of Sufism with electronica has taken the genre beyond its traditional boundaries and into a mainstream audience. He even doubles as a DJ with the stage name Arkin Allen, spinning hardcore house and techno beats at rave festivals in the US and Canada. Not surprisingly, one Turkish newspaper described him as a 'dervish for the modern world'.

Traditional Turkish folk music has also undergone a revival in recent years, as 'Türkü' – an updated, modern version often using electronic instruments coupled with traditional songs.

DANIEL BARENBOIM

No figure in the Middle Eastern arts has done as much to promote peace and understanding between Israelis and Palestinians as Daniel Barenboim (b 1942), the Israeli pianist and conductor. Barenboim is best known for having co-founded the West-Eastern Divan Orchestra, a collection of young, talented Israeli, Palestinian, Lebanese, Syrian, Jordanian and Egyptian classical musicians, with his friend, the late Palestinian intellectual Edward Said. From its base in Seville in Spain, the symphony orchestra (conducted by Barenboim) tours the world, including Israel and the Palestinian Territories. Back in Seville, the Barenboim-Said Foundation, which was set up to promote coexistence and dialogue and is funded by the local Andalusian government, holds summer workshops for young musicians from the Middle East, while it also supports a range of projects, including musical education programs in the Palestinian Territories.

But Barenboim has never been content to let his music alone do the talking. An outspoken critic of Israel's policies and an advocate of Palestinian rights, Barenboim has performed in the West Bank, including a piano recital he performed after secretly entering the Palestinian Territories under the cover of darkness when the Israeli government refused permission for the concert to go ahead. After a concert in Ramallah in January 2008, he accepted honorary Palestinian citizenship. In 2005, he also refused to be interviewed by uniformed reporters for Israeli Army Radio as a mark of respect for the Palestinians who were present. In 2011, he conducted an Orchestra for Gaza, with volunteers from major European orchestras in Gaza City, having entered the Gaza Strip secretly under UN protection.

To learn more about Barenboim and the West-Eastern Divan Orchestra, track down Paul Smaczny's documentary, *Knowledge is the Beginning*, which won an Emmy Award in 2006.

MIDDLE EASTERN MUSIC – OUR TOP 10 ALBUMS

» *The Lady & the Legend*, Fairouz (Lebanon)
» *Al-Atlaal*, Umm Kolthum (Egypt)
» *Awedony*, Amr Diab (Egypt)
» *Le Luth de Baghdad*, Nasseer Shamma (Iraq)
» *Asmar*, Yeir Dalal (Israel)
» *The Idan Raichel Project*, The Idan Raichel Project (Israel)
» *Nar with Secret Tribe*, Mercan Dede (Turkey)
» *Deli Kızın Türküsü*, Sezen Aksu (Turkey)
» *Les Plus Grands Classiques de la Musique Arabe*, various artists
» *Drab zeen*, Toufic Faroukh (Lebanon)

But Turkey's most pervasive soundtrack of choice is Turkish pop and its stars rank among the country's best-known celebrities. Sezen Aksu is not known as 'the Queen of Turkish music' for nothing; she launched the country's love affair with the genre with her first single in 1976. Combining Western influences and local folk music to create a thoroughly contemporary sound, she's also an independent spirit not afraid to speak out on environmental issues and Turkey's treatment of its minorities.

Other super-popular pop stars include Tarkan, 'arabesque' luminary İbrahim Tatlises, Çelik, Serdat Ortaç and Mustafa Sandal.

Relatively new to Turkey and with its roots in the Turkish diaspora of Germany, rap music has found a growing following within Turkey with a younger audience drawn to its counter-culture voice of protest. Many of the groups are based in Germany, among them Cartel (the first group to make it big), KMR and Aziza-A.

Israeli

Israeli's thriving music scene has, in recent years, begun to recognise the multinational origins of Israel's population. There has also been a drive to excavate distinctive Jewish rhythms from broader European traditions. The result is a deeper, more distinctive Israeli sound.

Perhaps the most successful example of this latter phenomenon is klezmer, which has taken the world-music scene by storm in recent years. With its foundations laid by the Jewish communities of Eastern Europe, klezmer's fast-paced, instrumental form was ideally suited to Jewish celebrations and it has sometimes been branded as Jewish jazz, in recognition of its divergence from established musical styles. The modern version has added vocals – almost always in Yiddish.

Songlines (www.song lines.co.uk) is the premier world music magazine. It features interviews with stars, extensive CD reviews and a host of other titbits that will broaden your horizons and prompt many additions to your CD collection.

If klezmer takes its inspiration from Jewish diaspora roots in Europe, the Idan Raichel Project (www.idanraichelproject.com), arguably Israel's most popular group, casts its net more widely. Israeli love songs are its forte, but it's the Ethiopian instruments, Jamaican rhythms and Yemeni vocals that mark the group out as something special. Although originally rejected by leading local record labels for being 'too ethnic', the Idan Raichel Project's building of bridges between Israel's now-multicultural musical traditions struck a chord with audiences at home and abroad.

Another artist to have adapted ancient musical traditions for a modern audience is Yasmin Levy, who sings in Ladino, the language of Sephardic Jews, who lived in Andalusia for centuries until 1492. The flamenco inflections in her music speak strongly of what she calls 'the musical memories of the old Moorish and Jewish-Spanish world'. Crossing frontiers of a different kind, Yair Dalal is an outstanding Israeli oud player who has collaborated with Palestinian and other Arab musicians.

Landscape & Environment

The Middle East faces some of the most pressing environmental issues of our time and there are few regions of the world where the human impact upon the environment has been quite so devastating. Further, as one of the world's largest oil-producing regions, the Middle East's size far outweighs its contribution to the gathering global environmental crisis. There *are* pockets of good news, but, it must be said, there aren't many.

Land

Wrapping itself around the eastern Mediterranean and with its feet on three continents, the Middle East is home to some suitably epic landforms, from the deserts that engulf much of the region and high mountain ranges of the north to some of history's most important rivers.

Desert Expeditions

» Western Oases, Egypt

» Sinai Desert, Egypt

» Wadi Rum, Jordan

» Negev, Israel and the Palestinian Territories

Deserts

Deserts consume the countries of the Middle East, covering 93% of Egypt, 77% of Jordanian and Iraqi territory, and 60% of Israel and the Palestinian Territories. Although deserts dominate much of the region, they're rarely home to the sandy landscapes of childhood imaginings. Apart from the Saharan sand seas in parts of Egypt, sand dunes worthy of the name are rare and stony gravel plains are the defining feature. Desert oases – such as Palmyra in Syria or Siwa in Egypt – have played an important role in the history of the region, serving as crucial watering points for caravans travelling the Silk Road and the Sahara.

Mountains

Mountains are as much a part of Middle Eastern landscapes as deserts, especially in Turkey and Lebanon. Eastern Turkey in particular is simply glorious with seriously high mountains rising above 5000m – the 5137m-high Mt Ararat (Ağrı Dağı) is the highest mountain in the countries covered by this book. Southeastern Anatolia offers windswept rolling steppe, jagged outcrops of rock that spill over into far-north Iraq. The vast, high plateau of rolling steppe and mountain ranges of Central Anatolia are similarly dramatic.

In Lebanon, the Mt Lebanon Range forms the backbone of the country: the highest peak, Qornet as-Sawda (3019m) rises southeast of Tripoli. Other Lebanese ranges include the beautiful Chouf Mountains, the Mt Lebanon Range and Bekaa Valley, and the Anti-Lebanon Range, a sheer arid massif averaging 2000m in height, which forms a natural border with Syria.

Rivers

It's difficult to overestimate the significance of the rivers that flow into and through the Middle East. The Nile, which runs for 6695km, 22% of it in Egypt, is the longest river on earth and along its banks flourished the glorious civilisation of ancient Egypt. Other Middle Eastern rivers resonate just as strongly with legends and empires past. According to the Bible, the Euphrates and Tigris are among the four rivers that flowed into the Garden of Eden and they would later provide the means for the cradle of civilisation in Mesopotamia. The Jordan River, the lowest river on earth, also features prominently in biblical texts. Even today, were it not for the rivers that run through these lands – hence providing a water source and narrow fertile agricultural zones close to the riverbanks – it's difficult to see how these regions could support life at all.

Wildlife

Animals

Occupying the junction of three natural zones, the Middle East was once a sanctuary for an amazing variety of mammals. Hardly any are left. And official government policies to protect wildlife are as rare as many of the animals. As a result, if you see anything more exciting than domesticated camels, donkeys and water buffaloes, you'll belong to a very small group of privileged Middle Eastern travellers.

The most famous exception to this otherwise gloomy outlook is the campaign to save the Arabian oryx, while the Israeli initiative known as Hai Bar (literally 'wildlife') is another small beacon of hope. Begun more than 45 years ago, the Hai Bar program set itself the most ambitious of aims: to reintroduce animals that roamed the Holy Land during biblical times by collecting a small pool of rare animals, breeding them, then reintroducing them to the wild. Consequently, the wild ass, beloved by the Prophet Isaiah, has turned the corner in Israel, though it's not likely to come off the endangered list any time soon. But the story of the Persian fallow deer is the one that really captured the public imagination. A small flock of the species was secretly flown in from Iran in 1978 on the last El Al flight to leave Tehran before the Islamic revolution. These shy animals have taken hold in the Galilee reserve of Akhziv and around the hills west of Jerusalem.

Casual wildlife sightings are extremely rare in the Middle East, although desert expeditions in Egypt's Sinai or Sahara offer the chance to see gazelle, rock hyraxes, fennec fox and even the graceful Nubian ibex.

In Lebanon, trekking in the Chouf Cedar Reserve, south of Beirut, might also yield a rare sighting of wolves, wild cats, ibex and gazelle.

But it's in Jordan where you've the best chance of spotting charismatic fauna. Oryx, ostrich, gazelle and Persian onager are all being reared for reintroduction to the wild and are on show at Jordan's Shaumari Wildlife Reserve in eastern Jordan. Jordan's striking caracal (Persian lynx), a feline with outrageous tufts of black hair on the tips of its outsized, pointy ears, is occasionally seen in Wadi Mujib and Dana Nature Reserves.

ENVIRONMENTAL PERFORMANCE

In the 132-country 2012 Environmental Performance Index, Egypt ranked highest among Middle Eastern countries at 60th, followed by Israel (61st), Lebanon (94th), Turkey (109th), Syria (113th), Jordan (117th) and Iraq (132nd).

Birds

In contrast to the region's dwindling number of high-profile mammals, the variety of bird life in the Middle East is exceptionally rich. As well as being home to numerous indigenous species, the Middle East, despite the critical loss of wetlands in Jordan and Iraq, continues to serve as a way station on migration routes between Asia, Europe and Africa. Twice a year, half a billion birds of every conceivable variety soar along the Syro-African rift, the largest avian fly way in the world, which is compressed into a narrow corridor along the eastern edge of Israel and the Palestinian Territories; indeed, Israel claims to be the world's second-largest flyway (after South America) for migratory birds.

At the disappearing wetlands of Azraq Wetland Reserve in Jordan, 347,000 birds were present on 2 February 1967. On the same date 33 years later there were just 1200.

At least one highly endangered bird species, the northern bald ibis, is not being allowed to migrate for its own safety. For more information, see the boxed text, p531.

Egypt's Sinai Peninsula and Al-Fayoum Oasis, and Wadi Araba in Jordan also receive an enormous and varied amount of ornithological traffic. Egypt alone has recorded sightings of over 430 different species.

For more information on the region's birdlife, contact the following organisations:

Birdlife International (www.birdlife.org/regional/middle_east/index.html)

International Birdwatching Center of the Jordan Valley (www.birdwatching.org.il)

International Center for the Study of Bird Migration (www.birds.org.il)

Society for the Protection of the Nature of Israel (SPNI; www.teva-tlv.org.il/english/)

Marine Life

The Red Sea teems with more than 1000 species of marine life, an amazing spectacle of colour and form. Fish, sharks, turtles, stingrays, dolphins, corals, sponges, sea cucumbers and molluscs all thrive in these waters. The rare loggerhead turtle nests on some of Turkey's Mediterranean beaches.

Coral is what makes a reef a reef – though thought for centuries to be some form of flowering plant, it is in fact an animal. Both hard and soft corals exist, their common denominator being that they are made up of polyps, which are tiny cylinders ringed by waving tentacles that sting their prey and draw it into their stomach. During the day corals retract into their tube, displaying their real colours only at night. Most of the bewildering variety of fish species in the Red Sea – including many that are found nowhere else – are closely associated with the coral reef, and live and breed in the reefs or nearby sea-grass beds.

SAVING THE ARABIAN ORYX

The Arabian oryx – sometimes said to be the unicorn of historical legend – is a majestic creature that stands about 1m high at the shoulder and has enormous horns that project over 50cm into the air. Adapted well to their desert environment, wild oryx once had an uncanny ability to sense rain on the wind. One herd is recorded as having travelled up to 155km, led by a dominant female, to rain. In times of drought, oryxes have been known to survive 22 months without water, obtaining moisture from plants and leaves.

Their white coats offered camouflage in the searing heat of the desert, providing a measure of protection from both heat and hunters, but the oryxes and their long, curved horns were highly prized and they were stalked relentlessly for them. In 1972, the last wild Arabian oryx was killed by hunters in Oman, which led officials to declare the oryx extinct in the wild. Nine oryxes left in captivity around the world were pooled and taken to the Arizona Zoo for a breeding program. They became known as the 'World Oryx Herd' and eventually grew to over 200 in number. As a result of programs to reintroduce the Arabian oryx into the wild across the region, an estimated 1000 oryxes were thought to survive in the wild in 2011, with the main viable populations in Israel and Saudi Arabia. There are also between 6000 and 7000 oryxes in captivity around the world.

The most accessible place to see an Arabian oryx (in captivity, but partly free-ranging) is in Jordan's Shaumari Wildlife Reserve.

It's well known that the world's coral reefs and other marine life are under threat from the effects of global warming, but there are plenty of local causes that threaten a more imminent death. This is especially the case in the Red Sea waters off Hurghada where, conservationists estimate, more than 1000 pleasure boats and almost as many fishing boats ply the waters. Twenty years ago, there was nothing to stop captains from anchoring to the coral, or snorkellers and divers breaking off a colourful chunk to take home. But in 1992, 12 of Hurghada's more reputable dive companies formed the **Hurghada Environmental Protection & Conservation Association** (Hepca; www.hepca.com). Working with the Egyptian National Parks Office, Hepca works to conserve the Red Sea's reefs through public-awareness campaigns, direct community action and lobbying of the Egyptian government to introduce appropriate laws. Thanks to these efforts, the whole coast south of Suez Governorate is now known as the Red Sea Protectorate. One of its earliest successes was to establish over 570 mooring buoys at popular dive sites around Hurghada. In 2009 the NGO also took over responsibility for waste management in the region, implementing door-to-door rubbish collection and recycling in Marsa Alam and Hurghada.

Plants

Middle Eastern flora tends to be at its lushest and most varied in the north, where the climate is less arid, although after millennia of woodcutting Turkey and Syria are now largely denuded. Only the Mediterranean coast west of Antalya and the Black Sea area and northeast Anatolia still have forests of considerable size.

In Lebanon, the Horsh Ehden Forest Nature Reserve is the last archetype of the ancient natural forests of Lebanon and is home to several species of rare orchids and other flowering plants. The cedars for which Lebanon is famous are now confined to a few mountain-top sites, most notably at the small grove at the Cedars ski resort (p369) and the Chouf Cedar Reserve (p376) in the Chouf Mountains. For more information about Lebanon's cedars see the boxed text, p370.

Notable National Parks & Reserves

- Ras Mohammed National Park, Egypt
- Shaumari Wildlife Reserve, Jordan
- Dana Biosphere Reserve, Jordan
- Azraq Wetland Reserve, Jordan
- Mujib Biosphere Reserve, Jordan
- Chouf Cedar Reserve, Lebanon
- Ein Gedi, Israel

National Parks & Wildlife Reserves

Although there are exceptions, most of the Middle East's officially protected areas exist in name only, and are poorly patrolled and poorly funded. Optimists may call them admirable statements of intent. The cynics would probably prefer to describe them as attempts to create token projects as a means of showing goodwill without having to do much at all to protect the environment. The truth, which varies from country to country, lies somewhere in between.

Syria and Iraq are bottom of the class when it comes to setting aside protected areas; Syria has one of the lowest ratios of protected areas to total land area of any country in the Mediterranean region. Next comes Egypt, which has set aside 23 'protected areas', although their status varies wildly and government funding is negligible.

Nearly 25 years ago the Jordanian government established 12 protected areas, totalling about 1200 sq km, amounting, in total, to just 1% of Jordan's territory. Some were abandoned, but the rest survive thanks to the impressive **Royal Society for the Conservation of Nature** (RSCN; www.rscn.org.jo), Jordan's major environmental agency.

Lebanon comes under the category of 'trying hard, but could do better'. Most national parks have a 'Friends Association', offering both environmental and practical information for visitors.

In recent years, thanks to EU aspirations, Turkey has stepped up its environmental protection practices. The growing number of protected

THE DEAD SEA IS DYING *DR ALON TAL*

The Dead Sea is the lowest place on earth and probably one of the hottest. The high resulting evaporation produces an astonishing salinity of 31%, about nine times higher than the oceans. The water's oily minerals also contain salubrious properties. German health insurance covers periodic visits to the Dead Sea for psoriasis patients to luxuriate in the healing waters.

Sadly, no natural resource in the Middle East shows more signs of impact from relentless population growth and economic development than the Dead Sea. Technically, the sea is a 'terminal lake' into which the Jordan River, along with other more arid watersheds, deposits its flow. In 1900, the river discharged 1.2 trillion litres a year into the Dead Sea. When Israeli and Jordanian farmers began to divert its water to produce a new agricultural economy in the 1950s, the flow was reduced to a putrid trickle and the Dead Sea began to dry up. Water levels in the river today are barely 10% of the natural flow. The Jordanian and Israeli potash industries in the southern, largely industrial Dead Sea region exacerbate the water loss by accelerating evaporation in their production processes. The impact is manifested in sinkholes, created when underground salt gets washed away by the infiltrating subsurface freshwater flow. Perhaps the most acute environmental consequence, though, is the 27m drop in the sea's water level and the long and discouraging walks now required to reach the edge of the retreating beach.

Among the suggested solutions to bring water back to the Dead Sea is a pipeline from the Gulf of Aqaba (Red Sea) to the Dead Sea's southern shore, producing hydroelectricity as well as a desalination plant that would provide water to Amman. The World Bank, however, recently decided that the US$5 billion project, dubbed the 'Peace Conduit', was sufficiently serious to justify a $15 million feasibility study.

For more on the Dead Sea, see the boxed text, p299.

Dr Alon Tal is a professor in the Desert Ecology Department at Israel's Ben-Gurion University.

areas includes 33 national parks, 16 nature parks and 35 nature reserves. It also includes 58 curiously named 'nature monuments', which are mostly protected trees, some as old as 1500 years. Sometimes the parks' regulations are carefully enforced, but at other times a blind eye is turned to such problems as litter-dropping picnickers. Visitor facilities are rare.

The Middle East's star environmental performer is undoubtedly Israel due to its strong regulation of hunting and a system of nature reserves comprising some 25% of the land. However, the parks are not without their problems. Many are minuscule in size and isolated, providing only limited protection for local species. Moreover, many of the reserves in the south are also used as military firing zones.

Columbia University's Water in the Middle East (http://library.columbia.edu/indiv/area/cuvl/middle_east_studies/water.html) hosts numerous links to articles on the Middle East's most pressing environmental issue.

Environmental Issues

Water

It's often said that the next great Middle Eastern war will be fought not over land but over water. Syria and Iraq have protested to Turkey because it is building dams at the headwaters of the Tigris and Euphrates. Egypt has threatened military action against Sudan or any other upstream country endangering its access to the waters of the Nile. And Jordan and Israel regularly spar over the waters of the shared Jordan River, which has now been reduced to a trickle, half of which is 50% raw sewage and effluent from fish farms.

To understand the extent of the Middle East's water-scarcity problem, consider Jordan, which has just 152.7 cu metres of renewable water per capita per year, compared to the UK's 2392. Jordan's figure is expected to fall to 90 cu metres by 2025. Anything less than 500 cu metres is considered to be a scarcity of water. Another study suggests that Jordan currently uses about 60% more water than is replenished from natural sources. By some estimates, Jordan will simply run out of water within 20 years. Dams on the Yarmouk River, water pipelines, plans to tap underground fossil water and desalination plants are all part of the projected (and extremely expensive) solution.

Desertification

Desertification, which is caused by overgrazing, deforestation, the overuse of off-road vehicles, wind erosion and drought, is another significant problem faced by all Middle Eastern countries, with the possible exception of Lebanon. The seemingly unstoppable encroachment of the desert onto previously fertile, inhabited and environmentally sensitive areas is resulting in millions of hectares of fertile land becoming infertile and, ultimately, uninhabitable. Jordan, Egypt and Iraq are on the frontline, but even largely desert-free Turkey is casting a worried eye on the future. While hotel owners in Cappadocia happily equip their rooms with Jacuzzis and mini-hammams, environmentalists fear that much of Turkey could be desert by 2025.

Pollution

Levels of waste – whether industrial outflow, sewage discharge or everyday rubbish – have reached critical levels across the region; recycling is almost nonexistent. At one level, the impact is devastating for local fishing industries, agricultural output, freshwater supplies and marine environments – Lebanon did not have functioning waste-water treatment plants until the mid-1990s, while up to 75% of Turkey's industrial waste is discharged without any treatment whatsoever. At another level, the great mounds of rubbish and airborne plastic bags provide an aesthetic assault on the senses for traveller and local alike.

The related issue of air pollution is also threatening to overwhelm in a region where the motor vehicle is king. In Cairo, for example, airborne smoke, soot, dust and liquid droplets from fuel combustion constantly exceed World Health Organization (WHO) standards (up to 260 micrograms per cu metre of air, when the international standard is 50), leading to skyrocketing instances of emphysema, asthma and cancer among the city's population. Cairo may be an extreme case, but it's a problem facing urban areas everywhere in the Middle East.

WATER

The Middle East is home to 4.5% of the world's population and around half of the world's oil supplies, but only receives 2% of the world's rainfall and possesses just 0.4% of the world's recoverable water supplies.

Survival Guide

Traveller Etiquette

Like anywhere else in the world, the people of the Middle East have particular ways of doing things and these customs can seem strange to first-time visitors. While you should always try to follow local customs, most people in the Middle East will be too polite to say anything if you break one of the region's taboos. In most cases, an apology and obvious goodwill will earn instant forgiveness.

Eating Etiquette

Middle Easterners can be a hospitable lot and it's not unusual for visitors to receive at least one invitation to eat in someone's home while travelling through the region. While each invitation needs to be assessed on its merits, our general advice would be that eating in a family home can be one of your most memorable travel experiences in the Middle East.

Homes

To avoid making your hosts feel uncomfortable, there are a few simple guidelines to follow.

» Bring a small gift of flowers, chocolates, pastries, fruit or honey.

» It's polite to be seen to wash your hands before a meal.

» Always remove your shoes before sitting down on a rug to eat or drink tea.

» Don't sit with your legs stretched out – it's considered rude during a meal.

» Always sit next to a person of the same sex at the dinner table unless your host(ess) suggests otherwise.

» Use only your right hand for eating or accepting food.

» When the meal begins, accept as much food as is offered to you. If you say 'no thanks' continually, it can offend the host.

» It's good manners to leave a little food on your plate at the end of the meal: traditionally, a clean plate was thought to invite famine.

» Your host will often lay the tastiest morsels in front of you; it's polite to accept them.

» The best part – such as the meat – is usually saved until last, so don't take it until offered.

Restaurants

There are fewer etiquette rules to observe in restaurants, but it's still worth trying to do so, particularly if you're eating as the guest of a local or sharing a table with locals.

» Picking teeth after a meal is quite acceptable and toothpicks are often provided.

» Be sure to leave the dining area and go outside or to the toilet before blowing your nose.

» Take food from your side of the table; stretching to the other side is considered impolite.

» It's polite to accept a cup of coffee after a meal and impolite to leave before it's served.

Religion

At some point during your travels in the Middle East, the conversation is likely to turn to religion. More specifically, you'll probably be asked, 'What's your religion?' Given that most foreign travellers come from secular Western traditions where religion is a private matter, the level of frankness in some of these discussions can come as a surprise. On one level, there's no better way of getting under the skin of a nation than talking about the things that matter most in life. So how do you go about answering this question?

It's usually easy to explain that you are Christian or, in some circumstances, Jewish, although in the company of Hamas militants or on the unfamiliar streets of Baghdad it is probably not wise to announce your Jewish faith. The overwhelming majority of Muslims won't bat an eyelid and may even welcome the opportunity to talk about the common origins and doctrines that Judaism and Islam share. Christians and Jews are respected as 'people of the book' who share the same God (see the boxed text, p581). In fact, many a Bedouin encounter begins with a celebration of that fact, with greetings such as 'Your God, my God same – *Salaam* (Peace)!'

The question of religion gets complicated when it comes to atheists. 'I don't believe in God' can call into question the very foundation of a Muslim's existence. If you are concerned your atheism will cause offence, perhaps say, 'I'm a seeker', suggesting you haven't quite made up your mind but may do so in the future. Be aware that Muslims may respond by explaining the merits of Islam to you. If that's not how you planned to spend your afternoon, try saying, 'I'm not religious'. This will likely lead to understanding nods and then, perhaps on subsequent meetings, an earnest attempt at conversion. Phrases like 'You'll find God soon, God-willing' are a measure of someone's affection for you and a reasonable response would be *shukran* (thank you).

General Etiquette

Tourism has the potential to improve the relationship between the Middle East and the West, but the gradual erosion of traditional life is the flipside of mass tourism. Sexual promiscuity, public drunkenness among tourists and the wearing of unsuitable clothing are all concerns to be aware of.

Try to have minimal impact on your surroundings. Create a positive precedent for those who follow you by keeping in mind the following:

» Don't hand out sweets or pens to children on the streets, since it encourages begging. Similarly, doling out medicines can encourage people not to seek proper medical advice and you have no control over whether the medicines are taken appropriately. A donation to a project, health centre or school is a far more constructive way to help.

» Buy your snacks, cigarettes, bubble gum etc from the enterprising grannies trying to make ends meet, rather than state-run stores. Also, use locally owned hotels and restaurants and buy locally made products.

» Try to give people a balanced perspective of life in the West. Try also to point out the strong points of the local culture, such as strong family ties and comparatively low crime.

» Make yourself aware of the human-rights situation, history and current affairs in the countries you travel through.

» If you're in a frustrating situation, be patient, friendly and considerate. Never lose your temper as a confrontational attitude won't go down well. For many Arabs, a loss of face is a serious and sensitive issue.

» Try to learn some of the standard greetings (see p640) – it will make a very good first impression.

» Always ask before taking photos of people. Don't worry if you don't speak the language – a smile and gesture will be appreciated. Never photograph someone if they don't want you to. If you agree to send someone a photo, make sure you follow through on it.

» Be respectful of Islamic traditions and don't wear revealing clothing; loose lightweight clothing is preferable. For more detailed advice on dress for women travellers, see p619.

» Men should shake hands when formally meeting other men, but not women, unless the woman extends her hand first. If you are a woman and uncomfortable with men extending their hand to you (they don't do this with local women), just put your hand over your heart and say hello.

» Public displays of physical affection are almost always likely to be misunderstood. Be discreet.

Safe Travel

Don't believe everything you read about the Middle East. Yes, there are regions that travellers would be ill advised to visit and you should, of course, always be careful while travelling in the region. But alongside the sometimes disturbing hard facts is more often a vast corpus of exaggeration, stereotyping and downright misrepresentation. We'll try and put this as simply as possible: there's every chance that you'll be safer in most parts of the Middle East than you would be back home.

Is it Safe?

Imagine somebody whose image of the USA was built solely on the 9/11 attacks, or who refused to visit Spain or the UK as a result of the terrorist attacks in Madrid and London in recent years. Just as the USA, the UK and Spain are rarely considered to be dangerous destinations, so too, day-to-day life in the Middle East very rarely involves shootings or explosions. There are trouble spots where violence persists, such as Syria and some regions of Iraq, and there are places where violence flares from time to time (such as in the Palestinian Territories or Lebanon). But such outbreaks of violence usually receive widespread media coverage, making it relatively easy to avoid these places until things settle down.

Terrorist incidents also do occur, and there have been attacks in Israel and the Palestinian Territories and the Red Sea resorts of Egypt's Sinai Peninsula in recent years. While such incidents are clearly major causes for concern, they are definitely the exception rather than the norm. The sad fact about modern terrorism is that you may face similar dangers anywhere in the world and that you're probably no more at risk in the Middle East than you may be in your home country. As one holidaymaker was reported saying in the wake of the 2005 Sharm el-Sheikh bombings: 'Actually, I live in central London. I don't really want to go home!'

As a foreigner, you may receive the occasional question ('Why does the West support Israel?'), but you'll rarely be held personally accountable for the policies of Western governments. Once in Tehran we stood, obviously Westerners, with cameras and pasty complexions, and watched a crowd march by chanting 'Death to America! Death to Britain!' Several marchers grinned, waved and broke off to come over and ask how we liked Iran.

So, while right now we'd advise against visits to Gaza, Hebron or Baghdad, don't let problems in some areas tar your image of the entire region. Keep abreast of current affairs, and if you need to phone your embassy for travel advice, then do so. Otherwise, just go.

Common Dangers

Road Accidents

Perhaps the most widespread threat to your safety comes from travelling on the region's roads. Road conditions vary, but driving standards are often poor and high speeds are common. Tips for minimising the risk of becoming a road statistic:

» Try to avoid night travel.

» A full-sized bus is usually safer than a minibus.

» If travelling in a shared taxi or minibus, avoid taking the seat next to the driver.

Political Unrest

The recent popular uprising against regimes from Cairo to Damascus has added a layer of uncertainty to travel in the region, although with the exception of Syria, the impact upon travellers has been minimal. Trouble spots in the region are usually well defined, and as long as you keep track of political developments, you're unlikely to come to any harm. Avoid political demonstrations or large gatherings and always ask the advice of locals if unsure.

Theft & Petty Crime

Crime rates are extremely low in most countries in the Middle East – theft is rarely a problem and robbery (mugging) even less of one. Even so, take the standard precautions. Always keep valuables with

GOVERNMENT TRAVEL ADVICE

The following government websites offer travel advisory services and information for travellers:

Australian Department of Foreign Affairs & Trade (www.smartraveller.gov.au)

Canadian Department of Foreign Affairs & International Trade (www.voyage.gc.ca)

French Ministère des Affaires et Étrangères Européennes (www.diplomatic.gouv.fr/fr/conseils-aux-voyageurs)

Italian Ministero degli Affari Esteri (www.viaggiaresicuri.mae.aci.it, in Italian)

UK Foreign & Commonwealth Office (www.fco.gov.uk)

US Department of State (www.travel.state.gov)

you or locked in a safe – never leave them in your room or in a car or bus. Use a money belt, a pouch under your clothes, a leather wallet attached to your belt, or internal pockets in your clothing. Keep a separate record of your passport, credit card and travellers cheque numbers; it won't cure problems, but it will make them easier to bear. We're sorry to say this, but beware of your fellow travellers; there are more than a few backpackers who make their money go further by helping themselves to other people's.

Country by Country

What follows is a high-level overview of the safety situation in the countries covered by this book. For more specific information, see individual country chapters.

Egypt

Egypt remains a relatively safe country to visit, but the turmoil that comes from the sudden overthrow of the old political order can have unpredictable consequences. Avoid political demonstrations (especially those in Cairo's Tahrir Sq) and be particularly wary in areas with mixed Muslim–Coptic Christian populations.

See p149 and the boxed text, p79.

Iraq

Much of Iraq remains off-limits to travellers, including Baghdad, southern, northern and central Iraq. Iraqi Kurdistan, however, is considered reasonably safe and is increasingly attracting both independent travellers and organised tours.

See p181.

Israel & the Palestinian Territories

Although the security situation has greatly improved in recent years, travellers should continue to exercise caution in Israel and the Palestinian Territories. You're unlikely to experience difficulties in most areas, although we strongly recommend against travel to the Gaza Strip. You should always keep your ear to the ground in Jerusalem, Hebron and other potential flashpoints.

See p271.

Jordan

Despite a constant if at times barely discernible rumble of discontent, Jordan has largely escaped the unrest arising from the Arab Spring and remains one of the safest countries in the region to visit.

Lebanon

Although the potential for political unrest and attendant violence remains a constant of Lebanese life, most of the country continues to be safe for travel. Hezbollah's ongoing war of words with Israel occasionally spills over into conflict, and particular care should be taken in southern Lebanon and Hezbollah's stronghold in the Bekaa Valley.

See the boxed text, p358.

Syria

While we hope the situation will change during the life of this book, at the time of writing we recommend against travel to Syria. The uprising against President Assad's regime threatens to spill over into full-scale civil war in a country that was for decades one of the Middle East's safest. As this book goes to press, it remains impossible to predict when Syria will again be safe to visit.

See p441.

Turkey

Turkey is possibly the safest country in the Middle East for travellers, with a stable and democratic political system and well-developed transport infrastructure. Always check the security situation, however, before you travel in areas close to the borders with Syria and Iraq.

Women Travellers

Despite the Middle East's reputation as difficult terrain for women travellers, there's no reason why women can't enjoy the region as much as their male counterparts. In fact, some seasoned women travellers to the Middle East consider their gender to be a help, not a hindrance.

For more information on the situation in specific countries, see the Women Travellers section in the Directory of each individual country chapter. And for general health advice, see p639.

Attitudes towards Women

For many people in the region, both men and women, the role of a woman is specifically defined: she is mother and matron of the household, while the man is the provider. Generalisations can, however, be misleading and the reality is often far more nuanced.

There are thousands of middle- and upper-middle-class professional women in the Arab World who, like their counterparts in the West, juggle work and family responsibilities. Among the working classes or in conservative rural areas where adherence to tradition is strongest, the ideal may be for women to concentrate on home and family, but economic reality means that millions of women are forced to work (but are still responsible for all domestic chores).

Contrary to stereotypes, the treatment of foreign women can be at its best in more conservative societies, providing, of course, you adhere to the prevailing social mores.

The treatment of women can also be due to age: older women will find they are greatly respected. One seasoned Middle Eastern expat and traveller told us she was so traumatised after travelling in Israel as a 21-year-old that she took up karate. Now in her forties, she's been going back to the region ever since. 'I realise the older I get, the less harassment I receive,' she said. She finds this a wonderful relief – 'I've reached that age where I can have a meaningful conversation with men without inviting other expectations. Having a husband is also immensely useful!'

Let's Talk About Sex

When it comes to sex, the differences between Western and Middle Eastern women become most apparent. Premarital sex (or, indeed, any sex outside marriage) is taboo in most of the region. With occasional exceptions among the upper classes, women are expected to be virgins when they marry and a family's reputation can rest upon this.

The presence of foreign women presents, in the eyes of some Middle Eastern men, a chance to get around these norms with ease and without consequences, a perception reinforced by distorted impressions gained from Western TV and the behaviour of a small number of women travellers. As one hopeful young man in Egypt remarked, when asked why he persisted in harassing every Western woman he saw: 'For every 10 that say no, there's one that says yes.'

Pros & Cons

Advantages

Women travellers are no different from their male counterparts in that meeting local people is a highlight of travelling in the Middle East. And unlike male travellers, they can meet Middle Eastern women without social restrictions, opening up a whole Middle Eastern world that men can never hope to see. Local women are as curious about life for women beyond the Middle East as you are about their lives, and they love to chat to women visitors. That said, local women are less likely than men to have had an education that included learning English – you'll find this to be the only major barrier to getting to meet and talk with them.

One other advantage, and one you should exploit to the

full, is that it's often perfectly acceptable for a woman to go straight to the front of a queue or ask to be served first before any men who may be waiting!

Disadvantages

Sexual harassment is a problem worldwide and the Middle East is no exception. Harassment can come in many forms: from stares, muttered comments and uncomfortably close contact on crowded public transport to the difficulty of eating in public on your own, where you may receive endless unwanted guests – even the wandering hands of waiters can be a problem. Women also report being followed and hissed at by unwanted male admirers on a fairly regular basis.

That said, although 'mild' harassment can be common in some countries, physical harassment is rare and sexual harassment is considered to be a serious crime in many Middle Eastern countries. In fact, incidents of sexual assault or rape are far lower in the region than in the West.

SURVIVAL STRATEGIES

Your experience of travelling in the region may depend partly on situations beyond your control, but there are some things you can try so as to minimise problems:

» Retain your self-confidence and sense of humour.

» Balance alertness with a certain detachment; ignoring stares and refusing to dignify suggestive remarks with a response generally stops unwanted advances in their tracks.

» Eat in a restaurant's family section, where one exists, or at places more used to tourists.

» If necessary, invent or borrow a husband, wear a wedding ring, even carry a photo of your 'kids'. While this may cause some consternation – what sort of mother/wife are you to have left your family to travel alone? – it will deter many suitors.

» Avoid direct eye contact with local men (dark sunglasses help), although a cold glare can also be an effective riposte if deployed at the right moment.

» Maximise your interaction with local women.

» In taxis, avoid sitting in the front seat unless the driver is female.

» On all forms of public transport, sit next to another woman whenever possible.

» You're lost? Try asking a local woman for directions.

» If nothing else works and you can't shake off a hanger-on, go to the nearest public place, such as a hotel lobby. If he persists, asking the receptionist to call the police usually frightens him off.

What to Wear

Fair or not, how women travellers dress will, considering the stereotypes at large in the region, go a long way towards determining how they're treated. To you, short pants and a tight top might be an expression of your right to do whatever the hell you want, but to many local men, your dress choice will send an entirely different message, confirming the worst views held of Western women.

The best way to tackle the stereotypes is to visibly debunk them: in other words, do as the locals do, dress and behave more modestly than you might at home and always err on the side of caution. As with anywhere, take your cues from those around you: if all the women are in long, concealing dresses, you should be conservatively dressed.

Dressing 'modestly' really means covering your upper legs and arms, shoulders and cleavage. A scarf is also useful, both to cover your neckline and to slip over your head when you want to look even more inconspicuous or when the occasion requires it (such as when visiting a mosque).

For all the inconvenience, dressing conservatively means you'll get a much warmer reception from the locals, you'll attract less unwanted attention, and you may feel more comfortable (long baggy clothes will keep you cooler under the fierce Middle Eastern sun).

Directory A–Z

This chapter provides a general overview of essential things you need to know about the Middle East, covering, in alphabetical order, everything from accommodation to volunteering. Each individual country chapter also has a Directory that includes more specific information about these subjects as they relate to each country. Please consult both when searching for information.

Accommodation

In most countries of the Middle East, you'll find accommodation that ranges from cheap and nasty to plush and palatial; most places sit comfortably somewhere in between. Throughout this book, accommodation is divided into price categories (budget, midrange and top end); within each category prices are listed in order of author preference. For the way these price categories are defined and the amenities you can expect from country to country, read the Accommodation section in the Directory section of each individual country chapter.

Generally Syria and Egypt have the cheapest accommodation, while Turkey, Jordan, Israel and the Palestinian Territories and Lebanon will cost a little more. However, travel through the Middle East is now such a well-worn path that in most major destinations covered by this book you'll find at least one high-quality place to suit your budget, whether you're travelling on a shoestring or an expense account.

Camping

Camping in the Middle East is possible, but stick to officially sanctioned campsites because many areas that are military or restricted zones aren't always marked as such and erecting a tent on an army firing range won't be a highlight of your trip. There are official camping grounds in Egypt, Lebanon, Turkey and Israel and the Palestinian Territories.

Hostels

There are youth hostels in Egypt, Israel and the Palestinian Territories. It's not usually necessary to hold a Hostelling International card to stay at these places, but it will usually get you a small discount.

Hotels

BUDGET

In hotels at the bottom end of the price scale, rooms are not always clean. In fact, let's be honest: they can be downright filthy. Very cheap hotels are just dormitories where you're crammed into a room with whoever else fronts up. The cheapest places are rarely suitable for women travelling alone.

That said, there are some places that stand out and while they may have no frills, nor do their shared bathrooms give any indication of the good health or otherwise of previous occupants. Some places treat you like a king even as you pay the price of a pauper. The happy (and most common) medium is usually a room devoid of character, but containing basic, well-maintained facilities.

MIDRANGE

In the midrange, rooms have private bathrooms, usually with hot water, fans to stir the air, a bit more space to swing a backpack and (sometimes) TVs promising international satellite channels.

TOP END

Hotels at the top end of the range have clean, self-contained rooms with hot showers and toilets that work all the time, not to mention

BOOK YOUR STAY ONLINE

For more accommodation reviews by Lonely Planet authors, check out http://hotels.lonelyplanet.com. You'll find independent reviews, as well as recommendations on the best places to stay. Best of all, you can book online.

satellite TV, shampoo and regularly washed towels in the bathrooms, air-con to provide refuge from the Middle Eastern sun and a few luxuries to lift the spirits.

An increasing (and entirely welcome) trend is the proliferation of tastefully designed boutique hotels that make a feature of traditional design. Prior to its implosion, Syria was leading the way with wonderful old courtyard homes and palaces converted into atmospheric hotels in Aleppo and Damascus.

GRAND OLD HOTELS OF THE MIDDLE EAST

If you're hankering after the Middle East of TE Lawrence and other stiff upper-lipped colonial types, a few grand old hotels from the era still exist. Some have been tarted up with only hints remaining of their former glories, but a few are fraying around the edges a little, perhaps adding to the appeal for nostalgia buffs.

» Windsor Hotel, Cairo (p66)

» Winter Palace Hotel, Luxor (p100)

» Palmyra Hotel, Baalbek (p378)

» Zenobia Cham Palace, Palmyra (p440)

» Baron Hotel, Aleppo (p426)

Business Hours

With just a few exceptions, the end-of-week holiday throughout the Middle East is Friday. In Israel and the Palestinian Territories it's Saturday (Shabbat), while in Lebanon and Turkey it's Sunday. In countries where Friday is the holiday, many embassies and offices are also closed on Thursday, although in areas where there are lots of tourists, many private businesses and shops are open on Thursday and many stores will reopen in the evening on Friday.

It's worth remembering that shops and businesses may have different opening hours for different times of the year – they tend to work shorter hours in winter and open earlier in summer to allow for a longer lunchtime siesta. During Ramadan (the month-long fast for Muslims), almost everything shuts down in the afternoon.

Customs Regulations

Customs regulations vary from country to country, but in most cases they aren't that different from what you'd expect in the West – a couple of hundred cigarettes and a couple of bottles of booze.

There was a time when electronics used to arouse interest when entering or leaving Egypt and Syria, but it's becoming increasingly rare. If they do pull you up, items such as laptop computers and especially video cameras may be written into your passport to ensure that they leave the country with you and are not sold. If you're carrying printed material that could be interpreted as being critical of the government, be discreet, although customs officials at major entry/departure points rarely search the bags of tourists.

Discount Cards

An International Student Identity Card (ISIC) can be useful in the Middle East. Egypt, Israel and the Palestinian Territories, Syria and Turkey have various (and often considerable) student discounts for admission to museums, archaeological sites and monuments. In Syria, it slashes admissions to almost all historical sites to about a 10th of the normal foreigners' price, while elsewhere discounts usually range from 25% to 50%. In Israel, cardholders also qualify for 10% reductions on some bus fares and 20% on rail tickets. Bear in mind that a student card issued by your own university or college may not be recognised elsewhere; it really should be an ISIC (www.isic.org).

Embassies & Consulates

It's important to realise what your own embassy can and can't do to help you if you get into trouble. Generally speaking, it won't be much help in emergencies if the trouble you're in is remotely your own fault. Remember that you are bound by the laws of the country you're in. Your embassy will not be sympathetic if you end up in jail after committing a crime locally, even if such actions are legal in your own country.

In genuine emergencies, you might get some limited assistance, but only if other channels have been exhausted. For example, if you need to get home urgently, a free ticket home is exceedingly unlikely – the embassy would expect you to have insurance. If all your money and documents are stolen, it might assist with getting a new passport, but a loan for onward travel is out of the question.

For the addresses and contact details of embassies and consulates in the Middle East, see the Directory sections in the individual country chapters.

Electricity

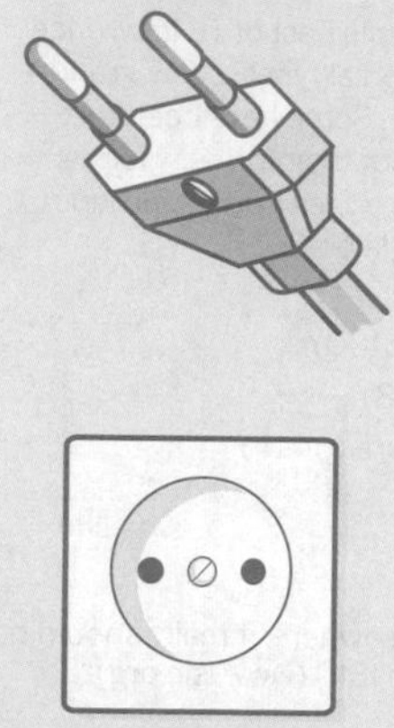

110V/220V/50Hz

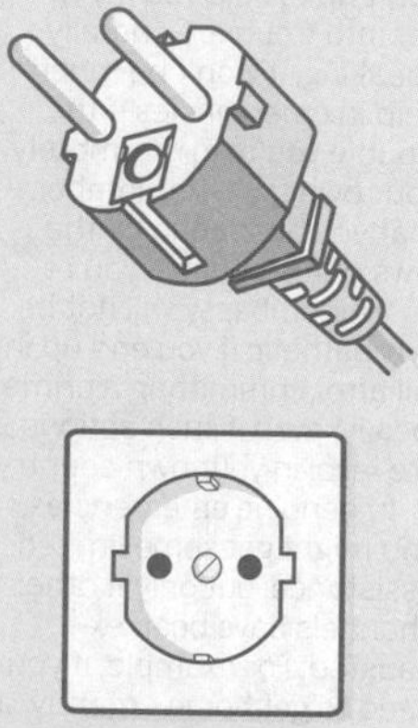

230V/50Hz

Gay & Lesbian Travellers

The situation for gay and lesbian travellers in the Middle East is more diverse than you might imagine. Israel is the best place in the region to be gay – homosexuality is legal, and Tel Aviv and Eilat in particular have thriving gay and lesbian scenes. The same doesn't apply to the Palestinian Territories, and hundreds of Palestinian gays have been forced to seek refuge in Israel.

Homosexuality is also legal in Turkey, with İstanbul and Ankara both home to a small but thriving gay culture. Turkey is, however, a Muslim country and discretion is key, while the local authorities have from time to time used morality laws to close down gay advocacy groups.

It is slightly more complicated in Egypt and Jordan, where, although the criminal code doesn't expressly forbid homosexual acts, laws regarding public decency have been used to prosecute gays, especially in Egypt; the Jordanian capital Amman nonetheless has a couple of gay-friendly spots. Homosexuality is illegal in Lebanon, Syria and Iraq, although Beirut takes a fairly liberal approach with a small but vibrant gay scene. In those countries where homosexuality is illegal or ambiguous in a legal sense, penalties include fines and/or imprisonment. That does not mean that gays aren't active, but it does mean that gay identity is generally expressed only in certain trusted, private spheres.

For more information on specific countries, see the Gay & Lesbian Travellers sections in the individual country chapters of this book.

Useful Resources

Gay Middle East (www.gaymiddleeast.com) A good rundown on the prevailing situation, including news updates, the legal situation and postings by locals and gay visitors.

Global Gayz (www.globalgayz.com) An excellent country-by-country rundown on the situation for gays and lesbians.

Spartacus International Gay Guide (www.spartacusworld.com/gayguide) Good for information on gay-friendly bars and hotels.

Insurance

Travel insurance covering theft, loss and medical problems is highly recommended. Some policies offer travellers lower and higher medical-expense options; the higher ones are chiefly for countries such as the USA, which have extremely high medical costs. Watch particularly for the small print as some policies specifically exclude 'dangerous activities', which can include scuba diving, motorcycling and even trekking.

For further details on health insurance, see p635, and for car insurance, see p632.

Internet Access

You're never too far from an internet cafe in all major cities and larger towns across the Middle East, although ones that last the distance are pretty rare. If you need to track one down and you're not close to one of those listed in this book, ask your hotel reception or head to the university district (if there is one) and ask around.

If you're travelling with a laptop, wireless internet access is increasingly the norm in most top-end hotels as well as many in the midrange categories. It's also getting easier to connect in upmarket cafes and restaurants.

Given its reputation for political censorship, there are surprisingly few websites that are blocked by governments in the region. That's not to say it doesn't happen.

Money

If we had to choose our preferred way of carrying our money to the Middle East, it would be a combination of withdrawing money from ATMs and carrying a supply of US dollars or euro cash.

See the Money section in the individual country chapters for more details.

ATMs

ATMs are now a way of life in most Middle Eastern countries and, with a few exceptions, it's possible to survive on cash advances. This is certainly the case in Turkey, Lebanon, Israel and the Palestinian Territories, Jordan and Egypt, where ATMs are everywhere and they're usually linked to one of the international networks (eg MasterCard, Maestro, Cirrus, Visa, Visa Electron or GlobalAccess systems). Syria increasingly has similar ATMs, but they've yet to reach beyond the major towns and most ATMs set a daily withdrawal limit of around US$50, making it more difficult to get by on this method alone. ATMs are appearing in Iraq, but they're still unreliable – bring US dollars cash.

Another thing to consider is whether the convenience of withdrawing money as you go is outweighed by the bank fees you'll be charged for doing so. It's a good idea to check the transaction fees both with your own bank back home and, if possible, with the banks whose machines you'll be using while you travel.

Cash

Although credit cards are increasingly accepted, cash remains king in the Middle East. And not just any cash. US dollars and, increasingly, euros are the currency of choice in most countries of the Middle East, and not just for changing money – many midrange and top-end hotels prefer their bills to be settled in either currency.

If your funds have run dry and you've no means of withdrawing money, Western Union (www.westernunion.com) has representatives in every country covered by this book.

The only danger in relying solely on travelling with cash is that if you lose it, it's lost forever – insurance companies simply won't believe that you had US$1000 in cash.

Credit Cards

Credit cards (especially Visa and MasterCard) are accepted by an ever-growing number of Middle Eastern hotels, top-end restaurants and handicraft shops, but the situation is still a long way from one where you could pay your way solely by flashing the card. Israel and the Palestinian Territories, Lebanon and Turkey are the most credit-card-friendly countries in the region, while Syria lags far behind – some Syrian businesses accept credit cards, and most still do so via Lebanese banks, which can add considerably to the cost of your purchase. You should always be wary of surcharges for paying by card, and not just in Syria – many Egyptian and Jordanian businesses also sting for commissions over and above the purchase price. Credit cards are still useless in Iraq.

Tipping

Tipping is expected to varying degrees in all Middle Eastern countries. Called baksheesh, it's more than just a reward for having rendered a service. Salaries and wages are much lower than in Western countries, so baksheesh is often regarded as an essential means of supplementing income. To a cleaner in a one- or two-star hotel who may earn the equivalent of US$50 per month, the accumulated daily dollar tips given by guests can constitute the mainstay of his or her salary.

For Western travellers who aren't used to continual tipping, demands for baksheesh for doing anything from opening doors to pointing out the obvious in museums can be quite irritating. But it is the accepted way. Don't be intimidated into paying baksheesh when you don't think the service warrants it, but remember that more things warrant baksheesh here than anywhere in the West. One hint: carry lots of small change with you, but keep it separate from bigger bills, so that baksheesh demands don't increase when they see that you can afford more.

Tipping is increasingly expected in midrange and top-end restaurants in Israel and the Palestinian Territories, Lebanon and Turkey. Check your bill closely, however, as many such restaurants include an additional charge for service, in which case a further tip is not necessary. One country where baksheesh or tipping isn't as prevalent is Jordan, where many locals feel irritated when tourists throw their money around, not least because some employers are known to deduct anticipated tips from their employees, resulting in even lower wages!

Other circumstances in which a tip is expected is where you've taken a tour either with a guide or a taxi driver or both. How much to leave depends on the length of the expedition and the helpfulness of the guide.

Travellers Cheques

If you're among the dwindling ranks of travellers still using travellers cheques, perhaps you should reconsider. Yes, they're secure and replaceable, but so too are most credit and other bank cards. However, the main reason for not using travellers cheques is that only a limited number of banks will change them, they'll always charge a commission for doing so and it always means you'll spend longer in the bank.

If you do take travellers cheques, carry a mix of high- and low denomination notes, as well as cheques, so that if you're about to leave a country, you can change just enough for a few days and not end up with too much local currency to get rid of.

Photography

Equipment

Memory cards are widely available in most countries of the Middle East, although you'll have a wider choice of brands in major cities. Expect prices to be broadly similar to what you'd pay back home. The situation for batteries is also similar, although for more professional cameras, you'd be better off bringing your own supply. When it comes to burning photos onto CDs, most internet cafes will do so without batting an eyelid.

Cameras and lenses collect dust quickly in desert areas. Lens paper, a dust brush and cleaners can be difficult to find in some countries, so bring your own.

Photographing People

As a matter of courtesy, never photograph people without first asking their permission. While that's a general rule for photography anywhere, it's especially important in the Middle East. In more conservative areas, including many rural areas, men should never photograph women and in most circumstances should never even ask. In countries where you can photograph women, show them the camera and make it clear that you want to take their picture. Digital cameras have the advantage of being able to show people their photo immediately after you've taken it, which is usually temptation enough for most people to say yes.

Restrictions

In most Middle Eastern countries, it is forbidden to photograph anything even vaguely military in nature (including bridges, train stations, airports, border crossings and other public works). The definition of what is 'strategic' differs from one country to the next, and signs are not always posted, so err on the side of caution and, if in doubt, ask your friendly neighbouring police officer for permission.

Photography is usually allowed inside religious and archaeological sites, unless signs indicate otherwise. As a rule, do not photograph inside mosques during a service. Many Middle Easterners are sensitive about the negative aspects of their country, so exercise discretion when taking photos in poorer areas.

Public Holidays

All Middle Eastern countries, save Israel, observe the main Islamic holidays listed below. Countries with a major Shiite population also observe Ashura, the anniversary of the martyrdom of Hussein, the third imam of the Shiites. Most of the countries in this book also observe both the Gregorian and the Islamic New Year holidays. Every country also has its own national days and other public holidays – for details refer to the individual country chapters. For Jewish holidays in Israel, see p270.

Eid al-Adha (Kurban Bayramı in Turkey) This feast marks the time that Muslims make the pilgrimage to Mecca.

Eid al-Fitr (Şeker Bayramı in Turkey) Another feast, this time to herald the end of Ramadan fasting; the celebrations last for three days.

Islamic New Year Also known as Ras as-Sana, it

ISLAMIC HOLIDAYS

Hejira year	New Year	Prophet's Birthday	Lailat al-Mi'raj	Ramadan begins	Eid al-Fitr	Eid al-Adha	Ashura
1433	29 Nov 2011	5 Feb 2012	18 May 2012	20 Jul 2012	20 Aug 2012	28 Oct 2012	6 Dec 2011
1434	18 Nov 2012	25 Jan 2013	7 May 2013	9 Jul 2013	9 Aug 2013	17 Oct 2013	26 Nov 2012
1435	7 Nov 2013	14 Jan 2014	27 April 2014	29 Jun 2014	30 Jul 2014	6 Oct 2014	15 Nov 2013
1436	26 Oct 2014	3 Jan 2015	16 Apr 2015	16 Jun 2015	19 Jul 2015	25 Sep 2015	4 Nov 2014
1437	15 Oct 2015	23 Dec 2015	5 Apr 2016	5 Jun 2016	8 Jul 2016	14 Sep 2016	24 Oct 2015
1438	4 Oct 2016	12 Dec 2016	25 Mar 2016	25 May 2017	27 Jun 2017	3 Sep 2017	13 Oct 2016

literally means 'the head of the year'.

Lailat al-Mi'raj This is the celebration of the Ascension of the Prophet Mohammed.

Prophet's Birthday This is also known as Moulid an-Nabi, 'the feast of the Prophet'.

Ramadan (Ramazan in Turkey) This is the ninth month of the Muslim calendar, when Muslims fast during daylight hours. Foreigners are not expected to follow suit, but it's considered impolite to smoke, drink or eat in public during Ramadan. As the sun sets each day, the fast is broken with *iftar* (the evening meal prepared to break the fast). See also p580 for further details.

Islamic Calendar

All Islamic holidays fall according to the Muslim calendar, while secular activities are planned according to the Christian system.

The Muslim year is based on the lunar cycle and is divided into 12 lunar months, each with 29 or 30 days. Consequently, the Muslim year is 10 or 11 days shorter than the Christian solar year, and the Muslim festivals gradually move around our year, completing the cycle in roughly 33 years. Actual dates may occur a day later, but probably not earlier, depending on western hemisphere moon sightings.

Telephone

In most countries of the Middle East, the cheapest way to make international calls is at your friendly local internet cafe for a fraction of the cost of calling on a normal landline. Staff at these cafes (most of which are equipped with webcams, microphones and headsets) are generally pretty tech-savvy, and can sell you the relevant card (there are usually a number of brands to choose from) and show you how to use it.

Most internet cafes will also let you use operators such as Skype (www.skype.com) – remember to take your sign-in details.

If you're a traditionalist, or if internet-connected phone calls aren't possible, head for the public telephone office, which usually sits adjacent to the post office. Here, you can generally make operator-connected calls or buy cards for use in phone booths around the city; kiosks dotted around most major cities generally sell the same cards. There are also privately run call centres (although many of these have three-minute call minimums), where you can make international calls and send faxes. Costs for international calls start at about US$3 per minute, and a few countries offer reduced rates at night.

Mobile Phones

Mobile networks in Middle Eastern countries all work on the GSM system, and it's extremely rare that your mobile brought from home won't automatically link up with a local operator. That's fine for receiving calls, but roaming charges can make for a nasty surprise back home if you've made a few calls on your trip. If you plan to be in a country for a while, your best option is to buy a local SIM card – an easy process in every country of the region.

See the Telephone section in the relevant country chapters for further details.

TIME

For more on time zones and daylight savings, please see the relevant sections of the individual country chapters.

	Time Zone	Daylight Saving
Egypt	GMT/UTC + two hours	yes
Iraq	GMT/UTC + three hours	yes
Israel & the Palestinian Territories	GMT/UTC + two hours	yes
Jordan	GMT/UTC + two hours	no
Lebanon	GMT/UTC + two hours	yes
Syria	GMT/UTC + two hours	yes
Turkey	GMT/UTC + two hours	yes

Toilets

Outside the midrange and top-end hotels and restaurants (where Western-style loos are the norm), visitors will encounter their fair share of Arab-style squat toilets (which, incidentally, according to physiologists, encourage a far more natural position than the Western-style invention!).

It's a good idea to carry an emergency stash of toilet paper with you for the times when you're caught short outside the hotel as most of these toilets have a water hose and bucket for the same purpose.

Tourist Information

Most countries in the region have tourist offices with branches in big towns and at tourist sights. That said, don't expect much. Usually, the most the offices can produce is a free map; help with booking accommodation or any other service is typically beyond the resources of the often-nonetheless-amiable staff. The exceptions to this rule are some of the offices in Israel and the Palestinian Territories, which are in fact very useful. Elsewhere, you'll usually get better results relying on the knowledge and resourcefulness of your hotel reception or a local guide. Tourist-office locations are given in the individual town and city sections throughout this book.

Travellers with Disabilities

Generally speaking, scant regard is paid to the needs of disabled travellers in the Middle East. Steps, high kerbs and other assorted obstacles are everywhere, streets are often badly rutted and uneven, roads are made virtually uncrossable by heavy traffic, and many doorways are low and narrow. Ramps and specially equipped lodgings and toilets are an extreme rarity. The exception is Israel and the Palestinian Territories; see p272 for details. Elsewhere, you'll have to plan your trip carefully and will probably be obliged to restrict yourself to luxury-level hotels and private, hired transport.

If it all sounds difficult, remember that where Middle Eastern governments have singularly failed to provide the necessary infrastructure, local officials, guides and hotel staff almost invariably do their best to help in any way they can.

Useful Resources

For further information about disabled travel contact the following:

Access-Able Travel Source (☎303-2322979; www.access-able.com; USA) Has lists of tour operators offering tours for travellers with disabilities.

Accessible Travel & Leisure (☎0145-272 9739; www.accessibletravel.co.uk) Claims to be the biggest UK travel agent dealing with travel for the disabled, including some options for Egypt. The company encourages the disabled to travel independently.

Royal Association for Disability & Rehabilitation (RADAR; ☎UK 020-7250 3222; www.radar.org.uk) Publishes a useful guide called *Holidays & Travel Abroad: A Guide for Disabled People*.

Society for Accessible Travel and Hospitality (☎212-447 7284; www.sath.org; USA)

Tourism for All (☎0303-303 0146; www.tourismforall.org.uk) Advice for disabled and less-mobile senior travellers.

Volunteering

There aren't many opportunities for volunteering in the Middle East – teaching English in Madaba in Jordan (see the boxed text, p307) or spending time on a kibbutz (p273) are two. Some international organisations (including some of the following) also have projects in the region:

Earthwatch (www.earthwatch.org)

Idealist.org (www.idealist.org)

International Volunteer Programs Association (www.volunteerinternational.org)

Worldwide Volunteering (www.wwv.org.uk)

Transport

GETTING THERE & AWAY

This section tells you how to reach the Middle East from other parts of the world, and outlines the routes for onward travel from the region. For details of travel between one country and its neighbours within the region, see the Getting There & Away section at the end of the relevant country chapter.

Flights, tours and rail tickets can be booked online at www.lonelyplanet.com/travel_services.

Entering the Middle East

Presuming all of your papers are in order, entering the Middle East is generally hassle free, although it can take quite a while to get across at busier border crossings, particularly if you're driving your own vehicle.

For detailed advice on visa requirements and border crossings, see p35, as well as each chapter's Transport section.

Passport

Please note that neither Israeli citizens nor anyone who has an Israeli stamp in their passport will be allowed to enter Iran, Iraq, Lebanon or Syria. For advice on how to get around this decades-old Middle Eastern conundrum, see the boxed text on p36.

Air

Airports & Airlines

The Middle East's main international airports are as follows. Please note that both Egypt and Turkey have additional airports that receive international flights – see the country chapters for details.

Atatürk International Airport (www.ataturkairport.com) Istanbul

Ben Gurion Airport (www.iaa.gov.il/Rashat/en-US/Airports/BenGurion) Tel Aviv

Cairo International Airport (www.cairo airport.com)

Damascus International Airport

Erbil Airport (www.erbilairport.net)

Queen Alia International Airport (www.aig.aero) Amman

Rafic Hariri International Airport (www.beirutairport.gov.lb) Beirut

The following airlines all fly into the Middle East:

Air Arabia (www.airarabia.com)

EgyptAir (www.egyptair.com.eg)

El Al (www.elal.co.il)

Emirates (www.emirates.com)

Gulf Air (www.gulfair.com)

Iraqi Airways (www.iraqiairways.co.uk)

Iran Air (www.iranair.com)

Jazeera Airways (www.jazeeraairways.com)

Middle East Airlines (www.mea.com.lb)

CLIMATE CHANGE & TRAVEL

Every form of transport that relies on carbon-based fuel generates CO_2, the main cause of human-induced climate change. Modern travel is dependent on aeroplanes, which might use less fuel per kilometre per person than most cars but travel much greater distances. The altitude at which aircraft emit gases (including CO_2) and particles also contributes to their climate change impact. Many websites offer 'carbon calculators' that allow people to estimate the carbon emissions generated by their journey and, for those who wish to do so, to offset the impact of the greenhouse gases emitted with contributions to portfolios of climate-friendly initiatives throughout the world. Lonely Planet offsets the carbon footprint of all staff and author travel.

Qatar Airways (www.qatarairways.com)

Royal Jordanian (www.rj.com)

SyrianAir (www.syriaair.com)

Turkish Airlines (www.turkishairlines.com)

Land

Border Crossings

AFRICA

Service taxis and occasional Cairo–Benghazi buses cross the border at Amsaad, 12km west of Sallum.

The **Nile River Valley Transport Corporation** (☎in Aswan 097-303 348, in Cairo 02-575 9058) runs one passenger ferry per week between Aswan in Egypt and Wadi Halfa in Sudan (16 to 24 hours). Options include 1st class with bed in a cabin, an airline seat and deck class. To board the ferry, you must have a valid Sudanese visa in your passport.

CAUCASUS

Armenia

The Turkish–Armenian border has been closed to travellers for years, so you'll need to travel via Georgia. Around three weekly buses depart from Trabzon's otogar heading for Yerevan.

Georgia

At least two daily buses depart from Trabzon's otogar for Tbilisi (19 hours).

EUROPE

It's fairly easy to get to İstanbul by direct train or bus from many points in Europe via Bulgaria; getting to Turkey overland is usually cheaper and faster by bus. Several Turkish bus lines offer reliable and quite comfortable services between İstanbul and Germany, Italy, Austria and Greece.

Bulgaria & Other Eastern European Countries

There are several bus departures daily to Sofia, and the coastal cities of Varna and Burgas in Bulgaria from İstanbul's otogar. There are also daily departures to Skopje, Tetovo and Gostivar in Macedonia, and to Constanta and Bucharest (Romania).

The daily *Bosphorus Express (Bosfor Ekspresi)* train runs from İstanbul to Bucharest, from where you can travel onwards by train to Moldova and Hungary. You can also catch the *Bosphorus Express* as far as Dimitrovgrad (Bulgaria) from where you can travel onwards to Sofia (Bulgaria) and on to Belgrade (Serbia). You'll need to take your own food and drinks as there are no restaurant cars on these trains.

Greece

At least six weekly buses travel from Athens' Peloponnese train station to İstanbul. You can also pick up the bus in Thessaloniki and at Alexandroupolis. Alternatively, you can make your own way to Alexandroupolis and take a service from the intercity bus station to the border town of Kipi. You can't walk across the border, but it's easy enough to hitch. Otherwise, take a bus to İpsala (5km east beyond the border) or Keşan (30km east beyond the border), from where there are many buses to the capital.

The best option for travelling by train between Greece and Turkey is the overnight train between Thessaloniki and İstanbul called the *Filia-Dostluk Express*. The 1400km journey takes 12 to 14 hours, including an hour or two's delay at the border, and accommodation is in comfy, air-conditioned sleeper cars. You can buy tickets at the train stations but not online. For more information see the websites of **Turkish State Railways** (TCDD; www.tcdd.gov.tr) or the **Hellenic Railways Organisation** (www.ose.gr).

IRAN

There are regular buses from İstanbul and Ankara to Tabriz and Tehran. There is also a direct bus running between Van (Turkey) and Orumiyeh (Iran). You may also want to consider taking a dolmuş from Doğubayazıt 35km east to the border at Gürbulak and then walking across the border. From Bazargan there are onward buses to Tabriz; from Sero there are buses to Orumiyeh.

The *Trans-Asya Ekspresi* train runs between Tehran and İstanbul, travelling via Tabriz, Van and Tatvan. Expect a comfortable journey on connecting Turkish and Iranian trains, a ferry ride across Lake Van, and no showers. Depending on the security situation in Syria, there may also be a weekly train service between Tehran (Iran) and Damascus (Syria) via Van, Malatya and Aleppo. See www.tcdd.gov.tr for more information.

Sea

Ferries shuttle reasonably regularly between southern Europe and Israel, Turkey and Egypt. There are other less-frequented routes connecting Egypt with Sudan and the Arabian Peninsula. In summer, you might also come across services operating between Cyprus and Syria, but these are highly seasonal and change from year to year.

Although vehicles can be shipped on most routes, bookings may have to be made some time in advance. The charge usually depends on the length or volume of the vehicle and should be checked with the carrier. As a rule, motorcycles cost almost nothing to ship while bicycles are free.

You're unlikely to regret taking an adequate supply of food and drink with you on any of these ships; even if it's available on board, you're pretty stuck if it doesn't agree with you or your budget.

Ferry Lines (www.ferrylines.com) is a good place to get started when looking at possible routes into the region.

Cyprus

If you have a multiple-entry visa for Turkey, you should be able to cross over to Northern Cyprus and back again without buying a new one. However, if your visa has expired, you should anticipate long queues at immigration.

Salamis Cruise Lines (www.varianostravel.com) From Limassol to Haifa (10 to 12 hours, 1 to 3 per month)

Akgünler (www.akgunler.com.tr) Girne to Taşucu, in Turkey (1½ hours, daily)

Fergün Shipping (www.fergun.net) Girne to Taşucu, in Turkey (2½ to 5 hours, up to two daily)

Greece

Private ferries link Turkey's Aegean coast and the Greek islands. Services are usually daily in summer, several times a week in spring and autumn, and perhaps just once a week in winter. Please note that all the information that follows covers travelling to Turkey from Greek cities and towns.

Car-ferry services operate between Greek ports and several Turkish ports, but not to İstanbul. Among the most important routes are Chios–Çeşme, Kastellorizo–Kaş, Kos–Bodrum, Lesvos–Ayvalık, Rhodes (Rhodos)–Bodrum, Rhodes (Rhodos)–Datça, Rhodes (Rhodos)–Marmaris and Samos–Kuşadası.

Russia & Ukraine

The following companies travel to and from Ukraine:

Sea Lines (www.sea-lines.net) Illichivsk to İstanbul (27 to 33 hours, twice weekly)

Gess Tour (www.gess-tour.com) From Odessa to İstanbul (40 hours, weekly)

The following each run five services a week (ranging from 4½ to 12 hours duration) from Sochi, in Russia, to Trabzon:

Olympia Line (www.olympia-line.ru)

Oz Star Denizcilik (www.al-port.com)

Sari Denizcilik (www.seaport-sochi.ru/lines)

Tours

International tour companies offer a host of possibilities for visiting the Middle East – everything from a package tour by the beach to a more gruelling six-week overland expedition.

For tour companies specialising in individual countries, see the Transport section of the relevant country chapter.

For a clearing house of sustainable tour options, visit www.responsibletravel.com.

Australia

Intrepid (www.intrepidtravel.com) Tours to every Middle Eastern country except Iraq.

Passport Travel (www.travelcentre.com.au) Tours to Turkey, Egypt, Jordan, Lebanon and Israel.

Italy, France & Germany

Antichi Splendori Viaggi (www.antichisplendori.it, in Italian) Experienced Italian operator.

Atalante (www.atalante.fr) French company with tours to Israel, Egypt and Jordan.

Dabuka Expeditions (www.dabuka.de) German expeditions into the Egyptian Sahara.

Terres d'Aventure (www.terdav.com) French operator that visits most countries in the region.

Zig-Zag Randonnées (www.zigzag-randonnees.com) Experienced French company that gets off the beaten track.

UK

Adventure Company (www.adventurecompany.co.uk) Egypt, Jordan, Lebanon and Syria with walking and even astronomy options.

Ancient World Tours (www.ancient.co.uk) Ancient Egypt specialists.

Andante Travels (www.andantetravels.co.uk) Archaeology tours, including to southeastern Turkey.

Crusader Travel (www.crusadertravel.com) Sinai treks and Red Sea diving.

Kumuka (www.kumuka.com) Small group tours throughout the region.

Wild Frontiers (www.silkroadandbeyond.co.uk) Tailor-made itineraries in Jordan and Lebanon.

USA

Bestway Tours & Safaris (www.bestway.com) All the usual tours plus Iraqi Kurdistan.

Yalla Tours (www.yallatours.com) Middle East specialists.

GETTING AROUND

This chapter should be used for general planning only. If you want to travel, for instance, between Turkey and Israel and the Palestinian Territories, it will give you a broad overview of the options: air, land or sea, train versus bus, and so on. Then, if you decide to go by bus from İstanbul to Damascus, you should begin by going to the Getting There & Away section at the back of the Turkey chapter for further details on buses to Syria, and so on.

Air

With no regional rail network to speak of, and distances that make the bus a discomforting test of endurance, flying is certainly the most user-friendly method of transport in the Middle East if your time is tight.

Flying isn't possible between Israel and the Palestinian Territories and other Middle Eastern countries, except for Egypt, Jordan and Turkey. But, these exceptions aside, almost every Middle Eastern capital is linked to each of the others.

Airlines

Until recently, most flights were operated by state airlines. Of these, when it comes to service, punctuality and safety, El Al (Israel), Royal Jordanian, Turkish Airlines and Middle East Airlines (Lebanon) are probably the pick of the bunch, while SyrianAir has a solid if unspectacular reputation.

The growth of private (usually low-cost) airlines, especially in Turkey and Israel, means that flying domestic routes within these countries has become a lot more feasible.

Detailed information on many airlines' safety records (including reams of statistics) can be found at www.airsafe.com/index.html.

For a list of airlines flying to and from the Middle East, see p627. Those that fly domestically within the Middle East:

Anadolujet (www.anadolujet.com) Turkey

Arkia Israel Airlines (www.arkia.co.il) Israel

Atlasjet (www.atlasjet.com) Turkey

Egypt Air (www.egyptair.com)

Onur Air (www.onurair.com.tr) Turkey

Pegasus Airlines (www.flypgs.com) Turkey

Sun Express (www.sunexpress.com) Turkey

Tarhan Tower Airlines (www.ttairlines.com) Turkey

Air Passes

Emirates (www.emirates.com) offers the 'Arabian Airpass' that allows cut-price travel around the Middle East. To qualify, you need to buy a flight to Dubai. Onward flight 'coupons' (a minimum of two, maximum of six) are then available to cities such as Cairo, Amman or Beirut. Prices are based upon zones, with the above cities coming within Zone C.

Bicycle

Although the numbers doing it are small, cycling round the Middle East is a viable proposition, provided that cyclists are self-sufficient and able to carry litres of extra water.

Most of the people we spoke to reckoned that the most enjoyable cycling was in Turkey and Syria. Although hilly, the scenery in Turkey is particularly fine and accommodation is fairly easy to come by, even in the smallest villages. This is definitely not the case elsewhere.

In Turkey, if you get tired of pedalling, it's also no problem to have your bike transported in the luggage hold of the big modern buses.

One big plus about cycling through the region is the fact that cyclists are usually given fantastic welcomes (a trademark of the Middle East in any case) and are showered with food and drinks. There are a couple of exceptions, with isolated reports of kids throwing stones at cyclists (maybe because of the cycling shorts, we don't know) along Jordan's King's Highway and in Sinai. But these are minor blips of annoyance.

By far the major difficulty cited by all cyclists was the heat. This is at its worst from June to August, and cycling in these summer months is definitely not recommended. May to mid-June and September through October are the best times. Even then, you're advised to make an early morning start and call it a day by early afternoon.

There are bicycle-repair shops in most major towns and the locals are excellent 'bush mechanics', with all but the most modern or sophisticated equipment.

The following additional tips may help:

- Carry a couple of extra chain links, a chain breaker, spokes, a spoke key, two inner tubes, tyre levers and a repair kit, a flat-head and Phillips-head screwdriver, and Allen keys and spanners to fit all the bolts on your bike.
- Check the bolts daily and carry spares.
- Fit as many water bottles to your bike as you can.
- Confine your panniers to a maximum weight of 15kg.
- Carrying the following equipment in your panniers is recommended: a two-person tent (weighing about 1.8kg) that can also accommodate the bike where security is a concern; a sleeping bag rated to 0°C and an inflatable

CYCLING CONTACTS

If you're considering cycling in the Middle East, but have a few pressing questions that first need answering, you can post your query on the Thorn Tree on Lonely Planet's website (www.lonelyplanet.com) under the Activities branch. There's a strong likelihood somebody will respond with the information that you're looking for.

Alternatively, you could contact the **Cyclists' Touring Club** (www.ctc.org.uk), a UK-based organisation that offers good tips and information sheets on cycling in different parts of the world; the website itself is quite useful.

mattress; a small camping stove; cooking pot; utensils; a water filter (two microns) and a compact torch.

» Wear cycling shorts with a chamois bum and cleated cycling shoes.

» Don't worry about filling the panniers with food, as there will be plentiful and fresh supplies along the route.

Boat

The most popular boat services are the two ferry services between Nuweiba in Egypt and Aqaba in Jordan. The fast-ferry service takes one hour, while the slow (and cheaper) ferry makes the journey in 2½ to three hours. Vehicles can usually be shipped on these routes, but advance arrangements may have to be made. For more information on these ferry services, see p340 and p152.

Bus

Buses are the workhorses of the Middle East, and in most places they're probably your only option for getting from A to B. Thankfully, most buses are reliable and comfortable.

The cost and comfort of bus travel vary enormously throughout the region. One typical nuisance is bus drivers' fondness (presumably shared by local passengers) for loud videos; sleep is almost always impossible. Another potential source of discomfort is that in most Middle Eastern countries, the concept of a 'nonsmoking bus' is not always observed.

Some sample journey times:

İstanbul–Damascus 30 hours

Damascus–Beirut four hours

Damascus–Amman seven hours

Amman–Cairo 16 hours

Amman–Baghdad 14 hours

Cairo–Tel Aviv 10 hours

Reservations

It's always advisable to book bus seats in advance at the bus station, which is usually the only ticket outlet and source of reliable information about current services. Reservations are a must over the Muslim weekend (Friday) as well as during public holidays (see p624).

Car & Motorcycle

Bringing your own car to the Middle East will give you a lot more freedom, but it's certainly not for everyone. For all the positives, it's difficult to imagine a route through the Middle East that would justify the expense and hassle of bringing a car and getting it out again.

Throughout the Middle East, motorcycles are fairly popular as a means of racing around in urban areas, but are little used as long-distance transport. If you do decide to ride a motorcycle through the region, try to take one of the more popular Japanese models if you want to stand any chance of finding spare parts. Even then, make sure your bike is in very good shape before setting out. Motorcycles can be shipped or, often, loaded as luggage onto trains.

Bringing Your Own Vehicle

Anyone planning to take their own vehicle with them needs to check in advance what spare parts and petrol are likely to be available.

A number of documents are also required (if you're unsure what to take, check with the automobile association in your home country):

Carnet de passage

Green card Issued by insurers. Insurance for some countries is only obtainable at the border.

International Driving Permit (IDP)

Vehicle registration documents In addition to carrying all ownership papers, check with your insurer whether you're covered for the countries you intend to visit and whether third-party cover is included.

Driving Licences

If you plan to drive, get an IDP from your local automobile association. An IDP is compulsory for foreign drivers and motorcyclists in Egypt, Iran, Iraq and Syria. Most foreign (or national) licences are acceptable in Israel and the Palestinian Territories, Lebanon and Turkey, and for foreign-registered vehicles in Jordan. However, even in these places an IDP is recommended. IDPs are valid for one year only.

Fuel & Spare Parts

Mechanical failure can be a problem as spare parts – or at least official ones – are often unobtainable. Fear not, ingenuity often compensates for factory parts; your mechanic back home will either have a heart attack or learn new techniques when you show them what's gone on under your hood in the Middle East.

Generally, Land Rovers, Volkswagens, Range Rovers, Mercedes and Chevrolets are the cars for which spare parts are most likely to be available, although in recent years Japan has been a particularly vigorous exporter of vehicles to the region. One tip is to ask your vehicle manufacturer for a list of any authorised service centres it has in the countries you plan to visit. The length of this list is likely to be a pretty good reflection of how easy it is to get parts on your travels.

Usually two grades of petrol are available; if in doubt get the more expensive one. Petrol stations are few and far between on many desert roads. Away from the main towns, it's advisable to fill up whenever you get the chance. Locally produced maps often indicate the locations of petrol stations. Diesel isn't readily available in every

CARNETS

A carnet de passage is like a passport for your car, a booklet that's stamped on arrival at and departure from a country to ensure that you export the vehicle again after you've imported it. It's usually issued by an automobile association in the country where the vehicle is registered. Most countries of the Middle East require a carnet although rules change frequently.

The sting in the tail with a carnet is that you usually have to lodge a deposit to secure it. If you default on the carnet – that is, you don't have an export stamp to match the import one – then the country in question can claim your deposit, which can be up to 300% of the new value of the vehicle. You can get around this problem with bank guarantees or carnet insurance, but you still have to fork out in the end if you default.

Should the worst occur and your vehicle is irretrievably damaged in an accident or catastrophic breakdown, you'll have to argue it out with customs officials. Having a vehicle stolen can be even worse, as you may be suspected of having sold it.

The carnet may also need to specify any expensive spare parts that you're planning to carry with you, such as a gearbox, which is designed to prevent any spare-part importation rackets. Contact your local automobile association for details about all necessary documentation at least three months in advance.

Middle Eastern country, nor is unleaded petrol.

Car Hire

International hire companies such as **Hertz** (www.hertz.com), **Avis** (www.avis.com) and **Europcar** (www.europcar.com) are represented in many large towns. Local companies are usually cheaper, but the cars of international companies are often better maintained and come with a better back-up service if problems arise. Local companies sometimes carry the advantage of including a driver for a similar cost to hiring the car alone. A good place to find competitive rates is **Imakoo Cars** (www.imakoocars.co.uk/directory-in.php/middle-east), a clearing house for cheap rates of international companies with services in all countries covered in this guide, except Egypt.

To hire a car, you'll need any or all of the following: a photocopy of your passport and visa; deposit or credit-card imprint; and your driving licence or IDP. The minimum age varies between 21 and 25 – the latter is most common, particularly with international companies.

Always make sure that insurance is included in the hire price and familiarise yourself with the policy – don't hire a car unless it's insured for every eventuality.

Insurance

Insurance is compulsory in most Middle Eastern countries, not to mention highly advisable. Given the large number of minor accidents, not to mention major ones, fully comprehensive insurance (as opposed to third-party) is strongly advised, both for your own and any hire vehicle.

Make certain you're covered for off-piste travel, as well as travel between Middle Eastern countries (if you're planning cross-border excursions).

In the event of an accident, make sure you submit the accident report as soon as possible to the insurance company or, if hiring, the car-hire company, and do so before getting the car repaired.

Road Conditions

Conditions across the Middle East vary enormously, but in almost all cases, they'll be worse than you're used to back home. The main roads are generally good, or at least reasonable, but there are plenty of unsurfaced examples, and the international roads are generally narrow and crowded. Turkey, Jordan and Israel and the Palestinian Territories probably have the best roads, but those in Lebanon and Syria adhere to the following rule: worse than they should be but probably better than you'd expect. Some of Egypt's roads are fine, others are bone-jarringly bad.

Road Hazards

Driving in the Middle East can be appalling by Western norms. Fatalism and high speed rule supreme. Car horns, used at the slightest provocation, take the place of caution and courtesy. Except in well-lit urban areas, try to avoid driving at night, as you may find your vehicle is the only thing on the road with lights.

In desert regions, particularly in Egypt, beware of wind-blown sand and wandering, free-range camels – the latter can be deadly at night.

Remember that an accident in the more remote parts of the region isn't always handled by your friendly insurance company. 'An eye for an eye' is likely to be the guiding principle of the other party and their relatives, whether you're in the wrong or not. In such cases, it may be more prudent to head for the nearest police station than to wait at the scene.

Road Rules

You're unlikely even to know what the speed limit is on a particular road, let alone be forced to keep to it – the rules exist more in theory than they are enforced in reality.

A warning triangle is required for vehicles (except motorcycles) in most Middle Eastern countries; in Turkey two triangles and a first-aid kit are compulsory.

In all countries, driving is on the right-hand side of the road and the rules of when to give way (at least officially) are those that apply in Continental Europe.

Hitching

Although many travellers hitchhike, it's never an entirely safe way of getting around and those who do so should understand that they are taking a small but potentially serious risk. There is no part of the Middle East where hitching can be recommended for unaccompanied women travellers. Just because we explain how hitching works, doesn't mean we recommend you do it.

Hitching as commonly understood in the West hardly exists in the Middle East (except in Israel and the Palestinian Territories). Although in most countries you'll often see people standing by the road hoping for a lift, they will nearly always expect (and be expected) to offer to pay. Hitching in the Middle Eastern sense is not so much an alternative to the public transport system as an extension of it, particularly in areas where there's no regular public transport. The going rate is often roughly the equivalent of the bus or shared taxi fare, but may be more if a driver takes you to an address or place off their route. You may well be offered free lifts from time to time, but you won't get very far if you set out deliberately to avoid paying for transport.

Throughout the Middle East a raised thumb is a vaguely obscene gesture. A common way of signalling that you want a lift is to extend your right hand, palm down.

Local Transport

Bus

In most cities and towns, a minibus or bus service operates. Fares are very cheap, and services are fast, regular and run on fixed routes with, in some cases, fixed stops. However, unless you're very familiar with the town, they can be difficult to get to grips with (few display their destinations and fewer still do so in English and they are often very crowded). Unless you can find a local who speaks your language to help you out, your best bet is to stand along the footpath (preferably at a bus stop if one exists) of a major thoroughfare heading in the direction you want to go, and call out the local name (or the name of a landmark close to where you're heading) into the drivers' windows when they slow down.

Taxi

In the West, taxis are usually considered a luxury. In the Middle East they're often unavoidable. Some cities have no other form of urban public transport, while there are also many rural routes that are only feasible in a taxi or private vehicle.

Taxis are seemingly everywhere you look and, if you can't see one, try lingering on the footpath next to a major road and, within no time, plenty of taxis will appear as if from nowhere and will soon toot their horns at you just in case you missed them, even if you're just trying to cross the street.

If you want to save money, it's important to be able to differentiate between the various kinds of taxis.

REGULAR TAXI

Regular taxis (variously known as 'agency taxis', 'telephone taxis', 'private taxis' or 'special taxis') are found in almost every Middle Eastern town or city. Unlike shared taxis, you pay to have the taxi to yourself, either to take you to a pre-agreed destination or for a specified period of time. They are primarily of use for transport within towns or on short rural trips, but in some countries hiring them for excursions of several hours is still cheap. They are also often the only way of reaching airports or seaports.

SHARED TAXI

A compromise between the convenience of a regular taxi and the economy of a bus, the shared taxi picks up and drops off passengers at points along its (generally fixed) route and runs to no particular schedule. It's known by different names – collect, collective or service taxi in English, *servees* in Arabic, sherut in Hebrew and dolmuş in Turkish. Most shared taxis take up to four or five passengers, but some seat up to about 12 and are indistinguishable for most purposes from minibuses.

Shared taxis are much cheaper than private taxis and, once you get the hang of them, can be just as convenient. They are dearer than buses, but more frequent and usually faster, because they don't stop so often or for so long. They also tend to operate for longer hours than buses. They can be used for urban, intercity or rural transport.

Fixed-route taxis wait at the point of departure until full or nearly full. Usually they pick up or drop off passengers anywhere en route, but in some places they have fixed halts or stations. Sometimes each service is allocated a number, which

TIPS FOR CATCHING TAXIS

On the whole, taxi drivers in the Middle East are helpful, honest and often humorous. Others – as in countries all over the world – find new arrivals too tempting a target for minor scams or a spot of overcharging. Here are a few tips:

» Not all taxi drivers speak English. Generally, in cities used to international travellers, they will (or know enough to get by), but not otherwise. If you're having trouble, ask a local for help.

» Always negotiate a fare (or insist that the meter is used if it works) before jumping in. This book quotes local rates but, if in doubt, inquire at your point of departure.

» Don't rely on street names (there are often several versions and the driver may recognise your pronunciation of none of them). If you're going to a well-known destination (such as a big hotel), find out if it's close to a local landmark and give the driver the local name for the landmark. Even better, get someone to write down the name in Arabic or whatever the local language is.

» Avoid using unlicensed cab drivers at airports or bus stations.

may be indicated on the vehicle. Generally, a flat fare applies for each route, but sometimes it's possible to pay a partial fare.

Fares depend largely on time and distance, but can also vary slightly according to demand.

Beware of boarding an empty one, as the driver may assume you want to hire the vehicle for your exclusive use and charge you accordingly. It's advisable to watch what other passengers pay and to hand over your fare in front of them. Passengers are expected to know where they are getting off. 'Thank you' in the local language is the usual cue for the driver to stop. Make it clear to the driver or other passengers if you want to be told when you reach your destination.

Train

There are train networks in Egypt, Israel and the Palestinian Territories, Syria and Turkey and these can represent the best transport option on some routes, such as between Cairo and Luxor in Egypt, or between Aleppo and Lattakia in Syria, for example. Levels of comfort vary from country to country – many of Egypt's trains are badly in need of an overhaul, while Syria and Turkey use new trains on some routes and the entire system is improving all the time.

In general, trains are less frequent and usually slower than buses, while many stations are some distance out of the town centres they serve.

In general, tickets are only sold at the station and reservations are either compulsory or highly recommended.

International train services between Damascus or Aleppo and neighbouring countries were suspended at the time of writing due to the deteriorating security situation in Syria.

Health

Prevention is the key to staying healthy while travelling in the Middle East. Infectious diseases can and do occur in the Middle East, but these are usually associated with poor living conditions and poverty and can be avoided with a few precautions. The most common reason for travellers needing medical help is as a result of accidents – cars are not always well maintained, seatbelts are rare and poorly lit roads are littered with potholes. Medical facilities can be excellent in large cities, but in remote areas may be more basic.

Before You Go

A little planning before departure can save you a lot of trouble later. See your dentist before a long trip; carry a spare pair of contact lenses and glasses (and take your optical prescription); and carry a first-aid kit with you.

It's tempting to leave it all to the last minute – don't! Many vaccines don't ensure immunity until two weeks, so visit a doctor four to eight weeks before departure. Ask your doctor for an International Certificate of Vaccination (otherwise known as the yellow booklet), which will list all the vaccinations you've received. This is mandatory for countries that require proof of yellow fever vaccination upon entry, but it's a good idea to carry it wherever you travel.

Travellers can register with the **International Association for Medical Advice to Travellers** (IMAT; www.iamat.org). Its website can help travellers to find a doctor with recognised training. Those heading off to very remote areas may like to do a first-aid course (Red Cross and St John Ambulance can help).

Bring medications in their original, clearly labelled containers. A signed and dated letter from your physician describing your medical conditions and medications, including generic names, is also a good idea. If carrying syringes or needles, be sure to have a physician's letter documenting their medical necessity.

Insurance

Find out in heaadvance if your insurance plan will make payments directly to providers or reimburse you later for overseas health expenditures (in many Middle Eastern countries doctors expect payment in cash). It's also worth making sure that your travel insurance will cover repatriation home or to better medical facilities elsewhere. Your insurance company may be able to locate the nearest source of medical help, or you can ask at your hotel. In an emergency, contact your embassy or consulate. Your travel insurance will not usually cover you for anything other than emergency dental treatment. Not all insurance covers emergency aeromedical evacuation home or to a hospital in a major city, which may be the only way to get medical attention for a serious emergency.

Recommended Vaccinations

The World Health Organization (WHO) recommends that all travellers, regardless of the region they are travelling in, should be covered for diphtheria, tetanus, measles, mumps, rubella and polio, as well as hepatitis B. While making preparations to travel, take the opportunity to ensure that all of your routine vaccination cover is complete. The consequences of these diseases can be severe and outbreaks do occur in the Middle East.

In the Middle East

Availability & Cost of Health Care

The health care systems in the Middle East are varied. Medical care can be excellent in Israel, with well-trained doctors and nurses, but can be patchier elsewhere. Reciprocal health arrangements with countries rarely exist and you should be prepared to pay for all medical and dental treatment.

Medical care is not always readily available outside major cities. Medicine, and even sterile dressings or intravenous fluids, may need to be bought from a local pharmacy. Nursing care may be limited or rudimentary as this is something families and friends are expected to provide.

Standards of dental care are variable throughout the region, and there is an increased risk of hepatitis B and HIV transmission via poorly sterilised equipment.

For minor illnesses such as diarrhoea, pharmacists can often provide valuable advice and sell over-the-counter medication. They can also advise as to whether more specialised help is needed.

Infectious Diseases

DIPHTHERIA

Diphtheria is spread through close respiratory contact. It causes a high temperature and severe sore throat. Sometimes a membrane forms across the throat requiring a tracheotomy to prevent suffocation. Vaccination is recommended for those likely to be in close contact with the local population in infected areas. The vaccine is given as an injection alone, or with tetanus, and lasts 10 years.

HEPATITIS A

Hepatitis A is spread through contaminated food (particularly shellfish) and water. It causes jaundice, and although it is rarely fatal, can cause prolonged lethargy and delayed recovery. Symptoms include dark urine, a yellow colour to the whites of the eyes, fever, and abdominal pain. Hepatitis A vaccine (Avaxim, VAQTA, Havrix) is given as an injection: a single dose will give protection for up to a year, while a booster 12 months later will provide a subsequent 10 years of protection.

HEPATITIS B

Infected blood, contaminated needles and sexual intercourse can all transmit hepatitis B. It can cause jaundice, and affects the liver, occasionally causing liver failure. All travellers should make this a routine vaccination. (Many countries now give hepatitis B vaccination as part of routine childhood vaccination.) A course will give protection for at least five years, and can be given over four weeks or six months.

LEISHMANIASIS

Spread through the bite of an infected sand fly, leishmaniasis can cause a slowly growing skin lump or ulcer. It may develop into a serious life-threatening fever usually accompanied by anaemia and weight loss. Sand fly bites should be avoided whenever possible. Infected dogs are also carriers. Leishmaniasis is present in Iraq, Israel and the Palestinian Territories, Jordan, Lebanon, Syria and Turkey.

MALARIA

The prevalence of malaria varies throughout the Middle East. Many areas are considered to be malaria free, while others have seasonal risks. The risk of malaria is minimal in most cities; however, check with your doctor if you are considering travelling to any rural areas. It is important to take antimalarial tablets if the risk is significant. For up-to-date information about the risk of contracting malaria in a specific country, contact your local travel health clinic.

POLIOMYELITIS

Generally spread through contaminated food and water, polio is present, though rare, throughout the Middle East. It is one of the vaccines given in childhood and should be boosted every 10 years, either

MEDICAL CHECKLIST

Following is a list of other items you should consider packing in your medical kit.

- ☐ acetaminophen/paracetamol (eg Tylenol) or aspirin
- ☐ adhesive or paper tape
- ☐ antibacterial ointment (eg Bactroban) for cuts and abrasions
- ☐ antibiotics (if travelling off the beaten track)
- ☐ antidiarrhoeal drugs (eg containing loperamide)
- ☐ antihistamines (for hay fever and allergic reactions)
- ☐ anti-inflammatory drugs (eg containing ibuprofen)
- ☐ bandages, gauze, gauze rolls
- ☐ insect repellent that contains DEET (for skin)
- ☐ insect spray that contains permethrin (for clothing, tents and bed nets)
- ☐ iodine tablets (for water purification)
- ☐ oral-rehydration salts
- ☐ pocket knife
- ☐ scissors, safety pins, tweezers
- ☐ steroid cream or cortisone (for allergic rashes)
- ☐ sunscreen
- ☐ syringes and sterile needles (if travelling to remote areas)
- ☐ thermometer

orally (a drop on the tongue), or as an injection. Polio may be carried asymptomatically, although it can cause a transient fever and, in rare cases, potentially permanent muscle weakness or paralysis.

RABIES

Spread through bites or licks on broken skin from an infected animal, rabies (present in all countries of the Middle East) is fatal. Animal handlers should be vaccinated, as should those travelling to remote areas where a reliable source of postbite vaccine is not available within 24 hours. Three injections are needed over a month. If you have not been vaccinated you will need a course of five injections starting within 24 hours or as soon as possible after the injury. Vaccination does not provide you with immunity, it merely buys you more time to seek appropriate medical treatment.

RIFT VALLEY FEVER

This haemorrhagic fever, which is found in Egypt, is spread through blood or blood products, including those from infected animals. It causes a flu-like illness with fever, joint pains and occasionally more serious complications. Complete recovery is possible.

SCHISTOSOMIASIS

Otherwise known as bilharzia, this is spread through the freshwater snail. It causes infection of the bowel and bladder, often with bleeding. It is caused by a fluke and is contracted through the skin from water contaminated with human urine or faeces. Paddling or swimming in suspect freshwater lakes or slow-running rivers should be avoided. There may be no symptoms. Possible symptoms include a transient fever and rash, and advanced cases of bilharzia may cause blood in the stool or in the urine. A blood test can detect antibodies if you have been exposed and treatment is then possible in specialist travel or infectious-disease clinics. Be especially careful in Egypt, Iraq and Syria.

TUBERCULOSIS (TB)

Tuberculosis is spread through close respiratory contact and occasionally through infected milk or milk products. BCG vaccine is recommended for those likely to be mixing closely with the local population. It is more important for those visiting family or planning on a long stay, and those employed as teachers and health care workers. TB can be asymptomatic, although symptoms can include coughing, weight loss or fever months or even years after exposure. An X-ray is the best way to confirm if you have TB. BCG gives a moderate degree of protection against TB. It causes a small permanent scar at the site of injection, and is usually only given in specialised chest clinics. As it's a live vaccine it should not be given to pregnant women or immunocompromised individuals. The BCG vaccine is not available in all countries.

TYPHOID

Typhoid is spread through food or water that has been contaminated by infected human faeces. The first symptom is usually fever or a pink rash on the abdomen. Septicaemia (blood poisoning) may also occur. Typhoid vaccine (typhim Vi, typherix) will give protection for three years. In some countries, the oral vaccine Vivotif is also available.

YELLOW FEVER

Yellow fever vaccination is not required for any areas of the Middle East. However, the mosquito that spreads yellow fever has been known to be present in some parts of the region. It is important to consult your local travel health clinic as part of your predeparture plans for the latest details. Any travellers from a yellow fever endemic area (eg parts of sub-Saharan Africa) will need to show proof of vaccination against yellow fever before entry.

Environmental Hazards

HEAT ILLNESS

Heat exhaustion occurs after heavy sweating and excessive fluid loss with inadequate replacement of fluids and salt. It is particularly common in hot climates when taking unaccustomed exercise before full acclimatisation. Symptoms include headache, dizziness and tiredness. Dehydration is already happening by the time you feel thirsty – aim to drink sufficient water so that you produce pale, diluted urine. The treatment of heat exhaustion consists of fluid replacement with water or fruit juice or both, and cooling by cold water and fans. The treatment of the salt-loss component consists of taking in salty fluids (such as soup or broth), and adding a little more table salt to foods than usual.

Heat stroke is much more serious. This occurs when the heat-regulating mechanism in the body breaks

WATER WARNING

Many locals don't drink the tap water and we recommend that you follow their lead. If you do decide to risk the local water, the safest places to do so are in Israel, Syria and Turkey. Don't even *think* of drinking from the tap in Egypt, Iraq, the Palestinian Territories or Lebanon. Cheap bottled water is readily available throughout the region.

down. An excessive rise in body temperature leads to sweating ceasing, irrational and hyperactive behaviour, and eventually loss of consciousness and death. Rapid cooling by spraying the body with water and fanning is an ideal treatment. Emergency fluid and electrolyte replacement by intravenous drip is usually also required.

INSECT BITES & STINGS

Mosquitoes may not carry malaria but can cause irritation and infected bites. Using DEET-based insect repellents will prevent bites. Mosquitoes also spread dengue fever.

Bees and wasps only cause real problems to those with a severe allergy (anaphylaxis). If you have a severe allergy to bee or wasp stings you should carry an adrenaline injection or similar.

Scorpions are frequently found in arid or dry climates. They can cause a painful sting, which is rarely life threatening.

Bed bugs are often found in hostels and cheap hotels. They lead to very itchy lumpy bites. Spraying the mattress with an appropriate insect killer will do a good job of getting rid of them.

Scabies are also frequently found in cheap accommodation. These tiny mites live in the skin, particularly between the fingers. They cause an intensely itchy rash. Scabies is easily treated with lotion available from pharmacies.

SNAKE BITES

Do not walk barefoot or stick your hand into holes or cracks. Half of those bitten by venomous snakes are not actually injected with poison (envenomed). If bitten by a snake, do not panic. Immobilise the bitten limb with a splint (eg a stick) and apply a bandage over the site using firm pressure, similar to a bandage over a sprain. Do not apply a tourniquet, or cut or suck the bite. Get the victim to medical help as soon as possible so that antivenene can be given if necessary.

TRAVELLER'S DIARRHOEA

To prevent diarrhoea, avoid tap water unless it has been boiled, filtered or chemically disinfected (with iodine tablets). Eat only fresh fruits or vegetables if cooked or if you have peeled them yourself, and avoid dairy products that may contain unpasteurised milk. Buffet meals are risky, as food should be piping hot; meals freshly cooked in front of you in a busy restaurant are more likely to be safe.

If you develop diarrhoea, be sure to drink plenty of fluids, preferably an oral rehydration solution containing salt and sugar. A few loose stools don't require treatment but, if you start having more than four or five stools a day, you should start taking an antibiotic (usually a quinolone drug) and an antidiarrhoeal agent (such as loperamide). If diarrhoea is bloody, persists for more than 72 hours, or is accompanied by fever, shaking chills or severe abdominal pain you should seek medical attention.

Travelling with Children

All travellers with children should know how to treat minor ailments and when to seek medical treatment. Make sure children are up to date with the routine vaccinations, and discuss possible travel vaccinations well before departure as some are not suitable for children aged under one year old.

In hot, moist climates any wound or break in the skin may lead to infection. The area should be cleaned and then kept dry and clean. Remember to avoid potentially contaminated food and water. If your child is vomiting or experiencing diarrhoea, lost fluid and salts must be replaced. It may be helpful to take rehydration powders for reconstituting with boiled water. Ask your doctor about this.

Children should be encouraged to avoid dogs or other mammals because of the risk of rabies and other diseases. Any bite, scratch or lick from a warm blooded, furry animal should immedi-

TRAVEL HEALTH WEBSITES

Lonely Planet (www.lonelyplanet.com) A good place to start.

Centers for Disease Control & Prevention (wwwnc.cdc.gov/travel/) A useful source of traveller health information.

MD Travel Health (www.mdtravelhealth.com) Complete travel health recommendations for every country, updated daily.

Travel Doctor (www.traveldoctor.co.uk) Another good source of travel health information.

WHO (www.who.int/ith/en) Publishes a good book, *International Travel and Health.*

It's also usually a good idea to consult your government's travel health website before departure.

Australia (www.smartraveller.gov.au)

UK (www.nhs.uk/Healthcareabroad)

USA (wwwn.cdc.gov/travel)

ately be thoroughly cleaned. If there is any possibility that the animal is infected with rabies, immediate medical assistance should be sought.

Women's Health

Emotional stress, exhaustion and travelling through different time zones can all contribute to an upset in the menstrual pattern. If using oral contraceptives, remember some antibiotics, diarrhoea and vomiting can stop the pill from working and lead to the risk of pregnancy – remember to take condoms with you just in case. Condoms should be kept in a cool, dry place or they may crack and perish.

Emergency contraception is most effective if taken within 24 hours after unprotected sex. The **International Planned Parent Federation** (www.ippf.org) can advise about the availability of contraception in different countries. Tampons and sanitary towels are not always available outside of major cities in the Middle East.

Travelling during pregnancy is usually possible, but there are important things to consider. Have a medical check-up before embarking on your trip. The most risky times for travel are during the first 12 weeks of pregnancy, when miscarriage is most likely, and after 30 weeks, when complications such as high blood pressure and premature delivery can occur. Most airlines will not accept a traveller after 28 to 32 weeks of pregnancy, and long-haul flights in the later stages can be very uncomfortable. Antenatal facilities vary greatly between countries in the Middle East and you should think carefully before travelling to a country with poor medical facilities or where there are major cultural and language differences compared with home. Taking written records of the pregnancy, including details of your blood group, is likely to be helpful if you need medical attention while away. Ensure your insurance policy covers pregnancy, delivery and postnatal care, but remember insurance policies are only as good as the facilities available.

Language

WANT MORE?

For in-depth language information and handy phrases, check out Lonely Planet's *Middle East Phrasebook*. You'll find it at **shop.lonelyplanet.com**, or you can buy Lonely Planet's iPhone phrasebooks at the Apple App Store.

ARABIC

The following phrases are in MSA (Modern Standard Arabic), which is the official language of the Arab world, used in schools, administration and the media, and understood across the Middle East. Note, though, that there are significant differences between MSA and the colloquial Arabic varieties spoken throughout the region. Egyptian, Gulf, Levantine and Tunisian Arabic are the most common spoken varieties, sometimes mutually unintelligible and with no official written form.

Arabic is written from right to left in Arabic script. Read our coloured pronunciation guides as if they were English and you should be understood. Note that a is pronounced as in 'act', aa as the 'a' in 'father', aw as in 'law', ay as in 'say', ee as in 'see', i as in 'hit', oo as in 'zoo', u as in 'put', gh is a throaty sound (like the Parisian French 'r'), r is rolled, dh is pronounced as in 'that', th as in 'thin' and kh as the 'ch' in the Scottish *loch*. The apostrophe (') indicates the glottal stop (like the pause in the middle of 'uh-oh'). The stressed syllables are indicated with italics. Masculine and feminine options are indicated with 'm' and 'f' respectively.

Basics

Hello.	السلام عليكم.	as·sa·*laa*·mu 'a·*lay*·kum
Goodbye.	إلى اللقاء.	*'i*·laa al·li·*kaa'*
Yes.	نعم.	*na*·'am
No.	لا.	laa
Excuse me.	عفواً.	*'af*·wan
Sorry.	آسف.	*'aa*·sif (m)
	آسفة.	*'aa*·si·fa (f)
Please.	لو سمحتَ.	law sa·*mah*·ta (m)
	لو سمحتِ.	law sa·*mah*·ti (f)
Thank you.	شكراً.	*shuk*·ran

How are you?

كيف حالكَ؟ *kay*·fa *haa*·lu·ka (m)
كيف حالكِ؟ *kay*·fa *haa*·lu·ki (f)

Fine, thanks. And you?

بخير شكراً. bi·*khay*·rin *shuk*·ran
وأنتَ/أنتِ؟ wa·*'an*·ta/wa·*'an*·ti (m/f)

What's your name?

ما اسمكَ؟ maa *'is*·mu·ka (m)
ما اسمكِ؟ maa *'is*·mu·ki (f)

My name is ...

اسمي ... *'is*·mee ...

Do you speak English?

هل تتكلّمُ/ تتكلّمينَ الإنجليزية؟ hal ta·ta·*kal*·la·mu/ ta·ta·kal·la·*mee*·na al·'inj·lee·*zee*·ya (m/f)

I don't understand.

أنا لا أفهم. *'a*·naa laa *'af*·ham

Accommodation

Where's a ...?	أين أجدُ ...؟	*'ay*·na *'a*·ji·du ...
campsite	مخيم	mu·*khay*·yam
guesthouse	بيت للضيوف	bayt li·du·*yoof*
hotel	فندق	*fun*·duk
youth hostel	فندق شباب	*fun*·duk sha·*baab*

Do you have a ... room?	هل عِندكم غرفةٌ ...؟	hal '*in*·da·kum *ghur*·fa·tun ...
single	بسرير منفرِدٍ	bi·sa·*ree*·rin *mun*·fa·rid
double	بسرير مزدوّجٍ	bi·sa·*ree*·rin muz·*daw*·waj
How much is it per ...?	كم ثمنه لِـ ...؟	kam *tha*·ma·nu·hu li ...
night	ليلةٍ واحدة	*lay*·la·tin *waa*·hid
person	شخصٍ واحدة	*shakh*·sin *waa*·hid

Eating & Drinking

Can you recommend a ...?	هل يمكنكَ أن توصي ...؟	hal yum·*ki*·nu·ka 'an too·see·ya ... (m)
	هل يمكنكِ أن توصي ...؟	hal yum·*ki*·nu·ki 'an *too*·see ... (f)
cafe	مقهىً	*mak*·han
restaurant	مطعمً	*mat*·'am

What would you recommend?	ماذا توصي؟	*maa*·dhaa *too*·see (m)
	ماذا توصينَ؟	*maa*·dhaa too·*see*·na (f)
What's the local speciality?	ما الوجبة الخاصّة لهذه المنطقة؟	maa al·*waj*·ba·tul *khaa*·sa li·*haa*·dhi·hil *man*·ta·ka
Do you have vegetarian food?	هل لديكم طعامٌ نباتيّ؟	hal la·*day*·ku·mu ta·'*aa*·mun na·*baa*·tee

I'd like the ..., please.	أريد ...، لو سمحتَ.	'u·*ree*·du ... law sa·*mah*·ta
bill	الحساب	hi·*saab*
menu	قائمة الطعام	*kaa*·'i·ma·tu at·ta·'*aam*

Emergencies

Help!	ساعدني!	saa·'*i*·du·nee (m)
	ساعديني!	*saa*·'i·*dee*·nee (f)
Go away!	اتركني!	'it·*ruk*·nee (m)
	اتركيني!	'it·ru·*kee*·nee (f)
Call ...!	اتّصلْ بـ ...!	'*it*·ta·sil bi (m)
	اتصلي بـ ...!	'it·*ta*·si·lee bi ... (f)
a doctor	طبيب	ta·*beeb*
the police	الشرطة	ash·*shur*·ta
I'm lost.	أنا ضائع.	'a·naa *daa*·'i' (m)
	أنا ضائعة.	'a·naa *daa*·'i·'a (f)
Where are the toilets?	أينَ دورات المياه؟	'*ay*·na daw·*raa*·tul mee·*yaah*
I'm sick.	أنا مريض.	'a·naa ma·*reed*

Signs – Arabic

Entrance	مدخل
Exit	مخرج
Open	مفتوح
Closed	مغلق
Information	معلومات
Prohibited	ممنوع
Toilets	دوراتُ المياه
Men	الرجال
Women	النساء

Shopping & Services

I'm looking for ...	أبحثُ عن ...	'*ab*·ha·thu 'an ...
Can I look at it?	هل يمكنني أن أراه؟	hal yum·*ki*·nu·nee 'an 'a·*raa*·hu
Do you have any others?	هل عندك غيره؟	hal '*in*·da·kum *ghay*·ru·hu
How much is it?	كم سعره؟	kam *si*'·ru·hu
That's too expensive.	هذا غالٍ جداً.	*haa*·dhaa *ghaa*·lin *jid*·dan
There's a mistake in the bill.	في خطأ في الحساب.	fee *kha*·ta' feel hi·*saab*
Where's an ATM?	أينَ جهاز الصرافة؟	'*ay*·na ji·*haaz* as·sar·*raa*·fa

Transport & Directions

Is this the ... to (Dubai)?	هل هذا الـ ... إلى (دبي)؟	hal *haa*·dhaa al ... '*i*·laa (*du*·ba·yee)
boat	سفينة	sa·*fee*·na
bus	باص	baas
plane	طائرة	*taa*·'i·ra
train	قطار	ki·*taar*

What time's the ... bus?	في أيّ ساعةٍ يغادرُ الباص الـ ...؟	fee '*ay*·yee *saa*·'a·tin yu·*ghaa*·di·ru al·*baas* al ...
first	أوّل	'*aw*·wal
last	آخر	'*aa*·khir

One ... ticket, please.	تذكرة ... واحدة، لو سمحت.	*tadh*·ka·ra·tu ... *waa*·hi·da law sa·*mah*·ta
one-way	ذهاب فقط	dha·*haa*·bu *fa*·kat
return	ذهاب وإياب	dha·*haa*·bu wa·'*ee*·*yaab*

Numbers – Arabic

1	١	واحد	*waa*·hid
2	٢	اثنان	'ith·*naan*
3	٣	ثلاثة	tha·*laa*·tha
4	٤	أربعة	*'ar*·ba·'a
5	٥	خمسة	*kham*·sa
6	٦	ستة	*sit*·ta
7	٧	سبعة	*sab*·'a
8	٨	ثمانية	tha·*maa*·ni·ya
9	٩	تسعة	*tis*·'a
10	١٠	عشرة	*'a*·sha·ra
100	١٠٠	مائة	*mi*·'a
1000	١٠٠٠	ألف	'alf

Note that Arabic numerals, unlike letters, are written from left to right.

How much is it to ...?
كم الأجرة إلى ...؟ kam al·*'uj*·ra·ti *'i*·laa ...

Please take me to (this address).
أوصلني عند 'aw·*sal*·nee 'ind
(هذا العنوان) (*haa*·dhaa al·'un·*waan*)
لو سمحت. law sa·*mah*·ta

Where's the (market)?
أين الـ (سوق)؟ *'ay*·na al (sook)

Can you show me (on the map)?
هل يمكنكَ أن hal yum·*ki*·nu·ka 'an
توضح لي tu·*wad*·da·ha lee
(على الخريطة)؟ (*'a*·laa al·kha·*ree*·ta) (m)
هل يمكنكِ أن hal yum·*ki*·nu·ki 'an
توضحي لي tu·*wad*·da·hee lee
(على الخريطة)؟ (*'a*·laa al·kha·*ree*·ta) (f)

What's the address?
ما هو العنوان؟ maa *hu*·wa al·'un·*waan*

HEBREW

Hebrew is the national language of Israel, with seven to eight million speakers worldwide. It's written from right to left in its own alphabet.

Most Hebrew sounds have equivalents in English. Just follow our pronunciation guides and you'll be understood. Note that a is pronounced as 'ah', ai as in 'aisle', e as in 'bet', i as the 'ea' in 'heat', o as 'oh' and u as the 'oo' in 'boot'. Both kh (like the 'ch' in the Scottish *loch*) and r (similar to the French 'r') are throaty sounds, pronounced at the back of the throat. The apostrophe (') indicates the glottal stop (like the pause in the middle of 'uh-oh'). The stressed syllables are indicated with italics. Masculine and feminine options are indicated by 'm' and 'f' respectively.

Basics

Hello.	שלום.	sha·*lom*
Goodbye.	להתראות.	le·hit·ra·*ot*
Yes.	כן.	ken
No.	לא.	lo
Please.	בבקשה.	be·va·ka·*sha*
Thank you.	תודה.	to·*da*
Excuse me./Sorry.	סליחה.	sli·*kha*

How are you?
מה נשמע? ma nish·*ma*

Fine, thanks. And you?
טוב, תודה. tov to·*da*
ואתה/ואת? ve·a·*ta*/ve·*at* (m/f)

What's your name?
איך קוראים לך? ekh kor·*im* le·*kha*/lakh (m/f)

My name is ...
שמי ... shmi ...

Do you speak English?
אתה מדבר אנגלית? a·*ta* me·da·*ber* ang·*lit* (m)
את מדברת אנגלית? at me·da·*be*·ret ang·*lit* (f)

I don't understand.
אני לא מבין/מבינה. a·*ni* lo me·*vin*/me·vi·*na* (m/f)

Accommodation

Where's a ...?	איפה ...?	e·fo ...
campsite	אתר הקמפינג	a·*tar* ha·*kemp*·ing
guesthouse	בית הארחה	bet ha·'a·ra·*kha*
hotel	בית המלון	bet ma·*lon*
youth hostel	אכסניית הנוער	akh·sa·ni·*yat* *no*·ar
Do you have a ... room?	יש לך חדר ...?	yesh le·*kha*/lakh *khe*·der ... (m/f)
single	ליחיד	le·ya·*khid*
double	זוגי	zu·*gi*

Signs – Hebrew

Entrance	כניסה
Exit	יציאה
Open	פתוח
Closed	סגור
Information	מודיעין
Prohibited	אסור
Toilets	שירותים
Men	גברים
Women	נשים

How much is it per ...?	כמה זה עולה ל ...?	*ka*·ma ze o·*le* le ...
night	לילה	*lai*·la
person	אדם	a·*dam*

Eating & Drinking

Can you recommend a ...?	אתה יכול להמליץ על ...?	a·*ta* ya·*khol* le·ham·*lits* al ... (m)
	את יכולה להמליץ על ...?	at ye·cho·*la* le·ham·*lits* al ... (f)
cafe	בית קפה	bet ka·*fe*
restaurant	מסעדה	mis·a·*da*

What would you recommend?
מה אתה ממליץ? ma a·*ta* mam·*lits* (m)
מה את ממליצה? ma at mam·li·*tsa* (f)

What's the local speciality?
מה המאכל המקומי? ma ha·ma·'a·*khal* ha·me·ko·*mi*

Do you have vegetarian food?
יש לכם אוכל צמחוני? yesh la·*khem* o·khel tsim·kho·*ni*

I'd like the ..., please.	אני צריך/צריכה את ..., בבקשה.	a·*ni* tsa·*rikh*/tsri·*kha* et ... be·va·ka·*sha* (m/f)
bill	החשבון	ha·khesh·*bon*
menu	התפריט	ha·taf·*rit*

Emergencies

Help!	הצילו!	ha·*tsi*·lu
Go away!	לך מפה!	lekh mi·*po*
Call ...!	תתקשר ל ...!	tit·ka·*sher* le ...
a doctor	רופא	ro·*fe*/ro·*fa* (m/f)
the police	משטרה	mish·ta·*ra*

I'm lost.
אני אבוד. a·*ni* a·*vud* (m)
אני אבודה. a·*ni* a·vu·*da* (f)

Where are the toilets?
איפה השירותים? e·fo ha·she·ru·*tim*

I'm sick.
אני חולה. a·*ni* kho·*le*/kho·*la* (m/f)

Shopping & Services

I'm looking for ...
אני מחפש ... a·*ni* me·kha·*pes* ... (m)
אני מחפשת ... a·*ni* me·kha·*pe*·set ... (f)

Can I look at it?
אפשר להסתכל על זה? ef·*shar* le·his·ta·*kel* al ze

Do you have any others?
יש לך אחרים? yesh le·*kha*/lakh a·khe·*rim* (m/f)

How much is it?
כמה זה עולה? *ka*·ma ze o·*le*

That's too expensive.
זה יקר מדי. ze ya·*kar* mi·*dai*

There's a mistake in the bill.
יש טעות בחשבון. yesh ta·*ut* ba·khesh·*bon*

Where's an ATM?
איפה יש כספומט? e·fo yesh kas·po·*mat*

Transport & Directions

Is this the ... to (Haifa)?	האם זה/זאת ה ... ל (חיפה)?	ha·*im* ze/zot ha ... le· (khai·*fa*) (m/f)
boat	אוניה	o·ni·*ya* (f)
bus	אוטובוס	o·to·bus (m)
plane	מטוס	ma·*tos* (m)
train	רכבת	ra·*ke*·vet (f)

What time's the ... bus?	באיזה שעה האוטובוס ה ...?	be·e·ze sha·*a* ha·o·to·bus ha ...
first	ראשון	ri·*shon*
last	אחרון	a·kha·*ron*

One ... ticket, please.	כרטיס אחד ... בבקשה.	kar·*tis* e·*khad* ... be·va·ka·*sha*
one-way	לכיוון אחד	le·ki·*vun* e·*khad*
return	הלוך ושוב	ha·*lokh* va·*shov*

How much is it to ...?
כמה זה ל ...? *ka*·ma ze le...

Numbers – Hebrew

1	אחת	a·*khat*
2	שתיים	*shta*·yim
3	שלוש	sha·*losh*
4	ארבע	*ar*·ba
5	חמש	kha·*mesh*
6	שש	shesh
7	שבע	*she*·va
8	שמונה	*shmo*·ne
9	תשע	*te*·sha
10	עשר	e·ser
100	מאה	*me*·a
1000	אלף	e·lef

Note that English numerals are used in modern Hebrew text.

Please take me to (this address).

תיקח/תיקחי אותי	ti·*kakh*/tik·*khi* o·*ti*
(לכתובת הזאת)	(lak·to·*vet* ha·*zot*)
בבקשה.	be·va·ka·*sha* (m/f)

Where's the (market)?

איפה ה (שוק)?	e·fo ha (shuk)

Can you show me (on the map)?

אתה/את יכול	a·*ta*/at ya·*khol*/ye·kho·*la*
להראות	le·har·*ot*
(לי על המפה)?	(li al ha·ma·*pa*) (m/f)

What's the address?

מה הכתובת?	ma hak·to·vet

TURKISH

Turkish is the official language of Turkey and co-official language of Cyprus (alongside Greek), with 70 million speakers worldwide.

Turkish vowels are generally shorter and slightly harsher than in English. When you see a double vowel in our pronunciation guides, eg sa·*at*, you need to pronounce it twice. Note also that a is pronounced as the 'u' in 'run', ai as in 'aisle', ay as in 'say', e as in 'bet', ee as in 'see', eu as the 'u' in 'nurse', ew as ee with rounded lips, o as in 'pot', oo as in 'zoo', uh as the 'a' in 'ago', zh as the 's' in 'pleasure', r is always rolled and v is softer than in English (pronounced between a 'v' and a 'w'). The stressed syllables are indicated with italics. Polite and informal options are indicated by 'pol' and 'inf' respectively.

Basics

Hello.	*Merhaba.*	*mer*·ha·ba
Goodbye. (when leaving)	*Hoşçakalın.* *Hoşçakal.*	hosh·*cha*·ka·luhn (pol) hosh·*cha*·kal (inf)
Goodbye. (when staying)	*Güle güle.*	gew·*le* gew·*le*
Yes.	*Evet.*	e·*vet*
No.	*Hayır.*	*ha*·yuhr
Please.	*Lütfen.*	*lewt*·fen
Thank you.	*Teşekkür.*	te·shek·*kewr*
Excuse me.	*Bakar mısınız?*	ba·*kar* muh·suh·*nuhz*
Sorry.	*Özür dilerim.*	er·*zewr* dee·*le*·reem

How are you?

Nasılsınız? (pol)	*na*·suhl·suh·nuhz
Nasılsın? (inf)	*na*·suhl·suhn

Fine. And you?

İyiyim.	ee·*yee*·yeem
Ya siz/sen? (pol/inf)	ya seez/sen

What's your name?

Adınız nedir?	a·duh·*nuhz ne*·deer (pol)
Adınız ne?	a·duh·*nuhz* ne (inf)

Signs – Turkish

Giriş	Entrance
Çıkış	Exit
Açık	Open
Kapalı	Closed
Danışma	Information
Yasak	Prohibited
Tuvaletler	Toilets
Erkek	Men
Kadın	Women

My name is ...

Benim adım ...	be·*neem* a·*duhm* ...

Do you speak English?

İngilizce konuşuyor musunuz?	een·gee·*leez*·je ko·noo·*shoo*·yor moo·soo·*nooz*

I don't understand.

Anlamıyorum.	an·*la*·muh·yo·room

Accommodation

Where's a ...?	*Buralarda nerede ... var?*	boo·ra·lar·*da* *ne*·re·de ... var
campsite	*kamp yeri*	kamp ye·*ree*
guesthouse	*misafirhane*	mee·*sa*·feer·ha·ne
hotel	*otel*	o·*tel*
youth hostel	*gençlik hosteli*	gench·*leek* hos·te·*lee*
Do you have a ... room?	*... odanız var mı?*	... o·da·*nuhz* var muh
single	*Tek kişilik*	tek kee·shee·*leek*
double	*İki kişilik*	ee·*kee* kee·shee·*leek*
How much is it per ...?	*... ne kadar?*	... ne ka·*dar*
night	*Geceliği*	ge·je·lee·*ee*
person	*Kişi başına*	kee·*shee* ba·shuh·*na*

Eating & Drinking

Can you recommend a ...?	*İyi bir ... tavsiye edebilir misiniz?*	ee·*yee* beer ... tav·see·*ye* e·*de*·bee·leer mee·see·*neez*
cafe	*kafe*	ka·*fe*
restaurant	*restoran*	res·to·*ran*

What would you recommend?

Ne tavsiye edersiniz?	ne tav·see·*ye* e·*der*·see·neez

Numbers – Turkish

1	*bir*	beer
2	*iki*	ee·*kee*
3	*üç*	ewch
4	*dört*	dert
5	*beş*	besh
6	*altı*	al·*tuh*
7	*yedi*	ye·*dee*
8	*sekiz*	se·*keez*
9	*dokuz*	do·*kooz*
10	*on*	on
100	*yüz*	yewz
1000	*bin*	been

What's the local speciality?
Bu yöreye has yiyecekler neler? — boo yeu·re·*ye* has yee·ye·jek·*ler* ne·*ler*

Do you have vegetarian food?
Vejeteryan yiyecekleriniz var mı? — ve·zhe·ter·*yan* yee·ye·jek·le·ree·*neez* var muh

I'd like the ..., please.	*... istiyorum.*	... ees·*tee*·yo·room
bill	*Hesabı*	he·sa·*buh*
menu	*Menüyü*	me·new·*yew*

Emergencies

Help!	*İmdat!*	*eem*·dat
Go away!	*Git burdan!*	geet boor·*dan*

Call ...!	*... çağırın!*	... cha·*uh*·ruhn
a doctor	*Doktor*	dok·*tor*
the police	*Polis*	po·*lees*

I'm lost.
Kayboldum. — kai·bol·*doom*

Where are the toilets?
Tuvaletler nerede? — too·va·let·*ler* ne·re·de

I'm sick.
Hastayım. — has·ta·*yuhm*

Shopping & Services

I'm looking for ...
... istiyorum. — ... ees·*tee*·yo·room

Can I look at it?
Bakabilir miyim? — ba·ka·bee·leer mee·*yeem*

Do you have any others?
Başka var mı? — bash·*ka* var muh

How much is it?
Ne kadar? — ne ka·*dar*

It's too expensive.
Bu çok pahalı. — boo chok pa·ha·*luh*

There's a mistake in the bill.
Hesapta bir yanlışlık var. — he·sap·*ta* beer yan·luhsh·*luhk* var

Where's an ATM?
Bankamatik nerede var? — ban·ka·ma·*teek* ne·re·de var

Transport & Directions

Is this the ... to (Sirkeci)?	*(Sirkeci'ye) giden ... bu mu?*	(*seer*·ke·jee·ye) gee·*den* ... boo moo
boat	*vapur*	va·*poor*
bus	*otobüs*	o·to·*bews*
plane	*uçak*	oo·*chak*
train	*tren*	tren

What time's the ... bus?	*... otobüs ne zaman?*	... o·to·*bews* ne za·*man*
first	*İlk*	eelk
next	*Sonraki*	son·ra·*kee*

One ... ticket, please.	*..., lütfen.*	... *lewt*·fen
one-way	*Bir gidiş bileti*	beer gee·*deesh* bee·le·*tee*
return	*Gidiş-dönüş bir bilet*	gee·deesh·deu·*newsh* beer bee·*let*

How much is it to ...?
... ne kadar? — ... ne ka·*dar*

Please take me to (this address).
Lütfen beni (bu adrese) götürün. — *lewt*·fen be·*nee* (boo ad·re·se) geu·*tew*·rewn

Where's the (market)?
(Pazar yeri) nerede? — (pa·*zar* ye·*ree*) *ne*·re·de

Can you show me (on the map)?
Bana (haritada) gösterebilir misiniz? — ba·*na* (ha·ree·ta·*da*) geus·te·*re*·bee·leer mee·seen·*neez*

What's the address?
Adresi nedir? — ad·re·*see* ne·*deer*

GLOSSARY

This glossary contains some English, Arabic (Ar), Egyptian (E), Farsi (Far), Hebrew (Heb), Jordanian (J), Kurdish (K), Lebanese (Leb) and Turkish (T) words and abbreviations you may encounter in this book. See p99 for useful words dealing with food. For other useful words and phrases, see Language (p640).

Abbasid dynasty – Baghdad-based successor dynasty to the *Umayyad dynasty*; ruled from AD 750 until the sacking of Baghdad by the Mongols in 1258
abu (Ar) – father or saint
acropolis – high city; hilltop citadel of a classic Hellenic city
agora – open space for commerce and politics in a classic Hellenic city, such as a marketplace or forum
ahwa (E) – see *qahwa*
Ashkenazi – a Jew of German or Eastern European descent
Ayyubid dynasty – Egyptian-based dynasty (AD 1169–1250) founded by *Saladin*

Ba'ath Party – secular, pan-Arab political party that ruled in Iraq until 2003 and still holds power in Syria
badia (J) – stone or basalt desert
bait – see *beit*
baksheesh – alms or tip
balad (Ar) – land or city
beit (Ar) – house; also *bait*

calèche (E) – horse-drawn carriage
caliph – Islamic ruler
cami(i) (T) – mosque
caravanserai – see *khan*
cardo – road running north–south through a Roman city
carnet de passage – permit allowing entry of a vehicle to a country without incurring taxes
çarşı (T) – market or bazaar
çay (T) – see *shai*
centrale – telephone office
chador (Ar) – black, one-piece, head-to-toe covering garment; worn by many Muslim women

Decapolis – league of 10 cities, including Damascus, in the northeast of ancient Palestine
decumanus – road running east–west through a Roman city
deir (Ar) – monastery or convent
dervish – Muslim mystic; see also *Sufi*
diaspora – community in dispersion or exile from its homeland
dolmuş (T) – minibus that sometimes runs to a timetable but more often sets off when it's full
döner kebap (T) – see *shwarma*

Eid al-Adha – Feast of Sacrifice marking the pilgrimage to Mecca
Eid al-Fitr – Festival of Breaking the Fast celebrated at the end of *Ramadan*
emir – literally 'prince'; Islamic ruler, military commander or governor
evi (T) – house

Fatimid dynasty – Shiite dynasty (AD 908–1171) from North Africa, later based in Cairo, claiming descent from Mohammed's daughter Fatima
felafel – deep-fried balls of chickpea paste with spices served in a piece of flat bread with tomatoes or pickled vegetables; *ta'amiyya* in Egypt
felucca – traditional wooden sailboat used on the Nile in Egypt
fuul – paste made from fava beans
gebel (E) – see *jebel*
gület (T) – traditional wooden yacht

hajj – annual Muslim pilgrimage to Mecca; one of the five pillars of Islam
hamam (T) – see *hammam*
Hamas – militant Islamic organisation that aims to create an Islamic state in the pre-1948 territory of Palestine; the word is an acronym (in Arabic) for Islamic Resistance Movement
hammam (Ar) – bathhouse; *hamam* in Turkish
han – see *khan*
haram – anything that is forbidden by Islamic law; also refers to the prayer hall of a mosque
hasid – (plural *hasidim*) member of an ultra-orthodox Jewish sect; also *hared*
Hejira – Mohammed's flight from Mecca to Medina in AD 622; the starting point of the Muslim era and the start of the Islamic calendar
Hezbollah – 'Party of God'; Lebanon-based organ of militant *Shiite* Muslims
hypostyle hall – hall in which the roof is supported by columns

imam – prayer leader or Muslim cleric
intifada – Palestinian uprising against Israeli authorities in the West Bank, Gaza and East Jerusalem; literally 'shaking off'
iwan – vaulted hall, opening into a central court in a *madrassa* or a mosque

jamaa – see *masjid*
jebel (Ar) – hill, mountain; *gebel* in Egypt
jihad – literally 'striving in the way of the faith'; holy war

kale(si) (T) – fortress
keffiyeh (Ar) – chequered scarf worn by Arabs
khan – travellers' inn, usually constructed on main trade routes, with accommodation on the 1st floor and stables and storage on the ground floor; also *caravanserai, han, wikala* in Egypt
kibbutz – (plural kibbutzim) Jewish communal settlement run cooperatively by its members
kilim – woven rug
kippa – skullcap
Knesset – Israeli parliament
konak (T) – mansion
Koran – see *Quran*
kosher – food prepared according to Jewish dietary law

Likud – Israeli right-wing political party
liman(ı) (T) – harbour
lokanta (T) – restaurant

madrassa – Muslim theological seminary; modern Arabic word for school; *medrese(si)* in Turkey
mahalle(si) (T) – neighbourhood, district of a city
Mamluk – slave-soldier dynasty that ruled out of Egypt from AD 1250–1517
masjid (Ar) – mosque; also *jamaa*
medina – city or town, especially the old quarter of a city
medrese(si) (T) – see *madrassa*
Mesopotamia – ancient name for Iraq from the Greek meaning 'between two rivers'
meydan(ı) – see *midan*
meyhane (T) – (plural meyhaneler) tavern
meze (T) – see *mezze*
mezze – a collection of appetisers or small plates of food; *meze* in Turkish
midan (Ar) – town or city square; *meydan(ı)* in Turkish (plural *meydanlar*)
midrahov (Heb) – pedestrian mall
mihrab – niche in a mosque indicating direction of Mecca
minbar – pulpit used for sermons in a mosque
mitzvah (Heb) – adherence to Jewish commandments
moshav (Heb) – cooperative settlement, with private and collective housing and industry
muezzin – cantor who sings the call to prayer
mullah – Muslim scholar, teacher or religious leader

nargileh (Ar) – water pipe used to smoke tobacco; *sheesha* in Egypt
norias – water wheels

obelisk – monolithic stone pillar with square sides tapering to a pyramidal top; used as a monument in ancient Egypt
otogar (T) – bus station
oud – pear-shaped, stringed instrument; the forerunner of the Western lute

pansiyon – pension, B&B or guesthouse
pasha – Ottoman governor appointed by the sultan in Constantinople
Peshmerga – Kurdish soldiers, literally 'those who face death'
PKK – Kurdistan Workers Party
PLO – Palestine Liberation Organisation
PTT (T) – Posta, Telefon, Telgraf; post, telephone and telegraph office
pylon – monumental gateway at the entrance to a temple

qahwa (Ar) – coffee, coffeehouse; *ahwa* in Egypt
qasr – castle or palace
Quran – the holy book of Islam; also *Koran*

Ramadan – ninth month of the lunar Islamic calendar during which Muslims fast from sunrise to sunset; Ramazan in Turkish
ras (Ar) – cape, headland or head

sahn (Ar) – courtyard of a mosque
Sala – the Muslim obligation of prayer, ideally to be performed five times a day; one of the five pillars of Islam
Saladin – (Salah ad-Din in Arabic) Kurdish warlord who retook Jerusalem from the Crusaders; founder of the *Ayyubid dynasty*
Sawm – the Muslim month of *Ramadan;* one of the five pillars of Islam
servees – shared taxi with a fixed route
settler – term used to describe Israelis who have created new communities on Arab territory, usually land captured from the Arabs during the 1967 war
Shabbat – Jewish Sabbath observed from sundown on Friday to one hour after sundown on Saturday
Shahada – Islam's basic tenet and profession of faith: 'There is no god but Allah, and Mohammed is the Prophet of Allah'; one of the five pillars of Islam
shai (Ar) – tea; *çay* in Turkish
sheesha (E) – see *nargileh*
sheikh – venerated religious scholar; also shaikh
sherut (Heb) – shared taxi with a fixed route
Shiite – one of the two main branches of Islam
shwarma – grilled meat sliced from a spit and served
in pita-type bread with salad; also *döner kebap* in Turkish
siq (Ar) – narrow passageway or defile such as the one at Petra
souq – market or bazaar
stele – (plural stelae) stone

or wooden commemorative slab or column decorated with inscriptions or figures

Sufi – follower of any of the Islamic mystical orders that emphasise dancing, chanting and trances in order to attain unity with God; see also *dervish*

sultan – absolute ruler of a Muslim state

Sunni – one of the two main branches of Islam

sura – chapter in the *Quran*

ta'amiyya (E) – see *felafel*

Talmud – a collection of 63 Jewish holy books that complement the *Torah*

tell – ancient mound created by centuries of urban rebuilding

Torah – five books of Moses, the first five Old Testament books; also called the Pentateuch

Umayyad dynasty – first great dynasty of Arab Muslim rulers, based in Damascus (AD 661–750); also Omayyad dynasty

wikala (E) – see *khan*

willayat – village

Zakat – the Muslim obligation to give alms to the poor; one of the five pillars of Islam

ziggurat (Far) – rectangular temple tower or tiered mound built in *Mesopotamia* by the Akkadians, Babylonians and Sumerians

behind the scenes

SEND US YOUR FEEDBACK

We love to hear from travellers – your comments keep us on our toes and help make our books better. Our well-travelled team reads every word on what you loved or loathed about this book. Although we cannot reply individually to postal submissions, we always guarantee that your feedback goes straight to the appropriate authors, in time for the next edition. Each person who sends us information is thanked in the next edition – the most useful submissions are rewarded with a selection of digital PDF chapters.

Visit **lonelyplanet.com/contact** to submit your updates and suggestions or to ask for help. Our award-winning website also features inspirational travel stories, news and discussions.

Note: We may edit, reproduce and incorporate your comments in Lonely Planet products such as guidebooks, websites and digital products, so let us know if you don't want your comments reproduced or your name acknowledged. For a copy of our privacy policy visit lonelyplanet.com/privacy.

OUR READERS

Many thanks to the travellers who used the last edition and wrote to us with helpful hints, useful advice and interesting anecdotes:

Shaarbek Amankul, Ben Auger, Graham Bambrough, Mohamed Bharmal, Marie Bodilsen, Philippe Boeglin, Gerard Browne, Jack Brumpton, Yuliono Budianto, Shane Campbell, Richard Cassem, Rodrigo Chia, Charles Clarke, Mark Coady, Damian Cohen, Jascha de Ridder, Jorge de Mello, Luigi de Angelis, Eva Dockery, Colin Doyle, David Edwards, Omar Gardener, Daniel Gregg, Andrew Hansen, Roy Hodgman, James Hodgson, Paul Hudson, Wei Hwu, Gerrit Jan Van Vliet, Sam Johnson, Peter Jones, Ravi Kaneriya, Nick Kembel, Greg King, Sebastian Kreft, Niklas Larsson, Laurie Mcadam, Jane Mcarthur, Barbara Mcleod, Julie Meilstrup, Curtis Miller, Laura Molins, Mauro Mondello, Aaron Nelson, Adam Paddick, Lisa Pascolo, Stephanie Powell, Michael Raffaele, Guy Raven & Carolein Kuijpers, Roberto Rojas Ortiz, Martin Schindl, Tom Smeenle, John Soar, Franciska Tillema, Will Todman, David Torrance, Bruno Vanbesien, Jeffrey Walker, Suzanne Wells, Cathy Wilson, Hilary Winchester

AUTHOR THANKS

Anthony Ham

Shukran to all of those from Cairo to İstanbul and most places in between who have, on every visit, reinforced my love affair with the region. A heartfelt thanks to Marina, Carlota and Valentina, my three girls who make coming home the greatest gift in the world. My work on this book is dedicated to Ron, whose visit to Damascus all those years ago made it a true place of the soul.

Stuart Butler

It takes a very understanding wife to agree to let you go gallivanting around Iraq, so firstly I'd like to thank my wife Heather for her continued support and for everything else she does. Further thanks to my young son who had to do without playing hide-and-seek with his daddy once again. Thanks to photographer Toby Adamson and Marion Poizeau for company on the road, and Haual Qaraman Rwandzy for patient driving along the Hamilton Road.

Zora O'Neill

A million thanks to my Cairo crew (Mandy, Amgad et al) and to my fellow authors on this title, as well as to *Egypt* authors Michael

Benanav, Anthony Sattin and Jess Lee for dealing with last-minute queries on their very well-researched contributions. Back at the head office, thanks to Anthony Ham, Kate Morgan (bon voyage!), Brigitte Ellemor and Adrian Persoglia for wrestling it all into shape.

Olivia Pozzan

Thanks to everyone who helped me discover the confusion and beauty of Lebanon: Pierre in Byblos for his generosity, Jamil in Beirut for his hospitality, and Ronnie for an entertaining walk through Beirut's chequered past. Warmest thanks to Pat, a true friend when I needed one.

Daniel Robinson

The countless people who showed great generosity with their time include (from north to south) Michael Benz, Kerstin Göring, Daniel Flatauer, David Friedman, Moshe Tov Kreps, Yair Moore, Maoz Yinon, the Fauzi Azar staff (especially Sami), Joseph Marotta, Sarah Yefet, Yafa Kfir and Amiram, Nissim Bados, Yaron Burgin, David Berger, Raz Zabar and Gil Shkedi. This project would not have been possible without the extraordinary backstopping and forbearance of my wife, Rachel Safman, and the patience of my mother-in-law, Edie Safman.

Anthony Sattin

I was unable to travel in Syria specifically for this book, but would like to thank the following people for help with recent journeys: Bashar al-Ash of Syriana Travel, Adli Qudsi of Friends of Aleppo Citadel, the directors of Damascus and Aleppo museums, Nabil Maleh, Yaser Al Saghrji and 1001 people who smoothed the way, helped me find what I wanted, brightened dull moments and assisted in various ways.

Paul Smith

Thanks to everybody I met on the road, particularly Amos Burr, Sebastian Silva, Joel Selby and Finn Robinson. Anthony, Kate and Brigitte all found time to help me with silly questions and Adrian was just as patient with the maps. Carol and Shawn always make sure that coming home is even more fun than travelling. Thanks to Mum and Dad for proof reading, and welcome to the family Tom! Margie, this one is for you. Miss you loads!

Jenny Walker

Returning to Jordan is always the greatest of pleasures, not just on account of the spectacular wonders of the country, but also because Jordanians continue to go out of their way to be hospitable – including His Excellency, Nayef Hmeidi al-Fayez, Minister of Tourism & Antiquities. While their assistance in researching this chapter is hugely appreciated, I reserve greatest thanks for my beloved husband, Sam Owen, who accompanied me during research and assisted immeasurably in resourcing further background information during write-up.

ACKNOWLEDGMENTS

Climate map data adapted from Peel MC, Finlayson BL & McMahon TA (2007) 'Updated World Map of the Köppen-Geiger Climate Classification', *Hydrology and Earth System Sciences*, 11, 163344.

Illustrations pp62-63, pp96-97 and pp138-139 by Javier Zarracina. Illustrations pp194-195 and pp314,315 by Michael Weldon.

Cover photograph: Camels at Giza, Egypt, Doug Pearson/AWL.Many of the images in this guide are available for licensing from Lonely Planet Images: www.lonelyplanetimages.com.

THIS BOOK

This 7th edition of Lonely Planet's *Middle East* guidebook was researched and written by Anthony Ham (coordinating author), Stuart Butler, Zora O'Neill, Olivia Pozzan, Daniel Robinson, Anthony Sattin, Paul Smith and Jenny Walker. Dr Caroline Evans wrote the text that formed the basis of the Health chapter. The previous edition of this book was also led by coordinating author Anthony Ham. This guidebook was commissioned in Lonely Planet's Melbourne office, and produced by the following:

Commissioning Editors Kate Morgan, Glenn van der Knijff

Coordinating Editor Bella Li

Coordinating Cartographer Valentina Kremenchutskaya

Coordinating Layout Designer Sandra Helou

Managing Editors Brigitte Ellemor, Bruce Evans

Managing Cartographers Adrian Persoglia, Mandy Sierp

Managing Layout Designer Chris Girdler

Assisting Editors Janet Austin, Andrew Bain, Gordon Farrer, Samantha Forge, Kate James, Kellie Langdon, Lucy Monie, Saralinda Turner, Jeanette Wall, Helen Yeates

Assisting Cartographer Csanad Csutoros

Assisting Layout Designer Wibowo Rusli

Cover Research Naomi Parker

Internal Image Research Aude Vauconsant

Language Content Branislava Vladisavljevic

Thanks to Shahara Ahmed, Frank Deim, Ryan Evans, Larissa Frost, Carol Jackson, Annelies Mertens, Trent Paton, Raphael Richards, Jacqui Saunders, Kerrianne Southway, John Taufa, Gerard Walker, Diana Von Holdt, Juan Winata

index

ABBREVIATIONS

E	Egypt
I	Iraq
I&PT	Israel & the Palestinian Territories
J	Jordan
L	Lebanon
S	Syria
T	Turkey

000 Map pages
000 Photo pages

000 Map pages
000 Photo pages

000 Map pages
000 Photo pages

N

O

P

000 Map pages
000 Photo pages

Q

R

S

U

V

W

000 Map pages
000 Photo pages

how to use this book

These symbols will help you find the listings you want:

- Sights
- Beaches
- Activities
- Courses
- Tours
- Festivals & Events
- Sleeping
- Eating
- Drinking
- Entertainment
- Shopping
- Information/ Transport

These symbols give you the vital information for each listing:

- Telephone Numbers
- Opening Hours
- Parking
- Nonsmoking
- Air-Conditioning
- Internet Access
- Wi-Fi Access
- Swimming Pool
- Vegetarian Selection
- English-Language Menu
- Family-Friendly
- Pet-Friendly
- Bus
- Ferry
- Metro
- Subway
- Tram
- Train

Reviews are organised by author preference.

Look out for these icons:

TOP CHOICE Our author's recommendation

FREE No payment required

A green or sustainable option

Our authors have nominated these places as demonstrating a strong commitment to sustainability – for example by supporting local communities and producers, operating in an environmentally friendly way, or supporting conservation projects.

Map Legend

Sights
- Beach
- Buddhist
- Castle
- Christian
- Hindu
- Islamic
- Jewish
- Monument
- Museum/Gallery
- Ruin
- Winery/Vineyard
- Zoo
- Other Sight

Activities, Courses & Tours
- Diving/Snorkelling
- Canoeing/Kayaking
- Skiing
- Surfing
- Swimming/Pool
- Walking
- Windsurfing
- Other Activity/ Course/Tour

Sleeping
- Sleeping
- Camping

Eating
- Eating

Drinking
- Drinking
- Cafe

Entertainment
- Entertainment

Shopping
- Shopping

Information
- Bank
- Embassy/ Consulate
- Hospital/Medical
- Internet
- Police
- Post Office
- Telephone
- Toilet
- Tourist Information
- Other Information

Transport
- Airport
- Border Crossing
- Bus
- Cable Car/ Funicular
- Cycling
- Ferry
- Metro
- Monorail
- Parking
- Petrol Station
- Taxi
- Train/Railway
- Tram
- Other Transport

Routes
- Tollway
- Freeway
- Primary
- Secondary
- Tertiary
- Lane
- Unsealed Road
- Plaza/Mall
- Steps
- Tunnel
- Pedestrian Overpass
- Walking Tour
- Walking Tour Detour
- Path

Geographic
- Hut/Shelter
- Lighthouse
- Lookout
- Mountain/Volcano
- Oasis
- Park
- Pass
- Picnic Area
- Waterfall

Population
- Capital (National)
- Capital (State/Province)
- City/Large Town
- Town/Village

Boundaries
- International
- State/Province
- Disputed
- Regional/Suburb
- Marine Park
- Cliff
- Wall

Hydrography
- River, Creek
- Intermittent River
- Swamp/Mangrove
- Reef
- Canal
- Water
- Dry/Salt/ Intermittent Lake
- Glacier

Areas
- Beach/Desert
- Cemetery (Christian)
- Cemetery (Other)
- Park/Forest
- Sportsground
- Sight (Building)
- Top Sight (Building)

Daniel Robinson
Israel & the Palestinian Territories Brought up in the San Francisco Bay Area and near Chicago, Daniel also spent part of his childhood in Jerusalem, a bit of his youth at Kibbutz Lotan and many years in Tel Aviv, where he worked on a PhD in late Ottoman history and covered suicide bombings for the Associated Press. A Lonely Planet author since 1989, he holds a BA in Near Eastern Studies from Princeton and an MA in Jewish History from Tel Aviv University.

Read more about Daniel at:
lonelyplanet.com/members/daniel_robinson

Anthony Sattin
Syria Anthony Sattin first fell for Syria more than twenty years ago. He has contributed to Lonely Planet's *Egypt*, *Morocco* and *Algeria* guides and to several anthologies, including *A House Somewhere*, which he edited. He contributes to a number of publications, including the *Sunday Times* and *Conde Nast Traveller* and presents documentaries for BBC radio. Anthony's highly acclaimed non-fiction includes *A Winter on the Nile*, *The Pharaoh's Shadow* and *Lifting the Veil*. Read more about Anthony at anthonysattin.com.

Paul Smith
Turkey From an early age, and with a vague and naive ambition to be the next David Attenborough, Paul dreamed of exploring the remotest areas of the globe in search of wildlife. While researching this edition Paul took a beating billed as a massage in a hamam, ate more than his own weight in *İskenders* and came to the realisation that there probably isn't another country on earth with more to offer the visitor than Turkey.

Jenny Walker
Jordan Jenny Walker's first involvement with the Middle East was as a student, contributing to her father's book on entomology in Saudi Arabia. Convinced she and her mum were the first Western women to brew tea in the desolate interior, she returned to university to see if that were true in a dissertation (BA Hons) and thesis on the Arabic Orient (MPhil, University of Oxford). Jenny has travelled in more than 100 countries. She is Associate Dean (PD) at Caledonian University College of Engineering, Oman.

OUR STORY

A beat-up old car, a few dollars in the pocket and a sense of adventure. In 1972 that's all Tony and Maureen Wheeler needed for the trip of a lifetime – across Europe and Asia overland to Australia. It took several months, and at the end – broke but inspired – they sat at their kitchen table writing and stapling together their first travel guide, *Across Asia on the Cheap*. Within a week they'd sold 1500 copies. Lonely Planet was born.

Today, Lonely Planet has offices in Melbourne, London and Oakland, with more than 600 staff and writers. We share Tony's belief that 'a great guidebook should do three things: inform, educate and amuse'.

OUR WRITERS

Anthony Ham

Coordinating Author Anthony first landed in Damascus in 1998 and couldn't bear to leave. He stayed three months and returns at every available opportunity. His first job for Lonely Planet was the Iraq chapter of this guide back in 1999, and he has since written or contributed to the guides to Jordan, Iran, Saudi Arabia and Libya, and five editions of this *Middle East* guide. He has also worked in Australia as a refugee lawyer, with clients from the Middle East, and has a Masters degree in Middle Eastern politics. Anthony is now based in Madrid and writes for magazines and newspapers around the world.

Stuart Butler

Iraq Hailing from southwest England, Stuart Butler has travelled widely throughout the Middle East. Visiting Iraq for Lonely Planet, though, was one of the most enjoyable travel experiences he has ever had – rarely has he encountered a country with such a genuinely friendly and welcoming population. Stuart's travels for Lonely Planet and various surf magazines have also taken him beyond Iraq – from the desert beaches of Yemen to the coastal jungles of Colombia. He lives in southwest France with his wife and son. Read about his travels at http://stuartbutler-journalist.blogspot.fr.

Read more about Stuart at:
lonelyplanet.com/members/stuartbutler

Zora O'Neill

Egypt Zora lived in Cairo in the 1990s while working on her Masters degree in Arabic literature and has contributed to more than a dozen guidebooks, including two editions of Lonely Planet's *Egypt*. She writes about food and travel for the *New York Times* and *Conde Nast Traveler*, and is currently working on a book about Arabic language and travel in the Middle East. She lives in Astoria, Queens, and blogs about her travels at www.rovinggastronome.com.

Read more about Zora at:
lonelyplanet.com/members/zoraoneill

Olivia Pozzan

Lebanon While working as a veterinarian for an Arabian Prince in the UAE, Olivia travelled extensively throughout the Gulf region and the Middle East, developing an affinity for its magnificent deserts and rugged landscapes. She has contributed to a dozen Lonely Planet guidebooks, from *Australia* to *Italy* and the *Middle East*. While researching Lebanon for this edition, she experienced an incredible hike through a night-time snowstorm. When not exploring the world's most exotic places, she lives the Aussie beach lifestyle and is a practising veterinarian.

Read more about Olivia at:
lonelyplanet.com/members/oliviapozzan

OVER PAGE MORE WRITERS

Published by Lonely Planet Publications Pty Ltd
ABN 36 005 607 983
7th edition – September 2012
ISBN 978 1 74179 670 4

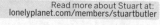

10 9 8 7 6 5 4 3 2 1
Printed in China